10 —

D0457585

THE MODERN LIBRARY
of the World's Best Books

>>

THE BASIC WRITINGS
OF SIGMUND FREUD

THE BASIC WRITINGS OF SIGMUND FREUD

TRANSLATED AND EDITED, WITH AN INTRODUCTION

By DR. A. A. BRILL

Psychopathology of Everyday Life
The Interpretation of Dreams
Three Contributions to the Theory of Sex
Wit and Its Relation to the Unconscious
Totem and Taboo
The History of the Psychoanalytic Movement

THE MODERN LIBRARY
NEW YORK

COPYRIGHT 1938 BY RANDOM HOUSE, INC.
COPYRIGHT RENEWED 1966 BY GIOIA B. BERNHEIM
AND EDMUND BRILL

THE MODERN LIBRARY
is published by RANDOM HOUSE, INC.
New York, New York
Manufactured in the United States of America

CONTENTS

v

THE BASIC WRITINGS
OF SIGMUND FREUD

INTRODUCTION

BY DR. A. A. BRILL

PSYCHOANALYSIS was unknown in this country until I introduced it in 1908. Ever since then, I have been translating, lecturing and writing on this subject both for physicians and laymen; and I am happy to say that today psychoanalysis, which has encountered so much opposition here, as it did abroad, is firmly established not only in medicine, but also in psychology, sociology, pedagogy and anthropology. It has not only permeated and transvalued the mental sciences, but indirectly also *belles lettres* and the cultural trends of the last generation.

At the beginning of the psychoanalytic movement in this country, its opponents and some of its lukewarm friends predicted that, like so many other discoveries in mental therapy, psychoanalysis was destined to be short-lived. They were poor prophets. The falsity of their prognosis can be seen in the fact that the psychoanalytic terminology, some of which I was the first to coin into English expressions, can now be found in all standard English dictionaries. Words like *abreaction, transference, repression, displacement, unconscious,* which I introduced as Freudian concepts, have been adopted and are used to give new meanings, new values to our knowledge of normal and abnormal behavior.

How did Freud come to discover psychoanalysis? Every contribution to the sum total of our knowledge has been consciously or unconsciously motivated by the wish to ameliorate the lot of mankind. Discoveries of this sort never come out of the clear sky; there is always a *vis a tergo,* which forms some definite nucleus in the mind of some genius, and this slowly grows until it attains sufficient proportions to make itself felt despite all obstacles. Freud has said that a human being is a resultant of constitution and fate, or heredity and environment. The constitution is brought along from all the past centuries and millenniums, but once here cannot be changed. A living being either comes into the world with a normal body and mind, and survives in the struggle for existence, or he is born defective and falls by the wayside. But, given an average being, his

3

further development, his future character or personality, depends on fate or environment. The same holds true for any scientific discovery.

The discoverer begins with some nucleus, some kernel of material, which for some unconscious reason takes possession of him. He then compulsively elaborates upon it through a long labor of trial and error until it is accepted by others—one might say, until he forces its acceptance by others. For no matter how true a thing may be, the world-at-large at first refuses to believe it. The world-at-large is the conservative old sage, who regularly objects to anything new and accepts it only after experience has demonstrated the *truth* of the discovery, and thus forces conviction upon him. I am presumptuous enough to feel that psychoanalysis is one of the greatest discoveries of our age. Freud has repeatedly been compared to Darwin, Spinoza, Newton, Einstein, and other great geniuses, whose works were at first combated and repudiated, but finally accepted. To give here even a short survey of the resistances and obstacles which Freud's teachings encountered would take too much space; I must refer the reader to the master's own history at the end of this volume.

Sigmund Freud was born in 1856 in Freiberg, Moravia, formerly Austria, now Czechoslovakia. He was brought up in Vienna, having lived there since the age of four. In his autobiography, he states: "My parents were Jews and I remained a Jew."

One of the arguments that has been hurled at psychoanalysis on a few occasions is that its originator was a Jew, implying thereby that the theories expressed by Freud do not apply to the rest of mankind. Such an argument, which, if accepted, would also invalidate Christianity, is too stupid to require refutation. Freud's works had the honor of forming part of the sacred pyre on Hitler's accession to power. The fact that the bulk of this pyre was composed of works of non-Jewish thinkers plainly shows that truth knows no creed or race. I feel, however, that Freud's Jewish descent—constitution—as well as the environment to which he was subjected because of it—fate—exerted considerable influence on his personality. One might say that only a Jewish genius, forged in the crucible of centuries of persecution, could have offered himself so willingly on the altar of public opprobrium for the sake of demonstrating the truths of psychoanalysis.

Freud tells us that in college he always stood first, and was hardly ever examined. Despite the very straitened financial condition of his family, his father wanted him to follow his own inclination in the selection of a vocation. He had no special love for medicine at that age, nor did he acquire it later, but rather he was stimulated by a sort of inquisitiveness directed to human relations and objects of nature. He was very much attracted to Darwin's theories because they offered the prospect of an extraordinary advance of human knowledge, and he finally decided to enter the medical school after he had read Goethe's beautiful essay, *Die Natur*.

In a number of his works Freud exposes his innermost feelings, so that he who reads will find there his real autobiography, and in some, notably, *The Interpretation of Dreams*, he touches on the Jewish problem. But his first encounter of this problem is described in his autobiography, where he states that he came face to face with it when he entered the university in 1873. It struck him as unreasonable that he was supposed to feel inferior and extra-national because he was a Jew. "I rejected the first," he states, "with all resoluteness. I could never grasp why I should be ashamed of my origin, or, as they began to say, of my 'race.' As to the nationality which was denied me, I gave this up without much regret." He felt that there would surely always be a bit of room for a zealous fellow worker within the sphere of mankind without the necessity of any enrollment. "But these first university impressions produced one very important result for the future. I became familiar early with my destiny—to belong to the opposition and to be proscribed from the 'compact majority.' A certain independence of judgment was in this way developed." [1]

While still in the university, he worked for a number of years in the physiological laboratory of the famous Ernst Brücke, who was his teacher and gave him as his first task the histology of the nervous system. With only a short interruption Freud worked in the Institute from 1876 until 1882. Then, he discovered, that with the exception of psychiatry, the other medical specialties did not attract him. He graduated from the medical school in 1881, and in 1882 he entered Vienna's well known *Allgemeine Krankenhaus* (general hospital). There, he went through the usual routine services, but continued his studies on the anatomy of the brain, in which he became very proficient. It is not generally known that in his early days Freud wrote a number of works on diseases of the nervous system, which were very highly regarded by his contemporaries. [2]

In 1885 he was attracted by the fame of Charcot, who was applying hypnotism to the study and treatment of hysteria and other functional nervous diseases. He remained for a year in Paris as a pupil and translator of this master's works. In 1886 he returned to his native Vienna and "married the girl who waited for me in a far-off city longer than four years." He then entered private practice, but continued as an instructor in the university.

What Freud saw in Charcot's Clinic made a very deep impression on him. While still a student, he also witnessed a performance of the "magnetiser," Hansen, in which a test person became deadly pale when she

---

[1] Freud: *Selbstdarstellung*, Meiner, Leipzig.
[2] See Smith Ely Jelliffe: *Sigmund Freud as a Neurologist*, Journal of Nervous and Mental Diseases, Vol. 85, No. 6, June, 1937.

merged into a cataleptic rigidity, and remained so during the whole duration of the catalepsy. This convinced Freud of the genuineness of hypnotic phenomena, a conviction which remained in him despite the fact
that the contemporary professors of psychiatry considered hypnosis
fraudulent and dangerous. From Charcot he learned that hypnosis could
produce hysterical symptoms as well as remove them, and that hysteria
could also occur in men; and from Liébault and Bernheim of the Nancy
School he learned that suggestion alone, without hypnotism, was as
efficacious as suggestion employed in hypnosis.

When Freud returned to Vienna and demonstrated what he had learned
from Charcot, he met with considerable opposition. It was the age of
physical therapy, when physicians knew nothing about the psychic factors in disease, when everything was judged by the formula, *Mens sana
in corpore sano* (a healthy mind in a healthy body). Every symptom was
explained on the basis of some organic lesion, and if nothing physical was
discovered, it was assumed that there must be something in the brain to
account for the disturbance. The treatment was based on this same deficient understanding; drugs, hydrotherapy, and electrotherapy were the
only agents that physicians could use. When the patient was excited, he
received some sedative; if he was depressed and felt fatigue, he was given
a tonic; and when drugs failed, electricity or cold baths were recommended. All these remedies gave only temporary alleviation, mainly
through suggestion. Most of the thoughtful physicians were fully cognizant of this helpless state, but there was nothing else to be done.

During the first few years of his private practice Freud relied mostly
on hypnotism and electrotherapy, but he soon realized that the latter
failed to benefit the patient, and that the whole idea of electric treatment
for functional nervous diseases was fantastic. He had some good results,
however, from hypnotic therapy; but he soon found that not every patient could be hypnotized, and that even those who could be, did not
remain permanently cured. Attributing such failures to a deficiency in
his technique, to an inability on his part to put every patient into a state
of somnambulism with its consequent amnesia, he spent some weeks in
Nancy with Liébault and Bernheim, to whom he took a recalcitrant patient for treatment. Bernheim made a number of efforts to produce a
deep hypnotic state in the patient, but finally had to admit failure. Freud,
though disappointed with the technique of hypnotism, learned a great
deal from the experiments witnessed there concerning the forceful psychic
forces which were still to be investigated. Very soon thereafter, he gradually gave up hypnotism and developed what he called "psychoanalysis."
In this connection he makes the following interesting statement: "The
importance of hypnotism for the history of the development of psychoanalysis must not be too lightly estimated. Both in theoretic as well as in

therapeutic aspects, psychoanalysis is the administrator of the estate left by hypnotism." [1]

In order to give a full account of the development of psychoanalysis, it will be necessary to go back a few years. While Freud still worked in Brücke's laboratory, he made the acquaintance of Dr. Josef Breuer, a prominent general practitioner of high scientific standing. Although Breuer was 14 years older than Freud, they soon became friends and frequently discussed their scientific views and experiences. Knowing Freud's interest in neurology and psychiatry, Breuer gave him an account of a very interesting case of hysteria which he had studied and cured by hypnosis from 1880 to 1882. [2] As this unique case was of the greatest importance to the development of psychoanalysis, it will be worth while to give a few details.

The patient concerned was a young girl of unusual education and talent, who had become ill while nursing her father to whom she was very much attached. Dr. Breuer states that when he took her as a patient she presented a variegated picture of paralyses with contractures, inhibitions and states of psychic confusion. Through an accidental observation Breuer discovered that the patient could be freed from such disturbances of consciousness if she could be enabled to give verbal expression to the affective phantasies which dominated her. Breuer elaborated this experience into a method of treatment. He hypnotized her and urged her to tell him what oppressed her at the time, and by this simple method he freed her from all her symptoms. The significance of the case lay in this fact, that in her waking state the patient knew nothing about the origin of her symptoms, but once hypnotized, she immediately knew the connection between her symptoms and some of her past experiences. All her symptoms were traceable to experiences during the time when she had nursed her sick father. Moreover, the symptoms were not arbitrary and senseless, but could be traced to definite experiences and forgotten reminiscences of that emotional situation.

A common feature of all the symptoms consisted in the fact that they had come into existence in situations in which an impulse to do something had to be foregone because other motives suppressed it. The symptom appeared as a substitute for the unperformed act. As a rule, the symptom was not the result of one single "traumatic" scene, but of a sum of many similar situations. If the patient in a state of hypnosis recalled hallucinatorily the act which she had suppressed in the past, and if she now brought it to conclusion under the stress of a freely generated affect, the symptom was wiped away never to return again. It was remarked that

[1] *Psychoanalysis: Exploring the Hidden Recesses of the Mind,* translated by A. A. Brill, Encyclopaedia Britannica.
[2] Breuer and Freud: *Studies in Hysteria,* p. 14, translated by A. A. Brill, Monograph Series.

the causes which had given origin to the symptom resembled the traumatic factors described by Charcot in his experimental cases. What was still more remarkable was that these traumatic causes with their concomitant psychic feelings had been entirely lost to the patient's memory, as if they had never happened, while their results—that is, the symptoms, had continued unchanged, as if unaffected by the wear and tear of time, until attacked by Breuer through hypnosis.

Although Breuer, as was mentioned above, told Freud about this wonderful discovery, he did not publish his findings. Freud could not understand why. The discovery seemed to him of inestimable value. But following his return from Nancy in 1889 with the cognition of hypnotic suggestive therapy, Freud decided to test Breuer's method in his own cases, and found ample corroboration of its efficacy during a period of many years. He then urged Breuer to report with him the results of his method, and in 1893 they jointly issued a preliminary communication, *On the Psychic Mechanisms of Hysterical Phenomena*.[1]

As can be seen, Breuer was the spiritual creator of this method of treatment and Freud always gave him full credit for it, although they differed from the very beginning in their basic interpretation of the symptoms. They called their treatment the "cathartic method" because they concluded that the efficacy of it rested on the mental and emotional purging, catharsis, which the patient went through during the treatment. The other conclusion drawn by the authors was that hysteria was a disease of the past, and that, as Freud put it later, the symptom was, as it were, a monument to *some* disagreeable and forgotten (repressed) episode from the patient's life. The patient, however, did not know the meaning of the monument any more than the average German would know the meaning of the Bunker Hill monument. This concept for the first time showed the importance of distinguishing between conscious and unconscious states, which was later amplified and developed by Freud as the psychology of the unconscious. New meaning was given to the affective or emotional factors of life, their fluctuations and dynamism. The symptom was the result of a dammed-up or strangulated affect. The patient could not give vent to the affect because the situation in question made this impossible, so that the idea was intentionally *repressed* from consciousness and excluded from associative elaboration. As a result of this repression, the sum of energy which could not be discharged took a wrong path to bodily innervation, and thus produced the symptom. In other words, the symptom was the result of a conversion of psychic energy into a physical manifestation, such as pain or paralysis. Thus, a pain in the face, diagnosed as neuralgia, might be due to an insult which would ordinarily evoke the thought, "I feel as if he had slapped me in the face." As this insult could

[1] l. c. D. I.

not be retaliated against, the strangulated energy remained in a state of repression and gave rise to "neuralgia." The cure or the discharge was effected through what the authors called the process of *abreaction*. The hypnotized patient was led back to the repressed episodes and allowed to give free vent in speech and action to the feelings which were originally kept out of consciousness.[1]

Breuer's and Freud's discoveries were not received as sympathetically as the authors expected. Their psychogenetic views of hysteria were interesting, but too revolutionary to be accepted by their older colleagues. On the other hand, in spite of much discussion, there was as yet, no real antagonism. That did not arise until later, when Freud began to stress the sexual factor in the neuroses. In his report of Anna O., Breuer stated: "The sexual element in her make-up was astonishingly undeveloped." [2] Throughout their book the sexual elements, of which there were many in every case, were treated no differently than the other factors in the patients' lives. How Freud happened to become interested in sex and then stress its importance in the etiology of the neuroses he tells us later.[3]

Very soon after the appearance of the *Studies in Hysteria,* Breuer withdrew from the field. He was, after all, unprepared for this specialty, and inasmuch as he enjoyed a stable and lucrative practice and a high reputation as a family physician, the storm which began to gather as his collaborator advanced deeper into the etiology of the neuroses more or less frightened him. Freud, therefore, continued alone to elaborate and perfect the instrument left by his erstwhile friend and collaborator; and as a result, the cathartic method underwent numerous modifications, the most important of which was the giving-up of hypnotism in favor of *free association.* As pointed out above, not everybody could be hypnotized, and since hypnotism was absolutely indispensable to the cathartic treatment at that time, many a worthy patient had had to be given up just because he or she could not be hypnotized. Freud was also dissatisfied with the therapeutic results of catharsis based on hypnotism. Although cures were often very striking, they were often of very short duration and depended mainly on the personal relation between the patient and physician. Moreover, Freud always entertained a feeling of antipathy to the application of hypnotism and suggestion to patients. Speaking of his visit to Bernheim in 1889, he states: "But I can remember even then a feeling of gloomy antagonism against this tyranny of suggestion. When a patient who did not prove to be yielding was shouted at: 'What are you doing? *Vous vous*

---

[1] To ab-react literally means to re-act or work off something repressed, thereby unburdening oneself of unconscious, strangulated feelings.
[2] l. c., p. 14.
[3] Cf. *The History of the Psychoanalytic Movement.*

contresuggestionnez !', I said to myself that this was an evident injustice
and violence." [1]

Yet his visit to Bernheim later helped him out of the dilemma of not
being able to hypnotize some patients. He recalled the following experiment which he had witnessed there, the object of which was to overcome
the post-hypnotic amnesia: On being awakened, the patient could not remember anything that had transpired during hypnosis, but when he was
urged to make an effort to recall what had been said to him, he eventually
remembered everything. Freud applied the same method to those patients
whom he could not hypnotize. He urged them to tell him everything that
came to their minds, to leave out nothing, regardless of whether they considered it relevant or not. He persuaded them to give up all conscious
reflection, abandon themselves to calm concentration, follow their spontaneous mental occurrences, and impart everything to him. In this way
he finally obtained those *free associations* which lead to the origin of
the symptoms. As he developed this method, he found that it was not as
simple as he had thought, that these so-called free associations were really
not *free,* but were determined by unconscious material which had to be
analyzed and interpreted. He therefore designated this new technique
psychoanalysis. The cathartic method, however, was ever preserved as a
sort of nucleus of psychoanalysis despite the expansions and modifications
which Freud gradually made as he proceeded with the new technique.

In the course of working with free associations, Freud gained a tremendous amount of insight into the play of forces of the human mind
which he could not have obtained through the former therapeutic procedure. The question as to how the patient could have forgotten so many
outer and inner experiences, which could be recalled only in a state of
hypnosis and which were difficult to bring to consciousness by means of
free association, soon became revealed to him. The forgotten material
represented something painful, something disagreeable, or something
frightful, obnoxious to the ego of the patient, which he did not like to
think of consciously. In order to make it conscious, the physician had to
exert himself mightily to overcome the patient's *resistance,* which kept
these experiences in a state of repression and away from consciousness.
The neurosis proved to be the result of a psychic conflict between two
dynamic forces, impulse and resistance, in the course of which struggle
the ego withdrew from the disagreeable impulse. As a result of this withdrawal, the obnoxious impulse was kept from access to consciousness as
well as from direct motor discharge, but it retained its impulsive energy.

This unconscious process actually is a primary defense mechanism,
comparable to an effort to fly away from something. But in order to keep

[1] Freud: *Massenpsychologie und Ich-Analyse,* p. 40, Int. Psycho-Verlag, Wien, 1921,
English translation by Strachey, London.

the disagreeable idea from consciousness, the ego has to contend against the constant thrust of the repressed impulse which is ever searching for expression. But despite constant exertion by the ego, the repressed, obnoxious impulse often finds an outlet through some by-path, and thus invalidates the intention of the repression. The repressed impulsive energy then settles by this indirect course on some organ or part of the body, and this innervation constitutes the symptom. Once this is established, the patient struggles against the symptom in the same way as he did against the originally repressed impulses.

To illustrate these mechanisms let us consider the case of an hysterical young woman. For some months she was courted by a young man proclaiming his ardent love for her. Suddenly one day he made an unsuccessful sexual assault upon her, and then disappeared, leaving her in a state of deep depression. She could not confide in her mother, because from the very beginning of the affair the mother had forbidden her to see the young man. Three years later I found her suffering from numerous hysterical conversion symptoms, and attacks of an epileptic character which had existed for some two and a half years. Analysis showed that the attacks represented symbolically what had taken place at the time of the abortive sexual assault. Every detail of the so-called epileptiform attack—every gesture, every movement—was a stereotyped repetition of the sexual attack which the patient was reproducing unconsciously. The other symptoms, too, were directly traceable to the love affair.

The whole process of this disease can readily be understood if we bear in mind the various steps of this love situation. The young woman was healthy and, biontically speaking, ready for mating; her primitive instinct of sex was striving for fulfillment. Consciously, she could think of love only in the modern sense of the term, in which the physical elements are deliberately kept out of sight. Her middle-class, religious environment precluded any illicit sexual activity as far as she was consciously concerned. But, behind it all, the sexual impulses were actively reaching out for maternity. She was sincerely in love with the man, but naturally thought of love as marriage, with everything that goes with it. The sudden shock of coming face to face with the physical elements of sex left a terrific impression on her mind: on the one hand, consciously, she rejected vehemently the lover's physical approaches, and on the other hand, unconsciously, she really craved them. For weeks afterwards she vividly lived over in her mind everything that had happened to her, and, now and then, even fancied herself as having yielded—a thought which was immediately rejected and replaced by feelings of reproach and disgust. Last, but not least, she actually missed the love-making, which she had enjoyed for months prior to the attempted assault. As she could not unburden herself to anyone, she tried very hard to forget everything, and finally seemingly succeeded. But a few weeks later she began to show the symptoms which finally developed into the pathogenic picture which was diagnosed as epilepsy or hystero-epilepsy. These symptoms were the symbolization, or, if you will, a dramatization of the conflict between her primitive self and her ethical self, between what Freud now calls the *Id* and the *Ego*.

To make ourselves more explicit, it will be necessary to say something about the elements of the psychic apparatus. According to Freud's formulation the child brings into the world an unorganized chaotic mentality called the *Id*, the sole aim of which is the gratification of all needs, the alleviation of hunger, self-preservation, and love, the preservation of the species. However, as the child grows older, that part of the id which comes in contact with the environment through the senses learns to know the inexorable reality of the outer world and becomes modified into what Freud calls the ego. This ego, possessing awareness of the environment, henceforth strives to curb the lawless id tendencies whenever they attempt to assert themselves incompatibly. The neurosis, as we see it here, was, therefore, *a conflict between the ego and the id*. The ego, aware of the forces of civilization, religion and ethics, refused to allow motor discharge to the powerful sexual impulses emanating from the lawless id, and thus blocked them from attainment of the object towards which they aimed. The ego then defended itself against these impulses by repressing them. The young lady in question seemingly forgot this whole episode. Had the repression continued unabated, she would have remained healthy. But the repressed material struggled against this fate, finally broke through as a substitutive formation on paths over which the ego had no control, and obtruded itself on the ego as symptoms. As a result of this process, the ego found itself more or less impoverished, its integrity was threatened and hurt, and hence it continued to combat the symptom in the same way as it had defended itself against the original id impulses.

This whole process constitutes the picture of the neuroses, or rather of the transference neuroses, which comprise hysteria, anxiety hysteria, and the compulsion neuroses, in contradistinction to the so-called narcistic neuroses, melancholic depressions, and to the psychoses, schizophrenia, paranoid conditions and paranoia proper, in which the underlying mechanisms are somewhat different. In a psychosis, as will be shown later, the illness results from *a conflict between the ego and the outer world,* and in the narcistic neurosis from *a conflict between the ego and the super-ego.* For just as the ego is a modified portion of the id as a result of contact with the outer world, the super-ego represents a modified part of the ego, formed through experiences absorbed from the parents, especially from the father. The super-ego is the highest mental evolution attainable by man, and consists of a precipitate of all prohibitions and inhibitions, all the rules of conduct which are impressed on the child by his parents and by parental substitutes. The feeling of *conscience* depends altogether on the development of the super-ego.[1]

From the description given here of the mechanism of the neurosis, scant as it is, one can already see the great rôle attributed by Freud to the unconscious factor of the mind. Psychoanalysis has been justly called the "psychology of depths" because it has emphasized the rôle of the unconscious mental processes. Unlike those psychologists and philosophers who use such terms as conscious, co-conscious, and sub-conscious in a very loose and confused manner, Freud conceives *consciousness* simply as an organ of perception. One is conscious or aware of those mental processes which occupy one at any given time. In contrast to this, the *unconscious* is utterly unknown and cannot be voluntarily recalled. No person can bring to light anything from his unconscious unless he is made to recall it by hypnosis, or unless it is interpreted for him by psychoanalysis. Midway between conscious and unconscious there is a *fore-conscious* or pre-conscious, which contains memories of which one is unaware, but which one can eventually recall with some effort.

This structure of a conscious fore-conscious, and an actual unconscious, is based on the attempt which Freud made to conceive the psychic apparatus as a composition of a number of forces or systems. It is a theoretical classification, which seems, however, to work well in practice. Bearing in mind these spatial divisions, we can state that whereas *the dream is the royal road to the unconscious,* most of the mechanisms discussed in the *Psychopathology of Everyday Life* belong to the fore-conscious system. This work was written after Freud became convinced that there is nothing arbitrary or accidental in psychic life, be it normal or abnormal. For the very unconscious forces which he found in the neuroses he also found in the common faulty actions of everyday life, like ordinary forgetting of familiar names, slips of the tongue, mistakes in reading or writing, which had hitherto been considered accidental and unworthy of explanation. Freud shows in the *Psychopathology of Everyday Life* that a rapid reflection or a short analysis always demonstrates the disturbing influence behind such slips, and conclusively proves that the same disturbances, differing only in degree, are found in every person, and that the gap between the neurotic and the so-called normal is, therefore, very narrow.

The dream, according to Freud, represents the hidden fulfillment of an unconscious wish. But the wishes which it represents as fulfilled are the very same unconscious wishes which are repressed in neuroses. Dreaming is a normal function of the mind; it is the guardian of sleep insofar as it strives to release tensions generated by unattainable wishes—tensions which, if not removed, might keep the person from sleeping. The dream is

[1] Freud: *The Ego and the Id,* translated by Joan Riviere, Hogarth Press, London.

not always successful in its efforts; sometimes it oversteps the limits of propriety; it goes too far; and then the dreamer is awakened by the super-ego.

Without going further into the psychology of the dream, enough has been said to show that these twin discoveries—that non-conscious psychic processes are active in every normal person, expressing themselves in inhibitions and other modifications of intentional acts, and that the dreams of mentally healthy persons are not differently constructed from neurotic or psychotic symptoms—gave rise not only to a New Psychology, but to fruitful investigations in many other fields of human knowledge. The ability to interpret the dreams of today made it possible also to interpret the dreams of yesterday. Freudian literature, therefore, abounds in studies throwing new light on mythology, folklore, fairy tales, and ethnology; and psychoanalysis has become as important to the non-medical sciences as to the therapy of the neuroses.

Returning now to the case of the virtuous young lady, we can understand better that her attacks should prove on analysis to be a detailed reproduction of the coitus which her lover had tried to force upon her. Employing the same distortions one finds in dreams, the patient reënacted everything that had happened at the last rendezvous with her lover. In fact, she went further; in her attacks she actually attained, or better, completed, what had been omitted in reality; she actually simulated coitus in all its physical manifestations. Despite distortion, the attack thus served as an unconscious compensation for the traumatic event. In the attack, the patient possessed her lost lover by playing both the masculine and the feminine rôle. Consciously, however, she knew nothing about it, and objected most vehemently when the meaning of her symptoms was made known to her. The treatment followed the same paths as the analysis of a dream. That the numerous implications of such a case are as important to psychology, sociology and pedagogy, as to mental medicine, is quite obvious.

I have always found it hard to understand why Freud's views on sex roused so much opposition. Freud did not enter that realm voluntarily, but was forced by a natural course of events into taking account of the sexual factor in neuroses. Following the discovery of the psychogenesis of hysterical symptoms, first through Breuer's cathartic method and later through the technique of "free association," Freud was led, step by step, to discover and explore the realm of *infantile sexuality*. This discovery was based entirely on empiric material. In probing for the origin of hysterical symptoms, in tracing them back as far as possible, even into childhood, Freud found physical and psychical activities of a definitely sexual nature in the earliest ages of childhood. The necessary conclusion was that the traumas underlying the symptoms were *invariably* of a sexual nature, since all his cases produced similar findings. Finally, therefore, he concluded that sexual activities in childhood could not be considered abnormal, but were on the contrary normal phenomena of the sexual instinct.

In following up these discoveries it was natural that he should also investigate the rôle of sexuality in the extensive syndrome of neurasthenia. To his surprise Freud found that *all* his so-called neurasthenics exhibited some sexual abuses such as *coitus interruptus, frustrated excitement, sexual abstinence, excessive masturbation,* etc. In the course of these investigations he was able to bring order into the field of neurasthenia—that "garbage can of medicine," as Forel aptly called it—by separating from others those cases which were mainly characterized by anxiety.[1] The results he embodied in his classic paper, *On the Right to Separate from Neurasthenia a Definite Symptom-Complex as "Anxiety Neurosis,"* [2] in which he called attention for the first time to the relation between anxiety and sex. The pursuit of studies in this direction [3] brought him at length to the conviction that all neuroses represent a general disturbance of the sexual functions; that the *actual neuroses* (neurasthenia and anxiety neuroses) result from a direct chemical or toxic disturbance, while the *psychoneuroses* (hysteria and compulsion neuroses) represent the psychic expression of these disturbances. This conclusion, based at first on explorations in the sexual life of adults, but reënforced and confirmed since 1908 through analyses of children, was finally compressed into the famous dictum that *"In a normal sex life no neurosis is possible."*

Freud was not the first to discover sexual difficulties in man. One need only think of literature throughout the ages to realize that there was abundant material on the subject long before the appearance of *Three Contributions to the Theory of Sex.* Freud's special merit lies in the fact that before him sex had been treated as an isolated phenomenon, or as (more or less) an abnormality, whereas he paid it the respect of considering it as a component of the normal personality. In the words of Dr. James J. Putnam, former professor of neurology at Harvard University, "Freud has made considerable addition to this stock of knowledge, but he has done also something of greater consequence than this. He has worked out, with incredible penetration, the part which the instinct plays in every phase of human life and in the development of human character, and has been able to establish on a firm footing the remarkable thesis that psychoneurotic illnesses never occur with a perfectly normal sexual life."

[1] Brill: *Diagnostic Errors in Neurasthenia;* Medical Review of Reviews, March, 1930.
[2] *Selected Papers on Hysteria and Other Psychoneuroses;* translated by Brill, Monograph Series.
[3] Freud: *Hemmung, Symptom und Angst; Gesammelte Schriften;* Int. Psychoanalytic Verlag. (*The Problem of Anxiety,* translated by H. A. Bunker, W. W. Norton, N. Y.)

Dr. Putnam wrote those words in his introduction to my first translation (1910) of Freud's three essays on sex, and I can think of no finer estimate of Freud's contribution to sexology.

In his study of sex, Freud kept steadily in mind the total human personality. His formulation of infantile sexuality has opened new fields of interest in the realm of child study and education which already are yielding good results. Another concept which has been enormously helpful to physicians and educators is Freud's *libido* theory. In psychoanalysis libido signifies that quantitatively changeable and not at present measurable energy of the sexual instinct which is usually directed to an outside object. It comprises all those impulses which deal with love in the broad sense. Its main component is sexual love; and sexual union is its aim; but it also includes self-love, love for parents and children, friendship, attachments to concrete objects, and even devotion to abstract ideas.

For those who are unacquainted with Freud's theories of the neuroses, it will not be amiss to add a few remarks on the paths taken by the libido in neurotic states. The homestead of the libido is the ego; in the child the whole libido is centered in the ego, and we designate it as *ego libido*. The child may be said to be purely egoistic at first; but as he grows older and reaches the narcistic stage of development, we speak of *narcistic libido*, because the former ego libido has now become erotically tinged. Still later, when the child has successfully passed through the early phases of development and can transfer his libido to objects outside himself, that is, when he is genitally pubescent, we speak of *object libido*. Libido thus can be directed to outside objects or can be withdrawn back to the ego. A great many normal and pathological states depend on the resulting interchanges between these two forces. The transference neuroses, hysteria and compulsion neuroses, are determined by some disturbance in the give-and-take of object libido, and hence are curable by psychoanalytic therapy, whereas the narcistic neuroses, or the psychoses which are mainly controlled by narcistic libido, can be studied and helped, but cannot as yet be cured by analysis. The psychotic is, as a rule, inaccessible to this treatment because he is unable to transfer sufficient libido to the analyst. The psychotic is either too suspicious or too interested in his own inner world to pay any attention to the physician.

But leaving this problem to the psychoanalytic therapist, one must agree with Freud that by broadening the term sex into love or libido, much is gained for the understanding of the sexual activity of the normal person, of the child, and of the pervert. As will be shown later, the activities of all three spring from the same source, but the manifestations of each depend on the accidental factors to which they have been subjected by their early environments. Moreover, the libido concept loosens sexuality from its close connection with the genitals and establishes it as a more comprehensive physical function, which strives for pleasure in general, and only secondarily enters into the service of propagation. It also adds to the sexual sphere those affectionate and friendly feelings to which we ordinarily apply the term love. To illustrate the application of the libido concept clinically, let us take the case of a nervous child, keeping in mind Freud's dictum that no neurosis is possible in a wholly normal sexual life —a teaching which has aroused more resistances against psychoanalysis than any other utterance of Freud.

An apparently normal girl of about four became very nervous, refused most of her food, had frequent crying spells and tantrums, with consequent loss of weight, malaise, and insomnia, so that her condition became quite alarming. After the ordinary medical measures had been found of no avail, I was consulted. The case was so simple that I could not understand why no one had thought of the cure before I came on the scene. The child had begun to show the symptoms enumerated above, about two months after her mother was separated from her, and she was cured soon after her mother returned to her. I cannot go into the many details of this interesting case, but one can readily see that it differed materially from the case of the young woman mentioned earlier. There we dealt with a disturbance of adult sexuality, here with an emotional disturbance based on a deprivation of mother love in a very sensitive or neurotic child. Nevertheless, it was a disturbance in the child's love life. For infantile sexuality consists of a gratification of partial impulses which are widely disseminated and not yet subservient to the primacy of the genitals. Here it was really a disturbance in the child's distribution of libido. When the mother was forced to leave her home, the libido which the child ordinarily transferred to the mother became detached and remained, as it were, floating in the air. She was unable to establish any new transference with the mother-substitutes which were offered to her, and was cured as soon as her love object was restored. In our hysterical young woman the situation was the same as far as the disposition of her libido was concerned. Here, too, there was a floating libido, detached from the lost love object, but it was *object libido* in the adult sense, in which the genitals participated. In the child genitality played no part because she was still depending on disseminated partial impulses and components, in which the mother played the leading part. We shall later hear that the child's relation to the mother is *anaclitic*.[1] Nevertheless, we feel justified in saying that in both cases there was a disturbance in the sexual life of the patient; in the child it was in the *infantile*, in the young woman it was in the *adult* sexual life.

The disseminated sexual activity of the child resembles in many ways

[1] Cf. *Three Contributions to the Theory of Sex.*

that of adult perverts, in that the latter, like children, can obtain sexual gratification from partial impulses apart from the genitals. The difference between them, however, is very marked. The child can obtain pleasure from the impulses of looking, touching, exhibitionism, etc., because these impulses have not yet undergone the normal evolution of partial repression, sublimation, and then subjection to the primacy of the genitals. In the pervert some partial impulses, so to say, withdraw from the primacy of the genitals and obtain pleasure independently as in the earliest period of the development of the libido. The *sadist*, the *masochist*, the *voyeur*, the *toucheur*, the *exhibitionist*, etc., gets his sexual pleasure from aggression, passivity, showing off, looking, or touching, with or without any direct genital participation.

The most frequent perversion, homosexuality, which is usually designated as an *inversion*, is very widespread in all strata of society. It has been estimated that from 1% to 3% of the male population suffers from this perversion. The prevailing idea that all perverts are mental degenerates is not borne out by investigation. Nor is it true, as some claim, that most homosexuals are intellectual giants.[1]

Concerning the relation of perversions to the neuroses, Freud claims that *the neurotic symptom is the negative of the perversion*. For reasons that the reader will find in the body of this volume, some people, instead of resorting to perverse looking, etc., suffer instead from neurotic disturbances of their eyesight. I have in mind a patient who was treated by numerous ophthalmologists for years. He complained of pains and blurred vision which could only temporarily be alleviated through medication or changing his eyeglasses. When he was analyzed, it was found that for many years he had alternated between scopophilia, which got him in conflict with the law on two occasions, and neurotic eye symptoms. During the summer months, when he endeavored to look through a telescope at bathing resorts, hoping to see some naked women, his eyesight was excellent, but as soon as this activity had to cease, his eyes began to disturb him. For over nine years this man struggled with a perversion for looking; he was a *voyeur* with conflicts which alternately afforded him perverse pleasure and made him suffer from neurotic symptoms, which were the negative of the perversion. In the negative periods, instead of experiencing pleasure, he suffered displeasure or pain. It is interesting to note that when this man was cured, he changed his former occupation and became a dealer in optical instruments. And through his new vocation he was able to *sublimate* the tendency for perverse looking. For *sublimation*, another term coined by Freud, is a process of deflecting libido or sexual-

---

[1] Those interested are referred to my paper, *Homoerotism and Paranoia*, American Journal of Psychiatry, March, 1934.

motive activity from human objects to new objects of a non-sexual, socially valuable nature.

Sublimation, too, gives justification for broadening the concept of sex; for investigation of cases of the type mentioned conclusively show that most of our so-called feelings of tenderness and affection, which color so many of our activities and relations in life, originally form part of pure sexuality, and are later inhibited and deflected to higher aims. Thus, I have in mind a number of benevolent people who contributed much of their time and money to the protection and conservation of animals, who were extremely aggressive in childhood and ruthless Nimrods as adults. Their accentuated aggression originally formed a part of their childhood sexuality; then, as a result of training, it was first inhibited and directed to animals, and later altogether repressed and changed into sympathy. Now and then, we encounter cases in which repression and sublimation do not follow each other in regular succession, owing to some weakness or *fixation* which obstructs the process of development. This may lead to paradoxical situations. For example, a man, who was notorious as a great lover of animals, suffered while riding his favorite pony from sudden attacks during which he beat the animal mercilessly until he was exhausted, and then felt extreme remorse and pity for the beast. He would then dismount, pat the horse, appeasing him with lumps of sugar, and walk him home—sometimes a distance of three or four miles. We cannot here go into any analysis of this interesting case; all we can say is that the horse represented a mother symbol, and that the attacks, in which cruelty alternated with compassion, represented the ambivalent feeling of love and hatred which the patient unconsciously felt for his mother.

This patient was entirely changed by analysis, and although he has not given up his interest in animals and still contributes much to their comfort, he is no longer known to the neighborhood boys as "the man who pays a dollar for a sick cat or sick dog." Psychoanalytic literature is rich in clinical material which demonstrates the great benefits accrued from Freud's amplification of the sex concept. It not only gives us an understanding of the broad ramifications of sexual energy hitherto undreamed of, but it has also furnished us with an instrument for treatment and adjustment of many unfortunates who are no more responsible for their perversions than is the victim of infantile paralysis for his malady.

In his effort to understand the mechanism of the expressions observable in those erroneous actions illustrated in the *Psychopathology of Everyday Life*, as well as the distortions in dreams, Freud discerned a remarkable resemblance between these distortions and those found in wit. The following slip of the tongue shows that a slight substitution of one letter not only uncovers the real truth, but also provokes mirth. It was related to

me many years ago by one of my patients. She was present at an evening
dance of a wealthy, but not too generous, host, which continued until about
midnight, when everybody expected a more or less substantial supper.
Instead, just sandwiches and lemonade were served. Theodore Roosevelt
was then running for President for the second time, under the slogan,
"He gave us a square deal." While they were disappointedly consuming
this modest repast, the guests were discussing the coming election with
the host, and one of them remarked, "There is one fine thing about
Teddy; he always gives you *a square meal.*"

This *lapsus linguae* not only disclosed unwittingly what the speaker
thought of the supper, discharging his hidden disappointment, but it also
provoked an outburst of laughter among the guests, for they, through
identification with the speaker, found outlet for their own disappointment. But unlike the speaker and the host, who were embarrassed by the
mistake, the others experienced a sudden relaxation of the tension generated by disappointment and resentment, which expressed itself in laughter. This slight distortion changed the whole atmosphere of the party.
Instead of resentful tension, the majority of the guests now felt relaxed
and pleased. There is no doubt that there is a definite connection between
faulty actions, dreams and wit. In all of them, the unconscious underlying thoughts are brought to consciousness in some sort of disguise, as if
to say, "The truth cannot always be told openly, but somehow it does
come out." Other authors have made valuable contributions to the subject of wit; yet most of them fail to grasp its basic function as emotional discharge. I am tempted to speak here of certain criticisms of
Freud's theories of wit, made by persons who have written on the subject
since my translation of his *Wit and Its Relation to the Unconscious* appeared in 1916; but, after rereading these superficial statements, I am
content to advise the authors thereof to *read* Freud's works.

Freud's interest in wit was a logical consequence of his free association technique. Once he became convinced that nothing must be ignored
—that whatever the patient expressed, be it in mimicry or in sounds,
formed part of an effort to release something indirectly because circumstances prevented direct expression—once this fact dawned upon him, it
was simply a question of classifying the various forms of distortion and
showing in what function of the psychic apparatus they were manifested.
The mechanisms of *condensation, displacement, substitution, illogical
thinking, absurdity, indirect expressions, elisions,* and *representation
through the opposite,* are all present in everyday conversation, but such
conventional inaccuracies glide by without any evident impediments.
When the thought in question meets with inner resistances, however, a
lapse of some kind occurs, which the speaker recognizes and at once excuses by some such expression as "I mean   . ." or "Oh, I made a mis-

take." The average person readily accepts such excuses, not realizing that by the slip of the tongue the speaker has unconsciously betrayed his resistance to something in the present situation. The disguises seen in the simple lapses of everyday life are even more evident in dreams because *censorship* is more or less abolished during sleep; but fundamentally they are the same. In wit these mental disguises are especially evident, but here they are utilized to produce pleasure. They, too, are products of the unconscious, and show that no matter how much restriction civilization imposes on the individual, he nevertheless finds some way to circumvent it. Wit is the best safety valve modern man has evolved; the more civilization, the more repression, the more need there is for wit. Only relatively civilized people have a sense of humor. The child and the true primitive show no such mechanisms. The child like the savage is still natural and frank. When the child begins to dream, which shows that repressive forces are already at work, he also shows the beginnings of a sense of humor.

The most pronounced psychopathological expressions which point to a deep-seated disturbance are *hallucinations* and *delusions*, which occur in adult psychotics and show a somewhat different kind of disguise. The hallucination as a verbal expression is neither witty nor in any other way distorted. The only thing peculiar about it is that the patient hears, sees, or feels something which is not perceived by anyone else. To be sure, the patient's statements do not concur with the objective facts; yet he is not lying; subjectively speaking, he actually perceives everything he says he does. But we know from Freud that hallucinations represent outward projections of inner feelings. Thus, a woman who has seemingly been living quite contentedly with her husband for five years, hears people say that she is a "bad woman," that her husband is divorcing her, and that she has had illicit relations with a well known movie star. At the same time she complains of peculiar feelings like pin-pricks and electricity in certain parts of her body. These statements could be true, but they are not. We, therefore, call them hallucinatory.

And indeed, the whole picture of the disease in this case showed that the woman suffered from hallucinations of hearing, sight, and sensation. Their meaning became plain when her mother informed me that her son-in-law had been impotent all these years, but that her daughter nevertheless loved him and would not consider leaving him. The hallucinations depicted the wish to be divorced and be married to a real man as a recompense for her drab existence. The annoyance and displeasure caused by "all that talk" and by the peculiar prickling sensations, represented the pangs of conscience, or the feeling of guilt which accompanied her erotic phantasies. The distortion in this whole picture consisted of a fusion of feelings and ideas which had played a part in the conflict in the mind of this sensitive patient. She could not decide one way or the other, so she tore herself entirely away from reality and behaved, as we say, *dereistically*.[1] She abandoned all logic and objectified her phantasies in disguised fashion.

However, no human being who has been brought up under the system of logic and morality which prevails in our civilization can disengage himself entirely from his or her past. The words and thoughts of hallucinations are not as distorted as the verbal expressions in wit or in slips of all kinds, but the fundamental disturbance is the same. The person who makes a mistake or laughs at a joke, or expresses a wish in a dream is still in contact with reality. No matter how bizarre the dream appears, one knows that it is only a dream; an injury inflicted by a joke is usually excused by "Can't you take a joke?"—and lapses are immediately recognized as mistakes by both the speaker and the hearer. Hallucinations and delusions are the only psychopathological expressions which are always taken seriously by the patient and sometimes even by others, because they represent an absolute *schizoidism* or splitting of the psychic apparatus. Unlike wit, dreams, and lapses, which are products of difficulties encountered in the effort to stick to reality at all cost, the hallucination represents an escape from reality.

The hallucinating patient would like to have nothing to do with reality; yet, as a matter of fact, this is hardly possible. Investigation shows that the patient can do this only imperfectly. In the case mentioned above, the deep struggle between the id tendencies and the forces of the ego were readily discernible. In the beginning of the psychosis she was very irritable and agitated; her hallucinations were very active and vivid, and in her effort to harmonize them with her past life, she frequently showed acute outbursts of violence. After a few months she became calmer; she paid little attention to anything; she just smiled and sometimes talked to herself inaudibly. When an effort was made to arouse her interest, she usually reacted to it with some irritation. The patient evidently refused to be affected by impressions from the outer world, and also ignored or depreciated everything that she remembered from her past, namely, her inner world.

As time went on, the patient developed the diagnostic characteristic of schizophrenia, namely, a marked apathy. She became indifferent to everything around her. Her relatives at first looked upon this behavior as an improvement in her general condition; but as a matter of fact, this was really a form of adjustment to the disease. What was actually happening was that the ego was gradually constructing for itself a new world in terms of the patient's infantile wish tendencies, in much the same way as kindred wishes are expressed in dreams, the turning away from reality being conditioned by the state of sleep.

[1] *De* (away from) *reor—ratio* (reason)—hence, *away from reason; unrealistically.*

It is now over six years since the first symptoms made their appearance. The patient has to be kept in a sanatorium because she is absolutely unable to care for herself. For the last few years she has given little trouble to her environment. She is usually calm and manageable, but behaves in every way like a little child. She talks in an embellished childish way, plays with toys, laughs and cries like a little girl of three or four years. There is no doubt that she is now living through her insuperable infantile wishes, to which she regressed because life did not grant her what her id tendencies craved. In terms of the psychic apparatus, it can be said that at first the ego strove to curb the id tendencies; the patient's hallucinations plainly demonstrated this; but as time went on, the ego weakened and was carried away from reality, from the outer world, by the id. In discussing the various forces of the mental apparatus, Freud compares the ego and the id to a rider and his horse. As a rule, the rider can curb the horse and force it to follow his will, but it sometimes happens that the horse runs away with the rider. To repeat what we said above, *the psychosis* in this case *represented a conflict between the ego and the outer world.*

It is quite clear that the distortions manifested in the psychoses are shown by the whole behavior of the person rather than through verbal expressions. Verbal distortions as seen in lapses, errors, blunders in speech and action, are immediate responses to a struggle between the ego and the id. No matter how anxious we are to hide our true nature in adjusting ourselves to the repressive forces of civilization, repression sometimes fails and our real desires come to the surface. The dream is a hidden fulfillment of a repressed wish, or a direct attempt to obtain in phantasy what is denied us in reality. Wit is a direct effort to make use of distortions in order to obtain pleasure from otherwise forbidden sources. Both lapses and dreams are momentary illusions which render a very quick and very brief service to the organism. Wit, on the other hand, is a conscious mechanism for the production of pleasure, the highest or latest development of civilization in this direction. We like to tell jokes and listen to them because for the moment we not only forget inexorable reality, but also obtain pleasure at the expense of our hardships.

But in all these phenomena we remain in touch with reality; the mistake, the dream and the joke amply demonstrate this. The psychosis exhibits alone no compromise with reality, turns its back on reality, as it were. Yet, even in a psychosis, symptoms show that there is a constant struggle between fancy and reality. A chronic schizophrenic may remain in a hospital for years in a state of indifference, but now and then he may suddenly act like a rational being. Sometimes a severe shock, such as an accident or illness which threatens his self-preservative instinct, brings the schizophrenic back to reality for a time. The latest form of

therapy for schizophrenics is based on this very idea. I am referring to
the insulin or, as it is called, the shock therapy, because the patient receives such a shock through the hypoglycemia that for a time at least he
gives up his phantasy world.[1] But it matters little whether hypoglycemia
cures or only produces a transient change; the fact that schizophrenics
occasionally return to normality spontaneously and then relapse, and the
fact that an accidental or experimental shock can drive them back to
reality at least for a time, clearly shows that the psychotic, too, is not
altogether detached from reality.

From what has been said thus far, Freud's great contribution to the
understanding of the psychoses can be fully realized; nevertheless, it
seems worthwhile to dwell on this phase of psychiatry a bit longer. To
show the influence of psychoanalysis on psychiatry I can do no better than
enumerate my own experiences in this field. For it is during the period of
my own psychiatric activity that this science has made the greatest progress, especially in this country.

When I entered the New York State Hospital service in 1903, psychiatry was on the threshold of a new epoch. Dr. Adolf Meyer had recently become director of what is now the New York Psychiatric Institute, and it was through his indomitable labor and perseverance that the
old New York insane asylums were eventually transformed into mental
hospitals. I was fortunate in being one among Dr. Meyer's first group of
students at the Psychiatric Institute, where he gave us a thorough ground-
ing in neuropathology and modern psychiatry in the form of lectures,
clinics, and abstracts of the teachings of prominent psychiatrists of the
German School.

After two years of neuropathology I turned to clinical psychiatry, and
I am presumptuous enough to feel that I made good use of the enormous
material at my disposal. I had charge of the so-called acute reception service at the Central Islip State Hospital, where I received and examined all
the new admissions from Manhattan and The Bronx. And yet, although I
enjoyed my work for a year or two, I then began to lose interest. Looking
back now, I can see that this was not due to a flagging of effort on my
part, but to the nature of the work itself. I followed the methods I had
learned from Dr. Meyer and from the original works of Kraepelin, Ziehen,
Wernicke, and other eminent psychiatrists. Upon receiving a patient, I
gave him the usual routine examination, the stenographic records of

[1] Notwithstanding many opinions to the contrary, that is all we can say at present
about this promising therapy. Professor Eugen Bleuler, the greatest authority on
schizophrenia, states in his last (6th) German edition of *The Textbook of Psychiatry:*
"This method, which has aroused great interest, is still in the experimental stage.
But, even now, it seems that it is possible thereby to calm and socialize many patients. But it has often failed, and it is a question whether it really exerts a curative
effect on the fundamental symptoms of the disease "

which covered on an average from 10 to 16 typewritten pages; the patient was thus classified and diagnosed. Once this was accomplished his future psychic condition depended mostly on himself, for there was nothing specific that we could do for him. We classified him symptomatically; we knew that if he was a manic-depressive, he would recover from the attack, and if he was a schizophrenic, he might improve to some degree or he might not. Everything was quite hopeless, and hence uninteresting.

It was at that time that my interest in psychotherapy awoke. Hypnotism was still in vogue, though only a few people practiced it here. I was much impressed by the works of Charcot, Forel, Loewenfeld, and others, and by our own Morton Prince and Boris Sidis, who both used hypnotism in treatment and experimentation and wrote on psychopathology. I began to employ hypnotism and suggestion, and obtained encouraging enough results. In 1906, Drs. Smith Ely Jelliffe and William A. White published an English translation of Dr. Dubois' *The Psychic Treatment of Mental Disorders,* which I read with alacrity and benefit; but the results of my psychotherapeutic procedures left much to be desired.

In my quest for new knowledge I took a two months' vacation in 1905, visiting some of the French, Austrian, and German clinics; and in the spring of 1907 I obtained a leave of absence from the hospital and went to Paris, where I imagined I could obtain all the psychotherapeutic knowledge that I wished as a preparation for private practice. I expected perhaps too much from Paris. I soon found that psychiatrically the French hospitals were below our standards in equipment and everything else. After looking around, I decided to work with Pierre Marie and entered his service in the Hospice de Bicêtre. He assigned me to study and then confer with him on a case of acromegaly. This was interesting enough, but this kind of work did not appeal to me. I had come to Paris to learn how to treat the borderline cases of mental disease, the psychoneuroses, and what I saw there was quite disappointing. It was then that the same man who had originally introduced me to the New York State Hospitals advised me to go to the Clinic of Psychiatry at Zurich, the Director of which was Professor Eugen Bleuler. In giving this advice to me, Dr. Frederick Peterson assured me that I would find the work there very interesting. He casually mentioned that he had spent a few months there and that they were applying Freud's theories in their work with the patients. Dr. Peterson was a great admirer of Freud at that time, and he was certainly right in prophesying that I would find the work at the Burghölzli Clinic interesting.

I was fortunate enough to arrive there at the beginning of a new era in psychiatry shortly after Professor Bleuler had recognized the value of Freud's theories and urged his assistants to learn and test them in the hospital. Professor Bleuler was the first orthodox psychiatrist to open his clinic to psychoanalysis. The first staff meeting at the hospital was an inspiring experience and it decided me to remain. The physicians who were there at the time have all played a great part in the history of the psychoanalytic movement. Besides Jung, who was the first assistant, there were also Riklin, Abraham and Meier. All of them worked for hours daily with the association technique which was especially designed to test Freud's theories experimentally. Within a month or so of my arrival Dr. Karl Abraham resigned to go into private practice in Berlin, and I was very happy when Professor Bleuler appointed me as his third assistant in the hospital to fill the vacancy. It would be impossible to describe now how I felt when I entered the ranks of this enthusiastic group. I repeat what I have often stated in the past—namely, that no such group of psychiatric workers ever existed before or since. Under the benevolent but penetrating eye of our "Herr Direktor" all of us worked zealously and assiduously to produce what the late Dr. George H. Kirby, former director of the New York Psychiatric Institute, later designated as "Interpretative Psychiatry."

Psychiatry as I had known it before had been barren of interest and hopeless in outlook despite my great interest in mental processes, an interest which I seemed to have displayed throughout my college and university years. To be sure, there had been plenty to do in the state hospital, neuropathologically and psychiatrically, but it had all come down to a few formulae, this or that form of dementia praecox, or this or that form of manic-depressive insanity, etc. In Burghölzli it was quite different: instead of diagnosing this or that form of dementia praecox, which could be done at sight after a little experience, we focussed our interest on the particular expressions of the patient. Instead of simply saying that the patient had hallucinations of hearing, we wished to know why he heard these particular voices, for following Freud, we invariably found that these particular hallucinations could be perceived only by this particular patient. They told the struggles of his wrecked individual mental life.

Jung was at that time the most ardent Freudian. Had I been better acquainted with the Freudian mechanisms, I could have foretold what was to happen a few years later. But now Jung brooked no disagreement with Freud's views; impulsive and bright, he refused to see the other side. Anyone who dared doubt what was certainly then new and revolutionary immediately aroused his anger. Nevertheless, psychoanalysis owes him much, his enthusiasm and brilliance soon placed him at the forefront of the battle line. He was my first, and, I might say, my most vehement teacher. I read the *Traumdeutung* under his guidance. The first analysis of one of my dreams was done by Jung and was extremely impressive. I still have a transcript of the dream with the analysis as we did it one morning in the laboratory after we had finished an association experiment with the galvanometer.

Jung's *Psychology of Dementia Praecox* [1] had appeared a few months before and I decided to put it into English. This book established Jung as the pioneer psychoanalyst in psychiatry. To be sure, Professor Bleuler was the man who had started everything and supervised and guided us all, but the appearance of Jung's book started the younger psychiatrists thinking and the older ones scolding.

In the hospital the spirit of Freud hovered over everything. Our conversation at meals was frequently punctuated with the word "complex," the special meaning of which was created at that time. No one could make a slip of any kind without immediately being called on to evoke free associations to explain it. It did not matter that women were present —wives and female voluntary internes—who might have curbed the frankness usually produced by free associations. The women were just as keen to discover the concealed mechanisms as their husbands. There was also a Psychoanalytic Circle, which met every month. Some of those who attended were far from agreeing with our views; but despite Jung's occasional impulsive intolerance, the meetings were very fruitful and successful in disseminating Freud's theories.

Meanwhile, I had been in active correspondence with Professor Freud, and when we met in the beginning of 1908, we both felt that we knew each other quite well. To make a long story, stretching over thirty years, short, I am happy to say that this friendship has continued ever since and has been the greatest experience of my life. It was during our first meeting that we agreed on the sequence in which I was to translate his works into English. I continued as his sole English•translator until after the World War, when I voluntarily gave up the task. All the works that I undertook in 1908 to translate are included in the present volume; but in addition, not included here, I translated some of his *Selected Papers on Hysteria and Psychoneuroses, Reflections on War and Death, Leonardo da Vinci, Psychoanalysis: Exploring the Hidden Recesses of the Mind* (which appeared in the Encyclopaedia Britannica), and the *Studies in Hysteria* which Freud had first published with Breuer. It was also during my first visit to Freud that I attended the first meeting of the Vienna Psychoanalytic Society. There I made the acquaintance of Freud's first disciples, some of whom, like the late Dr. Adler and Dr. Stekel, later chose to follow different paths. The reader will find a full account of these secessionists in Freud's own history of the psychoanalytic movement. It was also at that meeting that I met Dr. Fritz Wittels who came here in 1928 at the

[1] Translated by A. A. Brill, Monograph Series, Nervous and Mental Disease Publishing Co.

invitation of the New School for Social Research and has been practicing psychoanalysis in New York City ever since, and in Burghölzli I learned to know Dr. Herman Nunberg, then a medical student, who was invited to start a group in Philadelphia and has been practicing analysis in New York City for about six years.

I returned to New York in the spring of 1908 with my translation of Jung's book complete and some analytic material which I had collected during my sojourn in Burghölzli. I was full of enthusiasm about the prospects of psychoanalysis in the mental sciences, and I started at once to inform and convince others of the value of this new science. It was no easy task. At first I was listened to with interest; then opposition arose and became increasingly strong as time went on. During the first few years I was the only psychiatrist employing psychoanalysis in the United States, though in Toronto I had an ardent collaborator and friend in Dr. Ernest Jones of London. He and I had first met when he was visiting the Clinic of Psychiatry at Zurich. Being both of us enthusiastic students of psychoanalysis, we had soon become friends. Dr. Jones had joined the psychiatric department of the University of Toronto at the same time that I was beginning my work at the Vanderbilt Clinic at Columbia University, and we have worked together ever since. After a few years in Toronto, Dr. Jones returned to London, and has ever since been an active contributor to psychoanalytic thought and a most helpful leader of the movement.

In 1909 Professor Stanley Hall, President of Clark University, invited Professor Freud and Jung to attend the celebration of the 20th anniversary of Clark University. A full account of this most important event is given by Freud elsewhere in this volume; but I should like to mention a few facts that in my opinion had a decisive influence upon the course of psychoanalysis in this country. First, the academic psychologists heard for the first time the master himself, and whether they agreed with him or not, they were impressed by him. Second, the five lectures [1] which Freud delivered at this conference were translated by a Fellow in Psychology at Clark University, no less a person than Harry W. Chase, the present Chancellor of New York University. Third, that conference marked the beginning of a friendship between Freud and James J. Putnam, then professor of neurology at Harvard, which lasted until Dr. Putnam died. Up to the time of this meeting Dr. Putnam had been rather critical of analysis, but he later changed into a great admirer of Freud and was very active on behalf of psychoanalysis. Although Freud was not himself satisfied with his visit here, the impressions he made were very helpful to those of us who lived here. Both his and Jung's lectures [2] were well re-

---

[1] *The Origin and Development of Psychoanalysis,* American Journal of Psychology, Vol. XXI, p. 181–218.
[2] *The Association Method,* translated by A. A. Brill, American Journal of Psychology, Vol. XXI.

ceiveɑ ɒy tne conference, which was maınly composed of psychologists.

Jung later gave his impression of "America" before the Second Psychoanalytic Congress at Nürnberg (March 30–31, 1910), which I believe is of interest in the light of his later attitude toward Freud's views on sex. In his *auto-referat* he states: "The psychological peculiarities of the Americans evince features which are accessible to psychoanalytic investigation. These features point to energetic sexual repressions. The causes for the repression can be found in the specific American Complex, namely, in the living together with lower races, especially with Negroes. Living together with barbaric races exerts a suggestive effect on the laboriously tamed instinct of the white race and tends to. pull it down. Hence, the need for strongly developed defensive measures, which precisely show themselves in those specific features of American culture." [1]

It was only natural that I should have directed my first psychoanalytic expositions to the medical profession, and especially to psychiatrists. I have always felt that psychoanalysis as a therapy belonged to the medical profession, to psychiatry, and what I have learned during all these years has not changed my opinion. In holding this view, I am not forgetting that the principles of psychoanalysis are applicable to many non-medical sciences, that many lay analysts have made valuable contributions to analysis, and last but not least, that a psychiatrist without psychoanalytic training is not a psychoanalyst, and has no moral right to practice psychoanalysis. [2]

Soon after I began to present papers on psychoanalysis and published my first translation, a number of psychiatrists became interested and showed an eagerness for more knowledge of the subjecт. Some of them visited me regularly, and we spent hours together arguing and discussing the new views. After a number of such informal meetings, I founded the New York Psychoanalytic Society on February 11, 1911. I was naturally chosen as its first president, an office which I held on and off until 1936, when I retired to an honorary post in the Society. Looking over the list of those who were present at the first meeting and constituted the charter members, I find that some of them, like M. J. Karpas, George H. Kirby and others, have passed away; some resigned after they had assimilated as many as they could of Freud's views and could go no further; still others gradually lost their enthusiasm, but remained in the group as kindly onlookers. Only one of the original members, Dr. C. P. Oberndorf, has continued as an active, steadfast and reliable co-worker throughout all these years. As it is not my intention to give at this time a history of the psychoanalytic movement in the United States, I will merely add a

---

[1] Jahrbuch f. Psychoan. u. Psychopathol. Bd. II.
[2] It may be of interest to state that the requisites for the specialty of psychoanalysis as stipulated by the New York Psychoanalytic Institute are higher than those demanded for other medical specialties.

few facts to supplement Freud's general history, which he published in February, 1914.

Very soon after the New York Psychoanalytic Society was formed, we organized the American Psychoanalytic Association, with Dr. James J. Putnam as President and Dr. Ernest Jones as Secretary. The membership of this organization was made up of those who, living in various parts of the country, had no opportunity to belong to the New York Society. Among the charter members of the American Psychoanalytic Association one notes the following distinguished psychiatrists: Dr. Ross McC. Chapman, Dr. Isador Coriat, Dr. August Hoch, Dr. Richard H. Hutchings, Dr. Smith Ely Jelliffe, Dr. Adolf Meyer, Dr. William A. White and others. Most of the members of the New York Society were also members of the American Psychoanalytic Association. This association met annually in different cities until its complexion changed in 1932, because new groups had meanwhile been formed in Baltimore-Washington, Chicago and Boston. The American Psychoanalytic Association is now made up of the membership of these American groups and no longer functions as an independent organization.

The American Psychiatric Association, which is the largest psychiatric organization in the world, has always been fair-minded and kindly disposed toward psychoanalysis; although some of the members were naturally critical, I always found there a sympathetic forum. Since 1926 I had worked hard to establish a Section on Psychoanalysis in this organization, and with the help of the late William A. White, Ross McC. Chapman, C. C. Cheney, Richard H. Hutchings, George H. Kirby, and others, the council of this association finally recommended that a Section on Psychoanalysis be formed in the American Psychiatric Association. In my inaugural address at the first official meeting of this Section, I expressed my feelings in the following words: "You have listened for well-nigh a generation to papers and discussions on the subject of psychoanalysis. You have been more than kind for these many years in offering us hospitality, dispassionate consideration of our information, and the encouragement and very great assistance of your discussions and criticisms based on clinical experience. While the outside world was in doubt of our respectability and intentions, you invited us to come to your meetings and, so to speak, display our wares. You disregarded the cant and vituperations hurled against us by our unthinking, unfair, or actually stupid detractors. When you gave criticism, it was the criticism of sincere seekers for the truth, and as such it was generous encouragement." [1] This Section has been actively functioning since 1934.

[1] Remarks read at the nineteenth annual meeting of the American Psychiatric Association, Section on Psychoanalysis, New York City, May 28–June 1, 1934. American Journal of Psychiatry, Vol. 91, March, 1935.

With the help of generous friends I succeeded in raising a fund of about $50,000 for a New York Psychoanalytic Institute, which was founded in 1931. Dr. Sandor Rado, formerly of the Berlin Institute has been its educational director ever since. A year later a similar institute was opened in Chicago under the leadership of Dr. Franz Alexander, and another in Boston, headed by Dr. Hanns Sachs. Other groups and institutes are in the process of formation on the Pacific coast by Drs. Ernest Simmel and Siegfried Bernfeld. Other European analysts, who were invited to come as teachers and have settled here, are Drs. Felix and Helene Deutsch, Karen Horney, and J. H. W. Van Ophuijsen.

These groups and institutes are devoted mainly to the training of physicians in the psychoanalytic technique; I mean Freudian psychoanalytic technique. We have nothing to do with the so-called analysts of the other schools. Besides therapeutic analysis these institutes also offer courses in psychoanalytic anthropology, sociology and in other allied disciplines. One must not imagine, however, that the progress made by psychoanalysis in this country proceeded smoothly and peacefully. One could write an interesting chapter on the adjustment of psychoanalysts to the American environment, but this will have to be reserved for future consideration. Suffice it to say that we had to overcome great, and almost insurmountable vicissitudes, but I am happy to say that psychoanalysis is here to stay.

I could continue and give you an elaborate description of Freud's works and struggles since the publication of his history of the psychoanalytic movement in 1914. Basically, nothing of importance has happened within the movement besides the defection of Otto Rank, who, like Adler and Jung, left Professor Freud after having devoted many years of valuable work to psychoanalysis. Reflecting on the works of the Freudian secessionists, I feel that none of them has contributed anything of real value to mental science since they separated themselves from the master. All of them, however, have made contributions of a special kind to the literature of psychology. The master himself has actively continued his life's work despite the bad handicap of a severe illness for over fourteen years. Reading his productions which have appeared within the last few months, one is impressed with the same fluency, alertness and brilliancy that have always characterized his works. His disciples, of whom there are many the world over, have made impressive contributions to the mental sciences, but a deep study of these productions will show nothing that is so novel as not to have been anticipated or implied by the master himself. We who follow him realize this full well, and most of us feel that this state of affairs will continue until his thoughts shall have been better assimilated and more fully developed.

That the world which at first turned its back on him has now recognized his great services to science and culture is shown by the many honors that have been showered upon him within the last few years. To mention only one of many: His eightieth birthday was an international event. It was celebrated in Vienna at the *Wiener Konzerthaus* and was attended by distinguished scientists from Vienna and abroad. The birthday oration, which was delivered by Thomas Mann, is a masterpiece which has been translated into many languages.[1]

It was not my intention to present here a complete outline of Freud's theories of the neuroses as he has developed them up to the present time. I merely strove to introduce the reader to the works contained in this volume, because they are all, as it were, by-products of his original studies and treatment of neurotic disturbances. I am fully aware that what is here presented is a very fragmentary description of the neurotic mechanisms as they are related to the works of this volume, works that are more psychological than psychopathological. I feel, however, that my presentation will suffice to show the intimate connection of neurotic and psychotic symptoms to ordinary mistakes and errors, to dreams and wit. The essays on sex show that there is no absolute gap between the sexual life of the normal person and that of the neurotic, the pervert, and the child. These relations are all correlated in Freud's *Totem and Taboo*, in which he shows the resemblance between the ceremonials of the compulsion neurotic and the taboos of savages, thus throwing new light on the origin of most of our cultural institutions. I purposely have omitted to speak of Freud's later metapsychological works, which are of special interest to the psychoanalytic therapist, but are not in any way necessary for the understanding of dreams or wit.

New York,
March, 1938.

[1] Alas! As these pages are going to the printer we have been startled by the terrible news that the Nazi holocaust has suddenly encircled Vienna and that Professor Freud and his family are virtual prisoners in the hands of civilization's greatest scourge.

ONE

PSYCHOPATHOLOGY OF
EVERYDAY LIFE

1

FORGETTING OF PROPER NAMES

DURING the year 1898, I published a short essay, *On the Psychic Mechanism of Forgetfulness*.[1] I shall now repeat its contents and take it as a starting-point for further discussion. I have there undertaken a psychologic analysis of a common case of temporary forgetfulness of proper names, and from a pregnant example of my own observation, I have reached the conclusion that this frequent and practically unimportant occurrence of a failure of a psychic function—of memory—admits an explanation which goes beyond the customary utilization of this phenomenon.

If an average psychologist should be asked to explain how it happens that we often fail to recall a name which we are sure we know, he would probably content himself with the answer that proper names are more apt to be forgotten than any other content of memory. He might give plausible reasons for this "forgetting preference" for proper names, but he would not assume any deep determinant for the process.

I was led to examine exhaustively the phenomenon of temporary forgetfulness through the observation of certain peculiarities, which, although not general, can, nevertheless, be seen clearly in some cases. In these, there is not only *forgetfulness,* but also false *recollection;* he who strives for the escaped name brings to consciousness others—substitutive names—which, although immediately recognized as false, nevertheless obtrude themselves with great tenacity. The process which should lead to the reproduction of the lost name is, as it were, displaced, and thus brings one to an incorrect substitute.

Now it is my assumption that the displacement is not left to psychic arbitrariness, but that it follows lawful and rational paths. In other words, I assume that the substitutive name (or names) stands in direct relation to the lost name, and I hope, if I succeed in demonstrating this connection, to throw light on the origin of the forgetting of names.

In the example which I selected for analysis in 1898, I vainly strove to

[1] *Monatschrift f. Psychiatrie.*

recall the name of the master who made the imposing frescoes of the "Last Judgment" in the dome of *Orvieto*. Instead of the lost name—*Signorelli*—two other names of artists—*Botticelli* and *Boltraffio*—obtruded themselves, names which my judgment immediately and definitely rejected as being incorrect. When the correct name was imparted to me by an outsider, I recognized it at once without any hesitation. The examination of the influence and association paths which caused the displacement from *Signorelli* to *Botticelli* and *Boltraffio* led to the following results:

(a) The reason for the escape of the name *Signorelli* is neither to be sought in the strangeness in itself of this name nor in the psychologic character of the connection in which it was inserted. The forgotten name was just as familiar to me as one of the substitutive names—*Botticelli*—and somewhat more familiar than the other substitute—*Boltraffio*—of the possessor of which I could hardly say more than that he belonged to the Milanese School. The connection, too, in which the forgetting of the name took place appeared to me harmless, and led to no further explanation. I journeyed by carriage with a stranger from Ragusa, Dalmatia, to a station in Herzegovina. Our conversation drifted to travelling in Italy, and I asked my companion whether he had been in Orvieto and had seen there the famous frescoes of ——.

(b) The forgetting of the name could not be explained until after I had recalled the theme discussed immediately before this conversation. This forgetting then made itself known *as a disturbance of the newly emerging theme caused by the theme preceding it*. In brief, before I asked my travelling companion if he had been in Orvieto, we had been discussing the customs of the Turks living in *Bosnia* and *Herzegovina*. I had related what I heard from a colleague who was practising medicine among them, namely, that they show full confidence in the physician and complete submission to fate. When one is compelled to inform them that there is no help for the patient, they answer: *"Sir* (Herr), what can I say? I know that if he could be saved, you would save him." In these sentences alone we can find the words and names: *Bosnia, Herzegovina,* and *Herr* (Sir), which may be inserted in an association series between *Signorelli, Botticelli* and *Boltraffio*.

(c) I assume that the stream of thoughts concerning the customs of the Turks in Bosnia, etc., was able to disturb the next thought, because I withdrew my attention from it before it came to an end. For I recalled that I wished to relate a second anecdote which was next to the first in my memory. These Turks value sexual pleasure above all else, and at sexual disturbances merge into an utter despair which strangely contrasts with their resignation at the peril of losing their lives. One of my colleague's patients once told him: "For you know, Sir (Herr), if that ceases, life no longer has any charm."

I refrained from imparting this characteristic feature because I did not wish to touch upon such a delicate theme in conversation with a stranger. But I went still further; I also deflected my attention from the continuation of the thought which might have associated itself in me with the theme "Death and Sexuality." I was at that time under the after-effects of a message which I had received a few weeks before, during a brief sojourn in *Trafoi*. A patient on whom I had spent much effort had ended his life on account of an incurable sexual disturbance. I know positively that this sad event, and everything connected with it, did not come to my conscious recollection on that trip in Herzegovina. However, the agreement between *Trafoi* and *Boltraffio* forces me to assume that this reminiscence was at that time brought into activity despite all the intentional deviation of my attention.

(d) I can no longer conceive the forgetting of the name Signorelli as an accidental occurrence. I must recognize in this process the influence of a *motive*. There were motives which actuated the interruption in the communication of my thoughts (concerning the customs of the Turks, etc.), which later influenced me to exclude from my consciousness the thoughts connected with them, and which might have led to the message concerning the incident in Trafoi—that is, I wanted to forget something, I *repressed* something. To be sure, I wished to forget something other than the name of the master of Orvieto; but this other thought brought about an associative connection between itself and this name, so that my act of volition missed the aim, and *I forgot the one against my will*, while I *intentionally* wished to forget the other. The disinclination to recall directed itself against the one content; the inability to remember appeared in another. The case would have been obviously simpler if this disinclination and the inability to remember had concerned the same content. The substitutive names no longer seem so thoroughly unjustified as they seemed before this explanation. They remind me (after the form of a compromise) as much of what I wished to forget as of what I wished to remember, and show me that my object to forget something was neither a perfect success nor a failure.

(e) The nature of the association formed between the lost name and the repressed theme (death and sexuality, etc.), containing the names of Bosnia, Herzegovina and Trafoi, is also very strange. In the scheme inserted here, which originally appeared in 1898, an attempt is made to graphically represent these associations.

The name Signorelli was thus divided into two parts. One pair of syllables (*elli*) returned unchanged in one of the substitutions, while the other had gained, through the translation of *signor* (Sir, Herr), many and diverse relations to the name contained in the repressed theme, but was lost through it in the reproduction. Its substitution was formed in a way to suggest that a displacement took place along the same associations —"Herzegovina and Bosnia"—regardless of the sense and acoustic demarcation. The names were therefore treated in this process like the written pictures of a sentence which is to be transformed into a picture-puzzle (rebus). No information was given to consciousness concerning the whole process, which, instead of the name Signorelli, was thus changed to the substitutive names. At first sight, no relation is apparent between the theme that contained the name Signorelli and the repressed one which immediately preceded it.

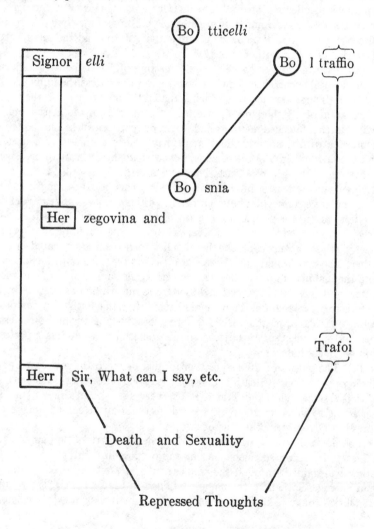

Perhaps it is not superfluous to remark that the given explanation does not contradict the conditions of memory reproduction and forgetting assumed by other psychologists, which they seek in certain relations and dispositions. Only in certain cases have we added another *motive* to the factors long recognized as causative in forgetting names, and have thus laid bare the mechanism of faulty memory. The assumed dispositions are indispensable also in our case, in order to make it possible for the repressed element to associatively gain control over the desired name and take it along into the repression. Perhaps this would not have occurred in another name having more favorable conditions of reproduction. For it is quite probable that a suppressed element continually strives to assert itself in some other way, but attains this success only where it meets with suitable conditions. At other times, the suppression succeeds without disturbance of function, or, as we may justly say, without symptoms.

When we recapitulate the conditions for forgetting a name with faulty recollection we find: (1) a certain disposition to forget the name; (2) a process of suppression which has taken place shortly before; and (3) the possibility of establishing an *outer* association between the concerned name and the element previously suppressed. The last condition will probably not have to be much overrated, for the slightest claim on the association is apt in most cases to bring it about. But it is a different and farther-reaching question whether such outer association can really furnish the proper condition to enable the suppressed element to disturb the reproduction of the desired name, or whether after all a more intimate connection between the two themes is not necessarily required. On superficial consideration, one may be willing to reject the latter requirement and consider the temporal meeting in perfectly dissimilar contents as sufficient. But on more thorough examination, one finds more and more frequently that the two elements (the repressed and the new one) connected by an outer association, possess besides a connection in content, and this can also be demonstrated in the example, *Signorelli.*

The value of the understanding gained through the analysis of the example *Signorelli* naturally depends on whether we must explain this case as a typical or as an isolated process. I must now maintain that the forgetting of a name associated with faulty recollection not uncommonly follows the same process as was demonstrated in the case of *Signorelli.* Almost every time that I observed this phenomenon in myself, I was able to explain it in the manner indicated above as being motivated by repression.

I must mention still another viewpoint in favor of the typical nature of our analysis. I believe that one is not justified in separating the cases of name-forgetting with faulty recollection from those in which incorrect substitutive names have not obtruded themselves. These substitutive names occur spontaneously in a number of cases; in other cases, where they do not come spontaneously, they can be brought to the surface by concentration of attention, and they then show the same relation to the repressed element and the lost name as those that come spontaneously. Two factors seem to play a part in bringing to consciousness the substitutive names: first, the effort of attention, and second, an inner determinant which adheres to the psychic material. I could find the latter in the greater or lesser facility which forms the required outer associations between the two elements. A great many of the cases of name-forgetting without faulty recollection therefore belong to the cases with substitutive name formation, the mechanism of which corresponds to the one in the example *Signorelli*. But I surely shall not venture to assert that all cases of name-forgetting belong to the same group. There is no doubt that there are cases of name-forgetting that proceed in a much simpler way. We shall represent this state of affairs carefully enough if we assert that *besides the simple forgetting of proper names, there is another forgetting which is motivated by repression.*

FORGETTING OF FOREIGN WORDS

THE ordinary vocabulary of our own language seems to be protected against forgetting within the limits of normal function, but it is quite different with words from a foreign language. The tendency to forget such words extends to all parts of speech. In fact, depending on our own general state and the degree of fatigue, the first manifestation of functional disturbance evinces itself in the irregularity of our control over foreign vocabulary. In a series of cases, this forgetting follows the same mechanism as the one revealed in the example *Signorelli* As a demonstration of this, I shall report a single analysis, characterized, however, by valuable features concerning the forgetting of a word, not a noun, from a Latin quotation. Before proceeding, allow me to give a full and clear account of this little episode.

Last summer, while journeying on my vacation, I renewed the acquaintance of a young man of academic education, who, as I soon noticed, was conversant with some of my works. In our conversation we drifted— I no longer remember how—to the social position of the race to which we both belonged. He, being ambitious, bemoaned the fact that his generation, as he expressed it, was destined to become stunted, that it was prevented from developing its talents and from gratifying its desires. He concluded his passionately felt speech with the familiar verse from Virgil: *Exoriare* ... in which the unhappy *Dido* leaves her vengeance upon *Aeneas* to posterity. Instead of "concluded," I should have said "wished to conclude," for he could not bring the quotation to an end, and attempted to conceal the open gap in his memory by transposing the words: "*Exoriar(e) ex nostris ossibus ultor!*" He finally became piqued and said: "Please don't make such a mocking face, as if you were gloating over my embarrassment, but help me. There is something missing in this verse. How does it read in its complete form?"

"With pleasure," I answered, and cited it correctly:
"*Exoriar(e) aliquis nostris ex ossibus ultor!*"
"It was too stupid to forget such a word," he said. "By the way, I un-

derstand you claim that forgetting is not without its reasons; I should be very curious to find out how I came to forget this indefinite pronoun *'aliquis'*."

I gladly accepted the challenge, as I hoped to get an addition to my collection, and said, "We can easily do this, but I must ask you to tell me frankly and without any criticism everything that occurs to your mind after you focus your attention, without any particular intention, on the forgotten word." [1]

"Very well, the ridiculous idea comes to me to divide the word in the following way: *a* and *liquis*."

"What does that mean?"

"I don't know."

"What else does that recall to you?"

"The thought goes on to *reliques—liquidation—liquidity—fluid*."

"Does that mean anything to you now?"

"No, not by a long shot."

"Just go ahead."

"I now think," he said, laughing sarcastically, "of Simon of Trent, whose relics I saw two years ago in a church in Trent. I think of the old accusation which has been brought against the Jews again, and of the work of *Kleinpaul*, who sees in these supposed sacrifices reincarnations or revivals, so to speak, of the Saviour."

"This stream of thoughts has some connection with the theme which we discussed before the Latin word escaped you."

"You are right. I now think of an article in an Italian journal which I have recently read. I believe it was entitled: 'What St. Augustine said Concerning Women.' What can you do with this?"

I waited.

"Now I think of something which surely has no connection with the theme."

"Oh, please abstain from all criticism, and—"

"Oh, I know! I recall a handsome old gentleman whom I met on my journey last week. He was really an *original* type. He looked like a big bird of prey. His name, if you care to know, is Benedict."

"Well, at least you give a grouping of saints and church fathers: *St. Simon, St. Augustine* and *St. Benedict.* I believe that there was a Church father named *Origines.* Three of these, moreover, are Christian names, like *Paul* in the name of *Kleinpaul*."

"Now I think of St. *Januarius* and his blood miracle—I find that the thoughts are running mechanically."

[1] This is the usual way of bringing to consciousness hidden ideas. Cf. *The Interpretation of Dreams*, pp. 191–194 of the present volume; also published in an edition by The Macmillan Company, New York, and Allen & Unwin, London. (1937).

"Just stop a moment; both St. Januarius and St. Augustine have something to do with the calendar. Will you recall to me the blood miracle?"

"Don't you know about it? The blood of St. Januarius is preserved in a phial in a church in Naples, and on a certain holiday, a miracle takes place causing it to liquefy. The people think a great deal of this miracle, and become very excited if the liquefying process is retarded, as happened once during the French occupation. The General in command—or Garibaldi, if I am not mistaken—then took the priest aside, and with a very significant gesture pointed out to him the soldiers arrayed without, and expressed his hope that the miracle would soon take place. And it actually took place. . . ."

"Well, what else comes to your mind? Why do you hesitate?"

"Something really occurred to me . . . but it is too intimate a matter to impart . . . besides, I see no connection and no necessiry for telling it."

"I will take care of the connection. Of course I cannot compel you to reveal what is disagreeable to you, but then you should not have demanded that I tell you why you forgot the word 'aliquis'."

"Really? Do you think so? Well, I suddenly thought of a woman from whom I could easily get a message that would be very annoying to us both."

"That she missed her courses?"

"How could you guess such a thing?"

"That was not very difficult. You prepared me for it long enough. Just think of the *saints of the calendar, the liquefying of the blood on a certain day, the excitement if the event does not take place, and the distinct threat that the miracle must take place.* . . . Indeed, you have elaborated the miracle of St. Januarius into a clever allusion to the courses of the woman."

"It was surely without my knowledge. And do you really believe that my inability to reproduce the word 'aliquis' was due to this anxious expectation?"

"That appears to me absolutely certain. Don't you recall dividing it into *a-liquis* and the associations: *reliques, liquidation, fluid?* Shall I also add to this connection the fact that St. Simon, to whom you got by way of *reliques*, was sacrificed as a child?"

"Please stop. I hope you do not take these thoughts—if I really entertained them—seriously. I will, however, confess to you that the lady is Italian, and that I visited Naples in her company. But may not all this be coincidental?"

"I must leave to your own judgment whether you can explain all these connections through the assumption of coincidence. I will tell you, however, that every similar case that you analyze will lead you to just such remarkable 'coincidences'!" [1]

I have more than one reason for valuing this little analysis, for which I am indebted to my travelling companion. First, because in this case, I was able to make use of a source which is otherwise inaccessible to me. Most of the examples of psychic disturbances of daily life that I have here compiled, I was obliged to take from observation of myself. I endeavored to evade the far richer material furnished me by my neurotic patients because I had to preclude the objection that the phenomena in question were only the result and manifestation of the neurosis. It was therefore of special value for my purpose to have a stranger free from a neurosis offer himself as a subject for such examination. This analysis is also important in other respects, inasmuch as it elucidates a case of word-forgetting *without* substitutive recollection, and thus confirms the principle formulated above, namely, that the appearance or nonappearance of incorrect substitutive recollections does not constitute an essential distinction.[2]

But the principal value of the example *aliquis* lies in another of its distinctions from the case *Signorelli*. In the latter example, the reproduction of the name becomes disturbed through the after-effects of a stream

---

[1] This small analysis has aroused much attention and evoked lively discussions in the literature. Through it, Bleuler attempted to prove mathematically the authenticity of psychoanalytic interpretation. He states: "It contains more probability value than thousands of unassailed medical 'cognitions,' and its peculiar position is only due to the fact that we are not yet in the habit of dealing in science with psychological probabilities."—Bleuler: *"Austistisch-Undiszipliniertes Denken,"* p. 142. Springer, Berlin, 1921.

[2] Finer observation reduces somewhat the contrast between the analyses of *Signorelli* and *aliquis* as far as the substitutive recollections are concerned. Here, too, the forgetting seems to be accompanied by substitutive formations. When I later asked my companion whether in his effort to recall the forgotten word, he did not think of some substitution, he informed me that he was at first tempted to put an *ab* into the verse: *nostris ab ossibus* (perhaps the disjointed part of *a-liquis*) and that later the word *exoriare* obtruded itself with particular distinctness and persistency. Being skeptical, he added that it was apparently due to the fact that it was the first word of the verse. But when I asked him to focus his attention on the associations to *exoriare*, he gave me the word *exorcism*. This makes me think that the reinforcement of *exoriare* in the reproduction has really the value of such substitution. It probably came through the association *exorcism* from the names of the saints. However, those are refinements upon which no value need be laid. It seems now quite possible that the appearance of any kind of substitutive recollection is a constant sign—perhaps only characteristic and misleading—of the purposive forgetting motivated by repression. This substitution might also exist in the reinforcement of an element akin to the thing forgotten, even where incorrect substitutive names fail to appear. Thus, in the example *Signorelli*, as long as the name of the painter remained inaccessible to me, I had more than a clear visual memory of the cycle of his frescoes, and of the picture of himself in the corner; at least it was more intensive than any of my other visual memory traces. In another case, also reported in my essay of 1898, I had hopelessly forgotten the street name and address connected with a disagreeable visit in a strange city, but—as if to mock me—the house number appeared especially vivid, whereas the memory of numbers usually causes me the greatest difficulty.

of thought which began shortly before and was interrupted, but whose content had no distinct relation to the new theme which contained the name Signorelli. Between the repression and the theme of the forgotten name, there existed only the relation of temporal contiguity, which reached the other in order that the two should be able to form a connection through an outer association.[1] On the other hand, in the example *aliquis*, one can note no trace of such an independent repressed theme which could occupy conscious thought immediately before and then re-echo as a disturbance. The disturbance of the reproduction proceeded here from the inner part of the theme touched upon, and was brought about by the fact that unconsciously a contradiction arose against the wish-idea represented in the quotation.

The origin must be construed in the following manner: The speaker deplored the fact that the present generation of his people was being deprived of its rights, and like Dido, he presaged that a new generation would take upon itself vengeance against the oppressors. He therefore expressed the wish for posterity. In this moment, he was interrupted by the contradictory thought: "Do you really wish so much for posterity? That is not true. Just think in what a predicament you would be if you should now receive the information that you must expect posterity from the quarter you have in mind! No, you want no posterity—as much as you need it for your vengeance." This contradiction asserts itself, just as in the example *Signorelli*, by forming an outer association between one of his ideation elements and an element of the repressed wish, but here it is brought about in a most strained manner through what seems an artificial detour of associations. Another important agreement with the example *Signorelli* results from the fact that the contradiction originates from repressed sources and emanates from thoughts which would cause a deviation of attention.

So much for the diversity and the inner relationship of both paradigms of the forgetting of names. We have learned to know a second mechanism of forgetting, namely, the disturbance of thought through an inner contradiction emanating from the repression. In the course of this discussion, we shall repeatedly meet with this process, which seems to me to be the more easily understood.

[1] I am not fully convinced of the lack of an inner connection between the two streams of thought in the case of *Signorelli*. In carefully following the repressed thought concerning the theme of death and sexual life, one does strike an idea which shows a near relation to the theme of the frescoes of Orvieto.

III

FORGETTING OF NAMES AND ORDER
OF WORDS

EXPERIENCES like those mentioned concerning the process of forgetting a part of the order of words from a foreign language may cause one to wonder whether the forgetting of the order of words in one's own language requires an essentially different explanation. To be sure, one is not wont to be surprised if after a while a formula or poem learned by heart can only be reproduced imperfectly, with variations and gaps. Still, as this forgetting does not affect equally all the things learned together, but seems to pick out therefrom definite parts, it may be worth our effort to investigate analytically some examples of such faulty reproductions.

Brill reports the following example:

"While conversing one day with a very brilliant young woman, she had occasion to quote from Keats. The poem was entitled 'Ode to Apollo,' and she recited the following lines:

" 'In thy western house of gold
Where thou livest in thy state,
Bards, that once sublimely told
Prosaic truths that came too late.'

She hesitated many times during the recitation, being sure that there was something wrong with the last line. To her great surprise, on referring to the book, she found that not only was the last line misquoted, but that there were many other mistakes. The correct lines read as follows:

ODE TO APOLLO
" 'In thy western *halls* of gold
When thou *sittest* in thy state,
Bards, that *erst* sublimely told
Heroic deeds and sang of fate.'

The words italicized are those that have been forgotten and replaced by others during the recitation.

46

"She was astonished at her many mistakes, and attributed them to a failure of memory. I could readily convince her, however, that there was no qualitative or quantitative disturbance of memory in her case, and recalled to her our conversation immediately before quoting these lines.

"We were discussing the over-estimation of personality among lovers, and she thought it was Victor Hugo who said that love is the greatest thing in the world because it makes an angel or a god out of a grocery clerk. She continued: 'Only when we are in love have we blind faith in humanity; everything is perfect, everything is beautiful, and . . . everything is so poetically unreal. Still, it is a wonderful experience; worth going through, notwithstanding the terrible disappointments that usually follow. It puts us on a level with the gods and incites us to all sorts of artistic activities. We become real poets; we not only memorize and quote poetry, but we often become Apollos ourselves.' She then quoted the lines given above.

"When I asked on what occasion she memorized the lines, she could not recall. As a teacher of elocution, she was wont to memorize so much and so often that it was difficult to tell just when she had memorized these lines. 'Judging by the conversation,' I suggested, 'it would seem that this poem is intimately associated with the idea of over-estimation of personality of one in love. Have you perhaps memorized this poem when you were in such a state?' She became thoughtful for a while and soon recalled the following facts: Twelve years before, when she was eighteen years old, she fell in love. She met the young man while participating in an amateur theatrical performance. He was, at the time, studying for the stage, and it was predicted that some day he would be a matinée idol. He was endowed with all the attributes needed for such a calling. He was well built, fascinating, impulsive, very clever and . . . very fickle-minded. She was warned against him, but she paid no heed, attributing it all to the envy of her counsellors. Everything went well for a few months, when she suddenly received word that her Apollo, for whom she had memorized these lines, had eloped with and married a very wealthy young woman. A few years later, she heard that he was living in a Western city, where he was taking care of his father-in-law's interests.

"The misquoted lines are now quite plain. The discussion about the over-estimation of personality among lovers unconsciously recalled to her a disagreeable experience, when she herself over-estimated the personality of the man she loved. She thought he was a god, but he turned out to be even worse than the average mortal. The episode could not come to the surface because it was determined by very disagreeable and painful thoughts, but the unconscious variations in the poem plainly showed her present mental state. The poetic expressions were not only changed to prosaic ones, but they clearly alluded to the whole episode."

Another example of forgetting the order of words of a poem well known to the person, I shall cite from Dr. C. G. Jung,[1] quoting the words of the author:

"A man wished to recite the familiar poem, 'A Pine Tree Stands Alone,' etc. In the line 'He felt drowsy' he became hopelessly stuck at the words 'with the white sheet.' This forgetting of such a well-known verse seemed to me rather peculiar, and I therefore asked him to reproduce what came to his mind when he thought of the words 'with the white sheet.' He gave the following series of associations: 'The white sheet makes one think of a white sheet on a corpse—a linen sheet with which one covers a dead body—(pause)—now I think of a near friend—his brother died quite recently—he is supposed to have died of heart disease—he was also very corpulent—my friend is corpulent, too, and I thought that he might meet the same fate—probably he doesn't exercise enough—when I heard of this death, I suddenly became frightened: the same thing might happen to me, as my own family is predisposed to obesity—my grandfather died of heart disease—I, also, am somewhat too corpulent, and for that reason, I began an obesity cure a few days ago.' "

Jung remarks: "The man had unconsciously identified himself with the pine tree which was covered with a white sheet."

For the following example of forgetting the order of words, I am indebted to my friend, Dr. Ferenczi, of Budapest. Unlike the former examples, it does not refer to a verse taken from poetry, but to a self-coined saying. It may also demonstrate to us the rather unusual case where the forgetting places itself at the disposal of discretion when the latter is in danger of yielding to a momentary desire. The mistake thus advances to a useful function. After we have sobered down, we justify that inner striving which at first could manifest itself only in some default, as in forgetting or psychic impotence.

"At a social gathering, some one quoted '*Tout comprendre c'est tout pardonner*,' to which I remarked that the first part of the sentence should suffice, as 'pardoning' is an exemption which must be left to God and the priest. One of the guests thought this observation very good, which in turn emboldened me to remark—probably to ensure myself of the good opinion of the well-disposed critic—that some time ago, I thought of something still better. But when I was about to repeat this clever idea, I was unable to recall it. Thereupon I immediately withdrew from the company and wrote my latent thoughts. I first recalled the name of the friend who had witnessed the birth of this (desired) thought, and of the street in Budapest where it took place, and then the name of another friend, whose name was Max, whom we usually called Maxie. That led me to the word 'maxim,' and to the thought that at that time, as in the present case,

[1] *The Psychology of Dementia Praecox*, translated by A. A. Brill.

it was a question of varying a well-known maxim. Strangely enough, I did not recall any maxim but the following sentence: *'God created man in His own image,'* and its changed conception, *'Man created God in his own image.'* Immediately I recalled the sought-for recollection.

"My friend said to me at that time in Andrassy Street, *'Nothing human is foreign to me.'* To which I remarked, basing it on psychoanalytic experience, 'You should go further and acknowledge *that nothing animal is foreign to you.'*

"But after I had finally found the desired recollection, I was even then prevented from telling it in this social gathering. The young wife of the friend whom I had reminded of the animality of the unconscious, was also among those present, and I was perforce reminded that she was not at all prepared for the reception of such unsympathetic views. The forgetting spared me a number of unpleasant questions from her and a hopeless discussion, and just that must have been the motive of the 'temporary amnesia.'

"It is interesting to note that as a concealing thought there emerged a sentence in which the deity is degraded to a human invention, while in the sought-for sentence, there was an allusion to the animal in the man. The *capitis diminutio* is therefore common to both. The whole matter was apparently only a continuation of the stream of thought concerning understanding and forgiving which was stimulated by the discussion.

"That the desired thought so rapidly appeared may also be due to the fact that I withdrew into a vacant room, away from the society in which it was censored."

I have since then analyzed a large number of cases of forgetting or faulty reproduction of the order of words, and the consistent result of these investigations led me to assume that the mechanisms of forgetting, as demonstrated in the examples *aliquis* and *Ode to Apollo,* are almost universally true. It is not always very convenient to report such analyses, for, just as those cited, they usually lead to intimate and painful things in the person analyzed; I shall therefore add no more to the number of such examples. What is common to all these cases, regardless of the material, is the fact that the forgotten or distorted material becomes connected through some associative path with an unconscious stream of thought which gives rise to the influence that comes to light as forgetting.

I am now returning to the forgetting of names, concerning which we have so far considered exhaustively neither the casuistic elements nor the motives. As this form of faulty acts can at times be abundantly observed in myself, I am not at a loss for examples. The slight attacks of migraine, from which I am still suffering, are wont to announce themselves hours before through the forgetting of names, and at the height of the attack, during which I am not forced, however, to give up my work, I am often unable to recall all proper names.

Still, just such cases as mine may furnish the cause for a strong objection to our analytic efforts. Should not one be forced to conclude from such observations that the causation of forgetfulness, especially forgetting of names, is to be sought in circulatory or functional disturbances of the brain, and spare himself the trouble of searching for psychologic explanations for these phenomena? Not at all; that would mean to substitute the mechanism of a process, which is the same in all cases, by a variable. But instead of an analysis, I shall cite a comparison which will settle the argument.

Let us assume that I was so reckless as to take a walk at night in an uninhabited neighborhood of a big city, and was attacked and robbed of my watch and purse. At the nearest police station I report the matter in the following words: "I was in this or that street, and was there robbed of my watch and purse by *lonesomeness* and *darkness*." Although these words would not express anything that is incorrect, I would, nevertheless, run the danger of being considered—judging from the wording of this report—as not quite right in the head. To be correct, the state of affairs could only be described by saying that, *favored* by the lonesomeness of the place and under *cover* of darkness, I was robbed of my valuables by *unknown malefactors*.

Now, then, the state of affairs in forgetting names need not be different. Favored by exhaustion, circulatory disturbances and intoxication, I am robbed by an unknown psychic force of the control over the proper names belonging to my memory; it is the same force which in other cases may bring about the same failure of memory during perfect health and mental capacity.

When I analyze those cases of name-forgetting in myself, I find almost regularly that the name withheld shows some relation to a theme which concerns my own person, and is apt to provoke in me strong and often painful emotions. Following the convenient and commendable practice of the Zürich School (Bleuler, Jung, Riklin), I might express the same thing in the following form: The name withheld has touched a "personal complex" in me. The relation of the name to my person is an unexpected one, and is mostly brought about through superficial associations (words of double meaning and of similar sounds); it may generally be designated as a side association. A few single examples will best illustrate the nature of the same:

(a) A patient requested me to recommend to him a sanatorium in the Riviera. I knew of such a place very near Genoa; I also recalled the name of the German colleague who was in charge of the place, but the place itself I could not name, well as I believed I knew it. There was nothing left to do but ask the patient to wait, and to appeal quickly to the women of the family.

"Just what is the name of the place near Genoa where Dr. X has his small institution in which Mrs. So-and-So remained so long under treatment?"

"Of course you would forget a name of that sort. The name is Nervi." To be sure, I have enough to do with nerves.

(b) Another patient spoke about a neighboring summer resort, and maintained that besides the two familiar inns, there was a third. I disputed the existence of any third inn, and referred to the fact that I had spent seven summers in the vicinity and therefore knew more about the place than he. Instigated by my contradiction, he recalled the name. The name of the third inn was "The Hochwartner." Of course, I had to admit it; indeed, I was forced to confess that for seven summers I had lived near this very inn, whose existence I had so strenuously denied. But why should I have forgotten the name and the object? I believe because the name sounded very much like that of a Vienna colleague who practised the same specialty as my own. It touched my "professional complex."

(c) On another occasion, when about to buy a railroad ticket on the *Reichenhall* station, I could not recall the very familiar name of the next big railroad station which I had so often passed. I was forced to look it up in the time-table. The name was *Rosehome* (*Rosenheim*). I soon discovered through what associations I lost it. An hour earlier, I had visited my sister in her home near Reichenhall; my sister's name is Rose, hence also a Rosehome. This name was taken away by my "family complex."

(d) This predatory influence of the "family complex," I can demonstrate in a whole series of complexes.

One day, I was consulted by a young man, a younger brother of one of my female patients, whom I saw any number of times, and whom I used to call by his first name. Later, while wishing to talk about his visit, I forgot his first name, in no way an unusual one, and could not recall it in any way. I walked into the street to read the business signs and recognized the name as soon as it met my eyes.

The analysis showed that I had formed a parallel between the visitor and my own brother which centered in the question: "Would my brother, in a similar case, have behaved like him or even more contrarily?" The outer connection between the thoughts concerning the stranger and my own family was rendered possible through the accident that the name of the mothers in each case was the same, Amelia. Subsequently, I also understood the substitutive names, Daniel and Frank, which obtruded themselves without any explanation. These names, as well as Amelia, belong to Schiller's play *The Robbers;* they are all connected with a joke of the Vienna pedestrian, Daniel Spitzer.

(e) On another occasion, I was unable to recall a patient's name which had a certain reference to my early life. The analysis had to be followed over a long devious road before the desired name was discovered. The patient expressed his apprehension lest he should lose his eyesight; this recalled a young man who became blind from a gunshot, and this again led to a picture of another youth who shot himself, and the latter bore the same name as my first patient, though not at all related to him. The name became known to me, however, only after the anxious apprehension from these two juvenile cases was transferred to a person of my own family.

Thus an incessant stream of "self-reference" flows through my thoughts concerning which I usually have no inkling, but which betrays itself through such name-forgetting. It seems as if I were forced to compare with my own person all that I hear about strangers, as if my personal complexes became stirred up by associations from without. It seems impossible that this should be an individual peculiarity of my own person; it must, on the contrary, point to the way we grasp outside matters in general. I have reasons to assume that other individuals meet with experiences quite similar to mine.

The best example of this kind was reported to me by a gentleman named Lederer as a personal experience. While on his wedding trip in Venice, he came across a man with whom he was but slightly acquainted, and whom he was obliged to introduce to his wife. As he forgot the name of the stranger, he got himself out of the embarrassment the first time by mumbling the name unintelligibly. But when he met the man a second time, as is inevitable in Venice, he took him aside and begged him to help him out of the difficulty by telling him his name, which he unfortunately had forgotten. The answer of the stranger pointed to a superior knowledge of human nature: "I readily believe that you did not grasp my name. My name is like yours—Lederer!"

One cannot suppress a slight feeling of unpleasantness on discovering his own name in a stranger. I had recently felt it very plainly when I was consulted during my office hours by a man named S. Freud. However, I am assured by one of my own critics that in this respect, he behaves in quite the opposite manner.

(f) The effect of personal relation can be recognized also in the following examples reported by Jung.[1]

"Mr. Y. falls in love with a lady who soon thereafter marries Mr. X. In spite of the fact that Mr. Y. was an old acquaintance of Mr. X., and had business relations with him, he repeatedly forgot the name, and on a number of occasions, when wishing to correspond with X., he was obliged to ask other people for his name."

However, the motivation for the forgetting is more evident in this case

[1] *The Psychology of Dementia Praecox*, p. 45.

than in the preceding ones, which were under the constellation of the personal reference. Here the forgetting is manifestly a direct result of the dislike of Y. for the happy rival; he does not wish to know anything about him.

(g) The following case, reported by Ferenczi, the analysis of which is especially instructive through the explanation of the substitutive thoughts (like *Botticelli-Boltraffio* to *Signorelli*), shows in a somewhat different way how self-reference leads to the forgetting of a name:

"A lady who heard something about psychoanalysis could not recall the name of the psychiatrist, Young (Jung).

"Instead, the following names occurred to her: Kl. (a name)—Wilde —Nietzsche—Hauptmann.

"I did not tell her the name and requested her to repeat her free associations to every thought.

"To Kl. she at once thought of Mrs. Kl., that she was an embellished and affected person who looked very well for her age. 'She does not age.' As a general and principal conception of Wilde and Nietzsche, she gave the association 'mental disease.' She continued: 'I cannot bear Wilde and Nietzsche. I do not understand them. I hear that they were both homosexual. Wilde has occupied himself with *young* people' (although she uttered in this sentence the correct name, she still could not remember it).

"To Hauptmann she associated the words *half* and *youth*, and only after I called her attention to the word *youth* did she become aware that she was looking for the name Young (Jung)."

It is clear that this lady, who had lost her husband at the age of thirty-nine, and had no prospect of marrying a second time, had cause enough to avoid reminiscences recalling youth or old age. The remarkable thing is that the concealing thoughts of the desired name came to the surface as simple associations of content without any sound-associations.

(h) Still different and very finely motivated is an example of name-forgetting which the person concerned has himself explained.

"While taking an examination in philosophy as a minor subject, I was questioned by the examiner about the teachings of *Epicurus*, and was asked whether I knew who took up his teachings centuries later. I answered that it was *Pierre Gassendi*, whom two days before, while in a café, I had happened to hear spoken of as a follower of Epicurus. To the question how I knew this, I boldly replied that I had taken an interest in *Gassendi* for a long time. This resulted in a certificate with a *magna cum laude*, but later, unfortunately, also in a persistent tendency to forget the name *Gassendi*. I believe that it is due to my guilty conscience that even now I cannot retain this name despite all efforts. I had no business knowing it at that time."

To have a proper appreciation of the intense repugnance entertained by our narrator against the recollection of this examination episode, one must have realized how highly he prizes his doctor's degree, and for how many other things this substitute must stand.

(i) I add here another example of forgetting the name of a city, an instance which is perhaps not as simple as those given before, but which will appear credible and valuable to those more familiar with such investigations. The name of an Italian city withdrew itself from memory on account of its far-reaching sound-similarity to a woman's first name, which was in turn connected with various emotional reminiscences which were surely not exhaustively treated in this report. Dr. S. Ferenczi, who observed this case of forgetting in himself, treated it—quite justly—as an analysis of a dream or a neurotic idea.

"Today I visited some old friends, and the conversation turned to cities of Northern Italy. Someone remarked that they still showed the Austrian influence. A few of these cities were cited. I, too, wished to mention one, but the name did not come to me, although I knew that I had spent two very pleasant days there; this, of course, does not quite concur with Freud's theory of forgetting. Instead of the desired name of the city, there obtruded themselves the following thoughts: '*Capua—Brescia*—the lion of Brescia.' This lion I saw objectively before me in the form of a marble statue, but I soon noticed that he resembled less the lion of the statue of liberty in Brescia (which I saw only in a picture) than the other marble lion which I saw in Lucerne on the monument in honor of the Swiss Guard fallen in the Tuileries. I finally thought of the desired name: it was Verona.

"I knew at once the cause of this amnesia. No other than a former servant of the family whom I visited at the time. Her name was Veronica; in Hungarian Verona. I felt a great antipathy for her on account of her repulsive physiognomy, as well as her hoarse, shrill voice and her unbearable self-assertion (to which she thought herself entitled on account of her long service). Also the tyrannical way in which she treated the children of the family was insufferable to me. Now I knew the significance of the substitutive thoughts.

"To Capua I immediately associated *caput mortuum*. I had often compared Veronica's head to a skull. The Hungarian word *kapzoi* (greed after money) surely furnished a determinant for the displacement. Naturally I also found those more direct associations which connected Capua and Verona as geographical ideas and as Italian words of the same rhythm.

"The same held true for Brescia; here, too, I found concealed sidetracks of associations of ideas.

"My antipathy at that time was so violent that I thought Veronica very ugly, and have often expressed my astonishment at the fact that anyone should love her: 'Why, to kiss her,' I said, 'must provoke nausea.'

"Brescia, at least in Hungary, is very often mentioned not in connection with the lion, but with another wild beast. The most hated name in this country, as well as in North Italy, is that of General Haynau, who is briefly referred to as the hyena of Brescia. From the hated tyrant Haynau, one stream of thought leads over Brescia to the city of Verona, and the other over the idea of the *grave-digging animal with the hoarse voice* (which corresponds to the thought of a monument to the dead), to the skull, and to the disagreeable organ of Veronica, which was so cruelly insulted in my unconscious mind. Veronica, in her time, ruled as tyrannically as did the Austrian General after the Hungarian and Italian struggles for liberty.

"Lucerne is associated with the idea of the summer which Veronica spent with her employers in a place near Lucerne. The Swiss Guard again recalls that she tyrannized not only the children, but also the adult members of the family, and thus played the part of the *'Garde-Dame.'*

"I expressly observe that this antipathy of mine against Veronica consciously belongs to things long overcome. Since that time, she has changed in her appearance and manner, very much to her advantage, so that I am able to meet her with sincere regard (to be sure, I hardly find such occasion). As usual, however, my unconscious sticks more tenaciously to those impressions; it is old in its resentment.

"The *Tuileries* represent an allusion to a second personality, an old French lady who actually 'guarded' the women of the house, and who was in high regard and somewhat feared by everybody. For a long time, I was her *élève* in French conversation. The word *élève* recalls that when I visited the brother-in-law of my present host in northern Bohemia, I had to laugh a great deal because the rural population referred to the *élèves* (pupils) of the school of forestry as *löwen* (lions). Also this jocose recollection might have taken part in the displacement of the hyena by the lion."

(j) The following example can also show how a personal complex swaying the person at the time being, may, by devious ways, bring about the forgetting of a name.[1]

Two men, an elder and a younger, who had travelled together in Sicily six months before, exchanged reminiscences of those pleasant and interesting days.

"Let's see, what was the name of that place," asked the younger, "where we passed the night before taking the trip to Selinunt? *Calatafini,* was it not?"

The elder rejected this by saying: "Certainly not; but I have forgotten the name, too, although I can recall perfectly all the details of the place. Whenever I hear someone forget a name, it immediately produces forget-

[1] *Zentralb. f. Psychoanalyse,* I. 9, 1911.

fulness in me. Let us look for the name. I cannot think of any other name except *Caltanisetta,* which is surely not correct."

"No," said the younger, "the name begins with, or contains, a *w.*"

"But the Italian language contains no *w,*" retorted the elder.

"I really meant a *v,* and I said *w* because I am accustomed to interchange them in my mother-tongue."

The elder, however, objected to the *v.* He added: "I believe that I have already forgotten many of the Sicilian names. Suppose we try to find out. For example, what is the name of the place situated on a height which was called *Enna* in antiquity?"

"Oh, I know that: *Castrogiovanni.*" In the next moment, the younger man discovered the lost name. He cried out *"Castelvetrano,"* and was pleased to be able to demonstrate the supposed *v.*

For a moment, the elder still lacked the feeling of recognition, but after he accepted the name, he was able to state why it had escaped him. He thought: "Obviously because the second half, *vetrano,* suggests *veteran.* I am aware that I am not quite anxious to think of ageing, and react peculiarly when I am reminded of it. Thus, *e.g.,* I had recently reminded a very esteemed friend in most unmistakable terms that he had 'long ago passed the years of youth,' because before this, he once remarked in the most flattering manner, 'I am no longer a young man.' That my resistance was directed against the second half of the name *Castelvetrano* is shown by the fact that the initial sound of the same returned in the substitutive name Caltanisetta."

"What about the name Caltanisetta itself?" asked the younger.

"That always seemed to me like a pet name of a young woman," admitted the elder.

Somewhat later he added: "The name for *Enna* was also only a substitutive name. And now it occurs to me that the name *Castrogiovanni,* which obtruded itself with the aid of a rationalization, alludes as expressly to *giovane,* young, as the last name, *Castelvetrano,* to *veteran.*"

The older man believed that he had thus accounted for his forgetting the name. What the motive was that led the young man to this memory failure was not investigated.

In some cases, one must have recourse to all the fineness of psychoanalytic technique in order to explain the forgetting of a name. Those who wish to read an example of such work, I refer to a communication by Professor Ernest Jones.[1]

Brill reports the following interesting example:

"Soon after I became an assistant in the Clinic of Psychiatry at Zürich,

[1] "Analyse eines Falles von Namenvergessen," *Zentralb. f. Psychoanalyse,* Jahrg. II, Heft 2, 1911.

I had an interesting experience in forgetting a name, which I may say, finally converted me to Freud's teachings. At that time, I was not fully convinced of his theories, and my attitude was skeptical, though by no means unsympathetic. I approached the whole subject in the spirit of an investigator and student who made every effort to discover and understand all the data before passing final judgment on his psychology. Spurred on by Professor Bleuler, all the physicians in the hospital were firm and ardent workers with the new theories. In fact, we were in the only hospital or clinic where the Freudian principles were applied in the study and treatment of patients. Those were the pioneer days of Freud among psychiatrists, and we observed and studied and noted whatever was done or said about us with unfailing patience and untiring interest and zeal. We made no scruples, for instance, of asking a man at table why he did not use his spoon in the proper way, or why he did such and such a thing in such and such a manner. It was impossible for one to show any degree of hesitation or make some abrupt pause in speaking without being at once called to account. We had to keep ourselves well in hand, ever ready and alert, for there was no telling when and where there would be a new attack. We had to explain why we whistled or hummed some particular tune or why we made some slip in talking or some mistake in writing. But we were glad to do this if for no other reason than to learn to face the truth.

"One afternoon, when I was off duty, I was reading about a certain case which recalled to my mind a similar one I had when I was in a hospital in New York. I am in the habit of making marginal notes and so I took up my pencil to write down the case, but when I came to note the name of the patient whom I had known for a number of months and in whom I had taken an unusual amount of interest, I found that I could not recall it. I tried very hard to bring it back to my mind, but without success. It was strange and puzzling; but as I knew definitely whom I meant, I finished the note. Now, according to Freud, I thought at once to myself, the name must be connected with something painful and unpleasant. I decided right there and then to find it by the Freudian free association method.

"Now, the patient whose name I could not recall, was the same man who, some years ago, attempted to set fire to the St. Patrick's Cathedral in New York; he gathered together some odds and ends before the entrance of the church and set fire to it. He was, of course, arrested, brought to the psychopathic pavilion in Bellevue and later to the State Hospital where he became my patient. I diagnosed him as a psychic epileptic. I decided that he suffered from a form of epilepsy which does not manifest itself in fits, as the general cases do, but rather in peculiar psychic actions which may last for a few minutes, hours, or perhaps for weeks, months or years. Nobody agreed with me in the diagnosis; my senior doctor held that the patient suffered from dementia praecox.

"Within a week or so, the patient recovered and was entirely normal, thus corroborating my diagnosis in every respect. The patient told us that this was his fifth attack and that in some of his previous ones, he had burned a railroad station, a church and several barns. He would run away from home, his wife and children, and wander off, scot-free, when one of these fits came upon him. He was an editor of a journal and newspaper in Canada, a man of considerable intelligence and refinement. On one of his attacks during the Boer War, he ran away from Canada and came to London, where, seeing calls for volunteers, he enlisted and was sent to South Africa. He fought bravely and was promoted to sergeant in a few weeks. When he came to himself, he was quite surprised to find himself a soldier and did not have the least idea how he got to South Africa. Previous experience told him, however, what his condition meant and upon reporting it to the physicians, he was honorably discharged. He sent a cable to his wife and returned home. He gave us various details about himself, the hospital where he found himself last, his former doctor, all of which we were soon able to corroborate. He had what we called a "fugue" or "poriomania." Cases like this have been reported where the person disappeared for as many as three years. Indeed, they are not as rare as you may suppose.

"Everybody congratulated me on my clever diagnosis, and I myself was greatly elated. The superintendent assured me that I had all good reason to be proud of myself and he went on to state, to my profound disappointment and displeasure, that he would report the case to a medical society. I had spent a tremendous amount of time and effort on it and desired to publish it as my first contribution to medical literature.

"A few days before the meeting, the superintendent changed his mind and asked me to read it. I was very much pleased at this and felt quite relieved. But the programs were already printed, and when I went before the society, everybody thought it was the superintendent's paper and that he sent me merely to read it for him. You may realize how deeply I felt about the whole affair.

"Now, I am dwelling quite at length on the phase of the situation because I would like you to note carefully that there was enough of the disagreeable and unpleasant associated with the whole experience to account for my forgetting the name of the patient.

"For hours on end, I sat there writing down the associations, but I was not a whit nearer to knowing the name than when I began. Various details and incidents came swarming into my mind and I had to write mighty rapidly to keep pace with them. I could see clearly how this New York patient looked, the color of his hair, the peculiar expression on his face.

I thought to myself, 'If that is the way to find
n method, I shall never be a Freudian.' It was
olleagues, surprised to find me indoors, asked
im inasmuch as I was not going out. I con-
of these Freudian labors. But when I was
ned to the associations with renewed inter-
still in as much darkness about the name as
u disheartened and thoroughly disgusted with the
At about four o'clock in the morning, I awoke and made a
eme effort to dismiss it from my mind, but in vain. *Nolens volens*, I
soon began to associate in bed, and finally, at about a little after five, the
long-sought name suddenly came to me. My joy and elation was not at
all free from a sense of relief; it was as if I had solved a long vexing problem. I have no doubt now that had I not been able to find it, I probably
would never have continued to take the slightest interest in Freud. I spent
so much time and effort in trying to ferret it out that I felt quite out of
humor with myself; but I was well compensated no less by the sense of
pleasure and satisfaction that went with the discovery, than by the fresh
conviction it gave me in Freudian psychology.

"Now, what was the situation? Let me say first that when you begin
to associate freely, you will soon be surprised to find that thousands of
associations begin pouring in upon consciousness. Sometimes, three or
four of these associations come at the same moment and you pause and
wonder which one to write down first. You soon make some selection and
continue. In my own case, I observed that a few very definite associations
kept on recurring continually. Every time I asked myself the name of this
New York patient, there would invariably come to my mind the case of
a real epileptic I then had in the Zürich hospital. His name was *Appenzeller;* he was just a Swiss peasant, and I explained the association on
the ground that they were both epileptics, the New York patient, as you
remember, being a psychic epileptic. Another continually recurring association was this: When I thought of the hospital on Long Island and all
that happened there during the five years I was connected with it, one
particular scene would stand out very clearly and prominently; my mind
would revert to it all the time. There were very often forest fires near the
hospital and on many occasions, we had to go out and check them lest
they reached our buildings. The particular scene was on a Friday; there
was a big fire raging near the hospital and we had to send out as many
doctors and nurses as we could possibly spare to help control it. I was
there to see that there was no confusion, that things were carried out
properly; I was chatting with a physician who was with me in the same
capacity. The fire was consuming a good deal of scrub pine; and now
and then, an attendant would succeed in shooting one of the rabbits that

were fleeing from the brush wood. As I was standing there, tendent came up to us, passed some remark or other, and the rabbit some distance away, asked one of the attendants for hi to try his skill, saying: 'Let's see if I can get that rabbit.' We all on knowingly, for we never had very much faith in the superinten marksmanship, and no mistake, he missed his aim and the rabbit escap He turned to me and declared somewhat uneasily, and by way of expl nation, that his fingers slipped, for it was beginning to rain. I seemingly concurred in the observation, but in my heart I smiled at his discomfiture. I could see him very plainly as he stood there, saying, 'Let's see if I can get that rabbit,' and he would then aim, shoot and miss it. Finally I saw the scene again in the morning, and with the words, 'Let's see if I can get that rabbit,' the name came to me. It was *Lapin*, the French word for rabbit. Later on, when I actually counted my associations, I found that this particular association came up twenty-eight times more than any of the others.

"This may seem strange to you, but that is exactly the way the mind works unconsciously. The name was symbolically represented by the scene; the whole situation was under repression and that is the manner in which the unconscious elaborated it. The repressed emotion attached itself to an actual occurrence: the superintendent fails to shoot the rabbit, *i.e.*, he fails to deprive me of the case. You can easily see also why I thought of Appenzeller. There was the sound association of the first part of Appenzeller, *Appen, Lapin;* and what is just as important, both patients were epileptics. You may thus see, first, that there was something distinctly disagreeable and painful associated with the name, and secondly, that there was a definite symbolic expression of it in the form of a repressed emotion."

I could multiply the examples of name-forgetting and prolong the discussion very much further if I did not wish to avoid elucidating here almost all the viewpoints which will be considered in later themes. I shall, however, take the liberty of comprehending in a few sentences the results of the analyses reported here.

The mechanism of forgetting, or rather of losing or temporary forgetting of a name, consists in the disturbance of the intended reproduction of the name through a strange stream of thought unconscious at the time. Between the disturbed name and the disturbing complex, there exists a connection either from the beginning or such a connection has been formed—perhaps by artificial means—through superficial (outer) associations.

The self-reference complex (personal, family or professional) proves to be the most effective of the disturbing complexes.

A name which, by virtue of its many meanings, belongs to a number of thought associations (complexes) is frequently disturbed in its connection to one series of thoughts through a stronger complex belonging to the other associations.

To avoid the awakening of pain through memory is one of the objects among the motives of these disturbances.

In general, one may distinguish two principal cases of name-forgetting; when the name itself touches something unpleasant, or when it is brought into connection with other associations which are influenced by such effects. Thus, names can be disturbed on their own account or on account of their nearer or more remote associative relations in the reproduction.

A review of these general principles readily convinces us that the temporary forgetting of a name is observed as the most frequent faulty action of our mental functions.

However, we are far from having described all the peculiarities of this phenomenon. I also wish to call attention to the fact that name-forgetting is extremely contagious. In a conversation between two persons, the mere mention of having forgotten this or that name by one often suffices to induce the same memory slip in the other. But wherever the forgetting is induced, the sought-for name easily comes to the surface.

There is also a continuous forgetting of names in which whole chains of names are withdrawn from memory. If, in the course of endeavoring to discover an escaped name, one finds others with which the latter is intimately connected, it often happens that these new names also escape. The forgetting thus jumps from one name to another, as if to demonstrate the existence of a hindrance not to be easily removed.

IV

CHILDHOOD AND CONCEALING MEMORIES

In a second essay,[1] I was able to demonstrate the purposive nature of our memories in an unexpected field. I started with the remarkable fact that the earliest recollections of a person often seemed to preserve the unimportant and accidental, whereas (frequently though not universally!) not a trace is found in the adult memory of the weighty and affective impressions of this period. As it is known that the memory exercises a certain selection among the impressions at its disposal, it would seem logical to suppose that this selection follows entirely different principles in childhood than at the time of intellectual maturity. However, close investigation points to the fact that such an assumption is superfluous. The indifferent childhood memories owe their existence to a process of displacement. It may be shown by psychoanalysis that in the reproduction they represent the substitute for other really significant impressions, whose direct reproduction is hindered by some resistance. As they do not owe their existence to their own contents, but to an associative relation of their contents to another repressed thought, they deserve the title of "concealing memories," by which I have designated them.

In the aforementioned essay I only touched upon, but in no way exhausted, the varieties in the relations and meanings of concealed memories. In the given example fully analyzed, I particularly emphasized a peculiarity in the temporal relation between the concealing memory and the contents of the memory concealed by it. The content of the concealing memory in that example belonged to one of the first years of childhood, while the thoughts represented by it, which remained practically unconscious, belonged to a later period of the individual in question. I called this form of displacement a retro-active or *regressive* one. Perhaps more often, one finds the reversed relation—that is, an indifferent impression of the most remote period becomes a concealing memory in consciousness, which simply owes its existence to an association with an earlier experience, against whose direct reproduction there are resistances. We would

[1] Published in the *Monatschrift f. Psychiatrie u. Neurologie,* 1899.

call these *encroaching* or *interposing* concealing memories. What most concerns the memory lies here chronologically beyond the concealing memory. Finally, there may be a third possible case, namely, the concealing memory may be connected with the impression it conceals, not only through its contents, but also through contiguity of time; this is the *contemporaneous* or *contiguous* concealing memory.

How large a portion of the sum total of our memory belongs to the category of concealing memories, and what part it plays in various neurotic hidden processes, these are problems into the value of which I have neither inquired, nor shall I enter here. I am concerned only with emphasizing the sameness between the forgetting of proper names with faulty recollection and the formation of concealing memories.

At first sight, it would seem that the diversities of both phenomena are far more striking than their exact analogies. There we deal with proper names, here with complete impressions experienced either in reality or in thought; there we deal with a manifest failure of the memory function, here with a memory act which appears strange to us. Again, there we are concerned with a momentary disturbance—for the name just forgotten could have been reproduced correctly a hundred times before, and will be so again from tomorrow on; here we deal with lasting possession without a failure, for the indifferent childhood memories seem to be able to accompany us through a great part of life. In both these cases, the riddle seems to be solved in an entirely different way. There it is the forgetting, while here it is the remembering which excites our scientific curiosity.

After deeper reflection, one realizes that, although there is a diversity in the psychic material and in the duration of time of the two phenomena, yet these are by far outweighed by the conformities between the two. In both cases we deal with the failure of remembering; what should be correctly reproduced by the memory fails to appear, and instead something else comes as a substitute. In the case of forgetting a name, there is no lack of memory function in the form of name substitution. The formation of a concealing memory depends on the forgetting of other important impressions. In both cases, we are reminded by an intellectual feeling of the intervention of a disturbance, which in each case takes a different form. In the case of forgetting of names, *we are aware* that the substitutive names are *incorrect*, while in concealing memories, we are surprised that we have them at all. Hence, if psychologic analysis demonstrates that the substitutive formation in each case is brought about in the same manner —that is, through displacement along a superficial association—we are justified in saying that the diversities in material, in duration of time, and in the centering of both phenomena serve to enhance our expectation, that we have discovered something that is important and of general value. This generality purports that the stopping and straying of the reproducing function indicates more often than we suppose that there is an intervention of a prejudicial factor, a tendency which favors one memory and, at the same time, works against another.

The subject of childhood memories appears to me so important and interesting that I would like to devote to it a few additional remarks which go beyond the views expressed so far.

How far back into childhood do our memories reach? I am familiar with some investigations on this question by V. and C. Henri [1] and Potwin.[2] They assert that such examinations show wide individual variations, inasmuch as some trace their first reminiscences to the sixth month of life, while others can recall nothing of their lives before the end of the sixth or even the eighth year. But what connection is there between these variations in the behavior of childhood reminiscences, and what significance may be ascribed to them? It seems that it is not enough to procure the material for this question by simple inquiry, but it must later be subjected to a study in which the person furnishing the information must participate.

I believe we accept too indifferently the fact of infantile amnesia—that is, the failure of memory for the first years of our lives—and fail to find in it a strange riddle. We forget of what great intellectual accomplishments and of what complicated emotions a child of four years is capable. We really ought to wonder why the memory of later years has, as a rule, retained so little of these psychic processes, especially as we have every reason for assuming that these same forgotten childhood activities have not glided off without leaving a trace in the development of the person, but that they have left a definite influence for all future time. Yet, in spite of this unparalleled effectiveness they were forgotten! This would suggest that there are particularly formed conditions of memory (in the sense of conscious reproduction) which have thus far eluded our knowledge. It is quite possible that the forgetting of childhood may give us the key to the understanding of those amnesias which, according to our newer studies, lie at the basis of the formation of all neurotic symptoms.

Of these retained childhood reminiscences, some appear to us readily comprehensible, while others seem strange or unintelligible. It is not difficult to correct certain errors in regard to both kinds. If the retained reminiscences of a person are subjected to an analytic test, it can be readily ascertained that a guarantee for their correctness does not exist. Some of the memory pictures are surely falsified and incomplete, or displaced in point of time and place. The assertions of persons examined, that their first memories reach back perhaps to their second year, are evidently unreliable. Motives can soon be discovered which explain the disfigurement and the displacement of these experiences, but they also demonstrate that these memory lapses are not the result of a mere unreliable memory. Powerful forces from a later period have moulded the memory capacity of our infantile experiences, and it is probably due to these same forces that the understanding of our childhood is generally so very strange to us.

The recollection of adults, as is known, proceeds through different psychic material. Some recall by means of visual pictures—their memories are of a visual character; other individuals can scarcely reproduce in memory the most paltry sketch of an experience; we call such persons *"auditifs"* and *"moteurs"* in contrast to the *"visuels,"* terms proposed by Charcot. These differences vanish in dreams; all our dreams are preponderatingly visual. But this development is also found in the childhood memories; the latter are plastic and visual, even in those people whose later memory lacks the visual element. The visual memory, therefore, preserves the type of the infantile recollections. Only my earliest childhood memories are of a visual character; they represent plastically depicted scenes, comparable only to stage settings.

In these scenes of childhood, whether they prove true or false, one usually sees his own childish person both in contour and dress. This circumstance must excite our wonder, for adults do not see their own persons in their recollections of later experiences.[1] It is, moreover, against our experiences to assume that the child's attention during his experiences is centered on himself rather than exclusively on outside impressions. Various sources force us to assume that the so-called earliest childhood recollections are not true memory traces but later elaborations of the same, elaborations which might have been subjected to the influences of many later psychic forces. Thus, the "childhood reminiscences" of individuals altogether advance to the signification of "concealing memories," and thereby form a noteworthy analogy to the childhood reminiscences as laid down in the legends and myths of nations.

Whoever has examined mentally a number of persons by the method of psychoanalysis must have gathered in this work numerous examples of concealing memories of every description. However, owing to the previously discussed nature of the relations of the childhood reminiscences to later life, it becomes extraordinarily difficult to report such examples. For, in order to attach the value of the concealing memory to an infantile reminiscence, it would be often necessary to present the entire life-history of the person concerned. Only seldom is it possible, as in the following

---

[1] I assert this as a result of certain investigations made by myself.

good example, to take out from its context and report a single childhood memory.

A twenty-four-year-old man preserved the following picture from the fifth year of his life: In the garden of a summer-house, he sat on a stool next to his aunt, who was engaged in teaching him the alphabet. He found difficulty in distinguishing the letter *m* from *n*, and he begged his aunt to tell him how to tell one from the other. His aunt called his attention to the fact that the letter *m* had one whole portion (a stroke) more than the letter *n*. There was no reason to dispute the reliability of this childhood recollection; its meaning, however, was discovered only later, when it showed itself to be the symbolic representation of another boyish inquisitiveness. For just as he wanted to know the difference between *m* and *n* at that time, so he concerned himself later about the difference between boy and girl, and he would have been willing that just this aunt should be his teacher. He also discovered that the difference was a similar one; that the boy again had one whole portion more than the girl, and at the time of this recognition, his memory awoke to the corresponding childish inquisitiveness.

The following interesting example is given by Brill:

"One of my patients informed me once that his memory went back to the time of his baptism, when he was about a week old. He maintained that he distinctly remembered the house and the stairway leading up to the first floor where he was supposed to have been baptized. He particularly recalled a lamp standing at the foot of the stairs and the minister who performed the baptism, a tall man in a black frock coat. He remembered vividly how his head was totally submerged in a basin of water. I was naturally skeptical and explained to him that I thought it was a concealing memory which probably hid something else of a much later date. He then informed me that he had entertained this memory for many years, but that when he imparted it to his mother, a few years ago, she laughed, declaring that there was no truth in it, that in the first place, he was not born in this particular house, but that he had merely lived there from the age of four to six, that she could not recall this particular lamp, that the minister who really baptized him was not tall, and what was more, that the baby's head is not submerged in a basin of water during baptism. Notwithstanding his mother's absolute denial, the patient continued to entertain this memory; he strongly felt that it was true despite all facts to the contrary.

"We then proceeded to analyze it. He stated that the most vivid element in the memory was the lamp, and so I asked him to concentrate his attention on it and give me his associations. He could see the lamp at the foot of the stairs, the stairway, and the room on the first floor. He then recalled that at the age of about five years, he was standing one afternoon in that room watching a Swedish servant who was either on a high chair or a step-ladder cleaning the chandelier. He became very inquisitive sexually and made a great effort to look under her clothes. She noticed it and gave him a very strong rebuke. He then recalled that a few years later, he watched through a keyhole to see his mother dress, and somehow she caught him and punished him very severely for it. He was very much humiliated, for she took him downstairs to the dining room and told his father and brother what he had done. At about the same age, probably a little before this episode with his mother, he was on the roof one evening and spied a woman undressing in a house across the street. In his great excitement, he ran down to call his brother, but when he returned, the woman had already slipped a nightgown on and was now pulling down the shades. He told me that for years he regretted that he went to call his brother. He kept on reproducing more scenes, all of which dealt with frustrated sexual looking.

"The lamp, therefore, represented a contrast association of darkness which stood in the way of his sexual inquisitiveness. That is why the lamp element was so accentuated in his memory.

"The question now presents itself, 'Why did he remember the fact of his baptism so vividly?' This young man is a good Christian; his parents are Christians, but his paternal grandfather was a Jew. He himself shows no traces of Semitism; the only thing he retains from his grandfather is the name. It is a German name which is often mistaken for a Jewish one, and for this reason, it has given him considerable trouble. He was refused, for instance, admission to a certain school because of his name. At college it was suspected that he was Jewish, and on that account he failed to be elected to a fraternity that admitted only Gentiles. The concealing memory of his baptism is thus a compensation for his suspected Judaism and that is why it retained its vividness, his mother's denial to the contrary. He had to be assured that he was baptized and, therefore, was a Christian. On the whole, the memory represents a religious scene in order to hide an immoral scene of marked affective content."

I would like to show by one more example the sense that may be gained by a childhood reminiscence through analytic work, although it may seem to contain no sense before. In my forty-third year, when I began to interest myself in what remained in my memory of my own childhood, a scene struck me which for a long time, as I afterwards believed, had repeatedly come to consciousness, and which through reliable identification could be traced to a period before the completion of my third year. I saw myself in front of a chest, the door of which was held open by my half-brother, twenty years my senior. I stood there demanding something and screaming; my mother, pretty and slender, then suddenly entered the room, as if returning from the street.

In these words I formulated this scene so vividly seen, which, however, furnished no other clue. Whether my brother wished to open or lock the chest (in the first explanation it was a "cupboard"), why I cried, and what bearing the arrival of my mother had, all these questions were dim to me; I was tempted to explain to myself that it dealt with the memory of a hoax by my older brother, which was interrupted by my mother. Such misunderstandings of childhood scenes retained in memory are not uncommon; we recall a situation, but it is not centralized; we do not know on which of the elements to place the psychic accent. Analytic effort led me to an entirely unexpected solution of the picture. I missed my mother and began to suspect that she was locked in this cupboard or chest, and therefore demanded that my brother should unlock it. As he obliged me and I became convinced that she was not in the chest, I began to cry; this is the moment firmly retained in the memory, which was directly followed by the appearance of my mother, who appeased my worry and anxiety.

But how did the child get the idea of looking for the absent mother in the chest? Dreams which occurred at the same time pointed dimly to a nurse, concerning whom other reminiscences were retained; as, for example, that she conscientiously urged me to deliver to her the small coins which I received as gifts, a detail which in itself may lay claim to the value of a concealing memory for later things. I then concluded to facilitate for myself this time the task of interpretation, and asked my now aged mother about that nurse. I found out all sorts of things, among others the fact that this shrewd but dishonest person had committed extensive robberies during the confinement of my mother, and that my half-brother was instrumental in bringing her to justice.

This information gave me the key to the scene from childhood, as through a sort of inspiration. The sudden disappearance of the nurse was not a matter of indifference to me; I had just asked this brother where she was, probably because I had noticed that he had played a part in her disappearance, and he, evasive and witty as he is to this day, answered that she was "boxed in." I understood this answer in the childish way, but asked no more, as there was nothing else to be discovered. When my mother left me shortly thereafter, I suspected that the naughty brother had treated her in the same way as he did the nurse, and therefore pressed him to open the chest.

I also understand now why in the translation of the visual childhood scene, my mother's slenderness was accentuated; she must have struck me as being newly restored. I am two-and-a-half years older than the sister born at that time, and when I was three years of age, I was separated from my half-brother.

V

MISTAKES IN SPEECH

ALTHOUGH the ordinary material of speech of our mother-tongue seems to be guarded against forgetting, its application, however, more often succumbs to another disturbance which is familiar to us as "slips of the tongue." What we observe in normal persons as slips of the tongue gives the same impression as the first step of the so-called "paraphasias" which manifest themselves under pathologic conditions.

I am in the exceptional position of being about to refer to a previous work on the subject. In the year 1895, Meringer and C. Mayer published a study on *Mistakes in Speech and Reading*, with whose viewpoints I do not agree. One of the authors, who is the spokesman in the text, is a philologist actuated by a linguistic interest to examine the rules governing those slips. He hoped to deduce from these rules the existence "of a definite psychic mechanism," "whereby the sounds of a word, of a sentence, and even the words themselves, would be associated and connected with one another in a quite peculiar manner" (p. 10).

The authors grouped the examples of speech-mistakes collected by them first, according to purely descriptive viewpoints, such as interchangings (*e.g.,* the Milo of Venus instead of the Venus of Milo), as anticipations (*e.g.,* the shoes made her sorft . . . the shoes made her feet sore), as echoes and post positions, as contaminations (*e.g.,* "I will soon him home," instead of "I will soon go home and I will see him"), and substitutions (*e.g.,* "he entrusted his money to a savings crank," instead of "a savings bank").[1] Besides these principal categories, there are some others of lesser importance (or of lesser significance for our purpose). In this grouping it makes no difference whether the transposition, disfigurement, fusion, etc., affects single sounds of the word or syllables, or whole words of the concerned sentence.

To explain the various forms of mistakes in speech, Meringer assumes a varied psychic value of phonetics. As soon as the innervation affects the first syllable of a word, or the first word of a sentence, the stimulating

[1] The examples are given by the editor.

process immediately strikes the succeeding sounds, and the following words, and in so far as these innervations are synchronous, they may effect some changes in one another. The stimulus of the psychically more intensive sound "rings" before or continues echoing, and thus disturbs the less important process of innervation. It is necessary therefore to determine which are the most important sounds of a word. Meringer states: "If one wishes to know which sound of a word possesses the greatest intensity, he should examine himself while searching for a forgotten word, for example, a name. That which first returns to consciousness invariably had the greatest intensity prior to the forgetting (p. 160). Thus the most important sounds are the initial sound of the root-syllable and the initial sound of the word itself, as well as one or another of the accentuated vowels" (p. 162).

Here, I cannot help voicing a contradiction. Whether or not the initial sound of the name belongs to the most important elements of the word, it is surely not true that in the case of the forgetting of the word it first returns to consciousness; the above rule is therefore of no use. When we observe ourselves during the search for a forgotten name, we are comparatively often forced to express the opinion that it begins with a certain letter. This conviction proves to be as often unfounded as founded. Indeed, I would even go so far as to assert that in the majority of cases, one reproduces a false initial sound. Also, in our example *Signorelli*, the substitutive name lacked the initial sound, and the principal syllables were lost; on the other hand, the less important pair of syllables *elli* returned to consciousness in the substitutive name *Botticelli*.

How little substitutive names respect the initial sound of the lost names may be learned from the following case. One day, I found it impossible to recall the name of the small country whose capital is *Monte Carlo*. The substitutive names were as follows: *Piedmont, Albania, Montevideo, Colico*. In place of Albania, *Montenegro* soon appeared, and then it struck me that the syllable *Mont* (pronounced *Mon*) occurred in all but the last of the substitutive names. It thus became easy for me to find from the name of Prince Albert the forgotten name *Monaco*. *Colico* practically imitates the syllabic sequence and rhythm of the forgotten name.

If we admit the conjecture that a mechanism similar to that pointed out in the forgetting of names may also play a part in the phenomena of speech-blunders, we are then led to a better-founded judgment of cases of speech-blunders. The speech disturbance which manifests itself as a speech-blunder may, in the first place, be caused by the influence of another component of the same speech; that is, through a fore-sound or an echo, or through another meaning within the sentence or context which differs from that which the speaker wishes to utter. In the second place, however, the disturbance could be brought about analogously to the process in the case *Signorelli,* through influences outside this word, sentence or context, from elements which we did not intend to express, and of whose incitement we became conscious only through the disturbance. In both modes of origin of the mistake in speech, the common element lies in the simultaneity of the stimulus, while the differentiating elements lie in the arrangement within or without the same sentence or context.

The difference does not at first appear as wide as when it is taken into consideration in certain conclusions drawn from the symptomatology of speech-mistakes. It is clear, however, that only in the first case, is there a prospect of drawing conclusions from the manifestations of speech-blunders concerning a mechanism which connects together sounds and words for the reciprocal influence of their articulation; that is, conclusions such as the philologist hopes to gain from the study of speech-blunders. In the case of disturbance through influence outside of the same sentence or context, it would before all be a question of becoming acquainted with the disturbing elements, and then the question would arise whether the mechanism of this disturbance cannot also suggest the probable laws of the formation of speech.

We cannot maintain that Meringer and Mayer have overlooked the possibility of speech disturbance through "complicated psychic influences," that is, through elements outside of the same word or sentence or the same sequence of words. Indeed, they must have observed that the theory of the psychic variation of sound applies, strictly speaking, only to the explanation of sound disturbances as well as to fore-sounds and after-sounds. Where the word disturbances cannot be reduced to sound disturbances, as, for example, in the substitutions and contaminations of words, they, too, have without hesitation sought the cause of the mistake in speech outside of the intended context, and proved this state of affairs by means of fitting examples.[1] According to the authors' own understanding, it is some similarity between a certain word in the intended sentence and some other not intended, which allows the latter to assert itself in consciousness by causing a disfigurement, a composition or a compromise formation (contamination).

Now, in my *Interpretation of Dreams,* I have shown the part played by the process of *condensation* in the origin of the so-called manifest contents of the dream from the latent thoughts of the dream. Any similarity of objects or of word-presentations between two elements of the unconscious material is taken as a cause for the formation of a third, which is a composite or compromise formation. This element represents both components in the dream content, and in view of this origin, it is frequently endowed with numerous contradictory individual determinants. The formation of substitutions and contaminations in speech-mistakes is, there

[1] Those who are interested are referred to pp. 62, 73 and 97 of these authors' work.

fore, the beginning of that work of condensation, which we find taking a most active part in the construction of the dream.

In a small essay destined for the general reader,[1] Meringer advanced a theory of very practical significance for certain cases of interchanging of words, especially for such cases where one word is substituted by another of opposite meaning. He says: "We may still recall the manner in which the President of the Austrian House of Deputies opened the session some time ago: 'Honored Sirs! I announce the presence of so and so many gentlemen, and therefore declare the session as "closed" ' !'" The general merriment first attracted his attention and he corrected his mistake. In the present case, the probable explanation is that the President wished himself in a position to close this session, from which he had little good to expect, and the thought broke through at least partially—a frequent manifestation—resulting in his use of "closed" in place of "opened," that is, the opposite of the statement intended. Numerous observations have taught me, however, that we frequently interchange contrasting words; they are already associated in our speech consciousness; they lie very close together and are easily incorrectly evoked.

Still, not in all cases of contrast substitution is it so simple as in the example of the President as to appear plausible that the speech-mistake occurs merely as a contradiction which arises in the inner thought of the speaker opposing the sentence uttered. We have found the analogous mechanism in the analysis of the example *aliquis;* there the inner contradiction asserts itself in the form of forgetting a word instead of a substitution through its opposite. But in order to adjust the difference, we may remark that the little word *aliquis* is incapable of a contrast similar to "closing" and "opening," and that the word "opening" cannot be subject to forgetting on account of its being a common component of speech.

Having been shown by the last examples of Meringer and Mayer that speech disturbance may be caused through the influence of fore-sounds, after-sounds, words from the same sentence that were intended for expression, as well as through the effect of words outside the sentence intended, *the stimulus of which would otherwise not have been suspected*, we shall next wish to discover two classes of mistakes in speech, and how we can distinguish the example of the one from a case of the other class.

But at this stage of the discussion, we must also think of the assertions of Wundt, who deals with the manifestations of speech-mistakes in his recent work on the development of language.[2] Psychic influences, according to Wundt, never lack in these as well as in other phenomena related to them. "The uninhibited stream of *sound* and *word associations* stimulated by spoken sounds belongs here, in the first place, as a positive

---

[1] *Neue Freie Presse,* August 23, 1900: "Wie man sich versprechen kann."
[2] *Völker psychologie,* vol. i., pt. i., p. 371, etc., 1900.

determinant. This is supported as a negative factor by the relaxation or suppression of the influences of the will which inhibit this stream, and by the active attention which is here a function of volition. Whether that play of associations manifests itself in the fact that a coming sound is anticipated or a preceding sound reproduced, or whether a familiar practised sound becomes intercalated between others, or finally, whether it manifests itself in the fact that altogether different sounds associatively related to the spoken sounds act upon these—all these questions designate only differences in the direction, and at most in the play of the occurring associations but not in the general nature of the same. In some cases, it may be also doubtful to which form a certain disturbance may be attributed, or whether it would not be more correct to refer such disturbance to a concurrence of many motives, *following the principle of the complication of causes*" [1] (cf. pp. 380-81).

I consider these observations of Wundt as absolutely justified and very instructive. Perhaps we could emphasize with even greater firmness than Wundt that the positive factor favoring mistakes in speech (the uninhibited stream of associations, and its negative, the relaxation of the inhibiting attention) regularly attain synchronous action, so that both factors become only different determinants of the same process. With the relaxation or, more unequivocally expressed, *through* this relaxation, of the inhibiting attention, the uninhibited stream of associations becomes active.

Among the examples of the mistakes in speech collected by me, I can scarcely find one in which I would be obliged to attribute the speech disturbance simply and solely to what Wundt calls "contact effect of sound." Almost invariably I discover besides this a disturbing influence of something *outside* of the intended speech. The disturbing element is either a single unconscious thought, which comes to light through the speech-blunder and can only be brought to consciousness through a searching analysis, or it is a more general psychic motive, which directs itself against the entire speech.

Example (a) Seeing my daughter make an unpleasant face while biting into an apple, I wished to quote the following couplet:

> "The ape he is a funny sight,
> When in the apple he takes a bite."

But I began: "*The apel* . . ." This seems to be a contamination of "*ape*" and "*apple*" (compromise formation), or it may be also conceived as an anticipation of the prepared "apple." The true state of affairs, however, was this: I began the quotation once before, and made no mistake

[1] Italics are mine.

the first time. I made the mistake only during the repetition, which was necessary because my daughter, having been distracted from another side, did not listen to me. This repetition with the added impatience to disburden myself of the sentence I must include in the motivation of the speech-blunder, which represented itself as a function of condensation.

(b) My daughter said, "I wrote to Mrs. Schresinger." The woman's name was Schlesinger. This speech-blunder may depend on the tendency to facilitate articulation. I must state, however, that this mistake was made by my daughter a few moments after I had said *apel* instead of *ape*. Mistakes in speech are in a great measure contagious; a similar peculiarity was noticed by Meringer and Mayer in the forgetting of names. I know of no reason for this psychic contagiousness.

(c) "I *sut* up like a pocket knife," said a patient in the beginning of treatment, instead of "I *shut* up." This suggests a difficulty of articulation which may serve as an excuse for the interchanging of sounds. When her attention was called to the speech-blunder, she promptly replied, "Yes, that happened because you said *'earnesht'* instead of *'earnest'*." As a matter of fact, I received her with the remark, "Today we shall be in earnest" (because it was the last hour before her discharge from treatment), and I jokingly changed the word into *earnesht*. In the course of the hour, she repeatedly made mistakes in speech, and I finally observed that it was not only because she imitated me but because she had a special reason in her unconscious to linger at the word earnest (Ernst) as a name.[1]

(d) A woman, speaking about a game invented by her children and called by them "the man in the box," said "the manx in the boc." I could readily understand her mistake. It was while analyzing her dream, in which her husband is depicted as very generous in money matters—just the reverse of reality—that she made this speech-blunder. The day before she had asked for a new set of furs, which her husband denied her, claiming that he could not afford to spend so much money. She upbraided him for his stinginess, "for putting away so much into the strongbox," and mentioned a friend whose husband has not nearly his income, and yet he presented his wife with a *mink* coat for her birthday. The mistake is now comprehensible. The word *manx (manks)* reduces itself to the "minks" which she longs for, and the *box* refers to her husband's stinginess.[2]

(e) A similar mechanism is shown in the mistake of another patient

[1] It turned out that she was under the influence of unconscious thoughts concerning pregnancy and prevention of conception. With the words "shut up like a pocket knife," which she uttered consciously as a complaint, she meant to describe the position of the child in the womb. The word "earnest" in my remark recalled to her the name (S. Ernst) of the well-known Vienna business firm in Kärthner Strasse, which used to advertise the sale of articles for the prevention of conception.
[2] Given by Editor.

whose memory deserted her in the midst of a long-forgotten childish reminiscence. Her memory failed to inform her on what part of the body the prying and lustful hand of another had touched her. Soon thereafter she visited one of her friends, with whom she discussed summer homes. Asked where her cottage in M. was located, she answered, "Near the *mountain loin*" instead of "*mountain lane.*"

(f) Another patient, whom I asked at the end of her visit how her uncle was, answered: "I don't know, I only see him now *in flagranti.*" The following day she said: "I am really ashamed of myself for having given you such a stupid answer yesterday. Naturally, you must have thought me a very uneducated person who always mistakes the meaning of foreign words. I wished to say *en passant.*" We did not know at the time where she got the incorrectly used foreign words, but during the same session, she reproduced a reminiscence as a continuation of the theme from the previous day, in which being caught *in flagranti* played the principal part. The mistake of the previous day had therefore anticipated the recollection, which, at that time, had not yet become conscious.

(g) "In discussing her summer plans, a patient said, 'I shall remain most of the summer in *Elberlon.*' She noted her mistake, and asked me to analyze it. The associations to *Elberlon* elicited: seashore on the Jersey coast—summer resort—vacation travelling. This recalled travelling in Europe with her cousin, a topic which we had discussed the day before during the analysis of a dream. The dream dealt with her dislike for this cousin, and she admitted that it was mainly due to the fact that the latter was the favorite of the man whom they met together while travelling abroad. During the dream analysis, she could not recall the name of the city in which they met this man, and I did not make any effort at the time to bring it to her consciousness, as we were engrossed in a totally different problem. When asked to focus her attention again on Elberlon and reproduce her associations, she said, 'It brings to mind *Elberlawn— lawn—field—*and *Elberfield.*' Elberfield was the lost name of the city in Germany. Here the mistake served to bring to consciousness in a concealed manner a memory which was connected with a painful feeling.

(h) "The following *lapsus linguae* was reported by the New York *Times* (October 7th, 1937):

" 'Delegates to the convention of the Georgia division of the United Daughters of the Confederacy listened appreciatively, while Mrs. Walter D. Lamar eulogized Jefferson Davis last night.

" 'The State Historian General concluded with warm enthusiasm: "Let the world know the wisdom, the kindness, the justice of the great and only President of the Confederate States of America—*Abraham Lincoln!*"

" 'Only after she had resumed her seat did a subdued gasp from her listeners make her realize her lapse.

" ' "It was just one of those slips that may happen at moments of enthusiasm," Mrs. Lamar said." '

"Yes! The speaker is right, but we must know that the process of enthusiasm is nothing but a heightened emotional state in which conscious attention is almost completely suspended. In such a state, one unwittingly displays his true feelings and as under the influence of alcohol, the truth comes out." [1]

(i) Before calling on me, a patient telephoned for an appointment and also wished to be informed about my consultation fee. He was told that the first consultation was ten dollars; after the examination was over, he again asked what he was to pay and added: "I don't like to owe money to anyone, especially to doctors; I prefer to pay right away." Instead of *pay* he said *play*. His last voluntary remarks and his mistake put me on my guard, but after a few more uncalled-for remarks, he set me at ease by taking money from his pocket. He counted four paper dollars and was very chagrined and surprised because he had no more money with him and promised to send me a cheque for the balance. I was sure that his mistake betrayed him, that he was only *playing* with me, but there was nothing to be done. At the end of a few weeks, I sent him a bill for the balance, and the letter was returned to me by the post office authorities marked "Not found."

(j) Miss X. spoke very warmly of Mr. Y., which was rather strange, as before this, she had always expressed her indifference, not to say her contempt, for him. On being asked about this sudden change of heart, she said: "I really never had anything against him; he was always nice to me, but I never gave him the chance to cultivate my acquaintance." She said "cuptivate." This neologism was a contamination of *cultivate* and *captivate,* and foretold the coming betrothal.

(k) An illustration of the mechanisms of contamination and condensation will be found in the following *lapsus linguae.* Speaking of Miss Z., Miss W. depicted her as a very "straitlaced" person who was not given to levity, etc. Miss X. thereupon remarked: "Yes, that is a very characteristic description, she always appealed to me as very *straicet-brazed.*" Here the mistake resolved itself into *straitlaced* and *brazenfaced,* which corresponded to Miss W.'s opinion of Miss Z.

(l) I was to give a lecture to a woman. Her husband, upon whose request this was done, stood behind the door listening. At the end of my sermonizing, which had made a visible impression, I said: "Goodbye, Sir!" To the experienced person, I thus betrayed the fact that the words were directed towards the husband, that I had spoken to oblige him.

[1] Given by Editor.

(m) Two women stopped in front of a drugstore, and one said to her companion, "If you will wait a few *moments,* I'll soon be back," but she said *movements* instead. She was on her way to buy some castoria for her child.

(n) Mr. L., who is fonder of being called on than of calling, spoke to me through the telephone from a nearby summer resort. He wanted to know when I would pay him a visit. I reminded him that it was his turn to visit me, and called his attention to the fact that, as he was the happy possessor of an automobile, it would be easier for him to call on me. (We were at different summer resorts, separated by about one half-hour's railway trip.) He gladly promised to call and asked: "How about Labor Day (September 1st), will it be convenient for you?" When I answered in the affirmative, he said, "Very well, then, put me down for *Election* Day" (November). His mistake was quite plain. He likes to visit me, but it was inconvenient to travel so far. In November, we would both be in the city. My analysis proved correct.

(o) A friend described to me a nervous patient and wished to know whether I could benefit him. I remarked: "I believe that in time I can remove all his symptoms by psychoanalysis, because it is a durable case," wishing to say "curable"!

(p) I repeatedly addressed my patient as "Mrs. Smith," her married daughter's name, when her real name is "Mrs. James." My attention having been called to it, I soon discovered that I had another patient of the same name who refused to pay for the treatment. Mrs. Smith was also my patient and paid her bills promptly.

(q) A *lapsus linguae* sometimes stands for a particular characteristic. A young woman, who is the dominating spirit in her home, said of her ailing husband, that he had consulted the doctor about a wholesome diet for himself, and then added: "The doctor said that diet has nothing to do with his ailments, and that he can eat and drink what *I* want."

(r) I cannot omit this excellent and instructive example, although, according to my authority, it is about twenty years old. A lady once expressed herself in society—the very words show that they were uttered with fervor and under the pressure of a great many secret emotions: "Yes, a woman must be pretty if she is to please the men. A man is much better off. As long as he has *five* straight limbs, he needs no more!"

This example affords us a good insight into the intimate mechanisms of a mistake in speech by means of condensation and contamination. It is quite obvious that we have here a fusion of two similar modes of expression:

"As long as he has his four *straight limbs.*"

"As long as he has all his *five senses.*"

Or the term "straight" may be the common element of the two intended expressions:

"As long as he has his *straight* limbs."

"All five should be *straight*."

It may also be assumed that both modes of expression—viz., those of the five senses and those of the straight five—have coöperated to introduce into the sentence about the straight limbs first a number and then the mysterious five instead of the simple four. But this fusion surely would not have succeeded if it had not expressed good sense in the form resulting from the mistake; if it had not expressed a cynical truth which, naturally, could not be uttered unconcealed, coming as it did from a woman.

Finally, we shall not hesitate to call attention to the fact that the woman's saying, following its wording, would just as well be an excellent witticism as a jocose speech-blunder. It is simply a question whether she uttered these words with conscious or unconscious intention. The behavior of the speaker in this case certainly speaks against the conscious intention, and thus excludes wit.

(s) Owing to similarity of material, I add here another case of speech-blunder, the interpretation of which requires less skill. A professor of anatomy strove to explain the nostril, which, as is known, is a very difficult anatomical structure. To his question whether his audience grasped his ideas, he received an affirmative reply. The professor, known for his self-esteem, thereupon remarked: "I can hardly believe this, for the number of people who understand the nostril, even in a city of millions like Vienna, can be counted *on a finger*—pardon me, I meant to say *on the fingers* of a hand."

In the psychotherapeutic procedure which I employ in the solution and removal of neurotic symptoms, I am often confronted with the task of discovering from the accidental utterances and fancies of the patient the thought contents, which, though striving for concealment, nevertheless unintentionally betray themselves. In doing this, the mistakes often perform the most valuable service, as I can show through most convincing and still most singular examples.

For example, patients speak of an aunt and later, without noting the mistake, call her "my mother," or designate a husband as a "brother." In this way, they attract my attention to the fact that they have "identified" these persons with each other, that they have placed them in the same category, which for their emotional life signifies the recurrence of the same type. Or, a young man of twenty years presents himself during my office hours with these words: "I am the father of N. N., whom you have treated—pardon me, I mean the brother; why, he is four years older than I." I understand through this mistake that he wishes to express that, like the brother, he, too, is ill through the fault of the father; like his brother he wishes to be cured, but that the father is the one most in need of treatment. At other times, an unusual arrangement of words, or a forced expression, is sufficient to disclose in the speech of a patient the participation of a repressed thought having a different motive.

Hence, in coarse as well as in finer speech disturbances, which may, nevertheless, be subsumed as "speech-blunders," I find that it is not the contact effects of the sound, but the thoughts outside the intended speech, which determine the origin of the speech-blunder, and also suffice to explain the newly formed mistakes in speech. I do not doubt the laws whereby the sounds produce changes upon one another; but they alone do not appear to me sufficiently forcible to mar the correct execution of speech. In those cases which I have studied and investigated more closely, they merely represent the preformed mechanism, which is conveniently utilized by a more remote psychic motive. The latter does not, however, form a part of the sphere of influence of these sound relations. *In a large number of substitutions caused by mistakes in talking, there is an entire absence of such phonetic laws.* In this respect, I am in full accord with Wundt, who likewise assumes that the conditions underlying speech-blunders are complex and go far beyond the contact effect of the sounds.

If I accept as certain "these more remote psychic influences," following Wundt's expression, there is still nothing to detain me from conceding also that in accelerated speech, with a certain amount of diverted attention, the causes of speech-blunder may be easily limited to the definite law of Meringer and Mayer. However, in a number of examples gathered by these authors, a more complicated solution is quite apparent.

In some forms of speech-blunders we may assume that the disturbing factor is the result of striking against obscene words and meanings. The purposive disfigurement and distortion of words and phrases, which is so popular with vulgar persons, aims at nothing else but the employing of a harmless motive as a reminder of the obscene, and this sport is so frequent that it would not be at all remarkable if it appeared unintentionally and contrary to the will.

I trust that the readers will not depreciate the value of these interpretations, for which there is no proof, and of these examples which I have myself collected and explained by means of analysis. But, if secretly I still cherish the expectation that even the apparently simple cases of speech-blunder will be traced to a disturbance caused by a half-repressed idea outside of the intended context, I am tempted to it by a noteworthy observation of Meringer. This author asserts that it is remarkable that nobody wishes to admit having made a mistake in speaking. There are many intelligent and honest people who are offended if we tell them that they made a mistake in speaking. I would not risk making this assertion as general as does Meringer, using the term "nobody." But the emotional trace which clings to the demonstration of the mistake, which manifestly belongs to the nature of shame, has its significance. It may be classed with the anger displayed at the inability to recall a forgotten name, and with the surprise at the tenaciousness of an apparently indifferent memory, and it invariably points to the participation of a motive in the formation of the disturbance.

The distorting of names amounts to an insult when done intentionally, and could have the same significance in a whole series of cases where it appears as unintentional speech-blunders. The person who, according to Mayer's report, once said "Freuder" instead of "Freud," because shortly before he pronounced the name "Breuer," and what at another time, spoke of the "Freuer-Breudian" method, was certainly not particularly enthusiastic over this method. Later, under the mistakes in writing, I shall report a case of name disfigurement which certainly admits of no other explanation.[1]

As a disturbing element in these cases, there is an intermingling of a criticism which must be omitted, because at the time being, it does not correspond to the intention of the speaker.

---

[1] It may be observed that aristocrats in particular very frequently distort the names of the physicians they consult, from which we may conclude that inwardly they slight them, in spite of the politeness with which they are wont to greet them. I shall cite here some excellent observations concerning the forgetting of names from the works of Dr. Ernest Jones: *Papers on Psychoanalysis*, Chap. iii., p. 49:

"Few people can avoid feeling a twinge of resentment when they find that their name has been forgotten, particularly if it is by someone with whom they had hoped or expected it would be remembered. They instinctively realize that if they had made a greater impression on the person's mind, he would certainly have remembered them again, for the name is an integral part of the personality. Similarly, few things are more flattering to most people than to find themselves addressed by name by a great personage where they could hardly have anticipated it. Napoleon, like most leaders of men, was a master of this art. In the midst of the disastrous campaign of France in 1814, he gave an amazing proof of his memory in this direction. When in a town near Craonne, he recollected that he had met the mayor, De Bussy, over twenty years ago in the La Fère Regiment. The delighted De Bussy at once threw himself into his service with extraordinary zeal. Conversely, there is no surer way of affronting someone than by pretending to forget his name; the insinuation is thus conveyed that the person is so unimportant in our eyes that we cannot be bothered to remember his name. This device is often exploited in literature. In Turgeniev's *Smoke* (p. 255) the following passage occurs: ' "So you still find Baden entertaining, M'sieur—Litvinov." Ratmirov always uttered Litvinov's surname with hesitation, every time, as though he had forgotten it, and could not at once recall it. In this way, as well as by the lofty flourish of his hat in saluting him, he meant to insult his pride.' The same author, in his *Fathers and Children* (p. 107), writes: 'The Governor invited Kirsanov and Bazarov to his ball, and within a few minutes invited them a second time, regarding them as brothers, and calling them Kisarov.' Here the forgetting that he had spoken to them, the mistake in the names and the inability to distinguish between the two young men, constitute a culmination of disparagement. Falsification of a name has the same signification as forgetting it; it is only a step towards complete amnesia."

A similar identification was reported to me concerning a young physician who timidly and reverently introduced himself to the celebrated Virchow with the following words: "I am Dr. Virchow." The surprised professor turned to him and asked, "Is your name also Virchow?" I do not know how the ambitious young man justified his speech-blunder, whether he thought of the charming excuse that he imagined himself so insignificant next to this big man that his own name slipped from him, or whether he had the courage to admit that he hoped that he, too, would some day be as great a man as Virchow, and that the professor should therefore not treat him in too disparaging a manner. One or both of these thoughts may have put this young man in an embarrassing position during the introduction.

Owing to very personal motives, I must leave it undecided whether a similar interpretation may also apply in the case to be cited. At the International Congress in Amsterdam, in 1907, my theories of hysteria were the subject of a lively discussion. One of my most violent opponents, in his diatribe against me, repeatedly made mistakes in speech in such a manner that he put himself in my place and spoke in my name. He said, for example, "Breuer and I, as is well known, have demonstrated," etc., when he wished to say "Breuer and Freud." The name of this opponent does not show the slightest sound similarity to my own. From this example, as well as from other cases of interchanging names in speech-blunders, we are reminded of the fact that the speech-blunder can fully forego the facility afforded to it through similar sounds, and can achieve its purpose if only supported in content by concealed relations.

In other and more significant cases, it is a self-criticism, an internal contradiction against one's own utterance, which causes the speech-blunder, and even forces a contrasting substitution for the one intended. We then observe with surprise how the wording of an assertion removes the purpose of the same, and how the error in speech lays bare the inner dishonesty. Here the *lapsus linguae* becomes a mimicking form of expression, often, indeed, for the expression of what one does not wish to say. It is thus a means of self-betrayal.

Brill relates: "I had recently been consulted by a woman who showed many paranoid trends, and as she had no relatives who could coöperate with me, I urged her to enter a State hospital as a voluntary patient. She was quite willing to do so, but on the following day, she told me that her friends, with whom she had leased an apartment, objected to her going to a hospital, as it would interfere with their plans, and so on. I lost patience and said: 'There is no use listening to your friends, who know nothing about your mental condition; you are quite *incompetent* to take care of your own affairs.' I meant to say 'competent.' Here, the *lapsus linguae* expressed my true opinion."

Favored by chance, the speech material often gives origin to examples of speech-blunders which serve to bring about an overwhelming revelation or a full comic effect, as shown by the following examples reported by Brill:

"A wealthy but not very generous host invited his friends for an evening dance. Everything went well until about 11:30 p.m., when there was an intermission, presumably for supper. To the great disappointment of most of the guests, there was no supper; instead, they were regaled with thin sandwiches and lemonade. As it was close to Election Day, the conversation centered on the different candidates; and as the discussion grew warmer, one of the guests, an ardent admirer of the Progressive Party candidate, remarked to the host: 'You may say what you please about Teddy, but there is one thing—he can always be relied upon, he always gives you a *square meal*,' wishing to say *square deal*. The assembled guests burst into a roar of laughter, to the great embarrassment of the speaker and the host, who fully understood each other."

"While writing a prescription for a woman who was especially weighed down by the financial burden of the treatment, I was interested to hear her say suddenly: 'Please do not give me *big bills*, because I cannot swallow them.' Of course, she meant to say *pills*."

The following example illustrates a rather serious case of self-betrayal through a mistake in talking. Some accessory details justify full reproduction as first printed by Dr. A. A. Brill.[1]

"While walking one night with Dr. Frink, we accidentally met a colleague, Dr. P., whom I had not seen for years, and of whose private life I knew nothing. We were naturally very pleased to meet again, and on my invitation, he accompanied us to a café, where we spent about two hours in pleasant conversation. To my question as to whether he was married, he gave a negative answer, and added, 'Why should a man like me marry?'

"On leaving the café, he suddenly turned to me and said: 'I should like to know what you would do in a case like this: I know a nurse who was named as co-respondent in a divorce case. The wife sued the husband for divorce and named her as co-respondent, and *he* got the divorce.' I interrupted him, saying, 'You mean *she* got the divorce.' He immediately corrected himself, saying, 'Yes, she got the divorce,' and continued to tell how the excitement of the trial had affected this nurse to such an extent that she became nervous and took to drink. He wanted me to advise him how to treat her.

"As soon as I had corrected his mistake, I asked him to explain it, but,

[1] *Zentralb. f. Psychoanalyse*, ii., Jahrg. i. Cf. also Brill's *Psychoanalysis: Its Theories and Practical Application*, p. 202. Saunders, Philadelphia and London.

as is usually the case, he was surprised at my question. He wanted to know whether a person had no right to make mistakes in talking. I explained to him that there is a reason for every mistake, and that if he had not told me that he was unmarried, I would say that he was the hero of the divorce case in question, and that the mistake showed that he wished he had obtained the divorce instead of his wife, so as not to be obliged to pay alimony and to be permitted to marry again in New York State.

"He stoutly denied my interpretation, but his emotional agitation, followed by loud laughter, only strengthened my suspicions. To my appeal that he should tell the truth 'for science' sake,' he said, 'Unless you wish me to lie, you must believe that I was never married, and hence, your psychoanalytic interpretation is all wrong.' He, however, added that it was dangerous to be with a person who paid attention to such little things. Then he suddenly remembered that he had another appointment and left us.

"Both Dr. Frink and I were convinced that my interpretation of his *lapsus linguae* was correct, and I decided to corroborate or disprove it by further investigation. The next day, I found a neighbor and old friend of Dr. P., who confirmed my interpretation in every particular. The divorce was granted to Dr. P.'s wife a few weeks before, and a nurse was named as co-respondent. A few weeks later, I met Dr. P., and he told me that he was thoroughly convinced of the Freudian mechanisms."

The self-betrayal is just as plain in the following case reported by Otto Rank:

A father who was devoid of all patriotic feeling and desirous of educating his children to be just as free from this superfluous sentiment, reproached his sons for participating in a patriotic demonstration, and rejected their reference to a similar behavior of their uncle with these words: "You are not obliged to imitate him; why, he is an *idiot*." The astonished features of the children at their father's unusual tone aroused him to the fact that he had made a mistake, and he remarked apologetically, "Of course, I wished to say *patriot*."

When such a speech-blunder occurs in a serious squabble and reverses the intended meaning of one of the disputants, at once it puts him at a disadvantage with his adversary—a disadvantage which the latter seldom fails to utilize.

This clearly shows that although people are unwilling to accept the theory of my conception and are not inclined to forego the convenience that is connected with the tolerance of a faulty action, they nevertheless interpret speech-blunders and other faulty acts in a manner similar to the one presented in this book. The merriment and derision which are sure to be evoked at the decisive moment through such linguistic mistakes, speak conclusively against the generally accepted convention that such a speech-blunder is a *lapsus linguae* and psychologically of no importance.

A nice example of speech-blunder, which aims not so much at the betrayal of the speaker as at the enlightenment of the listener outside the scene, is found in Wallenstein (*Piccolomini*, Act. I, Scene 5), and shows us that the poet, who here uses this means, is well-versed in the mechanism and intent of speech-blunders. In the preceding scene, Max Piccolomini was passionately in favor of the ducal party, and was enthusiastic over the blessings of the peace which became known to him in the course of a journey, while accompanying Wallenstein's daughter to the encampment. He leaves his father and the Court ambassador, Questenberg, in great consternation. The scene proceeds as follows:

QUESTENBERG. Woe unto us! Are matters thus? Friend, should we allow him to go there with this false opinion, and not recall him at once in order to open his eyes instantly?
OCTAVIO (*rousing himself from profound meditation*). He has already opened mine, and I see more than pleases me.
QUESTENBERG. What is it, friend?
OCTAVIO. A curse on that journey!
QUESTENBERG. Why? What is it?
OCTAVIO. Come! I must immediately follow the unlucky trail, must see with my own eyes—come . . . (*Wishes to lead him away.*)
QUESTENBERG. What is the matter? Where?
OCTAVIO. (*urging*). To *her!*
QUESTENBERG. To——?
OCTAVIO (*corrects himself*). To the duke! Let us go, *etc.*

The slight speech-blunder *to her* in place of *to him* is meant to betray to us the fact that the father has seen through his son's motive for espousing the other cause, while the courtier complains that "he speaks to him altogether in riddles."

Another example wherein a poet makes use of a speech-blunder was discovered by Otto Rank in Shakespeare. I quote Rank's report from the *Zentralblatt für Psychoanalyse*, I. 3.

"A poetic speech-blunder, very delicately motivated and technically remarkably well utilized, which, like the one pointed out by Freud in Wallenstein (*Zur Psychopathologie des Alltagslebens*, 2nd Edition, p. 48), not only shows that poets knew the mechanism and sense of this error, but also presupposes an understanding of it on the part of the hearer, can be found in Shakespeare's *Merchant of Venice* (Act III, Scene 2). By the will of her father, Portia was bound to select a husband through a lottery. She escaped all her distasteful suitors by lucky chance. When she finally found in Bassanio the suitor after her own heart, she had cause to fear lest he, too, should draw the unlucky lottery. In the scene, she would like to tell him that even if he chose the wrong casket, he might, nevertheless, be sure of her love. But she is hampered by her vow. In this mental conflict, the poet puts these words in her mouth, which were directed to the welcome suitor:

> "There is something tells me (but it is not love),
> I would not lose you; and you know yourself
> Hate counsels not in such a quality.
> But lest you should not understand me well
> (And yet a maiden hath no tongue but thought),
> I would detain you here some month or two,
> Before you venture for me. I could teach you
> How to choose right, but then I am forsworn;
> So will I never be; so may you miss me;
> But if you do, you'll make me wish a sin,
> That I had been forsworn. Beshrew your eyes,
> They have o'erlooked me, and divided me:
> *One half of me is yours, the other half yours—*
> *Mine own, I would say;* but if mine, then yours—
> And so all yours."

"Just the very thing which she would like to hint to him very gently, because really she should keep it from him, namely, that even before the choice, she is wholly his—that she loves him, the poet, with admirable psychologic sensitiveness, allows to come to the surface in the speech-blunder. It is through this artifice that he manages to allay the intolerable uncertainty of the lover as well as the like tension of the hearer concerning the outcome of the choice."

Some speech-blunders are clearly based on wishful thinking as shown by the following example reported by the *New York World-Telegram* (December 10, 1934):

"D., convicted murderer of a policeman, readily answered questions of interviewers in his cell last night. His impetus carried him past the query: 'How old are you?' 'I'll be twenty-nine next August,' D. replied. He stopped short in an embarrassed silence, for he was scheduled to die within two days in the electric chair." [1]

The conception of speech-blunders here defended can be readily verified in the smallest details. I have been able to demonstrate repeatedly that the most insignificant and most natural cases of speech-blunders have their good sense, and admit of the same interpretation as the more striking examples. A patient, who, contrary to my wishes but with firm personal

---

[1] Given by Editor.

motives, decided upon a short trip to Budapest, justified herself by saying that she was going for only three days, but she blundered and said for only three weeks. She betrayed her secret feeling that, to spite me, she preferred spending three weeks to three days in that society which I considered unfit for her.

One evening, wishing to excuse myself for not having called for my wife at the theater, I said: "I was at the theater at ten minutes after ten." I was corrected: "You meant to say before ten o'clock." Naturally, I wanted to say before ten. After ten would certainly be no excuse. I had been told that the theater program read, "Finished before ten o'clock." When I arrived at the theater, I found the foyer dark and the theater empty. Evidently the performance was over earlier and my wife did not wait for me. When I looked at the clock, it still wanted five minutes to ten. I determined to make my case more favorable at home, and say that it was ten minutes to ten. Unfortunately, the speech-blunder spoiled the intent and laid bare my dishonesty, in which I acknowledged more than there really was to confess.

This leads us to those speech disturbances which can no longer be described as speech-blunders, for they do not injure the individual word, but affect the rhythm and execution of the entire speech, as, for example, the stammering and stuttering of embarrassment. But here, as in the former cases, it is the inner conflict that is betrayed to us through the disturbance in speech. I really do not believe that anyone will make mistakes in talking in an audience with His Majesty, in a serious love declaration or in defending one's name and honor before a jury; in short, people make no mistakes where *they are all there*, as the saying goes. Even in criticizing an author's style, we are allowed and accustomed to follow the principle of explanation, which we cannot miss in the origin of a single speech-blunder. A clear and unequivocal manner of writing shows us that here, the author is in harmony with himself, but where we find a forced and involved expression, aiming at more than one target, as appropriately expressed, we can thereby recognize the participation of an unfinished and complicated thought, or we can hear through it the stifled voice of the author's self-criticism.[1]

---

[1] "Ce qu'on conçoit bien
S'énonce clairement,
Et les mots pour le dire
Arrivent aisément."
—Boileau, *Art Poétique.*

VI

MISTAKES IN READING AND WRITING

THAT the same viewpoints and observation should hold true for mistakes in reading and writing as for lapses in speech is not at all surprising when one remembers the inner relation of these functions. I shall here confine myself to the reports of several carefully analyzed examples and shall make no attempt to include all of the phenomena.

A. LAPSES IN READING

(a) While looking over a number of the *Leipziger Illustrierte,* which I was holding obliquely, I read as the title of the front-page picture, "A Wedding Celebration in the Odyssey." Astonished and with my attention aroused, I moved the page into the proper position only to read correctly, "A Wedding Celebration in the Ostsee (Baltic Sea)." How did this senseless mistake in reading come about?

Immediately my thoughts turned to a book by Ruth, *Experimental Investigations of "Music Phantoms,"* etc., with which I had recently been much occupied, as it closely touched the psychologic problems that are of interest to me. The author promised a work in the near future to be called *Analysis and Principles of Dream Phenomena.* No wonder that I, having just published an *Interpretation of Dreams,* awaited the appearance of this book with the most intense interest. In Ruth's work concerning music phantoms, I found an announcement in the beginning of the table of contents of the detailed inductive proof that the old Hellenic myths and traditions originated mainly from slumber and music phantoms, from dream phenomena and from deliria. Thereupon, I had immediately plunged into the text in order to find out whether he was also aware that the scene where Odysseus appears before Nausicaä was based upon the common dream of nakedness. One of my friends called my attention to the clever passage in G. Keller's *Grüne Heinrich,* which explains this episode in the Odyssey as an objective representation of the dream of the mariner straying far from home. I added to it the reference to the exhibition dream of nakedness.[1]

[1] *The Interpretation of Dreams.* See p. 292.

(b) A woman who is very anxious to have children always reads *storks* instead of *stocks*.

(c) One day, I received a letter which contained very disturbing news. I immediately called my wife and informed her that poor Mrs. Wm. H. was seriously ill and was given up by the doctors. There must have been a false ring to the words in which I expressed my sympathy, as my wife grew suspicious, asked to see the letter and expressed her opinion that it could not read as stated by me, because no one calls the wife by the husband's name. Moreover, the correspondent was well acquainted with the Christian name of the woman concerned. I defended my assertion obstinately and referred to the customary visiting cards, on which a woman designates herself by the Christian name of her husband. I was finally compelled to take up the letter and, as a matter of fact, we read therein "Poor W. M." What is more, I had even overlooked "Poor Dr. W. M." My mistake in reading signified a spasmodic effort, so to speak, to turn the sad news from the man towards the woman. The title between the adjective and the name did not go well with my claim that the woman must have been meant. That is why it was omitted in the reading. The motive for this falsifying was not that the woman was less an object of my sympathy than the man, but the fate of this poor man had excited my fears regarding another and nearer person who, I was aware, had the same disease.

(d) Both irritating and laughable is a lapse in reading to which I am frequently subject when I walk through the streets of a strange city during my vacation. I then read *antiquities* on every shop sign that shows the slightest resemblance to the word; this displays the questing spirit of the collector.

(e) In his important work,[1] Bleuler relates:

"While reading, I once had the intellectual feeling of seeing my name two lines below. To my astonishment, I found only the words *blood corpuscles*. Of the many thousands of lapses in reading in the peripheral as well as in the central field of vision that I have analyzed, this was the most striking case. Whenever I imagined that I saw my name, the word that induced this illusion usually showed a greater resemblance to my name than the word *bloodcorpuscles*. In most cases, all the letters of my name had to be close together before I could commit such an error. In this case, however, I could readily explain the delusion of reference and the illusion. What I had just read was the end of a statement concerning a form of bad style in scientific works, a tendency from which I am not entirely free."

[1] Bleuler, *Affectivity, Suggestibility, Paranoia,* page 121, Halle. Marhold, 1906.

B. LAPSES IN WRITING

(a) On a sheet of paper containing principally short daily notes of business interest, I found, to my surprise, the incorrect date, "Thursday, October 20th," bracketed under the correct date of the month of September. It was not difficult to explain this anticipation as the expression of a wish. A few days before, I had returned fresh from my vacation and felt ready for any amount of professional work, but as yet, there were few patients. On my arrival, I had found a letter from a patient announcing her arrival on the twentieth of October. As I wrote the same date in September, I may certainly have thought, "X. ought to be here already; what a pity about that whole month!" and with this thought, I pushed the current date a month ahead. In this case, the disturbing thought can scarcely be called unpleasant; therefore, after noticing this lapse in writing, I immediately knew the solution. In the fall of the following year, I experienced an entirely analogous and similarly motivated lapse in writing. Dr. Ernest Jones has made a study of similar cases, and found that most mistakes in writing dates are motivated.

(b) I received the proof sheets of my contribution to the annual report on neurology and psychiatry, and I was naturally obliged to review with special care the names of authors, which, because of the many different nationalities represented, offer the greatest difficulties to the compositor. As a matter of fact, I found some strange-sounding names still in need of correction; but, oddly enough, the compositor had corrected one single name in my manuscript, and with very good reason. I had written *Buckrhard*, which the compositor guessed to be *Burckhard*. I had praised the treatise of this obstetrician entitled *The Influence of Birth on the Origin of Infantile Paralysis*, and I was not conscious of the least enmity toward him. But an author in Vienna, who had angered me by an adverse criticism of my *Interpretation of Dreams*, bears the same name. It was as if in writing the name Burckhard, meaning the obstetrician, a wicked thought concerning the other Burckhard had obtruded itself. The twisting of the name, as I have already stated in regard to lapses in speech, often signifies a depreciation.[1]

(c) The following is seemingly a serious case of *lapsus calami*, which it would be equally correct to describe as an erroneously carried out action. I intended to withdraw from the postal savings bank the sum of 300 crowns, which I wished to send to an absent relative to enable him to

---

[1] A similar situation occurs in *Julius Caesar*, iii. 3:
"Cinna.   Truly, my name is Cinna.
"Burgher. Tear him to pieces! he is a conspirator.
"Cinna.   I am Cinna the poet! not Cinna the conspirator.
"Burgher. No matter; his name is Cinna; tear the name out of his heart and let him go."

take treatment at a watering-place. I noted that my account was 4,380 crowns, and I decided to bring it down to the round sum of 4,000 crowns, which was not to be touched in the near future. After making out the regular cheque, I suddenly noticed that I had written not 380 crowns, as I had intended, but exactly 438 crowns. I was frightened at the untrustworthiness of my action. I soon realized that my fear was groundless, as I had not grown poorer than I was before. But I had to reflect for quite a while in order to discover what influence diverted me from my first intention without making itself known to my consciousness.

First I got on a wrong track: I subtracted 380 from 438, but after that, I did not know what to do with the difference. Finally an idea occurred to me which showed me the true connection. Four hundred thirty-eight is exactly 10 per cent of the entire account of 4,380 crowns! But the bookseller, too, gives a 10 per cent discount! I recalled that a few days before, I had selected several books, in which I was no longer interested, in order to offer them to the bookseller for 300 crowns. He thought the price demanded too high, but promised to give me a final answer within the next few days. If he should accept my first offer, he would replace the exact sum that I was to spend on the sufferer. There is no doubt that I was sorry about this expenditure. The emotion at the realization of my mistakes can be more easily understood as a fear of growing poor through such outlays. But both the sorrow over this expense and the fear of poverty connected with it were entirely foreign to my consciousness; I did not regret this expense when I promised the sum, and would have laughed at the idea of any such underlying motive. I should probably not have assigned such feelings to myself had not my psychoanalytic practice made me quite familiar with the repressed elements of psychic life, and if I had not had a dream a few days before which brought forth the same solution.

(d) Although it is usually difficult to find the person responsible for printers' errors, the psychologic mechanisms underlying them are the same as in other mistakes. Typographical errors also well demonstrate the fact that people are not at all indifferent to such trivialities as "mistakes," and, judging by the indignant reactions of the parties concerned, one is forced to the conclusion that mistakes are not treated by the public at large as mere accidents. This state of affairs is very well summed up in the following editorial from the New York *Times*. Not the least interesting are the comments of the keen-witted editor, who does not seem to share our views:

"Behold what a fire a little word kindleth by its absence. The other day, not' dropped out of this sentence in an editorial in the first edition of the Sunday *Times*:

> 'For years and years Southern newspapers have asked
> Southern farmers to put all their hopes in one crop.'

"This error, exactly reversing the writer's intention, was corrected in subsequent editions. *Notless,* the sentence came to the Charleston *News and Courier,* organ of that stern and witty resenter of the universe as she is at present conducted, Mr. William W. Ball. There had been a grievous fault, and grievously must the sinner answer it. Severe is the rebuke and kindly, if a bit superfluous, the offer of 'information' to a darkened mind.

"Ordinarily, we shouldn't have noticed one of the expected and inevitable slips of most newspapers. 'Not' is an easy faller-by-the-way. All writers for the press know what pits they are liable to fall into any day. Why does a mistake that glares and gibbers at you in print hide itself so successfully in the copy or the proof? How do you come to set down 'eighteenth' century when you mean 'nineteenth'? How does Richard Grant White's 'heteronymy' so persecute you that you are capable of attributing 'Paradise Lost' to John Milton, the crazy sporting squire? Some students of demonology believe firmly in the constant presence and maleficence of the writer's devil." [1]

"We venture to doubt the editor's assumption of demonological influences. Examination of a great many typographical errors clearly shows that they are based on the mechanisms described here.

"The following two examples were reported from Berlin in the New York *Times*:

A typesetter was imprisoned because instead of ending an article with the official formula 'Heil Hitler,' he inadvertently permitted a '*t*' to attach itself to '*Heil*' so that it read 'Heilt Hitler,' meaning 'Heal Hitler' instead of 'Hail Hitler.' His pleading that it was a mistake was of no avail. It seems that the Nazis who burned Freud's works, nevertheless, recognize the truth of Freud's teachings. The mistake plainly showed the typesetter's view of Hitler's personality. His mistake unconsciously expresses his wish that the Lord may heal Hitler of his madness.

"The second example shows that even those who are nearest to the *Führer* and constantly sing his praises to the Germans, do not really believe what they say, as shown by the following wireless from Berlin to the New York *Times* (November 12, 1936), congratulating eighteen

---

[1] Given by the Editor.

hundred boys and girls of the Hitler Youth for taking part in the mightiest *Freiheitsbewegung* (movement of liberty) in German history. Rudolf Hess, the vice-leader of the Nazi party, used instead the word *Freiheitsberaubung* (robbery of liberty). The last word appeared in the *Lokalanzeiger* and caused the publishers no small amount of annoyance.

"Abstract statements of a highly moral content are not seldom changed erotically through a typographical mistake, as shown' by the following examples:

(e) "The teacher was giving an instruction paper on mathematical methods, and spoke of a plan 'for the instruction of youth that might be carried out *ad libidinem.*'

(f) "Some time ago, the following embarrassing misprint appeared in the *Detroit Educational Bulletin,* a high-quality journal devoted to parents and teachers: "Our immorality is the good that lives after us." The '*t*' was left out of the word "immortality" from Thomas A. Edison's quotation." [1]

(g) The "Wicked Bible" is so called from the fact that the negative was left out of the seventh commandment. This authorized edition of the Bible was published in London in 1631, and it is said that the printer had to pay a fine of two thousand pounds for the omission.

Another biblical misprint dates back to the year 1580, and is found in the Bible of the famous library of Wolfenbuttel in Hesse. In the passage in Genesis where God tells Eve that Adam shall be her master and shall rule over her, the German translation is *"Und er soll dein Herr sein."* The word *Herr* (master) was substituted by *Narr,* which means fool. Newly discovered evidence seems to show that the error was a conscious machination of the printer's suffragette wife, who refused to be ruled by her husband.

(h) Dr. Ernest Jones reports the following case concerning A. A. Brill: "Although by custom almost a teetotaler, he yielded to a friend's importunity one evening, in order to avoid offending him, and took a little wine. During the next morning, an exacerbation of an eye-strain headache gave him cause to regret this slight indulgence, and his reflection on the subject found expression in the following slip of the pen. Having occasion to write the name of a girl mentioned by a patient, he wrote not Ethel but Ethyl.[2] It happened that the girl in question was rather too fond of drink, and in Dr. Brill's mood at the time, this characteristic of hers stood out with conspicuous significance." [3]

(i) A woman wrote to her sister, felicitating her on the occasion of taking possession of a new and spacious residence. A friend who was

---

[1] Given by the Editor.
[2] Ethyl alcohol is, of course, the chemical name for ordinary alcohol.
[3] Jones, *Psychoanalysis,* p. 66.

present noticed that the writer put the wrong address on the letter, and what was still more remarkable was the fact that she did not address it to the previous residence, but to one long ago given up, but which her sister had occupied when she first married. When the friend called her attention to it, the writer remarked, "You are right; but what in the world made me do this?", to which her friend replied: "Perhaps you begrudge her the nice big apartment into which she has just moved because you yourself are cramped for space, and for that reason you put her back into her first residence, where she was no better off than yourself." "Of course I begrudge her the new apartment," she honestly admitted. As an after-thought she added, "It is a pity that one is so mean in such matters."

(k) Ernest Jones reports the following example given to him by Dr. A. A. Brill. In a letter to Dr. Brill, a patient tried to attribute his nervous-ness to business worries and excitement during the cotton crisis. He went on to say: "My trouble is all due to that d—— frigid wave; there isn't even any seed to be obtained for new crops." He referred to a cold wave which had destroyed the cotton crops, but instead of writing "wave" he wrote "wife." In the bottom of his heart, he entertained reproaches against his wife on account of her marital frigidity and childlessness, and he was not far from the cognition that the enforced abstinence played no little part in the causation of his malady.

(l) Another example of omission is the following related by Brill: "A prospective patient, who had corresponded with me relative to treatment, finally wrote for an appointment for a certain day. Instead of keeping his appointment, he sent regrets which began as follows: 'Owing to *foreseen* circumstances, I am unable to keep my appointment.' He naturally meant to write *unforeseen*. He finally came to me months later, and in the course of the analysis, I discovered that my suspicions at the time were justified; there were no unforeseen circumstances to prevent his coming at that time; he was advised not to come to me. The unconscious does not lie."

Wundt gives a most noteworthy proof for the easily ascertained fact that we more easily make mistakes in writing than in speaking (*loc. cit.,* p. 374). He states: "In the course of normal conversation, the inhibiting function of the will is constantly directed toward bringing into harmony the course of ideation with the movement of articulation. If the articula-tion following the ideas becomes retarded through mechanical causes, as in writing, such anticipations then readily make their appearance."

Observation of the determinants which favor lapses in reading gives rise to doubt, which I do not like to leave unmentioned, because I am of the opinion that it may become the starting-point of a fruitful investiga-tion. It is a familiar fact that in reading aloud, the attention of the reader often wanders from the text and is directed toward his own thoughts. The results of this deviation of attention are often such that when interrupted and questioned, he cannot even state what he has read. In other words, he has read automatically, although the reading was nearly always correct. I do not think that such conditions favor any noticeable increase in the mistakes. We are accustomed to assume concerning a whole series of functions that they are most precisely performed when done automatically, with scarcely any conscious attention. This argues that the conditions governing attention in mistakes in speaking, writing and reading must be differently determined than assumed by Wundt (cessation or diminution of attention). The examples which we have subjected to analysis have really not given us the right to take for granted a quantitative diminution of attention. We found what is probably not exactly the same thing, a disturbance of the attention through a strange obtruding thought.

VII

FORGETTING OF IMPRESSIONS AND RESOLUTIONS

IF ANYONE should be inclined to overrate the state of our present knowledge of mental life, all that would be needed to force him to assume a modest attitude would be to remind him of the function of memory. No psychologic theory has yet been able to account for the connection between the fundamental phenomena of remembering and forgetting; indeed, even the complete analysis of that which one can actually observe has as yet scarcely been grasped. Today, forgetting has perhaps grown more puzzling than remembering, especially since we have learned from the study of dreams and pathologic states that even what for a long time we believed forgotten may suddenly return to consciousness.

To be sure, we are in possession of some viewpoints which we hope will receive general recognition. Thus we assume that forgetting is a spontaneous process to which we may ascribe a certain temporal discharge. We emphasize the fact that, just as among the units of every impression or experience, in forgetting, too, a certain selection takes place among the existing impressions. We are acquainted with some of the conditions that underlie the tenaciousness of memory and the awakening of that which would otherwise remain forgotten. Nevertheless, we can observe in innumerable cases of daily life how unreliable and unsatisfactory our knowledge of the mechanism is. Thus we may listen to two persons exchanging reminiscences concerning the same outward impressions, say of a journey that they have taken together some time before. What remains most firmly in the memory of the one is often forgotten by the other, as if it had never occurred, even when there is not the slightest reason to assume that this impression is of greater psychic importance for the one than for the other. A great many of those factors which determine the selective power of memory are obviously still beyond our ken.

With the purpose of adding some small contribution to the knowledge of the conditions of forgetting, I was wont to subject to a psychologic analysis those cases in which forgetting concerned me personally. As a rule, I took up only a certain group of those cases, namely, those in which the forgetting astonished me, because, in my opinion, I should have remembered the experience in question. I wish further to remark that I am generally not inclined to forgetfulness (of things experienced, not of things learned), and that for a short period of my youth, I was able to perform extraordinary feats of memory. When I was a schoolboy, it was quite natural for me to be able to repeat from memory the page of a book which I had read; and shortly before I entered the University, I could write down practically verbatim the popular lectures on scientific subjects directly after hearing them. In the tension before the final medical examination, I must have made use of the remnant of this ability, for in certain subjects I gave the examiners apparently automatic answers, which proved to be exact reproductions of the text book, which I had skimmed through but once and then in greatest haste.

Since those days, I have steadily lost control over my memory; of late, however, I became convinced that with the aid of a certain artifice I can recall far more than I would otherwise credit myself with remembering. For example, when, during my office hours, a patient states that I have seen him before and I cannot recall either the fact or the time, then I help myself by guessing—that is, I allow a number of years, beginning from the present time, to come to my mind quickly. Whenever this could be controlled by records of definite information from the patient, it was always shown that in over ten years [1] I had seldom missed it by more than six months. The same thing happens when I meet a casual acquaintance and, from politeness, inquire about his small child. When he tells of its progress, I try to fancy how old the child now is. I control my estimate by the information given by the father, and at most, I make a mistake of a month, and in older children of three months. I cannot state, however, what basis I have for this estimate. Of late, I have grown so bold that I always offer my estimate spontaneously, and still run no risk of grieving the father by displaying my ignorance in regard to his offspring. Thus I extend my conscious memory by invoking my larger unconscious memory.

I shall report some *striking* examples of forgetting, which, for the most part, I have observed in myself. I distinguish forgetting of impressions and experiences, that is, the forgetting of knowledge, from forgetting of resolutions, that is, the forgetting of omissions. The uniform result of the entire series of observations I can formulate as follows: *The forgetting in all cases is proved to be founded on a motive of displeasure.*

[1] In the course of the conference, the details of the previous first visit return to consciousness.

A. FORGETTING OF IMPRESSIONS AND KNOWLEDGE

(a) During the summer, my wife once made me very angry, although the cause in itself was trifling. We sat in a restaurant opposite a gentleman from Vienna whom I knew, and who surely also remembered me. However, I had reasons for not wishing to renew his acquaintance. My wife, who had heard nothing except the reputed name of the man opposite her, showed by her actions that she was listening to his conversation with his neighbors, for, from time to time, she asked me questions which took up the thread of their discussion. I became impatient and finally irritated. A few weeks later, I complained to a relative about this behavior of my wife, but I was not able to recall even a single word of the conversation of the gentleman in question. As I am usually of a rather resentful nature and cannot forget a single incident of an episode that has annoyed me, my amnesia in this case was undoubtedly determined by respect for my wife.

A short time ago, I had a similar experience. I wished to make merry with an intimate friend over a statement made by my wife only a few hours earlier, but I found myself hindered by the noteworthy fact that I had entirely forgotten the statement. I had to ask my wife to recall it to me. It is easy to understand that my forgetting in this case may be analogous to the typical disturbance of judgment which dominates us when it concerns those nearest to us.

(b) To oblige a woman who was a stranger in Vienna, I had under- taken to procure a small iron safe for the preservation of documents and money. When I offered my services, the image of an establishment in the heart of the city where I was sure I had seen such safes floated before me with extraordinary visual vividness. To be sure, I could not recall the name of the street, but I felt certain that I would discover the store in a walk through the city, for my memory told me that I had passed it count- less times. To my chagrin, I could not find the store with the show-window with the safes, though I walked through the inner part of the city in every direction. I concluded that the only thing left to do was to search through a business directory, and if that failed, to try to identify the establishment in a second round of the city. It did not, however, require so much effort; among the addresses in the directory, I found one which immediately presented itself as that which had been forgotten. It was true that I had passed the show-window countless times, each time, however, when I had gone to visit the M. family, who have lived a great many years in this very building. After this intimate friendship had turned to an absolute estrangement, I had taken care to avoid the neighborhood as well as the house, though without ever thinking of the reason for my action. In my walk through the city searching for the safe in the show window, I had traversed every street in the neighborhood but the right one, and I had avoided this as if it were forbidden ground.

The motive of displeasure which was at the bottom of my disorientation is thus comprehensible. But the mechanism of forgetting is no longer so simple as in the former example. Here my aversion naturally does not extend to the vendor of safes, but to another person, concerning whom I wish to know nothing, and later, transfers itself from the latter to this incident where it brings about the forgetting. Similarly, in the case of *Burckhard* mentioned above, the grudge against the one brought about the error in writing the name of the other. The similarity of names which here established a connection between two essentially different streams of thought was accomplished in the showcase window instance by the contiguity of space and the inseparable environment. Moreover, this latter case was more closely knit together, for money played a great part in the causation of the estrangement from the family living in this house.

(c) The B. and R. Company requested me to pay a professional call on one of their officers. On my way to him, I was engrossed in the thought that I must already have been in the building occupied by the firm. It seemed as if I used to see their signboard in a lower story, while my professional visit was taking me to a higher story. I could not recall, however, which house it was nor when I had called there. Although the entire matter was indifferent and of no consequence, I nevertheless occupied myself with it, and at last learned in the usual roundabout way, by collecting the thoughts that occurred to me in this connection, that one story above the floor occupied by the firm B. and R., was the *Pension Fischer*, where I had frequently visited patients. Then I remembered the building which sheltered both the company and the *pension*.

I was still puzzled, however, as to the motive that entered into play in this forgetting. I found nothing disagreeable in my memory concerning the firm itself or the *Pension Fischer*, or the patients living there. I was also aware that it could not deal with anything very painful, otherwise I hardly would have been successful in tracing the thing forgotten in a roundabout way without resorting to external aid, as happened in the preceding example. Finally it occurred to me that a little before, while starting on my way to a new patient, a gentleman whom I had difficulty in recalling greeted me in the street. Some months previously, I had seen this man in an apparently serious condition and had made the diagnosis of general paresis, but later I had learned of his recovery; consequently my judgment had been incorrect. Was it not possible that we had in this case a remission, which one usually finds in *dementia paralytica*? In that contingency, my diagnosis would still be justified. The influence emanating from this meeting caused me to forget the neighborhood of the B. and R. Company, and my interest to discover the thing forgotten was transferred from this case of disputed diagnosis. But the associative connection in this loose inner relation was effected by means of a similarity of names: the man who recovered, contrary to expectation, was also an officer of a large company that recommends patients to me. And the physician with whom I had seen the supposed paretic bore the name of Fischer, the name of the *pension* in the house which I had forgotten.

(d) Mislaying a thing really has the same significance as forgetting where we have placed it. Like most people delving in pamphlets and books, I am well oriented about my desk, and can produce what I want with one lunge. What appears to others as disorder has become for me perfect order. Why, then, did I mislay a catalogue which was sent to me not long ago so that it could not be found? What is more, it had been my intention to order a book which I found announced therein entitled *Über die Sprache,* because it was written by an author whose spirited, vivacious style I like, whose insight into psychology and whose knowledge of the cultural world I have learned to appreciate. I believe that was just why I mislaid the catalogue. It was my habit to lend the books of this author among my friends for their enlightenment, and a few days before, on returning one, somebody had said: "His style reminds me altogether of yours, and his way of thinking is identical." The speaker did not know what he was stirring up with this remark. Years ago, when I was younger and in greater need of forming alliances, I was told practically the same thing by an older colleague, to whom I had recommended the writings of a familiar medical author. To put it in his words, "It is absolutely your style and manner." I was so influenced by these remarks that I wrote a letter to this author with the object of bringing about a closer relation, but a rather cool answer put me back "in my place." Perhaps still earlier discouraging experiences conceal themselves behind this last one, for I did not find the mislaid catalogue. Through this premonition, I was actually prevented from ordering the advertised book, although the disappearance of the catalogue formed no real hindrance, as I remembered well both the name of the book and the author.

(e) Another case of mislaying merits our interest on account of the conditions under which the mislaid object was rediscovered. A younger man narrates as follows: "Several years ago, there were some misunderstandings between me and my wife. I found her too cold, and though I fully appreciated her excellent qualities, we lived together without evincing any tenderness for each other. One day, on her return from a walk, she gave me a book which she had bought because she thought it would interest me. I thanked her for this mark of 'interest,' promised to read the book, put it away and did not find it again. So months passed, during which I occasionally remembered the lost book, and also tried in vain to find it.

"About six months later, my beloved mother, who was not living with us, became ill. My wife left home to nurse her mother-in-law. The patient's condition became serious and gave my wife the opportunity to show the best side of herself. One evening, I returned home full of enthusiasm over what my wife had accomplished, and felt very grateful to her. I stepped to my desk and, without definite intention but with the certainty of a somnambulist, I opened a certain drawer, and in the very top of it I found the long-missing, mislaid book."

(f) The following example of "misplacing" belongs to a type well known to every psychoanalyst. I must add that the patient who experienced this misplacing has himself found the solution of it.

This patient, whose psychoanalytic treatment had to be interrupted through the summer vacation when he was in a state of resistance and ill health, put away his keys in the evening in their usual place, or so he thought. He then remembered that he wished to take some things from his desk, where he also had put the money which he needed on the journey. He was to depart the next day, which was the last day of treatment and the date when the doctor's fee was due. But the keys had disappeared.

He began a thorough and systematic search through his small apartment. He became more and more excited over it, but his search was unsuccessful. As he recognized this "misplacement" as a symptomatic act—that is, as being intentional—he aroused his servant in order to continue his search with the help of an "unprejudiced" person. After another hour, he gave up the search and feared that he had lost his keys. The next morning, he ordered new keys from the desk factory, which were hurriedly made for him. Two acquaintances who had been with him in a cab even recalled hearing something fall to the ground as he stepped out of the cab, and he was therefore convinced that the keys had slipped from his pocket. They were found lying between a thick book and a thin pamphlet, the latter a work of one of my pupils, which he wished to take along as reading matter for his vacation; and they were so skillfully placed that no one would have supposed that they were there. He himself was unable to replace the keys in such a position as to render them invisible. The unconscious skill with which an object is misplaced on account of secret but strong motives reminds one of "somnambulistic sureness." The motive was naturally ill humor over the interruption of the treatment and the secret rage over the fact that he had to pay such a high fee when he felt so ill.

(g) Brill relates: [1] "A man was urged by his wife to attend a social function in which he really took no interest. Yielding to his wife's entreaties, he began to take his dress-suit from the trunk when he suddenly thought of shaving. After accomplishing this, he returned to the trunk

[1] Brill, *loc. cit.*, p. 197.

and found it locked. Despite a long, earnest search, the key could not be found. A locksmith could not be found on Sunday evening, so that the couple had to send their regrets. On having the trunk opened the next morning, the lost key was found within. The husband had absent-mindedly dropped the key into the trunk and sprung the lock. He assured me that this was wholly unintentional and unconscious, but we know that he did not wish to go to this social affair. The mislaying of the key therefore lacked no motive."

Ernest Jones noticed in himself that he was in the habit of mislaying his pipe whenever he suffered from the effects of over-smoking. The pipe was then found in some unusual place where it did not belong and which it normally did not occupy.

(h) In the summer of 1901, I once remarked to a friend with whom I was then actively engaged in exchanging ideas on scientific questions: "These neurotic problems can be solved only if we take the position of absolutely accepting an original bi-sexuality in every individual." To which he replied: "I told you that two and a half years ago, while we were taking an evening walk in Br. At that time, you wouldn't listen to it."

It is truly painful to be thus requested to renounce one's originality. I could neither recall such a conversation nor my friend's revelation. One of us must be mistaken; and according to the principle of the question *cui prodest?*, I must be the one. Indeed, in the course of the following weeks, everything came back to me just as my friend had recalled it. I myself remembered that at that time, I gave the answer: "I have not yet got so far, and I do not care to discuss it." But since this incident, I have grown more tolerant when I miss any mention of my name in medical literature in connection with ideas for which I deserve credit.

It is scarcely accidental that the numerous examples of forgetting which have been collected without any selection should require for their solution the introduction of such painful themes as exposing one's wife; a friendship that has turned into the opposite; a mistake in medical diagnosis; enmity on account of similar pursuits, or the borrowing of somebody's ideas. I am rather inclined to believe that every person who will undertake an inquiry into the motives underlying his forgetting will be able to fill up a similar sample card of vexatious circumstances. The tendency to forget the disagreeable seems to me to be quite general; the capacity for it is naturally differently developed in different persons. Certain *denials* which we encounter in medical practice can probably be ascribed to forgetting.[1] Our conception of such forgetting confines the distinction be-

---

[1] If we inquire of a person whether he suffered from leutic infection ten or fifteen years ago, we are only too apt to forget that psychically the patient has looked upon this disease in an entirely different manner than on, let us say, an acute attack of

tween this and that behavior to purely psychologic relations, and permits us to see in both forms of reaction the expression of the same motive. Of the numerous examples of denials of unpleasant recollection which I have observed in kinsmen of patients, one remains in my memory as especially singular.

A mother telling me of the childhood of her nervous son, now in his puberty, made the statement that, like his brothers and sisters, he was subject to bed-wetting throughout his childhood, a symptom which certainly has some significance in a history of a neurotic patient. Some weeks later, while seeking information regarding the treatment, I had occasion to call her attention to signs of a constitutional morbid predisposition in the young man, and at the same time, referred to the bed-wetting recounted in the anamnesis. To my surprise, she contested this fact concerning him, denying it as well for the other children, and asked me how I could possibly know this. Finally, I let her know that she herself had told me a short time before what she had thus forgotten.[1]

---

rheumatism. In the anamneses which parents give about their neurotic daughters, it is hardly possible to distinguish with any degree of certainty the portion forgotten from that hidden, for anything that stands in the way of the girl's future marriage is systematically set aside by the parents, that is, it becomes repressed. A man who had recently lost his beloved wife from an affection of the lungs reported to me the following case of misleading the doctor, which can only be explained by the theory of such forgetting. "As my poor wife's pleuritis had not disappeared after many weeks, Dr. P. was called in consultation. While taking the history, he asked among others the customary question whether there were any cases of lung trouble in my wife's family. My wife denied any such cases, and even I myself could not remember any. While Dr. P. was taking leave, the conversation accidentally turned to excursions, and my wife said: "Yes, even to Landgersdorf, where my poor brother lies buried, is a long journey." This brother died about fifteen years ago, after having suffered for years from tuberculosis. My wife was very fond of him, and often spoke about him. Indeed, I recall that when her malady was diagnosed as pleurisy, she was very worried and sadly remarked: 'My brother also died of lung trouble.' But the memory was so very repressed that even after the above-cited conversation about the trip to L., she found no occasion to correct her information concerning the diseases in her family. I myself was struck by this forgetting at the very moment she began to talk about Landgersdorf." A perfectly analogous experience is related by Ernest Jones in his work. A physician whose wife suffered from some obscure abdominal malady remarked to her: "It is comforting to think that there has been no tuberculosis in your family." She turned to him very astonished and said: "Have you forgotten that my mother died of tuberculosis, and that my sister recovered from it only after having been given up by the doctors?"

[1] During the days when I was first writing these pages, the following almost incredible case of forgetting happened to me. On the 1st of January, I examined my notes so that I could send out my bills. In the month of June, I came across the name M——l, and could not recall the person to whom it belonged. My surprise increased when I observed from my books that I treated the case in a sanatorium, and that for weeks, I had called on the patient daily. A patient treated under such conditions is rarely forgotten by a physician in six months. I asked myself if it could have been a man—a paretic—a case without interest? Finally the note about the fee received brought to my memory all the knowledge which strove to elude it. M——l was a fourteen-year-old girl, the most remarkable case of my latter years, a case which taught me a lesson I am not likely to forget ever, a case whose upshot

One also finds abundant indications which show that even in healthy, not neurotic persons, resistances are found against the memory of disagreeable impressions and the idea of painful thoughts.[1] But the full significance of this fact can be estimated only when we enter into the psychology of neurotic persons. One is forced to make such elementary defensive striving against ideas which can awaken painful feelings, a striving which can be put side by side only with the flight-reflex in painful stimuli, as the main pillar of the mechanism which carries the hysterical symptoms. One need not offer any objection to the acceptance of such defensive tendency on the ground that we frequently find it impossible to rid ourselves of painful memories which cling to us, or to banish such painful emotions as remorse and reproaches of conscience. No one maintains that this defensive tendency invariably gains the upper hand, that in the play of psychic forces, it may not strike against factors which stir up the contrary feeling for other purposes and bring it about in spite of it.

As the architectural principle of the psychic apparatus, we may conjecture a certain stratification or structure of instances deposited in strata. And it is quite possible that this defensive tendency belongs to a lower psychic instance, and is inhibited by higher instances. At all events, it speaks for the existence and force of this defensive tendency, when we can trace it to processes such as those found in our examples of forgetting. We see then that something is forgotten for its own sake, and where this is not possible, the defensive tendency misses the target and causes something else to be forgotten—something less significant, but which has fallen into associative connection with the disagreeable material.

The views here developed, namely, that painful memories merge into motivated forgetting with special ease, merits application in many spheres where as yet, it has found no, or scarcely any, recognition. Thus it seems to me that it has not yet been strongly enough emphasized in the estima-

---

gave me many painful hours. The child became afflicted with an unmistakable hysteria which quickly and thoroughly improved under my care. After this improvement, the child was taken away from me by the parents. She still complained of abdominal pains which had played the main part in the hysterical symptoms. Two months later she died of sarcoma of the abdominal glands. The hysteria to which she was greatly predisposed, took the tumor-formation as a provocative agent, and I, fascinated by the tumultuous but harmless manifestations of hysteria overlooked the first sign of the insidious and incurable disease.

[1] A. Pick (*"Zur Psychologie des Vergessens bei Geistes und Nervenkranken," Archiv. f. Kriminal-Anthropologie u. Kriminalistik,* von H. Gross) has recently collected a number of authors who realize the value of the influence of the affective factors on memory and who more or less clearly recognize that a defensive striving against pain can lead to forgetting. But none of us has been able to represent this phenomenon and its psychologic determination as exhaustively, and at the same time as effectively, as Nietzsche in one of his aphorisms (*Jenseits von Gut und Bösen, ii., Hauptstück* 68): " 'I have done that,' says my Memory. 'I could not have done that,' says my Pride, and remains inexorable. Finally, my Memory yields."

tion of testimony taken in court,[1] where the putting of a witness under oath obviously leads us to place too great a trust on the purifying influence of his psychic play of forces. It is universally admitted that in the origin of the traditions and folklore of a people, care must be taken to eliminate from memory such a motive as would be painful to the national feeling. Perhaps, on closer investigation, it may be possible to form a perfect analogy between the manner of development of national traditions and infantile reminiscences of the individual. The great Darwin has formulated a "golden rule" for the scientific worker from his insight into this pain-motive of forgetting.[2]

Almost exactly as in the forgetting of names, faulty recollections can also appear in the forgetting of impressions, and when finding credence, they may be designated as delusions of memory. The memory disturbance in pathologic cases (in paranoia, it actually plays the rôle of a constituting factor in the formation of delusions) has brought to light an extensive literature in which there is no reference whatever to its being motivated. As this theme also belongs to the psychology of the neuroses, it goes beyond our present treatment. Instead, I will give from my own experience, a curious example of memory disturbance, showing clearly enough its determination through unconscious repressed material and its connection with this material.

While writing the latter chapters of my volume on the interpretation of dreams, I happened to be in a summer resort without access to libraries and reference books, so that I was compelled to introduce into the manuscript all kinds of references and citations from memory. These I naturally reserved for future correction. In the chapter on day-dreams, I thought of the distinguished figure of the poor book-keeper in Alphonse Daudet's *Nabab*, through whom the author probably described his own day-dreams. I imagined that I distinctly remembered one phantasy of this man, whom I called Mr. Jocelyn, which he hatched while walking the streets of Paris, and I began to reproduce it from memory. This phantasy described how Mr. Jocelyn boldly hurled himself at a runaway horse and brought it to a standstill; how the carriage door opened and a great personage stepped from the coupé, pressed Mr. Jocelyn's hand and said: "You are my savior —I owe my life to you! What can I do for you?"

I assured myself that casual inaccuracies in the rendition of this phantasy could readily be corrected at home on consulting the book. But

[1] Cf. Hans Gross, *Kriminal Psychologie*, 1898.

[2] Ernest Jones quotes the following passage from Darwin's autobiography that does equal credit to his scientific honesty and his psychologic acumen: "I had, during many years, followed a golden rule, namely, that whenever a published fact, a new observation or thought, came across me which was opposed to my general results, to make a memorandum of it without fail and at once; for I had found by experience that such facts and thoughts were far more apt to escape from the memory than favorable ones" (Jones, *loc. cit.*, p. 38).

when I perused *Nabab* in order to compare it with my manuscript, I found, to my very great shame and consternation, that there was nothing to suggest such a dream by Mr. Jocelyn; indeed, the poor book-keeper did not even bear this name—he was called Mr. Joyeuse.

This second error then furnished the key for the solution of the first mistake, the faulty reminiscence. Joyeux, of which Joyeuse is the feminine form, was the only possible word which would translate my own name *Freud* into French. Whence, therefore, came this falsely remembered phantasy which I had attributed to Daudet? It could only be a product of my own, a day-dream which I myself had spun, and which did not become conscious, or which was once conscious and had since been absolutely forgotten. Perhaps I invented it myself in Paris, where frequently enough I walked the streets alone, and full of longing for a helper and protector, until Charcot took me into his circle. I had often met the author of *Nabab* in Charcot's house. But the provoking part of it all is the fact that there is scarcely anything to which I am so hostile as the thought of being someone's protégé. What we see of this sort of thing in our country spoils all desire for it, and my character is little suited to the rôle of a protected child. I have always entertained an immense desire to "be the strong man myself." And it had to happen that I should be reminded of such a, to be sure, never fulfilled day-dream! Besides, this incident is a good example of how the restraint relation to one's ego, which breaks forth triumphantly in paranoia, disturbs and entangles us in the objective grasp of things.

Another case of faulty recollection which can be satisfactorily explained resembles the *fausse reconnaissance* to be discussed later. I related to one of my patients, an ambitious and very capable man, that a young student had recently gained admittance into the circle of my pupils by means of an interesting work, *Der Künstler, Versuch einer Sexualpsychologie.* When, a year and a quarter later, this work lay before me in print, my patient maintained that he remembered with certainty having read somewhere, perhaps in a bookseller's advertisement, the announcement of the same book, even before I first mentioned it to him. He remembered that this announcement came to his mind at that time, and he ascertained besides that the author had changed the title, that it no longer read *"Versuch"* but *"Ansätze zu einer Sexualpsychologie."*

Careful inquiry of the author and comparison of all dates showed conclusively that my patient was trying to recall the impossible. No notice of this work had appeared anywhere before its publication, certainly not a year and a quarter before it went into print. However, I neglected to seek a solution for this false recollection until the same man brought about an equally valuable renewal of it. He thought that he had recently noticed a work on "agoraphobia" in the show window of a bookshop, and as he was now looking for it in all available catalogues, I was able to explain to him why his effort must remain fruitless. The work on agoraphobia existed only in his phantasy as an unconscious resolution to write such a book himself. His ambition to emulate that young man, and through such a scientific work, to become one of my pupils, had led him to the first as well as to the second false recollection. He also recalled later that the book-seller's announcement which had occasioned his false reminiscence dealt with a work entitled *Genesis, Das Gesetz der Zeugung* ("Genesis, The Law of Generation"). But the change in the title as mentioned by him was really instigated by me; I recalled that I myself had perpetrated the same inaccuracy in the repetition of the title by saying *"Ansätz"* in place of *"Versuch."*

B. FORGETTING OF INTENTIONS

No other group of phenomena is better qualified to demonstrate the thesis that lack of attention does not in itself suffice to explain faulty acts as the forgetting of intentions. An intention is an impulse for an action which has already found approbation, but whose execution is postponed for a suitable occasion. Now, in the interval thus created, sufficient change may take place in the motive to prevent the intention from coming to execution. It is not, however, forgotten, it is simply revised and omitted.

We are naturally not in the habit of explaining the forgetting of inten-tions which we daily experience in every possible situation as being due to a recent change in the adjustment of motives. We generally leave it unexplained, or we seek a psychologic explanation in the assumption that at the time of execution, the required attention for the action, which was an indispensable condition for the occurrence of the intention, and was then at the disposal of the same action, no longer exists. Obser-vation of our normal behavior towards intentions urges us to reject this tentative explanation as arbitrary. If I resolve in the morning to carry out a certain intention in the evening, I may be reminded of it several times in the course of the day, but it is not at all necessary that it should become conscious throughout the day. As the time for its execu-tion approaches, it suddenly occurs to me and induces me to make the necessary preparation for the intended action. If I go walking and take a letter with me to be posted, it is not at all necessary that I, as a normal, not nervous individual, should carry it in my hand and continually look for a letter-box. As a matter of fact, I am accustomed to put it in my pocket and give my thoughts free rein on my way, feeling confident that the first letter-box will attract my attention and cause me to put my hand in my pocket and draw out the letter.

This normal behavior in a formed intention corresponds perfectly with the experimentally produced conduct of persons who are under a so-called "post-hypnotic suggestion" to perform something after a certain time.[1] We are accustomed to describe the phenomenon in the following manner: the suggested intention slumbers in the person concerned until the time for its execution approaches. Then it awakes and excites the action.

In two situations of everyday life, even the layman is cognizant of the fact that forgetting of resolutions is by no means excusable on the basis of elementary phenomena no further reducible, but he realizes that it ultimately depends on unadmitted motives. I am referring to affairs of love and army service. A lover who is late at a rendezvous will vainly excuse himself to his sweetheart that unfortunately he has entirely forgotten their rendezvous. She will not hesitate to answer him: "A year ago, you would not have forgotten. Evidently you no longer care for me." Even if he should grasp the above cited psychologic explanation, and should wish to excuse his forgetting on the plea of important business, he would only elicit the answer from the lady—as keen-sighted as the physician in the psychoanalytic treatment—"How remarkable that such business disturbances did not occur before!" Of course, the lady does not wish to deny the possibility of forgetting; but she believes, and not without reason, that practically the same inference of a certain unwillingness may be drawn from the unintentional forgetting as from a conscious subterfuge.

Similarly, in military service, no distinction is recognized between an omission resulting from forgetting and one in consequence of intentional neglect. And rightly so. The soldier dares forget nothing that the service demands of him. If he forgets in spite of his knowledge of the requirements, then it is due to the fact that the motives which urge the fulfillment of the military exactions are opposed by contrary motives. Thus the soldier who at inspection pleads forgetting as an excuse for not having polished his buttons, is sure to be punished. But this punishment is small in comparison to the one he courts if he admits to his superiors that the motive for his negligence is that "I am entirely disgusted with the service." Owing to this saving of punishment for economic reasons, as it were, he makes use of forgetting as an excuse, or it is the result of a compromise.

Duties towards women (like army service) demand that nothing relating to them must be subject to forgetting, and thus imply that forgetting may be permissible in unimportant matters, but in weighty matters, its occurrence is an indication that one wishes to treat them as unimportant: that is, that their importance is disputed.[2] The viewpoint of psychic

---

[1] Cf. Bernheim, *Neue Studien über Hypnotismus, Suggestion und Psychotherapie*, 1892.

[2] In Bernard Shaw's *Caesar and Cleopatra*, Caesar's indifference to Cleopatra is depicted by his being vexed on leaving Egypt at having forgotten to do something. He finally recollected what he had forgotten—to take leave of Cleopatra—this, to be

validity is in fact not to be contested here. No person forgets to carry out actions that seem important to himself without exposing himself to the suspicion that he is suffering from some mental disturbance. Our investigations therefore can refer only to forgetting of more or less secondary resolutions, for no resolution is deemed absolutely indifferent, otherwise it would certainly never have been formed.

As in the former functional disturbances, I have collected the cases of neglect through forgetting which I have observed in myself, and endeavored to explain them. In doing so, I have found that they could invariably be traced to some interference of unknown and unadmitted motives—or, as may be said, they were due to a *counter-will*. In a number of these cases, I found myself in a position similar to that of being in some distasteful service: I was under a constraint to which I had not entirely resigned myself, so that I showed my protest in the form of forgetting. This accounts for the fact that I am particularly prone to forget to send congratulations on such occasions as birthdays, jubilees, wedding celebrations and promotions to higher rank. I continually make new resolutions not to forget them, but I am more than ever convinced that I shall not succeed. I am now on the point of dropping them altogether, and to admit consciously the striving motives. In a period of transition, I told a friend who asked me to send a congratulatory telegram for him, at a certain time when I was to send one myself, that I would probably forget both. It was not surprising that the prophecy came true. It is undoubtedly due to painful experiences in life that I am unable to manifest sympathy where this manifestation must necessarily appear exaggerated, for the small amount of my feeling does not admit the corresponding expression. Since I have learned that I often mistook the pretended sympathy of others for real, I am in rebellion against the conventions of expressing sympathy, the social expediency of which I naturally acknowledge. Condolences in cases of death are excepted from this divided feeling; once I determine to send them I do not neglect them. Wherever my emotional participation is no longer involved with social duty, its expression is never inhibited by forgetting.

Cases in which we forget to carry out actions which we have promised to do as a favor for others, can similarly be explained as antagonism to conventional duty and as an unfavorable inward opinion. Here, it regularly happens that only the patron believes in the excusing power of forgetfulness, while the petitioner has no doubt about the right answer: "He has no interest in this matter, otherwise he would not have forgotten it."

There are some who are noted as generally forgetful, and we excuse

---

sure, is in full accord with historical truth. How little Caesar thought of this little Egyptian princess! Cited from Jones, *loc. cit.*, p. 50.

their lapses in the same manner as we excuse those who are short-sighted when they do not greet us on the street.[1] Such persons forget all small promises which they have made; they leave unexecuted all orders which they have received; they prove themselves unreliable in little things; and at the same time, demand that we shall not take these slight offenses amiss —that is, they do not want us to attribute these failings to personal characteristics but to refer them to an organic peculiarity.[2] I am not one of these people myself, and have had no opportunity to analyze the actions of such a person in order to discover from the selection of forgetting the motive underlying the same. I cannot forego, however, the conjecture *per analogiam,* that here the motive is an unusually large amount of un-avowed disregard for others which exploits a constitutional factor for its purpose.[3]

In other cases, the motives for forgetting are less easy to discover, and when found, excite greater astonishment. Thus, in former years, I observed that of a great number of professional calls, I only forgot those that I was to make on patients whom I treated gratis or on colleagues. The mortification caused by this discovery led me to the habit of noting every morning the calls of the day in a form of resolution. I do not know if other physicians have come to the same practice by a similar road. Thus, we get an idea of what causes the so-called neurasthenic to make a memorandum of the communications he wishes to make to the doctor. He apparently lacks confidence in the reproductive capacity of his memory. This is true, but the scene usually proceeds in this manner. The patient has recounted his various complaints and inquiries at considerable length. After he has finished, he pauses for a moment, then he pulls out the memorandum and says apologetically, "I have made some notes because

[1] Women, with their fine understanding of unconscious mental processes, are, as a rule, more apt to take offense at not being recognized in the street, and hence not greeted, than to accept the most obvious explanation, namely, that the neglector is short-sighted or so engrossed in thought that he did not notice them. They conclude that they surely would have been noticed if he had considered them of any consequence.

[2] Dr. Ferenczi reports that he was an absent-minded person himself, and was considered peculiar by his friends on account of the frequency and strangeness of his failing. But the signs of this inattention have almost all disappeared since he began to practise psychoanalysis with patients, and was forced to turn his attention to the analysis of his own ego. He believes that one renounces these failings when one learns to extend by so much one's own responsibilities. He therefore justly maintains that distractedness is a state which depends on unconscious complexes, and is curable by psychoanalysis. One day, he was reproaching himself for having committed a technical error in the psychoanalysis of a patient, and on this day all his former distractions reappeared. He stumbled while walking in the street (a representation of that *faux pas* in the treatment), he forgot his pocket-book at home, he was a penny short in his car fare, he did not properly button his clothes, etc.

[3] E. Jones remarks regarding this: "Often the resistance is of a general order. Thus a busy man forgets to mail a letter entrusted to him—to his slight annoyance—by his wife, just as he may 'forget' to carry out her shopping orders."

I cannot remember anything." As a rule, he finds nothing new on the memorandum. He repeats each point and answers it himself: "Yes, I have already asked about that." By means of the memorandum, he probably only demonstrates one of his symptoms, the frequency with which his resolutions are disturbed through the interference of obscure motives.

I am touching, moreover, on an affliction to which even most of my healthy acquaintances are subject, when I admit that especially in former years, I had the habit of easily forgetting for a long time to return borrowed books, also that it very often happened that I deferred payments through forgetfulness. One morning, not long ago, I left the tobacco shop where I make my daily purchase of cigars without paying. It was a most harmless omission, as I am known there and could therefore expect to be reminded of my debt the next morning. But this slight neglect, the attempt to contract a debt, was surely not unconnected with reflections concerning the budget with which I had occupied myself throughout the preceding day. Even among the so-called respectable people, one can readily demonstrate a double behavior when it concerns the theme of money and possession. The primitive greed of the suckling which wishes to seize every object (in order to put it in its mouth) has generally been only imperfectly subdued through culture and training.[1]

I fear that in all the examples thus far given, I have grown quite commonplace. But it can be only a pleasure to me if I happen upon familiar matters which everyone understands, for my main object is to collect everyday material and utilize it scientifically. I cannot conceive why wisdom, which is, so to speak, the sediment of everyday experiences, should be denied admission among the acquisitions of knowledge. For it is not the diversity of objects but the stricter method of verification and the striving for far-reaching connections which make up the essential character of scientific work.

We have invariably found that resolutions of some importance are

[1] For the sake of the unity of the theme, I may here digress from the accepted classification, and add that the human memory evinces a particular partiality in regard to money matters. False reminiscences of having already paid something are often very obstinate, as I know from personal experience. When free sway is given to avaricious intent outside of the serious interests of life, when it is indulged in in the spirit of fun, as in card playing, we then find that the most honorable men show an inclination to errors, mistakes in memory and accounts, and without realizing how, they even find themselves involved in small frauds. Such liberties depend in no small part also on the psychically refreshing character of the play. The saying that in play we can learn a person's character may be admitted if we can add "his repressed character." If waiters ever make unintentional mistakes, they are apparently due to the same mechanism. Among merchants, we can frequently observe a certain delay in the paying out of sums of money, in payments of bills and the like, which brings the owner no profit and can be only understood psychologically as the expression of a counter-will against giving out money. Brill sums it up with epigrammatic keenness: "We are more apt to mislay letters containing bills and cheques." (Brill, *Psychoanalysis, its Theories and Practical Application*, p. 197.)

forgotten when obscure motives arise to disturb them. In still less important resolutions, we find a second mechanism of forgetting. Here a counter-will becomes transferred to the resolution from something else after an external association has been formed between the latter and the content of the resolution. The following example reported by Brill illustrates this: "A patient found that she had suddenly become very negligent in her correspondence. She was naturally punctual and usually took pleasure in letter-writing, but for the last few weeks, she simply could not bring herself to write a letter without exerting the greatest amount of effort. The explanation was quite simple. Some weeks before, she had received an important letter calling for a categorical answer. She was undecided what to say, and therefore did not answer it at all. This indecision in the form of inhibition was unconsciously transferred to other letters and caused the inhibition against letter-writing in general."

Direct counter-will and more remote motivation are found together in the following example of delaying: I had written a short treatise on the dream for the series *Grenzfragen des Nerven- und Seelenlebens,* in which I gave an abstract of my book, *The Interpretation of Dreams.* Bergmann, the publisher, had sent me the proof sheets and asked for a speedy return of the same as he wished to issue the pamphlet before Christmas. I corrected the sheets the same night, and placed them on my desk in order to take them to the post office the next morning. In the morning, I forgot all about it, and only thought of it in the afternoon at the sight of the paper cover on my desk. In the same way, I forgot the proofs that evening and the following morning, and until the afternoon of the second day, when I quickly took them to a letter-box, wondering what might be the basis of this procrastination. Obviously, I did not want to send them off, although I could find no explanation for such an attitude.

After posting the letter, I entered the shop of my Vienna publisher, who put out my *Interpretation of Dreams.* I left a few orders; then, as if impelled by a sudden thought, said, "You undoubtedly know that I have written the 'Dream' book a second time?" "Ah!" he exclaimed, "then I must ask you to——" "Calm yourself," I interposed; "it is only a short treatise for the Löwenfeld-Kurella collection." But still he was not satisfied; he feared that the abstract would hurt the sale of the book. I disagreed with him, and finally asked: "If I had come to you before, would you have objected to the publication?" "No; under no circumstances," he answered.

Personally, I believe I acted within my full rights and did nothing contrary to the general practice; still, it seems to me that a thought similar to that entertained by the publisher was the motive for my procrastination in dispatching the proof sheets.

This reflection leads back to a former occasion when another publisher raised some difficulties because I was obliged to take out several pages of the text from an earlier work on cerebral infantile paralysis, and put them unchanged into a work on the same theme in Nothnagel's handbook. There again the reproach received no recognition; that time also I had loyally informed my first publisher (the same who published *The Interpretation of Dreams*) of my intention.

However, if this series of recollections is followed back still farther, it brings to light a still earlier occasion relating to a translation from the French, in which I really violated the property rights that should be considered in a publication. I had added notes to the text without asking the author's permission, and some years later, I had cause to think that the author was dissatisfied with this arbitrary action.

There is a proverb which indicates the popular knowledge that the forgetting of intentions is not accidental. It says: "What one forgets once he will often forget again."

Indeed, we sometimes cannot help feeling that no matter what may be said about forgetting and faulty actions, the whole subject is already known to everybody as something self-evident. It is strange enough that it is still necessary to push before consciousness such well-known facts. How often I have heard people remark: "Please do not ask me to do this, I shall surely forget it." The coming true of this prophecy later is surely nothing mysterious in itself. He who speaks thus perceives the inner resolution not to carry out the request, and only hesitates to acknowledge it to himself.

Much light is thrown, moreover, on the forgetting of resolutions through something which could be designated as "forming false resolutions." I had once promised a young author to write a review of his short work, but on account of inner resistances, not unknown to me, I promised him that it would be done the same evening. I really had serious intentions of doing so, but I had forgotten that I had set aside that evening for the preparation of an expert testimony that could not be deferred. After I thus recognized my resolution as false, I gave up the struggle against my resistances and refused the author's request.

VIII

ERRONEOUSLY CARRIED-OUT ACTIONS

I SHALL give another passage from the above-mentioned work of Meringer and Mayer (p. 98):

"Lapses in speech do not stand entirely alone. They resemble the errors which often occur in our other activities and are quite foolishly termed 'forgetfulness.' "

I am therefore in no way the first to presume that there is a sense and purpose behind the slight functional disturbances of the daily life of healthy people.[1]

If the lapse in speech, which is without doubt a motor function, admits of such a conception, it is quite natural to transfer to the lapses of our other motor functions the same expectation. I have here formed two groups of cases; all these cases in which the faulty effect seems to be the essential element—that is, the deviation from the intention—I denote as erroneously carried-out actions or defaults; the others, in which the entire action appears rather inexpedient, I call "symptomatic and chance actions." Again, no distinct line of demarcation can be formed; indeed, we are forced to conclude that all divisions used in this treatise are of only descriptive significance and contradict the inner unity of the sphere of manifestation.

The psychologic understanding of erroneous actions apparently gains little in clearness when we place it under the head of "ataxia," and especially under "cortical ataxia." Let us rather try to trace the individual examples to their proper determinants. To do this, I shall again resort to personal observations, the opportunities for which I could not very frequently find in myself.

(a) In former years, when I made more calls at the homes of patients than I do at present, it often happened, when I stood before a door where I should have knocked or rung the bell, that I would pull the key of my own house from my pocket, only to replace it, quite abashed. When I in-

---

[1] A second publication of Meringer has later shown me how very unjust I was to this author when I attributed to him such understanding.

vestigated in what patients' homes this occurred, I had to admit that the faulty action—taking out my key instead of ringing the bell—signified paying a certain tribute to the house where the error occurred. It was equivalent to the thought "Here I feel at home," as it happened only where I possessed the patient's regard. (Naturally, I never rang my own doorbell.)

The default was therefore a symbolic representation of a definite thought which was not accepted consciously as serious; for in reality, the psychiatrist is well aware that the patient seeks him only so long as he expects to be benefited by him, and that his own excessively warm interest for his patient is evinced only as a means of psychic treatment.

That the senseful faulty handling of the keys is by no means peculiar to myself is readily shown by self-observation of others.

An almost identical repetition of my experience is described by A. Maeder ("Contrib. à la psychopathologie de la vie quotidienne," *Arch. de Psychol.*, vi., 1906); *"Il est arrivé à chacun de sortir son trousseau, en arrivant à la porte d'un ami particulièrement cher, de se surprendre pour ainsi dire, en train d'ouvrir avec sa clef comme chez soi. C'est un retard, puisqu'il faut sonner malgré tout, mais c'est une preuve qu'on se sent— ou qu'on voudrait se sentir—comme chez soi, auprès de cet ami."*

Jones speaks as follows about the use of keys: [1] "The use of keys is a fertile source of occurrences of this kind, of which two examples may be given. If I am disturbed in the midst of some engrossing work at home by having to go to the hospital to carry out some routine work, I am very apt to find myself trying to open the door of my laboratory there with the key of my desk at home, although the two keys are quite unlike each other. The mistake unconsciously demonstrates where I would rather be at the moment.

"Some years ago, I was acting in a subordinate position at a certain institution, the front door of which was kept locked, so that it was necessary to ring for admission. On several occasions, I found myself making serious attempts to open the door with my house key. Each one of the permanent visiting staff, of which I aspired to be a member, was provided with a key to avoid the trouble of having to wait at the door. My mistake thus expressed the desire to be on a similar footing and to be quite 'at home' there."

A similar experience is reported by Dr. Hans Sachs of Vienna: "I always carry two keys with me, one for the door of my office and one for my residence. They are not by any means easily interchanged, as the office key is at least three times as big as my house key. Besides, I carry the first in my trouser pocket and the other in my vest pocket. Yet it often happened that I noticed, on reaching the door, that while ascending the

[1] Jones, *loc. cit.*, p. 79.

stairs, I had taken out the wrong key. I decided to undertake a statistical examination; as I was daily in about the same emotional state when I stood before both doors, I thought that the interchanging of the two keys must show a regular tendency, if they were differently determined psychically. Observation of later occurrences showed that I regularly took out my house key before the office door. Only on one occasion was this reversed: I came home tired, knowing that I would find a guest there. I made an attempt to unlock the door, with the, naturally too big, office key."

(b) At a certain time twice a day for six years, I was accustomed to wait for admission before a door in the second story of the same house, and during this long period of time, it happened twice (within a short interval) that I climbed a story higher. On the first of these occasions, I was in an ambitious day-dream, which allowed me to "mount always higher and higher." In fact, at that time, I heard the door in question open as I put my foot on the first step of the third flight. On the other occasion, I again went too far, "engrossed in thought." As soon as I became aware of it, I turned back and sought to snatch the dominating phantasy; I found that I was irritated over a criticism of my works, in which the reproach was made that I "always went too far," which I replaced by the less respectful expression, "climbed too high."

(c) For many years, a reflex hammer and a tuning-fork lay side by side on my desk. One day, I hurried off at the close of my office hours, as I wished to catch a certain train, and, despite broad daylight, put the tuning-fork in my coat pocket in place of the reflex hammer. My attention was called to the mistake through the weight of the object drawing down my pocket. Anyone accustomed to reflect on such slight occurrences would, without hesitation, explain the faulty action by the hurry of the moment, and excuse it. In spite of that, I preferred to ask myself why I took the tuning-fork instead of the hammer. The haste could just as well have been a motive for carrying out the action properly in order not to waste time over the correction.

"Who last grasped the tuning-fork?" was the question which immediately flashed through my mind. It happened that only a few days ago, an idiotic child, whose attention to sensory impressions I was testing, had been so fascinated by the tuning-fork that I found it difficult to tear it away from him. Could it mean, therefore, that I was an idiot? To be sure, so it would seem, as the next thought which associated itself with the hammer was *chamer* (Hebrew for "ass").

But what was the meaning of this abusive language? We must here inquire into the situation. I hurried to a consultation to see a patient who, according to the anamnesis which I received by letter, had fallen from a balcony some months before, and since then, had been unable to walk. The physician who invited me wrote that he was still unable to say whether he was dealing with a spinal injury or traumatic neurosis—hysteria. That was what I was to decide. This could therefore be a reminder to be particularly careful in this delicate differential diagnosis. As it is, my colleagues think that hysteria is diagnosed far too carelessly where more serious matters are concerned. But the abuse is not yet justified. Yes, the next association was that the small railroad station is the same place in which, some years previous, I saw a young man who, after a certain emotional experience, could not walk properly. At that time, I diagnosed his malady as hysteria, and later put him under psychic treatment; but it afterward turned out that my diagnosis was neither incorrect nor correct. A large number of the patient's symptoms were hysterical, and they promptly disappeared in the course of treatment. But back of these, there was a visible remnant that could not be reached by therapy, and could be referred only to a multiple sclerosis. Those who saw the patient after me had no difficulty in recognizing the organic affection. I could scarcely have acted or judged differently; still, the impression was that of a serious mistake; the promise of a cure which I had given him could naturally not be kept.

The mistake in grasping the tuning-fork instead of the hammer could therefore be translated into the following words: "You fool, you ass, get yourself together this time, and be careful not to diagnose again a case of hysteria where there is an incurable disease, as you did in this place years ago in the case of that poor man!" And fortunately for this little analysis, even if unfortunately for my mood, this same man, now showing a very spastic gait, had been to my office a few days before, one day after the examination of the idiotic child.

We observe that this time it is the voice of self-criticism which makes itself perceptible through the mistake in grasping. The erroneously carried-out action is specially suited to express self-reproach. The present mistake attempts to represent the mistake which was committed elsewhere.

(d) It is quite obvious that grasping the wrong thing may also serve a whole series of other obscure purposes. Here is a first example: It is very seldom that I break anything. I am not particularly dexterous, but by virtue of the anatomic integrity of my nervous and muscular apparatus, there are apparently no grounds in me for such awkward movements with undesirable results. I can recall no object in my home which I have ever broken. Owing to the narrowness of my study, it has often been necessary for me to work in the most uncomfortable position among my numerous antique clay and stone objects, of which I have a small collection. So much is this true that onlookers have expressed fear lest I topple down something and shatter it. But it never happened. Then, why did I brush to the floor the cover of my simple inkwell so that it broke into pieces?

My inkstand is made of a flat piece of marble which is hollowed out for the reception of the glass inkwell; the inkwell has a marble cover with a knob of the same stone. A circle of bronze statuettes with small terra-cotta figures is set behind this inkstand. I seated myself at the desk to write; I made a remarkably awkward outward movement with the hand holding the pen-holder, and so swept the cover of the inkstand, which already lay on the desk, to the floor.

It is not difficult to find the explanation. Some hours before, my sister had been in the room to look at some of my new acquisitions. She found them very pretty, and then remarked: "Now the desk really looks very well, only the inkstand doesn't match. You must get a prettier one." I accompanied my sister out and did not return for several hours. But then, as it seems, I performed the execution of the condemned inkstand.

Did I perhaps conclude from my sister's words that she intended to present me with a prettier inkstand on the next festive occasion, and did I shatter the unsightly old one in order to force her to carry out her signified intention? If that be so, then my swinging motion was only apparently awkward; in reality, it was most skillful and designed, as it seemingly understood how to avoid all the valuable objects located near it.

I actually believe that we must accept this explanation for a whole series of seemingly accidental awkward movements. It is true that on the surface, these seem to show something violent and irregular, similar to spastic-ataxic movements, but on examination, they seem to be dominated by some intention, and they accomplish their aim with a certainty that cannot be generally credited to conscious arbitrary motions. In both characteristics, the force as well as the sure aim, they show besides a resemblance to the motor manifestations of the hysterical neurosis, and in part also to the motor accomplishments of somnambulism, which here as well as there, point to the same unfamiliar modification of the functions of innervation.

In latter years, since I have been collecting such observations, it has happened several times that I have shattered and broken objects of some value, but the examination of these cases convinced me that it was never the result of accident or of my unintentional awkwardness. Thus, one morning while in my bath-robe and straw slippers, I followed a sudden impulse as I passed a room, and hurled a slipper from my foot against the wall so that it brought down a beautiful little marble Venus from its bracket. As it fell to pieces, I recited quite unmoved the following verse from Busch:

"Ach! Die Venus ist perdü— [1]
Klickeradoms!—von Medici!"

This crazy action and my calmness at the sight of the damage are explained in the then existing situation. We had a very sick person in the family, of whose recovery I had personally despaired. That morning, I had been informed that there was a great improvement; I know that I had said to myself, "After all she will live." My attack of destructive madness served therefore as the expression of a grateful feeling toward fate, and afforded me the opportunity of performing an "act of sacrifice," just as if I had vowed, "If she gets well, I will give this or that as a sacrifice." That I chose the Venus of Medici as this sacrifice was only gallant homage to the convalescent. But even today, it is still incomprehensible to me that I decided so quickly, aimed so accurately and struck no other object in close proximity.

Another breaking, in which I utilized a penholder falling from my hand, also signified a sacrifice, but this time, it was a pious offering to avert some evil. I had once allowed myself to reproach a true and worthy friend for no other reason than certain manifestations which I interpreted from his unconscious activity. He took it amiss and wrote me a letter in which he bade me not to treat my friends by psychoanalysis. I had to admit that he was right and appeased him with my answer. While writing this letter, I had before me my latest acquisition—a small, handsome, glazed Egyptian figure. I broke it in the manner mentioned, and then immediately knew that I had caused this mischief to avert a greater one. Luckily, both the friendship and the figure could be so cemented that the break would not be noticed.

A third case of breaking had a less serious connection; it was only a disguised "execution," to use an expression from Th. Vischer's *Auch Einer,* of an object that no longer suited my taste. For quite a while, I had carried a cane with a silver handle; through no fault of mine, the thin silver plate was once damaged and poorly repaired. Soon after the cane was returned, I mirthfully used the handle to angle for the leg of one of my children. In that way, it naturally broke and I got rid of it.

The indifference with which we accept the resulting damage in all these cases may certainly be taken as evidence for the existence of an unconscious purpose in their execution.

(e) As can sometimes be demonstrated by analysis, the dropping of objects or the overturning and breaking of the same, are very frequently utilized as the expression of unconscious streams of thought, but more often, they serve to represent the superstitious or odd significances connected therewith in popular sayings. The meanings attached to the spill-

[1] Alas! The Venus of Medici is lost!

ing of salt, the overturning of a wineglass, the sticking of a knife dropped to the floor, and so on, are well known. I shall discuss later the right to investigate such superstitious interpretations; here I shall simply observe that the individual awkward acts do not by any means always have the same meaning, but, depending on the circumstances, they serve to represent now this or that purpose.

Recently, we passed through a period in my house, during which an unusual number of glass and china dishes were broken. I myself largely contributed to the damage. This little endemic was readily explained by the fact that it preceded the public betrothal of my eldest daughter. At such festivities, it is customary to break some dishes and utter at the same time some felicitating expression. This custom may signify a sacrifice or express any other symbolic sense.

When servants destroy fragile objects by letting them fall, we certainly do not think in the first place of a psychic motive for it; still, some obscure motives are not improbable even here. Nothing lies farther from the uneducated than the appreciation of art and works of art. Our servants are dominated by a foolish hostility against these productions, especially when the objects, whose worth they do not realize, become a source of a great deal of work for them. On the other hand, persons of the same education and origin employed in scientific institutions often distinguish themselves by great dexterity and reliability in the handling of delicate objects, as soon as they begin to identify themselves with their masters and consider themselves an essential part of the staff.

I shall here add the report of a young mechanical engineer, which gives some insight into the mechanism of damaging things.

"Some time ago, I worked with many others in the laboratory of the High School on a series of complicated experiments on the subject of elasticity. It was a work that we undertook of our own volition, but it turned out that it took up more of our time than we expected. One day, while going to the laboratory with F., he complained of losing so much time, especially on this day, when he had so many other things to do at home. I could only agree with him, and he added half jokingly, alluding to an incident of the previous week: 'Let us hope that the machine will refuse to work, so that we can interrupt the experiment and go home earlier.'

"In arranging the work, it happened that F. was assigned to the regulation of the pressure valve; that is, it was his duty to carefully open the valve and let the fluid under pressure flow from the accumulator into the cylinder of the hydraulic press. The leader of the experiment stood at the manometer and called a loud 'Stop!' when the maximum pressure was reached. At this command, F. grasped the valve and turned it with all his force—to the left (all valves, without any exception, are closed to the right). This caused a sudden full pressure in the accumulator of the press, and as there was no outlet, the connecting pipe burst. This was quite a trifling accident to the machine, but enough to force us to stop our work for the day and go home.

"It is characteristic, moreover, that some time later on discussing this occurrence, my friend F. could not recall the remark that I positively remember he had made."

Similarly, to fall, to make a misstep, or to slip need not always be interpreted as an entirely accidental miscarriage of a motor action. The linguistic double meaning of these expressions points to diverse hidden phantasies, which may present themselves through the giving up of bodily equilibrium. I recall a number of lighter nervous ailments in women and girls which made their appearance after falling without injury, and which were conceived as traumatic hysteria as a result of the shock of the fall. At that time, I already entertained the impression that these conditions had a different connection, that the fall was already a preparation of the neurosis, and an expression of the same unconscious phantasies of sexual content which may be taken as the moving forces behind the symptoms. Was not this very thing meant in the proverb which says, *"When a maiden falls, she falls on her back"*?

We can also add to these mistakes the case of one who gives a beggar a gold piece in place of a copper or a silver coin. The solution of such mishandling is simple: it is an act of sacrifice designed to mollify fate, to avert evil, and so on. If we hear a tender mother or an aunt express concern regarding the health of a child, immediately before taking a walk during which she displays her charity, contrary to her usual habit, we can hardly doubt the sense of this apparently undesirable accident. In this manner, our faulty acts make possible the practice of all those pious and superstitious customs which must shun the light of consciousness, because of the strivings against them of our unbelieving reason.

(f) That accidental actions are really intentional will find no greater credence in any other sphere than in sexual activity, where the border between the intention and accident hardly seems discernible. That an apparently clumsy movement may be utilized in a most refined way for sexual purposes, I can verify by a nice example from my own experience. In a friend's house, I met a young girl visitor who excited in me a feeling of fondness which I had long believed extinct, thus putting me in a jovial, loquacious and complaisant mood. At that time, I endeavored to find out how this came about, as a year before this same girl made no impression on me.

As the girl's uncle, a very old man, entered the room, we both jumped to our feet to bring him a chair which stood in the corner. She was more agile than I and also nearer the object, so that she was the first to take possession of the chair. She carried it with its back to her, holding both hands on the edge of the seat. As I got there later and did not give up the claim to carrying the chair, I suddenly stood directly back of her, and with both my arms was embracing her from behind, and for a moment, my hands touched her lap. I naturally solved the situation as quickly as it came about. Nor did it occur to anybody how dexterously I had taken advantage of this awkward movement.

Occasionally, I have had to admit to myself that the annoying, awkward stepping aside on the street, whereby for some seconds one steps here and there, yet always in the same direction as the other person, until finally both stop facing each other, that this "barring one's way" repeats an ill-mannered, provoking conduct of earlier times and conceals erotic purposes under the mask of awkwardness. From my psychoanalysis of neurotics, I know that the so-called naïveté of young people and children is frequently only such a mask employed in order that the subject may say or do the indecent without restraint.

(g) The effects which result from mistakes of normal persons are, as a rule, of a most harmless nature. Just for this reason, it would be particularly interesting to find out whether mistakes of considerable importance, which could be followed by serious results, as, for example, those of physicians or druggists, fall within the range of our point of view.

As I am seldom in a position to deal with active medical matters, I can only report one mistake from my own experience. I treated a very old woman, whom I visited twice daily for several years. My medical activities were limited to two acts, which I performed during my morning visits: I dropped a few drops of an eye lotion into her eyes and gave her a hypodermic injection of morphine. I prepared regularly two bottles—a blue one, containing the eye lotion, and a white one, containing the morphine solution. While performing these duties, my thoughts were mostly occupied with something else, for they had been repeated so often that the attention acted as if free. One morning, I noticed that the automaton worked wrong; I had put the dropper into the white instead of into the blue bottle, and had dropped into the eyes the morphine instead of the lotion. I was greatly frightened, but then calmed myself through the reflection that a few drops of a *two per cent* solution of morphine would not likely do any harm even if left in the conjunctival sac. The cause of the fright manifestly belonged elsewhere.

In attempting to analyze the slight mistake, I first thought of the phrase, "to seize the old woman by mistake," which pointed out the short way to the solution. I had been impressed by a dream which a young man had told me the previous evening, the contents of which could be explained only on the basis of sexual intercourse with his own mother.[1] The strangeness of the fact that the Oedipus legend takes no offense at the age of Queen Jocasta seemed to me to agree with the assumption that in being in love with one's mother, we never deal with the present personality, but with her youthful memory picture carried over from our childhood. Such incongruities always show themselves where one phantasy fluctuating between two periods is made conscious, and is then bound to one definite period.

Deep in thoughts of this kind, I came to my patient of over ninety; I must have been well on the way to grasp the universal character of the Oedipus fable as the correlation of the fate which the oracle pronounces, for I made a blunder in reference to or on the old woman. Here, again, the mistake was harmless; of the two possible errors, taking the morphine solution for the eye, or the eye lotion for the injection, I chose the one by far the least harmful. The question still remains open whether in mistakes in handling things which may cause serious harm, we can assume an unconscious intention as in the cases here discussed.

The following case from Brill's experience corroborates the assumption that even serious mistakes are determined by unconscious intentions: "A physician received a telegram informing him that his aged uncle was very sick. In spite of important family affairs at home, he at once repaired to that distant town because his uncle was really his father, who had cared for him since he was one and a half years old, when his own father had died. On reaching there, he found his uncle suffering from pneumonia, and, as the old man was an octogenarian, the doctors held out no hope for his recovery. 'It was simply a question of a day or two,' was the local doctor's verdict. Although a prominent physician in a big city, he refused to coöperate in the treatment, as he found that the case was properly managed by the local doctor, and he could not suggest anything to improve matters.

"Since death was daily expected, he decided to remain to the end. He waited a few days, but the sick man struggled hard, and although there was no question of any recovery, because of the many new complications which had arisen, death seemed to be deferred for a while. One night, before retiring, he went into the sickroom and took his uncle's pulse. As it was quite weak, he decided not to wait for the doctor, and administered a hypodermic injection. The patient grew rapidly worse and died within a few hours. There was something strange in the last symptoms, and on later attempting to replace the tube of hypodermic tablets into the case,

---

[1] The Oedipus dream, as I was wont to call it, because it contains the key to the understanding of the legend of King Oedipus. In the text of Sophocles, the relation of such a dream is put in the mouth of Jocasta. (Cf. *The Interpretation of Dreams* pp. 307–9, etc.)

he found, to his consternation, that he had taken out the wrong tube, and instead of a small dose of digitalis, he had given a large dose of hyoscine.

"This case was related to me by the doctor after he read my paper on the Oedipus Complex. We agreed that this mistake was determined not only by his impatience to get home to his sick child, but also by an old resentment and unconscious hostility toward his uncle (father)."

It is known that in the more serious cases of psychoneuroses one sometimes finds self-mutilations as symptoms of the disease. That the psychic conflict may end in suicide can never be excluded in these cases. Thus, I know from experience, which some day I shall support with convincing examples, that many apparently accidental injuries happening to such patients are really self-inflicted. This is brought about by the fact that there is a constantly lurking tendency to self-punishment, usually expressing itself in self-reproach, or contributing to the formation of a symptom, which skillfully makes use of an external situation. The required external situation may accidentally present itself or the punishment tendency may assist it until the way is open for the desired injurious effect.

Such occurrences are by no means rare even in cases of moderate severity, and they betray the portions of unconscious intention through a series of special features—for example, through the striking presence of mind which the patients show in the pretended accidents.[1]

I will report exhaustively one in place of many such examples from my professional experience. A young woman broke her leg below the knee in a carriage accident so that she was bedridden for weeks. The striking part of it was the lack of any manifestation of pain and the calmness with which she bore her misfortune. This calamity ushered in a long and serious neurotic illness, from which she was finally cured by psychotherapy. During the treatment I discovered the circumstances surrounding the accident, as well as certain impressions which preceded it. The young woman with her jealous husband spent some time on the farm of her married sister, in company with her numerous brothers and sisters with their wives and husbands. One evening, she gave an exhibition of one of her talents before this intimate circle; she danced artistically the "cancan," to the great delight of her relatives, but to the great annoyance of her husband, who afterward whispered to her, "Again you have behaved like a whore." The words took effect; we will leave it undecided whether it was just on account of the dance. That night she was restless in her sleep, and the next forenoon, she decided to go out driving. She

---

[1] The self-inflicted injury which does not entirely tend toward self-annihilation has, moreover, no other choice in our present state of civilization than to hide itself behind the accidental, or to break through in a simulation of spontaneous illness. Formerly, it was a customary sign of mourning; at other times, it expressed itself in ideas of piety and renunciation of the world.

chose the horses herself, refusing one team and demanding another. Her youngest sister wished to have her baby with its nurse accompany her, but she opposed this vehemently. During the drive, she was nervous; she reminded the coachman that the horses were getting skittish, and as the fidgety animals really produced a momentary difficulty, she jumped from the carriage in fright and broke her leg, while those remaining in the carriage were uninjured. Although after the disclosure of these details we can hardly doubt that this accident was really contrived, we cannot fail to admire the skill which forced the accident to mete out a punishment so suitable to the crime. For, as it happened, "cancan" dancing with her became impossible for a long time.

Concerning self-inflicted injuries of my own experience, I cannot report anything in calm times, but under extraordinary conditions, I do not believe myself incapable of such acts. When a member of my family complains that he or she has bitten his tongue, bruised her finger, and so on, instead of the expected sympathy, I put the question, "Why did you do that?" But I have most painfully squeezed my thumb, after a youthful patient acquainted me during the treatment with his intention (naturally not to be taken seriously) of marrying my eldest daughter, while I knew that she was then in a private hospital in extreme danger of losing her life.

One of my boys, whose vivacious temperament was wont to put difficulties in the management of nursing him in his illness, had a fit of anger one morning because he was ordered to remain in bed during the forenoon, and threatened to kill himself: a way out suggested to him by the newspapers. In the evening, he showed me a swelling on the side of his chest which was the result of bumping against the door knob. To my ironical question why he did it, and what he meant by it, the eleven-year-old child explained, "That was my attempt at suicide which I threatened this morning." However, I do not believe that my views on self-inflicted wounds were accessible to my children at that time.

Whoever believes in the occurrence of semi-intentional self-inflicted injury—if this awkward expression be permitted—will become prepared to accept through it the fact that aside from conscious intentional suicide, there also exists semi-intentional annihilation—with unconscious intention—which is capable of aptly utilizing a threat against life and masking it as a casual mishap. Such mechanisms are by no means rare. For the tendency to self-destruction exists to a certain degree in many more persons than in those who bring it to completion. Self-inflicted injuries are, as a rule, a compromise between this impulse and the forces working against it, and even where it really comes to suicide, the inclination has existed for a long time with less strength or as an unconscious and repressed tendency.

Even suicide consciously committed chooses its time, means and opportunity; it is quite natural that unconscious suicide should wait for a motive to take upon itself one part of the causation and thus free it from its oppression by taking up the defensive forces of the person.[1] These are in no way idle discussions which I here bring up; more than one case of apparently accidental misfortune has become known to me whose surrounding circumstances justified the suspicion of suicide.

For example, during an officers' horse-race one of the riders fell from his horse and was so seriously injured that a few days later he succumbed to his injuries. His behavior after regaining consciousness was remarkable in more than one way, and his conduct previous to the accident was still more remarkable. He had been greatly depressed by the death of his beloved mother, had crying spells in the society of his comrades, and to his trusted friend had spoken of the *taedium vitae*. He had wished to quit the service in order to take part in a war in Africa which had no interest for him.[2] Formerly a keen rider, he had later evaded riding whenever possible. Finally, before the horse-race, from which he could not withdraw, he expressed a sad foreboding; in the light of our conception, it is not surprising that his premonition came true. It may be contended that it is quite comprehensible without any further cause that a person in such a state of nervous depression cannot manage a horse as well as on normal days. I quite agree with that, only I should like to look for the mechanism of this motor inhibition through "nervousness" in the intention of self-destruction here emphasized.

Another analysis of an apparently accidental self-inflicted wound, detailed to me by an observer, recalls the saying, "He who digs a pit for others falls in himself."[3]

---

[1] The case is then identical with a sexual attack on a woman, in whom the attack of the man cannot be warded off through the full muscular strength of the woman because a portion of the unconscious feelings of the one attacked meets it with ready acceptance. To be sure, it is said that such a situation paralyzes the strength of a woman; we need only add the reasons for this paralysis. Insofar, the clever sentence of Sancho Panza, which he pronounced as governor of his island, is psychologically unjust (*Don Quixote*, vol. ii., chap. xlv). A woman haled before the judge a man who was supposed to have robbed her of her honor by force of violence. Sancho indemnified her with a full purse which he took from the accused, but after the departure of the woman, he gave the accused permission to follow her and snatch the purse from her. Both returned wrestling, the woman priding herself that the villain was unable to possess himself of the purse. Thereupon Sancho spoke: "Had you shown yourself so stout and valiant to defend your body (nay, but half so much) as you have done to defend your purse, the strength of Hercules could not have forced you."

[2] It is evident that the situation of a battlefield is such as to meet the requirement of conscious suicidal intent which, nevertheless, shuns the direct way. Cf. in *Wallenstein* the words of the Swedish captain concerning the death of Max Piccolomini: "They say he wished to die."

[3] "Selbstbestrafung wegen Abortus" by Dr. J. E. G. van Emden, Haag (Holland), *Zentralb. f. Psychoanalyse*, ii., 12.

"Mrs. X., belonging to a good middle-class family, is married and has three children. She is somewhat nervous, but never needed any strenuous treatment, as she could sufficiently adapt herself to life. One day, she sustained a rather striking though transitory disfigurement of her face in the following manner: She stumbled in a street that was in process of repair and struck her face against the house wall. The whole face was bruised, the eyelids blue and oedematous, and as she feared that something might happen to her eyes, she sent for the doctor. After she was calmed, I asked her, 'But why did you fall in such a manner?' She answered that just before this accident she warned her husband, who had been suffering for some months from a joint affection, to be very careful in the street, and she often had the experience that in some remarkable way those things occurred to her against which she warned others.

"I was not satisfied with this as the determination of her accident, and asked her whether she had not something else to tell me. 'Yes, just before the accident, she noticed a nice picture in a shop on the other side of the street, which she suddenly desired as an ornament for her nursery, and wished to buy it at once. She thereupon walked across to the shop without looking at the street, stumbled over a heap of stones, and fell with her face against the wall without making the slightest effort to shield herself with her hands. The intention to buy the picture was immediately forgotten, and she walked home in haste.'

" 'But why were you not more careful?' I asked.

" 'Oh!' she answered, 'perhaps it was only a punishment for that episode which I confided to you!'

" 'Has this episode still bothered you?'

" 'Yes, later I regretted it very much; I considered myself wicked, criminal and immoral, but at the time, I was almost crazy with nervousness.'

"She referred to an abortion which was started by a quack and had to be brought to completion by a gynecologist. This abortion was initiated with the consent of her husband, as both wished on account of their pecuniary circumstances to be spared from being additionally blessed with children.

"She said: 'I had often reproached myself with the words, "You really had your child killed," and I feared that such a crime could not remain unpunished. Now that you have assured me that there is nothing seriously wrong with my eyes, I am quite assured I have already been sufficiently punished.'

"This accident, therefore, was on the one hand a retribution for her sin, but on the other hand it may have served as an escape from a more dire punishment which she had feared for many months. In the moment that she ran to the shop to buy the picture, the memory of this whole history, with its fears (already quite active in her unconscious at the time she warned her husband), became overwhelming and could perhaps find expression in words like these: 'But why do you want an ornament for the nursery?—you who had your child killed! You are a murderer! The great punishment is surely approaching!'

"This thought did not become conscious, but instead of it she made use of the situation—I might say of the psychologic moment—to utilize in a commonplace manner the heap of stones to inflict upon herself this punishment. It was for this reason that she did not even attempt to put out her arms while falling and was not much frightened. The second, and probably lesser, determinant of her accident was obviously the self-punishment for her unconscious wish to be rid of her husband, who was an accessory to the crime in this affair. This was betrayed by her absolutely superfluous warning to be very careful in the street on account of the stones. For, just because her husband had a weak leg, he was very careful in walking."

If such a rage against one's own integrity and one's own life can be hidden behind apparently accidental awkwardness and motor insufficiency, then it is not a big step forward to grasp the possibility of transferring the same conception to mistakes which seriously endanger the life and health of others. What I can put forward as evidence for the validity of this conception was taken from my experience with neurotics, and hence, does not fully meet the demands of this situation. I will report a case in which it was not an erroneously carried-out action, but what may be more aptly termed a symbolic or chance action that gave me the clue which later made possible the solution of the patient's conflict.

I once undertook to improve the marriage relations of a very intelligent man, whose differences with his tenderly attached young wife could surely be traced to real causes, but as he himself admitted, could not be altogether explained through them. He continually occupied himself with the thought of a separation, which he repeatedly rejected because he dearly loved his two small children. In spite of this, he always returned to that resolution and sought no means to make the situation bearable to himself. Such an unsettlement of a conflict served to prove to me that there were unconscious and repressed motives which enforced the conflicting conscious thoughts, and in such cases, I always undertake to end the conflict by psychic analysis. One day, the man related to me a slight occurrence which had extremely frightened him. He was sporting with the older child, by far his favorite. He tossed it high in the air and repeated this tossing till finally he thrust it so high that its head almost struck the massive gas chandelier. Almost, but not quite, or say "just about!" Nothing happened to the child except that it became dizzy from fright. The father stood transfixed with the child in his arms, while the mother merged into an hysterical attack. The particular facility of this careless movement, with the violent reaction in the parents, suggested to me to look upon this accident as a symbolic action which gave expression to an evil intention toward the beloved child.

I could remove the contradiction to the actual tenderness of this father for his child by referring the impulse to injure it to the time when it was the only one, and so small, that as yet, the father had no occasion for tender interest in it. Then it was easy to assume that this man, so little pleased with his wife at that time, might have thought: "If this small being for whom I have no regard whatever should die, I would be free and could separate from my wife." The wish for the death of this much loved being must therefore have continued unconsciously. From here, it was easy to find the way to the unconscious fixation of this wish.

There was indeed a powerful determinant in a memory from the patient's childhood: it referred to the death of a little brother, which the mother laid to his father's negligence, and which led to serious quarrels with threats of separation between the parents. The continued course of my patient's life, as well as the therapeutic success, confirmed my analysis.

IX

SYMPTOMATIC AND CHANCE ACTIONS

THE actions described so far, in which we recognize the execution of an unconscious intention, appeared as disturbances of other unintended actions, and hid themselves under the pretext of awkwardness. Chance actions, which we shall now discuss, differ from erroneously carried-out actions only in that they disdain the support of a conscious intention and really need no pretext. They appear independently and are accepted because one does not credit them with any aim or purpose. We execute them "without thinking anything of them," "by mere chance," "just to keep the hands busy," and we feel confident that such information will be quite sufficient should one inquire as to their significance. In order to enjoy the advantage of this exceptional position, these actions which no longer claim awkwardness as an excuse must fulfill certain conditions: they must not be striking, and their effects must be insignificant.

I have collected a large number of such "chance actions" from myself and others, and after thoroughly investigating the individual examples, I believe that the name "symptomatic actions" is more suitable. They give expression to something which the actor himself does not suspect in them, and which, as a rule, he has no intention of imparting to others, but aims to keep to himself. Like the other phenomena considered so far, they thus play the part of symptoms.

The richest output of such chance or symptomatic actions is above all obtained in the psychoanalytic treatment of neurotics. I cannot deny myself the pleasure of showing by two examples of this nature how far and how delicately the determination of these plain occurrences is swayed by unconscious thoughts. The line of demarcation between the symptomatic actions and the erroneously carried-out actions is so indefinite that I could have disposed of these examples in the preceding chapter.

(a) During the analysis, a young woman reproduced this idea which suddenly occurred to her. Yesterday, while cutting her nails, "she had cut into the flesh while engaged in trimming the cuticle." This is of so little interest that we ask in astonishment why it is at all remembered and mentioned, and therefore come to the conclusion that we deal with a symptomatic action. It was really the finger upon which the wedding ring is worn which was injured through this slight awkwardness. It happened, moreover, on her wedding-day, which thus gives to the injury of the delicate skin a very definite and easily guessed meaning. At the same time, she also related a dream which alluded to the awkwardness of her husband and her feminine anesthesia. But why did she injure the ring finger of her left hand when the wedding ring is worn on the right? Her husband is a jurist, a "Doctor of Laws" (*Doktor der Rechte,* literally a Doctor of Rights), and her secret affection as a girl belonged to a physician who was jokingly called *Doktor der Linke* (literally Doctor of Left). Incidentally, a left-handed marriage has a definite meaning.

(b) A single young woman relates: "Yesterday, quite unintentionally, I tore a hundred-dollar note in two pieces and gave half to a woman who was visiting me. Is that, too, a symptomatic action?" After closer investigation, the matter of the hundred-dollar note elicited the following associations: She dedicated a part of her time and her fortune to charitable work. Together with another woman she was taking care of the rearing of an orphan. The hundred dollars was the contribution sent her by that woman, which she enclosed in an envelope and provisionally deposited on her writing-desk.

The visitor was a prominent woman with whom she was associated in another act of charity. This woman wished to note the names of a number of persons to whom she could apply for charitable aid. There was no paper, so my patient grasped the envelope from her desk, and without thinking of its contents, tore it in two pieces, one of which she kept and gave the other to her visitor.

Note the harmlessness of this aimless occurrence. It is known that a hundred-dollar note suffers no loss in value when it is torn, provided all the pieces are produced. That the woman would not throw away the piece of paper was assumed by the importance of the names on it, and there was just as little doubt that she would return the valuable content as soon as she noticed it.

But to what unconscious thought should this chance action, which was made possible through forgetfulness, give expression? The visitor in this case had a very definite relation to my patient and myself. It was she who at one time had recommended me as physician to the suffering girl, and if I am not mistaken, my patient considered herself indebted for this advice. Should this halved hundred-dollar note perhaps represent a fee for her mediation? That still remained enigmatic.

But other material was added to this beginning. Several days before, a woman mediator of a different sort had inquired of a relative whether the gracious young lady wished to make the acquaintance of a certain gentleman, and that morning, some hours before the woman's visit, the wooing letter of the suitor arrived, giving occasion for much mirth. When therefore the visitor opened the conversation with inquiries regarding the health of my patient, the latter could well have thought: "You certainly found the right doctor for me, but if you could assist me in obtaining the right husband (and a child), I should be still more grateful."

Both mediators became fused into one in this repressed thought, and she handed the visitor the fee which her phantasy was ready to give the other. This resolution became perfectly convincing when I add that I had told her of such chance or symptomatic actions only the previous evening. She then took advantage of the next occasion to produce an analogous action.

We can undertake a grouping of these extremely frequent chance and symptomatic actions according to their occurrence as habitual, regular under certain circumstances, and as isolated ones. The first group (such as playing with the watch-chain, fingering one's beard, and so on), which can almost serve as a characteristic of the person concerned, is related to the numerous tic movements, and certainly deserves to be dealt with in connection with the latter. In the second group, I place the playing with one's cane, the scribbling with one's pencil, the jingling of coin's in one's pocket, kneading dough and other plastic materials, all sorts of handling of one's clothing and many other actions of the same order.

These playful occupations during psychoanalytic treatment regularly conceal sense and meaning to which other expression is denied. Generally the person in question knows nothing about it; he is unaware whether he is doing the same thing or whether he has imitated certain modifications in his customary playing, and he also fails to see or hear the effects of these actions. For example, he does not hear the noise which is produced by the jingling of coins, and he is astonished and incredulous when his attention is called to it. Of equal significance to the physician, and worthy of his observation, is everything that one does with his clothing, often without noticing it. Every change in the customary attire, every little negligence, such as an unfastened button, every trace of exposure means to express something that the wearer of the apparel does not wish to say directly; usually he is entirely unconscious of it.

The interpretation of these trifling chance actions, as well as the proof for their interpretation, can be demonstrated every time with sufficient certainty from the surrounding circumstances during the treatment, from the themes under discussion, and from the ideas that come to the surface when attention is directed to the seeming accident. Because of this connection, I will refrain from supporting my assertions by reporting examples with their analyses; but I mention these matters because I believe that they have the same meaning in normal persons as in my patients.

I cannot, however, refrain from showing by at least one example how closely an habitually accomplished symbolic action may be connected with the most intimate and important part of the life of a normal individual.[1]

"As Professor Freud has taught us, the symbolism in the infantile life of the normal plays a greater rôle than was expected from earlier psychoanalytic experiences. In view of this, the following brief analysis may be of general interest, especially on account of its medical aspects.

"A doctor, on rearranging his, furniture in a new house, came across a straight, wooden stethoscope, and, after pausing to decide where he should put it, was impelled to place it on the side of his writing-desk in such a position that it stood exactly between his chair and the one reserved for his patients. The act in itself was certainly odd, for in the first place, the straight stethoscope served no purpose as he invariably used a binaural one; and in the second place, all his medical apparatus and instruments were always kept in drawers, with the sole exception of this one. However, he gave no thought to the matter until one day, it was brought to his notice by a patient who had never seen a wooden stethoscope, asking him what it was. On being told, she asked him why he kept it there. He answered in an offhand way that that place was as good as any other. This, however, started him thinking, and he wondered whether there had been an unconscious motive in his action. Being interested in the psychoanalytic method, he asked me to investigate the matter.

"The first memory that occurred to him was the fact that when a medical student, he had been struck by the habit his hospital interne had of always carrying a wooden stethoscope in his hand on his ward visits, although he never used it. He greatly admired this interne, and was much attached to him. Later on, when he himself became an interne, he contracted the same habit, and would feel very uncomfortable if by mistake he left the room without having the instrument to swing in his hand. The aimlessness of the habit was shown, not only by the fact that the only stethoscope he ever used was a binaural one, which he carried in his pocket, but also in that it was continued when he was a surgical interne and never needed any stethoscope at all.

"From this, it was evident that the idea of the instrument in question had in some way or other become invested with a greater psychic significance than normally belonged to it—in other words, that to the subject it stood for more than it does for other people. The idea must have become unconsciously associated with some other one which it symbolized, and from which it derived its additional fullness of meaning. I will forestall the rest of the analysis by saying what this secondary idea was—namely,

[1] "Beitrag zur Symbolik im Alltag" by Ernest Jones, Zentralb. f. Psychoanalyse, i. 3, 1911.

a phallic one; the way in which this curious association had been formed will presently be related. The discomfort he experienced in hospital on missing the instrument, and the relief and assurance the presence of it gave him, was related to what is known as a 'castration complex'—namely, a childhood fear, often continued in a disguised form into adult life, lest a private part of his body should be taken away from him, just as playthings so often were. The fear was due to paternal threats that it would be cut off if he were not a good boy, particularly in a certain direction. This is a very common complex, and accounts for a great deal of general nervousness and lack of confidence in later years.

"Then came a number of childhood memories relating to his family doctor. He had been strongly attached to this doctor as a child, and during the analysis, long-buried memories were recovered of a double phantasy he had in his fourth year concerning the birth of a younger sister—namely, that she was the child (1) of himself and his mother, the father being relegated to the background, and (2) of the doctor and himself; in this, he thus played both a masculine and feminine part.[1] At the time, when his curiosity was being aroused by the event, he could not help noticing the prominent share taken by the doctor in the proceedings, and the subordinate position occupied by the father: the significance of this for his later life will presently be pointed out.

"The stethoscope association was formed through many connections. In the first place, the physical appearance of the instrument—a straight, rigid, hollow tube, having a small bulbous summit at one extremity and a broad base at the other—and the fact of its being the essential part of the medical paraphernalia, the instrument with which the doctor performed his magical and interesting feats, were matters that attracted his boyish attention. He had had his chest repeatedly examined by the doctor at the age of six, and distinctly recollected the voluptuous sensation of feeling the latter's head near him pressing the wooden stethoscope into his chest, and of the rhythmic to-and-fro respiratory movement. He had been struck by the doctor's habit of carrying his stethoscope inside his hat; he found it interesting that the doctor should carry his chief instrument concealed about his person, always handy when he went to see patients, and that he only had to take off his hat (i.e., a part of his clothing) and 'pull it out.' At the age of eight, he was impressed by being told by an older boy that it was the doctor's custom to get into bed with his women patients. It is certain that the doctor, who was young and handsome, was extremely popular among the women of the neighborhood, including the subject's own mother. The doctor and his 'instrument' were therefore objects of great interest throughout his boyhood.

[1] Psychoanalytic research, with the penetration of infantile amnesia, has shown that this apparent precocity is a less abnormal occurrence than was previously supposed.

"It is probable that, as in many other cases, unconscious identification with the family doctor had been a main motive in determining the subject's choice of profession. It was here doubly conditioned (1) by the superiority on certain interesting occasions of the doctor to the father, of whom the subject was very jealous, and (2) by the doctor's knowledge of forbidden topics [1] and his opportunity for illicit indulgence. The subject admitted that he had on several occasions experienced erotic temptations in regard to his women patients; he had twice fallen in love with one, and finally had married one.

"The next memory was of a dream, plainly of a homosexual-masochistic nature; in it a man, who proved to be a replacement figure of the family doctor, attacked the subject with a 'sword.' The idea of a sword, as is so frequently the case in dreams, represented the same idea as was mentioned above to be associated with that of a wooden stethoscope. The thought of a sword reminded the subject of the passage in the *Nibelung Saga*, where Sigurd sleeps with his naked sword (*Gram*) between him and Brunhilda, an incident that had always greatly struck his imagination.

"The meaning of the symptomatic act now at last became clear. The subject had placed his wooden stethoscope between him and his patients, just as Sigurd had placed his sword (an equivalent symbol) between him and the maiden he was not to touch. The act was a compromise-formation; it served both to gratify in his imagination the repressed wish to enter into nearer relations with an attractive patient (interposition of phallus), and at the same time, to remind him that this wish was not to become a reality (interposition of sword). It was, so to speak, a charm against yielding to temptation.

"I might add that the following passage from Lord Lytton's *Richelieu* made a great impression on the boy:

> '*Beneath the rule of men entirely great*
> *The pen is mightier than the sword*,' [2]

and that he became a prolific writer and uses an unusually large fountain pen. When I asked him what need he had of this pen, he replied in a characteristic manner, 'I have so much to express.'

"This analysis reminds us of the profound views that are afforded us in the psychic life through the 'harmless' and 'senseless' actions, and how early in life the tendency to symbolization develops."

I can also relate an experience from my psychotherapeutic practice in which the hand, playing with a mass of bread-crumbs, gave evidence of an eloquent declaration. My patient was a boy not yet thirteen years of age, who had been very hysterical for two years. I finally took him for psycho-

---

[1] The term "medical questions" is a common periphrasis for "sexual" questions.
[2] Cf. Oldham's "I wear my pen as others do their sword."

analytic treatment, after a lengthy stay at a hydrotherapeutic institution had proved futile. My supposition was that he must have had sexual experiences, and that, corresponding to his age, he had been troubled by sexual questions; but I was cautious about helping him with explanations as I wished to test further my assumption. I was therefore curious as to the manner in which the desired material would evince itself in him.

One day, it struck me that he was rolling something between the fingers of his right hand; he would thrust it into his pocket and there continue playing with it, then would draw it out again, and so on. I did not ask what he had in his hand; but as he suddenly opened his hand, he showed it to me. It was bread-crumbs kneaded into a mass. At the next session, he again brought along a mass, and in the course of our conversation, although his eyes were closed, modelled a figure with an incredible rapidity which excited my interest. Without doubt, it was a manikin like the crudest prehistoric idols, with a head, two arms, two legs and an appendage between the legs which he drew out to a long point.

This was scarcely completed when he kneaded the manikin together again: later, he allowed it to remain, but modelled an identical appendage on the flat of the back and on other parts in order to veil the meaning of the first. I wished to show him that I had understood him, but at the same time, I wanted to deprive him of the evasion that he had thought of nothing while actively forming these figures. With this intention, I suddenly asked him whether he remembered the story of the Roman king who gave his son's envoy a pantomimic answer in his garden.

The boy did not wish to recall what he must have learned so much more recently than I. He asked if that was the story of the slave on whose bald skull the answer was written. I told him, "No, that belonged to Greek history," and related the following: "King Tarquinius Superbus had induced his son Sextus to steal into a Latin city. The son, who had later obtained a foothold in the city, sent a messenger to the king, asking what steps he should take next. The king gave no answer, but went into his garden, had the question repeated there, and silently struck off the heads of the largest and most beautiful poppies. All that the messenger could do was to report this to Sextus, who understood his father, and caused the most distinguished citizens of the city to be removed by assassination."

While I was speaking, the boy stopped kneading, and as I was relating what the king did in his garden, I noticed that at the words "silently struck" he tore off the head of the manikin with a movement as quick as lightning. He therefore understood me, and showed that he was also understood by me. Now I could question him directly, and gave him the information that he desired, and in a short time, the neurosis came to an end.

The symptomatic actions which we observe in inexhaustible abundance in healthy as well as in nervous people are worthy of our interest far more than one reason. To the physician, they often serve as valuable indications for orienting himself in new or unfamiliar conditions; to the keen observer, they often betray everything, occasionally even more than he cares to know. He who is familiar with its application sometimes feels like King Solomon, who, according to the Oriental legend, understood the language of animals.

One day, I was to examine a strange young man at his mother's home. As he came towards me, I was attracted by a large stain on his trousers, which by its peculiar stiff edges, I recognized as one produced by albumen. After a moment's embarrassment, the young man excused this stain by remarking that he was hoarse and therefore drank a raw egg, and that some of the slippery white of the egg had probably fallen on his clothes. To confirm his statements, he showed the eggshell which could still be seen on a small plate in the room. The suspicious spot was thus explained in this harmless way; but as his mother left us alone, I thanked him for having so greatly facilitated the diagnosis for me, and without further procedure, I took as the topic of our discussion his confession that he was suffering from the effects of masturbation.

Another time, I called on a woman as rich as she was miserly and foolish, who was in the habit of giving the physician the task of working his way through a heap of her complaints before he could reach the simple cause of her condition. As I entered, she was sitting at a small table engaged in arranging silver dollars in little piles: as she arose, she tumbled some of the pieces of money to the floor. I helped her pick them up, but interrupted the recitation of her misery by remarking: "Has your good son-in-law been spending so much of your money again?" She bitterly denied this, only to relate a few moments later the lamentable story of the aggravation caused by her son-in-law's extravagances. And she has not sent for me since. I cannot maintain that one always makes friends of those to whom he tells the meaning of their symptomatic actions.

He who observes his fellow-men while at table will be able to verify in them the nicest and most instructive symptomatic actions.

Dr. Hans Sachs relates the following:

"I happened to be present when an elderly couple related to me partook of their supper. The lady had stomach trouble and was forced to follow a strict diet. A roast was put before the husband, and he requested his wife, who was not allowed to partake of this food, to give him the mustard. The wife opened the closet and took out the small bottle of stomach drops, and placed it on the table before her husband. Between the barrel-shaped mustard glass and the small drop bottle, there was naturally no similarity through which the mishandling could be explained; yet the wife only noticed the mistake after her husband laughingly called her attention to it. The sense of this symptomatic action needs no explanation."

For an excellent example of this kind which was very skillfully utilized by the observer, I am indebted to Dr. Bernh. Dattner:

"I dined in a restaurant with my colleague H., a doctor of philosophy. He spoke about the injustice done to probationary students, and added that even before he finished his studies, he was placed as secretary to the ambassador, or rather the Minister plenipotentiary to Chile. 'But,' he added, 'the minister was afterwards transferred, and I did not make any effort to meet the newly appointed.' While uttering the last sentence, he was lifting a piece of pie to his mouth, but he let it drop as if out of awkwardness. I immediately grasped the hidden sense of this symptomatic action, and remarked to my colleague, who was unacquainted with psychoanalysis, 'You really allowed a very choice morsel to slip from you.' He did not realize, however, that my words could equally refer to his symptomatic action, and he repeated the same words I uttered with a peculiarly agreeable and surprising vividness, as if I had actually taken the words from his mouth: 'It was really a very choice morsel that I allowed to get away from me.' He then followed this remark with a detailed description of his clumsiness which has cost him this very remunerative position.

"The sense of this symbolic action becomes clearer if we remember that my colleague had scruples about telling me, almost a perfect stranger, concerning his precarious material situation, and his repressed thought took on the mask of symptomatic action which expressed symbolically what was meant to be concealed, and the speaker thus got relief from his unconscious."

Chance or symptomatic actions occurring in affairs of married life have often a most serious significance, and could lead those who do not concern themselves with the psychology of the unconscious to a belief in omens. It is not an auspicious beginning if a young woman loses her wedding ring on her wedding tour, even if it is only mislaid and soon found.

I know a woman, now divorced, who in the management of her business affairs frequently signed her maiden name many years before she actually resumed it.

Once I was the guest of a newly married couple and heard the young woman laughingly relate her latest experience, how, on the day succeeding her return from the wedding tour, she had sought out her single sister in order to go shopping with her as in former times, while her husband was attending business. Suddenly she noticed a man on the opposite side of the street; nudging her sister she said, "Why, that is surely Mr. L." She forgot that for some weeks this man had been her husband. I was chilled at this tale, but I did not dare draw any inferences. The little story came back to me only several years later, after this marriage had ended most unhappily.

A friend who has learned to observe signs related to me that the great actress Eleanore Duse introduced a symptomatic action into one of her rôles which shows very nicely from what depth she drew her acting. It was a drama dealing with adultery; she had just been in discussion with her husband and now stood soliloquizing before the seducer made his appearance. During this short interval, she played with her wedding ring; she pulled it off, replaced it and finally took it off again. She was now ready for the other.

I know of an elderly man who married a young girl, and instead of starting at once on his wedding tour, he decided to spend the night in a hotel. Scarcely had they reached the hotel, when he noticed with fright that he was without his wallet, in which he had the entire sum of money for the wedding tour; he must have mislaid or lost it. He was still able to reach his servant by telephone; the latter found the missing article in the coat discarded for the travelling clothes and brought it to the hotel to the waiting bridegroom, who had thus entered upon his marriage without means.

It is consoling to think that the "losing of objects" by people is merely an unsuspected extension of a symptomatic action, and is thus welcome at least to the secret intention of the loser. Often it is only an expression of slight appreciation of the lost article, a secret dislike for the same, or perhaps for the person from whom it came, or the desire to lose this object was transferred to it from other and more important objects through symbolic association. The loss of valuable articles serves as an expression of diverse feelings; it may either symbolically represent a repressed thought—that is, it may bring back a memory which one would rather not hear—or it may represent a sacrifice to the obscure forces of fate, the worship of which is not yet entirely extinct even with us.[1]

[1] Here is another small collection of various symptomatic actions in normal and neurotic persons. An elderly colleague who does not like to lose at cards had to pay one evening a large sum of money in consequence of his losses; he did this without complaint, but with a peculiarly constrained temper. After his departure, it was discovered that he had left practically everything he had with him at this place, spectacles, cigar case and handkerchief. That would be readily translated into the words: "You robbers, you have nicely plundered me." A man who suffers from occasional sexual impotence, which has its origin in the intimacy of his infantile relations to his mother, relates that he is in the habit of embellishing pamphlets and notes with an S, the initial of his mother's name. He cannot bear the idea of having letters from home come in contact with other unsanctified correspondence, and therefore finds it necessary to keep the former separate. A young woman suddenly flings open the door of the consulting room while her predecessor is still present. She excuses herself on the ground of "thoughtlessness"; it soon comes to light that she demonstrated her curiosity which caused her at an earlier time to intrude into the bedroom of her parents. Girls who are proud of their beautiful hair know so well how to manipulate combs and hairpins, that in the midst of conversation, their hair becomes loosened. During the

These as well as other similar experiences have caused me to think that the actions executed unintentionally must inevitably become the source of misunderstanding in human relations. The perpetrator of the act, who is unaware of any associated intention, takes no account of it, and does not hold himself responsible for it. On the other hand, the second party, having regularly utilized even such acts as those of his partner to draw conclusions as to their purpose and meaning, recognizes more of the stranger's psychic processes than the latter is ready either to admit or believe that he has imparted. He becomes indignant when these conclusions drawn from his symptomatic actions are held up to him; he declares them baseless because he does not see any conscious intention in their execution, and complains of being misunderstood by the other. Samuel Butler, whose psychological insight was truly remarkable, expressed the same views long before Professor Freud came on the scene.[1] Speaking of conscious and unconscious knowers, he states (*Life and Habit*, p. 27):

------

treatment (in a reclining position) some men scatter change from their pockets and thus pay for the hour of treatment; the amount scattered is in proportion to their estimation of the work. Whoever forgets articles in the doctor's office, such as eyeglasses, gloves, handbags, generally indicates that he cannot tear himself away and is anxious to return soon. Ernest Jones says: "One can almost measure the success with which a physician is practising psychotherapy, for instance, by the size of the collection of umbrellas, handkerchiefs, purses and so on, that he could make in a month. The slightest habits and acts performed with a minimum of attention, such as the winding of a clock before retiring to sleep, the putting out of lights before leaving the room and similar actions, are occasionally subject to disturbances which clearly demonstrate the influence of the unconscious complex, and what is thought to be the strongest habits."

In the journal, *Caenobium*, Maeder tells about a hospital physician who, on account of an important matter, desired to get to the city that evening, although he was on duty and had no right to leave the hospital. On his return, he noticed, to his surprise, that there was a light in his room. On leaving the room, he had forgotten to put it out, something that had never happened before. But he soon grasped the motive of this forgetting. The hospital superintendent who lived in the same house must have concluded from the light in the room that he was at home. A man overburdened with worries and subject to occasional depressions assured me that he regularly forgot to wind his watch on those evenings when life seemed too hard and unfriendly. In this omission to wind his watch, he symbolically expressed that it was a matter of indifference to him whether he lived to see the next day. Another man who was personally unknown to me wrote: "Having been struck by a terrible misfortune, life appeared so harsh and unsympathetic, that I imagined that I had not sufficient strength to live to see the next day. I then noticed that almost every day I forgot to wind my watch, something that I never omitted before. I had been in the habit of doing it regularly before retiring in an almost mechanical and unconscious manner. It was only very seldom that I thought of it, and that happened when I had something important for the next day which held my interest. Should this be considered a symptomatic action? I really cannot explain it." Whoever will take the trouble, like Jung (*The Psychology of Dementia Praecox*, translated by Brill), or Maeder ("*Une voie nouvelle en psychologie—Freud et son ècole*," *Caenobium*, Lugano, 1906), to pay attention to melodies which one hums to himself aimlessly and unconsciously, will regularly discover the relation of the melody's text to a theme which occupies the person at that time.

[1] Given by Editor.

"Another example may be taken from Bacon of the manner in which sayings which drop from men unconsciously, give the key of their inner thoughts to another person, though they themselves know not that they have such thoughts at all; much less that these thoughts are their only true convictions. In his Essay on Friendship the great philosopher writes: 'Reading good books on morality is a little flat and dead.' Innocent, not to say pathetic, as this passage may sound, it is pregnant with painful inferences concerning Bacon's moral character. For if he knew that he found reading good books on morality a little flat and dead, it follows he must have tried to read them; nor is he saved by the fact that he found them a little flat and dead; for though this does indeed show that he had begun to be so familiar with a few first principles as to find it more or less exhausting to have his attention directed to them further—yet his words prove that they were not so incorporate with him that he should feel the loathing for further discourse upon the matter which honest people commonly feel now. *It will be remembered that he took bribes when he came to be Lord Chancellor.*"

Close examination shows that such misunderstandings are based on the fact that the person is too fine an observer and understands too much. The more "nervous" two persons are, the more readily will they give each other cause for disputes, which are based on the fact that one as definitely denies about his own person what he is sure to accept about the other.

And this is, indeed, the punishment for the inner dishonesty to which people grant expression under the guise of "forgetting," of erroneous actions and accidental emotions, a feeling which they would do better to confess to themselves and others when they can no longer control it. As a matter of fact, it can be generally affirmed that everyone is continually practising psychoanalysis on his neighbors, and consequently, learns to know them better than each individual knows himself. The road following the admonition γνῶθι σεαυτὸν leads through the study of one's own apparently casual commissions and omissions.

X

ERRORS

ERRORS of memory are distinguished from forgetting and false recollections through one feature only, namely, that the error (false recollection) is not recognized as such but finds credence. However, the use of the expression "error" seems to depend on still another condition. We speak of "erring" instead of "falsely recollecting" where the character of the objective reality is emphasized in the psychic material to be reproduced—that is, where something other than a fact of my own psychic life is to be remembered, or rather something that may be confirmed or refuted through the memory of others. The reverse of the error in memory in this sense is formed by ignorance.

In my book *The Interpretation of Dreams*,[1] I was responsible for a series of errors in historical, and above all, in material facts, which I was astonished to discover after the appearance of the book. On closer examination, I found that they did not originate from my ignorance, but could be traced to errors of memory explainable by means of analysis.

(a) On page 431 [1] I indicated as *Schiller's* birthplace the city of *Marburg*, a name which recurs in *Styria*. The error is found in the analysis of a dream during a night journey from which I was awakened by the conductor calling out the name of the station *Marburg*. In the contents of the dream, inquiry is made concerning a book by *Schiller*. But *Schiller* was not born in the university town of *Marburg* but in the Swabian city of *Marbach*. I maintain that I always knew this.

(b) On page 260, *Hannibal's* father is called *Hasdrubal*. This error was particularly annoying to me, but it was most corroborative of my conception of such errors. Few readers of the book are better posted on the history of the *Barcides* than the author who wrote this error and overlooked it in three proofs. The name of Hannibal's father was *Hamilcar*

---

[1] Translated by A. A. Brill. The Macmillan Company, New York; Allen & Unwin, London; included in the present volume, pp. 180–549.
[2] This and succeeding page references to *The Interpretation of Dreams* are to this volume.

Barca; Hasdrubal was the name of *Hannibal's* brother as well as that of his brother-in-law and predecessor in command.

(c) On pages 303 and 547, I assert that *Zeus* emasculates his father *Kronos* and hurls him from the throne. This horror I have erroneously advanced by a generation; according to Greek mythology, it was *Kronos* who committed this on his father *Uranos*.[1]

How is it to be explained that my memory furnished me with false material on these points, while it usually places the most remote and unusual material at my disposal, as the readers of my books can verify? And, what is more, in three carefully executed proof-readings, I passed over these errors as if struck blind.

Goethe said of Lichtenberg: "Where he cracks a joke, there lies a concealed problem." Similarly we can affirm of these passages cited from my book: back of every error is a repression. More accurately stated: the error conceals a falsehood, a disfigurement which is ultimately based on repressed material. In the analysis of the dreams there reported, I was compelled by the very nature of the theme to which the dream thoughts related, on the one hand, to break off the analysis in some places before it had reached its completion, and on the other hand, to remove an indiscreet detail through a slight disfigurement of its outline. I could not act differently, and had no other choice if I was at all to offer examples and illustrations. My constrained position was necessarily brought about by the peculiarity of dreams, which give expression to repressed thoughts, or to material which is incapable of becoming conscious. In spite of this, it is said that enough material remained to offend the more sensitive souls. The disfigurement or concealment of the continuing thoughts known to me could not be accomplished without leaving some trace. What I wished to repress has often against my will obtruded itself on what I have taken up, and evinced itself in the matter as an unnoticeable error. Indeed, each of the three examples given is based on the same theme: the errors are the results of repressed thoughts which occupy themselves with my deceased father.

(*ad a*) Whoever reads through the dream analyzed on page 431 will find some parts unveiled; in some parts he will be able to divine through allusions that I have broken off the thoughts which would have contained an unfavorable criticism of my father. In the continuation of this line of thoughts and memories, there lies an annoying tale, in which books and a business friend of my father, named *Marburg*, play a part; it is the same name, the calling out of which in the southern railway station had aroused me from sleep. I wished to suppress this Mr. *Marburg* in the analysis from myself and my readers: he avenged himself by intruding where he

---

[1] This is not a perfect error. According to the orphic version of the myth, the emasculation was performed by Zeus on his father Kronos.

did not belong, and changed the name of Schiller's birthplace from *Marbach* to *Marburg*.

(*ad b*) The error *Hasdrubal* in place of *Hamilcar*, the name of the brother instead of that of the father, originated from an association which dealt with the Hannibal phantasies of my college years and my dissatisfaction with the conduct of my father towards the "enemies of our people." I could have continued and recounted how my attitude towards my father was changed by a visit to England, where I made the acquaintance of my half-brother, by a previous marriage of my father. My brother's eldest son was my age exactly. Thus the age relations were no hindrance to a phantasy which may be stated thus: how much pleasanter it would be had I been born the son of my brother instead of the son of my father! This suppressed phantasy then falsified the text of my book at the point where I broke off the analysis, by forcing me to put the name of the brother for that of the father.

(*ad c*) The influence of the memory of this same brother is responsible for my having advanced by a generation the mythological horror of the Greek deities. One of the admonitions of my brother has lingered long in my memory: "Do not forget one thing concerning your conduct in life," he said: "you belong not to the second but really to the third generation of your father." Our father had remarried at an advanced age, and was therefore an old man to his children by the second marriage. I commit the error mentioned where I discuss the piety between parents and children.

Several times, friends and patients have called my attention to the fact that in reporting their dreams or alluding to them in dream analyses, I have related inaccurately the circumstances experienced by us in common. These are also historic errors. On re-examining such individual cases, I have found that my recollection of the facts was unreliable only where I had purposely disfigured or concealed something in the analysis. Here again, we have *an unobserved error as a substitute for an intentional concealment or repression*.

From these errors, which originate from repression, we must sharply distinguish those which are based on actual ignorance. Thus, for example, it was ignorance when, on my excursion to Wachau, I believed that I had passed the resting-place of the revolutionary leader Fischof. Only the name is common to both places. *Fischof's Emmersdorf* is located in Kärnthen. But I did not know any better.

Here is another embarrassing but instructive error, an example of temporary ignorance, if you like. One day, a patient reminded me to give him the two books on Venice which I had promised him, as he wished to use them in planning his Easter tour. I answered that I had them ready and went into the library to fetch them, though the truth of the matter was that I had forgotten to look them up, since I did not quite approve of my patient's journey, looking upon it as an unnecessary interruption to the treatment, and as a material loss to the physician. Thereupon, I made a quick survey of the library for the books.

One was *Venedig als Kunststätte,* and besides this, I imagined I had an historic work of a similar order. Certainly there was *Die Mediceer (The Medici)*; I took them and brought them in to him; then, embarrassed, I confessed my error. Of course, I really knew that the Medici had nothing to do with Venice, but for a short time, it did not appear to me at all incorrect. Now I was compelled to practise justice; as I had so frequently interpreted my patient's symptomatic actions, I could save my prestige only by being honest and admitting to him the secret motives of my averseness to his trip.

It may cause general astonishment to learn how much stronger is the impulse to tell the truth than is usually supposed. Perhaps it is a result of my occupation with psychoanalysis that I can scarcely lie any more. As often as I attempt a distortion, I succumb to an error or some other faulty act, which betrays my dishonesty, as was manifest in this and in the preceding examples.

Of all faulty actions, the mechanism of the error seems to be the most superficial. That is, the occurrence of the error invariably indicates that the mental activity concerned had to struggle with some disturbing influence, although the nature of the error need not be determined by the quality of the disturbing idea, which may have remained obscure. It is not out of place to add that the same state of affairs may be assumed in many simple cases of lapses in speaking and writing. Every time we commit a lapse in speaking or writing, we may conclude that through mental processes, there has come a disturbance which is beyond our intention. It may be conceded, however, that lapses in speaking and writing often follow the laws of similarity and convenience, or the tendency to acceleration, without allowing the disturbing element to leave a trace of its own character in the error resulting from the lapses in speaking or writing. It is the responsiveness of the linguistic material which at first makes possible the determination of the error, but it also limits the same.

In order not to confine myself exclusively to personal errors, I will relate a few examples which could just as well have been ranged under "Lapses in Speech" or under "Erroneously Carried-out Actions," but as all these forms of faulty action have the same value, they may as well be reported here.

(a) I forbade a patient to speak on the telephone to his lady-love, with whom he himself was willing to break off all relations, as each conversation only renewed the struggling against it. He was to write her his final decision, although there were some difficulties in the way of delivering the letter to her. He visited me at one o'clock to tell me that he had found a way of avoiding these difficulties, and among other things, he asked me whether he might refer to me in my professional capacity.

At two o'clock, while he was engaged in composing the letter of refusal, he interrupted himself suddenly and said to his mother, "Well, I have forgotten to ask the Professor whether I may use his name in the letter." He hurried to the telephone, got the connection and asked the question, "May I speak to the Professor after his dinner?" In answer, he got an astonished "Adolf, have you gone crazy!" The answering voice was the very voice which, at my command, he had listened to for the last time. He had simply "made a mistake," and in place of the physician's number had called up that of his beloved.

(b) During a summer vacation, a school teacher, a poor but excellent young man, courted the daughter of a summer resident, until the girl fell passionately in love with him, and even prevailed upon her family to countenance the matrimonial alliance, in spite of the difference in position and race. One day, however, the teacher wrote his brother a letter in which he said: "Pretty, the lass is not at all, but she is very amiable, and so far so good. But whether I can make up my mind to marry a Jewess I cannot yet tell." This letter got into the hands of the fiancée, who put an end to the engagement, while at the same time, his brother was wondering at the protestations of love directed to him. My informer assured me that this was really an error and not a cunning trick.

I am familiar with another case in which a woman who was dissatisfied with her old physician, and still did not openly wish to discharge him, accomplished this purpose through the interchange of letters. Here, at least, I can assert confidently that it was error and not conscious cunning that made use of this familiar comedy-motive.

(c) Brill [1] tells of a woman who, inquiring about a mutual friend, erroneously called her by her maiden name. Her attention having been directed to this error, she had to admit that she disliked her friend's husband and had never been satisfied with her marriage.

A similar trick was played by me quite recently. I had promised my oldest brother to pay him a long-due visit at a seashore in England; as the time was short, I felt obliged to travel by the shortest route and without interruption. I begged for a day's sojourn in Holland, but he thought that I could stop there on my return trip. Accordingly, I journeyed from Munich through Cologne to Rotterdam—Hook of Holland—where I was to take the steamer at midnight to Harwich. In Cologne, I had to change cars; I left my train to go into the Rotterdam express, but it was not to be found. I asked various railway employees, was sent from one platform to another, got into an exaggerated state of despair, and could easily

[1] *Loc. cit.*, p. 191.

reckon that during this fruitless search, I had probably missed my connection.

After this was corroborated, I pondered whether or not I should spend the night in Cologne. This was favored by a feeling of piety, for according to an old family tradition, my ancestors were once expelled from this city during a persecution of the Jews. But eventually I came to another decision; I took a later train to Rotterdam, where I arrived late at night and was thus compelled to spend a day in Holland. This brought me the fulfillment of a long-fostered wish—the sight of the beautiful Rembrandt paintings at The Hague and in the Royal Museum at Amsterdam. Not before the next forenoon, while collecting my impressions during the railway journey in England, did I definitely remember that only a few steps from the place where I got off at the railroad station in Cologne, indeed, on the same platform, I had seen a large sign, "Rotterdam—Hook of Holland." There stood the train in which I should have continued my journey.

If one does not wish to assume that, contrary to my brother's orders, I had really resolved to admire the Rembrandt pictures on my way to him, then the fact that despite clear directions, I hurried away and looked for another train must be designated as an incomprehensible "blinding." Everything else—my well-acted perplexity, the emergence of the pious intention to spend the night in Cologne—was only a contrivance to hide my resolution until it had been fully accomplished.

One may possibly be disinclined to consider the class of errors which I have here explained as very numerous or particularly significant. But I leave it to your consideration whether there is no ground for extending the same points of view also to the more important errors of judgment, as evinced by people in life and science. Only for the most select and most balanced minds does it seem possible to guard the perceived picture of external reality against the distortion to which it is otherwise subjected in its transit through the psychic individuality of the one perceiving it.

XI

COMBINED FAULTY ACTS

Two of the last-mentioned examples, my error which transfers the Medici to Venice and that of the young man who knew how to circumvent a command against a conversation on the telephone with his lady-love, have really not been fully discussed, as after careful consideration they may be shown to represent a union of forgetting with an error. I can show the same union still more clearly in certain other examples.

(a) A friend related to me the following experience: "Some years ago, I consented to be elected to the committee of a certain literary society, as I supposed the organization might some time be of use to me in assisting me in the production of my drama. Although not much interested, I attended the meetings regularly every Friday. Some months ago, I was definitely assured that one of my dramas would be presented at the theater in F., and since that time, it regularly happened that I forgot the meeting of the association. As I read their program announcements I was ashamed of my forgetfulness. I reproached myself, feeling that it was certainly rude of me to stay away now when I no longer needed them, and determined that I would certainly not forget the next Friday. Continually I reminded myself of this resolution until the hour came and I stood before the door of the meeting-room. To my astonishment, it was locked; the meeting was already over. I had mistaken my day; it was already Saturday!

(b) The next example is the combination of a symptomatic action with a case of mislaying; it reached me by remote by-ways, but from a reliable source.

A woman travelled to Rome with her brother-in-law, a renowned artist. The visitor was highly honored by the German residents of Rome, and among other things, received a gold medal of antique origin. The woman was grieved that her brother-in-law did not sufficiently appreciate the value of this beautiful gift. After she had returned home, she discovered in unpacking that—without knowing how—she had brought the medal home with her. She immediately notified her brother-in-law of this by letter, and informed him that she would send it back to Rome the next day. The next day, however, the medal was so aptly mislaid that it could not be found and could not be sent back, and then it dawned on the woman what her "absent-mindedness" signified—namely, that she wished to keep the medal herself.

(c) Here are some cases in which the falsified action persistently repeats itself, and at the same time, also changes its mode of action:

Due to unknown motives, Jones [1] left a letter for several days on his desk, forgetting each time to post it. He ultimately posted it, but it was returned to him from the Dead-letter Office because he forgot to address it. After addressing and posting it a second time, it was again returned to him, this time without a stamp. He was then forced to recognize the unconscious opposition to the sending of the letter.

(d) A short account by Dr. Karl Weiss (Vienna) [1] of a case of forgetting impressively describes the futile effort to accomplish something in the face of opposition. "How persistently the unconscious activity can achieve its purpose if it has cause to prevent a resolution from being executed, and how difficult it is to guard against this tendency, will be illustrated by the following incident: An acquaintance requested me to lend him a book and bring it to him the next day. I immediately promised it, but perceived a distinct feeling of displeasure which I could not explain at the time. Later, it became clear to me: this acquaintance had owed me for years a sum of money which he evidently had no intention of returning. I did not give this matter any more thought, but I recalled it the following forenoon with the same feeling of displeasure, and at once said to myself: 'Your unconscious will see to it that you forget the book, but you don't wish to appear unobliging and will therefore do everything not to forget it.' I came home, wrapped the book in paper and put it near me on the desk while I wrote some letters.

"A little later I went away, but after a few steps, I recollected that I had left on the desk the letters which I wished to post. (By the way, one of the letters was written to a person who urged me to undertake something disagreeable.) I returned, took the letters and again left. While in the street-car, it occurred to me that I had undertaken to purchase something for my wife, and I was pleased at the thought that it would be only a small package. The association, 'small package,' suddenly recalled 'book' —and only then I noticed that I did not have the book with me. Not only had I forgotten it when I left my home the first time, but I had overlooked it again when I got the letters near which it lay."

I do not mean to assert that such cases of combined faulty actions can teach anything new that we have not already seen in the individual cases. But this change in form of the faulty action, which nevertheless attains

[1] *Loc. cit.*, p. 42.
[2] *Zentralb. f. Psychoanalyse*, ii. 9.

the same result, gives the plastic impression of a will working towards a definite end, and in a far more energetic way, contradicts the idea that the faulty action represents something fortuitous and requires no explanation. Not less remarkable is the fact that the conscious intention thoroughly fails to check the success of the faulty action. Despite all, my friend did not pay his visit to the meeting of the literary society, and the woman found it impossible to give up the medal. That unconscious something which worked against these resolutions found another outlet after the first road was closed to it. It requires something other than the conscious counter-resolution to overcome the unknown motive; it requires a psychic work which makes the unknown known to consciousness.

XII

DETERMINISM—CHANCE—AND
SUPERSTITIOUS BELIEFS

POINTS OF VIEW

As THE general result of the preceding separate discussions, we must put down the following principle: *Certain inadequacies of our psychic functions—whose common character will soon be more definitely determined—and certain performances which are apparently unintentional prove to be well motivated when subjected to psychoanalytic investigation, and are determined through the consciousness of unknown motives.*

In order to belong to the class of phenomena which can thus be explained, a faulty psychic action must satisfy the following conditions:

(a) It must not exceed a certain measure, which is firmly established through our estimation, and is designated by the expression "within normal limits."

(b) It must evince the character of the momentary and temporary disturbance. The same action must have been previously performed more correctly or we must always rely on ourselves to perform it more correctly; if we are corrected by others, we must immediately recognize the truth of the correction and the incorrectness of our psychic action.

(c) If we at all perceive a faulty action, we must not perceive in ourselves any motivation of the same, but must attempt to explain it through "inattention" or attribute it to an "accident."

Thus, there remain in this group the cases of forgetting, the errors, the lapses in speaking, reading, writing, the erroneously carried-out actions and the so-called chance actions. The explanations of these very definite psychic processes are connected with a series of observations which may in part arouse further interest.

I. By assuming that a part of our psychic function is unexplainable through purposive ideas, we ignore the realms of determinism in our mental life. Here, as in still other spheres, determinism reaches farther than we suppose. In the year 1900, I read an essay published in the *Zeit* written by the literary historian R. M. Meyer, in which he maintains and illustrates by examples, that it is impossible to compose nonsense intentionally and arbitrarily. For some time, I have been aware that it is impossible to think of a number, or even of a name, of one's own free will. If one investigates this seeming voluntary formation, let us say, of a number of many digits uttered in unrestrained mirth, it always proves to be so strictly determined that the determination seems impossible. I will now briefly discuss an example of an "arbitrarily chosen" first name, and then exhaustively analyze an analogous example of a "thoughtlessly uttered" number.

While preparing the history of one of my patients for publication, I considered what first name I should give her in the article. There seemed to be a wide choice; of course, certain names were at once excluded by me, in the first place the real name, then the names of members of my family to which I would have objected, also some female names having an especially peculiar pronunciation. But, excluding these, there should have been no need of being puzzled about such a name. It would be thought, and I myself supposed, that a whole multitude of feminine names would be placed at my disposal. Instead of this, only one sprang up, no other besides it; it was the name Dora.

I inquired as to its determination: "Who else is called Dora?" I wished to reject the next idea as incredulous; it occurred to me that the nurse of my sister's children was named Dora. But I possess so much self-control, or practice, in analysis, if you like, that I held firmly to the idea and proceeded. Then a slight incident of the previous evening soon flashed through my mind which brought the looked-for determinant. On my sister's dining room table, I noticed a letter bearing the address, "Miss Rosa W." Astonished, I asked whose name this was, and was informed that the right name of the supposed Dora was really Rosa, and that on accepting the position, she had to lay aside her name because Rosa would also refer to my sister. I said pityingly; "Poor people! They cannot even retain their own names!" I now recall that on hearing this, I became quiet for a moment and began to think of all sorts of serious matters which merged into obscurity, but which I could now easily bring into my consciousness. Thus, when I sought a name for a person *who could not retain her own name,* no other except "Dora" occurred to me. The exclusiveness here is based, moreover, on firmer internal associations, for in the history of my patient, it was a stranger in the house, the governess, who exerted a decisive influence on the course of the treatment.

This slight incident found its unexpected continuation many years later. While discussing in a lecture the long since published history of the girl called Dora, it occurred to me that one of my two women pupils had the very name Dora, which I was obliged to utter so often in the different associations of the case. I turned to the young student whom I knew personally with the apology that I had really not thought that she bore the same name, and that I was ready to substitute it in my lecture by another name.

I was now confronted with the task of rapidly choosing another name, and reflected that I must not now choose the first name of the other woman student, and so set a poor example to the class, who were already quite conversant with psychoanalysis. I was therefore well pleased when the name "Erna" occurred to me as the substitute for Dora, and Erna I used in the discourse. After the lecture, I asked myself whence the name "Erna" could possibly have originated and had to laugh as I observed that the feared possibility in the choice of the substitutive name had come to pass, in part at least. The other lady's family name was Lucerna, of which Erna was a part.

In a letter to a friend, I informed him that I had finished reading the proof sheets of *The Interpretation of Dreams,* and that I did not intend to make any further changes in it, "even if it contained 2,467 mistakes." I immediately attempted to explain to myself the number and added this little analysis as a postscript to the letter. It will be best to quote it now as I wrote it when I caught myself in this transaction:

"I will add hastily another contribution to the *Psychopathology of Everyday Life.* You will find in the letter the number 2,467 as a jocose and arbitrary estimation of the number of errors that may be found in the dream-book. I meant to write: no matter how large the number might be, and this one presented itself. But there is nothing arbitrary or undetermined in the psychic life. You will therefore rightly suppose that the unconscious hastened to determine the number which was liberated by consciousness. Just previous to this, I had read in the paper that General E. M. had been retired as Inspector-General of Ordnance. You must know that I am interested in this man. While I was serving as military medical student, he, then a colonel, once came into the hospital and said to the physician: 'You must make me well in eight days, as I have some work to do for which the Emperor is waiting.'

"At that time, I decided to follow this man's career, and just think, today (1899) he is at the end of it—Inspector-General of Ordnance and already retired. I wished to figure out in what time he had covered this road, and assumed that I had seen him in the hospital in 1882. That would make 17 years. I related this to my wife, and she remarked, 'Then you, too, should be retired.' And I protested, 'The Lord forbid!' After this conversation, I seated myself at the table to write to you. The previous train of thought continued, and for good reason. The figuring was incorrect; I had a definite recollection of the circumstances in my mind. I had celebrated my coming of age, my *24th* birthday, in the military prison (for being absent without permission). Therefore, I must have seen him in 1880, which makes it 19 years ago. You then have the number 24 in 2,467! Now take the number that represents my age, 43, and add 24 years to it and you get 67! That is, to the question whether I wished to retire, I had expressed the wish to work 24 years more. Obviously, I am annoyed that in the interval during which I followed Colonel M., I have not accomplished much myself, and still there is a sort of triumph in the fact that he is already finished, while I still have all before me. Thus we may justly say that not even the unintentionally thrown-out number 2,467 lacks its determination from the unconscious."

Since this first example of the interpretation of an apparently arbitrary choice of a number, I have repeated a similar test with the same result; but most cases are of such intimate content that they do not lend themselves to report.

It is for this reason that I shall not hesitate to add here a very interesting analysis of a "chance number" which Dr. Alfred Adler (Vienna) received from a "perfectly healthy" man.[1] Adler wrote to me: "Last night, I devoted myself to the *Psychopathology of Everyday Life,* and I would have read it all through, had I not been hindered by a remarkable coincidence. When I read that every number that we apparently conjure up quite arbitrarily in our consciousness has a definite meaning, I decided to test it. The number 1,734 occurred to my mind. The following associations then came up: $1,734 \div 17 = 102$; $102 \div 17 = 6$. I then separated the number into 17 and 34. I am 34 years old. I believe that I once told you that I consider 34 the last year of youth, and for this reason, I felt miserable on my last birthday. The end of my 17th year was the beginning of a very nice and interesting period of my development. I divide my life into periods of 17 years. What do the divisions signify? The number 102 recalls the fact that volume 102 of the Reclam Universal Library is Kotzebue's play *Menschenhass und Reue* (Human Hatred and Repentance).

"My present psychic state is 'human hatred and repentance.' Number 6 of the U. L. (I know a great many numbers by heart) is Mullner's *Schuld* (Fault). I am constantly annoyed at the thought that it is through my own fault that I have not become what I could have been with my abilities.

"I then asked myself, 'What is Number 17 of the U. L.?' But I could not recall it. But as I positively knew it before, I assumed that I wished to forget this number. All reflection was in vain. I wished to continue with my reading, but I read only mechanically without understanding a word, for I was annoyed by the number 17. I extinguished the light and continued my search. It finally came to me that number 17 must be a play

[1] Alfred Adler, "Drei Psychoanalysen von Zahlen einfällen und obsedierenden Zahlen," *Psych. Neur Wochenschr.,* No. 28, 1905.

by Shakespeare. But which one? I thought of Hero and Leander. Apparently, a stupid attempt of my will to distract me. I finally arose and consulted the catalogue of the U. L. Number 17 was *Macbeth*! To my surprise, I had to discover that I knew nothing of the play, despite the fact that it did not interest me any less than any other Shakespearean drama. I only thought of: murder, Lady Macbeth, witches, 'nice is ugly,' and that I found Schiller's version of *Macbeth* very nice. Undoubtedly, I also wished to forget the play. Then it occurred to me that 17 and 34 may be divided by 17 and result in 1 and 2. Numbers 1 and 2 of the U. L. is Goethe's *Faust*. Formerly, I found much of Faust in me."

We must regret that the discretion of the physician did not allow us to see the significance of ideas. Adler remarked that the man did not succeed in the synthesis of his analysis. His associations would hardly be worth reporting unless their continuation would bring out something that would give us the key to the understanding of the number 1,734 and the whole series of ideas.

To quote further: "To be sure, this morning I had an experience which speaks much for the correctness of the Freudian conception. My wife, whom I awakened through my getting up at night, asked me what I wanted with the catalogue of the U. L. I told her the story. She found it all pettifogging but—very interesting. *Macbeth*, which caused me so much trouble, she simply passed over. She said that nothing came to her mind when she thought of a number. I answered, 'Let us try it. She named the number 117. To this I immediately replied: '17 refers to what I just told you; furthermore, I told you yesterday that if a wife is in the 82nd year and the husband is in the 35th year, it must be a gross misunderstanding.' For the last few days, I have been teasing my wife by maintaining that she was a little old mother of 82 years. $82+35=117$."

The man who did not know how to determine his own number at once found the solution when his wife named a number which was apparently arbitrarily chosen. As a matter of fact, the woman understood very well from which complex the number of her husband originated, and chose her own number from the same complex, which was surely common to both, as it dealt in his case with their relative ages. Now, we can find it easy to interpret the number that occurred to the man. As Dr. Adler indicates, it expressed a repressed wish of the husband which, fully developed, would read: "For a man of 34 years as I am, only a woman of 17 would be suitable."

Lest one should think too lightly of such "playing," I will add that I was recently informed by Dr. Adler that a year after the publication of this analysis, the man was divorced from his wife.[1]

---

[1] As an explanation of *Macbeth*, number 17 of the U. L., I was informed by Dr. Adler that in his seventeenth year, this man had joined an anarchistic society whose aim was

Adler gives a similar explanation for the origin of obsessive numbers. Also the choice of so-called "favorite numbers" is not without relation to the life of the person concerned, and does not lack a certain psychologic interest. A gentleman who evinced a particular partiality for the numbers 17 and 19 could specify, after brief reflection, that at the age of 17, he attained the greatly longed-for academic freedom by having been admitted to the university, that at 19, he made his first long journey, and shortly thereafter, made his first scientific discovery. But the fixation of this preference followed later, after two questionable affairs, when the same numbers were invested with importance in his "love-life."

Indeed, even those numbers which we use in a particular connection extremely often and with apparent arbitrariness can be traced by analysis to an unexpected meaning. Thus, one day, it struck one of my patients that he was particularly fond of saying, "I have already told you this from 17 to 36 times." And he asked himself whether there was any motive for it. It soon occurred to him that he was born on the 27th day of the month, and that his younger brother was born on the 26th day of another month, and he had grounds for complaint that Fate had robbed him of so many of the benefits of life only to bestow them on his younger brother. Thus he represented this partiality of Fate by deducting 10 from the date of his birth and adding it to the date of his brother's birthday. "I am the elder and yet am so 'cut short.' "

I shall tarry a little longer at the analysis of chance numbers, for I know of no other individual observation which would so readily demonstrate the existence of highly organized thinking processes, of which consciousness has no knowledge. Moreover, there is no better example of analysis in which the suggestion of the position, a frequent accusation, is so distinctly out of consideration. I shall therefore report the analysis of a chance number of one of my patients (with his consent), to which I will only add that he is the youngest of many children and that he lost his beloved father in his young years.

While in a particularly happy mood, he let the number 426,718 come to his mind, and put to himself the question, "Well, what does it bring to your mind?" First came a joke he had heard: "If your catarrh of the nose is treated by a doctor, it lasts 42 days, if it is not treated, it lasts— 6 weeks." This corresponds to the first digit of the number ($42 = 6 \times 7$). During the blocking that followed this first solution, I called his attention to the fact that the number of six digits selected by him contains all the first numbers except 3 and 5. He at once found the continuation of the solution:

---

regicide. Probably this is why he forgot the content of the play *Macbeth*. The same person invented at that time a secret code in which numbers were substituted by letters.

"We were altogether 7 children, I was the youngest. Number 3 in the order of the children corresponds to my sister A., and 5 to my brother L.; both of them were my enemies. As a child, I used to pray to the Lord every night that He should take out of my life these two tormenting spirits. It seems to me that I have fulfilled for myself this wish: '3' and '5', the *evil* brother and the hated sister, are omitted."

"If the number stands for your sisters and brothers, what significance is there to 18 at the end? You were altogether only 7."

"I often thought if my father had lived longer, I should not have been the youngest child. If one more would have come, we should have been 8, and there would have been a younger child, toward whom I could have played the role of the older one."

With this, the number was explained, but we still wished to find the connection between the first part of the interpretation and the part following it. This came very readily from the condition required for the last digits —if the father had lived longer. $42 = 6 \times 7$ signifies the ridicule directed against the doctors who could not help the father, and in this way, expresses the wish for the continued existence of the father. The whole number really corresponds to the fulfillment of his two wishes in reference to his family circle—namely, that both the evil brother and sister should die and that another little child should follow him. Or, briefly expressed: *If only these two had died in place of my father!* [1]

Another analysis of numbers I take from Jones.[2] A gentleman of his acquaintance let the number 986 come to his mind, and defied him to connect it to anything of special interest in his mind. "Six years ago, on the hottest day he could remember, he had seen a joke in an evening newspaper, which stated that the thermometer had stood at 98.6° F., evidently an exaggeration of 98.6° F. We were at the time seated in front of a very hot fire, from which he had just drawn back, and he remarked, probably quite correctly, that the heat had aroused his dormant memory. However, I was curious to know why this memory had persisted with such vividness as to be so readily brought out, for with some people, it surely would have been forgotten beyond recall, unless it had become associated with some other mental experience of more significance.

He told me that on reading the joke, he had laughed uproariously, and that on many subsequent occasions, he had recalled it with great relish. As the joke was obviously of an exceedingly tenuous nature, this strengthened my expectation that more lay behind. His next thought was the general reflection that the conception of heat had always greatly impressed

---

[1] For the sake of simplicity, I have omitted some of the not less suitable thoughts of the patient.

[2] *Loc. cit.*, p. 36.

him, that heat was the most important thing in the universe, the source of all life, and so on. This remarkable attitude of a quite prosaic young man certainly needed some explanation, so I asked him to continue his free associations. The next thought was of a factory stack which he could see from his bedroom window. He often stood of an evening watching the flame and smoke issuing out of it, and reflecting on this deplorable waste of energy. Heat, flame, the source of life, the waste of vital energy issuing from an upright, hollow tube—it was not hard to divine from such associations that the ideas of heat and fire were unconsciously linked in his mind with the idea of love, as is so frequent in symbolic thinking, and that there was a strong masturbation complex present, a conclusion that he presently confirmed."

Those who wish to get a good impression of the way the material of numbers becomes elaborated in the unconscious thinking, I refer to two· papers by Jung [1] and Jones.[2]

In personal analysis of this kind, two things were especially striking. First, the absolute somnambulistic certainty with which I attacked the unknown objective point, merging into a mathematical train of thought, which later suddenly extended to the looked-for number, and the rapidity with which the entire subsequent work was performed. Secondly, the fact that the numbers were always at the disposal of my unconscious mind, when as a matter of fact, I am a poor mathematician and find it very difficult to consciously recall years, house numbers and the like. Moreover, in these unconscious mental operations with figures, I found a tendency to superstition, the origin of which had long remained unknown to me.

It will not surprise us to find that not only numbers, but also mental occurrences of different kinds of words regularly prove on analytic investigation to be well determined.

Brill relates: "While working on the English edition of this book, I was obsessed one morning with the strange word '*Cardillac.*' Busily intent on my work, I refused at first to pay attention to it, but, as is usually the case, I simply could not do anything else. '*Cardillac*' was constantly in my mind. Realizing that my refusal to recognize it was only a resistance, I decided to analyze it. The following associations occurred to me: *Cardillac, cardiac, carrefour, Cadillac.*

"*Cardiac*" recalled cardalgia—heartache—a medical friend who had recently told me confidentially that he feared that he had some attacks of pain in the region of his heart. Knowing him so well, I at once rejected his theory, and told him that his attacks were of a neurotic character, and that his other apparent physical ailments were also only the expression of his neurosis.

[1] "Ein Beitrag zur Kenntnis des Zahlentraumes," *Zentralb. f. Psychoanalyse,* i. 12.
[2] "Unconscious Manipulation of Numbers" (*ibid.,* ii. 5, 1912).

"I might add that just before telling me of his heart trouble, he spoke of a business matter of vital interest to him which had suddenly come to naught. Being a man of unbounded ambitions, he was very depressed because of late he had suffered many reverses. His neurotic conflicts, however, had become manifest a few months before this misfortune, soon after his father's death had left a big business on his hands. As the business could be continued only under his management, he was unable to decide whether to enter into commercial life or continue his chosen career. His great ambition was to become a successful physician, and although he had practised medicine successfully for many years, he was not altogether satisfied with the financial fluctuations of his professional income. On the other hand, his father's business promised him an assured, though limited, return. In brief, he was 'at a crossing and did not know which way to turn.'

"I then recalled the word *carrefour*, which is the French for 'crossing,' and it occurred to me that while working in a hospital in Paris, I lived near the 'Carrefour St. Lazare.' And now I could understand what relation all these associations had for me.

"When I resolved to leave the state hospital, I made the decision, first, because I desired to get married, and secondly, because I wished to enter private practice. This brought up a new problem. Although my State hospital service was an absolute success, judging by promotions and so on, I felt like a great many others in the same situation, namely, that my training was ill suited for private practice. To specialize in mental work was a daring undertaking for one without money and social connections. I also felt that the best I could do for patients, should they ever come my way, would be to commit them to one of the hospitals, as I had little confidence in the home treatment then in vogue. In spite of the substantial advances in mental work, the specialist was almost helpless when confronted with the average case of insanity. This was partially due to the fact that such cases were brought to him only after they had fully developed the psychosis when hospital treatment was imperative. Of the great army of milder mental disturbances, the so-called border-line cases, which make up the bulk of clinic and private practice, I knew very little. Such patients were only rarely seen in the state hospital, and what I knew concerning the treatment of neurasthenia, hysteria and psychasthenia hardly held out more hope for a successful private practice.

"It was in this state of mind that I came to Paris, where I hoped to learn enough about the psychoneuroses to enable me to continue my specialty in private practice, with a feeling that I could do something for my patients. What I saw in the Paris hospitals, however, did not help to change my state of mind. I was, therefore, seriously thinking of giving up my mental work for some other specialty. As can be seen, I was confronted with a situation similar to the one of my medical friend. I, too, was at a 'crossing' and did not know which way to turn. However, my suspense was soon ended. One day, I received a letter from my friend, Professor Peterson, who originally introduced me to the State hospital service, in which he urged me not to give up psychiatry and suggested that I visit the psychiatric clinic of Zurich.

"But what does *Cadillac* mean? Cadillac is the name of a hotel and of an automobile. A few days before, in a country place, my medical friend and I had been trying to hire an automobile, but there was none to be had. We both expressed the wish to own an automobile—again an unrealized ambition. I also recalled that the 'Carrefour St. Lazare' always impressed me as being one of the busiest thoroughfares in Paris. It was always congested with automobiles. Cadillac also recalled that only a few days ago, on the way to my clinic, I noticed a large sign over a building which announced that on a certain day, 'this building was to be occupied by the Cadillac,' etc. This at first made me think of the Cadillac Hotel, but on second sight, I noticed that it referred to the Cadillac motor-car. There was a sudden obstruction here for a few moments. The word Cadillac reappeared and by sound association the word *catalogue* occurred to me. This word brought back a very mortifying occurrence of recent origin, the motive of which was again blighted ambition.

"When one wishes to report any auto-analysis, he must be prepared to lay bare many intimate affairs of his own life. Anyone reading carefully Professor Freud's works cannot fail to become fully acquainted with him and his family life. I have often been asked by persons who claimed to have read and studied Freud's works such questions as: 'How old is Freud?' 'Is Freud married?' 'How many children has he?' etc. Such questions can only be asked by those who have not read Freud's works, or by very careless and superficial readers. All these questions and many more intimate ones are answered in Freud's works. Auto-analyses are autobiographies *par excellence;* but whereas the autobiographer may for definite reasons consciously and unconsciously hide many facts of his life, the auto-analyst not only tells the truth consciously, but perforce brings to light his whole intimate personality. It is for these reasons that one finds it very unpleasant to report his own auto-analyses. However, as we often report our patient's unconscious productions, it is but fair that we should now and then sacrifice ourselves on the altar of publicity. This is my apology for having thrust some of my personal affairs on the reader, and for being obliged to continue a little longer in the same strain.

"Before digressing with the last remarks, I mentioned that the word *Cadillac* brought the word association *catalogue*. This association brought back another important epoch in my life with which Professor Peterson was connected. When I was informed by the secretary of the faculty that

I was appointed chief of clinic of the department of psychiatry, I was exceedingly pleased to be so honored. It was the realization of an ambition which I dared entertain only in special euphoric states and, a compensation for the many unmerited criticisms from those who were blindly and unreasonably opposing my work as an expositor of Freud. Thereafter, I called on the stenographer of the faculty and spoke to her about a correction to be made in my name as it was printed in the catalogue. For some unknown reason (perhaps racial prejudice) this stenographer, a maiden lady, must have taken a dislike to me. For about three years I repeatedly requested her to have this correction made, but she paid no attention to me; she always promised to attend to it, but the mistake remained uncorrected.

"This time, I again reminded her of this correction, and also called her attention to the fact that as I had been appointed chief of clinic, I was especially anxious to have my name correctly printed in the catalogue. She apologized for her remissness and assured me that everything would be corrected as I requested, but on receiving the new catalogue, I found that while the correction had been made in my name, I was not listed as chief of clinic. When I spoke to her about it, she seemed puzzled; she said that she had no idea that I had been appointed chief of clinic. She had to consult the minutes of the faculty, written by herself, before she was convinced of it.[1] She was naturally very apologetic and said that she would at once write to the superintendent of the clinic to inform him of my appointment. I gained nothing by her regrets and apologies; the catalogue was already published and I was not listed as chief of clinic.

"Thus, the obsessive neologism *cardillac,* a condensation of *cardiac, Cadillac* and *catalogue,* contained some of the most important events of my medical career. When I was almost at the end of this analysis, I suddenly recalled a dream containing this neologism, cardillac, in which my wish was realized. My name appeared in its rightful place in the catalogue. The person who showed it to me in the dream was Professor Peterson. It was when I was at the first 'crossing' after I had graduated from the medical college that Professor Peterson advised me to enter the State hospital service. About five years later, when I was at the second crossing —the state of indecision described above—it was again Professor Peterson who directed me to the clinic of psychiatry at Zurich, where through Bleuler and Jung, I became acquainted with Professor Freud and his works, and it was also through the kind recommendation of Dr. Peterson that I was elevated to position of chief of clinic."

I am indebted to Dr. Hitschman for the solution of another case in

---

[1] This is another excellent example showing how a conscious intention was powerless to counteract an unconscious resistance.

which a line of poetry repeatedly obtruded itself on the mind in a certain place without showing any trace of its origin and relation.

Related by the jurist E.: "Six years ago, I travelled from Biarritz to San Sebastian. The railroad crosses over the Bidassao—a river which here forms the boundary between France and Spain. On the bridge one has a splendid view, on the one side of the broad valley and the Pyrenees and on the other of the sea. It was a beautiful, bright summer day; everything was filled with sun and light. I was on a vacation and pleased with my trip to Spain. Suddenly, the following words came to me: *'But the soul is already free, floating on a sea of light.'*

"At that time, I was trying to remember whence these lines came, but I could not remember; judging by the rhythm, the words must be a part of some poem, which, however, entirely escaped my memory. Later, when the verse repeatedly came to my mind, I asked many people about it without receiving any information.

"Last year, I crossed the same bridge on my return journey from Spain. It was a very dark night and it rained. I looked through the window to ascertain whether we had already reached the frontier station and noticed that we were on the Bidassao bridge. Immediately the above-cited verse returned to my memory and again I could not recall its origin.

"At home, many months later, I found Uhland's poems. I opened the volume and my glance fell upon the verse: *'But the soul is already free, floating on a sea of light,'* which were the concluding lines of the poem entitled 'The Pilgrim.' I read the poem and dimly recalled that I had known it many years ago. The scene of action is in Spain, and this seemed to me to be the only relation between the quoted verse and the place on the railroad journey described by me. I was only half satisfied with my discovery and mechanically continued to turn the pages of the book. On turning the next page, I found a poem, the title of which was *'Bidassao Bridge.'*

"I may add that the contents of this poem seemed even stranger to me than that of the first, and that its first verse read:

" 'On the Bidassao bridge stands a saint grey with age, he blesses to the right the Spanish mountain, to the left he blesses the French land.' "

II. This understanding of the determination of apparently arbitrarily selected names, numbers, and words may perhaps contribute to the solution of another problem. As is known, many persons argue against the assumption of an absolute psychic determinism by referring to an intense feeling of conviction that there is a free will. This feeling of conviction exists, but is not incompatible with the belief in determinism. Like all normal feelings, it must be justified by something. But, so far as I can observe, it does not manifest itself in weighty and important decisions; on these occasions, one has much more the feeling of a psychic compulsion and gladly falls back upon it. (Compare Luther's "Here I stand, I cannot do anything else.")

On the other hand, it is in trivial and indifferent decisions that one feels sure that he could just as easily have acted differently, that he acted of his own free will, and without any motives. From our analyses we therefore need not contest the right of the feeling of conviction that there is a free will. If we distinguish conscious from unconscious motivation, we are then informed by the feeling of conviction that the conscious motivation does not extend over all our motor resolutions. *Minima non curat praetor.* What is thus left free from the one side receives its motive from the other side, from the unconscious, and the determinism in the psychic realm is thus carried out uninterruptedly.[1]

III. Although conscious thought must be altogether ignorant of the motivation of the faulty actions described above, yet it would be desirable to discover a psychologic proof of its existence; indeed, reasons obtained through a deeper knowledge of the unconscious make it probable that such proofs are to be discovered somewhere. As a matter of fact, phenomena can be demonstrated in two spheres which seem to correspond to an unconscious and hence, to a displaced knowledge of these motives.

(a) It is a striking and generally recognized feature in the behavior of paranoiacs, that they attach the greatest significance to trivial details in the behavior of others. Details which are usually overlooked by others they interpret and utilize as the basis of far-reaching conclusions. For example, the last paranoiac seen by me concluded that there was a general understanding among people of his environment, because at his departure from the railway station, they made a certain motion with one hand. Another noticed how people walked on the street, how they brandished their walking-sticks, and the like.[2]

The category of the accidental, requiring no motivation, which the normal person lets pass as a part of his own psychic functions and faulty actions, is thus rejected by the paranoiac in his application to the psychic manifestations of others. All that he observes in others is full of meaning; all is explainable. But how does he come to look at it in this manner?

[1] These conceptions of strict determinism in seemingly arbitrary actions have already borne rich fruit for psychology—perhaps also for the administration of justice. Bleuler and Jung have in this way made intelligible the reaction in the so-called association experiments, wherein the test person answers to a given word with one occurring to him (stimulus-word reaction), while the time elapsing between the stimulus-word and answer is measured (reaction-time). Jung has shown in his *Diagnostische Assoziationsstudien*, 1906, what fine reagents for psychic occurrences we possess in this association-experiment. Three students of criminology, H. Gross, of Prague, and Wertheimer and Klein, have developed from these experiments a technique for the diagnosis of facts (*Tatbestands-Diagnostik*) in criminal cases, the examination of which is now tested by psychologists and jurists.

[2] Proceeding from other points of view, this interpretation of trivial and accidental acts by the patient has been designated as "delusions of reference."

Probably here, as in so many other cases, he projects into the mental life of others what exists in his own unconscious activity. Many things obtrude themselves on consciousness in paranoia, which in normal and neurotic persons can only be demonstrated through psychoanalysis as existing in their unconscious.[1] In a certain sense, the paranoiac behavior is justified; he perceives something that escapes the normal person; he sees clearer than one of normal intellectual capacity, but his knowledge becomes worthless when he imputes to others the state of affairs he thus recognizes. I hope that I shall not be expected to justify every paranoiac interpretation. But the point which we grant to paranoia in this conception of chance actions will facilitate for us the psychologic understanding of the conviction which the paranoiac attaches to all these interpretations. *There is certainly some truth to it;* even our errors of judgment, which are not designated as morbid, acquire their feeling of conviction in the same way. This feeling is justified for a certain part of the erroneous train of thought or for the source of its origin, and we shall later extend to it the remaining relationships.

(b) The phenomena of superstition furnish another indication of the unconscious motivation in chance and faulty actions. I will make myself clear through the discussion of a simple experience which gave me the starting-point to these reflections.

Having returned from my vacation, my thoughts immediately turned to the patients with whom I was to occupy myself in the beginning of my year's work. My first visit was to a very old woman (see above) for whom I had twice daily performed the same professional services for many years. Owing to this monotony, unconscious thoughts have often found expression on the way to the patient and during my occupation with her. She was over ninety years old; it was therefore pertinent to ask oneself at the beginning of each year how much longer she was likely to live.

On the day of which I speak, I was in a hurry and took a carriage to her house. Every coachman at the cabstand near my house knew the old woman's address, as each of them had often driven me there. This day, it happened that the driver did not stop in front of her house, but before one of the same number in a nearby and really similar-looking parallel street. I noticed the mistake and reproached the coachman, who apologized for it.

Is it of any significance when I am taken to a house where the old woman is not to be found? Certainly not to me; but were I *superstitious,*

---

[1] For example, the phantasies of the hysterical regarding sexual and cruel abuse which are made conscious by analysis often correspond in every detail with the complaints of persecuted paranoiacs. It is remarkable, but not altogether unexpected that we also meet the identical content as reality in the contrivances of perverts for the gratification of their desires.

I should see an omen in this incident, a hint of fate that this would be the last year for the old woman. A great many omens which have been preserved by history have been founded on no better symbolism. Of course, I explain the incident as an accident without further meaning.

The case would have been entirely different had I come on foot and, "absorbed in thought" or "through distraction," I had gone to the house in the parallel street instead of the correct one. I would not explain that as an accident, but as an action with unconscious intent requiring interpretation. My explanation of this "lapse in walking" would probably be that I expected that the time would soon come when I should no longer meet the old woman.

I therefore differ from a superstitious person in the following manner:

I do not believe that an occurrence in which my mental life takes no part can teach me anything hidden concerning the future shaping of reality; but I do believe that an unintentional manifestation of my own mental activity surely contains something concealed which belongs only to my mental life—that is, I believe in outer (real) chance, but not in inner (psychic) accidents. With the superstitious person, the case is reversed: he knows nothing of the motive of his chance and faulty actions; he believes in the existence of psychic contingencies; he is therefore inclined to attribute meaning to external chance, which manifests itself in actual occurrence, and to see in the accident a means of expression for something hidden outside of him. There are two differences between me and the superstitious person: first, he projects the motive to the outside, while I look for it in myself; second, he explains the accident by an event which I trace to a thought. What he considers hidden corresponds to the unconscious with me, and the compulsion not to let chance pass as chance, but to explain it as common to both of us.

Thus, I admit that this conscious ignorance and unconscious knowledge of the motivation of psychic accidentalness is one of the psychic roots of superstition. *Because* the superstitious person knows nothing of the motivation of his own accidental actions, and because the fact of this motivation strives for a place in his recognition, he is compelled to dispose of them by displacing them into the outer world. If such a connection exists, it can hardly be limited to this single case. As a matter of fact, I believe that a large portion of the mythological conception of the world which reaches far into the most modern religions, *is nothing but psychology projected to the outer world*. The dim perception (the endo-psychic perception, as it were) of psychic factors and relations [1] of the unconscious was taken as a model in the construction of a *transcendental reality*, which is destined to be changed again by science into *psychology of the unconscious*.

[1] Which naturally has nothing of the character of perception.

It is difficult to express it in other terms; the analogy to paranoia must here come to our aid. We venture to explain in this way the myths of paradise and the fall of man, of God, of good and evil, of immortality and the like—that is, to transform *metaphysics* into *meta-psychology*. The gap between the paranoiac's displacement and that of superstition is narrower than appears at first sight. When human beings began to think, they were obviously compelled to explain the outer world in an anthropomorphic sense by a multitude of personalities in their own image; the accidents which they explained superstitiously were thus actions and expressions of persons. In that regard, they behaved just like paranoiacs, who draw conclusions from insignificant signs which others give them, and like all normal persons, who justly take the unintentional actions of their fellow-beings as a basis for the estimation of their characters. Only in our modern, philosophical, but by no means finished views of life does superstition seem so much out of place: in the view of life of prescientific times and nations, it was justified and consistent.

The Roman who gave up an important undertaking because he sighted an ill-omened flock of birds was relatively right; his action was consistent with his principles. But if he withdrew from an undertaking because he had stumbled on his threshold (*un Romain retournerait*), he was absolutely superior even to us unbelievers. He was a better psychologist than we are striving to become. For his stumbling could demonstrate to him the existence of a doubt, an internal counter-current, the force of which could weaken the power of his intention at the moment of its execution. For only by concentrating all psychic forces on the desired aim can one be assured of perfect success. How does Schiller's Tell, who hesitated so long to shoot the apple from his son's head, answer the bailiff's question, why he had provided himself with a second arrow?

"With the second arrow I would have pierced you, had I struck my dear child—and truly, I should not have failed to reach you."

IV. Whoever has had the opportunity of studying the concealed feelings of persons by means of psychoanalysis can also tell something new concerning the quality of unconscious motives, which express themselves in superstition. Nervous persons afflicted with compulsive thinking and compulsive states, who are often very intelligent, show very plainly that superstition originates from repressed hostile and cruel impulses. The greater part of superstition signifies fear of impending evil, and he who has frequently wished evil to others, but because of a good bringing-up, has repressed the same into the unconscious, will be particularly apt to expect punishment for such unconscious evil in the form of a misfortune threatening him from without.

If we concede that we have by no means exhausted the psychology of superstition in these remarks, we must, on the other hand, at least touch upon the question whether real roots of superstition should be altogether denied, whether there are really no omens, prophetic dreams, telepathic experiences, manifestations of supernatural forces and the like. I am now far from willing to repudiate without anything further all these phenomena, concerning which we possess so many minute observations even from men of intellectual prominence, and which should certainly form a basis for further investigation. We may even hope that some of these observations will be explained by our present knowledge of the unconscious psychic processes without necessitating radical changes in our present aspect. If still other phenomena, as, for example, those maintained by the spiritualists, should be proven, we should then consider the modification of our "laws" as demanded by the new experience, without becoming confused in regard to the relation of things of this world.

In the sphere of these analyses, I can only answer the questions here proposed subjectively—that is, in accordance with my personal experience. I am sorry to confess that I belong to that class of unworthy individuals before whom the spirits cease their activities and the supernatural disappears, so that I have never been in position to experience anything personally that would stimulate belief in the miraculous. Like everybody else, I have had forebodings and experienced misfortunes; but the two evaded each other, so that nothing followed the foreboding, and the misfortune struck me unannounced. When as a young man, I lived alone in a strange city, I frequently heard my name suddenly pronounced by an unmistakable, dear voice, and I then made a note of the exact moment of the hallucination in order to inquire carefully of those at home what had occurred at that time. There was nothing to it. On the other hand, I later worked among my patients calmly and without foreboding while my child almost bled to death. Nor have I ever been able to recognize as unreal phenomena any of the forebodings reported to me by my patients.

The belief in prophetic dreams numbers many adherents, because it can be supported by the fact that some things really so happen in the future as they were previously foretold by the wish of the dream.[1] But in this, there is little to be wondered at, as many far-reaching deviations may be regularly demonstrated between a dream and the fulfillment which the credulity of the dreamer prefers to neglect.

A nice example, one which may be justly called prophetic, was once brought to me for exhaustive analysis by an intelligent and truth-loving patient. She related that she once dreamed that she had met a former friend and family physician in front of a certain store in a certain street, and next morning when she went downtown, she actually met him at the place named in the dream. I may observe that the significance of this wonderful coincidence was not proven to be due to any subsequent event

[1] Cf. Freud, *Traum und Telepathie* (Dream and Telepathy), G. S., Bd. III.

—that is, it could not be justified through future occurrences. Careful examination definitely established the fact that there was no proof that the woman recalled the dream in the morning following the night of the dream—that is, before the walk and before the meeting. She could offer no objection when this state of affairs was presented in a manner that robbed this episode of everything miraculous, leaving only an interesting psychologic problem. One morning, she had walked through this very street, had met her old family physician before that certain store, and on seeing him, received the conviction that during the preceding night, she had dreamed of this meeting at this place. The analysis then showed with great probability how she came to this conviction, to which, in accordance with the general rule, we cannot deny a certain right to credence. A meeting at a definite place following a previous expectation really describes the fact of a *rendezvous*. The old family physician awakened her memory of old times, when meetings with a *third person,* also a friend of the physician, were of marked significance to her. Since that time, she had continued her relations with this gentleman, and the day before the mentioned dream, she had waited for him in vain. If I could report in greater detail the circumstances here before us, I could easily show that the illusion of the prophetic dream at the sight of the friend of former times is perchance equivalent to the following speech: "Ah, doctor, you now remind me of bygone times, when I never had to wait in vain for N. when we had arranged a meeting."

I have observed in myself a simple and easily explained example, which is probably a good model for similar occurrences of those familiar "remarkable coincidences" wherein we meet a person of whom we were just thinking. During a walk through the inner city a few days after the title of "Professor" was bestowed on me, which carried with it a great deal of prestige even in monarchical cities, my thoughts suddenly turned to a childish revenge-phantasy against a certain married couple. Some months previous, this couple had called me to see their little daughter, who suffered from an interesting compulsive manifestation following the appearance of a dream. I took a great interest in the case, the genesis of which I believed I could surmise, but the parents were unfavorable to my treatment and gave me to understand that they thought of applying to a foreign authority who treated by hypnotism. I now fancied to myself that after the failure of this treatment, the parents begged me to take the patient under my care, saying that they now had full confidence in me, etc. But I answered: "Now that I have become a professor, you have confidence in me. The title has made no change in my ability; if you could not use me when I was instructor, you can get along without me now that I am a professor." At this point, my phantasy was interrupted by a loud "Good evening, Professor!" and as I looked up, there was the same couple on whom I had just taken this imaginary vengeance.

The next reflection destroyed all semblance of the miraculous. I was walking towards this couple on a straight, almost deserted street; glancing up hastily at a distance of perhaps twenty steps from me, I had seen and realized their stately personalities; but this perception, following the model of a negative hallucination, was set aside by certain emotionally accentuated motives and then asserted itself spontaneously as an emerging phantasy.

A similar experience is related by Brill, which also throws some light on the nature of telepathy.

"While engrossed in conversation during our customary Sunday evening dinner at one of the large New York restaurants, I suddenly stopped and irrelevantly remarked to my wife, 'I wonder how Dr. R. is doing in Pittsburgh.' She looked at me much astonished and said: 'Why, that is exactly what I have been thinking for the last few seconds! Either you have transferred this thought to me or I have transferred it to you. How can you otherwise explain this strange phenomenon?' I had to admit that I could offer no solution. Our conversation throughout the dinner showed not the remotest association to Dr. R., nor, so far as our memories went, had we heard or spoken of him for some time. Being a skeptic, I refused to admit that there was anything mysterious about it, although inwardly I felt quite uncertain. To be frank, I was somewhat mystified.

"But we did not remain very long in this state of mind, for on looking toward the cloak-room, we were surprised to see Dr. R. Closer inspection, however, showed our mistake, but we were struck by the remarkable resemblance of this stranger to Dr. R. From the position of the cloak-room, we were forced to conclude that this stranger had passed our table. Absorbed in our conversation, we had not noticed him consciously, but the visual image had stirred up the association of his double, Dr. R. That we should both have experienced the same thought is also quite natural. The last that we had heard from Dr. R. was that he had taken up private practice in Pittsburgh, and, being aware of the vicissitudes that beset the beginner in private practice, it was quite natural that we should wonder how he was getting along.

"What promised to be a supernatural manifestation was thus easily explained on a normal basis; but had we not noticed the stranger before he left the restaurant, it would have been impossible to exclude the mysterious. I venture to say that such simple mechanisms are at the basis of the most complicated telepathic manifestations; at least, that has been my experience in all those cases that were accessible to investigation."

To the category of the wonderful and uncanny, we may also add that strange feeling we perceive in certain moments and situations when it seems as if we had already had exactly the same experience, or had previously found ourselves in the same situation. Yet we are never successful in our efforts to recall clearly those former experiences and situations. I know that I follow only the loose colloquial expression when I designate that which stimulates us in such moments as a "feeling." We undoubtedly deal with a judgment, and, indeed, with a judgment of cognition; but these cases, nevertheless, have a character peculiar to themselves, and besides, we must not ignore the fact that we never recall what we are seeking.

I do not know whether this phenomenon of *Déjà vu* (having already seen this or that) was ever seriously offered as a proof of a former psychic existence of the individual; but it is certain that psychologists have taken an interest in it, and have attempted to solve the riddle in a multitude of speculative ways. None of the proposed tentative explanations seems right to me, because none takes account of anything but the accompanying manifestations and the conditions favoring the phenomenon. Those psychic processes which, according to my observation, are alone responsible for the explanation of the *Déjà vu* phenomenon—namely, the unconscious phantasies—are generally neglected by the psychologist even today.

I believe that it is wrong to designate the feeling of having experienced something before as an illusion. On the contrary, in such moments, something is really touched that we have already experienced, only we cannot consciously recall the latter because it never was conscious. In the latter, the feeling of *Déjà vu* corresponds to the memory of an unconscious phantasy. There are unconscious phantasies (or day-dreams) just as there are similar conscious creations, which everyone knows from personal experience.

I realize that the object is worthy of most minute study, but I will here give the analysis of only one case of *Déjà vu* in which the feeling was characterized by particular intensity and persistence. A woman of thirty-seven years asserted that she most distinctly remembered that at the age of twelve and a half, she paid her first visit to some school friends in the country, and as she entered the garden, she immediately had the feeling of having been there before. This feeling was repeated as she went through the living rooms, so that she believed she knew beforehand how big the next room was, what views one could have on looking out of it, etc. But the belief that this feeling of recognition might have its source in a previous visit to the house and garden, perhaps a visit paid in earliest childhood, was absolutely excluded and disproved by statements from her parents. The woman who related this sought no psychologic explanation, but saw in the appearance of this feeling a prophetic reference to the importance which these friends later assumed in her emotional life. On tak-

ing into consideration, however, the circumstance under which this phenomenon presented itself to her, we found the way to another conception.

When she decided on visiting her schoolmates, she knew that these girls
had an only brother who was then seriously ill. In the course of the visit,
she actually saw him. She found him looking very badly and thought to
herself that he would soon die. But it happened that her own only brother
had had a serious attack of diphtheria some months before, and during
his illness, she had lived for weeks with relatives far from her parental
home. She believed that her brother was taking part in this visit to the
country, imagined even that this·was his first long journey since his illness; still, her memory was remarkably indistinct in regard to these
points, whereas all other details, and particularly the dress which she
wore that day, remained most clearly before her eyes.

To the initiated, it will not be difficult to conclude from these indications that the expectation of her brother's death had played a great part
in the girl's mind at that time, and that either it never became conscious
or it was more energetically repressed after the favorable issue of the illness. Under other circumstances, she would have been compelled to wear
another dress—namely, mourning clothes. She found the analogous situation in her friends' home; their only brother was in danger of an early
death, an event that really came to pass in a short time. She might have
consciously remembered that she had lived through a similar situation
a few months previous, but instead of recalling what was inhibited through
repression, she transferred the memory feeling to the locality, to the
garden and the house and merged it into the *fausse reconnaissance*,
namely, that she had already seen everything exactly as it was.

From the fact of the repression, we may conclude that the former expectation of the death of her brother was not far from evincing the character of a wish-phantasy. She would then have become the only child. In
her later neurosis, she suffered in the most intense manner from the fear
of losing her parents, behind which the analysis disclosed, as usual, the
unconscious wish of the same content.

My own experience of *Déjà vu* I can trace in a similar manner to the
emotional constellation of the moment. It may be expressed as follows:
"That would be another occasion for awakening certain phantasies (unconscious and unknown) which were formed in me at one time or another
as a wish to improve my situation."

Dr. Ferenczi, to whom this edition is indebted for so many contributions, wrote to me concerning this: "I have been convinced, from my
experience as well as that of others, that the inexplicable feeling of
familiarity can be referred to unconscious phantasies of which we are unconsciously reminded in an actual situation. With one of my patients, the
process was apparently different, but in reality it was quite analogous.

This feeling returned to him very often, but showed itself regularly as originating in a forgotten (repressed) portion of a dream of the preceding night. Thus it appears that the *Déjà vu* can originate not only from daydreams but also from night dreams."

In 1915, I described another phenomenon which resembles much the *Déjà vu*. It is the *Déjà raconté* feeling, the illusion that something has already been related during the psychoanalytic treatment, which is especially interesting. The patient asserts with all subjective signs of certainty, that he previously related this definite episode. The physician, however, is sure of the contrary and, as a rule, can convince the patient of it. The explanation of this interesting phenomenon is undoubtedly based on the fact that the patient had the impulse and intention of imparting this memory, but failed to execute it, and that he now puts the memory of the first resolution as a substitute for the second feeling.

V. Recently, when I had occasion to recite to a colleague of a philosophical turn of mind some examples of name-forgetting with their analyses, he hastened to reply: "That is all very well, but with me the forgetting of a name proceeds in a different manner." Evidently, one cannot dismiss this question as simply as that; I do not believe that my colleague had ever thought of an analysis for the forgetting of a name, nor could he say how the process differed in him. But his remark, nevertheless, touches upon a problem which many would be inclined to place in the foreground. Does the solution given for faulty and chance actions apply in general or only in particular cases, and if only in the latter, what are the conditions under which it may also be employed in the explanation of the other phenomena?

In answer to this question, my experiences leave me in the lurch. I can only urge against considering the demonstrated connections as rare, for as often as I have made the test in myself and with my patients, it was always definitely demonstrated exactly as in the examples reported, or there were at least good reasons to assume this. One should not be surprised, however, when one does not succeed every time in finding the concealed meaning of the symptomatic action, as the amount of inner resistances ranging themselves against the solution must be considered a deciding factor. Also, it is not always possible to explain every individual dream of oneself or of patients. To substantiate the general validity of the theory, it is enough if one can penetrate only a certain distance into the hidden associations. The dream which proves refractory when the solution is attempted on the following day can often be robbed of its secret a week or a month later, when the psychic factors combating one another have been reduced as a consequence of a real change that has meanwhile taken place. The same applies to the solution of faulty and symptomatic actions. It would, therefore, be wrong to affirm of all cases which resist analysis that they are caused by another psychic mechanism than that here revealed; such assumption requires more than negative proofs; moreover, the readiness to believe in a different explanation of faulty and symptomatic actions, which probably exists universally in all normal persons, does not prove anything; it is obviously an expression of the same psychic forces which produced the secret, which therefore strives to protect and struggle against its elucidation.

On the other hand, we must not overlook the fact that the repressed thoughts and feelings are not independent in attaining expression in symptomatic and faulty actions. The technical possibility for such an adjustment of the innervations must be furnished independently of them, and this is then gladly utilized by the intention of the repressed material to come to conscious expression. In the case of linguistic faulty actions, an attempt has been made by philosophers and philologists to verify through minute observations what structural and functional relations enter into the service of such intention. If in the determinations of faulty and symptomatic actions, we separate the unconscious motive from its co-active physiological and psychophysical relations, the question remains whether there are still other factors within normal limits which, like the unconscious motive, or a substitute for it, can produce faulty and symptomatic actions on the path of these relations. It is not my task to answer this question.

To be sure, it is not my intention to exaggerate still more the differences, large as they are, between the psychoanalytic and the current concepts of faulty actions. I prefer to give cases in which these differences are not so marked. In the simplest and least striking examples of lapses in talking and writing, wherein perhaps only words are fused or words and letters omitted, there is no very complicated interpretation. Psychoanalytically, it can only be asserted, that in these cases one sees some disturbance of the intention, but one cannot say whence it originated and what its purpose is. It really produces nothing except a manifestation of its presence. In the same cases, one also observes that the faulty actions become effective through the undisputed favorable influences of sound relations and mediate psychological associations. But scientifically, it is only fair to demand that we judge such rudimentary cases of lapses in speech or writing by the more marked expressions, the investigations of which result in unequivocal explanations of the causation of faulty actions.

VI. Since the discussion of speech-blunders, we have been content to demonstrate that faulty actions have a concealed motive, and through the aid of psychoanalysis, we have traced our way to the knowledge of their motivation. The general nature and the peculiarities of the psychic factors brought to expression in these faulty actions, we have hitherto left almost without consideration; at any rate, we have not attempted to define them more accurately or to examine into their lawfulness. Nor will we now attempt a thorough elucidation of the subject, as the first steps have already taught us that it is more feasible to enter this structure from another side.[1] Here, we can put before ourselves certain questions which I will cite in their order. (1) What are the content and origin of the thoughts and feelings which show themselves through faulty and chance actions? (2) What are the conditions which force a thought or a feeling to make use of these occurrences as a means of expression and place it in a position to do so? (3) Can constant and definite associations be demonstrated between the manner of the faulty action and the qualities brought to expression through it?

I shall begin by bringing together some material for answering the last question. In the discussion of the examples of speech-blunders, we found it necessary to go beyond the contents of the intended speech, and we had to seek the cause of the speech disturbance outside the intention. The latter was quite clear in a series of cases, and was known to the consciousness of the speaker. In the example that seemed most simple and transparent, it was a similar sounding but different conception of the same thought, which disturbed its expression without anyone being able to say why the one succumbed and the other came to the surface (Meringer and Mayers' *Contaminations*).

In a second group of cases, one conception succumbed to a motive which did not, however, prove strong enough to cause complete submersion. The conception which was withheld was clearly presented to consciousness.

Only of the third group can we affirm unreservedly that the disturbing thought differed from the one intended, and it is obvious that it may establish an essential distinction. The disturbing thought is either connected with the disturbed one through a thought association (disturbance through inner contradiction), or it is substantially strange to it, and just the disturbed word is connected with the disturbing thought through a surprising outer association, which is frequently unconscious.

In the examples which I have given from my psychoanalyses, the entire speech is either under the influence of thoughts which have become active simultaneously, or under absolutely unconscious thoughts which betray themselves either through the disturbance itself, or which evince an indirect influence by making it possible for the individual parts of the unconsciously intended speech to disturb one another. The retained or

[1] This work should be considered popular. Through an accumulation of many examples, it wishes to pave the way for the necessary assumption of unconscious, yet effective, psychic processes. It wishes to avoid all theoretical discussions concerning the nature of this unconscious.

unconscious thoughts from which the disturbances in speech emanate are of most varied origin. A general survey does not reveal any definite direction.

Comparative examinations of examples of mistakes in reading and writing lead to the same conclusions. Isolated cases, as in speech-blunders, seem to owe their origin to an unmotivated work of condensation (*e.g.*, the *Apel*). But we should like to know whether special conditions must not be fulfilled in order that such condensation, which is considered regular in dream-work and faulty in our waking thoughts, should take place. No information concerning this can be obtained from the examples themselves. But I would refuse to draw the conclusion from this, that there are no such conditions, as, for instance, the relaxation of conscious attention; for I have learned elsewhere that automatic actions are especially characterized by correctness and reliability. I would rather emphasize the fact that here, as so frequently in biology, it is the normal relations, or those approaching the normal, that are less favorable objects for investigation than the pathological. What remains obscure in the explanation of these most simple disturbances will, according to my expectation, be made clear through the explanation of more serious disturbances.

Also, mistakes in reading and writing do not lack examples in which more remote and more complicated motivation can be recognized.

There is no doubt that the disturbances of the speech functions occur more easily and make less demand on the disturbing forces than other psychic acts.

But one is on different ground when it comes to the examination of forgetting in the literal sense—*i.e.*, the forgetting of past experiences. (To distinguish this forgetting from the others, we designate *sensu strictiori* the forgetting of proper names and foreign words, as in Chapters I and II, as "slips"; and the forgetting of resolutions as "omissions.") The principal conditions of the normal process in forgetting are unknown.[1]

[1] I can perhaps give the following outline concerning the mechanism of actual forgetting. The memory material succumbs in general to two influences, condensation and distortion. Distortion is the work of the tendencies dominating the psychic life and directs itself above all against the affective remnants of memory traces which maintain a more resistive attitude towards condensation. The traces which have grown indifferent, merge into a process of condensation without opposition; in addition, it may be observed that tendencies of distortion also feed on the indifferent material, because they have not been gratified where they wished to manifest themselves. As these processes of condensation and distortion continue for long periods, during which all fresh experiences act upon the transformation of the memory content, it is our belief that it is time that makes memory uncertain and indistinct. It is quite probable that in forgetting, there can really be no question of a direct function of time. From the repressed memory traces, it can be verified that they suffer no changes even in the longest periods. The unconscious, at all events, knows no time limit. The most important, as well as the most peculiar character of psychic fixation consists in the fact that all impressions are, on the one hand, retained in the same form as they were received, and also in the forms that they have assumed in their

We are also reminded of the fact that not all is forgotten which we believe to be. Our explanation deals here only with those cases in which the forgetting arouses our astonishment, in so far as it infringes upon the rule that the unimportant is forgotten, while the important matter is guarded by memory. Analysis of these examples of forgetting, which seems to demand a special explanation, shows that the motive of forgetting is always an unwillingness to recall something which may evoke painful feelings. We come to the conjecture that this motive universally strives for expression in psychic life, but is inhibited through other and contrary forces from regularly manifesting itself. The extent and significance of this dislike to recall painful impressions seems worthy of the most painstaking psychologic investigation. The question as to what special conditions render possible the universally resistant forgetting in individual cases cannot be solved from this further connection.

A different factor steps into the foreground in the forgetting of resolutions; the supposed conflict resulting in the repression of the painful memory becomes tangible, and in the analysis of the examples, one regularly recognizes a counter-will which opposes but does not put an end to the resolution. As in previously discussed faulty acts, we here also recognize two types of the psychic process: the counter-will either turns directly against the resolution (in intentions of some consequence) or it is substantially foreign to the resolution itself and establishes its connection with it through an outer association (in almost indifferent resolutions).

The same conflict governs the phenomena of erroneously carried-out actions. The impulse which manifests itself in the disturbances of the action is frequently a counter-impulse. Still oftener, it is altogether a strange impulse which only utilizes the opportunity to express itself through a disturbance in the execution of the action. The cases in which the disturbance is the result of an inner contradiction are the most significant ones, and also deal with the more important activities.

The inner conflict in the chance or symptomatic actions then withdraws into the background. Those motor expressions, which are least thought of, or are entirely overlooked by consciousness, serve as the expression of numerous unconscious or restrained feelings. For the most part, they represent symbolically wishes and phantasies.

The first question (as to the origin of the thoughts and emotions which find expression in faulty actions) we can answer by saying that in a series of cases, the origin of the disturbing thoughts can be readily traced to repressed emotions of the psychic life. Even in healthy persons, egotistic,

---

further development. This state of affairs cannot be elucidated by any comparison from any other sphere. By virtue of this theory, every former state of the memory content may thus be restored, even though all original relations have long been replaced by newer ones.

jealous and hostile feelings and impulses, burdened by the pressure of moral education, often utilize the path of faulty actions to express in some way their undeniably existing force which is not recognized by the higher psychic instances. Allowing these faulty and chance actions to continue, corresponds, in great part, to a comfortable toleration of the unmoral. The manifold sexual currents play no insignificant part in these repressed feelings. That they appear so seldom in the thoughts revealed by the analyses of my examples, is simply a matter of coincidence. As I have undertaken the analyses of numerous examples from my own psychic life, the selection was partial from the first, and aimed at the exclusion of sexual matters. At other times, it seemed that the disturbing thoughts originated from the most harmless objection and consideration.

We have now reached the answer to the second question—that is, what psychologic conditions are responsible for the fact that a thought must seek expression, not in its complete form, but, as it were, in parasitic form, as a modification and disturbance of another. From the most striking examples of faulty actions, it is quite obvious that this determinant should be sought in a relation to conscious capacity, or in the more or less firmly pronounced character of "repression." But an examination of this series of examples shows that this character consists of many indistinct elements. The tendency to overlook something because it is wearisome, or the reflection that the concerned thought does not really belong to the intended matter, seems to play the same rôle as motives for the reflection of a thought (which later depends for expression on the disturbance of another), as the moral condemnation of a rebellious emotional feeling, or as the origin of absolutely unconscious trains of thought. An insight into the general nature of the condition of faulty and chance actions cannot be gained in this way.

However, this investigation gives us one single significant fact; the more harmless the motivation of the faulty act, the less obnoxious and hence, the less incapable of consciousness, the thought to which it gives expression is; the easier also becomes the solution of the phenomenon after we have turned our attention toward it. The simplest cases of speech-blunders are immediately noticed and spontaneously corrected. Where one deals with motivation through actually repressed feelings, the solution requires a painstaking analysis, which may sometimes strike against difficulties or turn out unsuccessful.

One is therefore justified in taking the result of this last investigation as an indication of the fact that the satisfactory explanation of the psychological conditions of faulty and chance actions is to be acquired in another way and from another source. The indulgent reader can, therefore, see in these discussions the demonstration of the surfaces of fracture in which this theme was quite artificially evolved from a broader connection.

VII. Just a few words to indicate the direction of this broader connection. The mechanism of the faulty and chance actions, as we have learned to know it through the application of analysis, shows in the most essential points an agreement with the mechanism of dream formation, which I have discussed in the chapter "The Dream Work" of my book on the interpretation of dreams. Here, as there, one finds condensation and and compromise formation ("contaminations"); in addition, the situation is much the same, since unconscious thoughts find expression as modifications of other thoughts in unusual ways and through outer associations. The incongruities, absurdities and errors in the dream content, by virtue of which the dream is scarcely recognized as a psychic function, originate in the same way—to be sure, through freer usage of the existing material—as the common error of our every-day life; *here, as there, the appearance of the incorrect function is explained through the peculiar interference of two or more correct functions.*

An important conclusion can be drawn from this combination: the peculiar mode of operation, whose most striking function we recognize in the dream content, should not be attributed only to the sleeping state of the psychic life, when we possess abundant proof of its activity during the waking state in faulty actions. The same connection also forbids us from assuming that these psychic processes which impress us as abnormal and strange, are determined by deep-seated decay of psychic activity or by morbid state of function.[1]

The correct understanding of this strange psychic work, which allows the faulty actions to originate like the dream pictures, will only be possible after we have discovered that the psychoneurotic symptoms, particularly the psychic formations of hysteria and compulsion neurosis, repeat in their mechanisms all the essential features of this mode of operation. The continuation of our investigation would therefore have to begin at this point.

There is still another special interest for us in considering the faulty, chance and symptomatic actions in the light of this last analogy. If we compare them to the function of the psychoneuroses and the neurotic symptoms, two frequently recurring statements gain in sense and support —namely, that the border-line between the nervous, normal and abnormal states is indistinct, and that we are all slightly nervous. Regardless of all medical experience, one may construe various types of such barely suggested nervousness, the *formes frustes* of the neuroses. There may be cases in which only a few symptoms appear, or they may manifest them-

---

[1] Cf. here *The Interpretation of Dreams* (p. 540, this volume), p. 559. Macmillan, New York; and Allen & Unwin, London.

selves rarely or in mild forms; the extenuation may be transferred to the number, intensity, or to the temporal outbreak of the morbid manifestation. It may also happen that just this type, which forms the most frequent transition between health and disease, may never be discovered. The transition type, whose morbid manifestations come in the form of faulty and symptomatic actions, is characterized by the fact that the symptoms are transformed to the least important psychic activities, while everything that can lay claim to a higher psychic value, remains free from disturbance. When the symptoms are disposed of in a reverse manner— that is, when they appear in the most important individual and social activities in a manner to disturb the functions of nourishment and sexual relations, professional and social life—such disposition is found in the severe cases of neuroses, and is perhaps more characteristic of the latter than the multiformity or vividness of the morbid manifestations.

But the common character of the mildest, as well as the severest cases, to which the faulty and chance actions contribute, lies *in the ability to refer the phenomena to unwelcome, repressed, psychic material, which, though pushed away from consciousness, is nevertheless not robbed of all capacity to express itself.*

TWO

THE INTERPRETATION
OF DREAMS

"Flectere si nequeo Superos, Acheronta movebo."

FOREWORD

TO THE THIRD ENGLISH EDITION

In 1909, G. Stanley Hall invited me to Clark University, in Worcester, to give the first lectures on psychoanalysis. In the same year, Dr. Brill published the first of his translations of my writings, which were soon followed by further ones. If psychoanalysis now plays a role in American intellectual life, or if it does so in the future, a large part of this result will have to be attributed to this and other activities of Dr. Brill's.

His first translation of *The Interpretation of Dreams* appeared in 1913. Since then, much has taken place in the world, and much has been changed in our views about the neuroses. This book, with the new contribution to psychology which surprised the world when it was published (1900), remains essentially unaltered. It contains, even according to my present-day judgment, the most valuable of all the discoveries it has been my good fortune to make. Insight such as this falls to one's lot but once in a lifetime.

Vienna.   FREUD
March 15, 1931

THE SCIENTIFIC LITERATURE OF
DREAM-PROBLEMS (UP TO 1900)

IN THE following pages, I shall demonstrate that there is a psychological technique which makes it possible to interpret dreams, and that on the application of this technique, every dream will reveal itself as a psychological structure, full of significance, and one which may be assigned to a specific place in the psychic activities of the waking state. Further, I shall endeavor to elucidate the processes which underlie the strangeness and obscurity of dreams, and to deduce from these processes the nature of the psychic forces whose conflict or co-operation is responsible for our dreams. This done, my investigation will terminate, as it will have reached the point where the problem of the dream merges into more comprehensive problems, and to solve these, we must have recourse to material of a different kind.

I shall begin by giving a short account of the views of earlier writers on this subject, and of the status of the dream-problem in contemporary science; since in the course of this treatise, I shall not often have occasion to refer to either. In spite of thousands of years of endeavor, little progress has been made in the scientific understanding of dreams. This fact has been so universally acknowledged by previous writers on the subject that it seems hardly necessary to quote individual opinions. The reader will find, in many stimulating observations, and plenty of interesting material relating to our subject, but little or nothing that concerns the true nature of the dream, or that solves definitely any of its enigmas. The educated layman, of course, knows even less of the matter.

The conception of the dream that was held in prehistoric ages by primitive peoples, and the influence which it may have exerted on the formation of their conceptions of the universe, and of the soul, is a theme of such great interest that it is only with reluctance that I refrain from dealing with it in these pages. I will refer the reader to the well-known works of Sir John Lubbock (Lord Avebury), Herbert Spencer, E. B. Tylor and other writers; I will only add that we shall not realize the importance of these problems and speculations until we have completed the task of dream interpretation that lies before us.

A reminiscence of the concept of the dream that was held in primitive times seems to underlie the evaluation of the dream which was current among the peoples of classical antiquity.[1] They took it for granted that dreams were related to the world of the supernatural beings in whom they believed, and that they brought inspirations from the gods and demons. Moreover, it appeared to them that dreams must serve a special purpose in respect of the dreamer; that, as a rule, they predicted the future. The extraordinary variations in the content of dreams, and in the impressions which they produced on the dreamer, made it, of course, very difficult to formulate a coherent conception of them, and necessitated manifold differentiations and group-formations, according to their value and reliability. The valuation of dreams by the individual philosophers of antiquity naturally depended on the importance which they were prepared to attribute to manticism in general.

In the two works of Aristotle in which there is mention of dreams, they are already regarded as constituting a problem of psychology. We are told that the dream is not god-sent, that it is not of divine but of daimonic origin. For nature is really daimonic, not divine; that is to say, the dream is not a supernatural revelation, but is subject to the laws of the human spirit, which has, of course, a kinship with the divine. The dream is defined as the psychic activity of the sleeper, inasmuch as he is asleep. Aristotle was acquainted with some of the characteristics of the dream-life; for example, he knew that a dream converts the slight sensations perceived in sleep into intense sensations ("one imagines that one is walking through fire, and feels hot, if this or that part of the body becomes only quite slightly warm"), which led him to conclude that dreams might easily betray to the physician the first indications of an incipient physical change which escaped observation during the day.[1]

As has been said, those writers of antiquity who preceded Aristotle did not regard the dream as a product of the dreaming psyche, but as an inspiration of divine origin, and in ancient times, the two opposing tendencies which we shall find throughout the ages in respect of the evaluation of the dream-life, were already perceptible. The ancients distinguished between the true and valuable dreams which were sent to the dreamer as warnings, or to foretell future events, and the vain, fraudulent and empty dreams, whose object was to misguide him or lead him to destruction.

---

[1] The following remarks are based on Büchsenschütz's careful essay, *Traum und Traumdeutung im Altertum* (Berlin, 1868).

[2] The relationship between dreams and disease is discussed by Hippocrates in a chapter of his famous work.

Editor's Note

As the first chapter of this work is nothing but an introduction to the book proper, it was deemed best for the purposes of this collection of Freud's basic writings to omit most of it and to give only those parts that are in any way pertinent to the themes under later consideration. For it is of no particular interest or value to the general reader to know everything held by the ancients and moderns concerning the phenomena of dreams, up to the appearance of the first German edition of this work in 1900.[1]

The author summarizes these views as follows:

The pre-scientific conception of the dream which obtained among the ancients was, of course, in perfect keeping with their general conception of the universe, which was accustomed to project as an external reality that which possessed reality only in the life of the psyche. Further, it accounted for the main impression made upon the waking life by the morning memory of the dream; for in this memory the dream, as compared with the rest of the psychic content, seems to be something alien, coming, as it were, from another world. It would be an error to suppose that the theory of the supernatural origin of dreams lacks followers even in our own times; for quite apart from pietistic and mystical writers—who cling, as they are perfectly justified in doing, to the remnants of the once predominant realm of the supernatural until these remnants have been swept away by scientific explanation—we not infrequently find that quite intelligent persons, who in other respects are averse to anything of a romantic nature, go so far as to base their religious belief in the existence and co-operation of superhuman spiritual powers on the inexplicable nature of the phenomena of dreams (Haffner). The validity ascribed to the dream-life by certain schools of philosophy—for example, by the school of Schelling—is a distinct reminiscence of the undisputed belief in the divinity of dreams which prevailed in antiquity; and for some thinkers, the mantic or prophetic power of dreams is still a subject of debate. This is due to the fact that the explanations attempted by psychology are too inadequate to cope with the accumulated material, however strongly the scientific thinker may feel that such superstitious doctrines should be repudiated.

To write a history of our scientific knowledge of the dream problem is extremely difficult, because, valuable though this knowledge may be in certain respects, no real progress in a definite direction is as yet dis-

[1] Those who have a special interest in the subject may read *The Interpretation of Dreams,* translated by Brill. The Macmillan Co., New York; and Allen & Unwin, London, 1937.

cernible. No real foundation of verified results has hitherto been established on which future investigators might continue to build. Every new author approaches the same problems afresh, and from the very beginning. If I were to enumerate such authors in chronological order, giving a survey of the opinions which each has held concerning the problems of the dream, I should be quite unable to draw a clear and complete picture of the present state of our knowledge on the subject. I have therefore preferred to base my method of treatment on themes rather than on authors, and in attempting the solution of each problem of the dream, I shall cite the material found in the literature of the subject.

But as I have not succeeded in mastering the whole of this literature—for it is widely dispersed and interwoven with the literature of other subjects—I must ask my readers to rest content with my survey as it stands, provided that no fundamental fact or important point of view has been overlooked.

In a supplement to a later German edition, the author adds:

I shall have to justify myself for not extending my summary of the literature of dream problems to cover the period between the first appearance of this book and the publication of the second edition. This justification may not seem very satisfactory to the reader; none the less, to me it was decisive. The motives which induced me to summarize the treatment of dreams in the literature of the subject have been exhausted by the foregoing introduction; to have continued this would have cost me a great deal of effort and would not have been particularly useful or instructive. For the interval in question—a period of nine years—has yielded nothing new or valuable as regards the conception of dreams, either in actual material or in novel points of view. In most of the literature which has appeared since the publication of my own work, the latter has not been mentioned or discussed; it has, of course, received the least attention from the so-called "research workers on dreams," who have thus afforded a brilliant example of the aversion to learning anything new so characteristic of the scientist. *"Les savants ne sont pas curieux,"* said the scoffer, Anatole France. If there were such a thing in science as the right of revenge, I, in my turn, should be justified in ignoring the literature which has appeared since the publication of this book. The few reviews which have appeared in the scientific journals are so full of misconceptions and lack of comprehension that my only possible answer to my critics would be a request that they should read this book over again—or perhaps merely that they should read it!

And in a supplement to the fourth German edition which appeared in 1914, a year after I published the first English translation of this work, he writes:

Since then, the state of affairs has certainly undergone a change; my contribution to the "interpretation of dreams" is no longer ignored in the literature of the subject. But the new situation makes it even more impossible to continue the foregoing summary. *The Interpretation of Dreams* has evoked a whole series of new contentions and problems, which have been expounded by the authors in the most varied fashions. But I cannot discuss these works until I have developed the theories to which their authors have referred. Whatever has appeared to me as valuable in this recent literature, I have accordingly reviewed in the course of the following exposition.

THE METHOD OF
DREAM-INTERPRETATION

THE ANALYSIS OF A SPECIMEN DREAM

THE epigraph on the title-page of this volume indicates the tradition to which I prefer to ally myself in my conception of the dream. I am proposing to show that dreams are capable of interpretation; and any contributions to the solution of the problem which have already been discussed will emerge only as possible by-products in the accomplishment of my special task. On the hypothesis that dreams are susceptible of interpretation, I at once find myself in disagreement with the prevailing doctrine of dreams—in fact, with all the theories of dreams, excepting only that of Scherner, for "to interpret a dream" is to specify its "meaning," to replace it by something which takes its position in the concatenation of our psychic activities as a link of definite importance and value. But, as we have seen, the scientific theories of the dream leave no room for a problem of dream-interpretation; since, in the first place, according to these theories, dreaming is not a psychic activity at all, but a somatic process which makes itself known to the psychic apparatus by means of symbols. Lay opinion has always been opposed to these theories. It asserts its privilege of proceeding illogically, and although it admits that dreams are incomprehensible and absurd, it cannot summon up the courage to deny that dreams have any significance. Led by a dim intuition, it seems rather to assume that dreams have a meaning, albeit a hidden one; that they are intended as a substitute for some other thought-process, and that we have only to disclose this substitute correctly in order to discover the hidden meaning of the dream.

The unscientific world, therefore, has always endeavored to "interpret" dreams, and by applying one or the other of two essentially different methods. The first of these methods envisages the dream-content as a whole, and seeks to replace it by another content, which is intelligible and in certain respects analogous. This is symbolic dream-interpretation; and of course it goes to pieces at the very outset in the case of those dreams which are not only unintelligible but confused. The construction which the biblical Joseph placed upon the dream of Pharaoh furnishes an example of this method. The seven fat kine, after which came seven lean ones that devoured the former, were a symbolic substitute for seven years of famine in the land of Egypt, which according to the prediction were to consume all the surplus that seven fruitful years had produced. Most of the artificial dreams contrived by the poets [1] are intended for some such symbolic interpretation, for they reproduce the thought conceived by the poet in a guise not unlike the disguise which we are wont to find in our dreams.

The idea that the dream concerns itself chiefly with the future, whose form it surmises in advance—a relic of the prophetic significance with which dreams were once invested—now becomes the motive for translating into the future the meaning of the dream which has been found by means of symbolic interpretation.

A demonstration of the manner in which one arrives at such a symbolic interpretation cannot, of course, be given. Success remains a matter of ingenious conjecture, of direct intuition, and for this reason dream-interpretation has naturally been elevated into an art which seems to depend upon extraordinary gifts.[2] The second of the two popular methods of dream-interpretation entirely abandons such claims. It might be described as the "cipher method," since it treats the dream as a kind of secret code in which every sign is translated into another sign of known meaning, according to an established key. For example, I have dreamt of a letter, and also of a funeral or the like; I consult a "dream-book," and I find that "letter" is to be translated by "vexation" and "funeral" by "engagement." It now remains to establish a connection, which I am again to assume as pertaining to the future, by means of the rigmarole which I have deciphered. An interesting variant of this cipher procedure, a variant in which its character of purely mechanical transference is to a certain extent corrected, is presented in the work on dream-interpretation by Ar-

---

[1] In a novel *Gradiva*, by the poet, W. Jensen, I chanced to discover several fictitious dreams, which were perfectly correct in their construction, and could be interpreted as though they had not been invented, but had been dreamt by actual persons. The poet declared, upon my inquiry, that he was unacquainted with my theory of dreams. I have made use of this agreement between my investigations and the creations of the poet as a proof of the correctness of my method of dream-analysis (*Der Wahn und die Träume* in W. Jensen's *Gradiva*, vol. i of the *Schriften zur angewandten Seelenkunde*, 1906, edited by myself, *Ges. Schriften*, vol. ix).

[2] Aristotle expressed himself in this connection by saying that the best interpreter of dreams is he who can best grasp similarities. For dream-pictures, like pictures in water, are disfigured by the motion (of the water), so that he hits the target best who is able to recognize the true picture in the distorted one (Büchsenschütz, p. 65).

temidoros of Daldis.[1] Here not only the dream-content, but also the personality and social position of the dreamer are taken into consideration, so that the same dream-content has a significance for the rich man, the married man, or the orator, which is different from that which applies to the poor man, the bachelor, or, let us say, the merchant. The essential point, then, in this procedure is that the work of interpretation is not applied to the entirety of the dream, but to each portion of the dream-content severally, as though the dream were a conglomerate in which each fragment calls for special treatment. Incoherent and confused dreams are certainly those that have been responsible for the invention of the cipher method.[2]

[1] Artemidoros of Daldis, born probably in the beginning of the second century of our calendar, has furnished us with the most complete and careful elaboration of dream-interpretation as it existed in the Graeco-Roman world. As Gompertz has emphasized, he ascribed great importance to the consideration that dreams ought to be interpreted on the basis of observation and experience, and he drew a definite line between his own art and other methods, which he considered fraudulent. The principle of his art of interpretation is, according to Gompertz, identical with that of magic: *i.e.* the principle of association. The thing dreamed meant what it recalled to the memory—to the memory, of course, of the dream-interpreter! This fact—that the dream may remind the interpreter of various things, and every interpreter of different things—leads, of course, to uncontrollable arbitrariness and uncertainty. The technique which I am about to describe differs from that of the ancients in one essential point, namely, in that it imposes upon the dreamer himself the work of interpretation. Instead of taking into account whatever may occur to the dream-interpreter, it considers only what occurs to the dreamer in connection with the dream-element concerned. According to the recent records of the missionary, Tfinkdjit (*Anthropos*, 1913), it would seem that the modern dream-interpreters of the Orient likewise attribute much importance to the co-operation of the dreamer. Of the dream-interpreters among the Mesopotamian Arabs this writer relates as follows: *"Pour interpréter exactement un songe les oniromanciens les plus habiles s'informent de ceux qui les consultent de toutes les circonstances qu'ils regardent nécessaires pour la bonne explication. . . . En un mot, nos oniromanciens ne laissent aucune circonstance leur échapper et ne donnent l'interprétation désirée avant d'avoir parfaitement saisi et reçu toutes les interrogations désirables."* Among these questions one always finds demands for precise information in respect to near relatives (parents, wife, children) as well as the following formula: *habistine in hoc nocte copulam conjugalem ante vel post somnium?*—*"L'idée dominante dans l'interprétation des songes consiste à expliquer le rêve par son opposé."*

[2] Dr. Alfred Robitsek calls my attention to the fact that Oriental dream-books, of which ours are pitiful plagiarisms, commonly undertake the interpretation of dream-elements in accordance with the assonance and similarity of words. Since these relationships must be lost by translation into our language, the incomprehensibility of the equivalents in our popular "dream-books" is hereby explained. Information as to the extraordinary significance of puns and the play upon words in the old Oriental cultures may be found in the writings of Hugo Winckler. The finest example of a dream-interpretation which has come down to us from antiquity is based on a play upon words. Artemidoros relates the following (p. 225): "But it seems to me that Aristandros gave a most happy interpretation to Alexander of Macedon. When the latter held Tyros encompassed and in a state of siege, and was angry and depressed over the great waste of time, he dreamed that he saw a Satyr dancing on his shield. It happened that Aristandros was in the neighbourhood of Tyros, and in the escort of the king, who was waging war on the Syrians. By dividing the word Satyros into σὰ and τύϱος, he induced the king to become more aggressive in the siege. And thus

The worthlessness of both these popular methods of interpretation does not admit of discussion. As regards the scientific treatment of the subject, the symbolic method is limited in its application, and is not susceptible of a general exposition. In the cipher method everything depends upon whether the "key," the dream-book, is reliable, and for that all guarantees are lacking. So that one might be tempted to grant the contention of the philosophers and psychiatrists, and to dismiss the problem of dream-interpretation as altogether fanciful.[1]

I have, however, come to think differently. I have been forced to perceive that here, once more, we have one of those not infrequent cases where an ancient and stubbornly retained popular belief seems to have come nearer to the truth of the matter than the opinion of modern science. I must insist that the dream actually does possess a meaning, and that a scientific method of dream-interpretation is possible. I arrived at my knowledge of this method in the following manner:

For years I have been occupied with the resolution of certain psycho-pathological structures—hysterical phobias, obsessional ideas, and the like—with therapeutic intentions. I have been so occupied, in fact, ever since I heard the significant statement of Joseph Breuer, to the effect that in these structures, regarded as morbid symptoms, solution and treatment go hand in hand.[2] Where it has been possible to trace a pathological idea back to those elements in the psychic life of the patient to which it owed its origin, this idea has crumbled away, and the patient has been relieved of it. In view of the failure of our other therapeutic efforts, and in the face of the mysterious character of these pathological conditions, it seemed to me tempting, in spite of all the difficulties, to follow the method initiated by Breuer until a complete elucidation of the subject had been achieved. I shall have occasion elsewhere to give a detailed account of the form which the technique of this procedure has finally assumed, and of the results of my efforts. In the course of these psychoanalytic studies, I happened upon the question of dream-interpretation. My patients, after I had pledged them to inform me of all the ideas and thoughts which occurred to them in connection with a given theme, related their dreams, and thus taught me that a dream may be interpolated in the psychic con-

---

Alexander became master of the city." (Σὰ Τύρος = thine is Tyros.) The dream, indeed, is so intimately connected with verbal expression that Ferenczi justly remarks that every tongue has its own dream-language. A dream is, as a rule, not to be translated into other languages.

[1] After the completion of my manuscript, a paper by Stumpf came to my notice which agrees with my work in attempting to prove that the dream is full of meaning and capable of interpretation. But the interpretation is undertaken by means of an allegorizing symbolism, and there is no guarantee that the procedure is generally applicable.

[2] *Selected Papers on Hysteria and other Psychoneuroses.* Monograph series, Journ. Nerv. Mental Dis. Pub. Co.

catenation, which may be followed backwards from a pathological idea into the patient's memory. The next step was to treat the dream itself as a symptom, and to apply to it the method of interpretation which had been worked out for such symptoms.

For this a certain psychic preparation on the part of the patient is necessary. A twofold effort is made, to stimulate his attentiveness in respect of his psychic perceptions, and to eliminate the critical spirit in which he is ordinarily in the habit of viewing such thoughts as come to the surface. For the purpose of self-observation with concentrated attention it is advantageous that the patient should take up a restful position and close his eyes; he must be explicitly instructed to renounce all criticism of the thought-formations which he may perceive. He must also be told that the success of the psychoanalysis depends upon his noting and communicating everything that passes through his mind, and that he must not allow himself to suppress one idea because it seems to him unimportant or irrelevant to the subject, or another because it seems nonsensical. He must preserve an absolute impartiality in respect to his ideas; for if he is unsuccessful in finding the desired solution of the dream, the obsessional idea, or the like, it will be because he permits himself to be critical of them.

I have noticed in the course of my psychoanalytical work that the psychological state of a man in an attitude of reflection is entirely different from that of a man who is observing his psychic processes. In reflection there is a greater play of psychic activity than in the most attentive self-observation; this is shown even by the tense attitude and the wrinkled brow of the man in a state of reflection, as opposed to the mimic tranquillity of the man observing himself. In both cases there must be concentrated attention, but the reflective man makes use of his critical faculties, with the result that he rejects some of the thoughts which rise into consciousness after he has become aware of them, and abruptly interrupts others, so that he does not follow the lines of thought which they would otherwise open up for him; while in respect of yet other thoughts he is able to behave in such a manner that they do not become conscious at all —that is to say, they are suppressed before they are perceived. In self-observation, on the other hand, he has but one task—that of suppressing criticism; if he succeeds in doing this, an unlimited number of thoughts enter his consciousness which would otherwise have eluded his grasp. With the aid of the material thus obtained—material which is new to the self-observer—it is possible to achieve the interpretation of pathological ideas, and also that of dream-formations. As will be seen, the point is to induce a psychic state which is in some degree analogous, as regards the distribution of psychic energy (mobile attention), to the state of the mind before falling asleep—and also, of course, to the hypnotic state. On falling asleep the "undesired ideas" emerge, owing to the slackening of a certain arbitrary (and, of course, also critical) action, which is allowed to influence the trend of our ideas; we are accustomed to speak of fatigue as the reason of this slackening; the emerging undesired ideas are changed into visual and auditory images. In the condition which it utilized for the analysis of dreams and pathological ideas, this activity is purposely and deliberately renounced, and the psychic energy thus saved (or some part of it) is employed in attentively tracking the undesired thoughts which now come to the surface—thoughts which retain their identity as ideas (in which the condition differs from the state of falling asleep). *"Undesired ideas" are thus changed into "desired" ones.*

There are many people who do not seem to find it easy to adopt the required attitude toward the apparently "freely rising" ideas, and to renounce the criticism which is otherwise applied to them. The "undesired ideas" habitually evoke the most violent resistance, which seeks to prevent them from coming to the surface. But if we may credit our great poet-philosopher Friedrich Schiller, the essential condition of poetical creation includes a very similar attitude. In a certain passage in his correspondence with Körner (for the tracing of which we are indebted to Otto Rank), Schiller replies in the following words to a friend who complains of his lack of creative power: "The reason for your complaint lies, it seems to me, in the constraint which your intellect imposes upon your imagination. Here I will make an observation, and illustrate it by an allegory. Apparently it is not good—and indeed it hinders the creative work of the mind—if the intellect examines too closely the ideas already pouring in, as it were, at the gates. Regarded in isolation, an idea may be quite insignificant, and venturesome in the extreme, but it may acquire importance from an idea which follows it; perhaps, in a certain collocation with other ideas, which may seem equally absurd, it may be capable of furnishing a very serviceable link. The intellect cannot judge all these ideas unless it can retain them until it has considered them in connection with these other ideas. In the case of a creative mind, it seems to me, the intellect has withdrawn its watchers from the gates, and the ideas rush in pell-mell, and only then does it review and inspect the multitude. You worthy critics, or whatever you may call yourselves, are ashamed or afraid of the momentary and passing madness which is found in all real creators, the longer or shorter duration of which distinguishes the thinking artist from the dreamer. Hence your complaints of unfruitfulness, for you reject too soon and discriminate too severely" (letter of December 1, 1788).

And yet, such a withdrawal of the watchers from the gates of the intellect, as Schiller puts it, such a translation into the condition of uncritical self-observation, is by no means difficult.

Most of my patients accomplish it after my first instructions. I myself can do so very completely, if I assist the process by writing down the ideas that flash through my mind. The quantum of psychic energy by which the critical activity is thus reduced, and by which the intensity of self-observation may be increased, varies considerably according to the subject-matter upon which the attention is to be fixed.

The first step in the application of this procedure teaches us that one cannot make the dream as a whole the object of one's attention, but only the individual components of its content. If I ask a patient who is as yet unpractised: "What occurs to you in connection with this dream?" he is unable, as a rule, to fix upon anything in his psychic field of vision. I must first dissect the dream for him; then, in connection with each fragment, he gives me a number of ideas which may be described as the "thoughts behind" this part of the dream. In this first and important condition, then, the method of dream-interpretation which I employ diverges from the popular, historical and legendary method of interpretation by symbolism and approaches more nearly to the second or "cipher method." Like this, it is an interpretation in detail, not *en masse;* like this, it conceives the dream, from the outset, as something built up, as a conglomerate of psychic formations.

In the course of my psychoanalysis of neurotics I have already subjected perhaps more than a thousand dreams to interpretation, but I do not wish to use this material now as an introduction to the theory and technique of dream-interpretation. For quite apart from the fact that I should lay myself open to the objection that these are the dreams of neuropaths, so that the conclusions drawn from them would not apply to the dreams of healthy persons, there is another reason that impels me to reject them. The theme to which these dreams point is, of course, always the history of the malady that is responsible for the neurosis. Hence every dream would require a very long introduction, and an investigation of the nature and etiological conditions of the psychoneuroses, matters which are in themselves novel and exceedingly strange, and which would therefore distract attention from the dream-problem proper. My purpose is rather to prepare the way, by the solution of the dream-problem, for the solution of the more difficult problems of the psychology of the neuroses. But if I eliminate the dreams of neurotics, which constitute my principal material, I cannot be too fastidious in my treatment of the rest. Only those dreams are left which have been incidentally related to me by healthy persons of my acquaintance, or which I find given as examples in the literature of dream-life. Unfortunately, in all these dreams I am deprived of the analysis without which I cannot find the meaning of the dream. My mode of procedure is, of course, less easy than that of the popular cipher method, which translates the given dream-content by reference to an established key; I, on the contrary, hold that the same dream-content may conceal a different meaning in the case of different persons, or in different connections. I must, therefore, resort to my own dreams as a source of abundant and convenient material, furnished by a person who is more or less normal, and containing references to many incidents of everyday life. I shall certainly be confronted with doubts as to the trustworthiness of these "self-analyses," and it will be said that arbitrariness is by no means excluded in such analyses. In my own judgment, conditions are more likely to be favourable in self-observation than in the observation of others; in any case, it is permissible to investigate how much can be accomplished in the matter of dream-interpretation by means of self-analysis. There are other difficulties which must be overcome in my own inner self. One has a comprehensible aversion to exposing so many intimate details of one's own psychic life, and one does not feel secure against the misinterpretations of strangers. But one must be able to transcend such considerations. *"Tout psychologiste,"* writes Delbœuf, *"est obligé de faire l'aveu même de ses faiblesses s'il croît par là jeter du jour sur quelque problème obscur."* And I may assume for the reader that his initial interest in the indiscretions which I must commit will very soon give way to an exclusive engrossment in the psychological problems elucidated by them.[1]

I shall therefore select one of my own dreams for the purpose of elucidating my method of interpretation. Every such dream necessitates a preliminary statement; so that I must now beg the reader to make my interests his own for a time, and to become absorbed, with me, in the most trifling details of my life; for an interest in the hidden significance of dreams imperatively demands just such a transference.

PRELIMINARY STATEMENT

In the summer of 1895 I had treated psycho-analytically a young lady who was an intimate friend of mine and of my family. It will be understood that such complicated relations may excite manifold feelings in the physician, and especially the psychotherapist. The personal interest of the physician is greater, but his authority less. If he fails, his friendship with the patient's relatives is in danger of being undermined. In this case, however, the treatment ended in partial success; the patient was cured of her hysterical anxiety, but not of all her somatic symptoms. At that time I was not yet quite sure of the criteria which denote the final cure of an hysterical case, and I expected her to accept a solution which did not seem acceptable to her. In the midst of this disagreement we discontinued the treatment for the summer holidays. One day a younger

[1] However, I will not omit to mention, in qualification of the above statement, that I have practically never reported a complete interpretation of a dream of my own. And I was probably right not to trust too far to the reader's discretion.

colleague, one of my most intimate friends, who had visited the patient—Irma—and her family in their country residence, called upon me. I asked him how Irma was, and received the reply: "She is better, but not quite well." I realize that these words of my friend Otto's, or the tone of voice in which they were spoken, annoyed me. I thought I heard a reproach in the words, perhaps to the effect that I had promised the patient too much, and—rightly or wrongly—I attributed Otto's apparent "taking sides" against me to the influence of the patient's relatives, who, I assumed, had never approved of my treatment. This disagreeable impression, however, did not become clear to me, nor did I speak of it. That same evening I wrote the clinical history of Irma's case, in order to give it, as though to justify myself, to Dr. M., a mutual friend, who was at that time the leading personality in our circle. During the night (or rather in the early morning) I had the following dream, which I recorded immediately after waking:—[1]

Dream of July 23–24, 1895

A great hall—a number of guests, whom we are receiving—among them Irma, whom I immediately take aside, as though to answer her letter, and to reproach her for not yet accepting the "solution." I say to her: "If you still have pains, it is really only your own fault."—She answers: "If you only knew what pains I have now in the throat, stomach, and abdomen—I am choked by them." I am startled, and look at her. She looks pale and puffy. I think that after all I must be overlooking some organic affection. I take her to the window and look into her throat. She offers some resistance to this, like a woman who has a set of false teeth. I think, surely, she doesn't need them.—The mouth then opens wide, and I find a large white spot on the right, and elsewhere I see extensive grayish-white scabs adhering to curiously curled formations, which are evidently shaped like the turbinal bones of the nose.—I quickly call Dr. M., who repeats the examination and confirms it. . . . Dr. M. looks quite unlike his usual self; he is very pale, he limps, and his chin is clean-shaven. . . . Now my friend Otto, too, is standing beside her, and my friend Leopold percusses her covered chest, and says: "She has a dullness below, on the left," and also calls attention to an infiltrated portion of skin on the left shoulder (which I can feel, in spite of the dress). . . . M. says: "There's no doubt that it's an infection, but it doesn't matter; dysentery will follow and the poison will be eliminated." . . . We know, too, precisely how the infection originated. My friend Otto, not long ago, gave her, when she was feeling unwell, an injection of a preparation of propyl . . . propyls . . . propionic acid . . . trimethylamin (the formula of which I see before

[1] This is the first dream which I subjected to an exhaustive interpretation.

*me, printed in heavy type). . . . One doesn't give such injections so
rashly. . . . Probably, too, the syringe was not clean.*

This dream has an advantage over many others. It is at once obvious
to what events of the preceding day it is related, and of what subject it
treats. The preliminary statement explains these matters. The news of
Irma's health which I had received from Otto, and the clinical history,
which I was writing late into the night, had occupied my psychic activities even during sleep. Nevertheless, no one who had read the preliminary
report, and had knowledge of the content of the dream, could guess what
the dream signified. Nor do I myself know. I am puzzled by the morbid
symptoms of which Irma complains in the dream, for they are not the
symptoms for which I treated her. I smile at the nonsensical idea of an
injection of propionic acid, and at Dr. M.'s attempt at consolation.
Towards the end the dream seems more obscure and quicker in tempo than
at the beginning. In order to learn the significance of all these details I
resolve to undertake an exhaustive analysis.

ANALYSIS

The hall—a number of guests, whom we are receiving. We were living
that summer at *Bellevue,* an isolated house on one of the hills adjoining
the Kahlenberg. This house was originally built as a place of entertain-
ment, and therefore has unusually lofty, hall-like rooms. The dream was
dreamed in *Bellevue,* a few days before my wife's birthday. During the
day my wife had mentioned that she expected several friends, and among
them Irma, to come to us as guests for her birthday. My dream, then, an-
ticipates this situation: It is my wife's birthday, and we are receiving a
number of people, among them Irma, as guests in the large hall of *Bellevue.*

*I reproach Irma for not having accepted the "solution," I say, "If you
still have pains, it is really your own fault."* I might even have said this
while awake; I may have actually said it. At that time I was of the opinion
(recognized later to be incorrect) that my task was limited to informing
patients of the hidden meaning of their symptoms. Whether they then
accepted or did not accept the solution upon which success depended—
for that I was not responsible. I am grateful to this error, which, fortunately, has now been overcome, since it made life easier·for me at a
time when, with all my unavoidable ignorance, I was expected to effect
successful cures. But I note that in the speech which I make to Irma in
the dream I am above all anxious that I shall not be blamed for the pains
which she still suffers. If it is Irma's own fault, it cannot be mine. Should
the purpose of the dream be looked for in this quarter?

Irma's complaints—pains in the neck, abdomen, and stomach; she is choked by them. Pains in the stomach belonged to the symptom-complex of my patient, but they were not very prominent; she complained rather of qualms and a feeling of nausea. Pains in the neck and abdomen and constriction of the throat played hardly any part in her case. I wonder why I have decided upon this choice of symptoms in the dream; for the moment I cannot discover the reason.

She looks pale and puffy. My patient had always a rosy complexion. I suspect that here another person is being substituted for her.

I am startled at the idea that I may have overlooked some organic affection. This, as the reader will readily believe, is a constant fear with the specialist who sees neurotics almost exclusively, and who is accustomed to ascribe to hysteria so many manifestations which other physicians treat as organic. On the other hand, I am haunted by a faint doubt—I do not know whence it comes—whether my alarm is altogether honest. If Irma's pains are indeed of organic origin, it is not my duty to cure them. My treatment, of course, removes only hysterical pains. It seems to me, in fact, that I wish to find an error in the diagnosis; for then I could not be reproached with failure to effect a cure.

I take her to the window in order to look into her throat. She resists a little, like a woman who has false teeth. I think to myself, she does not need them. I had never had occasion to inspect Irma's oral cavity. The incident in the dream reminds me of an examination, made some time before, of a governess who at first produced an impression of youthful beauty, but who, upon opening her mouth, took certain measures to conceal her denture. Other memories of medical examinations, and of petty secrets revealed by them, to the embarrassment of both physician and patient, associate themselves with this case.—"She surely does not need them," is perhaps in the first place a compliment to Irma; but I suspect yet another meaning. In a careful analysis one is able to feel whether or not the *arrière-pensées* which are to be expected have all been exhausted. The way in which Irma stands at the window suddenly reminds me of another experience. Irma has an intimate woman friend of whom I think very highly. One evening, on paying her a visit, I found her at the window in the position reproduced in the dream, and her physician, the same Dr. M., declared that she had a diphtheritic membrane. The person of Dr. M. and the membrane return, indeed, in the course of the dream. Now it occurs to me that during the past few months I have had every reason to suppose that this lady too is hysterical. Yes, Irma herself betrayed the fact to me. But what do I know of her condition? Only the one thing, that like Irma in the dream she suffers from hysterical choking. Thus, in the dream I have replaced my patient by her friend. Now I remember that I have often played with the supposition that this lady, too, might ask me to relieve her of her symptoms. But even at the time I thought it improbable, since she is extremely reserved. She *resists,* as the dream shows. Another explanation might be that *she does not need it;* in fact, until now she has shown herself strong enough to master her condition without outside help. Now only a few features remain, which I can assign neither to Irma nor to her friend; pale, puffy, false teeth. The false teeth led me to the governess; I now feel inclined to be satisfied with bad teeth. Here another person, to whom these features may allude, occurs to me. She is not my patient, and I do not wish her to be my patient, for I have noticed that she is not at her ease with me, and I do not consider her a docile patient. She is generally pale, and once, when she had not felt particularly well, she was puffy.[1] I have thus compared my patient Irma with two others, who would likewise resist treatment. What is the meaning of the fact that I have exchanged her for her friend in the dream? Perhaps that I wish to exchange her; either her friend arouses in me stronger sympathies, or I have a higher regard for her intelligence. For I consider Irma foolish because she does not accept my solution. The other woman would be more sensible, and would thus be more likely to yield. *The mouth then opens readily;* she would tell more than Irma.[2]

What I see in the throat: a white spot and scabby turbinal bones. The white spot recalls diphtheria, and thus Irma's friend, but it also recalls the grave illness of my eldest daughter two years earlier, and all the anxiety of that unhappy time. The scab on the turbinal bones reminds me of my anxiety concerning my own health. At that time I frequently used cocaine in order to suppress distressing swellings in the nose, and I had heard a few days previously that a lady patient who did likewise had contracted an extensive necrosis of the nasal mucous membrane. In 1885 it was I who had recommended the use of cocaine, and I had been gravely reproached in consequence. A dear friend, who had died before the date of this dream, had hastened his end by the misuse of this remedy.

I quickly call Dr. M., who repeats the examination. This would simply correspond to the position which M. occupied among us. But the word "quickly" is striking enough to demand a special examination. It reminds me of a sad medical experience. By continually prescribing a drug (sulphonal), which at that time was still considered harmless, I was once responsible for a condition of acute poisoning in the case of a woman

---

[1] The complaint of pains in the abdomen, as yet unexplained, may also be referred to this third person. It is my own wife, of course, who is in question; the abdominal pains remind me of one of the occasions on which her shyness became evident to me. I must admit that I do not treat Irma and my wife very gallantly in this dream, but let it be said, in my defence, that I am measuring both of them against the ideal of the courageous and docile female patient.

[2] I suspect that the interpretation of this portion has not been carried far enough to follow every hidden meaning. If I were to continue the comparison of the three women, I should go far afield. Every dream has at least one point at which it is unfathomable; a central point, as it were, connecting it with the unknown.

patient, and hastily turned for assistance to my older and more experienced colleague. The fact that I really had this case in mind is confirmed by a subsidiary circumstance. The patient, who succumbed to the toxic effects of the drug, bore the same name as my eldest daughter. I had never thought of this until now; but now it seems to me almost like a retribution of fate—as though the substitution of persons had to be continued in another sense: this Matilda for that Matilda; an eye for an eye, a tooth for a tooth. It is as though I were seeking every opportunity to reproach myself for a lack of medical conscientiousness.

Dr. M. is pale; his chin is shaven, and he limps. Of this so much is correct, that his unhealthy appearance often arouses the concern of his friends. The other two characteristics must belong to another person. An elder brother living abroad occurs to me, for he, too, shaves his chin, and if I remember him rightly, the M. of the dream bears on the whole a certain resemblance to him. And some days previously the news arrived that he was limping on account of an arthritic affection of the hip. There must be some reason why I fuse the two persons into one in my dream. I remember that, in fact, I was on bad terms with both of them for similar reasons. Both had rejected a certain proposal which I had recently made them.

My friend Otto is now standing next to the patient, and my friend Leopold examines her and calls attention to a dulness low down on the left side. My friend Leopold also is a physician, and a relative of Otto's. Since the two practise the same speciality, fate has made them competitors, so that they are constantly being compared with one another. Both of them assisted me for years, while I was still directing a public clinic for neurotic children. There, scenes like that reproduced in my dream had often taken place. While I would be discussing the diagnosis of a case with Otto, Leopold would examine the child anew and make an unexpected contribution towards our decision. There was a difference of character between the two men like that between Inspector Brasig and his friend Karl. Otto was remarkably prompt and alert; Leopold was slow and thoughtful, but thorough. If I contrast Otto and the cautious Leopold in the dream I do so, apparently, in order to extol Leopold. The comparison is like that made above between the disobedient patient Irma and her friend, who was believed to be more sensible. I now become aware of one of the tracks along which the association of ideas in the dream proceeds: from the sick child to the children's clinic. Concerning the dulness low on the left side, I have the impression that it corresponds with a certain case of which all the details were similar, a case in which Leopold impressed me by his thoroughness. I thought vaguely, too, of something like a metastatic affection, but it might also be a reference to the patient whom I should have liked to have in Irma's place. For this lady, as far as I can gather, exhibited symptoms which imitated tuberculosis.

An infiltrated portion of skin on the left shoulder. I know at once that this is my own rheumatism of the shoulder, which I always feel if I lie awake long at night. The very phrasing of the dream sounds ambiguous: "Something which I can feel, as he does, in spite of the dress." "Feel on my own body" is intended. Further, it occurs to me how unusual the phrase "infiltrated portion of skin" sounds. We are accustomed to the phrase: "an infiltration of the upper posterior left"; this would refer to the lungs, and thus, once more, to tuberculosis.

In spite of the dress. This, to be sure, is only an interpolation. At the clinic the children were, of course, examined undressed; here we have some contrast to the manner in which adult female patients have to be examined. The story used to be told of an eminent physician that he always examined his patients through their clothes. The rest is obscure to me; I have, frankly, no inclination to follow the matter further.

Dr. M. says: "It's an infection, but it doesn't matter; dysentery will follow, and the poison will be eliminated." This, at first, seems to me ridiculous; nevertheless, like everything else, it must be carefully analysed; more closely observed it seems after all to have a sort of meaning. What I had found in the patient was a local diphtheritis. I remember the discussion about diphtheritis and diphtheria at the time of my daughter's illness. Diphtheria is the general infection which proceeds from local diphtheritis. Leopold demonstrates the existence of such a general infection by the dulness, which also suggests a metastatic focus. I believe, however, that just this kind of metastasis does not occur in the case of diphtheria. It reminds me rather of pyaemia.

It doesn't matter is a consolation. I believe it fits in as follows: The last part of the dream has yielded a content to the effect that the patient's sufferings are the result of a serious organic affection. I begin to suspect that by this I am only trying to shift the blame from myself. Psychic treatment cannot be held responsible for the continued presence of a diphtheritic affection. Now, indeed, I am distressed by the thought of having invented such a serious illness for Irma, for the sole purpose of exculpating myself. It seems so cruel. Accordingly, I need the assurance that the outcome will be benign, and it seems to me that I made a good choice when I put the words that consoled me into the mouth of Dr. M. But here I am placing myself in a position of superiority to the dream; a fact which needs explanation.

But why is this consolation so nonsensical?

Dysentery. Some sort of far-fetched theoretical notion that the toxins of disease might be eliminated through the intestines. Am I thereby trying to make fun of Dr. M.'s remarkable store of far-fetched explanations, his habit of conceiving curious pathological relations? Dysentery suggests something else. A few months ago I had in my care a young man who was suffering from remarkable intestinal troubles; a case which had been treated by other colleagues as one of "anaemia with malnutrition." I realized that it was a case of hysteria; I was unwilling to use my psychotherapy on him, and sent him off on a sea-voyage. Now a few days previously I had received a despairing letter from him; he wrote from Egypt, saying that he had had a fresh attack, which the doctor had declared to be dysentery. I suspect that the diagnosis is merely an error on the part of an ignorant colleague, who is allowing himself to be fooled by the hysteria; yet I cannot help reproaching myself for putting the invalid in a position where he might contract some organic affection of the bowels in addition to his hysteria. Furthermore, dysentery sounds not unlike diphtheria, a word which does not occur in the dream.

Yes, it must be the case that with the consoling prognosis, "Dysentery will develop, etc.," I am making fun of Dr. M., for I recollect that years ago he once jestingly told a very similar story of a colleague. He had been called in to consult with him in the case of a woman who was very seriously ill, and he felt obliged to confront his colleague, who seemed very hopeful, with the fact that he found albumen in the patient's urine. His colleague, however, did not allow this to worry him, but answered calmly: "*That does not matter,* my dear sir; the albumen will soon be excreted!" Thus I can no longer doubt that this part of the dream expresses derision for those of my colleagues who are ignorant of hysteria. And, as though in confirmation, the thought enters my mind: "Does Dr. M. know that the appearances in Irma's friend, his patient, which gave him reason to fear tuberculosis, are likewise due to hysteria? Has he recognized this hysteria, or has he allowed himself to be fooled?"

But what can be my motive in treating this friend so badly? That is simple enough: Dr. M. agrees with my solution as little as does Irma herself. Thus, in this dream I have already revenged myself on two persons: on Irma in the words, "If you still have pains, it is your own fault," and on Dr. M. in the wording of the nonsensical consolation which has been put into his mouth.

We know precisely how the infection originated. This precise knowledge in the dream is remarkable. Only a moment before this we did not yet know of the infection, since it was first demonstrated by Leopold.

My friend Otto gave her an·injection not long ago, when she was feeling unwell. Otto had actually related during his short visit to Irma's family that he had been called in to a neighbouring hotel in order to give an injection to someone who had been suddenly taken ill. Injections remind me once more of the unfortunate friend who poisoned himself with cocaine. I had recommended the remedy for internal use only during the withdrawal of morphia; but he immediately gave himself injections of cocaine.

With a preparation of propyl . . . propyls . . . propionic acid. How on earth did this occur to me? On the evening of the day after I had written the clinical history and dreamed about the case, my wife opened a bottle of liqueur labelled "Ananas," [1] which was a present from our friend Otto. He had, as a matter of fact, a habit of making presents on every possible occasion; I hope he will some day be cured of this by a wife. [2] This liqueur smelt so strongly of fusel oil that I refused to drink it. My wife suggested: "We will give the bottle to the servants," and I, more prudent, objected, with the philanthropic remark: "They shan't be poisoned either." The smell of fusel oil (amyl . . .) has now apparently awakened my memory of the whole series: propyl, methyl, etc., which furnished the preparation of propyl mentioned in the dream. Here, indeed, I have effected a substitution: I dreamt of propyl after smelling amyl; but substitutions of this kind are perhaps permissible, especially in organic chemistry.

Trimethylamin. In the dream I see the chemical formula of this substance—which at all events is evidence of a great effort on the part of my memory—and the formula is even printed in heavy type, as though to distinguish it from the context as something of particular importance. And where does trimethylamin, thus forced on my attention, lead me? To a conversation with another friend, who for years has been familiar with all my germinating ideas, and I with his. At that time he had just informed me of certain ideas concerning a sexual chemistry, and had mentioned, among others, that he thought he had found in trimethylamin one of the products of sexual metabolism. This substance thus leads me to sexuality, the factor to which I attribute the greatest significance in respect of the origin of these nervous affections which I am trying to cure. My patient Irma is a young widow; if I am required to excuse my failure to cure her, I shall perhaps do best to refer to this condition, which her admirers would be glad to terminate. But in what a singular fashion such a dream is fitted together! The friend who in my dream becomes my patient in Irma's place is likewise a young widow.

I surmise why it is that the formula of trimethylamin is so insistent in the dream. So many important things are centred about this one word: trimethylamin is an allusion, not merely to the all-important factor of sexuality, but also to a friend whose sympathy I remember with satisfaction whenever I feel isolated in my opinions. And this friend, who plays such a large part in my life: will he not appear yet again in the concatena-

[1] "Ananas," moreover, has a remarkable assonance with the family name of my patient Irma.
[2] In this the dream did not turn out to be prophetic. But in another sense it proved correct, for the "unsolved" stomach pains, for which I did not want to be blamed, were the forerunners of a serious illness, due to gall-stones.

tion of ideas peculiar to this dream? Of course; he has a special knowledge of the results of affections of the nose and the sinuses, and has revealed to science several highly remarkable relations between the turbinal bones and the female sexual organs. (The three curly formations in Irma's throat.) I got him to examine Irma, in order to determine whether her gastric pains were of nasal origin. But he himself suffers from suppurative rhinitis, which gives me concern, and to this perhaps there is an allusion in pyaemia, which hovers before me in the metastasis of the dream.

One doesn't give such injections so rashly. Here the reproach of rashness is hurled directly at my friend Otto. I believe I had some such thought in the afternoon, when he seemed to indicate, by word and look, that he had taken sides against me. It was, perhaps: "How easily he is influenced; how irresponsibly he pronounces judgment." Further, the above sentence points once more to my deceased friend, who so irresponsibly resorted to cocaine injections. As I have said, I had not intended that injections of the drug should be taken. I note that in reproaching Otto I once more touch upon the story of the unfortunate Matilda, which was the pretext for the same reproach against me. Here, obviously, I am collecting examples of my conscientiousness, and also of the reverse.

Probably too the syringe was not clean. Another reproach directed at Otto, but originating elsewhere. On the previous day I happened to meet the son of an old lady of eighty-two, to whom I am obliged to give two injections of morphia daily. At present she is in the country, and I have heard that she is suffering from phlebitis. I immediately thought that this might be a case of infiltration caused by a dirty syringe. It is my pride that in two years I have not given her a single infiltration; I am always careful, of course, to see that the syringe is perfectly clean. For I am conscientious. From the phlebitis I return to my wife, who once suffered from thrombosis during a period of pregnancy, and now three related situations come to the surface in my memory, involving my wife, Irma, and the dead Matilda, whose identity has apparently justified my putting these three persons in one another's places.

I have now completed the interpretation of the dream.[1] In the course of this interpretation I have taken great pains to avoid all those notions which must have been suggested by a comparison of the dream-content with the dream-thoughts hidden behind this content. Meanwhile the "meaning" of the dream has dawned upon me. I have noted an intention which is realized through the dream, and which must have been my motive in dreaming. The dream fulfils several wishes, which were awakened

[1] Even if I have not, as might be expected, accounted for everything that occurred to me in connection with the work of interpretation.

within me by the events of the previous evening (Otto's news, and the writing of the clinical history). For the result of the dream is, that it is not I who am to blame for the pain which Irma is still suffering, but that Otto is to blame for it. Now Otto has annoyed me by his remark about Irma's imperfect cure; the dream avenges me upon him, in that it turns the reproach upon himself. The dream acquits me of responsibility for Irma's condition, as it refers this condition to other causes (which do, indeed, furnish quite a number of explanations). The dream represents a certain state of affairs, such as I might wish to exist; *the content of the dream is thus the fulfilment of a wish; its motive is a wish.*

This much is apparent at first sight. But many other details of the dream become intelligible when regarded from the standpoint of wish-fulfilment. I take my revenge on Otto, not merely for too readily taking sides against me, in that I accuse him of careless medical treatment (the injection), but I revenge myself also for the bad liqueur which smells of fusel oil, and I find an expression in the dream which unites both these reproaches: the injection of a preparation of propyl. Still I am not satisfied, but continue to avenge myself by comparing him with his more reliable colleague. Thereby I seem to say: "I like him better than you." But Otto is not the only person who must be made to feel the weight of my anger. I take my revenge on the disobedient patient, by exchanging her for a more sensible and more docile one. Nor do I pass over Dr. M.'s contradiction; for I express, in an obvious allusion, my opinion of him: namely, that his attitude in this case is that of an ignoramus ("Dysentery will develop, etc."). Indeed, it seems as though I were appealing from him to someone better informed (my friend, who told me about trimethylamin), just as I have turned from Irma to her friend, and from Otto to Leopold. It is as though I were to say: Rid me of these three persons, replace them by three others of my own choice, and I shall be rid of the reproaches which I am not willing to admit that I deserve! In my dream the unreasonableness of these reproaches is demonstrated for me in the most elaborate manner. Irma's pains are not attributable to me, since she herself is to blame for them, in that she refuses to accept my solution. They do not concern me, for being as they are of an organic nature, they cannot possibly be cured by psychic treatment.—Irma's sufferings are satisfactorily explained by her widowhood (trimethylamin!); a state which I cannot alter.—Irma's illness has been caused by an incautious injection administered by Otto, an injection of an unsuitable drug, such as I should never have administered.—Irma's complaint is the result of an injection made with an unclean syringe, like the phlebitis of my old lady patient, whereas my injections have never caused any ill effects. I am aware that these explanations of Irma's illness, which unite in acquitting me, do not agree with one another; that they even exclude one another. The whole plea—for this dream is nothing else—recalls vividly the defence offered by a man who was accused by his neighbour of having returned a kettle in a damaged condition. In the first place, he said, he had returned the kettle undamaged; in the second place it already had holes in it when he borrowed it; and in the third place, he had never borrowed it at all. A complicated defence, but so much the better; if only one of these three lines of defence is recognized as valid, the man must be acquitted.

Still other themes play a part in the dream, and their relation to my non-responsibility for Irma's illness is not so apparent: my daughter's illness, and that of a patient with the same name; the harmfulness of cocaine; the affection of my patient, who was traveling in Egypt; concern about the health of my wife; my brother, and Dr. M.; my own physical troubles, and anxiety concerning my absent friend, who is suffering from suppurative rhinitis. But if I keep all these things in view, they combine into a single train of thought, which might be labelled: concern for the health of myself and others; professional conscientiousness. I recall a vaguely disagreeable feeling when Otto gave me the news of Irma's condition. Lastly, I am inclined, after the event, to find an expression of this fleeting sensation in the train of thoughts which forms part of the dream. It is as though Otto had said to me: "You do not take your medical duties seriously enough; you are not conscientious; you do not perform what you promise." Thereupon this train of thought placed itself at my service, in order that I might give proof of my extreme conscientiousness, of my intimate concern about the health of my relatives, friends and patients. Curiously enough, there are also some painful memories in this material, which confirm the blame attached to Otto rather than my own exculpation. The material is apparently impartial, but the connection between this broader material, on which the dream is based, and the more limited theme from which emerges the wish to be innocent of Irma's illness, is, nevertheless, unmistakable.

I do not wish to assert that I have entirely revealed the meaning of the dream, or that my interpretation is flawless.

I could still spend much time upon it; I could draw further explanations from it, and discuss further problems which it seems to propound. I can even perceive the points from which further mental associations might be traced; but such considerations as are always involved in every dream of one's own prevent me from interpreting it farther. Those who are over-ready to condemn such reserve should make the experiment of trying to be more straightforward. For the present I am content with the one fresh discovery which has just been made: If the method of dream-interpretation here indicated is followed, it will be found that dreams do really possess a meaning, and are by no means the expression of a disintegrated cerebral activity, as the writers on the subject would have us believe. *When the work of interpretation has been completed the dream can be recognized as a wish-fulfilment.*

III

THE DREAM AS WISH-FULFILMENT

WHEN, after passing through a narrow defile, one suddenly reaches a height beyond which the ways part and a rich prospect lies outspread in different directions, it is well to stop for a moment and consider whither one shall turn next. We are in somewhat the same position after we have mastered this first interpretation of a dream. We find ourselves standing in the light of a sudden discovery. The dream is not comparable to the irregular sounds of a musical instrument, which, instead of being played by the hand of a musician, is struck by some external force; the dream is not meaningless, not absurd, does not presuppose that one part of our store of ideas is dormant while another part begins to awake. It is a perfectly valid psychic phenomenon, actually a wish-fulfilment; it may be enrolled in the continuity of the intelligible psychic activities of the waking state; it is built up by a highly complicated intellectual activity. But at the very moment when we are about to rejoice in this discovery a host of problems besets us. If the dream, as this theory defines it, represents a fulfilled wish, what is the cause of the striking and unfamiliar manner in which this fulfilment is expressed? What transformation has occurred in our dream-thoughts before the manifest dream, as we remember it on waking, shapes itself out of them? How has this transformation taken place? Whence comes the material that is worked up into the dream? What causes many of the peculiarities which are to be observed in our dream-thoughts; for example, how is it that they are able to contradict one another? (see the analogy of the kettle, p. 667). Is the dream capable of teaching us something new concerning our internal psychic processes, and can its content correct opinions which we have held during the day? I suggest that for the present all these problems be laid aside, and that a single path be pursued. We have found that the dream represents a wish as fulfilled. Our next purpose should be to ascertain whether this is a general characteristic of dreams, or whether it is only the accidental content of the particular dream ("the dream about Irma's injection") with which we have begun our analysis; for even if we conclude that every dream has a meaning and psychic value, we must nevertheless allow for the possibility that this meaning may not be the same in every dream. The first dream which we have considered was the fulfilment of a wish; another may turn out to be the realization of an apprehension; a third may have a reflection as its content; a fourth may simply reproduce a reminiscence. Are there, then, dreams other than wish-dreams; or are there none but wish-dreams?

It is easy to show that the wish-fulfilment in dreams is often undisguised and easy to recognize, so that one may wonder why the language of dreams has not long since been understood. There is, for example, a dream which I can evoke as often as I please, experimentally, as it were. If, in the evening, I eat anchovies, olives, or other strongly salted foods, I am thirsty at night, and therefore I wake. The waking, however, is preceded by a dream, which has always the same content, namely, that I am drinking. I am drinking long draughts of water; it tastes as delicious as only a cool drink can taste when one's throat is parched; and then I wake, and find that I have an actual desire to drink. The cause of this dream is thirst, which I perceive when I wake. From this sensation arises the wish to drink, and the dream shows me this wish as fulfilled. It thereby serves a function, the nature of which I soon surmise. I sleep well, and am not accustomed to being waked by a bodily need. If I succeed in appeasing my thirst by means of the dream that I am drinking, I need not wake up in order to satisfy that thirst. It is thus a *dream of convenience*. The dream takes the place of action, as elsewhere in life. Unfortunately, the need of water to quench the thirst cannot be satisfied by a dream, as can my thirst for revenge upon Otto and Dr. M., but the intention is the same. Not long ago I had the same dream in a somewhat modified form. On this occasion I felt thirsty before going to bed, and emptied the glass of water which stood on the little chest beside my bed. Some hours later, during the night, my thirst returned, with the consequent discomfort. In order to obtain water, I should have had to get up and fetch the glass which stood on my wife's bed-table. I thus quite appropriately dreamt that my wife was giving me a drink from a vase; this vase was an Etruscan cinerary urn, which I had brought home from Italy, and had since given away. But the water in it tasted so salt (apparently on account of the ashes) that I was forced to wake. It may be observed how conveniently the dream is capable of arranging matters. Since the fulfilment of a wish is its only purpose, it may be perfectly egoistic. Love of comfort is really not compatible with consideration for others. The introduction of the cinerary urn is probably once again the fulfilment of a wish; I regret that I no longer possess this vase; it, like the glass of water at my wife's side, is inaccessible to me. The cinerary urn is appropriate also in connection with the sensation of an increasingly salty taste, which I know will compel me to wake.[1]

Such convenience-dreams came very frequently to me in my youth. Accustomed as I had always been to working until late at night, early waking was always a matter of difficulty. I used then to dream that I was out of bed and standing at the wash-stand. After a while I could no longer shut out the knowledge that I was not yet up; but in the meantime I had continued to sleep. The same sort of lethargy-dream was dreamed by a young colleague of mine, who appears to share my propensity for sleep. With him it assumed a particularly amusing form. The landlady with whom he was lodging in the neighbourhood of the hospital had strict orders to wake him every morning at a given hour, but she found it by no means easy to carry out his orders. One morning sleep was especially sweet to him. The woman called into his room: "Herr Pepi, get up; you've got to go to the hospital." Whereupon the sleeper dreamt of a room in the hospital, of a bed in which he was lying, and of a chart pinned over his head, which read as follows: "Pepi M., medical student, 22 years of age." He told himself in the dream: "If I am already at the hospital, I don't have to go there," turned over, and slept on. He had thus frankly admitted to himself his motive for dreaming.

Here is yet another dream of which the stimulus was active during sleep: One of my women patients, who had been obliged to undergo an unsuccessful operation on the jaw, was instructed by her physicians to wear by day and night a cooling apparatus on the affected cheek; but she was in the habit of throwing it off as soon as she had fallen asleep. One day I was asked to reprove her for doing so; she had again thrown the apparatus on the floor. The patient defended herself as follows: "This time I really couldn't help it; it was the result of a dream which I had during the night. In the dream I was in a box at the opera, and was taking a lively interest in the performance. But Herr Karl Meyer was lying in the sanatorium and complaining pitifully on account of pains in his jaw. I said to myself, 'Since I haven't the pains, I don't need the apparatus

[1] The facts relating to dreams of thirst were known also to Weygandt, who speaks of them as follows: "It is just this sensation of thirst which is registered most accurately of all; it always causes a representation of quenching the thirst. The manner in which the dream represents the act of quenching the thirst is manifold, and is specified in accordance with some recent recollection. A universal phenomenon noticeable here is the fact that the representation of quenching the thirst is immediately followed by disappointment in the inefficacy of the imagined refreshment." But he overlooks the universal character of the reaction of the dream to the stimulus. If other persons who are troubled by thirst at night awake without dreaming beforehand, this does not constitute an objection to my experiment, but characterizes them as persons who sleep less soundly. Cf. here *Isaiah xxix*. 8: "It shall even be as when an hungry man dreameth, and, behold, he eateth; but he awaketh, and his soul is empty: or as when a thirsty man dreameth, and, behold he drinketh; but he awaketh, and, behold, he is faint. . . ."

either'; that's why I threw it away." The dream of this poor sufferer reminds me of an expression which comes to our lips when we are in a disagreeable situation: "Well, I can imagine more amusing things!" The dream presents these "more amusing things!" Herr Karl Meyer, to whom the dreamer attributed her pains, was the most casual acquaintance of whom she could think.

It is quite as simple a matter to discover the wish-fulfilment in several other dreams which I have collected from healthy persons. A friend who was acquainted with my theory of dreams, and had explained it to his wife, said to me one day: "My wife asked me to tell you that she dreamt yesterday that she was having her menses. You will know what that means." Of course I know: if the young wife dreams that she is having her menses, the menses have stopped. I can well imagine that she would have liked to enjoy her freedom a little longer, before the discomforts of maternity began. It was a clever way of giving notice of her first pregnancy. Another friend writes that his wife had dreamt not long ago that she noticed milk-stains on the front of her blouse. This also is an indication of pregnancy, but not of the first one; the young mother hoped she would have more nourishment for the second child than she had for the first.

A young woman who for weeks had been cut off from all society because she was nursing a child who was suffering from an infectious disease dreamt, after the child had recovered, of a company of people in which Alphonse Daudet, Paul Bourget, Marcel Prévost and others were present; they were all very pleasant to her and amused her enormously. In her dream these different authors had the features which their portraits give them. M. Prévost, with whose portrait she is not familiar, looked like the man who had disinfected the sickroom the day before, the first outsider to enter it for a long time. Obviously the dream is to be translated thus: "It is about time now for something more entertaining than this eternal nursing."

Perhaps this collection will suffice to prove that frequently, and under the most complex conditions, dreams may be noted which can be understood only as wish-fulfilments, and which present their content without concealment. In most cases these are short and simple dreams, and they stand in pleasant contrast to the confused and overloaded dream-compositions which have almost exclusively attracted the attention of the writers on the subject. But it will repay us if we give some time to the examination of these simple dreams. The simplest dreams of all are, I suppose, to be expected in the case of children whose psychic activities are certainly less complicated than those of adults. Child psychology, in my opinion, is destined to render the same services to the psychology of adults as a study of the structure or development of the lower animals renders to the investigation of the structure of the higher orders of animals. Hitherto but few deliberate efforts have been made to make use of the psychology of the child for such a purpose.

The dreams of little children are often simple fulfilments of wishes, and for this reason are, as compared with the dreams of adults, by no means interesting. They present no problem to be solved, but they are invaluable as affording proof that the dream, in its inmost essence, is the fulfilment of a wish. I have been able to collect several examples of such dreams from the material furnished by my own children.

For two dreams, one that of a daughter of mine, at that time eight and a half years of age, and the other that of a boy of five and a quarter, I am indebted to an excursion to Hallstatt in the summer of 1896. I must first explain that we were living that summer on a hill near Aussee, from which, when the weather was fine, we enjoyed a splendid view of the Dachstein. With a telescope we could easily distinguish the Simony hut. The children often tried to see it through the telescope—I do not know with what success. Before the excursion I had told the children that Hallstatt lay at the foot of the Dachstein. They looked forward to the outing with the greatest delight. From Hallstatt we entered the valley of Eschern, which enchanted the children with its constantly changing scenery. One of them, however, the boy of five, gradually became discontented. As often as a mountain came into view, he would ask: "Is that the Dachstein?" whereupon I had to reply: "No, only a foot-hill." After this question had been repeated several times he fell quite silent, and did not wish to accompany us up the steps leading to the waterfall. I thought he was tired. But the next morning he came to me, perfectly happy, and said: "Last night I dreamt that we went to the Simony hut." I understood him now; he had expected, when I spoke of the Dachstein, that on our excursion to Hallstatt he would climb the mountain, and would see at close quarters the hut which had been so often mentioned when the telescope was used. When he learned that he was expected to content himself with foot-hills and a waterfall he was disappointed, and became discontented. But the dream compensated him for all this. I tried to learn some details of the dream; they were scanty. "You go up steps for six hours," as he had been told.

On this excursion the girl of eight and a half had likewise cherished wishes which had to be satisfied by a dream. We had taken with us to Hallstatt our neighbour's twelve-year-old boy; quite a polished little gentleman, who, it seemed to me, had already won the little woman's sympathies. Next morning she related the following dream: "Just think, I dreamt that Emil was one of the family, that he said 'papa' and 'mamma' to you, and slept at our house, in the big room, like one of the boys. Then mamma came into the room and threw a handful of big bars of chocolate, wrapped in blue and green paper, under our beds." The girl's brothers, who evidently had not inherited an understanding of dream-interpretation, declared, just as the writers we have quoted would have done: "That dream is nonsense." The girl defended at least one part of the dream, and from the standpoint of the theory of the neuroses it is interesting to learn which part it was that she defended: "That Emil was one of the family was nonsense, but that about the bars of chocolate wasn't." It was just this latter part that was obscure to me, until my wife furnished the explanation. On the way home from the railway-station the children had stopped in front of a slot-machine, and had wanted exactly such bars of chocolate, wrapped in paper with a metallic lustre, such as the machine, in their experience, provided. But the mother thought, and rightly so, that the day had brought them enough wish-fulfilments, and therefore left this wish to be satisfied in the dream. This little scene had escaped me. That portion of the dream which had been condemned by my daughter I understood without any difficulty. I myself had heard the well-behaved little guest enjoining the children, as they were walking ahead of us, to wait until 'papa' or 'mamma' had come up. For the little girl the dream turned this temporary relationship into a permanent adoption. Her affection could not as yet conceive of any other way of enjoying her friend's company permanently than the adoption pictured in her dream, which was suggested by her brothers. Why the bars of chocolate were thrown under the bed could not, of course, be explained without questioning the child.

From a friend I have learned of a dream very much like that of my little boy. It was dreamed by a little girl of eight. Her father, accompanied by several children, had started on a walk to Dornbach, with the intention of visiting the Rohrer hut, but had turned back, as it was growing late, promising the children to take them some other time. On the way back they passed a signpost which pointed to the Hameau. The children now asked him to take them to the Hameau, but once more, and for the same reason, they had to be content with the promise that they should go there some other day. Next morning the little girl went to her father and told him, with a satisfied air: "Papa, I dreamed last night that you were with us at the Rohrer hut, and on the Hameau." Thus, in the dream her impatience had anticipated the fulfilment of the promise made by her father.

Another dream, with which the picturesque beauty of the Aussee inspired my daughter, at that time three and a quarter years of age, is equally straightforward. The little girl had crossed the lake for the first time, and the trip had passed too quickly for her. She did not want to leave the boat at the landing, and cried bitterly. The next morning she told us: "Last night I was sailing on the lake." Let us hope that the duration of this dream-voyage was more satisfactory to her.

My eldest boy, at that time eight years of age, was already dreaming of the realization of his fancies. He had ridden in a chariot with Achilles, with Diomedes as charioteer. On the previous day he had shown a lively interest in a book on the myths of Greece which had been given to his elder sister.

If it can be admitted that the talking of children in their sleep belongs to the sphere of dreams, I can relate the following as one of the earliest dreams in my collection: My youngest daughter, at that time nineteen months old, vomited one morning, and was therefore kept without food all day. During the night she was heard to call excitedly in her sleep: "Anna F(r)eud, *st'awbewy, wild st'awbewy, om'lette, pap!*" She used her name in this way in order to express the act of appropriation; the menu presumably included everything that would seem to her a desirable meal; the fact that two varieties of strawberry appeared in it was a demonstration against the sanitary regulations of the household, and was based on the circumstance, which she had by no means overlooked, that the nurse had ascribed her indisposition to an over-plentiful consumption of strawberries; so in her dream she avenged herself for this opinion which met with her disapproval.[1]

When we call childhood happy because it does not yet know sexual desire, we must not forget what a fruitful source of disappointment and renunciation, and therefore of dream-stimulation, the other great vital impulse may be for the child.[2] Here is a second example. My nephew, twenty-two months of age, had been instructed to congratulate me on my birthday, and to give me a present of a small basket of cherries, which at that time of the year were scarce, being hardly in season. He seemed to find the task a difficult one, for he repeated again and again: "Cherries in it," and could not be induced to let the little basket go out of his hands. But he knew how to indemnify himself. He had, until then, been in the habit of telling his mother every morning that he had dreamt of the "white soldier," an officer of the guard in a white cloak, whom he had once admired in the street. On the day after the sacrifice on my birthday

[1] The dream afterwards accomplished the same purpose in the case of the child's grandmother, who is older than the child by about seventy years. After she had been forced to go hungry for a day on account of the restlessness of her floating kidney, she dreamed, being apparently translated into the happy years of her girlhood, that she had been "asked out," invited to lunch and dinner, and had at each meal been served with the most delicious titbits.

[2] A more searching investigation into the psychic life of the child teaches us, of course, that sexual motives, in infantile forms, play a very considerable part, which has been too long overlooked, in the psychic activity of the child. This permits us to doubt to some extent the happiness of the child, as imagined later by adults. Cf. *Three Contributions to the Theory of Sex.*

he woke up joyfully with the announcement, which could have referred only to a dream: *"He[r] man eaten all the cherries!"* [1]

What animals dream of I do not know. A proverb for which I am indebted to one of my pupils professes to tell us, for it asks the question: "What does the goose dream of?" and answers: "Of maize." [2] The whole theory that the dream is the fulfilment of a wish is contained in these two sentences. [3]

---

[1] It should be mentioned that young children often have more complex and obscure dreams, while, on the other hand, adults, in certain circumstances, often have dreams of a simple and infantile character. How rich in unsuspected content the dreams of children no more than four or five years of age may be is shown by the examples in my *Analyse der Phobie eines fünfjährigen Knaben (Jahrbuch von Bleuler-Freud,* vol. i, 1909), and Jung's "Experiences Concerning the Psychic Life of the Child," translated by Brill, *American Journal of Psychology,* April, 1910. For analytically interpreted dreams of children, see also von Hug-Hellmuth, Putnam, Raalte, Spielrein, and Tausk; others by Banchieri, Busemann, Doglia, and especially Wigam, who emphasizes the wish-fulfilling tendency of such dreams. On the other hand, it seems that dreams of an infantile type reappear with especial frequency in adults who are transferred into the midst of unfamiliar conditions. Thus Otto Nordenskjöld, in his book, *Antarctic* (1904, vol. i, p. 336), writes as follows of the crew who spent the winter with him: "Very characteristic of the trend of our inmost thoughts were our dreams, which were never more vivid and more numerous. Even those of our comrades with whom dreaming was formerly exceptional had long stories to tell in the morning, when we exchanged our experiences in the world of phantasy. They all had reference to that outside world which was now so far removed from us, but they often fitted into our immediate circumstances. An especially characteristic dream was that in which one of our comrades believed himself back at school, where the task was assigned to him of skinning miniature seals, which were manufactured especially for purposes of instruction. Eating and drinking constituted the pivot around which most of our dreams revolved. One of us, who was especially fond of going to big dinner-parties, was delighted if he could report in the morning 'that he had had a three-course dinner.' Another dreamed of tobacco, whole mountains of tobacco; yet another dreamed of a ship approaching on the open sea under full sail. Still another dream deserves to be mentioned: The postman brought the post and gave a long explanation of why it was so long delayed; he had delivered it at the wrong address, and only with great trouble was he able to get it back. To be sure, we were often occupied in our sleep with still more impossible things, but the lack of phantasy in almost all the dreams which I myself dreamed, or heard others relate, was quite striking. It would certainly have been of great psychological interest if all these dreams could have been recorded. But one can readily understand how we longed for sleep. That alone could afford us everything that we all most ardently desired." I will continue by a quotation from Du Prel (p. 231): "Mungo Park, nearly dying of thirst on one of his African expeditions, dreamed constantly of the well-watered valleys and meadows of his home. Similarly Trenck, tortured by hunger in the fortress of Magdeburg, saw himself surrounded by copious meals. And George Back, a member of Franklin's first expedition, when he was on the point of death by starvation, dreamed continually and invariably of plenteous meals."

[2] A Hungarian proverb cited by Ferenczi states more explicitly that "the pig dreams of acorns, the goose of maize." A Jewish proverb asks: "Of what does the hen dream?"—"Of millet" (*Sammlung jüd. Sprichw. u. Redensarten.,* edit. by Bernstein, 2nd ed., p. 116).

[3] I am far from wishing to assert that no previous writer has ever thought of tracing a dream to a wish. (Cf. the first passages of the next chapter.) Those interested in the subject will find that even in antiquity the physician Herophilos, who lived under the First Ptolemy, distinguished between three kinds of dreams: dreams sent by the

We now perceive that we should have reached our theory of the hidden meaning of dreams by the shortest route had we merely consulted the vernacular. Proverbial wisdom, it is true, often speaks contemptuously enough of dreams—it apparently seeks to justify the scientists when it says that "dreams are bubbles"; but in colloquial language the dream is predominantly the gracious fulfiller of wishes. "I should never have imagined that in my wildest dreams," we exclaim in delight if we find that the reality surpasses our expectations.

---

gods; natural dreams—those which come about whenever the soul creates for itself an image of that which is beneficial to it, and will come to pass; and mixed dreams— those which originate spontaneously from the juxtaposition of images, when we see that which we desire. From the examples collected by Scherner, J. Stärcke cites a dream which was described by the author himself as a wish-fulfilment (p. 239). Scherner says: "The phantasy immediately fulfills the dreamer's wish, simply because this existed vividly in the mind." This dream belongs to the "emotional dreams." Akin to it are dreams due to "masculine and feminine erotic longing," and to "irritable moods." As will readily be seen, Scherner does not ascribe to the wish any further significance for the dream than to any other psychic condition of the waking state; least of all does he insist on the connection between the wish and the essential nature of the dream.

DISTORTION IN DREAMS

IF I now declare that wish-fulfilment is the meaning of *every* dream, so that there cannot be any dreams other than wish-dreams, I know before-hand that I shall meet with the most emphatic contradiction. My critics will object: "The fact that there are dreams which are to be understood as fulfilments of wishes is not new, but has long since been recognized by such writers as Radestock, Volkelt, Purkinje, Griesinger and others.[1] That there *can* be no other dreams than those of wish-fulfilments is yet one more unjustified generalization; which, fortunately, can be easily refuted. Dreams which present the most painful content, and not the least trace of wish-fulfilment, occur frequently enough. The pessimistic philosopher, Eduard von Hartmann, is perhaps most completely opposed to the theory of wish-fulfilment. In his *Philosophy of the Unconscious*, Part II (Stereotyped German edition, s. 344), he says: 'As regards the dream, with it all the troubles of waking life pass over into the sleeping state; all save the one thing which may in some degree reconcile the cultured person with life—scientific and artistic enjoyment. . . .' But even less pessimistic observers have emphasized the fact that in our dreams pain and disgust are more frequent than pleasure (Scholz, p. 33; Volkelt, p. 80, *et al.*). Two ladies, Sarah Weed and Florence Hallam, have even worked out, on the basis of their dreams, a numerical value for the preponderance of distress and discomfort in dreams. They find that 58 per cent. of dreams are disagreeable, and only 28.6 per cent. positively pleasant. Besides those dreams that convey into our sleep the many painful emotions of life, there are also anxiety-dreams, in which this most terrible of all the painful emotions torments us until we wake. Now it is precisely by these anxiety-dreams that children are so often haunted (cf. Debacker on *Pavor nocturnus*); and yet it was in children that you found the wish-fulfilment dream in its most obvious form."

The anxiety-dream does really seem to preclude a generalization of the

---

[1] Already Plotinus, the neo-Platonist, said: "When desire bestirs itself, then comes phantasy, and presents to us, as it were, the object of desire" (Du Prel, p. 276).

thesis deduced from the examples given in the last chapter, that dreams are wish-fulfilments, and even to condemn it as an absurdity.

Nevertheless, it is not difficult to parry these apparently invincible objections. It is merely necessary to observe that our doctrine is not based upon the estimates of the obvious dream-content, but relates to the thought-content, which, in the course of interpretation, is found to lie behind the dream. Let us compare and contrast the *manifest* and the *latent dream-content*. It is true that there are dreams the manifest content of which is of the most painful nature. But has anyone ever tried to interpret these dreams—to discover their latent thought-content? If not, the two objections to our doctrine are no longer valid; for there is always the possibility that even our painful and terrifyng dreams may, upon interpretation, prove to be wish-fulfilments.[1]

In scientific research it is often advantageous, if the solution of one problem presents difficulties, to add to it a second problem; just as it is easier to crack two nuts together instead of separately. Thus, we are confronted not only with the problem: How can painful and terrifying dreams be the fulfilments of wishes? but we may add to this a second problem which arises from the foregoing discussion of the general problem of the dream: Why do not the dreams that show an indifferent content, and yet turn out to be wish-fulfilments, reveal their meaning without disguise? Take the exhaustively treated dream of Irma's injection: it is by no means of a painful character, and it may be recognized, upon interpretation, as a striking wish-fulfilment. But why is an interpretation necessary at all? Why does not the dream say directly what it means? As a matter of fact, the dream of Irma's injection does not at first produce the impression that it represents a wish of the dreamer's as fulfilled. The reader will not have received this impression, and even I myself was not aware of the fact until I had undertaken the analysis. If we call this peculiarity of dreams—namely, that they need elucidation—the phenomenon of distortion in dreams, a second question then arises: What is the origin of this distortion in dreams?

If one's first thoughts on this subject were consulted several possible

[1] It is quite incredible with what obstinacy readers and critics have excluded this consideration and disregarded the fundamental differentiation between the manifest and the latent dream-content. Nothing in the literature of the subject approaches so closely to my own conception of dreams as a passage in J. Sully's essay: *Dreams as a Revelation* (and it is not because I do not think it valuable that I allude to it here for the first time). *"It would seem then, after all, that dreams are not the utter nonsense they have been said to be by such authorities as Chaucer, Shakespeare, and Milton. The chaotic aggregations of our night-fancy have a significance and communicate new knowledge. Like some letter in cipher, the dream-inscription when scrutinized closely loses its first look of balderdash and takes on the aspect of a serious, intelligible message. Or, to vary the figure slightly, we may say that, like some palimpsest the dream discloses beneath its worthless surface-characters traces of an old and precious communication"* (p. 364).

solutions might suggest themselves: for example, that during sleep one is incapable of finding an adequate expression for one's dream-thoughts. The analysis of certain dreams, however, compels us to offer another explanation. I shall demonstrate this by means of a second dream of my own, which again involves numerous indiscretions, but which compensates for this personal sacrifice by affording a thorough elucidation of the problem.

Preliminary Statement.—In the spring of 1897 I learnt that two professors of our university had proposed me for the title of *Professor Extraordinarius* (assistant professor). The news came as a surprise to me, and pleased me considerably as an expression of appreciation on the part of two eminent men which could not be explained by personal interest. But I told myself immediately that I must not expect anything to come of their proposal. For some years past the Ministry had disregarded such proposals, and several colleagues of mine, who were my seniors, and at least my equals in desert, had been waiting in vain all this time for the appointment. I had no reason to suppose that I should fare any better. I resolved, therefore, to resign myself to disappointment. I am not, so far as I know, ambitious, and I was following my profession with gratifying success even without the recommendation of a professorial title. Whether I considered the grapes to be sweet or sour did not matter, since they undoubtedly hung too high for me.

One evening a friend of mine called to see me; one of those colleagues whose fate I had regarded as a warning. As he had long been a candidate for promotion to the professorate (which in our society makes the doctor a demigod to his patients), and as he was less resigned than I, he was accustomed from time to time to remind the authorities of his claims in the hope of advancing his interests. It was after one of these visits that he called on me. He said that this time he had driven the exalted gentleman into a corner, and had asked him frankly whether considerations of religious denomination were not really responsible for the postponement of his appointment. The answer was: His Excellency had to admit that in the present state of public opinion he was not in a position, etc. "Now at least I know where I stand," my friend concluded his narrative, which told me nothing new, but which was calculated to confirm me in my resignation. For the same denominational considerations would apply to my own case.

On the morning after my friend's visit I had the following dream, which was notable also on account of its form. It consisted of two thoughts and two images, so that a thought and an image emerged alternately. But here I shall record only the first half of the dream, since the second half has no relation to the purpose for which I cite the dream.

I. *My friend R. is my uncle—I have a great affection for him.*

II. *I see before me his face, somewhat altered. It seems to be elongated; a yellow beard, which surrounds it, is seen with peculiar distinctness.*

Then follow the other two portions of the dream, again a thought and an image, which I omit.

The interpretation of this dream was arrived at in the following manner:

When I recollected the dream in the course of the morning, I laughed outright and said, "The dream is nonsense." But I could not get it out of my mind, and I was pursued by it all day, until at last, in the evening, I reproached myself in these words: "If in the course of a dream-interpretation one of your patients could find nothing better to say than 'That is nonsense,' you would reprove him, and you would suspect that behind the dream there was hidden some disagreeable affair, the exposure of which he wanted to spare himself. Apply the same thing to your own case; your opinion that the dream is nonsense probably signifies merely an inner resistance to its interpretation. Don't let yourself be put off." I then proceeded with the interpretation.

"R. is my uncle." What can that mean? I had only one uncle, my uncle Joseph.[1] His story, to be sure, was a sad one. Once, more than thirty years ago, hoping to make money, he allowed himself to be involved in transactions of a kind which the law punishes severely, and paid the penalty. My father, whose hair turned grey with grief within a few days, used always to say that uncle Joseph had never been a bad man, but, after all, he was a simpleton. If, then, my friend R. is my uncle Joseph, that is equivalent to saying: R. is a simpleton." Hardly credible, and very disagreeable! But there is the face that I saw in the dream, with its elongated features and its yellow beard. My uncle actually had such a face—long, and framed in a handsome yellow beard. My friend R. was extremely swarthy, but when black-haired people begin to grow grey they pay for the glory of their youth. Their black beards undergo an unpleasant change of colour, hair by hair; first they turn a reddish brown, then a yellowish brown, and then definitely grey. My friend R.'s beard is now in this stage; so, for that matter, is my own, a fact which I note with regret. The face that I see in my dream is at once that of my friend R. and that of my uncle. It is like one of those composite photographs of Galton's; in order to emphasize family resemblances Galton had several faces photographed on the same

---

[1] It is astonishing to see how my memory here restricts itself—in the waking state! —for the purposes of analysis. I have known five of my uncles and I loved and honoured one of them. But at the moment when I overcame my resistance to the interpretation of the dream, I said to myself: "I have only one uncle, the one who is intended in the dream."

plate. No doubt is now possible; it is really my opinion that my friend R. is a simpleton—like my uncle Joseph.

I have still no idea for what purpose I have worked out this relationship. It is certainly one to which I must unreservedly object. Yet it is not very profound, for my uncle was a criminal, and my friend R. is not, except in so far as he was once fined for knocking down an apprentice with his bicycle. Can I be thinking of this offence? That would make the comparison ridiculous. Here I recollect another conversation, which I had some days ago with another colleague, N.; as a matter of fact, on the same subject. I met N. in the street; he, too, has been nominated for a professorship, and having heard that I had been similarly honoured he congratulated me. I refused his congratulations, saying: "You are the last man to jest about the matter, for you know from your own experience what the nomination is worth." Thereupon he said, though probably not in earnest: "You can't be sure of that. There is a special objection in my case. Don't you know that a woman once brought a criminal accusation against me? I need hardly assure you that the matter was put right. It was a mean attempt at blackmail, and it was all I could do to save the plaintiff from punishment. But it may be that the affair is remembered against me at the Ministry. You, on the other hand, are above reproach." Here, then, I have the criminal, and at the same time the interpretation and tendency of my dream. My uncle Joseph represents both of my colleagues who have not been appointed to the professorship—the one as a simpleton, the other as a criminal. Now, too, I know for what purpose I need this representation. If denominational considerations are a determining factor in the postponement of my two friends' appointment, then my own appointment is likewise in jeopardy. But if I can refer the rejection of my two friends to other causes, which do not apply to my own case, my hopes are unaffected. This is the procedure followed by my dream: it makes the one friend, R., a simpleton, and the other, N., a criminal. But since I am neither one nor the other, there is nothing in common between us. I have a right to enjoy my appointment to the title of professor, and have avoided the distressing application to my own case of the information which the official gave to my friend R.

I must pursue the interpretation of this dream still farther; for I have a feeling that it is not yet satisfactorily elucidated. I still feel disquieted by the ease with which I have degraded two respected colleagues in order to clear my own way to the professorship. My dissatisfaction with this procedure has, of course, been mitigated since I have learned to estimate the testimony of dreams at its true value. I should contradict anyone who suggested that I really considered R. a simpleton, or that I did not believe N.'s account of the blackmailing incident. And of course I do not believe that Irma has been made seriously ill by an injection of a preparation of propyl administered by Otto. Here, as before, what the dream expresses is only my *wish that things might be so*. The statement in which my wish is realized sounds less absurd in the second dream than in the first; it is here made with a skilful use of actual points of support in establishing something like a plausible slander, one of which one could say that "there is something in it." For at that time my friend R. had to contend with the adverse vote of a university professor of his own department, and my friend N. had himself, all unsuspectingly, provided me with material for the calumny. Nevertheless, I repeat, it still seems to me that the dream requires further elucidation.

I remember now that the dream contained yet another portion which has hitherto been ignored by the interpretation. After it occurred to me that my friend R. was my uncle, I felt in the dream a great affection for him. To whom is this feeling directed? For my uncle Joseph, of course, I have never had any feelings of affection. R. has for many years been a dearly loved friend, but if I were to go to him and express my affection for him in terms approaching the degree of affection which I felt in the dream, he would undoubtedly be surprised. My affection, if it was for him, seems false and exaggerated, as does my judgment of his intellectual qualities, which I expressed by merging his personality in that of my uncle; but exaggerated in the opposite direction. Now, however, a new state of affairs dawns upon me. The affection in the dream does not belong to the latent content, to the thoughts behind the dream; it stands in opposition to this content; it is calculated to conceal the knowledge conveyed by the interpretation. Probably this is precisely its function. I remember with what reluctance I undertook the interpretation, how long I tried to postpone it, and how I declared the dream to be sheer nonsense. I know from my psychoanalytic practice how such a condemnation is to be interpreted. It has no informative value, but merely expresses an affect. If my little daughter does not like an apple which is offered her, she asserts that the apple is bitter, without even tasting it. If my patients behave thus, I know that we are dealing with an idea which they are trying to *repress*. The same thing applies to my dream. I do not want to interpret it because there is something in the interpretation to which I object. After the interpretation of the dream is completed, I discover what it was to which I objected; it was the assertion that R. is a simpleton. I can refer the affection which I feel for R. not to the latent dream-thoughts, but rather to this unwillingness of mine. If my dream, as compared with its latent content, is disguised at this point, and actually misrepresents things by producing their opposites, then the manifest affection in the dream serves the purpose of the misrepresentation; in other words, the distortion is here shown to be intentional—it is a means of *disguise*. My dream-thoughts of R. are derogatory, and so that I may not become aware of this the very opposite of defamation—a tender affection for him—enters into the dream.

This discovery may prove to be generally valid. As the examples in Chapter III have demonstrated, there are, of course, dreams which are undisguised wish-fulfilments. Wherever a wish-fulfilment is unrecognizable and disguised there must be present a tendency to defend oneself against this wish, and in consequence of this defence the wish is unable to express itself save in a distorted form. I will try to find a parallel in social life to this occurrence in the inner psychic life. Where in social life can a similar misrepresentation be found? Only where two persons are concerned one of whom possesses a certain power while the other has to act with a certain consideration on account of this power. The second person will then distort his psychic actions; or, as we say, he will *mask* himself. The politeness which I practise every day is largely a disguise of this kind; if I interpret my dreams for the benefit of my readers, I am forced to make misrepresentations of this kind. The poet even complains of the necessity of such misrepresentation: *Das Beste, was du wissen kannst, darfst du den Buben doch nicht sagen:* "The best that thou canst know thou mayst not tell to boys."

The political writer who has unpleasant truths to tell to those in power finds himself in a like position. If he tells everything without reserve, the Government will suppress them—retrospectively in the case of a verbal expression of opinion, preventively if they are to be published in the Press. The writer stands in fear of the censorship; he therefore moderates and disguises the expression of his opinions. He finds himself compelled, in accordance with the sensibilities of the censor, either to refrain altogether from certain forms of attack, or to express himself in allusions instead of by direct assertions; or he must conceal his objectionable statement in an apparently innocent disguise. He may, for instance, tell of a contretempt between two Chinese mandarins, while he really has in mind the officials of his own country. The stricter the domination of the censorship, the more thorough becomes the disguise, and, often enough, the more ingenious the means employed to put the reader on the track of the actual meaning.

The detailed correspondence between the phenomena of censorship and the phenomena of dream-distortion justifies us in presupposing similar conditions for both. We should then assume that in every human being there exist, as the primary cause of dream-formation, two psychic forces (tendencies or systems), one of which forms the wish expressed by the dream, while the other exercises a censorship over this dream-wish, thereby enforcing on it a distortion. The question is, what is the nature of the authority of this second agency by virtue of which it is able to exercise its censorship? If we remember that the latent dream-thoughts are not conscious before analysis, but that the manifest dream-content emerging from them is consciously remembered, it is not a far-fetched assumption that admittance to the consciousness is the prerogative of the second agency. Nothing can reach the consciousness from the first system which has not previously passed the second instance; and the second instance lets nothing pass without exercising its rights, and forcing such modifications as are pleasing to itself upon the candidates for admission to consciousness. Here we arrive at a very definite conception of the "essence" of consciousness; for us the state of becoming conscious is a special psychic act, different from and independent of the process of becoming fixed or represented, and consciousness appears to us as a sensory organ which perceives a content proceeding from another source. It may be shown that psychopathology simply cannot dispense with these fundamental assumptions. But we shall reserve for another time a more exhaustive examination of the subject.

If I bear in mind the notion of the two psychic instances and their relation to the consciousness, I find in the sphere of politics a perfectly appropriate analogy to the extraordinary affection which I feel for my friend R., who is so disparaged in the dream-interpretation. I refer to the political life of a State in which the ruler, jealous of his rights, and an active public opinion are in mutual conflict. The people, protesting against the actions of an unpopular official, demand his dismissal. The autocrat, on the other hand, in order to show his contempt for the popular will, may then deliberately confer upon the official some exceptional distinction which otherwise would not have been conferred. Similarly, my second instance, controlling the access to my consciousness, distinguishes my friend R. with a rush of extraordinary affection, because the wish-tendencies of the first system, in view of a particular interest on which they are just then intent, would like to disparage him as a simpleton.[1]

We may now perhaps begin to suspect that dream-interpretation is capable of yielding information concerning the structure of our psychic apparatus which we have hitherto vainly expected from philosophy. We shall not, however, follow up this trail, but shall return to our original

[1] Such hypocritical dreams are not rare, either with me or with others. While I have been working at a certain scientific problem I have been visited for several nights, at quite short intervals, by a somewhat confusing dream which has as its content a reconciliation with a friend dropped long ago. After three or four attempts I finally succeeded in grasping the meaning of this dream. It was in the nature of an encouragement to give up the remnant of consideration still surviving for the person in question, to make myself quite free from him, but it hypocritically disguised itself in its antithesis. I have recorded a "hypocritical Oedipus dream" in which the hostile feelings and death-wishes of the dream-thoughts were replaced by manifest tenderness ("Typisches Beispiel eines verkappten Oedipusträumes," *Zentralblatt für Psychoanalyse*, Bd. i, Heft i-ii, 1910). Another class of hypocritical dreams will be recorded in another place (see Chap. vi, *The Dream-Work*).

problem as soon as we have elucidated the problem of dream-distortion. The question arose, how dreams with a disagreeable content can be analysed as wish-fulfilments. We see now that this is possible where a dream-distortion has occurred, when the disagreeable content serves only to disguise the thing wished for. With regard to our assumptions respecting the two psychic instances, we can now also say that disagreeable dreams contain, as a matter of fact, something which is disagreeable to the second instance, but which at the same time fulfils a wish of the first instance. They are wish-dreams in so far as every dream emanates from the first instance, while the second instance behaves towards the dream only in a defensive, not in a constructive manner.[1] Were we to limit ourselves to a consideration of what the second instance contributes to the dream we should never understand the dream, and all the problems which the writers on the subject have discovered in the dream would have to remain unsolved.

That the dream actually has a secret meaning, which proves to be a wish-fulfilment, must be proved afresh in every case by analysis. I will therefore select a few dreams which have painful contents, and endeavour to analyse them. Some of them are dreams of hysterical subjects, which therefore call for a long preliminary statement, and in some passages an examination of the psychic processes occurring in hysteria. This, though it will complicate the presentation, is unavoidable.

When I treat a psychoneurotic patient analytically, his dreams regularly, as I have said, become a theme of our conversations. I must therefore give him all the psychological explanations with whose aid I myself have succeeded in understanding his symptoms. And here I encounter unsparing criticism, which is perhaps no less shrewd than that which I have to expect from my colleagues. With perfect uniformity my patients contradict the doctrine that dreams are the fulfilments of wishes. Here are several examples of the sort of dream-material which is adduced in refutation of my theory.

"You are always saying that a dream is a wish fulfilled," begins an intelligent lady patient. "Now I shall tell you a dream in which the content is quite the opposite, in which a wish of mine is not fulfilled. How do you reconcile that with your theory? The dream was as follows: *I want to give a supper, but I have nothing available except some smoked salmon. I think I will go shopping, but I remember that it is Sunday afternoon, when all the shops are closed. I then try to ring up a few caterers, but the telephone is out of order. Accordingly I have to renounce my desire to give a supper.*"

I reply, of course, that only the analysis can decide the meaning of this

[1] Later on we shall become acquainted with cases in which, on the contrary, the dream expresses a wish of this second instance.

dream, although I admit that at first sight it seems sensible and coherent and looks like the opposite of a wish-fulfilment. "But what occurrence gave rise to this dream?" I ask. "You know that the stimulus of a dream always lies among the experiences of the preceding day."

Analysis.—The patient's husband, an honest and capable meat sales-man, had told her the day before that he was growing too fat, and that he meant to undergo treatment for obesity. He would rise early, take physi-cal exercise, keep to a strict diet, and above all accept no more invitations to supper.—She proceeds jestingly to relate how her husband, at a *table d'hôte*, had made the acquaintance of an artist, who insisted upon paint-ing his portrait, because he, the painter, had never seen such an expressive head. But her husband had answered in his downright fashion, that while he was much obliged, he would rather not be painted; and he was quite convinced that a bit of a pretty young girl's posterior would please the artist better than his whole face.[1]—She is very much in love with her hus-band, and teases him a good deal. She has asked him not to give her any caviar. What can that mean?

As a matter of fact, she had wanted for a long time to eat a caviare sandwich every morning, but had grudged the expense. Of course she could get the caviar from her husband at once if she asked for it. But she has, on the contrary, begged him not to give her any caviar, so that she might tease him about it a little longer.

(To me this explanation seems thin. Unconfessed motives are wont to conceal themselves behind just such unsatisfying explanations. We are reminded of the subjects hypnotized by Bernheim, who carried out a post-hypnotic order, and who, on being questioned as to their motives, instead of answering: "I do not know why I did that," had to invent a reason that was obviously inadequate. There is probably something similar to this in the case of my patient's caviar. I see that in waking life she is compelled to invent an unfulfilled wish. Her dream also shows her the non-fulfilment of her wish. But why does she need an unfulfilled wish?)

The ideas elicited so far are insufficient for the interpretation of the dream. I press for more. After a short pause, which corresponds to the overcoming of a resistance, she reports that the day before she had paid a visit to a friend of whom she is really jealous because her husband is always praising this lady so highly. Fortunately this friend is very thin and lanky, and her husband likes full figures. Now of what did this thin friend speak? Of course, of her wish to become rather plumper. She also asked my patient: "When are you going to invite us again? You always have such good food."

[1] To sit for the painter.
Goethe: "And if he has no backside,
How can the nobleman sit?"

Now the meaning of the dream is clear. I am able to tell the patient: "It is just as though you had thought at the moment of her asking you that: 'Of course, I'm to invite you so that you can eat at my house and get fat and become still more pleasing to my husband! I would rather give no more suppers!' The dream then tells you that you cannot give a supper, thereby fulfilling your wish not to contribute anything to the rounding out of your friend's figure. Your husband's resolution to accept no more invitations to supper in order that he may grow thin teaches you that one grows fat on food eaten at other people's tables." Nothing is lacking now but some sort of coincidence which will confirm the solution. The smoked salmon in the dream has not yet been traced.—"How did you come to think of salmon in your dream?"—"Smoked salmon is my friend's favorite dish," she replied. It happens that I know the lady, and am able to affirm that she grudges herself salmon just as my patient grudges herself caviar.

This dream admits of yet another and more exact interpretation—one which is actually necessitated only by a subsidiary circumstance. The two interpretations do not contradict one another, but rather dovetail into one another, and furnish an excellent example of the usual ambiguity of dreams, as of all other psychopathological formations. We have heard that at the time of her dream of a denied wish the patient was impelled to deny herself a real wish (the wish to eat caviar sandwiches). Her friend, too, had expressed a wish, namely, to get fatter, and it would not surprise us if our patient had dreamt that this wish of her friend's—the wish to increase in weight—was not to be fulfilled. Instead of this, however, she dreamt that one of her own wishes was not fulfilled. The dream becomes capable of a new interpretation if in the dream she does not mean herself, but her friend, if she has put herself in the place of her friend, or, as we may say, has *identified* herself with her friend.

I think she has actually done this, and as a sign of this identification she has created for herself in real life an unfulfilled wish. But what is the meaning of this hysterical identification? To elucidate this a more exhaustive exposition is necessary. Identification is a highly important motive in the mechanism of hysterical symptoms; by this means patients are enabled to express in their symptoms not merely their own experiences, but the experiences of quite a number of other persons; they can suffer, as it were, for a whole mass of people, and fill all the parts of a drama with their own personalities. It will here be objected that this is the well-known hysterical imitation, the ability of hysterical subjects to imitate all the symptoms which impress them when they occur in others, as though pity were aroused to the point of reproduction. This, however, only indicates the path which the psychic process follows in hysterical imitation. But the path itself and the psychic act which follows this path are two different matters. The act itself is slightly more complicated than we are prone to believe the imitation of the hysterical to be; it corresponds to an unconscious end-process, as an example will show. The physician who has, in the same ward with other patients, a female patient suffering from a particular kind of twitching, is not surprised if one morning he learns that this peculiar hysterical affection has found imitators. He merely tells himself: The others have seen her, and have imitated her; this is psychic infection.—Yes, but psychic infection occurs somewhat in the following manner: As a rule, patients know more about one another than the physician knows about any one of them, and they are concerned about one another when the doctor's visit is over. One of them has an attack to-day: at once it is known to the rest that a letter from home, a recrudescence of lovesickness, or the like, is the cause. Their sympathy is aroused, and although it does not emerge into consciousness they form the following conclusion: "If it is possible to suffer such an attack from such a cause, I too may suffer this sort of an attack, for I have the same occasion for it." If this were a conclusion capable of becoming conscious, it would perhaps express itself in *dread* of suffering a like attack; but it is formed in another psychic region, and consequently ends in the realization of the dreaded symptoms. Thus identification is not mere imitation, but an assimilation based upon the same etiological claim; it expresses a "just like," and refers to some common condition which has remained in the unconscious.

In hysteria identification is most frequently employed to express a sexual community. The hysterical woman identifies herself by her symptoms most readily—though not exclusively—with persons with whom she has had sexual relations, or who have had sexual intercourse with the same persons as herself. Language takes cognizance of this tendency: two lovers are said to be "one." In hysterical phantasy, as well as in dreams, identification may ensue if one simply thinks of sexual relations; they need not necessarily become actual. The patient is merely following the rules of the hysterical processes of thought when she expresses her jealousy of her friend (which, for that matter, she herself admits to be unjustified) by putting herself in her friend's place in her dream, and identifying herself with her by fabricating a symptom (the denied wish). One might further elucidate the process by saying: In the dream she puts herself in the place of her friend, because her friend has taken her own place in relation to her husband, and because she would like to take her friend's place in her husband's esteem.[1]

---

[1] I myself regret the inclusion of such passages from the psychopathology of hysteria, which, because of their fragmentary presentation, and because they are torn out of their context, cannot prove to be very illuminating. If these passages are capable of throwing any light upon the intimate relations between dreams and the psychoneuroses, they have served the intention with which I have included them.

The contradiction of my theory of dreams on the part of another female patient, the most intelligent of all my dreamers, was solved in a simpler fashion, though still in accordance with the principle that the non-fulfilment of one wish signified the fulfillment of another. I had one day explained to her that a dream is a wish-fulfilment. On the following day she related a dream to the effect that she was travelling with her mother-in-law to the place in which they were both to spend the summer. Now I knew that she had violently protested against spending the summer in the neighbourhood of her mother-in-law. I also knew that she had fortunately been able to avoid doing so, since she had recently succeeded in renting a house in a place quite remote from that to which her mother-in-law was going. And now the dream reversed this desired solution. Was not this a flat contradiction of my theory of wish-fulfilment? One had only to draw the inferences from this dream in order to arrive at its interpretation. According to this dream, I was wrong; *but it was her wish that I should be wrong, and this wish the dream showed her as fulfilled.* But the wish that I should be wrong, which was fulfilled in the theme of the country house, referred in reality to another and more serious matter. At that time I had inferred, from the material furnished by her analysis, that something of significance in respect to her illness must have occurred at a certain time in her life. She had denied this, because it was not present in her memory. We soon came to see that I was right. Thus her wish that I should prove to be wrong, which was transformed into the dream that she was going into the country with her mother-in-law, corresponded with the justifiable wish that those things which were then only suspected had never occurred.

Without an analysis, and merely by means of an assumption, I took the liberty of interpreting a little incident in the life of a friend, who had been my companion through eight classes at school. He once heard a lecture of mine, delivered to a small audience, on the novel idea that dreams are wish-fulfilments. He went home, dreamt *that he had lost all his lawsuits*—he was a lawyer—and then complained to me about it. I took refuge in the evasion: "One can't win all one's cases"; but I thought to myself: "If, for eight years, I sat as *primus* on the first bench, while he moved up and down somewhere in the middle of the class, may he not naturally have had the wish, ever since his boyhood, that I too might for once make a fool of myself?"

Yet another dream of a more gloomy character was offered me by a female patient in contradiction of my theory of the wish-dream. This patient, a young girl, began as follows: "You remember that my sister has now only one boy, Charles. She lost the elder one, Otto, while I was still living with her. Otto was my favourite; it was I who really brought him up. I like the other little fellow, too, but, of course, not nearly as much as his dead brother. Now I dreamt last night that I *saw Charles lying dead before me. He was lying in his little coffin, his hands folded; there were candles all about; and, in short, it was just as it was at the time of little Otto's death, which gave me such a shock.* Now tell me, what does this mean? You know me—am I really so bad as to wish that my sister should lose the only child she has left? Or does the dream mean that I wish that Charles had died rather than Otto, whom I liked so much better?"

I assured her that this latter interpretation was impossible. After some reflection, I was able to give her the interpretation of the dream, which she subsequently confirmed. I was able to do so because the whole previous history of the dreamer was known to me.

Having become an orphan at an early age, the girl had been brought up in the home of a much older sister, and had met, among the friends and visitors who frequented the house, a man who made a lasting impression upon her affections. It looked for a time as though these barely explicit relations would end in marriage, but this happy culmination was frustrated by the sister, whose motives were never completely explained. After the rupture the man whom my patient loved avoided the house; she herself attained her independence some time after the death of little Otto, to whom, meanwhile, her affections had turned. But she did not succeed in freeing herself from the dependence due to her affection for her sister's friend. Her pride bade her avoid him, but she found it impossible to transfer her love to the other suitors who successively presented themselves. Whenever the man she loved, who was a member of the literary profession, announced a lecture anywhere, she was certain to be found among the audience; and she seized every other opportunity of seeing him unobserved. I remembered that on the previous day she had told me that the Professor was going to a certain concert, and that she too was going, in order to enjoy the sight of him. This was on the day before the dream; and the concert was to be given on the day on which she told me the dream. I could now easily see the correct interpretation, and I asked her whether she could think of any particular event which had occurred after Otto's death. She replied immediately: "Of course; the Professor returned then, after a long absence, and I saw him once more beside little Otto's coffin." It was just as I had expected. I interpreted the dream as follows: "If now the other boy were to die, the same thing would happen again. You would spend the day with your sister; the Professor would certainly come to offer his condolences, and you would see him once more under the same circumstances as before. The dream signifies nothing more than this wish of yours to see him again—a wish against which you are fighting inwardly. I know that you have the ticket for to-day's concert in your bag. Your dream is a dream of impatience; it has anticipated by several hours the meeting which is to take place to-day."

In order to disguise her wish she had obviously selected a situation in which wishes of the sort are commonly suppressed—a situation so sorrowful that love is not even thought of. And yet it is entirely possible that even in the actual situation beside the coffin of the elder, more dearly loved boy, she had not been able to suppress her tender affection for the visitor whom she had missed for so long.

A different explanation was found in the case of a similar dream of another patient, who in earlier life had been distinguished for her quick wit and her cheerful disposition, and who still displayed these qualities, at all events in the free associations which occurred to her during treatment. In the course of a longer dream, it seemed to this lady that she saw her fifteen-year-old daughter lying dead before her in a box. She was strongly inclined to use this dream-image as an objection to the theory of wish-fulfilment, although she herself suspected that the detail of the box must lead to a different conception of the dream.[1] For in the course of the analysis it occurred to her that on the previous evening the conversation of the people in whose company she found herself had turned on the English word "box," and upon the numerous translations of it into German such as *Schachtel* (box), *Loge* (box at the theatre), *Kasten* (chest), *Ohrfeige* (box on the ear), etc. From other components of the same dream it was now possible to add the fact that the lady had guessed at the relationship between the English word "box" and the German *Büchse*, and had then been haunted by the recollection that *Büchse* is used in vulgar parlance to denote the female genitals. It was therefore possible, treating her knowledge of topographical anatomy with a certain indulgence, to assume that the child in the box signified a child in the mother's womb. At this stage of the explanation she no longer denied that the picture in the dream actually corresponded with a wish of hers. Like so many other young women, she was by no means happy on finding that she was pregnant, and she had confessed to me more than once the wish that her child might die before its birth; in a fit of anger, following a violent scene with her husband, she had even struck her abdomen with her fists, in order to injure the child within. The dead child was, therefore, really the fulfilment of a wish, but a wish which had been put aside for fifteen years, and it is not surprising that the fulfilment of the wish was no longer recognized after so long an interval. For there had been many changes in the meantime.

The group of dreams (having as content the death of beloved relatives) to which belong the last two mentioned will be considered again under the head of "Typical Dreams." I shall then be able to show by new examples that in spite of their undesirable content all these dreams must be interpreted as wish-fulfilments. For the following dream, which again was told me in order to deter me from a hasty generalization of my theory, I am indebted, not to a patient, but to an intelligent jurist of my acquaintance.

[1] As in the dream of the deferred supper and the smoked salmon.

"I dream," my informant tells me, *"that I am walking in front of my house with a lady on my arm. Here a closed carriage is waiting; a man steps up to me, shows me his authorization as a police officer, and requests me to follow him. I ask only for time in which to arrange my affairs."* The jurist then asks me: "Can you possibly suppose that it is my wish to be arrested?"—"Of course not," I have to admit. "Do you happen to know upon what charge you were arrested?"—"Yes; I believe for infanticide." —"Infanticide? But you know that only a mother can commit this crime upon her new-born child?"—"That is true." [1]—"And under what circumstances did you dream this? What happened on the evening before?"— "I would rather not tell you—it is a delicate matter."—"But I need it, otherwise we must forgo the interpretation of the dream."—"Well, then, I will tell you. I spent the night, not at home, but in the house of a lady who means a great deal to me. When we awoke in the morning, something again passed between us. Then I went to sleep again, and dreamt what I have told you."—"The woman is married?"—"Yes."—"And you do not wish her to conceive?"—"No; that might betray us."—"Then you do not practice normal coitus?"—"I take the precaution to withdraw before ejaculation."—"Am I to assume that you took this precaution several times during the night, and that in the morning you were not quite sure whether you had succeeded?"—"That might be so."—"Then your dream is the fulfilment of a wish. By the dream you are assured that you have not begotten a child, or, what amounts to the same thing, that you have killed the child. I can easily demonstrate the connecting-links. Do you remember, a few days ago we were talking about the troubles of matrimony, and about the inconsistency of permitting coitus so long as no impregnation takes place, while at the same time any preventive act committed after the ovum and the semen meet and a foetus is formed is punished as a crime? In this connection we recalled the medieval controversy about the moment of time at which the soul actually enters into the foetus, since the concept of murder becomes admissible only from that point onwards. Of course, too, you know the gruesome poem by Lenau, which puts infanticide and birth-control on the same plane."—"Strangely enough, I happened, as though by chance, to think of Lenau this morning."—"Another echo of your dream. And now I shall show you yet another incidental wish-fulfilment in your dream. You walk up to your house with the lady on your arm. So you take her home, instead of spending the night at her house, as you did in reality. The fact that the wish-fulfilment, which is the essence of the dream, disguises itself in such an unpleasant form, has

---

[1] If often happens that a dream is told incompletely, and that a recollection of the omitted portions appears only in the course of the analysis. These portions, when subsequently fitted in, invariably furnish the key to the interpretation. Cf. Chapter VII, on forgetting in dreams.

perhaps more than one explanation. From my essay on the etiology of anxiety neurosis, you will see that I note *coitus interruptus* as one of the factors responsible for the development of neurotic fear. It would be consistent with this if, after repeated coitus of this kind, you were left in an uncomfortable frame of mind, which now becomes an element of the composition of your dream. You even make use of this uncomfortable state of mind to conceal the wish-fulfilment. At the same time, the mention of infanticide has not yet been explained. Why does this crime, which is peculiar to females, occur to you?"—"I will confess to you that I was involved in such an affair years ago. I was responsible for the fact that a girl tried to protect herself from the consequences of a *liaison* with me by procuring an abortion. I had nothing to do with the carrying out of her plan, but for a long time I was naturally worried in case the affair might be discovered."—"I understand. This recollection furnished a second reason why the supposition that you had performed *coitus interruptus* clumsily must have been painful to you."

A young physician, who heard this dream related in my lecture-room, must have felt that it fitted him, for he hastened to imitate it by a dream of his own, applying its mode of thinking to another theme. On the previous day he had furnished a statement of his income; a quite straightforward statement, because he had little to state. He dreamt that an acquaintance of his came from a meeting of the tax commission and informed him that all the other statements had passed unquestioned, but that his own had aroused general suspicion, with the result that he would be punished with a heavy fine. This dream is a poorly disguised fulfilment of the wish to be known as a physician with a large income. It also calls to mind the story of the young girl who was advised against accepting her suitor because he was a man of quick temper, who would assuredly beat her after their marriage. Her answer was: "I wish he *would* strike me!" Her wish to be married was so intense that she had taken into consideration the discomforts predicted for this marriage; she had even raised them to the plane of a wish.

If I group together the very frequent dreams of this sort, which seem flatly to contradict my theory, in that they embody the denial of a wish or some occurrence obviously undesired, under the head of "counter-wish-dreams," I find that they may all be referred to two principles, one of which has not yet been mentioned, though it plays a large part in waking as well as dream-life. One of the motives inspiring these dreams is the wish that I should appear in the wrong. These dreams occur regularly in the course of treatment whenever the patient is in a state of resistance; indeed, I can with a great degree of certainty count on evoking such a dream once I have explained to the patient my theory that the dream is a wish-fulfilment.[1] Indeed, I have reason to expect that many of my readers will have such dreams, merely to fulfil the wish that I may prove to be wrong. The last dream which I shall recount from among those occurring in the course of treatment once more demonstrates this very thing. A young girl who had struggled hard to continue my treatment, against the will of her relatives and the authorities whom they had consulted, dreamt the following dream: *At home she is forbidden to come to me any more. She then reminds me of the promise I made her to treat her for nothing if necessary, and I tell her: "I can show no consideration in money matters."*

It is not at all easy in this case to demonstrate the fulfilment of a wish, but in all cases of this kind there is a second problem, the solution of which helps also to solve the first. Where does she get the words which she puts into my mouth? Of course, I have never told her anything of the kind; but one of her brothers, the one who has the greatest influence over her, has been kind enough to make this remark about me. It is then the purpose of the dream to show that her brother is right; and she does not try to justify this brother merely in the dream; it is her purpose in life and the motive of her illness.

A dream which at first sight presents peculiar difficulties for the theory of wish-fulfilment was dreamed by a physician (Aug. Stärcke) and interpreted by him: *"I have and see on the last phalange of my left forefinger a primary syphilitic affection."*

One may perhaps be inclined to refrain from analysing this dream, since it seems clear and coherent, except for its unwished-for content. However, if one takes the trouble to make an analysis, one learns that "primary affection" reduces itself to *"prima affectio"* (first love), and that the repulsive sore, in the words of Stärke, proves to be "the representative of wish-fulfilments charged with intense emotion."[2]

The other motive for counter-wish-dreams is so clear that there is a danger of overlooking it, as happened in my own case for a long time. In the sexual constitution of many persons there is a masochistic component, which has arisen through the conversion of the aggressive, sadistic component into its opposite. Such people are called "ideal" masochists if they seek pleasure not in the bodily pain which may be inflicted upon them, but in humiliation and psychic chastisement. It is obvious that such persons may have counter-wish-dreams and disagreeable dreams, yet these are for them nothing more than wish-fulfilments, which satisfy their masochistic inclinations. Here is such a dream: A young

---

[1] Similar "counter-wish-dreams" have been repeatedly reported to me within the last few years, by those who attend my lectures, as their reaction to their first encounter with the "wish-theory of dreams."

[2] *Zentralblatt für Psychoanalyse*, Jahrg. II, 1911-12.

man, who in earlier youth greatly tormented his elder brother, toward whom he was homosexually inclined, but who has since undergone a complete change of character, has the following dream, which consists of three parts: (1) *He is "teased" by his brother.* (2) *Two adults are caressing each other with homosexual intentions.* (3) *His brother has sold the business the management of which the young man had reserved for his own future.* From this last dream he awakens with the most unpleasant feelings; and yet it is a masochistic wish-dream, which might be translated: It would serve me right if my brother were to make that sale against my interests. It would be my punishment for all the torments he has suffered at my hands.

I hope that the examples given above will suffice—until some further objection appears—to make it seem credible that even dreams with a painful content are to be analysed as wish-fulfilments.[1] Nor should it be considered a mere matter of chance that in the course of interpretation one always happens upon subjects about which one does not like to speak or think. The disagreeable sensation which such dreams arouse is of course precisely identical with the antipathy which would, and usually does, restrain us from treating or discussing such subjects—an antipathy which must be overcome by all of us if we find ourselves obliged to attack the problem of such dreams. But this disagreeable feeling which recurs in our dreams does not preclude the existence of a wish; everyone has wishes which he would not like to confess to others, which he does not care to admit even to himself. On the other hand, we feel justified in connecting the unpleasant character of all these dreams with the fact of dream-distortion, and in concluding that these dreams are distorted, and that their wish-fulfilment is disguised beyond recognition, precisely because there is a strong revulsion against—a will to repress—the subject-matter of the dream, or the wish created by it. Dream-distortion, then, proves in reality to be an act of the censorship. We shall have included everything which the analysis of disagreeable dreams has brought to light if we re-word our formula thus: *The dream is the (disguised) fulfilment of a (suppressed, repressed) wish.*[2]

[1] I will here observe that we have not yet disposed of this theme; we shall discuss it again later.

[2] A great contemporary poet, who, I am told, will hear nothing of psychoanalysis and dream-interpretation, has nevertheless derived from his own experience an almost identical formula for the nature of the dream: "Unauthorized emergence of suppressed yearnings under false features and names" (C. Spitteler, *Meine frühesten Erlebnisse,* in *Süddeutsche Monatshefte,* October, 1913).

I will here anticipate by citing the amplification and modification of this fundamental formula propounded by Otto Rank: "On the basis of and with the aid of repressed infantile-sexual material, dreams regularly represent as fulfilled current, and as a rule also erotic, wishes in a disguised and symbolic form" (*Ein Traum, der sick selbst deutet*).

Now there still remain to be considered, as a particular sub-order of dreams with painful content, the anxiety-dreams, the inclusion of which among the wish-dreams will be still less acceptable to the uninitiated. But I can here deal very cursorily with the problem of anxiety-dreams; what they have to reveal is not a new aspect of the dream-problem; here the problem is that of understanding neurotic anxiety in general. The anxiety which we experience in dreams is only apparently explained by the dream-content. If we subject that content to analysis, we become aware that the dream-anxiety is no more justified by the dream-content than the anxiety in a phobia is justified by the idea to which the phobia is attached. For example, it is true that it is possible to fall out of a window, and that a certain care should be exercised when one is at a window, but it is not obvious why the anxiety in the corresponding phobia is so great, and why it torments its victims more than its cause would warrant. The same explanation which applies to the phobia applies also to the anxiety-dream. In either case the anxiety is only *fastened on to* the idea which accompanies it, and is really derived from another source.

On account of this intimate relation of dream-anxiety to neurotic anxiety, the discussion of the former obliges me to refer to the latter. In a little essay on *Anxiety Neurosis*,[1] written in 1895, I maintain that neurotic anxiety has its origin in the sexual life, and corresponds to a libido which has been deflected from its object and has found no employment. The accuracy of this formula has since then been demonstrated with ever-increasing certainty. From it we may deduce the doctrine that anxiety-dreams are dreams of sexual content, and that the libido appertaining to this content has been transformed into anxiety. Later on I shall have an opportunity of confirming this assertion by the analysis of several dreams

---

Nowhere have I said that I have accepted this formula of Rank's. The shorter version contained in the text seems to me sufficient. But the fact that I merely mentioned Rank's modification was enough to expose psychoanalysis to the oft-repeated reproach that it asserts that *all dreams have a sexual content*. If one understands this sentence as it is intended to be understood, it only proves how little conscientiousness our critics are wont to display, and how ready our opponents are to overlook statements if they do not accord with their aggressive inclinations. Only a few pages back I mentioned the manifold wish-fulfilments of children's dreams (to make an excursion on land or water, to make up for an omitted meal, etc.). Elsewhere I have mentioned dreams excited by thirst and the desire to evacuate, and mere comfort- or convenience-dreams. Even Rank does not make an absolute assertion. He says "as a rule also erotic wishes," and this can be completely confirmed in the case of most dreams of adults.

The matter has, however, a different aspect if we employ the word "sexual" in the sense of "Eros," as the word is understood by psychoanalysts. But the interesting problem of whether all dreams are not produced by "libidinal" motives (in opposition to "destructive" ones) has hardly been considered by our opponents.

[1] *Selected Papers on Hysteria and other Psychoneuroses*, p. 133, translated by A. A. Brill, *Journal of Nervous and Mental Diseases*, Monograph Series.

of neurotics. In my further attempts to arrive at a theory of dreams I shall again have occasion to revert to the conditions of anxiety-dreams and their compatibility with the theory of wish-fulfilment.

V

THE MATERIAL AND SOURCES OF DREAMS

HAVING realized, as a result of analysing the dream of Irma's injection, that the dream was the fulfilment of a wish, we were immediately interested to ascertain whether we had thereby discovered a general characteristic of dreams, and for the time being we put aside every other scientific problem which may have suggested itself in the course of the interpretation. Now that we have reached the goal on this one path, we may turn back and select a new point of departure for exploring dream-problems, even though we may for a time lose sight of the theme of wish-fulfilment, which has still to be further considered.

Now that we are able, by applying our process of interpretation, to detect a *latent* dream-content whose significance far surpasses that of the *manifest* dream-content, we are naturally impelled to return to the individual dream-problems, in order to see whether the riddles and contradictions which seemed to elude us when we had only the manifest content to work upon may not now be satisfactorily solved.

The opinions of previous writers on the relation of dreams to waking life, and the origin of the material of dreams, have not been given here. We may recall however three peculiarities of the memory in dreams, which have been often noted, but never explained:—

1. That the dream clearly prefers the impressions of the last few days (Robert, Strümpell, Hildebrandt; also Weed-Hallam);
2. That it makes a selection in accordance with principles other than those governing our waking memory, in that it recalls not essential and important, but subordinate and disregarded things;
3. That it has at its disposal the earliest impressions of our childhood, and brings to light details from this period of life, which, again, seem trivial to us, and which in waking life were believed to have been long since forgotten.[1]

---

[1] It is evident that Robert's idea—that the dream is intended to rid our memory of the useless impressions which it has received during the day—is no longer tenable if indifferent memories of our childhood appear in our dreams with some degree of

These peculiarities in the dream's choice of material have, of course, been observed by previous writers in the manifest dream-content.

A. RECENT AND INDIFFERENT IMPRESSIONS
IN THE DREAM

If I now consult my own experience with regard to the origin of the elements appearing in the dream-content, I must in the first place express the opinion that in every dream we may find some reference to the experiences of the *preceding day*. Whatever dream I turn to, whether my own or someone else's, this experience is always confirmed. Knowing this, I may perhaps begin the work of interpretation by looking for the experience of the preceding day which has stimulated the dream; in many cases this is indeed the quickest way. With the two dreams which I subjected to a close analysis in the last chapter (the dreams of Irma's injection, and of the uncle with the yellow beard) the reference to the preceding day is so evident that it needs no further elucidation. But in order to show how constantly this reference may be demonstrated, I shall examine a portion of my own dream-chronicle. I shall relate only so much of the dreams as is necessary for the detection of the dream-source in question.

1. *I pay a call at a house to which I gain admittance only with difficulty, etc., and meanwhile I am keeping a woman waiting for me.*
Source: A conversation during the evening with a female relative to the effect that she would have to wait for a remittance for which she had asked, until . . . etc.

2. *I have written a monograph on a species (uncertain) of plant.*
Source: In the morning I had seen in a bookseller's window a *mono¹ graph* on the genus Cyclamen.

3. *I see two women in the street, mother and daughter, the latter being a patient.*
Source: A female patient who is under treatment had told me in the evening what difficulties her *mother* puts in the way of her continuing the treatment.

4. *At S. and R.'s bookshop I subscribe to a periodical which costs 20 florins annually.*
Source: During the day my wife has reminded me that I still owe her *20 florins* of her weekly allowance.

5. *I receive a communication from the Social Democratic Committee, in which I am addressed as a member.*

---

frequency. We should be obliged to conclude that our dreams generally perform their prescribed task very inadequately.

Source: I have received simultaneous *communications* from the Liberal Committee on Elections and from the president of the Humanitarian Society, of which latter I am actually a member.

6. *A man on a steep rock rising from the sea, in the manner of Böcklin.*
Source: Dreyfus on Devil's Island; also news from my relatives in *England,* etc.

The question might be raised, whether a dream invariably refers to the events of the preceding day only, or whether the reference may be extended to include impressions from a longer period of time in the immediate past. This question is probably not of the first importance, but I am inclined to decide in favour of the exclusive priority of the day before the dream (the dream-day). Whenever I thought I had found a case where an impression two or three days old was the source of the dream, I was able to convince myself after careful investigation that this impression had been remembered the day before; that is, that a demonstrable reproduction on the day before had been interpolated between the day of the event and the time of the dream; and further, I was able to point to the recent occasion which might have given rise to the recollection of the older impression. On the other hand, I was unable to convince myself that a regular interval of biological significance (H. Swoboda gives the first interval of this kind as eighteen hours) elapses between the dream-exciting daytime impression and its recurrence in the dream.

I believe, therefore, that for every dream a dream-stimulus may be found among those experiences "on which one has not yet slept."

Havelock Ellis, who has likewise given attention to this problem, states that he has not been able to find any such periodicity of reproduction in his dreams, although he has looked for it. He relates a dream in which he found himself in Spain; he wanted to travel to a place called *Daraus, Varaus,* or *Zaraus.* On awaking he was unable to recall any such place-names, and thought no more of the matter. A few months later he actually found the name Zaraus; it was that of a railway-station between San Sebastian and Bilbao, through which he had passed in the train eight months (250 days) before the date of the dream.

Thus the impressions of the immediate past (with the exception of the day before the night of the dream) stands in the same relation to the dream-content as those of periods indefinitely remote. The dream may select its material from any period of life, provided only that a chain of thought leads back from the experiences of the day of the dream (the "recent" impressions) of that earlier period.

But why this preference for recent impressions? We shall arrive at some conjectures on this point if we subject one of the dreams already mentioned to a more precise analysis. I select the

Dream of the Botanical Monograph

*I have written a monograph on a certain plant. The book lies before me;
I am just turning over a folded coloured plate. A dried specimen of the
plant, as though from a herbarium, is bound up with every copy.*

Analysis:

In the morning I saw in a bookseller's window a volume entitled *The
Genus Cyclamen,* apparently a monograph on this plant.

The cyclamen is my wife's favourite flower. I reproach myself for re
membering so seldom to bring her flowers, as she would like me to do. In
connection with the theme of giving her flowers, I am reminded of a story
which I recently told some friends of mine in proof of my assertion that
we often forget in obedience to a purpose of the unconscious, and that
forgetfulness always enables us to form a deduction about the secret dis
position of the forgetful person. A young woman who has been accustomed to receive a bouquet of flowers from her husband on her birthday
misses this token of affection on one of her birthdays, and bursts into
tears. The husband comes in, and cannot understand why she is crying
until she tells him: "To-day is my birthday." He claps his hand to his
forehead, and exclaims: "Oh, forgive me, I had completely forgotten it!"
and proposes to go out immediately in order to get her flowers. But she
refuses to be consoled, for she sees in her husband's forgetfulness a proof
that she no longer plays the same part in his thoughts as she formerly did.
This Frau L. met my wife two days ago, told her that she was feeling
well, and asked after me. Some years ago she was a patient of mine.

Supplementary facts: I did once actually write something like a monograph on a plant, namely, an essay on the coca plant, which attracted the
attention of K. Koller to the anaesthetic properties of cocaine. I had
hinted that the alkaloid might be employed as an anaesthetic, but I was
not thorough enough to pursue the matter farther. It occurs to me, too,
that on the morning of the day following the dream (for the interpretation of which I did not find time until the evening) I had thought of
cocaine in a kind of day-dream. If I were ever afflicted with glaucoma, I
would go to Berlin, and there undergo an operation, incognito, in the
house of my Berlin friend, at the hands of a surgeon whom he would
recommend. The surgeon, who would not know the name of his patient,
would boast, as usual, how easy these operations had become since the
introduction of cocaine; and I should not betray the fact that I myself
had a share in this discovery. With this phantasy were connected thoughts
of how awkward it really is for a physician to claim the professional
services of a colleague. I should be able to pay the Berlin eye specialist,
who did not know me, like anyone else. Only after recalling this day-

dream do I realize that there is concealed behind it the memory of a definite event. Shortly after Koller's discovery, my father contracted glaucoma; he was operated on by my friend Dr. Koenigstein, the eye specialist. Dr. Koller was in charge of the cocaine anaesthetization, and he made the remark that on this occasion all the three persons who had been responsible for the introduction of cocaine had been brought together.

My thoughts now pass on to the time when I was last reminded of the history of cocaine. This was a few days earlier, when I received a *Festschrift*, a publication in which grateful pupils had commemorated the jubilee of their teacher and laboratory director. Among the titles to fame of persons connected with the laboratory I found a note to the effect that the discovery of the anaesthetic properties of cocaine had been due to K. Koller. Now I suddenly become aware that the dream is connected with an experience of the previous evening. I had just accompanied Dr. Koenigstein to his home, and had entered into a discussion of a subject which excites me greatly whenever it is mentioned. While I was talking with him in the entrance-hall Professor Gärtner and his young wife came up. I could not refrain from congratulating them both upon their *blooming* appearance. Now Professor Gärtner is one of the authors of the *Festschrift* of which I have just spoken, and he may well have reminded me of it. And Frau L., of whose birthday disappointment I spoke a little way back, had been mentioned, though of course in another connection, in my conversation with Dr. Koenigstein.

I shall now try to elucidate the other determinants of the dream-content. A *dried specimen* of the plant accompanies the monograph, as though it were a *herbarium*. And herbarium reminds me of the "gymnasium." The director of our "gymnasium" once called the pupils of the upper classes together, in order that they might examine and clean the "gymnasium" herbarium. Small insects had been found—*book-worms*. The director seemed to have little confidence in my ability to assist, for he entrusted me with only a few of the pages. I know to this day that there were crucifers on them. My interest in botany was never very great. At my preliminary examination in botany I was required to identify a crucifer, and failed to recognize it; had not my theoretical knowledge come to my aid, I should have fared badly indeed. Crucifers suggest composites. The artichoke is really a composite, and in actual fact one which I might call my *favourite flower*. My wife, more thoughtful than I, often brings this favourite flower of mine home from the market.

I see the monograph which I have written lying before me. Here again there is an association. My friend wrote to me yesterday from Berlin: "I am thinking a great deal about your dream-book. I see it lying before me, completed, and I turn the pages." How I envied him this power of vision! If only I could see it lying before me, already completed!

The folded coloured plate. When I was a medical student I suffered a sort of craze for studying monographs exclusively. In spite of my limited means, I subscribed to a number of the medical periodicals, whose *coloured plates* afforded me much delight. I was rather proud of this inclination to thoroughness. When I subsequently began to publish books myself, I had to draw the plates for my own treatises, and I remember one of them turned out so badly that a well-meaning colleague ridiculed me for it. With this is associated, I do not exactly know how, a very early memory of my childhood. My father, by way of a jest, once gave my elder sister and myself a book containing *coloured plates* (the book was a narrative of a journey through Persia) in order that we might destroy it. From an educational point of view this was hardly to be commended. I was at the time five years old, and my sister less than three, and the picture of us two children blissfully tearing the book to pieces (I should add, like an *artichoke*, leaf by leaf), is almost the only one from this period of my life which has remained vivid in my memory. When I afterwards became a student, I developed a conspicuous fondness for collecting and possessing books (an analogy to the inclination for studying from monographs, a hobby alluded to in my dream-thoughts, in connection with cyclamen and artichoke). I became a *book-worm* (cf. *herbarium*). Ever since I have been engaged in introspection I have always traced this earliest passion of my life to this impression of my childhood: or rather, I have recognized in this childish scene a "screen or concealing memory" for my subsequent bibliophilia.[1] And of course I learned at an early age that our passions often become our misfortunes. When I was seventeen, I ran up a very considerable account at the bookseller's, with no means with which to settle it, and my father would hardly accept it as an excuse that my passion was at least a respectable one. But the mention of this experience of my youth brings me back to my conversation with my friend Dr. Koenigstein on the evening preceding the dream; for one of the themes of this conversation was the same old reproach—that I am much too absorbed in my *hobbies.*

For reasons which are not relevant here I shall not continue the interpretation of this dream, but will merely indicate the path which leads to it. In the course of the interpretation I was reminded of my conversation with Dr. Koenigstein, and, indeed, of more than one portion of it. When I consider the subjects touched upon in this conversation, the meaning of the dream immediately becomes clear to me. All the trains of thought which have been started—my own inclinations, and those of my wife, the cocaine, the awkwardness of securing medical treatment from one's own

[1] Cf. *The Psychopathology of Everyday Life.*

colleagues, my preference for monographical studies, and my neglect of certain subjects, such as botany—all these are continued in and lead up to one branch or another of this widely-ramified conversation. The dream once more assumes the character of a justification, of a plea for my rights (like the dream of Irma's injection, the first to be analysed); it even continues the theme which that dream introduced, and discusses it in association with the new subject-matter which has been added in the interval between the two dreams. Even the dream's apparently indifferent form of expression at once acquires a meaning. Now it means: "I am indeed the man who has written that valuable and successful treatise (on cocaine)," just as previously I declared in self-justification: "I am after all a thorough and industrious student"; and in both instances I find the meaning: "I can allow myself this." But I may dispense with the further interpretation of the dream, because my only purpose in recording it was to examine the relation of the dream-content to the experience of the previous day which arouses it. As long as I know only the manifest content of this dream, only one relation to any impression of the day is obvious; but after I have completed the interpretation, a second source of the dream becomes apparent in another experience of the same day. The first of these impressions to which the dream refers is an indifferent one, a subordinate circumstance. I see a book in a shop window whose title holds me for a moment, but whose contents would hardly interest me. The second experience was of great psychic value; I talked earnestly with my friend, the eye specialist, for about an hour; I made allusions in this conversation which must have ruffled the feelings of both of us, and which in me awakened memories in connection with which I was aware of a great variety of inner stimuli. Further, this conversation was broken off unfinished, because some acquaintances joined us. What, now, is the relation of these two impressions of the day to one another, and to the dream which followed during the night?

In the manifest dream-content I find merely an illusion to the indifferent impression, and I am thus able to reaffirm that the dream prefers to take up into its content experiences of a non-essential character. In the dream-interpretation, on the contrary, everything converges upon the important and justifiably disturbing event. If I judge the sense of the dream in the only correct way, according to the latent content which is brought to light in the analysis, I find that I have unwittingly lighted upon a new and important discovery. I see that the puzzling theory that the dream deals only with the worthless odds and ends of the day's experiences has no justification; I am also compelled to contradict the assertion that the psychic life of the waking state is not continued in the dream, and that hence, the dream wastes our psychic energy on trivial material. The very opposite is true; what has claimed our attention during the day dominates our dream-thoughts also, and we take pains to dream only in connection with such matters as have given us food for thought during the day.

Perhaps the most immediate explanation of the fact that I dream of the indifferent impression of the day, while the impression which has with good reason excited me causes me to dream, is that here again we are dealing with the phenomenon of dream-distortion, which we have referred to as a psychic force playing the part of a censorship. The recollection of the monograph on the genus cyclamen is utilized as though it were an *allusion* to the conversation with my friend, just as the mention of my patient's friend in the dream of the deferred supper is represented by the allusion "smoked salmon." The only question is, by what intermediate links can the impression of the monograph come to assume the relation of allusion to the conversation with the eye specialist, since such a relation is not at first perceptible? In the example of the deferred supper the relation is evident at the outset; "smoked salmon," as the favourite dish of the patient's friend, belongs to the circle of ideas which the friend's personality would naturally evoke in the mind of the dreamer. In our new example we are dealing with two entirely separate impressions, which at first glance seem to have nothing in common, except indeed that they occur on the same day. The monograph attracts my attention in the morning: in the evening I take part in the conversation. The answer furnished by the analysis is as follows: Such relations between the two impressions as do not exist from the first are established subsequently between the idea-content of the one impression and the idea-content of the other. I have already picked out the intermediate links emphasized in the course of writing the analysis. Only under some outside influence, perhaps the recollection of the flowers missed by Frau L., would the idea of the monograph on the cyclamen have attached itself to the idea that the cyclamen is my wife's favourite flower. I do not believe that these inconspicuous thoughts would have sufficed to evoke a dream.

> "*There needs no ghost, my lord, come from the grave*
>   *To tell us this,*"

as we read in Hamlet. But behold! in the analysis I am reminded that the name of the man who interrupted our conversation was *Gärtner* (gardener), and that I thought his wife looked *blooming;* indeed, now I even remember that one of my female patients, who bears the pretty name of *Flora,* was for a time the main subject of our conversation. It must have happened that by means of these intermediate links from the sphere of botanical ideas the association was effected between the two events of the day, the indifferent one and the stimulating one. Other relations were then established, that of cocaine for example, which can with perfect appropriateness form a link between the person of Dr. Koenigstein and the botanical monograph which I have written, and thus secure the fusion of the two circles of ideas, so that now a portion of the first experience may be used as an allusion to the second.

I am prepared to find this explanation attacked as either arbitrary or artificial. What would have happened if Professor Gärtner and his blooming wife had not appeared, and if the patient who was under discussion had been called, not Flora, but Anna? And yet the answer is not hard to find. If these thought-relations had not been available, others would probably have been selected. It is easy to establish relations of this sort, as the jocular questions and conundrums with which we amuse ourselves suffice to show. The range of wit is unlimited. To go a step farther: if no sufficiently fertile associations between the two impressions of the day could have been established, the dream would simply have followed a different course; another of the indifferent impressions of the day, such as come to us in multitudes and are forgotten, would have taken the place of the monograph in the dream, would have formed an association with the content of the conversation, and would have represented this in the dream. Since it was the impression of the monograph and no other that was fated to perform this function, this impression was probably that most suitable for the purpose. One need not, like Lessing's *Hänschen Schlau,* be astonished that "only the rich people of the world possess the most money."

Still, the psychological process by which, according to our exposition, the indifferent experience substitutes itself for the psychologically important one seems to us odd and open to question. In a later chapter we shall undertake the task of making the peculiarities of this seemingly incorrect operation more intelligible. Here we are concerned only with the result of this process, which we were compelled to accept by constantly recurring experiences in the analysis of dreams. In this process it is as though, in the course of the intermediate steps, a *displacement* occurs—let us say, of the psychic accent—until ideas of feeble potential, by taking over the charge from ideas which have a stronger initial potential, reach a degree of intensity which enables them to force their way into consciousness. Such displacements do not in the least surprise us when it is a question of the transference of affective magnitudes or of motor activities. That the lonely spinster transfers her affection to animals, that the bachelor becomes a passionate collector, that the soldier defends a scrap of coloured cloth—his flag—with his life-blood, that in a love-affair a clasp of the hands a moment longer than usual evokes a sensation of bliss, or that in *Othello* a lost handkerchief causes an outburst of rage—all these are examples of psychic displacements which to us seem incontestable. But if, by the same means, and in accordance with the same fundamental principles, a decision is made as to what is to reach our consciousness and what is to be withheld from it—that is to say, what we are to think—this gives us the impression of morbidity, and if it occurs in waking life we call it an error of thought. We may here anticipate the result of a discussion which will be undertaken later, namely, that the psychic process which we have recognized in dream-displacement proves to be not a morbidly deranged process, but one merely differing from the normal, one of a more *primary* nature.

Thus we interpret the fact that the dream-content takes up remnants of trivial experiences as a manifestation of *dream-distortion* (by displacement), and we thereupon remember that we have recognized this dream-distortion as the work of a censorship operating between the two psychic instances. We may therefore expect that dream-analysis will constantly show us the real and psychically significant source of the dream in the events of the day, the memory of which has transferred its accentuation to some indifferent memory. This conception is in complete opposition to Robert's theory, which consequently has no further value for us. The fact which Robert was trying to explain simply does not exist; its assumption is based on a misunderstanding, on a failure to substitute the real meaning of the dream for its apparent meaning. A further objection to Robert's doctrine is as follows: If the task of the dream were really to rid our memory, by means of a special psychic activity, of the "slag" of the day's recollections, our sleep would perforce be more troubled, engaged in more strenuous work, than we can suppose it to be, judging by our waking thoughts. For the number of the indifferent impressions of the day against which we should have to protect our memory is obviously immeasurably large; the whole night would not be long enough to dispose of them all. It is far more probable that the forgetting of the indifferent impressions takes place without any active interference on the part of our psychic powers.

Still, something cautions us against taking leave of Robert's theory without further consideration. We have left unexplained the fact that one of the indifferent impressions of the day—indeed, even of the previous day—constantly makes a contribution to the dream-content. The relations between this impression and the real source of the dream in the unconscious do not always exist from the outset; as we have seen, they are established subsequently, while the dream is actually at work, as though to serve the purpose of the intended displacement. Something, therefore, must necessitate the opening up of connections in the direction of the recent but indifferent impression; this impression must possess some quality that gives it a special fitness. Otherwise it would be just as easy for the dream-thoughts to shift their accentuation to some inessential component of their own sphere of ideas.

Experiences such as the following show us the way to an explanation: If the day has brought us two or more experiences which are worthy to evoke a dream, the dream will blend the allusion of both into a single whole: it obeys *a compulsion to make them into a single whole*. For example: One summer afternoon I entered a railway carriage in which I found two acquaintances of mine who were unknown to one another. One of them was an influential colleague, the other a member of a distinguished family which I had been attending in my professional capacity. I introduced the two gentlemen to each other; but during the long journey they conversed with each other through me, so that I had to discuss this or that topic now with one, now with the other. I asked my colleague to recommend a mutual acquaintance who had just begun to practise as a physician. He replied that he was convinced of the young man's ability, but that his undistinguished appearance would make it difficult for him to obtain patients in the upper ranks of society. To this I rejoined: "That is precisely why he needs recommendation." A little later, turning to my other fellow-traveller, I inquired after the health of his aunt—the mother of one of my patients—who was at this time prostrated by a serious illness. On the night following this journey I dreamt that the young friend whom I had asked one of my companions to recommend was in a fashionable drawing-room, and with all the bearing of a man of the world was making—before a distinguished company, in which I recognized all the rich and aristocratic persons of my acquaintance—a funeral oration over the old lady (who in my dream had already died) who was the aunt of my second fellow-traveller. (I confess frankly that I had not been on good terms with this lady.) Thus my dream had once more found the connection between the two impressions of the day, and by means of the two had constructed a unified situation.

In view of many similar experiences I am persuaded to advance the proposition that a dream works under a kind of compulsion which forces it to combine into a unified whole all the sources of dream-stimulation which are offered to it.[1] In a subsequent chapter (on the function of dreams) we shall consider this impulse of combination as part of the process of condensation, another primary psychic process.

I shall now consider the question whether the dream-exciting source to which our analysis leads us must always be a recent (and significant) event, or whether a subjective experience—that is to say, the recollection of a psychologically significant event, a train of thought—may assume the rôle of a dream-stimulus. The very definite answer, derived from numerous analyses, is as follows: The stimulus of the dream may be a

---

[1] The tendency of the dream at work to blend everything present of interest into a single transaction has already been noticed by several authors, for instance, by Delage and Delbœuf.

subjective transaction, which has been made recent, as it were, by the mental activity of the day.

And this is perhaps the best time to summarize in schematic form the different conditions under which the dream-sources are operative.

The source of a dream may be:—

(a) A recent and psychologically significant event which is directly' represented in the dream.[1]

(b) Several recent and significant events, which are combined by the dream into a single whole.[2]

(c) One or more recent and significant events, which are represented in the dream-content by allusion to a contemporary but indifferent event.[3]

(d) A subjectively significant experience (recollection, train of thought), which is *constantly* represented in the dream by allusion to a recent but indifferent impression.[4]

As may be seen, in dream-interpretation the condition is always ful-filled that one component of the dream-content repeats a recent impression of the day of the dream. The component which is destined to be represented in the dream may either belong to the same circle of ideas as the dream-stimulus itself (as an essential or even an inessential element of the same), or it may originate in the neighbourhood of an indifferent impression, which has been brought by more or less abundant associations into relation with the sphere of the dream-stimulus. The apparent multiplicity of these conditions results merely from the *alternative*, that a *displacement has or has not occurred*, and it may here be noted that this alternative enables us to explain the contrasts of the dream quite as readily as the medical theory of the dream explains the series of states from the partial to the complete waking of the brain cells.

In considering this series of sources we note further that the psychologically significant but not recent element (a train of thought, a recollection) may be replaced for the purposes of dream-formation by a recent but psychologically indifferent element, provided the two following conditions are fulfilled: (1) the dream-content preserves a connection with things recently experienced; (2) the dream-stimulus is still a psychologically significant event. In one single case (a) both these conditions are fulfilled by the same impression. If we now consider that these same indifferent impressions, which are utilized for the dream as long as they are recent, lose this qualification as soon as they are a day (or at most several days) older, we are obliged to assume that the very freshness of an impression gives it a certain psychological value for dream-formation,

[1] The dream of Irma's injection; the dream of the friend who is my uncle.
[2] The dream of the funeral oration delivered by the young physician.
[3] The dream of the botanical monograph.
[4] The dreams of my patients during analysis are mostly of this kind.

somewhat equivalent to the value of emotionally accentuated memories or trains of thought. Later on, in the light of certain psychological considerations, we shall be able to divine the explanation of this importance of *recent* impressions in dream-formation.[1]

Incidentally our attention is here called to the fact that at night, and unnoticed by our consciousness, important changes may occur in the material comprised by our ideas and memories. The injunction that before making a final decision in any matter one should sleep on it for a night is obviously fully justified. But at this point we find that we have passed from the psychology of dreaming to the psychology of sleep, a step which there will often be occasion to take.

At this point there arises an objection which threatens to invalidate the conclusions at which we have just arrived. If indifferent impressions can find their way into the dream only so long as they are of recent origin, how does it happen that in the dream-content we find elements also from earlier periods of our lives, which at the time when they were still recent possessed, as Strümpell puts it, no psychic value, and which, therefore, ought to have been forgotten long ago; elements, that is, which are neither fresh nor psychologically significant?

This objection can be disposed of completely if we have recourse to the results of the psychoanalysis of neurotics. The solution is as follows: The process of shifting and rearrangement which replaces material of psychic significance by material which is indifferent (whether one is dreaming or thinking) has already taken place in these earlier periods of life, and has since become fixed in the memory. Those elements which were originally indifferent are in fact no longer so, since they have acquired the value of psychologically significant material. That which has actually remained indifferent can never be reproduced in the dream.

From the foregoing exposition the reader may rightly conclude that I assert that there are no indifferent dream-stimuli, and therefore no guileless dreams. This I absolutely and unconditionally believe to be the case, apart from the dreams of children, and perhaps the brief dream-reactions to nocturnal sensations. Apart from these exceptions, whatever one dreams is either plainly recognizable as being psychically significant, or it is distorted and can be judged correctly only after complete interpretation, when it proves after all to be of psychic significance. The dream never concerns itself with trifles; we do not allow sleep to be disturbed by trivialities.[2] Dreams which are apparently guileless turn out to be the reverse of innocent if one takes the trouble to interpret them; if I may be

[1] Cf. Chap. VII on *Transference.*

[2] Havelock Ellis, a kindly critic of *The Interpretation of Dreams*, writes in *The World of Dreams* (p. 169): "From this point on, not many of us will be able to follow F." But Mr. Ellis has not undertaken any analyses of dreams, and will not believe how unjustifiable it is to judge them by the manifest dream-content.

permitted the expression, they all show "the mark of the beast." Since this is another point on which I may expect contradiction, and since I am glad of an opportunity to show dream-distortion at work, I shall here subject to analysis a number of "guileless dreams" from my collection.

I

An intelligent and refined young woman, who in real life is distinctly reserved, one of those people of whom one says that "still waters run deep," relates the following dream: *"I dreamt that I arrived at the market too late, and could get nothing from either the butcher or the greengrocer woman."* Surely a guileless dream, but as it has not the appearance of a real dream I induce her to relate it in detail. Her report then runs as follows: *She goes to the market with her cook, who carries the basket. The butcher tells her, after she has asked him for something: "That is no longer to be obtained," and wants to give her something else, with the remark: "That is good, too." She refuses, and goes to the greengrocer woman. The latter tries to sell her a peculiar vegetable, which is bound up in bundles, and is black in colour. She says: "I don't know that, I won't take it."*

The connection of the dream with the preceding day is simple enough. She had really gone to the market too late, and had been unable to buy anything. *The meatshop was already closed,* comes into one's mind as a description of the experience. But wait, is not that a very vulgar phrase which—or rather, the opposite of which—denotes a certain neglect with regard to a man's clothing? [1] The dreamer has not used these words; she has perhaps avoided them; but let us look for the interpretation of the details contained in the dream.

When in a dream something has the character of a spoken utterance—that is, when it is said or heard, not merely thought—and the distinction can usually be made with certainty—then it originates in the utterances of waking life, which have, of course, been treated as raw material, dismembered, and slightly altered, and above all removed from their context.[2] In the work of interpretation we may take such utterances as our starting-point. Where, then, does the butcher's statement, *That is no longer to be obtained,* come from? From myself; I had explained to her some days previously "that the oldest experiences of childhood are *no longer to be obtained* as such, but will be replaced in the analysis by 'transferences' and dreams." Thus, I am the butcher; and she refuses to accept these transferences to the present of old ways of thinking and

---

[1] Its meaning is: "Your fly is undone." (TRANS.)

[2] Cf. what is said of speech in dreams in the chapter on *The Dream-Work*. Only one of the writers on the subject—Delbœuf—seems to have recognized the origin of the speeches heard in dreams, he compares them with *clichés*.

feeling. Where does her dream utterance, *I don't know that, I won't take it,* come from? For the purposes of the analysis this has to be dissected. "I don't know that" she herself had said to her cook, with whom she had a dispute on the previous day, but she had then added: *Behave yourself decently.* Here a displacement is palpable; of the two sentences which she spoke to her cook, she included the insignificant one in her dream; but the suppressed sentence, "Behave yourself decently!" alone fits in with the rest of the dream-content. One might use the words to a man who was making indecent overtures, and had neglected "to close his meat-shop." That we have really hit upon the trail of the interpretation is proved by its agreement with the allusions made by the incident with the green-grocer woman. A vegetable which is sold tied up in bundles (a longish vegetable, as she subsequently adds), and is also black: what can this be but a dream-combination of asparagus and black radish? I need not interpret asparagus to the initiated; and the other vegetable, too (think of the exclamation: "Blacky, save yourself!"), seems to me to point to the sexual theme at which we guessed in the beginning, when we wanted to replace the story of the dream by "the meat-shop is closed." We are not here concerned with the full meaning of the dream; so much is certain, that it is full of meaning and by no means guileless.[1]

II

Another guileless dream of the same patient, which in some respects is a pendant to the above. *Her husband asks her: "Oughtn't we to have the piano tuned?" She replies: "It's not worth while, the hammers would have to be rebuffed as well."* Again we have the reproduction of an actual event of the preceding day. Her husband had asked her such a question, and she had answered it in such words. But what is the meaning of her dreaming it? She says of the piano that it is a *disgusting* old box which has a bad tone; it *belonged* to her husband before they were married,[2] etc., but the key to the true solution lies in the phrase: *It isn't worth while.* This has its origin in a call paid yesterday to a woman friend. She was asked to take off her coat, but declined, saying: "Thanks, it isn't worth

---

[1] For the curious, I may remark that behind the dream there is hidden a phantasy of indecent, sexually provoking conduct on my part, and of repulsion on the part of the lady. If this interpretation should seem preposterous, I would remind the reader of the numerous cases in which physicians have been made the object of such charges by hysterical women, with whom the same phantasy has not appeared in a distorted form as a dream, but has become undisguisedly conscious and delusional.—With this dream the patient began her psychoanalytical treatment. It was only later that I learned that with this dream she repeated the initial trauma in which her neurosis originated, and since then I have noticed the same behaviour in other persons who in their childhood were victims of sexual attacks, and now, as it were, wish in their dreams for them to be repeated.

[2] A substitution by the opposite, as will be clear after analysis.

while, I must go in a moment." At this point I recall that yesterday, during the analysis, she suddenly took hold of her coat, of which a button had come undone. It was as though she meant to say: "Please don't look in, it isn't worth while." Thus *box* becomes *chest*, and the interpretation of the dream leads to the years when she was growing out of her childhood, when she began to be dissatisfied with her figure. It leads us back, indeed, to earlier periods, if we take into consideration the *disgusting* and the *bad tone*, and remember how often in allusions and in dreams the two small hemispheres of the female body take the place—as a substitute and an antithesis—of the large ones.

III

I will interrupt the analysis of this dreamer in order to insert a short, innocent dream which was dreamed by a young man. *He dreamt that he was putting on his winter overcoat again; this was terrible.* The occasion for this dream is apparently the sudden advent of cold weather. On more careful examination we note that the two brief fragments of the dream do not fit together very well, for what could be terrible about wearing a thick or heavy coat in cold weather? Unfortunately for the innocency of this dream, the first association, under analysis, yields the recollection that yesterday a lady had confidentially confessed to him that her last child owed its existence to the splitting of a condom. He now reconstructs his thoughts in accordance with this suggestion: A thin condom is dangerous, a thick one is bad. The condom is a "pullover" (*Ueberzieher*= literally pullover), for it is pulled over something: and *Ueberzieher* is the German term for a light overcoat. An experience like that related by the lady would indeed be "terrible" for an unmarried man.

We will now return to our other innocent dreamer.

IV

She puts a candle into a candlestick; but the candle is broken, so that it does not stand up. The girls at school say she is clumsy; but she replies that it is not her fault.

Here, too, there is an actual occasion for the dream; the day before she had actually put a candle into a candlestick; but this one was not broken. An obvious symbolism has here been employed. The candle is an object which excites the female genitals; its being broken, so that it does not stand upright, signifies impotence on the man's part (*it is not her fault*). But does this young woman, carefully brought up, and a stranger to all obscenity, know of such an application of the candle? By chance she is able to tell how she came by this information. While paddling a canoe on the Rhine, a boat passed her which contained some students, who were

singing rapturously, or rather yelling: "When the Queen of Sweden, behind closed shutters, with the candles of Apollo. . . ."

She does not hear or else understand the last word. Her husband was
asked to give her the required explanation. These verses are then replaced
in the dream-content by the innocent recollection of a task which she
once performed *clumsily* at her boarding-school, because of the *closed
shutters*. The connection between the theme of masturbation and that of
impotence is clear enough. "Apollo" in the latent dream-content connects
this dream with an earlier one in which the virgin Pallas figured. All this
is obviously not innocent.

V

Lest it may seem too easy a matter to draw conclusions from dreams
concerning the dreamer's real circumstances, I add another dream originating with the same person, which once more appears innocent. *"I dreamt
of doing something,"* she relates, *"which I actually did during the day,
that is to say, I filled a little trunk so full of books that I had difficulty in
closing it. My dream was just like the actual occurrence."* Here the
dreamer herself emphasizes the correspondence between the dream and
the reality. All such criticisms of the dream, and comments on the dream,
although they have found a place in the waking thoughts, properly belong
to the latent dream-content, as further examples will confirm. We are
told, then, that what the dream relates has actually occurred during the
day. It would take us too far afield to show how we arrive at the idea of
making use of the English language to help us in the interpretation of
this dream. Suffice it to say that it is again a question of a little box (cf.
p. 231, the dream of the dead child in the box) which has been filled so
full that nothing can go into it.

In all these "innocent" dreams the sexual factor as the motive of the
censorship is very prominent. But this is a subject of primary significance,
which we must consider later.

B. INFANTILE EXPERIENCES AS
THE SOURCE OF DREAMS

As the third of the peculiarities of the dream-content, we have adduced
the fact, in agreement with all other writers on the subject (excepting
Robert), that impressions from our childhood may appear in dreams,
which do not seem to be at the disposal of the waking memory. It is, of
course, difficult to decide how seldom or how frequently this occurs, because after waking the origin of the respective elements of the dream is
not recognized. The proof that we are dealing with impressions of our
childhood must thus be adduced objectively, and only in rare instances

do the conditions favour such proof. The story is told by A. Maury, as being particularly conclusive, of a man who decides to visit his birthplace after an absence of twenty years. On the night before his departure he dreams that he is in a totally unfamiliar locality, and that he there meets a strange man with whom he holds a conversation. Subsequently, upon his return home, he is able to convince himself that this strange locality really exists in the vicinity of his home, and the strange man in the dream turns out to be a friend of his dead father's, who is living in the town. This is, of course, a conclusive proof that in his childhood he had seen both the man and the locality. The dream, moreover, is to be interpreted as a dream of impatience, like the dream of the girl who carries in her pocket her ticket for a concert, the dream of the child whose father had promised him an excursion to the Hameau (p. 213), and so forth. The motives which reproduce just these impressions of childhood for the dreamer cannot, of course, be discovered without analysis.

One of my colleagues, who attended my lectures, and who boasted that his dreams were very rarely subject to distortion, told me that he had sometime previously seen, in a dream, *his former tutor in bed with his nurse,* who had remained in the household until his eleventh year. The actual location of this scene was realized even in the dream. As he was greatly interested, he related the dream to his elder brother, who laughingly confirmed its reality. The brother said that he remembered the affair very distinctly, for he was six years old at the time. The lovers were in the habit of making him, the elder boy, drunk with beer whenever circumstances were favourable to their nocturnal intercourse. The younger child, our dreamer, at that time three years of age, slept in the same room as the nurse, but was not regarded as an obstacle.

In yet another case it may be definitely established, without the aid of dream-interpretation, that the dream contains elements from childhood—namely, if the dream is a so-called *perennial* dream, one which, being first dreamt in childhood, recurs again and again in adult years. I may add a few examples of this sort to those already known, although I have no personal knowledge of perennial dreams. A physician, in his thirties, tells me that a yellow lion, concerning which he is able to give the precisest information, has often appeared in his dream-life, from his earliest childhood up to the present day. This lion, known to him from his dreams, was one day discovered *in natura,* as a long-forgotten china animal. The young man then learned from his mother that the lion had been his favourite toy in early childhood, a fact which he himself could no longer remember.

If we now turn from the manifest dream-content to the dream-thoughts which are revealed only on analysis, the experiences of childhood may be found to recur even in dreams whose content would not have led us to suspect anything of the sort. I owe a particularly delightful and instructive example of such a dream to my esteemed colleague of the "yellow lion." After reading Nansen's account of his polar expedition, he dreamt that he was giving the intrepid explorer electrical treatment on an ice-floe for the sciatica of which the latter complained! During the analysis of this dream he remembered an incident of his childhood, without which the dream would be wholly unintelligible. When he was three or four years of age he was one day listening attentively to the conversation of his elders; they were talking of exploration, and he presently asked his father whether exploration was a bad illness. He had apparently confounded *Reisen* (journey, trips) with *Reissen* (gripes, tearing pains), and the derision of his brothers and sisters prevented his ever forgetting the humiliating experience.

We have a precisely similar case when, in the analysis of the dream of the monograph on the genus cyclamen, I stumble upon a memory, retained from childhood, to the effect that when I was five years old my father allowed me to destroy a book embellished with coloured plates. It will perhaps be doubted whether this recollection really entered into the composition of the dream-content, and it may be suggested that the connection was established subsequently by the analysis. But the abundance and intricacy of the associative connections vouch for the truth of my explanation: cyclamen—favourite flower—favourite dish—artichoke; to pick to pieces like an artichoke, leaf by leaf (a phrase which at that time one heard daily, *à propos* of the dividing up of the Chinese empire); herbarium—bookworm, whose favourite food is books. I can further assure the reader that the ultimate meaning of the dream, which I have not given here, is most intimately connected with the content of the scene of childish destruction.

In another series of dreams we learn from analysis that the very wish which has given rise to the dream, and whose fulfilment the dream proves to be, has itself originated in childhood, so that one is astonished to find that *the child with all his impulses survives in the dream.*

I shall now continue the interpretation of a dream which has already proved instructive: I refer to the dream in which my friend R. is my uncle. We have carried its interpretation far enough for the wish-motive —the wish to be appointed professor—to assert itself palpably; and we have explained the affection felt for my friend R. in the dream as the outcome of opposition to, and defiance of, the two colleagues who appear in the dream-thoughts. The dream was my own; I may, therefore, continue the analysis by stating that I did not feel quite satisfied with the solution arrived at. I knew that my opinion of these colleagues, who were so badly treated in my dream-thoughts, would have been expressed in very different language in my waking life; the intensity of the wish that

I might not share their fate as regards the appointment seemed to me too slight fully to account for the discrepancy between my dream-opinion and my waking opinion. If the desire to be addressed by another title were really so intense it would be proof of a morbid ambition, which I do not think I cherish, and which I believe I was far from entertaining. I do not know how others who think they know me would judge me; perhaps I really was ambitious; but if I was, my ambition has long since been transferred to objects other than the rank and title of *Professor extraordinarius*.

Whence, then, the ambition which the dream has ascribed to me? Here I am reminded of a story which I heard often in my childhood, that at my birth an old peasant woman had prophesied to my happy mother (whose first-born I was) that she had brought a great man into the world. Such prophecies must be made very frequently; there are so many happy and expectant mothers, and so many old peasant women, and other old women who, since their mundane powers have deserted them, turn their eyes toward the future; and the prophetess is not likely to suffer for her prophecies. Is it possible that my thirst for greatness has originated from this source? But here I recollect an impression from the later years òf my childhood, which might serve even better as an explanation. One evening, at a restaurant on the Prater, where my parents were accustomed to take me when I was eleven or twelve years of age, we noticed a man who was going from table to table and, for a small sum, improvising verses upon any subject that was given him. I was sent to bring the poet to our table, and he showed his gratitude. Before asking for a subject he threw off a few rhymes about myself, and told us that if he could trust his inspiration I should probably one day become a "minister." I can still distinctly remember the impression produced by this second prophecy. It was in the days of the "bourgeois Ministry"; my father had recently brought home the portraits of the bourgeois university graduates, Herbst, Giskra, Unger, Berger and others, and we illuminated the house in their honour. There were even Jews among them; so that every diligent Jewish schoolboy carried a ministerial portfolio in his satchel. The impression of that time must be responsible for the fact that until shortly before I went to the university I wanted to study jurisprudence, and changed my mind only at the last moment. A medical man has no chance of becoming a minister. And now for my dream: It is only now that I begin to see that it translates me from the sombre present to the hopeful days of the bourgeois Ministry, and completely fulfils what was then my youthful ambition. In treating my two estimable and learned colleagues, merely because they are Jews, so badly, one as though he were a simpleton, and the other as though he were a criminal, I am acting as though I were the Minister; I have put myself in his place. What a revenge I take upon his

Excellency! He refuses to appoint me *Professor extraordinarius*, and so in my dream I put myself in his place.

In another case I note the fact that although the wish that excites the dream is a contemporary wish it is nevertheless greatly reinforced by memories of childhood. I refer to a series of dreams which are based on the longing to go to Rome. For a long time to come I shall probably have to satisfy this longing by means of dreams, since at the season of the year when I should be able to travel Rome is to be avoided for reasons of health.[1] Thus I once dreamt that I saw the Tiber and the bridge of Sant' Angelo from the window of a railway carriage; presently the train started, and I realized that I had never entered the city at all. The view that appeared in the dream was modelled after a well-known engraving which I had casually noticed the day before in the drawing-room of one of my patients. In another dream someone took me up a hill and showed me Rome half shrouded in mist, and so distant that I was astonished at the distinctness of the view. The content of this dream is too rich to be fully reported here. The motive, "to see the promised land afar," is here easily recognizable. The city which I thus saw in the mist is Lübeck; the original of the hill is the Gleichenberg. In a third dream I am at last in Rome. To my disappointment the scenery is anything but urban: it consists of *a little stream of black water, on one side of which are black rocks, while on the other are meadows with large white flowers. I notice a certain Herr Zucker (with whom I am superficially acquainted), and resolve to ask him to show me the way into the city.* It is obvious that I am trying in vain to see in my dream a city which I have never seen in my waking life. If I resolve the landscape into its elements, the white flowers point to Ravenna, which is known to me, and which once, for a time, replaced Rome as the capital of Italy. In the marshes around Ravenna we had found the most beautiful water-lilies in the midst of black pools of water; the dream makes them grow in the meadows, like the narcissi of our own Aussee, because we found it so troublesome to cull them from the water. The black rock so close to the water vividly recalls the valley of the Tepl at Karlsbad. "Karlsbad" now enables me to account for the peculiar circumstance that I ask Herr Zucker to show me the way. In the material of which the dream is woven I am able to recognize two of those amusing Jewish anecdotes which conceal such profound and, at times, such bitter worldly wisdom, and which we are so fond of quoting in our letters and conversation. One is the story of the "constitution"; it tells how a poor Jew sneaks into the Karlsbad express without a ticket; how he is detected, and is treated more and more harshly by the conductor at each succeeding

[1] I long ago learned that the fulfilment of such wishes only called for a little courage, and I then became a zealous pilgrim to Rome.

call for tickets; and how, when a friend whom he meets at one of the stations during his miserable journey asks him where he is going, he an- swers: "To Karlsbad—if my constitution holds out." Associated in memory with this is another story about a Jew who is ignorant of French, and who has express instructions to ask in Paris for the Rue Richelieu. Paris was for many years the goal of my own longing, and I regarded the satisfaction with which I first set foot on the pavements of Paris as a warrant that I should attain to the fulfilment of other wishes also. More- over, asking the way is a direct allusion to Rome, for, as we know, "all roads lead to Rome." And further, the name Zucker (sugar) again points to Karlsbad, whither we send persons afflicted with the *constitutional* disease, diabetes (*Zuckerkrankheit*, sugar-disease). The occasion for this dream was the proposal of my Berlin friend that we should meet in Prague at Easter. A further association with sugar and diabetes might be found in the matters which I had to discuss with him.

A fourth dream, occurring shortly after the last-mentioned, brings me back to Rome. I see a street corner before me, and am astonished that so many German placards should be posted there. On the previous day, when writing to my friend, I had told him, with truly prophetic vision, that Prague would probably not be a comfortable place for German travellers. The dream, therefore, expressed simultaneously the wish to meet him in Rome instead of in the Bohemian capital, and the desire, which probably originated during my student days, that the German language might be accorded more tolerance in Prague. As a matter of fact, I must have un- derstood the Czech language in the first years of my childhood, for I was born in a small village in Moravia, amidst a Slav population. A Czech nursery rhyme, which I heard in my seventeenth year, became, without effort on my part, so imprinted upon my memory that I can repeat it to this day, although I have no idea of its meaning. Thus in these dreams also there is no lack of manifold relations to the impressions of my early childhood.

During my last Italian journey, which took me past Lake Trasimenus, I at length discovered, after I had seen the Tiber, and had reluctantly turned back some fifty miles from Rome, what a reinforcement my long- ing for the Eternal City had received from the impressions of my child- hood. I had just conceived a plan of travelling to Naples via Rome the following year when this sentence, which I must have read in one of our German classics, occurred to me: [1] "It is a question which of the two paced to and fro in his room the more impatiently after he had conceived the plan of going to Rome—Assistant Headmaster Winckelmann or the great General Hannibal." I myself had walked in Hannibal's footsteps; like him I was destined never to see Rome, and he too had gone to Cam-

[1] The writer in whose works I found this passage was probably Jean Paul Richter.

pania when all were expecting him in Rome. Hannibal, with whom I had achieved this point of similarity, had been my favourite hero during my years at the "gymnasium"; like so many boys of my age, I bestowed my sympathies in the Punic war not on the Romans, but on the Carthaginians. Moreover, when I finally came to realize the consequences of belonging to an alien race, and was forced by the anti-Semitic feeling among my class-mates to take a definite stand, the figure of the Semitic commander assumed still greater proportions in my imagination. Hannibal and Rome symbolized, in my youthful eyes, the struggle between the tenacity of the Jews and the organization of the Catholic Church. The significance for our emotional life which the anti-Semitic movement has since assumed helped to fix the thoughts and impressions of those earlier days. Thus the desire to go to Rome has in my dream-life become the mask and symbol for a number of warmly cherished wishes, for whose realization one had to work with the tenacity and single-mindedness of the Punic general, though their fulfilment at times seemed as remote as Hannibal's lifelong wish to enter Rome.

And now, for the first time, I happened upon the youthful experience which even to-day still expresses its power in all these emotions and dreams. I might have been ten or twelve years old when my father began to take me with him on his walks, and in his conversation to reveal his views on the things of this world. Thus it was that he once told me the following incident, in order to show me that I had been born into happier times than he: "When I was a young man, I was walking one Saturday along the street in the village where you were born; I was well-dressed, with a new fur cap on my head. Up comes a Christian, who knocks my cap into the mud, and shouts, 'Jew, get off the pavement!' "—"And what did you do?"—"I went into the street and picked up the cap," he calmly replied. That did not seem heroic on the part of the big, strong man who was leading me, a little fellow, by the hand. I contrasted this situation, which did not please me, with another, more in harmony with my sentiments—the scene in which Hannibal's father, Hamilcar Barcas, made his son swear before the household altar to take vengeance on the Romans.[1] Ever since then Hannibal has had a place in my phantasies.

I think I can trace my enthusiasm for the Carthaginian general still further back into my childhood, so that it is probably only an instance of an already established emotional relation being transferred to a new vehicle. One of the first books which fell into my childish hands after I learned to read was Thiers' *Consulate and Empire*. I remember that I pasted on the flat backs of my wooden soldiers little labels bearing the names of the Imperial marshals, and that at that time Masséna (as a Jew,

---

[1] In the first edition of this book I gave here the name "Hasdrubal," an amazing error, which I explained in my *Psychopathology of Everyday Life*.

Menasse) was already my avowed favourite.[1] This preference is doubt-less also to be explained by the fact of my having been born, a hundred years later, on the same date. Napoleon himself is associated with Han-nibal through the crossing of the Alps. And perhaps the development of this martial ideal may be traced yet farther back, to the first three years of my childhood, to wishes which my alternately friendly and hostile relations with a boy a year older than myself must have evoked in the weaker of the two playmates.

The deeper we go into the analysis of dreams, the more often are we put on to the track of childish experiences which play the part of dream-sources in the latent dream-content.

We have learned that dreams very rarely reproduce memories in such a manner as to constitute, unchanged and unabridged, the sole manifest dream-content. Nevertheless, a few authentic examples which show such reproduction have been recorded, and I can add a few new ones, which once more refer to scenes of childhood. In the case of one of my patients a dream once gave a barely distorted reproduction of a sexual incident, which was immediately recognized as an accurate recollection. The mem-ory of it had never been completely lost in the waking life, but it had been greatly obscured, and it was revivified by the previous work of analysis. The dreamer had at the age of twelve visited a bedridden schoolmate, who had exposed himself, probably only by a chance movement in bed. At the sight of the boy's genitals he was seized by a kind of compulsion, exposed himself, and took hold of the member of the other boy who, however, looked at him in surprise and indignation, whereupon he became embar-rassed and let it go. A dream repeated this scene twenty-three years later, with all the details of the accompanying emotions, changing it, however, in this respect, that the dreamer played the passive instead of the active rôle, while the person of the schoolmate was replaced by a contemporary.

As a rule, of course, a scene from childhood is represented in the mani-fest dream-content only by an illusion, and must be disentangled from the dream by interpretation. The citation of examples of this kind cannot be very convincing, because any guarantee that they are really experiences of childhood is lacking; if they belong to an earlier period of life, they are no longer recognized by our memory. The conclusion that such childish experiences recur at all in dreams is justified in psychoanalytic work by a great number of factors, which in their combined results appear to be sufficiently reliable. But when, for the purposes of dream-interpretation, such references to childish experiences are torn out of their context, they may not perhaps seem very impressive, especially where I do not even give all the material upon which the interpretation is based. However, I shall not let this deter me from giving a few examples.

[1] The Jewish descent of the Marshal is somewhat doubtful.

I

With one of my female patients all dreams have the character of "hurry"; she is hurrying so as to be in time, so as not to miss her train, and so on. In one dream *she has to visit a girl friend; her mother had told her to ride and not walk; she runs, however, and keeps on calling.* The material that emerged in the analysis allowed one to recognize a memory of childish romping, and, especially for one dream, went back to the popular childish game of rapidly repeating the words of a sentence as though it was all one word. All these harmless jokes with little friends were remembered because they replaced other less harmless ones.[1]

II

The following dream was dreamed by another female patient: *She is in a large room in which there are all sorts of machines; it is rather like what she would imagine an orthopaedic institute to be. She hears that I am pressed for time, and that she must undergo treatment along with five others. But she resists, and is unwilling to lie down on the bed—or whatever it is—which is intended for her. She stands in a corner, and waits for me to say "It is not true." The others, meanwhile, laugh at her, saying it is all foolishness on her part. At the same time, it is as though she were called upon to make a number of little squares.*

The first part of the content of this dream is an allusion to the treatment and to the transference [2] to myself. The second contains an allusion to a scene of childhood; the two portions are connected by the mention of the bed. The orthopaedic institute is an allusion to one of my talks, in which I compared the treatment, with regard to its duration and its nature, to an orthopaedic treatment. At the beginning of the treatment I had to tell her that *for the present I had little time to give her,* but that later on I would devote a whole hour to her daily. This aroused in her the old sensitiveness, which is a leading characteristic of children who are destined to become hysterical. Their desire for love is insatiable. My patient was the youngest of six brothers and sisters (hence, *with five others*), and as such her father's favourite, but in spite of this she seems to have felt that her beloved father devoted far too little time and attention to her. Her waiting for me to say "It is not true" was derived as follows: A little tailor's apprentice had brought her a dress, and she had given him the money for it. Then she asked her husband whether she would have to pay the money again if the boy were to lose it. To tease her, her husband answered "Yes" (the *teasing* in the dream), and she asked again and again,

---

[1] [In the original this paragraph contains many plays on the word "Hetz" (hurry, chase, scurry, game, etc.).—TRANS.]

[2] [This word is here used in the psychoanalytical sense.—TRANS.]

and *waited for him to say "It is not true."* The thought of the latent dream-content may now be construed as follows: Will she have to pay me double the amount when I devote twice as much time to her?—a thought which is stingy or *filthy* (the uncleanliness of childhood is often replaced in dreams by greed for money; the word "filthy" here supplies the bridge). If all the passage referring to her waiting until I say "It is not true" is intended in the dream as a circumlocution for the word "dirty," *the stand-ing-in-the-corner and not lying-down-on-the-bed* are in keeping with this word, as component parts of a scene of her childhood in which she had soiled her bed, in punishment for which *she was put into the corner*, with a warning that papa would not love her any more, whereupon her brothers and sisters laughed at her, etc. The little squares refer to her young niece, who showed her the arithmetical trick of writing figures in nine squares (I think) in such a way that on being added together in any direction they make fifteen.

III

Here is a man's dream: *He sees two boys tussling with each other; they are cooper's boys, as he concludes from the tools which are lying about; one of the boys has thrown the other down; the prostrate boy is wearing ear-rings with blue stones. He runs towards the assailant with lifted cane, in order to chastise him. The boy takes refuge behind a woman, as though she were his mother, who is standing against a wooden fence. She is the wife of a day-labourer, and she turns her back to the man who is dreaming. Finally she turns about and stares at him with a horrible look, so that he runs away in terror; the red flesh of the lower lid seems to stand out from her eyes.*

This dream has made abundant use of trivial occurrences from the previous day, in the course of which he actually saw two boys in the street, one of whom threw the other down. When he walked up to them in order to settle the quarrel, both of them took to their heels. Cooper's boys—this is explained only by a subsequent dream, in the analysis of which he used the proverbial expression: *"To knock the bottom out of the barrel."* Ear-rings with blue stones, according to his observation, are worn chiefly by *prostitutes*. This suggests a familiar doggerel rhyme about two boys: "The other boy was called Marie": that is, he was a girl. The woman standing by the fence: after the scene with the two boys he went for a walk along the bank of the Danube and, taking advantage of being alone, urinated *against a wooden fence*. A little farther on a respectably dressed, elderly lady smiled at him very pleasantly, and wanted to hand him her card with her address.

Since, in the dream, the woman stood as he had stood while urinating, there is an allusion to a woman urinating, and this explains the "horrible look" and the prominence of the red flesh, which can only refer to the genitals gaping in a squatting posture; seen in childhood, they had appeared in later recollection as *"proud flesh,"* as a *"wound."* The dream unites two occasions upon which, as a little boy, the dreamer was enabled to see the genitals of little girls, once by throwing the little girl down, and once while the child was *urinating*; and, as is shown by another association, he had retained in his memory the punishment administered or threatened by his father on account of these manifestations of sexual curiosity.

IV

A great mass of childish memories, which have been hastily combined into a phantasy, may be found behind the following dream of an elderly lady: *She goes out in a hurry to do some shopping. On the Graben* [1] *she sinks to her knees as though she had broken down. A number of people collect around her, especially cab-drivers, but no one helps her to get up. She makes many vain attempts; finally she must have succeeded, for she is put into a cab which is to take her home. A large, heavily laden basket (something like a market-basket) is thrown after her through the window.*

This is the woman who is always harassed in her dreams, just as she used to be harassed when a child. The first situation of the dream is apparently taken from the sight of a fallen horse, just as "broken down" points to horse-racing. In her youth she was a rider; still earlier she was probably also a *horse*. With the idea of falling down is connected her first childish reminiscence of the seventeen-year-old son of the hall porter, who had an epileptic seizure in the street and was brought home in a cab. Of this, of course, she had only heard, but the idea of epileptic fits, of *falling down*, acquired a great influence over her phantasies, and later on influenced the form of her own hysterical attacks. When a person of the female sex dreams of falling, this almost always has a sexual significance; she becomes a *"fallen woman,"* and, for the purpose of the dream under consideration, this interpretation is probably the least doubtful, for she falls in the Graben, the street in Vienna which is known as the concourse of prostitutes. The *market-basket* admits of more than one interpretation; in the sense of refusal (German, *Korb* = basket = snub, refusal) it reminds her of the many snubs which she at first administered to her suitors and which, she thinks, she herself received later. This agrees with the detail: *no one will help her up*, which she herself interprets as "being disdained." Further, the *market-basket* recalls phantasies which have already appeared in the course of analysis, in which she imagines that she has married far beneath her station and now goes to the market as a market-

---

[1] [A street in Vienna.—TRANS.]

woman. Lastly, the market-basket might be interpreted as the mark of a *servant*. This suggests further memories of her childhood—of a *cook* who was discharged because she stole; she, too, *sank to her knees* and begged for mercy. The dreamer was at that time twelve years of age. Then emerges a recollection of a chamber-maid, who was dismissed because she had an affair with the coachman of the household, who, incidentally, married her afterwards. This recollection, therefore, gives us a clue to the cab-drivers in the dream (who, in opposition to the reality, do not stand by the fallen woman). But there still remains to be explained the throwing of the basket; in particular, why is it thrown *through the window?* This reminds her of the forwarding of luggage by rail, to the custom of *Fensterln* [1] in the country, and to trivial impressions of a summer resort, of a gentleman who threw some blue plums into the window of a lady's room, and of her little sister, who was frightened because an idiot who was passing looked in at the window. And now, from behind all this emerges an obscure recollection from her tenth year of a nurse in the country to whom one of the menservants made love (and whose conduct the child may have noticed), and who was "sent packing," "thrown out," together with her lover (in the dream we have the expression: "thrown into"); an incident which we have been approaching by several other paths. The luggage or box of a servant is disparagingly described in Vienna as "seven plums." "Pack up your seven plums and get out!"

My collection, of course, contains a plethora of such patients' dreams, the analysis of which leads back to impressions of childhood, often dating back to the first three years of life, which are remembered obscurely, or not at all. But it is a questionable proceeding to draw conclusions from these and apply them to dreams in general, for they are mostly dreams of neurotic, and especially hysterical, persons; and the part played in these dreams by childish scenes might be conditioned by the nature of the neurosis, and not by the nature of dreams in general. In the interpretation of my own dreams, however, which is assuredly not undertaken on account of grave symptoms of illness, it happens just as frequently that in the latent dream-content I am unexpectedly confronted with a scene of my childhood, and that a whole series of my dreams will suddenly converge upon the paths proceeding from a single childish experience. I have already given examples of this, and I shall give yet more in different connections. Perhaps I cannot close this chapter more fittingly than by citing

[1] [*Fensterln* is the custom, now falling into disuse, found in rural districts of the German Schwarzwald, of lovers who woo their sweethearts at their bedroom windows, to which they ascend by means of a ladder, enjoying such intimacy that the relation practically amounts to a trial marriage. The reputation of the young woman never suffers on account of *Fensterln,* unless she becomes intimate with too many suitors.—TRANS.]

several dreams of my own, in which recent events and long-forgotten experiences of my childhood appear together as dream-sources.

I. After I have been travelling, and have gone to bed hungry and tired, the prime necessities of life begin to assert their claims in sleep, and I dream as follows: *I go into a kitchen in order to ask for some pudding. There three women are standing, one of whom is the hostess; she is rolling something in her hands, as though she were making dumplings. She replies that I must wait until she has finished* (not distinctly as a speech). *I become impatient, and go away affronted. I want to put on an overcoat; but the first I try on is too long. I take it off, and am somewhat astonished to find that it is trimmed with fur. A second coat has a long strip of cloth with a Turkish design sewn into it. A stranger with a long face and a short, pointed beard comes up and prevents me from putting it on, declaring that it belongs to him. I now show him that it is covered all over with Turkish embroideries. He asks: "How do the Turkish (drawings, strips of cloth . . .) concern you?" But we soon become quite friendly.*

In the analysis of this dream I remember, quite unexpectedly, the first novel which I ever read, or rather, which I began to read from the end of the first volume, when I was perhaps thirteen years of age. I have never learned the name of the novel, or that of its author, but the end remains vividly in my memory. The hero becomes insane, and continually calls out the names of the three women who have brought the greatest happiness and the greatest misfortune into his life. Pélagie is one of these names. I still do not know what to make of this recollection during the analysis. Together with the three women there now emerge the three Parcae, who spin the fates of men, and I know that one of the three women, the hostess in the dream, is the mother who gives life, and who, moreover, as in my own case, gives the child its first nourishment. Love and hunger meet at the mother's breast. A young man—so runs an anecdote—who became a great admirer of womanly beauty, once observed, when the conversation turned upon the handsome wet-nurse who had suckled him as a child, that he was sorry that he had not taken better advantage of his opportunities. I am in the habit of using the anecdote to elucidate the factor of retrospective tendencies in the mechanism of the psychoneuroses.—One of the Parcae, then, is rubbing the palms of her hands together, as though she were making dumplings. A strange occupation for one of the Fates, and urgently in need of explanation! This explanation is furnished by another and earlier memory of my childhood. When I was six years old, and receiving my first lessons from my mother, I was expected to believe that we are made of dust, and must, therefore, return to dust. But this did not please me, and I questioned the doctrine. Thereupon my mother rubbed the palms of her hands together—just as in making dumplings, except that there was no dough between them—and showed me the blackish scales of *epidermis* which were thus rubbed off, as a proof that it is of dust that we are made. Great was my astonishment at this demonstration *ad oculos,* and I acquiesced in the idea which I was later to hear expressed in the words: "Thou owest nature a death." [1] Thus the women to whom I go in the kitchen, as I so often did in my childhood when I was hungry and my mother, sitting by the fire, admonished me to wait until lunch was ready, are really the Parcae. And now for the dumplings! At least one of my teachers at the University—the very one to whom I am indebted for my *histological* knowledge (*epidermis*)—would be reminded by the name *Knödl* (*Knödl* means dumpling), of a person whom he had to prosecute for *plagiarising* his writings. Committing a plagiarism, taking anything one can lay hands on, even though it belongs to another, obviously leads to the second part of the dream, in which I am treated like the *overcoat thief* who for some time plied his trade in the lecture-halls. I have written the word *plagiarism*—without definite intention—because it occurred to me, and now I see that it must belong to the latent dream-content and that it will serve as a bridge between the different parts of the manifest dream-content. The chain of associations—*Pélagie—plagiarism—plagiostomi* [2] (sharks)—*fish-bladder*—connects the old novel with the affair of Knödl and the overcoats (German: *Überzieher* = pull over, overcoat or condom), which obviously refer to an appliance appertaining to the technique of sex. This, it is true, is a very forced and irrational connection, but it is nevertheless one which I could not have established in waking life if it had not already been established by the dream-work. Indeed, as though nothing were sacred to this impulse to enforce associations, the beloved name, *Brücke* (bridge of words, see above), now serves to remind me of the very institute in which I spent my happiest hours as a student, wanting for nothing. "So will you at the *breasts* of Wisdom every day more pleasure find"), in the most complete contrast to the desires which plague me (German: *plagen*) while I dream. And finally, there emerges the recollection of another dear teacher, whose name once more sounds like something edible (*Fleischl—Fleisch* = meat —like *Knödl* = dumplings), and of a pathetic scene in which the scales of epidermis play a part (mother—hostess), and mental derangement (the novel), and a remedy from the Latin pharmacopeia (*Küche* = kitchen) which numbs the sensation of *hunger,* namely, cocaine.

In this manner I could follow the intricate trains of thought still farther, and could fully elucidate that part of the dream which is lacking in the

---

[1] Both the affects pertaining to these childish scenes—astonishment and resignation to the inevitable—appeared in a dream of slightly earlier date, which first reminded me of this incident of my childhood.

[2] I do not bring in the plagiostomi arbitrarily; they recall a painful incident of disgrace before the same teacher.

analysis; but I must refrain, because the personal sacrifice which this would involve is too great. I shall take up only one of the threads, which will serve to lead us directly to one of the dream-thoughts that lie at the bottom of the medley. The stranger with the long face and pointed beard, who wants to prevent me from putting on the overcoat, has the features of a tradesman of Spalato, of whom my wife bought a great deal of *Turkish* cloth. His name was *Popović*, a suspicious name, which even gave the humorist Stettenheim a pretext for a suggestive remark: "He told me his name, and blushingly shook my hand." [1] For the rest, I find the same misuse of names as above in the case of *Pélagie, Knödl, Brücke, Fleischl*. No one will deny that such playing with names is a childish trick; if I indulge in it the practice amounts to an act of retribution, for my own name has often enough been the subject of such feeble attempts at wit. Goethe once remarked how sensitive a man is in respect to his name, which he feels that he fills even as he fills his skin; Herder having written the following lines on his name:—

"Der du von Göttern abstammst, von Gothen oder vom Kote."
"So seid ihr Götterbilder auch zu Staub."

"Thou who art born of the gods, of the Goths, or of the mud."
"Thus are thy godlike images even dust."

I realize that this digression on the misuse of names was intended merely to justify this complaint. But here let us stop. . . . The purchase at Spalato reminds me of another purchase at Cattaro, where I was too cautious, and missed the opportunity of making an excellent bargain. (Missing an opportunity at the breast of the wet-nurse; see above.) One of the dream-thoughts occasioned by the sensation of hunger really amounts to this: We should let nothing escape; we should take what we can get, even if we do a little wrong; we should never let an opportunity go by; life is so short, and death inevitable. Because this is meant even sexually, and because desire is unwilling to check itself before the thought of doing wrong, this philosophy of *carpe diem* has reason to fear the censorship, and must conceal itself behind a dream. And so all sorts of counter-thoughts find expression, with recollections of the time when *spiritual nourishment* alone was sufficient for the dreamer, with hindrances of every kind and even threats of disgusting sexual punishments.

II. A second dream requires a longer preliminary statement:

I had driven to the Western Station in order to start on a holiday trip to the Aussee, but I went on to the platform in time for the Ischl train, which leaves earlier. There I saw Count Thun, who was again going to see the Emperor at Ischl. In spite of the rain he arrived in an open carriage,

[1] *Popo* = backside, in German nursery language.

came straight through the entrance-gate for the local trains, and with a curt gesture and not a word of explanation he waved back the gatekeeper, who did not know him and wanted to take his ticket. After he had left in the Ischl train, I was asked to leave the platform and return to the waiting-room; but after some difficulty I obtained permission to remain. I passed the time noting how many people bribed the officials to secure a compartment; I fully intended to make a complaint—that is, to demand the same privilege. Meanwhile I sang something to myself, which I afterwards recognized as the aria from *The Marriage of Figaro:*—

> "If my lord Count would tread a measure, tread a measure,
>> Let him but say his pleasure,
>> And I will play the tune."

(Possibly another person would not have recognized the tune.)

The whole evening I was in a high-spirited, pugnacious mood; I chaffed the waiter and the cab-driver, I hope without hurting their feelings; and now all kinds of bold and revolutionary thoughts came into my mind, such as would fit themselves to the words of Figaro, and to memories of Beaumarchais' comedy, of which I had seen a performance at the *Comédie Française*. The speech about the great men who have taken the trouble to be born; the seigneurial right which Count Almaviva wishes to exercise with regard to Susanne; the jokes which our malicious Opposition journalists make on the name of Count Thun (German, *thun* = do), calling him Graf Nichtsthun, Count-Do-Nothing. I really do not envy him; he now has a difficult audience with the Emperor before him, and it is I who am the real Count-Do-Nothing, for I am going off for a holiday. I make all sorts of amusing plans for the vacation. Now a gentleman arrives whom I know as a Government representative at the medical examinations, and who has won the flattering nickname of "the Governmental bed-fellow" (literally, "by-sleeper") by his activities in this capacity. By insisting on his official status he secured half a first-class compartment, and I heard one guard say to another: "Where are we going to put the gentleman with the first-class half-compartment?" A pretty sort of favouritism! I am paying for a whole first-class compartment. I did actually get a whole compartment to myself, but not in a through carriage, so there was no lavatory at my disposal during the night. My complaints to the guard were fruitless; I revenged myself by suggesting that at least a hole be made in the floor of this compartment, to serve the possible needs of passengers. At a quarter to three in the morning I wake, with an urgent desire to urinate, from the following dream:—

A crowd, a students' meeting. . . . A certain Count (Thun or Taaffe) is making a speech. Being asked to say something about the Germans, he declares, with a contemptuous gesture, that their favourite flower is colts-

foot, and he then puts into his buttonhole something like a torn leaf, really the crumpled skeleton of a leaf. I jump up, and I jump up,[1] *but I am surprised at my implied attitude.* Then, more indistinctly: *It seems as though this were the vestibule (Aula); the exits are thronged, and one must escape. I make my way through a suite of handsomely appointed rooms, evidently ministerial apartments, with furniture of a colour between brown and violet, and at last I come to a corridor in which a housekeeper, a fat, elderly woman, is seated. I try to avoid speaking to her, but she apparently thinks I have a right to pass this way, because she asks whether she shall accompany me with the lamp. I indicate with a gesture, or tell her, that she is to remain standing on the stairs, and it seems to me that I am very clever, for after all I am evading detection. Now I am downstairs, and I find a narrow, steeply rising path, which I follow.*

Again indistinctly: *It is as though my second task were to get away from the city, just as my first was to get out of the building. I am riding in a one-horse cab, and I tell the driver to take me to a railway station.* "*I can't drive with you on the railway line itself,*" *I say, when he reproaches me as though I had tired him out. Here it seems as though I had already made a journey in his cab which is usually made by rail. The stations are crowded; I am wondering whether to go to Krems or to Znaim, but I reflect that the Court will be there, and I decide in favour of Graz or some such place. Now I am seated in the railway carriage, which is rather like a tram, and I have in my buttonhole a peculiar long braided thing, on which are violet-brown violets of stiff material, which makes a great impression on people.* Here the scene breaks off.

I am once more in front of the railway station, but I am in the company of an elderly gentleman. I think out a scheme for remaining unrecognized, but I see this plan already being carried out. Thinking and experiencing are here, as it were, the same thing. He pretends to be blind, at least in one eye, and I hold before him a male glass urinal (which we have to buy in the city, or have bought). I am thus a sick-nurse, and have to give him the urinal because he is blind. If the conductor sees us in this position, he must pass us by without drawing attention to us. At the same time the position of the elderly man, and his urinating organ, is plastically perceived. Then I wake with a desire to urinate.

The whole dream seems a sort of phantasy, which takes the dreamer back to the year of revolution, 1848, the memory of which had been revived by the jubilee of 1898, as well as by a little excursion to Wachau, on which I visited *Emmersdorf*, the refuge of the student leader Fischof,[2]

---

[1] This repetition has crept into the text of the dream, apparently through absent-mindedness, and I have left it because analysis shows that it has a meaning.

[2] This is an error and not a slip, for I learned later that the Emmersdorf in Wachau is not identical with the refuge of the revolutionist Fischof, a place of the same name.

to whom several features of the manifest dream-content might refer. The association of ideas then leads me to England, to the house of my brother, who used in jest to twit his wife with the title of Tennyson's poem *Fifty Years Ago*, whereupon the children were used to correct him: *Fifteen Years Ago*. This phantasy, however, which attaches itself to the thoughts evoked by the sight of Count Thun, is, like the façade of an Italian church, without organic connection with the structure behind it, but unlike such a façade it is full of gaps, and confused, and in many places portions of the interior break through. The first situation of the dream is made up of a number of scenes, into which I am able to dissect it. The arrogant attitude of the Count in the dream is copied from a scene at my school which occurred in my fifteenth year. We had hatched a conspiracy against an unpopular and ignorant teacher; the leading spirit in this conspiracy was a schoolmate who since that time seems to have taken Henry VIII of England as his model. It fell to me to carry out the *coup d'état*, and a discussion of the importance of the Danube (German, *Donau*) to Austria (Wachau!) was the occasion of an open revolt. One of our fellow-conspirators was our only aristocratic schoolmate—he was called "the giraffe" on account of his conspicuous height—and while he was being reprimanded by the tyrant of the school, the professor of the *German* language, he stood just as the Count stood in the dream. The explanation of the *favourite* flower, and the putting into a buttonhole of something that must have been a flower (which recalls the orchids which I had given that day to a friend, and also a rose of Jericho) prominently recalls the incident in Shakespeare's historical play which opens the civil wars of the *Red* and the *White* Roses; the mention of Henry VIII has paved the way to this reminiscence. Now it is not very far from roses to red and white carnations. (Meanwhile two little rhymes, the one German, the other Spanish, insinuate themselves into the analysis: *Rosen, Tulpen, Nelken, alle Blumen welken,* and *Isabelita, no llores, que se marchitan las flores.* The Spanish line occurs in *Figaro*.) Here in Vienna white carnations have become the badge of the *Anti-Semites*, red ones of the *Social Democrats*. Behind this is the recollection of an anti-Semitic challenge during a railway journey in beautiful Saxony (Anglo-Saxon). The third scene contributing to the formation of the first situation in the dream dates from my early student days. There was a debate in a *German* students' club about the relation of philosophy to the general sciences. Being a green youth, full of materialistic doctrines, I thrust myself forward in order to defend an extremely one-sided position. Thereupon a sagacious older fellow-student, who has since then shown his capacity for leading men and organizing the masses, and who, moreover, bears a name belonging to the animal kingdom, rose and gave us a thorough dressing-down; he too, he said, had herded swine in his youth, and had then returned repentant to his father's house. I *jumped up* (as in the dream), became *piggishly rude,* and retorted that since I knew he had herded *swine,* I *was not surprised* at the tone of his discourse. (In the dream I am *surprised* at my German Nationalistic feelings.) There was a great commotion, and an almost general demand that I should retract my words, but I stood my ground. The insulted student was too sensible to take the advice which was offered him, that he should send me a *challenge,* and let the matter drop.

The remaining elements of this scene of the dream are of more remote origin. What does it mean that the Count should make a scornful reference to coltsfoot? Here I must question my train of associations. Coltsfoot (German: *Huflattich*), *Lattice* (lettuce), *Salathund* (the dog that grudges others what he cannot eat himself). Here plenty of opprobrious epithets may be discerned: *Gir-affe* (German: *Affe* = monkey, ape), *pig, sow, dog;* I might even arrive, by way of the name, at *donkey,* and thereby pour contempt upon an academic professor. Furthermore, I translate coltsfoot (*Huflattich*)—I do not know whether I do so correctly—by *pisse-en-lit.* I get this idea from Zola's *Germinal,* in which some children are told to bring some dandelion salad with them. The dog—*chien*—has a name sounding not unlike the verb for the major function (*chier,* as *pisser* stands for the minor one). Now we shall soon have the indecent in all its three physical categories, for in the same *Germinal,* which deals with the future revolution, there is a description of a very peculiar contest, which relates to the production of the gaseous excretions known as *flatus.*[1] And now I cannot but observe how the way to this *flatus* has been prepared a long while since, beginning with the *flowers,* and proceeding to the Spanish rhyme of *Isabelita,* to *Ferdinand* and *Isabella,* and, by way of Henry VIII, to English history at the time of the Armada, after the victorious termination of which the English struck a medal with the inscription: *Flavit et dissipati sunt,* for the storm had scattered the Spanish fleet.[2] I had thought of using this phrase, half jestingly, as the title of a chapter on "Therapy," if I should ever succeed in giving a detailed account of my conception and treatment of hysteria.

I cannot give so detailed an interpretation of the second scene of the dream, out of sheer regard for the censorship. For at this point I put myself in the place of a certain eminent gentleman of the revolutionary pe-

[1] Not in *Germinal,* but in *La Terre*—a mistake of which I became aware only in the analysis.—Here I would call attention to the identity of letters in *Huflattich* and *Flatus.*

[2] An unsolicited biographer, Dr. F. Wittels, reproaches me for having omitted the name of Jehovah from the above motto. The English medal contains the name of the Deity, in Hebrew letters, on the background of a cloud, and placed in such a manner that one may equally well regard it as part of the picture or as part of the inscription.

riod, who had an adventure with an eagle (German: *Adler*) and who is
said to have suffered from incontinence of the bowels, *incontinentia alvi*,
etc.; and here I believe that I *should not be justified* in passing the censorship, even though it was an *aulic* councillor (*aula, consiliarius aulicus*)
who told me the greater part of this history. The suite of rooms in the
dream is suggested by his Excellency's private saloon carriage, into which
I was able to glance; but it means, as it so often does in dreams, a woman
(*Frauenzimmer*, German, *Zimmer*—room, is appended to *Frauen*—
woman, in order to imply a slight contempt [1]). The personality of the
housekeeper is an ungrateful allusion to a witty old lady, which ill repays
her for the good times and the many good stories which I have enjoyed in
her house. The incident of the lamp goes back to *Grillparzer*, who notes
a charming experience of a similar nature, of which he afterwards made
use in *Hero and Leander* (the *waves* of the *sea* and of love—the Armada
and the *storm*).

I must forego a detailed analysis of the two remaining portions of the
dream; I shall single out only those elements which lead me back to the
two scenes of my childhood for the sake of which alone I have selected the
dream. The reader will rightly assume that it is sexual material which
necessitates the suppression; but he may not be content with this explanation. There are many things of which one makes no secret to oneself, but which must be treated as secrets in addressing others, and here
we are concerned not with the reasons which induce me to conceal the
solution, but with the motive of the inner censorship which conceals the
real content of the dream even from myself. Concerning this, I will confess that the analysis reveals these three portions of the dream as im-
pertinent boasting, the exuberance of an absurd megalomania, long ago
suppressed in my waking life, which, however, dares to show itself, with
individual ramifications, even in the manifest dream-content (*it seems
to me that I am a cunning fellow*), making the high-spirited mood of the
evening before the dream perfectly intelligible. Boasting of every kind,
indeed; thus, the mention of Graz points to the phrase: "What price
Graz?" which one is wont to use when one feels unusually wealthy.
Readers who recall Master Rabelais's inimitable description of the life
and deeds of Gargantua and his son Pantagruel will be able to enroll even
the suggested content of the first portion of the dream among the boasts
to which I have alluded. But the following belongs to the two scenes of
childhood of which I have spoken: I had bought a *new* trunk for this
journey, the colour of which, a *brownish violet*, appears in the dream
several times (violet-brown violets of a stiff cloth, on an object which is
known as a "girl-catcher"—the furniture in the ministerial chambers).
Children, we know, believe that one *attracts people's attention with any-*

[1] [Translator's Note.]

thing new. Now I have been told of the following incident of my childhood; my recollection of the occurrence itself has been replaced by my
recollection of the story. I am told that at the age of two I still used
occasionally to wet my bed, and that when I was reproved for doing so I
consoled my father by promising to buy him a beautiful *new red* bed in
N. (the nearest large town). Hence, the interpolation in the dream, that
we *had bought the urinal in the city or had to buy it;* one must keep one's
promises. (One should note, moreover, the association of the male urinal
and the woman's trunk, *box.*) All the megalomania of the child is contained in this promise. The significance of dreams of urinary difficulties
in the case of children has already been considered in the interpretation
of an earlier dream (cf. the dream on p. 241). The psychoanalysis of
neurotics has taught us to recognize the intimate connection between
wetting the bed and the character trait of ambition.

Then, when I was seven or eight years of age another domestic incident
occurred which I remember very well. One evening, before going to bed,
I had disregarded the dictates of discretion, and had satisfied my needs
in my parents' bedroom, and in their presence. Reprimanding me for this
delinquency, my father remarked: "That boy will never amount to anything." This must have been a terrible affront to my ambition, for allusions to this scene recur again and again in my dreams, and are constantly
coupled with enumerations of my accomplishments and successes, as
though I wanted to say: "You see, I have amounted to something after
all." This childish scene furnishes the elements for the last image of the
dream, in which the rôles are interchanged, of course for the purpose of
revenge. The elderly man, obviously my father, for the blindness in one
eye signifies his one-sided glaucoma,[1] is now urinating before me as I
once urinated before him. By means of the glaucoma I remind my father
of cocaine, which stood him in good stead during his operation, as though
I had thereby fulfilled my promise. Besides, I make sport of him; since
he is blind, I must hold the *glass* in front of him, and I delight in allusions
to my knowledge of the theory of hysteria, of which I am proud.[2]

[1] Another interpretation: He is one-eyed like Odin, the father of the gods—Odin's
consolation. The consolation in the childish scene: I will buy him a new bed.
[2] Here is some more material for interpretation: Holding the urine-glass recalls the
story of a peasant (illiterate) at the optician's, who tried on now one pair of spectacles, now another, but was still unable to read.—(Peasant-catcher—girl-catcher in
the preceding portion of the dream.)—The peasants' treatment of the feeble-
minded father in Zola's *La Terre.*—The tragic atonement, that in his last days my
father soiled his bed like a child; hence, I am his nurse in the dream.—"Thinking and
experiencing are here, as it were, identical"; this recalls a highly revolutionary closet
drama by Oscar Panizza, in which God, the Father, is ignominiously treated as a
palsied greybeard. With Him will and deed are one, and in the book he has to be
restrained by His archangel, a sort of Ganymede, from scolding and swearing, because His curses would immediately be fulfilled.—Making plans is a reproach against
my father, dating from a later period in the development of the critical faculty, much

If the two childish scenes of urination are, according to my theory, closely associated with the desire for greatness, their resuscitation on the journey to the Aussee was further favoured by the accidental circumstance that my compartment had no lavatory, and that I must be prepared to postpone relief during the journey, as actually happened in the morning when I woke with the sensation of a bodily need. I suppose one might be inclined to credit this sensation with being the actual stimulus of the dream; I should, however, prefer a different explanation, namely, that the dream-thoughts first gave rise to the desire to urinate. It is quite unusual for me to be disturbed in sleep by any physical need, least of all at the time when I woke on this occasion—a quarter to four in the morning. I would forestall a further objection by remarking that I have hardly ever felt a desire to urinate after waking early on other journeys made under more comfortable circumstances. However, I can leave this point undecided without weakening my argument.

Further, since experience in dream-analysis has drawn my attention to the fact that even from dreams the interpretation of which seems at first sight complete, because the dream-sources and the wish-stimuli are easily demonstrable, important trains of thought proceed which reach back into the earliest years of childhood, I had to ask myself whether this characteristic does not even constitute an essential condition of dreaming. If it were permissible to generalize this notion, I should say that every dream is connected through its manifest content with recent experiences, while through its latent content it is connected with the most remote experiences; and I can actually show in the analysis of hysteria that these remote experiences have in a very real sense remained recent right up to

---

as the whole rebellious content of the dream, which commits *lèse majesté* and scorns authority, may be traced to a revolt against my father. The sovereign is called the father of his country (*Landesvater*), and the father is the first and oldest, and for the child the only authority, from whose absolutism the other social authorities have evolved in the course of the history of human civilization (in so far as "mother-right" does not necessitate a qualification of this doctrine).—The words which occurred to me in the dream, "thinking and experiencing are the same thing," refer to the explanation of hysterical symptoms, with which the male urinal (glass) is also associated.—I need not explain the principle of *Gschnas* to a Viennese; it consists in constructing objects of rare and costly appearance out of trivial, and preferably comical and worthless material—for example, making suits of armour out of kitchen utensils, wisps of straw and *Salzstangeln* (long rolls), as our artists are fond of doing at their jolly parties. I had learned that hysterical subjects do the same thing; besides what really happens to them, they unconsciously conceive for themselves horrible or extravagantly fantastic incidents, which they build up out of the most harmless and commonplace material of actual experience. The symptoms attach themselves primarily to these phantasies, not to the memory of real events, whether serious or trivial. This explanation had helped me to overcome many difficulties, and afforded me much pleasure. I was able to allude to it by means of the dream-element "male urine-glass," because I had been told that at the last *Gschnas* evening a poison-chalice of Lucretia Borgia's had been exhibited, the chief constituent of which had consisted of a glass urinal for men, such as is used in hospitals.

the present. But I still find it very difficult to prove this conjecture; I shall have to return to the probable rôle in dream-formation of the earliest experiences of our childhood in another connection (Chapter VII).

Of the three peculiarities of the dream-memory considered above, one —the preference for the unimportant in the dream-content—has been satisfactorily explained by tracing it back to dream-distortion. We have succeeded in establishing the existence of the other two peculiarities—the preferential selection of recent and also of infantile material—but we have found it impossible to derive them from the motives of the dream. Let us keep in mind these two characteristics, which we still have to explain or evaluate; a place-will have to be found for them elsewhere, either in the discussion of the psychology of the sleeping state, or in the consideration of the structure of the psychic apparatus—which we shall undertake later after we have seen that by means of dream-interpretation we are able to glance as through an inspection-hole into the interior of this apparatus.

But here and now I will emphasize another result of the last few dream-analyses. The dream often appears to have several meanings; not only may several wish-fulfilments be combined in it, as our examples show, but one meaning or one wish-fulfilment may conceal another, until in the lowest stratum one comes upon the fulfilment of a wish from the earliest period of childhood; and here again it may be questioned whether the word "often" at the beginning of this sentence may not more correctly be replaced by "constantly." [1]

C. THE SOMATIC SOURCES OF DREAMS

If we attempt to interest a cultured layman in the problems of dreams, and if, with this end in view, we ask him what he believes to be the source of dreams, we shall generally find that he feels quite sure he knows at least this part of the solution. He thinks immediately of the influence exercised on the formation of dreams by a disturbed or impeded digestion ("Dreams come from the stomach"), an accidental position of the body, a trifling occurrence during sleep. He does not seem to suspect that even after all these factors have been duly considered something still remains to be explained.

In the introductory chapter [2] we examined at length the opinion of sci-

[1] The stratification of the meanings of dreams is one of the most delicate but also one of the most fruitful problems of dream-interpretation. Whoever forgets the possibility of such stratification is likely to go astray and to make untenable assertions concerning the nature of dreams. But hitherto this subject has been only too imperfectly investigated. So far, a fairly orderly stratification of symbols in dreams due to urinary stimulus has been subjected to a thorough evaluation only by Otto Rank.
[2] This part has been omitted from this text. Those who have a special interest in the subject may read the original translation published by Macmillan Co., N. Y. and Allen & Unwin, London.

entific writers on the rôle of somatic stimuli in the formation of dreams, so that here we need only recall the results of this inquiry. We have seen that three kinds of somatic stimuli will be distinguished: the objective sensory stimuli which proceed from external objects, the inner states of excitation of the sensory organs, having only a subjective reality, and the bodily stimuli arising within the body; and we have also noticed that the writers on dreams are inclined to thrust into the background any psychic sources of dreams which may operate simultaneously with the somatic stimuli, or to exclude them altogether. In testing the claims made on behalf of these somatic stimuli we have learned that the significance of the objective excitation of the sensory organs—whether accidental stimuli operating during sleep, or such as cannot be excluded from the dormant relation of these dream-images and ideas to the internal bodily stimuli and confirmed by experiment; that the part played by the subjective sensory stimuli appears to be demonstrated by the recurrence of hypnagogic sensory images in dreams; and that, although the broadly accepted relation of these dream-images and ideas to the internal bodily stimuli cannot be exhaustively demonstrated, it is at all events confirmed by the well-known influence which an excited state of the digestive, urinary and sexual organs exercises upon the content of our dreams.

"Nerve stimulus" and "bodily stimulus" would thus be the anatomical sources of dreams; that is, according to many writers, the sole and exclusive sources of dreams.

But we have already considered a number of doubtful points, which seem to question not so much the correctness of the somatic theory as its adequacy.

However confident the representatives of this theory may be of its factual basis—especially in respect of the accidental and external nerve-stimuli, which may without difficulty be recognized in the dream-content—nevertheless they have all come near to admitting that the rich content of ideas found in dreams cannot be derived from the external nerve-stimuli alone. In this connection Miss Mary Whiton Calkins tested her own dreams, and those of a second person, for a period of six weeks, and found that the element of external sensory perception was demonstrable in only 13.2 per cent. and 6.7 per cent. of these dreams respectively. Only two dreams in the whole collection could be referred to organic sensations. These statistics confirm what a cursory survey of our own experience would already have led us to suspect.

A distinction has often been made between "nerve-stimulus dreams" which have already been thoroughly investigated, and other forms of dreams. Spitta, for example, divided dreams into nerve-stimulus dreams and association-dreams. But it was obvious that this solution remained unsatisfactory unless the link between the somatic sources of dreams and their ideational content could be indicated.

In addition to the first objection, that of the insufficient frequency of the external sources of stimulus, a second objection presents itself, namely, the inadequacy of the explanations of dreams afforded by this category of dream-sources. There are two things which the representatives of this theory have failed to explain: firstly, why the true nature of the external stimulus is not recognized in the dream, but is constantly mistaken for something else; and secondly, why the result of the reaction of the perceiving mind to this misconceived stimulus should be so indeterminate and variable. We have seen that Strümpell, in answer to these questions, asserts that the mind, since it turns away from the outer world during sleep, is not in a position to give the correct interpretation of the objective sensory stimulus, but is forced to construct illusions on the basis of the indefinite stimulation arriving from many directions. In his own words (*Die Natur und Entstehung der Träume*, p. 108):—

"When by an external or internal nerve-stimulus during sleep a feeling, or a complex of feelings, or any sort of psychic process arises in the mind, and is perceived by the mind, this process calls up from the mind perceptual images belonging to the sphere of the waking experiences, that is to say, earlier perceptions, either unembellished, or with the psychic values appertaining to them. It collects about itself, as it were, a greater or lesser number of such images, from which the impression resulting from the nerve-stimulus receives its psychic value. In this connection it is commonly said, as in ordinary language we say of the waking procedure, that the mind *interprets* in sleep the impressions of nervous stimuli. The result of this interpretation is the so-called *nerve-stimulus dream*—that is, a dream the components of which are conditioned by the fact that a nerve-stimulus produces its psychical effect in the life of the mind in accordance with the laws of reproduction."

In all essential points identical with this doctrine is Wundt's statement that the concepts of dreams proceed, at all events for the most part, from sensory stimuli, and especially from the stimuli of general sensation, and are therefore mostly phantastic illusions—probably only to a small extent pure memory-conceptions raised to the condition of hallucinations. To illustrate the relation between dream-content and dream-stimuli which follows from this theory, Strümpell makes use of an excellent simile. It is "as though the ten fingers of a person ignorant of music were to stray over the keyboard of an instrument." The implication is that the dream is not a psychic phenomenon, originating from psychic motives, but the result of a physiological stimulus, which expresses itself in psychic symptomatology because the apparatus affected by the stimulus is not capable of any other mode of expression. Upon a similar assumption is based the explanation of obsessions which Meynert attempted in his famous simile of the dial on which individual figures are most deeply embossed.

Popular though this theory of the somatic dream-stimuli has become, and seductive though it may seem, it is none the less easy to detect its weak point. Every somatic dream-stimulus which provokes the psychic apparatus in sleep to interpretation by the formation of illusions may evoke an incalculable number of such attempts at interpretation. It may consequently be represented in the dream-content by an extraordinary number of different concepts.[1] But the theory of Strümpell and Wundt cannot point to any sort of motive which controls the relation between the external stimulus and the dream-concept chosen to interpret it, and therefore it cannot explain the "peculiar choice" which the stimuli "often enough make in the course of their productive activity" (Lipps, *Grundtatsachen des Seelenlebens*, p. 170). Other objections may be raised against the fundamental assumption behind the theory of illusions—the assumption that during sleep the mind is not in a condition to recognize the real nature of the objective sensory stimuli. The old physiologist Burdach shows us that the mind is quite capable even during sleep of a correct interpretation of the sensory impressions which reach it, and of reacting in accordance with this correct interpretation, inasmuch as he demonstrates that certain sensory impressions which seem important to the individual may be excepted from the general neglect of the sleeping mind (as in the example of nurse and child), and that one is more surely awakened by one's own name than by an indifferent auditory impression; all of which presupposes, of course, that the mind discriminates between sensations, even in sleep. Burdach infers from these observations that we must not assume that the mind is incapable of interpreting sensory stimuli in the sleeping state, but rather *that it is not sufficiently interested in them.* The arguments which Burdach employed in 1830 reappear unchanged in the works of Lipps (in the year 1883), where they are employed for the purpose of attacking the theory of somatic stimuli. According to these arguments the mind seems to be like the sleeper in the anecdote, who, on being asked, "Are you asleep?" answers "No," and on being again addressed with the words: "Then lend me ten florins," takes refuge in the excuse: "I am asleep."

The inadequacy of the theory of somatic dream-stimuli may be further demonstrated in another way. Observation shows that external stimuli do

---

[1] I would advise everyone to read the exact and detailed records (collected in two volumes) of the dreams experimentally produced by Mourly Vold in order to convince himself how little the conditions of the experiments help to explain the content of the individual dream, and how little such experiments help us towards an understanding of the problems of dreams.

not oblige me to dream, even though these stimuli appear in the dream-content as soon as I begin to dream—supposing that I do dream. In response to a touch- or pressure-stimulus experienced while I am asleep, a variety of reactions are at my disposal. I may overlook it, and find on waking that my leg has become uncovered, or that I have been lying on an arm; indeed, pathology offers me a host of examples of powerfully exciting sensory and motor stimuli of different kinds which remain ineffective during sleep. I may perceive the sensation during sleep, and through my sleep, as it were, as constantly happens in the case of pain stimuli, but without weaving the pain into the texture of a dream. And thirdly, I may wake up in response to the stimulus, simply in order to avoid it. Still another, fourth, reaction is possible: namely, that the nerve-stimulus may cause me to dream; but the other possible reactions occur quite as frequently as the reaction of dream-formation. This, however, would not be the case *if the incentive to dreaming did not lie outside the somatic dream-sources.*

Appreciating the importance of the above-mentioned lacunae in the explanation of dreams by somatic stimuli, other writers—Scherner, for example, and, following him, the philosopher Volkelt—endeavoured to determine more precisely the nature of the psychic activities which cause the many-coloured images of our dreams to proceed from the somatic stimuli, and in so doing they approached the problem of the essential nature of dreams as a problem of psychology, and regarded dreaming as a psychic activity. Scherner not only gave a poetical, vivid and glowing description of the psychic peculiarities which unfold themselves in the course of dream-formation, but he also believed that he had hit upon the principle of the method the mind employs in dealing with the stimuli which are offered to it. The dream, according to Scherner, in the free activity of the phantasy, which has been released from the shackles imposed upon it during the day, strives to represent symbolically the nature of the organ from which the stimulus proceeds. Thus there exists a sort of dream-book, a guide to the interpretation of dreams, by means of which bodily sensations, the conditions of the organs, and states of stimulation, may be inferred from the dream-images. "Thus the image of a cat expressed extreme ill-temper, the image of pale, smooth pastry the nudity of the body. The human body as a whole is pictured by the phantasy of the dream as a house, and the individual organs of the body as parts of the house. In 'toothache-dreams' a vaulted vestibule corresponds to the mouth, and a staircase to the descent from the pharynx to the oesophagus; in the 'headache-dream' a ceiling covered with disgusting toad-like spiders is chosen to denote the upper part of the head." "Many different symbols are employed by our dreams for the same organ: thus the breathing lung finds its symbol in a roaring stove, filled with flames, the heart in empty boxes and baskets, and the bladder in round, bag-shaped or merely hollow objects. It is of particular significance that at the close of the dream the stimulating organ or its function is often represented without disguise, and usually on the dreamer's own body. Thus the 'toothache-ache dream' commonly ends by the dreamer drawing a tooth out his mouth." It cannot be said that this theory of dream-interpretation has found much favour with other writers. It seems, above all, extravagant; and so Scherner's readers have hesitated to give it even the small amount of credit to which it is, in my opinion, entitled. As will be seen, it tends to a revival of dream-interpretation by means of *symbolism*, a method employed by the ancients; only the province from which the interpretation is to be derived is restricted to the human body. The lack of a scientifically comprehensible technique of interpretation must seriously limit the applicability of Scherner's theory. Arbitrariness in the interpretation of dreams would appear to be by no means excluded, especially since in this case also a stimulus may be expressed in the dream-content by several representative symbols; thus even Scherner's follower Volkelt was unable to confirm the representation of the body as a house. Another objection is that here again the dream-activity is regarded as a useless and aimless activity of the mind, since, according to this theory, the mind is content with merely forming phantasies around the stimulus with which it is dealing, without even remotely attempting to abolish the stimulus.

Scherner's theory of the symbolization of bodily stimuli by the dream is seriously damaged by yet another objection. These bodily stimuli are present at all times, and it is generally assumed that the mind is more accessible to them during sleep than in the waking state. It is therefore impossible to understand why the mind does not dream continuously all night long, and why it does not dream every night about all the organs. If one attempts to evade this objection by positing the condition that special excitations must proceed from the eye, the ear, the teeth, the bowels, etc., in order to arouse the dream-activity, one is confronted with the difficulty of proving that this increase of stimulation is objective; and proof is possible only in a very few cases. If the dream of flying is a symbolization of the upward and downward motion of the pulmonary lobes, either this dream, as has already been remarked by Strümpell, should be dreamt much oftener, or it should be possible to show that respiration is more active during this dream. Yet a third alternative is possible—and it is the most probable of all—namely, that now and again special motives are operative to direct the attention to the visceral sensations which are constantly present. But this would take us far beyond the scope of Scherner's theory.

The value of Scherner's and Volkelt's disquisitions resides in their calling our attention to a number of characteristics of the dream-content which are in need of explanation, and which seem to promise fresh discoveries. It is quite true that symbolizations of the bodily organs and functions do occur in dreams: for example, that water in a dream often signifies a desire to urinate, that the male genital organ may be represented by an upright staff, or a pillar, etc. With dreams which exhibit a very animated field of vision and brilliant colours, in contrast to the dimness of other dreams, the interpretation that they are "dreams due to visual stimulation" can hardly be dismissed, nor can we dispute the participation of illusion-formation in dreams which contain noise and a medley of voices. A dream like that of Scherner's, that two rows of fair handsome boys stood facing one another on a bridge, attacking one another, and then resuming their positions, until finally the dreamer himself sat down on a bridge and drew a long tooth from his jaw; or a similar dream of Volkelt's, in which two rows of drawers played a part, and which again ended in the extraction of a tooth; dream-formations of this kind, of which both writers relate a great number, forbid our dismissing Scherner's theory as an idle invention without seeking the kernel of truth which may be contained in it. We are therefore confronted with the task of finding a different explanation of the supposed symbolization of the alleged dental stimulus.

Throughout our consideration of the theory of the somatic sources of dreams, I have refrained from urging the argument which arises from our analyses of dreams. If by a procedure which has not been followed by other writers in their investigation of dreams we can prove that the dream possesses intrinsic value as psychic action, that a wish supplies the motive of its formation, and that the experiences of the previous day furnish the most obvious material of its content, any other theory of dreams which neglects such an important method of investigation—and accordingly makes the dream appear a useless and enigmatical psychic reaction to somatic stimuli—may be dismissed without special criticism. For in this case there would have to be—and this is highly improbable—two entirely different kinds of dreams, of which only one kind has come under our observation, while the other kind alone has been observed by the earlier investigators. It only remains now to find a place in our theory of dreams for the facts on which the current doctrine of somatic dream-stimuli is based.

We have already taken the first step in this direction in advancing the thesis that the dream-work is under a compulsion to elaborate into a unified whole all the dream-stimuli which are simultaneously present (p. 248). We have seen that when two or more experiences capable of making an impression on the mind have been left over from the previous day, the wishes that result from them are united into one dream; similarly, that the impressions possessing psychic value and the indifferent experiences of the previous day unite in the dream-material, provided that connecting ideas between the two can be established. Thus the dream appears to be a reaction to everything which is simultaneously present as actual in the sleeping mind. As far as we have hitherto analysed the dream-material, we have discovered it to be a collection of psychic remnants and memory-traces, which we were obliged to credit (on account of the preference shown for recent and for infantile material) with a character of psychological actuality, though the nature of this actuality was not at the time determinable. We shall now have little difficulty in predicting what will happen when to these actualities of the memory fresh material in the form of sensations is added during sleep. These stimuli, again, are of importance to the dream because they are actual; they are united with the other psychic actualities to provide the material for dream-formation. To express it in other words, the stimuli which occur during sleep are elaborated into a wish-fulfilment, of which the other components are the psychic remnants of daily experience with which we are already familiar. This combination, however, is not inevitable; we have seen that more than one kind of behaviour toward the physical stimuli received during sleep is possible. Where this combination is effected, a conceptual material for the dream-content has been found which will represent both kinds of dream-sources, the somatic as well as the psychic.

The nature of the dream is not altered when somatic material is added to the psychic dream-sources; it still remains a wish-fulfilment, no matter how its expression is determined by the actual material available.

I should like to find room here for a number of peculiarities which are able to modify the significance of external stimuli for the dream. I imagine that a co-operation of individual, physiological and accidental factors, which depend on the circumstances of the moment, determines how one will behave in individual cases of more intensive objective stimulation during sleep; habitual or accidental profundity of sleep, in conjunction with the intensity of the stimulus, will in one case make it possible so to suppress the stimulus that it will not disturb the sleeper, while in another case it will force the sleeper to wake, or will assist the attempt to subdue the stimulus by weaving it into the texture of the dream. In accordance with the multiplicity of these constellations, external objective stimuli will be expressed more rarely or more frequently in the case of one person than in that of another. In my own case, since I am an excellent sleeper, and obstinately refuse to allow myself to be disturbed during sleep on any pretext whatever, this intrusion of external causes of excitation into my dreams is very rare, whereas psychic motives apparently cause me to dream very easily. Indeed, I have noted only a single dream in which an objective, painful source of stimulation is demonstrable, and it will be highly instructive to see what effect the external stimulus had in this particular dream.

I am riding a gray horse, at first timidly and awkwardly, as though I were merely carried along. Then I meet a colleague, P., also on horseback, and dressed in rough frieze; he is sitting erect in the saddle; he calls my attention to something (probably to the fact that I have a very bad seat). Now I begin to feel more and more at ease on the back of my highly intelligent horse; I sit more comfortably, and I find that I am quite at home up here. My saddle is a sort of pad, which completely fills the space between the neck and the rump of the horse. I ride between two vans, and just manage to clear them. After riding up the street for some distance, I turn round and wish to dismount, at first in front of a little open chapel which is built facing on to the street. Then I do really dismount in front of a chapel which stands near the first one; the hotel is in the same street; I might let the horse go there by itself, but I prefer to lead it thither. It seems as though I should be ashamed to arrive there on horseback. In front of the hotel there stands a page-boy, who shows me a note of mine which has been found, and ridicules me on account of it. On the note is written, doubly underlined, "Eat nothing," and then a second sentence (indistinct): something like "Do not work"; at the same time a hazy idea that I am in a strange city, in which I do no work.

It will not at once be apparent that this dream originated under the influence, or rather under the compulsion, of a pain-stimulus. The day before, however, I had suffered from boils, which made every movement a torture, and at last a boil had grown to the size of an apple at the root of the scrotum, and had caused me the most intolerable pains at every step; a feverish lassitude, lack of appetite, and the hard work which I had nevertheless done during the day, had conspired with the pain to upset me. I was not altogether in a condition to discharge my duties as a physician, but in view of the nature and the location of the malady, it was possible to imagine something else for which I was most of all unfit, namely riding. Now it is this very activity of riding into which I am plunged by the dream; it is the most energetic denial of the pain which imagination could conceive. As a matter of fact, I cannot ride; I do not dream of doing so; I never sat on a horse but once—and then without a saddle—and I did not like it. But in this dream I ride as though I had no boil on the perineum; or rather, *I ride, just because I want to have none.* To judge from the description, my saddle is the poultice which has enabled me to fall asleep. Probably, being thus comforted, I did not feel anything of my pain during the first few hours of my sleep. Then the painful sensations made themselves felt, and tried to wake me; whereupon the dream came and said to me, soothingly: "Go on sleeping, you are not going to wake! You have no boil, for you are riding on horseback, and with a boil just there no one could ride!" And the dream was successful; the pain was stifled, and I went on sleeping.

But the dream was not satisfied with "suggesting away" the boil by tenaciously holding fast to an idea incompatible with the malady (thus behaving like the hallucinatory insanity of a mother who has lost her child, or of a merchant who has lost his fortune). In addition, the details of the sensation denied and of the image used to suppress it serve the dream also as a means to connect other material actually present in the mind with the situation in the dream, and to give this material representation. I am riding on a *gray* horse—the colour of the horse exactly corresponds with the *pepper-and-salt* suit in which I last saw my colleague P. in the country. I have been warned that highly seasoned food is the cause of boils, and in any case it is preferable as an etiological explanation to *sugar,* which might be thought of in connection with furunculosis. My friend P. likes to *"ride the high horse"* with me ever since he took my place in the treatment of a female patient, in whose case I had performed great feats (*Kunststücke*: in the dream I sit the horse at first sideways, like a trick-rider, *Kunstreiter*), but who really, like the horse in the story of the Sunday equestrian, led me wherever she wished. Thus the horse comes to be a symbolic representation of a lady patient (in the dream it is *highly intelligent*). *"I feel quite at home"* refers to the position which I occupied in the patient's household until I was replaced by my colleague P. "I thought you were safe in the saddle up there," one of my few well-wishers among the eminent physicians of the city recently said to me, with reference to the same household. And it was a *feat* to practise psychotherapy for eight to ten hours a day, while suffering such pain, but I know that I cannot continue my peculiarly strenuous work for any length of time without perfect physical health, and the dream is full of dismal allusions to the situation which would result if my illness continued (the note, such as neurasthenics carry and show to their doctors): *Do not work, do not eat.* On further interpretation I see that the dream-activity has succeeded in finding its way from the wish-situation of riding to some very early childish quarrels which must have occurred between myself and a nephew, who is a year older than I, and is now living in England. It has also taken up elements from my journeys in Italy; the street in the dream is built up out of impressions of Verona and Siena. A still deeper interpretation leads to sexual dream-thoughts, and I recall what the dream-allusions to that beautiful country were supposed to mean in the dream of a female patient who had never been to Italy (*to Italy,* German: *gen Italien = Genitalien = genitals*); at the same time there are references to the house in which I preceded my friend P. as physician, and to the place where the boil is located.

In another dream I was similarly successful in warding off a threatened disturbance of my sleep; this time the threat came from a sensory stimulus. It was only chance, however, that enabled me to discover the connection between the dream and the accidental dream-stimulus, and in this way to understand the dream. One midsummer morning in a Tyrolese mountain resort I woke with the knowledge that I had dreamed: *The Pope is dead.* I was not able to interpret this short, non-visual dream. I could remember only one possible basis of the dream, namely, that shortly before this the newspapers had reported that His Holiness was slightly indisposed. But in the course of the morning my wife asked me: "Did you hear the dreadful tolling of the church bells this morning?" I had no idea that I had heard it, but now I understood my dream. It was the reaction of my need for sleep to the noise by which the pious Tyroleans were trying to wake me. I avenged myself on them by the conclusion which formed the content of my dream, and continued to sleep, without any further interest in the tolling of the bells.

Among the dreams mentioned in the previous chapters there are several which might serve as examples of the elaboration of so-called nerve-stimuli. The dream of drinking in long draughts is such an example; here the somatic stimulus seems to be the sole source of the dream, and the wish arising from the sensation—thirst—the only motive for dreaming. We find much the same thing in other simple dreams, where the somatic stimulus is able of itself to generate a wish. The dream of the sick woman who throws the cooling apparatus from her cheek at night is an instance of an unusual manner of reacting to a pain-stimulus with a wish-fulfilment; it seems as though the patient had temporarily succeeded in making herself analgesic, and accompanied this by ascribing her pains to a stranger.

My dream of the three Parcae is obviously a hunger-dream, but it has contrived to shift the need for food right back to the child's longing for its mother's breast, and to use a harmless desire as a mask for a more serious one that cannot venture to express itself so openly. In the dream of Count Thun we were able to see by what paths an accidental physical need was brought into relation with the strongest, but also the most rigorously repressed impulses of the psychic life. And when, as in the case reported by Garnier, the First Consul incorporates the sound of an exploding infernal machine into a dream of battle before it causes him to wake, the true purpose for which alone psychic activity concerns itself with sensations during sleep is revealed with unusual clarity. A young lawyer, who is full of his first great bankruptcy case, and falls asleep in the afternoon, behaves just as the great Napoleon did. He dreams of a certain G. Reich in *Hussiatyn,* whose acquaintance he has made in connection with the bankruptcy case, but *Hussiatyn* (German: *husten,* to cough) forces itself upon his attention still further; he is obliged to wake, only to hear his wife—who is suffering from bronchial catarrh—violently coughing.

Let us compare the dream of Napoleon I—who, incidentally, was an excellent sleeper—with that of the sleepy student, who was awakened by his landlady with the reminder that he had to go to the hospital, and who thereupon dreamt himself into a bed in the hospital, and then slept on, the underlying reasoning being as follows: If I am already in the hospital, I needn't get up to go there. This is obviously a convenience-dream; the sleeper frankly admits to himself his motive in dreaming; but he thereby reveals one of the secrets of dreaming in general. In a certain sense, all dreams are *convenience-dreams;* they serve the purpose of continuing to sleep instead of waking. *The dream is the guardian of sleep, not its disturber.* In another place we shall have occasion to justify this conception in respect to the psychic factors that make for waking; but we can already demonstrate its applicability to the objective external stimuli. Either the mind does not concern itself at all with the causes of sensations during sleep, if it is able to carry this attitude through as against the intensity of the stimuli, and their significance, of which it is well aware; or it employs the dream to deny these stimuli; or, thirdly, if it is obliged to recognize the stimuli, it seeks that interpretation of them which will represent the actual sensation as a component of a desired situation which is compatible with sleep. The actual sensation is woven into the dream *in order to deprive it of its reality.* Napoleon is permitted to go on sleeping; it is only a dream-memory of the thunder of the guns at Arcole which is trying to disturb him.[1]

The wish to sleep, to which the conscious ego has adjusted itself, and which (together with the dream-censorship and the "secondary elaboration" to be mentioned later) represents the ego's contribution to the dream, must thus always be taken into account as a motive of dream-formation, and every successful dream is a fulfilment of this wish. The relation of this general, constantly present, and unvarying sleep-wish to the other wishes of which now one and now another is fulfilled by the dream-content, will be the subject of later consideration. In the wish to sleep we have discovered a motive capable of supplying the deficiency in the theory of Strümpell and Wundt, and of explaining the perversity and capriciousness of the interpretaton of the external stimulus. The correct interpretation, of which the sleeping mind is perfectly capable, would involve active interest, and would require the sleeper to wake; hence, of those interpretations which are possible at all only such are admitted as are acceptable to the dictatorial censorship of the sleep-wish. The logic

[1] The two sources from which I know of this dream do not entirely agree as to its content.

of dream situations would run, for example: "It is the nightingale, and not the lark." For if it is the lark, love's night is at an end. From among the interpretations of the stimulus which are thus admissible, that one is selected which can secure the best connection with the wish-impulses that are lying in wait in the mind. Thus everything is definitely determined, and nothing is left to caprice. The misinterpretation is not an illusion, but—if you will—an excuse. Here again, as in substitution by displacement in the service of the dream-censorship, we have an act of deflection of the normal psychic procedure.

If the external nerve-stimuli and the inner bodily stimuli are sufficiently intense to compel psychic attention, they represent—that is, if they result in dreaming at all, and not in waking—a fixed point for dream-formation, a nucleus in the dream-material, for which an appropriate wish-fulfilment is sought, just as (see above) mediating ideas between two psychical dream-stimuli are sought. To this extent it is true of a number of dreams that the somatic element dictates the dream-content. In this extreme case even a wish that is not actually present may be aroused for the purpose of dream-formation. But the dream cannot do otherwise than represent a wish in some situation as fulfilled; it is, as it were, confronted with the task of discovering what wish can be represented as fulfilled by the given sensation. Even if this given material is of a painful or disagreeable character, yet it is not unserviceable for the purposes of dream-formation. The psychic life has at its disposal even wishes whose fulfilment evokes displeasure, which seems a contradiction, but becomes perfectly intelligible if we take into account the presence of two sorts of psychic instance and the censorship that subsists between them.

In the psychic life there exist, as we have seen, *repressed* wishes, which belong to the first system, and to whose fulfilment the second system is opposed. We do not mean this in a historic sense—that such wishes have once existed and have subsequently been destroyed. The doctrine of *repression*, which we need in the study of psychoneuroses, asserts that such repressed wishes still exist, but simultaneously with an inhibition which weighs them down. Language has hit upon the truth when it speaks of the "suppression" (sub-pression, or pushing under) of such impulses. The psychic mechanism which enables such suppressed wishes to force their way to realization is retained in being and in working order. But if it happens that such a suppressed wish is fulfilled, the vanquished inhibition of the second system (which is capable of consciousness) is then expressed as discomfort. And, in order to conclude this argument: If sensations of a disagreeable character which originate from somatic sources are present during sleep, this constellation is utilized by the dream-activity to procure the fulfilment—with more or less maintenance of the censorship—of an otherwise suppressed wish.

This state of affairs makes possible a certain number of anxiety-dreams, while others of these dream-formations which are unfavourable to the wish-theory exhibit a different mechanism. For the anxiety in dreams may of course be of a psychoneurotic character, originating in psycho-sexual excitation, in which case, the anxiety corresponds to repressed libido. Then this anxiety, like the whole anxiety-dream, has the signifi-cance of a neurotic symptom, and we stand at the dividing-line where the wish-fulfilling tendency of dreams is frustrated. But in other anxiety-dreams the feeling of anxiety comes from somatic sources (as in the case of persons suffering from pulmonary or cardiac trouble, with occasional difficulty in breathing), and then it is used to help such strongly sup-pressed wishes to attain fulfilment in a dream, the dreaming of which from psychic motives would have resulted in the same release of anxiety. It is not difficult to reconcile these two apparently contradictory cases. When two psychic formations, an affective inclination and a conceptual content, are intimately connected, either one being actually present will evoke the other, even in a dream; now the anxiety of somatic origin evokes the suppressed conceptual content, now it is the released conceptual con-tent, accompanied by sexual excitement, which causes the release of anxiety. In the one case it may be said that a somatically determined affect is psychically interpreted; in the other case all is of psychic origin, but the content which has been suppressed is easily replaced by a somatic interpretation which fits the anxiety. The difficulties which lie in the way of understanding all this have little to do with dreams; they are due to the fact that in discussing these points we are touching upon the problems of the development of anxiety and of repression.

The general aggregate of bodily sensation must undoubtedly be in-cluded among the dominant dream-stimuli of internal bodily origin. Not that it is capable of supplying the dream-content; but it forces the dream-thoughts to make a choice from the material destined to serve the purpose of representation in the dream-content, inasmuch as it brings within easy reach that part of the material which is adapted to its own character, and holds the rest at a distance. Moreover, this general feeling, which sur-vives from the preceding day, is of course connected with the psychic residues that are significant for the dream. Moreover, this feeling itself may be either maintained or overcome in the dream, so that it may, if it is painful, veer round into its opposite.

If the somatic sources of excitation during sleep—that is, the sensa-tions of sleep—are not of unusual intensity, the part which they play in dream-formation is, in my judgment, similar to that of those impressions of the day which are still recent, but of no great significance. I mean that they are utilized for the dream-formation if they are of such a kind that they can be united with the conceptual content of the psychic dream-source, but not otherwise. They are treated as a cheap ever-ready material, which can be used whenever it is needed, and not as valuable material which itself prescribes the manner in which it must be utilized. I might suggest the analogy of a connoisseur giving an artist a rare stone, a piece of onyx, for example, in order that it may be fashioned into a work of art. Here the size of the stone, its colour, and its markings help to decide what head or what scene shall be represented; while if he is dealing with a uniform and abundant material such as marble or sandstone, the artist is guided only by the idea which takes shape in his mind. Only in this way, it seems to me, can we explain the fact that the dream-content furnished by physical stimuli of somatic origin which are not unusually accentuated does not make its appearance in all dreams and every night.[1]

Perhaps an example which takes us back to the interpretation of dreams will best illustrate my meaning. One day I was trying to understand the significance of the sensation of being inhibited, of not being able to move from the spot, of not being able to get something done, etc., which occurs so frequently in dreams, and is so closely allied to anxiety. That night I had the following dream: *I am very incompletely dressed, and I go from a flat on the ground-floor up a flight of stairs to an upper story. In doing this I jump up three stairs at a time, and I am glad to find that I can mount the stairs so quickly. Suddenly I notice that a servant-maid is coming down the stairs—that is, towards me. I am ashamed, and try to hurry away, and now comes this feeling of being inhibited; I am glued to the stairs, and cannot move from the spot.*

Analysis: The situation of the dream is taken from an every-day reality. In a house in Vienna I have two apartments, which are connected only by the main staircase. My consultation-rooms and my study are on the raised ground-floor, and my living-rooms are on the first floor. Late at night, when I have finished my work downstairs, I go upstairs to my bedroom. On the evening before the dream I had actually gone this short distance with my garments in disarray—that is, I had taken off my collar, tie and cuffs; but in the dream this had changed into a more advanced, but, as usual, indefinite degree of undress. It is a habit of mine to run up two or three steps at a time; moreover, there was a wish-fulfilment recognized even in the dream, for the ease with which I run upstairs reassures me as to the condition of my heart. Further, the manner in which I run upstairs is an effective contrast to the sensation of being inhibited, which occurs in the second half of the dream. It shows me—what needed no proof—that dreams have no difficulty in representing motor actions fully and completely carried out; think, for example, of flying in dreams!

[1] Rank has shown, in a number of studies, that certain awakening-dreams provoked by organic stimuli (dreams of urination and ejaculation) are especially calculated to demonstrate the conflict between the need for sleep and the demands of the organic need, as well as the influence of the latter on the dream-content.

But the stairs up which I go are not those of my own house; at first I do not recognize them; only the person coming towards me informs me of their whereabouts. This woman is the maid of an old lady whom I visit twice daily in order to give her hypodermic injections; the stairs, too, are precisely similar to those which I have to climb twice a day in this old lady's house.

How do these stairs and this woman get into my dream? The shame of not being fully dressed is undoubtedly of a sexual character; the servant of whom I dream is older than I, surly, and by no means attractive. These questions remind me of the following incident: When I pay my morning visit at this house I am usually seized with a desire to clear my throat; the sputum falls on the stairs. There is no spittoon on either of the two floors, and I consider that the stairs should be kept clean not at my expense, but rather by the provision of a spittoon. The housekeeper, another elderly, curmudgeonly person, but, as I willingly admit, a woman of cleanly instincts, takes a different view of the matter. She lies in wait for me, to see whether I shall take the liberty referred to, and if she sees that I do I can distinctly hear her growl. For days thereafter, when we meet, she refuses to greet me with the customary signs of respect. On the day before the dream the housekeeper's attitude was reinforced by that of the maid. I had just finished my usual hurried visit to the patient when the servant confronted me in the ante-room, observing: "You might as well have wiped your shoes to-day, doctor, before you came into the room. The red carpet is all dirty again from your feet." This is the only justification for the appearance of the stairs and the maid in my dream.

Between my leaping upstairs and my spitting on the stairs there is an intimate connection. Pharyngitis and cardiac troubles are both supposed to be punishments for the vice of smoking, on account of which vice my own housekeeper does not credit me with excessive tidiness, so that my reputation suffers in both the houses which my dream fuses into one.

I must postpone the further interpretation of this dream until I can indicate the origin of the typical dream of being incompletely clothed. In the meantime, as a provisional deduction from the dream just related, I note that the dream-sensation of inhibited movement is always aroused at a point where a certain connection requires it. A peculiar condition of my motor system during sleep cannot be responsible for this dream-content, since a moment earlier I found myself, as though in confirmation of this fact, skipping lightly up the stairs.

D. TYPICAL DREAMS

Generally speaking, we are not in a position to interpret another person's dream if he is unwilling to furnish us with the unconscious thoughts which lie behind the dream-content, and for this reason the practical applicability of our method of dream-interpretation is often seriously restricted.[1] But there are dreams which exhibit a complete contrast to the individual's customary liberty to endow his dream-world with a special individuality, thereby making it inaccessible to an alien understanding: there are a number of dreams which almost every one has dreamed in the same manner, and of which we are accustomed to assume that they have the same significance in the case of every dreamer. A peculiar interest attaches to these typical dreams, because, no matter who dreams them, they presumably all derive from the same sources, so that they would seem to be particularly fitted to provide us with information as to the sources of dreams.

With quite special expectations, therefore, we shall proceed to test our technique of dream-interpretation on these typical dreams, and only with extreme reluctance shall we admit that precisely in respect of this material our method is not fully verified. In the interpretation of typical dreams we as a rule fail to obtain those associations from the dreamer which in other cases have led us to comprehension of the dream, or else these associations are confused and inadequate, so that they do not help us to solve our problem.

Why this is the case, and how we can remedy this defect in our technique, are points which will be discussed in a later chapter. The reader will then understand why I can deal with only a few of the group of typical dreams in this chapter, and why I have postponed the discussion of the others.

(a) The Embarrassment-Dream of Nakedness

In a dream in which one is naked or scantily clad in the presence of strangers, it sometimes happens that one is not in the least ashamed of one's condition. But the dream of nakedness demands our attention only when shame and embarrassment are felt in it, when one wishes to escape or to hide, and when one feels the strange inhibition of being unable to stir from the spot, and of being utterly powerless to alter the painful situation. It is only in this connection that the dream is typical; otherwise the nucleus of its content may be involved in all sorts of other connections, or may be replaced by individual amplifications. The essential point is that one has a painful feeling of shame, and is anxious to hide one's nakedness, usually by means of locomotion, but is absolutely un-

---

[1] The statement that our method of dream-interpretation is inapplicable when we have not at our disposal the dreamer's association-material must be qualified. In one case our work of interpretation is independent of these associations: namely, when the dreamer makes use of *symbolic* elements in his dream. We then employ what is, strictly speaking, a second or *auxiliary* method of dream-interpretation (*vid. inf.*).

able to do so. I believe that the great majority of my readers will at some time have found themselves in this situation in a dream.

The nature and manner of the exposure is usually rather vague. The dreamer will say, perhaps, "I was in my chemise," but this is rarely a clear image; in most cases the lack of clothing is so indeterminate that it is described in narrating the dream by an alternative: "I was in my chemise or my petticoat." As a rule the deficiency in clothing is not serious enough to justify the feeling of shame attached to it. For a man who has served in the army, nakedness is often replaced by a manner of dressing that is contrary to regulations. "I was in the street without my sabre, and I saw some officers approaching," or "I had no collar," or "I was wearing checked civilian trousers," etc.

The persons before whom one is ashamed are almost always strangers, whose faces remain indeterminate. It never happens, in the typical dream, that one is reproved or even noticed on account of the lack of clothing which causes one such embarrassment. On the contrary, the people in the dream appear to be quite indifferent; or, as I was able to note in one particularly vivid dream, they have stiff and solemn expressions. This gives us food for thought.

The dreamer's embarrassment and the spectator's indifference constitute a contradiction such as often occurs in dreams. It would be more in keeping with the dreamer's feelings if the strangers were to look at him in astonishment, or were to laugh at him, or be outraged. I think, however, that this obnoxious feature has been displaced by wish-fulfilment, while the embarrassment is for some reason retained, so that the two components are not in agreement. We have an interesting proof that the dream which is partially distorted by wish-fulfilment has not been properly understood; for it has been made the basis of a fairy-tale familiar to us all in Andersen's version of *The Emperor's New Clothes*, and it has more recently received poetical treatment by Fulda in *The Talisman*. In Andersen's fairy-tale we are told of two impostors who weave a costly garment for the Emperor, which shall, however, be visible only to the good and true. The Emperor goes forth clad in this invisible garment, and since the imaginary fabric serves as a sort of touchstone, the people are frightened into behaving as though they did not notice the Emperor's nakedness.

But this is really the situation in our dream. It is not very venturesome to assume that the unintelligible dream-content has provided an incentive to invent a state of undress which gives meaning to the situation present in the memory. This situation is thereby robbed of its original meaning, and made to serve alien ends. But we shall see that such a misunderstanding of the dream-content often occurs through the conscious activity of a second psychic system, and is to be recognized as a factor of the final form of the dream; and further, that in the development of obsessions and phobias similar misunderstandings—still, of course, within the same psychic personality—play a decisive part. It is even possible to specify whence the material for the fresh interpretation of the dream is taken. The impostor is the dream, the Emperor is the dreamer himself, and the moralizing tendency betrays a hazy knowledge of the fact that there is a question, in the latent dream-content, of forbidden wishes, victims of repression. The connection in which such dreams appear during my analyses of neurotics proves beyond a doubt that a memory of the dreamer's earliest childhood lies at the foundation of the dream. Only in our childhood was there a time when we were seen by our relatives, as well as by strange nurses, servants and visitors, in a state of insufficient clothing, and at that time we were not ashamed of our nakedness.[1] In the case of many rather older children it may be observed that being undressed has an exciting effect upon them, instead of making them feel ashamed. They laugh, leap about, slap or thump their own bodies; the mother, or whoever is present, scolds them, saying: "Fie, that is shameful—you mustn't do that!" Children often show a desire to display themselves; it is hardly possible to pass through a village in country districts without meeting a two- or three-year-old child who lifts up his or her blouse or frock before the traveller, possibly in his honour. One of my patients has retained in his conscious memory a scene from his eighth year, in which, after undressing for bed, he wanted to dance into his little sister's room in his shirt, but was prevented by the servant. In the history of the childhood of neurotics exposure before children of the opposite sex plays a prominent part; in paranoia the delusion of being observed while dressing and undressing may be directly traced to these experiences; and among those who have remained perverse there is a class in whom the childish impulse is accentuated into a symptom: the class of *exhibitionists*.

This age of childhood, in which the sense of shame is unknown, seems a paradise when we look back upon it later, and paradise itself is nothing but the mass-phantasy of the childhood of the individual. This is why in paradise men are naked and unashamed, until the moment arrives when shame and fear awaken; expulsion follows, and sexual life and cultural development begin. Into this paradise dreams can take us back every night; we have already ventured the conjecture that the impressions of our earliest childhood (from the prehistoric period until about the end of the third year) crave reproduction for their own sake, perhaps without further reference to their content, so that their repetition is a wish-fulfilment. Dreams of nakedness, then, are *exhibition-dreams*.[2]

[1] The child appears in the fairy-tale also, for there a little child suddenly cries out: "But he hasn't anything on at all!"
[2] Ferenczi has recorded a number of interesting dreams of nakedness in women which

The nucleus of an exhibition-dream is furnished by one's own person, which is seen not as that of a child, but as it exists in the present, and by the idea of scanty clothing which emerges indistinctly, owing to the superimposition of so many later situations of being partially clothed, or out of consideration for the censorship; to these elements are added the persons in whose presence one is ashamed. I know of no example in which the actual spectators of these infantile exhibitions reappear in a dream; for a dream is hardly ever a simple recollection. Strangely enough, those persons who are the objects of our sexual interest in childhood are omitted from all reproductions, in dreams, in hysteria or in obsessional neurosis; paranoia alone restores the spectators, and is fanatically convinced of their presence, although they remain unseen. The substitute for these persons offered by the dream, the "number of strangers" who take no notice of the spectacle offered them, is precisely the *counter-wish* to that single intimately-known person for whom the exposure was intended. "A number of strangers," moreover, often occur in dreams in all sorts of other connections; as a *counter-wish* they always signify "a secret." [1] It will be seen that even that restitution of the old state of affairs that occurs in paranoia complies with this counter-tendency. One is no longer alone; one is quite positively being watched; but the spectators are "a number of strange, curiously indeterminate people."

Furthermore, repression finds a place in the exhibition-dream. For the disagreeable sensation of the dream is, of course, the reaction on the part of the second psychic instance to the fact that the exhibitionistic scene which has been condemned by the censorship has nevertheless succeeded in presenting itself. The only way to avoid this sensation would be to refrain from reviving the scene.

In a later chapter we shall deal once again with the feeling of inhibition. In our dreams it represents to perfection *a conflict of the will, a denial*. According to our unconscious purpose, the exhibition is to proceed; according to the demands of the censorship, it is to come to an end.

The relation of our typical dreams to fairy-tales and other fiction and poetry is neither sporadic nor accidental. Sometimes the penetrating insight of the poet has analytically recognized the process of transformation of which the poet is otherwise the instrument, and has followed it up in the reverse direction; that is to say, has traced a poem to a dream. A friend has called my attention to the following passage in G. Keller's *Der Grüne Heinrich*: "I do not wish, dear Lee, that you should ever

---

were without difficulty traced to the infantile delight in exhibitionism, but which differ in many features from the "typical" dream of nakedness discussed above.
[1] For obvious reasons the presence of "the whole family" in the dream has the same significance.

come to realize from experience the exquisite and piquant truth in the situation of Odysseus, when he appears, naked and covered with mud, before Nausicaä and her playmates! Would you like to know what it means? Let us for a moment consider the incident closely. If you are ever parted from your home, and from all that is dear to you, and wander about in a strange country; if you have seen much and experienced much; if you have cares and sorrows, and are, perhaps, utterly wretched and forlorn, you will some night inevitably dream that you are approaching your home; you will see it shining and glittering in the loveliest colours; lovely and gracious figures will come to meet you; and then you will suddenly discover that you are ragged, naked, and covered with dust. An indescribable feeling of shame and fear overcomes you; you try to cover yourself, to hide, and you wake up bathed in sweat. As long as humanity exists, this will be the dream of the care-laden, tempest-tossed man, and thus Homer has drawn this situation from the profoundest depths of the eternal nature of humanity."

What are the profoundest depths of the eternal nature of humanity, which the poet commonly hopes to awaken in his listeners, but these stirrings of the psychic life which are rooted in that age of childhood, which subsequently becomes prehistoric? Childish wishes, now suppressed and forbidden, break into the dream behind the unobjectionable and permissibly conscious wishes of the homeless man, and it is for this reason that the dream which is objectified in the legend of Nausicaä regularly develops into an anxiety-dream.

My own dream of hurrying upstairs, which presently changed into being glued to the stairs, is likewise an exhibition-dream, for it reveals the essential ingredients of such a dream. It must therefore be possible to trace it back to experiences in my childhood, and the knowledge of these should enable us to conclude how far the servant's behaviour to me (*i.e.* her reproach that I had soiled the carpet) helped her to secure the position which she occupies in the dream. Now I am actually able to furnish the desired explanation. One learns in a psychoanalysis to interpret temporal proximity by material connection; two ideas which are apparently without connection, but which occur in immediate succession, belong to a unity which has to be deciphered; just as an *a* and a *b*, when written in succession, must be pronounced as one syllable, *ab*. It is just the same with the interrelations of dreams. The dream of the stairs has been taken from a series of dreams with whose other members I am familiar, having interpreted them. A dream included in this series must belong to the same context. Now, the other dreams of the series are based on the memory of a nurse to whom I was entrusted for a season, from the time when I was still at the breast to the age of two and a half, and of whom a hazy recollection has remained in my consciousness. Accord-

ing to information which I recently obtained from my mother, she was old
and ugly, but very intelligent and thorough; according to the inferences
which I am justified in drawing from my dreams, she did not always treat
me quite kindly, but spoke harshly to me when I showed insufficient understanding of the necessity for cleanliness. Inasmuch as the maid endeavoured to continue my education in this respect, she is entitled to be
treated, in my dream, as an incarnation of the prehistoric old woman. It
is to be assumed, of course, that the child was fond of his teacher in spite
of her harsh behaviour.[1]

(b) Dreams of the Death of Beloved Persons

Another series of dreams which may be called typical are those whose content is that a beloved relative, a parent, brother, sister, child, or the like,
has died. We must at once distinguish two classes of such dreams: those
in which the dreamer remains unmoved, and those in which he feels profoundly grieved by the death of the beloved person, even expressing this
grief by shedding tears in his sleep.

We may ignore the dreams of the first group; they have no claim to be
reckoned as typical. If they are analysed, it is found that they signify
something that is not contained in them, that they are intended to mask
another wish of some kind. This is the case in the dream of the aunt who
sees the only son of her sister lying on a bier (p. 229). The dream does
not mean that she desires the death of her little nephew; as we have
learned, it merely conceals the wish to see a certain beloved person again
after a long separation—the same person whom she had seen after as
long an interval at the funeral of another nephew. This wish, which is
the real content of the dream, gives no cause for sorrow, and for that reason no sorrow is felt in the dream. We see here that the feeling contained
in the dream does not belong to the manifest, but to the latent dream-
content, and that the affective content has remained free from the distortion which has befallen the conceptual content.

It is otherwise with those dreams in which the death of a beloved relative is imagined, and in which a painful affect is felt. These signify, as
their content tells us, the wish that the person in question might die; and
since I may here expect that the feelings of all my readers and of all who
have had such dreams will lead them to reject my explanation, I must
endeavour to rest my proof on the broadest possible basis.

We have already cited a dream from which we could see that the wishes

[1] A supplementary interpretation of this dream: To spit (*spucken*) on the stairs,
since *spuken* (to haunt) is the occupation of spirits (cf. English, spook), led me by
a free translation to *esprit d'escalier.* "Stair-wit" means unreadiness at repartee,
(*Schlagfertigkeit* = literally: readiness to hit out) with which I really have to reproach myself. But was the nurse deficient in *Schlagfertigkeit?*

represented as fulfilled in dreams are not always current wishes. They may also be bygone, discarded, buried and repressed wishes, which we must nevertheless credit with a sort of continued existence, merely on account of their reappearance in a dream. They are not dead, like persons who have died, in the sense that we know death, but are rather like the shades in the Odyssey which awaken to a certain degree of life so soon as they have drunk blood. The dream of the dead child in the box (p. 231) contained a wish that had been present fifteen years earlier, and which had at that time been frankly admitted as real. Further—and this, perhaps, is not unimportant from the standpoint of the theory of dreams—a recollection from the dreamer's earliest childhood was at the root of this wish also. When the dreamer was a little child—but exactly when cannot be definitely determined—she heard that her mother, during the pregnancy of which she was the outcome, had fallen into a profound emotional depression, and had passionately wished for the death of the child in her womb. Having herself grown up and become pregnant, she was only following the example of her mother.

If anyone dreams that his father or mother, his brother or sister, has died, and his dream expresses grief, I should never adduce this as proof that he wishes any of them dead *now*. The theory of dreams does not go as far as to require this; it is satisfied with concluding that the dreamer has wished them dead at some time or other during his childhood. I fear, however, that this limitation will not go far to appease my critics; probably they will just as energetically deny the possibility that they ever had such thoughts, as they protest that they do not harbour them now. I must, therefore, reconstruct a portion of the submerged infantile psychology on the basis of the evidence of the present.[1]

Let us first of all consider the relation of children to their brothers and sisters. I do not know why we presuppose that it must be a loving one, since examples of enmity among adult brothers and sisters are frequent in everyone's experience, and since we are so often able to verify the fact that this estrangement originated during childhood, or has always existed. Moreover, many adults who to-day are devoted to their brothers and sisters, and support them in adversity, lived with them in almost continuous enmity during their childhood. The elder child ill-treated the younger, slandered him, and robbed him of his toys; the younger was consumed with helpless fury against the elder, envied and feared him, or his earliest impulse toward liberty and his first revolt against injustice were directed against his oppressor. The parents say that the children do not agree,

[1] Cf. also: *Analyse der Phobie eines fünfjährigen Knaben* in the *Jahrbuch für psychoanal und psychopath. Forschungen*, Bd. i, 1909 (*Ges. Schriften*, Bd. viii), and *Über Infantile Sexualtheorien*, in the *Sammlung kleiner Schriften zur Neurosenlehre* (*Ges. Schriften*, Bd. v).

and cannot find the reason for it. It is not difficult to see that the character even of a well-behaved child is not the character we should wish to find in an adult. A child is absolutely egoistical; he feels his wants acutely, and strives remorselessly to satisfy them, especially against his competitors, other children, and first of all against his brothers and sisters. And yet we do not on that account call a child "wicked"—we call him "naughty"; he is not responsible for his misdeeds, either in our own judgment or in the eyes of the law. And this is as it should be; for we may expect that within the very period of life which we reckon as childhood, altruistic impulses and morality will awake in the little egoist, and that, in the words of Meynert, a secondary ego will overlay and inhibit the primary ego. Morality, of course, does not develop simultaneously in all its departments, and furthermore, the duration of the amoral period of childhood differs in different individuals. Where this morality fails to develop we are prone to speak of "degeneration"; but here the case is obviously one of arrested development. Where the primary character is already overlaid by the later development it may be at least partially uncovered again by an attack of hysteria. The correspondence between the so-called hysterical character and that of a naughty child is positively striking. The obsessional neurosis, on the other hand, corresponds to a super-morality, which develops as a strong reinforcement against the primary character that is threatening to revive.

Many persons, then, who now love their brothers and sisters, and who would feel bereaved by their death, harbour in their unconscious hostile wishes, survivals from an earlier period, wishes which are able to realize themselves in dreams. It is, however, quite especially interesting to observe the behaviour of little children up to their third and fourth year towards their younger brothers or sisters. So far the child has been the only one; now he is informed that the stork has brought a new baby. The child inspects the new arrival, and expresses his opinion with decision: "The stork had better take it back again!" [1]

I seriously declare it as my opinion that a child is able to estimate the disadvantages which he has to expect on account of a new-comer. A connection of mine, who now gets on very well with a sister, who is four years her junior, responded to the news of this sister's arrival with the reservation: "But I shan't give her my red cap, anyhow." If the child should come to realize only at a later stage that its happiness may be prejudiced

---

[1] Hans, whose phobia was the subject of the analysis in the above-mentioned publication, cried out at the age of three and a half, while feverish, shortly after the birth of a sister: "But I don't want to have a little sister." In his neurosis, eighteen months later, he frankly confessed the wish that his mother should drop the child into the bath while bathing it, in order that it might die. With all this, Hans was a good-natured, affectionate child, who soon became fond of his sister, and took her under his special protection.

by a younger brother or sister, its enmity will be aroused at this period. I know of a case where a girl, not three years of age, tried to strangle an infant in its cradle, because she suspected that its continued presence boded her no good. Children at this time of life are capable of a jealousy that is perfectly evident and extremely intense. Again, perhaps the little brother or sister really soon disappears, and the child once more draws to himself the whole affection of the household; then a new child is sent by the stork; is it not natural that the favourite should conceive the wish that the new rival may meet the same fate as the earlier one, in order that he may be as happy as he was before the birth of the first child, and during the interval after his death? [1] Of course, this attitude of the child towards the younger brother or sister is, under normal circumstances, a mere function of the difference of age. After a certain interval the maternal instincts of the older girl will be awakened towards the helpless new-born infant.

Feelings of hostility towards brothers and sisters must occur far more frequently in children than is observed by their obtuse elders.[2]

In the case of my own children, who followed one another rapidly, I missed the opportunity of making such observations, I am now retrieving it, thanks to my little nephew, whose undisputed domination was disturbed after fifteen months by the arrival of a feminine rival. I hear, it is true, that the young man behaves very chivalrously toward his little sister, that he kisses her hand and strokes her; but in spite of this I have convinced myself that even before the completion of his second year he is using his new command of language to criticize this person, who, to him, after all, seems superfluous. Whenever the conversation turns upon her he chimes in, and cries angrily: "Too (l)ittle, too (l)ittle!" During the last few months, since the child has outgrown this disparagement, owing to her splendid development, he has found another reason for his insistence that she does not deserve so much attention. He reminds us, on every suitable pretext: "She hasn't any teeth." [3] We all of us recollect the case of the

---

[1] Such cases of death in the experience of children may soon be forgotten in the family, but psychoanalytical investigation shows that they are very significant for a later neurosis.

[2] Since the above was written a great many observations relating to the originally hostile attitude of children toward their brothers and sisters, and toward one of their parents, have been recorded in the literature of psychoanalysis. One writer, Spitteler, gives the following peculiarly sincere and ingenuous description of this typical childish attitude as he experienced it in his earliest childhood: "Moreover, there was now a second Adolf. A little creature whom they declared was my brother, but I could not understand what he could be for, or why they should pretend he was a being like myself. I was sufficient unto myself: what did I want with a brother? And he was not only useless, he was also even troublesome. When I plagued my grandmother, he too wanted to plague her; when I was wheeled about in the baby-carriage he sat opposite me, and took up half the room, so that we could not help kicking one another."

[3] The three-and-a-half-year-old Hans embodied his devastating criticism of his little

eldest daughter of another sister of mine. The child, who was then six years of age, spent a full half-hour in going from one aunt to another with the question: "Lucie can't understand that yet, can she?" Lucie was her rival—two and a half years younger.

I have never failed to come across this dream of the death of brothers or sisters, denoting an intense hostility, e.g. I have met it in all my female patients. I have met with only one exception, which could easily be interpreted into a confirmation of the rule. Once, in the course of a sitting, when I was explaining this state of affairs to a female patient, since it seemed to have some bearing on the symptoms under consideration that day, she answered, to my astonishment, that she had never had such dreams. But another dream occurred to her, which presumably had nothing to do with the case—a dream which she had first dreamed at the age of *four*, when she was the youngest child, and had since then dreamed repeatedly. *"A number of children, all her brothers and sisters with her boy and girl cousins, were romping about in a meadow. Suddenly they all grew wings, flew up, and were gone."* She had no idea of the significance of this dream; but we can hardly fail to recognize it as a dream of the death of all the brothers and sisters, in its original form, and but little influenced by the censorship. I will venture to add the following analysis of it: on the death of one out of this large number of children—in this case the children of two brothers were brought up together as brothers and sisters—would not our dreamer, at that time not yet four years of age, have asked some wise, grown-up person: "What becomes of children when they are dead?" The answer would probably have been: "They grow wings and become angels." After this explanation, all the brothers and sisters and cousins in the dream now have wings, like angels and— this is the important point—they fly away. Our little angel-maker is left alone: just think, the only one out of such a crowd! That the children romp about a meadow, from which they fly away, points almost certainly to butterflies—it is as though the child had been influenced by the same association of ideas which led the ancients to imagine Psyche, the soul, with the wings of a butterfly.

Perhaps some readers will now object that the inimical impulses of children toward their brothers and sisters may perhaps be admitted, but how does the childish character arrive at such heights of wickedness as to desire the death of a rival or a stronger playmate, as though all misdeeds could be atoned for only by death? Those who speak in this fashion forget that the child's idea of "being dead" has little but the word in common with our own. The child knows nothing of the horrors of decay, of

---

sister in these identical words (*loc. cit.*). He assumed that she was unable to speak on account of her lack of teeth.

shivering in the cold grave, of the terror of the infinite Nothing, the thought of which the adult, as all the myths of the hereafter testify, finds so intolerable. The fear of death is alien to the child; and so he plays with the horrid word, and threatens another child: "If you do that again, you will die, just like Francis died;" at which the poor mother shudders, unable perhaps to forget that the greater proportion of mortals do not survive beyond the years of childhood. Even at the age of eight, a child returning from a visit to a natural history museum may say to her mother: "Mamma, I do love you so; if you ever die, I am going to have you stuffed and set you up here in the room, so that I can always, always see you!" So different from our own is the childish conception of being dead.[1]

Being dead means, for the child, who has been spared the sight of the suffering that precedes death, much the same as "being gone," and ceasing to annoy the survivors. The child does not distinguish the means by which this absence is brought about, whether by distance, or estrangement, or death.[2] If, during the child's prehistoric years, a nurse has been dismissed, and if his mother dies a little while later, the two experiences, as we discover by analysis, form links of a chain in his memory. The fact that the child does not very intensely miss those who are absent has been realized, to her sorrow, by many a mother, when she has returned home from an absence of several weeks, and has been told, upon inquiry: "The children have not asked for their mother once." But if she really departs to "that undiscovered country from whose bourne no traveller returns," the children seem at first to have forgotten her, and only *subsequently* do they begin to remember their dead mother.

While, therefore, the child has its motives for desiring the absence of another child, it is lacking in all those restraints which would prevent it from clothing this wish in the form of a death-wish; and the psychic reaction to dreams of a death-wish proves that, in spite of all the differences of content, the wish in the case of the child is after all identical with the corresponding wish in an adult.

[1] To my astonishment, I was told that a highly intelligent boy of ten, after the sudden death of his father, said: "I understand that father is dead, but I can't see why he does not come home to supper." Further material relating to this subject will be found in the section *Kinderseele,* edited by Frau Dr. von Hug-Hellmuth, in *Imago,* Bd. i–v, 1912–18.

[2] The observation of a father trained in psychoanalysis was able to detect the very moment when his very intelligent little daughter, aged four, realized the difference between "being away" and "being dead." The child was being troublesome at table, and noted that one of the waitresses in the *pension* was looking at her with an expression of annoyance. "Josephine ought to be dead," she thereupon remarked to her father. "But why dead?" asked the father, soothingly. "Wouldn't it be enough if she went away?" "No," replied the child, "then she would come back again." To the uncurbed self-love (*narcissism*) of the child every inconvenience constitutes the crime of *lèse majesté,* and, as in the Draconian code, the child's feelings prescribe for all such crimes the one invariable punishment.

If, then, the death-wish of a child in respect of his brothers and sisters is explained by his childish egoism, which makes him regard his brothers and sisters as rivals, how are we to account for the same wish in respect of his parents, who bestow their love on him, and satisfy his needs, and whose preservation he ought to desire for these very egoistical reasons? Towards a solution of this difficulty we may be guided by our knowledge that the very great majority of dreams of the death of a parent refer to the parent of the same sex as the dreamer, so that a man generally dreams of the death of his father, and a woman of the death of her mother. I do not claim that this happens constantly; but that it happens in a great majority of cases is so evident that it requires explanation by some factor of general significance.[1] Broadly speaking, it is as though a sexual preference made itself felt at an early age, as though the boy regarded his father, and the girl her mother, as a rival in love—by whose removal he or she could but profit.

Before rejecting this idea as monstrous, let the reader again consider the actual relations between parents and children. We must distinguish between the traditional standard of conduct, the filial piety expected in this relation, and what daily observation shows us to be the fact. More than one occasion for enmity lies hidden amidst the relations of parents and children; conditions are present in the greatest abundance under which wishes which cannot pass the censorship are bound to arise. Let us first consider the relation between father and son. In my opinion the sanctity with which we have endorsed the injunctions of the Decalogue dulls our perception of the reality. Perhaps we hardly dare permit ourselves to perceive that the greater part of humanity neglects to obey the fifth commandment. In the lowest as well as in the highest strata of human society, filial piety towards parents is wont to recede before other interests. The obscure legends which have been handed down to us from the primeval ages of human society in mythology and folklore give a deplorable idea of the despotic power of the father, and the ruthlessness with which it was exercised. Kronos devours his children, as the wild boar devours the litter of the sow; Zeus emasculates his father [2] and takes his place as ruler. The more tyrannically the father ruled in the ancient family, the more surely must the son, as his appointed successor, have assumed the position of an enemy, and the greater must have been his impatience to attain to supremacy through the death of his father. Even in our own middle-class families

---

[1] The situation is frequently disguised by the intervention of a tendency to punishment, which, in the form of a moral reaction, threatens the loss of the beloved parent.
[2] At least in some of the mythological accounts. According to others, emasculation was inflicted only by Kronos on his father Uranos.

With regard to the mythological significance of this motive, cf. Otto Rank's *Der Mythus von der Geburt des Helden*, in Heft v of *Schriften zur angew. Seelenkunde*, 1909, and *Das Inzestmotiv in Dichtung und Sage*, 1912, chap. ix, 2.

the father commonly fosters the growth of the germ of hatred which is naturally inherent in the paternal relation, by refusing to allow the son to be a free agent or by denying him the means of becoming so. A physician often has occasion to remark that a son's grief at the loss of his father cannot quench his gratification that he has at last obtained his freedom. Fathers, as a rule, cling desperately to as much of the sadly antiquated *potestas patris familias* as still survives in our modern society, and the poet who, like Ibsen, puts the immemorial strife between father and son in the foreground of his drama is sure of his effect. The causes of conflict between mother and daughter arise when the daughter grows up and finds herself watched by her mother when she longs for real sexual freedom, while the mother is reminded by the budding beauty of her daughter that for her the time has come to renounce sexual claims.

All these circumstances are obvious to everyone, but they do not help us to explain dreams of the death of their parents in persons for whom filial piety has long since come to be unquestionable. We are, however, prepared by the foregoing discussion to look for the origin of a death-wish in the earliest years of childhood.

In the case of psychoneurotics, analysis confirms this conjecture beyond all doubt. For analysis tells us that the sexual wishes of the child—in so far as they deserve this designation in their nascent state—awaken at a very early age, and that the earliest affection of the girl-child is lav-- ished on the father, while the earliest infantile desires of the boy are directed upon the mother. For the boy the father, and for the girl the mother, becomes an obnoxious rival, and we have already shown, in the case of brothers and sisters, how readily in children this feeling leads to the death-wish. As a general rule, sexual selection soon makes its appearance in the parents; it is a natural tendency for the father to spoil his little daughters, and for the mother to take the part of the sons, while both, so long as the glamour of sex does not prejudice their judgment, are strict in training the children. The child is perfectly conscious of this partiality, and offers resistance to the parent who opposes it. To find love in an adult is for the child not merely the satisfaction of a special need; it means also that the child's will is indulged in all other respects. Thus the child is obeying its own sexual instinct, and at the same time reinforcing the stimulus proceeding from the parents, when its choice between the parents corresponds with their own.

The signs of these infantile tendencies are for the most part overlooked; and yet some of them may be observed even after the early years of childhood. An eight-year-old girl of my acquaintance, whenever her mother is called away from the table, takes advantage of her absence to proclaim herself her successor. "Now I shall be Mamma; Karl, do you want some more vegetables? Have some more, do," etc. A particularly clever and lively little girl, not yet four years of age, in whom this trait of child psychology is unusually transparent, says frankly: "Now mummy can go away; then daddy must marry me, and I will be his wife." Nor does this wish by any means exclude the possibility that the child may most tenderly love its mother. If the little boy is allowed to sleep at his mother's side whenever his father goes on a journey, and if after his father's return he has to go back to the nursery, to a person whom he likes far less, the wish may readily arise that his father might always be absent, so that he might keep his place beside his dear, beautiful mamma; and the father's death is obviously a means for the attainment of this wish; for the child's experience has taught him that "dead" folks, like grandpapa, for example, are always absent; they never come back.

While such observations of young children readily accommodate themselves to the interpretation suggested, they do not, it is true, carry the complete conviction which is forced upon a physician by the psychoanalysis of adult neurotics. The dreams of neurotic patients are communicated with preliminaries of such a nature that their interpretation as wish-dreams becomes inevitable. One day I find a lady depressed and weeping. She says: "I do not want to see my relatives any more; they must shudder at me." Thereupon, almost without any transition, she tells me that she has remembered a dream, whose significance, of course, she does not understand. She dreamed it when she was four years old, and it was this: *A fox or a lynx is walking about the roof; then something falls down, or she falls down, and after that, her mother is carried out of the house—dead;* whereat the dreamer weeps bitterly. I have no sooner informed her that this dream must signify a childish wish to see her mother dead, and that it is because of this dream that she thinks that her relatives must shudder at her, than she furnishes material in explanation of the dream. "Lynx-eye" is an opprobrious epithet which a street boy once bestowed on her when she was a very small child; and when she was three years old a brick or tile fell on her mother's head, so that she bled profusely.

I once had occasion to make a thorough study of a young girl who was passing through various psychic states. In the state of frenzied confusion with which her illness began, the patient manifested a quite peculiar aversion for her mother; she struck her and abused her whenever she approached the bed, while at the same period she was affectionate and submissive to a much older sister. Then there followed a lucid but rather apathetic condition, with badly disturbed sleep. It was in this phase that I began to treat her and to analyse her dreams. An enormous number of these dealt, in a more or less veiled fashion, with the death of the girl's mother; now she was present at the funeral of an old woman, now she saw herself and her sister sitting at a table, dressed in mourning; the meaning of the dreams could not be doubted. During her progressive improvement hysterical phobias made their appearance, the most distressing of which was the fear that something had happened to her mother. Wherever she might be at the time, she had then to hurry home in order to convince herself that her mother was still alive. Now this case, considered in conjunction with the rest of my experience, was very instructive; it showed, in polyglot translations, as it were, the different ways in which the psychic apparatus reacts to the same exciting idea. In the state of confusion, which I regard as an overthrow of the second psychic instance by the first instance, at other times suppressed, the unconscious enmity towards the mother gained the upper hand, and found physical expression; then, when the patient became calmer, the insurrection was suppressed, and the domination of the censorship restored, and this enmity had access only to the realms of dreams, in which it realized the wish that the mother might die; and after the normal condition had been still further strengthened it created the excessive concern for the mother as a hysterical counter-reaction and defensive phenomenon. In the light of these considerations, it is no longer inexplicable why hysterical girls are so often extravagantly attached to their mothers.

On another occasion I had an opportunity of obtaining a profound insight into the unconscious psychic life of a young man for whom an obsessional neurosis made life almost unendurable, so that he could not go into the streets, because he was tormented by the fear that he would kill everyone he met. He spent his days in contriving evidence of an alibi in case he should be accused of any murder that might have been committed in the city. It goes without saying that this man was as moral as he was highly cultured. The analysis—which, by the way, led to a cure—revealed, as the basis of this distressing obsession, murderous impulses in respect of his rather overstrict father—impulses which, to his astonishment, had consciously expressed themselves when he was seven years old, but which, of course, had originated in a much earlier period of his childhood. After the painful illness and death of his father, when the young man was in his thirty-first year, the obsessive reproach made its appearance, which transferred itself to strangers in the form of this phobia. Anyone capable of wishing to push his own father from a mountain-top into an abyss cannot be trusted to spare the lives of persons less closely related to him; he therefore does well to lock himself into his room.

According to my already extensive experience, parents play a leading part in the infantile psychology of all persons who subsequently become psychoneurotics. Falling in love with one parent and hating the other forms part of the permanent stock of the psychic impulses which arise in early childhood, and are of such importance as the material of the subsequent neurosis. But I do not believe that psychoneurotics are to be

sharply distinguished in this respect from other persons who remain normal—that is, I do not believe that they are capable of creating something
absolutely new and peculiar to themselves. It is far more probable—and
this is confirmed by incidental observations of normal children—that in
their amorous or hostile attitude toward their parents, psychoneurotics
do no more than reveal to us, by magnification, something that occurs less
markedly and intensively in the minds of the majority of children. Antiquity has furnished us with legendary matter which corroborates this
belief, and the profound and universal validity of the old legends is explicable only by an equally universal validity of the above-mentioned
hypothesis of infantile psychology.

I am referring to the legend of King Oedipus and the *Oedipus Rex* of
Sophocles. Oedipus, the son of Laius, king of Thebes, and Jocasta, is exposed as a suckling, because an oracle had informed the father that his
son, who was still unborn, would be his murderer. He is rescued, and grows
up as a king's son at a foreign court, until, being uncertain of his origin,
he, too, consults the oracle, and is warned to avoid his native place, for he
is destined to become the murderer of his father and the husband of his
mother. On the road leading away from his supposed home he meets King
Laius, and in a sudden quarrel strikes him dead. He comes to Thebes,
where he solves the riddle of the Sphinx, who is barring the way to the
city, whereupon he is elected king by the grateful Thebans, and is rewarded with the hand of Jocasta. He reigns for many years in peace and
honour, and begets two sons and two daughters upon his unknown mother,
until at last a plague breaks out—which causes the Thebans to consult
the oracle anew. Here Sophocles' tragedy begins. The messengers bring
the reply that the plague will stop as soon as the murderer of Laius is
driven from the country. But where is he?

> "Where shall be found,
> Faint, and hard to be known, the trace of the ancient guilt?"

The action of the play consists simply in the disclosure, approached
step by step and artistically delayed (and comparable to the work of a
psychoanalysis) that Oedipus himself is the murderer of Laius, and that
he is the son of the murdered man and Jocasta. Shocked by the abominable
crime which he has unwittingly committed, Oedipus blinds himself, and
departs from his native city. The prophecy of the oracle has been fulfilled.

The *Oedipus Rex* is a tragedy of fate; its tragic effect depends on the
conflict between the all-powerful will of the gods and the vain efforts of
human beings threatened with disaster; resignation to the divine will, and
the perception of one's own impotence is the lesson which the deeply
moved spectator is supposed to learn from the tragedy. Modern authors
have therefore sought to achieve a similar tragic effect by expressing the

same conflict in stories of their own invention. But the playgoers have looked on unmoved at the unavailing efforts of guiltless men to avert the fulfilment of curse or oracle; the modern tragedies of destiny have failed of their effect.

If the *Oedipus Rex* is capable of moving a modern reader or playgoer no less powerfully than it moved the contemporary Greeks, the only possible explanation is that the effect of the Greek tragedy does not depend upon the conflict between fate and human will, but upon the peculiar nature of the material by which this conflict is revealed. There must be a voice within us which is prepared to acknowledge the compelling power of fate in the *Oedipus,* while we are able to condemn the situations occurring in *Die Ahnfrau* or other tragedies of fate as arbitrary inventions. And there actually is a motive in the story of King Oedipus which explains the verdict of this inner voice. His fate moves us only because it might have been our own, because the oracle laid upon us before our birth the very curse which rested upon him. It may be that we were all destined to direct our first sexual impulses toward our mothers, and our first impulses of hatred and violence toward our fathers; our dreams convince us that we were. King Oedipus, who slew his father Laius and wedded his mother Jocasta, is nothing more or less than a wish-fulfilment—the fulfilment of the wish of our childhood. But we, more fortunate than he, in so far as we have not become psychoneurotics, have since our childhood succeeded in withdrawing our sexual impulses from our mothers, and in forgetting our jealousy of our fathers. We recoil from the person for whom this primitive wish of our childhood has been fulfilled with all the force of the repression which these wishes have undergone in our minds since childhood. As the poet brings the guilt of Oedipus to light by his investigation, he forces us to become aware of our own inner selves, in which the same impulses are still extant, even though they are suppressed. The antithesis with which the chorus departs:—

> ". . . Behold, this is Oedipus,
> Who unravelled the great riddle, and was first in power,
> Whose fortune all the townsmen praised and envied;
> See in what dread adversity he sank!"

—this admonition touches us and our own pride, us who since the years of our childhood have grown so wise and so powerful in our own estimation. Like Oedipus, we live in ignorance of the desires that offend morality, the desires that nature has forced upon us and after their unveiling we may well prefer to avert our gaze from the scenes of our childhood.[1]

[1] None of the discoveries of psychoanalytical research has evoked such embittered contradiction, such furious opposition, and also such entertaining acrobatics of criticism, as this indication of the incestuous impulses of childhood which survive in the

In the very text of Sophocles' tragedy there is an unmistakable reference to the fact that the Oedipus legend had its source in dream-material of immemorial antiquity, the content of which was the painful disturbance of the child's relations to its parents caused by the first impulses of sexuality. Jocasta comforts Oedipus—who is not yet enlightened, but is troubled by the recollection of the oracle—by an allusion to a dream which is often dreamed, though it cannot, in her opinion, mean anything:—

> "For many a man hath seen himself in dreams
> His mother's mate, but he who gives no heed
> To suchlike matters bears the easier life."

The dream of having sexual intercourse with one's mother was as common then as it is to-day with many people, who tell it with indignation and astonishment. As may well be imagined, it is the key to the tragedy and the complement to the dream of the death of the father. The Oedipus fable is the reaction of fantasy to these two typical dreams, and just as such a dream, when occurring to an adult, is experienced with feelings of aversion, so the content of the fable must include terror and self-chastisement. The form which it subsequently assumed was the result of an uncomprehending secondary elaboration of the material, which sought to make it serve a theological intention.[1] The attempt to reconcile divine omnipotence with human responsibility must, of course, fail with this material as with any other.

Another of the great poetic tragedies, Shakespeare's *Hamlet*, is rooted in the same soil as *Oedipus Rex*. But the whole difference in the psychic life of the two widely separated periods of civilization, and the progress, during the course of time, of repression in the emotional life of humanity, is manifested in the differing treatment of the same material. In *Oedipus Rex* the basic wish-phantasy of the child is brought to light and realized as it is in dreams; in *Hamlet* it remains repressed, and we learn of its existence—as we discover the relevant facts in a neurosis—only through the inhibitory effects which proceed from it. In the more modern drama, the curious fact that it is possible to remain in complete uncertainty as to the character of the hero has proved to be quite consistent with the overpowering effect of the tragedy. The play is based upon Hamlet's hesita-

---

unconscious. An attempt has even been made recently, in defiance of all experience, to assign only a "symbolic" significance to incest. Ferenczi has given an ingenious reinterpretation of the Oedipus myth, based on a passage in one of Schopenhauer's letters, in *Imago*, i, 1912. The "Oedipus complex," which was first alluded to here in *The Interpretation of Dreams*, has through further study of the subject, acquired an unexpected signficance for the understanding of human history and the evolution of religion and morality. See *Totem und Taboo*.

[1] Cf. the dream-material of exhibitionism, p. 294-5.

tion in accomplishing the task of revenge assigned to him; the text does not give the cause or the motive of this hesitation, nor have the manifold attempts at interpretation succeeded in doing so. According to the still prevailing conception, a conception for which Goethe was first responsible, Hamlet represents the type of man whose active energy is paralysed by excessive intellectual activity: "Sicklied o'er with the pale cast of thought." According to another conception, the poet has endeavoured to portray a morbid, irresolute character, on the verge of neurasthenia. The plot of the drama, however, shows us that Hamlet is by no means intended to appear as a character wholly incapable of action. On two separate occasions we see him assert himself: once in a sudden outburst of rage, when he stabs the eavesdropper behind the arras, and on the other occasion when he deliberately, and even craftily, with the complete unscruplousness of a prince of the Renaissance, sends the two courtiers to the death which was intended for himself. What is it, then, that inhibits him in accomplishing the task which his father's ghost has laid upon him? Here the explanation offers itself that it is the peculiar nature of this task. Hamlet is able to do anything but take vengeance upon the man who did away with his father and has taken his father's place with his mother— the man who shows him in realization the repressed desires of his own childhood. The loathing which should have driven him to revenge is thus replaced by self-reproach, by concientious scruples, which tell him that he himself is no better than the murderer whom he is required to punish. I have here translated into consciousness what had to remain unconscious in the mind of the hero; if anyone wishes to call Hamlet an hysterical subject I cannot but admit that this is the deduction to be drawn from my interpretation. The sexual aversion which Hamlet expresses in conversation with Ophelia is perfectly consistent with this deduction—the same sexual aversion which during the next few years was increasingly to take possession of the poet's soul, until it found its supreme utterance in *Timon of Athens*. It can, of course, be only the poet's own psychology with which we are confronted in *Hamlet*; and in a work on Shakespeare by Georg Brandes (1896) I find the statement that the drama was composed immediately after the death of Shakespeare's father (1601)—that is to say, when he was still mourning his loss, and during a revival, as we may fairly assume, of his own childish feelings in respect of his father. It is known, too, that Shakespeare's son, who died in childhood, bore the name of Hamnet (identical with Hamlet). Just as *Hamlet* treats of the relation of the son to his parents, so *Macbeth*, which was written about the same period, is based upon the theme of childlessness. Just as all neurotic symptoms, like dreams themselves, are capable of hyper-interpretation, and even require such hyper-interpretation before they become perfectly intelligible, so every genuine poetical creation must have proceeded from more than one motive, more than one impulse in the mind of the poet, and must admit of more than one interpretation. I have here attempted to interpret only the deepest stratum of impulses in the mind of the creative poet.[1]

With regard to typical dreams of the death of relatives, I must add a few words upon their significance from the point of view of the theory of dreams in general. These dreams show us the occurrence of a very unusual state of things; they show us that the dream-thought created by the repressed wish completely escapes the censorship, and is transferred to the dream without alteration. Special conditions must obtain in order to make this possible. The following two factors favour the production of these dreams: first, this is the last wish that we could credit ourselves with harbouring; we believe such a wish "would never occur to us even in a dream"; the dream-censorship is therefore unprepared for this monstrosity, just as the laws of Solon did not foresee the necessity of establishing a penalty for patricide. Secondly, the repressed and unsuspected wish is, in this special case, frequently met half-way by a residue from the day's experience, in the form of some *concern* for the life of the beloved person. This anxiety cannot enter into the dream otherwise than by taking advantage of the corresponding wish; but the wish is able to mask itself behind the concern which has been aroused during the day. If one is inclined to think that all this is really a very much simpler process, and to imagine that one merely continues during the night, and in one's dream, what was begun during the day, one removes the dreams of the death of those dear to us out of all connection with the general explanation of dreams, and a problem that may very well be solved remains a problem needlessly.

It is instructive to trace the relation of these dreams to anxiety-dreams. In dreams of the death of those dear to us the repressed wish has found a way of avoiding the censorship—and the distortion for which the censorship is responsible. An invariable concomitant phenomenon, then, is that painful emotions are felt in the dream. Similarly, an anxiety-dream occurs only when the censorship is entirely or partially overpowered, and on the other hand, the overpowering of the censorship is facilitated when

[1] These indications in the direction of an analytical understanding of *Hamlet* were subsequently developed by Dr. Ernest Jones, who defended the above conception against others which have been put forward in the literature of the subject (*The Problem of Hamlet and the Oedipus Complex*, 1911). The relation of the material of Hamlet to the "myth of the birth of the hero" has been demonstrated by O. Rank. Further attempts at an analysis of *Macbeth* will be found in my essay on *Einige Charaktertypen, aus der psychoanalytischen Arbeit*, in *Imago*, iv, 1916 (*Ges. Schriften*, Bd. x), in L. Jekels's *Shakespeare's Macbeth*, in *Imago*, v. 1918; and in *The Oedipus Complex as an Explanation of Hamlet's Mystery: a Study in Motive* (*American Journal of Psychology*, 1910, vol. xxi).

the actual sensation of anxiety is already present from somatic sources. It thus becomes obvious for what purpose the censorship performs its office and practises dream-distortion; it does so *in order to prevent the development of anxiety or other forms of painful affect.*

I have spoken in the foregoing sections of the egoism of the child's psyche, and I now emphasize this peculiarity in order to suggest a connection, for dreams too have retained this characteristic. All dreams are absolutely egoistical; in every dream the beloved ego appears, even though in a disguised form. The wishes that are realized in dreams are invariably the wishes of this ego; it is only a deceptive appearance if interest in another person is believed to have evoked a dream. I will now analyse a few examples which appear to contradict this assertion.

I

A boy not yet four years of age relates the following dream: *He saw a large garnished dish, on which was a large joint of roast meat; and the joint was suddenly—not carved—but eaten up. He did not see the person who ate it.*[1]

Who can he be, this strange person, of whose luxurious repast the little fellow dreams? The experience of the day must supply the answer. For some days past the boy, in accordance with the doctor's orders, had been living on a milk diet; but on the evening of the "dream-day" he had been naughty, and, as a punishment, had been deprived of his supper. He had already undergone one such hunger-cure, and had borne his deprivation bravely. He knew that he would get nothing, but he did not even allude to the fact that he was hungry. Training was beginning to produce its effect; this is demonstrated even by the dream, which reveals the beginnings of dream-distortion. There is no doubt that he himself is the person whose desires are directed toward this abundant meal, and a meal of roast meat at that. But since he knows that this is forbidden him, he does not dare, as hungry children do in dreams (cf. my little Anna's dream about strawberries, p. 214), to sit down to the meal himself. The person remains anonymous.

---

[1] Even the large, over-abundant, immoderate and exaggerated things occurring in dreams may be a childish characteristic. A child wants nothing more intensely than to grow big, and to eat as much of everything as grown-ups do; a child is hard to satisfy; he knows no such word as "enough," and insatiably demands the repetition of whatever has pleased him or tasted good to him. He learns to practise moderation, to be modest and resigned, only through training. As we know, the neurotic also is inclined to immoderation and excess.

II

One night I dream that I see on a bookseller's counter a new volume of one of those collectors' series, which I am in the habit of buying (monographs on artistic subjects, history, famous artistic centres, etc.). *The new collection is entitled "Famous Orators" (or Orations), and the first number bears the name of Dr. Lecher.*

On analysis it seems to me improbable that the fame of Dr. Lecher, the long-winded speaker of the German Opposition, should occupy my thoughts while I am dreaming. The fact is that a few days ago I undertook the psychological treatment of some new patients, and am now forced to talk for ten to twelve hours a day. Thus I myself am a long-winded speaker.

III

On another occasion I dream that a university lecturer of my acquaintance says to me: *"My son, the myopic."* Then follows a dialogue of brief observations and replies. A third portion of the dream follows, in which I and my sons appear, and so far as the latent dream-content is concerned, the father, the son, and Professor M., are merely lay figures, representing myself and my eldest son. Later on I shall examine this dream again, on account of another peculiarity.

IV

The following dream gives an example of really base, egoistical feelings, which conceal themselves behind an affectionate concern:

My friend Otto looks ill; his face is brown and his eyes protrude.

Otto is my family physician, to whom I owe a debt greater than I can ever hope to repay, since he has watched for years over the health of my children, has treated them successfully when they have been ill, and, moreover, has given them presents whenever he could find any excuse for doing so. He paid us a visit on the day of the dream, and my wife noticed that he looked tired and exhausted. At night I dream of him, and my dream attributes to him certain of the symptoms of Basedow's disease. If you were to disregard my rules for dream-interpretation you would understand this dream to mean that I am concerned about the health of my friend, and that this concern is realized in the dream. It would thus constitute a contradiction not only of the assertion that a dream is a wish-fulfilment, but also of the assertion that it is accessible only to egoistical impulses. But will those who thus interpret my dream explain why I should fear that Otto has Basedow's disease, for which diagnosis his appearance does not afford the slightest justification? My analysis, on the other hand, furnishes the following material, deriving from an incident which had occurred six years earlier. We were driving—a small party of us, including Professor R.—in the dark through the forest of N., which lies at a distance of some hours from where we were staying in the country. The driver, who was not quite sober, overthrew us and the carriage down a bank, and it was only by good fortune that we all escaped unhurt. But we were forced to spend the night at the nearest inn, where the news of our mishap aroused great sympathy. A certain gentleman, who showed unmistakable symptoms of *morbus Basedowii*—the brownish colour of the skin of the face and the protruding eyes, but no goitre—placed himself entirely at our disposal, and asked what he could do for us. Professor R. answered in his decisive way, "Nothing, except lend me a nightshirt." Whereupon our generous friend replied: "I am sorry, but I cannot do that," and left us.

In continuing the analysis, it occurs to me that Basedow is the name not only of a physician, but also of a famous pedagogue. (Now that I am wide awake, I do not feel quite sure of this fact.) My friend Otto is the person whom I have asked to take charge of the physical education of my children—especially during the age of puberty (hence the nightshirt) in case anything should happen to me. By seeing Otto in my dream with the morbid symptoms of our above-mentioned generous helper, I clearly mean to say: "If anything happens to me, he will do just as little for my children as Baron L. did for us, in spite of his amiable offers." The egoistical flavour of this dream should now be obvious enough.[1]

But where is the wish-fulfilment to be found in this? Not in the vengeance wreaked on my friend Otto (who seems to be fated to be badly treated in my dreams), but in the following circumstance: Inasmuch as in my dream I represented Otto as Baron L., I likewise identified myself with another person, namely, with Professor R.; for I have asked something of Otto, just as R. asked something of Baron L. at the time of the incident I have described. And this is the point. For Professor R. has gone his way independently, outside academic circles, just as I myself have done, and has only in his later years received the title which he had

---

[1] While Dr. Ernest Jones was delivering a lecture before an American scientific society, and was speaking of egoism in dreams, a learned lady took exception to this unscientific generalization. She thought the lecturer was entitled to pronounce such a verdict only on the dreams of Austrians, but had no right to include the dreams of Americans. As for herself, she was sure that all her dreams were strictly altruistic.

In justice to this lady with her national pride it may, however, be remarked that the dogma: "the dream is wholly egoistic" must not be misunderstood. For inasmuch as everything that occurs in preconscious thinking may appear in dreams (in the content as well as the latent dream-thoughts) the altruistic feelings may possibly occur. Similarly, affectionate or amorous feelings for another person, if they exist in the unconscious, may occur in dreams. The truth of the assertion is therefore restricted to the fact that among the unconscious stimuli of dreams one very often finds egoistical tendencies which seem to have been overcome in the waking state.

earned long before. Once more, then, I want to be a professor! The very phrase "in his later years" is a wish-fulfilment, for it means that I shall live long enough to steer my boys through the age of puberty myself.

Of other typical dreams, in which one flies with a feeling of ease or falls in terror, I know nothing from my own experience, and whatever I have to say about them I owe to my psycho-analyses. From the information thus obtained one must conclude that these dreams also reproduce impressions made in childhood—that is, that they refer to the games involving rapid motion which have such an extraordinary attraction for children. Where is the uncle who has never made a child fly by running with it across the room with outstretched arms, or has never played at falling with it by rocking it on his knee and then suddenly straightening his leg, or by lifting it above his head and suddenly pretending to withdraw his supporting hand? At such moments children shout with joy, and insatiably demand a repetition of the performance, especially if a little fright and dizziness are involved in the game; in after years they repeat their sensations in dreams, but in dreams they omit the hands that held them, so that now they are free to float or fall. We know that all small children have a fondness for such games as rocking and see-sawing; and if they see gymnastic performances at the circus their recollection of such games is refreshed.[1] In some boys a hysterical attack will consist simply in the reproduction of such performances, which they accomplish with great dexterity. Not infrequently sexual sensations are excited by these games of movement, which are quite neutral in themselves.[2] To express the matter in a few words: the "exciting" games of childhood are repeated in dreams of flying, falling, reeling and the like, but the voluptuous feelings are now transformed into anxiety. But, as every mother knows, the excited play of children often enough culminates in quarrelling and tears.

I have therefore good reason for rejecting the explanation that it is the state of our dermal sensations during sleep, the sensation of the move-

---

[1] Psychoanalytic investigation has enabled us to conclude that in the predilection shown by children for gymnastic performances, and in the repetition of these in hysterical attacks, there is, besides the pleasure felt in the organ, yet another factor at work (often unconscious): namely, a memory-picture of sexual intercourse observed in human beings or animals.

[2] A young colleague, who is entirely free from nervousness, tells me, in this connection: "I know from my own experience that while swinging, and at the moment at which the downward movement was at its maximum, I used to have a curious feeling in my genitals, which, although it was not really pleasing to me, I must describe as a voluptuous feeling." I have often heard from patients that the first erections with voluptuous sensations which they can remember to have had in boyhood occurred while they were climbing. It is established with complete certainty by psychoanalysis that the first sexual sensations often have their origin in the scufflings and wrestlings of childhood.

ments of the lungs, etc., that evokes dreams of flying and falling. I see that these very sensations have been reproduced from the memory to which the dream refers—and that they are, therefore, dream-content and not dream-sources.

I do not for a moment deny, however, that I am unable to furnish a full explanation of this series of typical dreams. Precisely here my material leaves me in the lurch. I must adhere to the general opinion that all the dermal and kinetic sensations of these typical dreams are awakened as soon as any psychic motive of whatever kind has need of them, and that they are neglected when there is no such need of them. The relation to infantile experiences seems to be confirmed by the indications which I have obtained from the analyses of psychoneurotics. But I am unable to say what other meanings might, in the course of the dreamer's life, have become attached to the memory of these sensations—different, perhaps, in each individual, despite the typical appearance of these dreams—and I should very much like to be in a position to fill this gap with careful analyses of good examples. To those who wonder why I complain of a lack of material, despite the frequency of these dreams of flying, falling, tooth-drawing, etc., I must explain that I myself have never experienced any such dreams since I have turned my attention to the subject of dream-interpretation. The dreams of neurotics which are at my disposal, however, are not all capable of interpretation, and very often it is impossible to penetrate to the farthest point of their hidden intention; a certain psychic force which participated in the building up of the neurosis, and which again becomes active during its dissolution, opposes interpretation of the final problem.

(c) The Examination-Dream

Everyone who has received his certificate of matriculation after passing his final examination at school complains of the persistence with which he is plagued by anxiety-dreams in which he has failed, or must go through his course again, etc. For the holder of a university degree this typical dream is replaced by another, which represents that he has not taken his doctor's degree, to which he vainly objects, while still asleep, that he has already been practising for years, or is already a university lecturer or the senior partner of a firm of lawyers, and so on. These are the ineradicable memories of the punishments we suffered as children for misdeeds which we had committed—memories which were revived in us on the *dies irae, dies illa* of the gruelling examination at the two critical junctures in our careers as students. The "examination-anxiety" of neurotics is likewise intensified by this childish fear. When our student days are over it is no longer our parents or teachers who see to our punishment; the inexorable chain of cause and effect of later life has taken over our further education. Now we dream of our matriculation, or the examination for the doctor's degree—and who has not been faint-hearted on such occasions?—whenever we fear that we may be punished by some unpleasant result because we have done something carelessly or wrongly, because we have not been as thorough as we might have been—in short, whenever we feel the burden of responsibility.

For a further explanation of examination-dreams I have to thank a remark made by a colleague who had studied this subject, who once stated, in the course of a scientific discussion, that in his experience the examination-dream occurred only to persons who had passed the examination, never to those who had flunked." We have had increasing confirmation of the fact that the anxiety-dream of examination occurs when the dreamer is anticipating a responsible task on the following day, with the possibility of disgrace; recourse will then be had to an occasion in the past on which a great anxiety proved to have been without real justification, having, indeed, been refuted by the outcome. Such a dream would be a very striking example of the way in which the dream-content is misunderstood by the waking instance. The exclamation which is regarded as a protest against the dream: "But I am already a doctor," etc., would in reality be the consolation offered by the dream, and should, therefore, be worded as follows: "Do not be afraid of the morrow; think of the anxiety which you felt before your matriculation; yet nothing happened to justify it, for now you are a doctor," etc. But the anxiety which we attribute to the dream really has its origin in the residues of the dream-day.

The tests of this interpretation which I have been able to make in my own case, and in that of others, although by no means exhaustive, were entirely in its favour.[1] For example, I failed in my examination for the doctor's degree in medical jurisprudence; never once has the matter worried me in my dreams, while I have often enough been examined in botany, zoology, and chemistry, and I sat for the examinations in these subjects with well-justified anxiety, but escaped disaster, through the clemency of fate, or of the examiner. In my dreams of school examinations I am always examined in history, a subject in which I passed brilliantly at the time, but only, I must admit, because my good-natured professor— my one-eyed benefactor in another dream did not overlook the fact that on the examination-paper which I returned to him I had crossed out with my fingernail the second of three questions, as a hint that he should not insist on it. One of my patients, who withdrew before the matricula-

[1] See also pp. 334–5.

tion examination, only to pass it later, but failed in the officer's examination, so that he did not become an officer, tells me that he often dreams of the former examination, but never of the latter.

W. Stekel, who was the first to interpret the "matriculation dream," maintains that this dream invariably refers to sexual experiences and sexual maturity. This has frequently been confirmed in my experience.

VI

THE DREAM-WORK

ALL other previous attempts to solve the problems of dreams have concerned themselves directly with the manifest dream-content as it is retained in the memory. They have sought to obtain an interpretation of the dream from this content, or, if they dispensed with an interpretation, to base their conclusions concerning the dream on the evidence provided by this content. We, however, are confronted by a different set of data; for us a new psychic material interposes itself between the dream-content and the results of our investigations: the *latent* dream-content, or dream-thoughts, which are obtained only by our method. We develop the solution of the dream from this latent content, and not from the manifest dream-content. We are thus confronted with a new problem, an entirely novel task—that of examining and tracing the relations between the latent dream-thoughts and the manifest dream-content, and the processes by which the latter has grown out of the former.

The dream-thoughts and the dream-content present themselves as two descriptions of the same content in two different languages; or, to put it more clearly, the dream-content appears to us as a translation of the dream-thoughts into another mode of expression, whose symbols and laws of composition we must learn by comparing the origin with the translation. The dream-thoughts we can understand without further trouble the moment we have ascertained them. The dream-content is, as it were, presented in hieroglyphics, whose symbols must be translated, one by one, into the language of the dream-thoughts. It would of course, be incorrect to attempt to read these symbols in accordance with their values as pictures, instead of in accordance with their meaning as symbols. For instance, I have before me a picture-puzzle (rebus)—a house, upon whose roof there is a boat; then a single letter; then a running figure, whose head has been omitted, and so on. As a critic I might be tempted to judge this composition and its elements to be nonsensical. A boat is out of place on the roof of a house, and a headless man cannot run; the man, too, is larger than the house, and if the whole thing is meant to represent a landscape the single letters of the alphabet have no right in it, since they do not occur in nature. A correct judgment of the picture-puzzle is possibly only if I make no such objections to the whole and its parts, and if, on the contrary, I take the trouble to replace each image by a syllable or word which it may represent by virtue of some allusion or relation. The words thus put together are no longer meaningless, but might constitute the most beautiful and pregnant aphorism. Now a dream is such a picture-puzzle, and our predecessors in the art of dream-interpretation have made the mistake of judging the *rebus* as an artistic composition. As such, of course, it appears nonsensical and worthless.

A. CONDENSATION

The first thing that becomes clear to the investigator when he compares the dream-content with the dream-thoughts is that a tremendous *work of condensation* has been accomplished. The dream is meagre, paltry and laconic in comparison with the range and copiousness of the dream-thoughts. The dream, when written down, fills half a page; the analysis, which contains the dream-thoughts, requires six, eight, twelve times as much space. The ratio varies with different dreams; but in my experience it is always of the same order. As a rule, the extent of the compression which has been accomplished is under-estimated, owing to the fact that the dream-thoughts which have been brought to light are believed to be the whole of the material, whereas a continuation of the work of interpretation would reveal still further thoughts hidden in the dream. We have already found it necessary to remark that one can never be really sure that one has interpreted a dream completely; even if the solution seems satisfying and flawless, it is always possible that yet another meaning has been manifested by the same dream. Thus the *degree of condensation* is—strictly speaking—indeterminable. Exception may be taken—and at first sight the objection seems perfectly plausible—to the assertion that the disproportion between dream-content and dream-thoughts justifies the conclusion that a considerable condensation of psychic material occurs in the formation of dreams. For we often have the feeling that we have been dreaming a great deal all night, and have then forgotten most of what we have dreamed. The dream which we remember on waking would thus *appear* to be merely a remnant of the total dream-work, which would surely equal the dream-thoughts in range if only we could remember it completely. To a certain extent this is undoubtedly true; there is no getting away from the fact that a dream is most accurately reproduced if we try to remember it immediately after waking, and that the recollection of it becomes more and more defective as the day goes on. On the other hand, it has to be recognized that the impression that we have dreamed a good deal more than we are able to reproduce is very often based on an illusion, the origin of which we shall explain later on. Moreover, the assumption of a condensation in the dream-work is not affected by the possibility of forgetting a part of dreams, for it may be demonstrated by the multitude of ideas pertaining to those individual parts of the dream which do remain in the memory. If a large part of the dream has really escaped the memory, we are probably deprived of access to a new series of dream-thoughts. We have no justification for expecting that those portions of the dream which have been lost should likewise have referred only to those thoughts which we know from the analysis of the portions which have been preserved.[1]

In view of the very great number of ideas which analysis elicits for each individual element of the dream-content, the principal doubt in the minds of many readers will be whether it is permissible to count everything that subsequently occurs to the mind during analysis as forming part of the dream-thoughts—in other words, to assume that all these thoughts have been active in the sleeping state, and have taken part in the formation of the dream. Is it not more probable that new combinations of thoughts are developed in the course of analysis, which did not participate in the formation of the dream? To this objection I can give only a conditional reply. It is true, of course, that separate combinations of thoughts make their first appearance during the analysis; but one can convince oneself every time this happens that such new combinations have been established only between thoughts which have already been connected in other ways in the dream-thoughts; the new combinations are, so to speak, corollaries, short-circuits, which are made possible by the existence of other, more fundamental modes of connection. In respect of the great majority of the groups of thoughts revealed by analysis, we are obliged to admit that they have already been active in the formation of the dream, for if we work through a succession of such thoughts, which at first sight seem to have played no part in the formation of the dream, we suddenly come upon a thought which occurs in the dream-content, and is indispensable to its interpretation, but which is nevertheless inaccessible except through this chain of thoughts. The reader may here turn to the dream of the botanical monograph, which is obviously the result of an astonishing degree of condensation, even though I have not given the complete analysis.

But how, then, are we to imagine the psychic condition of the sleeper which precedes dreaming? Do all the dream-thoughts exist side by side, or do they pursue one another, or are there several simultaneous trains of thought, proceeding from different centres, which subsequently meet? I do not think it is necessary at this point to form a plastic conception of the

---

[1] References to the condensation in dreams are to be found in the works of many writers on the subject. Du Prel states in his *Philosophie der Mystik* that he is absolutely certain that a condensation-process of the succession of ideas had occurred.

psychic condition at the time of dream-formation. But let us not forget that we are concerned with *unconscious* thinking, and that the process may easily be different from that which we observe in ourselves in deliberate contemplation accompanied by consciousness.

The fact, however, is irrefutable that dream-formation is based on a process of condensation. How, then, is this condensation effected?

Now, if we consider that of the dream-thoughts ascertained only the most restricted number are represented in the dream by means of one of their conceptual elements, we might conclude that the condensation is accomplished by means of omission, inasmuch as the dream is not a faithful translation or projection, point by point, of the dream-thoughts, but a very incomplete and defective reproduction of them. This view, as we shall soon perceive, is a very inadequate one. But for the present let us take it as a point of departure, and ask ourselves: If only a few of the elements of the dream-thoughts make their way into the dream-content, what are the conditions that determine their selection?

In order to solve this problem, let us turn our attention to those elements of the dream-content which must have fulfilled the conditions for which we are looking. The most suitable material for this investigation will be a dream to whose formation a particularly intense condensation has contributed. I select the dream, cited on page 241, of the botanical monograph.

I

Dream-content: *I have written a monograph upon a certain (indeterminate) species of plant. The book lies before me. I am just turning over a folded coloured plate. A dried specimen of the plant is bound up in this copy, as in a herbarium.*

The most prominent element of this dream is the *botanical monograph.* This is derived from the impressions of the dream-day; I had actually seen a *monograph on the genus Cyclamen* in a bookseller's window. The mention of this genus is lacking in the dream-content; only the monograph and its relation to botany have remained. The "botanical monograph" immediately reveals its relation to the *work on cocaine* which I once wrote; from cocaine the train of thought proceeds on the one hand to a *Festschrift,* and on the other to my friend, the oculist, Dr. *Koenigstein,* who was partly responsible for the introduction of cocaine as a local anaesthetic. Moreover, Dr. Koenigstein is connected with the recollection of an interrupted conversation I had had with him on the previous evening, and with all sorts of ideas relating to the remuneration of medical and surgical services among colleagues. This conversation, then, is the actual dream-stimulus; the monograph on cyclamen is also a real incident, but one of an indifferent nature; as I now see, the "botanical monograph" of the dream proves to be a *common mean* between the two experiences of the day, taken over unchanged from an indifferent impression, and bound up with the psychically significant experience by means of the most copious associations.

Not only the combined idea of the *botanical monograph,* however, but also each of its separate elements, *"botanical"* and *"monograph,"* penetrates farther and farther, by manifold associations, into the confused tangle of the dream-thoughts. To *botanical* belong the recollections of the person of Professor Gärtner (German: Gärtner = gardener), of his *blooming* wife, of my patient, whose name is *Flora,* and of a lady concerning whom I told the story of the forgotten *flowers. Gärtner,* again, leads me to the laboratory and the conversation with *Koenigstein;* and the allusion to the two female patients belongs to the same conversation. From the lady with the flowers a train of thoughts branches off to the favourite flowers of my wife, whose other branch leads to the title of the hastily seen monograph. Further, *botanical* recalls an episode at the "Gymnasium", and a university examination; and a fresh subject—that of my hobbies—which was broached in the above-mentioned conversation, is linked up, by means of what is humorously called my *favourite flower,* the artichoke, with the train of thoughts proceeding from the forgotten flowers; behind "artichoke" there lies, on the one hand, a recollection of Italy, and on the other a reminiscence of a scene of my childhood, in which I first formed an acquaintance—which has since then grown so intimate—with books. *Botanical,* then, is a veritable nucleus, and, for the dream, the meeting-point of many trains of thought; which, I can testify, had all really been brought into connection by the conversation referred to. Here we find ourselves in a thought-factory, in which, as in *The Weaver's Masterpiece:*—

> "The little shuttles to and fro
> Fly, and the threads unnoted flow;
> One throw links up a thousand threads."

Monograph in the dream, again, touches two themes: the one-sided nature of my studies, and the costliness of my hobbies.

The impression derived from this first investigation is that the elements "botanical" and "monograph" were taken up into the dream-content because they were able to offer the most numerous points of contact with the greatest number of dream-thoughts, and thus represented *nodal points* at which a great number of the dream-thoughts met together, and because they were of *manifold* significance in respect of the meaning of the dream. The fact upon which this explanation is based may be expressed in another form: Every element of the dream-content proves to be *over-determined*—that is, it appears several times over in the dream-thoughts.

We shall learn more if we examine the other components of the dream in respect of their occurrence in the dream-thoughts. The *coloured plate* refers (cf. the analysis on p. 242) to a new subject, the criticism passed upon my work by colleagues, and also to a subject already represented in the dream—my hobbies—and, further, to a memory of my childhood, in which I pull to pieces a book with coloured plates; the dried specimen of the plant relates to my experience with the herbarium at the "Gymnasium", and gives this memory particular emphasis. Thus I perceive the nature of the relation between the dream-content and dream-thoughts: Not only are the elements of the dream determined several times over by the dream-thoughts, but the individual dream-thoughts are represented in the dream by several elements. Starting from an element of the dream, the path of the association leads to a number of dream-thoughts; and from a single dream-thought to several elements of the dream. In the process of dream-formation, therefore, it is not the case that a single dream-thought, or a group of dream-thoughts, supplies the dream-content with an abbreviation of itself as its representative, and that the next dream-thought supplies another abbreviation as its representative (much as representatives are elected from among the population); but rather that the whole mass of the dream-thoughts is subjected to a certain elaboration, in the course of which those elements that receive the strongest and completest support stand out in relief; so that the process might perhaps be likened to election by the *scrutin du liste*. Whatever dream I may subject to such a dissection, I always find the same fundamental principle confirmed—that the dream-elements have been formed out of the whole mass of the dream-thoughts, and that every one of them appears, in relation to the dream-thoughts, to have a multiple determination.

It is certainly not superfluous to demonstrate this relation of the dream-content to the dream-thoughts by means of a further example, which is distinguished by a particularly artful intertwining of reciprocal relations. The dream is that of a patient whom I am treating for claustrophobia (fear of enclosed spaces). It will soon become evident why I feel myself called upon to entitle this exceptionally clever piece of dream-activity:

II. "A Beautiful Dream"

The dreamer is driving with a great number of companions in X-street, where there is a modest hostelry (which is not the case). *A theatrical performance is being given in one of the rooms of the inn. He is first spectator, then actor. Finally the company are told to change their clothes, in order to return to the city. Some of the company are shown into rooms on the ground floor, others to rooms on the first floor. Then a dispute arises. The people upstairs are annoyed because those downstairs have not yet finished changing, so that they cannot come down. His brother is upstairs; he is downstairs; and he is angry with his brother be-cause they are so hurried.* (This part obscure.) *Besides, it was already decided, upon their arrival, who was to go upstairs and who down. Then he goes alone up the hill towards the city, and he walks so heavily, and with such difficulty, that he cannot move from the spot. An elderly gentle-man joins him and talks angrily of the King of Italy. Finally, towards the top of the hill, he is able to walk much more easily.*

The difficulty experienced in climbing the hill was so distinct that for some time after waking he was in doubt whether the experience was a dream or the reality.

Judged by the manifest content, this dream can hardly be eulogized. Contrary to the rules, I shall begin the interpretation with that portion to which the dreamer referred as being the most distinct.

The difficulty dreamed of, and probably experienced during the dream —difficulty in climbing, accompanied by dyspnoea—was one of the symp-toms which the patient had actually exhibited some years before, and which, in conjunction with other symptoms, was at the time attributed to tuberculosis (probably hysterically simulated). From our study of ex-hibition-dreams we are already acquainted with this sensation of being inhibited in motion, peculiar to dreams, and here again we find it utilized as material always available for the purposes of any other kind of repre-sentation. The part of the dream-content which represents climbing as difficult at first, and easier at the top of the hill, made me think, while it was being related, of the well-known masterly introduction to Daudet's *Sappho.* Here a young man carries the woman he loves upstairs; she is at first as light as a feather, but the higher he climbs the more she weighs; and this scene is symbolic of the progress of their relation, in describing which Daudet seeks to admonish young men not to lavish an earnest affection upon girls of humble origin and dubious antecedents.[1] Although I knew that my patient had recently had a love-affair with an actress, and had broken it off, I hardly expected to find that the interpretation which had occurred to me was correct. The situation in Sappho is actually the *reverse* of that in the dream; for in the dream climbing was difficult at the first and easy later on; in the novel the symbolism is pertinent only if what was at first easily carried finally proves to be a heavy burden. To my astonishment, the patient remarked that the interpretation fitted in very well with the plot of a play which he had seen the previous evening. The play was called *Rund um Wien* ("Round about Vienna"), and treated of the career of a girl who was at first respectable, but who sub-sequently lapsed into the *demi-monde,* and formed relations with highly-

[1] In estimating the significance of this passage we may recall the meaning of dreams of climbing stairs, as explained in the chapter on Symbolism.

placed lovers, thereby *climbing*, but finally she *went downhill* faster and faster. This play reminded him of another, entitled *Von Stufe zu Stufe* ("From Step to Step"), the poster advertising which had depicted *a flight of stairs*.

To continue the interpretation: The actress with whom he had had his most recent and complicated affair had lived in X-street. There is no inn in this street. However, while he was spending part of the summer in Vienna for the sake of this lady, he had lodged (German: *abgestiegen* = stopped, literally *stepped off*) at a small hotel in the neighbourhood. When he was leaving the hotel, he said to the cab-driver: "I am glad at all events that I didn't get any vermin here!" (Incidentally, the dread of vermin is one of his phobias.) Whereupon the cab-driver answered: "How could anybody stop there! That isn't a hotel at all, it's really nothing but a *pub!*"

The "pub" immediately reminded him of a quotation:

> "Of a wonderful host
> I was lately a guest."

But the host in the poem by Uhland is an *apple-tree*. Now a second quotation continues the train of thought:

> FAUST: (*dancing with the young witch*).
>
> "A lovely dream once came to me;
> I then beheld an apple-tree,
> And there two fairest apples shone:
> They lured me so, I *climbed thereon*."
>
> THE FAIR ONE:
>
> "Apples have been desired by you,
> Since first in Paradise they grew;
> And I am moved with joy to know
> That such within my garden grow." [1]

There is not the slightest doubt what is meant by the apple-tree and the apples. A beautiful bosom stood high among the charms by which the actress had bewitched our dreamer.

Judging from the context of the analysis, we had every reason to assume that the dream referred to an impression of the dreamer's childhood. If this is correct, it must have referred to the wet-nurse of the dreamer, who is now a man of nearly thirty years of age. The bosom of the nurse is in reality an inn for the child. The nurse, as well as Daudet's *Sappho,* appears as an allusion to his recently abandoned mistress.

---

[1] Translated by Bayard Taylor.

The (elder) brother of the patient also appears in the dream-content; he is *upstairs*, while the dreamer himself is *downstairs*. This again is an inversion, for the brother, as I happen to know, has lost his social position, while my patient has retained his. In relating the dream-content, the dreamer avoided saying that his brother was upstairs and that he himself was downstairs. This would have been too obvious an expression, for in Austria we say that a man is *on the ground floor* when he has lost his fortune and social position, just as we say that he has *come down*. Now the fact that at this point in the dream something is represented as inverted must have a meaning; and the inversion must apply to some other relation between the dream-thoughts and the dream-content. There is an indication which suggests how this inversion is to be understood. It obviously applies to the end of the dream, where the circumstances of climbing are the *reverse* of those described in *Sappho*. Now it is evident what inversion is meant: In *Sappho* the man carries the woman who stands in a sexual relation to him; in the dream-thoughts, conversely, there is a reference to a woman carrying a man; and, as this could occur only in childhood, the reference is once more to the nurse who carries the heavy child. Thus the final portion of the dream succeeds in representing Sappho and the nurse in the same allusion.

Just as the name *Sappho* has not been selected by the poet without reference to a Lesbian practice, so the portions of the dream in which people are busy *upstairs* and *downstairs*, "above" and "beneath," point to fancies of a sexual content with which the dreamer is occupied, and which, as suppressed cravings, are not unconnected with his neurosis. Dream-interpretation itself does not show that these are fancies and not memories of actual happenings; it only furnishes us with a set of thoughts and leaves it to us to determine their actual value. In this case real and imagined happenings appear at first as of equal value—and not only here, but also in the creation of more important psychic structures than dreams. A large company, as we already know, signifies a secret. The brother is none other than a representative, drawn into the scenes of childhood by "fancying backwards," of all of the subsequent rivals for women's favours. Through the medium of an experience indifferent in itself, the episode of the gentleman who talks angrily of the King of Italy refers to the intrusion of people of low rank into aristocratic society. It is as though the warning which Daudet gives to young men were to be supplemented by a similar warning applicable to a suckling child.[1]

---

[1] The fantastic nature of the situation relating to the dreamer's wet-nurse is shown by the circumstance, objectively ascertained, that the nurse in this case was his mother. Further, I may call attention to the regret of the young man in the anecdote related on p. 266 (that he had not taken better advantage of his opportunities with his wet-nurse) as the probable source of this dream.

In the two dreams here cited I have shown by italics where one of the elements of the dream recurs in the dream-thoughts, in order to make the multiple relations of the former more obvious. Since, however, the analysis of these dreams has not been carried to completion, it will probably be worth while to consider a dream with a full analysis, in order to demonstrate the manifold determination of the dream-content. For this purpose I shall select the dream of Irma's injection (see p. 195). From this example we shall readily see that the condensation-work in the dream-formation has made use of more means than one.

The chief person in the dream-content is my patient Irma, who is seen with the features which belong to her in waking life, and who therefore, in the first instance, represents herself. But her attitude, as I examine her at the window, is taken from a recollection of another person, of the lady for whom I should like to exchange my patient, as is shown by the dream-thoughts. Inasmuch as Irma has a diphtheritic membrane, which recalls my anxiety about my eldest daughter, she comes to represent this child of mine, behind whom, connected with her by the identity of their names, is concealed the person of the patient who died from the effects of poison. In the further course of the dream the significance of Irma's personality changes (without the alteration of her image as it is seen in the dream): she becomes one of the children whom we examine in the public dispensaries for children's diseases, where my friends display the differences in their mental capacities. The transition was obviously effected by the idea of my little daughter. Owing to her unwillingness to open her mouth, the same Irma constitutes an allusion to another lady who was once examined by me, and, also in the same connection, to my wife. Further, in the morbid changes which I discover in her throat I have summarized allusions to quite a number of other persons.

All these people whom I encounter as I follow up the associations suggested by "Irma" do not appear personally in the dream; they are concealed behind the dream-person "Irma," who is thus developed into a collective image, which, as might be expected, has contradictory features. Irma comes to represent these other persons, who are discarded in the work of condensation, inasmuch as I allow anything to happen to her which reminds me of these persons, trait by trait.

For the purposes of dream-condensation I may construct a *composite person* in yet another fashion, by combining the actual features of two or more persons in a single dream-image. It is in this fashion that the Dr. M. of my dream was constructed; he bears the name of Dr. M., and he speaks and acts as Dr. M. does, but his bodily characteristics and his malady belong to another person, my eldest brother; a single feature, paleness, is doubly determined, owing to the fact that it is common to both persons. Dr. R., in my dream about my uncle, is a similar composite person. But here the dream-image is constructed in yet another fashion. I have not united features peculiar to the one person with the features of the other, thereby abridging by certain features the memory-picture of each; but I have adopted the method employed by Galton in producing family portraits; namely, I have superimposed the two images, so that the common features stand out in stronger relief, while those which do not coincide neutralize one another and become indistinct. In the dream of my uncle the *fair beard* stands out in relief, as an emphasized feature, from a physiognomy which belongs to two persons, and which is consequently blurred; further, in its reference to growing grey the beard contains an allusion to my father and to myself.

The construction of collective and composite persons is one of the principal methods of dream-condensation. We shall presently have occasion to deal with this in another connection.

The notion of *dysentery* in the dream of Irma's injection has likewise a multiple determination; on the one hand, because of its paraphasic assonance with diphtheria, and on the other because of its reference to the patient whom I sent to the East, and whose hysteria had been wrongly diagnosed.

The mention of *propyls* in the dream proves again to be an interesting case of condensation. Not *propyls* but *amyls* were included in the dream-thoughts. One might think that here a simple displacement had occurred in the course of dream-formation. This is in fact the case, but the displacement serves the purposes of the condensation, as is shown from the following supplementary analysis: If I dwell for a moment upon the word *propylen* (German) its assonance with the word *propylaeum* suggests itself to me. But a *propylaeum* is to be found not only in Athens, but also in Munich. In the latter city, a year before my dream, I had visited a friend who was seriously ill, and the reference to him in *trimethylamin*, which follows closely upon *propyls*, is unmistakable.

I pass over the striking circumstance that here, as elsewhere in the analysis of dreams, associations of the most widely differing values are employed for making thought-connections as though they were equivalent, and I yield to the temptation to regard the procedure by which *amyls* in the dream-thoughts are replaced in the dream-content by *propyls* as a sort of plastic process.

On the one hand, here is the group of ideas relating to my friend Otto, who does not understand me, thinks I am in the wrong, and gives me the liqueur that smells of amyls; on the other hand, there is the group of ideas—connected with the first by contrast—relating to my Berlin friend who does understand me, who would always think that I was right, and to whom I am indebted for so much valuable information concerning the chemistry of sexual processes.

What elements in the Otto group are to attract my particular attention are determined by the recent circumstances which are responsible for the dream; *amyls* belong to the element so distinguished, which are predestined to find their way into the dream-content. The large group of ideas centering upon William is actually stimulated by the contrast between William and Otto, and those elements in it are emphasized which are in tune with those already stirred up in the "Otto" group. In the whole of this dream I am continually recoiling from somebody who excites my displeasure towards another person with whom I can at will confront the first; trait by trait I appeal to the friend as against the enemy. Thus "amyls" in the Otto group awakes recollections in the other group, also belonging to the region of chemistry; "trimethylamin," which receives support from several quarters, finds its way into the dream-content. "Amyls," too, might have got into the dream-content unchanged, but it yields to the influence of the "William" group, inasmuch as out of the whole range of recollections covered by this name an element is sought out which is able to furnish a double determination for "amyls." "Propyls" is closely associated with "amyls"; from the "William" group comes Munich with its propylaeum. Both groups are united in "propyls—propylaeum." As though by a compromise, this intermediate element then makes its way into the dream-content. Here a common mean which permits of a multiple determination has been created. It thus becomes palpable that a multiple determination must facilitate penetration into the dream-content. For the purpose of this mean-formation a displacement of the attention has been unhesitatingly effected from what is really intended to something adjacent to it in the associations.

The study of the dream of Irma's injection has now enabled us to obtain some insight into the process of condensation which occurs in the formation of dreams. We perceive, as peculiarities of the condensing process, a selection of those elements which occur several times over in the dream-content, the formation of new unities (composite persons, mixed images), and the production of common means. The purpose which is served by condensation, and the means by which it is brought about, will be investigated when we come to study in all their bearings the psychic processes at work in the formation of dreams. Let us for the present be content with establishing the fact of dream-condensation as a relation between the dream-thoughts and the dream-content which deserves attention.

The condensation-work of dreams becomes most palpable when it takes words and means as its objects. Generally speaking, words are often treated in dreams as things, and therefore undergo the same combinations as the ideas of things. The results of such dreams are comical and bizarre word-formations.

1. A colleague sent an essay of his, in which he had, in my opinion, overestimated the value of a recent physiological discovery, and had expressed himself, moreover, in extravagant terms. On the following night I dreamed a sentence which obviously referred to this essay: "That is a truly *norekdal* style." The solution of this word-formation at first gave me some difficulty; it was unquestionably formed as a parody of the superlatives "colossal," "pyramidal"; but it was not easy to say where it came from. At last the monster fell apart into the two names *Nora* and *Ekdal,* from two well-known plays by Ibsen. I had previously read a newspaper article on Ibsen by the writer whose latest work I was now criticizing in my dream.

2. One of my female patients dreams that *a man with a fair beard and a peculiar glittering eye is pointing to a sign-board attached to a tree which reads: uclamparia—wet.*[1]

Analysis.—The man was rather authoritative-looking, and his peculiar glittering eye at once recalled the church of San Paolo, near Rome, where she had seen the mosaic portraits of the Popes. One of the early Popes had a golden eye (this is really an optical illusion, to which the guides usually call attention). Further associations showed that the general physiognomy of the man corresponded with her own clergyman (pope), and the shape of the fair beard recalled her doctor (myself), while the stature of the man in the dream recalled her father. All these persons stand in the same relation to her; they are all guiding and directing the course of her life. On further questioning, the golden eye recalled gold—money—the rather expensive psychoanalytic treatment, which gives her a great deal of concern. Gold, moreover, recalls the gold cure for alcoholism—Herr D., whom she would have married, if it had not been for his clinging to the disgusting alcohol habit—she does not object to anyone's taking an occasional drink; she herself sometimes drinks beer and liqueurs. This again brings her back to her visit to San Paolo (*fuori la mura*) and its surroundings. She remembers that in the neighbouring monastery of the *Tre Fontane* she drank a liqueur made of *eucalyptus* by the Trappist monks of the monastery. She then relates how the monks transformed this malarial and swampy region into a dry and wholesome neighbourhood by planting numbers of *eucalyptus* trees. The word *"uclamparia"* then resolves itself into *eucalyptus* and *malaria,* and the word *wet* refers to the former swampy nature of the locality. Wet also suggests dry. *Dry* is actually the name of the man whom she would have married but for his over-indulgence in alcohol. The peculiar name of *Dry* is of Germanic origin (*drei* = three) and hence, alludes to the monastery of the Three (*drei*) Fountains. In talking of Mr. Dry's habit she used the strong expression: "He could drink a fountain." Mr. Dry jocosely refers to his habit by saying: "You

[1] Given by translator, as the author's example could not be translated.

know I must drink because I am always *dry*" (referring to his name). The *eucalyptus* refers also to her neurosis, which was at first diagnosed as *malaria*. She went to Italy because her attacks of anxiety, which were accompanied by marked rigors and shivering, were thought to be of malarial origin. She bought some eucalyptus oil from the monks, and she maintains that it has done her much good.

The condensation *uclamparia—wet* is therefore the point of junction for the dream as well as for the neurosis.

3. In a rather long and confused dream of my own, the apparent nucleus of which is a sea-voyage, it occurs to me that the next port is *Hearsing,* and next after that *Fliess.* The latter is the name of my friend in B., to which city I have often journeyed. But *Hearsing* is put together from the names of the places in the neighbourhood of Vienna, which so frequently end in "ing": *Hietzing, Liesing, Moedling* (the old Medelitz, *"meæ deliciæ,"* "my joy"; that is, my own name, the German for "joy" being *Freude*), and the English *hearsay,* which points to calumny, and establishes the relation to the indifferent dream-stimulus of the day—a poem in *Fliegende Blätter* about a slanderous dwarf, "Sagter Hatergesagt" (Saidhe Hashesaid). By the combination of the final syllable *ing* with the name *Fliess, Vlissingen* is obtained, which is a real port through which my brother passes when he comes to visit us from England. But the English for *Vlissingen* is *Flushing,* which signifies *blushing,* and recalls patients suffering from *erythrophobia* (fear of blushing), whom I sometimes treat, and also a recent publication of Bechterew's, relating to this neurosis, the reading of which angered me.[1]

4. Upon another occasion I had a dream which consisted of two separate parts. The first was the vividly remembered word *"Autodidasker"*: the second was a faithful reproduction in the dream-content of a short and harmless fancy which had been developed a few days earlier, and which was to the effect that I must tell Professor N., when I next saw him: "The

---

[1] The same analysis and synthesis of syllables—a veritable chemistry of syllables—serves us for many a jest in waking life. "What is the cheapest method of obtaining silver? You go to a field where silver-berries are growing and pick them; then the berries are eliminated and the silver remains in a free state." [Translator's example] The first person who read and criticized this book made the objection—with which other readers will probably agree—"that the dreamer often appears too witty." That is true, so long as it applies to the dreamer; it involves a condemnation only when its application is extended to the interpreter of the dream. In waking reality I can make very little claim to the predicate "witty"; if my dreams appear witty, this is not the fault of my individuality, but of the peculiar psychological conditions under which the dream is fabricated, and is intimately connected with the theory of wit and the comical. The dream becomes witty because the shortest and most direct way to the expression of its thoughts is barred for it; the dream is under constraint. My readers may convince themselves that the dreams of my patients give the impression of being quite as witty (at least, in intention), as my own, and even more so. Nevertheless, this reproach impelled me to compare the technique of wit with th• dream-work.

patient about whose condition I last consulted you is really suffering from a neurosis, just as you suspected." So not only must the newly-coined *"Autodidasker"* satisfy the requirement that it should contain or represent a compressed meaning, but this meaning must have a valid connection with my resolve—repeated from waking life—to give Professor N. due credit for his diagnosis.

Now *Autodidasker* is easily separated into *author* (German, *Autor*), *autodidact*, and *Lasker*, with whom is associated the name *Lasalle*. The first of these words leads to the occasion of the dream—which this time is significant. I had brought home to my wife several volumes by a well-known author who is a friend of my brother's, and who, as I have learned, comes from the same neighbourhood as myself (J. J. David). One evening she told me how profoundly impressed she had been by the pathetic sadness of a story in one of David's novels (a story of wasted talents), and our conversation turned upon the signs of talent which we perceive in our own children. Under the influence of what she had just read, my wife expressed some concern about our children, and I comforted her with the remark that precisely such dangers as she feared can be averted by training. During the night my thoughts proceeded farther, took up my wife's concern for the children, and interwove with it all sorts of other things. Something which the novelist had said to my brother on the subject of marriage showed my thoughts a by-path which might lead to representation in the dream. This path led to Breslau; a lady who was a very good friend of ours had married and gone to live there. I found in Breslau *Lasker* and *Lasalle*, two examples to justify the fear lest our boys should be ruined by women, examples which enabled me to represent simultaneously two ways of influencing a man to his undoing.[1] The *Cherchez la femme,* by which these thoughts may be summarized, leads me, if taken in another sense, to my brother, who is still unmarried and whose name is *Alexander*. Now I see that *Alex*, as we abbreviate the name, sounds almost like an inversion of *Lasker*, and that this fact must have contributed to send my thoughts on a *détour* by way of Breslau.

But the playing with names and syllables in which I am here engaged has yet another meaning. It represents the wish that my brother may enjoy a happy family life, and this in the following manner: In the novel of artistic life, *L'Œuvre*, which, by virtue of its content, must have been in association with my dream-thoughts, the author, as is well-known, has incidentally given a description of his own person and his own domestic happiness, and appears under the name of *Sandoz*. In the metamorphosis of his name he probably went to work as follows: *Zola*, when inverted

---

[1] Lasker died of progressive paralysis; that is, of the consequences of an infection caught from a woman (syphilis); Lasalle, also a syphilitic, was killed in a duel which he fought on account of the lady whom he had been courting.

(as children are fond of inverting names) gives *Aloz*. But this was still too undisguised; he therefore replaced the syllable *Al*, which stands at the beginning of the name Alexander, by the third syllable of the same name, *sand*, and thus arrived at *Sandoz*. My *autodidasker* originated in a similar fashion.

My phantasy—that I am telling Professor N. that the patient whom we have both seen is suffering from a neurosis—found its way into the dream in the following manner: Shortly before the close of my working year I had a patient in whose case my powers of diagnosis failed me. A serious organic trouble—possibly some alterative degeneration of the spinal cord—was to be assumed, but could not be conclusively demonstrated. It would have been tempting to diagnose the trouble as a neurosis, and this would have put an end to all my difficulties, but for the fact that the sexual anamnesis, failing which I am unwilling to admit a neurosis, was so energetically denied by the patient. In my embarrassment I called to my assistance the physician whom I respect most of all men (as others do also), and to whose authority I surrender most completely. He listened to my doubts, told me he thought them justified, and then said: "Keep on observing the man, it is probably a neurosis." Since I know that he does not share my opinions concerning the etiology of the neuroses, I refrained from contradicting him, but I did not conceal my scepticism. A few days later I informed the patient that I did not know what to do with him, and advised him to go to someone else. Thereupon, to my great astonishment, he began to beg my pardon for having lied to me; he had felt so ashamed; and now he revealed to me just that piece of sexual etiology which I had expected, and which I found necessary for assuming the existence of a neurosis. This was a relief to me, but at the same time a humiliation; for I had to admit that my consultant, who was not disconcerted by the absence of anamnesis, had judged the case more correctly. I made up my mind to tell him, when next I saw him, that he had been right and I had been wrong.

This is just what I do in the dream. But what sort of a wish is fulfilled if I acknowledge that I am mistaken? This is precisely my wish; I wish to be mistaken as regards my fears—that is to say, I wish that my wife, whose fears I have appropriated in my dream-thoughts, may prove to be mistaken. The subject to which the fact of being right or wrong is related in the dream is not far removed from that which is really of interest to the dream-thoughts. We have the same pair of alternatives, of either organic or functional impairment caused by a woman, or actually by the sexual life—either tabetic paralysis or a neurosis—with which latter the nature of Lasalle's undoing is indirectly connected.

In this well-constructed (and on careful analysis quite transparent) dream, Professor N. appears not merely on account of this analogy, and my wish to be proved mistaken, or the associated references to Breslau and to the family of our married friend who lives there, but also on account of the following little dialogue which followed our consultation: After he had acquitted himself of his professional duties by making the above-mentioned suggestion, Dr. N. proceeded to discuss personal matters. "How many children have you now?"—"Six."—A thoughtful and respectful gesture.—"Girls, boys?"—"Three of each. They are my pride and my riches."—"Well, you must be careful; there is no difficulty about the girls, but the boys are a difficulty later on as regards their upbringing." I replied that until now they had been very tractable; obviously this prognosis of my boys' future pleased me as little as his diagnosis of my patient, whom he believed to be suffering only from a neurosis. These two impressions, then, are connected by their contiguity, by their being successively received; and when I incorporate the story of the neurosis into the dream, I substitute it for the conversation on the subject of upbringing, which is even more closely connected with the dream-thoughts, since it touches so closely upon the anxiety subsequently expressed by my wife. Thus, even my fear that N. may prove to be right in his remarks on the difficulties to be met with in bringing up boys is admitted into the dream-content, inasmuch as it is concealed behind the representation of my wish that I may be wrong to harbour such apprehensions. The same phantasy serves without alteration to represent both the conflicting alternatives.

Examination-dreams present the same difficulties to interpretation that I have already described as characteristic of most typical dreams. The associative material which the dreamer supplies only rarely suffices for interpretation. A deeper understanding of such dreams has to be accumulated from a considerable number of examples. Not long ago I arrived at a conviction that reassurances like "But you already are a doctor," and so on, not only convey a consolation but imply a reproach as well. This would have run: "You are already so old, so far advanced in life, and yet you still commit such follies, are guilty of such childish behaviour." This mixture of self-criticism and consolation would correspond with the examination-dreams. After this it is no longer surprising that the reproaches in the last analysed examples concerning "follies" and "childish behaviour" should relate to repetitions of reprehensible sexual acts.

The verbal transformations in dreams are very similar to those which are known to occur in paranoia, and which are observed also in hysteria and obsessions. The linguistic tricks of children, who at a certain age actually treat words as objects, and even invent new languages and artificial syntaxes, are a common source of such occurrences both in dreams and in the psychoneuroses.

The analysis of nonsensical word-formations in dreams is particularly well suited to demonstrate the degree of condensation effected in the dream-work. From the small number of the selected examples here considered it must not be concluded that such material is seldom observed or is at all exceptional. It is, on the contrary, very frequent, but owing to the dependence of dream-interpretation on psychoanalytic treatment very few examples are noted down and reported, and most of the analyses which are reported are comprehensible only to the specialist in neuropathology.

When a spoken utterance, expressly distinguished as such from a thought, occurs in a dream, it is an invariable rule that the dream-speech has originated from a remembered speech in the dream-material. The wording of the speech has either been preserved in its entirety or has been slightly altered in expression; frequently the dream-speech is pieced together from different recollections of spoken remarks; the wording has remained the same, but the sense has perhaps become ambiguous, or differs from the wording. Not infrequently the dream-speech serves merely as an allusion to an incident in connection with which the remembered speech was made.[1]

B. THE WORK OF DISPLACEMENT

Another and probably no less significant relation must have already forced itself upon our attention while we were collecting examples of dream-condensation. We may have noticed that these elements which obtrude themselves in the dream-content as its essential components do not by any means play this same part in the dream-thoughts. As a corollary to this, the converse of this statement is also true. That which is obviously the essential content of the dream-thoughts need not be represented at all in the dream. The dream is, as it were, *centred elsewhere;* its content is arranged about elements which do not constitute the central point of the dream-thoughts. Thus, for example, in the dream of the botanical monograph the central point of the dream-content is evidently the element "botanical"; in the dream-thoughts we are concerned with the complications and conflicts resulting from services rendered between colleagues which place them under mutual obligations; later on with the reproach that I am in the habit of sacrificing too much time to my hobbies; and the element "botanical" finds no place in this nucleus of the dream-thoughts, unless it is loosely connected with it by antithesis, for botany was never among my favourite subjects. In the Sappho-dream of

---

[1] In the case of a young man who was suffering from obsessions, but whose intellectual functions were intact and highly developed, I recently found the only exception to this rule. The speeches which occurred in his dreams did not originate in speeches which he had heard or had made himself, but corresponded to the undistorted verbal expression of his obsessive thoughts, which came to his waking consciousness only in an altered form.

my patient, ascending and descending, being upstairs and down, is made the central point; the dream, however, is concerned with the danger of sexual relations with persons of "low" degree; so that only one of the elements of the dream-thoughts seems to have found its way into the dream-content, and this is unduly expanded. Again, in the dream of my uncle, the fair beard, which seems to be its central point, appears to have no rational connection with the desire for greatness which we have recognized as the nucleus of the dream-thoughts. Such dreams very naturally give us an impression of a "displacement." In complete contrast to these examples, the dream of Irma's injection shows that individual elements may claim the same place in dream-formation as that which they occupy in the dream-thoughts. The recognition of this new and utterly inconstant relation between the dream-thoughts and the dream-content will probably astonish us at first. If we find in a psychic process of normal life that one idea has been selected from among a number of others, and has acquired a particular emphasis in our consciousness, we are wont to regard this as proof that a peculiar psychic value (a certain degree of interest) attaches to the victorious idea. We now discover that this value of the individual element in the dream-thoughts is not retained in dream-formation, or is not taken into account. For there is no doubt which of the elements of the dream-thoughts are of the highest value; our judgment informs us immediately. In dream-formation the essential elements, those that are emphasized by intensive interest, may be treated as though they were subordinate, while they are replaced in the dream by other elements, which were certainly subordinate in the dream-thoughts. It seems at first as though the psychic intensity [1] of individual ideas were of no account in their selection for dream-formation, but only their greater or lesser multiplicity of determination. One might be inclined to think that what gets into the dream is not what is important in the dream-thoughts, but what is contained in them several times over; but our understanding of dream-formation is not much advanced by this assumption; to begin with, we cannot believe that the two motives of multiple determination and intrinsic value can influence the selection of the dream otherwise than in the same direction. Those ideas in the dream-thoughts which are most important are probably also those which recur most frequently, since the individual dream-thoughts radiate from them as centres. And yet the dream may reject these intensively emphasized and extensively reinforced elements, and may take up into its content other elements which are only extensively reinforced.

This difficulty may be solved if we follow up yet another impression received during the investigation of the over-determination of the dream-

---

[1] The psychic intensity or value of an idea—the emphasis due to interest—is of course to be distinguished from perceptual or conceptual intensity.

content. Many readers of this investigation may already have decided, in their own minds, that the discovery of the multiple determination of the dream-elements is of no great importance, because it is inevitable. Since in analysis we proceed from the dream-elements, and register all the ideas which associate themselves with these elements, is it any wonder that these elements should recur with peculiar frequency in the thought-material obtained in this manner? While I cannot admit the validity of this objection, I am now going to say something that sounds rather like it: Among the thoughts which analysis brings to light are many which are far removed from the nucleus of the dream, and which stand out like artificial interpolations made for a definite purpose. Their purpose may readily be detected; they establish a connection, often a forced and far-fetched connection, between the dream-content and the dream-thoughts, and in many cases, if these elements were weeded out of the analysis, the components of the dream-content would not only not be over-determined, but they would not be sufficiently determined. We are thus led to the conclusion that multiple determination, decisive as regards the selection made by the dream, is perhaps not always a primary factor in dream-formation, but is often a secondary product of a psychic force which is as yet unknown to us. Nevertheless, it must be of importance for the entrance of the individual elements into the dream, for we may observe that in cases where multiple determination does not proceed easily from the dream-material it is brought about with a certain effort.

It now becomes very probable that a psychic force expresses itself in the dream-work which, on the one hand, strips the elements of the high psychic value of their intensity and, on the other hand, *by means of over-determination*, creates new significant values from elements of slight value, which new values then make their way into the dream-content. Now if this is the method of procedure, there has occurred in the process of dream-formation a *transference and displacement of the psychic intensities* of the individual elements, from which results the textual difference between the dream-content and the thought-content. The process which we here assume to be operative is actually the most essential part of the dream-work; it may fitly be called *dream-displacement. Dream-displacement and dream-condensation* are the two craftsmen to whom we may chiefly ascribe the structure of the dream.

I think it will be easy to recognize the psychic force which expresses itself in dream-displacement. The result of this displacement is that the dream-content no longer has any likeness to the nucleus of the dream-thoughts, and the dream reproduces only a distorted form of the dream-wish in the unconscious. But we are already acquainted with dream-distortion; we have traced it back to the censorship which one psychic instance in the psychic life exercises over another. Dream-displacement is one of the chief means of achieving this distortion. *Is fecit, cui profuit*. We must assume that dream-displacement is brought about by the influ- ence of this censorship, the endopsychic defence.[1]

The manner in which the factors of displacement, condensation and over-determination interact with one another in dream-formation—which is the ruling factor and which the subordinate one—all this will be re- served as a subject for later investigation. In the meantime, we may state, as a second condition which the elements that find their way into the dream must satisfy, that *they must be withdrawn from the resistance of the censorship*. But henceforth, in the interpretation of dreams, we shall reckon with dream-displacement as an unquestionable fact.

C. THE MEANS OF REPRESENTATION IN DREAMS

Besides the two factors of *condensation* and *displacement* in dreams, which we have found to be at work in the transformation of the latent dream-material into the manifest dream-content, we shall, in the course of this investigation, come upon two further conditions which exercise an unquestionable influence over the selection of the material that even- tuality appears in the dream. But first, even at the risk of seeming to interrupt our progress, I shall take a preliminary glance at the processes by which the interpretation of dreams is accomplished. I do not deny that the best way of explaining them, and of convincing the critic of their

[1] Since I regard the attribution of dream-distortion to the censorship as the central point of my conception of the dream, I will here quote the closing passage of a story, *Träumen wie Wachen*, from *Phantasien eines Realisten*, by Lynkeus (Vienna, sec- ond edition, 1900), in which I find this chief feature of my doctrine reproduced:

"Concerning a man who possesses the remarkable faculty of never dreaming non- sense. . . ."

"Your marvellous faculty of dreaming as if you were awake is based upon your virtues, upon your goodness, your justice, and your love of truth; it is the moral clarity of your nature which makes everything about you intelligible to me."

"But if I really give thought to the matter," was the reply, "I almost believe that all men are made as I am, and that no one ever dreams nonsense! A dream which one remembers so distinctly that one can relate it afterwards, and which, there- fore, is no dream of delirium, *always* has a meaning; why, it cannot be otherwise! For that which is in contradiction to itself can never be combined into a whole. The fact that time and space are often thoroughly shaken up, detracts not at all from the real content of the dream, because both are without any significance whatever for its essential content. We often do the same thing in waking life; think of fairy-tales, of so many bold and pregnant creations of fantasy, of which only a foolish person would say: 'That is nonsense! For it isn't possible.' "

"If only it were always possible to interpret dreams correctly, as you have just done with mine!" said the friend.

"That is certainly not an easy task, but with a little attention it must always be possible to the dreamer.—You ask why it is generally impossible? In your case there seems to be something veiled in your dreams, something unchaste in a special and exalted fashion, a certain secrecy in your nature, which it is difficult to fathom; and that is why your dreams so often seem to be without meaning, or even nonsensical. But in the profoundest sense, this is by no means the case; indeed it cannot be, for a man is always the same person, whether he wakes or dreams."

reliability, would be to take a single dream as an example, to detail its
interpretation, as I did (in Chapter II) in the case of the dream of Irma's
injection, but then to assemble the dream-thoughts which I had discovered, and from them to reconstruct the formation of the dream—that is
to say, to supplement dream-analysis by dream-synthesis. I have done
this with several specimens for my own instruction; but I cannot undertake to do it here, as I am prevented by a number of considerations (relating to the psychic material necessary for such a demonstration) such as
any right-thinking person would approve. In the analysis of dreams these
considerations present less difficulty, for an analysis may be incomplete
and still retain its value, even if it leads only a little way into the structure of the dream. I do not see how a synthesis, to be convincing, could
be anything short of complete. I could give a complete synthesis only of
the dreams of such persons as are unknown to the reading public. Since,
however, neurotic patients are the only persons who furnish me with the
means of making such a synthesis, this part of the description of dreams
must be postponed until I can carry the psychological explanation of the
neuroses far enough to demonstrate their relation to our subject.[1] This
will be done elsewhere.

From my attempts to construct dreams synthetically from their dream-
thoughts, I know that the material which is yielded by interpretation
varies in value. Part of it consists of the essential dream-thoughts, which
would completely replace the dream and would in themselves be a sufficient substitute for it, were there no dream-censorship. To the other part
one is wont to ascribe slight importance, nor does one set any value on the
assertion that all these thoughts have participated in the formation of
the dream; on the contrary, they may include notions which are associated with experiences that have occurred subsequently to the dream, between the dream and the interpretation. This part comprises not only all
the connecting-paths which have led from the manifest to the latent
dream-content, but also the intermediate and approximating associations
by means of which one has arrived at a knowledge of these connecting-
paths during the work of interpretation.

At this point we are interested exclusively in the essential dream-
thoughts. These commonly reveal themselves as a complex of thoughts
and memories of the most intricate possible construction, with all the
characteristics of the thought-processes known to us in waking life. Not
infrequently they are trains of thought which proceed from more than

---

[1] I have since given the complete analysis and synthesis of two dreams in the *Bruch-
stück einer Hysterieanalyse*, 1905 (*Ges. Schriften*, Bd. viii). Fragment of an Analysis
of a Case of Hysteria, translated by Strachey, Collected Papers, vol. iii, Hogarth
Press, London. O. Rank's analysis, *Ein Traum der sich selbst deutet*, deserves mention as the most complete interpretation of a comparatively long dream.

one centre, but which are not without points of contact; and almost invariably we find, along with a train of thought, its contradictory counterpart, connected with it by the association of contrast.

The individual parts of this complicated structure naturally stand in the most manifold logical relations to one another. They constitute foreground and background, digressions, illustrations, conditions, lines of argument and objections. When the whole mass of these dream-thoughts is subjected to the pressure of the dream-work, during which the fragments are turned about, broken up and compacted, somewhat like drifting ice, the question arises, what becomes of the logical ties which had hitherto provided the framework of the structure? What representation do "if," "because," "as though," "although," "either—or" and all the other conjunctions, without which we cannot understand a phrase or a sentence, receive in our dreams?

To begin with, we must answer that the dream has at its disposal no means of representing these logical relations between the dream-thoughts. In most cases it disregards all these conjunctions, and undertakes the elaboration only of the material content of the dream-thoughts. It is left to the interpretation of the dream to restore the coherence which the dream-work has destroyed.

If dreams lack the ability to express these relations, the psychic material of which they are wrought must be responsible for this defect. As a matter of fact, the representative arts—painting and sculpture—are similarly restricted, as compared with poetry, which is able to employ speech; and here again the reason for this limitation lies in the material by the elaboration of which the two plastic arts endeavour to express something. Before the art of painting arrived at an understanding of the laws of expression by which it is bound, it attempted to make up for this deficiency. In old paintings little labels hung out of the mouths of the persons represented, giving in writing the speech which the artist despaired of expressing in the picture.

Here, perhaps an objection will be raised, challenging the assertion that our dreams dispense with the representation of logical relations. There are dreams in which the most complicated intellectual operations take place; arguments for and against are adduced, jokes and comparisons are made, just as in our waking thoughts. But here again appearances are deceptive; if the interpretation of such dreams is continued it will be found that *all these things are dream-material, not the representation of intellectual activity in the dream.* The *content* of the dream-thoughts is reproduced by the apparent thinking in our dreams, but not *the relations of the dream-thoughts to one another,* in the determination of which relations thinking consists. I shall give some examples of this. But the fact which is most easily established is that all speeches which occur in dreams, and which are expressly designated as such, are unchanged or only slightly modified replicas of speeches which occur likewise among the memories in the dream-material. Often the speech is only an allusion to an event contained in the dream-thoughts; the meaning of the dream is quite different.

However, I shall not dispute the fact that even critical thought-activity, which does not simply repeat material from the dream-thoughts, plays a part in dream-formation. I shall have to explain the influence of this factor at the close of this discussion. It will then become clear that this thought activity is evoked not by the dream-thoughts, but by the dream itself, after it is, in a certain sense, already completed.

Provisionally, then, it is agreed that the logical relations between the dream-thoughts do not obtain any particular representation in the dream. For instance, where there is a contradiction in the dream, this is either a contradiction directed against the dream itself or a contradiction contained in one of the dream-thoughts; a contradiction in the dream corresponds with a contradiction *between* the dream-thoughts only in the most indirect and intermediate fashion.

But just as the art of painting finally succeeded in depicting, in the persons represented, at least the intentions behind their words—tenderness, menace, admonition, and the like—by other means than by floating labels, so also the dream has found it possible to render an account of certain of the logical relations between its dream-thoughts by an appropriate modification of the peculiar method of dream-representation. It will be found by experience that different dreams go to different lengths in this respect; while one dream will entirely disregard the logical structure of its material, another attempts to indicate it as completely as possible. In so doing the dream departs more or less widely from the text which it has to elaborate; and its attitude is equally variable in respect to the temporal articulation of the dream-thoughts, if such has been established in the unconscious (as, for example, in the dream of Irma's injection).

But what are the means by which the dream-work is enabled to indicate those relations in the dream-material which are difficult to represent? I shall attempt to enumerate these, one by one.

In the first place, the dream renders an account of the connection which is undeniably present between all the portions of the dream-thoughts by combining this material into a unity as a situation or a proceeding. It reproduces *logical connection* in the form of *simultaneity;* in this case it behaves rather like the painter who groups together all the philosophers or poets in a picture of the School of Athens, or Parnassus. They never were assembled in any hall or on any mountain-top, although to the reflective mind they do constitute a community.

The dream carries out in detail this mode of representation. Whenever it shows two elements close together, it vouches for a particularly intimate connection between their corresponding representatives in the dream-thoughts. It is as in our method of writing: *to* signifies that the two letters are to be pronounced as one syllable; while *t* with *o* following a blank space indicates that *t* is the last letter of one word and *o* the first letter of another. Consequently, dream-combinations are not made up of arbitrary, completely incongruous elements of the dream-material, but of elements that are pretty intimately related in the dream-thoughts also.

For representing *causal relations* our dreams employ two methods, which are essentially reducible to one. The method of representation more frequently employed—in cases, for example, where the dream-thoughts are to the effect: "Because this was thus and thus, this and that must happen"—consists in making the subordinate clause a prefatory dream and joining the principal clause on to it in the form of the main dream. If my interpretation is correct, the sequence may likewise be reversed. The principal clause always corresponds to that part of the dream which is elaborated in the greatest detail.

An excellent example of such a representation of causality was once provided by a female patient, whose dream I shall subsequently give in full. The dream consisted of a short prologue, and of a very circumstantial and very definitely centred dream-composition. I might entitle it "Flowery language." The preliminary dream is as follows: *She goes to the two maids in the kitchen and scolds them for taking so long to prepare "a little bite of food." She also sees a very large number of heavy kitchen utensils in the kitchen turned upside down in order to drain, even heaped up in stacks. The two maids go to fetch water, and have, as it were, to climb into a river, which reaches up to the house or into the courtyard.*

Then follows the main dream, which begins as follows: *She is climbing down from a height over a curiously shaped trellis, and she is glad that her dress doesn't get caught anywhere, etc.* Now the preliminary dream refers to the house of the lady's parents. The words which are spoken in the kitchen are words which she has probably often heard spoken by her mother. The piles of clumsy pots and pans are taken from an unpretentious hardware shop located in the same house. The second part of this dream contains an allusion to the dreamer's father, who was always pestering the maids, and who during a flood—for the house stood close to the bank of the river—contracted a fatal illness. The thought which is concealed behind the preliminary dream is something like this: "Because I was born in this house, in such sordid and unpleasant surroundings . . ." The main dream takes up the same thought, and presents it in a form that has been altered by a wish-fulfilment: "I am of exalted origin." Properly then: "Because I am of such humble origin, the course of my life has been so and so."

As far as I can see, the division of a dream into two unequal portions does not always signify a causal relation between the thoughts of the two portions. It often seems as though in the two dreams the same material were presented from different points of view; this is certainly the case when a series of dreams, dreamed the same night, end in a seminal emission, the somatic need enforcing a more and more definite expression. Or the two dreams have proceeded from two separate centres in the dream-material, and they overlap one another in the content, so that the subject which in one dream constitutes the centre co-operates in the other as an allusion, and *vice versa*. But in a certain number of dreams the division into short preliminary dreams and long subsequent dreams actually signifies a causal relation between the two portions. The other method of representing the causal relation is employed with less comprehensive material, and consists in the transformation of an image in the dream into another image, whether it be of a person or a thing. Only where this transformation is actually seen occurring in the dream shall we seriously insist on the causal relation; not where we simply note that one thing has taken the place of another. I said that both methods of representing the causal relation are really reducible to the same method; in both cases *causation* is represented by succession, sometimes by the succession of dreams, sometimes by the immediate transformation of one image into another. In the great majority of cases, of course, the causal relation is not represented at all, but is effaced amidst the succession of elements that is unavoidable even in the dream-process.

Dreams are quite incapable of expressing the alternative "either—or"; it is their custom to take both members of this alternative into the same context, as though they had an equal right to be there. A classic example of this is contained in the dream of Irma's injection. Its latent thoughts obviously mean: I am not responsible for the persistence of Irma's pains; the responsibility rests *either* with her resistance to accepting the solution *or* with the fact that she is living under unfavourable sexual conditions, which I am unable to change, *or* her pains are not hysterical at all, but organic. The dream, however, carries out all these possibilities, which are almost mutually exclusive, and is quite ready to add a fourth solution derived from the dream-wish. After interpreting the dream, I then inserted the *either—or* in its context in the dream-thoughts.

But when in narrating a dream the narrator is inclined to employ the alternative *either—or:* "It was either a garden or a living-room," etc., there is not really an alternative in the dream-thoughts, but an "and"—a simple addition. When we use *either—or* we are as a rule describing a quality of vagueness in some element of the dream, but a vagueness which may still be cleared up. The rule to be applied in this case is as follows: The individual members of the alternative are to be treated as equal and connected by an "and." For instance, after waiting long and vainly for the address of a friend who is travelling in Italy, I dream that I receive a telegram which gives me the address. On the telegraph form I see printed in blue letters: the first word is blurred—perhaps *via*

> or *villa;* the second is distinctly *Sezerno,*
> or even (*Casa*).

The second word, which reminds me of Italian names, and of our discussions on etymology, also expresses my annoyance in respect of the fact that my friend has kept his address a secret from me; but each of the possible first three words may be recognized on analysis as an independent and equally justifiable starting-point in the concatenation of ideas.

During the night before the funeral of my father I dreamed of a printed placard, a card or poster rather like the notices in the waiting-rooms of railway stations which announce that smoking is prohibited. The sign reads either:—

> *You are requested to shut the eyes*

> or

> *You are requested to shut one eye*

an alternative which I am in the habit of representing in the following form:

> *the*
> You are requested to shut   eye(s).
> *one*

Each of the two versions has its special meaning, and leads along particular paths in the dream-interpretation. I had made the simplest possible funeral arrangements, for I knew what the deceased thought about such matters. Other members of the family, however, did not approve of such puritanical simplicity; they thought we should feel ashamed in the presence of the other mourners. Hence one of the wordings of the dream asks for the "shutting of one eye," that is to say, it asks that people should show consideration. The significance of the vagueness, which is here represented by an *either—or,* is plainly to be seen. The dream-work has not succeeded in concocting a coherent and yet ambiguous wording for the dream-thoughts. Thus the two principal trains of thought are separated from each other, even in the dream-content.

In some few cases the division of a dream into two equal parts expresses the alternative which the dream finds it so difficult to present.

The attitude of dreams to the category of *antithesis* and *contradiction* is very striking. This category is simply ignored; the word "No" does not seem to exist for a dream. Dreams are particularly fond of reducing antitheses to uniformity, or representing them as one and the same thing. Dreams likewise take the liberty of representing any element whatever by its desired opposite, so that it is at first impossible to tell, in respect of any element which is capable of having an opposite, whether it is contained in the dream-thoughts in the negative or the positive sense.[1] In one of the recently cited dreams, whose introductory portion we have already interpreted ("because my origin is so and so"), the dreamer climbs down over a trellis, and holds a blossoming bough in her hands. Since this picture suggests to her the angel in paintings of the Annunciation (her own name is Mary) bearing a lily-stem in his hand, and the white-robed girls walking in procession on Corpus Christi Day, when the streets are decorated with green boughs, the blossoming bough in the dream is quite clearly an allusion to sexual innocence. But the bough is thickly studded with red blossoms, each of which resembles a camellia. At the end of her walk (so the dream continues) the blossoms are already beginning to fall; then follow unmistakable allusions to menstruation. But this very bough, which is carried like a lily-stem and as though by an innocent girl, is also an allusion to Camille, who, as we know, usually wore a white camellia, but a red one during menstruation. The same blossoming bough ("the flower of maidenhood" in Goethe's songs of the miller's daughter) represents at once sexual innocence and its opposite. Moreover, the same dream, which expresses the dreamer's joy at having succeeded in passing through life unsullied, hints in several places (as in the falling of the blossom) at the opposite train of thought, namely, that she had been guilty of various sins against sexual purity (that is, in her childhood). In the analysis of the dream we may clearly distinguish the two trains of thought, of which the comforting one seems to be superficial, and the reproachful one more profound. The two are diametrically opposed to each other, and their similar yet contrasting elements have been represented by identical dream-elements.

The mechanism of dream-formation is favourable in the highest degree to only one of the logical relations. This relation is that of similarity, agreement, contiguity, "just as"; a relation which may be represented in our dreams, as no other can be, by the most varied expedients. The

[1] From a work of K. Abel's, *Der Gegensinn der Urworte*, 1884, (see my review of it in the Bleuler-Freud *Jahrbuch*, ii, 1910 (*Ges. Schriften*, Bd. x). I learned the surprising fact, which is confirmed by other philologists, that the oldest languages behaved just as dreams do in this regard. They had originally only one word for both extremes in a series of qualities or activities (strong—weak, old—young, far—near, bind—separate), and formed separate designations for the two opposites only secondarily, by slight modifications of the common primitive word. Abel demonstrates a very large number of those relationships in ancient Egyptian, and points to distinct remnants of the same development in the Semitic and Indo-Germanic languages.

"screening" which occurs in the dream-material, or the cases of "just as," are the chief points of support for dream-formation, and a not inconsiderable part of the dream-work consists in creating new "screenings" of this kind in cases where those that already exist are prevented by the resistance of the censorship from making their way into the dream. The effort towards condensation evinced by the dream-work facilitates the representation of a relation of similarity.

Similarity, agreement, community, are quite generally expressed in dreams by contraction into a *unity,* which is either already found in the dream-material or is newly created. The first case may be referred to as *identification,* the second as *composition.* Identification is used where the dream is concerned with persons, composition where things constitute the material to be unified; but compositions are also made of persons. Localities are often treated as persons.

Identification consists in giving representation in the dream-content to only one of two or more persons who are related by some common feature, while the second person or other persons appear to be suppressed as far as the dream is concerned. In the dream this one "screening" person enters into all the relations and situations which derive from the persons whom he screens. In cases of composition, however, when persons are combined, there are already present in the dream-image features which are characteristic of, but not common to, the persons in question, so that a new unity, a composite person, appears as the result of the union of these features. The combination itself may be effected in various ways. Either the dream-persons bears the name of one of the persons to whom he refers—and in this case we simply know, in a manner that is quite analogous to knowledge in waking life, that this or that person is intended—while the visual features belong to another person; or the dream-image itself is compounded of visual features which in reality are derived from the two. Also, in place of the visual features, the part played by the second person may be represented by the attitudes and gestures which are usually ascribed to him by the words he speaks, or by the situations in which he is placed. In this latter method of characterization the sharp distinction between the identification and the combination of persons begins to disappear. But it may also happen that the formation of such a composite person is unsuccessful. The situations or actions of the dream are then attributed to one person, and the other—as a rule the more important—is introduced as an inactive spectator. Perhaps the dreamer will say: "My mother was there too" (Stekel). Such an element of the dream-content is then comparable to a determinative in hieroglyphic script which is not meant to be expressed, but is intended only to explain another sign.

The common feature which justifies the union of two persons—that is to say, which enables it to be made—may either be represented in the dream or it may be absent. As a rule identification or composition of persons actually serves to avoid the necessity of representing this common feature. Instead of repeating: "A is ill-disposed towards me, and so is B," I make, in my dream, a composite person of A and B; or I conceive A as doing something which is alien to his character, but which is characteristic of B. The dream-person obtained in this way appears in the dream in some new connection, and the fact that he signifies both A and B justifies my inserting that which is common to both persons—their hostility towards me—at the proper place in the dream-interpretation. In this manner I often achieve a quite extraordinary degree of condensation of the dream-content; I am able to dispense with the direct representation of the very complicated relations belonging to one person, if I can find a second person who has an equal claim to some of these relations. It will be readily understood how far this representation by means of identification may circumvent the censoring resistance which sets up such harsh conditions for the dream-work. The thing that offends the censorship may reside in those very ideas which are connected in the dream-material with the one person; I now find a second person, who likewise stands in some relation to the objectionable material, but only to a part of it. Contact at that one point which offends the censorship now justifies my formation of a composite person, who is characterized by the indifferent features of each. This person, the result of combination or identification, being free of the censorship, is now suitable for incorporation in the dream-content. Thus, by the application of dream-condensation, I have satisfied the demands of the dream-censorship.

When a common feature of two persons is represented in a dream, this is usually a hint to look for another concealed common feature, the representation of which is made impossible by the censorship. Here a displacement of the common feature has occurred, which in some degree facilitates representation. From the circumstance that the composite person is shown to me in the dream with an indifferent common feature, I must infer that another common feature which is by no means indifferent exists in the dream-thoughts.

Accordingly, the identification or combination of persons serves various purposes in our dreams; in the first place, that of representing a feature common to two persons; secondly, that of representing a *displaced* common feature; and, thirdly, that of expressing a community of features which is merely *wished for*. As the wish for a community of features in two persons often coincides with the *interchanging* of these persons, this relation also is expressed in dreams by identification. In the dream of Irma's injection I wish to exchange one patient for another—that is to say, I wish this other person to be my patient, as the former person has been; the dream deals with this wish by showing me a person who is called

Irma, but who is examined in a position such as I have had occasion to see only the other person occupy. In the dream about my uncle this substitution is made the centre of the dream; I identify myself with the minister by judging and treating my colleagues as shabbily as he does. It has been my experience—and to this I have found no exception—that every dream treats of oneself. Dreams are absolutely egoistic.[1] In cases where not my ego but only a strange person occurs in the dream-content, I may safely assume that by means of identification my ego is concealed behind that person. I am permitted to supplement my ego. On other occasions, when my ego appears in the dream, the situation in which it is placed tells me that another person is concealing himself, by means of identification, behind the ego. In this case I must be prepared to find that in the interpretation I should transfer something which is connected with this person—the hidden common feature—to myself. There are also dreams in which my ego appears together with other persons who, when the identification is resolved, once more show themselves to be my ego. Through these identifications I shall then have to connect with my ego certain ideas to which the censorship has objected. I may also give my ego multiple representation in my dream, either directly or by means of identification with other people. By means of several such identifications an extraordinary amount of thought material may be condensed.[2] That one's ego should appear in the same dream several times or in different forms is fundamentally no more surprising than that it should appear, in conscious thinking, many times and in different places or in different relations: as, for example, in the sentence: "When *I* think what a healthy child *I* was."

Still easier than in the case of persons is the resolution of identifications in the case of localities designated by their own names, as here the disturbing influence of the all-powerful ego is lacking. In one of my dreams of Rome (p. 259) the name of the place in which I find myself is *Rome;* I am surprised, however, by a large number of German placards at a street corner. This last is a wish-fulfilment, which immediately suggests *Prague;* the wish itself probably originated at a period of my youth when I was imbued with a German nationalistic spirit which to-day is quite subdued. At the time of my dream I was looking forward to meeting a friend in *Prague;* the identification of Rome with Prague is therefore explained by a desired common feature; I would rather meet my friend in Rome than in Prague; for the purpose of this meeting I should like to exchange Prague for Rome.

---

[1] Cf. here the observations made on pp. 313–14.

[2] If I do not know behind which of the persons appearing in the dream I am to look for my ego, I observe the following rule: That person in the dream who is subject to an emotion which I am aware of while asleep is the one that conceals my ego.

The possibility of creating composite formations is one of the chief causes of the fantastic character so common in dreams, in that it introduces into the dream-content elements which could never have been objects of perception. The psychic process which occurs in the creation of composite formations is obviously the same as that which we employ in conceiving or figuring a dragon or a centaur in our waking senses. The only difference is that in the fantastic creations of waking life the impression intended is itself the decisive factor, while the composite formation in the dream is determined by a factor—the common feature in the dream-thoughts—which is independent of its form. Composite formations in dreams may be achieved in a great many different ways. In the most artless of these methods only the properties of the one thing are represented, and this representation is accompanied by a knowledge that they refer to another object also. A more careful technique combines features of the one object with those of the other in a new image, while it makes skilful use of any really existing resemblances between the two objects. The new creation may prove to be wholly absurd, or even successful as a fantasy, according as the material and the wit employed in constructing it may permit. If the objects to be condensed into a unity are too incongruous, the dream-work is content with creating a composite formation with a comparatively distinct nucleus, to which are attached more indefinite modifications. The unification into one image has here been to some extent unsuccessful; the two representations overlap one another, and give rise to something like a contest between the visual images. Similar representations might be obtained in a drawing if one were to attempt to give form to a unified abstraction of disparate perceptual images.

Dreams naturally abound in such composite formations; I have given several examples of these in the dreams already analysed, and will now cite more such examples. In the dream on p. 305, which describes the career of my patient "in flowery language," the dream-ego carries a spray of blossom in her hand which, as we have seen, signifies at once sexual innocence and sexual transgression. Moreover, from the manner in which the blossoms are set on, they recall *cherry*-blossom; the blossoms themselves, considered singly, are *camellias*, and finally the whole spray gives the dreamer the impression of an *exotic* plant. The common feature in the elements of this composite formation is revealed by the dream-thoughts. The blossoming spray is made up of allusions to presents by which she was induced or was to have been induced to behave in a manner agreeable to the giver. So it was with cherries in her childhood, and with a camellia-tree in her later years; the exotic character is an allusion to a much-travelled naturalist, who sought to win her favour by means of a drawing of a flower. Another female patient contrives a composite mean out of *bathing machines* at a seaside resort, country *privies,* and the *attics* of our city dwelling-houses. A reference to human nakedness and exposure is common to the first two elements; and we may infer from their connection with the third element that (in her childhood) the garret was likewise the scene of bodily exposure. A dreamer of the male sex makes a composite locality out of two places in which "treatment" is given—my office and the assembly rooms in which he first became acquainted with his wife. Another, a female patient, after her elder brother has promised to regale her with caviare, dreams that his legs are *covered all over with black beads of caviare.* The two elements, *"taint"* in a moral sense and the recollection of a cutaneous eruption in childhood which made her legs look as though studded over with *red* instead of black spots, have here been combined with the beads of *caviare* to form a new idea— the idea of *"what she gets from her brother."* In this dream parts of the human body are treated as objects, as is usually the case in dreams. In one of the dreams recorded by Ferenczi there occurs a composite formation made up of the person of a *physician* and a *horse,* and this composite being wears a *nightshirt.* The common feature in these three components was revealed in the analysis, after the nightshirt had been recognized as an allusion to the father of the dreamer in a scene of childhood. In each of the three cases there was some object of her sexual curiosity. As a child she had often been taken by her nurse to the army stud, where she had the amplest opportunity to satisfy her curiosity, at that time still uninhibited.

I have already stated that the dream has no means of expressing the relation of contradiction, contrast, negation. I shall now contradict this assertion for the first time. A certain number of cases of what may be summed up under the word "contrast" obtain representation, as we have seen, simply by means of identification—that is, when an exchange, a substitution, can be bound up with the contrast. Of this we have cited repeated examples. Certain other of the contrasts in the dream-thoughts, which perhaps come under the category of *"inverted, turned into the opposite,"* are represented in dreams in the following remarkable manner, which may almost be described as witty. The "inversion" does not itself make its way into the dream-content, but manifests its presence in the material by the fact that a part of the already formed dream-content which is, for other reasons, closely connected in context is—as it were subsequently—*inverted.* It is easier to illustrate this process than to describe it. In the beautiful "Up and Down" dream (p. 324) the dream-representation of ascending is an inversion of its prototype in the dream-thoughts: that is, of the introductory scene of Daudet's *Sappho;* in the dream climbing is difficult at first and easy later on, whereas in the novel it is easy at first, and later becomes more and more difficult. Again, "above" and "below," with reference to the dreamer's brother, are re-versed in the dream. This points to a relation of inversion or contrast be-tween two parts of the material in the dream-thoughts, which indeed we found in them, for in the childish phantasy of the dreamer he is carried by his nurse, while in the novel, on the contrary, the hero carries his be-loved. My dream of *Goethe's* attack on Herr M. (to be cited later) like-wise contains an inversion of this sort, which must be set right before the dream can be interpreted. In this dream Goethe attacks a young man, Herr M.; the reality, as contained in the dream-thoughts, is that an eminent man, a friend of mine, has been attacked by an unknown young author. In the dream I reckon time from the date of Goethe's death; in reality the reckoning was made from the year in which the paralytic was born. The thought which influences the dream-material reveals itself as my opposition to the treatment of Goethe as though he were a lunatic. "It is the other way about," says the dream; "if you don't understand the book it is you who are feeble-minded, not the author." All these dreams of inversion, moreover, seem to me to imply an allusion to the contemptu-ous phrase, "to turn one's back upon a person" (German: *einem die Kehrseite zeigen,* lit. to show a person one's backside): cf. the inversion in respect of the dreamer's brother in the Sappho dream. It is further worth noting how frequently inversion is employed in precisely those dreams which are inspired by repressed homosexual impulses.

Moreover, inversion, or transformation into the opposite, is one of the most favoured and most versatile methods of representation which the dream-work has at its disposal. It serves, in the first place, to enable the wish-fulfilment to prevail against a definite element of the dream-thoughts. "If only it were the other way about!" is often the best expres-sion for the reaction of the ego against a disagreeable recollection. But inversion becomes extraordinarily useful in the service of the censorship, for it effects, in the material to be represented, a degree of distortion which at first simply paralyses our understanding of the dream. It is therefore always permissible, if a dream stubbornly refuses to surrender its meaning, to venture on the experimental inversion of definite portions of its manifest content. Then, not infrequently, everything becomes clear.

Besides the inversion of content, the temporal inversion must not be overlooked. A frequent device of dream-distortion consists in presenting the final issue of the event or the conclusion of the train of thought at the beginning of the dream, and appending at the end of the dream the prem-ises of the conclusion, or the causes of the event. Anyone who forgets this technical device of dream-distortion stands helpless before the problem of dream-interpretation.[1]

---

[1] The hysterical attack often employs the same device of temporal inversion in order to conceal its meaning from the observer. The attack of a hysterical girl, for

In many cases, indeed, we discover the meaning of the dream only when we have subjected the dream-content to a multiple inversion, in accordance with the different relations. For example, in the dream of a young patient who is suffering from obsessional neurosis, the memory of the childish death-wish directed against a dreaded father concealed itself behind the following words: *His father scolds him because he comes home so late,* but the context of the psychoanalytic treatment and the impressions of the dreamer show that the sentence must be read as follows: *He is angry with his father,* and further, that his father always *came home too early* (i.e. too soon). He would have preferred that his father should not come home at all, which is identical with the wish (see p. 304) that his father would die. As a little boy, during the prolonged absence of his father, the dreamer was guilty of a sexual aggression against another child, and was punished by the threat: "Just you wait until your father comes home!"

If we should seek to trace the relations between the dream-content and the dream-thoughts a little farther, we shall do this best by making the dream itself our point of departure, and asking ourselves: What do certain formal characteristics of the dream-presentation signify in relation to the dream-thoughts? First and foremost among the formal characteristics which are bound to impress us in dreams are the differences in the sensory intensity of the single dream-images, and in the distinctness of various parts of the dream, or of whole dreams as compared with one another. The differences in the intensity of individual dream-images cover the whole gamut, from a sharpness of definition which one is inclined—although without warrant—to rate more highly than that of reality, to a provoking indistinctness which we declare to be characteristic of dreams, because it really is not wholly comparable to any of the degrees of indistinctness which we occasionally perceive in real objects. Moreover, we usually describe the impression which we receive of an indistinct object in a dream as "fleeting," while we think of the more distinct dream-images as having been perceptible also for a longer period of time. We must now ask ourselves by what conditions in the dream-material these differences in the distinctness of the individual portions of the dream-content are brought about.

---

example, consists in enacting a little romance, which she has imagined in the unconscious in connection with an encounter in a tram. A man, attracted by the beauty of her foot, addresses her while she is reading, whereupon she goes with him and a passionate love-scene ensues. Her attack begins with the representation of this scene by writhing movements of the body (accompanied by movements of the lips and folding of the arms to signify kisses and embraces), whereupon she hurries into the next room, sits down on a chair, lifts her skirt in order to show her foot, acts as though she were about to read a book, and speaks to me (answers me). Cf. the observation of Artemidorus: "In interpreting dream-stories one must consider them the first time from the beginning to the end, and the second time from the end to the beginning."

Before proceeding farther, it is necessary to deal with certain expectations which seem to be almost inevitable. Since actual sensations experienced during sleep may constitute part of the dream-material, it will probably be assumed that these sensations, or the dream-elements resulting from them, are emphasized by a special intensity, or conversely, that anything which is particularly vivid in the dream can probably be traced to such real sensations during sleep. My experience, however, has never confirmed this. It is not true that those elements of a dream which are derivatives of real impressions perceived in sleep (nerve stimuli) are distinguished by their special vividness from others which are based on memories. The factor of reality is inoperative in determining the intensity of dream-images.

Further, it might be expected that the sensory intensity (vividness) of single dream-images is in proportion to the psychic intensity of the elements corresponding to them in the dream-thoughts. In the latter, intensity is identical with psychic value; the most intense elements are in fact the most significant, and these constitute the central point of the dream-thoughts. We know, however, that it is precisely these elements which are usually not admitted to the dream-content, owing to the vigilance of the censorship. Still, it might be possible for their most immediate derivatives, which represent them in the dream, to reach a higher degree of intensity without, however, for that reason constituting the central point of the dream-representation. This assumption also vanishes as soon as we compare the dream and the dream-material. The intensity of the elements in the one has nothing to do with the intensity of the elements in the other; as a matter of fact, a complete *"transvaluation of all psychic values"* takes place between the dream-material and the dream. The very element of the dream which is transient and hazy, and screened by more vigorous images, is often discovered to be the one and only direct derivative of the topic that completely dominates the dream-thoughts.

The intensity of the dream-elements proves to be determined in a different manner: that is, by two factors which are mutually independent. It will readily be understood that those elements by means of which the wish-fulfilment expresses itself are those which are intensely represented. But analysis tells us that from the most vivid elements of the dream the greatest number of trains of thought proceed, and that those which are most vivid are at the same time those which are best determined. No change of meaning is involved if we express this latter empirical proposition in the following formula: The greatest intensity is shown by those elements of the dream for whose formation the most extensive *condensation-work* was required. We may, therefore, expect that it will be possible to express this condition, as well as the other condition of the wish-fulfilment in a single formula.

I must utter a warning that the problem which I have just been considering—the causes of the greater or lesser intensity or distinctness of single elements in dreams—is not to be confounded with the other problem—that of variations in the distinctness of whole dreams or sections of dreams. In the former case the opposite of distinctness is haziness; in the latter, confusion. It is, of course, undeniable that in both scales the two kinds of intensities rise and fall in unison. A portion of the dream which seems clear to us usually contains vivid elements; an obscure dream, on the contrary, is composed of less vivid elements. But the problem offered by the scale of definition, which ranges from the apparently clear to the indistinct or confused, is far more complicated than the problem of the fluctuations in vividness of the dream-elements. For reasons which will be given later, the former cannot at this stage be further discussed. In isolated cases one observes, not without surprise, that the impression of distinctness or indistinctness produced by a dream has nothing to do with the dream-structure, but proceeds from the dream-material, as one of its ingredients. Thus, for example, I remember a dream which on waking seemed so particularly well-constructed, flawless and clear that I made up my mind, while I was still in a somnolent state, to admit a new category of dreams—those which had not been subject to the mechanism of condensation and distortion, and which might thus be described as "phantasies during sleep." A closer examination, however, proved that this unusual dream suffered from the same structural flaws and breaches as exist in all other dreams; so I abandoned the idea of a category of "dream-phantasies." [1] The content of the dream, reduced to its lowest terms, was that I was expounding to a friend a difficult and long-sought theory of bisexuality, and the wish-fulfilling power of the dream was responsible for the fact that this theory (which, by the way, was not communicated in the dream) appeared to be so lucid and flawless. Thus, what I believed to be a judgment as regards the finished dream was a part, and indeed the most essential part, of the dream-content. Here the dream-work reached out, as it were, into my first waking thoughts, and presented to me, in the form of a *judgment* of the dream, that part of the dream-material which it had failed to represent with precision in the dream. I was once confronted with the exact counterpart of this case by a female patient who at first absolutely declined to relate a dream which was necessary for the analysis "because it was so hazy and confused," and who finally declared, after repeatedly protesting the inaccuracy of her description, that it seemed to her that several persons—herself, her husband, and her father —had occurred in the dream, and that she had not known whether her husband was her father, or who really was her father, or something of that sort. Comparison of this dream with the ideas which occurred to the

[1] I do not know to-day whether I was justified in doing so.

dreamer in the course of the sitting showed beyond a doubt that it dealt with the rather commonplace story of a maidservant who has to confess that she is expecting a child, and hears doubts expressed as to "who the father really is." [1] The obscurity manifested by this dream, therefore, was once more a portion of the dream-exciting material. A fragment of this material was represented in the *form* of the dream. *The form of the dream or of dreaming is employed with astonishing frequency to represent the concealed content.*

Glosses on the dream, and seemingly harmless comments on it, often serve in the most subtle manner to conceal—although, of course, they really betray—a part of what is dreamed. As, for example, when the dreamer says: *Here the dream was wiped out,* and the analysis gives an infantile reminiscence of listening to someone cleaning himself after defecation. Or another example, which deserves to be recorded in detail: A young man has a very distinct dream, reminding him of phantasies of his boyhood which have remained conscious. He found himself in a hotel at a seasonal resort; it was night; he mistook the number of his room, and entered a room in which an elderly lady and her two daughters were undressing to go to bed. He continues: *"Then there are some gaps in the dream;* something is missing; and at the end there was a man in the room, who wanted to throw me out, and with whom I had to struggle."* He tries in vain to recall the content and intention of the boyish phantasy to which the dream obviously alluded. But we finally become aware that the required content had already been given in his remarks concerning the indistinct part of the dream. The "gaps" are the genital apertures of the women who are going to bed: "Here something is missing" describes the principal characteristic of the female genitals. In his young days he burned with curiosity to see the female genitals, and was still inclined to adhere to the infantile sexual theory which attributes a male organ to women.

A very similar form was assumed in an analogous reminiscence of another dreamer. He dreamed: *I go with Fräulein K. into the restaurant of the Volksgarten* . . . then comes a dark place, an interruption . . . *then I find myself in the salon of a brothel, where I see two or three women, one in a chemise and drawers.*

Analysis.—Fräulein K. is the daughter of his former employer; as he himself admits, she was a sister-substitute. He rarely had the opportunity of talking to her, but they once had a conversation in which "one recognized one's sexuality, so to speak, as though one were to say: I am a man and you are a woman." He had been only once to the above-mentioned restaurant, when he was accompanied by the sister of his brother-in-law,

---

[1] Accompanying hysterical symptoms; amenorrhoea and profound depression were the chief troubles of this patient.

a girl to whom he was quite indifferent. On another occasion he accompanied three ladies to the door of the restaurant. The ladies were his sister, his sister-in-law, and the girl already mentioned. He was perfectly indifferent to all three of them, but they all belonged to the "sister category." He had visited a brothel but rarely, perhaps two or three times in his life.

The interpretation is based on the "dark place," the "interruption" in the dream, and informs us that on occasion, but in fact only rarely, obsessed by his boyish curiosity, he had inspected the genitals of his sister, a few years his junior. A few days later the misdemeanor indicated in the dream recurred to his conscious memory.

All dreams of the same night belong, in respect of their content, to the same whole; their division into several parts, their grouping and number, are all full of meaning and may be regarded as pieces of information about the latent dream-thoughts. In the interpretation of dreams consisting of several main sections, or of dreams belonging to the same night, we must not overlook the possibility that these different and successive dreams mean the same thing, expressing the same impulses in different material. That one of these homologous dreams which comes first in time is usually the most distorted and most bashful, while the next dream is bolder and more distinct.

Even Pharaoh's dream of the ears and the kine, which Joseph interpreted, was of this kind. It is given by Josephus in greater detail than in the Bible. After relating the first dream, the King said: "After I had seen this vision I awaked out of my sleep, and, being in disorder, and considering with myself what this appearance should be, I fell asleep again, and saw another dream much more wonderful than the foregoing, which still did more affright and disturb me." After listening to the relation of the dream, Joseph said: "This dream, O King, although seen under two forms, signifies one and the same event of things." [1]

Jung, in his *Beitrag zur Psychologie des Gerüchtes*, relates how a veiled erotic dream of a schoolgirl was understood by her friends without interpretation, and continued by them with variations, and he remarks, with reference to one of these narrated dreams, "that the concluding idea of a long series of dream-images had precisely the same content as the first image of the series had endeavoured to represent. The censorship thrust the complex out of the way as long as possible by a constant renewal of symbolic screenings, displacements, transformations into something harmless, etc." Scherner was well acquainted with this peculiarity of dream-representation, and describes it in his *Leben des Traumes* (p.

---

[1] Josephus; *Antiquities of the Jews,* book ii, chap. v, trans. by Wm. Whiston, David McKay, Philadelphia.

166) in terms of a special law in the Appendix to his doctrine of organic stimulation: "But finally, in all symbolic dream-formations emanating from definite nerve stimuli, the phantasy observes the general law that at the beginning of the dream it depicts the stimulating object only by the remotest and freest allusions, but towards the end, when the graphic impulse becomes exhausted, the stimulus itself is nakedly represented by its appropriate organ or its function; whereupon the dream, itself describing its organic motive, achieves its end. . . ."

A pretty confirmation of this law of Scherner's has been furnished by Otto Rank in his essay: *Ein Traum, der sich selbst deutet*. This dream, related to him by a girl, consisted of two dreams of the same night, separated by an interval of time, the second of which ended with an orgasm. It was possible to interpret this orgastic dream in detail in spite of the few ideas contributed by the dreamer, and the wealth of relations between the two dream-contents made it possible to recognize that the first dream expressed in modest language the same thing as the second, so that the latter—the orgastic dream—facilitated a full explanation of the former. From this example, Rank very justifiably argues the significance of orgastic dreams for the theory of dreams in general.

But in my experience it is only in rare cases that one is in a position to translate the lucidity or confusion of a dream, respectively, into a certainty or doubt in the dream-material. Later on I shall have to disclose a hitherto unmentioned factor in dream-formation, upon whose operation this qualitative scale in dreams is essentially dependent.

In many dreams in which a certain situation and environment are preserved for some time, there occur interruptions which may be described in the following words: "But then it seemed as though it were, at the same time, another place, and there such and such a thing happened." In these cases what interrupts the main action of the dream, which after a while may be continued again, reveals itself in the dream-material as a subordinate clause, an interpolated thought. Conditionally in the dream-thoughts is represented by simultaneity in the dream-content (*wenn* or *wann* = if or when, while).

We may now ask, What is the meaning of the sensation of inhibited movement which so often occurs in dreams, and is so closely allied to anxiety? One wants to move, and is unable to stir from the spot; or wants to accomplish something, and encounters obstacle after obstacle. The train is about to start, and one cannot reach it; one's hand is raised to avenge an insult, and its strength fails, etc. We have already met with this sensation in exhibition-dreams, but have as yet made no serious attempt to interpret it. It is convenient, but inadequate, to answer that there is motor paralysis in sleep, which manifests itself by means of the sensation alluded to. We may ask: "Why is it, then, that we do not dream continually of such inhibited movements?" And we may permissibly suspect that this sensation, which may at any time occur during sleep, serves some sort of purpose for representation, and is evoked only when the need of this representation is present in the dream-material.

Inability to do a thing does not always appear in the dream as a sensation; it may appear simply as part of the dream-content. I think one case of this kind is especially fitted to enlighten us as to the meaning of this peculiarity. I shall give an abridged version of a dream in which I seem to be accused of dishonesty. *The scene is a mixture made up of a private sanatorium and several other places. A manservant appears, to summon me to an inquiry. I know in the dream that something has been missed, and that the inquiry is taking place because I am suspected of having appropriated the lost article. Analysis shows that inquiry is to be taken in two senses; it includes the meaning of medical examination. Being conscious of my innocence, and my position as consultant in this sanatorium, I calmly follow the manservant. We are received at the door by another manservant, who says, pointing at me, "Have you brought him? Why, he is a respectable man." Thereupon, and unattended, I enter a great hall where there are many machines, which reminds me of an inferno with its hellish instruments of punishment. I see a colleague strapped to an appliance; he has every reason to be interested in my appearance, but he takes no notice of me. I understand that I may now go. Then I cannot find my hat, and cannot go after all.*

The wish that the dream fulfils is obviously the wish that my honesty shall be acknowledged, and that I may be permitted to go; there must therefore be all sorts of material in the dream-thoughts which comprise a contradiction of this wish. The fact that I may go is the sign of my absolution; if, then, the dream provides at its close an event which prevents me from going, we may readily conclude that the suppressed material of the contradiction is asserting itself in this feature. The fact that I cannot find my hat therefore means: "You are not after all an honest man." The inability to do something in the dream is *the expression of a contradiction, a "No"*; so that our earlier assertion, to the effect that the dream is not capable of expressing a negation, must be revised accordingly.[1]

---

[1] A reference to an experience of childhood emerges, in the complete analysis, through the following connecting-links: "The Moor has done his duty, the Moor can go." And then follows the waggish question: "How old is the Moor when he has done his duty?"—"A year, then he can go (walk)." (It is said that I came into the world with so much black curly hair that my young mother declared that I was a little Moor.) The fact that I cannot find my hat is an experience of the day which has been exploited in various senses. Our servant, who is a genius at stowing things away, had hidden the hat. A rejection of melancholy thoughts of death is concealed behind the conclusion of the dream: "I have not nearly done my duty yet; I cannot go yet."

In other dreams in which the inability to do something occurs, not merely as a situation, but also as a sensation, the same contradiction is more emphatically expressed by the sensation of inhibited movement, or a will to which a counter-will is opposed. Thus the sensation of inhibited movement represents *a conflict of will*. We shall see later on that this very motor paralysis during sleep is one of the fundamental conditions of the psychic process which functions during dreaming. Now an impulse which is conveyed to the motor system is none other than the will, and the fact that we are certain that this impulse will be inhibited in sleep makes the whole process extraordinarily well-adapted to the representation of a *will* towards something and of a *"No"* which opposes itself thereto. From my explanation of anxiety, it is easy to understand why the sensation of the inhibited will is so closely allied to anxiety, and why it is so often connected with it in dreams. Anxiety is a libidinal impulse which emanates from the unconscious and is inhibited by the preconscious.[1] Therefore, when a sensation of inhibition in the dream is accompanied by anxiety, the dream must be concerned with a volition which was at one time capable of arousing libido; there must be a sexual impulse.

As for the judgment which is often expressed during a dream: "Of course, it is only a dream," and the psychic force to which it may be ascribed, I shall discuss these questions later on. For the present I will merely say that they are intended to depreciate the importance of what is being dreamed. The interesting problem allied to this, as to what is meant if a certain content in the dream is characterized in the dream itself as having been "dreamed"—the riddle of a "dream within a dream"—has been solved in a similar sense by W. Stekel, by the analysis of some convincing examples. Here again the part of the dream "dreamed" is to be depreciated in value and robbed of its reality; that which the dreamer continues to dream after waking from the "dream within a dream" is what the dream-wish desires to put in place of the obliterated reality. It may therefore be assumed that the part "dreamed" contains the representation of the reality, the real memory, while, on the other hand, the continued dream contains the representation of what the dreamer merely wishes. The inclusion of a certain content in "a dream within a dream" is therefore equivalent to the wish that what has been characterized as a dream had never occurred. In other words: when a particular incident is represented by the dream-work in a "dream," it signifies the strongest confirmation of the reality of this incident, the most emphatic *affirmation* of it. The dream-work utilizes the dream itself as a form of repudiation, and thereby confirms the theory that a dream is a wish-fulfilment.

Birth and death together—as in the dream of Goethe and the paralytic, which was a little earlier in date.

[1] This theory is not in accordance with more recent views.

D. REGARD FOR REPRESENTABILITY

We have hitherto been concerned with investigating the manner in which our dreams represent the relations between the dream-thoughts, but we have often extended our inquiry to the further question as to what alterations the dream-material itself undergoes for the purposes of dream-formation. We now know that the dream-material, after being stripped of a great many of its relations, is subjected to compression, while at the same time displacements of the intensity of its elements enforce a psychic transvaluation of this material. The displacements which we have considered were shown to be substitutions of one particular idea for another, in some way related to the original by its associations, and the displacements were made to facilitate the condensation, inasmuch as in this manner, instead of two elements, a common mean between them found its way into the dream. So far no mention has been made of any other kind of displacement. But we learn from the analyses that displacement of another kind does occur, and that it manifests itself in *an exchange of the verbal expression* for the thought in question. In both cases we are dealing with a displacement along a chain of associations, but the same process takes place in different psychic spheres, and the result of this displacement in the one case is that one element is replaced by another, while in the other case an element exchanges its verbal shape for another.

This second kind of displacement occurring in dream-formation is not only of great theoretical interest, but is also peculiarly well-fitted to explain the appearance of phantastic absurdity in which dreams disguise themselves. Displacement usually occurs in such a way that a colourless and abstract expression of the dream-thought is exchanged for one that is pictorial and concrete. The advantage, and along with it the purpose, of this substitution is obvious. Whatever is pictorial is *capable of representation* in dreams and can be fitted into a situation in which abstract expression would confront the dream-representation with difficulties not unlike those which would arise if a political leading article had to be represented in an illustrated journal. Not only the possibility of representation, but also the interests of condensation and of the censorship, may be furthered by this exchange. Once the abstractly expressed and unserviceable dream-thought is translated into pictorial language, those contacts and identities between this new expression and the rest of the dream-material which are required by the dream-work, and which it contrives whenever they are not available, are more readily provided, since in every language concrete terms, owing to their evolution, are richer in associations than are abstract terms. It may be imagined that a good part of the intermediate work in dream-formation, which seeks to reduce the separate dream-thoughts to the tersest and most unified expression in the dream, is effected in this manner, by fitting paraphrases of the various thoughts. The one thought whose mode of expression has perhaps been determined by other factors will therewith exert a distributive and selective influence on the expressions available for the others, and it may even do this from the very start, just as it would in the creative activity of a poet. When a poem is to be written in rhymed couplets, the second rhyming line is bound by two conditions: it must express the meaning allotted to it, and its expression must permit of a rhyme with the first line. The best poems are, of course, those in which one does not detect the effort to find a rhyme, and in which both thoughts have as a matter of course, by mutual induction, selected the verbal expression which, with a little subsequent adjustment, will permit of the rhyme.

In some cases the change of expression serves the purposes of dream-condensation more directly, in that it provides an arrangement of words which, being ambiguous, permits of the expression of more than one of the dream-thoughts. The whole range of verbal wit is thus made to serve the purpose of the dream-work. The part played by words in dream-formation ought not to surprise us. A word, as the point of junction of a number of ideas, possesses, as it were, a predestined ambiguity, and the neuroses (obsessions, phobias) take advantage of the opportunities for condensation and disguise afforded by words quite as eagerly as do dreams.[1] That dream-distortion also profits by this displacement of expression may be readily demonstrated. It is indeed confusing if one ambiguous word is substituted for two with single meanings, and the replacement of sober, everyday language by a plastic mode of expression baffles our understanding, especially since a dream never tells us whether the elements presented by it are to be interpreted literally or metaphorically, whether they refer to the dream-material directly, or only by means of interpolated expressions. Generally speaking, in the interpretation of any element of a dream it is doubtful whether it

(a) is to be accepted in the negative or the positive sense (contrast relation);
(b) is to be interpreted historically (as a memory);
(c) is symbolic; or whether
(d) its valuation is to be based upon its wording.

In spite of this versatility, we may say that the representation effected by the dream-work, *which was never even intended to be understood,* does not impose upon the translator any greater difficulties than those that the ancient writers of hieroglyphics imposed upon their readers.

I have already given several examples of dream-representations which

---

[1] Cf. *Wit and its Relation to the Unconscious.*

are held together only by ambiguity of expression ("her mouth opens without difficulty," in the dream of Irma's injection; "I cannot go yet after all," in the last dream related, etc.). I shall now cite a dream in the analysis of which plastic representation of the abstract thoughts plays a greater part. The difference between such dream-interpretation and the interpretation by means of symbols may nevertheless be clearly defined; in the symbolic interpretation of dreams the key to the symbolism is selected arbitrarily by the interpreter, while in our own cases of verbal disguise these keys are universally known and are taken from established modes of speech. Provided one hits on the right idea on the right occasion, one may solve dreams of this kind, either completely or in part, independently of any statements made by the dreamer.

A lady, a friend of mine, dreams: *She is at the opera. It is a Wagnerian performance, which has lasted until 7.45 in the morning. In the stalls and pit there are tables, at which people are eating and drinking. Her cousin and his young wife, who have just returned from their honeymoon, are sitting at one of these tables; beside them is a member of the aristocracy. The young wife is said to have brought him back with her from the honeymoon quite openly, just as she might have brought back a hat. In the middle of the stalls there is a high tower, on the top of which there is a platform surrounded by an iron railing. There, high overhead, stands the conductor, with the features of Hans Richter, continually running round behind the railing, perspiring terribly; and from this position he is conducting the orchestra, which is arranged round the base of the tower. She herself is sitting in a box with a friend of her own sex* (known to me). *Her younger sister tries to hand her up, from the stalls, a large lump of coal, alleging that she had not known that it would be so long, and that she must by this time be miserably cold. (As though the boxes ought to have been heated during the long performance.)*

Although in other respects the dream gives a good picture of the situation, it is, of course, nonsensical enough: the tower in the middle of the stalls, from which the conductor leads the orchestra, and above all the coal which her sister hands up to her. I purposely asked for no analysis of this dream. With some knowledge of the personal relations of the dreamer, I was able to interpret parts of it independently of her. I knew that she had felt intense sympathy for a musician whose career had been prematurely brought to an end by insanity. I therefore decided to take the tower in the stalls *verbally*. It then emerged that the man whom she wished to see in the place of Hans Richter *towered* above all the other members of the orchestra. This tower must be described as a *composite formation by means of apposition;* by its substructure it represents the greatness of the man, but by the railing at the top, behind which he runs round like a prisoner or an animal in a cage (an allusion to the name of the unfortunate man),[1] it represents his later fate. "Lunatic-tower" is perhaps the expression in which the two thoughts might have met.

Now that we have discovered the dream's method of representation, we may try, with the same key, to unlock the meaning of the second apparent absurdity, that of the coal which her sister hands up to the dreamer. "Coal" should mean "secret love."

> "No fire, no coal so hotly glows
> As the secret love of which no one knows."

She and her friend *remain seated* [2] while her younger sister, who still has a prospect of marrying, hands her up the coal "because she did not know *that it would be so long.*" What would be so long is not told in the dream. If it were an anecdote, we should say "the performance"; but in the dream we may consider the sentence as it is, declare it to be ambiguous, and add "before she married." The interpretation "secret love" is then confirmed by the mention of the cousin who is sitting with his wife in the stalls, and by the *open love-affair* attributed to the latter. The contrasts between secret and open love, between the dreamer's fire and the coldness of the young wife, dominate the dream. Moreover, here once again there is a person *"in a high position"* as a middle term between the aristocrat and the musician who is justified in raising high hopes.

In the above analysis we have at last brought to light a third factor, whose part in the transformation of the dream-thoughts into the dream-content is by no means trivial: namely, consideration of the *suitability of the dream-thoughts for representation in the particular psychic material of which the dream makes use*—that is, for the most part in visual images. Among the various subordinate ideas associated with the essential dream-thoughts, those will be preferred which permit of visual representation, and the dream-work does not hesitate to recast the intractable thoughts into another verbal form, even though this is a more unusual form, provided it makes representation possible, and thus puts an end to the psychological distress caused by strangulated thinking. This pouring of the thought-content into another mould may at the same time serve the work of condensation, and may establish relations with another thought which otherwise would not have been established. It is even possible that this second thought may itself have previously changed its original expression for the purpose of meeting the first one half-way.

Herbert Silberer [3] has described a good method of directly observing the transformation of thoughts into images which occurs in dream-forma-

---

[1] Hugo Wolf.
[2] [The German "sitzen gelieben" is often applied to women who have not succeeded in getting married.—TRANS.]
[3] Bleuler-Freud *Jahrbuch*, i, 1909.

tion, and has thus made it possible to study in isolation this one factor of the dream-work. If while in a state of fatigue and somnolence he imposed upon himself a mental effort, it frequently happened that the thought escaped him, and in its place there appeared a picture in which he could recognize the substitute for the thought. Not quite appropriately, Silberer described this substitution as "auto-symbolic." I shall cite here a few examples from Silberer's work, and on account of certain peculiarities of the phenomena observed I shall refer to the subject later on.

"*Example* 1.—I remember that I have to correct a halting passage in an essay.

"*Symbol.*—I see myself planing a piece of wood.

"*Example* 5.—I endeavour to call to mind the aim of certain metaphysical studies which I am proposing to undertake.

"This aim, I reflect, consists in working one's way through, while seeking for the basis of existence, to ever higher forms of consciousness or levels of being.

"*Symbol.*—I run a long knife under a cake as though to take a slice out of it.

"*Interpretation.*—My movement with the knife signifies 'working one's way through.' . . . The explanation of the basis of the symbolism is as follows: At table it devolves upon me now and again to cut and distribute a cake, a business which I perform with a long, flexible knife, and which necessitates a certain amount of care. In particular, the neat extraction of the cut slices of cake presents a certain amount of difficulty; the knife must be carefully pushed *under* the slices in question (the slow 'working one's way through' in order to get to the bottom). But there is yet more symbolism in the picture. The cake of the symbol was really a 'dobos-cake'—that is, a cake in which the knife has to cut through several *layers* (the levels of consciousness and thought).

"*Example* 9.—I lost the thread in a train of thought. I make an effort to find it again, but I have to recognize that the point of departure has completely escaped me.

"*Symbol.*—Part of a form of type, the last lines of which have fallen out."

In view of the part played by witticisms, puns, quotations, songs, and proverbs in the intellectual life of educated persons, it would be entirely in accordance with our expectations to find disguises of this sort used with extreme frequency in the representation of the dream-thoughts. Only in the case of a few types of material has a generally valid dream-symbolism established itself on the basis of generally known allusions and verbal equivalents. A good part of this symbolism, however, is common to the psychoneuroses, legends, and popular usages as well as to dreams.

In fact, if we look more closely into the matter, we must recognize that in employing this kind of substitution the dream-work is doing nothing at all original. For the achievement of its purpose, which in this case is representation without interference from the censorship, it simply follows the paths which it finds already marked out in unconscious thinking, and gives the preference to those transformations of the repressed material which are permitted to become conscious also in the form of witticisms and allusions, and with which all the phantasies of neurotics are replete. Here we suddenly begin to understand the dream-interpretations of Scherner, whose essential correctness I have vindicated elsewhere. The preoccupation of the imagination with one's own body is by no means peculiar to or characteristic of the dream alone. My analyses have shown me that it is constantly found in the unconscious thinking of neurotics, and may be traced back to sexual curiosity, whose object, in the adolescent youth or maiden, is the genitals of the opposite sex, or even of the same sex. But, as Scherner and Volkelt very truly insist, the house does not constitute the only group of ideas which is employed for the symbolization of the body, either in dreams or in the unconscious phantasies of neurosis. To be sure, I know patients who have steadily adhered to an architectural symbolism for the body and the genitals (sexual interest, of course, extends far beyond the region of the external genital organs)— patients for whom posts and pillars signify legs (as in the *Song of Songs*), to whom every door suggests a bodily aperture ("hole"), and every waterpipe the urinary system, and so on. But the groups of ideas appertaining to plant-life, or to the kitchen, are just as often chosen to conceal sexual images [1]; in respect of the former everyday language, the sediment of imaginative comparisons dating from the remotest times, has abundantly paved the way (the "vineyard" of the Lord, the "seed" of Abraham, the "garden" of the maiden in the *Song of Songs*). The ugliest as well as the most intimate details of sexual life may be thought or dreamed of in apparently innocent allusions to culinary operations, and the symptoms of hysteria will become absolutely unintelligible if we forget that sexual symbolism may conceal itself behind the most commonplace and inconspicuous matters as its safest hiding-place. That some neurotic children cannot look at blood and raw meat, that they vomit at the sight of eggs and macaroni, and that the dread of snakes, which is natural to mankind, is monstrously exaggerated in neurotics—all this has a definite sexual meaning. Wherever the neurosis employs a disguise of this sort, it treads the paths once trodden by the whole of humanity in the early stages of

---

[1] A mass of corroborative material may be found in the three supplementary volumes of Edward Fuchs's *Illustrierte Sittengeschichte;* privately printed by A. Lange, Munich.

civilization—paths to whose thinly veiled existence our idiomatic expressions, proverbs, superstitions, and customs testify to this day.

I here insert the promised "flower-dream" of a female patient, in which I shall print in Roman type everything which is to be sexually interpreted. This beautiful dream lost all its charm for the dreamer once it had been interpreted.

(a) Preliminary dream: *She goes to the two maids in the kitchen and scolds them for taking so long to prepare "a little bite of food." She also sees a very large number of heavy kitchen utensils in the kitchen, heaped into piles and turned upside down in order to drain.* Later addition: *The two maids go to fetch water, and have, as it were, to climb into a river which reaches up to the house or into the courtyard.*[1]

(b) Main dream [2]: *She is descending from a height* [3] *over curiously constructed railings, or a fence which is composed of large square trellis-work hurdles with small square apertures.*[4] *It is really not adapted for climbing; she is constantly afraid that she cannot find a place for her foot, and she is glad that her dress doesn't get caught anywhere, and that she is able to climb down it so respectably.*[5] *As she climbs she is carrying* a big branch *in her hand,*[6] *really like a tree, which is thickly studded with* red flowers; *a spreading branch, with many twigs.*[7] *With this is connected the idea of cherry-blossoms* (Blüten = flowers), *but they look like fully opened* camellias, *which of course do not grow on trees. As she is descending, she first has one, then suddenly two, and then again only one.*[8] *When she has reached the ground the lower* flowers *have already begun to fall. Now that she has reached the bottom she sees an "odd man" who is combing—as she would like to put it—just such a tree, that is, with a piece of wood he is scraping* thick bunches of hair *from it, which hang from it like moss. Other men have chopped off such branches in a garden, and have flung them into the road, where they are lying about, so that* a number of people *take some of them. But she asks whether this is right, whether she may take one, too.*[9] *In the garden there stands a young* man

---

[1] For the interpretation of this preliminary dream, which is to be regarded as "causal," *see* p. 343.

[2] Her career.

[3] Exalted origin, the wish-contrast to the preliminary dream.

[4] A composite formation, which unites two localities, the so-called garret (German: *Boden* = floor, garret) of her father's house, in which she used to play with her brother, the object of her later phantasies, and the farm of a malicious uncle, who used to tease her.

[5] Wish-contrast to an actual memory of her uncle's farm, to the effect that she used to expose herself while she was asleep.

[6] Just as the angel bears a lily-stem in the Annunciation.

[7] For the explanation of this composite formation, *see* p. 346; innocence, menstruation, *La Dame aux Camélias*.

[8] Referring to the plurality of the persons who serve her phantasies.

[9] Whether it is permissible to masturbate. ["*Sich einen herunterreissen*" means "to pull off" and colloquially "to masturbate."—Trans.]

(he is a foreigner, and known to her) toward whom she goes in order to ask him how it is possible to transplant such branches in her own garden.[1] *He embraces her, whereupon she struggles and asks him what he is thinking of, whether it is permissible to embrace her in such a manner. He says there is nothing wrong in it, that it is permitted.*[2] *He then declares himself willing to go with her into the other garden, in order to show her how to put them in, and he says something to her which she does not quite understand: "Besides this I need three metres (later she says: square metres) or three fathoms of ground." It seems as though he were asking her for something in return for his willingness, as though he had the intention of indemnifying (reimbursing) himself in her garden, as though he wanted to evade some law or other, to derive some advantage from it without causing her an injury. She does not know whether or not he really shows her anything.*

The above dream, which has been given prominence on account of its symbolic elements, may be described as a "biographical" dream. Such dreams occur frequently in psychoanalysis, but perhaps only rarely outside it.[3]

I have, of course, an abundance of such material, but to reproduce it here would lead us too far into the consideration of neurotic conditions. Everything points to the same conclusion, namely, that we need not assume that any special symbolizing activity of the psyche is operative in dream-formation; that, on the contrary, the dream makes use of such symbolizations as are to be found ready-made in unconscious thinking, since these, by reason of their ease of representation, and for the most part by reason of their being exempt from the censorship, satisfy more effectively the requirements of dream-formation.

E. REPRESENTATION IN DREAMS BY SYMBOLS: SOME FURTHER TYPICAL DREAMS

The analysis of the last biographical dream shows that I recognized the symbolism in dreams from the very outset. But it was only little by little that I arrived at a full appreciation of its extent and significance, as the result of increasing experience, and under the influence of the works of W. Stekel, concerning which I may here fittingly say something.

This author, who has perhaps injured psychoanalysis as much as he has benefited it, produced a large number of novel symbolic translations, to which no credence was given at first, but most of which were later confirmed and had to be accepted. Stekel's services are in no way belittled by

[1] The branch (*Ast*) has long been used to represent the male organ, and, moreover, contains a very distinct allusion to the family name of the dreamer.
[2] Refers to matrimonial precautions, as does that which immediately follows.
[3] An analogous "biographical" dream is recorded on p. 378, among the examples of dream symbolism.

the remark that the sceptical reserve with which these symbols were received was not unjustified. For the examples upon which he based his
interpretations were often unconvincing, and, moreover, he employed a
method which must be rejected as scientifically unreliable. Stekel found
his symbolic meanings by way of intuition, by virtue of his individual
faculty of immediately understanding the symbols. But such an art cannot be generally assumed; its efficiency is immune from criticism, and its
results have therefore no claim to credibility. It is as though one were
to base one's diagnosis of infectious diseases on the olfactory impressions
received beside the sick-bed, although of course there have been clinicians
to whom the sense of smell—atrophied in most people—has been of
greater service than to others, and who really have been able to diagnose a
case of abdominal typhus by their sense of smell.

The progressive experience of psychoanalysis has enabled us to discover patients who have displayed in a surprising degree this immediate
understanding of dream-symbolism. Many of these patients suffered from
dementia praecox, so that for a time there was an inclination to suspect
that all dreamers with such an understanding of symbols were suffering
from that disorder. But this did not prove to be the case; it is simply a
question of a personal gift or idiosyncrasy without perceptible pathological significance.

When one has familiarized oneself with the extensive employment of
symbolism for the representation of sexual material in dreams, one naturally asks oneself whether many of these symbols have not a permanently established meaning, like the signs in shorthand; and one even
thinks of attempting to compile a new dream-book on the lines of the
cipher method. In this connection it should be noted that symbolism does
not appertain especially to dreams, but rather to the unconscious imagination, and particularly to that of the people, and it is to be found in a
more developed condition in folklore, myths, legends, idiomatic phrases,
proverbs, and the current witticisms of a people than in dreams. We
should have, therefore, to go far beyond the province of dream-interpretation in order fully to investigate the meaning of symbolism, and to discuss the numerous problems—for the most part still unsolved—which
are associated with the concept of the symbol.[1] We shall here confine ourselves to saying that representation by a symbol comes under the heading of the indirect representations, but that we are warned by all sorts of
signs against indiscriminately classing symbolic representation with the

---

[1] Cf. the works of Bleuler and his Zürich disciples, Maeder, Abraham, and others,
and of the non-medical authors (Kleinpaul and others) to whom they refer. But
the most pertinent things that have been said on the subject will be found in the
work of O. Rank and H. Sachs, *Die Bedeutung der Psychoanalyse für die Geistes-
wissenschaft*, 1913, chap. i; also E. Jones, *Die Theorie der Symbolik Intern. Zeitschr.
für Psychoanalyse*, v, 1919.

other modes of indirect representation before we have clearly conceived its distinguishing characteristics. In a number of cases the common quality shared by the symbol and the thing which it represents is obvious, in others it is concealed; in these latter cases the choice of the symbol appears to be enigmatic. And these are the very cases that must be able to elucidate the ultimate meaning of the symbolic relation; they point to the fact that it is of a genetic nature. What is to-day symbolically connected was probably united, in primitive times, by conceptual and linguistic identity.[1] The symbolic relationship seems to be a residue and reminder of a former identity. It may also be noted that in many cases the symbolic identity extends beyond the linguistic identity, as had already been asserted by Schubert (1814).[2]

Dreams employ this symbolism to give a disguised representation to their latent thoughts. Among the symbols thus employed there are, of course, many which constantly, or all but constantly, mean the same thing. But we must bear in mind the curious plasticity of psychic material. Often enough a symbol in the dream-content may have to be interpreted not symbolically but in accordance with its proper meaning; at other times the dreamer, having to deal with special memory-material, may take the law into his own hands and employ anything whatever as a sexual symbol, though it is not generally so employed. Wherever he has the choice of several symbols for the representation of a dream-content, he will decide in favour of that symbol which is in addition objectively related to his other thought-material; that is to say, he will employ an individual motivation besides the typically valid one.

Although since Scherner's time the more recent investigations of dream-problems have definitely established the existence of dream-symbolism—even Havelock Ellis acknowledges that our dreams are indubitably full of symbols—it must yet be admitted that the existence of symbols in dreams has not only facilitated dream-interpretation, but has also made it more difficult. The technique of interpretation in accordance with the dreamer's free associations more often than otherwise leaves us in the lurch as far as the symbolic elements of the dream-content are concerned. A return to the arbitrariness of dream-interpretation as it was practised

---

[1] This conception would seem to find an extraordinary confirmation in a theory advanced by Hans Sperber (*Über den Einfluss sexueller momente auf Entstehung und Entwicklung der Sprache*, in *Imago*, i, 1912). Sperber believes that primitive words denoted sexual things exclusively, and subsequently lost their sexual significance and were applied to other things and activities, which were compared with the sexual.

[2] For example, a ship sailing on the sea may appear in the urinary dreams of Hungarian dreamers, despite the fact that the term of "to ship," for "to urinate," is foreign to this language (Ferenczi). In the dreams of the French and the other romance peoples "room" serves as a symbolic representation for "woman," although these peoples have nothing analogous to the German *Frauenzimmer*. Many symbols are as old as language itself, while others are continually being coined (e.g. the aeroplane, the Zeppelin).

in antiquity, and is seemingly revived by Stekel's wild interpretations, is contrary to scientific method. Consequently, those elements in the dream-content which are to be symbolically regarded compel us to employ a combined technique, which on the one hand is based on the dreamer's associations, while on the other hand the missing portions have to be supplied by the interpreter's understanding of the symbols. Critical circumspection in the solution of the symbols must coincide with careful study of the symbols in especially transparent examples of dreams in order to silence the reproach of arbitrariness in dream-interpretation. The uncertainties which still adhere to our function as dream-interpreters are due partly to our imperfect knowledge (which, however, can be progressively increased) and partly to certain peculiarities of the dream-symbols themselves. These often possess many and varied meanings, so that, as in Chinese script, only the context can furnish the correct meaning. This multiple significance of the symbol is allied to the dream's faculty of admitting over-interpretations, of representing, in the same content, various wish-impulses and thought-formations, often of a widely divergent character.

After these limitations and reservations I will proceed. The Emperor and the Empress (King and Queen) [1] in most cases really represent the dreamer's parents; the dreamer himself or herself is the prince or princess. But the high authority conceded to the Emperor is also conceded to great men, so that in some dreams, for example, Goethe appears as a father-symbol (Hitschmann).—All elongated objects, sticks, tree-trunks, umbrellas (on account of the opening, which might be likened to an erection), all sharp and elongated weapons, knives, daggers, and pikes, represent the male member. A frequent, but not very intelligible symbol for the same is a nail-file (a reference to rubbing and scraping?).—Small boxes, chests, cupboards, and ovens correspond to the female organ; also cavities, ships, and all kinds of vessels.—A room in a dream generally represents a woman; the description of its various entrances and exits is scarcely calculated to make us doubt this interpretation.[2] The interest

---

[1] [In the U.S.A. the father is represented in dreams as "the President," and even more often as "the Governor"—a title which is frequently applied to the parent in everyday life.—TRANS.]

[2] "A patient living in a boarding-house dreams that he meets one of the servants, and asks her what her number is; to his surprise she answers: 14. He has in fact entered into relations with the girl in question, and has often had her in his bedroom. She feared, as may be imagined, that the landlady suspected her, and had proposed, on the day before the dream, that they should meet in one of the unoccupied rooms. In reality this room had the number 14, while in the dream the woman bore this number. A clearer proof of the identification of woman and room could hardly be imagined." (Ernest Jones, *Intern. Zeitschr. f. Psychoanalyse*, ii, 1914). (Cf. Artemidorus, *The Symbolism of Dreams* [German version by F. S. Krauss, Vienna, 1881, p. 110]: "Thus, for example, the bedroom signifies the wife, supposing one to be in the house.")

as to whether the room is "open" or "locked" will be readily understood in this connection. (Cf. Dora's dream in *Fragment of an Analysis of Hysteria*.) There is no need to be explicit as to the sort of key that will unlock the room; the symbolism of "lock and key" has been gracefully if broadly employed by Uhland in his song of the *Graf Eberstein*.—The dream of walking through a suite of rooms signifies a brothel or a harem. But, as H. Sachs has shown by an admirable example, it is also employed to represent marriage (contrast). An interesting relation to the sexual investigations of childhood emerges when the dreamer dreams of two rooms which were previously one, or finds that a familiar room in a house of which he dreams has been divided into two, or the reverse. In childhood the female genitals and anus (the "behind" [1]) are conceived of as a single opening according to the infantile cloaca theory, and only later is it discovered that this region of the body contains two separate cavities and openings. Steep inclines, ladders, and stairs, and going up or down them, are symbolic representations of the sexual act. [2] Smooth walls over which one climbs, façades of houses, across which one lets oneself down—often with a sense of great anxiety—correspond to erect human bodies, and probably repeat in our dreams childish memories of climbing up parents or nurses. "Smooth" walls are men; in anxiety dreams one often holds firmly to "projections" on houses. Tables, whether bare or covered, and boards, are women, perhaps by virtue of contrast, since they have no protruding contours. "Wood," generally speaking, seems, in accordance with its linguistic relations, to represent feminine matter (*Materie*). The name of the island Madeira means "wood" in Portuguese. Since "bed and board" (*mensa et thorus*) constitute marriage, in dreams the latter is often substituted for the former, and as far as practicable the sexual representation-complex is transposed to the eating-complex.—Of articles of dress, a woman's hat may very often be interpreted with certainty as the male genitals. In the dreams of men

---

[1] Cf. "the *cloaca* theory" in *Three Contributions to the Theory of Sex.*

[2] I may here repeat what I have said in another place (*Die Zukünftigen Chancen der psychoanalytischen Therapie, Zentralblatt für Psychoanalyse*, i, No. 1 and 2, 1910, and *Ges. Schriften*, Bd. vi): "Some time ago I learned that a psychologist who is unfamiliar with our work remarked to one of my friends that we were surely overestimating the secret sexual significance of dreams. He stated that his most frequent dream was that of climbing a flight of stairs, and that there was surely nothing sexual behind this. Our attention having been called to this objection, we directed our investigations to the occurrence in dreams of flights of stairs, ladders, and steps, and we soon ascertained that stairs (or anything analogous to them) represent a definite symbol of coitus. The basis for this comparison is not difficult to find; with rhythmical intervals and increasing breathlessness one reaches a height, and may then come down again in a few rapid jumps. Thus the rhythm of coitus is reproduced in climbing stairs. Let us not forget to consider the colloquial usage. This tells us that 'mounting' is, without further addition, used as a substitutive designation for the sexual act. In French, the step of a staircase is called *la marche; un vieux marcheur* corresponds exactly to the German, *ein alter Steiger*."

one often finds the necktie as a symbol for the penis; this is not only because neckties hang down in front of the body, and are characteristic of men, but also because one can select them at pleasure, a freedom which nature prohibits as regards the original of the symbol. Persons who make use of this symbol in dreams are very extravagant in the matter of ties, and possess whole collections of them.[1] All complicated machines and appliances are very probably the genitals—as a rule the male genitals—in the description of which the symbolism of dreams is as indefatigable as human wit. It is quite unmistakable that all weapons and tools are used as symbols for the male organ: e.g. ploughshare, hammer, gun, revolver, dagger, sword, etc. Again, many of the landscapes seen in dreams, especially those that contain bridges or wooded mountains, may be readily recognized as descriptions of the genitals. Marcinowski collected a series of examples in which the dreamer explained his dream by means of drawings, in order to represent the landscapes and places appearing in it. These drawings clearly showed the distinction between the manifest and the latent meaning of the dream. Whereas, naïvely regarded, they seemed to represent plans, maps, and so forth, closer investigation showed that they were representations of the human body, of the genitals, etc., and only after conceiving them thus could the dream be understood.[2] Finally, where one finds incomprehensible neologisms one may suspect combinations of components having a sexual significance.—Children, too, often signify the genitals, since men and women are in the habit of fondly referring to their genital organs as "little man," "little woman," "little thing." The "little brother" was correctly recognized by Stekel as the penis. To play with or to beat a little child is often the dream's representation of masturbation. The dream-work represents castration by baldness, haircutting, the loss of teeth, and beheading. As an insurance against castration, the dream uses one of the common symbols of the penis in double or multiple form; and the appearance in a dream of a lizard—an animal whose tail, if pulled off, is regenerated by a new growth—has the same meaning. Most of those animals which are utilized as genital symbols in mythology and folklore play this part also in dreams: the fish, the snail, the cat, the mouse (on account of the hairiness of the genitals), but above all the snake, which is the most important symbol of the male member. Small animals and vermin are substitutes for little children, e.g. undesired sisters or brothers. To be infected with vermin is often the equiva-

[1] Cf. in the *Zentralblatt für Psychoanalyse*, ii, 675, the drawing of a nineteen-year-old manic patient: a man with a snake as a neck-tie, which is turning towards a girl. Also the story *Der Schamhaftige* (*Anthropophyteia*, vi, 334): A woman entered a bathroom, and there came face to face with a man who hardly had time to put on his shirt. He was greatly embarrassed, but at once covered his throat with the front of his shirt, and said: "Please excuse me, I have no necktie."
[2] Cf. Pfister's works on cryptography and picture-puzzles.

lent for pregnancy.—As a very recent symbol of the male organ I may mention the airship, whose employment is justified by its relation to flying, and also, occasionally, by its form.—Stekel has given a number of other symbols, not yet sufficiently verified, which he has illustrated by examples. The works of this author, and especially his book: *Die Sprache des Traumes,* contain the richest collection of interpretations of symbols, some of which were ingeniously guessed and were proved to be correct upon investigation, as, for example, in the section on the symbolism of death. The author's lack of critical reflection, and his tendency to generalize at all costs, make his interpretations doubtful or inapplicable, so that in making use of his works caution is urgently advised. I shall therefore restrict myself to mentioning a few examples.

Right and *left,* according to Stekel, are to be understood in dreams in an ethical sense. "The right-hand path always signifies the way to righteousness, the left-hand path the path to crime. Thus the left may signify homosexuality, incest, and perversion, while the right signifies marriage, relations with a prostitute, etc. The meaning is always determined by the individual moral standpoint of the dreamer" (loc. cit., p. 466). *Relatives* in dreams generally stand for the genitals (p. 473). Here I can confirm this meaning only for the son, the daughter, and the younger sister—that is, wherever "little thing" could be employed. On the other hand, verified examples allow us to recognize *sisters* as symbols of the breasts, and *brothers* as symbols of the larger hemispheres. To be unable to overtake a carriage is interpreted by Stekel as regret at being unable to catch up with a difference in age (p. 479). The *luggage* of a traveller is the burden of sin by which one is oppressed (*ibid.*). But a traveller's luggage often proves to be an unmistakable symbol of one's own genitals. To numbers, which frequently occur in dreams, Stekel has assigned a fixed symbolic meaning, but these interpretations seem neither sufficiently verified nor of universal validity, although in individual cases they can usually be recognized as plausible. We have, at all events, abundant confirmation that the figure three is a symbol of the male genitals. One of Stekel's generalizations refers to the double meaning of the genital symbols. "Where is there a symbol," he asks, "which (if in any way permitted by the imagination) may not be used simultaneously in the masculine and the feminine sense?" To be sure, the clause in parenthesis retracts much of the absolute character of this assertion, for this double meaning is not always permitted by the imagination. Still, I think it is not superfluous to state that in my experience this general statement of Stekel's requires elaboration. Besides those symbols which are just as frequently employed for the male as for the female genitals, there are others which preponderantly, or almost exclusively, designate one of the sexes, and there are yet others which, so far as we know, have only the male or only the female signification. To use long, stiff objects and weapons as symbols of the female genitals, or hollow objects (chests, boxes, etc.) as symbols of the male genitals, is certainly not permitted by the imagination.

It is true that the tendency of dreams, and of the unconscious phantasy, to employ the sexual symbols bisexually, reveals an archaic trait, for in childhood the difference in the genitals is unknown, and the same genitals are attributed to both sexes. One may also be misled as regards the significance of a bisexual symbol if one forgets the fact that in some dreams a general reversal of sexes takes place, so that the male organ is represented by the female, and *vice versa*. Such dreams express, for example, the wish of a woman to be a man.

The genitals may even be represented in dreams by other parts of the body: the male member by the hand or the foot, the female genital orifice by the mouth, the ear, or even the eye. The secretions of the human body —mucus, tears, urine, semen, etc.—may be used in dreams interchangeably. This statement of Stekel's, correct in the main, has suffered a justifiable critical restriction as the result of certain comments of R. Reitler's (*Internat. Zeitschr. für Psych.*, i, 1913). The gist of the matter is the replacement of an important secretion, such as the semen, by an indifferent one.

These very incomplete indications may suffice to stimulate others to make a more painstaking collection.[1] I have attempted a much more detailed account of dream-symbolism in my *Introductory Lectures on Psychoanalysis* (trans. by Joan Riviere. Allen & Unwin, London).

I shall now append a few instances of the use of such symbols, which will show how impossible it is to arrive at the interpretation of a dream if one excludes dream-symbolism, but also how in many cases it is imperatively forced upon one. At the same time, I must expressly warn the investigator against overestimating the importance of symbols in the interpretation of dreams, restricting the work of dream-translation to the translation of symbols, and neglecting the technique of utilizing the associations of the dreamer. The two techniques of dream-interpretation must supplement one another; practically, however, as well as theoretically, precedence is retained by the latter process, which assigns the final significance to the utterances of the dreamer, while the symbol-translation which we undertake play an auxiliary part.

1. The hat as the symbol of a man (of the male genitals):[2] (A frag-

[1] In spite of all the differences between Scherner's conception of dream-symbolism and the one developed here, I must still insist that Scherner should be recognized as the true discoverer of symbolism in dreams, and that the experience of psychoanalysis has brought his book (published in 1861) into posthumous repute.

[2] From *Nachträge zur Traumdeutung* in *Zentralblatt für Psychoanalyse*, i, Nos. 5 and 6, 1911.

ment from the dream of a young woman who suffered from agoraphobia as the result of her fear of temptation.)

"*I am walking in the street in summer; I am wearing a straw hat of peculiar shape, the middle piece of which is bent upwards, while the side pieces hang downwards (here the description hesitates), and in such a fashion that one hangs lower than the other. I am cheerful and in a confident mood, and as I pass a number of young officers I think to myself: You can't do anything to me.*"

As she could produce no associations to the hat, I said to her: "The hat is really a male genital organ, with its raised middle piece and the two downward-hanging side pieces." It is perhaps peculiar that her hat should be supposed to be a man, but after all one says: *Unter die Haube kommen* (to get under the cap) when we mean: to get married. I intentionally refrained from interpreting the details concerning the unequal dependence of the two side pieces, although the determination of just such details must point the way to the interpretation. I went on to say that if, therefore, she had a husband with such splendid genitals she would not have to fear the officers; that is, she would have nothing to wish from them, for it was essentially her temptation-phantasies which prevented her from going about unprotected and unaccompanied. This last explanation of her anxiety I had already been able to give her repeatedly on the basis of other material.

It is quite remarkable how the dreamer behaved after this interpretation. She withdrew her description of the hat, and would not admit that she had said that the two side pieces were hanging down. I was, however, too sure of what I had heard to allow myself to be misled, and so I insisted that she did say it. She was quiet for a while, and then found the courage to ask why it was that one of her husband's testicles was lower than the other, and whether it was the same with all men. With this the peculiar detail of the hat was explained, and the whole interpretation was accepted by her.

The hat symbol was familiar to me long before the patient related this dream. From other but less transparent cases I believed that I might assume the hat could also stand for the female genitals.[1]

2. The "little one" as the genital organ. Being run over as a symbol of sexual intercourse.

(Another dream of the same agoraphobic patient.)

"*Her mother sends away her little daughter so that she has to go alone. She then drives with her mother to the railway station, and sees her little one walking right along the track, so that she is bound to be run over.*"

---

[1] Cf. Kirchgraber for a similar example (*Zentralblatt für Psychoanalyse*, iii, 1912, p. 95). Stekel reported a dream in which the hat with an obliquely-standing feather in the middle symbolized the (impotent) man.

She hears the bones crack. (At this she experiences a feeling of discomfort but no real horror.) She then looks out through the carriage window, to see whether the parts cannot be seen behind. Then she reproaches her mother for allowing the little one to go out alone."
Analysis.—It is not an easy matter to give here a complete interpretation of the dream. It forms part of a cycle of dreams, and can be fully understood only in connection with the rest. For it is not easy to obtain the material necessary to demonstrate the symbolism in a sufficiently isolated condition. The patient at first finds that the railway journey is to be interpreted historically as an allusion to a departure from a sanatorium for nervous diseases, with whose director she was of course in love. Her mother fetched her away, and before her departure the physician came to the railway station and gave her a bunch of flowers; she felt uncomfortable because her mother witnessed this attention. Here the mother, therefore, appears as the disturber of her tender feelings, a rôle actually played by this strict woman during her daughter's girlhood.—The next association referred to the sentence: "She then looks to see whether the parts cannot be seen behind." In the dream-façade one would naturally be compelled to think of the pieces of the little daughter who had been run over and crushed. The association, however, turns in quite a different direction. She recalls that she once saw her father in the bath-room, naked, from behind; she then begins to talk about sex differences, and remarks that in the man the genitals can be seen from behind, but in the woman they cannot. In this connection she now herself offers the interpretation that "the little one" is the genital organ, and her little one (she has a four-year-old daughter) her own organ. She reproaches her mother for wanting her to live as though she had no genitals, and recognizes this reproach in the introductory sentence of the dream: the mother sends her little one away, so that she has to go alone. In her phantasy, going alone through the streets means having no man, no sexual relations (*coire* = to go together), and this she does not like. According to all her statements, she really suffered as a girl through her mother's jealousy, because her father showed a preference for her.

The deeper interpretation of this dream depends upon another dream of the same night, in which the dreamer identifies herself with her brother. She was a "tomboy," and was always being told that she should have been born a boy. This identification with the brother shows with especial clearness that "the little one" signifies the genital organ. The mother threatened him (her) with castration, which could only be understood as a punishment for playing with the genital parts, and the identification, therefore, shows that she herself had masturbated as a child, though she had retained only a memory of her brother's having done so. An early knowledge of the male genitals, which she lost later, must, according to the assertions of this second dream, have been acquired at this time. Moreover, the second dream points to the infantile sexual theory that girls originate from boys as a result of castration. After I had told her of this childish belief, she at once confirmed it by an anecdote in which the boy asks the girl: "Was it cut off?" to which the girl replies: "No, it's always been like that."

Consequently the sending away of "the little one," of the genital organ, in the first dream refers also to the threatened castration. Finally, she blames her mother for not having borne her as a boy.

That "being run over" symbolizes sexual intercourse would not be evident from this dream if we had not learned it from many other sources.

3. Representation of the genitals by buildings, stairs, and shafts. (Dream of a young man inhibited by a father complex.)

"He is taking a walk with his father in a place which is certainly the Prater, for one can see the Rotunda, in front of which there is a small vestibule to which there is attached a captive balloon; the balloon, however, seems rather limp. His father asks him what this is all for; he is surprised at it, but he explains it to his father. They come into a courtyard in which lies a large sheet of tin. His father wants to pull off a big piece of this, but first looks round to see if anyone is watching. He tells his father that all he needs to do is to speak to the overseer, and then he can take as much as he wants to without any more ado. From this courtyard a flight of stairs leads down into a shaft, the walls of which are softly upholstered, rather like a leather arm-chair. At the end of this shaft there is a long platform, and then a new shaft begins . . ."

Analysis.—This dreamer belonged to a type of patient which is not at all promising from a therapeutic point of view; up to a certain point in the analysis such patients offer no resistance whatever, but from that point onwards they prove to be almost inaccessible. This dream he analysed almost independently. "The Rotunda," he said, "is my genitals, the captive balloon in front is my penis, about whose flaccidity I have been worried." We must, however, interpret it in greater detail: the Rotunda is the buttocks, constantly associated by the child with the genitals; the smaller structure in front is the scrotum. In the dream his father asks him what this is all for—that is, he asks him about the purpose and arrangement of the genitals. It is quite evident that this state of affairs should be reversed, and that he ought to be the questioner. As such questioning on the part of the father never occurred in reality, we must conceive the dream-thought as a wish, or perhaps take it conditionally, as follows. "If I had asked my father for sexual enlightenment . . ." The continuation of this thought we shall presently find in another place.

The courtyard in which the sheet of tin is spread out is not to be conceived symbolically in the first instance, but originates from his father's place of business. For reasons of discretion I have inserted the tin for another material in which the father deals without, however, changing anything in the verbal expression of the dream. The dreamer had entered his father's business, and had taken a terrible dislike to the somewhat questionable practices upon which its profit mainly depended. Hence the continuation of the above dream-thought ("if I had asked him") would be: "He would have deceived me just as he does his customers." For the "pulling off," which serves to represent commercial dishonesty, the dreamer himself gives a second explanation, namely, masturbation. This is not only quite familiar to us (see above, p. 367), but agrees very well with the fact that the secrecy of masturbation is expressed by its opposite (one can do it quite openly). Thus, it agrees entirely with our expectations that the autoerotic activity should be attributed to the father, just as was the questioning in the first scene of the dream. The shaft he at once interprets as the vagina, by referring to the soft upholstering of the walls. That the action of coition in the vagina is described as a going down instead of in the usual way as a going up agrees with what I have found in other instances.[1]

The details—that at the end of the first shaft there is a long platform, and then a new shaft—he himself explains biographically. He had for some time had sexual intercourse with women, but had given it up on account of inhibitions, and now hopes to be able to begin it again with the aid of the treatment. The dream, however, becomes indistinct towards the end, and to the experienced interpreter it becomes evident that in the second scene of the dream the influence of another subject has already begun to assert itself; which is indicated by his father's business, his dishonest practices, and the vagina represented by the first shaft, so that one may assume a reference to his mother.

4. The Male Organ symbolized by Persons and the Female by a Landscape.

(Dream of a woman of the lower class, whose husband is a policeman, reported by B. Dattner.)

". . . *Then someone broke into the house and she anxiously called for a policeman. But he went peacefully with two tramps into a church,[2] to which a great many steps led up*[3]*; behind the church there was a mountain*[4] *on top of which there was a dense forest.*[5] *The policeman was provided with a helmet, a gorget, and a cloak.*[6] *The two vagrants, who went*

[1] Cf. comment in the *Zentralblatt für Psychoanalyse*, i; and see above, p. 367, note 9.
[2] Or chapel = vagina.
[3] Symbol of coitus.
[4] Mons Veneris.
[5] Crines pubis.
[6] Demons in cloaks and hoods are, according to the explanation of a specialist, of a phallic character.

along with the policeman quite peaceably, had sack-like aprons tied round their loins.[1] *A road led from the church to the mountain. This road was overgrown on each side with grass and brushwood, which became thicker and thicker as it reached the top of the mountain, where it spread out into quite a forest."*

5. Castration Dreams of children.

(a) *"A boy aged three years and five months, for whom his father's return from military service is clearly inconvenient, wakes one morning in a disturbed and excited state, and constantly repeats the question: Why did Daddy carry his head on a plate? Last night Daddy carried his head on a plate."*

(b) *"A student who is now suffering from a severe obsessional neurosis remembers that in his sixth year he repeatedly had the following dream: He goes to the barber to have his hair cut. Then a large woman with severe features comes up to him and cuts off his head. He recognizes the woman as his mother."*

6. A modified staircase dream.

To one of my patients, a sexual abstainer, who was very ill, whose phantasy was fixated upon his mother, and who repeatedly dreamed of climbing stairs while accompanied by his mother, I once remarked that moderate masturbation would probably have been less harmful to him than his enforced abstinence. The influence of this remark provoked the following dream:

His piano teacher reproaches him for neglecting his piano-playing, and for not practicing the Études *of Moscheles and Clementi's* Gradus ad Parnassum. With reference to this he remarked that the *Gradus*, too, is a stairway, and that the piano itself is a stairway, as it has a scale.

It may be said that there is no class of ideas which cannot be enlisted in the representation of sexual facts and wishes.

7. The Sensation of Reality and the Representation of Repetition.

A man, now thirty-five, relates a clearly remembered dream which he claims to have had when he was four years of age: *The notary with whom his father's will was deposited*—he had lost his father at the age of three—*brought two large Emperor-pears, of which he was given one to eat. The other lay on the window-sill of the living-room.* He woke with the conviction of the reality of what he had dreamt, and obstinately asked his mother to give him the second pear; it was, he said, still lying on the window-sill. His mother laughed at this.

Analysis.—The notary was a jovial old gentleman who, as he seems to remember, really sometimes brought pears with him. The window-sill was as he saw it in the dream. Nothing else occurs to him in this connection, except, perhaps, that his mother has recently told him a dream.

[1] The two halves of the scrotum.

She has two birds sitting on her head; she wonders when they will fly away, but they do not fly away, and one of them flies to her mouth and sucks at it.

The dreamer's inability to furnish associations justifies the attempt to interpret it by the substitution of symbols. The two pears—*pommes ou poires*—are the breasts of the mother who nursed him; the window-sill is the projection of the bosom, analogous to the balconies in the dream of houses. His sensation of reality after waking is justified, for his mother had actually suckled him for much longer than the customary term, and her breast was still available. The dream is to be translated: "Mother, give (show) me the breast again at which I once used to drink." The "once" is represented by the eating of the one pear, the "again" by the desire for the other. *The temporal repetition* of an act is habitually represented in dreams by *the numerical multiplication of an object.*

It is naturally a very striking phenomenon that symbolism should already play a part in the dream of a child of four, but this is the rule rather than the exception. One may say that the dreamer has command of symbolism from the very first.

The early age at which people make use of symbolic representation, even apart from the dream-life, may be shown by the following uninfluenced memory of a lady who is now twenty-seven: *She is in her fourth year. The nursemaid is driving her, with her brother, eleven months younger, and a cousin, who is between the two in age, to the lavatory, so that they can do their little business there before going for their walk. As the oldest, she sits on the seat and the other two on chambers. She asks her (female) cousin: Have you a purse, too? Walter has a little sausage, I have a purse. The cousin answers: Yes, I have a purse, too. The nursemaid listens, laughing, and relates the conversation to the mother, whose reaction is a sharp reprimand.*

Here a dream may be inserted whose excellent symbolism permitted of interpretation with little assistance from the dreamer:

8. The Question of Symbolism in the Dreams of Normal Persons.[1]

An objection frequently raised by the opponents of psychoanalysis—and recently also by Havelock Ellis [2]—is that, although dream-symbolism may perhaps be a product of the neurotic psyche, it has no validity whatever in the case of normal persons. But while psychoanalysis recognizes no essential distinctions, but only quantitative differences, between the psychic life of the normal person and that of the neurotic, the analysis of those dreams in which, in sound and sick persons alike, the repressed complexes display the same activity, reveals the absolute identity of the mechanisms as well as of the symbolism. Indeed, the natural dreams of

[1] Alfred Robitsek in the *Zentralblatt für Psychoanalyse*, ii, 1911, p. 340.
[2] *The World of Dreams*, London, 1911, p. 168.

healthy persons often contain a much simpler, more transparent, and more characteristic symbolism than those of neurotics, which, owing to the greater strictness of the censorship and the more extensive dream-distortion resulting therefrom, are frequently troubled and obscured, and are therefore more difficult to translate. The following dream serves to illustrate this fact. This dream comes from a non-neurotic girl of a rather prudish and reserved type. In the course of conversation I found that she was engaged to be married, but that there were hindrances in the way of the marriage which threatened to postpone it. She related spontaneously the following dream:

I arrange the centre of a table with flowers for a birthday. On being questioned she states that in the dream she seemed to be at home (she has no home at the time) and experienced a feeling of happiness.

The "popular" symbolism enables me to translate the dream for myself. It is the expression of her wish to be married: the table, with the flowers in the centre, is symbolic of herself and her genitals. She represents her future wishes as fulfilled, inasmuch as she is already occupied with thoughts of the birth of a child; so the wedding has taken place long ago.

I call her attention to the fact that "the centre of a table" is an unusual expression, which she admits; but here, of course, I cannot question her more directly. I carefully refrain from suggesting to her the meaning of the symbols, and ask her only for the thoughts which occur to her mind in connection with the individual parts of the dream. In the course of the analysis her reserve gave way to a distinct interest in the interpretation, and a frankness which was made possible by the serious tone of the conversation.—To my question as to what kind of flowers they had been, her first answer is *"expensive flowers; one has to pay for them";* then she adds that they were *lilies-of-the-valley, violets, and pinks or carnations.* I took the word *lily* in this dream in its popular sense, as a symbol of chastity; she confirmed this, as purity occurred to her in association with *lily. Valley* is a common feminine dream-symbol. The chance juxtaposition of the two symbols in the name of the flower is made into a piece of dream-symbolism, and serves to emphasize the preciousness of her virginity—*expensive flowers; one has to pay for them*—and expresses the expectation that her husband will know how to appreciate its value. The comment, *expensive flowers,* etc., has, as will be shown, a different meaning in every one of the three different flower-symbols.

I thought of what seemed to me a venturesome explanation of the hidden meaning of the apparently quite asexual word *violets* by an unconscious relation to the French *viol.* But to my surprise the dreamer's association was the English word *violate.* The accidental phonetic similarity of the two words *violet* and *violate* is utilized by the dream to express in "the language of flowers" the idea of the violence of defloration (another word which makes use of flower-symbolism), and perhaps also to give expression to a masochistic tendency on the part of the girl.—An excellent example of the word bridges across which run the paths to the unconscious. *"One has to pay for them"* here means life, with which she has to pay for becoming a wife and a mother.

In association with *pinks,* which she then calls *carnations,* I think of *carnal.* But her association is *colour,* to which she adds that *carnations* are the flowers which her fiancé gives her frequently and in large quantities. At the end of the conversation she suddenly admits, spontaneously, that she has not told me the truth; the word that occurred to her was not *colour,* but *incarnation,* the very word I expected. Moreover, even the word "colour" is not a remote association; it was determined by the meaning of *carnation* (i.e. *flesh-colour*)—that is, by the complex. This lack of honesty shows that the resistance here is at its greatest because the symbolism is here most transparent, and the struggle between libido and repression is most intense in connection with this phallic theme. The remark that these flowers were often given her by her fiancé is, together with the double meaning of *carnation,* a still further indication of their phallic significance in the dream. The occasion of the present of flowers during the day is employed to express the thought of a sexual present and a return present. She gives her virginity and expects in return for it a rich love-life. But the words: *"expensive flowers; one has to pay for them"* may have a real, financial meaning.—The flower-symbolism in the dream thus comprises the virginal female, the male symbol, and the reference to violent defloration. It is to be noted that sexual flower-symbolism, which, of course, is very widespread, symbolizes the human sexual organs by flowers, the sexual organs of plants; indeed, presents of flowers between lovers may perhaps have this unconscious significance.

The birthday for which she is making preparations in the dream probably signifies the birth of a child. She identifies herself with the bridegroom, and represents him preparing her for a birth (having coitus with her). It is as though the latent thoughts were to say: "If I were he, I would not wait, but I would deflower the bride without asking her; I would use violence." Indeed, the word *violate* points to this. Thus even the sadistic libidinal components find expression.

In a deeper stratum of the dream the sentence *I arrange,* etc., probably has an auto-erotic, that is, an infantile significance.

She also has a knowledge—possible only in the dream—of her physical need; she sees herself flat like a table, so that she emphasizes all the more her virginity, the costliness of the *centre* (another time she calls it *a centre-piece of flowers*). Even the horizontal element of the table may contribute something to the symbol.—The concentration of the dream is worthy of remark; nothing is superfluous, every word is a symbol.

Later on she brings me a supplement to this dream: *"I decorate the flowers with green crinkled paper."* She adds that it was *fancy paper* of the sort which is used to disguise ordinary flower-pots. She says also: "To hide untidy things, whatever was to be seen which was not pretty to the eye; there is a gap, a little space in the flowers. The paper looks like velvet or moss." With *decorate* she associates *decorum*, as I expected. The green colour is very prominent, and with this she associates *hope*, yet another reference to pregnancy.—In this part of the dream the identification with the man is not the dominant feature, but thoughts of shame and frankness express themselves. She makes herself beautiful for him; she admits physical defects, of which she is ashamed and which she wishes to correct. The associations *velvet* and *moss* distinctly point to *crines pubis*.

The dream is an expression of thoughts hardly known to the waking state of the girl; thoughts which deal with the love of the senses and its organs; she is "prepared for a birth-day," i.e. she has coitus; the fear of defloration and perhaps the pleasurably toned pain find expression; she admits her physical defects and over-compensates them by means of an over-estimation of the value of her virginity. Her shame excuses the emerging sensuality by the fact that the aim of it all is the child. Even material considerations, which are foreign to the lover, find expression here. The affect of the simple dream—the feeling of bliss—shows that here strong emotional complexes have found satisfaction.

I close with the

9. Dream of a Chemist.

(A young man who has been trying to give up his habit of masturbation by substituting intercourse with a woman.)

Preliminary statement: On the day before the dream he had been instructing a student as to *Grignard's* reaction, in which magnesium is dissolved in absolutely pure ether under the catalytic influence of iodine. Two days earlier there had been an explosion in the course of the same reaction, in which someone had burned his hand.

Dream I. *He is going to make phenylmagnesiumbromide; he sees the apparatus with particular distinctness, but he has substituted himself for the magnesium. He is now in a curious, wavering attitude. He keeps on repeating to himself: "This is the right thing, it is working, my feet are beginning to dissolve, and my knees are getting soft." Then he reaches down and feels for his feet, and meanwhile (he does not know how) he takes his legs out of the carboy, and then again he says to himself: "That can't be . . . Yes, it has been done correctly." Then he partially wakes, and repeats the dream to himself, because he wants to tell it to me. He is positively afraid of the analysis of the dream. He is much excited during this state of semi-sleep, and repeats continually: "Phenyl, phenyl."*

II. *He is in . . . with his whole family. He is supposed to be at the Schottentor at half-past eleven in order to keep an appointment with the lady in question, but he does not wake until half-past eleven. He says to himself: "It is too late now; when you get there it will be half-past twelve." The next moment he sees the whole family gathered about the table—his mother and the parlourmaid with the soup-tureen with peculiar distinctness. Then he says to himself: "Well, if we are sitting down to eat already, I certainly can't get away."*

Analysis.—He feels sure that even the first dream contains a reference to the lady whom he is to meet at the place of rendezvous (the dream was dreamed during the night before the expected meeting). The student whom he was instructing is a particularly unpleasant fellow; the chemist had said to him: "That isn't right, because the magnesium was still unaffected," and the student had answered, as though he were quite unconcerned: "Nor it is." He himself must be this student; he is as indifferent to his *analysis* as the student is to his *synthesis;* the *he* in the dream, however, who performs the operation, is myself. How unpleasant he must seem to me with his indifference to the result!

Again, he is the material with which the analysis (synthesis) is made. For the question is the success of the treatment. The legs in the dream recall an impression of the previous evening. He met a lady at a dancing class of whom he wished to make a conquest; he pressed her to him so closely that she once cried out. As he ceased to press her legs he felt her firm, responding pressure against his lower thighs as far as just above the knees, the spot mentioned in the dream. In this situation, then, the woman is the magnesium in the retort, which is at last working. He is feminine towards me, as he is virile towards the woman. If he succeeds with the woman, the treatment will also succeed. Feeling himself and becoming aware of his knees refers to masturbation, and corresponds to his fatigue of the previous day . . . The rendezvous had actually been made for half-past eleven. His wish to oversleep himself and to keep to his sexual object at home (that is, masturbation) corresponds to his resistance.

He says, in respect to the repetition of the name phenyl, that all these radicals ending in *yl* have always been pleasing to him; they are very convenient to use: benzyl, acetyl, etc. That, however, explained nothing. But when I proposed the root *Schlemihl* [1] he laughed heartily, and told me that during the summer he had read a book by Prévost which contained a chapter: *Les exclus de l'amour,* and in this there was some mention of

[1] [This Hebrew word is well known in German-speaking countries, even among Gentiles, and signifies an unlucky, awkward person.—TRANS.]

Schlemiliés; and in reading of these outcasts he said to himself: "That is my case." He would have played the *Schlemihl* if he had missed the appointment.

It seems that the sexual symbolism of dreams has already been directly confirmed by experiment. In 1912 Dr. K. Schrötter, at the instance of H. Swoboda, produced dreams in deeply hypnotized persons by suggestions which determined a large part of the dream-content. If the suggestion proposed that the subject should dream of normal or abnormal sexual relations, the dream carried out these orders by replacing sexual material by the symbols with which psychoanalytic dream-interpretation has made us familiar. Thus, following the suggestion that the dreamer should dream of homosexual relations with a lady friend, this friend appeared in the dream carrying a shabby travelling-bag, upon which there was a label with the printed words: "For ladies only." The dreamer was believed never to have heard of dream-symbolization or of dream-interpretation. Unfortunately, the value of this important investigation was diminished by the fact that Dr. Schrötter shortly afterwards committed suicide. Of his dream-experiments he gave us only a preliminary report in the *Zentralblatt für Psychoanalyse.*

Similar results were reported in 1923 by G. Roffenstein. Especially interesting were the experiments performed by Betlheim and Hartmann, because they eliminated hypnosis. These authors told stories of a crude sexual content to confused patients suffering from Korsakoff's psychosis, and observed the distortions which appeared when the material related was reproduced.[1] It was shown that the reproduced material contained symbols made familiar by the interpretation of dreams (climbing stairs, stabbing and shooting as symbols of coitus, knives and cigarettes as symbols of the penis). Special value was attached to the appearance of the symbol of climbing stairs, for, as the authors justly observed, "a symbolization of this sort could not be effected by a conscious wish to distort."

Only when we have formed a due estimate of the importance of symbolism in dreams can we continue the study of the *typical dreams* which was interrupted in an earlier chapter (p. 311). I feel justified in dividing these dreams roughly into two classes; first, those which always really have the same meaning, and second, those which despite the same or a similar content must nevertheless be given the most varied interpretations. Of the typical dreams belonging to the first class I have already dealt fairly fully with the examination-dream.

On account of their similar affective character, the dreams of missing a train deserve to be ranked with the examination-dreams; moreover, their interpretation justifies this approximation. They are consolation-

[1] *Über Fehlreaktionen bei der Korsakoffschen Psychose, Arch. f. Psychiatrie,* Bd. lxxii, 1924.

dreams, directed against another anxiety perceived in dreams—the fear of death. "To depart" is one of the most frequent and one of the most readily established of the death-symbols. The dream therefore says consolingly: "Reassure yourself, you are not going to die (to depart)," just as the examination-dream calms us by saying: "Don't be afraid; this time, too, nothing will happen to you." The difficulty in understanding both kinds of dreams is due to the fact that the anxiety is attached precisely to the expression of consolation.

The meaning of the "dreams due to dental stimulus" which I have often enough had to analyse in my patients escaped me for a long time because, much to my astonishment, they habitually offered too great a resistance to interpretation. But finally an overwhelming mass of evidence convinced me that in the case of men nothing other than the masturbatory desires of puberty furnish the motive power of these dreams. I shall analyse two such dreams, one of which is also a "flying dream." The two dreams were dreamed by the same person—a young man of pronounced homosexuality which, however, has been inhibited in life.

He is witnessing a performance of Fidelio *from the stalls of the opera-house; he is sitting next to L., whose personality is congenial to him, and whose friendship he would like to have. Suddenly he flies diagonally right across the stalls; he then puts his hand in his mouth and draws out two of his teeth.*

He himself describes the flight by saying that it was as though he were thrown into the air. As the opera performed was *Fidelio*, he recalls the words:—

"He who a charming wife acquires. . . ."

But the acquisition of even the most charming wife is not among the wishes of the dreamer. Two other lines would be more appropriate:—

"He who succeeds in the lucky (big) throw
The friend of a friend to be. . . ."

The dream thus contains the "lucky (big) throw," which is not, however, a wish-fulfilment only. For it conceals also the painful reflection that in his striving after friendship he has often had the misfortune to be "thrown out," and the fear lest this fate may be repeated in the case of the young man by whose side he has enjoyed the performance of *Fidelio*. This is now followed by a confession, shameful to a man of his refinement, to the effect that once, after such a rejection on the part of a friend, his profound sexual longing caused him to masturbate twice in succession.

The other dream is as follows: *Two university professors of his acquaintance are treating him in my place. One of them does something to his penis; he is afraid of an operation. The other thrusts an iron bar against his mouth, so that he loses one or two teeth. He is bound with four silk handkerchiefs.*

The sexual significance of this dream can hardly be doubted. The silk handkerchiefs allude to an identification with a homosexual of his acquaintance. The dreamer, who has never achieved coition (nor has he ever actually sought sexual intercourse) with men, conceives the sexual act on the lines of masturbation with which he was familiar during puberty.

I believe that the frequent modifications of the typical dream due to dental stimulus—that, for example, in which another person draws the tooth from the dreamer's mouth—will be made intelligible by the same explanation.[1] It may, however, be difficult to understand how "dental stimulus" can have come to have this significance. But here I may draw attention to the frequent "displacement from below to above" which is at the service of sexual repression, and by means of which all kinds of sensations and intentions occurring in hysteria, which ought to be localized in the genitals, may at all events be realized in other, unobjectionable parts of the body. We have a case of such displacement when the genitals are replaced by the face in the symbolism of unconscious thought. This is corroborated by the fact that verbal usage relates the buttocks to the cheeks,[2] and the *labia minora* to the lips which enclose the orifice of the mouth. The nose is compared to the penis in numerous allusions, and in each case the presence of hair completes the resemblance. Only one feature —the teeth—is beyond all possibility of being compared in this way; but it is just this coincidence of agreement and disagreement which makes the teeth suitable for purposes of representation under the pressure of sexual repression.

I will not assert that the interpretation of dreams due to dental stimulus as dreams of masturbation (the correctness of which I cannot doubt) has been freed of all obscurity.[3] I carry the explanation as far as I am able, and must leave the rest unsolved. But I must refer to yet another relation indicated by a colloquial expression. In Austria there is in use an indelicate designation for the act of masturbation, namely: "To pull one out," or "to pull one off." [4] I am unable to say whence these colloquial-

---

[1] The extraction of a tooth by another is usually to be interpreted as castration (cf. hair-cutting; Stekel). One must distinguish between dreams due to dental stimulus and dreams referring to the dentist, such as have been recorded, for example, by Coriat (*Zentralblatt für Psychoanalyse*, iii, 440).

[2] [In German "*Backen*" = cheeks and "*Hinterbacken*" (lit. "hind-cheeks") = buttocks.—TRANS.]

[3] According to C. G. Jung, dreams due to dental stimulus in the case of women have the significance of parturition dreams. E. Jones has given valuable confirmation of this. The common element of this interpretation with that represented above may be found in the fact that in both cases (castration-birth) there is a question of removing a part from the whole body.

[4] Cf. the "biographical" dream on pp. 367-8.

isms originate, or on what symbolisms they are based; but the teeth would very well fit in with the first of the two.

Dreams of pulling teeth, and of teeth falling out, are interpreted in popular belief to mean the death of a connection. Psychoanalysis can admit of such a meaning only at the most as a joking allusion to the sense already indicated.

To the second group of typical dreams belong those in which one is flying or hovering, falling, swimming, etc. What do these dreams signify? Here we cannot generalize. They mean, as we shall learn, something different in each case; only, the sensory material which they contain always comes from the same source.

We must conclude from the information obtained in psychoanalysis that these dreams also repeat impressions of our childhood—that is, that they refer to the games involving movement which have such an extraordinary attraction for children. Where is the uncle who has never made a child fly by running with it across the room, with outstretched arms, or has never played at falling with it by rocking it on his knee and then suddenly straightening his leg, or by lifting it above his head and suddenly pretending to withdraw his supporting hand? At such moments children shout with joy and insatiably demand a repetition of the performance, especially if a little fright and dizziness are involved in it. In after years they repeat their sensations in dreams, but in dreams they omit the hands that held them, so that now they are free to float or fall. We know that all small children have a fondness for such games as rocking and see-sawing; and when they see gymnastic performances at the circus their recollection of such games is refreshed. In some boys the hysterical attack consists simply in the reproduction of such performances, which they accomplish with great dexterity. Not infrequently sexual sensations are excited by these games of movement, innocent though they are in themselves. To express the matter in a few words: it is these romping games of childhood which are being repeated in dreams of flying, falling, vertigo, and the like, but the pleasurable sensations are now transformed into anxiety. But, as every mother knows, the romping of children often enough ends in quarrelling and tears.

I have therefore good reason for rejecting the explanation that it is the condition of our cutaneous sensations during sleep, the sensation of the movements of the lungs, etc., that evoke dreams of flying and falling. As I see it, these sensations have themselves been reproduced from the memory to which the dream refers—that they are therefore dream-content, and not dream-sources.[1]

This material, consisting of sensations of motion, similar in character,

[1] This passage, dealing with dreams of motion, is repeated on account of the context. Cf. p. 315.

and originating from the same sources, is now used for the representation of the most manifold dream-thoughts. Dreams of flying or hovering, for the most part pleasurably toned, will call for the most widely differing interpretations—interpretations of a quite special nature in the case of some dreamers, and interpretations of a typical nature in that of others. One of my patients was in the habit of dreaming very frequently that she was hovering a little way above the street without touching the ground. She was very short of stature, and she shunned every sort of contamination involved by intercourse with human beings. Her dream of suspension —which raised her feet above the ground and allowed her head to tower into the air—fulfilled both of her wishes. In the case of other dreamers of the same sex, the dream of flying had the significance of the longing: "If only I were a little bird!" Similarly, others become angels at night, because no one has ever called them angels by day. The intimate connection between flying and the idea of a bird makes it comprehensible that the dream of flying, in the case of male dreamers, should usually have a coarsely sensual significance [1]; and we should not be surprised to hear that this or that dreamer is always very proud of his ability to fly.

Dr. Paul Federn (Vienna) has propounded the fascinating theory that a great many flying dreams are erection dreams, since the remarkable phenomenon of erection, which constantly occupies the human phantasy, cannot fail to be impressive as an apparent suspension of the laws of gravity (cf. the winged phalli of the ancients).

It is a noteworthy fact that a prudent experimenter like Mourly Vold, who is really averse to any kind of interpretation, nevertheless defends the erotic interpretation of the dreams of flying and hovering.[2] He describes the erotic element as "the most important motive factor of the hovering dream," and refers to the strong sense of bodily vibration which accompanies this type of dream, and the frequent connection of such dreams with erections and emissions.

Dreams of *falling* are more frequently characterized by anxiety. Their interpretation, when they occur in women, offers no difficulty, because they nearly always accept the symbolic meaning of falling, which is a circumlocution for giving way to an erotic temptation. We have not yet exhausted the infantile sources of the dream of falling; nearly all children have fallen occasionally, and then been picked up and fondled; if they fell out of bed at night, they were picked up by the nurse and taken into her bed.

People who dream often, and with great enjoyment, of *swimming*, cleaving the waves, etc., have usually been bed-wetters, and they now repeat in

---

[1] [A reference to the German slang word *"vögeln"* (to copulate) from *"Vogel"* (a bird).—TRANS.]

[2] *Über den Traum*, Ges. Schriften, Bd. iii.

the dream a pleasure which they have long since learned to forgo. We shall soon learn, from one example or another, to what representations dreams of swimming easily lend themselves.

The interpretation of dreams of *fire* justifies a prohibition of the nursery, which forbids children to "play with fire" so that they may not wet the bed at night. These dreams also are based on reminiscences of the *enuresis nocturna* of childhood. In my *Fragment of an Analysis of Hysteria* [1] I have given the complete analysis and synthesis of such a dream of fire in connection with the infantile history of the dreamer, and have shown for the representation of what maturer impulses this infantile material has been utilized.

It would be possible to cite quite a number of other "typical" dreams, if by such one understands dreams in which there is a frequent recurrence, in the dreams of different persons, of the same manifest dream-content. For example: dreams of passing through narrow alleys, or a whole suite of rooms; dreams of burglars, in respect of whom nervous people take measures of precaution before going to bed; dreams of being chased by wild animals (bulls, horses); or of being threatened with knives, daggers, and lances. The last two themes are characteristic of the manifest dream-content of persons suffering from anxiety, etc. A special investigation of this class of material would be well worth while. In lieu of this I shall offer two observations, which do not, however, apply exclusively to typical dreams.

The more one is occupied with the solution of dreams, the readier one becomes to acknowledge that the majority of the dreams of adults deal with sexual material and give expression to erotic wishes. Only those who really analyse dreams, that is, those who penetrate from their manifest content to the latent dream-thoughts, can form an opinion on this subject; but never those who are satisfied with registering merely the manifest content (as, for example, Näcke in his writings on sexual dreams). Let us recognize at once that there is nothing astonishing in this fact, which is entirely consistent with the principles of dream-interpretation. No other instinct has had to undergo so much suppression, from the time of childhood onwards, as the sexual instinct in all its numerous components: [2]— from no other instinct are so many and such intense unconscious wishes left over, which now, in the sleeping state, generate dreams. In dream-interpretation this importance of the sexual complexes must never be forgotten, though one must not, of course, exaggerate it to the exclusion of all other factors.

Of many dreams it may be ascertained, by careful interpretation, that

[1] *Collected Papers*, vol. iii, trans. by Alix and James Strachey. Hogarth Press, London.
[2] Cf. *Three Contributions to the Theory of Sex.*

they may even be understood bisexually, inasmuch as they yield an indisputable over-interpretation, in which they realize homosexual impulses—that is, impulses which are contrary to the normal sexual activity of the dreamer. But that all dreams are to be interpreted bisexually, as Stekel [1] maintains, and Adler,[2] seems to me to be a generalization as insusceptible of proof as it is improbable, and one which, therefore, I should be loth to defend; for I should, above all, be at a loss to know how to dispose of the obvious fact that there are many dreams which satisfy other than erotic needs (taking the word in the widest sense), as, for example, dreams of hunger, thirst, comfort, etc. And other similar assertions, to the effect that "behind every dream one finds a reference to death" (Stekel), or that every dream shows "an advance from the feminine to the masculine line" (Adler), seem to me to go far beyond the admissible in the interpretation of dreams. The assertion that *all dreams call for a sexual interpretation,* against which there is such an untiring polemic in the literature of the subject, is quite foreign to my *Interpretation of Dreams.* It will not be found in any of the eight editions of this book, and is in palpable contradiction to the rest of its contents.

We have stated elsewhere that dreams which are conspicuously *innocent* commonly embody crude erotic wishes, and this we might confirm by numerous further examples. But many dreams which appear indifferent, in which we should never suspect a tendency in any particular direction, may be traced, according to the analysis, to unmistakably sexual wish-impulses, often of an unsuspected nature. For example, who, before it had been interpreted, would have suspected a sexual wish in the following dream? The dreamer relates: *Between two stately palaces there stands, a little way back, a small house, whose doors are closed. My wife leads me along the little bit of road leading to the house and pushes the door open, and then I slip quickly and easily into the interior of a courtyard that slopes steeply upwards.*

Anyone who has had experience in the translating of dreams will, of course, at once be reminded that penetration into narrow spaces and the opening of locked doors are among the commonest of sexual symbols, and will readily see in this dream a representation of attempted coition from behind (between the two stately buttocks of the female body). The narrow, steep passage is, of course, the vagina; the assistance attributed to the wife of the dreamer requires the interpretation that in reality it is only consideration for the wife which is responsible for abstention from such an attempt. Moreover, inquiry shows that on the previous day a young girl

[1] W. Stekel, *Die Sprache des Traumes,* 1911.
[2] Alf. Adler, *Der Psychische Hermaphroditismus im Leben und in der Neurose,* in *Fortschritte der Medizin,* 1910, No. 16, and later papers in the *Zentralblatt für Psychoanalyse,* i, 1910–11.

had entered the household of the dreamer; she had pleased him, and had given him the impression that she would not be altogether averse to an approach of this sort. The little house between the two palaces is taken from a reminiscence of the Hradschin in Prague, and once more points to the girl, who is a native of that city.

If, in conversation with my patients, I emphasize the frequency of the Oedipus dream—the dream of having sexual intercourse with one's mother —I elicit the answer: "I cannot remember such a dream." Immediately afterwards, however, there arises the recollection of another, an unrecognizable, indifferent dream, which the patient has dreamed repeatedly, and which on analysis proves to be a dream with this very content—that is, yet another Oedipus dream. I can assure the reader that disguised dreams of sexual intercourse with the dreamer's mother are far more frequent than undisguised dreams to the same effect.[1]

---

[1] I have published a typical example of such a disguised Oedipus dream in No. 1 of the *Zentralblatt für Psychoanalyse* (see below); another, with a detailed analysis, was published in No. 4 of the same journal by Otto Rank. For other disguised Oedipus dreams in which the *eye* appears as a symbol, see Rank (*Int. Zeitschr. für Ps.A.*, i, 1913). Papers upon eye dreams and eye symbolism by Eder, Ferenczi, and Reitler will be found in the same issue. The blinding in the Oedipus legend and elsewhere is a substitute for castration. The ancients, by the way, were not unfamiliar with the symbolic interpretation of the undisguised Oedipus dream (*see* O. Rank, *Jahrb.* ii, p. 534: "Thus, a dream of Julius Caesar's of sexual relations with his mother has been handed down to us, which the oneiroscopists interpreted as a favourable omen signifying his taking possession of the earth (Mother Earth). Equally well known is the oracle delivered to the Tarquinii, to the effect that that one of them would become the ruler of Rome who should be the first to kiss his mother (*osculum matri tulerit*), which Brutus conceived as referring to Mother Earth (*terram osculo contigit, scilicet quod ea communis mater omnium mortalium esset*, Livy, I, lxi). Cf. here the dream of Hippias in Heredotus, VI, 107: "But Hippias led the barbarians to Marathon after he had had the following dream-vision the previous night. It had seemed to Hippias that he was sleeping with his own mother. He concluded from this dream that he would return home to Athens, and would regain power, and that he would die in his fatherland in his old age." These myths and interpretations point to a correct psychological insight. I have found that those persons who consider themselves preferred or favoured by their mothers manifest in life that confidence in themselves, and that unshakable optimism, which often seem heroic, and not infrequently compel actual success.

Typical example of a disguised Oedipus dream:—

A man dreams: *He has a secret affair with a woman whom another man wishes to marry. He is concerned lest the other should discover this relation and abandon the marriage; he therefore behaves very affectionately to the man; he nestles up to him and kisses him.*—The facts of the dreamer's life touch the dream-content only at one point. He has a secret affair with a married woman, and an equivocal expression of her husband, with whom he is on friendly terms, aroused in him the suspicion that he might have noticed something of this relationship. There is, however, in reality, yet another factor, the mention of which was avoided in the dream, and which alone gives the key to it. The life of the husband is threatened by an organic malady. His wife is prepared for the possibility of his sudden death, and our dreamer consciously harbours the intention of marrying the young widow after her husband's decease. It is through this objective situation that the dreamer finds himself transferred into the constellation of the Oedipus dream; his wish is to be enabled to kill the man, so that he may win the woman for his wife; his dream

There are dreams of landscapes and localities in which emphasis is always laid upon the assurance: "I have been here before." But this *"Déjà vu"* has a special significance in dreams. In this case the locality is always the genitals of the mother; of no other place can it be asserted with such certainty that one "has been here before." I was once puzzled by the account of a dream given by a patient afflicted with obsessional neurosis. He dreamed that he called at a house where he had been *twice* before. But this very patient had long ago told me of an episode of his sixth year. At that time he shared his mother's bed, and had abused the occasion by inserting his finger into his mother's genitals while she was asleep.

A large number of dreams, which are frequently full of anxiety, and often have for content the traversing of narrow spaces, or staying long in the water, are based upon phantasies concerning the intra-uterine life, the sojourn in the mother's womb, and the act of birth. I here insert the dream of a young man who, in his phantasy, has even profited by the intra-uterine opportunity of spying upon an act of coition between his parents.

"He is in a deep shaft, in which there is a window, as in the Semmering tunnel. Through this he sees at first an empty landscape, and then he composes a picture in it, which is there all at once and fills up the empty space. The picture represents a field which is being deeply tilled by an implement, and the wholesome air, the associated idea of hard work, and the bluish-black clods of earth make a pleasant impression on him. He then goes on and sees a work on education lying open . . . and is surprised that so much attention is devoted in it to the sexual feelings (of children), which makes him think of me."

Here is a pretty water-dream of a female patient, which was turned to special account in the course of treatment.

At her usual holiday resort on the . . . Lake, she flings herself into the dark water at a place where the pale moon is reflected in the water.

Dreams of this sort are parturition dreams; their interpretation is effected by reversing the fact recorded in the manifest dream-content; thus, instead of "flinging oneself into the water," read "coming out of the water" —that is, "being born." [1] The place from which one is born may be recognized if one thinks of the humorous sense of the French *"la lune."* The pale moon thus becomes the white "bottom," which the child soon guesses to be the place from which it came. Now what can be the meaning of the patient's wishing to be born at a holiday resort? I asked the dreamer this,

---

gives expression to the wish in a hypocritical distortion. Instead of representing her as already married to the other man, it represents the other man only as wishing to marry her, which indeed corresponds with his own secret intention, and the hostile wishes directed against the man are concealed under demonstrations of affection, which are reminiscences of his childish relations to his father.

[1] For the mythological meaning of water-birth, *see* Rank: *Der Mythus von der Geburt des Helden,* 1909.

and she replied without hesitation: "Hasn't the treatment made me as though I were *born again?*" Thus the dream becomes an invitation to continue the treatment at this summer resort—that is, to visit her there; perhaps it also contains a very bashful allusion to the wish to become a mother herself.[1]

Another dream of parturition, with its interpretation, I take from a paper by E. Jones. *"She stood at the seashore watching a small boy, who seemed to be hers, wading into the water. This he did till the water covered him and she could only see his head bobbing up and down near the surface. The scene then changed to the crowded hall of an hotel. Her husband left her, and she 'entered into conversation with' a stranger.*

"The second half of the dream was discovered in the analysis to represent flight from her husband, and the entering into intimate relations with a third person, behind whom was plainly indicated Mr. X.'s brother, mentioned in a former dream. The first part of the dream was a fairly evident birth-phantasy. In dreams, as in mythology, the delivery of a child from the uterine waters is commonly represented, by way of distortion, as the entry of the child into water; among many other instances, the births of Adonis, Osiris, Moses, and Bacchus are well-known illustrations of this. The bobbing up and down of the head in the water at once recalled to the patient the sensation of quickening which she had experienced in her only pregnancy. Thinking of the boy going into the water induced a reverie in which she saw herself taking him out of the water, carrying him into the nursery, washing and dressing him, and installing him in her household.

"The second half of the dream, therefore, represents thoughts concerning the elopement, which belonged to the first half of the underlying latent content; the first half of the dream corresponded with the second half of the latent content, the birth phantasy. Besides this inversion in the order, further inversions took place in each half of the dream. In the first half the child entered the water, and then his head bobbed; in the underlying dream-thoughts the quickening occurred first, and then the child left the water (a double inversion). In the second half her husband left her; in the dream-thoughts she left her husband."

Another parturition dream is related by Abraham—the dream of a young woman expecting her first confinement: *From one point of the floor of the room a subterranean channel leads directly into the water (path of parturition—amniotic fluid). She lifts up a trap in the floor, and there im-*

---

[1] It was not for a long time that I learned to appreciate the significance of the phantasies and unconscious thoughts relating to life in the womb. They contain the explanation of the curious dread, felt by so many people, of being buried alive, as well as the profoundest unconscious reason for the belief in a life after death, which represents only the projection into the future of this mysterious life before birth. *The act of birth, moreover, is the first experience attended by anxiety, and is thus, the source and model of the affect of anxiety.*

mediately appears a creature dressed in brownish fur, which almost resembles a seal. This creature changes into the dreamer's younger brother, to whom her relation has always been maternal in character.

Rank has shown from a number of dreams that parturition-dreams employ the same symbols as micturition-dreams. The erotic stimulus expresses itself in these dreams as an urethral stimulus. The stratification of meaning in these dreams corresponds with a change in the significance of the symbol since childhood.

We may here turn back to the interrupted theme (see p. 210) of the part played by organic, sleep-disturbing stimuli in dream-formation. Dreams which have come into existence under these influences not only reveal quite frankly the wishfulfilling tendency, and the character of convenience-dreams, but they very often display a quite transparent symbolism as well, since waking not infrequently follows a stimulus whose satisfaction in symbolic disguise has already been vainly attempted in the dream. This is true of emission dreams as well as those evoked by the need to urinate or defecate. The peculiar character of emission dreams permits us directly to unmask certain sexual symbols already recognized as typical, but nevertheless violently disputed, and it also convinces us that many an apparently innocent dream-situation is merely the symbolic prelude to a crudely sexual scene. This, however, finds *direct* representation, as a rule, only in the comparatively infrequent emission dreams, while it often enough turns into an anxiety-dream, which likewise leads to waking.

The symbolism of *dreams due to urethral stimulus* is especially obvious, and has always been divined. Hippocrates had already advanced the theory that a disturbance of the bladder was indicated if one dreamt of fountains and springs (Havelock Ellis). Scherner, who has studied the manifold symbolism of the urethral stimulus, agrees that "the powerful urethral stimulus always turns into the stimulation of the sexual sphere and its symbolic imagery. . . . The dream due to urethral stimulus is often at the same time the representative of the sexual dream."

O. Rank, whose conclusions (in his paper on *Die Symbolschichtung im Wecktraum*) I have here followed, argues very plausibly that a large number of "dreams due to urethral stimulus" are really caused by sexual stimuli, which at first seek to gratify themselves by way of regression to the infantile form of urethral erotism. Those cases are especially instructive in which the urethral stimulus thus produced leads to waking and the emptying of the bladder, whereupon, in spite of this relief, the dream is continued, and expresses its need in undisguisedly erotic images.[1]

---

[1] "The same symbolic representations which in the infantile sense constitute the basis of the vesical dream appear in the 'recent' sense in purely sexual significance: water = urine = semen = amniotic fluid; ship = 'to pump ship' (urinate) = seed-capsule; getting wet = enuresis = coitus = pregnancy; swimming = full bladder = dwelling-place of the unborn; rain = urination = symbol of fertili-

In a quite analogous manner dreams due to *intestinal stimulus* disclose the pertinent symbolism, and thus confirm the relation, which is also amply verified by ethno-psychology, of *gold* and *feces*.[1] "Thus, for example, a woman, at a time when she is under the care of a physician on account of an *intestinal disorder*, dreams of a digger for hidden treasure who is burying a treasure in the vicinity of a little wooden shed which looks like a rural *privy*. A second part of the dream has as its content how she *wipes* the *posterior* of her child, a little girl, who has *soiled herself*."

Dreams of "rescue" are connected with parturition dreams. To rescue, especially to rescue from the water, is, when dreamed by a woman, equivalent to giving birth; this sense is, however, modified when the dreamer is a man.[2]

Robbers, burglars, and ghosts, of which we are afraid before going to bed, and which sometimes even disturb our sleep, originate in one and the same childish reminiscence. They are the nightly visitors who have waked the child in order to set it on the chamber, so that it may not wet the bed, or have lifted the coverlet in order to see clearly how the child is holding its hands while sleeping. I have been able to induce an exact recollection of the nocturnal visitor in the analysis of some of these anxiety-dreams. The robbers were always the father; the ghosts more probably corresponded to female persons in white night-gowns.

F. EXAMPLES—ARITHMETIC AND SPEECH IN DREAMS

Before I proceed to assign to its proper place the fourth of the factors which control the formation of dreams, I shall cite a few examples from my collection of dreams, partly for the purpose of illustrating the co-operation of the three factors with which we are already acquainted, and partly for the purpose of adducing evidence for certain unsupported assertions which have been made, or of bringing out what necessarily follows from them. It has, of course, been difficult in the foregoing account of the dream-work to demonstrate my conclusions by means of examples. Examples in support of isolated statements are convincing only when considered in the context of an interpretation of a dream as a whole; when they are

---

zation; traveling (journeying—alighting) = getting out of bed = having sexual intercourse (honeymoon journey); urinating = sexual ejaculation" (Rank, I, c.).

[1] Freud, *Charakter und Analerotik*; Rank, *Die Symbolschictung*, etc.; Dattner, *Intern. Zeitschr. f. Psych.* i, 1913; Reik, *Intern. Zeitschr.*, iii, 1915.

[2] For such a dream see Pfister, *Ein Fall von psychoanalytischer Seelensorge und Seelenheilung*, in *Evangelische Freiheit*, 1909. Concerning the symbol of "rescuing," see my paper, *Die Zukünftigen Chancender psychoanalytischen Therapie*, in *Zentralblatt für Psychoanalyse*, No. I, 1910. Also *Beitrage zur Psychologie des Liebeslebens*, i. *Über einen besonderen Typus der objektwahl beim Manne*, in *Jahrbuch für Ps.A.*, Bd. ii, 1910 (*Ges. Schriften*, Bd. v). Also Rank, *Beilege zur Rettungs-phantasie* in the *Zentralblatt für Psychoanalyse*, i, 1910, p. 331; Reik, *Zur Rettungssymbolic*; ibid., p. 299.

wrested from their context, they lose their value; on the other hand, a dream-interpretation, even when it is by no means profound, soon becomes so extensive that it obscures the thread of the discussion which it is intended to illustrate. This technical consideration must be my excuse if I now proceed to mix together all sorts of things which have nothing in common except their reference to the text of the foregoing chapter.

We shall first consider a few examples of very peculiar or unusual methods of representation in dreams. A lady dreamed as follows: *A servant-girl is standing on a ladder as though to clean the windows, and has with her a chimpanzee and a gorilla cat* (later corrected, *angora cat*). *She throws the animals on to the dreamer; the chimpanzee nestles up to her, and this is very disgusting.* This dream has accomplished its purpose by a very simple means, namely, by taking a mere figure of speech literally, and representing it in accordance with the literal meaning of its words. "Monkey," like the names of animals in general, is an opprobrious epithet, and the situation of the dream means merely *"to hurl invectives."* This same collection will soon furnish us with further examples of the employment of this simple artifice in the dream-work.

Another dream proceeds in a very similar manner: *A woman with a child which has a conspicuously deformed cranium; the dreamer has heard that the child acquired this deformity owing to its position in its mother's womb. The doctor says that the cranium might be given a better shape by means of compression, but that this would injure the brain. She thinks that because it is a boy it won't suffer so much from deformity.* This dream contains a plastic representation of the abstract concept: "Childish impressions," with which the dreamer has become familiar in the course of the treatment.

In the following example the dream-work follows rather a different course. The dream contains a recollection of an excursion to the Hilmteich, near Graz: *There is a terrible storm outside; a miserable hotel—the water is dripping from the walls, and the beds are damp.* (The latter part of the content was less directly expressed than I give it.) The dream signifies *"superfluous."* The abstract idea occurring in the dream-thoughts is first made equivocal by a certain abuse of language; it has perhaps been replaced by "overflowing," or by "fluid" and "super-fluid (-fluous)," and has then been brought to representation by an accumulation of like impressions. Water within, water without, water in the beds in the form of dampness—everything fluid and "super" fluid. That for the purposes of dream-representation the spelling is much less considered than the sound of words ought not to surprise us when we remember that rhyme exercises a similar privilege.

The fact that language has at its disposal a great number of words which were originally used in a pictorial and concrete sense, but are at present used in a colourless and abstract fashion, has, in certain other cases, made it very easy for the dream to represent its thoughts. The dream has only to restore to these words their full significance, or to follow their change of meaning a little way back. For example, a man dreams that his friend, who is struggling to get out of a very tight place, calls upon him for help. The analysis shows that the tight place is a hole, and that the dreamer symbolically uses these very words to his friend: "Be careful, or you'll get yourself into a hole." [1] Another dreamer climbs a mountain from which he obtains an extraordinarily extensive view. He identifies himself with his brother, who is editing a "review" dealing with the Far East.

In a dream in *Der Grüne Heinrich* a spirited horse is plunging about in a field of the finest oats, every grain of which is really "a sweet almond, a raisin and a new penny" wrapped in red silk and tied with a bit of pig's bristle." The poet (or the dreamer) immediately furnishes the meaning of this dream, for the horse felt himself pleasantly tickled, so that he exclaimed: "The oats are pricking me" ("I feel my oats").

In the old Norse sagas (according to Henzen) prolific use is made in dreams of colloquialisms and witty expressions; one scarcely finds a dream without a double meaning or a play upon words.

It would be a special undertaking to collect such methods of representation and to arrange them in accordance with the principles upon which they are based. Some of the representations are almost witty. They give one the impression that one would have never guessed their meaning if the dreamer himself had not succeeded in explaining it.

1. A man dreams *that he is asked for a name, which, however, he cannot recall*. He himself explains that this means: "I shouldn't dream of it."

2. A female patient relates a dream in which *all the persons concerned were singularly large*. "That means," she adds, "that it must deal with an episode of my early childhood, for at that time all grown-up people naturally seemed to me immensely large." She herself did not appear in the dream.

The transposition into childhood is expressed differently in other dreams—by the translation of time into space. One sees persons and scenes as though at a great distance, at the end of a long road, or as though one were looking at them through the wrong end of a pair of opera-glasses.

3. A man who in waking life shows an inclination to employ abstract and indefinite expressions, but who otherwise has his wits about him, dreams, in a certain connection, *that he reaches a railway station just as a train is coming in. But then the platform moves towards the train, which stands still;* an absurd inversion of the real state of affairs. This detail, again, is nothing more than an indication to the effect that something else

[1] [Given by translator, as the author's example could not be translated.]

in the dream must be inverted. The analysis of the same dream leads to recollections of picture-books in which men were represented standing on their heads and walking on their hands.

4. The same dreamer, on another occasion, relates a short dream which almost recalls the technique of a rebus. *His uncle gives him a kiss in an automobile.* He immediately adds the interpretation, which would never have occurred to me: it means *auto-erotism.* In the waking state this might have been said in jest.

5. At a New Year's Eve dinner the host, the patriarch of the family, ushered in the New Year with a speech. One of his sons-in-law, a lawyer, was not inclined to take the old man seriously, especially when in the course of his speech he expressed himself as follows: "When I open the ledger for the Old Year and glance at its pages I see everything on the asset side and nothing, thank the Lord, on the side of liability; all you children have been a great *asset,* none of you a *liability.*" On hearing this the young lawyer thought of X., his wife's brother, who was a cheat and a liar, and whom he had recently extricated from the entanglements of the law. That night, in a dream, he saw the New Year's celebration once more, and heard the speech, or rather saw it. Instead of speaking, the old man actually opened the ledger, and on the side marked "assets" he saw his name amongst others, but on the other side, marked "liability," there was the name of his brother-in-law, X. However, the word "Liability" was changed into "Lie-Ability," which he regarded as X.'s main characteristic.[1]

6. A dreamer *treats another person for a broken bone.* The analysis shows that the fracture represents a *broken marriage vow, etc.*

7. In the dream-content the time of day often represents a certain period of the dreamer's childhood. Thus, for example, 5.15 a.m. means to one dreamer the age of five years and three months; when he was that age, a younger brother was born.

8. Another representation of *age* in a dream: *A woman is walking with two little girls; there is a difference of fifteen months in their ages.* The dreamer cannot think of any family of her acquaintance in which this is the case. She herself interprets it to mean that the two children represent her own person, and that the dream reminds her that the two traumatic events of her childhood were separated by this period of time ($3\frac{1}{2}$ and $4\frac{3}{4}$ years).

9. It is not astonishing that persons who are undergoing psychoanalytic treatment frequently dream of it, and are compelled to give expression in their dreams to all the thoughts and expectations aroused by it. The image chosen for the treatment is as a rule that of a journey, usually in a motor-car, this being a modern and complicated vehicle; in the reference to the speed of the car the patient's ironical humour is given free play. If the

[1] Reported by Brill in his *Fundamental Conceptions of Psychoanalysis.*

"unconscious," as an element of waking thought, is to be represented in the dream, it is replaced, appropriately enough, by *subterranean* localities, which at other times, when there is no reference to analytic treatment, have represented the female body or the womb. *Below* in the dream very often refers to the genitals, and its opposite, *above,* to the face, mouth or breast. By *wild beasts* the dream-work usually symbolizes passionate impulses; those of the dreamer, and also those of other persons of whom the dreamer is afraid; or thus, by means of a very slight displacement, the persons who experience these passions. From this it is not very far to the totemistic representation of the dreaded *father* by means of vicious animals, dogs, wild horses, etc. One might say that wild beasts serve to represent the *libido,* feared by the ego, and combated by repression. Even the neurosis itself, the *sick person,* is often separated from the dreamer and exhibited in the dream as an independent person.

One may go so far as to say that the dream-work makes use of all the means accessible to it for the visual representation of the dream-thoughts, whether these appear admissible or inadmissible to waking criticism, and thus exposes itself to the doubt as well as the derision of all those who have only hearsay knowledge of dream-interpretation, but have never themselves practised it. Stekel's book, *Die Sprache des Traumes,* is especially rich in such examples, but I avoid citing illustrations from this work as the author's lack of critical judgment and his arbitrary technique would make even the unprejudiced observer feel doubtful.

10. From an essay by V. Tausk (*Kleider und Farben im Dienste der Traumdarstellung,* in *Interna. Zeitschr. für Ps.A.,* ii, 1914):—

(*a*) A. dreams that *he sees his former governess wearing a dress of black lustre, which fits closely over her buttocks.*—That means he declares this woman to be *lustful.*

(*b*) C. in a dream *sees a girl on the road to X, bathed in a white light and wearing a white blouse.*

The dreamer began an affair with a Miss White on this road.

11. In an analysis which I carried out in the French language I had to interpret a dream in which I appeared as an elephant. I naturally had to ask why I was thus represented. *"Vous me trompez,"* answered the dreamer (*Trompe* = trunk).

The dream-work often succeeds in representing very refractory material, such as proper names, by means of the forced exploitation of very remote relations. In one of my dreams *old Brücke has set me a task. I make a preparation, and pick something out of it which looks like crumpled tinfoil.* (I shall return to this dream later.) The corresponding association, which is not easy to find, is *stanniol,* and now I know that I have in mind the name of the author *Stannius,* which appeared on the title-page of a treatise on the nervous system of fishes, which in my youth I regarded with reverence. The first scientific problem which my teacher set me did actually relate to the nervous system of a fish—the *Ammocoetes*. Obviously, this name could not be utilized in the picture-puzzle.

Here I must not fail to include a dream with a curious content, which is worth noting also as the dream of a child, and which is readily explained by analysis. A lady tells me: "I can remember that when I was a child I repeatedly dreamed that *God wore a conical paper hat on His head*. They often used to make me wear such a hat at table, so that I shouldn't be able to look at the plates of the other children and see how much they had received of any particular dish. Since I had heard that God was omniscient, the dream signified that I knew everything in spite of the hat which I was made to wear."

What the dream-work consists in, and its unceremonious handling of its material, the dream-thoughts, may be shown in an instructive manner by the numbers and calculations which occur in dreams. Superstition, by the way, regards numbers as having a special significance in dreams. I shall therefore give a few examples of this kind from my collection.

1. From the dream of a lady, shortly before the end of her treatment:—

She wants to pay for something or other; her daughter takes 3 florins 65 kreuzer from her purse; but the mother says: "What are you doing? It costs only 21 kreuzer." This fragment of the dream was intelligible without further explanation owing to my knowledge of the dreamer's circumstances. The lady was a foreigner, who had placed her daughter at school in Vienna, and was able to continue my treatment as long as her daughter remained in the city. In three weeks the daughter's scholastic year would end, and the treatment would then stop. On the day before the dream the principal of the school had asked her whether she could not decide to leave the child at school for another year. She had then obviously reflected that in this case she would be able to continue the treatment for another year. Now, this is what the dream refers to, for a year is equal to *365* days; the three weeks remaining before the end of the scholastic year, and of the treatment, are equivalent to *21* days (though not to so many hours of treatment). The numerals, which in the dream-thoughts refer to periods of time, are given money values in the dream, and simultaneously a deeper meaning finds expression—for *"time is money."* *365* kreuzer, of course, are *3 florins 65 kreuzer*. The smallness of the sums which appear in the dream is a self-evident wish-fulfilment; the wish has reduced both the cost of the treatment and the year's school fees.

2. In another dream the numerals are involved in even more complex relations. A young lady, who has been married for some years, learns that an acquaintance of hers, of about the same age, Elise L., has just become

engaged. Thereupon she dreams: *She is sitting in the theatre with her husband, and one side of the stalls is quite empty. Her husband tells her that Elise L. and her fiancé had also wished to come to the theatre, but that they only could have obtained poor seats; three for 1 florin 50 kreuzer, and of course they could not take those. She thinks they didn't lose much, either.*

What is the origin of the *1 florin 50 kreuzer*? A really indifferent incident of the previous day. The dreamer's sister-in-law had received *150* florins as a present from her husband, and hastened to get rid of them by buying some jewellery. Let us note that 150 florins is *100 times* 1 florin 50 kreuzer. But whence the *3* in connection with the seats in the theatre? There is only one association for this, namely, that the fiancé is three months younger than herself. When we have ascertained the significance of the fact that one side of the stalls is empty we have the solution of the dream. This feature is an undisguised allusion to a little incident which had given her husband a good excuse for teasing her. She had decided to go to the theatre that week; she had been careful to obtain tickets a few days beforehand, and had had to pay the advance booking-fee. When they got to the theatre they found that one side of the house was almost empty; so that she certainly *need not have been in such a hurry*.

I shall now substitute the dream-thoughts for the dream: "It surely was nonsense to marry so early; there was *no need for* my being in such a hurry. From Elise L.'s example I see that I should have got a husband just the same—and one a *hundred times* better—if I had only waited (antithesis to the *haste* of her sister-in-law), I could have bought *three* such men for the money (the dowry)!"—Our attention is drawn to the fact that the numerals in this dream have changed their meanings and their relations to a much greater extent than in the one previously considered. The transforming and distorting activity of the dream has in this case been greater—a fact which we interpret as meaning that these dream-thoughts had to overcome an unusual degree of endo-psychic resistance before they attained to representation. And we must not overlook the fact that the dream contains an absurd element, namely, that *two* persons are expected to take *three seats*. It will throw some light on the question of the interpretation of absurdity in dreams if I remark that this absurd detail of the dream-content is intended to represent the most strongly emphasized of the dream-thoughts: "It was *nonsense* to marry so early." The figure *3*, which occurs in a quite subordinate relation between the two persons compared (three months' difference in their ages), has thus been adroitly utilized to produce the idea of nonsense required by the dream. The reduction of the actual 150 florins to 1 florin 50 kreuzer corresponds to the dreamer's disparagement of her husband in her suppressed thoughts.

3. Another example displays the arithmetical powers of dreams, which have brought them into such disrepute. A man dreams: *He is sitting in the B.'s house* (the B.'s are a family with which he was formerly acquainted), *and he says: "It was nonsense that you didn't give me Amy for my wife." Thereupon, he asks the girl: "How old are you?" Answer: I was born in 1882." "Ah, then you are 28 years old."*

Since the dream was dreamed in the year 1898, this is obviously bad arithmetic, and the inability of the dreamer to calculate may, if it cannot be otherwise explained, be likened to that of a general paralytic. My patient was one of those men who cannot help thinking about every woman they see. The patient who for some months came next after him in my consulting-room was a young lady; he met this lady after he had constantly asked about her, and he was very anxious to make a good impression on her. This was the lady whose age he estimated at *28.* So much for explaining the result of his apparent calculation. But *1882* was the year in which he had married. He had been unable to refrain from entering into conversation with the two other women whom he met at my house—the two by no means youthful maids who alternately opened the door to him—and as he did not find them very responsive, he had told himself that they probably regarded him as elderly and "serious."

Bearing in mind these examples, and others of a similar nature (to follow), we may say: The dream-work does not calculate at all, whether correctly or incorrectly; it only strings together, in the *form* of a sum, numerals which occur in the dream-thoughts, and which may serve as allusions to material which is insusceptible of representation. It thus deals with figures, as material for expressing its intentions, just as it deals with all other concepts, and with names and speeches which are only verbal images.

For the dream-work cannot compose a new speech. No matter how many speeches and answers, which may in themselves be sensible or absurd, may occur in dreams, analysis always shows us that the dream has merely taken from the dream-thoughts fragments of speeches which have really been delivered or heard, and has dealt with them in the most arbitrary fashion. It has not only torn them from their context and mutilated them, accepting one fragment and rejecting another, but it has often fitted them together in a novel manner, so that the speech which seems coherent in a dream is dissolved by analysis into three or four components. In this new application of the words the dream has often ignored the meaning which they had in the dream-thoughts, and has drawn an entirely new meaning from them.[1] Upon closer inspection the more distinct

[1] Analyses of other numerical dreams have been given by Jung, Marcinowski and others. Such dreams often involve very complicated arithmetical operations, which are none the less solved by the dreamer with astonishing confidence. Cf. also Ernest

and compact ingredients of the dream-speech may be distinguished from others, which serve as connectives, and have probably been supplied, just as we supply omitted letters and syllables in reading. The dream-speech thus has the structure of *breccia*, in which the larger pieces of various material are held together by a solidified cohesive medium.

Strictly speaking, of course, this description is correct only for those dream-speeches which have something of the sensory character of a speech, and are described as "speeches." The others, which have not, as it were, been perceived as heard or spoken (which have no accompanying acoustic or motor emphasis in the dream) are simply thoughts, such as occur in our waking life, and find their way unchanged into many of our dreams. Our reading, too, seems to provide an abundant and not easily traceable source for the indifferent speech-material of dreams. But anything that is at all conspicuous as a speech in a dream can be referred to actual speeches which have been made or heard by the dreamer.

We have already found examples of the derivation of such dream-speeches in the analyses of dreams which have been cited for other purposes. Thus, in the "innocent market-dream" (p. 251) where the speech: *That is no longer to be had* serves to identify me with the butcher, while a fragment of the other speech: *I don't· know that, I don't take that,* precisely fulfils the task of rendering the dream innocent. On the previous day the dreamer, replying to some unreasonable demand on the part of her cook, had waved her aside with the words: *I don't know that, behave yourself properly,* and she afterwards took into the dream the first, indifferent-sounding part of the speech in order to allude to the latter part, which fitted well into the phantasy underlying the dream, but which might also have betrayed it.

Here is one of many examples which all lead to the same conclusion:—

A large courtyard in which dead bodies are being burned. The dreamer says, "I'm going, I can't stand the sight of it." (Not a distinct speech.) Then he meets two butcher boys and asks, "Well, did it taste good?" And one of them answers, "No, it wasn't good." As though it had been human flesh.

The innocent occasion of this dream is as follows: After taking supper with his wife, the dreamer pays a visit to his worthy but by no means

---

Jones, *Über unbewusste Zahlenbehandlung Zentralb. für Psychoanalyse,* 4, ii, 1912, p. 241).

Neurosis behaves in the same fashion. I know a patient who—involuntarily and unwillingly—hears (hallucinates) songs or fragments of songs without being able to understand their significance for her psychic life. She is certainly not a paranoiac. Analysis shows that by exercising a certain license she gave the text of these songs a false application. "Oh, thou blissful one! Oh, thou happy one!" This is the first line of Christmas carol, but by not continuing it to the word, Christmastide, she turns it into a bridal song, etc. The same mechanism of distortion may operate, without hallucination, merely in association.

appetizing neighbour. The hospitable old lady is just sitting down to her own supper, and *presses* him (among men a composite, sexually significant word is used jocosely in the place of this word) to taste it. He declines, saying that he has no appetite. She replies: *"Go on with you, you can manage it all right,"* or something of the kind. The dreamer is thus forced to taste and praise what is offered him. "But that's good!" When he is alone again with his wife, he complains of his neighbour's importunity, and of the quality of the food which he has tasted. "I can't stand the sight of it," a phrase that in the dream, too, does not emerge as an actual speech, is a thought relating to the physical charms of the lady who invites him, which may be translated by the statement that he has no desire to look at her.

The analysis of another dream—which I will cite at this stage for the sake of a very distinct speech, which constitutes its nucleus, but which will be explained only when we come to evaluate the affects in dreams—is more instructive. I dream very vividly: *I have gone to Brücke's laboratory at night, and on hearing a gentle knocking at the door, I open it to (the deceased) Professor Fleischl, who enters in the company of several strangers, and after saying a few words sits down at his table.* Then follows a second dream: *My friend Fl. has come to Vienna, unobtrusively, in July; I meet him in the street, in conversation with my (deceased) friend P., and I go with them somewhere, and they sit down facing each other as though at a small table, while I sit facing them at the narrow end of the table. Fl. speaks of his sister, and says: "In three-quarters of an hour she was dead,"* and then something like *"That is the threshold."* As *P. does not understand him, Fl. turns to me, and asks me how much I have told P. of his affairs. At this, overcome by strange emotions, I try to tell Fl. that P. (cannot possibly know anything, of course, because he) is not alive. But noticing the mistake myself, I say:* "Non vixit." *Then I look searchingly at P., and under my gaze he becomes pale and blurred, and his eyes turn a sickly blue—and at last he dissolves. I rejoice greatly at this; I now understand that Ernst Fleischl, too, is only an apparition, a revenant, and I find that it is quite possible that such a person should exist only so long as one wishes him to, and that he can be made to disappear by the wish of another person.*

This very pretty dream unites so many of the enigmatical characteristics of the dream-content—the criticism made in the dream itself, inasmuch as I myself notice my mistake in saying *Non vixit* instead of *Non vivit*, the unconstrained intercourse with deceased persons, whom the dream itself declares to be dead, the absurdity of my conclusion, and the intense satisfaction which it gives me—that "I would give my life" to expound the complete solution of the problem. But in reality I am incapable of doing what I do in the dream, i.e. of sacrificing such intimate friends to my ambition. And if I attempted to disguise the facts, the true meaning of the dream, with which I am perfectly familiar, would be spoiled. I must therefore be content to select a few of the elements of the dream for interpretation, some here, and some at a later stage.

The scene in which I annihilate P. with a glance forms the centre of the dream. His eyes become strange and weirdly blue, and then he dissolves. This scene is an unmistakable imitation of a scene that was actually experienced. I was a demonstrator at the Physiological Institute; I was on duty in the morning, and Brücke learned that on several occasions I had been unpunctual in my attendance at the students' laboratory. One morning, therefore, he arrived at the hour of opening, and waited for me. What he said to me was brief and to the point; but it was not what he said that mattered. What overwhelmed me was the terrible gaze of his blue eyes, before which I melted away—as P. does in the dream, for P. has exchanged rôles with me, much to my relief. Anyone who remembers the eyes of the great master, which were wonderfully beautiful even in his old age, and has ever seen him angered, will readily imagine the emotions of the young transgressor on that occasion.

But for a long while I was unable to account for the *Non vixit* with which I pass sentence in the dream. Finally, I remembered that the reason why these two words were so distinct in the dream was not because they were heard or spoken, but because they were *seen*. Then I knew at once where they came from. On the pedestal of the statue of the Emperor Joseph in the Vienna Hofburg are inscribed the following beautiful words:—

> *Saluti patriae v i x i t*
> *n o n diu sed totus.*[1]

From this inscription I had taken what fitted one inimical train of thought in my dream-thoughts, and which was intended to mean: "That fellow has nothing to say in the matter, he is not really alive." And I now recalled that the dream was dreamed a few days after the unveiling of the memorial to Fleischl, in the cloisters of the University, upon which occasion I had once more seen the memorial to Brücke, and must have thought with regret (in the unconscious) how my gifted friend P., with all his devotion to science, had by his premature death forfeited his just claim

---

[1] The inscription in fact reads:—

> *Saluti p u b l i c a e vixit*
> *non diu sed totus.*

The motive of the mistake: *patriae* for *publicae*, has probably been correctly divined by Wittels.

to a memorial in these halls. So I set up this memorial to him in the dream; Josef is my friend P.'s baptismal name.[1]

According to the rules of dream-interpretation, I should still not be justified in replacing *non vivit*, which I need, by *non vixit*, which is placed at my disposal by the recollection of the Kaiser Josef memorial. Some other element of the dream-thoughts must have contributed to make this possible. Something now calls my attention to the fact that in the dream scene two trains of thought relating to my friend P. meet, one hostile, the other affectionate—the former on the surface, the latter covered up—and both are given representation in the same words: *non vixit*. As my friend P. has deserved well of science, I erect a memorial to him; as he has been guilty of a malicious wish (expressed at the end of the dream), I annihilate him. I have here constructed a sentence with a special cadence, and in doing so I must have been influenced by some existing model. But where can I find a similar antithesis, a similar parallel between two opposite reactions to the same person, both of which can claim to be wholly justified, and which nevertheless do not attempt to affect one another? Only in one passage which, however, makes a profound impression upon the reader—Brutus's speech of justification in Shakespeare's *Julius Caesar:* "As Caesar loved me, I weep for him; as he was fortunate, I rejoice at it; as he was valiant, I honour him; but as he was ambitious, I slew him." Have we not here the same verbal structure, and the same antithesis of thought, as in the dream-thoughts? So I am playing Brutus in my dream. If only I could find in my dream-thoughts another collateral connection to confirm this! I think it might be the following: "My friend Fl. comes to Vienna in July." This detail is not the case in reality. To my knowledge, my friend has never been in Vienna in July. But the month of *July* is named after *Julius Caesar*, and might therefore very well furnish the required allusion to the intermediate thought—that I am playing the part of Brutus.[2]

Strangely enough, I once did actually play the part of Brutus. When I was a boy of fourteen, I presented the scene between Brutus and Caesar in Schiller's poem to an audience of children: with the assistance of my nephew, who was a year older than I, and who had come to us from England—and was thus a *revenant*—for in him I recognized the playmate of my early childhood. Until the end of my third year we had been inseparable; we had loved each other and fought each other and, as I have already hinted, this childish relation has determined all my later feelings in my intercourse with persons of my own age. My nephew John

---

[1] As an example of over-determination: My excuse for coming late was that after working late into the night, in the morning I had to make the long journey from Kaiser-Josef-Strasse to Währinger Strasse.

[2] And also, *Caesar = Kaiser*.

has since then had many incarnations, which have revivified first one and then another aspect of a character that is ineradicably fixed in my unconscious memory. At times he must have treated me very badly, and I must have opposed my tyrant courageously, for in later years I was often told of a short speech in which I defended myself when my father—his grandfather—called me to account: "Why did you hit John?" "*I hit him because he hit me.*" It must be this childish scene which causes *non vivit* to become *non vixit*, for in the language of later childhood striking is known as *wichsen* (German: *wichsen* = to polish, to wax, i.e. to thrash); and the dream-work does not disdain to take advantage of such associations. My hostility towards my friend P., which has so little foundation in reality—he was greatly my superior, and might therefore have been a new edition of my old playmate—may certainly be traced to my complicated relations with John during our childhood. I shall, as I have said, return to this dream later on.

G. ABSURD DREAMS—INTELLECTUAL PERFORMANCES IN DREAMS

I

Hitherto, in our interpretation of dreams, we have come upon the element of *absurdity* in the dream-content so frequently that we must no longer postpone the investigation of its cause and its meaning. We remember, of course, that the absurdity of dreams has furnished the opponents of dream-interpretation with their chief argument for regarding the dream as merely the meaningless product of an attenuated and fragmentary activity of the psyche.

I will begin with a few examples in which the absurdity of the dream-content is apparent only, disappearing when the dream is more thoroughly examined. These are certain dreams which—accidentally, one begins by thinking—are concerned with the dreamer's dead father.

1. Here is the dream of a patient who had lost his father six years before the date of the dream:—

His father had been involved in a terrible accident. He was travelling by the night express when the train was derailed, the seats were telescoped, and his head was crushed from side to side. The dreamer sees him lying on his bed; from his left eyebrow a wound runs vertically upwards. The dreamer is surprised that his father should have met with an accident (since he is dead already, as the dreamer adds in relating his dream). His father's eyes are so clear.

According to the prevailing standards of dream-criticism, this dream-content would be explained as follows: At first, while the dreamer is picturing his father's accident, he has forgotten that his father has already been many years in his grave; in the course of the dream this *memory* awakens, so that he is surprised at his own dream even while he is dreaming it. Analysis, however, tells us that it is quite superfluous to seek for such explanations. The dreamer had commissioned a sculptor to make a *bust* of his father, and he had inspected the bust two days before the dream. It is this which seems to him to have come to grief (the German word means "gone wrong" or "met with an accident"). The sculptor has never seen his father, and has had to work from photographs. On the very day before the dream the son had sent an old family servant to the studio in order to see whether he, too, would pass the same judgment upon the marble bust—namely, that it was *too narrow between the temples*. And now follows the memory-material which has contributed to the formation of the dream: The dreamer's father had a habit, whenever he was harassed by business cares or domestic difficulties, of pressing his temples between his hands, as though his head was growing too large and he was trying to compress it. When the dreamer was four years old, he was present when a pistol was accidentally discharged, and his father's eyes were blackened (*his eyes are so clear*). When his father was thoughtful or depressed, he had a deep furrow in his forehead just where the dream shows his wound. The fact that in the dream this wrinkle is replaced by a wound points to the second occasion for the dream. The dreamer had taken a photograph of his little daughter; the plate had fallen from his hand, and when he picked it up it revealed a crack which ran like a vertical furrow across the child's forehead, extending as far as the eyebrow. He could not help feeling a superstitious foreboding, for on the day before his mother's death the negative of her portrait had been cracked.

Thus, the absurdity of this dream is simply the result of a carelessness of verbal expression, which does not distinguish between the bust or the photograph and the original. We are all accustomed to making remarks like: "Don't you think it's exactly your father?" The appearance of absurdity in this dream might, of course, have been easily avoided. If it were permissible to form an opinion on the strength of a single case, one might be tempted to say that this semblance of absurdity is admitted or even desired.

II

Here is another example of the same kind from my own dreams (I lost my father in the year 1896):—

After his death my father has played a part in the political life of the Magyars, and has united them into a political whole; and here I see, indistinctly, a little picture: *a number of men, as though in the Reichstag; a man is standing on one or two chairs; there are others round about him. I remember that on his death-bed he looked so like Garibaldi, and I am glad that this promise has really come true.*

Certainly this is absurd enough. It was dreamed at the time when the Hungarians were in a state of anarchy, owing to Parliamentary *obstruction*, and were passing through the crisis from which Koloman *Széll* subsequently delivered them. The trivial circumstance that the scenes beheld in dreams consist of such little pictures is not without significance for the elucidation of this element. The customary visual dream-representations of our thoughts present images that impress us as being life-size; my dream-picture, however, is the reproduction of a wood-cut inserted in the text of an illustrated history of Austria, representing Maria Theresa in the Reichstag of Pressburg—the famous scene of *Moriamur pro rege nostro*.[1] Like Maria Theresa, my father, in my dream, is surrounded by the multitude; but he is standing on one or two chairs (*Stühlen*), and is thus, like a *Stuhlrichter* (presiding judge). (He has *united* them; here the intermediary is the phrase: "We shall need no *judge*.") Those of us who stood about my father's death-bed did actually notice that he looked very like Garibaldi. He had a *post-mortem* rise of temperature; his cheeks shone redder and redder . . . involuntarily we continue: "And behind him, in unsubstantial (radiance), lay that which subdues us all—the common fate."

This uplifting of our thoughts prepares us for the fact that we shall have to deal with this "common fate." The *post-mortem* rise in temperature corresponds to the words "after his death" in the dream-content. The most agonizing of his afflictions had been a complete paralysis of the intestines (*obstruction*) during the last few weeks of his life. All sorts of disrespectful thoughts associate themselves with this. One of my contemporaries, who lost his father while still at the "gymnasium"—upon which occasion I was profoundly moved, and tendered him my friendship—once told me, derisively, of the distress of a relative whose father had died in the street, and had been brought home, when it appeared, upon undressing the corpse, that at the moment of death, or *post-mortem*, an evacuation of the bowels (*Stuhlentleerung*) had taken place. The daughter was deeply distressed by this circumstance, because this ugly detail would inevitably spoil her memory of her father. We have now penetrated to the wish that is embodied in this dream. To stand after one's death before one's children great and undefiled: who would not wish that? What now has become of the absurdity of this dream? The appearance of absurdity was due only to the fact that a perfectly permissible figure of speech, in which we are accustomed to ignore any absurdity that may exist as between its components, has been faithfully represented in the

---

[1] I have forgotten in what author I found a reference to a dream which was overrun with unusually small figures, the source of which proved to be one of the engravings of Jacques Callot, which the dreamer had examined during the day. These engravings contain an enormous number of very small figures; a whole series of them deals with the horrors of the Thirty Years War.

dream. Here again we can hardly deny that the appearance of absurdity is desired and has been purposely produced.

The frequency with which dead persons appear in our dreams as living and active and associating with us has evoked undue astonishment, and some curious explanations, which afford conspicuous proof of our misunderstanding of dreams. And yet the explanation of these dreams is close at hand. How often it happens that we say to ourselves: "If my father were still alive, what would he say to this?" The dream can express this *if* in no other way than by his presence in a definite situation. Thus, for instance, a young man whose grandfather has left him a great inheritance dreams that the old man is alive, and calls his grandson to account, reproaching him for his lavish expenditure. What we regard as an objection to the dream on account of our better knowledge that the man is already dead, is in reality the consoling thought that the dead man does not need to learn the truth, or satisfaction over the fact that he can no longer have a say in the matter.

Another form of absurdity found in dreams of deceased relatives does not express scorn and derision; it serves to express the extremest repudiation, the representation of a suppressed thought which one would like to believe the very last thing one would think of. Dreams of this kind appear to be capable of solution only if we remember that a dream makes no distinction between desire and reality. For example, a man who nursed his father during his last illness, and who felt his death very keenly, dreamed some time afterwards the following senseless dream: *His father was again living, and conversing with him as usual, but* (and this was the remarkable thing) *he had nevertheless died, though he did not know it.* This dream is intelligible if, after "he had nevertheless died," we insert *in consequence of the dreamer's wish,* and if after "but he did not know it," we add *that the dreamer had entertained this wish.* While nursing him, the son had often wished that his father was dead; that is, he had had the really compassionate thought that it would be a good thing if death would at last put an end to his sufferings. While he was mourning his father's death, even this compassionate wish became an unconscious reproach, as though it had really contributed to shorten the sick man's life. By the awakening of the earliest infantile feelings against his father, it became possible to express this reproach as a dream; and it was precisely because of the extreme antithesis between the dream-instigator and the day-thoughts that this dream had to assume so absurd a form.[1]

As a general thing, the dreams of a deceased person of whom the dreamer has been fond confront the interpreter with difficult problems, the solution of which is not always satisfying. The reason for this may be

---

[1] Cf. *Formulierungen über die zwei Prinzipien des seelischen Geschehens,* in *Jahrbuch f. Ps.A.,* iii, 1, 1911 (*Ges. Schriften,* Bd. v).

sought in the especially pronounced ambivalence of feeling which controls the relation of the dreamer to the dead person. In such dreams it is
quite usual for the deceased person to be treated at first as living; then it
suddenly appears that he is dead; and in the continuation of the dream
he is once more living. This has a confusing effect. I at last divined that
this alternation of death and life is intended to represent the *indifference*
of the dreamer ("It is all one to me whether he is alive or dead"). This
indifference, of course, is not real, but wished; its purpose is to help the
dreamer to deny his very intense and often contradictory emotional attitudes, and so it becomes the dream-representation of his *ambivalence*.
For other dreams in which one meets with deceased persons the following
rule will often be a guide: If in the dream the dreamer is not reminded
that the dead person is dead, he sets himself on a par with the dead; he
dreams of his own death. The sudden realization or astonishment in the
dream ("but he has long been dead!") is a protest against this identification, and rejects the meaning that the dreamer is dead. But I will admit
that I feel that dream-interpretation is far from having elicited all the
secrets of dreams having this content.

III

In the example which I shall now cite, I can detect the dream-work in the
act of purposely manufacturing an absurdity for which there is no occasion whatever in the dream-material. It is taken from the dream which I
had as a result of meeting Count Thun just before going away on a holiday. "*I am driving in a cab, and I tell the driver to drive to a railway
station. 'Of course, I can't drive with you on the railway track itself,' I
say, after the driver has reproached me, as though I had worn him out;
at the same time, it seems as though I had already made with him a journey that one usually makes by train.*" Of this confused and senseless
story analysis gives the following explanation: During the day I had
hired a cab to take me to a remote street in Dornbach. The driver, however, did not know the way, and simply kept on driving, in the manner of
such worthy people, until I became aware of the fact and showed him the
way, indulging in a few derisive remarks. From this driver a train of
thought led to the aristocratic personage whom I was to meet later on.
For the present, I will only remark that one thing that strikes us middle-
class plebeians about the aristocracy is that they like to put themselves
in the driver's seat. Does not Count Thun guide the Austrian "car of
State"? The next sentence in the dream, however, refers to my brother,
whom I thus also identify with the cab-driver. I had refused to go to Italy
with him this year ("Of course, I can't drive with you on the railway
track itself"), and this refusal was a sort of punishment for his accustomed complaint that I usually *wear him out* on this tour (this finds its

way into the dream unchanged) by rushing him too quickly from place to place, and making him see too many beautiful things in a single day. That evening my brother had accompanied me to the railway station, but shortly before the carriage had reached the Western station of the Metropolitan Railway he had jumped out in order to take the train to Purkersdorf. I suggested to him that he might remain with me a little longer, as he did not travel to Purkersdorf by the Metropolitan but by the Western Railway. This is why, in my dream, I made in the cab a journey which one usually makes by train. In reality, however, it was the other way about: what I told my brother was: "The distance which you travel on the Metropolitan Railway you could travel in my company on the Western Railway." The whole confusion of the dream is therefore due to the fact that in my dream I replace "Metropolitan Railway" by "cab," which, to be sure, does good service in bringing the driver and my brother into conjunction. I then elicit from the dream some nonsense which is hardly disentangled by elucidation, and which almost constitutes a contradiction of my earlier speech ("Of course, I cannot drive with you on the railway track itself"). But as I have no excuse whatever for confronting the Metropolitan Railway with the cab, I must intentionally have given the whole enigmatical story this peculiar form in my dream.

But with what intention? We shall now learn what the absurdity in the dream signifies, and the motives which admitted it or created it. In this case the solution of the mystery is as follows: In the dream I need an absurdity, and something incomprehensible, in connection with "driving" (*Fahren* = riding, driving) because in the dream-thoughts I have a certain opinion that demands representation. One evening, at the house of the witty and hospitable lady who appears, in another scene of the same dream, as the "housekeeper," I heard two riddles which I could not solve. As they were known to the other members of the party, I presented a somewhat ludicrous figure in my unsuccessful attempts to find the solutions. They were two puns turning on the words *Nachkommen* (to obey orders—offspring) and *Vorfahren* (to drive—forefathers, ancestry). They ran, I believe, as follows:—

> "The coachman does it
>   At the master's behests;
> Everyone has it;
>   In the grave it rests."
>
> (*Vorfahren*)

A confusing detail was that the first halves of the two riddles were identical:

> "The coachman does it
>   At the master's behests;

Not everyone has it,
In the cradle it rests."

(*Nachkommen*)

When I saw Count Thun drive up (*vorfahren*) in state, and fell into the
Figaro-like mood, in which one finds that the sole merit of such aristocratic gentlemen is that they have taken the trouble to be born (to become *Nachkommen*), these two riddles became intermediary thoughts
for the dream-work. As aristocrats may readily be replaced by coachmen,
and since it was once the custom to call a coachman "Herr Schwäger"
(brother-in-law), the work of condensation could involve my brother in
the same representation. But the dream-thought at work in the background is as follows: It is nonsense to be proud of one's ancestors (*Vorfahren*). I would rather be an ancestor (*Vorfahr*) myself. On account of
this opinion, "it is nonsense," we have the nonsense in the dream. And
now the last riddle in this obscure passage of the dream is solved—
namely that I have driven before (*vorher gefahren, vorgefahren*) with
this driver.

Thus, a dream is made absurd if there occurs in the dream-thoughts, as
one of the elements of the contents, the opinion: "That is nonsense";
and, in general, if criticism and derision are the motives of one of the
dreamer's unconscious trains of thought. Hence absurdity is one of the
means by which the dream-work represents contradiction; another means
is the inversion of material relation between the dream-thoughts and the
dream-content; another is the employment of the feeling of motor inhibition. But the absurdity of a dream is not to be translated by a simple
"no"; it is intended to reproduce the tendency of the dream-thoughts to
express laughter or derision simultaneously with the contradiction. Only
with this intention does the dream-work produce anything ridiculous.
Here again it transforms a part of the latent content into a manifest
form.[1]

As a matter of fact, we have already cited a convincing example of this
significance of an absurd dream. The dream (interpreted without analysis) of the Wagnerian performance which lasted until 7.45 a.m., and in
which the orchestra is conducted from a tower, etc. (see p. 363), is obviously saying: It is a crazy world and an insane society. He who deserves

---

[1] Here the dream-work parodies the thought which it qualifies as ridiculous, in
that it creates something ridiculous in relation to it. Heine does the same thing when
he wishes to deride the bad rhymes of the King of Bavaria. He does it by using even
worse rhymes:—

"Herr Ludwig ist ein grosser Poet
Und singt er, so stürzt Apollo
Vor ihm auf die Knie und bittet und fleht,
Halt ein, ich werde sonst toll, oh!"

a thing doesn't get it, and he who doesn't care for it does get it. In this way the dreamer compares her fate with that of her cousin. The fact that dreams of a dead father were the first to furnish us with examples of absurdity in dreams is by no means accidental. The conditions for the creation of absurd dreams are here grouped together in a typical fashion. The authority proper to the father has at an early age evoked the criticism of the child, and the strict demands which he has made have caused the child, in self-defence, to pay particularly close attention to every weakness of his father's; but the piety with which the father's personality is surrounded in our thoughts, especially after his death, intensifies the censorship which prevents the expression of this criticism from becoming conscious.

<h2 style="text-align:center">IV</h2>

Here is another absurd dream of a deceased father:—

I receive a communication from the town council of my native city concerning the cost of accommodation in the hospital in the year 1851. This was necessitated by a seizure from which I was suffering. I make fun of the matter for, in the first place, I was not yet born in 1851, and in the second place, my father, to whom the communication might refer, is already dead. I go to him in the adjoining room, where he is lying in bed, and tell him about it. To my surprise he remembers that in the year 1851 he was once drunk and had to be locked up or confined. It was when he was working for the firm of T. "Then you, too, used to drink?" I ask. "You married soon after?" I reckon that I was born in 1856, which seems to me to be immediately afterwards.

In the light of the foregoing exposition, we shall translate the insistence with which this dream exhibits its absurdities as a sure sign of a particularly embittered and passionate polemic in the dream-thoughts. All the greater, then, is our astonishment when we perceive that in this dream the polemic is waged openly, and that my father is denoted as the person who is made a laughing-stock. Such frankness seems to contradict our assumption of a censorship controlling the dream-work. The explanation is that here the father is only an interposed figure, while the quarrel is really with another person, who appears in the dream only in a single allusion. Whereas a dream usually treats of revolt against other persons, behind whom the father is concealed, here it is the other way about: the father serves as the man of straw to represent another, and hence the dream dares to concern itself openly with a person who is usually hallowed, because there is present the certain knowledge that he is not in reality intended. We learn of this condition of affairs by considering the occasion of the dream. It was dreamed after I had heard that an older colleague, whose judgment was considered infallible, had expressed disapproval and astonishment on hearing that one of my patients had already been undergoing psychoanalytic treatment at my hands for five years. The introductory sentences of the dream allude in a transparently disguised manner to the fact that this colleague had for a time taken over the duties which my father could no longer perform (statement of expenses, accommodation in the hospital); and when our friendly relations began to alter for the worse I was thrown into the same emotional conflict as that which arises in the case of a misunderstanding between father and son (by reason of the part played by the father, and his earlier functions). The dream-thoughts now bitterly resent the reproach that I am not making better progress, which extends itself from the treatment of this patient to other things. Does my colleague know anyone who can get on any faster? Does he not know that conditions of this sort are usually incurable and last for life? What are four or five years in comparison to a whole lifetime, especially when life has been made so much easier for the patient during the treatment?

The impression of absurdity in this dream is brought about largely by the fact that sentences from different divisions of the dream-thoughts are strung together without any reconciling transition. Thus, the sentence, *I go to him in the adjoining room,* etc., leaves the subject from which the preceding sentences are taken, and faithfully reproduces the circumstances under which I told my father that I was engaged to be married. Thus the dream is trying to remind me of the noble disinterestedness which the old man showed at that time, and to contrast this with the conduct of another newly-introduced person. I now perceive that the dream is allowed to make fun of my father because in the dream-thoughts, in the full recognition of his merits, he is held up as an example to others. It is in the nature of every censorship that one is permitted to tell untruths about forbidden things rather than the truth. The next sentence, to the effect that my father remembers that he was *once drunk,* and was *locked up* in consequence, contains nothing that really relates to my father any more. The person who is screened by him is here a no less important personage than the great Meynert, in whose footsteps I followed with such veneration, and whose attitude towards me, after a short period of favouritism, changed into one of undisguised hostility. The dream recalls to me his own statement that in his youth he had at one time formed the habit of *intoxicating himself with chloroform,* with the result that he had to *enter a sanatorium;* and also my second experience with him, shortly before his death. I had an embittered literary controversy with him in reference to masculine hysteria, the existence of which he denied, and when I visited him during his last illness, and asked him how he felt, he described his condition at some length, and concluded with the words: "You know, I have always been one of the prettiest cases of masculine hysteria." Thus, to my satisfaction, and to my astonishment, he admitted what he so long and so stubbornly denied. But the fact that in this scene of my dream I can use my father to screen Meynert is explained not by any discovered analogy between the two persons, but by the fact that it is the brief yet perfectly adequate representation of á conditional sentence in the dream-thoughts which, if fully expanded, would read as follows: "Of course, if I belonged to the second generation, if I were the son of a professor or a privy councillor, I should have progressed more rapidly." In my dream I make my father a professor and a privy councillor. The most obvious and most annoying absurdity of the dream lies in the treatment of the date 1851, which seems to me to be indistinguishable from 1856, *as though a difference of five years meant nothing whatever*. But it is just this one of the dream-thoughts that requires expression. Four or five years—that is precisely the length of time during which I enjoyed the support of the colleague mentioned at the outset; but it is also the duration of time I kept my fiancée waiting before I married her; and by a coincidence that is eagerly exploited by the dream-thoughts, it is also the time I have kept my oldest patient waiting for a complete cure. "What are five years?" ask the dream-thoughts. *"That is no time at all to me, that isn't worth consideration.* I have time enough ahead of me, and just as what you wouldn't believe came true at last, so I shall accomplish this also." Moreover, the number *51*, when considered apart from the number of the century, is determined in yet another manner and in an opposite sense; for which reason it occurs several times over in the dream. It is the age at which man seems particularly exposed to danger; the age at which I have seen colleagues die suddenly, among them one who had been appointed a few days earlier to a professorship for which he had long been waiting.

V

Another absurd dream which plays with figures:—

An acquaintance of mine, Herr M., has been attacked in an essay by no less a person than Goethe and, as we all think, with unjustifiable vehemence. Herr M. is, of course, crushed by this attack. He complains of it bitterly at a dinner-party; but his veneration for Goethe has not suffered as a result of this personal experience. I try to elucidate the temporal relations a little, as they seem improbable to me. Goethe died in 1832; since his attack upon M. must, of course, have taken place earlier, M. was at the time quite a young man. It seems plausible to me that he was 18 years old. But I do not know exactly what the date of the present year is, and so the whole calculation lapses into obscurity. The attack, by the way, is contained in Goethe's well-known essay on "Nature."

We shall soon find the means of justifying the nonsense of this dream.

Herr M., with whom I became acquainted *at a dinner-party*, had recently asked me to examine his brother, who showed signs of *general paralysis*. The conjecture was right; the painful thing about this visit was that the patient gave his brother away by alluding to his *youthful pranks*, though our conversation gave him no occasion to do so. I had asked the patient to tell me the year of his birth, and had repeatedly got him to make trifling calculations in order to show the weakness of his memory—which tests, by the way, he passed quite well. Now I can see that I behave like a paralytic in the dream (*I do not know exactly what the date of the present year is*). Other material of the dream is drawn from another recent source. The editor of a medical periodical, a friend of mine, had accepted for his paper a very unfavourable *"crushing"* review of the last book of my Berlin friend, Fl., the critic being a very *youthful reviewer*, who was not very competent to pass judgment. I thought I had a right to interfere, and called the editor to account; he greatly regretted his acceptance of the review, but he would not promise any redress. I thereupon broke off my relations with the periodical, and in my letter of resignation I expressed the hope that *our personal relations would not suffer* as a result of the incident. The third source of this dream is an account given by a female patient—it was fresh in my memory at the time—of the psychosis of her brother who had fallen into a frenzy crying *"Nature, Nature."* The physicians in attendance thought that the cry was derived from a reading of Goethe's beautiful *essay*, and that it pointed to the patients' overwork in the study of natural philosophy. I thought, rather, of the sexual meaning in which even our less cultured people use the word "Nature," and the fact that the unfortunate man afterwards mutilated his genitals seems to show that I was not far wrong. Eighteen years was the age of this patient at the time of this access of frenzy.

If I add, further, that the book of my so severely criticized friend ("One asks oneself whether the author or oneself is crazy" had been the opinion of another critic) treats of the *temporal conditions* of life, and refers the duration of Goethe's life to the multiple of a number significant from the biological point of view, it will readily be admitted that in my dream I am putting myself in my friend's place. (*I try to elucidate the temporal relations a little.*) But I behave like a paretic, and the dream revels in absurdity. This means that the dream-thoughts say, ironically: "Naturally, he is the fool, the lunatic, and you are the clever people who know better. Perhaps, however, it is the other way about?" Now, *"the other way about"* is abundantly represented in my dream, inasmuch as Goethe has attacked the young man, which is absurd, while it is perfectly possible even to-day for a young fellow to attack the immortal Goethe.

and inasmuch as I reckon from the *year of Goethe's death,* while I made the paretic reckon from the *year of his birth.*

But I have further promised to show that no dream is inspired by other than egoistical motives. Accordingly, I must account for the fact that in this dream I make my friend's cause my own, and put myself in his place. My critical conviction in waking life would not justify my doing so. Now, the story of the eighteen-year-old patient, and the divergent interpretations of his cry, *"Nature,"* allude to the fact that I have put myself into opposition to the majority of physicians by claiming a sexual etiology for the psychoneuroses. I may say to myself: "You will meet with the same kind of criticism as your friend; indeed you have already done so to some extent"; so that I may now replace the "he" in the dream-thoughts by "we." "Yes, you are right; we two are the fools." That *mea res agitur* is clearly shown by the mention of the short, incomparably beautiful essay of Goethe's, for it was a popular lecture on this essay which induced me to study the natural sciences when I left the gymnasium, and was still undecided as to my future.

VI

I have to show that yet another dream in which my ego does not appear is none the less egoistic. On p. 313 I referred to a short dream in which Professor M. says: "My son, the myopic . . ."; and I stated that this was only a preliminary dream, preceding another in which I play a part. Here is the main dream, previously omitted, which challenges us to explain its absurd and unintelligible word-formation.

On account of something or other that is happening in Rome it is necessary for the children to flee, and this they do. The scene is then laid before a gate, a double gate in the ancient style (the Porta Romana in Siena, as I realize while I am dreaming). I am sitting on the edge of a well, and I am greatly depressed; I am almost weeping. A woman—a nurse, a nun—brings out the two boys and hands them over to their father, who is not myself. The elder is distinctly my eldest son, but I do not see the face of the other boy. The woman asks the eldest boy for a parting kiss. She is remarkable for a red nose. The boy refuses her the kiss, but says to her, extending her his hand in parting, "Auf Geseres," and to both of us (or to one of us) "Auf Ungeseres." I have the idea that this indicates a preference.

This dream is built upon a tangle of thoughts induced by a play I saw at the theatre, called *Das neue Ghetto* ("The New Ghetto"). The Jewish question, anxiety as to the future of my children, who cannot be given a fatherland, anxiety as to educating them so that they may enjoy the privileges of citizens—all these features may easily be recognized in the accompanying dream-thoughts.

"By the waters of Babylon we sat down and wept." Siena, like Rome, is famous for its beautiful fountains. In the dream I have to find some sort of substitute for Rome (cf. p. 259) from among localities which are known to me. Near the Porta Romana of Siena we saw a large, brightly-lit building, which we learned was the *Manicomio,* the insane asylum. Shortly before the dream I had heard that a co-religionist had been forced to resign a position, which he had secured with great effort, in a State asylum.

Our interest is aroused by the speech: *"Auf Geseres,"* where one might expect, from the situation continued throughout the dream, *"Auf Wieder-sehen"* (*Au revoir*), and by its quite meaningless antithesis: *"Auf Un-geseres."* (*"Un"* is a prefix meaning "not.")

According to information received from Hebrew scholars, *Geseres* is a genuine Hebrew word, derived from the verb *goiser,* and may best be rendered by "ordained sufferings, fated disaster." From its employment in the Jewish jargon one would take it to mean "wailing and lamenta-tion." *Ungeseres* is a coinage of my own, and is the first to attract my attention, but for the present it baffles me. The little observation at the end of the dream—that *Ungeseres* indicates an advantage over *Geseres*—opens the way to the associations, and therewith to understanding. This relation holds good in the case of caviare; the *unsalted kind*[1] is more highly prized than the salted. "Caviare to the general"—"noble pas-sions." Herein lies concealed a jesting allusion to a member of my house-hold, of whom I hope—for she is younger than I—that she will watch over the future of my children; this, too, agrees with the fact that an-other member of my household, our worthy nurse, is clearly indicated by the nurse (or nun) of the dream. But a connecting-link is wanting be-tween the pair, *salted—unsalted* and *Geseres—Ungeseres.* This is to be found in *gesauert* and *ungesauert* (leavened and unleavened). In their flight or exodus from Egypt the children of Israel had not time to allow their dough to become leavened, and in commemoration of this event they eat unleavened bread at Passover to this day. Here, too, I can find room for the sudden association which occurred to me in this part of the analy-sis. I remembered how we, my friend from Berlin and myself, had strolled about the streets of Breslau, a city which was strange to us, during the last days of Easter. A little girl asked me the way to a certain street; I had to tell her that I did not know it; I then remarked to my friend, "I hope that later on in life the child will show more perspicacity in select-ing the persons whom she allows to direct her." Shortly afterwards a sign caught my eye: "Dr. *Herod,* consulting hours . . ." I said to myself:

---

[1] [Note the resemblance of *Geseres* and *Ungeseres* to the German words for salted and unsalted—*gesalzen* and *ungesalzen;* also to the words *gesauert* and *ungesauert,* leavened and unleavened.—TRANS.]

"I hope this colleague does not happen to be a children's specialist."
Meanwhile, my friend had been developing his views on the biological
significance of *bilateral symmetry,* and had begun a sentence with the
words: "If we had only one eye in the middle of the forehead, like
Cyclops . . ." This leads us to the speech of the professor in the preliminary dream: *"My son, the myopic."* And now I have been led to the
chief source for *Geseres.* Many years ago, when this son of Professor M.'s,
who is to-day an independent thinker, was still sitting on his school-
bench, he contracted an affection of the eye which, according to the doctor, gave some cause for anxiety. He expressed the opinion that so long
as it was confined *to one eye* it was of no great significance, but that if
it should extend to the other eye it would be serious. The affection subsided in the one eye without leaving any ill effects; shortly afterwards,
however, the same symptoms did actually appear in the other eye. The
boy's terrified mother immediately summoned the physician to her distant home in the country. But the doctor was now of a different opinion
(took *the other side). "What sort of 'Geseres' is this you are making?"*
he asked the mother, impatiently. *"If one side got well, the other will,
too."* And so it turned out.

And now as to the connection between this and myself and my family.
The *school-bench* upon which Professor M.'s son learned his first lessons
has become the property of my eldest son; it was given to him by the
boy's mother, and it is into his mouth that I put the words of farewell in
the dream. One of the wishes that may be connected with this transference may now be readily guessed. This school-bench is intended by its
construction to guard the child from becoming *shortsighted* and *one-
sided.* Hence *myopia* (and behind it the Cyclops), and the discussion
about *bilateralism.* The fear of one-sidedness has a twofold significance;
it might mean not only physical one-sidedness, but intellectual one-sidedness also. Does it not seem as though the scene in the dream, with all its
craziness, were contradicting precisely this anxiety? When *on the one
hand* the boy has spoken his words of farewell, *on the other hand* he calls
out the very opposite, as though to establish an equilibrium. He is acting, as it were, in obedience to bilateral symmetry!

Thus, a dream frequently has the profoundest meaning in the places
where it seems most absurd. In all ages those who have had something
to say and have been unable to say it without danger to themselves have
gladly donned the cap and bells. He for whom the forbidden saying was
intended was more likely to tolerate it if he was able to laugh at it, and
to flatter himself with the comment that what he disliked was obviously
absurd. Dreams behave in real life as does the prince in the play who is
obliged to pretend to be a madman, and hence we may say of dreams
what Hamlet said of himself, substituting an unintelligible jest for the

actual truth: "I am but mad north-north-west; when the wind is southerly I know a hawk from a handsaw" (Act II, sc. ii).[1]

Thus, my solution of the problem of absurdity in dreams is that the dream-thoughts are never absurd—at least, not those of the dreams of sane persons—and that the dream-work produces absurd dreams, and dreams with individually absurd elements, when the dream-thoughts contain criticism, ridicule, and derision, which have to be given expression. My next concern is to show that the dream-work is exhausted by the co-operation of the three factors enumerated—and of a fourth which has still to be mentioned—that it does no more than translate the dream-thoughts, observing the four conditions prescribed, and that the question whether the mind goes to work in dreams with all its intellectual faculties, or with only part of them, is wrongly stated, and does not meet the actual state of affairs. But since there are plenty of dreams in which judgments are passed, criticisms made, and facts recognized in which astonishment at some individual element of the dream appears, and explanations are attempted, and arguments adduced, I must meet the objections deriving from these occurrences by the citation of selected examples.

My answer is as follows: *Everything in dreams which occurs as the apparent functioning of the critical faculty is to be regarded, not as the intellectual performance of the dream-work, but as belonging to the substance of the dream-thoughts, and it has found its way from these, as a completed structure, into the manifest dream-content.* I may go even farther than this! I may even say that the judgments which are passed upon the dream as it is remembered *after waking,* and the feelings which are aroused by the reproduction of the dream, belong largely to the latent dream-content, and must be fitted into place in the interpretation of the dream.

1. One striking example of this has already been given. A female patient does not wish to relate her dream *because it was too vague.* She saw a person in the dream, and does not know *whether it was her husband or her father.* Then follows a second dream-fragment, in which there occurs a "manure-pail," with which the following reminiscence is associated. As a young housewife she once declared jestingly, in the presence of a young male relative who frequented the house, that her next business would be to procure a new manure-pail. Next morning one was sent to her, but it was filled with lilies of the valley. This part of the dream

---

[1] This dream furnishes a good example in support of the universally valid doctrine that dreams of the same night, even though they are separated in the memory, spring from the same thought-material. The dream-situation in which I am rescuing my children from the city of Rome, moreover, is distorted by a reference back to an episode of my childhood. The meaning is that I envy certain relatives who years ago had occasion to transplant their children to the soil of another country.

served to represent the phrase, "Not grown on my own manure." [1] If we complete the analysis, we find in the dream-thoughts the after-effect of a story heard in youth; namely, that a girl had given birth to a child, and that *it was not clear who was the father*. The dream-representation here overlaps into the waking thought, and allows one of the elements of the dream-thoughts to be represented by a judgment, formed in the waking state, of the whole dream.

2. A similar case: One of my patients has a dream which strikes him as being an interesting one, for he says to himself, immediately after waking: *"I must tell that to the doctor."* The dream is analysed, and shows the most distinct allusion to an affair in which he had become involved during the treatment, and of which he had decided *to tell me nothing*.[2]

3. Here is a third example from my own experience:—

I go to the hospital with P., through a neighbourhood in which there are houses and gardens. Thereupon I have an idea that I have already seen this locality several times in my dreams. I do not know my way very well; P. shows me a way which leads round a corner to a restaurant (indoor); here I ask for Frau Doni, and I hear that she is living at the back of the house, in a small room, with three children. I go there, and on the way I meet an undefined person with my two little girls. After I have been with them for a while, I take them with me. A sort of reproach against my wife for having left them there.

On waking I am conscious of a great *satisfaction*, whose motive seems to be the fact that I shall now learn from the analysis what is meant by *"I have already dreamed of this."* [3] But the analysis of the dream tells me nothing about this; it shows me only that the satisfaction belongs to the latent dream-content, and not to a judgment of the dream. It is *satisfaction concerning the fact that I have had children by my marriage*. P.'s path through life and my own ran parallel for a time; now he has outstripped me both socially and financially, but his marriage has remained childless. Of this the two occasions of the dream give proof on complete analysis. On the previous day I had read in the newspaper the obituary notice of a certain Frau *Dona* A——y (which I turn into Doni), who had died in childbirth; I was told by my wife that the dead woman had been nursed by the same midwife whom she herself had employed at the birth

---

[1] [This German expression is equivalent to our saying: "I am not responsible for that," "That's not my funeral," or "That's not due to my own efforts."—TRANS.]

[2] The injunction or resolve already contained in the dream: *"I must tell that to the doctor,"* when it occurs in dreams during psychoanalytic treatment, is constantly accompanied by a great resistance to confessing the dream, and is not infrequently followed by the forgetting of the dream.

[3] A subject which has been extensively discussed in recent volumes of the *Revue Philosophique* (paramnesia in dreams).

of our two youngest boys. The name *Dona* had caught my attention, for I had recently met with it for the first time in an English novel. The other occasion for the dream may be found in the date on which it was dreamed; this was the night before the birthday of my eldest boy, who, it seems, is poetically gifted.

4. The same satisfaction remained with me after waking from the absurd dream that my father, after his death, had played a political rôle among the Magyars. It is motivated by the persistence of the feeling which accompanied the last sentence of the dream: *"I remember that on his deathbed he looked so like Garibaldi, and* I am glad *that it has really come true. . . ."* (*Followed by a forgotten continuation.*) I can now supply from the analysis what should fill this gap. It is the mention of my second boy, to whom I have given the baptismal name of an eminent historical personage who attracted me greatly during my boyhood, especially during my stay in England. I had to wait for a year before I could fulfill my intention of using this name if the next child should be a son, and with great *satisfaction* I greeted him by this name as soon as he was born. It is easy to see how the father's suppressed desire for greatness is, in his thoughts, transferred to his children; one is inclined to believe that this is one of the ways by which the suppression of this desire (which becomes necessary in the course of life) is effected. The little fellow won his right to inclusion in the text of this dream by virtue of the fact that the same accident—that of soiling his clothes (quite pardonable in either a child or in a dying person)—had occurred to him. Compare with this the allusion *Stuhlrichter* (presiding judge) and the wish of the dream: to stand before one's children *great* and *undefiled*.

5. If I should now have to look for examples of judgments or expressions of opinion which remain in the dream itself, and are not continued in, or transferred to, our waking thoughts, my task would be greatly facilitated were I to take my examples from dreams which have already been cited for other purposes. The dream of Goethe's attack on Herr M. appears to contain quite a number of acts of judgment. *I try to elucidate the temporal relations a little, as they seem improbable to me.* Does not this look like a critical impulse directed against the nonsensical idea that Goethe should have made a literary attack upon a young man of my acquaintance? *"It seems plausible to me that he was 18 years old."* That sounds quite like the result of a calculation, though a silly one; and the *"I do not know exactly what is the date of the present year"* would be an example of uncertainty or doubt in dreams.

But I know from analysis that these acts of judgment, which seem to have been performed in the dream for the first time, admit of a different construction, in the light of which they become indispensable for interpreting the dream, while at the same time all absurdity is avoided. With the sentence "*I try to elucidate the temporal relations a little,*" I put my-self in the place of my friend, who is actually trying to elucidate the temporal relations of life. The sentence then loses its significance as a judgment which objects to the nonsense of the previous sentences. The interposition, "*Which seems improbable to me,*" belongs to the follow-ing: "*It seems plausible to me.*" With almost these identical words I re-plied to the lady who told me of her brother's illness: "It seems improb-able to me" that the cry of "Nature, Nature," was in any way connected with Goethe; it seems much more plausible to me that it has the sexual significance which is known to you. In this case, it is true, a judgment was expressed, but in reality, not in a dream, and on an occasion which is remembered and utilized by the dream-thoughts. The dream-content ap-propriates this judgment like any other fragment of the dream-thoughts.

The number 18 with which the judgment in the dream is meaninglessly connected still retains a trace of the context from which the real judg-ment was taken. Lastly, the "*I do not know exactly what is the date of the present year*" is intended for no other purpose than that of my identi-fication with the paralytic, in examining whom this particular fact was established.

In the solution of these apparent acts of judgment in dreams, it will be well to keep in mind the above-mentioned rule of interpretation, which tells us that we must disregard the coherence which is established in the dream between its constituent parts as an unessential phenomenon, and that every dream-element must be taken separately and traced back to its source. The dream is a compound, which for the purposes of investiga-tion must be broken up into its elements. On the other hand, we become alive to the fact that there is a psychic force which expresses itself in our dreams and establishes this apparent coherence; that is, the material ob-tained by the dream-work undergoes a secondary elaboration. Here we have the manifestations of that psychic force which we shall presently take into consideration as the fourth of the factors which co-operate in dream-formation.

6. Let us now look for other examples of acts of judgment in the dreams which have already been cited. In the absurd dream about the communi-cation from the town council, I ask the question, "*You married soon after?*" I reckon that I was born in 1856, which seems to me to be directly afterwards. This certainly takes the form of an *inference*. My father mar-ried shortly after his attack, in the year 1851. I am the eldest son, born in 1856; so this is correct. We know that this inference has in fact been falsi-fied by the wish-fulfilment, and that the sentence which dominates the dream-thoughts is as follows: *Four or five years—that is no time at all—that need not be counted.* But every part of this chain of reasoning may be seen to be otherwise determined from the dream-thoughts, as regards

both its content and its form. It is the patient of whose patience my colleague complains who intends to marry immediately the treatment is ended. The manner in which I converse with my father in this dream reminds me of an *examination* or *cross-examination*, and thus of a university professor who was in the habit of compiling a complete docket of personal data when entering his pupils' names: You were born when?— 1856.—*Patre?*—Then the applicant gave the Latin form of the baptismal name of the father and we students assumed that the Hofrat drew inferences from the father's name which the baptismal name of the candidate would not always have justified. Hence, the *drawing of inferences* in the dream would be merely the repetition of the *drawing of inferences* which appears as a scrap of material in the dream-thoughts. From this we learn something new. If an inference occurs in the dream-content, it assuredly comes from the dream-thoughts; but it may be contained in these as a fragment of remembered material, or it may serve as the logical connective of a series of dream-thoughts. In any case, an inference in the dream represents an inference taken from the dream-thoughts.[1]

It will be well to continue the analysis of this dream at this point. With the inquisition of the professor is associated the recollection of an index (in my time published in Latin) of the university students; and further, the recollection of my own course of study. The *five years* allowed for the study of medicine were, as usual, too little for me. I worked unconcernedly for some years longer; my acquaintances regarded me as a loafer, and doubted whether I should "get through." Then, suddenly, I decided to take my examinations, and I "got through" *in spite of the postponement*. A fresh confirmation of the dream-thoughts with which I defiantly meet my critics: "Even though you won't believe it, because I am taking my time, I shall reach the *conclusion* (German, *Schluss* = end, conclusion, *inference*). It has often happened like that."

In its introductory portion this dream contains several sentences which, we can hardly deny, are of the nature of an argument. And this argument is not at all absurd; it might just as well occur in my waking thoughts. *In my dream I make fun of the communication from the town council, for in the first place I was not yet born in 1851, and in the second place my father, to whom it might refer, is already dead.* Not only is each of these statements perfectly correct in itself, but they are the very arguments that I should employ if I received such a communication. We know from the foregoing analysis (p. 416) that this dream has sprung from the soil of deeply embittered and scornful dream-thoughts; and if we may also assume that the motive of the censorship is a very powerful one, we shall

---

[1] These results correct at several points my earlier statements concerning the representation of logical relations (p. 341). These described the general procedure of the dream-work, but overlooked its most delicate and most careful operations.

understand that the dream-thought has every occasion to create *a flaw-less refutation of an unreasonable demand,* in accordance with the pattern contained in the dream-thoughts. But the analysis shows that in this case the dream-work has not been required to make a free imitation, but that material taken from the dream-thoughts had to be employed for the purpose. It is as though in an algebraic equation there should occur, besides the figures, plus and minus signs, and symbols of powers and of roots, and as though someone, in copying this equation, without understanding it, should copy both the symbols and the figures, and mix them all up together. The two arguments may be traced to the following material: It is painful to me to think that many of the hypotheses upon which I base my psychological solution of the psychoneuroses will arouse scepticism and ridicule when they first become known. For instance, I shall have to assert that impressions of the second year of life, and even the first, leave an enduring trace upon the emotional life of subsequent neuropaths, and that these impressions—although greatly distorted and exaggerated by the memory—may furnish the earliest and profoundest basis of a hysterical symptom. Patients to whom I explain this at a suitable moment are wont to parody my explanation by offering to search for reminiscences of the period *when they were not yet born.* My disclosure of the unsuspected part played by the father in the earliest sexual impulses of female patients may well have a similar reception. (Cf. the discussion on p. 304.) Nevertheless, it is my well-founded conviction that both doctrines are true. In confirmation of this I recall certain examples in which the death of the father occurred when the child was very young, and subsequent incidents, otherwise inexplicable, proved that the child had unconsciously preserved recollections of the person who had so early gone out of its life. I know that both my assertions are based upon *inferences* whose validity will be attacked. It is the doing of the wish-fulfilment that precisely the material of those inferences, which I fear will be contested, should be utilized by the dream-work for establishing *incontestable conclusions.*

7. In one dream, which I have hitherto only touched upon, astonishment at the subject emerging is distinctly expressed at the outset.

"The elder Brücke must have set me some task or other; strangely enough, it relates to the preparation of the lower part of my own body, the pelvis and legs, which I see before me as though in the dissecting-room, but without feeling the absence of part of my body, and without a trace of horror. Louise N. is standing beside me, and helps me in the work. The pelvis is eviscerated; now the upper, now the lower aspect is visible, and the two aspects are commingled. Large fleshy red tubercles are visible (which, even in the dream, make me think of haemorrhoids). Also something lying over them had to be carefully picked off; it looked like

crumpled tinfoil.[1] Then I was once more in possession of my legs, and I made a journey through the city, but I took a cab (as I was tired). To my astonishment, the cab drove into the front door of a house, which opened and allowed it to pass into a corridor, which was broken off at the end, and eventually led on into the open.[2] Finally I wandered through changing landscapes, with an Alpine guide, who carried my things. He carried me for some distance, out of consideration for my tired legs. The ground was swampy; we went along the edge; people were sitting on the ground, like Red Indians or gypsies; among them a girl. Until then I had made my way along on the slippery ground, in constant astonishment that I was so well able to do so after making the preparation. At last we came to a small wooden house with an open window at one end. Here the guide set me down, and laid two planks, which stood in readiness, on the window-sill so as to bridge the chasm which had to be crossed from the window. Now I grew really alarmed about my legs. Instead of the expected crossing, I saw two grown-up men lying upon wooden benches which were fixed on the walls of the hut, and something like two sleeping children next to them; as though not the planks but the children were intended to make the crossing possible. I awoke with terrified thoughts.

Anyone who has been duly impressed by the extensive nature of dream-condensation will readily imagine what a number of pages the exhaustive analysis of this dream would fill. Fortunately for the context, I shall make this dream only the one example of astonishment in dreams, which makes its appearance in the parenthetical remark, "*strangely enough.*" Let us consider the occasion of the dream. It is a visit of this lady, Louise N., who helps me with my work in the dream. She says: "Lend me something to read." I offer her *She*, by Rider Haggard. "A *strange* book, but full of hidden meaning," I try to explain; "the eternal feminine, the immortality of our emotions——" Here she interrupts me: "I know that book already. Haven't you something of your own?" "No, my own immortal works are still unwritten." "Well, when are you going to publish your so-called 'latest revelations,' which, you promised us, even we should be able to read?" she asks, rather sarcastically. I now perceive that she is a mouthpiece for someone else, and I am silent. I think of the effort it cost me to make public even my work on dreams, in which I had to surrender so much of my own intimate nature. ("The best that you know you can't tell the boys.") The preparation of *my own body* which I am ordered to make in my dream is thus the *self-analysis* involved in the communication of my dreams. The elder Brücke very properly finds a place here; in the first years of my scientific work it

---

[1] Stanniol, allusion to *Stannius;* the nervous system of fishes; cf. p. 401.
[2] The place in the corridor of my apartment-house where the perambulators of the other tenants stand; it is also otherwise hyper-determined several times over.

so happened that I neglected the publication of a certain discovery until his insistence forced me to publish it. But the further trains of thought, proceeding from my conversation with Louise N., go too deep to become conscious; they are side-tracked by way of the material which has been incidentally awakened in me by the mention of Rider Haggard's *She*. The comment *"strangely enough"* applies to this book, and to another by the same author, *The Heart of the World*; and numerous elements of the dream are taken from these two fantastic romances. The swampy ground over which the dreamer is carried, the chasm which has to be crossed by means of planks, come from *She;* the Red Indians, the girl, and the wooden house, from *The Heart of the World*. In both novels a woman is the leader, and both treat of perilous wandering; *She* has to do with an adventurous journey to an undiscovered country, a place almost untrodden by the foot of man. According to a note which I find in my record of the dream, the fatigue in my legs was a real sensation from those days. Probably a weary mood corresponded with this fatigue, and the doubting question: "How much farther will my legs carry me?" In *She* the end of the adventure is that the heroine meets her death in the mysterious central fire, instead of winning immortality for herself and for others. Some related anxiety has mistakably arisen in the dream-thoughts. The "wooden house" is assuredly also a *coffin*—that is, the grave. But in representing this most unwished-for of all thoughts by means of a wish-fulfilment, the dream-work has achieved its masterpiece. I was once in a grave, but it was an empty Etruscan grave near Orvieto—a narrow chamber with two stone benches on the walls, upon which were lying the skeletons of two adults. The interior of the wooden house in the dream looks exactly like this grave, except that stone has been replaced by wood. The dream seems to say: "If you must already sojourn in your grave, let it be this Etruscan grave," and by means of this interpolation it transforms the most mournful expectation into one that is really to be desired. Unfortunately, as we shall learn, the dream is able to change into its opposite only the idea accompanying an affect, but not always the affect itself. Hence, I awake with "thoughts of terror," even after the idea that perhaps my children will achieve what has been denied to their father has forced its way to representation: a fresh allusion to the strange romance in which the identity of a character is preserved through a series of generations covering two thousand years.

8. In the context of another dream there is a similar expression of astonishment at what is experienced in the dream. This, however, is connected with such a striking, far-fetched, and almost intellectual attempt at explanation that if only on this account I should have to subject the whole dream to analysis, even if it did not possess two other interesting features. On the night of the eighteenth of July I was travelling on the

Southern Railway, and in my sleep I heard someone call out: *"Hollthurn, 10 minutes." I immediately think of Holothuria—of a natural history museum—that here is a place where valiant men have vainly resisted the domination of their overlord.—Yes, the counter-reformation in Austria! —As though it were a place in Styria or the Tyrol. Now I see indistinctly a small museum, in which the relics or the acquisitions of these men are preserved. I should like to leave the train, but I hesitate to do so. There are women with fruit on the platform; they squat on the ground, and in that position invitingly hold up their baskets.—I hesitated, in doubt as to whether we have time, but here we are still stationary.—I am suddenly in another compartment, in which the leather and the seats are so narrow that one's spine directly touches the back.[1] I am surprised at this, but I may have changed carriages while asleep. Several people, among them an English brother and sister; a row of books plainly on a shelf on the wall. —I see "The Wealth of Nations," and "Matter and Motion" (by Maxwell), thick books bound in brown linen. The man asks his sister about a book of Schiller's, whether she has forgotten it. These books seem to belong now to me, now to them. At this point I wish to join in the conversation in order to confirm or support what is being said. . . . I wake sweat-* ing all over, because all the windows are shut. The train stops at *Marburg.*

While writing down the dream, a part of it occurs to me which my memory wished to pass over. *I tell the brother and sister (in English), referring to a certain book: "It is from . . ." but I correct myself: "It is by . . ." The man remarks to his sister: "He said it correctly."*

The dream begins with the name of a station, which seems to have almost waked me. For this name, which was *Marburg,* I substitute *Hollthurn.* The fact that I heard Marburg the first, or perhaps the second time it was called out, is proved by the mention of Schiller in the dream; he was born in Marburg, though not the Styrian Marburg.[2] Now on this occasion, although I was travelling first class, I was doing so under very disagreeable circumstances. The train was overcrowded; in my compartment I had come upon a lady and gentleman who seemed very fine people, and had not the good breeding, or did not think it worth while, to conceal their displeasure at my intrusion. My polite greeting was not returned, and although they were sitting side by side (with their backs to the engine), the woman before my eyes hastened to pre-empt the seat oppo-

---

[1] This description is not intelligible even to myself, but I follow the principle of reproducing the dream in those words which occur to me while I am writing it down. The wording itself is a part of the dream-representation.

[2] Schiller was not born in one of the *Marburgs,* but in *Marbach,* as every German schoolboy knows, and as I myself knew. This again is one of those errors (cf. p. 260) which creep in as substitutes for an intentional falsification in another place and which I have endeavoured to explain in *The Psychopathology of Everyday Life.*

site her, and next to the window, with her umbrella; the door was immediately closed, and pointed remarks about the opening of windows were
exchanged. Probably I was quickly recognized as a person hungry for
fresh air. It was a hot night, and the atmosphere of the compartment,
closed on both sides, was almost suffocating. My experience as a traveller
leads me to believe that such inconsiderate and overbearing conduct
marks people who have paid for their tickets only partly, or not at all.
When the conductor came round, and I presented my dearly bought
ticket, the lady exclaimed haughtily and almost threateningly: "My husband has a pass." She was an imposing-looking person, with a discontented expression, in age not far removed from the autumn of feminine
beauty; the man had no chance to say anything; he sat there motionless.
I tried to sleep. In my dream I take a terrible revenge on my disagreeable travelling companions; no one would suspect what insults and hu-
miliations are concealed behind the disjointed fragments of the first half
of the dream. After this need has been satisfied, the second wish, to exchange my compartment for another, makes itself felt. The dream changes
its scene so often, and without making the slightest objection to such
changes, that it would not have seemed at all remarkable had I at once,
from my memories, replaced my travelling companions by more agreeable persons. But here was a case where something or other opposes the
change of scene, and finds it necessary to explain it. How did I suddenly
get into another compartment? I could not positively remember having
changed carriages. So there was only one explanation: *I must have left
the carriage while asleep*—an unusual occurrence, examples of which,
however, are known to neuropathologists. We know of persons who undertake railway journeys in a crepuscular state, without betraying their
abnormal condition by any sign whatever, until at some stage of their
journey they come to themselves, and are surprised by the gap in their
memory. Thus, while I am still dreaming, I declare my own case to be
such a case of *automatisme ambulatoire*.

Analysis permits of another solution. The attempt at explanation,
which so surprises me if I am to attribute it to the dream-work, is not
original, but is copied from the neurosis of one of my patients. I have
already spoken in another chapter of a highly cultured and kindly man
who began, shortly after the death of his parents, to accuse himself of
murderous tendencies, and who was distressed by the precautionary
measures which he had to take to secure himself against these tendencies.
His was a case of severe obsessional ideas with full insight. To begin
with, it was painful to him to walk through the streets, as he was obsessed
by the necessity of accounting for all the persons he met; he had to know
whither they had disappeared; if one of them suddenly eluded his pursuing glance, he was left with a feeling of distress and the idea that he

might possibly have made away with the man. Behind this obsessive idea was concealed, among other things, a Cain-phantasy, for "all men are brothers." Owing to the impossibility of accomplishing this task, he gave up going for walks, and spent his life imprisoned within his four walls. But reports of murders which had been committed in the world outside were constantly reaching his room by way of the newspapers, and his conscience tormented him with the doubt that he might be the murderer for whom the police were looking. The certainty that he had not left the house for weeks protected him for a time against these accusations, until one day there dawned upon him the possibility that *he might have left his house while in an unconscious state,* and might thus have committed murder without knowing anything about it. From that time onwards he locked his front door, and gave the key to his old housekeeper, strictly forbidding her to give it into his hands, even if he demanded it.

This, then, is the origin of the attempted explanation that I may have changed carriages while in an unconscious state; it has been taken into the dream ready-made, from the material of the dream-thoughts, and is evidently intended to identify me with the person of my patient. My memory of this patient was awakened by natural association. My last night journey had been made a few weeks earlier in his company. He was cured, and we were going into the country together to his relatives, who had sent for me; as we had a compartment to ourselves, we left all the windows open throughout the night, and for as long as I remained awake we had a most interesting conversation. I knew that hostile impulses to-wards his father in childhood, in a sexual connection, had been at the root of his illness. By identifying myself with him I wanted to make an analogous confession to myself. The second scene of the dream really resolves itself into a wanton phantasy to the effect that my two elderly travelling companions had acted so uncivilly towards me because my arrival on the scene had prevented them from exchanging kisses and embraces during the night, as they had intended. This phantasy, however, goes back to an early incident of my childhood when, probably impelled by sexual curiosity, I had intruded into my parents' bedroom, and was driven thence by my father's emphatic command.

I think it would be superfluous to multiply such examples. They would all confirm what we have learned from those already cited: namely, that an act of judgment in a dream is merely the repetition of an original act of judgment in the dream-thoughts. In most cases it is an unsuitable repetition, fitted into an inappropriate context; occasionally, however, as in our last example, it is so artfully applied that it may almost give one the impression of independent intellectual activity in the dream. At this point we might turn our attention to that psychic activity which, though it does not appear to co-operate constantly in the formation of dreams, yet endeavours to fuse the dream-elements of different origin into a flawless and significant whole. We consider it necessary, however, first of all to consider the expressions of affect which appear in dreams, and to compare these with the affects which analysis discovers in the dream-thoughts.

H. THE AFFECTS IN DREAMS

A shrewd remark of Stricker's called our attention to the fact that the expressions of affects in dreams cannot be disposed of in the contemptuous fashion in which we are wont to shake off the dream-content after we have waked. "If I am afraid of robbers in my dreams, the robbers, to be sure, are imaginary, but the fear of them is real"; and the same thing is true if I rejoice in my dream. According to the testimony of our feelings, an affect experienced in a dream is in no way inferior to one of like intensity experienced in waking life, and the dream presses its claim to be accepted as part of our real psychic experiences, by virtue of its affective rather than its ideational content. In the waking state we do not put the one before the other, since we do not know how to evaluate an affect psychically except in connection with an ideational content. If an affect and an idea are ill-matched as regards their nature or their intensity, our waking judgment becomes confused.

The fact that in dreams the ideational content does not always produce the affective result which in our waking thoughts we should expect as its necessary consequence has always been a cause of astonishment. Strümpell declared that ideas in dreams are stripped of their psychic values. But there is no lack of instances in which the reverse is true; when an intensive manifestation of affect appears in a content which seems to offer no occasion for it. In my dream I may be in a horrible, dangerous, or disgusting situation, and yet I may feel no fear or aversion; on the other hand, I am sometimes terrified by harmless things, and sometimes delighted by childish things.

This enigma disappeared more suddenly and more completely than perhaps any other dream-problem if we pass from the manifest to the latent content. We shall then no longer have to explain it, for it will no longer exist. Analysis tells us that *the ideational contents have undergone displacements and substitutions, while the affects have remained unchanged.* No wonder, then, that the ideational content which has been altered by dream-distortion no longer fits the affect which has remained intact; and no cause for wonder when analysis has put the correct content into its original place.[1]

---

[1] If I am not greatly mistaken, the first dream which I was able to elicit from my grandson (aged 20 months) points to the fact that the dream-work had succeeded in transforming its material into a wish-fulfilment, while the affect which belonged

In a psychic complex which has been subjected to the influence of the resisting censorship, the affects are the unyielding constituent, which alone can guide us to the correct completion. This state of affairs is revealed in the psychoneuroses even more distinctly than in dreams. Here the affect is always in the right, at least as regards its quality; its intensity may, of course, be increased by displacement of the neurotic attention. When the hysterical patient wonders that he should be so afraid of a trifle, or when the sufferer from obsessions is astonished that he should reproach himself so bitterly for a mere nothing, they are both in error, inasmuch as they regard the conceptual content—the trifle, the mere nothing—as the essential thing, and they defend themselves in vain, because they make this conceptual content the starting-point of their thought-work. Psychoanalysis, however, puts them on the right path, inasmuch as it recognizes that, on the contrary, it is the affect that is justified, and looks for the concept which pertains to it, and which has been repressed by a substitution. All that we need assume is that the liberation of affect and the conceptual content do not constitute the indissoluble organic unity as which we are wont to regard them, but that the two parts may be welded together, so that analysis will separate them. Dream-interpretation shows that this is actually the case.

I will first of all give an example in which analysis explains the apparent absence of affect in a conceptual content which ought to compel a liberation of affect.

I

The dreamer sees three lions in a desert, one of which is laughing, but she is not afraid of them. Then, however, she must have fled from them, for she is trying to climb a tree. But she finds that her cousin, the French teacher, is already up in the tree, etc.

The analysis yields the following material: The indifferent occasion of dream was a sentence in the dreamer's English exercise: "The *lion's* greatest adornment is his mane." Her father used to wear a beard which encircled his face like a *mane*. The name of her English teacher is Miss *Lyons*. An acquaintance of hers had sent her the ballads of *Loewe* (*Loewe* = lion). These, then, are the three lions; why should she be afraid of them? She has read a story in which a negro who has incited his

---

to it remained unchanged even in the sleeping state. The night before its father was to return to the front the child cried out, sobbing violently: "Papa, Papa—Baby." That may mean: Let Papa and Baby still be together; while the weeping takes cognizance of the imminent departure. The child was at the time very well able to express the concept of separation. "Fort" (= away, replaced by a peculiarly accented, long-drawn-out *ooooh*) had been his first word, and for many months before this first dream he had played at "away" with all his toys; which went back to his early self-conquest in allowing his mother to go away.

fellows to revolt is hunted with bloodhounds, and climbs a tree to save himself. Then follow fragmentary recollections in the merriest mood, such as the following directions for catching lions (from *Die Fliegende Blätter*): "Take a desert and put it through a sieve; the lions will be left behind." Also a very amusing, but not very proper anecdote about an official who is asked why he does not take greater pains to win the favour of his chief, and who replies that he has been trying to creep into favour, but that his immediate superior was *already up there*. The whole matter becomes intelligible as soon as one learns that on the dream-day the lady had received a visit from her husband's superior. He was very polite to her, and kissed her hand, and *she was not at all afraid of him*, although he is a "big bug" (*Grosses Tier* = big animal) and plays the part of a "*social lion*" in the capital of her country. This lion is, therefore, like the lion in *A Midsummer Night's Dream*, who is unmasked as Snug the joiner; and of such stuff are all the dream-lions of which one is not afraid.

II

As my second example, I will cite the dream of the girl who saw her sister's little son lying as a corpse in his coffin, but who, it may be added, was conscious of no pain or sorrow. Why she was unmoved we know from the analysis. The dream only disguised her wish to see once more the man she loved; the affect had to be attuned to the wish, and not to its disguisement. There was thus no occasion for sorrow.

In a number of dreams the affect does at least remain connected with the conceptual content which has replaced the content really belonging to it. In others, the dissolution of the complex is carried farther. The affect is entirely separated from the idea belonging to it, and finds itself accommodated elsewhere in the dream, where it fits into the new arrangement of the dream-elements. We have seen that the same thing happens to acts of judgment in dreams. If an important inference occurs in the dream-thoughts, there is one in the dream also; but the inference in the dream may be displaced to entirely different material. Not infrequently this displacement is effected in accordance with the principle of antithesis.

I will illustrate the latter possibility by the following dream, which I have subjected to the most exhaustive analysis.

III

A castle by the sea; afterwards it lies not directly on the coast, but on a narrow canal leading to the sea. A certain Herr P. is the governor of the castle. I stand with him in a large salon with three windows, in front of which rise the projections of a wall, like battlements of a fortress. I belong to the garrison, perhaps as a volunteer naval officer. We fear the arrival of enemy warships, for we are in a state of war. Herr P. intends to leave the castle; he gives me instructions as to what must be done if what we fear should come to pass. His sick wife and his children are in the threatened castle. As soon as the bombardment begins, the large hall is to be cleared. He breathes heavily, and tries to get away; I detain him, and ask him how I am to send him news in case of need. He says something further, and immediately afterwards he sinks to the floor dead. I have probably taxed him unnecessarily with my questions. *After his death, which makes no further impression upon me, I consider whether the widow is to remain in the castle, whether I should give notice of the death to the higher command, whether I should take over the control of the castle as the next in command. I now stand at the window, and scrutinize the ships as they pass by; they are cargo steamers, and they rush by over the dark water; several with more than one funnel, other with bulging decks* (these are very like the railway stations in the preliminary dream, which has not been related). *Then my brother is standing beside me, and we both look out of the window on to the canal. At the sight of one ship we are alarmed, and call out:* "Here comes the warship!" *It turns out, however, that they are only the ships which I have already seen, returning. Now comes a small ship, comically truncated, so that it ends amidships; on the deck one sees curious things like cups or little boxes. We call out as with one voice:* "That is the breakfast ship."

The rapid motion of the ships, the deep blue of the water, the brown smoke of the funnels—all these together produce an intense and gloomy impression.

The localities in this dream are compiled from several journeys to the Adriatic (Miramare, Duino, Venice, Aquileia). A short but enjoyable Easter trip to Aquileia with my brother, a few weeks before the dream, was still fresh in my memory; also the *naval war* between America and Spain, and, associated with this my anxiety as to the fate of my relatives in America, play a part in the dream. Manifestations of affect appear at two places in this dream. In one place an affect that would be expected is lacking: it is expressly emphasized that the death of the governor makes no impression upon me; at another point, when I see the warships, I am *frightened*, and experience all the sensations of fright in my sleep. The distribution of affects in this well-constructed dream has been effected in such a way that any obvious contradiction is avoided. For there is no reason why I should be frightened at the governor's death, and it is fitting that, as the commander of the castle, I should be alarmed by the sight of the warship. Now analysis shows that Herr P. is nothing but a substitute for my own ego (in the dream I am his substitute). I am the governor who suddenly dies. The dream-thoughts deal with the future of my family after my premature death. No other disagreeable thought is to be found among the dream-thoughts. The alarm which goes with the sight of the warship must be transferred from it to this disagreeable thought. Inversely, the analysis shows that the region of the dream-thoughts from which the warship comes is laden with most cheerful reminiscences. In Venice, a year before the dream, one magically beautiful day, we stood at the windows of our room on the Riva Schiavoni and looked out over the blue lagoon, on which there was more traffic to be seen than usual. Some English ships were expected; they were to be given a festive reception; and suddenly my wife cried, happy as a child: *"Here comes the English warship!"* In the dream I am frightened by the very same words; once more we see that speeches in dreams have their origin in speeches in real life. I shall presently show that even the element "English" in this speech has not been lost for the dream-work. Here, then, between the dream-thoughts and the dream-content, I turn joy into fright, and I need only point to the fact that by means of this transformation I give expression to part of the latent dream-content. The example shows, however, that the dream-work is at liberty to detach the occasion of an affect from its connections in the dream-thoughts, and to insert it at any other place it chooses in the dream-content.

I will take the opportunity which is here incidentally offered of subjecting to a closer analysis the "breakfast ship," whose appearance in the dream so absurdly concludes a situation that has been rationally adhered to. If I look more closely at this dream-object, I am impressed after the event by the fact that it was black, and that by reason of its truncation at its widest beam it achieved, at the truncated end, a considerable resemblance to an object which had aroused our interest in the museums of the Etruscan cities. This object was a rectangular cup of black clay, with two handles, upon which stood things like coffee-cups or tea-cups, very similar to our modern service for the *breakfast table*. Upon inquiry we learned that this was the toilet set of an Etruscan lady, with little boxes for rouge and powder; and we told one another jestingly that it would not be a bad idea to take a thing like that home to the lady of the house. The dream-object, therefore, signifies a *"black toilet"* (*toilette=* dress), or mourning, and refers directly to a death. The other end of the dream-object reminds us of the "boat" (German, *Nachen*, from the Greek root, νεχυς, as a philological friend informs me), upon which corpses were laid in prehistoric times, and were left to be buried by the sea. This is associated with the return of the ships in the dream.

"Silently on his rescued boat the old man drifts into harbour."

It is the return voyage after the ship*wreck* (German: *Schiff-bruch =* ship-*breaking*); the breakfast ship looks as though it were *broken* off amidships. But whence comes the name "breakfast" ship? This is where "English" comes in, which we have left over from the warships. *Break-*

fast, a *breaking of the fast*. *Breaking* again belongs to shipwreck *(Schiff-bruch)*, and *fasting* is associated with the black (mourning).

But the only thing about this breakfast ship which has been newly created by the dream is its name. The thing existed in reality, and recalls to me one of the merriest moments of my last journey. As we distrusted the fare in Aquileia, we took some food with us from Goerz, and bought a bottle of the excellent Istrian wine in Aquileia; and while the little mail-steamer slowly travelled through the *canale delle Mee* and into the lonely expanse of lagoon in the direction of Grado, we had breakfast on deck in the highest spirits—we were the only passengers—and it tasted to us as few breakfasts have ever tasted. This, then, was the *"breakfast ship,"* and it is behind this very recollection of the gayest *joie de vivre* that the dream hides the saddest thoughts of an unknown and mysterious future.

The detachment of affects from the groups of ideas which have occasioned their liberation is the most striking thing that happens to them in dream-formation, but it is neither the only nor even the most essential change which they undergo on the way from the dream-thoughts to the manifest dream. If the affects in the dream-thoughts are compared with those in the dream, one thing at once becomes clear: Wherever there is an affect in the dream, it is to be found also in the dream-thoughts; the converse, however, is not true. In general, a dream is less rich in affects than the psychic material from which it is elaborated. When I have reconstructed the dream-thoughts, I see that the most intense psychic impulses are constantly striving in them for self-assertion, usually in conflict with others which are sharply opposed to them. Now, if I turn back to the dream, I often find it colourless and devoid of any very intensive affective tone. Not only the content, but also the affective tone of my thoughts is often reduced by the dream-work to the level of the indifferent. I might say that a *suppression of the affects* has been accomplished by the dream-work. Take, for example, the dream of the botanical monograph. It corresponds to a passionate plea for my freedom to act as I am acting, to arrange my life as seems right to me, and to me alone. The dream which results from this sounds indifferent; I have written a monograph; it is lying before me; it is provided with coloured plates, and dried plants are to be found in each copy. It is like the peace of a deserted battlefield; no trace is left of the tumult of battle.

But things may turn out quite differently; vivid expressions of affect may enter into the dream itself; but we will first of all consider the unquestioned fact that so many dreams appear indifferent, whereas it is never possible to go deeply into the dream-thoughts without deep emotion.

The complete theoretical explanation of this suppression of affects during the dream-work cannot be given here; it would require a most careful investigation of the theory of the affects and of the mechanism of repression. Here I can put forward only two suggestions. I am forced—for other reasons—to conceive the liberation of affects as a centrifugal process directed towards the interior of the body, analogous to the processes of motor and secretory innervation. Just as in the sleeping state the emission of motor impulses towards the outer world seems to be suspended, so the centrifugal awakening of affects by unconscious thinking during sleep may be rendered more difficult. The affective impulses which occur during the course of the dream-thoughts may thus in themselves be feeble, so that those that find their way into the dream are no stronger. According to this line of thought, the "suppression of the affects" would not be a consequence of the dream-work at all, but a consequence of the state of sleep. This may be so, but it cannot possibly be all the truth. We must remember that all the more complex dreams have revealed themselves as the result of a compromise between conflicting psychic forces. On the one hand, the wish-forming thoughts have to oppose the contradiction of a censorship; on the other hand, as we have often seen, even in unconscious thinking, every train of thought is harnessed to its contradictory counterpart. Since all these trains of thought are capable of arousing affects, we shall, broadly speaking, hardly go astray if we conceive the suppression of affects as the result of the inhibition which the contrasts impose upon one another, and the censorship upon the urges which it has suppressed. *The inhibition of affects would accordingly be the second consequence of the dream-censorship, just as dream-distortion was the first consequence.*

I will here insert an example of a dream in which the indifferent emotional tone of the dream-content may be explained by the antagonism of the dream-thoughts. I must relate the following short dream, which every reader will read with disgust.

IV

Rising ground, and on it something like an open-air latrine; a very long bench, at the end of which is a wide aperture. The whole of the back edge is thickly covered with little heaps of excrement of all sizes and degrees of freshness. A thicket behind the bench. I urinate upon the bench; a long stream of urine rinses everything clean, the patches of excrement come off easily and fall into the opening. Nevertheless, it seems as though something remained at the end.

Why did I experience no disgust in this dream?

Because, as the analysis shows, the most pleasant and gratifying thoughts have co-operated in the formation of this dream. Upon analysing it, I immediately think of the *Augean stables* which were cleansed by Hercules. I am this Hercules. The rising ground and the thicket belong to Aussee, where my children are now staying. I have discovered the infantile etiology of the neuroses, and have thus guarded my own children from falling ill. The bench (omitting the aperture, of course) is the faithful copy of a piece of furniture of which an affectionate female patient has made me a present. This reminds me how my patients honour me. Even the museum of human excrement is susceptible of a gratifying interpretation. However much it digusts me, it is a souvenir of the beautiful land of Italy, where in the small cities, as everyone knows, the privies are not equipped in any other way. The stream of urine that washes everything clean is an unmistakable allusion to greatness. It is in this manner that *Gulliver* extinguishes the great fire in Lilliput; to be sure, he thereby incurs the displeasure of the tiniest of queens. In this way, too, Gargantua, the superman of Master Rabelais, takes vengeance upon the Parisians, straddling Notre-Dame and training his stream of urine upon the city. Only yesterday I was turning over the leaves of Garnier's illustrations to Rabelais before I went to bed. And, strangely enough, here is another proof that I am the superman! The platform of Notre-Dame was my favourite nook in Paris; every free afternoon I used to go up into the towers of the cathedral and there clamber about between the monsters and gargoyles. The circumstance that all the excrement vanishes so rapidly before the stream of urine corresponds to the motto: *Afflavit et dissipati sunt*, which I shall some day make the title of a chapter on the therapeutics of hysteria.

And now as to the affective occasion of the dream. It had been a hot summer afternoon; in the evening, I had given my lecture on the connection between hysteria and the perversions, and everything which I had to say displeased me thoroughly, and seemed utterly valueless. I was tired; I took not the least pleasure in my difficult work, and longed to get away from this rummaging in human filth; first to see my children, and then to revisit the beauties of Italy. In this mood I went from the lecture-hall to a café to get some little refreshment in the open air, for my appetite had forsaken me. But a member of my audience went with me; he begged for permission to sit with me while I drank my coffee and gulped down my roll, and began to say flattering things to me. He told me how much he had learned from me, that he now saw everything through different eyes, that I had cleansed the *Augean stables* of error and prejudice, which encumbered the theory of the neuroses—in short, that I was a very great man. My mood was ill-suited to his hymn of praise; I struggled with my disgust, and went home earlier in order to get rid of him; and before I went to sleep I turned over the leaves of *Rabelais*, and read a short story by C. F. Meyer entitled *Die Leiden eines Knaben* (The Sorrows of a Boy).

The dream had originated from this material, and Meyer's novel had supplied the recollections of scenes of childhood.[1] The day's mood of an-

---

[1] Cf. the dream about Count Thun, last scene.

noyance and disgust is continued in the dream, inasmuch as it is permitted to furnish nearly all the material for the dream-content. But during the night the opposite mood of vigorous, even immoderate self-assertion awakened and dissipated the earlier mood. The dream had to assume such a form as would accommodate both the expressions of self-depreciation and exaggerated self-glorification in the same material. This compromise-formation resulted in an ambiguous dream-content, but, owing to the mutual inhibition of the opposites, in an indifferent emotional tone.

According to the theory of wish-fulfilment, this dream would not have been possible had not the opposed, and indeed suppressed, yet pleasure-emphasized megalomaniac train of thought been added to the thoughts of disgust. For nothing painful is intended to be represented in dreams; the painful elements of our daily thoughts are able to force their way into our dreams only if at the same time they are able to disguise a wish-fulfilment.

The dream-work is able to dispose of the affects of the dream-thoughts in yet another way than by admitting them or reducing them to zero. *It can transform them into their opposites.* We are acquainted with the rule that for the purposes of interpretation every element of the dream may represent its opposite, as well as itself. One can never tell beforehand which is to be posited; only the context can decide this point. A suspicion of this state of affairs has evidently found its way into the popular consciousness; the dream-books, in their interpretations, often proceed according to the principle of contraries. This transformation into the contrary is made possible by the intimate associative ties which in our thoughts connect the idea of a thing with that of its opposite. Like every other displacement, this serves the purposes of the censorship, but it is often the work of wish-fulfilment, for wish-fulfilment consists in nothing more than the substitution of an unwelcome thing by its opposite. Just as concrete images may be transformed into their contraries in our dreams, so also may the affects of the dream-thoughts, and it is probable that this inversion of affects is usually brought about by the dream-censorship. The *suppression and inversion of affects* is useful even in social life, as is shown by the familiar analogy of the dream-censorship and, above all, hypocrisy. If I am conversing with a person to whom I must show consideration while I should like to address him as an enemy, it is almost more important that I should conceal the expression of my affect from him than that I should modify the verbal expression of my thoughts. If I address him in courteous terms, but accompany them by looks or gestures of hatred and disdain, the effect which I produce upon him is not very different from what it would have been had I cast my unmitigated contempt into his face. Above all, then, the censorship bids me suppress my affects, and if I am a master of the art of dissimulation I can hypocritically display the opposite affect—smiling where I should like to be angry, and pretending affection where I should like to destroy.

We have already had an excellent example of such an inversion of affect in the service of the dream-censorship. In the dream "of my uncle's beard" I feel great affection for my friend R., while (and because) the dream-thoughts berate him as a simpleton. From this example of the in-version of affects we derived our first proof of the existence of the censorship. Even here it is not necessary to assume that the dream-work creates a counter-affect of this kind that is altogether new; it usually finds it lying ready in the material of the dream-thoughts, and merely intensifies it with the psychic force of the defence-motives until it is able to predominate in the dream-formation. In the dream of my uncle, the affectionate counter-affect probably has its origin in an infantile source (as the continuation of the dream would suggest), for owing to the peculiar nature of my earliest childhood experiences the relation of uncle and nephew has become the source of all my friendships and hatreds (cf. analysis on p. 408).

An excellent example of such a reversal of affect is found in a dream recorded by Ferenczi.[1] "An elderly gentleman was awakened at night by his wife, who was frightened because he laughed so loudly and uncontrollably in his sleep. The man afterwards related that he had had the following dream: *I lay in my bed, a gentleman known to me came in, I wanted to turn on the light, but I could not; I attempted to do so repeatedly, but in vain. Thereupon my wife got out of bed, in order to help me, but she, too, was unable to manage it; being ashamed of her négligé in the presence of the gentleman, she finally gave it up and went back to her bed; all this was so comical that I had to laugh terribly. My wife said: 'What are you laughing at, what are you laughing at?' but I continued to laugh until I woke.* The following day the man was extremely depressed, and suffered from headache: 'From too much laughter, which shook me up,' he thought.

"Analytically considered, the dream looks less comical. In the latent dream-thoughts the 'gentleman known' to him who came into the room is the image of death as the 'great unknown,' which was awakened in his mind on the previous day. The old gentleman, who suffers from arteriosclerosis, had good reason to think of death on the day before the dream. The uncontrollable laughter takes the place of weeping and sobbing at the idea that he has to die. It is the light of life that he is no longer able to turn on. This mournful thought may have associated itself with a failure to effect sexual intercourse, which he had attempted shortly before this, and in which the assistance of his wife *en négligé* was of no avail; he realized that he was already on the decline. The dream-work knew how to transform the sad idea of impotence and death into a comic scene, and the sobbing into laughter."

There is one class of dreams which has a special claim to be called "hypocritical," and which severely tests the theory of wish-fulfilment. My attention was called to them when Frau Dr. M. Hilferding proposed for discussion by the Psychoanalytic Society of Vienna a dream recorded by Rosegger, which is here reprinted:—

In *Waldheimat,* vol. xi, Rosegger writes as follows in his story, *Fremd gemacht* (p. 303):—

"I usually enjoy healthful sleep, yet I have gone without repose on many a night; in addition to my modest existence as a student and literary man, I have for long years dragged out the shadow of a veritable tailor's life—like a ghost from which I could not become divorced.

"It is not true that I have occupied myself very often or very intensely with thoughts of my past during the day. A stormer of heaven and earth who has escaped from the hide of the Philistine has other things to think about. And as a gay young fellow, I hardly gave a thought to my nocturnal dreams; only later, when I had formed the habit of thinking about everything, or when the Philistine within me began to assert itself a little, did it strike me that—when I dreamed at all—I was always a journeyman tailor, and that in that capacity I had already worked in my master's shop for a long time without any pay. As I sat there beside him, and sewed and pressed, I was perfectly well aware that I no longer belonged there, and that as a burgess of the town I had other things to attend to; but I was always on a holiday, or away in the country, and so I sat beside my master and helped him. I often felt far from comfortable about it, and regretted the waste of time which I might have employed for better and more useful purposes. If anything was not quite correct in measure and cut I had to put up with a scolding from my master. Of wages there was never a question. Often, as I sat with bent back in the dark workshop, I decided to give notice and make myself scarce. Once I actually did so, but the master took no notice of me, and next time I was sitting beside him again and sewing.

"How happy I was when I woke up after such weary hours! And I then resolved that, if this intrusive dream should ever occur again, I would energetically throw it off, and would cry aloud: 'It is only a delusion, I am lying in bed, and I want to sleep' . . . And the next night I would be sitting in the tailor's shop again.

"So it went on for years, with dismal regularity. Once, when the master and I were working at Alpelhofer's, at the house of the peasant with whom I began my apprenticeship, it happened that my master was particularly dissatisfied with my work. 'I should like to know where in the world your thoughts are?' he cried, and looked at me sullenly. I thought the most sensible thing to do would be to get up and explain to the master that I was working with him only as a favour, and then take my leave. But I did not do this. I even submitted when the master engaged an apprentice, and ordered me to make room for him on the bench. I moved into the corner, and kept on sewing. On the same day another journeyman was engaged; a bigoted fellow; he was the Bohemian who had worked for us nineteen years earlier, and then had fallen into the lake on his way home from the public-house. When he tried to sit down there was no room for him. I looked at the master inquiringly, and he said to me: 'You have no talent for tailoring; *you may go; you're a stranger henceforth.*' My fright on that occasion was so overpowering that I woke.

"The grey of morning glimmered through the clear windows of my familiar home. *Objets d'art* surrounded me; in the tasteful bookcase stood the eternal Homer, the gigantic Dante, the incomparable Shakespeare, the glorious Goethe—all radiant and immortal. From the adjoining room resounded the clear little voices of the children, who were waking up and prattling to their mother. I felt as though I had rediscovered that idyllically sweet, peaceful, poetical and spiritualized life in which I have so often and so deeply been conscious of contemplative human happiness. And yet I was vexed that I had not given my master notice first, but had been dismissed by him.

"And how remarkable this seems to me: since that night, when my master 'made a stranger' of me, I have enjoyed restful sleep; I no longer dream of my tailoring days, which now lie in the remote past; which in their unpretentious simplicity were really so cheerful, but which, none the less, have cast a long shadow over the later years of my life."

In this series of dreams of a poet who, in his younger years, had been a journeyman tailor, it is hard to recognize the domination of the wish-fulfilment. All the delightful things occurred in his waking life, while the dream seemed to drag along with it the ghost-like shadow of an unhappy existence which had long been forgotten. Dreams of my own of a similar character enable me to give some explanation of such dreams. As a young doctor, I worked for a long time in the Chemical Institute without being able to accomplish anything in that exacting science, so that in the waking state I never think about this unfruitful and actually somewhat humiliating period of my student days. On the other hand, I have a recurring dream to the effect that I am working in the laboratory, making analyses, and experiments, and so forth; these dreams, like the examination-dreams, are disagreeable, and they are never very distinct. During the analysis of one of these dreams my attention was directed to the word *"analysis,"* which gave me the key to an understanding of them. Since then I have become an "analyst." I make analyses which are greatly praised—psychoanalyses, of course. Now I understand: when I feel proud of these analyses in my waking life, and feel inclined to boast of my achievements, my dreams hold up to me at night those other, unsuccessful analyses, of which I have no reason to be proud; they are the punitive dreams of the upstart, like those of the journeyman tailor who became a celebrated poet. But how is it possible for a dream to place itself at the service of self-criticism in its conflict with parvenu pride, and to take as its content a rational warning instead of a prohibited wish-fulfilment? I have already hinted that the answer to this question presents many difficulties. We may conclude that the foundation of the dream consisted at first of an arrogant phantasy of ambition; but that in its stead only its suppression and abasement has reached the dream-content. One must remember that there are masochistic tendencies in mental life to which such an inversion might be attributed. I see no objection to regarding such dreams as *punishment-dreams,* as distinguished from wish-fulfilling dreams. I should not see in this any limitation of the theory of dreams hitherto as presented, but merely a verbal concession to the point of view to which the convergence of contraries seems strange. But a more thorough investigation of individual dreams of this class allows us to recognize yet another element. In an indistinct, subordinate portion of one of my laboratory dreams, I was just at the age which placed me in the most gloomy and most unsuccessful year of my professional career; I still had no position, and no idea how I was going to support myself, when I suddenly found that I had the choice of several women whom I might marry! I was, therefore, young again and, what is more, she was young again— the woman who has shared with me all these difficult years. In this way, one of the wishes which constantly gnaws at the heart of the ageing man was revealed as the unconscious dream-instigator. The conflict raging in other psychic strata between vanity and self-criticism had certainly determined the dream-content, but the more deeply-rooted wish for youth had alone made it possible as a dream. One often says to oneself even in the waking state: "To be sure, things are going well with you to-day, and once you found life very hard; but, after all, life was sweet in those days, when you were still so young." [1]

Another group of dreams, which I have often myself experienced, and which I have recognized to be hypocritical, have as their content a reconciliation with persons with whom one has long ceased to have friendly relations. The analysis constantly discovers an occasion which might well induce me to cast aside the last remnants of consideration for these former friends, and to treat them as strangers or enemies. But the dream chooses to depict the contrary relation.

[1] Ever since psychoanalysis has dissected the personality into an ego and a super-ego (*Group Psychology and the Analysis of the Ego,* trans. by James Strachey. Intern. Psychoanalytic Press, London) it has been easy to recognize in these punishment-dreams wish-fulfilments of the super-ego.

In considering dreams recorded by a novelist or poet, we may often enough assume that he has excluded from the record those details which he felt to be disturbing and regarded as unessential. His dreams thus set us a problem which could be readily solved if we had an exact reproduction of the dream-content.

O. Rank has called my attention to the fact that in Grimm's fairy-tale of the valiant little tailor, or *Seven at one Stroke,* there is related a very similar dream of an upstart. The tailor, who has become a hero, and has married the king's daughter, dreams one night while lying beside the princess, his wife, about his trade; having become suspicious, on the following night she places armed guards where they can listen to what is said by the dreamer, and arrest him. But the little tailor is warned, and is able to correct his dream.

The complicated processes of removal, diminution, and inversion by which the affects of the dream-thoughts finally become the affects of the dream may be very well surveyed in suitable syntheses of completely analysed dreams. I shall here discuss a few examples of affective manifestations in dreams which will, I think, prove this conclusively in some of the cases cited.

V

In the dream about the odd task which the elder Brücke sets me—that of preparing my own pelvis—I am aware in the dream itself of not feeling *appropriate horror.* Now this is a wish-fulfilment in more senses than one. The preparation signifies the self-analyses which I perform, as it were, by publishing my book on dreams, which I actually found so painful that I postponed the printing of the completed manuscript for more than a year. The wish now arises that I may disregard this feeling of aversion, and for that reason I feel no horror (*Grauen,* which also means "to grow grey") in the dream. I should much like to escape "Grauen" in the other sense too, for I am already growing quite grey, and the grey in my hair warns me to delay no longer. For we know that at the end of the dream this thought secures representation: "I shall have to leave my children to reach the goal of their difficult journey without my help."

In the two dreams that transfer the expression of satisfaction to the moments immediately after waking, this satisfaction is in the one case motivated by the expectation that I am now going to learn what is meant by "I have already dreamed of this," and refers in reality to the birth of my first child, and in the other case it is motivated by the conviction that "that which has been announced by a premonitory sign" is now going to happen, and the satisfaction is that which I felt on the arrival of my second son. Here the same affects that dominated in the dream-thoughts have remained in the dream, but the process is probably not quite so simple as this in any dream. If the two analyses are examined a little more closely it will be seen that this satisfaction, which does not succumb to the censorship, receives reinforcement from a source which must fear the censorship, and whose affect would certainly have aroused opposition if it had not screened itself by a similar and readily admitted affect of satisfaction from the permitted source, and had, so to speak, sneaked in behind it. I am unfortunately unable to show this in the case of the actual dream, but an example from another situation will make my meaning intelligible. I will put the following case: Let there be a person near me whom I hate so strongly that I have a lively impulse to rejoice should anything happen to him. But the moral side of my nature does not give way to this impulse; I do not dare to express this sinister wish, and when something does happen to him which he does not deserve I suppress my satisfaction, and force myself to thoughts and expressions of regret. Everyone will at some time have found himself in such a position. But now let it happen that the hated person, through some transgression of his own, draws upon himself a well-deserved calamity; I shall now be allowed to give free rein to my satisfaction at his being visited by a just punishment, and I shall be expressing an opinion which coincides with that of other impartial persons. But I observe that my satisfaction proves to be more intense than that of others, for it has received reinforcement from another source—from my hatred, which was hitherto prevented by the inner censorship from furnishing the affect, but which, under the altered circumstances, is no longer prevented from doing so. This case generally occurs in social life when antipathetic persons or the adherents of an unpopular minority have been guilty of some offence. Their punishment is then usually commensurate not with their guilt, but with their guilt plus the ill-will against them that has hitherto not been put into effect. Those who punish them doubtless commit an injustice, but they are prevented from becoming aware of it by the satisfaction arising from the release within themselves of a suppression of long standing. In such cases the quality of the affect is justified, but not its degree; and the self-criticism that has been appeased in respect of the first point is only too ready to neglect to scrutinize the second point. Once you have opened the doors more people enter than it was your original intention to admit.

A striking feature of the neurotic character, namely, that in it causes capable of evoking affect produce results which are qualitatively justified but quantitatively excessive, is to be explained on these lines, in so far as it admits of a psychological explanation at all. But the excess of affect proceeds from unconscious and hitherto suppressed affective sources which are able to establish an associative connection with the actual occasion, and for whose liberation of affect the unprotested and permitted source of affects opens up the desired path. Our attention is thus called to the fact that the relation of mutual inhibition must not be regarded as the only relation obtaining between the suppressed and the suppressing psychic institution. The cases in which the two institutions bring about a pathological result by co-operation and mutual reinforcement deserve just as much attention. These hints regarding the psychic mechanism will contribute to our understanding of the expressions of affects in dreams. A gratification which makes its appearance in a dream, and which, of course, may readily be found in its proper place in the dream-thoughts, may not always be fully explained by means of this reference. As a rule, it is necessary to search for a second source in the dream-thoughts, upon which the pressure of the censorship rests, and which, under this pressure, would have yielded not gratification but the contrary affect, had it not been enabled by the presence of the first dream-source to free its gratification-affect from repression, and reinforce the gratification springing from the other source. Hence affects which appear in dreams appear to be formed by the confluence of several tributaries, and are over-determined in respect of the material of the dream-thoughts. *Sources of affect which are able to furnish the same affect combine in the dream-work in order to produce it.*[1]

Some insight into these involved relations is gained from the analysis of the admirable dream in which *"Non vixit"* constitutes the central point (cf. p. 406). In this dream expressions of affect of different qualities are concentrated at two points in the manifest content. Hostile and painful impulses (in the dream itself we have the phrase "overcome by strange emotions") overlap one another at the point where I destroy my antagonistic friend with a couple of words. At the end of the dream I am greatly pleased, and am quite ready to believe in a possibility which I recognize as absurd when I am awake, namely, that there are *revenants* who can be swept away by a mere wish.

I have not yet mentioned the occasion of this dream. It is an important one, and leads us far down into the meaning of the dream. From my friend in Berlin (whom I have designated as Fl.) I had received the news that he was about to undergo an operation, and that relatives of his living in Vienna would inform me as to his condition. The first few messages after the operation were not very reassuring, and caused me great anxiety. I should have liked to go to him myself, but at that time I was afflicted with a painful complaint which made every movement a torment. I now learn from the dream-thoughts that I feared for this dear friend's life. I knew that his only sister, with whom I had never been acquainted, had died young, after a very brief illness. (*In the dream Fl. tells me about his sister, and says: "In three-quarters of an hour she was dead."*) I must

---

[1] I have since explained the extraordinary effect of pleasure produced by tendency wit on analogous lines.

have imagined that his own constitution was not much stronger, and that I should soon be travelling, in spite of my health, in response to far worse news—and that I should arrive too late, for which I should eternally reproach myself.[1] This reproach, that I should arrive too late, has become the central point of the dream, but it has been represented in a scene in which the revered teacher of my student years—Brücke—reproaches me for the same thing with a terrible look from his blue eyes. What brought about this alteration of the scene will soon become apparent: the dream cannot reproduce the scene itself as I experienced it. To be sure, it leaves the blue eyes to the other man, but it gives me the part of the annihilator, an inversion which is obviously the work of the wish-fulfilment. My concern for the life of my friend, my self-reproach for not having gone to him, my shame (*he had come to me in Vienna unobtrusively*), my desire to consider myself excused on account of my illness—all this builds up an emotional tempest which is distinctly felt in my sleep, and which rages in that region of the dream-thoughts.

But there was another thing in the occasion of the dream which had quite the opposite effect. With the unfavourable news during the first days of the operation I received also an injunction to speak to no one about the whole affair, which hurt my feelings, for it betrayed an unnecessary distrust of my discretion. I knew, of course, that this request did not proceed from my friend, but that it was due to clumsiness or excessive timidity on the part of the messenger; yet the concealed reproach affected me very disagreeably, because it was not altogether unjustified. As we know, only reproaches which "have something in them" have the power to hurt. Years ago, when I was younger than I am now, I knew two men who were friends, and who honoured me with their friendship; and I quite superfluously told one of them what the other had said of him. This incident, of course, had nothing to do with the affairs of my friend Fl., but I have never forgotten the reproaches to which I had to listen on that occasion. One of the two friends between whom I made trouble was Professor Fleischl; the other one I will call by his baptismal name, Josef, a name which was borne also by my friend and antagonist P., who appears in this dream.

In the dream the element unobtrusively points to the reproach that I cannot keep anything to myself, and so does the question of Fl. as to *how much of his affairs I have told P*. But it is the intervention of that old memory which transposes the reproach for arriving too late from the present to the time when I was working in Brücke's laboratory; and by

[1] It is this fancy from the unconscious dream-thoughts which peremptorily demands *non vivit* instead of *non vixit*. "You have come too late, he is no longer alive." The fact that the manifest situation of the dream aims at the *non vivit* has been mentioned on page 407.

replacing the second person in the annihilation scene of the dream by a Josef, I enable this scene to represent not only the first reproach—that I have arrived too late—but also that other reproach, more strongly affected by the repression, to the effect that I do not keep secrets. The work of condensation and displacement in this dream, as well the motives for it, are now obvious.

My present trivial annoyance at the injunction not to divulge secrets draws reinforcement from springs that flow far beneath the surface, and so swells to a stream of hostile impulses towards persons who are in reality dear to me. The source which furnishes the reinforcement is to be found in my childhood. I have already said that my warm friendships as well as my enmities with persons of my own age go back to my childish relations to my nephew, who was a year older than I. In these he had the upper hand, and I early learned how to defend myself; we lived together, were inseparable, and loved one another, but at times, as the statements of older persons testify, we used to squabble and *accuse* one another. In a certain sense, all my friends are incarnations of this first figure; they are all *revenants*. My nephew himself returned when a young man, and then we were like Caesar and Brutus. An intimate friend and a hated enemy have always been indispensable to my emotional life; I have always been able to create them anew, and not infrequently my childish ideal has been so closely approached that friend and enemy have coincided in the same person; but not simultaneously, of course, nor in constant alternation, as was the case in my early childhood.

How, when such associations exist, a recent occasion of emotion may cast back to the infantile occasion and substitute this as a cause of affect, I shall not consider now. Such an investigation would properly belong to the psychology of unconscious thought, or a psychological explanation of the neuroses. Let us assume, for the purposes of dream-interpretation, that a childish recollection presents itself, or is created by the phantasy with, more or less, the following content: We two children quarrel on account of some object—just what we shall leave undecided, although the memory, or illusion of memory, has a very definite object in view—and each claims that *he got there first*, and therefore has the first right to it. We come to blows; Might comes before Right; and, according to the indications of the dream, I must have known that I was in the wrong (*noticing the error myself*); but this time I am the stronger, and take possession of the battlefield; the defeated combatant hurries to my father, his grandfather, and accuses me, and I defend myself with the words, which I have heard from my father: "*I hit him because he hit me.*" Thus, this recollection, or more probably phantasy, which forces itself upon my attention in the course of the analysis—without further evidence I myself do not know how—becomes a central item of the dream-thoughts, which collects the affective impulses prevailing in the dream-thoughts, as the bowl of a fountain collects the water that flows into it. From this point the dream-thoughts flow along the following channels: "It serves you right that you have had to make way for me; why did you try to push me off? I don't need you; I'll soon find someone else to play with," etc. Then the channels are opened through which these thoughts flow back again into the dream-representation. For such an *"ôte-toi que je m'y mette"* I once had to reproach my deceased friend Josef. He was next to me in the line of promotion in Brücke's laboratory, but advancement there was very slow. Neither of the two assistants budged from his place, and youth became impatient. My friend, who knew that his days were numbered, and was bound by no intimate relation to his superior, sometimes gave free expression to his impatience. As this superior was a man seriously ill, the wish to see him removed by promotion was susceptible of an obnoxious secondary interpretation. Several years earlier, to be sure, I myself had cherished, even more intensely, the same wish—to obtain a post which had fallen vacant; wherever there are gradations of rank and promotion the way is opened for the suppression of covetous wishes. Shakespeare's Prince Hal cannot rid himself of the temptation to see how the crown fits, even at the bedside of his sick father. But, as may readily be understood, the dream inflicts this inconsiderate wish not upon me, but upon my friend.[1]

"As he was ambitious, I slew him." As he could not expect that the other man would make way for him, the man himself has been put out of the way. I harbour these thoughts immediately after attending the unveiling of the memorial to the other man at the University. Part of the satisfaction which I feel in the dream may therefore be interpreted: A just punishment; it serves you right.

At the funeral of this friend a young man made the following remark, which seemed rather out of place: "The preacher talked as though the world could no longer exist without this one human being." Here was a stirring of revolt in the heart of a sincere man, whose grief had been disturbed by exaggeration. But with this speech are connected the dream-thoughts: "No one is really irreplaceable; how many men have I already escorted to the grave! But I am still alive; I have survived them all; I claim the field." Such a thought, at the moment when I fear that if I make a journey to see him I shall find my friend no longer among the living, permits only of the further development that I am glad once more to have survived someone; that it is not *I* who have died but he; that I am master

[1] It will have been obvious that the name *Josef* plays a great part in my dreams (see the dream about my uncle). It is particularly easy for me to hide my ego in my dreams behind persons of this name, since Joseph was the name of the dream-interpreter in the Bible.

of the field, as once I was in the imagined scene of my childhood. This satisfaction, infantile in origin, at the fact that I am master of the field, covers the greater part of the affect which appears in the dream. I am glad that I am the survivor; I express this sentiment with the naïve egoism of the husband who says to his wife: "If one of us dies, I shall move to Paris." My expectation takes it as a matter of course that I am not the one to die.

It cannot be denied that great self-control is needed to interpret one's dreams and to report them. One has to reveal oneself as the sole villain among all the noble souls with whom one shares the breath of life. Thus, I find it quite comprehensible that *revenants* should exist only as long as one wants them, and that they can be obliterated by a wish. It was for this reason that my friend Josef was punished. But the *revenants* are the successive incarnations of the friend of my childhood; I am also gratified at having replaced this person for myself over and over again, and a substitute will doubtless soon be found even for the friend whom I am now on the point of losing. No one is irreplaceable.

But what has the dream-censorship been doing in the meantime? Why does it not raise the most emphatic objection to a train of thoughts characterized by such brutal selfishness, and transform the satisfaction inherent therein into extreme discomfort? I think it is because other unobjectionable trains of thought referring to the same persons result also in satisfaction, and with their affect cover that proceeding from the forbidden infantile sources. In another stratum of thought I said to myself, at the ceremony of unveiling the memorial: "I have lost so many dear friends, some through death, some through the dissolution of friendship; is it not good that substitutes have presented themselves, that I have gained a friend who means more to me than the others could, and whom I shall now always retain, at an age when it is not easy to form new friendships?" The gratification of having found this substitute for my lost friend can be taken over into the dream without interference, but behind it there sneaks in the hostile feeling of malicious gratification from the infantile source. Childish affection undoubtedly helps to reinforce the rational affection of to-day; but childish hatred also has found its way into the representation.

But besides this, there is in the dream a distinct reference to another train of thoughts which may result in gratification. Some time before this, after long waiting, a little daughter was born to my friend. I knew how he had grieved for the sister whom he had lost at an early age, and I wrote to him that I felt that he would transfer to this child the love he had felt for her, that this little girl would at last make him forget his irreparable loss.

Thus this train also connects up with the intermediary thoughts of the latent dream-content, from which paths radiate in the most contrary directions: "No one is irreplaceable. See, here are only *revenants;* all those whom one has lost return." And now the bonds of association between the contradictory components of the dream-thoughts are more tightly drawn by the accidental circumstance that my friend's little daughter bears the same name as the girl playmate of my own youth, who was just my own age, and the sister of my oldest friend and antagonist. I heard the name "Pauline" with *satisfaction,* and in order to allude to this coincidence I replaced one Josef in the dream by another Josef, and found it impossible to suppress the identical initials in the name Fleischl and Fl. From this point a train of thought runs to the naming of my own children. I insisted that the names should not be chosen according to the fashion of the day, but should be determined by regard for the memory of those dear to us. The children's names make them *"revenants."* And, finally, is not the procreation of children for all men the only way of access to immortality?

I shall add only a few observations as to the affects of dreams considered from another point of view. In the psyche of the sleeper an affective tendency—what we call a mood—may be contained as its dominating element, and may induce a corresponding mood in the dream. This mood may be the result of the experiences and thoughts of the day, or it may be of somatic origin; in either case it will be accompanied by the corresponding trains of thought. That this ideational content of the dream-thoughts should at one time determine the affective tendency primarily, while at another time it is awakened in a secondary manner by the somatically determined emotional disposition, is indifferent for the purposes of dream-formation. This is always subject to the restriction that it can represent only a wish-fulfilment, and that it may lend its psychic energy to the wish alone. The mood actually present will receive the same treatment as the sensation which actually emerges during sleep (cf. p. 288), which is either neglected or reinterpreted in the sense of a wish-fulfilment. Painful moods during sleep become the motive force of the dream, inasmuch as they awake energetic wishes which the dream has to fulfil. The material in which they inhere is elaborated until it is serviceable for the expression of the wish-fulfilment. The more intense and the more dominating the element of the painful mood in the dream-thoughts, the more surely will the most strongly suppressed wish-impulses take advantage of the opportunity to secure representation; for thanks to the actual existence of discomfort, which otherwise they would have to create spontaneously, they find that the more difficult part of the work necessary to ensure representation has already been accomplished; and with these observations we touch once more upon the problem of anxiety-dreams, which will prove to be the boundary-case of dream-activity.

I. THE SECONDARY ELABORATION

We will at last turn our attention to the fourth of the factors participating in dream-formation.

If we continue our investigation of the dream-content on the lines already laid down—that is, by examining the origin in the dream-thoughts of conspicuous occurrences—we come upon elements that can be explained only by making an entirely new assumption. I have in mind cases where one manifests astonishment, anger, or resistance in a dream, and that, too, in respect of part of the dream-content itself. Most of these impulses of criticism in dreams are not directed against the dream-content, but prove to be part of the dream-material, taken over and fittingly applied, as I have already shown by suitable examples. There are, however, criticisms of this sort which are not so derived: their correlatives cannot be found in the dream-material. What, for instance, is meant by the criticism not infrequent in dreams: "After all, it's only a dream"? This is a genuine criticism of the dream, such as I might make if I were awake. Not infrequently it is only the prelude to waking; even oftener it is preceded by a painful feeling, which subsides when the actuality of the dream-state has been affirmed. The thought: "After all, it's only a dream" in the dream itself has the same intention as it has on the stage on the lips of Offenbach's *Belle Hélène;* it seeks to minimize what has just been experienced, and to secure indulgence for what is to follow. It serves to lull to sleep a certain mental agency which at the given moment has every occasion to rouse itself and forbid the continuation of the dream, or the scene. But it is more convenient to go on sleeping and to tolerate the dream, "because, after all, it's only a dream." I imagine that the disparaging criticism: "After all, it's only a dream," appears in the dream at the moment when the censorship, which is never quite asleep, feels that it has been surprised by the already admitted dream. It is too late to suppress the dream, and the agency therefore meets with this remark the anxiety or painful emotion which rises into the dream. It is an expression of the *esprit d'escalier* on the part of the psychic censorship.

In this example we have incontestable proof that everything which the dream contains does not come from the dream-thoughts, but that a psychic function, which cannot be differentiated from our waking thoughts, may make contributions to the dream-content. The question arises, does this occur only in exceptional cases, or does the psychic agency which is otherwise active only as the censorship play a constant part in dream-formation?

One must decide unhesitatingly for the latter view. It is indisputable that the censoring agency, whose influence we have so far recognized only in the restrictions of and omissions in the dream-content, is likewise responsible for interpolations in and amplifications of this content. Often these interpolations are readily recognized; they are introduced with hesitation, prefaced by an "as if"; they have no special vitality of their own, and are constantly inserted at points where they may serve to connect two portions of the dream-content or create a continuity between two sections of the dream. They manifest less ability to adhere in the memory than do the genuine products of the dream-material; if the dream is forgotten, they are forgotten first, and I strongly suspect that our frequent complaint that although we have dreamed so much we have forgotten most of the dream, and have remembered only fragments, is explained by the immediate falling away of just these cementing thoughts. In a complete analysis these interpolations are often betrayed by the fact that no material is to be found for them in the dream-thoughts. But after careful examination I must describe this case as the less usual one; in most cases the interpolated thoughts can be traced to material in the dream-thoughts which can claim a place in the dream neither by its own merits nor by way of over-determination. Only in the most extreme cases does the psychic function in dream-formation which we are now considering rise to original creation; whenever possible it makes use of anything appropriate that it can find in the dream-material.

What distinguishes this part of the dream-work, and also betrays it, is its tendency. This function proceeds in a manner which the poet maliciously attributes to the philosopher: with its rags and tatters it stops up the breaches in the structure of the dream. The result of its efforts is that the dream loses the appearance of absurdity and incoherence, and approaches the pattern of an intelligible experience. But the effort is not always crowned with complete success. Thus, dreams occur which may, upon superficial examination, seem faultlessly logical and correct; they start from a possible situation, continue it by means of consistent changes, and bring it—although this is rare—to a not unnatural conclusion. These dreams have been subjected to the most searching elaboration by a psychic function similar to our waking thought; they seem to have a meaning, but this meaning is very far removed from the real meaning of the dream. If we analyse them, we are convinced that the secondary elaboration has handled the material with the greatest freedom, and has retained as little as possible of its proper relations. These are the dreams which have, so to speak, already been once interpreted before we subject them to waking interpretation. In other dreams this tendencious elaboration has succeeded only up to a point; up to this point consistency seems to prevail, but then the dream becomes nonsensical or confused; but perhaps before it concludes it may once more rise to a semblance of rationality. In yet other dreams the elaboration has failed completely; we find ourselves helpless, confronted with a senseless mass of fragmentary contents.

I do not wish to deny to this fourth dream-forming power, which will soon become familiar to us—it is in reality the only one of the four dream-creating factors which is familiar to us in other connections—I do not wish to deny to this fourth factor the faculty of creatively making new contributions to our dreams. But its influence is certainly exerted, like that of the other factors, mainly in the preference and selection of psychic material already formed in the dream-thoughts. Now there is a case where it is to a great extent spared the work of building, as it were, a façade to the dream by the fact that such a structure, only waiting to be used, already exists in the material of the dream-thoughts. I am accustomed to describe the element of the dream-thoughts which I have in mind as "phantasy"; I shall perhaps avoid misunderstanding if I at once point to the *day-dream* as an analogy in waking life.[1] The part played by this element in our psychic life has not yet been fully recognized and revealed by psychiatrists; though M. Benedikt has, it seems to me, made a highly promising beginning. Yet the significance of the day-dream has not escaped the unerring insight of the poets; we are all familiar with the description of the day-dreams of one of his subordinate characters which Alphonse Daudet has given us in his *Nabab*. The study of the psycho-neuroses discloses the astonishing fact that these phantasies or day-dreams are the immediate predecessors of symptoms of hysteria—at least, of a great many of them; for hysterical symptoms are dependent not upon actual memories, but upon the phantasies built up on a basis of memories. The frequent occurrence of conscious day-phantasies brings these formations to our ken; but while some of these phantasies are conscious, there is a superabundance of unconscious phantasies, which must perforce remain unconscious on account of their content and their origin in repressed material. A more thorough examination of the character of these day-phantasies shows with what good reason the same name has been given to these formations as to the products of nocturnal thought—*dreams*. They have essential features in common with nocturnal dreams; indeed, the investigation of day-dreams might really have afforded the shortest and best approach to the understanding of nocturnal dreams.

Like dreams, they are wish-fulfilments; like dreams, they are largely based upon the impressions of childish experiences; like dreams, they obtain a certain indulgence from the censorship in respect of their creations. If we trace their formation, we become aware how the wish-motive which has been operative in their production has taken the material of which they are built, mixed it together, rearranged it, and fitted it together into a new whole. They bear very much the same relation to the

[1] *Rêve, petit roman* = day-dream, story.

childish memories to which they refer as many of the baroque palaces of Rome bear to the ancient ruins, whose hewn stones and columns have furnished the material for the structures built in the modern style.

In the "secondary elaboration" of the dream-content which we have ascribed to our fourth dream-forming factor, we find once more the very same activity which is allowed to manifest itself, uninhibited by other influences, in the creation of day-dreams. We may say, without further preliminaries, that this fourth factor of ours seeks to construct *something like* a day-dream from the material which offers itself. But where such a day-dream has already been constructed in the context of the dream-thoughts, this factor of the dream-work will prefer to take possession of it, and contrive that it gets into the dream-content. There are dreams that consist merely of the repetition of a day-phantasy, which has perhaps remained unconscious—as, for instance, the boy's dream that he is riding in a war-chariot with the heroes of the Trojan war. In my *"Autodidasker"* dream the second part of the dream at least is the faithful repetition of a day-phantasy—harmless in itself—of my dealings with Professor N. The fact that the exciting phantasy forms only a part of the dream, or that only a part of it finds its way into the dream-content, is due to the complexity of the conditions which the dream must satisfy at its genesis. On the whole, the phantasy is treated like any other component of the latent material; but it is often still recognizable as a whole in the dream. In my dreams there are often parts which are brought into prominence by their producing a different impression from that produced by the other parts. They seem to me to be in a state of flux, to be more coherent and at the same time more transient than other portions of the same dream. I know that these are unconscious phantasies which find their way into the context of the dream, but I have never yet succeeded in registering such a phantasy. For the rest, these phantasies, like all the other component parts of the dream-thoughts, are jumbled together, condensed, superimposed, and so on; but we find all the transitional stages, from the case in which they may constitute the dream-content, or at least the dream-façade, unaltered, to the most contrary case, in which they are represented in the dream-content by only one of their elements, or by a remote allusion to such an element. The fate of the phantasies in the dream-thoughts is obviously determined by the advantages they can offer as against the claims of the censorship and the pressure of condensation.

In my choice of examples for dream-interpretation I have, as far as possible, avoided those dreams in which unconscious phantasies play a considerable part, because the introduction of this psychic element would have necessitated an extensive discussion of the psychology of unconscious thought. But even in this connection I cannot entirely avoid the "phantasy," because it often finds its way into the dream complete, and still more often perceptibly glimmers through it. I might mention yet one more dream, which seems to be composed of two distinct and opposed phantasies, overlapping here and there, of which the first is superficial, while the second becomes, as it were, the interpretation of the first.[1]

The dream—it is the only one of which I possess no careful notes—is roughly to this effect: *The dreamer—a young unmarried man—is sitting in his favourite inn, which is seen correctly; several persons come to fetch him, among them someone who wants to arrest him. He says to his table companions, "I will pay later, I am coming back." But they cry, smiling scornfully: "We know all about that; that's what everybody says." One guest calls after him: "There goes another one." He is then led to a small place where he finds a woman with a child in her arms. One of his escorts says: "This is Herr Müller." A commissioner or some other official is running through a bundle of tickets or papers, repeating Müller, Müller, Müller. At last the commissioner asks him a question, which he answers with a "Yes." He then takes a look at the woman, and notices that she has grown a large beard.*

The two component parts are here easily separable. What is superficial is the *phantasy of being arrested;* this seems to be newly created by the dream-work. But behind it the *phantasy of marriage* is visible, and this material, on the other hand, has been slightly modified by the dream-work, and the features which may be common to the two phantasies appear with special distinctness, as in Galton's composite photographs. The promise of the young man, who is at present a bachelor, to return to his place at his accustomed table—the scepticism of his drinking companions, made wise by their many experiences—their calling after him: "There goes (marries) another one"—are all features easily susceptible of the other interpretation, as is the affirmative answer given to the official. Running through a bundle of papers and repeating the same name corresponds to a subordinate but easily recognized feature of the marriage ceremony—the reading aloud of the congratulatory telegrams which have arrived at irregular intervals, and which, of course, are all addressed to the same name. In the personal appearance of the bride in this dream the marriage phantasy has even got the better of the arrest phantasy which screens it. The fact that this bride finally wears a beard I can explain from information received—I had no opportunity of making an

[1] I have analysed an excellent example of a dream of this kind, having its origin in the stratification of several phantasies, in the *Fragment of an Analysis of a Case of Hysteria* (*Collected Papers,* vol. iii). I undervalued the significance of such phantasies for dream-formation as long as I was working principally on my own dreams, which were rarely based upon day-dreams but most frequently upon discussions and mental conflicts. With other persons it is often much easier to prove the *complete analogy between the nocturnal dream and the day-dream.* In hysterical patients an attack may often be replaced by a dream; it is then obvious that the day-dream phantasy is the first step for both these psychic formations.

analysis. The dreamer had, on the previous day, been crossing the street with a friend who was just as hostile to marriage as himself, and had called his friend's attention to a beautiful brunette who was coming towards them. The friend had remarked: "Yes, if only these women wouldn't get beards as they grow older, like their fathers."

Of course, even in this dream there is no lack of elements with which the dream-distortion has done deep work. Thus, the speech, "I will pay later," may have reference to the behaviour feared on the part of the father-in-law in the matter of a dowry. Obviously all sorts of misgivings are preventing the dreamer from surrendering himself with pleasure to the phantasy of marriage. One of these misgivings—that with marriage he might lose his freedom—has embodied itself in the transformation of a scene of arrest.

If we once more return to the thesis that the dream-work prefers to make use of a ready-made phantasy, instead of first creating one from the material of the dream-thoughts, we shall perhaps be able to solve one of the most interesting problems of the dream. I have related the dream of Maury, who is struck on the back of the neck by a small board, and wakes after a long dream—a complete romance of the period of the French Revolution. Since the dream is produced in a coherent form, and completely fits the explanation of the waking stimulus, of whose occurrence the sleeper could have had no forboding, only one assumption seems possible, namely, that the whole richly elaborated dream must have been composed and dreamed in the short interval of time between the falling of the board on Maury's cervical vertebrae and the waking induced by the blow. We should not venture to ascribe such rapidity to the mental operations of the waking state, so that we have to admit that the dream-work has the privilege of a remarkable acceleration of its issue.

To this conclusion, which rapidly became popular, more recent authors (Le Lorrain, Egger, and others) have opposed emphatic objections; some of them doubt the correctness of Maury's record of the dream, some seek to show that the rapidity of our mental operations in waking life is by no means inferior to that which we can, without reservation, ascribe to the mental operations in dreams. The discussion raises fundamental questions, which I do not think are at all near solution. But I must confess that Egger's objections, for example, to Maury's dream of the guillotine, do not impress me as convincing. I would suggest the following explanation of this dream: Is it so very improbable that Maury's dream may have represented a phantasy which had been preserved for years in his memory, in a completed state, and which was awakened—I should like to say, alluded to—at the moment when he became aware of the waking stimulus? The whole difficulty of composing so long a story, with all its details, in the exceedingly short space of time which is here at the dreamer's disposal then disappears; the story was already composed. If the board had struck Maury's neck when he was awake, there would perhaps have been time for the thought: "Why, that's just like being guillotined." But as he is struck by the board while asleep, the dream-work quickly utilizes the incoming stimulus for the construction of a wish-fulfilment, *as if* it thought (this is to be taken quite figuratively): "Here is a good opportunity to realize the wish-phantasy which I formed at such and such a time while I was reading." It seems to me undeniable that this dream-romance is just such a one as a young man is wont to construct under the influence of exciting impressions. Who has not been fascinated—above all, a Frenchman and a student of the history of civilization—by descriptions of the Reign of Terror, in which the aristocracy, men and women, the flower of the nation, showed that it was possible to die with a light heart, and preserved their ready wit and the refinement of their manners up to the moment of the last fateful summons? How tempting to fancy oneself in the midst of all this, as one of these young men who take leave of their ladies with a kiss of the hand, and fearlessly ascend the scaffold! Or perhaps ambition was the ruling motive of the phantasy—the ambition to put oneself in the place of one of those powerful personalities who, by their sheer force of intellect and their fiery eloquence, ruled the city in which the heart of mankind was then beating so convulsively; who were impelled by their convictions to send thousands of human beings to their death, and were paving the way for the transformation of Europe; who, in the meantime, were not sure of their own heads, and might one day lay them under the knife of the guillotine, perhaps in the rôle of a Girondist or the hero Danton? The detail preserved in the memory of the dream, "accompanied by an enormous crowd," seems to show that Maury's phantasy was an ambitious one of just this character.

But the phantasy prepared so long ago need not be experienced again in sleep; it is enough that it should be, so to speak, "touched off." What I mean is this: If a few notes are struck, and someone says, as in *Don Juan:* "That is from *Figaro's Wedding* by Mozart," memories suddenly surge up within me, none of which I can recall to consciousness a moment later. The phrase serves as a point of irruption from which a complete whole is simultaneously put into a condition of stimulation. It may well be the same in unconscious thinking. Through the waking stimulus the psychic station is excited which gives access to the whole guillotine phantasy. This phantasy, however, is not run through in sleep, but only in the memory of the awakened sleeper. Upon waking, the sleeper remembers in detail the phantasy which was transferred as a whole into the dream. At the same time, he has no means of assuring himself that he is really remembering something which was dreamed. The same explanation—namely, that one is dealing with finished phantasies which have been evoked as wholes by the waking stimulus—may be applied to other dreams which are adapted to the waking stimulus—for example, to Napoleon's dream of a battle before the explosion of a bomb. Among the dreams collected by Justine Tobowolska in her dissertation on the apparent duration of time in dreams,[1] I think the most corroborative is that related by Macario (1857) as having been dreamed by a playwright, Casimir Bonjour. Bonjour intended one evening to witness the first performance of one of his own plays, but he was so tired that he dozed off in his chair behind the scenes just as the curtain was rising. In his sleep he went through all the five acts of his play, and observed all the various signs of emotion which were manifested by the audience during each individual scene. At the close of the performance, to his great satisfaction, he heard his name called out amidst the most lively manifestations of applause. Suddenly he woke. He could hardly believe either his eyes or his ears; the performance had not gone beyond the first lines of the first scene; he could not have been asleep for more than two minutes. As for the dream, the running through the five acts of the play and the observing the attitude of the public towards each individual scene need not, we may venture to assert, have been something new, produced while the dreamer was asleep; it may have been a repetition of an already completed work of the phantasy. Tobowolska and other authors have emphasized a common characteristic of dreams that show an accelerated flow of ideas: namely, that they seem to be especially coherent, and not at all like other dreams, and that the dreamer's memory of them is summary rather than detailed. But these are precisely the characteristics which would necessarily be exhibited by ready-made phantasies touched off by the dream-work—a conclusion which is not, of course, drawn by these authors. I do not mean to assert that all dreams due to a waking stimulus admit of this explanation, or that the problem of the accelerated flux of ideas in dreams is entirely disposed of in this manner.

And here we are forced to consider the relation of this secondary elaboration of the dream-content to the other factors of the dream-work. May not the procedure perhaps be as follows? The dream-forming factors, the efforts at condensation, the necessity of evading the censorship, and the regard for representability by the psychic means of the dream first of all create from the dream-material a provisional dream-content, which is subsequently modified until it satisfies as far as possible the exactions of a secondary agency.—No, this is hardly probable. We must rather assume that the requirements of this agency constitute from the very first one of the conditions which the dream must satisfy, and that this condition, as well as the conditions of condensation, the opposing censorship,

---

[1] Tobowolska, Justine. *Étude sur les illusions de temps dans les rêves du sommeil normal,* 1900, p. 53.

and representability, simultaneously influence, in an inductive and selective manner, the whole mass of material in the dream-thoughts. But of the four conditions necessary for dream-formation, the last recognized is that whose exactions appear to be least binding upon the dream. The following consideration makes it seem very probable that this psychic function, which undertakes the so-called secondary elaboration of the dream-content, is identical with the work of our waking thought: Our waking (preconscious) thought behaves towards any given perceptual material precisely as the function in question behaves towards the dream-content. It is natural to our waking thought to create order in such material, to construct relations, and to subject it to the requirements of an intelligible coherence. Indeed, we go rather too far in this respect; the tricks of conjurers befool us by taking advantage of this intellectual habit of ours. In the effort to combine in an intelligible manner the sensory impressions which present themselves we often commit the most curious mistakes, and even distort the truth of the material before us. The proofs of this fact are so familiar that we need not give them further consideration here. We overlook errors which make nonsense of a printed page because we imagine the proper words. The editor of a widely read French journal is said to have made a bet that he could print the words "from in front" or "from behind" in every sentence of a long article without any of his readers noticing it. He won his bet. Years ago I came across a comical example of false association in a newspaper. After the session of the French Chamber in which Dupuy quelled the panic, caused by the explosion of a bomb thrown by an anarchist, with the courageous words, "La séance continue," the visitors in the gallery were asked to testify as to their impressions of the outrage. Among them were two provincials. One of these said that immediately after the end of a speech he had heard a detonation, but that he had thought that it was the parliamentary custom to fire a shot whenever a speaker had finished. The other, who had apparently already listened to several speakers, had got hold of the same idea, but with this variation, that he supposed the shooting to be a sign of appreciation following a specially successful speech.

Thus, the psychic agency which approaches the dream-content with the demand that it must be intelligible, which subjects it to a first interpretation, and in doing so leads to the complete misunderstanding of it, is none other than our normal thought. In our interpretation the rule will be, in every case, to disregard the apparent coherence of the dream as being of suspicious origin and, whether the elements are confused or clear, to follow the same regressive path to the dream-material.

At the same-time, we note those factors upon which the above-mentioned (p. 353) scale of quality in dreams—from confusion to clearness — is essentially dependent. Those parts of the dream seem to us clear in which the secondary elaboration has been able to accomplish something; those seem confused where the powers of this performance have failed. Since the confused parts of the dream are often likewise those which are less vividly presented, we may conclude that the secondary dream-work is responsible also for a contribution to the plastic intensity of the individual dream-structures.

If I seek an object of comparison for the definitive formation of the dream, as it manifests itself with the assistance of normal thinking, I can think of none better than those mysterious inscriptions with which *Die Fliegende Blätter* has so long amused its readers. In a certain sentence which, for the sake of contrast, is in dialect, and whose significance is as scurrilous as possible, the reader is led to expect a Latin inscription. For this purpose the letters of the words are taken out of their syllabic groupings, and are rearranged. Here and there a genuine Latin word results; at other points, on the assumption that letters have been obliterated by weathering, or omitted, we allow ourselves to be deluded about the significance of certain isolated and meaningless letters. If we do not wish to be fooled we must give up looking for an inscription, must take the letters as they stand, and combine them, disregarding their arrangement, into words of our mother tongue.

The secondary elaboration is that factor of the dream-work which has been observed by most of the writers on dreams, and whose importance has been duly appreciated. Havelock Ellis gives an amusing allegorical description of its performances: "As a matter of fact, we might even imagine the sleeping consciousness as saying to itself: 'Here comes our master, Waking Consciousness, who attaches such mighty importance to reason and logic and so forth. Quick! gather things up, put them in order —any order will do—before he enters to take possession.' " [1]

The identity of this mode of operation with that of waking thought is very clearly stated by Delacroix in his *Sur la structure logique du rêve* (p. 526): *"Cette fonction d'interprétation n'est pas particulière au rêve; c'est le même travail de coordination logique que nous faisons sur nos sensations pendant la veille."*

J. Sully is of the same opinion; and so is Tobowolska: *"Sur ces successions incohérentes d'hallucinations, l'esprit s'efforce de faire le même travail de coordination logique qu'il fait pendant la veille sur les sensations. Il relie entre elles par un lien imaginaire toutes ces images décousues et bouche les écarts trop grands qui se trouvaient entre elles"* (p. 93).

Some authors maintain that this ordering and interpreting activity begins even in the dream and is continued in the waking state. Thus Paulhan (p. 547): *"Cependant j'ai souvent pensé qu'il pouvait y avoir une certain déformation, ou plutôt reformation du rêve dans le souvenir. . . . La*

[1] *The World of Dreams*, pp. 10, 11, London, 1911.

tendence systématisante de l'imagination pourrait fort bien achever après le réveil ce qu'elle a ébauché pendant le sommeil. De la sorte, la rapidité réelle de la pensée serait augmentée en apparence par les perfectionnements dûs à l'imagination éveillée."

Leroy and Tobowolska (p. 592): *"Dans le rêve, au contraire, l'interprétation et la coordination se font non seulement à l'aide des données du rêve, mais encore à l'aide de celles de la veille. . . ."*

It was therefore inevitable that this one recognized factor of dream-formation should be over-estimated, so that the whole process of creating the dream was attributed to it. This creative work was supposed to be accomplished at the moment of waking, as was assumed by Goblot, and with deeper conviction by Foucault, who attributed to waking thought the faculty of creating the dream out of the thoughts which emerged in sleep.

In respect to this conception Leroy and Tobowolska express themselves as follows: *"On a cru pouvoir placer le rêve au moment du reveil et ils ont attribué à la pensée de la veille la fonction de construire le rêve avec les images présentes dans la pensée du sommeil."*

To this estimate of the secondary elaboration I will add the one fresh contribution to the dream-work which has been indicated by the sensitive observations of H. Silberer. Silberer has caught the transformation of thoughts into images *in flagranti*, by forcing himself to accomplish intellectual work while in a state of fatigue and somnolence. The elaborated thought vanished, and in its place there appeared a vision which proved to be a substitute for—usually abstract—thoughts. In these experiments it so happened that the emerging image, which may be regarded as a dream-element, represented something other than the thoughts which were waiting for elaboration: namely, the exhaustion itself, the difficulty or distress involved in this work; that is, the subjective state and the manner of functioning of the person exerting himself rather than the object of his exertions. Silberer called this case, which in him occurred quite often, the "functional phenomenon," in contradistinction to the "material phenomenon" which he expected.

"For example: one afternoon I am lying, extremely sleepy, on my sofa, but I nevertheless force myself to consider a philosophical problem. I endeavour to compare the views of Kant and Schopenhauer concerning time. Owing to my somnolence I do not succeed in holding on to both trains of thought, which would have been necessary for the purposes of comparison. After several vain efforts, I once more exert all my will-power to formulate for myself the Kantian deduction in order to apply it to Schopenhauer's statement of the problem. Thereupon, I directed my attention to the latter, but when I tried to return to Kant, I found that he had again escaped me, and I tried in vain to fetch him back. And now this fruitless endeavour to rediscover the Kantian documents mislaid some-where in my head suddenly presented itself, my eyes being closed, as in a dream-image, in the form of a visible, plastic symbol: *I demand informa-tion of a grumpy secretary, who, bent over a desk, does not allow my urgency to disturb him; half straightening himself, he gives me a look of angry refusal.*" [1]

Other examples, which relate to the fluctuation between sleep and waking:—

"Example No. 2.—Conditions: Morning, while awaking. While to a certain extent asleep (crepuscular state), thinking over a previous dream, in a way repeating and finishing it, I feel myself drawing nearer to the waking state, yet I wish to remain in the crepuscular state.

"Scene: *I am stepping with one foot over a stream, but I at once pull it back again and resolve to remain on this side.*" [2]

"Example No. 6.—Conditions the same as in Example No. 4 (he wishes to remain in bed a little longer without oversleeping). I wish to indulge in a little longer sleep.

"Scene: *I am saying good-bye to somebody, and I agree to meet him (or her) again before long.*"

I will now proceed to summarize this long disquisition on the dream-work. We were confronted by the question whether in dream-formation the psyche exerts all its faculties to their full extent, without inhibition, or only a fraction of them, which are restricted in their action. Our in-vestigations lead us to reject such a statement of the problem as wholly inadequate in the circumstances. But if, in our answer, we are to remain on the ground upon which the question forces us, we must assent to two conceptions which are apparently opposed and mutually exclusive. The psychic activity in dream-formation resolves itself into two achievements: the production of the dream-thoughts and the transformation of these into the dream-content. The dream-thoughts are perfectly accurate, and are formed with all the psychic profusion of which we are capable; they belong to the thoughts which have not become conscious, from which our conscious thoughts also result by means of a certain transposition. There is doubtless much in them that is worth knowing, and also mysterious, but these problems have no particular relation to our dreams, and cannot claim to be treated under the head of dream-problems.[3] On the other

---

[1] *Jahrb.*, i, p. 514.
[2] *Jahrb.*, iii, p. 625.
[3] Formerly I found it extraordinarily difficult to accustom my readers to the dis-tinction between the manifest dream-content and the latent dream-thoughts. Over and over again arguments and objections were adduced from the uninterpreted

hand we have the process which changes the unconscious thoughts into the dream-content, which is peculiar to the dream-life and characteristic of it. Now, this peculiar dream-work is much farther removed from the pattern of waking thought than has been supposed by even the most decided depreciators of the psychic activity in dream-formation. It is not so much that it is more negligent, more incorrect, more forgetful, more incomplete than waking thought; it is something altogether different, qualitatively, from waking thought, and cannot therefore be compared with it. It does not think, calculate, or judge at all, but limits itself to the work of transformation. It may be exhaustively described if we do not lose sight of the conditions which its product must satisfy. This product, the dream, has above all to be withdrawn from the censorship, and to this end the dream-work makes use of the *displacement of psychic intensities*, even to the transvaluation of all psychic values; thoughts must be exclusively or predominantly reproduced in the material of visual and acoustic memory-traces, and from this requirement there proceeds the *regard of the dream-work for representability*, which it satisfies by fresh displacements. Greater intensities have (probably) to be produced than are at the disposal of the night dream-thoughts, and this purpose is served by the extensive *condensation* to which the constituents of the dream-thoughts are subjected. Little attention is paid to the logical relations of the thought-material; they ultimately find a veiled representation in the *formal* peculiarities of the dream. The affects of the dream-thoughts undergo slighter alterations than their conceptual content. As a rule, they are suppressed; where they are preserved, they are freed from the concepts and combined in accordance with their similarity. Only one part of the dream-work—the revision, variable in amount, which is effected by the partially awakened conscious thought—is at all consistent with the conception which the writers on the subject have endeavoured to extend to the whole performance of dream-formation.

dream as it was retained in the memory, and the necessity of interpreting the dream was ignored. But now, when the analysts have at least become reconciled to substituting for the manifest dream its meaning as found by interpretation, many of them are guilty of another mistake, to which they adhere just as stubbornly. They look for the essence of the dream in this latent content, and thereby overlook the distinction between latent dream-thoughts and the dream-work. The dream is fundamentally nothing more than a special *form* of our thinking, which is made possible by the conditions of the sleeping state. It is the dream-work which produces this form, and it alone is the essence of dreaming—the only explanation of its singularity. I say this in order to correct the reader's judgment of the notorious "prospective tendency" of dreams. That the dream should concern itself with efforts to perform the tasks with which our psychic life is confronted is no more remarkable than that our conscious waking life should so concern itself, and I will only add that this work may be done also in the preconscious, a fact already familiar to us.

THE PSYCHOLOGY OF THE DREAM-
PROCESSES

AMONG the dreams which have been communicated to me by others there is one which is at this point especially worthy of our attention. It was told me by a female patient who had heard it related in a lecture on dreams. Its original source is unknown to me. This dream evidently made a deep impression upon the lady, since she went so far as to imitate it, i.e. to repeat the elements of this dream in a dream of her own; in order, by this transference, to express her agreement with a certain point in the dream.

The preliminary conditions of this typical dream were as follows: A father had been watching day and night beside the sick-bed of his child. After the child died, he retired to rest in an adjoining room, but left the door ajar so that he could look from his room into the next, where the child's body lay surrounded by tall candles. An old man, who had been installed as a watcher, sat beside the body, murmuring prayers. After sleeping for a few hours the father dreamed that *the child was standing by his bed, clasping his arm and crying reproachfully: "Father, don't you see that I am burning?"* The father woke up and noticed a bright light coming from the adjoining room. Rushing in, he found that the old man had fallen asleep, and the sheets and one arm of the beloved body were burnt by a fallen candle.

The meaning of this affecting dream is simple enough, and the explanation given by the lecturer, as my patient reported it, was correct. The bright light shining through the open door on to the sleeper's eyes gave him the impression which he would have received had he been awake: namely, that a fire had been started near the corpse by a falling candle. It is quite possible that he had taken into his sleep his anxiety lest the aged watcher should not be equal to his task.

We can find nothing to change in this interpretation; we can only add that the content of the dream must be overdetermined, and that the speech of the child must have consisted of phrases which it had uttered while still alive, and which were associated with important events for the father. Perhaps the complaint, "I am burning," was associated with the fever from which the child died, and "Father, don't you see?" to some other affective occurrence unknown to us.

Now, when we have come to recognize that the dream has meaning, and can be fitted into the context of psychic events, it may be surprising that a dream should have occurred in circumstances which called for such an immediate waking. We shall then note that even this dream is not lacking in a wish-fulfilment. The dead child behaves as though alive; he warns his father himself; he comes to his father's bed and clasps his arm, as he probably did in the recollection from which the dream obtained the first part of the child's speech. It was for the sake of this wish-fulfilment that the father slept a moment longer. The dream was given precedence over waking reflection because it was able to show the child still living. If the father had waked first, and had then drawn the conclusion which led him into the adjoining room, he would have shortened the child's life by this one moment.

There can be no doubt about the peculiar features in this brief dream which engage our particular interest. So far, we have endeavoured mainly to ascertain wherein the secret meaning of the dream consists, how it is to be discovered, and what means the dream-work uses to conceal it. In other words, our greatest interest has hitherto been centred on the problems of interpretation. Now, however, we encounter a dream which is easily explained, and the meaning of which is without disguise; we note that nevertheless this dream preserves the essential characteristics which conspicuously differentiate a dream from our waking thoughts, and this difference demands an explanation. It is only when we have disposed of all the problems of interpretation that we feel how incomplete is our psychology of dreams.

But before we turn our attention to this new path of investigation, let us stop and look back, and consider whether we have not overlooked something important on our way hither. For we must understand that the easy and comfortable part of our journey lies behind us. Hitherto, all the paths that we have followed have led, if I mistake not, to light, to explanation, and to full understanding; but from the moment when we seek to penetrate more deeply into the psychic processes in dreaming, all paths lead into darkness. It is quite impossible to *explain* the dream as a psychic process, for to explain means to trace back to the known, and as yet we have no psychological knowledge to which we can refer such explanatory fundamentals as may be inferred from the psychological investigation of dreams. On the contrary, we shall be compelled to advance a number of new assumptions, which do little more than conjecture the structure of the psychic apparatus and the play of the energies active in it; and we shall have to be careful not to go too far beyond the simplest logical construction, since otherwise its value will be doubtful. And even if we should be unerring in our inferences, and take cognizance of all the logical possibilities, we should still be in danger of arriving at a completely mistaken result, owing to the probable incompleteness of the preliminary statement of our elementary data. We shall not be able to arrive at any conclusions as to the structure and function of the psychic instrument from even the most careful investigation of dreams, or of any other *isolated* activity; or, at all events, we shall not be able to confirm our conclusions. To do this we shall have to collate such phenomena as the comparative study of a whole series of psychic activities proves to be reliably constant. So that the psychological assumptions which we base on the analysis of the dream-processes will have to mark time, as it were, until they can join up with the results of other investigations which, proceeding from another starting-point, will seek to penetrate to the heart of the same problem.

A. THE FORGETTING OF DREAMS

I propose, then, that we shall first of all turn our attention to a subject which brings us to a hitherto disregarded objection, which threatens to undermine the very foundation of our efforts at dream-interpretation. The objection has been made from more than one quarter that the dream which we wish to interpret is really unknown to us, or, to be more precise, that we have no guarantee that we know it as it really occurred.

What we recollect of the dream, and what we subject to our methods of interpretation, is, in the first place, mutilated by the unfaithfulness of our memory, which seems quite peculiarly incapable of retaining dreams, and which may have omitted precisely the most significant parts of their content. For when we try to consider our dreams attentively, we often have reason to complain that we have dreamed much more than we remember; that unfortunately we know nothing more than this one fragment, and that our recollection of even this fragment seems to us strangely uncertain. Moreover, everything goes to prove that our memory reproduces the dream not only incompletely but also untruthfully, in a falsifying manner. As, on the one hand, we may doubt whether what we dreamed was really as disconnected as it is in our recollections, so on the other hand we may doubt whether a dream was really as coherent as our account of it; whether in our attempted reproduction we have not filled in the gaps which really existed, or those which are due to forgetfulness, with new and arbitrarily chosen material; whether we have not embellished the dream, rounded it off and corrected it, so that any conclusion as to its real content becomes impossible. Indeed, one writer (Spitta) [1] surmises that all that is orderly and coherent is really first put into the dream

---

[1] Similar views are expressed by Foucault and Tannery.

during the attempt to recall it. Thus we are in danger of being deprived
of the very object whose value we have undertaken to determine.

In all our dream-interpretations we have hitherto ignored these warnings. On the contrary, indeed, we have found that the smallest, most
insignificant, and most uncertain components of the dream-content invited interpretations no less emphatically than those which were distinctly and certainly contained in the dream. In the dream of Irma's
injection we read: "I *quickly* called in Dr. M," and we assumed that even
this small addendum would not have got into the dream if it had not
been susceptible of a special derivation. In this way we arrived at the
history of that unfortunate patient to whose bedside I "quickly" called
my older colleague. In the seemingly absurd dream which treated the
difference between fifty-one and fifty-six as a *quantité négligeable* the
number fifty-one was mentioned repeatedly. Instead of regarding this as
a matter of course, or a detail of indifferent value, we proceeded from
this to a second train of thought in the latent dream-content, which led
to the number fifty-one, and by following up this clue we arrived at the
fears which proposed fifty-one years as the term of life in the sharpest
opposition to a dominant train of thought which was boastfully lavish
of the years. In the dream *"Non vixit"* I found, as an insignificant interpolation, that I had at first overlooked the sentence: *"As P. does not understand him, Fl. asks me,"* etc. The interpretation then coming to a standstill, I went back to these words, and I found through them the way to the
infantile phantasy which appeared in the dream-thoughts as an intermediate point of junction. This came about by means of the poet's
verses:—

> "Selten habt ihr mich *verstanden,*
> Selten auch verstand ich Euch,
> Nur wenn wir im *Kot* uns fanden
> So verstanden wir uns gleich!"

> "(Seldom have you *understood* me,
> Seldom have I understood you,
> But when we found ourselves in the *mire,*
> We at once understood each other!)"

Every analysis will afford evidence of the fact that the most insignificant
features of the dream are indispensable to interpretation, and will show
how the completion of the task is delayed if we postpone our examination of them. We have given equal attention, in the interpretation of
dreams, to every nuance of verbal expression found in them; indeed,
whenever we were confronted by a senseless or insufficient wording, as
though we had failed to translate the dream into the proper version, we

have respected even these defects of expression. In brief, what other writers have regarded as arbitrary improvisations, concocted hastily to avoid confusion, we have treated like a sacred text. This contradiction calls for explanation.

It would appear, without doing any injustice to the writers in question, that the explanation is in our favour. From the standpoint of our newly-acquired insight into the origin of dreams, all contradictions are completely reconciled. It is true that we distort the dream in our attempt to reproduce it; we once more find therein what we have called the secondary and often misunderstanding elaboration of the dream by the agency of normal thinking. But this distortion is itself no more than a part of the elaboration to which the dream-thoughts are constantly subjected as a result of the dream-censorship. Other writers have here suspected or observed that part of the dream-distortion whose work is manifest; but for us this is of little consequence, as we know that a far more extensive work of distortion, not so easily apprehended, has already taken the dream for its object from among the hidden dream-thoughts. The only mistake of these writers consists in believing the modification effected in the dream by its recollection and verbal expression to be arbitrary, incapable of further solution, and consequently liable to lead us astray in our cognition of the dream. They underestimate the determination of the dream in the psyche. Here there is nothing arbitrary. It can be shown that in all cases a second train of thought immediately takes over the determination of the elements which have been left undetermined by the first. For example, I wish quite arbitrarily to think of a number; but this is not possible; the number that occurs to me is definitely and necessarily determined by thoughts within me which may be quite foreign to my momentary purpose.[1] The modifications which the dream undergoes in its revision by the waking mind are just as little arbitrary. They preserve an associative connection with the content, whose place they take, and serve to show us the way to this content, which may itself be a substitute for yet another content.

In analysing the dreams of patients I impose the following test of this assertion, and never without success. If the first report of a dream seems not very comprehensible, I request the dreamer to repeat it. This he rarely does in the same words. But the passages in which the expression is modified are thereby made known to me as the weak points of the dream's disguise; they are what the embroidered emblem on Siegfried's raiment was to Hagen. These are the points from which the analysis may start. The narrator has been admonished by my announcement that I intend to take special pains to solve the dream, and immediately, obedient to the urge of resistance, he protects the weak points of the dream's

[1] Cf. *The Psychopathology of Everyday Life.*

disguise, replacing a treacherous expression by a less relevant one. He thus calls my attention to the expressions which he has discarded. From the efforts made to guard against the solution of the dream, I can also draw conclusions about the care with which the raiment of the dream has been woven.

The writers whom I have mentioned are, however, less justified when they attribute so much importance to the doubt with which our judgment approaches the relation of the dream. For this doubt is not intellectually warranted; our memory can give no guarantees, but nevertheless we are compelled to credit its statements far more frequently than is objectively justifiable. Doubt concerning the accurate reproduction of the dream, or of individual data of the dream, is only another offshoot of the dream-censorship, that is, of resistance to the emergence of the dream-thoughts into consciousness. This resistance has not yet exhausted itself by the displacements and substitutions which it has effected, so that it still clings, in the form of doubt, to what has been allowed to emerge. We can recognize this doubt all the more readily in that it is careful never to attack the intensive elements of the dream, but only the weak and indistinct ones. But we already know that a transvaluation of all the psychic values has taken place between the dream-thoughts and the dream. The distortion has been made possible only by devaluation; it constantly manifests itself in this way and sometimes contents itself therewith. If doubt is added to the indistinctness of an element of the dream-content, we may, following this indication, recognize in this element a direct offshoot of one of the outlawed dream-thoughts. The state of affairs is like that obtaining after a great revolution in one of the republics of antiquity or the Renaissance. The once powerful, ruling families of the nobility are now banished; all high posts are filled by upstarts; in the city itself only the poorer and most powerless citizens, or the remoter followers of the vanquished party, are tolerated. Even the latter do not enjoy the full rights of citizenship. They are watched with suspicion. In our case, instead of suspicion we have doubt. I must insist, therefore, that in the analysis of a dream one must emancipate oneself from the whole scale of standards of reliability; and if there is the slightest possibility that this or that may have occurred in the dream, it should be treated as an absolute certainty. Until one has decided to reject all respect for appearances in tracing the dream-elements, the analysis will remain at a standstill. Disregard of the element concerned has the psychic effect, in the person analysed, that nothing in connection with the unwished ideas behind this element will occur to him. This effect is really not self-evident; it would be quite reasonable to say, "Whether this or that was contained in the dream I do not know for certain; but the following ideas happen to occur to me." But no one ever does say so; it is precisely the disturbing effect of doubt in the analysis that permits it to be unmasked as an offshoot and instrument of the psychic resistance. Psychoanalysis is justifiably suspicious. One of its rules runs: Whatever disturbs the progress of the work is a resistance.[1]

The forgetting of dreams, too, remains inexplicable until we seek to explain it by the power of the psychic censorship. The feeling that one has dreamed a great deal during the night and has retained only a little of it may have yet another meaning in a number of cases: it may perhaps mean that the dream-work has continued in a perceptible manner throughout the night, but has left behind it only one brief dream. There is, however, no possible doubt that a dream is progressively forgotten on waking. One often forgets it in spite of a painful effort to recover it. I believe, however, that just as one generally overestimates the extent of this forgetting, so also one overestimates the lacunae in our knowledge of the dream due to the gaps occurring in it. All the dream-content that has been lost by forgetting can often be recovered by analysis; in a number of cases, at all events, it is possible to discover from a single remaining fragment, not the dream, of course—which, after all, is of no importance—but the whole of the dream-thoughts. It requires a greater expenditure of attention and self-suppression in the analysis; that is all; but it shows that the forgetting of the dream is not innocent of hostile intention.[2]

---

[1] This peremptory statement: "Whatever disturbs the progress of the work is a resistance" might easily be misunderstood. It has, of course, the significance merely of a technical rule, a warning for the analyst. It is not denied that during an analysis events may occur which cannot be ascribed to the intention of the person analysed. The patient's father may die in other ways than by being murdered by the patient, or a war may break out and interrupt the analysis. But despite the obvious exaggeration of the above statement there is still something new and useful in it. Even if the disturbing event is real and independent of the patient, the extent of the disturbing influence does often depend only on him, and the resistance reveals itself unmistakably in the ready and immoderate exploitation of such an opportunity.

[2] As an example of the significance of doubt and uncertainty in a dream with a simultaneous shrinking of the dream-content to a single element I will cite from my *Introductory Lectures on Psychoanalysis* the following dream, the analysis of which was successful, despite a short postponement:—

"*A sceptical lady patient has a rather long dream, in which it happens that certain persons tell her of my book on* Wit, *and praise it highly. Then something is said about a 'channel,' perhaps another book in which 'channel' occurs, or something else to do with 'channel' . . . she doesn't know; it is quite vague.*"

"You will, of course, be inclined to think that the element 'channel' will resist analysis, because it is so indeterminate. You are right in assuming this difficulty, but it is not difficult because it is vague; it is vague for the reason that makes the interpretation difficult. The dreamer could associate nothing with 'channel'; and of course I could not suggest anything. A little while later—the following day, to be precise—she stated that something did occur to her which *perhaps* referred to 'channel.' It was, as a matter of fact, a witticism which she had heard someone repeat. On a steamer running between Dover and Calais a well-known writer was talking to an Englishman, who in a certain connection quoted the aphorism: *Du sublime au ridicule il n'y a qu'un pas.* The writer retorted: *Oui, le pas de Calais,* whereby he wished to imply that he thought France sublime and England ridiculous. But the *Pas de Calais*

A convincing proof of the tendencious nature of dream-forgetting—of the fact that it serves the resistance—is obtained on analysis by investigating a preliminary stage of forgetting.[1] It often happens that in the midst of an interpretation an omitted fragment of the dream suddenly emerges which is described as having been previously forgotten. This part of the dream that has been wrested from forgetfulness is always the most important part. It lies on the shortest path to the solution of the dream, and for that very reason it was most exposed to the resistance. Among the examples of the dreams that I have included in the text of this treatise, it once happened that I had subsequently to interpolate a fragment of dream-content. The dream is a dream of travel, which revenges itself on two unamiable travelling companions; I have left it almost entirely uninterpreted, as part of its content is crudely obscene. The part omitted reads: *"I said, referring to a book of Schiller's: 'It is from . . .' but corrected myself, as I realized my mistake: 'It is by . . .' Whereupon the man remarked to his sister, 'Yes, he said it correctly.'"* [2]

Self-correction in dreams, which to some writers seems so wonderful, does not really call for consideration. But I will draw from my own memory an instance typical of verbal errors in dreams. I was nineteen years of age when I visited England for the first time, and I spent a day on the shore of the Irish Sea. Naturally enough, I amused myself by picking up the marine animals left on the beach by the tide, and I was just examining a starfish (the dream begins with *Hollthurn—Holothurian*) when a pretty little girl came up to me and asked me: *"Is it a starfish? Is it alive?"* I replied, *"Yes, he is alive,"* but then felt ashamed of my mistake, and repeated the sentence correctly. For the grammatical mistake which I then made, the dream substitutes another which is quite common among German people. *"Das Buch ist von Schiller"* is not to be trans-

---

is a channel, the *Canal la Manche* (the sleeve channel). Do I think that this association has anything to do with the dream? I certainly do; it really furnishes the solution of this enigmatical dream-element. Can you doubt that this witticism already existed, before the dream, as the unconscious of the element 'channel'; can you assume that it was subsequently invented as an association? The association testifies to the scepticism concealed behind her obtrusive admiration, and the resistance is, of course, the common reason for both her hesitation in finding an association and the indefinite character of the corresponding dream-element. Note the relation of the dream-element to the unconscious in this case. It is like a fragment of this unconscious, like an allusion to it; by its isolation it has become quite unintelligible."

[1] Concerning the intention of forgetting in general, see my *The Psychopathology of Everyday Life.*

[2] Such corrections in the use of foreign languages are not rare in dreams, but they are usually attributed to foreigners. Maury (p. 143), while he was studying English, once dreamed that he informed someone that he had called on him the day before in the following words: "I called for you yesterday." The other answered, correctly: "You mean: I called on you yesterday."

lated by "*the book is from,*" but by "*the book is by.*" That the dream-work accomplishes this substitution, because the word *from*, owing to its consonance with the German adjective *fromm* (pious, devout) makes a remarkable condensation possible, should no longer surprise us after all that we have heard of the intentions of the dream-work and its uncrupulous selection of means. But what relation has this harmless recollection of the seashore to my dream? It explains, by means of a very innocent example, that I have used the word—the word denoting gender, or *sex* or the *sexual* (*he*)—in the wrong place. This is surely one of the keys to the solution of the dream. Those who have heard of the derivation of the book-title *Matter and Motion* (*Molière in Le Malade Imaginaire: La Matière est-elle laudable?—A Motion of the bowels*) will readily be able to supply the missing parts.

Moreover, I can prove conclusively, by a *demonstratio ad oculos*, that the forgetting of the dream is in a large measure the work of the resistance. A patient tells me that he has dreamed, but that the dream has vanished without leaving a trace, as if nothing had happened. We set to work, however; I come upon a resistance which I explain to the patient; encouraging and urging him, I help him to become reconciled to some disagreeable thought; and I have hardly succeeded in doing so when he exclaims: "Now I can recall what I dreamed!" The same resistance which that day disturbed him in the work of interpretation caused him also to forget the dream. By overcoming this resistance I have brought back the dream to his memory.

In the same way the patient, having reached a certain part of the work, may recall a dream which occurred three, four, or more days ago, and which has hitherto remained in oblivion.[1]

Psychoanalytical experience has furnished us with yet another proof of the fact that the forgetting of dreams depends far more on the resistance than on the mutually alien character of the waking and sleeping states, as some writers have believed it to depend. It often happens to me, as well as to other analysts, and to patients under treatment, that we are waked from sleep by a dream, as we say, and that immediately thereafter, while in full possession of our mental faculties, we begin to interpret the dream. Often in such cases I have not rested until I have achieved a full understanding of the dream, and yet it has happened that after waking I have forgotten the interpretation-work as completely as I have forgotten the dream-content itself, though I have been aware that I have dreamed and that I had interpreted the dream. The dream has far more frequently taken the result of the interpretation with it into forget-

---

[1] Ernest Jones describes an analogous case of frequent occurrence; during the analysis of one dream another dream of the same night is often recalled which until then was not merely forgotten, but was not even suspected.

fulness than the intellectual faculty has succeeded in retaining the dream in the memory. But between this work of interpretation and the waking thoughts there is not that psychic abyss by which other writers have sought to explain the forgetting of dreams.—When Morton Prince objects to my explanation of the forgetting of dreams on the ground that it is only a special case of the amnesia of dissociated psychic states, and that the impossibility of applying my explanation of this special amnesia to other types of amnesia makes it valueless even for its immediate purpose, he reminds the reader that in all his descriptions of such dissociated states he has never attempted to discover the dynamic explanation underlying these phenomena. For had he done so, he would surely have discovered that repression (and the resistance produced thereby) is the cause not of these dissociations merely, but also of the amnesia of their psychic content.

That dreams are as little forgotten as other psychic acts, that even in their power of impressing themselves on the memory they may fairly be compared with the other psychic performances, was proved to me by an experiment which I was able to make while preparing the manuscript of this book. I had preserved in my notes a great many dreams of my own which, for one reason or another, I could not interpret, or, at the time of dreaming them, could interpret only very imperfectly. In order to obtain material to illustrate my assertion, I attempted to interpret some of them a year or two later. In this attempt I was invariably successful; indeed, I may say that the interpretation was effected more easily after all this time than when the dreams were of recent occurrence. As a possible explanation of this fact, I would suggest that I had overcome many of the internal resistances which had disturbed me at the time of dreaming. In such subsequent interpretations I have compared the old yield of dream-thoughts with the present result, which has usually been more abundant, and I have invariably found the old dream-thoughts unaltered among the present ones. However, I soon recovered from my surprise when I reflected that I had long been accustomed to interpret dreams of former years that had occasionally been related to me by my patients as though they had been dreams of the night before; by the same method, and with the same success. In the section on anxiety-dreams I shall include two examples of such delayed dream-interpretations. When I made this experiment for the first time I expected, not unreasonably, that dreams would behave in this connection merely like neurotic symptoms. For when I treat a psychoneurotic, for instance, an hysterical patient, by psychoanalysis, I am compelled to find explanations for the first symptoms of the malady, which have long since disappeared, as well as for those still existing symptoms which have brought the patient to me; and I find the former problem easier to solve than the more exigent one of today. In the *Studies in Hysteria*,[1] published as early as 1895, I was able to give the explanation of a first hysterical attack which the patient, a woman over forty years of age, had experienced in her fifteenth year.[2]

I will now make a few rather unsystematic remarks relating to the interpretations of dreams, which will perhaps serve as a guide to the reader who wishes to test my assertions by the analysis of his own dreams.

He must not expect that it will be a simple and easy matter to interpret his own dreams. Even the observation of endoptic phenomena, and other sensations which are commonly immune from attention, calls for practice, although this group of observations is not opposed by any psychic motive. It is very much more difficult to get hold of the "unwished ideas." He who seeks to do so must fulfil the requirements laid down in this treatise, and while following the rules here given, he must endeavour to restrain all criticism, all preconceptions, and all affective or intellectual bias in himself during the work of analysis. He must be ever mindful of the precept which Claude Bernard held up to the experimenter in the physiological laboratory: *"Travailler comme une bête"*—that is, he must be as enduring as an animal, and also as disinterested in the results of his work. He who will follow this advice will no longer find the task a difficult one. The interpretation of a dream cannot always be accomplished in one session; after following up a chain of associations you will often feel that your working capacity is exhausted; the dream will not tell you anything more that day; it is then best to break off, and to resume the work the following day. Another portion of the dream-content then solicits your attention, and you thus obtain access to a fresh stratum of the dream-thoughts. One might call this the "fractional" interpretation of dreams.

It is most difficult to induce the beginner in dream-interpretation to recognize the fact that his task is not finished when he is in possession of a complete interpretation of the dream which is both ingenious and coherent, and which gives particulars of all the elements of the dream-content. Besides this, another interpretation, an over-interpretation of the same dream, one which has escaped him, may be possible. It is really not easy to form an idea of the wealth of trains of unconscious thought striving for expression in our minds, or to credit the adroitness displayed by the dream-work in killing—so to speak—seven flies at one stroke, like the

[1] Translated by A. A. Brill, Journal of Nervous and Mental Diseases Publishing Co., New York.
[2] Dreams which have occurred during the first years of childhood, and which have sometimes been retained in the memory for decades with perfect sensorial freshness, are almost always of great importance for the understanding of the development and the neurosis of the dreamer. The analysis of them protects the physician from errors and uncertainties which might confuse him even theoretically.

journeyman tailor in the fairy-tale, by means of its ambiguous modes of expression. The reader will constantly be inclined to reproach the author for a superfluous display of ingenuity, but anyone who has had personal experience of dream-interpretation will know better than to do so.

On the other hand, I cannot accept the opinion first expressed by H. Silberer, that every dream—or even that many dreams, and certain groups of dreams—calls for two different interpretations, between which there is even supposed to be a fixed relation. One of these, which Silberer calls the *psychoanalytic* interpretation, attributes to the dream any meaning you please, but in the main an infantile sexual one. The other, the more important interpretation, which he calls the *anagogic* interpretation, reveals the more serious and often profound thoughts which the dream-work has used as its material. Silberer does not prove this assertion by citing a number of dreams which he has analysed in these two directions. I am obliged to object to this opinion on the ground that it is contrary to facts. The majority of dreams require no over-interpretation, and are especially insusceptible of an anagogic interpretation. The influence of a tendency which seeks to veil the fundamental conditions of dream-formation and divert our interest from its instinctual roots is as evident in Silberer's theory as in other theoretical efforts of the last few years. In a number of cases I can confirm Silberer's assertions; but in these the analysis shows me that the dream-work was confronted with the task of transforming a series of highly abstract thoughts, incapable of direct representation, from waking life into a dream. The dream-work attempted to accomplish this task by seizing upon another thought-material which stood in loose and often *allegorical* relation to the abstract thoughts, and thereby diminished the difficulty of representing them. The abstract interpretation of a dream originating in this manner will be given by the dreamer immediately, but the correct interpretation of the substituted material can be obtained only by means of the familiar technique.

The question whether every dream can be interpreted is to be answered in the negative. One should not forget that in the work of interpretation one is opposed by the psychic forces that are responsible for the distortion of the dream. Whether one can master the inner resistances by one's intellectual interest, one's capacity for self-control, one's psychological knowledge, and one's experience in dream-interpretation depends on the relative strength of the opposing forces. It is always possible to make some progress; one can at all events go far enough to become convinced that a dream has meaning, and generally far enough to gain some idea of its meaning. It very often happens that a second dream enables us to confirm and continue the interpretation assumed for the first. A whole series of dreams, continuing for weeks or months, may have a common basis, and should therefore be interpreted as a continuity. In dreams that follow one another we often observe that one dream takes as its central point something that is only alluded to in the periphery of the next dream, and conversely, so that even in their interpretations the two supplement each other. That different dreams of the same night are always to be treated, in the work of interpretation, as a whole, I have already shown by examples.

In the best interpreted dreams we often have to leave one passage in obscurity because we observe during the interpretation that we have here a tangle of dream-thoughts which cannot be unravelled, and which furnishes no fresh contribution to the dream-content. This, then, is the keystone of the dream, the point at which it ascends into the unknown. For the dream-thoughts which we encounter during the interpretation commonly have no termination, but run in all directions into the net-like entanglement of our intellectual world. It is from some denser part of this fabric that the dream-wish then arises, like the mushroom from its mycelium.

Let us now return to the facts of dream-forgetting. So far, of course, we have failed to draw any important conclusion from them. When our waking life shows an unmistakable intention to forget the dream which has been formed during the night, either as a whole, immediately after waking, or little by little in the course of the day, and when we recognize as the chief factor in this process of forgetting the psychic resistance against the dream which has already done its best to oppose the dream at night, the question then arises: What actually has made the dream-formation possible against this resistance? Let us consider the most striking case, in which the waking life has thrust the dream aside as though it had never happened. If we take into consideration the play of the psychic forces, we are compelled to assert that the dream would never have come into existence had the resistance prevailed at night as it did by day. We conclude, then, that the resistance loses some part of its force during the night; we know that it has not been discontinued, as we have demonstrated its share in the formation of dreams—namely, the work of distortion. We have therefore to consider the possibility that at night the resistance is merely diminished, and that dream-formation becomes possible because of this slackening of the resistance; and we shall readily understand that as it regains its full power on waking it immediately thrusts aside what it was forced to admit while it was feeble. Descriptive psychology teaches us that the chief determinant of dream-formation is the dormant state of the psyche; and we may now add the following explanation: *The state of sleep makes dream-formation possible by reducing the endopsychic censorship.*

We are certainly tempted to look upon this as the only possible conclusion to be drawn from the facts of dream-forgetting, and to develop from this conclusion further deductions as to the comparative energy operative in the sleeping and waking states. But we shall stop here for the present. When we have penetrated a little farther into the psychology of dreams we shall find that the origin of dream-formation may be differently conceived. The resistance which tends to prevent the dream-thoughts from becoming conscious may perhaps be evaded without suffering reduction. It is also plausible that both the factors which favour dream-formation, the reduction as well as the evasion of the resistance, may be simultaneously made possible by the sleeping state. But we shall pause here, and resume the subject a little later.

We must now consider another series of objections against our procedure in dream-interpretation. For we proceed by dropping all the directing ideas which at other times control reflection, directing our attention to a single element of the dream, noting the involuntary thoughts that associate themselves with this element. We then take up the next component of the dream-content, and repeat the operation with this; and, regardless of the direction taken by the thoughts, we allow ourselves to be led onwards by them, rambling from one subject to another. At the same time, we harbour the confident hope that we may in the end, and without intervention on our part, come upon the dream-thoughts from which the dream originated. To this the critic may make the following objection: That we arrive somewhere if we start from a single element of the dream is not remarkable. Something can be associatively connected with every idea. The only thing that is remarkable is that one should succeed in hitting upon the dream-thoughts in this arbitrary and aimless excursion. It is probably a self-deception; the investigator follows the chain of associations from the one element which is taken up until he finds the chain breaking off, whereupon he takes up a second element; it is thus only natural that the originally unconfined associations should now become narrowed down. He has the former chain of associations still in mind, and will therefore in the analysis of the second dream-idea hit all the more readily upon single associations which have something in common with the associations of the first chain. He then imagines that he has found a thought which represents a point of junction between two of the dream-elements. As he allows himself all possible freedom of thought-connection, excepting only the transitions from one idea to another which occur in normal thinking, it is not difficult for him finally to concoct out of a series of "intermediary thoughts," something which he calls the dream-thoughts; and without any guarantee, since they are otherwise unknown, he palms these off as the psychic equivalent of the dream. But all this is a purely arbitrary procedure, an ingenious-looking exploitation of chance, and anyone who will go to this useless trouble can in this way work out any desired interpretation for any dream whatever.

If such objections are really advanced against us, we may in defense refer to the impression produced by our dream-interpretations, the surprising connections with other dream-elements which appear while we are following up the individual ideas, and the improbability that anything which so perfectly covers and explains the dream as do our dream-interpretations could be achieved otherwise than by following previously established psychic connections. We might also point to the fact that the procedure in dream-interpretation is identical with the procedure followed in the resolution of hysterical symptoms, where the correctness of the method is attested by the emergence and disappearance of the symptoms—that is, where the interpretation of the text is confirmed by the interpolated illustrations. But we have no reason to avoid this problem—namely, how one can arrive at a pre-existent aim by following an arbitrarily and aimlessly maundering chain of thoughts—since we shall be able not to solve the problem, it is true, but to get rid of it entirely.

For it is demonstrably incorrect to state that we abandon ourselves to an aimless excursion of thought when, as in the interpretation of dreams, we renounce reflection and allow the involuntary ideas to come to the surface. It can be shown that we are able to reject only those directing ideas which are known to us, and that with the cessation of these the unknown—or, as we inexactly say, unconscious—directing ideas immediately exert their influence, and henceforth determine the flow of the involuntary ideas. Thinking without directing ideas cannot be ensured by any influence we ourselves exert on our own psychic life; neither do I know of any state of psychic derangement in which such a mode of thought establishes itself.[1] The psychiatrists have here far too prema-

---

[1] Only recently has my attention been called to the fact that Ed. von Hartmann took the same view with regard to this psychologically important point: Incidental to the discussion of the rôle of the unconscious in artistic creation (*Philos. d. Unbew.*, Bd. 1, Abschn. B., Kap. V) Eduard von Hartmann clearly enunciated the law of association of ideas which is directed by unconscious directing ideas, without however realizing the scope of this law. With him it was a question of demonstrating that "every combination of a sensuous idea when it is not left entirely to chance, but is directed to a definite end, is in need of help from the unconscious," and that the conscious interest in any particular thought-association is a stimulus for the unconscious to discover from among the numberless possible ideas the one which corresponds to the directing idea. "It is the unconscious that selects, and appropriately, in accordance with the aims of the interest: and this holds true *for the associations in abstract thinking (as sensible representations and artistic combinations as well as for flashes of wit)*." Hence, a limiting of the association of ideas to ideas that evoke and are evoked in the sense of pure association-psychology is untenable. Such a restriction "would be justified only if there were states in human life in which man was free not only from any conscious purpose, but also from the domination or cooperation of any unconscious interest, any passing mood. But such a state hardly ever comes to pass, *for even if one leaves one's train of thought seemingly altogether*

turely relinquished the idea of the solidity of the psychic structure. I know that an unregulated stream of thoughts, devoid of directing ideas, can occur as little in the realm of hysteria and paranoia as in the formation or solution of dreams. Perhaps it does not occur at all in the endogenous psychic affections, and, according to the ingenious hypothesis of Lauret, even the deliria observed in confused psychic states have meaning and are incomprehensible to us only because of omissions. I have had the same conviction whenever I have had an opportunity of observing such states. The deliria are the work of a censorship which no longer makes any effort to conceal its sway, which, instead of lending its support to a revision that is no longer obnoxious to it, cancels regardlessly anything to which it objects, thus causing the remnant to appear disconnected. This censorship proceeds like the Russian censorship on the frontier, which allows only those foreign journals which have had certain passages blacked out to fall into the hands of the readers to be protected.

The free play of ideas following any chain of associations may perhaps occur in cases of destructive organic affections of the brain. What, however, is taken to be such in the psychoneuroses may always be explained as the influence of the censorship on a series of thoughts which have been pushed into the foreground by the concealed directing ideas.[1] It has been considered an unmistakable sign of free association unencumbered by directing ideas if the emerging ideas (or images) appear to be connected by means of the so-called superficial associations—that is, by assonance, verbal ambiguity, and temporal coincidence, without inner relationship of meaning; in other words, if they are connected by all those associations which we allow ourselves to exploit in wit and in playing upon words. This distinguishing mark holds good with associations which lead us from the elements of the dream-content to the intermediary thoughts, and from these to the dream-thoughts proper; in many analyses of dreams we have found surprising examples of this. In these no con-

---

to chance, or if one surrenders oneself entirely to the involuntary dreams of phantasy, yet always other leading interests, dominant feelings and moods prevail at one time rather than another, and these will always exert an influence on the association of ideas." (Philos. d. Unbew., 11e Aufl. i, 246). In semi-conscious dreams there always appear only such ideas as correspond to the (unconscious) momentary main interest. By rendering prominent the feelings and moods over the free thought-series, the methodical procedure of psycho-analysis is thoroughly justified even from the standpoint of Hartmann's Psychology (N. E. Pohorilles, Internat. Zeitschrift. f. Ps.A., l, 1913, p. 605).—Du Prel concludes from the fact that a name which we vainly try to recall suddenly occurs to the mind that there is an unconscious but none the less purposeful thinking, whose result then appears in consciousness (Philos. d. Mystik, p. 107).

[1] Jung has brilliantly corroborated this statement by analyses of dementia praecox. (Cf. The Psychology of Dementia Praecox, translated by A. A. Brill. Monograph Series, Journal of Nervous and Mental Diseases Publishing Co., New York.)

nection was too loose and no witticism too objectionable to serve as a bridge from one thought to another. But the correct understanding of such surprising tolerance is not far to seek. *Whenever one psychic element is connected with another by an obnoxious and superficial association, there exists also a correct and more profound connection between the two, which succumbs to the resistance of the censorship.*

The correct explanation for the predominance of the superficial associations is the pressure of the censorship, and not the suppression of the directing ideas. Whenever the censorship renders the normal connective paths impassable, the superficial associations will replace the deeper ones in the representation. It is as though in a mountainous region a general interruption of traffic, for example an inundation, should render the broad highways impassable: traffic would then have to be maintained by steep and inconvenient tracks used at other times only by the hunter.

We can here distinguish two cases which, however, are essentially one. In the first case, the censorship is directed only against the connection of two thoughts which, being detached from one another, escape its opposition. The two thoughts then enter successively into consciousness; their connection remains concealed; but in its place there occurs to us a superficial connection between the two which would not otherwise have occurred to us, and which as a rule connects with another angle of the conceptual complex instead of that from which the suppressed but essential connection proceeds. Or, in the second case, both thoughts, owing to their content, succumb to the censorship; both then appear not in their correct form but in a modified, substituted form; and both substituted thoughts are so selected as to represent, by a superficial association, the essential relation which existed between those that they have replaced. *Under the pressure of the censorship, the displacement of a normal and vital association by one superficial and apparently absurd has thus occurred in both cases.*

Because we know of these displacements, we unhesitatingly rely upon even the superficial associations which occur in the course of dream-interpretation.[1]

The psychoanalysis of neurotics makes abundant use of the two principles: that with the abandonment of the conscious directing ideas the control over the flow of ideas is transferred to the concealed directing ideas; and that superficial associations are only a displacement-substitute

---

[1] The same considerations naturally hold good of the case in which superficial associations are exposed in the dream-content, as, for example, in both the dreams reported by Maury (p. 50, *pélerinage—pelletier—pelle, kilometer—kilograms—gilolo, Lobelia—Lopez—Lotto*). I know from my work with neurotics what kind of reminiscence is prone to represent itself in this manner. It is the consultation of encyclopedias by which most people have satisfied their need of an explanation of the sexual mystery when obsessed by the curiosity of puberty.

for suppressed and more profound ones. Indeed, psychoanalysis makes these two principles the foundation-stones of its technique. When I request a patient to dismiss all reflection, and to report to me whatever comes into his mind, I firmly cling to the assumption that he will not be able to drop the directing idea of the treatment, and I feel justified in concluding that what he reports, even though it may seem to be quite ingenuous and arbitrary, has some connection with his morbid state. Another directing idea of which the patient has no suspicion is my own personality. The full appreciation, as well as the detailed proof of both these explanations, belongs to the description of the psychoanalytic technique as a therapeutic method. We have here reached one of the junctions, so to speak, at which we purposely drop the subject of dream-interpretation.[1]

Of all the objections raised, only one is justified and still remains to be met: namely, that we ought not to ascribe all the associations of the interpretation-work to the nocturnal dream-work. By interpretation in the waking state we are actually opening a path running back from the dream-elements to the dream-thoughts. The dream-work has followed the contrary direction, and it is not at all probable that these paths are equally passable in opposite directions. On the contrary, it appears that during the day, by means of new thought-connections, we sink shafts that strike the intermediary thoughts and the dream-thoughts now in this place, now in that. We can see how the recent thought-material of the day forces its way into the interpretation-series, and how the additional resistance which has appeared since the night probably compels it to make new and further detours. But the number and form of the collaterals which we thus contrive during the day are, psychologically speaking, indifferent, so long as they point the way to the dream-thoughts which we are seeking.

B. REGRESSION

Now that we have defended ourselves against the objections raised, or have at least indicated our weapons of defence, we must no longer delay entering upon the psychological investigations for which we have so long been preparing. Let us summarize the main results of our recent investigations: The dream is a psychic act full of import; its motive power is invariably a wish craving fulfilment; the fact that it is unrecognizable as a wish, and its many peculiarities and absurdities, are due to the influence of the psychic censorship to which it has been subjected during its formation. Besides the necessity of evading the censorship, the following

[1] The above statements, which when written sounded very improbable, have since been corroborated and applied experimentally by Jung and his pupils in the *Diagnostiche Assoziationsstudien.*

factors have played a part in its formation: first, a need for condensing the psychic material; second, regard for representability in sensory images; and third (though not constantly), regard for a rational and intelligible exterior of the dream-structure. From each of these propositions a path leads onward to psychological postulates and assumptions. Thus, the reciprocal relation of the wish-motives, and the four conditions, as well as the mutual relations of these conditions, must now be investigated; the dream must be inserted in the context of the psychic life.

At the beginning of this section we cited a certain dream in order that it might remind us of the problems that are still unsolved. The interpretation of this dream (of the burning child) presented no difficulties, although in the analytical sense it was not given in full. We asked ourselves why, after all, it was necessary that the father should dream instead of waking, and we recognized the wish to represent the child as living as a motive of the dream. That there was yet another wish operative in the dream we shall be able to show after further discussion. For the present, however, we may say that for the sake of the wish-fulfilment the thought-process of sleep was transformed into a dream.

If the wish-fulfilment is cancelled out, only one characteristic remains which distinguishes the two kinds of psychic events. The dream-thought would have been: "I see a glimmer coming from the room in which the body is lying. Perhaps a candle has fallen over, and the child is burning!" The dream reproduces the result of this reflection unchanged, but represents it in a situation which exists in the present and is perceptible by the senses like an experience of the waking state. This, however, is the most common and the most striking psychological characteristic of the dream; a thought, usually the one wished for, is objectified in the dream, and represented as a scene, or—as we think—experienced.

But how are we now to explain this characteristic peculiarity of the dream-work, or—to put it more modestly—how are we to bring it into relation with the psychic processes?

On closer examination, it is plainly evident that the manifest form of the dream is marked by two characteristics which are almost independent of each other. One is its representation as a present situation with the omission of "perhaps"; the other is the translation of the thought into visual images and speech.

The transformation to which the dream-thoughts are subjected because the expectation is put into the present tense is, perhaps, in this particular dream not so very striking. This is probably due to the special and really subsidiary rôle of the wish-fulfilment in this dream. Let us take another dream, in which the dream-wish does not break away from the continuation of the waking thoughts in sleep; for example, the dream of Irma's injection. Here the dream-thought achieving representation is in the conditional: "If only Otto could be blamed for Irma's illness!" The dream suppresses the conditional, and replaces it by a simple present tense: "Yes, Otto is to blame for Irma's illness." This, then, is the first of the transformations which even the undistorted dream imposes on the dream-thoughts. But we will not linger over this first peculiarity of the dream. We dispose of it by a reference to the conscious phantasy, the day-dream, which behaves in a similar fashion with its conceptual content. When Daudet's M. Joyeuse wanders unemployed through the streets of Paris while his daughter is led to believe that he has a post and is sitting in his office, he dreams, in the present tense, of circumstances that might help him to obtain a recommendation and employment. The dream, then, employs the present tense in the same manner and with the same right as the day-dream. The present is the tense in which the wish is represented as fulfilled.

The second quality peculiar to the dream alone, as distinguished from the day-dream, is that the conceptual content is not thought, but is transformed into visual images, to which we give credence, and which we believe that we experience. Let us add, however, that not all dreams show this transformation of ideas into visual images. There are dreams which consist solely of thoughts, but we cannot on that account deny that they are substantially dreams. My dream "Autodidasker—the day-phantasy about Professor N." is of this character; it is almost as free of visual elements as though I had thought its content during the day. Moreover, every long dream contains elements which have not undergone this transformation into the visual, and which are simply thought or known as we are wont to think or know in our waking state. And we must here reflect that this transformation of ideas into visual images does not occur in dreams alone, but also in hallucinations and visions, which may appear spontaneously in health, or as symptoms in the psychoneuroses. In brief, the relation which we are here investigating is by no means an exclusive one; the fact remains, however, that this characteristic of the dream, whenever it occurs, seems to be its most noteworthy characteristic, so that we cannot think of the dream-life without it. To understand it, however, requires a very exhaustive discussion.

Among all the observations relating to the theory of dreams to be found in the literature of the subject, I should like to lay stress upon one as being particularly worthy of mention. The famous G. T. H. Fechner makes the conjecture,[1] in a discussion as to the nature of the dreams, *that the dream is staged elsewhere than in the waking ideation.* No other assumption enables us to comprehend the special peculiarities of the dream-life.

The idea which is thus put before us is one of *psychic locality.* We shall wholly ignore the fact that the psychic apparatus concerned is

[1] *Psychophysik,* Part II, p. 520.

known to us also as an anatomical preparation, and we shall carefully avoid the temptation to determine the psychic locality in any anatomical sense. We shall remain on psychological ground, and we shall do no more than accept the invitation to think of the instrument which serves the psychic activities much as we think of a compound microscope, a photographic camera, or other apparatus. The psychic locality, then, corresponds to a place within such an apparatus in which one of the preliminary phases of the image comes into existence. As is well known, there are in the microscope and the telescope such ideal localities or planes, in which no tangible portion of the apparatus is located. I think it superfluous to apologize for the imperfections of this and all similar figures. These comparisons are designed only to assist us in our attempt to make intelligible the complication of the psychic performance by dissecting it and referring the individual performances to the individual components of the apparatus. So far as I am aware, no attempt has yet been made to divine the construction of the psychic instrument by means of such dissection. I see no harm in such an attempt; I think that we should give free rein to our conjectures, provided we keep our heads and do not mistake the scaffolding for the building. Since for the first approach to any unknown subject we need the help only of auxiliary ideas, we shall prefer the crudest and most tangible hypothesis to all others.

Accordingly, we conceive the psychic apparatus as a compound instrument, the component parts of which we shall call *instances*, or, for the sake of clearness, *systems*. We shall then anticipate that these systems may perhaps maintain a constant spatial orientation to one another, very much as do the different and successive systems of lenses of a telescope. Strictly speaking, there is no need to assume an actual spatial arrangement of the psychic system. It will be enough for our purpose if a definite sequence is established, so that in certain psychic events the system will be traversed by the excitation in a definite temporal order. This order may be different in the case of other processes; such a possibility is left open. For the sake of brevity, we shall henceforth speak of the component parts of the apparatus as "ψ-systems."

The first thing that strikes us is the fact that the apparatus composed of ψ-systems has a direction. All our psychic activities proceed from (inner or outer) stimuli and terminate in innervations. We thus ascribe to the apparatus a sensory and a motor end; at the sensory end we find a system which receives the perceptions, and at the motor end another which opens the sluices of motility. The psychic process generally runs from the perceptive end to the motor end. The most general scheme of the psychic apparatus has therefore the following appearance as shown in Fig. 1 on page 489. But this is only in compliance with the requirement, long familiar to us, that the psychic apparatus must be constructed like a reflex apparatus. The reflex act remains the type of every psychic activity as well.

We now have reason to admit a first differentiation at the sensory end. The percepts that come to us leave in our psychic apparatus a trace, which we may call a *memory-trace*. The function related to this memory-trace we call "the memory." If we hold seriously to our resolution to connect the psychic processes into systems, the memory-trace can consist only of lasting changes in the elements of the systems. But, as has already

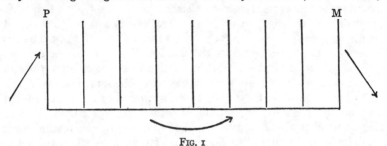

Fig. 1

been shown elsewhere, obvious difficulties arise when one and the same system is faithfully to preserve changes in its elements and still to remain fresh and receptive in respect of new occasions of change. In accordance with the principle which is directing our attempt, we shall therefore ascribe these two function to two different systems. We assume that an initial system of this apparatus receives the stimuli of perception but retains nothing of them—that is, it has no memory; and that behind this there lies a second system, which transforms the momentary excitation of the first into lasting traces. The following would then be the diagram of our psychic apparatus:—

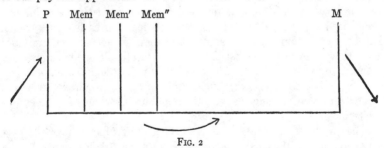

Fig. 2

We know that of the percepts which act upon the P-system, we retain permanently something else as well as the content itself. Our percepts prove also to be connected with one another in the memory, and this is especially so if they originally occurred simultaneously. We call this the fact of *association*. It is now clear that, if the *P*-system is entirely lacking in memory, it certainly cannot preserve traces for the associations; the individual *P*-elements would be intolerably hindered in their functioning if a residue of a former connection should make its influence felt against a new perception. Hence we must rather assume that the memory-system is the basis of association. The fact of association, then, consists in this— that in consequence of a lessening of resistance and a smoothing of the ways from one of the *mem*-elements, the excitation transmits itself to a second rather than to a third *mem*-element.

On further investigation we find it necessary to assume not one but many such *mem*-systems, in which the same excitation transmitted by the *P*-elements undergoes a diversified fixation. The first of these *mem*-systems will in any case contain the fixation of the association through simultaneity, while in those lying farther away the same material of excitation will be arranged according to other forms of combination; so that relationships of similarity, etc., might perhaps be represented by these later systems. It would, of course, be idle to attempt to express in words the psychic significance of such a system. Its characteristic would lie in the intimacy of its relations to elements of raw material of memory— that is (if we wish to hint at a more comprehensive theory) in the gradations of the conductive resistance on the way to these elements.

An observation of a general nature, which may possibly point to something of importance, may here be interpolated. The *P*-system, which possesses no capacity for preserving changes, and hence no memory, furnishes to consciousness the complexity and variety of the sensory qualities. Our memories, on the other hand, are unconscious in themselves; those that are most deeply impressed form no exception. They can be made conscious, but there is no doubt that they unfold all their activities in the unconscious state. What we term our character is based, indeed, on the memory-traces of our impressions, and it is precisely those impressions that have affected us most strongly, those of our early youth, which hardly ever become conscious. But when memories become conscious again they show no sensory quality, or a very negligible one in comparison with the perceptions. If, now, it can be confirmed *that for consciousness memory and quality are mutually exclusive in the ψ-systems,* we have gained a most promising insight into the determinations of the neuron-excitations.[1]

What we have so far assumed concerning the composition of the psychic apparatus at the sensible end has been assumed regardless of dreams and of the psychological explanations which we have hitherto derived from them. Dreams, however, will serve as a source of evidence for our

[1] Since writing this, I have thought that consciousness occurs actually *in the locality* of the memory-trace. (Cf. *Notiz über den Wünderblock,* 1925, *Ges Schriften,* Bd. vi.)

knowledge of another part of the apparatus. We have seen that it was impossible to explain dream-formation unless we ventured to assume two psychic "instances," one of which subjected the activities of the other to criticism, the result of which was exclusion from consciousness.

We have concluded that the criticizing "instance" maintains closer relations with the consciousness than the "instance" criticized. It stands between the latter and the consciousness like a screen. Further, we have found that there is reason to identify the criticizing "instance" with that which directs our waking life and determines our voluntary conscious activities. If, in accordance with our assumptions, we now replace these "instances" by systems, the criticizing system will therefore be moved to the motor end. We now enter both systems in our diagram, expressing, by the names given them, their relation to consciousness.

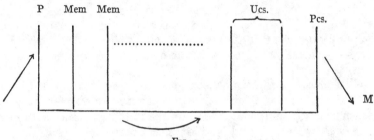

FIG. 3

The last of the systems at the motor end we call the *preconscious* (*Pcs.*) to denote that the exciting processes in this system can reach consciousness without any further detention, provided certain other conditions are fulfilled, *e.g.* the attainment of a definite degree of intensity, a certain apportionment of that function which we must call attention, etc. This is at the same time the system which holds the keys of voluntary motility. The system behind it we call the *unconscious* (*Ucs.*), because it has no access to consciousness *except through the preconscious*, in the passage through which the excitation-process must submit to certain changes.[1]

In which of these systems, then, do we localize the impetus to dream-formation? For the sake of simplicity, let us say in the system *Ucs.* We shall find, it is true, in subsequent discussions, that this is not altogether correct; that dream-formation is obliged to make connection with dream-thoughts which belong to the system of the preconscious. But we shall learn elsewhere, when we come to deal with the dream-wish, that the

[1] The further elaboration of this linear diagram will have to reckon with the assumption that the system following the *Pcs.* represents the one to which we must attribute consciousness (*Cs.*), so that $P = Cs.$

motive-power of the dream is furnished by the *Ucs.*, and on account of this factor we shall assume the unconscious system as the starting-point for dream-formation. This dream-excitation, like all the other thought-structures, will now strive to continue itself in the *Pcs.*, and thence to gain admission to the consciousness.

Experience teaches us that the path leading through the preconscious to consciousness is closed to the dream-thoughts during the day by the resisting censorship. At night they gain admission to consciousness; the question arises, In what way and because of what changes? If this admission were rendered possible to the dream-thoughts by the weakening, during the night, of the resistance watching on the boundary between the unconscious and the preconscious, we should then have dreams in the material of our ideas, which would not display the hallucinatory character that interests us at present.

The weakening of the censorship between the two systems, *Ucs.* and *Pcs.*, can explain to us only such dreams as the "Autodidasker" dream, but not dreams like that of the burning child, which—as will be remembered—we stated as a problem at the outset in our present investigations.

What takes place in the hallucinatory dream we can describe in no other way than by saying that the excitation follows a retrogressive course. It communicates itself not to the motor end of the apparatus, but to the sensory end, and finally reaches the system of perception. If we call the direction which the psychic process follows from the unconscious into the waking state *progressive,* we may then speak of the dream as having a *regressive* character.[1]

This *regression* is therefore assuredly one of the most important psychological peculiarities of the dream-process; but we must not forget that it is not characteristic of the dream alone. Intentional recollection and other component processes of our normal thinking likewise necessitate a retrogression in the psychic apparatus from some complex act of ideation to the raw material of the memory-traces which underlie it. But during the waking state this turning backwards does not reach beyond the memory-images; it is incapable of producing the hallucinatory revival of the perceptual images. Why is it otherwise in dreams? When we spoke of the condensation-work of the dream we could not avoid the assumption that by the dream-work the intensities adhering to the ideas

[1] The first indication of the element of regression is already encountered in the writings of Albertus Magnus. According to him the *imaginatio* constructs the dream out of the tangible objects which it has retained. The process is the converse of that operating in the waking state. Hobbes states (*Leviathan,* 1651): "In sum our dreams are the reverse of our imagination, the motion, when we are awake, beginning at one end, and when we dream at another" (quoted by Havelock Ellis, *loc. cit.,* p. 112).

are completely transferred from one to another. It is probably this modification of the usual psychic process which makes possible the cathexis [1] of the system of P to its full sensory vividness in the reverse direction to thinking.

I hope that we are not deluding ourselves as regards the importance of this present discussion. We have done nothing more than give a name to an inexplicable phenomenon. We call it regression if the idea in the dream is changed back into the visual image from which it once originated. But even this step requires justification. Why this definition if it does not teach us anything new? Well, I believe that the word *regression* is of service to us, inasmuch as it connects a fact familiar to us with the scheme of the psychic apparatus endowed with direction. At this point, and for the first time, we shall profit by the fact that we have constructed such a scheme. For with the help of this scheme we shall perceive, without further reflection, another peculiarity of dream-formation. If we look upon the dream as a process of regression within the hypothetical psychic apparatus, we have at once an explanation of the empirically proven fact that all thought-relations of the dream-thoughts are either lost in the dream-work or have difficulty in achieving expression. According to our scheme, these thought-relations are contained not in the first *mem*-systems, but in those lying farther to the front, and in the regression to the perceptual images they must forfeit expression. *In regression the structure of the dream-thoughts breaks up into its raw material.*

But what change renders possible this regression which is impossible during the day? Let us here be content with an assumption. There must evidently be changes in the cathexis of the individual systems, causing the latter to become more accessible or inaccessible to the discharge of the excitation; but in any such apparatus the same effect upon the course of the excitation might be produced by more than one kind of change. We naturally think of the sleeping state, and of the many cathectic changes which this evokes at the sensory end of the apparatus. During the day there is a continuous stream flowing from the ψ-system of the P toward the motility end; this current ceases at night, and can no longer block the flow of the current of excitation in the opposite direction. This would appear to be that "seclusion from the outer world" which according to the theory of some writers is supposed to explain the psychological character of the dream. In the explanation of the regression of the dream we shall, however, have to take into account those other regressions which occur during morbid waking states. In these other forms of regression the explanation just given plainly leaves us in the lurch. Regression occurs in spite of the uninterrupted sensory current in a progressive direction.

[1] [From the Greek *Kathexo*, to occupy, used here in place of the author's term *Besetzung*, to signify a charge or investment of energy.—TRANS.]

The hallucinations of hysteria and paranoia, as well as the visions of mentally normal persons, I would explain as corresponding, in fact, to regressions, i.e. to thoughts transformed into images; and would assert that only such thoughts undergo this transformation as are in intimate connection with suppressed memories, or with memories which have remained unconscious. As an example I will cite the case of one of my youngest hysterical patients—a boy of twelve, who was prevented from falling asleep by "green faces with red eyes," which terrified him. The source of this manifestation was the suppressed, but once conscious memory of a boy whom he had often seen four years earlier, and who offered a warning example of many bad habits, including masturbation, for which he was now reproaching himself. At that time his mother had noticed that the complexion of this ill-mannered boy was *greenish* and that he had *red* (i.e. red-rimmed) *eyes*. Hence his terrifying vision, which merely determined his recollection of another saying of his mother's, to the effect that such boys become demented, are unable to learn anything at school, and are doomed to an early death. A part of this prediction came true in the case of my little patient; he could not get on at school, and, as appeared from his involuntary associations, he was in terrible dread of the remainder of the prophecy. However, after a brief period of successful treatment his sleep was restored, his anxiety removed, and he finished his scholastic year with an excellent record.

Here I may add the interpretation of a vision described to me by an hysterical woman of forty, as having occurred when she was in normal health. One morning she opened her eyes and saw her brother in the room, although she knew him to be confined in an insane asylum. Her little son was asleep by her side. Lest the child *should be frightened* on seeing his *uncle*, and *fall into convulsions*, she pulled the sheet over his face. This done, the phantom disappeared. This apparition was the revision of one of her childish memories, which, although conscious, was most intimately connected with all the unconscious material in her mind. Her nurserymaid had told her that her mother, who had died young (my patient was then only eighteen months old), had suffered from epileptic or hysterical convulsions, which dated back to a fright caused by her brother (the patient's *uncle*) who appeared to her disguised as a spectre with a *sheet* over his head. The vision contains the same elements as the reminiscence, viz. the appearance of the brother, the sheet, the fright, and its effect. These elements, however, are arranged in a fresh context, and are transferred to other persons. The obvious motive of the vision, and the thought which it replaced, was her solicitude lest her little son, who bore a striking resemblance to his uncle, should share the latter's fate.

Both examples here cited are not entirely unrelated to the state of sleep, and may for that reason be unfitted to afford the evidence for the sake of which I have cited them. I will, therefore, refer to my analysis of an hallucinatory paranoic woman patient [1] and to the results of my hitherto unpublished studies on the psychology of the psychoneuroses, in order to emphasize the fact that in these cases of regressive thought-transformation one must not overlook the influence of a suppressed memory, or one that has remained unconscious, this being usually of an infantile character. This memory draws into the regression, as it were, the thoughts with which it is connected, and which are kept from expression by the censorship—that is, into that form of representation in which the memory itself is psychically existent. And here I may add, as a result of my studies of hysteria, that if one succeeds in bringing to consciousness infantile scenes (whether they are recollections or phantasies) they appear as hallucinations, and are divested of this character only when they are communicated. It is known also that even in persons whose memories are not otherwise visual, the earliest infantile memories remain vividly visual until late in life.

If, now, we bear in mind the part played in the dream-thoughts by the infantile experiences, or by the phantasies based upon them, and recollect how often fragments of these re-emerge in the dream-content, and how even the dream-wishes often proceed from them, we cannot deny the probability that in dreams, too, the transformation of thoughts into visual images may be the result of the *attraction* exercised by the visually represented memory, striving for resuscitation, upon the thoughts severed from consciousness and struggling for expression. Pursuing this conception, we may further describe the dream as the *substitute for the infantile scene modified by transference to recent material*. The infantile scene cannot enforce its own revival, and must therefore be satisfied to return as a dream.

This reference to the significance of the infantile scenes (or of their phantastic repetitions) as in a certain degree furnishing the pattern for the dream-content renders superfluous the assumption made by Scherner and his pupils concerning inner sources of stimuli. Scherner assumes a state of "visual excitation," of internal excitation in the organ of sight, when the dreams manifest a special vividness or an extraordinary abundance of visual elements. We need raise no objection to this assumption; we may perhaps content ourselves with assuming such a state of excitation only for the psychic perceptive system of the organ of vision; we shall, however, insist that this state of excitation is a reanimation by the memory of a former actual visual excitation. I cannot, from my own experience, give a good example showing such an influence of an infantile memory; my own dreams are altogether less rich in perceptual elements

[1] *Selected Papers on Hysteria and other Psychoneuroses*, p. 165, translated by A. A. Brill, Monograph Series, Journal of Nervous and Mental Diseases Publishing Co.

than I imagine those of others to be; but in my most beautiful and most vivid dream of late years I can easily trace the hallucinatory distinctness of the dream-contents to the visual qualities of recently received impressions. On page 437 I mentioned a dream in which the dark blue of the water, the brown of the smoke issuing from the ship's funnels, and the sombre brown and red of the buildings which I saw made a profound and lasting impression upon my mind. This dream, if any, must be attributed to visual excitation, but what was it that had brought my organ of vision into this excitable state? It was a recent impression which had joined itself to a series of former impressions. The colours I beheld were in the first place those of the toy blocks with which my children had erected a magnificent building for my admiration, on the day preceding the dream. There was the sombre red on the large blocks, the blue and brown on the small ones. Joined to these were the colour impressions of my last journey in Italy: the beautiful blue of the Isonzo and the lagoons, the brown hue of the Alps. The beautiful colours seen in the dream were but a repetition of those seen in memory.

Let us summarize what we have learned about this peculiarity of dreams: their power of recasting their idea-content in visual images. We may not have explained this character of the dream-work by referring it to the known laws of psychology, but we have singled it out as pointing to unknown relations, and have given it the name of the *regressive* character. Wherever such regression has occurred, we have regarded it as an effect of the resistance which opposes the progress of thought on its normal way to consciousness, and of the simultaneous attraction exerted upon it by vivid memories.[1] The regression in dreams is perhaps facilitated by the cessation of the progressive stream flowing from the sense-organs during the day; for which auxiliary factor there must be some compensation, in the other forms of regression, by the strengthening of the other regressive motives. We must also bear in mind that in pathological cases of regression, just as in dreams, the process of energy-transference must be different from that occurring in the regressions of normal psychic life, since it renders possible a full hallucinatory cathexis of the perceptive system. What we have described in the analysis of the dream-work as "regard for representability" may be referred to the *selective attraction* of visually remembered scenes touched by the dream-thoughts.

As to the regression, we may further observe that it plays a no less important part in the theory of neurotic symptom-formation than in the theory of dreams. We may therefore distinguish a threefold species of

---

[1] In a statement of the theory of repression it should be explained that a thought passes into repression owing to the co-operation of two of the factors which influence it. On the one side (the censorship of *Cs.*) it is pushed, and from the other side (the *Ucs.*) it is pulled, much as one is helped to the top of the Great Pyramid. (Cf. the Chapter *Die Verdrängung* in *Ges. Schriften*, Bd. v.)

regression: (*a*) a *topical* one, in the sense of the scheme of the ψ-systems here expounded; (*b*) a *temporal* one, in so far as it is a regression to older psychic formations; and (*c*) a *formal* one, when primitive modes of expression and representation take the place of the customary modes. These three forms of regression are, however, basically one, and in the majority of cases they coincide, for that which is older in point of time is at the same time formally primitive and, in the psychic topography, nearer to the perception-end.

We cannot leave the theme of regression in dreams without giving utterance to an impression which has already and repeatedly forced itself upon us, and which will return to us reinforced after a deeper study of the psychoneuroses: namely, that dreaming is on the whole an act of regression to the earliest relationships of the dreamer, a resuscitation of his childhood, of the impulses which were then dominant and the modes of expression which were then available. Behind this childhood of the individual we are then promised an insight into the phylogenetic childhood, into the evolution of the human race, of which the development of the individual is only an abridged repetition influenced by the fortuitous circumstances of life. We begin to suspect that Friedrich Nietzsche was right when he said that in a dream "there persists a primordial part of humanity which we can no longer reach by a direct path," and we are encouraged to expect, from the analysis of dreams, a knowledge of the archaic inheritance of man, a knowledge of psychical things in him that are innate. It would seem that dreams and neuroses have preserved for us more of the psychical antiquities than we suspected; so that psychoanalysis may claim a high rank among those sciences which endeavour to reconstruct the oldest and darkest phases of the beginnings of mankind.

It is quite possible that we shall not find this first part of our psychological evaluation of dreams particularly satisfying. We must, however, console ourselves with the thought that we are, after all, compelled to build out into the dark. If we have not gone altogether astray, we shall surely reach approximately the same place from another starting-point, and then, perhaps, we shall be better able to find our bearings.

C. THE WISH-FULFILMENT

The dream of the burning child (cited above) affords us a welcome opportunity for appreciating the difficulties confronting the theory of wishfulfilment. That a dream should be nothing but a wish-fulfilment must undoubtedly seem strange to us all—and not only because of the contradiction offered by the anxiety-dream. Once our first analyses had given us the enlightenment that meaning and psychic value are concealed behind our dreams, we could hardly have expected so unitary a determination of this meaning. According to the correct but summary definition of Aristotle, the dream is a continuation of thinking in sleep. Now if, during the day, our thoughts perform such a diversity of psychic acts—judgments, conclusions, the answering of objections, expectations, intentions, etc.— why should they be forced at night to confine themselves to the production of wishes only? Are there not, on the contrary, many dreams that present an altogether different psychic act in dream-form—for example, anxious care—and is not the father's unusually transparent dream of the burning child such a dream? From the gleam of light that falls upon his eyes while he is asleep the father draws the apprehensive conclusion that a candle has fallen over and may be burning the body; he transforms this conclusion into a dream by embodying it in an obvious situation enacted in the present tense. What part is played in this dream by the wish-fulfilment? And how can we possibly mistake the predominance of the thought continued from the waking state or evoked by the new sensory impression?

All these considerations are justified, and force us to look more closely into the rôle of the wish-fulfillment in dreams, and the significance of the waking thoughts continued in sleep.

It is precisely the wish-fulfillment that has already caused us to divide all dreams into two groups. We have found dreams which were plainly wish-fulfillments; and others in which the wish-fulfillment was unrecognizable and was often concealed by every available means. In this latter class of dreams we recognized the influence of the dream-censorship. The undisguised wish-dreams were found chiefly in children; *short*, frank wish-dreams *seemed* (I purposely emphasize this word) to occur also in adults.

We may now ask whence in each case does the wish that is realized in the dream originate? But to what opposition or to what diversity do we relate this "whence"? I think to the opposition between conscious daily life and an unconscious psychic activity which is able to make itself perceptible only at night. I thus, find a threefold possibility for the origin of a wish. Firstly, it may have been excited during the day, and owing to external circumstances may have remained unsatisfied; there is thus left for the night an acknowledged and unsatisfied wish. Secondly, it may have emerged during the day, only to be rejected; there is thus left for the night an unsatisfied but suppressed wish. Thirdly, it may have no relation to daily life, but may belong to those wishes which awake only at night out of the suppressed material in us. If we turn to our scheme of the psychic apparatus, we can localize a wish of the first order in the system *Pcs*. We may assume that a wish of the second order has been forced back from the *Pcs*. system into the *Ucs*. system, where alone, if anywhere, can it maintain itself; as for the wish-impulse of the third order, we believe that it is wholly incapable of leaving the *Ucs*. system. Now, have the wishes arising from these different sources the same value for the dream, the same power to incite a dream?

On surveying the dreams at our disposal with a view to answering this question, we are at once moved to add as a fourth source of the dream-wish the actual wish-impetus which arises during the night (for example, the stimulus of thirst, and sexual desire). It then seems to us probable that the source of the dream-wish does not affect its capacity to incite a dream. I have in mind the dream of the child who continued the voyage that had been interrupted during the day, and the other children's dreams cited in the same chapter; they are explained by an unfulfilled but unsuppressed wish of the daytime. That wishes suppressed during the day assert themselves in dreams is shown by a great many examples. I will mention a very simple dream of this kind. A rather sarcastic lady, whose younger friend has become engaged to be married, is asked in the daytime by her acquaintances whether she knows her friend's fiancé, and what she thinks of him. She replies with unqualified praise, imposing silence on her own judgment, although she would have liked to tell the truth, namely, that he is a *commonplace fellow—one meets such by the dozen (Dutzendmensch)*. The following night she dreams that the same question is put to her, and that she replies with the formula: *"In case of subsequent orders, it will suffice to mention the reference number."* Finally, as the result of numerous analyses, we learn that the wish in all dreams that have been subject to distortion has its origin in the unconscious, and could not become perceptible by day. At first sight, then, it seems that in respect of dream-formation all wishes are of equal value and equal power.

I cannot prove here that this is not really the true state of affairs, but I am strongly inclined to assume a stricter determination of the dream-wish. Children's dreams leave us in no doubt that a wish unfulfilled during the day may instigate a dream. But we must not forget that this is, after all, the wish of a child; that it is a wish-impulse of the strength peculiar to childhood. I very much doubt whether a wish unfulfilled in the daytime would suffice to create a dream in an adult. It would rather seem that as we learn to control our instinctual life by intellection we more and more renounce as unprofitable the formation or retention of such intense wishes as are natural to childhood. In this, indeed, there may be individual variations; some retain the infantile type of the psychic processes longer than others; just as we find such differences in the gradual decline of the originally vivid visual imagination. In general, however, I am of the opinion that unfulfilled wishes of the day are insufficient to produce a dream in adults. I will readily admit that the wish-impulses originating in consciousness contribute to the instigation of dreams, but they probably do no more. The dream would not occur if the preconscious wish were not reinforced from another source.

That source is the unconscious. I believe that *the conscious wish becomes effective in exciting a dream only when it succeeds in arousing a similar unconscious wish which reinforces it*. From the indications obtained in the psychoanalysis of the neuroses, I believe that these unconscious wishes are always active and ready to express themselves whenever they find an opportunity of allying themselves with an impulse from consciousness, and transferring their own greater intensity to the lesser intensity of the latter.[1] It must, therefore, seem that the conscious wish alone has been realized in the dream; but a slight peculiarity in the form of the dream will put us on the track of the powerful ally from the unconscious. These ever-active and, as it were, immortal wishes of our unconscious recall the legendary Titans who, from time immemorial, have been buried under the mountains which were once hurled upon them by the victorious gods, and even now quiver from time to time at the convulsions of their mighty limbs. These wishes, existing in repression, are themselves of infantile origin, as we learn from the psychological investigation of the neuroses. Let me, therefore, set aside the view previously expressed, that it matters little whence the dream-wish originates, and replace it by another, namely: *the wish manifested in the dream must be an infantile wish*. In the adult it originates in the *Ucs.*, while in the child, in whom no division and censorship exist as yet between the *Pcs.* and *Ucs.*, or in whom these are only in process of formation, it is an unfulfilled and unrepressed wish from the waking state. I am aware that this conception cannot be generally demonstrated, but I maintain that it can often be demonstrated even where one would not have suspected it, and that it cannot be generally refuted.

In dream-formation, the wish-impulses which are left over from the conscious waking life are, therefore, to be relegated to the background. I cannot admit that they play any part except that attributed to the material of actual sensations during sleep in relation to the dream-content. If I now take into account those other psychic instigations left over from the waking life of the day, which are not wishes, I shall merely be adhering to the course mapped out for me by this line of thought. We may succeed in provisionally disposing of the energetic

---

[1] They share this character of indestructibility with all other psychic acts that are really unconscious—that is, with psychic acts belonging solely to the system *Ucs.* These paths are opened once and for all; they never fall into disuse; they conduct the excitation-process to discharge as often as they are charged again with unconscious excitation. To speak metaphorically, they suffer no other form of annihilation than did the shades of the lower regions in the *Odyssey*, who awoke to new life the moment they drank blood. The processes depending on the preconscious system are destructible in quite another sense. The psychotherapy of the neuroses is based on this difference.

cathexis of our waking thoughts by deciding to go to sleep. He is a good sleeper who can do this; Napoleon I is reputed to have been a model of this kind. But we do not always succeed in doing it, or in doing it completely. Unsolved problems, harassing cares, overwhelming impressions, continue the activity of our thought even during sleep, maintaining psychic processes in the system which we have termed the preconscious. The thought-impulses continued into sleep may be divided into the following groups:—

1. Those which have not been completed during the day, owing to some accidental cause.
2. Those which have been left uncompleted because our mental powers have failed us, i.e. unsolved problems.
3. Those which have been turned back and suppressed during the day. This is reinforced by a powerful fourth group:—
4. Those which have been excited in our *Ucs.* during the day by the workings of the *Pcs.*; and finally we may add a fifth, consisting of:—
5. The indifferent impressions of the day, which have therefore been left unsettled.

We need not underrate the psychic intensities introduced into sleep by these residues of the day's waking life, especially those emanating from the group of the unsolved issues. It is certain that these excitations continue to strive for expression during the night, and we may assume with equal certainty that the state of sleep renders impossible the usual continuance of the process of excitation in the preconscious and its termination in becoming conscious. In so far as we can become conscious of our mental processes in the ordinary way, even during the night, to that extent we are simply not asleep. I cannot say what change is produced in the *Pcs.* system by the state of sleep,[1] but there is no doubt that the psychological characteristics of sleep are to be sought mainly in the cathectic changes occurring just in this system, which dominates, moreover, the approach to motility, paralysed during sleep. On the other hand, I have found nothing in the psychology of dreams to warrant the assumption that sleep produces any but secondary changes in the conditions of the *Ucs.* system. Hence, for the nocturnal excitations in the *Pcs.* there remains no other path than that taken by the wish-excitations from the *Ucs.*; they must seek reinforcement from the *Ucs.*, and follow the detours of the unconscious excitations. But what is the relation of the preconscious day-residues to the dream? There is no doubt that they penetrate abundantly into

[1] I have endeavoured to penetrate farther into the relations of the sleeping state and the conditions of hallucination in my essay, Metapsychological Supplement to the Theory of Dreams. *Collected Papers*, vol. iv, p. 137 (*Metapsychologische Ergänzung zur Traumlehre. Int. Zeitschr. f. Ps.A.* iv, 1916–18, *Ges. Schriften*, Bd. v, p. 520).

the dream; that they utilize the dream-content to obtrude themselves upon consciousness even during the night; indeed, they sometimes even dominate the dream-content, and impel it to continue the work of the day; it is also certain that the day-residues may just as well have any other character as that of wishes. But it is highly instructive, and for the theory of wish-fulfillment of quite decisive importance, to see what conditions they must comply with in order to be received into the dream.

Let us pick out one of the dreams cited above, *e.g.* the dream in which my friend Otto seems to show the symptoms of *Basedow's disease* (p. 313). Otto's appearance gave me some concern during the day, and this worry, like everything else relating to him, greatly affected me. I may assume that this concern followed me into sleep. I was probably bent on finding out what was the matter with him. During the night my concern found expression in the dream which I have recorded. Not only was its content senseless, but it failed to show any wish-fulfilment. But I began to search for the source of this incongruous expression of the solicitude felt during the day, and analysis revealed a connection. I identified my friend Otto with a certain Baron L. and myself with a Professor R. There was only one explanation of my being impelled to select just this substitute for the day-thought. I must always have been ready in the *Ucs.* to identify myself with Professor R., as this meant the realization of one of the immortal infantile wishes, viz. the wish to become great. Repulsive ideas respecting my friend, ideas that would certainly have been repudiated in a waking state, took advantage of the opportunity to creep into the dream; but the worry of the day had likewise found some sort of expression by means of a substitute in the dream-content. The day-thought, which was in itself not a wish, but on the contrary a worry, had in some way to find a connection with some infantile wish, now unconscious and suppressed, which then allowed it—duly dressed up—to "arise" for consciousness. The more domineering the worry the more forced could be the connection to be established; between the content of the wish and that of the worry there need be no connection, nor was there one in our example.

It would perhaps be appropriate, in dealing with this problem, to inquire how a dream behaves when material is offered to it in the dream-thoughts which flatly opposes a wish-fulfilment; such as justified worries, painful reflections and distressing realizations. The many possible results may be classified as follows: (*a*) The dream-work succeeds in replacing all painful ideas by contrary ideas, and suppressing the painful affect belonging to them. This, then, results in a pure and simple satisfaction-dream, a palpable "wish-fulfilment," concerning which there is nothing more to be said. (*b*) The painful ideas find their way into the manifest dream-content, more or less modified, but nevertheless quite recognizable.

This is the case which raises doubts about the wish-theory of dreams, and thus calls for further investigation. Such dreams with a painful content may either be indifferent in feeling, or they may convey the whole painful affect, which the ideas contained in them seem to justify, or they may even lead to the development of anxiety to the point of waking.

Analysis then shows that even these painful dreams are wish-fulfilments. An unconscious and repressed wish, whose fulfilment could only be felt as painful by the dreamer's ego, has seized the opportunity offered by the continued cathexis of painful day-residues, has lent them its support, and has thus made them capable of being dreamed. But whereas in case (a) the unconscious wish coincided with the conscious one, in case (b) the discord between the unconscious and the conscious—the repressed material and the ego—is revealed, and the situation in the fairy-tale, of the three wishes which the fairy offers to the married couple, is realized (see below, p. 520). The gratification in respect of the fulfilment of the repressed wish may prove to be so great that it balances the painful affects adhering to the day-residues; the dream is then indifferent in its affective tone, although it is on the one hand the fulfilment of a wish, and on the other the fulfilment of a fear. Or it may happen that the sleep ego plays an even more extensive part in the dream-formation, that it reacts with violent resentment to the accomplished satisfaction of the repressed wish, and even goes so far as to make an end of the dream by means of anxiety. It is thus not difficult to recognize that dreams of pain and anxiety are, in accordance with our theory, just as much wish-fulfilments as are the straightforward dreams of gratification.

Painful dreams may also be "punishment dreams." It must be admitted that the recognition of these dreams adds something that is, in a certain sense, new to the theory of dreams. What is fulfilled by them is once more an unconscious wish—the wish for the punishment of the dreamer for a repressed, prohibited wish-impulse. To this extent these dreams comply with the requirement here laid down: that the motive-power behind the dream-formation must be furnished by a wish belonging to the unconscious. But a finer psychological dissection allows us to recognize the difference between this and the other wish-dreams. In the dreams of group (b) the unconscious dream-forming wish belonged to the repressed material. In the punishment-dreams it is likewise an unconscious wish, but one which we must attribute not to the repressed material but to the "ego."

Punishment-dreams point, therefore, to the possibility of a still more extensive participation of the ego in dream-formation. The mechanism of dream-formation becomes indeed in every way more transparent if in place of the antithesis "conscious" and "unconscious," we put the antithesis: "ego" and "repressed." This, however, cannot be done without taking into account what happens in the psychoneuroses, and for this reason it has not been done in this book. Here I need only remark that the occurrence of punishment-dreams is not generally subject to the presence of painful day-residues. They originate indeed most readily if the contrary is true, if the thoughts which are day-residues are of a gratifying nature, but express illicit gratifications. Of these thoughts nothing then finds its way into the manifest dream except their contrary, just as was the case in the dreams of group (*a*). Thus it would be the essential characteristic of punishment-dreams that in them it is not the unconscious wish from the repressed material (from the system *Ucs.*) that is responsible for dream-formation, but the punitive wish reacting against it, a wish pertaining to the ego, even though it is unconscious (i.e. preconscious).[1]

I will elucidate some of the foregoing observations by means of a dream of my own, and above all I will try to show how the dream-work deals with a day-residue involving painful expectation:

Indistinct beginning. *I tell my wife I have some news for her, something very special. She becomes frightened, and does not wish to hear it. I assure her that on the contrary it is something which will please her greatly, and I begin to tell her that our son's Officers' Corps has sent a sum of money (5,000 k.?) . . . something about honourable mention . . . distribution . . . at the same time I have gone with her into a small room, like a store-room, in order to fetch something from it. Suddenly I see my son appear; he is not in uniform but rather in a tight-fitting sports suit (like a seal?) with a small cap. He climbs on to a basket which stands to one side near a chest, in order to put something on this chest. I address him; no answer. It seems to me that his face or forehead is bandaged, he arranges something in his mouth, pushing something into it. Also his hair shows a glint of grey. I reflect: Can he be so exhausted? And has he false teeth? Before I can address him again I awake without anxiety, but with palpitations. My clock points to 2.30 a.m.*

To give a full analysis is once more impossible. I shall therefore confine myself to emphasizing some decisive points. Painful expectations of the day had given occasion for this dream; once again there had been no news for over a week from my son, who was fighting at the Front. It is easy to see that in the dream-content the conviction that he has been killed or wounded finds expression. At the beginning of the dream one can observe an energetic effort to replace the painful thoughts by their contrary. I have to impart something very pleasing, something about sending money, honourable mention, and distribution. (The sum of money originates in a gratifying incident of my medical practice; it is therefore trying to lead

---

[1] Here one may consider the idea of the super-ego which was later recognized by psychoanalysis.

the dream away altogether from its theme.) But this effort fails. The boy's mother has a presentiment of something terrible and does not wish to listen. The disguises are too thin; the reference to the material to be suppressed shows through everywhere. If my son is killed, then his comrades will send back his property; I shall have to distribute whatever he has left among his sisters, brothers and other people. Honourable mention is frequently awarded to an officer after he has died the "hero's death." The dream thus strives to give direct expression to what it at first wished to deny, whilst at the same time the wish-fulfilling tendency reveals itself by distortion. (The change of locality in the dream is no doubt to be understood as threshold symbolism, in line with Silberer's view.) We have indeed no idea what lends it the requisite motive-power. But my son does not appear as "falling" (on the field of battle) but "climbing."—He was, in fact, a daring mountaineer.—He is not in uniform, but in a sports suit; that is, the place of the fatality now dreaded has been taken by an accident which happened to him at one time when he was ski-running, when he fell and fractured his thigh. But the nature of his costume, which makes him look like a seal, recalls immediately a younger person, our comical little grandson; the grey hair recalls his father, our son-in-law, who has had a bad time in the War. What does this signify? But let us leave this: the locality, a pantry, the chest, from which he wants to take something (in the dream, to put something on it), are unmistakable allusions to an accident of my own, brought upon myself when I was between two and three years of age. I climbed on a foot-stool in the pantry, in order to get something nice which was on a chest or table. The foot-stool tumbled over and its edge struck me behind the lower jaw. I might very well have knocked all my teeth out. At this point, an admonition presents itself: it serves you right—like a hostile impulse against the valiant warrior. A profounder analysis enables me to detect the hidden impulse, which would be able to find satisfaction in the dreaded mishap to my son. It is the envy of youth which the elderly man believes that he has thoroughly stifled in actual life. There is no mistaking the fact that it was the very intensity of the painful apprehension lest such a misfortune should really happen that searched out for its alleviation such a repressed wish-fulfilment.

I can now clearly define what the unconscious wish means for the dream. I will admit that there is a whole class of dreams in which the *incitement* originates mainly or even exclusively from the residues of the day; and returning to the dream about my friend Otto, I believe that even my desire to become at last a *professor extraordinarius* would have allowed me to sleep in peace that night, had not the day's concern for my friend's health continued active. But this worry alone would not have produced a dream; the *motive-power* needed by the dream had to be contributed by a wish, and it was the business of my concern to find such a wish for itself, as the motive power of the dream. To put it figuratively, it is quite possible that a day-thought plays the part of the *entrepreneur* in the dream; but the *entrepreneur*, who, as we say, has the idea, and feels impelled to realize it, can do nothing without *capital*; he needs a *capitalist* who will defray the expense, and this capitalist, who contributes the psychic expenditure for the dream, is invariably and indisputably, whatever the nature of the waking thoughts, *a wish from the unconscious.*

In other cases the capitalist himself is the *entrepreneur;* this, indeed, seems to be the more usual case. An unconscious wish is excited by the day's work, and this now creates the dream. And the dream-processes provide a parallel for all the other possibilities of the economic relationship here used as an illustration. Thus the *entrepreneur* may himself contribute a little of the capital, or several *entrepreneurs* may seek the aid of the same capitalist, or several capitalists may jointly supply the capital required by the *entrepreneurs.* Thus there are dreams sustained by more than one dream-wish, and many similar variations, which may be readily imagined, and which are of no further interest to us. What is still lacking to our discussion of the dream-wish we shall only be able to complete later on.

The *tertium comparationis* in the analogies here employed, the quantitative element of which an allotted amount is placed at the free disposal of the dream, admits of a still closer application to the elucidation of the dream-structure. As shown on p. 338, we can recognize in most dreams a centre supplied with a special sensory intensity. This is as a rule the direct representation of the wish-fulfilment; for if we reverse the displacements of the dream-work we find that the psychic intensity of the elements in the dream-thoughts is replaced by the *sensory* intensity of the elements in the dream-content. The elements in the neighbourhood of the wish-fulfilment have often nothing to do with its meaning, but prove to be the offshoots of painful thoughts which are opposed to the wish. But owing to their connection with the central element, often artificially established, they secure so large a share of its intensity as to become capable of representation. Thus, the representative energy of the wish-fulfillment diffuses itself over a certain sphere of association, within which all elements are raised to representation, including even those that are in themselves without resources. In dreams containing several dynamic wishes we can easily separate and delimit the spheres of the individual wish-fulfilments, and we shall find that the gaps in the dream are often of the nature of boundary-zones.

Although the foregoing remarks have restricted the significance of the day-residues for the dream, they are none the less deserving of some further attention. For they must be a necessary ingredient in dream-formation, inasmuch as experience reveals the surprising fact that every dream shows in its content a connection with a recent waking impression, often of the most indifferent kind. So far we have failed to understand the necessity for this addition to the dream-mixture (p. 249). This necessity becomes apparent only when we bear in mind the part played by the unconscious wish, and seek further information in the psychology of the neuroses. We shall then learn that an unconscious idea, as such, is quite incapable of entering into the preconscious, and that it can exert an influence there only by establishing touch with a harmless idea already belonging to the preconscious, to which it transfers its intensity, and by which it allows itself to be screened. This is the fact of *transference*, which furnishes the explanation of so many surprising occurrences in the psychic life of neurotics. The transference may leave the idea from the preconscious unaltered, though the latter will thus acquire an unmerited intensity, or it may force upon this some modification derived from the content of the transferred idea. I trust the reader will pardon my fondness for comparisons with daily life, but I feel tempted to say that the situation for the repressed idea is like that of the American dentist in Austria, who may not carry on his practice unless he can get a duly installed doctor of medicine to serve him as a signboard and legal "cover." Further, just as it is not exactly the busiest physicians who form such alliances with dental practitioners, so in the psychic life the choice as regards covers for repressed ideas does not fall upon such preconscious or conscious ideas as have themselves attracted enough of the attention active in the preconscious. The unconscious prefers to entangle with its connections either those impressions and ideas of the preconscious which have remained unnoticed as being indifferent or those which have immediately had attention withdrawn from them again (by rejection). It is a well-known proposition of the theory of associations, confirmed by all experience, that ideas which have formed a very intimate connection in one direction assume a negative type of attitude towards whole groups of new connections. I have even attempted at one time to base a theory of hysterical paralysis on this principle.

If we assume that the same need of transference on the part of the repressed ideas, of which we have become aware through the analysis of the neurosis, makes itself felt in dreams also, we can at once explain two of the problems of the dream: namely, that every dream-analysis reveals an interweaving of a recent impression, and that this recent element is often of the most indifferent character. We may add what we have already learned elsewhere, that the reason why these recent and indifferent elements so frequently find their way into the dream-content as substitutes for the very oldest elements of the dream-thoughts is that they have the least to fear from the resisting censorship. But while this freedom from censorship explains only the preference shown to the trivial elements, the constant presence of recent elements points to the necessity for transference. Both groups of impressions satisfy the demand of the repressed ideas for material still free from associations, the indifferent ones because they have offered no occasion for extensive associations, and the recent ones because they have not had sufficient time to form such associations.

We thus, see that the day-residues, among which we may now include the indifferent impressions, not only borrow something from the *Ucs.* when they secure a share in dream-formation—namely, the motive-power at the disposal of the repressed wish—but they also offer to the unconscious something that is indispensable to it, namely, the points of attachment necessary for transference. If we wished to penetrate more deeply into the psychic processes, we should have to throw a clearer light on the play of excitations between the preconscious and the unconscious, and indeed the study of the psychoneuroses would impel us to do so; but dreams, as it happens, give us no help in this respect.

Just one further remark as to the day-residues. There is no doubt that it is really these that disturb our sleep, and not our dreams which, on the contrary, strive to guard our sleep. But we shall return to this point later.

So far we have discussed the dream-wish; we have traced it back to the sphere of the *Ucs.*, and have analysed its relation to the day-residues, which, in their turn, may be either wishes, or psychic impulses of any other kind, or simply recent impressions. We have thus found room for the claims that can be made for the dream-forming significance of our waking mental activity in all its multifariousness. It might even prove possible to explain, on the basis of our train of thought, those extreme cases in which the dream, continuing the work of the day, brings to a happy issue an unsolved problem of waking life. We merely lack a suitable example to analyse, in order to uncover the infantile or repressed source of wishes, the tapping of which has so successfully reinforced the efforts of the preconscious activity. But we are not a step nearer to answering the question: Why is it that the unconscious can furnish in sleep nothing more than the motive-power for a wish-fulfilment? The answer to this question must elucidate the psychic nature of the state of wishing: and it will be given with the aid of the notion of the psychic apparatus.

We do not doubt that this apparatus, too, has only arrived at its present perfection by a long process of evolution. Let us attempt to restore it as it existed in an earlier stage of capacity. From postulates to be confirmed in other ways we know that at first the apparatus strove to keep itself as free from stimulation as possible, and therefore, in its early structure, adopted the arrangement of a reflex apparatus, which enabled it promptly to discharge by the motor paths any sensory excitation reaching it from without. But this simple function was disturbed by the exigencies of life, to which the apparatus owes the impetus toward further development. The exigencies of life first confronted it in the form of the great physical needs. The excitation aroused by the inner need seeks an outlet in motility, which we may describe as "internal change" or "expression of the emotions." The hungry child cries or struggles helplessly. But its situation remains unchanged; for the excitation proceeding from the inner need has not the character of a momentary impact, but of a continuing pressure. A change can occur only if, in some way (in the case of the child by external assistance), there is an *experience of satisfaction,* which puts an end to the internal excitation. An essential constituent of this experience is the appearance of a certain percept (of food in our example), the memory-image of which is henceforth associated with the memory-trace of the excitation arising from the need. Thanks to the established connection, there results, at the next occurrence of this need, a psychic impulse which seeks to revive the memory-image of the former percept, and to re-evoke the former percept itself; that is, it actually seeks to re-establish the situation of the first satisfaction. Such an impulse is what we call a wish; the reappearance of the perception constitutes the wish-fulfilment, and the full cathexis of the perception, by the excitation springing from the need, constitutes the shortest path to the wish-fulfilment. We may assume a primitive state of the psychic apparatus in which this path is actually followed, i.e. in which the wish ends in hallucination. This first psychic activity therefore aims at an identity of perception: that is, at a repetition of that perception which is connected with the satisfaction of the need.

This primitive mental activity must have been modified by bitter practical experience into a secondary and more appropriate activity. The establishment of identity of perception by the short regressive path within the apparatus does not produce the same result in another respect as follows upon cathexis of the same perception coming from without. The satisfaction does not occur, and the need continues. In order to make the internal cathexis equivalent to the external one, the former would have to be continuously sustained, just as actually happens in the hallucinatory psychoses and in hunger-phantasies, which exhaust their performance in *maintaining their hold* on the object desired. In order to attain to more appropriate use of the psychic energy, it becomes necessary to suspend the full regression, so that it does not proceed beyond the memory-image, and thence can seek other paths, leading ultimately to the production of the desired identity from the side of the outer world.[1] This inhibition, as well as the subsequent deflection of the excitation, becomes the task of a second system, which controls voluntary motility, i.e.

[1] In other words: the introduction of a "test of reality" is recognized as necessary.

a system whose activity first leads on to the use of motility for purposes remembered in advance. But all this complicated mental activity, which works its way from the memory-image to the production of identity of perception via the outer world, merely represents *a roundabout way to wish-fulfillment* made necessary by experience.[1] Thinking is indeed nothing but a substitute for the hallucinatory wish; and if the dream is called a wish-fulfillment, this becomes something self-evident, since nothing but a wish can impel our psychic apparatus to activity. The dream, which fulfills its wishes by following the short regressive path, has thereby simply preserved for us a specimen of the *primary* method of operation of the psychic apparatus, which has been abandoned as inappropriate. What once prevailed in the waking state, when our psychic life was still young and inefficient, seems to have been banished into our nocturnal life; just as we still find in the nursery those discarded primitive weapons of adult humanity, the bow and arrow. *Dreaming is a fragment of the superseded psychic life of the child.* In the psychoses those modes of operation of the psychic apparatus which are normally suppressed in the waking state reassert themselves, and thereupon betray their inability to satisfy our demands in the outer world.[2]

The unconscious wish-impulses evidently strive to assert themselves even during the day, and the fact of transference, as well as the psychoses, tells us that they endeavour to force their way through the preconscious system to consciousness and the command of motility. Thus, in the censorship between *Ucs.* and *Pcs.*, which the dream forces us to assume, we must recognize and respect the guardian of our psychic health. But is it not carelessness on the part of this guardian to diminish his vigilance at night, and to allow the suppressed impulses of the *Ucs.* to achieve expression, thus again making possible the process of hallucinatory regression? I think not, for when the critical guardian goes to rest—and we have proof that his slumber is not profound—he takes care to close the gate to motility. No matter what impulses from the usually inhibited *Ucs.* may bustle about the stage, there is no need to interfere with them; they remain harmless, because they are not in a position to set in motion the motor apparatus which alone can operate to produce any change in the outer world. Sleep guarantees the security of the fortress which has to be guarded. The state of affairs is less harmless when a displacement of

---

[1] Le Lorrain justly extols the wish-fulfilments of dreams: *"Sans fatigue sérieuse, sans être obligé de recourir à cette lutte opiniâtre et longue qui use et corrode les jouissances poursuivies."*

[2] I have further elaborated this train of thought elsewhere, where I have distinguished the two principles involved as the pleasure-principle and the reality-principle. "Formulations regarding the Two Principles in Mental Functioning," *Collected Papers*, vol. iv, p. 13 (*Formulierungen über die zwei Prinzipien des psychischen Geschehens* in *Ges. Schriften*, Bd. v, s. 409).

energies is produced, not by the decline at night in the energy put forth by the critical censorship, but by the pathological enfeeblement of the latter, or the pathological reinforcement of the unconscious excitations, and this while the preconscious is cathected and the gates of motility are open. The guardian is then overpowered; the unconscious excitations subdue the *Pcs.*, and from the *Pcs.* they dominate our speech and action, or they enforce hallucinatory regressions, thus directing an apparatus not designed for them by virtue of the attraction exerted by perceptions on the distribution of our psychic energy. We call this condition psychosis.

We now find ourselves in the most favourable position for continuing the construction of our psychological scaffolding, which we left after inserting the two systems, *Ucs.* and *Pcs.* However, we still have reason to give further consideration to the wish as the sole psychic motive-power in the dream. We have accepted the explanation that the reason why the dream is in every case a wish-fulfilment is that it is a function of the system *Ucs.*, which knows no other aim than wish-fulfilment, and which has at its disposal no forces other than the wish-impulses. Now if we want to continue for a single moment longer to maintain our right to develop such far-reaching psychological speculations from the facts of dream-interpretation, we are in duty bound to show that they insert the dream into a context which can also embrace other psychic structures. If there exists a system of the *Ucs.*—or something sufficiently analogous for the purposes of our discussion—the dream cannot be its sole manifestation; every dream may be a wish-fulfilment, but there must be other forms of abnormal wish-fulfilment as well as dreams. And in fact the theory of all psychoneurotic symptoms culminates in the one proposition *that they, too, must be conceived as wish-fulfillments of the unconscious.*[1] Our explanation makes the dream only the first member of a series of the greatest importance for the psychiatrist, the understanding of which means the solution of the purely psychological part of the psychiatric problem.[2] But in other members of this group of wish-fulfilments—for example, in the hysterical symptoms—I know of one essential characteristic which I have so far failed to find in the dream. Thus, from the investigations often alluded to in this treatise, I know that the formation of a hysterical symptom needs a junction of both the currents of our psychic life. The symptom is not merely the expression of a realized unconscious wish; the latter must be joined by another wish from the preconscious, which is fulfilled by the same symptom; so that the symptom is at least doubly determined,

---

[1] Expressed more exactly: One portion of the symptom corresponds to the unconscious wish-fulfillment, while the other corresponds to the reaction-formation opposed to it.
[2] Hughlings Jackson has expressed himself as follows: "Find out all about dreams, and you will have found out all about insanity."

once by each of the conflicting systems. Just as in dreams, there is no limit to further over-determination. The determination which does not derive from the *Ucs.* is, as far as I can see, invariably a thought-stream of reaction against the unconscious wish; for example, a self-punishment. Hence I can say, quite generally, that *a hysterical symptom originates only where two contrary wish-fulfillments, having their source in different psychic systems, are able to meet in a single expression.*[1] Examples would help us but little here, as nothing but a complete unveiling of the complications in question can carry conviction. I will therefore content myself with the bare assertion, and will cite one example, not because it proves anything, but simply as an illustration. The hysterical vomiting of a female patient proved, on the one hand, to be the fulfilment of an unconscious phantasy from the years of puberty—namely, the wish that she might be continually pregnant, and have a multitude of children; and this was subsequently supplemented by the wish that she might have them by as many fathers as possible. Against this immoderate wish there arose a powerful defensive reaction. But as by the vomiting the patient might have spoilt her figure and her beauty, so that she would no longer find favour in any man's eyes, the symptom was also in keeping with the punitive trend of thought, and so, being admissible on both sides, it was allowed to become a reality. This is the same way of acceding to a wish-fulfilment as the queen of the Parthians was pleased to adopt in the case of the triumvir Crassus. Believing that he had undertaken his campaign out of greed for gold, she caused molten gold to be poured into the throat of the corpse. "Here thou hast what thou hast longed for!"

Of the dream we know as yet only that it expresses a wish-fulfilment of the unconscious; and apparently the dominant preconscious system permits this fulfilment when it has compelled the wish to undergo certain distortions. We are, moreover, not in fact in a position to demonstrate regularly the presence of a train of thought opposed to the dream-wish, which is realized in the dream as well as its antagonist. Only now and then have we found in dream-analyses signs of reaction-products as, for instance, my affection for my friend R. in the "dream of my uncle" (p. 220). But the contribution from the preconscious which is missing here may be found in another place. The dream can provide expression for a wish from the *Ucs.* by means of all sorts of distortions, once the dominant system has withdrawn itself into the *wish to sleep,* and has realized this wish by producing the changes of cathexis within the psychic apparatus

---

[1] Cf. my latest formulation of the origin of hysterical symptoms in the treatise on "Hysterical Phantasies and their Relation to Bisexuality," *Collected Papers,* vol. ii, p. 51. This forms Chapter X in the English edition of *Selected Papers on Hysteria and Other Psychoneuroses.*

which are within its power; thereupon holding on to the wish in question for the whole duration of sleep.[1]

Now this persistent wish to sleep on the part of the preconscious has a quite general facilitating effect on the formation of dreams. Let us recall the dream of the father who, by the gleam of light from the death-chamber, was led to conclude that his child's body might have caught fire. We have shown that one of the psychic forces decisive in causing the father to draw this conclusion in the dream instead of allowing himself to be awakened by the gleam of light was the wish to prolong the life of the child seen in the dream by one moment. Other wishes originating in the repressed have probably escaped us, for we are unable to analyse this dream. But as a second source of motive-power in this dream we may add the father's desire to sleep, for, like the life of the child, the father's sleep is prolonged for a moment by the dream. The underlying motive is: "Let the dream go on, or I must wake up." As in this dream, so in all others, the wish to sleep lends its support to the unconscious wish. On page 209 we cited dreams which were manifestly dreams of convenience. But in truth all dreams may claim this designation. The efficacy of the wish to go on sleeping is most easily recognized in the awakening dreams, which so elaborate the external sensory stimulus that it becomes compatible with the continuance of sleep; they weave it into a dream in order to rob it of any claims it might make as a reminder of the outer world. But this wish to go on sleeping must also play its part in permitting all other dreams, which can only act as disturbers of the state of sleep from within. "Don't worry; sleep on; it's only a dream," is in many cases the suggestion of the *Pcs.* to consciousness when the dream gets too bad; and this describes in a quite general way the attitude of our dominant psychic activity towards dreaming, even though the thought remains unuttered. I must draw the conclusion that *throughout the whole of our sleep we are just as certain that we are dreaming as we are certain that we are sleeping.* It is imperative to disregard the objection that our consciousness is never directed to the latter knowledge, and that it is directed to the former knowledge only on special occasions, when the censorship feels, as it were, taken by surprise. On the contrary, there are persons in whom the retention at night of the knowledge that they are sleeping and dreaming becomes quite manifest, and who are thus apparently endowed with the conscious faculty of guiding their dream-life. Such a dreamer, for example, is dissatisfied with the turn taken by a dream; he breaks it off without waking, and begins it afresh, in order to continue it along different lines, just like a popular author who, upon request, gives a happier ending to his play. Or on another occasion, when the dream places him in

[1] This idea has been borrowed from the theory of sleep of Liébault, who revived hypnotic research in modern times (*Du Sommeil provoqué*, etc., Paris, 1889).

a sexually exciting situation, he thinks in his sleep: "I don't want to continue this dream and exhaust myself by an emission; I would rather save it for a real situation."

The Marquis Hervey (Vaschide) declared that he had gained such power over his dreams that he could accelerate their course at will, and turn them in any direction he wished. It seems that in him the wish to sleep had accorded a place to another, a preconscious wish, the wish to observe his dreams and to derive pleasure from them. Sleep is just as compatible with such a wish-resolve as it is with some proviso as a condition of waking up (wet-nurse's sleep). We know, too, that in all persons an interest in dreams greatly increases the number of dreams remembered after waking.

Concerning other observations as to the guidance of dreams, Ferenczi states: "The dream takes the thought that happens to occupy our psychic life at the moment, and elaborates it from all sides. It lets any given dream-picture drop when there is a danger that the wish-fulfilment will miscarry, and attempts a new kind of solution, until it finally succeeds in creating a wish-fulfilment that satisfies in one compromise both instances of the psychic life."

D. WAKING CAUSED BY DREAMS. THE FUNCTION OF DREAMS. THE ANXIETY-DREAM

Now that we know that throughout the night the preconscious is orientated to the wish to sleep, we can follow the dream-process with proper understanding. But let us first summarize what we already know about this process. We have seen that day-residues are left over from the waking activity of the mind, residues from which it has not been possible to withdraw all cathexis. Either one of the unconscious wishes has been aroused through the waking activity during the day or it so happens that the two coincide; we have already discussed the multifarious possibilities. Either already during the day or only on the establishment of the state of sleep the unconscious wish has made its way to the day-residues, and has effected a transference to them. Thus there arises a wish transferred to recent material; or the suppressed recent wish is revived by a reinforcement from the unconscious. This wish now endeavours to make its way to consciousness along the normal path of the thought processes, through the preconscious, to which indeed it belongs by virtue of one of its constituent elements. It is, however, confronted by the censorship which still subsists, and to whose influence it soon succumbs. It now takes on the distortion for which the way has already been paved by the transference to recent material. So far it is on the way to becoming something resembling an obsession, a delusion, or the like, i.e. a thought reinforced by a transference, and distorted in expression owing to the censorship. But its further progress is now checked by the state of sleep of the preconscious; this system has presumably protected itself against invasion by diminishing its excitations. The dream-process, therefore, takes the regressive course, which is just opened up by the peculiarity of the sleeping state, and in so doing follows the attraction exerted on it by memory-groups, which are, in part only, themselves present as visual cathexis, not as translations into the symbols of the later systems. On its way to regression it acquires representability. The subject of compression will be discussed later. The dream-process has by this time covered the second part of its contorted course. The first part threads its way progressively from the unconscious scenes or phantasies to the preconscious, while the second part struggles back from the boundary of the censorship to the tract of the perceptions. But when the dream-process becomes a perception-content, it has, so to speak, eluded the obstacle set up in the Pcs. by the censorship and the sleeping state. It succeeds in drawing attention to itself, and in being remarked by consciousness. For consciousness, which for us means a sense-organ for the apprehension of psychic qualities, can be excited in waking life from two sources: firstly, from the periphery of the whole apparatus, the perceptive system; and secondly, from the excitations of pleasure and pain which emerge as the sole psychic qualities yielded by the transpositions of energy in the interior of the apparatus. All other procesesses in the ψ-systems, even those in the preconscious, are devoid of all psychic quality, and are therefore not objects of consciousness, inasmuch as they do not provide either pleasure or pain for its perception. We shall have to assume that *these releases of pleasure and pain automatically regulate the course of the cathectic processes.* But in order to make possible more delicate performances, it subsequently proved necessary to render the flow of ideas more independent of pain-signals. To accomplish this, the Pcs. system needed qualities of its own which could attract consciousness, and most probably received them through the connection of the preconscious processes with the memory-system of speech-symbols, which was not devoid of quality. Through the qualities of this system, consciousness, hitherto only a sense-organ for perceptions, now becomes also a sense-organ for a part of our thought-processes. There are now, as it were, two sensory surfaces, one turned toward perception and the other toward the preconscious thought-processes.

I must assume that the sensory surface of consciousness which is turned to the preconscious is rendered far more unexcitable by sleep than the surface turned toward the P-system. The giving up of interest in the nocturnal thought-process is, of course, an appropriate procedure. Nothing is to happen in thought; the preconscious wants to sleep. But once the dream becomes perception, it is capable of exciting consciousness through the qualities now gained. The sensory excitation performs what is in fact its function; namely, it directs a part of the cathectic energy available in the *Pcs.* to the exciting cause in the form of attention. We must therefore admit that the dream always has a *waking* effect—that is, it calls into activity part of the quiescent energy of the *Pcs.* Under the influence of this energy, it now undergoes the process which we have described as secondary elaboration with a view to coherence and comprehensibility. This means that the dream is treated by this energy like any other perception-content; it is subjected to the same anticipatory ideas as far, at least, as the material allows. As far as this third part of the dream-process has any direction, this is once more progressive.

To avoid misunderstanding, it will not be amiss to say a few words as to the temporal characteristics of these dream-processes. In a very interesting discussion, evidently suggested by Maury's puzzling guillotine dream, Goblot tries to demonstrate that a dream takes up no other time than the transition period between sleeping and waking. The process of waking up requires time; during this time the dream occurs. It is supposed that the final picture of the dream is so vivid that it forces the dreamer to wake; in reality it is so vivid only because when it appears the dreamer is already very near waking. *"Un rêve, c'est un réveil qui commence."*

It has already been pointed out by Dugas that Goblot, in order to generalize his theory, was forced to ignore a great many facts. There are also dreams from which we do not awaken; for example, many dreams in which we dream that we dream. From our knowledge of the dream-work, we can by no means admit that it extends only over the period of waking. On the contrary, we must consider it probable that the first part of the dream-work is already begun during the day, when we are still under the domination of the preconscious. The second phase of the dream-work, viz. the alteration by the censorship, the attraction exercised by unconscious scenes, and the penetration to perception, continues probably all through the night, and accordingly we may always be correct when we report a feeling that we have been dreaming all night, even although we cannot say what we have dreamed. I do not, however, think that it is necessary to assume that up to the time of becoming conscious the dream-processes really follow the temporal sequence which we have described; viz. that there is first the transferred dream-wish, then the process of distortion due to the censorship, and then the change of direction to regression, etc. We were obliged to construct such a sequence for the sake of description; in reality, however, it is probably rather a question of simultaneously trying this path and that, and of the excitation fluctuating to and fro, until finally, because it has attained the most apposite concentration, one particular grouping remains in the field. Certain personal experiences even incline me to believe that the dream-work often requires more than one day and one night to produce its result, in which case the extraordinary art manifested in the construction of the dream is shorn of its miraculous character. In my opinion, even the regard for the comprehensibility of the dream as a perceptual event may exert its influence before the dream attracts consciousness to itself. From this point, however, the process is accelerated, since the dream is henceforth subjected to the same treatment as any other perception. It is like fire works, which require hours for their preparation and then flare up in a moment.

Through the dream-work, the dream-process now either gains sufficient intensity to attract consciousness to itself and to arouse the preconscious (quite independently of the time or profundity of sleep), or its intensity is insufficient, and it must wait in readiness until attention, becoming more alert immediately before waking, meets it half-way. Most dreams seem to operate with relatively slight psychic intensities, for they wait for the process of waking. This, then, explains the fact that as a rule we perceive something dreamed if we are suddenly roused from a deep sleep. Here, as well as in spontaneous waking, our first glance lights upon the perception-content created by the dream-work, while the next falls on that provided by the outer world.

But of greater theoretical interest are those dreams which are capable of waking us in the midst of our sleep. We may bear in mind the purposefulness which can be demonstrated in all other cases, and ask ourselves why the dream, that is, the unconscious wish, is granted the power to disturb our sleep, *i.e.* the fulfilment of the preconscious wish. The explanation is probably to be found in certain relations of energy which we do not yet understand. If we did so, we should probably find that the freedom given to the dream and the expenditure upon it of a certain detached attention represent a saving of energy as against the alternative case of the unconscious having to be held in check at night just as it is during the day. As experience shows, dreaming, even if it interrupts our sleep several times a night, still remains compatible with sleep. We wake up for a moment, and immediately fall asleep again. It is like driving off a fly in our sleep; we awake *ad hoc*. When we fall asleep again we have removed the cause of disturbance. The familiar examples of the sleep of wet-nurses, etc., show that the fulfilment of the wish to sleep is quite compatible with the maintenance of a certain amount of attention in a given direction.

But we must here take note of an objection which is based on a greater knowledge of the unconscious processes. We have ourselves described the unconscious wishes as always active, whilst nevertheless asserting that in the daytime they are not strong enough to make themselves perceptible. But when the state of sleep supervenes, and the unconscious wish has shown its power to form a dream, and with it to awaken the preconscious, why does this power lapse after cognisance has been taken of the dream? Would it not seem more probable that the dream should continually renew itself, like the disturbing fly which, when driven away, takes pleasure in returning again and again? What justification have we for our assertion that the dream removes the disturbance to sleep?

It is quite true that the unconscious wishes are always active. They represent paths which are always practicable, whenever a quantum of excitation makes use of them. It is indeed an outstanding peculiarity of the unconscious processes that they are indestructible. Nothing can be brought to an end in the unconscious; nothing is past or forgotten. This is impressed upon us emphatically in the study of the neuroses, and especially of hysteria. The unconscious path of thought which leads to the discharge through an attack is forthwith passable again when there is a sufficient accumulation of excitation. The mortification suffered thirty years ago operates, after having gained access to the unconscious sources of affect, during all these thirty years as though it were a recent experience. Whenever its memory is touched, it revives, and shows itself to be cathected with excitation which procures a motor discharge for itself in an attack. It is precisely here that psychotherapy must intervene, its task being to ensure that the unconscious processes are settled and forgotten. Indeed, the fading of memories and the weak affect of impressions which are no longer recent, which we are apt to take as self-evident, and to explain as a primary effect of time on our psychic memory-residues, are in reality secondary changes brought about by laborious work. It is the preconscious that accomplishes this work; *and the only course which psychotherapy can pursue is to bring the Ucs. under the dominion of the Pcs.*

There are, therefore, two possible issues for any single unconscious excitation-process. Either it is left to itself, in which case it ultimately breaks through somewhere and secures, on this one occasion, a discharge for its excitation into motility, or it succumbs to the influence of the preconscious, and through this its excitation becomes *bound* instead of being *discharged. It is the latter case that occurs in the dream-process.* The cathexis from the *Pcs.* which goes to meet the dream once this has attained to perception, because it has been drawn thither by the excitation of consciousness, binds the unconscious excitation of the dream and renders it harmless as a disturber of sleep. When the dreamer wakes up for a moment, he has really chased away the fly that threatened to disturb his sleep. We may now begin to suspect that it is really more expedient and economical to give way to the unconscious wish, to leave clear its path to regression so that it may form a dream, and then to bind and dispose of this dream by means of a small outlay of preconscious work, than to hold the unconscious in check throughout the whole period of sleep. It was, indeed, to be expected that the dream, even if originally it was not a purposeful process, would have seized upon some definite function in the play of forces of the psychic life. We now see what this function is. The dream has taken over the task of bringing the excitation of the *Ucs.*, which had been left free, back under the domination of the preconscious; it thus discharges the excitation of the *Ucs.*, acts as a safety-valve for the latter, and at the same time, by a slight outlay of waking activity, secures the sleep of the preconscious. Thus, like the other psychic formations of its group, the dream offers itself as a compromise, serving both systems simultaneously, by fulfilling the wishes of both, in so far as they are mutually compatible. A glance at Robert's "elimination theory" will show that we must agree with this author on his main point, namely, the determination of the function of dreams, though we differ from him in our general presuppositions and in our estimation of the dream-process.[1]

The above qualification—*in so far as the two wishes are mutually compatible*—contains a suggestion that there may be cases in which the function of the dream fails. The dream-process is, to begin with, admitted as a wish-fulfilment of the unconscious, but if this attempted wish-fulfilment disturbs the preconscious so profoundly that the latter can no longer maintain its state of rest, the dream has broken the compromise, and has failed to perform the second part of its task. It is then at once broken off, and replaced by complete awakening. But even here it is not really the fault of the dream if, though at other times the guardian, it has now to appear as the disturber of sleep, nor need this prejudice us against

---

[1] Is this the only function which we can attribute to dreams? I know of no other. A. Maeder, to be sure, has endeavoured to claim for the dream yet other "secondary" functions. He started from the just observation that many dreams contain attempts to provide solutions of conflicts, which are afterwards actually carried through. They thus behave like preparatory practice for waking activities. He therefore drew a parallel between dreaming and the play of animals and children, which is to be conceived as a training of the inherited instincts, and a preparation for their later serious activity, thus setting up a *fonction ludique* for the dream. A little while before Maeder, Alfred Adler likewise emphasized the function of "thinking ahead" in the dream. (An analysis which I published in 1905 contained a dream which may be conceived as a resolution-dream, which was repeated night after night until it was realized.)

But an obvious reflection must show us that this "secondary" function of the dream has no claim to recognition within the framework of any dream-interpretation. Thinking ahead, making resolutions, sketching out attempted solutions which can then perhaps be realized in waking life—these and many more performances are functions of the unconscious and preconscious activities of the mind which continue as "day-residues" in the sleeping state, and can then combine with an unconscious wish to form a dream (*see* p. 507). The function of "thinking ahead" in the dream is thus rather a function of preconscious waking thought, the result of which may be disclosed to us by the analysis of dreams or other phenomena. After the dream has so long been fused with its manifest content, one must now guard against confusing it with the latent dream-thoughts.

its averred purposive character. This is not the only instance in the organism in which a contrivance that is usually to the purpose becomes inappropriate and disturbing so soon as something is altered in the conditions which engender it; the disturbance, then, at all events serves the new purpose of indicating the change, and of bringing into play against it the means of adjustment of the organism. Here, of course, I am thinking of the anxiety-dream, and lest it should seem that I try to evade this witness against the theory of wish-fulfilment whenever I encounter it, I will at least give some indications as to the explanation of the anxiety-dream.

That a psychic process which develops anxiety may still be a wish-fulfilment has long ceased to imply any contradiction for us. We may explain this occurrence by the fact that the wish belongs to one system (the *Ucs.*), whereas the other system (the *Pcs.*) has rejected and suppressed it.[1] The subjection of the *Ucs.* by the *Pcs.* is not thoroughgoing even in perfect psychic health; the extent of this suppression indicates the degree of our psychic normality. Neurotic symptoms indicate to us that the two systems are in mutual conflict; the symptoms are the result of a compromise in this conflict, and they temporarily put an end to it. On the one hand they afford the *Ucs.* a way out for the discharge of its excitation—they serve it as a kind of sally-gate—while, on the other hand, they give the *Pcs.* the possibility of dominating the *Ucs.* in some degree. It is instructive to consider, for example, the significance of a hysterical phobia, or of agoraphobia. A neurotic is said to be incapable of crossing

[1] "A second consideration, much more important and far-reaching, but equally overlooked by the laity, is the following. A wish-fulfillment must certainly bring some pleasure; but we go on to ask; 'To whom?' Of course to the person who has the wish. But we know that the attitude of the dreamer towards his wishes is a peculiar one: he rejects them, censors them, in short, he will have none of them. Their fulfillment, then, can afford him no pleasure, rather the opposite, and here experience shows that this 'opposite,' which has still to be explained, takes the form of *anxiety*. The dreamer, where his wishes are concerned, is like two separate people closely linked together by some important thing in common. Instead of enlarging upon this I will remind you of a well-known fairy-tale in which you will see these relationships repeated. A good fairy promised a poor man and his wife to fulfill their first three wishes. They were delighted, and made up their minds to choose the wishes carefully. But the woman was tempted by the smell of some sausages being cooked in the next cottage and wished for two like them. Lo! and behold, there they were—and the first wish was fulfilled. With that, the man lost his temper and in his resentment wished that the sausages might hang on the tip of his wife's nose. This also came to pass, and the sausages could not be removed from their position; so the second wish was fulfilled, but it was the man's wish and its fulfilment was most unpleasant for the woman. You know the rest of the story: as they were after all man and wife the third wish had to be that the sausages should come off the end of the woman's nose. We might make use of this fairy-tale many times over in other contexts, but here it need only serve to illustrate the fact that it is possible for the fulfilment of one person's wish to be very disagreeable to someone else, unless the two people are entirely at one!" *Introductory Lectures on Psycho-Analysis*, London, 1929, pp. 182–183.

the street alone, and this we should rightly call a "symptom." Let someone now remove this symptom by constraining him to this action which
he deems himself incapable of performing. The result will be an attack
of anxiety, just as an attack of anxiety in the street has often been the
exciting cause of the establishment of an agoraphobia. We thus, learn
that the symptom has been constituted in order to prevent the anxiety
from breaking out. The phobia is thrown up before the anxiety like a
frontier fortress.

We cannot enlarge further on this subject unless we examine the rôle
of the affects in these processes, which can only be done here imperfectly.
We will therefore affirm the proposition that the principal reason why
the suppression of the *Ucs.* becomes necessary is that if the movement
of ideas in the *Ucs.* were allowed to run its course, it would develop an
affect which originally had the character of pleasure, but which, since
the process of *repression,* bears the character of pain. The aim, as well as
the result, of the suppression is to prevent the development of this pain.
The suppression extends to the idea-content of the *Ucs.*, because the
liberation of pain might emanate from this idea-content. We here take as
our basis a quite definite assumption as to the nature of the development
of affect. This is regarded as a motor or secretory function, the key to the
innervation of which is to be found in the ideas of the *Ucs.* Through the
domination of the *Pcs.* these ideas are as it were strangled, that is, inhibited from sending out the impulse that would develop the affect. The
danger which arises if cathexis by the *Pcs.* ceases thus consists in the
fact that the unconscious excitations would liberate an affect that—in
consequence of the repression that has previously occurred—could only
be felt as pain or anxiety.

This danger is released if the dream-process is allowed to have its
own way. The conditions for its realization are, that repressions shall
have occurred, and that the suppressed wish-impulses can become sufficiently strong. They, therefore, fall entirely outside the psychological
framework of dream-formation. Were it not for the fact that our theme
is connected by just one factor with the theme of the development of
anxiety, namely, by the setting free of the *Ucs.* during sleep, I could
refrain from the discussion of the anxiety-dream altogether, and thus
avoid all the obscurities involved in it.

The theory of the anxiety-dream belongs, as I have already repeatedly stated, to the psychology of the neuroses. I might further add
that anxiety in dreams is an anxiety-problem and not a dream-problem.
Having once exhibited the point of contact of the psychology of the
neuroses with the theme of the dream-process, we have nothing further
to do with it. There is only one thing left which I can do. Since I have
asserted that neurotic anxiety has its origin in sexual sources, I can sub-

ject anxiety-dreams to analysis in order to demonstrate the sexual material in their dream-thoughts.

For good reasons I refrain from citing any of the examples so abundantly placed at my disposal by neurotic patients, and prefer to give some anxiety-dreams of children.

Personally, I have had no real anxiety-dream for decades, but I do recall one from my seventh or eighth year which I subjected to interpretation some thirty years later. The dream was very vivid, and showed me *my beloved mother, with a peculiarly calm, sleeping countenance, carried into the room and laid on the bed by two (or three) persons with birds' beaks.* I awoke crying and screaming, and disturbed my parents' sleep. The peculiarly draped, excessively tall figures with beaks I had taken from the illustrations of Philippson's Bible; I believe they represented deities with the heads of sparrowhawks from an Egyptian tomb-relief. The analysis yielded, however, also the recollection of a house-porter's boy, who used to play with us children on a meadow in front of the house; I might add that his name was Philip. It seemed to me then that I first heard from this boy the vulgar word signifying sexual intercourse, which is replaced among educated persons by the Latin word *coitus,* but which the dream plainly enough indicates by the choice of the birds' heads.[1] I must have guessed the sexual significance of the word from the look of my worldly-wise teacher. My mother's expression in the dream was copied from the countenance of my grandfather, whom I had seen a few days before his death snoring in a state of coma. The interpretation of the secondary elaboration in the dream must therefore have been that my *mother* was dying; the *tomb*-relief, too, agrees with this. I awoke with this anxiety, and could not calm myself until I had waked my parents. I remember that I suddenly became calm when I saw my mother; it was as though I had needed the assurance: then she is not dead. But this secondary interpretation of the dream had only taken place when the influence of the developed anxiety was already at work. I was not in a state of anxiety because I had dreamt that my mother was dying; I interpreted the dream in this manner in the preconscious elaboration because I was already under the domination of the anxiety. The latter, however, could be traced back, through the repression to a dark, plainly sexual craving, which had found appropriate expression in the visual content of the dream.

A man twenty-seven years of age, who had been seriously ill for a year, had repeatedly dreamed, between the ages of eleven and thirteen, dreams attended with great anxiety, to the effect that *a man with a hatchet was running after him; he wanted to run away, but seemed to be paralysed,*

---

[1] [The German of the word *bird* is "*Vogel,*" which gives origin to the vulgar expression *vögeln,* denoting sexual intercourse.—Trans.]

and could not move from the spot. This may be taken as a good and typical example of a very common anxiety-dream, free from any suspicion of a sexual meaning. In the analysis, the dreamer first thought of a story told him by his uncle (chronologically later than the dream), viz. that he was attacked at night in the street by a suspicious-looking individual; and he concluded from this association that he might have heard of a similar episode at the time of the dream. In association with the hatchet, he recalled that during this period of his life he once hurt his hand with a *hatchet* while chopping wood. This immediately reminded him of his relations with his younger brother, whom he used to maltreat and knock down. He recalled, in particular, one occasion when he hit his brother's head with his boot and made it bleed, and his mother said: "I'm afraid he will kill him one day." While he seemed to be thus held by the theme of *violence,* a memory from his ninth year suddenly emerged. His parents had come home late and had gone to bed, whilst he was pretending to be asleep. He soon heard panting, and other sounds that seemed to him mysterious, and he could also guess the position of his parents in bed. His further thoughts showed that he had established an analogy between this relation between his parents and his own relation to his younger brother. He subsumed what was happening between his parents under the notion of *"an act of violence and a fight."* The fact that he had frequently noticed *blood in his mother's bed* corroborated this conception.

That the sexual intercourse of adults appears strange and alarming to children who observe it, and arouses anxiety in them, is, I may say, a fact established by everyday experience. I have explained this anxiety on the ground that we have here a sexual excitation which is not mastered by the child's understanding, and which probably also encounters repulsion because their parents are involved, and is therefore transformed into anxiety. At a still earlier period of life the sexual impulse towards the parent of opposite sex does not yet suffer repression, but as we have seen (pp. 249–51) expresses itself freely.

For the night terrors with hallucinations (*pavor nocturnus*) so frequent in children I should without hesitation offer the same explanation. These, too, can only be due to misunderstood and rejected sexual impulses which, if recorded, would probably show a temporal periodicity, since an intensification of sexual *libido* may equally be produced by accidentally exciting impressions and by spontaneous periodic processes of development.

I have not the necessary observational material for the full demonstration of this explanation.[1] On the other hand, pediatrists seem to lack the point of view which alone makes intelligible the whole series of phenom-

---

[1] This material has since been provided in abundance by the literature of psychoanalysis.

ena, both from the somatic and from the psychic side. To illustrate by a comical example how closely, if one is made blind by the blinkers of medical mythology, one may pass by the understanding of such cases, I will cite a case which I found in a thesis on *pavor nocturnus* (Debacker, 1881, p. 66).

A boy of thirteen, in delicate health, began to be anxious and dreamy; his sleep became uneasy, and once almost every week it was interrupted by an acute attack of anxiety with hallucinations. The memory of these dreams was always very distinct. Thus he was able to relate that the devil had shouted at him: "Now we have you, now we have you!" and then there was a smell of pitch and brimstone, and the fire burned his skin. From this dream he woke in terror; at first he could not cry out; then his voice came back to him, and he was distinctly heard to say: "No, no, not me; I haven't done anything," or: "Please, don't; I will never do it again!" At other times he said: "Albert has never done that!" Later he avoided undressing, "because the fire attacked him only when he was undressed." In the midst of these evil dreams, which were endangering his health, he was sent into the country, where he recovered in the course of eighteen months. At the age of fifteen he confessed one day: *"Je n'osais pas l'avouer, mais j'éprouvais continuellement des picotements et des surexcitations aux* parties; [1] *à la fin, cela m'énervait tant que plusieurs fois j'ai pensé me jeter par la fenêtre du dortoir."*

It is, of course, not difficult to guess: 1. That the boy had practised masturbation in former years, that he had probably denied it, and was threatened with severe punishment for his bad habit. (His confession: *Je ne le ferai plus;* his denial: *Albert n'a jamais fait ça.*) 2. That under the advancing pressure of puberty the temptation to masturbate was re-awakened through the titillation of the genitals. 3. That now, however, there arose within him a struggle for repression, which suppressed the libido and transformed it into anxiety, and that this anxiety now gathered up the punishments with which he was originally threatened.

Let us, on the other hand, see what conclusions were drawn by the author (p. 69):

"1. It is clear from this observation that the influence of puberty may produce in a boy of delicate health a condition of extreme weakness, and that this may lead to a *very marked cerebral anaemia.*[2]

"2. This cerebral anaemia produces an alteration of character, demonomaniacal hallucinations, and very violent nocturnal, and perhaps also diurnal, states of anxiety.

"3. The demonomania and the self-reproaches of the boy can be traced

---

[1] The emphasis is my own, though the meaning is plain enough without it.
[2] The italics are mine.

to the influences of a religious education which had acted upon him as a child.

"4. All manifestations disappeared as a result of a lengthy sojourn in the country, bodily exercise, and the return of physical strength after the termination of puberty.

"5. Possibly an influence predisposing to the development of the boy's cerebral state may be attributed to heredity and to the father's former syphilis."

Then finally come the concluding remarks: *"Nous avons fait entrer cette observation dans le cadre délires apyrétiques d'inanition, car c'est à l'ischémie cérébrale que nous rattachons cet état particulier."*

E. THE PRIMARY AND SECONDARY PROCESSES. REPRESSION

In attempting to penetrate more profoundly into the psychology of the dream-processes, I have undertaken a difficult task, to which, indeed, my powers of exposition are hardly adequate. To reproduce the simultaneity of so complicated a scheme in terms of a successive description, and at the same time to make each part appear free from all assumptions, goes fairly beyond my powers. I have now to atone for the fact that in my exposition of the psychology of dreams I have been unable to follow the historic development of my own insight. The lines of approach to the comprehension of the dream were laid down for me by previous investigations into the psychology of the neuroses, to which I should not refer here, although I am constantly obliged to do so; whereas I should like to work in the opposite direction, starting from the dream, and then proceeding to establish its junction with the psychology of the neuroses. I am conscious of all the difficulties which this involves for the reader, but I know of no way to avoid them.

Since I am dissatisfied with this state of affairs, I am glad to dwell upon another point of view, which would seem to enhance the value of my efforts. As was shown in the introductory section, I found myself confronted with a theme which had been marked by the sharpest contradictions on the part of those who had written on it. In the course of our treatment of the problems of the dream, room has been found for most of these contradictory views. We have been compelled to take decided exception to two only of the views expressed: namely, that the dream is a meaningless process, and that it is a somatic process. Apart from these, we have been able to find a place for the truth of all the contradictory opinions at one point or another of the complicated tissue of the facts, and we have been able to show that each expressed something genuine and correct. That our dreams continue the impulses and interests of waking life has been generally confirmed by the discovery of the hidden dream-thoughts. These concern themselves only with things that seem to us important and of great interest. Dreams never occupy themselves with trifles. But we have accepted also the opposite view, namely, that the dream gathers up the indifferent residues of the day, and cannot seize upon any important interest of the day until it has in some measure withdrawn itself from waking activity. We have found that this holds true of the dream-content, which by means of distortion gives the dream-thought an altered expression. We have said that the dream-process, owing to the nature of the mechanism of association, finds it easier to obtain possession of recent or indifferent material, which has not yet been put under an embargo by our waking mental activity; and that on account of the censorship it transfers the psychic intensity of the significant but also objectionable material to the indifferent. The hypermnesia of the dream and its ability to dispose of infantile material have become the main foundations of our doctrine; in our theory of dreams we have assigned to a wish of infantile origin the part of the indispensable motive-power of dream-formation. It has not, of course, occurred to us to doubt the experimentally demonstrated significance of external sensory stimuli during sleep; but we have placed this material in the same relation to the dream-wish as the thought-residues left over from our waking activity. We need not dispute the fact that the dream interprets objective sensory stimuli after the manner of an illusion; but we have supplied the motive for this interpretation, which has been left indeterminate by other writers. The interpretation proceeds in such a way that the perceived object is rendered harmless as a source of disturbance of sleep, whilst it is made usable for the wish-fulfilment. Though we do not admit as a special source of dreams the subjective state of excitation of the sensory organs during sleep (which seems to have been demonstrated by Trumbull Ladd), we are, nevertheless, able to explain this state of excitation by the regressive revival of the memories active behind the dream. As to the internal organic sensations, which are wont to be taken as the cardinal point of the explanation of dreams, these, too, find a place in our conception, though indeed a more modest one. These sensations—the sensations of falling, of soaring, or of being inhibited—represent an ever-ready material, which the dream-work can employ to express the dream-thought as often as need arises.

That the dream-process is a rapid and momentary one is, we believe, true as regards the perception by consciousness of the preformed dream-content; but we have found that the preceding portions of the dream-process probably follow a slow, fluctuating course. As for the riddle of the superabundant dream-content compressed into the briefest moment of time, we have been able to contribute the explanation that the dream seizes upon ready-made formations of the psychic life. We have found that it is true that dreams are distorted and mutilated by the memory, but that this fact presents no difficulties, as it is only the last manifest portion of a process of distortion which has been going on from the very beginning of the dream-work. In the embittered controversy, which has seemed irreconcilable, whether the psychic life is asleep at night, or can make the same use of all its faculties as during the day, we have been able to conclude that both sides are right, but that neither is entirely so. In the dream-thoughts we found evidence of a highly complicated intellectual activity, operating with almost all the resources of the psychic apparatus; yet it cannot be denied that these dream-thoughts have originated during the day, and it is indispensable to assume that there is a sleeping state of the psychic life. Thus, even the doctrine of partial sleep received its due, but we have found the characteristic feature of the sleeping state not in the distintegration of the psychic system of connections, but in the special attitude adopted by the psychic system which is dominant during the day—the attitude of the wish to sleep. The deflection from the outer world retains its significance for our view, too; though not the only factor at work, it helps to make possible the regressive course of the dream-representation. The abandonment of voluntary guidance of the flow of ideas is incontestable; but psychic life does not thereby become aimless, for we have seen that upon relinquishment of the voluntary directing ideas, involuntary ones take charge. On the other hand, we have not only recognized the loose associative connection of the dream, but have brought a far greater area within the scope of this kind of connection than could have been suspected; we have, however, found it merely an enforced substitute for another, a correct and significant type of association. To be sure, we too have called the dream absurd, but examples have shown us how wise the dream is when it simulates absurdity. As regards the functions that have been attributed to the dream, we are able to accept them all. That the dream relieves the mind, like a safety-valve, and that, as Robert has put it, all kinds of harmful material are rendered harmless by representation in the dream, not only coincides exactly with our own theory of the twofold wish-fulfilment in the dream, but in its very wording becomes more intelligible for us than it is for Robert himself. The free indulgence of the psyche in the play of its faculties is reproduced in our theory as the non-interference of the preconscious activity with the dream. The "return to the embryonal standpoint of psychic life in the dream," and Havelock Ellis's remark that the dream is *"an archaic world of vast emotions and imperfect thoughts,"* appear to us as happy anticipations of our own exposition, which asserts that *primitive* modes of operations that are suppressed during the day play a part in the formation of dreams. We can fully identify ourselves with Sully's statement, that "our dreams bring back again our earlier and successively developed personalities, our old ways of regarding things, with impulses and modes of reaction which ruled us long ago"; and for us, as for Delage, the *suppressed* material becomes the mainspring of the dream.

We have fully accepted the rôle that Scherner ascribes to the dream-phantasy, and his own interpretations, but we have been obliged to transpose them, as it were, to another part of the problem. It is not the dream that creates the phantasy, but the activity of unconscious phantasy that plays the leading part in the formation of the dream-thoughts. We remain indebted to Scherner for directing us to the source of the dream-thoughts, but almost everything that he ascribes to the dream-work is attributable to the activity of the unconscious during the day, which instigates dreams no less than neurotic symptoms. The dream-work we had to separate from this activity as something quite different and far more closely controlled. Finally, we have by no means renounced the relation of the dream to psychic disturbances, but have given it, on new ground, a more solid foundation.

Held together by the new features in our theory as by a superior unity, we find the most varied and most contradictory conclusions of other writers fitting into our structure; many of them are given a different turn, but only a few of them are wholly rejected. But our own structure is still unfinished. For apart from the many obscure questions in which we have involved ourselves by our advance into the dark regions of psychology, we are now, it would seem, embarrassed by a new contradiction. On the one hand, we have made it appear that the dream-thoughts proceed from perfectly normal psychic activities, but on the other hand we have found among the dream-thoughts a number of entirely abnormal mental processes, which extend also to the dream-content, and which we reproduce in the interpretation of the dream. All that we have termed the "dream-work" seems to depart so completely from the psychic processes which we recognize as correct and appropriate that the severest judgments expressed by the writers mentioned as to the low level of psychic achievement of dreams must appear well founded.

Here, perhaps, only further investigations can provide an explanation and set us on the right path. Let me pick out for renewed attention one of the constellations which lead to dream-formation.

We have learned that the dream serves as a substitute for a number of thoughts derived from our daily life, and which fit together with perfect logic. We cannot, therefore, doubt that these thoughts have their own origin in our normal mental life. All the qualities which we value in our thought-processes, and which mark them out as complicated performances of a high order, we shall find repeated in the dream-thoughts. There is, however, no need to assume that this mental work is performed during sleep; such an assumption would badly confuse the conception of the psychic state of sleep to which we have hitherto adhered. On the contrary, these thoughts may very well have their origin in the daytime, and, unremarked by our consciousness, may have gone on from their first stimulus until, at the onset of sleep, they have reached completion. If we are to conclude anything from this state of affairs, it can only be that it proves *that the most complex mental operations are possible without the coöperation of consciousness*—a truth which we have had to learn anyhow from every psychoanalysis of a patient suffering from hysteria or obsessions. These dream-thoughts are certainly not in themselves incapable of consciousness; if we have not become conscious of them during the day, this may have been due to various reasons. The act of becoming conscious depends upon a definite psychic function—attention—being brought to bear. This seems to be available only in a determinate quantity, which may have been diverted from the train of thought in question by other aims. Another way in which such trains of thought may be withheld from consciousness is the following: From our conscious reflection we know that, when applying our attention, we follow a particular course. But if that course leads us to an idea which cannot withstand criticism, we break off and allow the cathexis of attention to drop. Now, it would seem that the train of thought thus started and abandoned may continue to develop without our attention returning to it, unless at some point it attains a specially high intensity which compels attention. An initial conscious rejection by our judgment, on the ground of incorrectness or uselessness for the immediate purpose of the act of thought, may, therefore, be the cause of a thought-process going on unnoticed by consciousness until the onset of sleep.

Let us now recapitulate: We call such a train of thought a *preconscious* train, and we believe it to be perfectly correct, and that it may equally well be a merely neglected train or one that has been interrupted and suppressed. Let us also state in plain terms how we visualize the movement of our thought. We believe that a certain quantity of excitation, which we call "cathectic energy," is displaced from a purposive idea along the association paths selected by this directing idea. A "neglected" train of thought has received no such cathexis, and the cathexis has been withdrawn from one that was "suppressed" "or rejected"; both have thus been left to their own excitations. The train of thought cathected by some aim becomes able under certain conditions to attract the attention of consciousness, and by the mediation of consciousness it then receives *"hypercathexis."* We shall be obliged presently to elucidate our assumptions as to the nature and function of consciousness.

A train of thought thus incited in the *Pcs.* may either disappear spontaneously, or it may continue. The former eventuality we conceive as follows: it diffuses its energy through all the association paths emanating from it, and throws the entire chain of thoughts into a state of excitation, which continues for a while, and then subsides, through the excitation which had called for discharge being transformed into dormant cathexis. If this first eventuality occurs, the process has no further significance for dream-formation. But other directing ideas are lurking in our preconscious, which have their source in our unconscious and ever-active wishes. These may gain control of the excitation in the circle of thoughts thus left to itself, establish a connection between it and the unconscious wish, and *transfer* to it the energy inherent in the unconscious wish. Henceforth the neglected or suppressed train of thought is in a position to maintain itself, although this reinforcement gives it no claim to access to consciousness. We may say, then, that the hitherto preconscious train of thought *has been drawn into the unconscious.*

Other constellations leading to dream-formation might be as follows: The preconscious train of thought might have been connected from the beginning with the unconscious wish, and for that reason might have met with rejection by the dominating aim-cathexis. Or an unconscious wish might become active for other (possibly somatic) reasons, and of its own accord seek a transference to the psychic residues not cathected by the *Pcs.* All three cases have the same result: there is established in the preconscious a train of thought which, having been abandoned by the preconscious cathexis, has acquired cathexis from the unconscious wish.

From this point onward the train of thought is subjected to a series of transformations which we no longer recognize as normal psychic processes, and which give a result that we find strange, a psychopathological formation. Let us now emphasize and bring together these transformations:—

1. The intensities of the individual ideas become capable of discharge in their entirety, and pass from one idea to another, so that individual ideas are formed which are endowed with great intensity. Through the repeated occurrence of this process, the intensity of an entire train of thought may ultimately be concentrated in a single conceptual unit. This is the fact of *compression* or *condensation* with which we became acquainted when investigating the dream-work. It is condensation that is mainly responsible for the strange impression produced by dreams, for we know of nothing analogous to it in the normal psychic life that is accessible to consciousness. We get here, too, ideas which are of great psychic significance as nodal points or as end-results of whole chains of thought, but this value is not expressed by any character *actually manifest* for our internal perception; what is represented in it is not in any way made more intensive. In the process of condensation the whole set of psychic connections becomes transformed into the *intensity* of the idea-content. The situation is the same as when in the case of a book I

italicize or print in heavy type any word to which I attach outstanding value for the understanding of the text. In speech I should pronounce the same word loudly and deliberately and with emphasis. The first simile points immediately to one of the examples which were given of the dream-work (trimethylamine in the dream of Irma's injection). Historians of art call our attention to the fact that the most ancient sculptures known to history follow a similar principle, in expressing the rank of the persons represented by the size of the statues. The king is made two or three times as tall as his retinue or his vanquished enemies. But a work of art of the Roman period makes use of more subtle means to accomplish the same end. The figure of the Emperor is placed in the centre, erect and in his full height, and special care is bestowed on the modelling of this figure; his enemies are seen cowering at his feet; but he is no longer made to seem a giant among dwarfs. At the same time, in the bowing of the subordinate to his superior, even in our own day, we have an echo of this ancient principle of representation.

The direction followed by the condensations of the dream is prescribed on the one hand by the true preconscious relations of the dream-thoughts, and on the other hand by the attraction of the visual memories in the unconscious. The success of the condensation-work produces those intensities which are required for penetration to the perception-system.

2. By the free transference of intensities, and in the service of the condensation, *intermediary ideas*—compromises, as it were—are formed (cf. the numerous examples). This, also, is something unheard of in the normal movement of our ideas, where what is of most importance is the selection and the retention of the right conceptual material. On the other hand, composite and compromise formations occur with extraordinary frequency when we are trying to find verbal expression for preconscious thoughts; these are considered "slips of the tongue."

3. The ideas which transfer their intensities to one another are *very loosely connected*, and are joined together by such forms of association as are disdained by our serious thinking, and left to be exploited solely by wit. In particular, assonances and punning asociations are treated as equal in value to any other associations.

4. Contradictory thoughts do not try to eliminate one another, but continue side by side, and often combine to form condensation-products, *as though no contradiction existed;* or they form compromises for which we should never forgive our thought, but which we frequently sanction in our action.

These are some of the most conspicuous abnormal processes to which the dream-thoughts which have previously been rationally formed are subjected in the course of the dream-work. As the main feature of these processes, we may see that the greatest importance is attached to rendering the cathecting energy mobile and *capable of discharge;* the content and the intrinsic significance of the psychic elements to which these cathexes adhere become matters of secondary importance. One might perhaps assume that condensation and compromise-formation are effected only in the service of regression, when the occasion arises for changing thoughts into images. But the analysis—and still more plainly the synthesis—of such dreams as show no regression towards images, *e.g.* the dream "Autodidasker: Conversation with Professor N.," reveals the same processes of displacement and condensation as do the rest.

We cannot, therefore, avoid the conclusion that two kinds of essentially different psychic processes participate in dream-formation; one forms perfectly correct and fitting dream-thoughts, equivalent to the results of normal thinking, while the other deals with these thoughts in a most astonishing and, as it seems, incorrect way. The latter process we have already set apart in Chapter VI as the dream-work proper. What can we say now as to the derivation of this psychic process?

It would be impossible to answer this question here if we had not penetrated a considerable way into the psychology of the neuroses, and especially of hysteria. From this, however, we learn that the same "incorrect" psychic processes—as well as others not enumerated—control the production of hysterical symptoms. In hysteria, too, we find at first a series of perfectly correct and fitting thoughts, equivalent to our conscious ones, of whose existence in this form we can, however, learn nothing, *i.e.* which we can only subsequently reconstruct. If they have forced their way anywhere to perception, we discover from the analysis of the symptom formed that these normal thoughts have been subjected to abnormal treatment, and *that by means of condensation and compromise-formation, through superficial associations which cover up contradictions, and eventually along the path of regression, they have been conveyed into the symptom.* In view of the complete identity between the peculiarities of the dream-work and those of the psychic activity which issues in psychoneurotic symptoms, we shall feel justified in transferring to the dream the conclusions urged upon us by hysteria.

From the theory of hysteria we borrow the proposition that *such an abnormal psychic elaboration of a normal train of thought takes place only when the latter has been used for the transference of an unconscious wish which dates from the infantile life and is in a state of repression.* Complying with this proposition, we have built up the theory of the dream on the assumption that the actuating dream-wish invariably originates in the unconscious; which, as we have ourselves admitted, cannot be universally demonstrated, even though it cannot be refuted. But in order to enable us to say just what *repression* is, after employing this term so freely, we shall be obliged to make a further addition to our psy-chological scaffolding.

We had elaborated the fiction of a primitive psychic apparatus, the work of which is regulated by the effort to avoid accumulation of excita-tion, and as far as possible to maintain itself free from excitation. For this reason it was constructed after the plan of a reflex apparatus; motility, in the first place as the path to changes within the body, was the channel of discharge at its disposal. We then discussed the psychic results of experi-ences of gratification, and were able at this point to introduce a second assumption, namely, that the accumulation of excitation—by processes that do not concern us here—is felt as pain, and sets the apparatus in operation in order to bring about again a state of gratification, in which the diminution of excitation is perceived as pleasure. Such a current in the apparatus, issuing from pain and striving for pleasure, we call a wish. We have said that nothing but a wish is capable of setting the apparatus in motion and that the course of any excitation in the apparatus is regu-lated automatically by the perception of pleasure and pain. The first oc-currence of wishing may well have taken the form of a hallucinatory cathexis of the memory of gratification. But this hallucination, unless it could be maintained to the point of exhaustion, proved incapable of bring-ing about a cessation of the need, and consequently of securing the pleas-ure connected with gratification.

Thus, there was required a second activity—in our terminology the activity of a second system—which would not allow the memory-cathexis to force its way to perception and thence to bind the psychic forces, but would lead the excitation emanating from the need-stimulus by a detour, which by means of voluntary motility would ultimately so change the outer world as to permit the real perception of the gratifying object. Thus far we have already elaborated the scheme of the psychic apparatus; these two systems are the germ of what we set up in the fully developed apparatus as the *Ucs.* and the *Pcs.*

To change the outer world appropriately by means of motility requires the accumulation of a large total of experiences in the memory-systems, as well as a manifold consolidation of the relations which are evoked in this memory-material by various directing ideas. We will now proceed further with our assumptions. The activity of the second system, groping in many directions, tentatively sending forth cathexes and retracting them, needs on the one hand full command over all memory-material, but on the other hand it would be a superfluous expenditure of energy were it to send along the individual thought-paths large quantities of cathexis, which would then flow away to no purpose and thus diminish the quantity needed for changing the outer world. Out of a regard for purposiveness, therefore, I postulate that the second system succeeds in maintaining the greater part of the energic cathexes in a state of rest, and in using only a small portion for its operations of displacement. The mechanics of these processes is entirely unknown to me; anyone who seriously wishes to follow up these ideas must address himself to the physical analogies, and find some way of getting a picture of the sequence of motions which ensues on the excitation of the neurones. Here I do no more than hold fast to the idea that the activity of the first ψ-system aims at *the free outflow of the quantities of excitation,* and that the second system, by means of the cathexes emanating from it, effects an *inhibition* of this outflow, a transformation into dormant cathexis, probably with a rise of potential. I therefore assume that the course taken by any excitation under the control of the second system is bound to quite different mechanical conditions from those which obtain under the control of the first system. After the second system has completed its work of experimental thought, it removes the inhibition and damming up of the excitations and allows them to flow off into motility.

An interesting train of thought now presents itself if we consider the relations of this inhibition of discharge by the second system to the process of regulation by the pain-principle. Let us now seek out the counterpart of the primary experience of gratification, namely, the *objective experience of fear.* Let a perception-stimulus act on the primitive apparatus and be the source of a pain-excitation. There will then ensue uncoordinated motor manifestations, which will go on until one of these withdraws the apparatus from perception, and at the same time from the pain. On the reappearance of the percept this manifestation will immediately be repeated (perhaps as a movement of flight), until the percept has again disappeared. But in this case no tendency will remain to recathect the perception of the source of pain by hallucination or otherwise. On the contrary, there will be a tendency in the primary apparatus to turn away again from this painful memory-image immediately if it is in any way awakened, since the overflow of its excitation into perception would, of course, evoke (or more precisely, begin to evoke) pain. This turning away from a recollection, which is merely a repetition of the former flight from perception, is also facilitated by the fact that, unlike the perception, the recollection has not enough quality to arouse consciousness, and thereby to attract fresh cathexis. This effortless and regular turning away of the psychic process from the memory of anything that had once been painful gives us the prototype and the first example of *psychic repression.* We all know how much of this turning away from the painful, the tactics of the ostrich, may still be shown as present even in the normal psychic life of adults.

In obedience to the pain-principle, therefore, the first ψ-system is quite incapable of introducing anything unpleasant into the thought-nexus. The system cannot do anything but wish. If this were to remain so, the activity of thought of the second system, which needs to have at its disposal all the memories stored up by experience, would be obstructed. But two paths are now open: either the work of the second system frees itself completely from the pain-principle, and continues its course, paying no heed to the pain attached to given memories, or it contrives to cathect the memory of the pain in such a manner as to preclude the liberation of pain. We can reject the first possibility, as the pain-principle also proves to act as a regulator of the cycle of excitation in the second system; we are therefore thrown back upon the second possibility, namely, that this system cathects a memory in such a manner as to inhibit any outflow of excitation from it, and hence, also, the outflow, comparable to a motor-innervation, needed for the development of pain. And thus, setting out from two different starting-points, i.e. from regard for the pain-principle, and from the principle of the least expenditure of innervation, we are led to the hypothesis that cathexis through the second system is at the same time an inhibition of the discharge of excitation. Let us, however, keep a close hold on the fact—for this is the key to the theory of repression—*that the second system can only cathect an idea when it is in a position to inhibit any pain emanating from this idea.* Anything that withdrew itself from this inhibition would also remain inaccessible for the second system, i.e. would immediately be given up by virtue of the pain-principle. The inhibition of pain, however, need not be complete; it must be permitted to begin, since this indicates to the second system the nature of the memory, and possibly its lack of fitness for the purpose sought by the process of thought.

The psychic process which is alone tolerated by the first system I shall now call the *primary process;* and that which results under the inhibiting action of the second system I shall call the *secondary process.* I can also show at another point for what purpose the second system is obliged to correct the primary process. The primary process strives for discharge of the excitation in order to establish with the quantity of excitation thus collected *an identity of perception;* the secondary process has abandoned this intention, and has adopted instead the aim of an *identity of thought.* All thinking is merely a detour from the memory of gratification (taken as a purposive idea) to the identical cathexis of the same memory, which is to be reached once more by the path of motor experiences. Thought must concern itself with the connecting-paths between ideas without allowing itself to be misled by their intensities. But it is obvious that condensations of ideas and intermediate or compromise-formations are obstacles to the attainment of the identity which is aimed at; by substituting one idea for another they swerve away from the path which would have led onward from the first idea. Such procedures are, therefore, carefully avoided in our secondary thinking. It will readily be seen, moreover, that the pain-principle, although at other times it provides the thought-process with its most important clues, may also put difficulties in its way in the pursuit of indentity of thought. Hence, the tendency of the thinking process must always be to free itself more and more from exclusive regulation by the pain-principle, and to restrict the development of affect through the work of thought to the very minimum which remains effective as a signal. This refinement in functioning is to be achieved by a fresh hyper-cathexis, effected with the help of consciousness. But we are aware that this refinement is seldom completely successful, even in normal psychic life, and that our thinking always remains liable to falsification by the intervention of the pain-principle.

This, however, is not the breach in the functional efficiency of our psychic apparatus which makes it possible for thoughts representing the result of the secondary thought-work to fall into the power of the primary psychic process; by which formula we may now describe the operations resulting in dreams and the symptoms of hysteria. This inadequacy results from the converging of two factors in our development, one of which pertains solely to the psychic apparatus, and has exercised a determining influence on the relation of the two systems, while the other operates fluctuatingly, and introduces motive forces of organic origin into the psychic life. Both originate in the infantile life, and are a precipitate of the alteration which our psychic and somatic organism has undergone since our infantile years.

When I termed one of the psychic processes in the psychic apparatus the *primary* process, I did so not only in consideration of its status and function, but was also able to take account of the temporal relationship actually involved. So far as we know, a psychic apparatus possessing only the primary process does not exist, and is to that extent a theoretical fiction; but this at least is a fact: that the primary processes are present in the apparatus from the beginning, while the secondary processes only take shape gradually during the course of life, inhibiting and overlaying the primary, whilst gaining complete control over them perhaps only in the prime of life. Owing to this belated arrival of the secondary processes, the essence of our being, consisting of unconscious wish-impulses, remains something which cannot be grasped or inhibited by the preconscious; and its part is once and for all restricted to indicating the most appropriate paths for the wish-impulses originating in the unconscious. These unconscious wishes represent for all subsequent psychic strivings a compulsion to which they must submit themselves, although they may perhaps endeavour to divert them and to guide them to superior aims. In consequence of this retardation, an extensive region of the memory-material remains in fact inaccessible to preconscious cathexis.

Now among these wish-impulses originating in the infantile life, indestructible and incapable of inhibition, there are some the fulfilments of which have come to be in contradiction with the purposive ideas of our secondary thinking. The fulfilment of these wishes would no longer produce an affect of pleasure, but one of pain; *and it is just this conversion of affect that constitutes the essence of what we call "repression."* In what manner and by what motive forces such a conversion can take place constitutes the problem of repression, which we need here only touch upon in passing. It will suffice to note the fact that such a conversion of affect occurs in the course of development (one need only think of the emergence of disgust, originally absent in infantile life), and that it is connected with the activity of the secondary system. The memories from which the unconscious wish evokes a liberation of affect have never been accessible to the *Pcs.*, and for that reason this liberation cannot be inhibited. It is precisely on account of this generation of affect that these ideas are not now accessible even by way of the preconscious thoughts to which they have transferred the energy of the wishes connected with them. On the contrary, the pain-principle comes into play, and causes the *Pcs.* to turn away from these transference-thoughts. These latter are left to themselves, are "repressed," and thus, the existence of a store of infantile memories, withdrawn from the beginning from the *Pcs.*, becomes the preliminary condition of repression.

In the most favourable case, the generation of pain terminates so soon as the cathexis is withdrawn from the transference-thoughts in the *Pcs.*, and this result shows that the intervention of the pain-principle is appropriate. It is otherwise, however, if the repressed unconscious wish receives an organic reinforcement which it can put at the service of its transference-thoughts, and by which it can enable them to attempt to break through with their excitation, even if the cathexis of the *Pcs.* has been taken away from them. A defensive struggle then ensues, inasmuch as the *Pcs.* reinforces the opposite to the repressed thoughts (counter-cathexis), and the eventual outcome is that the transference-thoughts (the carriers of the unconscious wish) break through in some form of compromise through symptom-formation. But from the moment that the repressed thoughts are powerfully cathected by the unconscious wish-impulse, but forsaken by the preconscious cathexis, they succumb to the primary psychic process, and aim only at motor discharge; or, if the way is clear, at hallucinatory revival of the desired identity of perception. We have already found, empirically, that the "incorrect" processes described are enacted only with thoughts which are in a state of repression. We are now in a position to grasp yet another part of the total scheme of the facts. These "incorrect" processes are the *primary* processes of the psychic apparatus; they occur wherever ideas abandoned by the preconscious cathexis are left to themselves and can become filled with the uninhibited energy which flows from the unconscious and strives for discharge. There are further facts which go to show that the processes described as "incorrect" are not really falsifications of our normal procedure, or defective thinking, but the modes of operation of the psychic apparatus when freed from inhibition. Thus we see that the process of conveyance of the preconscious excitation to motility occurs in accordance with the same procedure, and that in the linkage of preconscious ideas with words we may easily find manifested the same displacements and confusions (which we ascribe to inattention). Finally, a proof of the increased work made necessary by the inhibition of these primary modes of procedure might be found in the fact that we achieve a *comical effect,* a surplus to be discharged through *laughter, if we allow these modes of thought to come to consciousness.*

The theory of the psychoneuroses asserts with absolute certainty that it can only be sexual wish-impulses from the infantile life, which have undergone repression (affect-conversion) during the developmental period of childhood, which are capable of renewal at later periods of development (whether as a result of our sexual constitution, which has, of course, grown out of an original bi-sexuality, or in consequence of unfavourable influences in our sexual life); and which therefore supply the motive-power for all psychoneurotic symptom-formation. It is only by the introduction of these sexual forces that the gaps still demonstrable in the theory of repression can be filled. Here, I will leave it undecided whether the postulate of the sexual and infantile holds good for the theory of dreams as well; I am not completing the latter, because in assuming that the dream-wish invariably originates in the unconscious I have already gone a step beyond the demonstrable.[1] Nor will I inquire further

---

[1] Here, as elsewhere, there are gaps in the treatment of the subject, which I have deliberately left, because to fill them up would, on the one hand, require excessive labour, and, on the other hand, I should have to depend on material which is foreign to the dream. Thus, for example, I have avoided stating whether I give the word "suppressed" a different meaning from that of the word "repressed." No doubt, however, it will have become clear that the latter emphasizes more than the former the relation to the unconscious. I have not gone into the problem which obviously arises, of why the dream-thoughts undergo distortion by the censorship even when they abandon the progressive path to consciousness, and choose the path of regression. And so with other similar omissions. I have, above all, sought to give some idea of the problems to which the further dissection of the dream-work leads, and to indicate the other themes with which these are connected. It was, however, not always easy to decide just where the pursuit should be discontinued.—That I have not treated exhaustively the part which the psycho-sexual life plays in the dream, and have avoided the interpretation of dreams of an obviously sexual content, is due to a special reason—which may not perhaps be that which the reader would expect. It is absolutely alien to my views and my neuropathological doctrines to regard the sexual life as a *pudendum* with which neither the physician nor the scientific investigator should concern himself. To me, the moral indignation which prompted the trans-

into the nature of the difference between the play of psychic forces in dream-formation and in the formation of hysterical symptoms, since there is missing here the needed fuller knowledge of one of the two things to be compared. But there is another point which I regard as important, and I will confess at once that it was only on account of this point that I entered upon all the discussions concerning the two psychic systems, their modes of operation, and the fact of repression. It does not greatly matter whether I have conceived the psychological relations at issue with approximate correctness, or, as is easily possible in such a difficult matter, wrongly and imperfectly. However our views may change about the interpretation of the psychic censorship or the correct and the abnormal elaboration of the dream-content, it remains certain that such processes are active in dream-formation, and that in their essentials they reveal the closest analogy with the processes observed in the formation of hysterical symptoms. Now the dream is not a pathological phenomenon; it does not presuppose any disturbance of our psychic equilibrium; and it does not leave behind it any weakening of our efficiency or capacities. The objection that no conclusions can be drawn about the dreams of healthy persons from my own dreams and from those of my neurotic patients may be rejected without comment. If, then, from the nature of the given phenomena we infer the nature of their motive forces, we find that the psychic mechanism utilized by the neuroses is not newly-created by a morbid disturbance that lays hold of the psychic life, but lies in readiness in the normal structure of our psychic apparatus. The two psychic systems, the frontier-censorship between them, the inhibition and overlaying of the one activity by the other, the relations of both to consciousness—or whatever may take the place of these concepts on a juster interpretation of the actual relations—all these belong to the normal structure of our psychic instrument, and the dream shows us one of the paths which lead to a knowledge of this structure. If we wish to be content with a minimum of perfectly assured additions to our knowledge, we shall say that the dream affords proof that *the suppressed material continues to exist even in the normal person and remains capable of psychic activity*. Dreams are one of the manifestations of this suppressed material; theoretically, this is true in all cases; and in tangible experience, it has been found true in at least a great number of cases, which happen to display most plainly the more striking features of the dream-life. The suppressed psychic material,

lator of Artemidorus of Daldis to keep from the reader's knowledge the chapter on sexual dreams contained in the *Symbolism of Dreams* is merely ludicrous. For my own part, what decided my procedure was solely the knowledge that in the explanation of sexual dreams I should be bound to get deeply involved in the still unexplained problems of perversion and bisexuality; it was for this reason that I reserved this material for treatment elsewhere.

which in the waking state has been prevented from expression and cut off from internal perception *by the mutual neutralization of contradictory attitudes,* finds ways and means, under the sway of compromise-formations, of obtruding itself on consciousness during the night.

Flectere si nequeo Superos, Acheronta movebo.

At any rate, *the interpretation of dreams is the via regia to a knowledge of the unconscious element in our psychic life.*

By the analysis of dreams we obtain some insight into the composition of this most marvellous and most mysterious of instruments; it is true that this only takes us a little way, but it gives us a start which enables us, setting out from the angle of other (properly pathological) formations, to penetrate further in our disjoining of the instrument. For disease —at all events that which is rightly called functional—does not necessarily presuppose the destruction of this apparatus, or the establishment of new cleavages in its interior; it can be explained *dynamically* by the strengthening and weakening of the components of the play of forces, so many of the activities of which are covered up in normal functioning. It might be shown elsewhere how the fact that the apparatus is a combination of two instances also permits of a refinement of its normal functioning which would have been impossible to a single system.[1]

F. THE UNCONSCIOUS AND CONSCIOUSNESS. REALITY

If we look more closely, we may observe that the psychological considerations examined in the foregoing chapter require us to assume, not the existence of two systems near the motor end of the psychic apparatus, but *two kinds of processes or courses taken by excitation.* But this does not disturb us; for we must always be ready to drop our auxiliary ideas, when we think we are in a position to replace them by something which comes closer to the unknown reality. Let us now try to correct certain views which may have taken a misconceived form as long as we regarded the two systems, in the crudest and most obvious sense, as two localities within the psychic apparatus—views which have left a precipitate in the terms "repression" and "penetration." Thus, when we say that an unconscious thought strives for translation into the preconscious in order subsequently to penetrate through to consciousness, we do not mean that a second idea has to be formed, in a new locality, like a paraphrase, as it were, whilst

---

[1] The dream is not the only phenomenon that permits us to base our psycho-pathology on psychology. In a short unfinished series of articles in the *Monatsschrift für Psychiatrie und Neurologie* (*Über den psychischen Mechanismus der Vergesslichkeit,* 1898, and *Über Deckerinnerungen,* 1899) I attempted to interpret a number of psychic manifestations from everyday life in support of the same conception. (These and other articles on "Forgetting," "Lapses of Speech," etc., have now been published in the *Psychopathology of Everyday Life.*)

the original persists by its side; and similarly, when we speak of penetration into consciousness, we wish carefully to detach from this notion any idea of a change of locality. When we say that a preconscious idea is repressed and subsequently absorbed by the unconscious, we might be tempted by these images, borrowed from the idea of a struggle for a particular territory, to assume that an arrangement is really broken up in the one psychic locality and replaced by a new one in the other locality. For these comparisons we will substitute a description which would seem to correspond more closely to the real state of affairs; we will say that an energic cathexis is shifted to or withdrawn from a certain arrangement, so that the psychic formation falls under the domination of a given instance or is withdrawn from it. Here again we replace a topographical mode of representation by a dynamic one; it is not the psychic formation that appears to us as the mobile element, but its innervation.[1]

Nevertheless, I think it expedient and justifiable to continue to use the illustrative idea of the two systems. We shall avoid any abuse of this mode of representation if we remember that ideas, thoughts, and psychic formations in general must not in any case be localized in organic elements of the nervous system but, so to speak, *between them,* where resistances and association-tracks form the correlate corresponding to them. Everything that can become an object of internal perception is *virtual,* like the image in the telescope produced by the crossing of light-rays. But we are justified in thinking of the systems—which have nothing psychic in themselves, and which never become accessible to our psychic perception—as something similar to the lenses of the telescope, which project the image. If we continue this comparison, we might say that the censorship between the two systems corresponds to the refraction of rays on passing into a new medium.

Thus far, we have developed our psychology on our own responsibility; it is now time to turn and look at the doctrines prevailing in modern psychology, and to examine the relation of these to our theories. The problem of the unconscious in psychology is, according to the forcible statement of Lipps,[2] less *a* psychological problem than *the* problem of psychology. As long as psychology disposed of this problem by the verbal explanation that the "psychic" is the "conscious," and that "unconscious psychic occurrences" are an obvious contradiction, there was no possibility of a physician's observations of abnormal mental states being turned to any psychological account. The physician and the philosopher can meet

---

[1] This conception underwent elaboration and modification when it was recognized that the essential character of a preconscious idea was its connection with the residues of verbal ideas (The Unconscious, *Collected Papers,* vol. iv, p. 98).

[2] *Der Begriff des Unbewussten in der Psychologie.* Lecture delivered at the Third International Psychological Congress at Munich, 1897.

only when both acknowledge that "unconscious psychic processes" is "the appropriate and justified expression for an established fact." The physician cannot but reject, with a shrug of his shoulders, the assertion that "consciousness is the indispensable quality of the psychic"; if his respect for the utterances of the philosophers is still great enough, he may perhaps assume that he and they do not deal with the same thing and do not pursue the same science. For a single intelligent observation of the psychic life of a neurotic, a single analysis of a dream, must force upon him the unshakable conviction that the most complicated and the most accurate operations of thought, to which the name of psychic occurrences can surely not be refused, may take place without arousing consciousness.[1] The physician, it is true, does not learn of these unconscious processes until they have produced an effect on consciousness which admits of communication or observation. But this effect on consciousness may show a psychic character which differs completely from the unconscious process, so that internal perception cannot possibly recognize in the first a substitute for the second. The physician must reserve himself the right to penetrate, by a *process of deduction,* from the effect on consciousness to the unconscious psychic process; he learns in this way that the effect on consciousness is only a remote psychic product of the unconscious process, and that the latter has not become conscious as such, and has, moreover, existed and operated without in any way betraying itself to consciousness.

A return from the over-estimation of the property of consciousness is the indispensable preliminary to any genuine insight into the course of psychic events. As Lipps has said, the unconscious must be accepted as the general basis of the psychic life. The unconscious is the larger circle which includes the smaller circle of the conscious; everything conscious has a preliminary unconscious stage, whereas the unconscious can stop at this stage, and yet claim to be considered a full psychic function. The unconscious is the true psychic reality; *in its inner nature it is just as much unknown to us as the reality of the external world, and it is just as imperfectly communicated to us by the data of consciousness as is the external world by the reports of our sense-organs.*

We get rid of a series of dream-problems which have claimed much at-

---

[1] I am happy to be able to point to an author who has drawn from the study of dreams the same conclusion as regards the relation between consciousness and the unconscious.

Du Prel says: "The problem: what is the psyche, manifestly requires a preliminary examination as to whether ·consciousness and psyche are identical. But it is just this preliminary question which is answered in the negative by the dream, which shows that the concept of the psyche extends beyond that of consciousness, much as the gravitational force of a star extends beyond its sphere of luminosity" (*Philos. d. Mystik,* p. 47).

"It is a truth which cannot be sufficiently emphasized that the concepts of consciousness and of the psyche are not co-extensive" (p. 306).

tention from earlier writers on the subject when the old antithesis between conscious life and dream-life is discarded, and the unconscious psychic assigned to its proper place. Thus, many of the achievements which are a matter for wonder in a dream are now no longer to be attributed to dreaming, but to unconscious thinking, which is active also during the day. If the dream seems to make play with a symbolical representation of the body, as Scherner has said, we know that this is the work of certain unconscious phantasies, which are probably under the sway of sexual impulses and find expression not only in dreams, but also in hysterical phobias and other symptoms. If the dream continues and completes mental work begun during the day, and even brings valuable new ideas to light, we have only to strip off the dream-disguise from this, as the contribution of the dream-work, and a mark of the assistance of dark powers in the depths of the psyche (cf. the devil in Tartini's sonata-dream). The intellectual achievement as such belongs to the same psychic forces as are responsible for all such achievements during the day. We are probably much too inclined to overestimate the conscious character even of intellectual and artistic production. From the reports of certain writers who have been highly productive, such as Goethe and Helmholtz, we learn, rather, that the most essential and original part of their creations came to them in the form of inspirations, and offered itself to their awareness in an almost completed state. In other cases, where there is a concerted effort of all the psychic forces, there is nothing strange in the fact that conscious activity, too, lends its aid. But it is the much-abused privilege of conscious activity to hide from us all other activities wherever it participates.

It hardly seems worth while to take up the historical significance of dreams as a separate theme. Where, for instance, a leader has been impelled by a dream to engage in a bold undertaking, the success of which has had the effect of changing history, a new problem arises only so long as the dream is regarded as a mysterious power and contrasted with other more familiar psychic forces. The problem disappears as soon as we regard the dream as *a form of expression* for impulses to which a resistance was attached during the day, whilst at night they were able to draw reinforcement from deep-lying sources of excitation.[1] But the great respect with which the ancient peoples regarded dreams is based on a just piece of psychological divination. It is a homage paid to the unsubdued and indestructible element in the human soul, to the *daemonic* power which furnishes the dream-wish, and which we have found again *in our unconscious*.

It is not without purpose that I use the expression *in our unconscious*,

[1] Cf. here (p. 190) the dream (Σά-τύρος) of Alexander the Great at the siege of Tyre.

for what we so call does not coincide with the unconscious of the philosophers, nor with the unconscious of Lipps. As they use the term, it merely
means the opposite of the conscious. That there exist not only conscious
but also unconscious psychic processes is the opinion at issue, which is so
hotly contested and so energetically defended. Lipps enunciates the more
comprehensive doctrine that everything psychic exists as unconscious, but
that some of it may exist also as conscious. But it is not to prove *this* doctrine that we have adduced the phenomena of dreams and hysterical
symptom-formation; the observation of normal life alone suffices to establish its correctness beyond a doubt. The novel fact that we have learned
from the analysis of psycho-pathological formations, and indeed from the
first member of the group, from dreams, is that the unconscious—and
hence all that is psychic—occurs as a function of two separate systems,
and that as such it occurs even in normal psychic life. There are consequently *two kinds of unconscious,* which have not as yet been distinguished by psychologists. Both are unconscious in the psychological
sense; but in our sense the first, which we call *Ucs.,* is likewise *incapable
of consciousness;* whereas the second we call *Pcs.* because its excitations,
after the observance of certain rules, are capable of reaching consciousness; perhaps not before they have again undergone censorship, but
nevertheless regardless of the *Ucs. system.* The fact that in order to attain consciousness the excitations must pass through an unalterable series,
a succession of instances, as is betrayed by the changes produced in them
by the censorship, has enabled us to describe them by analogy in spatial
terms. We described the relations of the two systems to each other and to
consciousness by saying that the system *Pcs.* is like a screen between the
system *Ucs.* and consciousness. The system *Pcs.* not only bars access to
consciousness, but also controls the access to voluntary motility, and has
control of the emission of a mobile cathectic energy, a portion of which is
familiar to us as attention.[1]

We must also steer clear of the distinction between the *super-conscious*
and the *subconscious,* which has found such favour in the more recent
literature on the psychoneuroses, for just such a distinction seems to emphasize the equivalence of what is psychic and what is conscious.

What rôle is now left, in our representation of things, to the phenomenon of consciousness, once so all-powerful and over-shadowing all else?
None other than *than of a sense-organ for the perception of psychic qualities.* According to the fundamental idea of our schematic attempt we can
regard conscious perception only as the function proper to a special system for which the abbreviated designation *Cs.* commends itself. This

---

[1] Cf. here my remarks in the *Proceedings of the Society for Psychical Research,* vol.
xxvi, in which the descriptive, dynamic and systematic meanings of the ambiguous
word "Unconscious" are distinguished from one another.

system we conceive to be similar in its mechanical characteristics to the perception-system P, and hence excitable by qualities, and incapable of retaining the trace of changes: i.e. devoid of memory. The psychic apparatus which, with the sense-organ of the P-systems, is turned to the outer world, is itself the outer world for the sense-organ of $Cs.$, whose teleological justification depends on this relationship. We are here once more confronted with the principle of the succession of instances which seems to dominate the structure of the apparatus. The material of excitation flows to the sense-organ $Cs.$ from two sides: first from the P-system, whose excitation, qualitatively conditioned, probably undergoes a new elaboration until it attains conscious perception; and, secondly, from the interior of the apparatus itself, whose quantitative processes are perceived as a qualitative series of pleasures and pains once they have reached consciousness after undergoing certain changes.

The philosophers, who became aware that accurate and highly complicated thought-structures are possible even without the co-operation of consciousness, thus found it difficult to ascribe any function to consciousness; it appeared to them a superfluous mirroring of the completed psychic process. The analogy of our $Cs.$ system with the perception-systems relieves us of this embarrassment. We see that perception through our sense-organs results in directing an attention-cathexis to the paths along which the incoming sensory excitation diffuses itself; the qualitative excitation of the P-system serves the mobile quantity in the psychic apparatus as a regulator of its discharge. We may claim the same function for the overlying sense-organ of the $Cs.$ system. By perceiving new qualities, it furnishes a new contribution for the guidance and suitable distribution of the mobile cathexis-quantities. By means of perceptions of pleasure and pain, it influences the course of the cathexes within the psychic apparatus, which otherwise operates unconsciously and by the displacement of quantities. It is probable that the pain-principle first of all regulates the displacements of cathexis automatically, but it is quite possible that consciousness contributes a second and more subtle regulation of these qualities, which may even oppose the first, and perfect the functional capacity of the apparatus, by placing it in a position contrary to its original design, subjecting even that which induces pain to cathexis and to elaboration. We learn from neuro-psychology that an important part in the functional activity of the apparatus is ascribed to these regulations by the qualitative excitations of the sense-organs. The automatic rule of the primary pain-principle, together with the limitation of functional capacity bound up with it, is broken by the sensory regulations, which are themselves again automatisms. We find that repression, which, though originally expedient, nevertheless finally brings about a harmful lack of inhibition and of psychic control, overtakes memories much more easily than it does perceptions, because in the former there is no additional cathexis from the excitation of the psychic sense-organs. Whilst an idea which is to be warded off may fail to become conscious because it has succumbed to repression, it may on other occasions come to be repressed simply because it has been withdrawn from conscious perception on other grounds. These are clues which we make use of in therapy in order to undo accomplished repressions.

The value of the hyper-cathexis which is produced by the regulating influence of the *Cs.* sense-organs on the mobile quantity is demonstrated in a teleological context by nothing more clearly than by the creation of a new series of qualities, and consequently a new regulation, which constitutes the prerogative of man over the animals. For the mental processes are in themselves unqualitative except for the excitations of pleasure and pain which accompany them: which, as we know, must be kept within limits as possible disturbers of thought. In order to endow them with quality, they are associated in man with verbal memories, the qualitative residues of which suffice to draw upon them the attention of consciousness, which in turn endows thought with a new mobile cathexis.

It is only on a dissection of hysterical mental processes that the manifold nature of the problems of consciousness becomes apparent. One then receives the impression that the transition from the preconscious to the conscious cathexis is associated with a censorship similar to that between *Ucs.* and *Pcs.* This censorship, too, begins to act only when a certain quantitative limit is reached, so that thought-formations which are not very intense escape it. All possible cases of detention from consciousness and of penetration into consciousness under certain restrictions are included within the range of psychoneurotic phenomena; all point to the intimate and twofold connection between the censorship and consciousness. I shall conclude these psychological considerations with the record of two such occurrences.

On the occasion of a consultation a few years ago, the patient was an intelligent-looking girl with a simple, unaffected manner. She was strangely attired; for whereas a woman's dress is usually carefully thought out to the last pleat, one of her stockings was hanging down and two of the buttons of her blouse were undone. She complained of pains in one of her legs, and exposed her calf without being asked to do so. Her chief complaint, however, was as follows: She had a feeling in her body *as though something were sticking into it which moved to and fro and shook her through and through.* This sometimes seemed to make her whole body *stiff.* On hearing this, my colleague in consultation looked at me; the trouble was quite obvious to him. To both of us it seemed peculiar that this suggested nothing to the patient's mother, though she herself must repeatedly have been in the situation described by her child. As for the girl, she had no idea of the import of her words, or she would never have allowed them to pass her lips. Here the censorship had been hoodwinked so successfully that under the mask of an innocent complaint a phantasy was admitted to consciousness which otherwise would have remained in the preconscious.

Another example: I began the psychoanalytic treatment of a boy of fourteen who was suffering from *tic convulsif*, hysterical vomiting, headache, etc., by assuring him that after closing his eyes he would see pictures or that ideas would occur to him, which he was to communicate to me. He replied by describing pictures. The last impression he had received before coming to me was revived visually in his memory. He had been playing a game of checkers with his uncle, and now he saw the checkerboard before him. He commented on various positions that were favourable or unfavourable, on moves that were not safe to make. He then saw a dagger lying on the checker-board—an object belonging to his father, but which his phantasy laid on the checker-board. Then a sickle was lying on the board; a scythe was added; and finally, he saw the image of an old peasant mowing the grass in front of his father's house far away. A few days later I discovered the meaning of this series of pictures. Disagreeable family circumstances had made the boy excited and nervous. Here was a case of a harsh, irascible father, who had lived unhappily with the boy's mother, and whose educational methods consisted of threats; he had divorced his gentle and delicate wife, and remarried; one day he brought home a young woman as the boy's new mother. The illness of the fourteen-year-old boy developed a few days later. It was the suppressed rage against his father that had combined these images into intelligible allusions. The material was furnished by a mythological reminiscence. The sickle was that with which Zeus castrated his father; the scythe and the image of the peasant represented Kronos, the violent old man who devours his children, and upon whom Zeus wreaks his vengeance in so unfilial a manner. The father's marriage gave the boy an opportunity of returning the reproaches and threats which the child had once heard his father utter because he *played* with his genitals (the draught-board; the prohibited moves; the dagger with which one could kill). We have here long-impressed memories and their unconscious derivatives which, *under the guise of meaningless pictures,* have slipped into consciousness by the devious paths opened to them.

If I were asked what is the theoretical value of the study of dreams, I should reply that it lies in the additions to psychological knowledge and the beginnings of an understanding of the neuroses which we thereby obtain. Who can foresee the importance a thorough knowledge of the structure and functions of the psychic apparatus may attain, when even our present state of knowledge permits of successful therapeutic intervention in the curable forms of the psychoneuroses? But, it may be asked, what of the practical value of this study in regard to a knowledge of the psyche and discovery of the hidden peculiarities of individual character? Have not the unconscious impulses revealed by dreams the value of real forces in the psychic life? Is the ethical significance of the suppressed wishes to be lightly disregarded, since, just as they now create dreams, they may some day create other things?

I do not feel justified in answering these questions. I have not followed up this aspect of the problem of dreams. In any case, however, I believe that the Roman Emperor was in the wrong in ordering one of his subjects to be executed because the latter had dreamt that he had killed the Emperor. He should first of all have endeavoured to discover the significance of the man's dream; most probably it was not what it seemed to be. And even if a dream of a different content had actually had this treasonable meaning, it would still have been well to recall the words of Plato—that the virtuous man contents himself with dreaming of that which the wicked man does in actual life. I am therefore of the opinion that dreams should be acquitted of evil. Whether any *reality* is to be attributed to the unconscious wishes, I cannot say. Reality must, of course, be denied to all transitory and intermediate thoughts. If we had before us the unconscious wishes, brought to their final and truest expression, we should still do well to remember that *psychic reality* is a special form of existence which must not be confounded with *material reality*. It seems, therefore, unnecessary that people should refuse to accept the responsibility for the immorality of their dreams. With an appreciation of the mode of functioning of the psychic apparatus, and an insight into the relations between conscious and unconscious, all that is ethically offensive in our dream-life and the life of phantasy for the most part disappears.

"What a dream has told us of our relations to the present (reality) we will then seek also in our consciousness, and we must not be surprised if we discover that the monster we saw under the magnifying-glass of the analysis is a tiny little infusorian" (H. Sachs).

For all practical purposes in judging human character, a man's actions and conscious expressions of thought are in most cases sufficient. Actions, above all, deserve to be placed in the front rank; for many impulses which penetrate into consciousness are neutralized by real forces in the psychic life before they find issue in action; indeed, the reason why they frequently do not encounter any psychic obstacle on their path is because the unconscious is certain of their meeting with resistances later. In any case, it is highly instructive to learn something of the intensively tilled soil from which our virtues proudly emerge. For the complexity of human character, dynamically moved in all directions, very rarely accommodates itself to the arbitrament of a simple alternative, as our antiquated moral philosophy would have it.

And what of the value of dreams in regard to our knowledge of the future? That, of course, is quite out of the question. One would like to substitute the words: "in regard to our knowledge of the past." For in every sense a dream has its origin in the past. The ancient belief that dreams reveal the future is not indeed entirely devoid of truth. By representing a wish as fulfilled the dream certainly leads us into the future; but this future, which the dreamer accepts as his present, has been shaped in the likeness of the past by the indestructible wish.

THREE

THREE CONTRIBUTIONS TO
THE THEORY OF SEX

THE SEXUAL ABERRATIONS[1]

THE fact of sexual need in man and animal is expressed in biology by the assumption of a "sexual instinct." This instinct is made analogous to the instinct of taking nourishment, and to hunger. The sexual expression corresponding to hunger not being found colloquially, science uses the expression, "libido." [2]

Popular conception makes definite assumptions concerning the nature and qualities of this sexual instinct. It is supposed to be absent during childhood and to commence about the time of and in connection with the maturing process of puberty; it is assumed that it manifests itself in irresistible attractions exerted by one sex upon the other, and that its aim is sexual union or at least such actions as would lead to that union.

But we have every reason to see in these assumptions a very untrustworthy picture of reality. Closer examination shows that they are based on errors, inaccuracies and hasty conclusions.

Let us introduce two terms, the *sexual object, i.e.,* the person from whom the sexual attraction emanates, and the *sexual aim, i.e.,* the aim towards which the instinct strives. Our experience then shows us that there are many deviations in reference to both sexual object and sexual aim, which require thorough investigation.

I. DEVIATION IN REFERENCE TO THE SEXUAL OBJECT

The popular theory of the sexual instinct corresponds closely to the poetic fable of dividing the person into two halves—man and woman—who

---

[1] The facts contained in the first "Contribution" have been gathered from the familiar publications of Krafft-Ebing, Moll, Moebius, Havelock Ellis, Schrenk-Notzing, Löwenfeld, Eulenberg, I. Bloch, and M. Hirschfeld, and from the later works published in the *Jahrbuch für sexuelle Zwischenstufen.* As these publications also mention the other literature bearing on this subject, I may forbear giving detailed references.

The conclusions reached through the psychoanalytic investigation of sexual inverts are all based on the reports of J. Sadger and on my own experience.

[2] The single adequate or fitting word of the German language, "Lust," unfortunately has many meanings and signifies the sensation of needs as well as that of satisfaction. "Libido" is the motor force of sexual life. It is a quantitative energy directed to an object. (*Vide infra.*)

strive to become reunited through love. It is, therefore, very surprising to find that there are men for whom the sexual object is not woman but man, and that there are women for whom it is not man but woman. Such *persons* are designated as contrary sexuals, or better, inverts, and the situation of such a relationship is called inversion. The number of such individuals is considerable, although it is difficult to estimate them accurately.[1]

A. Inversion

The Behavior of Inverts. The above-mentioned persons behave in many ways quite differently.

(a) Some are absolutely inverted; *i.e.*, their sexual object must be always of the same sex, while the opposite sex can never be to them an object of sexual longing; on the contrary, it leaves them indifferent or may even evoke repugnance. As men they are unable, on account of this repugnance, to perform the normal sexual act or miss all pleasure in its performance.

(b) They are amphigenously inverted (psychosexually hermaphroditic); *i.e.*, their sexual object may belong indifferently to either the same or to the other sex. The inversion lacks here the character of exclusiveness.

(c) Some are occasionally inverted. Under certain conditions, chiefly when the normal sexual object is inaccessible, or through imitation, they are able to take as the sexual object a person of the same sex and thus find sexual gratification.

The inverts also manifest a manifold behavior in their judgment of the peculiarities of their sexual instinct. Some consider the inversion as a matter of course, just as a normal person looks upon his libido, and firmly demand the same rights as the normal. Others, however, struggle against their inversion and perceive in it a morbid compulsion.[2]

Other variations deal with temporal relations. The characteristics of the inversion in any individual may date back as far as his memory goes, or they may become manifest to him at a definite period before or after puberty.[3] The inverted character may either be retained throughout life,

---

[1] For the difficulties entailed in the attempt to ascertain the proportional number of inverts, compare the work of M. Hirschfeld in the Jahrbuch für sexuelle Zwischenstufen, 1904. (Cf. also Brill, The Conception of Homosexuality, Journal of the A.M.A., August 2, 1913.)

[2] Such a struggle against the compulsion to inversion may offer a favorable condition for treatment through suggestion or psychoanalysis.

[3] Many have justly emphasized the fact that the autobiographic statements of inverts, as to the time of the appearance of their tendency to inversion, are untrustworthy as they may have repressed from memory any evidences of heterosexual feelings. Psychoanalysis has confirmed this suspicion in all cases of inversion accessible to study and has decidedly changed their histories by filling up the infantile amnesias.

or it may occasionally recede, or it may represent an episode on the path of normal development. A periodical fluctuation between the desire for the normal and that of the inverted sexual object has also been observed. Of special interest are those cases in which the libido changes and assumes the character of inversion after a painful experience with the normal sexual object.

These different categories of variation generally exist independently of one another. In the most extreme cases it can regularly be assumed that the inversion has existed at all times and that the person feels contented with his peculiar state.

Many authors will hesitate to gather into a unit all the cases enumerated here and will prefer to emphasize the differences rather than the common traits of these groups, a view which corresponds with their judgment of inversions. But no matter how classifications are justified, it cannot be overlooked that all transitions are abundantly encountered, so that group formations, as it were, unwittingly obtrude themselves.

Conception of Inversion. The first studies of the inversion gave rise to the assumption that it was a sign of innate nervous degeneration. This harmonized with the fact that physicians first observed it among nervous persons, or among those giving such an impression. There are two elements which should be considered independently in this characterization: the congenitality, and the degeneration.

Degeneration. The term, *degeneration,* is open to the objections which may be urged against the promiscuous use of this particular term. It has, in fact, become customary to designate all morbid manifestations not of traumatic or infectious origin as degenerative. Indeed, Magnan's classification of degenerates makes it possible to apply the concept of degeneration to the most general forms of nervous activity. Under such circumstances, it may be asked whether the idea of "degeneration" is still of any use, or whether it has a new meaning. It would seem more appropriate not to speak of degeneration: (1) where there are not many marked deviations from the normal; (2) where the capacity for working and living do not in general appear markedly impaired.[1]

That inverts are not degenerates in this qualified sense can be seen from the following facts:

[1] With what reserve the diagnosis of degeneration should be made and what slight practical significance can be attributed to it may be gathered from the remarks of Moebius (Ueber Entartung; Grenzfragen des Nerven—und Seelenlebens, No. III, 1900). He says: "If we review the wide sphere of degeneration upon which we have here turned some light, we can conclude without further ado that it is really of little value to diagnose degeneration."

1. The inversion is found in people who otherwise show no marked deviation from the normal.

2. It is found also in people whose mental capacities are not disturbed, who on the contrary are distinguished· by especially high intellectual development and ethical culture.[1]

3. If one disregards the patients of one's own practice and strives to comprehend a wider field of experience, he will encounter facts in two directions, which will prevent him from considering inversion as a sign of degeneration.

(a) It must be remembered that inversion was a frequent manifestation among the ancient nations at the height of their culture. It was an institution endowed with important functions. (b) It is found to be widely prevalent among savages and primitive races, whereas the term, degeneration, is generally applied to higher civilization (I. Bloch). Even among the most civilized nations of Europe, climate and race have a most powerful influence on the distribution of, and attitude toward, inversion.[2]

Innateness. Only for the first and most extreme class of inverts, as can be imagined, has innateness been claimed, and this on their own assurance that at no time in their life has their sexual instinct followed a different course. The fact of the existence of two other classes, especially of the third, is difficult to reconcile with the assumption that inversion is congenital. Hence, the desire of those holding the view to separate the absolute inverts from the others results in the rejection of the general conception of inversion. Accordingly in a number of cases the inversion would be of a congenital character, while in others it might originate from other causes.

In contrast to this is the concept which assumes the inversion as an *acquired* characteristic of the sexual instinct. This view is based on the following facts:

(1) In many inverts (even absolute ones) an early affective sexual impression can be demonstrated, as a result of which the homosexual tendency developed.

(2) In many others external influences of life of a promoting and inhibiting nature can be demonstrated, which in earlier or later life led to a fixation of the inversion (exclusive relations with the same sex, companionship in war, detention in prison, dangers of heterosexual intercourse, celibacy, genital weakness, etc.).

---

[1] We must agree with the spokesman of "Uranism" (I. Bloch) that some of the most prominent men known have been inverts and perhaps absolute inverts.

[2] In the conception of inversion the pathological features have been separated from the anthropological. For this credit is due to I. Bloch (Beiträge zur Ätiologie der Psychopathia Sexualis, 2 Teile, 1902–3), who has also brought into prominence the existence of inversion in the civilized races of antiquity.

(3) Hypnotic suggestion may remove the inversion, which would be surprising, if it were of a congenital character.

From the viewpoint of these assumptions, the certainty of the existence of congenital inversion can certainly be questioned. It may be disputed on the ground that a more accurate examination of those claiming to be congenital inverts will probably show that the direction of the libido was determined by a definite experience of early childhood, which has not been retained in the conscious memory of the person, but which can be brought back to memory by proper influences (Havelock Ellis). According to these authors inversion could be designated only as a frequent variation of the sexual instinct, which may be determined by a number of external circumstances of life.

The apparent certainty thus reached can, however, be overthrown by the retort that there are obviously many persons who experience even in their early youth those very sexual influences (seduction, mutual mastur-bation) without becoming inverts, or without continuing so. Hence, one is forced to assume that the alternatives congenital and acquired are either incomplete or do not cover the circumstances present in inversions.

Explanation of Inversions. The nature of inversion is explained neither by the assumption that it is congenital nor that it is acquired. In the first case, we need to be told what there is in it of the congenital, unless we are satisfied with the roughest explanation, namely, that a person brings along a congenital sexual instinct connected with a definite sexual object. In the second case it is a question whether the manifold accidental influ-ences suffice to explain the acquisition, unless there is something in the individual to meet it half way. The negation of this last factor is inadmis-sible according to our former conclusions.

The Approach to Homosexuality. Since the time of Frank Lydston, Kiernan, and Chevalier, a new series of ideas has been introduced for the explanation of the possibility of sexual inversion. These contain a new contradiction to the popular belief which assumes that a human being is either a man or a woman. For science shows cases in which the sexual characteristics appear blurred so that the sexual distinction is difficult, especially on an anatomical basis. The genitals of such persons unite the male and female characteristics (hermaphroditism). In rare cases both parts of the sexual apparatus are well developed (true hermaphroditism), but usually both are stunted.[1]

---

[1] Compare the last detailed discussion of somatic hermaphroditism (Taruffi: Her-maphroditismus und Zeugungsunfähigkeit, German edit. by R. Teuscher, 1903), and the works of Neugebauer in many volumes of the Jahrbuch für sexuelle Zwischen-stufen.

The importance of these abnormalities lies in the fact that they unexpectedly facilitate the understanding of the normal formation. A certain degree of anatomical hermaphroditism really belongs to the normal. In no normally formed male or female are traces of the apparatus of the other sex lacking; these either continue functionless as rudimentary organs, or they are transformed for the purpose of assuming other functions.

The conception which we gather from this long known anatomical fact is that there is an original predisposition to bisexuality, that in the course of development this changes to monosexuality, leaving only slight remnants of the stunted sex.

It was natural to transfer this view to the psychic sphere and to conceive the inversion in its aberrations as an expression of psychic hermaphroditism. To bring the question to a decision, it only needed one other regular concurrence of the inversion with the psychic and somatic signs of hermaphroditism.

But this second expectation was not realized. The relations between the assumed psychical and the demonstrable anatomical androgyny should never be conceived as being so close. In inverts one frequently finds a general diminution of the sexual instinct (H. Ellis) and a slight anatomical stunting of the organs. This, however, is found frequently but by no means regularly or preponderantly. We must, therefore, admit that inversion and somatic hermaphroditism are totally independent of each other.

Great importance has also been attached to the so-called secondary and tertiary sex characteristics, and their aggregate occurrence in inverts has been emphasized (H. Ellis). There is much truth in this, but it should not be forgotten that the secondary and tertiary sex characteristics very frequently appear in the other sex, which indicates androgyny without, however, involving changes in the sexual object in the sense of an inversion.

Psychic hermaphroditism would gain in substantiality if parallel with the inversion of the sexual object there should be at least a change in the other psychic qualities, such as in the impulses and distinguishing traits characteristic of the other sex. But such inversion of character can be expected with some regularity only in female inverts; in men the most perfect psychic manliness may be united with the inversion. If one firmly adheres to the hypothesis of a psychic hermaphroditism, one must add that its manifestations in various spheres show only a very slight indication of contrary determination. The same also holds true in the somatic androgyny. According to Halban, the appearance of individual stunted organs and secondary sex characteristics are quite independent of each other.[1]

A spokesman for the masculine inverts stated the bisexual theory in its crudest form in the following words: "It is a female brain in a male body." But we do not know the characteristics of a "female brain." The substitution of the anatomical for the psychological is as frivolous as it is unjustified. The tentative explanation by Krafft-Ebing seems to be more accurately formulated than that of Ulrich but does not essentially differ from it. Krafft-Ebing thinks that the bisexual predisposition supplies the individual with male and female brain centers just as somatic sexual organs. These centers develop first towards puberty mostly under the influence of the independent sex glands. We can, however, say the same of the male and female "centers" as of the male and female brains. More-over, we do not even know whether we can assume for the sexual func-tions separate brain locations ("centers") in the same way as for the speech function.

After this discussion, two ideas, as it were, remain: first, that a bisexual predisposition may also be presumed for the inversion, though we do not know of what it consists beyond the anatomical formations; and, sec-ondly, that we are dealing with disturbances which are experienced by the sexual instinct during its development.[2]

The Sexual Object of the Invert. The theory of psychic hermaphroditism presupposed that the sexual object of the inverted is the reverse of the

[1] J. Halban, "Die Entstehung der Geschlechtscharaktere," Arch. für Gynäkologie, Bd. 70, 1903. See also there the literature on the subject.

[2] According to a report in Vol. 6 of the Jahrbuch f. sexuelle Zwischenstufen, E. Gley is supposed to have been the first to mention bisexuality as an explanation of inver-sion. He published a paper (*Les abérrations de l'instinct sexuel*) in the Revue Phi-losophique as early as January, 1884. It is moreover noteworthy that the majority of authors who trace inversion back to bisexuality assume this factor not only for the inverts but also for those who have developed normally, and justly interpret the inversion as a result of disturbance in development. Among these authors are Cheva-lier (*Inversion sexuelle*, 1893), and Krafft-Ebing ("*Zur Erklärung der konträren Sexualempfindung*," Jahrbücher f. Psychiatrie u. Nervenheilkunde, XIII), who states that there are a number of observations "from which at least the virtual and continued existence of this second center (of the underlying sex) results." A Dr. Arduin (Die Frauenfrage und die sexuellen Zwischenstufen, Vol. II of the Jahrbuch f. sexuelle Zwischenstufen, 1900) states that "in every man there exist male and female elements." See also the same Jahrbuch, Bd. 1, 1899 ("Die objektive Diagnose der Homosexualität," by M. Hirschfeld, pp. 8-9). In the determination of sex, as far as heterosexual persons are concerned, some are disproportionately more strongly developed than others. G. Herman is firm in his belief "that in every woman there are male, and in every man there are female germs and qualities." (Genesis, das Gesetz der Zeugung, 9 Bd., Libido und Manie, 1903). As recently as 1906, W. Fliess (Der Ablauf des Lebens) has claimed ownership of the idea of bisexuality (in the sense of double sex). In uninformed circles the assertion is made that the philosopher, O. Weininger, is the authority for the human bisexuality conception since this idea is made the foundation of his rather hasty work, Geschlecht und Charakter, 1903 (translated into English). The above citations show how unfounded is such a claim.

normal. The male invert, like the woman, succumbs to the charms emanating from manly qualities of body and mind; he feels himself like a woman and seeks a man.

But however true this may be for a great number of inverts, it by no means describes the general character of inversion. There is no doubt that a large number of male inverts have retained the psychic character of virility, that proportionately they show but little of the secondary characteristics of the other sex, and that they look for real feminine psychic features in their sexual object. If that were not so, it would be incomprehensible why masculine prostitution, in offering itself to inverts, copies in all its exterior, today as in antiquity, the female dress and female behavior. This imitation would otherwise be an insult to the ideal of the inverts. Among the Greeks, where the most virile men were found among inverts, it is quite obvious that it was not the masculine character of the boy, which kindled the love of man, but it was his physical resemblance to woman as well as his feminine psychic qualities, such as shyness, demureness and the need of instruction and help. As soon as the boy himself became a man, he ceased to be a sexual object for men and in turn became a lover of boys. The sexual object in this case as in many others is therefore not of the same sex, but a union of both sex characteristics, a compromise between the impulses striving for the man and for the woman, but firmly conditioned by the masculinity of body (the genitals).[1]

---

[1] Although psychoanalysis has not yet given us a full explanation for the origin of inversion, it has revealed the psychic mechanism of its genesis and has essentially enriched the problems in question. In all the cases examined we have ascertained that the later inverts go through in their childhood a phase of very intense but short-lived fixation on the woman (usually on the mother) and after overcoming it, they identify themselves with the woman and take themselves as the sexual object; that is, proceeding on a narcissistic basis, they look for young men resembling themselves in persons whom they wish to love as their mother has loved them. We have, moreover, frequently found that alleged inverts are by no means indifferent to the charms of women, but the excitation evoked by the woman is always transferred to a male object. They thus repeat through life the mechanism which gave origin to their inversion. Their obsessive striving for the man proves to be determined by their restless flight from the woman. Psychoanalytic research very strongly opposes the attempt to separate homosexuals from other persons as a group of a special nature. By also studying sexual excitations different than those manifestly overt, it discovers that all men are capable of homosexual object selection and actually accomplish this in the unconscious. Indeed, attachments of libidinous feelings to persons of the same sex play no small rôle as factors in normal psychic life, and as causative factors of disease they play a greater rôle than those belonging to the opposite sex. According to psychoanalysis, it rather seems that it is the independence of the object, selection of the sex of the object, the same free disposal over male and female objects, as observed in childhood, in primitive states and in prehistoric times, which forms the origin from which the normal as well as the inversion types developed, following restrictions in this or that direction. In the psychoanalytic sense the exclusive sexual interest of the man for the woman is also a problem requiring an explanation, and is not something that is self-evident and explainable on the basis of chemical attraction. The determination as to the definite sexual behavior does not occur until after puberty and is the result of a series of as yet not observable factors, some of which

The conditions in the woman are more definite; here the active inverts show with special frequency the somatic and psychic characteristics of man and desire femininity in their sexual object; though even here greater variation will be found on more intimate investigation.

The Sexual Aim of the Invert. The important fact to bear in mind is that no uniformity of the sexual aim can be attributed to inversion. Intercourse *per anum* in men by no means goes with inversion; masturbation

---

are of a constitutional, while some are of an accidental nature. Certainly some of these factors can turn out to be so enormous that by their character they influence the result. In general, however, the multiplicity of the determining factors is reflected by the manifoldness of the outcomes in the manifest sexual behavior of the person. In the inversion types it can be ascertained that they are altogether controlled by an archaic constitution and by primitive psychic mechanisms. The importance of the *narcissistic object selection* and the *clinging* to the erotic significance of the *anal* zone seem to be their most essential characteristics. But one gains nothing by separating the most extreme inversion types from the others on the basis of such constitutional peculiarities. What is found in the latter as seemingly an adequate determinant can also be demonstrated only in lesser force, in the constitution of transitional types, and in manifestly normal persons. The differences in the results may be of a qualitative nature, but analysis shows that the differences in the determinants are only quantitative. As a remarkable factor among the accidental influences of object selection, we found the sexual rejection or the early sexual intimidation, and our attention was also called to the fact that the existence of both parents plays an important rôle in the child's life. The disappearance of a strong father in childhood not infrequently favors the inversion. Finally, one can put forth the claim that the inversion of the sexual object should notionally be strictly separated from the mixing of the sex characteristics in the subject. A certain degree of independence is unmistakable also in this relation. A series of important points of view concerning the question of inversion have been brought forward by Ferenczi (in a contribution, Zur Nosologie der männlichen Homosexualität—Homoerotic—. (Int. Zeit. f. Psa., 2, 1914.) (In English, in Contribution to Psychoanalysis, i., Badger, Boston, 1916.) Ferenczi correctly criticizes the fact that under the term Homosexuality (which term he would replace by the better one Homoerotic) a number of different conditions are grouped which are of quite variable significance both from an organic as well as psychical point of view because the one symptom of inversion is present. He shows that there are but four very marked differences at least between two types of subject-homoerotics, who feel and act like women, and the object-homoerotic who is masculine throughout and has only (mistakenly) exchanged a female object against one of the same sex. The first he recognizes as a true "intermediary sexual stage" in the sense of Magnus Hirschfeld; the second he terms—less fortunately—a compulsion neurotic. The striving against the tendency to inversion as well as the possibility of psychical influence is only possible with the object-homoerotic. It may also be added, that after the recognition of these two types, one finds that in many individuals a certain amount of subject-homoeroticism is mixed with a portion of object-homoeroticism.

Of recent years biological workers, especially Eugen Steinach, have thrown a clear light upon the organic conditionings of homoerotism as well as upon sexual characters. Through the experimental procedure of castration followed by implanting the gonads of the opposite sex, he was able in different mammals to change males into females and vice versa. The change concerns more or less completely the somatic sexual characters and the psychosexual behavior (as subject- and object-erotic). The carriers of this sex determining power are not that portion of the sexual glands which builds up the sexual cells but the so-called interstitial cells of the organs (the puberty glands).

is just as frequently the exclusive aim; and the limitation of the sexual aim to mere effusion of feelings is here even more frequent than in heterosexual love. In women, too, the sexual aims of the inverts are manifold, among which contact with the mucous membrane of the mouth seems to be preferred.

In one case, the sexual alteration took place in a man whose testicles had been damaged by tuberculosis. In his sexual life he had behaved as a passive homosexual woman, and showed very clearly marked secondary female sexual characters (hair distribution, nature of facial hair, fatty mammae and female hips). Following the implanation of a cryptorchids testicle, this man began to behave as a man and directed his libido towards the female in the normal manner. At the same time, the somatic female sex character disappeared. (A. Lipschütz, Die Pubertätsdrüse und ihre Wirkungen, Bern, 1919).

It would be unjust to maintain that the knowledge of inversion is placed on a new basis, and it would be premature to expect from it directly a way to the cure of homosexuality. W. Fliess has correctly accented the fact that this experimental experience does not solve the problem of the general bisexual *Anlage* of the higher animals. It seems to me much more probable that a direct confirmation of the accepted bisexuality will come from such and further investigation.

Conclusion. Although we are by no means in a position to explain satisfactorily from the material on hand the origin of inversion, we can say that through this investigation we have obtained an insight which can become of greater significance to us than the solution of the above problem. Our attention is called to the fact that we have assumed a too close connection between the sexual instinct and the sexual object. The experience gained from the so-called abnormal cases teaches us that a connection exists between the sexual instinct and the sexual object which we are in danger of overlooking in the uniformity of normal states where the instinct seems to bring with it the object. We are thus, instructed to separate this connection between the instinct and the object. The sexual instinct is probably entirely independent of its object and is not originated by the stimuli proceeding from the object.

B. The Sexually Immature and Animals as Sexual Objects

Whereas those sexual inverts whose sexual object does not belong to the normally adapted sex, appear to the observer as a collective number of perhaps otherwise normal individuals, the cases who choose immature sexual objects (children) apparently represent from the beginning sporadic aberrations. Only exceptionally are children taken as exclusive sexual objects. They are mostly drawn into this rôle if a faint-hearted and impotent individual happens to be in contact with such substitutes, or if an impulsive urge (uncontrollable at the time) cannot secure the proper object. Still, it throws some light on the nature of the sexual instinct, that it should permit such great variations and depreciation of its object, something which hunger, adhering more energetically to its object, would allow only in the most extreme cases. The same may be said of sexual relations with animals—a thing not at all rare among farmers—where the sexual attraction goes beyond the limits of the species.

For esthetic reasons one would gladly attribute this and other excessive aberrations of the sexual instinct to the insane, but this would not accord with the facts. Experience teaches that among the latter no disturbances of the sexual instinct can be found other than those observed among the sane, or among whole races and classes. Thus, we find with gruesome frequency sexual abuse of children by teachers and servants merely because they have the best opportunity for it. The insane present the aforesaid aberration only in a somewhat intensified form; or what is of special significance is the fact that the aberration becomes exclusive and takes the place of the normal sexual gratification.

This very remarkable relation of sexual variations ranging from the normal to the insane gives material for reflection. It seems to me that the fact to be explained would show that the impulses of the sexual life belong to those which even normally are most poorly controlled by the higher psychic activities. He who is in any way psychically abnormal, be it in social or ethical conditions, is, according to my experience, regularly so in his sexual life. But many are abnormal in their sexual life who in every other respect correspond to the average; they have kept abreast of the human cultural development, but their sexuality remained as their weak point.

As a general result of these discussions we come to see that, under numerous conditions and in a surprising number of individuals, the nature and value of the sexual object steps into the background. There is something else in the sexual instinct which is the essential and constant element.[1]

2. DEVIATION IN REFERENCE TO THE SEXUAL AIM

The union of the genitals in the characteristic act of copulation is taken as the normal sexual aim. It serves to diminish the sexual tension and to quench temporarily the sexual desire (gratification analogous to satisfac-

---

[1] The most pronounced difference between the love life of antiquity and ours lies in the fact that the ancients placed the emphasis on the instinct itself, while we put it on its object. The ancients extolled the instinct and were ready to ennoble through it even an inferior object, while we disparage the activity of the instinct as such and only countenance it on account of the merits of the object.

tion of hunger). Yet, even in the most normal sexual act, certain addenda are distinguishable, the development of which may lead to aberrations described as *perversions*. Thus, certain intermediary relations to the sexual object connected with copulation, such as touching and looking, are recognized as preliminaries to the sexual aim. These activities are on the one hand pleasurable as such, and on the other hand, they enhance the excitement which persists until the definite sexual aim is attained. One special form of contact, which consists of mutual approximation of the mucous membranes of the lips in the kiss, has received a sexual value among the civilized nations, though the parts of the body do not belong to the sexual apparatus and merely form the entrance to the digestive tract. These addenda, therefore, supply the factors which allow us to bring the perversions into relation to the normal sexual life, and are available also for classification. The perversions represent either (a) anatomical *transgressions* of the bodily regions destined for sexual union, or (b) a *lingering* at the intermediary relations to the sexual object which should normally be rapidly passed, on the way to the definite sexual aim.

(a) Anatomical Transgression

Overestimation of the Sexual Object. The psychic estimation in which the sexual object shares as a goal of the sexual instinct is only in the rarest cases limited to the genitals; generally it embraces the whole body and tends to include all sensations emanating from the sexual object. The same overestimation extends to the psychic sphere and manifests itself as a logical blinding (diminished judgment) concerning the psychic attainments and perfections of the sexual object, and in a credulous yielding to the judgments emanating from the latter. The absolute faith inspired by love thus becomes an important, if not the primordial source of authority.[1]

It is this sexual overvaluation, which is so incompatible with the restriction of the sexual aim to the union of the genitals only, and which raises other parts of the body to sexual aims.[2]

[1] I must mention here that the blind obedience evinced by the hypnotized subject to the hypnotist causes me to think that the nature of hypnosis is to be found in the unconscious fixation of the libido on the person of the hypnotizer (by means of the masochistic component of the sexual instinct). Ferenczi has connected this character of suggestibility with the "parent complex." (Jahrbuch für psychoanalytische und psychopathologische Forschungen, 1, 1909).

[2] At the same time it is to be observed that sexual overestimation is not developed by all of the mechanisms of object choice, and that we will later learn of another and more direct explanation of the sexual rôle of the other bodily parts. The factor of "excitement hunger" which Hoche and I. Bloch have offered as explanation of the spreading of the sexual interests to other parts of the body than the genitals does not seem to me to deserve this significance. The different paths along which the libido moves, behave one to another from the beginning like communicating pipes, and one must therefore take into account the phenomenon of collateral streaming.

The significance of the factor of sexual overestimation can be best studied in the male, in whom alone the sexual life is accessible to investigation, whereas in the woman it is veiled in impenetrable darkness, partly because of cultural stunting and partly on account of the conventional reticence and insincerity of women.[1]

Sexual Utilization of the Mucous Membrane of the Lips and Mouth. The employment of the mouth as a sexual organ is considered as a perversion if the lips (tongue) of the one are brought into contact with the genitals of the other, but not when the mucous membrane of the lips of both touch each other. In the latter exception we find the connection with the normal. He who abhors the former as perversions, though since antiquity these have been common practices among mankind, yields to a distinct *feeling of loathing* which restrains him from adopting such sexual aims. The limit of such loathing is frequently purely conventional; he who kisses fervently the lips of a pretty girl will perhaps be able to use her tooth-brush only with a sense of loathing, though there is no reason to assume that his own oral cavity for which he entertains no loathing is cleaner than that of the girl. Our attention is here called to the factor of loathing which stands in the way of the libidinous overestimation of the sexual aim, but which may in turn be vanquished by the libido. In loathing we may observe one of the forces which have brought about the restrictions of the sexual aim. As a rule, these forces halt at the genitals; there is, however, no doubt that even the genitals of the other sex may themselves be an object of loathing. Such behavior is characteristic of all hysterics, especially women. The force of the sexual instinct prefers to occupy itself with the overcoming of this loathing (see later).

Sexual Utilization of the Anal Opening. It is even more obvious than in the former case, that it is loathing which stamps as a perversion the use of the anus as a sexual aim. But it should not be interpreted as espousing a cause when I observe that the basis of this loathing—namely, that this part of the body serves for the excretion and comes into contact with the loathsome excrement—is not more plausible than the basis which hysterical girls have for the disgust which they entertain for the male genital because it serves for urination.

The sexual rôle of the mucous membrane of the anus is by no means limited to intercourse between men; the preference for it is not at all a characteristic of inverted feeling. On the contrary, it seems that *pedicatio* in men owes its rôle to its analogy with the act in the woman, whereas

[1] In typical cases, the wife permits this sexual-overvaluation of the male to pass by but almost always makes up for it in the child born to her.

among inverts it is mutual masturbation which is the most common sexual aim.

The Significance of Other Parts of the Body. Sexual infringement on the other parts of the body, in all its variations, offers nothing new; it adds nothing to our knowledge of the sexual instinct which thereby only announces its intention to dominate the sexual object in every way. Besides the sexual overvaluation, a second and generally unknown factor may be mentioned among the anatomical transgressions. Certain parts of the body, like the mucous membrane of the mouth and anus, which repeatedly appear in such practices, lay claim, as it were, to be considered and treated as genitals. We shall hear how this claim is justified by the development of the sexual instinct and how it is fulfilled in the symptomatology of certain morbid conditions.

Unfit Substitutes for the Sexual Object. Fetichism. We are especially impressed by those cases in which the normal sexual object is substituted for another, which, though related to it, is totally unfit for the normal sexual aim. According to our scheme of classification, it would have been better to have mentioned this most interesting group of aberrations of the sexual instinct among the deviations in reference to the sexual object, but we have postponed it until we became acquainted with the factor of *sexual exaggeration,* upon which these manifestations depend, as they are all connected with a giving up of the sexual aim.

The substitute for the sexual object is generally a part of the body but little adapted for sexual purposes, such as the foot or hair or some inanimate object (fragments of clothing, underwear), which has some demonstrable relation to the sexual person, preferably to the sexuality of the same. This substitute is not unjustly compared with the fetich in which the savage sees the embodiment of his god.

The transition to cases of fetichism, with a renunciation of a normal, or of a perverted sexual aim, is formed in cases where a fetichistic condition is required in the sexual object—in the form of special color of hair, clothes, or even body blemishes—if the sexual aim is to be attained. No other variation of the sexual instinct verging on the pathological is as generally clear to us as this one, despite the peculiarity of the manifestations occasioned by it. A certain depreciation in the striving for the normal sexual aim may be presupposed in all these cases (executive weakness of the sexual apparatus).[1] Its association to the normal is effected by

---

[1] This weakness corresponds to the constitutional predisposition. The early sexual intimidation which pushes the person away from the normal sexual aim and urges him to seek a substitute, has been demonstrated by psychoanalysis, as an accidental determinant.

the psychologically necessary overestimation of the sexual object, which inevitably transcends everything associatively related to the sexual object. A certain degree of such fetishism is, therefore, regularly found in the normal, especially during those stages of wooing when the normal sexual aim seems inaccessible or when its realization is unduly deferred.

"Get me a handkerchief from her bosom—a garter of my love."

—Faust.

The case becomes pathological only when the striving for the fetich fixes itself beyond such determinations and takes the place of the normal sexual aim; or again, when the fetich disengages itself from the person concerned and itself becomes a sexual object. These are the general determinants for the transition of mere variations of the sexual instinct to pathological aberrations.

The persistent influence of a sexual impression mostly received in early childhood often shows itself in the selection of a fetich. This was first asserted by Binet and was later proven by many illustrations—a fact which may be placed parallel to the proverbial adhesion to a first love in the normal (*"On revient toujours à ses premiers amours"*). Such a connection is especially seen in cases showing a simple fetichistic conditioning of the sexual object. The significance of early sexual impressions will be met again in other places.[1]

In other cases, it is mostly a symbolic mental association, which is unconscious to the person concerned, which leads to the substitution of the object by a fetich. The paths of these connections can not always be definitely demonstrated. The foot is a very primitive sexual symbol already found in myths.[2] Fur is used as a fetich probably on account of its association with the hairiness of the *mons veneris*. Such symbolism seems often to depend on sexual experiences in childhood.[3]

---

[1] Deeper penetrating psychoanalytic investigation has led to a more authoritative critique of Binet's assertion. All observations dealing with this subject show that there is a first encounter with the fetich, wherein it already shows itself to be in possession of a sexual interest. From the accompanying circumstances one cannot, however, understand how it came into possession of this interest. Moreover, all these "early" sexual impressions occur after the fifth to sixth year whereas psychoanalysis permits itself to doubt whether such pathological fixations can take place as new formations at so late a date. The actual facts are that behind the first memories of the appearance of the fetich there lies a submerged and forgotten phase of the sexual development for which the fetich acts as a substitute or as a "cover memory," the remnant and precipitate of which is also represented by the fetich. The changing of the phase of fetichism which takes place during the first years of childhood as well as the choice of the fetich itself is constitutionally determined.

[2] The shoe or slipper is accordingly a symbol for the female genitals.

[3] Psychoanalysis has filled up the gap in the understanding of fetichisms by showing that the selection of the fetich depends on a coprophilic smell-desire which has been lost by repression. Feet and hair are strong-smelling objects which are raised to fetiches after the renouncing of the now unpleasant sensation of smell. Accordingly, only the filthy and ill-smelling foot is the sexual object in the perversion which cor-

(b) Fixation of Precursory Sexual Aims

The Appearance of New Intentions. All the outer and inner determinations which impede or hold at a distance the attainment of the normal sexual aim, such as impotence, costliness of the sexual object, and dangers of the sexual act, will conceivably strengthen the inclination to linger at the preparatory acts, and to form them into new sexual aims to take the place of the normal. On closer investigation it is always seen that indications of what seems the most peculiar of these new aims have already existed in the normal sexual act.

Touching and Looking. At least a certain amount of touching is indispensable for a person in order to attain the normal sexual aim. It is also generally known that touching of the skin of the sexual object causes much pleasure and produces a supply of new excitement. Hence, the lingering at touching can hardly be considered a perversion if the sexual act is forthwith accomplished.

The same holds true in the end with looking, which is analogous to touching. The manner in which the libidinous excitement is frequently awakened is by optical impressions, and selection takes account of this circumstance—if this teleological mode of thinking be permitted—by making the sexual object a thing of beauty. Covering of the body, which keeps abreast with civilization, continuously arouses sexual curiosity and serves to supplement the sexual object by uncovering the hidden parts. This can be turned into the artistic ("sublimation") if the interest is turned from the genitals to the form of the body.[1] The tendency to linger at this intermediary sexual aim of the sexually accentuated looking is found to a certain degree in most normals; indeed, it gives them the possibility of directing a certain amount of their libido to a higher artistic aim. On the other hand, the desire for looking becomes a perversion (a) when it is exclusively limited to the genitals; (b) when it becomes connected with the overcoming of loathing (voyeurs and onlookers at the functions of excretion); and (c) when instead of preparing for the normal

---

responds to the foot fetichism. Another contribution to the explanation of the fetichistic preference of the foot is found in the Infantile Sexual Theories (see later). The foot replaces the penis, which is so much missed in the woman. In some cases of foot fetichism it could be shown that the desire for looking originally directed to the genitals, which strove to reach its object from below, was stopped on the way by prohibition and repression, and, therefore, adhered to the foot or shoe as a fetich. In conformity with infantile expectation, the female genital was hereby imagined as a male genital.

[1] I have no doubt that the concept of "beauty" is rooted in the soil of sexual stimulation and signified originally that which is sexually exciting. The more remarkable, therefore, is the fact that the genitals, the sight of which provokes the greatest sexual excitement, can really never be considered "beautiful."

sexual aim, it suppresses it. The latter, if I may draw conclusions from a single analysis, is in a most pronounced way true of exhibitionists, who expose their genitals with the idea of bringing to view the genitals of others.[1]

In the perversion which consists in striving to look and be looked at, we are confronted with a very remarkable peculiarity which will occupy us even more intensively in the following aberration. The sexual aim exists here in a two-fold formation, in an *active* and a *passive* form.

The force which opposes the desire for looking and through which the latter is eventually abolished is *shame* (like the former loathing).

Sadism and Masochism. The tendency to cause pain to the sexual object and its opposite, the most frequent and most significant of all perversions, was designated in its two forms by Krafft-Ebing as sadism for the active form, and masochism for the passive form. Other authors prefer the narrower term, *algolagnia,* which emphasizes the pleasure in pain and cruelty, whereas the terms selected by Krafft-Ebing place the pleasure secured in all kinds of humility and submission in the foreground.

The roots of active algolagnia, sadism, can be readily demonstrable in the normal individual. The sexuality of most men shows an admixture of aggression, of a desire to subdue, the biological significance of which lies in the necessity for overcoming the resistance of the sexual object by actions other than mere *courting.* Sadism would then correspond to an aggressive component of the sexual instinct which has become independent and exaggerated and has been brought to the foreground by displacement.

The concept of sadism fluctuates in everyday speech from a mere active or impetuous attitude towards the sexual object to an absolute attachment of the gratification to the subjection and maltreatment of the object. Strictly speaking, only the last extreme case can claim the name of perversion.

Similarly, the designation masochism comprises all passive attitudes to the sexual life and to the sexual object; in its most extreme form the gratification is connected with suffering of physical or mental pain at the hands of the sexual object. Masochism as a perversion seems further removed from the normal sexual goal than its opposite. It may even be doubted whether it ever is primary and whether it does not more often originate through transformation from sadism.[2] It can often be recog-

---

[1] Analysis reveals that this perversion—just as most others—has an unexpected multiplicity of motivations and meanings. Exhibitionism, for instance, is strongly dependent upon the castration complex; it would emphasize again the integrity of one's own (male) genitals and repeats the infantile satisfaction of the lack of the penis in the female.

[2] Later reflections which can be supported by definite evidence concerning the struc-

nized that masochism is nothing but a continuation of sadism directed against one's own person in which the latter at first takes the place of the sexual object. Clinical analysis of extreme cases of masochistic perversions show that there is a cooperation of a large series of factors which exaggerate and fix the original passive sexual attitude (castration complex, guilt).

The pain which is here overcome ranks with the loathing and shame which are the resistances opposed to the libido.

Sadism and masochism occupy a special place in the perversions, for the contrast of activity and passivity lying at their bases belong to the common traits of the sexual life.

That cruelty and the sexual instinct are most intimately connected is beyond doubt taught by the history of civilization, but in the explanation of this connection no one has gone beyond the accentuation of the aggressive factors of the libido. The aggression which is mixed with the sexual instinct is, according to some authors, a remnant of cannibalistic lust—that is, a participation of the domination apparatus, which serves also for the gratification of the other ontogenetically older great need.[1] It has also been claimed that every pain contains in itself the possibility of a pleasurable sensation. Let us be satisfied with the impression that the explanation given concerning this perversion is by no means satisfactory and that it is possible that many psychic strivings unite herein into one effect.[2]

The most striking peculiarity of this perversion lies in the fact that its active and passive forms are regularly encountered together in the same person. He who experiences pleasure by causing pain to others in sexual relations is also capable of experiencing pain in sexual relations as pleasure. A sadist is simultaneously a masochist, though either the active or the passive side of the perversion may be more strongly developed in him and thus, represent his preponderant sexual activity.[3]

---

ture of the mental systems and of the activities of instincts therein, have changed my judgment concerning masochism very widely. I have been led to recognize a primary erotogenic masochism from which there develops two later forms, a feminine, and a moral masochism. Through a turning back of an unconsumed sadism directed against oneself during life there arises a secondary masochism which is added to the primary masochism. (See Freud, Das ökonomische Problem des Masochismus, Int. Zeit. f. Psa., 10, 121, 1924. Translated into English in Collected Papers, Vol. 2, p. 255. Hogarth Press.)

[1] Cf. here the later studies on the pregenital phases of the sexual development, in which this view is confirmed.

[2] From the researches just cited, the contrasting pair, sadism-masochism, originates from a special source of impulses and is to be differentiated from the other "perversions."

[3] Instead of substantiating this statement by many examples, I will merely cite Havelock Ellis (The Sexual Impulse, 1903): "All known cases of sadism and masochism, even those cited by Krafft-Ebing always show (as has already been shown

We, thus, see that certain perverted tendencies regularly appear in contrasting pairs, which, in view of the material to be produced later, is of great theoretical value.[1] It is furthermore clear that the existence of the contrast, sadism and masochism, can not readily be attributed to the mixture of aggression. On the other hand, one may be tempted to connect such synchronously existing contrasts with the united contrast of male and female in bi-sexuality, the significance of which is reduced in psychoanalysis to the contrast of activity and passivity.

3. GENERAL STATEMENTS APPLICABLE TO ALL PERVERSIONS

Variation and Disease. The physicians who at first studied the *perversions* in pronounced cases and under peculiar conditions were naturally inclined to attribute to them the characteristic of morbidity or degeneracy similar to the *inversions*. This view, however, is easier to refute here than in the former case. Everyday experience has shown that most of these transgressions, at least the milder ones, are seldom lacking as components of the sexual life of normals who look upon them as upon other intimacies. Wherever the conditions are favorable, even a normal person may for a long time substitute such a perversion for the normal sexual aim or may put it side by side with it. In no normal person does the normal sexual aim lack some addenda which could be designated as perverse; a universality in itself shows the futility of applying opprobrious names to perversions. In the realm of the sexual life one is sure to meet with exceptional difficulties which are at present really unsolvable, if one wishes to draw a sharp line between the mere variations within physiological limits and morbid symptoms.

Nevertheless, the quality of the new sexual aim in some of these perversions is such as to require special consideration. Some of the perversions are so remote in content from the normal that we cannot help calling them "morbid." This is especially true of those in which the sexual instinct, in overcoming the resistances (shame, loathing, fear, and pain), has brought about surprising results (licking of feces and violation of cadavers). Yet, even in these cases one cannot feel certain of regularly finding among the perpetrators of such acts persons of pronounced abnormalities or insane minds. We cannot lose sight of the fact that persons who otherwise behave normally are sometimes recorded as sick in the realm of the sexual life, where they are dominated by the most unbridled of all instincts. On the other hand, a manifest abnormality in other relations of life will always show an undercurrent of abnormal sexual behavior.

---

by Colin, Scott, and Fere) traces of both groups of manifestations in the same individual."
[1] See later discussion of "Ambivalence."

In the majority of cases we are able to find the morbid character of the perversion not in the content of the new sexual aim, but in its relation to the normal. It is morbid if the perversion does not appear beside the normal (sexual aim and sexual object), where favorable circumstances promote it and unfavorable impede the normal, or if it has under all circumstances repressed and supplanted the normal. The *exclusiveness* and *fixation* of the perversion justifies us in considering it a morbid symptom.

The Psychic Participation in the Perversions. Perhaps, it is precisely that we must recognize the most prolific psychic participation for the transformation of the sexual instinct. In these cases a piece of psychic work has been accomplished in which, in spite of its gruesome success, the value of an idealization of the instinct cannot be disputed. The omnipotence of love nowhere perhaps shows itself stronger than in this one of her aberrations. The highest and lowest in sexuality are everywhere most intimately connected. ("From heaven through the world to hell.")

Two Results. In the study of perversions we have gained an insight into the fact that the sexual instinct has to struggle against certain psychic forces, resistances, among which shame and loathing are most prominent. We may presume that these forces are employed to restrict the instinct to the accepted normal limits, and as they have developed in the individual before the sexual instinct has attained its full strength, it is really they which have directed his course of development.[1]

We have, furthermore, remarked that some of the examined perversions can be comprehended only by assuming a union of many motives. If they are amenable to analysis—disintegration—they invariably show a composite nature. This may give us a hint that the sexual instinct itself may not be something simple, that it may, on the contrary, be composed of many components, some of which detach themselves to form perversions. Our clinical observation thus calls our attention to fusions, which have lost their expression in the uniform normal behavior.[2]

---

[1] On the other hand, the restricting forces of sexual evolution—disgust, shame, morality—must also be looked upon as historical precipitates of the outer inhibitions which the sexual instinct experienced in the psychogenesis of humanity. One can observe that they appear during the development of the individual as if they were spontaneously at the call of education and other influences.

[2] I wish to make a preliminary comment about the origin of the perversions. A disposition to normal sexual development exists before their fixation, exactly as in the case of fetichism. Analytical study has thus far been able to show in individual cases that the perversion is an arrest in the development of the Oedipus complex and following its repression—depending on their constitution, the strongest components of the sexual instinct reappear.

4. THE SEXUAL INSTINCT OF NEUROTICS

Psychoanalysis. A proper contribution to the knowledge of the sexual instinct in persons who are at least related to the normal can be gained only from one source, and is accessible only by one definite path. There is only one way to obtain a thorough and unerring solution of problems in the sexual life of so-called psychoneurotics (hysteria, obsessions, the wrongly named neurasthenia, and surely also dementia praecox and paranoia), and that is by subjecting them to that cathartic or psychoanalytic investigation, discovered by J. Breuer and me.[1]

I must repeat what I have said in other publications, that these psychoneuroses, as far as my experience goes, are based on motive powers of the sexual instinct. I do not mean that the energy of the sexual instinct merely contributes to the forces supporting the morbid manifestations (symptoms), but I advisedly maintain that this contribution supplies the only constant and most important source of energy in the neurosis. The sexual life of neurotics manifests itself either exclusively, preponderantly, or partially in these symptoms. As I have already stated in different places, the symptoms are the sexual activities of the patient. The proof for this assertion I have obtained from an increasing number of hysterics and other neurotics during a period of forty years. In individual cases I have already given these results in detail in other communications and hope to report other cases.[2]

Psychoanalysis abrogates the symptoms of hysteria on the supposition that they are the substitutes—the transcriptions as it were—for a series of emotionally accentuated psychic processes, wishes, and desires, to which a path of discharge through the conscious psychic activities has been closed by a special process (repression). These mental formations which are restricted to the unconscious state, strive for expression; that is, for *discharge,* in conformity to their affective value, and find such in hysteria through a process of *conversion* into somatic phenomena—the hysterical symptoms. If, *lege artis,* and with the aid of a special technique, retrogressive transformations of the symptoms into the affectual and conscious thoughts can be effected, it then becomes possible to get the most accurate information about the nature and origin of these previously unconscious psychic formations.

Results of Psychoanalysis. In this manner it has been discovered that the symptoms represent a substitute for strivings which received their force

[1] Breuer and Freud: Studies in Hysteria, translated by A. A. Brill.
[2] It is to add to rather than detract from this statement when I modify it as follows: Nervous symptoms depend on the one hand upon the claims of the libidinal impulses, on the other upon the protest of the Ego and its reactions against the same.

from the sexual instinct. This fully concurs with what we know of the character of hysterics, which we have taken as models for all psychoneurotics, before they have become sick, and with what we know concerning the causes of the disease. The hysterical character shows a fragment of *sexual repression,* which reaches beyond the normal limits. It is an exaggeration of the resistances against the sexual instinct which became known to us as shame and loathing. It is an instinctive flight from intellectual occupation with the sexual problem, the consequence of which in pronounced cases is a complete sexual ignorance, which is preserved until the age of sexual maturity is attained.[1]

This feature, so characteristic of hysteria, is not seldom concealed in crude observation by the existence of the second constitutional factor of hysteria, namely, an enormous development of sexual craving. But psychological analysis will always reveal it and thus solve the very contradictory enigma of hysteria by proving the existence of the contrasting pair, an immense sexual desire and a very exaggerated sexual rejection.

The provocation of the disease in hysterically predisposed persons is brought about, if in consequence of their progressive maturity or external conditions of life they are earnestly confronted with the real sexual demand. Between the pressure of the craving and the opposition of the sexual rejection an outlet for the disease results, which does not remove the conflict, but seeks to elude it by transforming the libidinal strivings into symptoms. It is an exception only in appearance if a hysterical person, say a man, becomes subject to some banal emotional disturbance, to a conflict in the center of which there is no sexual interest. Psychoanalysis will regularly show that it is the sexual components of the conflicts which make the disease possible by withdrawing the psychic processes from normal adjustment.

Neurosis and Perversion. A great part of the opposition to this assertion of mine is explained by the fact that the sexuality from which I deduce the psychoneurotic symptoms is thought of as coincident with the normal sexual instinct. But psychoanalysis teaches us more than that. It shows that the symptoms do not by any means result at the expense only of the so-called normal sexual instinct (at least not exclusively or preponderately), but they represent the converted expression of impulses which in a broader sense might be designated as *perverse* if they could manifest themselves directly in phantasies and acts without deviating from consciousness. The symptoms are, therefore, partially formed at the cost of

[1] Studies in Hysteria (Nervous and Mental Disease Monograph Series, No. 40), J. Breuer tells of the patient with whom he first practised the cathartic method: "The sexual factor was surprisingly undeveloped."

abnormal sexuality. *The neurosis is, so to say, the negative of the perversion.*[1]

The sexual instinct of the psychoneurotic shows all the aberrations which we have studied as variations of the normal and as manifestations of morbid sexual life.

(a) In all neurotics we find without exception in the unconscious psychic life feelings of inversion and fixation of libido on persons of the same sex. Without a deep and searching discussion, it is impossible adequately to appreciate the significance of this factor for the formation of the picture of the disease; I can only assert that the unconscious tendency to inversion is never wanting, and renders the greatest service, especially in the explanation of male hysteria.[2]

(b) All the tendencies to anatomical transgression can be demonstrated in psychoneurotics in the unconscious, and as symptom-creators. Of special frequency and intensity are those which impart to the mouth and the mucous membrane of the anus the rôle of genitals.

(c) The partial impulses which usually appear in contrasting pairs play a very prominent rôle in the symptom-formations of the psychoneuroses. We have learned to know them as carriers of new sexual aims, such as a mania for looking, exhibitionism, and the actively and passively formed impulses of cruelty. The contribution of the last is indispensable for the understanding of the morbid nature of the symptoms; it almost regularly controls some portion of the social behavior of the patient. The transformation of love into hatred, of tenderness into hostility, which is characteristic of a large number of neurotic cases and apparently of all cases of paranoia, takes place by means of the union of cruelty with libido.

The interest in these deductions will be more heightened by certain peculiarities of the actual facts.

a. Wherever such impulse is found in the unconscious which can be paired with a contrast, one can regularly demonstrate that the latter, too, is effective. Every "active" perversion is here accompanied by its passive counterpart. He who in the unconscious is an exhibitionist is at the same time a voyeur, he who suffers from sadistic feelings as a result of repres-

---

[1] The well known fancies of perverts which under favorable conditions may be changed into actions, the delusional fears of paranoiacs which are in a hostile manner projected on others, and the unconscious fancies of hysterics which are discovered in their symptoms by psychoanalysis, agree as to content in the minutest details.
[2] A psychoneurosis very often associates itself with a manifest inversion, in which the heterosexual feeling becomes subjected to complete repression.—It is but just to state that the necessity of a general recognition of the tendency to inversion in psychoneurotics was first imparted to me personally by Wilh. Fliess of Berlin, after I had myself discovered it in some cases. This fact, not sufficiently valued, must markedly influence all theories of homosexuality.

sion will also show another reinforcement of the symptoms from the source of masochistic tendencies. The perfect concurrence with the behavior of the corresponding positive perversions is certainly very noteworthy. In the picture of the disease, however, the preponderant rôle is played by either one or the other of the opposing tendencies.

b. In a pronounced case of psychoneurosis we seldom find the development of one single perverted impulse; usually, there are many and regularly there are traces of all perversions. The individual impulse, however, on account of its intensity, is independent of the development of the others, but the study of the positive perversions gives us the accurate counterparts.

5. PARTIAL IMPULSES AND EROGENOUS ZONES

Keeping in mind what we have learned from the examination of the positive and negative perversions, it becomes quite obvious that they be traced back to a number of "partial impulses," which are not, however, primary, but can be subjected to further analysis. By an "instinct" we can understand in the first place nothing but the psychic representative of a continually flowing inner somatic source of stimulation which is to be distinguished from a "stimulus" which comes from combined external excitations. "Instinct" is, thus, one of the concepts marking the limits between the psychic and the physical. The simplest and most obvious assumption concerning the nature of instincts would be that in themselves they possess no quality but only manifest themselves as a measure of laborious effort in the psychic life. What distinguishes the instincts from one another and furnishes them with specific attributes is their relation to their somatic sources and to their *aims*. The source of the instinct is an exciting process in an organ, and the immediate aim of the instinct lies in the release of this organic stimulus.[1]

A further provisional assumption in the theory of the instincts, which we cannot relinquish, states that from the bodily organs two kinds of excitation arise which are founded upon differences of a chemical nature. One of these forms of overstimulation can be designated as specifically sexual, and the concerned organ as an *erogenous zone*, while the sexual element emanating from it is a partial impulse.[2]

[1] The science of the instincts is the most significant, but the most incomplete part of the psychoanalytic theory. In my later works (Jenseits des Lustprinzips—Beyond the Pleasure Principle—English trans., Boni and Liveright, N. Y., and Das Ich und Das Es, 1925, The Ego and the Id, English trans., Internat. Psychoanalytic Press, London), I have developed further contributions to the study of the instincts.
[2] It is not easy to justify here these assumptions which are taken from a definite class of neurotic diseases. On the other hand, it would be impossible to assert anything definite concerning the instincts if one did not take the trouble of mentioning these presuppositions.

In the perversions which claim sexual significance for the oral cavity and the anal opening, the part played by the erogenous zones is quite obvious. The latter behave in every way like a part of the sexual apparatus. In hysteria these parts of the body, as well as the tracts of mucous membrane proceeding from them, become the seat of new sensations and innervating changes in a manner similar to the real genitals when under the excitement of normal sexual processes.

In the psychoneuroses the significance of the erogenous zones as additional apparatus and substitutes for the genitals, appears to be most prominent in hysteria though that does not signify that it is of lesser validity in the other morbid forms. It is not so recognizable in compulsion neurosis and paranoia because their symptom formation takes place in regions of the psychic apparatus which lie at a great distance from the central locations for bodily control. What is more remarkable in the compulsion neurosis is the significance of the impulses which create new sexual aims and appear independently of the erogenous zones. Nevertheless, the eye corresponds to an erogenous zone in the looking and exhibition mania, while the skin takes on the same part in the pain and cruelty components of the sexual instinct. The skin, which in special parts of the body has become differentiated as sensory organs and changed to mucous membrane, is the erogenous zone, κατ ἐξοχήν.[1]

6. EXPLANATION OF THE SEEMING PREPONDERANCE OF SEXUAL PERVERSIONS IN THE PSYCHONEUROSES

The sexuality of psychoneurotics has perhaps been placed in a false light by the above discussions. It appears that the sexual behavior of the psychoneurotic approaches in predisposition to the pervert and deviates by just as much from the normal. Nevertheless, it is very possible that the constitutional disposition of these patients besides containing an immense amount of sexual repression and a predominant force of sexual instinct also possesses an unusual tendency to perversions in the broadest sense. However, an examination of milder cases shows that the last assumption is not an absolute requisite, or at least that in pronouncing judgment on the morbid effects one ought to discount the effect of one of the factors. In most psychoneurotics, the disease first appears after puberty following the demands of the normal sexual life. Against these the repression above all directs itself. Or the disease comes on later, owing to the fact that the libido is unable to attain normal sexual gratification. In both cases the libido behaves like a stream, the principal bed of which is dammed; it fills the collateral roads which until now perhaps have been empty. Thus,

[1] One should think here of Moll's assertion, which divides the sexual instinct into the impulses of *contrectation* and detumescence. *Contrectation* signifies a desire to touch the skin.

the manifestly great (though to be sure negative) tendency to perversion in psychoneurotics may be collaterally increased. The fact of the matter is that sexual repression has to be added as an inner factor to such external ones as restriction of freedom, inaccessibility to the normal sexual object, dangers of the normal sexual act, etc., which cause the origin of perversions in individuals who might have otherwise remained normal.

In individual cases of neurosis the behavior may be different; now the congenital force of the tendency to perversion may be more decisive, and at other times more influence may be exerted by the collateral increase of the same through the deviation of the libido from the normal sexual aim and object. It would be unjust to construe where a coöperation exists. The greatest results are at all times produced in a neurosis if constitution and experience coöperate in the same direction. A pronounced constitution may perhaps be able to dispense with the assistance of life's impressions, while a profound disturbance in life may perhaps bring on a neurosis even in an average constitution. These views similarly hold true in the etiological importance of congenital and accidental experiences in other spheres.

If, however, preference is given to the assumption that an especially formed tendency to perversions is characteristic of the psychoneurotic constitution, there is a prospect of being able to distinguish a multiformity of such constitutions in accordance with the congenital preponderance of this or that erogenous zone, or of this or that partial impulse. Whether there is a special relationship between the predisposition to perversions and the selection of the morbid picture has not, like many other things in this realm, been investigated.

7. REFERENCE TO THE INFANTILISM OF SEXUALITY

By demonstrating perverted feelings as symptom-formations in psychoneurotics, we have enormously increased the number of persons who can be added to the classification or group of perverts. This is not only because neurotics represent a very large proportion of humanity, but we must consider also that the neuroses in all their gradations run in an uninterrupted series to the normal state. Moebius was quite justified in saying that we are all somewhat hysterical. Hence, the very wide dissemination of perversions is no rare peculiarity, but must form a part of the normally accepted constitution.

We have heard that it is a question whether perversions may be referred to congenital determinants or whether they can originate from accidental experiences, just as Binet showed in fetichisms. Now we are forced to the conclusion that there is indeed something congenital at the basis of perversions, but it is something *which is congenital in all persons;* which as a predisposition may fluctuate in intensity, and that it is brought into prominence by influences of life. We deal here with congenital roots in the constitution of the sexual instinct, which in one series of cases develop into real carriers of sexual activity (perverts); while in other cases they undergo an insufficient suppression (repression), so that as morbid symptoms they are capable of attracting to themselves in a roundabout way a considerable part of the sexual energy; while again in favorable cases between the two extremes, they give origin to the normal sexual life through effective restrictions and other elaborations.

But we must also remember that the assumed constitution which shows the roots of all perversions will be demonstrable only in the child, albeit all impulses manifest themselves in him only in moderate intensity. If we are led to suppose that neurotics conserve the infantile state of their sexuality or return to it, our interest must then turn to the sexual life of the child, and we will then follow the play of influences which control the processes of development of the infantile sexuality up to its termination in a perversion, a neurosis or a normal sexual life.

CONTRIBUTION II

INFANTILE SEXUALITY

The Neglect of the Infantile. It is a part of popular belief about the sexual instinct that it is absent in childhood and that it first appears in the period of life known as puberty. This, though a common error, is serious in its consequences and is chiefly due to our ignorance of the fundamental principles of the sexual life. A comprehensive study of the sexual manifestations of childhood would probably reveal to us the essential features of the sexual instinct and would show us its development and its composition from various sources.

It is quite remarkable that those writers who endeavor to explain the qualities and reactions of the adult individual have given so much more attention to the ancestral period than to the period of the individual's own existence—that is, they have attributed more influence to heredity than to childhood. As a matter of fact, it might well be supposed that the influence of the latter period would be easier to understand, and that it would be entitled to more consideration than heredity.[1] To be sure, one occasionally finds in medical literature notes on the premature sexual activities of small children, about erections and masturbation and even reactions resembling coitus, but these are referred to merely as exceptional occurrences, as curiosities, or as deterring examples of premature perversity. No author has, to my knowledge, recognized the normality of the sexual instinct in childhood, and in the numerous writings on the development of the child the chapter on "Sexual Development" is usually passed over.[2]

---

[1] For it is hardly possible to have a correct knowledge of the part belonging to heredity without first understanding the part belonging to childhood.

[2] On revision, this assertion seemed even to myself so bold that I decided to test its correctness by again reviewing the literature. The result of this second review did not warrant any change in my original statement. The scientific elaboration of the physical as well as the psychic phenomena of the infantile sexuality is still in its initial stages. One author (S. Bell, "A Preliminary Study of the Emotions of Love Between the Sexes," American Journal of Psychology, XIII, 1902) says: "I know of no scientist who has given a careful analysis of the emotion as it is seen in the adolescent." The only attention given to somatic sexual manifestations occurring

Infantile Amnesia. The reason for this remarkable negligence I seek partly in conventional considerations, which influence writers because of their own bringing up, and partly to a psychic phenomenon which thus far has remained unexplained. I refer to the peculiar amnesia which veils from most people (not from all) the first years of their childhood, usually the first six or eight years. So far, it has not occurred to us that this amnesia should surprise us, though we have good reasons for it. For we are informed that during those years which have left nothing except a few incomprehensible memory fragments, we have vividly reacted to impressions, that we have manifested human pain and pleasure and that we have expressed love, jealousy and other passions as they then affected us. Indeed, we are told that we have uttered remarks which proved to grownups that we possessed understanding and a budding power of judgment. Still we know nothing of all this when we become older. Why does our memory lag behind all our other psychic activities? We really have reason to believe that at no time of life are we more capable of impressions and reproductions than during the years of childhood.[1]

On the other hand we must assume, or we may convince ourselves through psychological observations on others, that the very impressions which we have forgotten have nevertheless left the deepest traces in our

---

before the age of puberty have been in connection with degenerative manifestations, and these were referred to as signs of degeneration. A chapter on the sexual life of children is not to be found in all the representative psychologies of this age which I have read. Among these works I can mention the following: Preyer, Baldwin (The Development of the Mind in the Child and in the Race, 1898); Perez, (L'enfant de 3–7 ans, 1894); Strümpell (Die pädagogische Pathologie, 1899); Karl Groos (Das Seelenleben des Kindes, 1904); Th. Heller (Grundriss der Heilpädagogik, 1904); Sully (Observations Concerning Childhood, 1897); and others. The best impression of the present situation of this sphere can be obtained from the journal Die Kinderfehler (issued since 1896).—On the other hand, one gains the impression that the existence of love in childhood is in no need of demonstration. Perez (l.c.) speaks for it', K. Groos (Die Spiele der Menschen, 1899) states that some children are very early subject to sexual emotions, and show a desire to touch the other sex (p. 336); S. Bell observed the earliest appearance of sex-love in a child during the middle part of its third year. See also Havelock Ellis, The Sexual Impulse. Appendix II.

The above-mentioned judgment concerning the literature of infantile sexuality no longer holds true since the appearance of the great and important work of G. Stanley Hall (Adolescence, Its Psychology and its Relation to Physiology, Anthropology, Sociology, Sex, Crime, Religion and Education, 2 vols., New York, 1908). The recent book of A. Moll, Das Sexualleben des Kindes, Berlin, 1909, offers no occasion for such a modification. See, on the other hand, Bleuler, Sexuelle Abnormitäten der Kinder (Jahrbuch der Schweizerischen Gesellschaft für Schulgesundheitsflege, IX, 1908). A book by Mrs. Dr. H. v. Hug-Hellmuth, Aus dem Seelenleben des Kindes (1913), has taken full account of the neglected sexual factors. (Translated in Monograph Series, No. 29.)

However, since Freud's ideas have been spread in English-speaking countries, many works made their appearance which deal directly or indirectly with the sexual life of the child. (Editor's note.)

[1] I have attempted to solve the problems presented by the earliest infantile recollections in *The Psychopathology of Everyday Life.*

psychic life, and acted as determinants for our whole future development. We conclude therefore that we do not deal with a real forgetting of infantile impressions but rather with an amnesia similar to that observed in neurotics for later experiences, the nature of which consists in their being kept away from consciousness (repression). But what forces bring about this repression of the infantile impressions? He who can solve this riddle will also explain hysterical amnesia.

We shall not, however, hesitate to assert that the existence of the infantile amnesia gives us a new point of comparison between the psychic states of the child and those of the psychoneurotic. We have already encountered another point of comparison when confronted by the fact that the sexuality of the psychoneurotic preserves the infantile character or has returned to it. May there not be an ultimate connection between the infantile and the hysterical amnesias?

The connection between infantile and hysterical amnesias is really more than a mere play of wit. Hysterical amnesia which serves the repression can only be explained by the fact that the individual already possesses a sum of memories which were withdrawn from conscious disposal and which by associative connection now seize that which is acted upon by the repelling forces of the repression emanating from consciousness.[1] We may say that without infantile amnesia there would be no hysterical amnesia.

I therefore believe that the infantile amnesia which causes the individual to look upon his childhood as if it were a *prehistoric* time and conceals from him the beginning of his own sexual life—that this amnesia, is responsible for the fact that one does not usually attribute any value to the infantile period in the development of the sexual life. One single observer cannot fill the gap which has been thus produced in our knowledge. As early as 1896, I had already emphasized the significance of childhood for the origin of certain important phenomena connected with the sexual life, and since then I have not ceased to put into the foreground the importance of the infantile factor for sexuality.

THE SEXUAL LATENCY PERIOD OF CHILDHOOD AND ITS INTERRUPTIONS

The extraordinary frequent discoveries of apparently abnormal and exceptional sexual manifestations in childhood, as well as the discovery of infantile reminiscences in neurotics, which were hitherto unconscious, allow us to sketch the following picture of the sexual behavior of child-

[1] One cannot understand the mechanism of repression if one takes into consideration only one of the two coöperating processes. As a comparison one may think of the way the tourist is despatched to the top of the great pyramid of Gizeh; he is pushed from below and pulled from above.

hood.[1] It seems certain that the newborn child brings with it the germs of sexual feelings which continue to develop for some time and then succumb to a progressive suppression, which may in turn be broken through by the regular advances of the sexual development or may be checked by individual idiosyncrasies. Nothing is known concerning the laws and periodicity of this oscillating course of development. It seems, however, that the sexual life of the child mostly manifests itself in the third or fourth year in some form accessible to observation.[2]

Sexual Inhibition. It is during this period of total or at least partial latency that the psychic forces develop which later act as inhibitions on the sexual life, and narrow its direction like dams. These psychic forces are loathing, shame, and moral and esthetic ideal demands. We may gain the impression that the erection of these dams in the civilized child is the work of education; and surely education contributes much to it. In reality, however, this development is organically determined and can occasionally be produced without the help of education. Indeed education remains properly within its assigned domain if it strictly follows the path laid out by the organic, and only imprints it somewhat cleaner and deeper.

[1] The use of the latter material is justified by the fact that the years of childhood of those who are later neurotics need not necessarily differ from those who are later normal except in intensity and distinctness.

[2] An anatomic analogy to the behavior of the infantile sexual function formulated by me is perhaps given by Bayer (Deutsches Archiv. für klinische Medizin, Bd. 73) who claims that the internal genitals (uterus) are regularly larger in newborn than in older children. However, Halban's conception, that after birth there is also an involution of the other parts of the sexual apparatus, has not been verified. According to Halban (Zeitschrift für Geburtshilfe u. Gynäkologie, LIII, 1904), this process of involution ends after a few weeks of extra-uterine life. The authors who regard the interstitial portions of the sex glands as the sex-determining organs have been led through their anatomical study to discuss for their part infantile sexuality and the sexual latency periods.

I cite from page 20 of Lipschütz's book on the Puberty Glands. "One would more correctly represent the facts by saying that the maturing of the sexual characteristics as seen fully in puberty, depends upon the increasingly rapid development of processes which have begun much earlier—according to our opinion even in embryonal life." (p. 169). *"What one heretofore has designated—and badly—as puberty, is probably only a second great phase of puberty which sets in in the middle of the second decade of life.*—Childhood reckoned from birth to the second great phase we can thus designate as an intermediary phase of puberty."—In a *referat* of Ferenczi (Int. Zeit. f. Psa., 6, 1920) this general correspondence between anatomical finding and psychological observation is disturbed by the one statement that the *"first apex"* of development of the sexual organs takes place in the earliest embryonal time, whereas the early blossoming of the sexual life of the child is to be found in the third and fourth year. The complete synchronization of anatomical preparation and psychical development is naturally not necessary. The pertinent investigations have still to be made upon the gonads of humans. Since in animals there is no latency period in the psychological sense, much is still to be learned as to whether the anatomical findings upon which foundations the authors assume two points of apical growth in the sexual development, can be demonstrated also on the other higher animals.

Reaction Formation and Sublimation. What are the means that accomplish these very important constructions so important for the later personal culture and normality? They are probably brought about at the cost of the infantile sexuality itself. The influx of this sexuality does not stop even in this latency period, but its energy is deflected either wholly or partially from sexual utilization and conducted to other aims. The historians of civilization seem to be unanimous in the opinion that such deflection of sexual motive powers from sexual aims to new aims, a process which merits the name of *sublimation,* has furnished powerful components for all cultural accomplishments. We will, therefore, add that the same process acts in the development of every individual, and that it begins to act in the sexual latency period.[1]

We can also venture an opinion about the mechanisms of such sublimation. The sexual feelings of these infantile years would on the one hand be unusable, since the procreating functions are postponed—this is the chief character of the latency period; on the other hand, they would as such be perverse, as they would emanate from erogenous zones and from impulses which in the individual's course of development could only evoke a feeling of displeasure. They, therefore, awaken psychic counterforces (feelings of reaction), which build up the already mentioned psychical dams of disgust, shame and morality.[2]

The Interruptions of the Latency Period. Without deluding ourselves as to the hypothetical nature and deficient clearness of our understanding regarding the infantile period of latency and delay, we will return to reality and state that such a utilization of the infantile sexuality represents an ideal bringing up from which the development of the individual usually deviates in some measure, often very considerably. A part of the sexual manifestation which has withdrawn from sublimation occasionally breaks through, or a sexual activity remains throughout the whole duration of the latency period until the reinforced breaking through of the sexual instinct in puberty. In so far as they have paid any attention to infantile sexuality, the educators behave as if they shared our views concerning the formation of the moral defense forces at the cost of sexuality. They seem to know that sexual activity makes the child uneducable, for they consider all sexual manifestations of the child as an "evil" in the face of which little can be accomplished. We have, however, every reason for directing our attention to those phenomena so much feared by the

---

[1] The expression, "sexual latency period," I have borrowed from W. Fliess.
[2] In the case here discussed, sublimation of the sexual motive powers proceeds on the road of reaction formations. But in general, it is necessary to separate sublimation from reaction formation. They are two diverse processes. Sublimation may also result through other and simpler mechanisms.

educators, for we expect to find in them the solution of the primary structure of the sexual instinct.

THE MANIFESTATIONS OF INFANTILE SEXUALITY

Thumbsucking. For reasons which we shall discuss later, we will take as a model of the infantile sexual manifestations thumbsucking, to which the Hungarian pediatrist, Lindner, has devoted an excellent essay.[1]

Thumbsucking, which manifests itself in the nursing baby and which may be continued till maturity or throughout life, consists in a rhythmic repetition of sucking contact with the mouth (the lips), wherein the purpose of taking nourishment is excluded. A part of the lip itself, the tongue, which is another preferable skin region within reach, and even the big toe —may be taken as objects for sucking. Simultaneously, there is also a desire to grasp things, which manifests itself in a rhythmical pulling of the ear lobe and which may cause the child to grasp a part of another person (generally the ear) for the same purpose. The pleasure-sucking is connected with a full absorption of attention and leads to sleep or even to a motor reaction in the form of an orgasm.[2] Pleasure-sucking is often combined with a rubbing contact with certain sensitive parts of the body, such as the breast and external genitals. It is by this path that many children go from thumbsucking to masturbation.

Lindner himself clearly recognized the sexual nature of this activity and openly emphasized it. In the nursery, thumbsucking is often treated in the same way as any other sexual "naughtiness" of the child. A very strong objection was raised against this view by many pediatrists and neurologists, which in part is certainly due to the confusion between the terms "sexual" and "genital." This contradiction raises the difficult question, which cannot be avoided, namely, in what general traits do we wish to recognize the sexual expression of the child. I believe that the association of the manifestations into which we have gained an insight through psychoanalytic investigation justifies us in claiming thumbsucking as a sexual activity. Through thumbsucking we can study directly the essential features of infantile sexual activities.[3]

[1] Jahrbuch für Kinderheilkunde, N. F., XIV, 1879.

[2] This already shows what holds true for the whole life, namely, that sexual gratification is the best hypnotic. Most nervous insomnias are traced to lack of sexual gratification. It is also known that unscrupulous nurses calm crying children to sleep by stroking their genitals.

[3] In 1919, a Dr. Galant (Neurol. Zentralb., No. 20), under the title "Das Lütscherli," published the confession of a grown-up girl who had not given up this childish sexual activity and described the pleasure of thumbsucking as completely analogous to a sexual gratification, especially to that of a kiss from her lover. "Not all kisses equal thumbsucking, no, no, by no means all. One cannot describe the enjoyment that goes through the entire body when one sucks one's thumb: one is far from this world; one is absolutely satisfied and supremely happy. It is a wonderful feeling. One only

Autoerotism. It is our duty here to devote more time to this manifestation. Let us emphasize the most striking character of this sexual activity which is, that the impulse is not directed to other persons but that the child gratifies himself on his own body; to use the happy term invented by Havelock Ellis, we will say that he is *autoerotic.*[1]

It is, moreover, clear that the action of the thumbsucking child is determined by the fact that he seeks a pleasure which he has already experienced and now remembers. Through the rhythmic sucking on a portion of the skin or mucous membrane, he finds gratification in the simplest way. It is also easy to conjecture on what occasions the child first experienced this pleasure which he now strives to renew. The first and most important activity in the child's life, the sucking from the mother's breast (or its substitute), must have acquainted him with this pleasure. We would say that the child's lips behaved like an *erogenous zone,* and that the stimulus from the warm stream of milk was really the cause of the pleasurable sensation. To be sure, the gratification of the erogenous zone was at first united with the gratification of the need for nourishment. The sexual activity leans first on one of the self-preservative functions and only later makes itself independent of it. He who sees a satiated child sink back from the mother's breast and fall asleep with reddened cheeks and blissful smile, will have to admit that this picture remains as typical of the expression of sexual gratification in later life. But the desire for repetition of sexual gratification is then separated from the desire for taking nourishment; a separation which becomes unavoidable with the appearance of teeth when the nourishment is no longer sucked but chewed. The child does not make use of a strange object for sucking but prefers his own skin, because it is more convenient, because it thus makes himself independent of the outer world which he cannot control, and because in this way he creates for himself, as it were, a second, even if an inferior, erogenous zone. This inferiority of this second region urges him later to seek the same parts, the lips of another person. ("It is a pity that I cannot kiss myself," might be attributed to him.)

Not all children suck their thumbs. It may be assumed that it is found only in children in whom the erogenous significance of the lip-zone is constitutionally reinforced. If the latter is retained in some children, they develop into kissing epicures with a tendency to perverse kissing, or as men, they show a strong desire for drinking and smoking. But should

---

wishes quiet; quiet that nothing can interrupt. It is simply indescribably wonderful; one feels no pain, no sorrow, and oh! one is transported into another world."

[1] H. Ellis has utilized the term *autoerotic* somewhat differently. He expresses the idea of a stimulus which does not come from the outside, but rather from within. For psychoanalysis it is not the genesis but the relationship to the object which is of most significance.

repression come into play, they then show disgust for eating and evince hysterical vomiting. By virtue of the community of the lip-zone, the repression encroaches upon the instinct of nourishment. Many of my female patients showing disturbances in eating, such as *hysterical globus,* choking sensations and vomiting have been energetic thumbsuckers in infancy.

In thumbsucking or pleasure-sucking, we are already able to observe the three essential characters of an infantile sexual manifestation. It has its origin in an *anaclitic* [1] relation to a physical function which is very important for life; it does not yet know any sexual object, that is, it is *autoerotic,* and its sexual aim is under the control of an *erogenous zone.* Let us assume for the present that these characteristics also hold true for most of the other activities of the infantile sexual instinct.

THE SEXUAL AIM OF THE INFANTILE SEXUALITY

Characteristic Erogenous Zones. From the example of thumbsucking, we may gather a great many points useful for distinguishing an erogenous zone. It is a portion of skin or mucous membrane in which stimuli produce a feeling of pleasure of definite quality. There is no doubt that the pleasure-producing stimuli are governed by special conditions; as yet we do not know them. The rhythmic characters must play some part and this strongly suggests an analogy to tickling. It does not, however, appear so certain whether the character of the pleasurable feeling evoked by the stimulus can be designated as "peculiar," and in what part of this peculiarity the sexual factor consists. Psychology is still groping in the dark when it concerns matters of pleasure and pain, and the most cautious assumption is therefore the most advisable. We may perhaps later come upon reasons which seem to support the peculiar quality of the sensation of pleasure.

The erogenous quality may adhere most notably to definite regions of the body. As is shown by the example of thumbsucking, there are predestined erogenous zones. But the same example also shows that any other region of skin or mucous membrane may assume the function of an erogenous zone, hence it must bring along a certain adaptability for it. The production of the sensation of pleasure therefore depends more on the quality of the stimulus than on the nature of the bodily region. The thumbsucking child looks around on his body and selects any portion of it for pleasure-sucking, and becoming accustomed to this particular part, he then prefers it. If he accidentally strikes upon a predestined region, such as breast, nipple or genitals, it naturally gets the preference. A very analogous tendency to displacement is again found in the symptomatology

---

[1] From the verb, *anaclino,* leaning on.

ɔf hysteria. In this neurosis, the repression mostly affects the genital zones proper, and they in turn transmit their excitability to the other zones which are usually dormant in adult life, but then behave exactly like genitals. But besides this, just as in thumbsucking, any other region of the body may become endowed with the excitation of the genitals and raised to an erogenous zone. Erogenous and hysterogenous zones show the same characters.[1]

The Infantile Sexual Aim. The sexual aim of the infantile impulse consists in the production of gratification through the proper excitation of this or that selected erogenous zone. To have a desire for its repetition, this gratification must have been previously experienced, and we may be sure that nature has devised definite means so as not to leave this experience of gratification to mere chance.[2] The arrangement which has fulfilled this purpose for the lip-zone, we have already discussed; it is the simultaneous connection of this part of the body with the taking of nourishment. We shall also meet other similar mechanisms as sources of sexuality. The state of desire for repetition of gratification can be recognized through a peculiar feeling of tension which in itself is rather of a painful character, and through a *centrally-conditioned* feeling of itching or sensitiveness which is projected into the peripheral erogenous zone. The sexual aim may therefore be formulated by stating that the main object is to substitute for the projected feeling of sensitiveness in the erogenous zone that outer stimulus which removes the feeling of sensitiveness by evoking the feeling of gratification. This external stimulus consists usually in ɑ manipulation which is analogous to sucking.

It is in full accord with our physiological knowledge, if the need happens to be awakened also peripherally, through an actual change in the erogenous zone. The action is puzzling only to some extent, as one stimulus ⁿeems to want another applied to the same place for its own abrogation.

THE MASTURBATIC SEXUAL MANIFESTATIONS [3]

It is a matter of great satisfaction to know that there is nothing further of great importance to learn about the sexual activity of the child, after the impulse of one erogenous zone has become comprehensible to us. The most pronounced differences are found in the action necessary for the

---

[1] Further reflection and evaluation of other observations lead me to attribute the quality of erotism to all parts of the body and inner organs. See later on narcissism.
[2] The use of teleological forms of thought in biological explanations can hardly be avoided even though it is recognized that in individual cases, one is not secure against error.
[3] Compare here the very comprehensive but confusing literature on masturbation, e.g., Rohleder, *Die Masturbation*, 1899. Cf. also the pamphlet, *Die Onanie*, which contains the discussion of the Vienna Psychoanalytic Society, Wiesbaden, 1912.

gratification, which consists in sucking for the lip-zone, and which must be replaced by other muscular actions in the other zones, depending on their situation and nature.

The Activity of the Anal Zone. Like the lip-zone, the anal zone is, through its position, adapted to produce an anaclisis of sexuality to other func-tions of the body. It should be assumed that the erogenous significance of this region of the body was originally very strong. Through psychoanaly-sis, one finds, not without surprise, the many transformations that nor-mally take place in the sexual excitations emanating from here, and that this zone often retains for life a considerable fragment of genital irrita-bility.[1] The intestinal catarrhs which occur quite frequently during in-fancy, produce sensitive irritations in this zone, and we often hear it said that intestinal catarrh at this delicate age causes "nervousness." In later neurotic diseases, they exert a definite influence on the symptomatic ex-pression of the neurosis, placing at its disposal the whole sum of intes-tinal disturbances. Considering the erogenous significance of the anal zone which has been retained at least in transformation, one should not laugh at the hemorrhoidal influences to which the old medical literature attached so much weight in the explanation of neurotic states.

Children utilizing the erogenous sensitiveness of the anal zone, can be recognized by their holding back of fecal masses until through accumu-lation there result violent muscular contractions; the passage of these masses through the anus is apt to produce a marked irritation of the mucous membrane. Besides the pain, this must also produce a sensation of pleasure. One of the surest premonitions of later eccentricity or nerv-ousness is when an infant obstinately refuses to empty his bowel when placed on the chamber by the nurse, and controls this function at his own pleasure. It naturally does not concern him that he will soil his bed; all he cares for is not to lose the subsidiary pleasure in defecating. Educators have again shown the right inkling when they designate children who withhold these functions as naughty.

The content of the bowel which acts as a stimulus to the sexually sensi-tive surface of mucous membrane, behaves like the precursor of another organ which does not become active until after the phase of childhood. In addition, it has other important meanings to the nursling. It is evi-dently treated as an additional part of the body; it represents the first "donation," the disposal of which expresses the pliability while the re-tention of it can express the spite of the little being towards his environ-

---

[1] Compare here my essay on *Charakter und Analerotik* and *Ueber Triebsumsetz-ungen insbesondere der Analerotik* (G. S. 5). Both in English in Collected Papers II, Hogarth Press, London. Cf. also Brill, *Psychoanalysis,* Chap. XIII, *Anal Eroticism and Character,* W. B. Saunders, Philadelphia.

ment. From the idea of "donation," he later derives the meaning of the "babe," which according to one of the infantile sexual theories, is supposed to be acquired through eating, and born through the bowel. The retention of fecal masses, which is at first intentional in order to utilize them, as it were, for masturbatic excitation of the anal zone, is at least one of the roots of constipation so frequent in neurotics. The whole significance of the anal zone is mirrored in the fact that there are but few neurotics who have not their special scatologic customs, ceremonies, etc., which they retain with cautious secrecy.

Real masturbatic irritation of the anal zone by means of the fingers, evoked through either centrally or peripherally supported itching, is not at all rare in older children.

The Activity of the Genital Zone. Among the erogenous zones of the child's body, there is one which certainly does not play the first rôle, and which cannot be the carrier of the earliest sexual feeling, which, however, is destined for great things in later life. In both male and female, it is connected with the voiding of urine (penis, clitoris), and in the former, it is enclosed in a sack of mucous membrane, probably in order not to miss the irritations caused by the secretions which may arouse sexual excitement at an early age. The sexual activities of this erogenous zone, which belongs to the real genitals, are the beginning of the later "normal" sexual life.

Owing to the anatomical position, the overflowing of secretions, the washing and rubbing of the body, and to certain accidental excitements (the wandering of intestinal worms in the girl), it happens that the pleasurable feeling which these parts of the body are capable of producing makes itself noticeable to the child, even during the sucking age, and thus awakens a desire for repetition. When we consider the sum of all these arrangements and bear in mind that the measures for cleanliness hardly produce a different result than uncleanliness, we can scarcely ignore the fact that the infantile masturbation from which hardly anyone escapes, forms the foundation for the future primacy of this erogenous zone for sexual activity. The action of removing the stimulus and setting free the gratification consists in a rubbing contiguity with the hand or in a certain previously-formed pressure reflex, effected by the closure of the thighs. The latter procedure seems to be the more common in girls. The preference for the hand in boys already indicates what an important part of the male sexual activity will be accomplished in the future by the mastery impulse (Bemächtigungstrieb).[1]

---

[1] Unusual techniques in the performance of masturbation in later years seem to point to the influence of a prohibition against masturbation which has been overcome.

I can only make it clearer if I state that the infantile masturbation should be divided into three phases. The first phase belongs to the nursing period, the second to the short flourishing period of sexual activity at about the fourth year, and only the third corresponds to the one which is often considered exclusively as masturbation of puberty.

Second Phase of Childhood Masturbation. Infantile masturbation seems to disappear after a brief time, but it may continue uninterruptedly till puberty and thus represent the first marked deviation from that development which is desirable for civilized man. At some time during childhood after the nursing period, the sexual instinct of the genitals re-awakens and continues active for some time until it is again suppressed, or it may continue without interruption. The possible relations are very diverse and can only be elucidated through a more precise analysis of individual cases. The details, however, of this *second* infantile sexual activity leave behind the profoundest (unconscious) impressions in the person's memory; if the individual remains healthy they determine his character and if he becomes sick after puberty, they determine the symptomatology of his neurosis.[1] In the latter case, it is found that this sexual period is forgotten and the conscious reminiscences pointing to it is displaced; I have already mentioned that I would like to connect the normal infantile amnesia with this infantile sexual activity. By psychoanalytic investigation, it is possible to bring to consciousness the forgotten material and thereby to remove a compulsion which emanates from the unconscious psychic material.

The Return of Infantile Masturbation. The sexual excitation of the nursing period returns during the designated years of childhood as a centrally determined tickling sensation demanding masturbatic gratification, or as a pollution-like process which, analogous to the pollution of maturity, may attain gratification without the aid of any action. The latter case is more frequent in girls and in the second half of childhood; its determinants are not well understood, but it often, though not regularly, seems to have as a basis a period of early active masturbation. The symptomatology of this sexual manifestation is poor; the genital apparatus is still undeveloped and all signs are therefore displayed by the urinary apparatus which is, so to say, the guardian of the genital apparatus. Most of the so-called bladder disturbances of this period are of a sexual nature; when-

[1] Why neurotics, when conscience-stricken, regularly connect it with their masturbatic activity, as was recognized by Bleuler, is a problem which still awaits an exhaustive analysis. The coarsest and most important factor of this condition may well be due to the fact that masturbation truly represents the executive part of the entire infantile sexuality and is therefore capable of taking over this fixated sense of guilt.

ever the *enuresis nocturna* does not represent an epileptic attack, it corresponds to a pollution.

The return of the sexual activity is determined by inner and outer causes, which can be conjectured from the formation of the neurotic symptoms and can be definitely revealed by psychoanalytic investigations. The internal causes will be discussed later; the accidental outer causes attain at this time a great and permanent importance. As the first outer cause, there is the influence of seduction which prematurely treats the child as a sexual object; under conditions favoring impressions, this teaches the child the gratification of the genital zones and thus, usually forces it to repeat this gratification in masturbation. Such influences can come from adults or other children. I cannot admit that I overestimated its frequency or its significance in my contributions to the etiology of hysteria,[1] though I did not know then that normal individuals may have the same experiences in their childhood, and hence placed a higher value on seductions than on the factors found in the sexual constitution and development.[2] It is quite obvious that no seduction is necessary to awaken the sexual life of the child, that such an awakening may come on spontaneously from inner sources.

Polymorphous-Perverse Disposition. It is instructive to know that under the influence of seduction, the child may become polymorphous-perverse and may be misled into all sorts of transgressions. This goes to show that the child carries along the adaptation for them in his disposition. The formation of such perversions meets but slight resistance because the psychic dams against sexual transgressions, such as shame, loathing and morality—which depend on the age of the child—are not yet erected or are only in the process of formation. In this respect, the child perhaps does not behave differently from the average uncultured woman in whom the same polymorphous-perverse disposition exists. Such a woman may remain sexually normal under usual conditions, but under the guidance of a clever seducer, she will find pleasure in every perversion and will retain it as her sexual activity. The same polymorphous or infantile disposition fits the prostitute for her professional activity, still it is absolutely impossible not to recognize in the uniform disposition to all perversions,

---

[1] Freud, *Selected Papers on Hysteria and Other Psychoneuroses,* 3rd edition, translated by A. A. Brill, N. Y. Nervous and Mental Disease Monograph Series, No. 4.
[2] Havelock Ellis, in an appendix to his study on the Sexual Impulse, gives a number of autobiographic reports of normal persons dealing with their first sexual feelings in childhood and the causes of the same. These reports naturally show the deficiencies due to infantile amnesia; they do not cover the prehistoric time in the sexual life and therefore must be supplemented by psychoanalysis of individuals who became neurotic. These reports are, nevertheless, valuable in more than one respect, and information of a similar nature has caused me to modify the etiological assumption mentioned in the text.

as shown by an enormous number of prostitutes and by many women who do not necessarily follow this calling, a universal and primitive human tendency.

Partial Impulses. For the rest, the influence of seduction does not aid us in unravelling the original relations of the sexual instinct, but rather confuses our understanding of the same, inasmuch as it prematurely supplies the child with a sexual object at a time when the infantile sexual instinct does not yet evince any desire for it. We must admit, however, that the infantile sexual life, though mainly under the control of erogenous zones, also shows components which from the very beginning point to other persons as sexual objects. Among these, we may mention the impulses for looking, showing off, and for cruelty, which manifest themselves somewhat independently of the erogenous zones and only later enter into intimate relationship with the sexual life; but along with the erogenous sexual activity they are noticeable even in the infantile years, as separate and independent strivings. The little child is, above all, shameless, and during his early years, he evinces definite pleasure in displaying his body and especially his sex organs. A counterpart to this perverse desire, the curiosity to see other persons' genitals, probably appears first in the later years of childhood when the hindrance of the feeling of shame has already reached a certain development. Under the influence of seduction, the looking perversion may attain great importance for the sexual life of the child. Still, from my investigations of the childhood years of normal and neurotic patients, I must conclude that the impulse for looking can appear in the child as a spontaneous sexual manifestation. Small children, whose attention has once been directed to their own genitals—usually by masturbation—are wont to progress in this direction without outside interference and to develop a vivid interest in the genitals of their playmates. As the occasion for the gratification of such curiosity is generally afforded during the gratification of both excrementitious needs, such children become *voyeurs* and are zealous spectators at the voiding of urine and feces of others. After this tendency has been repressed, the curiosity to see the genitals of others (one's own or those of the other sex) remains as a tormenting desire which in some neurotic cases, furnishes the strongest motive-power for the formation of symptoms.

The cruelty component of the sexual instinct develops in the child with still greater independence of those sexual activities which are connected with erogenous zones. Cruelty is intimately related to the childish character, since the inhibition which restrains the mastery impulse before it causes pain to others—that is, the capacity for sympathy—develops comparatively late. As we know that a thorough psychological analysis of this impulse has not as yet been successfully done, we may assume that the feelings of cruelty emanate from the mastery impulse and appear at a period in the sexual life before the genitals have taken on their later rôle. This feeling then dominates a phase of the sexual life which we shall later describe as the pregenital organization. Children who are distinguished for evincing especial cruelty to animals and playmates may be justly suspected of an intensive and a premature sexual activity which emanates from the erogenous zones. But in a simultaneous prematurity of all sexual impulses, the erogenous sexual activity surely seems to be primary. The absence of the barrier of sympathy carries with it the danger that a connection formed in childhood between cruelty and the erogenous impulses will not be broken in later life.

An erogenous source of the passive impulse for cruelty (masochism) is found in the painful irritation of the gluteal region, which is familiar to all educators since the confessions of J. J. Rousseau. This has justly caused them to demand that physical punishment, which is usually directed to this part of the body, should be withheld from all children in whom the libido might be forced into collateral roads by the later demands of cultural education.[1]

STUDY OF INFANTILE SEXUAL INVESTIGATION

Inquisitiveness. About the same time as the sexual life of the child reaches its first rich development, from the age of three to the age of five, there appear the beginnings of that activity which are ascribed to the impulse for knowledge and investigation. The desire for knowledge can neither be reckoned among the elementary instinctive components, nor can it be altogether subsumed under sexuality. Its activity corresponds, on the one hand, to a sublimated form of acquisition, and on the other hand, the energy with which it works comes from the looking impulse. Its relation

[1] The assertions here mentioned concerning infantile sexuality were justified in 1905, mainly through psychoanalytic investigations in adults. Direct observation of the child could not at the time be utilized to its full extent and resulted only in individual indications and valuable confirmations. Since then, it has become possible through the analysis of some cases of nervous disease in the delicate age of childhood to gain a direct understanding of the infantile psychosexuality. I can point with satisfaction to the fact that direct observation has fully confirmed the conclusion drawn from psychoanalysis, and thus furnish good evidence for the reliability of the latter method of investigation. Moreover, the "Analysis of a Phobia in a Five-year-old Boy" (Jahrbuch, Bd. I—G. S. VIII—, English trans. in Collected Papers, Vol III, Hogarth Press, London) has taught us something new for which psychoanalysis had not prepared us, to wit, that sexual symbolism, the representation of the sexual by nonsexual objects and relations—reaches back into the years when the child is first learning to master language. My attention has also been directed to a deficiency in the above-cited statement which for the sake of clearness described any conceivable separation between the two phases of *autoerotism* and *object love* as a temporal separation. From the cited analysis (as well as from the above-mentioned work of Bell, see p. 580n) we learn that children from three to five are capable of evincing a very strong *object-selection* which is accompanied by strong affects.

to the sexual life, however, is of particular importance, for we have learned from psychoanalysis that the inquisitiveness of children is directed to sexual problems unusually early and in an unexpectedly intensive manner; indeed, curiosity may perhaps first be awakened by sexual problems.

The Riddle of the Sphinx. It is not theoretical but practical interests, which start the work of the child's investigation activity. The menace to the conditions of his existence through the actual or expected arrival of a new child, the fear of losing the care and love which is connected with this event, cause the child to become thoughtful and sagacious. Corresponding with the history of this awakening, the first problem with which he occupies himself is not the question as to the difference between the sexes, but the riddle: Where do children come from? In a distorted form which can easily be unravelled, this is the same riddle which was proposed by the Theban Sphinx. The fact of the two sexes is usually first accepted by the child without struggle and hesitation. It is quite natural for the male child to presuppose in all persons he knows a genital like his own, and to find it impossible to harmonize the lack of it with his conception of others.

The Castration Complex and Penis Envy. This conviction is energetically adhered to by the boy and stubbornly defended against the contradictions which soon result, and is only given up after severe internal struggles (castration complex). The substitute formations of this lost penis on the part of the woman play a great rôle in the formation of many perversions.[1]

The assumption of the same (male) genital in all persons is the first of the remarkable and consequential infantile sexual theories. It is of little help to the child when biological science agrees with his preconceptions and recognizes the feminine clitoris as the real substitute for the penis. The little girl does not react with similar rejections when she sees the differently formed genital of the boy. She is immediately prepared to recognize it and soon becomes envious of the penis; this envy reaches its highest point in the consequentially important wish that she also should be a boy.

Birth Theories. Many people can remember distinctly how intensely they interested themselves, in the prepubescent period, in the question of where children came from. The anatomical solutions at that time read very

[1] One has the right to speak also of a castration complex in women. Male and female children form the theory that originally the woman, too, had a penis, which has been lost through castration. The conviction finally won that the woman has no penis often produces in the male a lasting depreciation of the other sex.

differently; the children come out of the breast or are cut out of the body, or the naval opens itself to let them out.[1] Outside of analysis, one only seldom remembers this investigation from early childhood years, for it had long since merged into repression; its results, however, are thoroughly uniform. One gets children by eating something special (as in the fairy tale) or they are born through the bowel, like a passage. These infantile theories recall the structures in the animal kingdom, especially the *cloaca* of those animals which are on a lower scale than mammals.

Sadistic Conception of the Sexual Act. If children at so tender an age witness the sexual act between adults, for which an occasion is furnished by the conviction of the adults that little children cannot understand anything sexual, they cannot help conceiving the sexual act as a kind of maltreating or overpowering; that is, it impresses them in a sadistic sense. Psychoanalysis teaches us also that such an early childhood impression contributes much to the disposition for a later sadistic displacement of the sexual aim. Besides this, children also occupy themselves with the problem of what the sexual act consists, or, as they grasp it, of what marriage consists, and seek the solution to the mystery usually in an intimacy carried on through the functions of urination and defecation.

The Typical Failure of the Infantile Sexual Investigation. It can be stated in general about infantile sexual theories that they are models of the child's own sexual constitution, and that despite their grotesque mistakes, they show more understanding of the sexual processes than is credited to their creators. Children also notice the pregnancy of their mother and know how to interpret it correctly. The stork fable is very often related before auditors who respond with a deep, but mostly mute suspicion. Inasmuch as two elements remain unknown to infantile sexual investigation, namely, the rôle of the fructifying semen and the existence of the female genital opening—precisely the same points in which the infantile organization is still backward—the effort of the infantile mind regularly remains fruitless and ends in a rejection, which not infrequently leaves a lasting injury to the desire for knowledge. The sexual investigation of these early childhood years is always conducted alone; it signifies the first step towards an independent orientation of the world, and causes a marked estrangement between the child and the persons of his environment who formerly enjoyed his full confidence.

---

[1] The wealth of sexual theories in these later years of childhood is very great. Only a few examples are given in this text.

DEVELOPMENTAL PHASES OF THE SEXUAL ORGANIZATION

As characteristics of the infantile sexuality, we have hitherto emphasized the fact that it is essentially autoerotic (he finds his object in his own body), and that the individual partial impulses, which on the whole are unconnected and independent of one another, are striving for the acquisition of pleasure. The goal of this development forms the so-called normal sexual life of the adult in whom the acquisition of pleasure has been put into the service of the function of propagation. The partial impulses, which are then under the primacy of one single erogenous zone, form a firm organization for the attainment of the sexual aim in a strange sexual object.

Pregenital Organizations. The study, with the help of psychoanalysis, of the inhibitions and disturbances in this course of development now permits us to recognize additions and primary stages of such organization of the partial impulses, which likewise furnish a sort of sexual regime. These phases of the sexual organization normally pass smoothly, and can only be recognizable by mere suggestions. Only in pathological cases do they become active and discernible to gross observation.

We will call the organizations of the sexual life in which the genital zones have not yet assumed the dominating role, the *pregenital phase.* So far, we have become acquainted with two of them which recall reversions to early animal states.

One of the first of such pregenital sexual organizations is the *oral,* or if one will, the cannibalistic. Here the sexual activity is not yet separated from the taking of nourishment and the contrasts within it are not yet differentiated. The object of the one activity is also that of the other; the sexual aim then consists in the *incorporation* of the object into one's own body, the prototype of *identification,* which later plays such an important psychic rôle. As a remnant of this fictitious phase of organization forced on us by pathology, we can consider thumbsucking. Here the sexual activity became separated from the nourishment activity and the strange object was given up in favor of one from his own body.[1]

A second pregenital phase is the *sadistic-anal* organization. Here the contrasts which run through the whole sexual life are already developed, but cannot yet be designated as *masculine* and *feminine,* but must be

---

[1] Cf. concerning remnants of this phase in adult neurotics, the work of Abraham, "Investigations regarding the Earliest Pregenital Stage of Development of the Libido" (Inter. Zeitschr. f. Psychoanalyse, IV, 1916). In a later work ("Versuch einer Entwicklungsgeschichte der Libido," 1924) Abraham subdivided both this oral phase and the later sadistic-anal one into two parts, for which the different behavior toward the object is characteristic. (In English in "Selected Papers," Int. Psa. Library, 13, Hogarth Press, 1927.)

called *active* and *passive*. The activity is supplied by the musculature of the body through the mastery impulse; the erogenous mucous membrane of the bowel manifests itself above all as an organ with a passive sexual aim; for both strivings there are objects present, which, however, do not merge together. Besides them, there are other partial impulses which are active in an autoerotic manner. The sexual polarity and the strange object can thus already be demonstrated in this phase. The organization and subordination under the function of propagation are still lacking.[1]

Ambivalence. This form of the sexual organization can already maintain itself throughout life and draws to itself a large part of sexual activity. The dominance of sadism and the rôle of the cloaca of the anal zone stamps it with an exquisitely archaic impression. As another characteristic belonging to it, we can mention the fact that the contrasting pair of impulses are developed in almost the same manner, a situation which was happily designated by Bleuler by the term *ambivalence.*

The assumption of the pregenital organizations of the sexual life rests on the analysis of the neuroses and can scarcely be appreciated without a knowledge of these. We have a right to expect that continued analytic efforts will furnish us with still more disclosures concerning the structure and development of the normal sexual function.

To complete the picture of the infantile sexual life, one must add, that frequently or regularly an object selection takes place even in childhood which is as characteristic as the one we have represented for the phase of development of puberty. This object selection proceeds in such a manner that all the sexual strivings proceed in the direction of one person in whom they wish to attain their aim. This is then the nearest approach to the definitive formation of the sexual life after puberty, that is possible in childhood. It differs from puberty only in the fact that the collection of the partial impulses and their subordination to the primacy of the genitals is very imperfectly or not at all accomplished in childhood. The establishment of this primacy in the service of reproduction, is therefore the last phase through which sexual development passes.[2]

[1] In the second of the two studies, Abraham calls attention to the fact that the anus arises from the primitive mouth of the embryonic form which appears as a biological prototype of the psychosexual development.
[2] I later (1925) altered this in that I interpolated a third phase into the development of the child after the two pregenital organizations, one which indeed deserves the name of a genital, one which reveals a sexual object and a measure of convergence of the sexual strivings upon this object, but which differs in one essential point from the definitive organization of sexual maturity. That is, it knows only one sort of genital, the male. I have therefore called it the *phallic* stage of organization ("Die infantile Genitalorganisation," Inter. Zeitschr. f. Psychoanalyse, IX, 1925; G. S., Vol. V). Its biological prototype according to Abraham is the homogeneous genital *Anlage* of the embryo undifferentiated for either sex.

The Two Periods of Object Selection. That the object selection takes place in two periods, or in two shifts, can be spoken of as a typical occurrence. The first shift has its origin between the age of three and five years and is brought to a stop or to regression by the latency period; it is characterized by the infantile nature of its sexual aims. The second shift starts with puberty and determines the definite formation of the sexual life.

The fact of the two period object selection, which is essentially due to the effect of the latency period, becomes most significant for the disturbance of this terminal state. The results of the infantile object selection reach into the later period; they are either preserved as such or are even refreshed at the time of puberty. But due to the development of the repression which takes place between the two phases, they become unusable. Their sexual aims have become softened and now represent what we can designate as the *tender* stream of the sexual life. Only psychoanalytic investigation can demonstrate that behind this tenderness, such as honoring and esteeming, there is concealed the old sexual strivings of the infantile partial impulses which have now become useless. The object selection of the pubescent period must renounce the infantile objects and begin anew as a sensuous stream. The fact that the two streams do not concur, often enough results in the fact that one of the ideals of the sexual life, namely, the union of all desires in one object, cannot be attained.

THE SOURCES OF INFANTILE SEXUALITY

In our effort to follow up the origins of the sexual instinct, we have thus far found that sexual excitement originates (a) as an imitation of a gratification which has been experienced in conjunction with other organic processes; (b) as the appropriate peripheral stimulation of erogenous zones; (c) and as an expression of some "impulse," like the looking and cruelty impulses, the origin of which we do not yet fully understand. Psychoanalytic investigation of later life which leads back to childhood and the contemporary observation of the child itself now coöperate to reveal to us still other regularly-flowing sources of sexual excitement. Observation of childhood has the disadvantage of dealing with easily misunderstood material, while psychoanalysis is made difficult by the fact that it can reach its objects and conclusions only by great detours; still the united efforts of both methods achieve a sufficient degree of positive understanding.

In investigating the erogenous zones, we have already found that these skin regions merely show the special exaggeration of a form of sensitiveness which is, to a certain degree, found over the whole surface of the skin. It will therefore not surprise us to learn that certain forms of general sensitiveness in the skin can be ascribed to very distinct erogenous action. Among these, we will above all mention temperature sensitiveness, which will perhaps prepare us for the understanding of the therapeutic effects of warm baths.

Mechanical Excitation. We must, moreover, describe here the production of sexual excitation by means of rhythmic mechanical shaking of the body. There are three kinds of exciting influences: those acting on the skin and those acting on the deeper parts, such as the muscles and joints. The sexual excitation produced by these influences seems to be of a pleasurable nature. It is worth emphasizing that for some time, we shall continue to use indiscriminately the terms "sexual excitement" and "gratification," leaving the search for an explanation of the terms to a later time. That such pleasure is produced by mechanical stimulation is proved by the fact that children are fond of play involving passive motion, like swinging or flying in the air, and repeatedly demand its repetition,[1] and we also know that rocking is regularly used in putting restless children to sleep. Shaking sensations experienced in wagons and railroad trains exert such a fascinating influence on older children that all boys, at least at one time in their lives, wish to become conductors and drivers. They are wont to ascribe to railroad activities an extraordinary and mysterious interest, and during the age of phantastic activity (shortly before puberty) they utilize these as a nucleus for exquisite sexual symbolisms. The desire to connect railroad travelling with sexuality apparently originates from the pleasurable character of the sensation of motion. When repression later sets in and changes so many of the childish likes into their opposites, these same persons as adolescents and adults then react to rocking and rolling with nausea, and become terribly exhausted by a railroad journey. Or they show a tendency to attacks of anxiety during the journey, and by becoming obsessed with railroad phobia, they protect themselves against a repetition of this painful experience.

This also fits in with the fact not yet understood, namely, that the concurrence of fear through mechanical shaking produces the severest hysterical forms of traumatic neurosis. It may at least be assumed that inasmuch as even a slight intensity of these influences becomes a source of sexual excitement, the action of an excessive amount of the same, will produce a profound disorder of the sexual mechanism.

Muscular Activity. It is well known that the child has a need for much muscular activity, from the gratification of which it draws extraordinary pleasure. Whether this pleasure has anything to do with sexuality, whether it includes in itself sexual satisfaction, or can cause sexual excitement; all this may be refuted by critical consideration which will

[1] Some persons can recall that the contact of the moving air in swinging caused them direct sexual pleasure in the genitals.

probably be directed also to the position just taken, namely, that the pleasure in the sensations of passive movement are of sexual character, or that they are sexually exciting. The fact remains, however, that a number of persons report that they have experienced the first signs of excitement in their genitals during fighting or wrestling with playmates, in which situation, besides the general muscular exertion, there is also an intensive contact with the opponent's skin. The desire for muscular contest with a definite person, like the desire for word contest in later years, is a good sign that this person has been selected as a love object. *"Was sich liebt, das neckt sich."* [1] In the promotion of sexual excitement through muscular activity, we might recognize one of the sources of the sadistic impulse. The infantile connection between fighting and sexual excitement acts in many persons as a determinant for the future pre-ferred course of their sexual impulse. [2]

Affective Processes. The other sources of sexual excitement in the child are open to less doubt. Through contemporary observations, as well as through later investigations, it is easy to ascertain that all more intensive affective processes, even excitements of a terrifying nature, encroach upon sexuality. This can at all events furnish us with a contribution to the understanding of the pathogenic action of such emotions. In the schoolchild, fear of a coming examination or exertion expended in the solution of a difficult school task, can become significant for the breaking through of sexual manifestations as well as for his relations to the school. Under such excitements, a sensation often occurs which impels him to touch the genitals, or it may lead to a pollution-like process with all its disagreeable consequences. The behavior of children at school, which is so often mysterious to the teacher, should surely be considered in relation to their germinating sexuality. The sexually-exciting influence of some painful affects, such as fear, shuddering and horror is felt by a great many people throughout life and readily explains why so many people seek opportunities to experience such sensations, provided that certain accessory circumstances (as under imaginary circumstances, in reading or in the theater) suppress the earnestness of the painful feeling.

If we could assume that very painful feelings can also attain the same erogenous result, especially if the pain be toned down or held in abeyance by a subsidiary condition, such a situation would then contain the main

[1] "Those who love each other tease each other."
[2] The analyses of neurotic disturbances of walking and of agoraphobia remove all doubt as to the sexual nature of the pleasure of motion. As everybody knows, modern cultural education utilizes sports to a great extent in order to turn away the youth from sexual activity; it would be more proper to say that it replaces the sexual pleasure by motion pleasure and forces the sexual activity back upon one of its autoerotic components.

roots of the sado-masochistic impulse, into the manifold composition of which we are gradually gaining some insight.[1]

Intellectual Work. Finally, it is evident that mental application or concentration of attention on an intellectual accomplishment will result, especially in youthful persons, but in older persons as well, in a simultaneous sexual excitement. This may be looked upon as the only justified basis for the otherwise so doubtful etiology of nervous disturbances from mental "overwork."

If we now, in conclusion, review the evidences and indications of the sources of the infantile sexual excitement, which have been reported neither completely nor exhaustively, we may lay down the following general laws as suggested or established. It seems to be provided in the most generous manner that the process of sexual excitement—the nature of which certainly remains quite mysterious to us—should be set in motion. The factor making this provision in a more or less direct way is the excitation of the sensible surfaces of the skin and sensory organs, while the most immediate exciting influences are exerted on certain parts which are designated as erogenous zones. The criterion in all these sources of sexual excitement is really the quality of the stimuli, though the factor of intensity (in pain) is not entirely unimportant. But in addition to this, there are arrangements in the organism which induce sexual excitement as a subsidiary action in a large number of inner processes as soon as the intensity of these processes has risen above certain quantitative limits. What we have designated as the partial impulses of sexuality are either directly derived from these inner sources of sexual excitation or composed of contributions from such sources, and from erogenous zones. It is possible that nothing of any considerable significance occurs in the organism that does not also contribute its components to the excitement of the sexual instinct.

It seems to me at present impossible to shed more light and certainty on these general propositions, and for this I hold two factors responsible: first, the novelty of this manner of investigation, and secondly, the fact that the nature of the sexual excitement is entirely unfamiliar to us. Nevertheless, I will not forbear speaking about two points which promise to open wide prospects in the future.

Diverse Sexual Constitutions. (a) We have considered above the possibility of establishing the manifold character of congenital sexual constitutions through the diverse formation of the erogenous zones; we may now attempt to do the same in dealing with the indirect sources of sexual

---

[1] The so-called "erogenic" masochism.

excitement. We may assume that, although these different sources furnish contributions in all individuals, they are not all equally strong in all persons; and that a further contribution to the differentiation of the diverse sexual constitution will be found in the preferred development of the individual sources of sexual excitement.[1]

The Paths of Opposite Influences. (b) Since we are now dropping the figurative manner of expression hitherto employed, by which we spoke of *sources* of sexual excitement, we may now assume that all the connecting paths leading from other functions to sexuality must also be passable in the reverse direction. For example, if the lip-zone, the common possession of both functions, is responsible for the fact that sexual gratification originates during the intake of nourishment, the same factor offers also an explanation for the disturbances in the taking of nourishment if the erogenous functions of the common zone are disturbed. As soon as we know that concentration of attention may produce sexual excitement, it is quite natural to assume that acting on the same path, but in a reverse direction, the state of sexual excitement may be able to influence the availability of voluntary attention. A good part of the symptomatology of the neuroses which I trace to disturbance of sexual processes manifests itself in disturbances of the other non-sexual bodily functions, and this hitherto incomprehensible action becomes less mysterious if it only represents the counterpart of the influences controlling the production of the sexual excitement.

However, the same paths through which sexual disturbances encroach upon the other functions of the body, must in health be supposed to serve another important function. It must be through these paths that the attraction of the sexual motive-powers to other than sexual aims, the sublimation of sexuality, is accomplished. We must conclude, with the admission that very little is definitely known concerning the paths beyond the fact that they exist and that they are probably passable in both directions.

---

[1] An undeniable result of these outlines is that every individual may be spoken of as oral-, anal-, urethral-erotic, etc., and that the finding of these psychical complexes entails no judgment as to abnormality or a neurosis. That which separates the normal from the abnormal is but a relative increase in a single component of the sexual instinct and what course it may take during development.

THE TRANSFORMATIONS OF PUBERTY

WITH the beginning of puberty, changes set in, which transform the infantile sexual life into its definite normal form. Hitherto, the sexual instinct has been preponderantly autoerotic; it now finds the sexual object. Thus far, it has manifested itself in single impulses and in erogenous zones seeking a certain pleasure as a single sexual aim. A new sexual aim now appears for the production of which all partial impulses coöperate, while the erogenous zones subordinate themselves to the primacy of the genital zone.[1] As the new sexual aim assigns very different functions to the two sexes, their sexual developments now part company. The male sexual development is more consistent and easier to understand, while in the woman a sort of regression seems to appear. The normality of the sexual life is guaranteed only by the exact concurrence of the two streams directed to the sexual object and sexual aim. It is like the piercing of a tunnel from opposite sides.

The new sexual aim in the man consists in the discharge of the sexual products. This is not contradictory to the former sexual aim, which is that of obtaining pleasure; on the contrary, the height of all pleasure is connected with this final act in the sexual process. The sexual instinct now enters into the service of the function of propagation; it becomes, so to say, altruistic. If this transformation is to succeed, its process must be adjusted to the original dispositions and all the peculiarities of the impulses.

Just as on every other occasion where new associations and compositions are to be formed in complicated mechanisms, here, too, there is a possibility for morbid disturbances if the new order of things does not get itself established. All morbid disturbances of the sexual life may justly be considered as inhibitions of development.

[1] The differences will be emphasized in the schematic representation given in the text. To what extent the infantile sexuality approaches the definitive sexual organization through its object selection has been discussed previously.

From the course of development just described, we can clearly see the issue and the end aim. The intermediary transitions are still quite obscure and many a riddle will have to be left unsolved.

The most striking process of puberty has been selected as its most characteristic; it is the manifest growth of the external genitals which have shown a relative inhibition of growth during the latency period of childhood. Simultaneously the inner genitals develop to such an extent as to be able to furnish sexual products or to receive them for the purpose of forming a new living being. A most complicated apparatus has thus been formed for future use.

This apparatus can be set in motion by stimuli, and observation teaches that the stimuli can effect it in three ways: from the outer world through the familiar erogenous zones; from the inner organic world by ways still to be investigated; and from the psychic life, which merely represents a depository of external impressions and a receptacle of inner excitations. The same result is, thus, evoked by three paths and forms a state which can be designated as "sexual excitation," and which manifests itself in psychic and somatic signs. The psychic sign consists of a peculiar feeling of tension of a most urgent character, and among the manifold somatic signs, the many changes in the genitals are uppermost. They have a definite meaning—namely, that of readiness, and constitute a preparation for the sexual act (the erection of the penis and the glandular activity of the vagina).

Sexual Tension. The character of the tension of sexual excitement is connected with a problem, the solution of which is as difficult as it would be important for the conception of the sexual process. Despite all divergence of opinion regarding it in psychology, I must firmly maintain that a feeling of tension must carry with it the character of displeasure. I consider it conclusive that such a feeling carries with it the impulse to alter the psychic situation and thus acts incitingly, which is quite contrary to the nature of the perceived pleasure. But if we ascribe the tension of the sexual excitation to the feelings of displeasure we are confronted by the fact that it is undoubtedly pleasurably perceived. The tension produced by sexual excitation is everywhere accompanied by pleasure; even in the preparatory changes of the genitals, there is a distinct feeling of gratification. What relation is there between this unpleasant tension and this feeling of pleasure?

Everything relating to the problem of pleasure and pain touches one of the weakest spots of present-day psychology. We shall try, if possible, to learn something from the condition of the case in question, and we shall avoid encroaching on the problem as a whole. Let us first glance at the manner in which the erogenous zones adjust themselves to the new order of things.[1] An important rôle devolves upon them in the preparation of the sexual excitation. The eye, which is very remote from the sexual object, is most often in position, during the relations of object wooing, to become attracted by that particular quality of excitation, the motive of which we designate as beauty in the sexual object. The excellencies of the sexual object are therefore also called "attractions." This attraction is on the one hand already connected with pleasure, and on the other hand, it either results in an increase of the sexual excitation or in an evocation of it where it is still wanting. The effect is the same if the excitation of another erogenous zone, e.g., the touch of the hand, is added to it. There is on the one hand the feeling of pleasure which soon becomes enhanced by the pleasure from the preparatory changes, and on the other hand, there is a further increase of the sexual tension which soon changes into a most distinct feeling of displeasure if it cannot proceed to more pleasure.

Another case will perhaps be clearer; let us, for example, take the case where an erogenous zone, such as a woman's breast, is excited by touching in a person who is not sexually excited at the time. This touching in itself evokes a feeling of pleasure, but it is also best adapted to awaken sexual excitement which demands still more pleasure. How it happens that the perceived pleasure evokes the desire for greater pleasure, that is the real problem.

Fore-pleasure Mechanism. But the rôle which devolves upon the erogenous zone is clear. What applies to one applies to all. They are all utilized to furnish a certain amount of pleasure through their own proper excitation; this pleasure increases the tension, and in turn serves to produce the necessary motor energy for the completion of the sexual act. The last part but one, of this act is again a suitable excitation of an erogenous zone; i.e., the genital zone proper of the glans penis is excited by the object most fit for it, the mucous membrane of the vagina, and through the pleasure furnished by this excitation, it now produces reflexly the motor energy which conveys to the surface the sexual substance. This last pleasure is highest in intensity and differs from the earliest ones in its mechanism. It is entirely produced through the discharge and it is altogether gratification pleasure; the tension of the libido temporarily subsides with it.

It does not seem to me unjustified to fix by name this distinction in the

---

[1] See an effort towards the solution of this question in the introductory discussion of my paper, Das ökonomische Problem der Masochismus," 1924 (Int. Zeit. f. Psa., G. S. V.). (English in Vol. II, Collected Papers, Hogarth Press, London.)

nature of the pleasures, the one resulting from the excitation of the erogenous zones, and the other, from the discharge of the sexual substance. In contrast to the end-pleasure, or pleasure of gratification of the sexual act, we can properly designate the first as *fore-pleasure*. The fore-pleasure is thus the same as that which could already be furnished by the infantile sexual instinct, albeit on a reduced scale; while the *end-pleasure* is new and is probably associated with conditions which first appear at puberty. The formula for the new function of the erogenous zones then reads: The erogenous zones are utilized for the purpose of producing greater gratification pleasure through the fore-pleasure, which they already furnished in infantile life.

I have recently been able to elucidate another example from a quite different realm of the psychic life, in which, too, a greater feeling of pleasure is obtained through a lesser, which, thus, acts therein as an alluring premium. There, too, we had the opportunity of going more deeply into the nature of pleasure.[1]

Dangers of the Fore-pleasure. However, the association of fore-pleasure with the infantile life is strengthened by the pathogenic rôle which it may assume. In the mechanism through which the fore-pleasure is expressed, there exists an obvious danger to the attainment of the normal sexual aim. This might happen if there should be too much fore-pleasure and too little tension in any part of the preparatory sexual process. The motive power for the further continuation of the sexual process may become dissipated, and the whole road shortened, so that the preparatory action could then take the place of the normal sexual aim. Experience shows that such a harmful circumstance is conditioned by the fact that the concerned erogenous zone or the corresponding partial impulse had already contributed an unusual amount of pleasure in infantile life. If other factors favoring fixation are added, a compulsion readily results for the later life which prevents the fore-pleasure from merging into the new combination. Indeed, the mechanism of many perversions is of such a nature; the perversion merely represents a lingering at a preparatory act of the sexual process.

The failure of the function of the sexual mechanism through a faulty fore-pleasure is generally avoided if the primacy of the genital zones has already been laid out in infantile life. The preparations of the second half of childhood (from the eighth year to puberty) really seem to favor this. During these years the genital zones behave almost as at the age of maturity. They are the seat of exciting sensations, and subject to prepara-

---

[1] See *Wit and Its Relation to the Unconscious*, (p. 726): "The fore-pleasure gained by the technique of wit is utilized for the purpose of setting free a greater pleasure by the removal of inner inhibitions."

tory changes if any kind of pleasure is experienced through the gratification of other erogenous zones. To be sure, the effect thus produced remains aimless, *i.e.*, it contributes nothing to the continuation of the sexual process. Besides the pleasure of gratification, a certain amount of sexual tension appears even in infancy, though it is less constant and less abundant. We can now also understand why we had a perfectly good reason for saying, in the discussion of the sources of sexuality, that the process in question acts as sexual gratification as well as sexual excitement. We note that on our way towards the truth we have at first enormously exaggerated the distinction between the infantile and the mature sexual life, and we, therefore, supplement what has been said with a correction. The infantile manifestations of sexuality not only condition the deviations from the normal sexual life, but also the normal formations of the same.

THE PROBLEM OF SEXUAL EXCITEMENT

It remains entirely unexplained whence the sexual tension comes which originates simultaneously with the gratification of erogenous zones, and what its nature is.[1] The obvious supposition that this tension originates in some way from the pleasure itself is not only improbable but untenable, inasmuch as during the greatest pleasure which is connected with the voiding of sexual substance there is no production of tension, but rather a removal of all tension. Hence, pleasure and sexual tension can be only indirectly connected.

The Rôle of Sexual Substances. Aside from the fact that only the discharge of the sexual substance can normally put an end to the sexual excitement, there are other essential facts which bring the sexual tension into relation with the sexual products. In a state of continence, the sexual apparatus is wont to disburden itself of the sexual substance nocturnally through pleasurable dream hallucinations of a sexual act; this discharge appears sporadically, but not at entirely irregular periods. The following interpretation of this process—the nocturnal pollution—can hardly be rejected, viz., that the sexual tension which brings about a substitute for the sexual act by the short hallucinatory road is a function of the accumulated semen in the reservoirs for the sexual products. Experiences with the exhaustibility of the sexual mechanism speak for the same thing. Where there is no stock of semen, it is not only impossible to accomplish the sexual act, but there is also a lack of excitability in the erogenous

---

[1] It is extremely informing that the German language in the use of the word, "Lust," takes cognizance of the rôle of preparatory sexual excitement, here mentioned, which at the same time delivers a part of satisfaction and a share of the sexual tension. "Lust" has a double meaning and signifies not only the sensation of sexual tension (*Ich habe Lust*—I have the desire—*ich möchte; ich verspüre den Drang*—I would like to, I am aware of the tension), but also that of its gratification.

zones, so that their appropriate excitation cannot evoke any pleasure. We, thus, discover incidentally that a certain amount of sexual tension is alone necessary for the excitability of the erogenous zones.

One would thus be forced to the assumption, which, if I am not mistaken, is quite generally accepted, namely, that the accumulation of sexual substance produces the sexual tension and maintains it. The pressure of these products on the walls of their receptacles acts as an excitant on the spinal center, the state of which is then perceived by the higher centers, which in turn produce in consciousness the familiar feeling of tension. If the excitation of erogenous zones increases the sexual tension, it can only be due to the fact that the erogenous zones are connected with these centers by previously formed anatomical connections. There they increase the tone of the excitation, and with sufficient sexual tension, they set in motion the sexual act, but with insufficient tension, they merely stimulate a production of the sexual substance.

The weakness of the theory which one finds adopted, e.g., in Krafft-Ebing's description of the sexual process, lies in the fact that it was based on the sexual activity of the mature man and pays too little heed to three kinds of relationships which should have been also considered. We refer to the relations existing in the child, in the woman, and in the castrated male. In none of the three cases can we speak of an accumulation of sexual products in the same sense as in the average man, which naturally renders difficult the general application of this scheme. It may, however, be admitted without any further ado that ways can be found to justify the subordination of even these cases. One, however, should be cautious about burdening the factor of accumulation of sexual products with actions which it seems incapable of supporting.

Overestimation of the Internal Genitals. That sexual excitement can be independent to a considerable extent of the production of sexual substance seems to be shown by observations on castrated males, in whom the libido sometimes escapes the injury caused by the operation, although the opposite behavior, which is really the motive for the operation, is usually the rule. It is, therefore, not at all surprising, as C. Rieger puts it, that the loss of the male germ glands in maturer age should exert no new influence on the psychic life of the individual. The germ glands do not really represent the sexuality of a person. For experience with castrated males only verifies what we had long before learned from the removal of the ovaries, namely, that it is impossible to do away with the sexual character by removing the germ glands. To be sure, castration performed at a tender age, before puberty, comes nearer to this aim, but it would seem in this case that besides the loss of the sexual glands, we must also consider the inhibition of development and other factors which are connected with that loss.

Chemical Theories. Animal experimentation through the removal of the gonads (testicles and ovaries) and a variety of corresponding transplantations of such new organs in vertebrates (see Lipschütz's work, *l.c.*) have at last thrown some light upon the origins of sexual excitement and have, thereby, minimized still more the importance of an eventual accumulation of cellular sexual products. Experimentally it has been possible (E. Steinach) to change a male into a female and vice-versa, whereby the psychosexual behavior of the animal corresponds to the somatic sexual characters and simultaneously changes with them. This sex determining influence does not, however, proceed from those portions of the gonads concerned with the production of spermatozoa or ovules, but rather from the interstitial cells, which are, therefore, designated (by Lipschütz) as "puberty glands." It is quite possible that further research will show that the puberty glands are hermaphroditic, in which case the doctrine concerning the bi-sexuality of higher animals may be anatomically grounded. And, furthermore, it is still possible that they are not the only organs which have to do with the production of sexual excitement and with the sexual characters. At all events, these newer findings correspond to what we already know of the rôle played by the thyroid in sexuality. We may now believe that in the interstitial tissues of the gonads special chemical substances are produced which, when taken up in the blood stream, charge definite parts of the central nervous system with sexual tension. Such a transformation of a toxic stimulus into a particular organic stimulus we are already familiar with from other toxic products introduced into the body from without.

To treat, if only hypothetically, the complexities of the pure toxic and physiologic stimulations which result in the sexual processes is not now our appropriate task. To be sure, I attach no value to this special assumption and I shall be quite ready to give it up in favor of another, provided its original character, *i.e.*, the emphasis on the sexual chemism, were preserved. For this apparently arbitrary statement is supported by a fact which, though little heeded, is most noteworthy. The neuroses which can only be traced to disturbances of the sexual life show the greatest clinical resemblance to the phenomena of intoxication and abstinence, which result from the habitual introduction of pleasure-producing poisonous substances (alkaloids).

THE LIBIDO THEORY

The assumptions concerning the chemical basis of the sexual excitement are in full accord with the auxiliary conceptions which we formed for the purpose of mastering the psychic manifestations of the sexual life. We have laid down the concept of libido as a force of variable quantity by which processes and transformations in the spheres of sexual excitement can be measured. This libido we distinguished from the energy which is at the basis of the psychic processes in general as far as their special origin is concerned, and we thus attribute to it also a qualitative character. In separating libidinal from other psychic energy, we give expression to the assumption that the sexual processes of the organism are differentiated from the nutritional processes through a special chemism. The analyses of perversions and psychoneuroses have taught us that this sexual excitement is furnished not only from the so-called sexual parts alone, but from all organs of the body. We thus formulate for ourselves the concept of a *libido-quantum*, the psychic representative of which we designate as the *ego-libido*. The production, increase, distribution, and displacement of this ego-libido, thus offer the possible explanation for the manifest psychosexual phenomena.

But this ego-libido can only become conveniently accessible to psychoanalytic study if its psychic energy is invested or occupied (cathexis)[1] in sexual objects; that is, if it becomes object-libido. We can then see it as it concentrates and fixes itself on objects, or as it leaves those objects and passes over to others, from which position it directs the individual's sexual activity; that is, as it leads to partial and temporary extinction of the libido. Psychoanalysis of the so-called transference neuroses (hysteria and compulsion neurosis) offers us here a reliable insight.

Concerning the fates of the object-libido, we can also state that it may be withdrawn from the object, that it may be preserved in a floating state in special states of tension, and that it may finally be taken back into the ego and again change into ego-libido as *narcissistic libido*. Through psychoanalysis, we look as if over a boundary, which we are not permitted to pass, into the activity of this narcissistic libido, and thus, form an idea of the relations between the two.[2] The narcissistic or ego-libido appears to us as the great reservoir from which all object cathexis is sent out, and into which it is drawn back again, while the narcissistic libido-cathexis of the ego appears to us as the realized primal state in the first childhood, which only becomes hidden by the later emissions of libido, and is retained at the bottom behind them.

The task of a libido theory on neurotic and psychotic disturbances would have for its object to express in terms of libido-economics all observed phenomena and disclosed processes. It is easy to divine that greater

[1] From the Greek, *cathexo*, to occupy.
[2] This limitation is not as valid as it once was, inasmuch as other neuroses besides the "transference neuroses" have become to a greater degree accessible to psychoanalysis.

importance would be attached to the destinies of the ego-libido, especially where it would be a question of explaining the deeper psychotic disturbances. The difficulty then lies in the fact that the means of our investigation, psychoanalysis, at present gives us definite information [1] only concerning the transformation of object-libido, but cannot distinguish, without further study, the ego-libido from the other effective energies in the ego.[2] The libido theory may, therefore, for the present be pursued only by the path of speculation. All that has been gained thus far from psychoanalytic observation would be lost if, following C. G. Jung, one would subtilize the very concept of libido to the extent of making it synonymous with psychic instinctive energy in general.

The separation of the sexual instinctive excitements from the others and with it the restriction of the concept libido to the former, finds strong support in the assumption of a special chemism of the sexual function, which was discussed before.

DIFFERENTIATION BETWEEN MAN AND WOMAN

It is known that the sharp division between the male and female character is established at puberty; a contrast, which, more than any other factor, decisively influences the later development of the human being. To be sure, the male and female dispositions are already well recognizable in childhood. Thus, the development of sexual inhibitions (shame, loathing, sympathy, etc.) proceeds earlier and with less resistance in the little girl than in the little boy. The tendency to sexual repression certainly seems here much greater, and where partial impulses of sexuality are noticed, they show a preference for the passive form. However, the autoerotic activity of the erogenous zones is the same in both sexes, and it is this agreement that removes the possibility of a sex differentiation in childhood as it appears after puberty. In respect to the autoerotic and masturbatic sexual manifestations, it may be asserted that the sexuality of the little girl has altogether a male character. Indeed, if one could give a more definite content to the terms, "masculine" and "feminine," one might advance the opinion that the libido is regularly and lawfully of a masculine nature, whether in the man or in the woman; and if we consider its object, we can say that it may be either male or female.[3]

---

[1] See previous citations.

[2] Cf. Zur Einführung des Narzismus, Jahrbuch der Psychoanalyse, VI, 1913. The term, narcissism, was not coined, as was incorrectly stated, by Naecke, but by H. Ellis.

[3] It is necessary to make clear that the conceptions, "masculine" and "feminine", whose content seems so unequivocal to the ordinary meaning, belong to the most confused terms in science and can be cut up into at least three paths. One uses masculine and feminine at times in the sense of *activity* and *passivity*, again, in the *biological* sense, and then also in the *sociological* sense. The first of these three meanings is the most essential and the only one utilizable in psychoanalysis. It agrees with

Since I became acquainted with the problem of bisexuality, I have felt that this factor was very important here, and it is my belief that without taking into account the factor of bisexuality, it will hardly be possible to understand the sexual manifestations of man and woman, which must actually be observed.

The Leading Zones in Man and Woman. Besides this, I can only add the following. The chief erogenous zone in the female child is the clitoris, which is homologous to the male penis. All that I have been able to discover about masturbation in little girls refers to the clitoris, and not to the other external genitals which are so important for the future sexual functions. With few exceptions, I, myself, doubt whether the female child can be seduced to anything but clitoris masturbation. The frequent spontaneous discharges of sexual excitement in little girls manifest themselves in a twitching of the clitoris, and its frequent erections enable the girl to understand correctly even without any instructions the sexual manifestations of the other sex; girls simply transfer to the boys the sensations of their own sexual processes.

If one wishes to understand how the little girl becomes a woman, he must follow up the further destinies of this clitoris excitation. Puberty, which brings to the boy a great advance of libido, distinguishes itself in the girl by a new wave of repression, which especially concerns the clitoris sexuality. It is a part of the male sexual life that sinks into repression. The reënforcement of the sexual inhibitions produced in the woman by the repression of puberty produces a stimulus in the libido of the man and forces him to increase his activities. With the height of the libido there occurs a rise in the overestimation of the sexual object, which attains its full force only in that woman who hesitates and denies her sexuality. If the woman finally submits to the sexual act, the clitoris becomes stimulated and its rôle is to conduct the excitement to the adjacent genital

the masculine designation of the libido in the text above, for the libido is always active, even when it is directed to a passive aim. The second, the biological significance of masculine and feminine is the one which permits the clearest determination. Masculine and feminine are here characterized by the presence of semen or ovum and through the functions emanating from them. The activity and its secondary manifestations, like stronger developed muscles, aggression, a greater intensity of libido, are as a rule soldered to the biological masculinity, but not necessarily connected with it, for there are species of animals in whom these qualities are attributed to the female. The third, the sociological meaning, receives its content through the observation of the actual existing male and female individuals. The result of this in man is that there is no pure masculinity or femininity either in the biological or psychological sense. On the contrary, every individual person shows a mixture of his own biological sex characteristics with the biological traits of the other sex and a union of activity and passivity; this is the case whether these psychological characteristic features depend on biological elements or whether they are independent of them.

parts; it acts here like a chip of pinewood, which is utilized to set fire to the harder wood. It often takes some time before this transference is accomplished, and during this transition the young wife remains anesthetic. This anesthesia may become permanent if the clitoric zone refuses to give up its excitability; a condition brought on by profuse sexual activities in infantile life. It is known that anesthesia in women is often only apparent and local. They are anesthetic at the vaginal entrance, but not at all unexcitable through the clitoris or even through other zones. Besides these erogenous causes of anesthesia, there are also psychic causes, likewise determined by the repression.

If the transference of the erogenous excitability from the clitoris to the vaginal entrance succeeds, the woman then changes her leading zone for the future sexual activity; the man, on the other hand, retains his from childhood. The main determinants for the woman's preference for neuroses, especially for hysteria, lie in this change of the leading zone as well as in the repression of puberty. These determinants are, therefore, most intimately connected with the nature of femininity.

OBJECT-FINDING

While the primacy of the genital zones is being established through the processes of puberty, and the erected penis in the man imperiously points towards the new sexual aim, *i.e.* towards the penetration of a cavity which excites the genital zone, object-finding, for which also preparations have been made since early childhood, becomes consummated on the psychic side. When the very incipient sexual gratifications were still connected with the taking of nourishment, the sexual instinct had a sexual object outside one's own body, in the mother's breast. This object is later lost, perhaps at the very time when it becomes possible for the child to form a general picture of the person to whom the organ granting him the gratification belongs. The sexual instinct later regularly becomes autoerotic, and only after overcoming the latency period is the original relation reestablished. It is not without good reason that the suckling of the child at the mother's breast has become a model for every love relation. Object-finding is really a re-finding.[1]

The Sexual Object of the Nursing Period. However, even after the separation of the sexual activity from the taking of nourishment, there still remains an important share from this first and most important of all sex-

[1] Psychoanalysis teaches that there are two paths of object-finding: the first is the one discussed in the text, which is *anaclitic, i.e.,* it follows the early infantile prototypes. The second is the *narcissistic,* which seeks its own body and finds it in someone else. The latter is of particularly great significance for the pathological outcomes, but does not fit into the relations treated here.

ual relations, which prepares for object selection and assists in re-establishing the lost happiness. Throughout the latency period, the child learns to love other persons who assist him in his helplessness and gratify his wants; all this follows the model of the child's infantile relations to his wet nurse and is a continuation of it. One may perhaps hesitate to identify the tender feelings and esteem of the child for his foster-parents with sexual love; I believe, however, that a more thorough psychological investigation will establish this identify beyond any doubt. The intercourse between the child and his foster-parents is for the former an inexhaustible source of sexual excitation and gratification of erogenous zones, especially since the parents—as a rule, the mother—supplies the child with feelings which originate from her own sexual life; she pats him, kisses him and rocks him, plainly taking him as a substitute for a perfectly valid sexual object.[1] The mother would probably be terrified if it were explained to her that her tenderness awakens the child's sexual instinct and prepares its future intensity. She considers her actions as a sexually "pure" love, for she carefully avoids causing more irritation to the genitals of the child than is indispensable in caring for the body. But, as we know, the sexual instinct is not awakened by the excitation of genital zones alone. What we call tenderness will sooner or later surely exert some influence on the genital zones also. If the mother better understood the high significance of the sexual instinct for the whole psychic life and for all ethical and psychic activities, she would spare herself all reproaches even after the enlightenment. For by teaching the child to love, she only fulfills her task. As a matter of fact, it is desirable that the child should become a capable man with energetic sexual needs, and accomplish in life everything which his instinct impells him to do. Excessive parental tenderness surely becomes harmful, because it accelerates sexual maturity, and also because it "spoils" the child and makes him unfit to renounce love temporarily, or to be satisfied with a smaller amount of love in later life. One of the surest premonitions of later nervousness is when a child shows itself insatiable in its demands for parental tenderness. On the other hand, neuropathic parents, who usually display excessive tenderness, often awaken in the child with their caressing a disposition for neurotic diseases. This example at least shows that neuropathic parents have nearer ways than inheritance by which they can transfer their disturbances to their children.

Infantile Anxiety. The children themselves behave from their early childhood as if their attachment to their foster-parents were of the nature of

---

[1] Those to whom this conception appears "wicked" may read Havelock Ellis' treatise on the relations between mother and child, which expresses the same ideas (The Sexual Impulse, p. 16).

sexual love. Fear displayed by children is originally nothing but an expression for the fact that they miss the beloved person. They, therefore, meet every stranger with fear, they are afraid of the dark because they cannot see the beloved person and are calmed if they can grasp that person's hand. One overestimates the effect of child fears and of the terrifying stories told by nurses if one blames the latter for producing these fears in children. Children who are predisposed to fear absorb these stories which make no impression whatsoever upon others; and only those children are predisposed to fear whose sexual instinct is excessively or prematurely developed, or who are exigent in manner as a result of pampering. The child behaves here like the adult; that is, he changes his libido into fear when he cannot bring it to gratification, and the grown-up who becomes neurotic on account of ungratified libido behaves in his anxiety like a child; he fears when he is alone, *i.e.*, when he is without a person of whose love he feels sure, who can calm his fears by means of the most childish measures.[1]

If the tenderness of the parents for the child has luckily failed to awaken the sexual instinct of the child prematurely, *i.e.*, before the physical conditions of puberty appear, and if that awakening has not gone so far as to cause an unmistakable breaking through of the psychic excitement into the genital system, it can then fulfill its task and direct the child at the age of maturity in the selection of the sexual object. It would, of course, be most natural for the child to select as the sexual object that person whom it has loved since childhood with, so to speak, a dampened libido.[2] But owing to the delay of sexual maturity, time has been gained for the erection beside the sexual inhibitions of the incest barrier, that moral prescription which explicitly excludes from object selection the beloved person of infancy, or blood relations. The observance of this barrier is above all a demand of cultural society, which must guard against the absorption by the family of those interests which it needs for the production of higher social units. Society, therefore, uses all means to loosen

---

[1] For the explanation of the origin of the infantile fear, I am indebted to a three-year-old boy whom I once heard calling from a dark room: "Auntie, talk to me, I am afraid because it is dark." "How will that help you," answered the aunt, "you cannot see anyhow." "That's nothing," answered the child, "if someone talks, then it becomes light."—He was, as we see, not afraid of darkness, but he was afraid because he missed the person he loved, and he promised to calm down as soon as he was assured of her presence. That neurotic anxiety originates from libido, representing a transformation product of the same, and behaves to it as vinegar to wine, is one of the most significant results of psychoanalytic research. For further discussion of these problems, see my *Introductory Lectures to Psychoanalysis* (translation by Joan Riviere, London, 1922), in which no final explanation has been given.

[2] Cf. here what was said earlier concerning object selection of the child; the "tender stream."

those family ties in every individual, especially in the boy, which are only important in childhood.[1]

However, object selection is first accomplished in the imagination, for the sexual life of the maturing youth hardly finds any escape except through an indulgence in phantasies; that is, in ideas which are not destined to be brought to execution.[2] In the phantasies of all persons, the infantile tendencies, now reënforced by somatic emphasis, reappear, and among them one finds in regular frequency and in the first place, the sexual feeling of the child for the parents. Usually, this has already been differentiated by sexual attraction, namely, the attraction of the son for the mother, and of the daughter for the father.[3] Simultaneously with the overcoming and rejection of these distinctly incestuous phantasies, there occurs one of the most important as well as one of the most painful psychic accomplishments of puberty; it is the breaking away from the

[1] The incest barrier probably belongs to the historical acquisitions of humanity and, like other moral taboos, it must be fixed in many individuals through organic heredity. (Cf. Totem and Taboo.) Psychoanalytic studies show, however, how intensively the individual struggles with the incest temptations during his development and how frequently he puts them into phantasies and even into reality.

[2] The phantasies of puberty associate themselves with the infantile sexual investigation abandoned in childhood, perhaps also reach back a little into the latency period. They may be retained wholly or in great part unconsciously, and, therefore, frequently do not permit of exact location in time. They are of great significance in the origin of many symptoms, inasmuch as they furnish precisely the preliminary stages of these; that is, they determine the forms in which the repressed libido components find their gratification. In the same way, they are the patterns for the night phantasies, which come into consciousness as dreams. Dreams are often nothing else than revivals of such phantasies under the influence of a day stimulus left over from the waking life ("day remnants") upon which they lean.

Certain of the sexual phantasies of puberty stand out distinguished as quite universal in occurrence and to a very great degree independent of the experience of the individual. Thus, the sexual phantasies of spying upon parental coitus; of early seduction through beloved persons; of the threat of castration; phantasies of the mother's womb, whose content is the being within the womb and the things experienced there; and the so-called "family romance," in which the growing child reacts to the difference in his attitude toward the parents now and in childhood. O. Rank has shown ("The Myth or the Birth of the Hero," 1909) the close relations of these phantasies to myths. (English translation by Jelliffe in Monograph Series, No. 18).

One says rightly that the Oedipus complex is the nuclear complex of the neuroses, that it represents the essential part in the content of the neuroses. It is the culminating point of infantile sexuality, which through its after-effects decisively influences the sexuality of the adult. The task before each new human being is to master the Oedipus complex; one who cannot do this falls into a neurosis. Progress in psychoanalytic work has resulted in an ever clearer picture of the significance of the Oedipus complex; its recognition has become the shibboleth which distinguishes the followers of psychoanalysis from its opponents.

In another work (Das Trauma der Geburt, 1924) Rank has carried the fixation to the mother back to the embryonic past and so pointed out the biological foundation of the Oedipus complex. He derives the incest barrier, differing from what has just been said, from the traumatic effect of the birth anxiety.

[3] Compare the description concerning the inevitable relation in the Oedipus legend (The Interpretation of Dreams, pp. 307-9).

parental authority, through which alone is formed that opposition between the new and old generations, which is so important for cultural
progress. Many persons are detained at each of the stations in the course
of development through which the individual must pass; and accordingly,
there are persons who never overcome the parental authority and never,
or very imperfectly, withdraw their affection from their parents. They
are mostly girls, who, to the delight of their parents, retain their full infantile love far beyond puberty, and it is instructive to find that in their
married life these girls are incapable of fulfilling their duties to their husbands. They make cold wives and remain sexually anesthetic. This shows
that the apparently nonsexual love for parents and sexual love are nourished from the same source, *i.e.*, that the first merely corresponds to an
infantile fixation of the libido.

The more we penetrate into the deeper disturbances of the psycho-
sexual development, the more easily we can recognize the evident significance of incestuous object-selection. As a result of sexual rejection, there
remains in the unconscious of the psychoneurotic a great part, or the
whole, of the psychosexual activity for object-finding. Girls with an excessive need for affection and an equal horror for the real demands of the
sexual life experience an uncontrollable temptation, on the other hand,
to realize in life the ideal of a sexual love, and, on the other hand, to conceal their libido under an affection which they may manifest without self-
reproach; this they do by clinging for life to that infantile attraction for
their parents or brothers or sisters, which has been repressed in puberty.
With the help of the symptoms and other morbid manifestations, psychoanalysis can trace their unconscious thoughts and translate them into the
conscious, and thus easily show to such persons that they are in love with
their consanguineous relations, in the popular meaning of the term. Likewise, when a once healthy person falls sick after an unhappy love affair,
the mechanism of the disease can distinctly be explained as a return of his
libido to the persons preferred in his infancy.

The After Effects of the Infantile Object Selection. Even those who have
happily eluded the incestuous fixation of their libido have not completely
escaped in its influence. It is a distinct echo of this phase of development,
that the first serious love of the young man is often for a mature woman,
and that of the girl for an older man equipped with authority—*i.e.*, for
persons who can revive in them the image of the mother and father.[1] Generally speaking, object selection unquestionably follows more freely these
prototypes. The man seeks above all the memory picture of his mother as
it has dominated him since the beginning of childhood; this is quite con-

[1] See my study, Ueber einen besondern Typus der Objektwahl beim Manne," 1910.
English translation by Joan Riviere, Collected Papers IV, Hogarth Press, London,

sistent with the fact that the mother, if still living, strives against this, her renewal, and meets it with hostility. In view of this significance of the infantile relation to the parents for the later selection of the sexual object, it is easy to understand that every disturbance of this infantile relation brings to a head the most serious results for the sexual life after puberty. Jealousy of the lover, too, never lacks infantile sources or at least infantile reinforcement. Quarrels between parents and unhappy marital relations between the same, determine the severest predispositions for disturbed sexual development or neurotic diseases in children.

The infantile desire for the parents is, to be sure, the most important, but not the only trace revived in puberty which points the way to object selection. Other dispositions of the same origin permit the man, still supported by his infancy, to develop more than one single sexual series and to form various conditions for object selection.[1]

Prevention of Inversion. One of the tasks imposed in object selection consists in not missing the opposite sex. This, as we know, is not solved without some difficulty. The first feelings after puberty often enough go astray, though not with any permanent injury. Dessoir has correctly called attention to the regularity of enthusiastic friendships formed by boys and girls with their own sex. The greatest force which guards against a permanent inversion of the sexual object, is surely the attraction exerted by the opposite sex characteristics on each other. For this phenomenon we can give no explanation in connection with these discussions.[2] This factor, however, does not in itself suffice to exclude the inversion; besides this, there are surely many other supporting factors.

Above all, there is the authoritative inhibition of society; experience shows that where the inversion is not considered a crime, it fully corresponds perfectly to the sexual inclinations of many persons. Moreover it may be assumed that in the man, the infantile memories of the mother's tenderness, as well as that of other females who cared for him as a child, energetically assist in directing his selection to the woman, while the early sexual intimidation experienced through the father and the attitude of rivalry existing between them deflects the boy from the same sex. Both factors also hold true in the case of the girl whose sexual activity is under the special care of the mother. This results in a hostile relation to the same sex, which decisively influences selection in the normal sense.

---

[1] Innumerable peculiarities of the human love-life, as well as the compulsiveness of being in love itself, can surely only be understood through a reference to childhood or as an effective remnant of the same.

[2] Here is the place to call attention to a certain phantastic but at the same time very penetrating study by Ferenczi (Versuch einer Genitaltheorie, 1924, translated by Bunker), in which the sexual life of higher animals is traced back to their biological evolutionary stages.

The bringing up of boys by male persons (slaves in the ancient times) seems to favor homosexuality; the frequency of inversion in the present day nobility is probably explained by their employment of male servants, and by the scant care that mothers of that class give to their children. It sometimes happens in hysterics that one of the parents disappears (through death, divorce or estrangement), thus enabling the other parent to absorb all the love of the child; such a state of affairs may establish the determinants for the sex of the person to be selected later as the sexual object, and with it a permanent inversion.

SUMMARY

It is now time to attempt a summing up. We have started from the aberrations of the sexual instinct in reference to its object and aim and have encountered the question whether these originate from a congenital predisposition, or whether they are acquired in consequence of influences from life. The answer to this question was reached through a psychoanalytic investigation of the relations of the sexual life of psychoneurotics, a numerous group not very different from the normal. We have thus found that a tendency to all perversions could be demonstrated in these persons in the form of unconscious forces, which betray themselves as symptom creators, and we could say that the neurosis is, as it were, the negative of the perversion. In view of the now recognized great diffusion of tendencies to perversion, the idea forced itself upon us that the disposition to perversions is a primitive and universal disposition of the human sexual instinct, from which the normal sexual behavior develops in consequence of organic changes and psychic inhibitions in the course of maturity. We hoped to be able to demonstrate the original disposition in the infantile life, and among the forces restraining the direction of the sexual instinct we have mentioned shame, loathing, sympathy, and the social constructions of morality and authority.

We have thus been forced to perceive in every fixed aberration from the normal sexual life, a fragment of inhibited development and infantilism. The significance of the variations of the original dispositions had to be put into the foreground, but between them and the influences of life, we had to assume a relation of co-operation and not of opposition. On the other hand, as the original disposition must have been a complex one, the sexual instinct itself appeared to us as something composed of many factors, which in the perversions becomes separated, as it were, into its components. The perversions thus prove themselves to be, on the one hand, inhibitions, and on the other, dissociations from the normal development. Both conceptions are united in the assumption that the sexual instinct of the adult, due to the composition of the diverse feelings of the infantile life, is formed into one unit, one striving, with one single aim.

We also added an explanation for the preponderance of perversive tendencies in the psychoneurotics, by recognizing in these tendencies collateral fillings of side branches caused by the shifting of the main river bed through repression, and we then turned our examination to the sexual life of the infantile period.[1] We found it regrettable that the existence of a sexual life in infancy has been disputed, and that the sexual manifestations which have often been observed in children have been described as abnormal occurrences. It rather seemed to us that the child brings along into the world germs of sexual activity and that even while taking nourishment, it at the same time also enjoys a sexual gratification which it then seeks again to procure for itself through the familiar activity of "thumbsucking." The sexual activity of the child, however, does not develop in the same measure as his other functions, but merges first into the so-called latency period from the age of three to the age of five years. The production of sexual excitation by no means ceases at this period but continues to furnish a stock of energy, the greater part of which is utilized for aims other than sexual. On the one hand, it is used for the delivery of sexual components for social feelings, and on the other hand (by means of repression and reaction formation), for the erection of the future sex barriers. Accordingly, the forces which are destined to hold the sexual instinct in certain tracks are built up in infancy with the help of education at the expense of the greater part of the perverse sexual feelings. Another part of the infantile sexual manifestations escapes this utilization and may manifest itself as sexual activity. It can then be discovered that the sexual excitation of the child flows from diverse sources. Above all, gratifications originate through the adapted sensible excitation of so-called erogenous zones. For these probably any skin region or sensory organ may serve; but there are certain distinguished erogenous zones, the excitation of which by certain organic mechanisms, is assured from the beginning. Moreover, sexual excitation originates in the organism, as it were, as a by-product in a greater number of processes, as soon as they attain a certain intensity; this especially takes place in all strong emotional excitements, even if they be of a painful nature. The excitations from all these sources do not yet unite, but they pursue their aim individually—this aim consisting merely in the gaining of a certain pleasure. The sexual instinct of childhood is therefore objectless or *autoerotic*.

[1] This was true not only of the "negative" tendencies to perversion appearing in the neurosis, but also of the so-called positive perversions. The latter are not only to be attributed to the fixation of the infantile tendencies, but also to regression to these tendencies owing to the misplacement of other paths of the sexual stream. Hence, the positive perversions are also accessible to psychoanalytic therapy. (Cf. the works of Sadger, Ferenczi and Brill.)

Still during infancy the erogenous zone of the genitals begins to make itself noticeable, either by the fact that like any other erogenous zone, it furnishes gratification through a suitable sensible stimulus, or because in some incomprehensible way, the gratification from other sources causes at the same time the sexual excitement which has a special connection with the genital zone. We found cause to regret that an adequate explanation of the relations between sexual gratification and sexual excitement, as well as between the activity of the genital zone and the remaining sources of sexuality, was not to be attained.

We have noticed through the study of neurotic disturbances that from the very beginning, tendencies toward an organization of the sexual instinctive components may be recognized in infantile sexual life. *Oral erotism* stands in the foreground in a first, very early phase; a second of these "pregenital" organizations is characterized by the predominance of *sadism* and *anal erotism,* and only in a third phase (which the child develops merely as far as the primacy of the *phallus*) is the sexual life determined also through the participation of the true genital zones.

We have then been compelled to affirm as one of the most striking discoveries, that this early flowering of the infantile sexual life (from the second to the fifth year) also brings to maturity an object choice with all its rich psychic activities. The phase joined to this and corresponding to it (despite the imperfect amalgamation of the individual instinctive components and the lack of certainty in the sexual aim) must therefore be valued as the important precursor of the later and final sexual organization.

The fact that sexual development in man shows *two different periods,* namely, the interruption of this development by the latency period, has seemed to us to deserve special consideration. It appears to contain one of the conditions for fitting man to develop to a higher culture, but also for his tendency to neurosis. So far as we know, nothing analogous is demonstrable in man's animal kin. The origin of this human peculiarity would have to be sought in the primal history of the human species.

We were unable to state what amount of sexual activity in childhood might be designated as normal, to the extent of being incapable of further development. The character of the sexual manifestation showed itself to be preponderantly masturbatic. We, moreover, verified from experience the belief that the external influences of seduction might produce premature breaches in the latency period, even to the extent of suppressing it, and that the sexual instinct of the child really shows itself to be polymorphous-perverse; furthermore, that every such premature sexual activity impairs the educability of the child.

Despite the incompleteness of our examinations of the infantile sexual life, we were subsequently forced to attempt to study the serious changes produced by the appearance of puberty. We selected two of the same as criteria, namely, the subordination of all other sources of the sexual feeling to the primacy of the genital zones, and the process of object-finding. Both of them are already developed in childhood. The first is accomplished through the mechanism of utilizing the fore-pleasure, whereby the former independent sexual acts connected with pleasure and excitement become preparatory acts for the new sexual aim, namely, the voiding of the sexual products, the attainment of which under enormous pleasure, puts an end to the sexual feeling. At the same time, we had to consider the differentiation of the sexual nature of man and woman, and we found that in order to become a woman, a new repression is required which abolishes a piece of infantile masculinity and prepares the woman for the change of the leading genital zone. We found lastly object selection, as we were led through the infantile signs of sexual desire of the child for the parents and foster-parents, which are revived in puberty but deflected, by the incest barriers which had been erected in the meantime, from these persons and directed to others resembling them. Let us finally add that during the transition period of puberty the somatic and psychic processes of development proceed side by side, but separately, until with the breaking through of an intense psychic love-stimulus for the innervation of the genitals, the normally demanded unification of the erotic function is established.

Factors Disturbing the Development. As we have already shown by different examples, every step on this long path of development may become a point of fixation and every joint in this complicated structure may afford opportunity for a dissociation of the sexual instinct. It still remains for us to review the various inner and outer factors which disturb this development, and to mention the part of the mechanism affected by the disturbance emanating from them. The factors which we mention here in a series, of course, cannot all be in themselves of equal validity, and we must expect to meet with difficulties in assigning to the individual factors their due importance.

Constitution and Heredity. In the first place, we must mention here the congenital *variation of the sexual constitution,* upon which the greatest weight probably falls, but the existence of which, as may be easily understood, can be established only through its later manifestations, and even then not always with great certainty. We understand by it a preponderance of one or another of the manifold sources of sexual excitement, and we believe that such a difference of disposition must always come to expression in the final result, even if it should remain within normal limits. Of course, we can also imagine certain variations of the original disposition, which even without further aid, must necessarily lead to the formation of an abnormal sexual life. One can call these "degenerative," and consider them as an expression of hereditary deterioration. In this connection, I have to report a remarkable fact. In more than half of the severe cases of hysteria, compulsion neuroses, etc., which I have treated by psychotherapy, I have succeeded in positively demonstrating that their fathers have gone through an attack of syphilis before marriage; they have either suffered from tabes or general paresis, or there was a definite history of lues. I expressly add, that the children who were later neurotic, showed absolutely no signs of hereditary lues, so that the abnormal sexual constitution was to be considered as the last off-shoot of the luetic heredity. As far as it is now from my thoughts to put down a descent from syphilitic parents as a regular and indispensable etiological determination of the neuropathic constitution, I nevertheless maintain that the coincidence observed by me is not accidental and not without significance.

The hereditary relations of the positive perverts are not so well known because they know how to evade inquiry, but we have every reason to believe that what is true of the neuroses is also true of the perversions. We often find perversions and psychoneuroses in the different sexes of the same family, so distributed that the male members, or one of them, is a positive pervert, while the females, following the repressive tendencies of their sex, are negative perverts or hysterics. This is a good example of the intimate relations between the two disturbances discovered by us.

Further Elaborations. We cannot, however, maintain that with the addition of the diverse components of the sexual constitution, we have fully finished the structure of the sexual life. On the contrary, the hypothesis continues and new possibilities arise, which depend upon the fate experienced by the sexual streams which originate from the individual sources. This *further elaboration* is evidently final and decisive, whereas the one described in accordance with the same constitution may lead to three final issues. If all the dispositions assumed as abnormal retain their relative proportion, and are strengthened with maturity, the ultimate result can only be a perverse sexual life. The analysis of such abnormally constituted dispositions has not yet been thoroughly undertaken, but we already know of cases that can be readily explained in the light of these theories. Some believe, for example, of a whole series of fixation perversions, that they must of necessity have been predisposed to the aberration by a congenital weakness of the sexual instinct. This statement seems to me untenable in this form, but it becomes very sensible if it refers to a constitutional weakness of one factor of the sexual instinct, namely, the genital zone, which later takes charge of the sum of the individual sexual activities as the function of propagation. That being the case, the summation necessary in puberty must fail and the strongest of the other sexual components then force through its activity as a perversion.[1]

Repression. Another issue results if, in the course of development, certain powerful components experience a *repression*—which we must carefully note is not a suspension. The excitations in question are produced as usual but are prevented from attaining their aim through psychic hindrances. They are then driven into many other paths until they finally express themselves in symptoms. The result may be an almost normal sexual life—usually a restricted one—but supplemented by a psychoneurotic disease. It is these cases that become so familiar to us through psychoanalytic investigation of neurotics. The sexual life of such persons begins like that of perverts. A considerable part of their childhood is filled up with perverse sexual activity which occasionally extends far beyond the period of maturity. However, owing to inner reasons, a repressive change then results—usually before puberty, but now and then even much later —so that, without any extinction of the old feelings, there later appears a neurosis instead of a perversion. One may recall here the saying: *"Junge Hure, alte Betschwester,"* (In youth a whore, a devotee in old age)—except that here, youth has turned out to be much too short. The substitution of the perversion by the neurosis in the life of the same person, as well as the above mentioned distribution of perversion and hysteria in different persons of the same family, must be placed side by side with the fact that the neurosis is the negative of the perversion.

Sublimation. The third issue in abnormal constitutional dispositions is made possible by the process of "sublimation," through which the excessive excitations from individual sexual sources are discharged and utilized in other spheres, so that no small enhancement of mental capacity results from a predisposition which is dangerous as such. This forms one of the sources of artistic activity, and, depending on whether such sublimation is complete or incomplete, the analysis of the character of highly gifted, especially of artistically disposed persons, will show every kind of proportionate blending between productive ability, perversion and neurosis. A lower form of sublimation is the suppression through *reaction-formation,* which, as we have found, begins early in the latency period of infancy, and may continue throughout life in favorable cases. What we call the *character* of the person is built up to a large extent from the material of sexual excitations; it is composed of impulses fixed since infancy

[1] Here one often sees that at first a normal sexual stream begins at the age of puberty, but owing to its inner weakness, it breaks down at the first outer hindrance, and then changes through regression to a perverse fixation.

and won through sublimation, and of such structures as are destined to suppress effectually those perverse feelings which are recognized as useless.[1] The general perverse sexual disposition of childhood can therefore be esteemed as a source of a number of our virtues, insofar as it incites their creation through the formation of reactions.[2]

Accidental Experiences. All other influences lose much in significance when compared with the sexual discharges, shifts of repressions, and sublimations, despite the fact that the inner determinants of the last two processes are totally unknown to us. He who includes repressions and sublimations among constitutional predispositions, and considers them as the living manifestations of the same, has surely the right to maintain that the final structure of the sexual life is, above all, the result of the congenital constitution. No intelligent person, however, will dispute that in such a coöperation of factors there is also room for modifying influences of accidental factors both from experience in childhood and from later life. It is not easy to estimate the effectiveness of the constitutional and of the accidental factors in their relation to each other. Theory is always inclined to overestimate the first, while therapeutic practice renders prominent the importance of the latter. By no means should it be forgotten, however, that between the two there exists a relation of coöperation and not of exclusion. The constitutional factor must wait for experiences which bring it to the surface, while the accidental factor needs the support of the constitutional factor in order to become effective. For the majority of cases, one can imagine a so-called "etiological group" in which the declining intensities of one factor become balanced by the rise in the others, but there is no reason to deny the existence of extreme cases at the ends of the series.

It would be still more in harmony with psychoanalytic investigations if the experiences of early childhood would get a place of preference among the accidental factors. The one etiological series would then become split up into two, and might be designated *dispositional* and *definitive*. Constitution and accidental infantile experiences are just as coöperative in the first series as disposition and later traumatic experiences in the second. All the factors which injure the sexual development show their effect in

---

[1] Certain character traits are known to stand in relationship to definite erogenous components. Thus obstinacy, stinginess, and orderliness are traceable to anal erotism. Ambition is determined through a marked urethral disposition.

[2] That keen observer of human nature, E. Zola, describes a girl in his book, "La Joie de Vivre," who in cheerful self-renunciation offers all she has in possession or expectation, her fortune and her life's hopes, to those she loves without thought of return. The childhood of this girl was dominated by an insatiable desire for love which, when she once was thwarted, caused her to plunge into a fit of cruelty against another girl.

that they produce a *regression,* or a return to a former phase of development.

We may now continue with our task of enumerating the factors which have become known to us as influential for the sexual development, whether they be active forces or merely manifestations of the same.

Prematurity. Such a factor is the spontaneous sexual *prematurity* which can be definitely demonstrated at least in the etiology of the neuroses, though in itself it is as little adequate for causation as the other factors. It manifests itself in a breaking through, shortening or suspending of the infantile latency period and becomes a cause of disturbances inasmuch as it provokes sexual manifestations which, either on account of the unready state of the sexual inhibitions or because of the undeveloped state of the genital system, can only manifest the character of perversions. These tendencies to perversion may either remain as such, or after the repression sets in, they may act as motive powers for neurotic symptoms. Be that as it may, sexual prematurity renders difficult the desirable later control of the sexual instinct by the higher psychic influences, and enhances the compulsive-like character which, even without this prematurity, forms part of the psychic representatives of the instinct. Sexual prematurity often runs parallel with premature intellectual development; it is found as such in the infantile history of the most distinguished and most productive individuals, and in such cases it does not seem to act as pathogenically as when it appears isolated.

Temporal Factors. Just like prematurity, other factors, which under the designation of *temporal* can be added to prematurity, also demand consideration. It seems to be established phylogenetically in what sequence the individual impulsive feelings become activated, and how long they can manifest themselves before they succumb to the influence of a newly appearing active impulse or to a typical repression. But variations seem to occur, both in this temporal succession as well as in the duration of the same, and these must exercise a conditioning influence on the end result. It cannot be a matter of indifference whether a certain stream appears earlier or later than its counterstream, for the effect of a repression cannot be made retrogressive; a temporal deviation in the composition of the components regularly alters the result. On the other hand, instinctive impulses appearing with special intensity often run a surprisingly swift course, *e.g.,* a heterosexual attachment of later manifest homosexuals. The strivings of childhood which manifest themselves most impetuously do not justify the fear that they will lastingly dominate the character of the grown-up; one has as much right to expect that they will disappear in order to make room for their counterparts. (Harsh masters do not rule long.) To what one may attribute such temporal confusions of the processes of development, we are hardly able to suggest. A view is opened here to a deeper phalanx of biological, and perhaps also historical problems, which we have not yet approached within fighting distance.

Adhesion. The significance of all premature sexual manifestations is enhanced by a psychic factor of unknown origin, which at present can be put down only as a psychological preliminary. I believe that it is the *heightened adhesion* or *fixedness* of these impressions of the sexual life which in later neurotics, as well as in perverts, must be added as a supplement to the existing facts. For the same premature sexual manifestations in other persons cannot impress themselves deeply enough to act compulsively on repetition, and to lay out the path of the sexual instinct for the whole future. A partial explanation for this adhesion is perhaps found in another psychic factor which we cannot miss in the causation of the neuroses, namely, in the preponderance which in the psychic life falls to the share of memory traces in comparison to those of recent impressions. This factor apparently depends on intellectual development and grows with the height of personal culture. In contrast to this, the savage has been characterized as the "unfortunate child of the moment." [1] Due to the hostile relation which exists between culture and the free development of sexuality, the results of which may be traced far into the formation of our life, the problem how the sexual life of the child evolves is of very little importance for the later life in the lower states of culture and civilization, but of very great importance in the higher states of civilization.

Fixation. The influence of the psychic factors just mentioned favor the development of the accidental stimuli of the infantile sexuality. The latter (especially in the form of seductions through other children or through adults) produce the material which, with the help of the former, may become fixed as permanent disturbances. A considerable number of the deviations from normal sexual life observed later have very early been established in this way in neurotics and perverts through impressions received during the alleged sexually free period of childhood. The responsiveness of the constitution, the prematurity, the quality of heightened adhesion, and the accidental stimuli of the sexual instinct through outside influence, all participate in the etiology of the symptoms.

The unsatisfactory conclusions which have resulted from this investigation of the disturbances of the sexual life are due to the fact that as yet

[1] It is possible that the heightened adhesion is only the result of the special intensive somatic sexual manifestation of former years.

we know too little concerning the biological processes of which the nature of sexuality consists, to form from our desultory views a satisfactory theory for the explanation of what is normal or pathological.

FOUR

WIT AND ITS RELATION TO THE UNCONSCIOUS

A. ANALYSIS

I

INTRODUCTION

WHOEVER has had occasion to examine that part of the literature of aesthetics and psychology dealing with the nature and affinities of wit, will, no doubt, concede that our philosophical inquiries have not awarded to wit the important rôle that it plays in our mental life. One can recount only a small number of thinkers who have penetrated at all deeply into the problems of wit. To be sure, among the authors on wit, one finds the illustrious names of the poet Jean Paul (Fr. Richter), and of the philosophers Th. Vischer, Kuno Fischer and Th. Lipps. But even these writers put the subject of wit in the background while their chief interest centers around the more comprehensive and more alluring problems of the comic.

In the main, this literature gives the impression that it is altogether impractical to study wit except when treated as a part of the comic.

PRESENTATION OF THE SUBJECT BY OTHER AUTHORS

According to Th. Lipps (*Komik und Humor*, 1898 [1]) wit is "essentially the subjective side of the comic; *i.e.*, it is that part of the comic which we ourselves create, which colors our conduct as such, and to which our relation is that of Superior Subject, never of Object, certainly not Voluntary Object" (p. 80). The following comment might also be added: In general, we designate as wit "every conscious and clever evocation of the comic, whether the comic element lies in the viewpoint or in the situation itself" (p. 78).

K. Fischer explains the relation between wit and the comic by the aid of caricature, which, according to the exposition, comes midway between the two (*Über den Witz*, 1889). The subject of the comic is the hideous element in any of its manifestations. "Where it is concealed it must be disclosed in the light of the comic view; where it is not at all or but

---

[1] *Beiträge zur Aesthetik*, edited by Theodor Lipps and Richard Maria Werner, VI,—a book to which I am indebted for the courage and capacity to undertake this attempt.

slightly noticeable, it must be rendered conspicuous and elucidated in such a manner that it becomes clear and intelligible. Thus arises caricature" (p. 45). "Our entire psychic world, the intellectual realm of our thoughts and conceptions, does not reveal itself to us on superficial consideration. It cannot be visualized directly either figuratively or intuitively, moreover it contains inhibitions, weak points, disfigurements, and an abundance of ludicrous and comical contrasts. In order to bring it out and to make it accessible to aesthetic examination, a force is necessary which is capable not only of reflecting upon these conceptions and elucidating them—namely, a force capable of clarifying thought. This force is nothing but judgment. The judgment which produces the comic contrast is wit. In caricature, wit has played its part unnoticed, but only in judgment does it attain its own individual form and the free domain of its evolution."

As can be seen, Lipps assigns the determining factor which classifies wit as part of the comic, to the activity or to the active behavior of the subject, whereas K. Fischer characterizes wit by its relation to its object, in which characterization he accentuates the hidden hideous element in the realm of thought. One cannot put to test the cogency of these definitions of wit; one can, in fact, hardly understand them unless one studies the text from which they were taken. One is thus forced to work his way through the author's descriptions of the comic in order to learn anything about wit. From other passages, however, one discovers that the same authors attribute to wit essential characteristics of general validity in which they disregard its relation to the comic.

K. Fischer's characterization of wit which seems to be most satisfactory to this author, runs as follows: "Wit is a *playful* judgment" (p. 51). For an elucidation of this expression, we are referred to the analogy: "How aesthetic freedom consists in the playful contemplation of objects" (p. 50). In another place (p. 20), the aesthetic attitude towards an object is characterized by the condition that we expect nothing from this object—especially no gratification of our serious needs—but that we content ourselves with the pleasure of contemplating the same. In contrast to labor, the aesthetic attitude is *playful*. "It may be that from aesthetic freedom there also results a kind of judgment, freed from the conventional restrictions and rule of conduct, which, in view of its genesis, I will call the *playful* judgment. This conception contains the first condition and possibly the entire formula for the solution of our problem. 'Freedom begets wit and wit begets freedom,' says Jean Paul. Wit is nothing but a free play of ideas" (p. 24).

Since time immemorial, a favorite definition of wit has been the ability to discover similarities in dissimilarities, *i.e.*, to find hidden similarities. Jean Paul has jocosely expressed this idea by saying that "wit is the disguised priest who unites every couple." Th. Vischer adds the postscript: "He likes best to unite those couples whose marriage the relatives refuse to sanction." Vischer refutes this, however, by remarking that in some witticisms, there is no question of comparison or discovery of similarities. Hence, with very little deviation from Jean Paul's definition, he defines wit as the skill to combine with surprising quickness many ideas, which through inner content and connections are foreign to one another. K. Fischer then calls attention to the fact that in a large number of these witty judgments, one does not find similarities, but contrasts; and Lipps further remarks that these definitions refer to the wit that the humorist possesses and not to the wit that he produces.

Other viewpoints, in some measure connected with one another, which have been mentioned in defining and describing wit are: *"the contrast of ideas," "sense in nonsense,"* and *"confusion and clearness."*

Definitions like those of Kraepelin lay stress upon the contrast of ideas. Wit is "the voluntary combination or linking of two ideas which in some way are contrasted with each other, usually through the medium of speech association." For a critic like Lipps, it would not be difficult to reveal the utter inadequacy of this formula, but he himself does not exclude the element of contrast—he merely assigns it elsewhere. "The contrast remains, but is not formed in a manner to show the ideas connected with the words, rather it shows the contrast or contradiction in the meaning and lack of meaning of the words" (p. 87). Examples show the better understanding of the latter. "A contrast arises first through the fact that we adjudge a meaning to its words which after all, we cannot ascribe to them."

In the further development of this last condition, the antithesis of "sense in nonsense" becomes obvious. "What we accept one moment as senseful, we later perceive as perfect nonsense. Thereby arises, in this case, the operation of the comic element" (p. 85). "A saying appears witty when we ascribe to it a meaning through psychological necessity and, while doing so, retract it. It may thus have many meanings. We lend a meaning to an expression, knowing that logically it does not belong to it. We find in it a truth, however, which later we fail to find because it is foreign to our laws of experience or usual modes of thinking. We endow it with a logical or practical inference which transcends its true content, only to contradict this inference as soon as we finally grasp the nature of the expression itself. The psychological process evoked in us by the witty expression which gives rise to the sense of the comic, depends in every case on the immediate transition from the borrowed feeling of truth and conviction to the impression or consciousness of relative nullity."

As impressive as this exposition sounds, one cannot refrain from questioning whether the contrast between the senseful and senseless upon which the comic depends, does not also contribute to the definition of wit in so far as it is distinguished from the comic. Also the factor of "confusion and clearness" leads one deeply into the problem of the relation of wit to the comic. Kant, speaking of the comic element in general, states that one of its remarkable attributes is the fact that it can delude us for a moment only. Heymans (*Zeitschr. f. Psychologie*, XI, 1896) explains how the mechanism of wit is produced through the succession of confusion and clearness. He illustrates his meaning by an excellent witticism from Heine, who causes one of his figures, the poor lottery agent, Hirsch-Hyacinth, to boast that the great Baron Rothschild treated him as an equal or quite FAMILLIONAIRE. Here, the word which acts as the carrier of the witticism appears in the first place simply as a faulty word-formation, as something incomprehensible, inconceivable and enigmatic. It is for these reasons that it is confusing. The comic element results from the solution of the enigma and from the understanding of the word. Lipps adds that the first stage of enlightenment, showing that the confusing word means this or that, is followed by a second stage in which one perceives that this nonsensical word has first deluded us and then given us the true meaning. Only this second enlightenment, the realization that it is all due to a word that is meaningless in ordinary usage—this reduction to nothingness produces the comic effect (p. 95).

Whether or not either the one or the other of these two conceptions may seem clearer, we are brought nearer to a definite insight through the discussion of the processes of confusion and enlightenment. If the comic effect of Heine's *famillionaire* depends upon the solution of the seemingly senseless word, then the wit would have to be attributed to the formation of this word and to the character of the word so formed.

In addition to the associations of the viewpoints just discussed, there is another characteristic of wit which is recognized as peculiar to it by all authors. "Brevity alone is the body and soul of wit," declares Jean Paul (*Vorschule der Aesthetik*, I, 45), and modifies it with a speech of the old tongue-wagger, Polonius. from Shakespeare's *Hamlet* (Act II, Scene 2):

> "Therefore, since brevity is the soul of wit,
> And tediousness the limbs and outward flourishes,
> I will be brief."

Lipps's description (p. 90) of the brevity of wit is also significant. He states that wit says what it does say, not always in few, but always in too few words; this is: "It expresses itself in words that will not stand the test of strict logic or of the ordinary mode of thought and expression. In fine, it can express itself by leaving the thing unsaid."

That "wit must unearth something hidden and concealed"—to quote

K. Fischer (p. 51)—we have already been taught from the grouping of wit with caricature. I re-emphasize this determinant because it also has more to do with the nature of wit than with its relation to the comic. I am well aware that the foregoing scanty quotations from the works of the authors on wit cannot do justice to the excellence of these works. In view of the difficulties that confront one in reproducing clearly such complicated and such delicately shaded streams of thought, I cannot spare inquiring minds the trouble of searching for the desired information in the original sources. However, I do not know whether they will return fully satisfied. For the criteria and attributes of wit mentioned by these authors, such as—activity, the relation of the content of wit to our thoughts, the character of the playful judgment, the union of dissimilarities, contrasting ideas, "sense in nonsense," the succession of confusion and clearness, the sudden emergence of the hidden and the peculiar brevity of wit—seems to us, at first glance, so very pertinent and so easily demonstrable by examples that we cannot succumb to the danger of underestimating the value of such ideas. But they are only disjointed fragments which we should like to see welded into an organic whole. In the end, they contribute no more to the knowledge of wit than a number of anecdotes teach us of the true characteristics of a personality whose biography interests us. We do not at all understand the connection that is supposed to exist between the individual conditions; for instance, what the brevity of wit may have to do with that side of wit exhibited in the playful judgment; besides we do not know whether wit must satisfy all or only some of these conditions in order to form real wit; which of them may be replaced and which ones are indispensable. We should also like a grouping and classification of wit in respect to its essential attributes. The classification as given by the authors is based, on the one hand, on the technical means, and on the other hand, on the utilization of wit in speech (sound-wit, play on words, the wit of caricature, characterization wit and witty repartee).

Accordingly, we should not find ourselves in a dilemma when it comes to pointing out goals for a further effort to explain wit. In order to look forward to success, we must either introduce new viewpoints into the work, or try to penetrate further by concentrating our attention or by broadening the scope of our interest. We can prescribe for ourselves the task of at least not permitting any lack along the latter lines. To be sure, it is rather remarkable how few examples of recognized witticisms suffice the authors for their investigations and how each one accepts the ones used by his predecessors. We need not shirk the responsibility of analyzing the same examples which have already served the classical authors, but we contemplate new material besides to lay a broader foundation for our deductions. It is quite natural that we should select such examples of wit as objects for our investigation as have produced the deepest impression upon our own lives and which have caused us the greatest amount of laughter.

Some may inquire whether the subject of wit is worthy of such effort. In my opinion, there is no doubt about it, for even if I disregard the personal motives to be revealed during the development of this theme (the motives which drove me to gain an insight into the problem of wit), I can refer to the fact that there is an intimate connection between all psychic occurrences; a connection which promises to furnish a psychological insight into a sphere which, although remote, will nevertheless be of considerable value to the other spheres. One may also be reminded what a peculiar, overwhelmingly fascinating charm wit offers in our society. A new joke operates almost as an event of universal interest. It is passed on from one person to another, just like the news of the latest conquest. Even prominent men who consider it worth while relating how they attained fame, what cities and countries they have seen, and with what celebrated persons they have consorted, do not disdain to dwell in their autobiographies upon this and that excellent joke which they have heard.[1]

[1] J. V. Falke: *Lebenserinnerungen*, 1897.

II

THE TECHNIQUE OF WIT

WE FOLLOW the beckoning of chance and take up as our first example of wit one which has already come to our notice in the previous chapter.

In that part of the *Reisebilder* entitled "Die Bäder von Lucca," Heine introduces the precious character, Hirsch-Hyacinth, the Hamburg lottery agent and curer of corns, who, boasting to the poet of his relationship with the rich Baron Rothschild, ends thus: "And as true as I pray that the Lord may grant me all good things, I sat next to Solomon Rothschild, who treated me just as if I were his equal, quite *famillionaire*."

It is by means of this excellent and very funny example, that Heymans and Lipps have illustrated the origin of the comic effect of wit from the succession of "confusion and clearness." However, we shall pass over this question and put to ourselves the following inquiry: What is it that causes the speech of Hirsch-Hyacinth to become witty? It can be only one of two things; either it is the thought expressed in the sentence which carries in itself the character of the witticism; or the witticism adheres to the mode of expression which clothes the thought. On whichever side the nature of the wit may lie, there we shall follow it farther and endeavor to elucidate it.

In general, a thought may be expressed in different forms of speech—that is, in different words—which may repeat it in its original accuracy. In the speech of Hirsch-Hyacinth, we have before us a definite form of thought expressed which seems to us especially peculiar and not very readily comprehensible. Let us attempt to express as exactly as is possible the same thought in other words. Lipps, indeed, has already done this and has thus, to some degree, elucidated the meaning of the poet. He says (p. 87), "We understand that Heine wishes to say that the reception was on a familiar basis, that is, that it was of the friendly sort." We change nothing in the sense when we assume a different interpretation which perhaps fits better into the speech of Hirsch-Hyacinth: "Rothschild treated me quite as his equal, in a very *familiar* way; that is, as far as this can be done by a *millionaire*." We would only add, "The condescension of a rich man always carries something embarrassing for the one experiencing it." [1]

Whether we shall remain content with this or with another equivalent formulation of the thought, we can see that the question which we have put to ourselves is already answered. The character of the wit in this example does not adhere to the thought. It is a correct and ingenious remark that Heine puts into the mouth of Hirsch-Hyacinth—a remark of indubitable bitterness, as is easily understood in the case of the poor man confronted with so much wealth; but we should not care to call it witty. Now, if anyone who cannot forget the poet's meaning in the interpretation should insist that the thought in itself is also witty, we can refer him to the definite fact that the witty character is lost in the interpretation. It is true that Hirsch-Hyacinth's speech made us laugh loudly, but though Lipps's or our own accurate rendering may please us and cause us to reflect, yet it cannot make us laugh.

But if the witty character of our example does not belong to the thought, then it must be sought in the form of expression in the wording. We have only to study the peculiarity of this mode of expression to realize what one may term word- or form-technique. Also we may discover the things that are intimately related to the very nature of wit, since the character as well as the effect of wit disappears when one set of expressions is changed for others. At all events, we are in full accord with our authors when we put so much value upon the verbal form of the wit. Thus, K. Fischer (p. 72) says: "It is, in the first place, the naked form which is responsible for the perception of wit, and one is reminded of a saying of Jean Paul's which affirms and proves this nature of wit in the same expression. 'Thus the mere position conquers, be it that of warriors or of sentences.'"

FORMATION OF MIXED WORDS

Now wherein lies the "technique" of this wit? What has occurred to the thought, in our own conception, that it became changed into wit and caused us to laugh heartily? The comparison of our conception with the text of the poet teaches us that two processes took place. In the first place, there occurred an important abbreviation. In order to express fully the thought contained in the witticism, we had to append to the words "Rothschild treated me just as an equal, on a familiar basis," an additional sentence which in its briefest form reads: *i.e.*, so far as a millionaire can do this. Even then, we feel the necessity of an additional explanatory sentence.[2] The poet expresses it in terser terms as follows: "Rothschild

---

[1] Since this joke will occupy us again and we do not wish to disturb the discussion following here, we shall find occasion later to point out a correction in Lipps's given interpretation which follows our own.

[2] The same holds true for Lipps's interpretation.

treated me just like an equal, quite *famillionaire.*" The entire restriction, which the second sentence imposes on the first, thus verifying the familiar treatment, has been lost in the jest. But it has not been so entirely lost as not to leave a substitute from which it can be reconstructed. A second change has also taken place. The word "familiar" in the witless expression of the thought has been transformed into *"famillionaire"* in the text of the wit, and there is no doubt that the witty character and ludicrous effect of the joke depends directly upon this word-formation. The newly formed word is identical in its first part with the word "familiar" of the first sentence, and its terminal syllables correspond to the word "millionaire" of the second sentence. In this manner, it puts us in a position to conjecture the second sentence which was omitted in the text of the wit. It may be described as a composite of two constituents "familiar" and "millionaire," and one is tempted to depict its origin from the two words graphically:

FAMIL I A R
MILLIONAIRE
_____

FAMILLIONAIRE

The process, then, which has carried the thought into the witticism can be represented in the following manner, which, although at first rather fantastic, nevertheless furnishes exactly the actual existing result: "Rothschild treated me quite familiarly, *i.e.,* as well as a millionaire can do that sort of thing."

Now imagine that a compressing force is acting upon these sentences and assume that for some reason or other, the second sentence is of lesser resistance. It is accordingly forced toward the vanishing point, but its important component, the word "millionaire," which strives against the compressing power, is pushed, as it were, into the first sentence and becomes fused with the very similar element, the word "familiar" of this sentence. It is just this possibility, provided by chance to save the essential part of the second sentence, which favors the disappearance of the other less important components. The jest then takes shape in this manner: "Rothschild treated me in a very famillionaire way."
(mili) (aire)

Apart from such a compressing force, which is really unknown to us, we may describe the origin of the wit-formation, that is, the technique of the wit in this case, as a *condensation with substitutive formation.* In our example, the substitutive formation consists in the formation of a mixed word. This fused word "famillionaire," incomprehensible in itself but instantly understood in its context and recognized as senseful, is now the carrier of the mirth-provoking stimulus of the jest, whose mechanism, to be sure, is in no way clearer to us through the discovery of the technique. To what extent can a linguistic process of condensation with substitutive formation produce pleasure through a fused word and force us to laugh? We make note of the fact that this is a different problem, the treatment of which we can postpone until we shall find access to it later. For the present, we shall continue to busy ourselves with the technique of wit.

Our expectation that the technique of wit cannot be considered an indifferent factor in the examination of the nature of wit prompts us to inquire next whether there are other examples of wit formed like Heine's "famillionaire." Not many of these exist, but enough to constitute a small group which may be characterized as the blend-word formations or fusions. Heine himself produced a second witticism, as it were, when he speaks of a "millionarr" (*Ideen*, Chap. XIV). This is a visible condensation of "millionaire" and "narr" (fool) and, like the first example, expresses a suppressed by-thought. Other examples of a similar nature are as follows:

In an excellent chapter on this same theme, Brill gives the following example.[1]

"Disraeli once remarked that old persons are apt to fall into 'anecdotage.' " The word *anecdotage,* though in itself incomprehensible, can be readily analyzed to show its original full sense; and on analysis we find that it is made up of two words, *anecdote* and *dotage.* That is, instead of saying that old persons are apt to fall into dotage and that old persons are fond of telling anecdotes, Disraeli fuses the two words into a neologism, *anecdotage,* and thus simultaneously expresses both ideas. The technique, therefore, lies in the fusion of the two words. Such a fusion of words is called *condensation.* Condensation is a substitutive formation, *i.e.,* instead of *anecdote* and *dotage* we have *anecdotage.*

"In a short story which I have recently read, one of the characters, a 'sport,' speaks of the Christmas season as the *alcoholidays.* By reduction, it can be easily seen that we have here a compound word, a combination of *alcohol* and *holidays* which can be graphically represented as follows:

$$a \; l \; c \; o \; HOL$$
$$HOL \; i \; d \; a \; y \; s$$

ALCOHOLIDAYS

"Here, the condensation expresses the idea that holidays are conducive to alcoholic indulgence. In other words, we have here a fused word, which, though strange in appearance, can be easily understood in its proper context. The witticism may be described as a *condensation with substitution.*

[1] *Psychoanalysis: Its Theories and Application,* 2nd Ed., p. 331.

"The same mechanism is found in the following: The famous dramatic critic, Mr. George Jean Nathan, summarizing three paragraphs to the effect that most plays then produced in New York City were violently emotional and hysterical, remarked: 'Thespis has taken up his home in *Dramatteawan*.' The last word is a condensation of *drama* and *Matteawan*. The substitution not only expressed the critic's idea that most of the plays at that time produced in New York were violent, emotional and hysterical, that is, insane, but it also contains a clever allusion to the nature of the problem presented by most of these plays. Matteawan is a state hospital for criminal insane. Most of the plays were not only insane, but also criminal since they treated of murders, divorces, robberies, scandals, etc."

During a conversation with a lady, I unintentionally furnished the material for a jest. I spoke to her about the great merits of an investigator whom I considered unjustly ignored. She remarked, "But the man really deserves a monument." "Perhaps he will get one some day," I answered, "but at the moment his success is very limited." "Monument" and "moment" are contrasts. The lady then united these contrasts and said: "Well, let us wish him a *monumentary* success."

If, at this stage, the reader should become displeased with a viewpoint which threatens to destroy his pleasure in wit without explaining the source of this pleasure, I must beg him to be patient for a while, because we are now confronted with the technique of wit, the examination of which promises many revelations if only we enter into it far enough. Besides the analysis of the examples thus far cited, which show simply a process of condensation, there are others in which the changed expressions manifest themselves in other ways.

CONDENSATION WITH MODIFICATION AND SUBSTITUTION

The following witticisms of Mr. N. will serve as illustrations.

"I was driving with him tête-à-bête." Nothing is simpler than the reduction of this jest. Evidently, it can only mean: I was driving tête-à-tête with Mr. X. and X. is a stupid ass (beast).

Neither of these two sentences is witty nor is there any wit if one combines them into this one: "I was out driving tête-à-tête" with that stupid ass (beast)." The wit appears when the words "stupid ass" are omitted and when, as a substitute for them, the first "t" of the second "tête" is changed to "b." This slight modification brings back to expression the suppressed "bête." The technique of this group of witticisms may be described as "condensation with a slight modification." And it would seem that the more insignificant the substitutive modification, the better is the wit.

Quite similar, although not without its complications, is the technique of another form of witticism. During a discussion about a person in whom there was something to praise and much to criticise, N. remarked: "Yes, vanity is one of his four heels of Achilles." [1] This modification consists in the fact that instead of the one vulnerable heel which was attributed to Achilles, we have here four heels. Four heels means four feet and that number is only found on animals. The two thoughts condensed in the witticism are as follows: Except for his vanity, he is an admirable fellow; still I do not care for him, for he is more of an animal than a human being.[2]

A similar but simpler joke I heard *statu nascendi* in a family circle. One of two brothers who were attending college was an excellent scholar, while the other was only an average student. It so happened that the model boy had a setback in school. The mother discussed this matter and expressed her fear lest this event be the beginning of a lasting deterioration. The boy, who until then had been overshadowed by his brother, gladly grasped this opportunity to remark: "Yes, Carl is going backward on all fours."

Here, the modification consists in a small addition as an assurance that in his judgment, his brother is going backward. This modification takes the place of a passionate plea for his own cause which may be expressed as follows: After all, you must not think that he is so much cleverer than I am simply because he has more success in school. He is really a stupid ass, *i.e.*, much more stupid than I am.

A good illustration of condensation with slight modification is furnished by a well-known witty jest of Mr. N., who remarked about a character in public life that he had a *"great future behind him."* The butt of this joke was a young man, whose ancestry, rearing and personal qualities seemed to have destined him for the leadership of a great party. But times changed and the party became politically incompetent. It could readily be foreseen that the man who was predestined to become its leader would come to nothing. The briefest reduction of the meaning by which one could replace this joke would be: The man has had a great future before him, but that is now past. Instead of "has had" and the appended afterthought, there is small change in the main sentence in which "before" is replaced by its opposite "behind." [3]

---

[1] This same witticism was supposed to have been coined before by Heine concerning Alfred de Musset.

[2] One of the complications involved in the technique of this example lies in the fact that the modification through which the omitted abuse is substituted is to be taken as an allusion to the latter, for it leads to it only through a process of deduction.

[3] Another factor which I shall mention later on is also effective in the technique of this witticism. It has to do with the inner character of the modification (representation through the opposite—contradiction). The technique of wit does not hesitate to make use simultaneously of several means, with which, however, we can only become acquainted in their sequential order.

Mr. N. made use of almost the same modification in the case of the nobleman who was appointed minister of agriculture for no other reason than that he was interested in agriculture. Public opinion had an opportunity to find out that he was the most incompetent man who had ever been intrusted with this office. When, however, he had relinquished his portfolio and had withdrawn to his agricultural pursuits, Mr. N. said of him: *"Like Cincinnatus of old he has returned to his place in front of the plough."*

That Roman, who was likewise called to his office from his farm, returned to his place behind the plough. In those days, just as in the present time, in front of the plough walked—the ox.

We could easily increase these examples by many others, but I am of the opinion that we are in need of no more cases in order to grasp this second group—*condensation with modification.* If we now compare the second group with the first, the technique of which consisted in condensation with a mixed word-formation, we readily see that the differences are not vital and that the lines of demarcation are indistinct. The mixed word-formation, like the modification, became subordinated to the idea of substitutive formation, and if we desired, we could also describe the mixed word-formation as a modification of the parent word through the second elements.

We may make our first pause here and ask ourselves with what known factor in the literature of wit our first result, either in whole or in part, coincides. It obviously agrees with the factor of brevity which Shakespeare calls the soul of wit. But brevity alone is not wit, else every laconism would be witty. The brevity of wit must be of a special kind. We recall that Lipps has attempted to describe more fully the peculiarity of the brevity of wit. Here, our investigation started and demonstrated that the brevity of wit is often the result of a special process which has left a second trace—substitutive formation—in the wording of the wit. By applying the process of reduction, which aims to cause a retrogression in the peculiar process of condensation, we find also that wit depends only upon the verbal expression which was produced by the process of condensation. Naturally, our entire interest now centers upon this peculiar and hitherto almost neglected mechanism. Furthermore, we cannot yet comprehend how it gave origin to all that is valuable in wit; namely, the resultant pleasure.

CONDENSATION IN DREAMS

Have processes similar to those here described as the technique of wit already been noted in another sphere of our psychic life? To be sure, in one apparently remote sphere. In *The Interpretation of Dreams*, the attempt to trace the dream to normal psychic operations is made. I contrast there the manifest and often peculiar dream-content with the latent but real thoughts of the dream from which it originated. I also investigated the psychological forces which participated in this transposition. The sum of the transforming processes I designated as the dream-work and, as a part of this dream-work, I described the process of condensation. This process has a striking similarity to the technique of wit and, like the latter, it leads to abbreviations and brings about substitutive formations of like character.

From recollections of his own dreams, the reader will be familiar with the compositions of persons and objects that appear in them; indeed, the dream makes similar compositions of words which can be reduced by analysis (*e.g.*, Autodidasker—Autodidakt and Lasker).[1] On other occasions and even much more frequently, the condensation work of the dream produces no compositions, but pictures which closely resemble an object or person up to a certain addition or variation which comes from another source, like the modifications in the witticisms of Mr. N. We cannot doubt that in this case, as in the other, we deal with a similar psychic process which is recognizable by identical results. Such a far-reaching analogy between wit-technique and dream-work surely arouses our interest in the former and stimulates our expectation of finding some explanation of wit from a comparison with the dream. We hesitate, however, to enter into this work, bearing in mind that we have investigated the technique of wit in only a very small number of witty jests. We shall therefore postpone the comparison of wit with the dream and again take up the technique of wit, leaving, however, at this place of our investigation a visible thread, as it were, which we shall take up again later.

WIT FORMED BY WORD-DIVISION

The next point to discuss is whether the process of condensation with substitutive formation is demonstrable in all witticisms so that it may be designated as a universal character of the technique of wit. I recall a joke which has clung to my mind because of certain peculiar circumstances. One of the great teachers of my youth, whom we considered unable to appreciate a joke—he had never told us a single joke hitherto—came into the Institute laughing. With an unwonted readiness, he explained the cause of his good humor. "I have read an excellent joke," he said. "*A young man who claimed to be a relative of the great J. J. Rousseau, and who bore his name, was introduced into a Parisian drawing-room. It should be added that he was decidedly red-headed. He behaved in such an awkward manner that the hostess ventured this criticism to the gentleman who had introduced him—'Vous m'avez fait connâitre un jeune homme roux et sot, mais pas un Rousseau.'*"

[1] *The Interpretation of Dreams*, p. 332.

At this point, our teacher started to laugh again. According to the nomenclature of our authors, this is sound-wit and a poor kind at that, since it plays with a proper name.

But what is the technique of this wit? It is quite clear that the character which we had perhaps hoped to demonstrate universally leaves us in the lurch in the first new example. Here, there is no omission and scarcely an abbreviation. In the witticism, the lady expresses almost everything that we can ascribe to the thoughts. "You have made me look forward to meeting a relative of J. J. Rousseau. I expected that he was perhaps even mentally related to him. Imagine my surprise to find this red-haired foolish boy, a *roux et sot*." To be sure, I was able to add and insert something, but this attempt at reduction does not annul the wit. It remains fixed and attached to the sound similarity of Rousseau. This proves that

$$\frac{\text{roux sot}}{}$$

condensation with substitution plays no part in the production of this witticism.

What else must we consider here? New attempts at reduction taught me that the joke will persistently continue until the name Rousseau is replaced by another. If, *e.g.*, I substitute the name Racine for it, I find that although the lady's criticism is just as feasible as before, it immediately loses every trace of wit. Now I know where I can look for the technique of this joke although I still hesitate to formulate it. I shall make the following attempt: The technique of the witticism lies in the fact that one and the same word—the name—is used in a twofold application, once as a whole and once divided into its syllables like a charade.

I can mention a few examples of identical technique. A witticism of this sort was utilized by an Italian lady to avenge a tactless remark made to her by the first Napoleon. Pointing to her compatriots at a court ball, he said: "*Tutti gli Italiani danzano si male*" (All Italians dance so badly). To which she quickly replied: "*Non tutti, ma buona parte*" (Not all, but a great many)—Buona parte.[1] Brill reports still another example in which

$$\frac{\text{Buonaparte.}}{}$$

the wit depends on the twofold application of a name: "*Hood once remarked that he had to be a lively Hood for a livelihood.*"[2]

MANIFOLD APPLICATION OF THE SAME MATERIAL

In these examples, which will suffice for this species of wit, the technique is the same. A name is made use of twice; first, as a whole, and then divided into its syllables—and in their divided state the syllables yield a different meaning.[3] The manifold application of the same word, once as

[1] Cited by Brill: *Psychoanalysis*, p. 335.
[2] L. c., p. 334.
[3] The excellence of these jokes depends upon the fact that they, at the same time, present another technical means of a much higher order.

a whole and then as the component syllables into which it divides itself, was the first case that came to our attention in which technique deviated from that of condensation. Upon brief reflection, however, we must divine from the abundance of examples that come to us that the newly discovered technique can hardly be limited to this single means. Obviously, there are any number of hitherto unobserved possibilities wherein one can utilize the same word or the same material of words in manifold application *in one sentence.* May not all these possibilities furnish technical means for wit? It would seem so, judging by the following examples.

"Two witty statesmen, X and Y, met at a dinner. X, acting as toast-master, introduced Y as follows: 'My friend, Y, is a very wonderful man. All you have to do is to open his mouth, put in a dinner, and a speech appears, etc.' Responding to the speaker, Y said: 'My friend, the toast-master, told you what a wonderful man I am, that all you have to do is to open my mouth, put in a dinner, and a speech appears. Now let me tell you what a wonderful man he is. All you have to do is open anybody's mouth, put in his speech, and the dinner appears.' " [1]

In examples of this sort, one can use the same material of words and simply change slightly their order. The slighter the change, the more one gets the impression that different sense was expressed with the same words, the better is the technical means of wit. And how simple are the means of its production! *"Put in a dinner and a speech appears—put in a speech and a dinner appears."* This is really nothing but a change of places of these two phrases whereby what was said of Y becomes differentiated from what is said of X. To be sure, this is not the whole technique of the joke.[2]

Great latitude is afforded the technique of wit if one so extends the *"manifold application of the same material"* that the word—or the words—upon which the wit depends may be used first unchanged and then with a slight modification. An example is another joke of Mr. N. He heard a gentleman, who himself was born a Jew, utter a malicious statement about Jewish character. "Mr. Councilor," said he, "I am familiar with your *antesemitism,* but your *antisemitism* is new to me."

Here only one single letter is changed, the modification of which could hardly be noticed in careless pronunciation. This example reminds one of the other modification jokes of Mr. N., but it differs from them by lack of condensation. Everything that was to be said has been told in the joke. "I know that you yourself were formerly a Jew, therefore I am surprised that you should rail against the Jew."

[1] This joke is attributed to the late Chauncey M. Depew. (Editor's example.)
[2] This resembles an excellent joke of Oliver Wendell Holmes cited by Brill: "Put not your trust in money, but put your money in trust." A contradiction is here announced which does not appear. At all events, it is a good example of the untranslatableness of the witticisms of such technique.

An excellent example of such wit modification is also the familiar exclamation: "Traduttore—Traditore." [1]

The similarity between the two words, almost approaching identity, results in a very impressive repesentation of the inevitability by which a translator becomes a transgressor—in the eyes of the author.

Words are plastic and may be moulded into almost any shape. There are some words which have lost their true original meaning in certain usages which they still enjoy in other applications. In one of Lichtenberg's jokes, precisely those conditions have been selected in which the blurred words have regained their meaning.

"How goes it?" asked the blind of the lame one. "As you see," replied the lame one to the blind.

Language is replete with words which taken in one sense are full of meaning and in another are colorless. There may be two different derivatives from the same root, one of which may develop into a word with a full meaning while the other may become a colorless suffix or prefix, and yet both may have the same sound. The similarity of sound between a word having full meaning and one whose meaning is colorless may also be accidental. In both cases, the technique of wit can make use of such relationship of the speech material. The following examples illustrate some of these points.

"Do you call a man kind who remits nothing to his family while away?" asked an actor. *"Call that kindness?" "Yes, unremitting kindness,"* was the reply of Douglas Jerrold. The wit here depends on the first syllable *un* of the word *unremitting. Un* is usually a prefix denoting "not," but by adding it to "remitting," a new relationship is unexpectedly established which changes the meaning of the context. *"An undertaker is one who always carries out what he undertakes."* [2] The striking character upon which the wit here depends is the manifold application of the words *undertaker* and *carry out*. Undertaker commonly denotes one who manages funerals. Only when taken in this sense and using the words *carry out* literally is the sentence witty. The wit lies in the manifold application of the same words.

DOUBLE MEANING AND PLAY ON WORDS

If we delve more deeply into the variety of "manifold application" of the same word, we suddenly notice that we are confronted with forms of "double meaning" or "plays on words" which have been known a long time and which are universally acknowledged as belonging to the technique of wit. Then, why have we bothered our brains about discovering

---

[1] Brill cites a very analogous modification wit: *Amantes—Amentes* (lovers—lunatics).
[2] Translator's examples.

something new when we could just as well have gleaned it from the most superficial treatise on wit? We can say in self-defense only that we are presenting another side of the same phenomena of verbal expressions. What the authors call the "playful" character of wit, we treat from the point of view of "manifold application."

Further examples of manifold application which may also be designated under a new and third group, the class of double meaning, may be divided into subdivisions. These, to be sure, are not essentially differentiated from one another any more than the whole third group from the second. In the first place, we have:

(a) Cases of double meaning of a name and its verbal significance: e.g., *"Discharge thyself of our company, Pistol"* (Henry IV, Act II). *"For Suffolk's duke may he suffocate"* (Henry IV, Act I). Heine says, *"Here in Hamburg rules not the rascally Macbeth, but Banko* (Banquo)."

(b) Cases where a double meaning is obtained by using a word which has both a verbal and metaphoric sense, furnish an abundant source for the technique of wit. A medical colleague, who was well known for his wit, once said to Arthur Schnitzler, the writer: *"I am not at all surprised that you became a great poet. Your father had already held up the mirror to his contemporaries."* The mirror used by the father of the writer, the famous Dr. Schnitzler, was the laryngoscope. According to the well-known quotation from *Hamlet* (Act III, Scene 2), the object of the play, as well as the writer who creates it, is to "hold, as 't were, the mirror up to nature; to show virtue her own feature, scorn her own image, and the very age and body of the time his form and pressure."

(c) Cases of actual double meaning or play on words—the ideal case, as it were, of manifold application. Here, no violence is done to the word. It is not torn into syllables. It need not undergo any modifications. It need not exchange its own particular sphere, say as a proper name, for another. Thanks to certain circumstances, it can express two meanings just as it stands in the structure of the sentence. Many examples are at our disposal.

One of the first royal acts of the last Napoleon was, as is well known, the confiscation of the estates belonging to the House of Orleans. *"C'est le premier vol de l'aigle"* was an excellent play on words current at that time. "Vol" means both flight and theft. Louis XV, wishing to test the wit of one of his courtiers, of whose talent in that direction he had heard, seized the first opportunity to command the cavalier to concoct a joke at his (the king's) expense. He wanted to be the "subject" of the witticism The courtier answered him with the clever *bon mot, "Le roi n'est pas sujet."* "Subject" also means "vassal." (Taken from K. Fischer.)

A physician, leaving the sick-bed of a wife, whose husband accompanied him, exclaimed doubtfully: "I do not like her looks." "I have not

liked her looks for a long time," was the quick rejoinder of the husband.
The physician, of course, referred to the condition of the wife, but he
expressed his apprehension about the patient in such words as to afford
the husband the means of utilizing them to assert his conjugal aversion.
Concerning a satirical comedy Heine remarked: *"This satire would not
have been so biting had the author of it had more to bite."* This jest is a
better example of metaphoric and common double meaning than of real
play upon words, but at present we are not concerned about such strict
lines of demarcation. *Charles Matthews, the elder, one of England's greatest actors, was asked what he was going to do with his son* (the young
man was destined for architecture). *"Why,"* answered the comedian, *"he
is going to draw houses like his father." Foote once asked a man why he
forever sang one tune. "Because it haunts me," replied the man. "No
wonder," said Foote, "you are continually murdering it."*

*A gentleman had shown much ingenuity in evading a notorious bor-
rower whom he had sent away many times with the request to call when
he was "in." One day, however, the borrower eluded the servant at the
door and cornered his victim.*

"Ah," said the host, seeing there was no way out of it, "at last I am in."

*"No," returned the borrower in anticipation, "at last I am in and you
are out."*

Heine said in the *Harzreise: "I cannot recall at the moment the names
of all the students, and of the professors there are some who have no
name as yet."*

Dr. Johnson said of the University of St. Andrews in Scotland, which
was poor in purse, but prolific in the distribution of its degrees: *"Let it
persevere in its present plan and it may become rich by degrees."* Here,
the wit depends more on the manifold application than on the play on
words.

The keen-witted writer, Horatio Winslow, sums up the only too-
familiar history of some American families as follows:

A TALE OF TWO AMERICAN GENERATIONS

Gold Mine
Gold Spoon
Gold Cure

The last couplet, gold cure, refers to the familiar cure for alcoholism.
This wit is an excellent example of unification—everything is, as it were,
of gold. The manifold meanings of the adjective, which do not very strikingly contrast with one another, make possible this "manifold application."

AMBIGUITY

Another play on words will facilitate the transition to a new subdivision of the technique of double meaning. The witty colleague who was responsible for the joke mentioned earlier is likewise answerable for this joke, current during the trial of Dreyfus:

"This girl reminds me of Dreyfus. The army does not believe in her innocence."

The word innocence, whose double meaning furnishes the basis of the witticism, has in one connection the customary meaning which is the opposite of guilt or transgression, while in the other connection, it has a sexual sense, the opposite of which is sexual experience. There are very many such examples of double meaning and in each one, the point of the joke refers especially to a sexual sense. The group could be designated as "ambiguous." *A good example to illustrate this is the story told of a wealthy but elderly gentleman who showed his devotion to a young actress by many lavish gifts. Being a respectable girl, she took the first opportunity to discourage his attentions by telling him that her heart was already given to another man. "I never aspired as high as that," was his polite answer.*

If one compares this example of double-meaning-with-ambiguity with other examples, one cannot help noticing a difference which is not altogether inconsequential to the technique. In the joke about "innocence" one meaning of the word is just as good for our understanding of it as the other. One can really not decide whether the sexual or non-sexual significance of the word is more applicable and more familiar. But it is different with the other example mentioned. Here, the final sense of the words, "I never aspired as high as that," is by far more obtrusive and covers and conceals, as it were, the sexual sense which could easily escape the unsuspecting person. In sharp contrast to this, let us examine another example of double meaning in which there is no attempt made to veil its sexual significance—e.g., Heine's characterization of a complaisant lady:
"She could pass (abschlagen) nothing except her water." It sounds like an obscene joke and the wit in it is scarcely noticed.[1] But the peculiarity that both senses of the double meaning are not equally manifested can occur also in witticisms without sexual reference providing that one sense is more common or that it is preferred on account of its connection with the other parts of the sentence (e.g., *c'est le premier vol de l'aigle*). All these examples I propose to call double meaning with allusion.

We have by this time become familiar with such a large number of

[1] Compare here K. Fischer (p. 85), who applies the term "double meaning" to those witticisms in which both meanings are not equally prominent, but where one overshadows the other. I have applied this term differently. Such a nomenclature is a matter of choice. Usage of speech has rendered no definite decision about them.

different techniques of wit that I am afraid we may lose sight of them. Let us, therefore, attempt to make a summary.

I. CONDENSATION
    (a) With mixed word-formation.
    (b) With modification.

II. THE APPLICATION OF THE SAME MATERIAL
    (c) The whole and the part.
    (d) Change of order.
    (e) Slight modification.
    (f) The same words used in their full or colorless sense.

III. DOUBLE MEANING
    (g) Name and verbal significance.
    (h) Metaphorical and verbal meaning.
    (i) True double meaning (play on words).
    (j) Ambiguous meaning.
    (k) Double meaning with allusion.

This variety causes confusion. It might vex us because we have devoted so much time to the consideration of the technical means of wit, and the stress laid on the forms might possibly arouse our suspicions that we are overvaluing their importance so far as the knowledge of the nature of wit is concerned. But this conjecture is met by the one irrefutable fact: namely, that the wit invariably disappears when we remove the effect of these techniques, in the expressions. We are thus directed to search for the unity in this variety. It must be possible to bring all these techniques under one head. As we have remarked before, it is not difficult to unite the second and third groups, for the double meaning, the play on words, is nothing but the ideal case of utilizing the same material. The latter is here apparently the more comprehensive conception. The examples of dividing, changing the order of the same material, manifold application with slight modifications (c, d, e)—all these could, without difficulty, be subordinated under the conception of double meaning. But what community exists between the technique of the first group—condensation with substitutive formation—and the two other goups—manifold application of the same material?

THE TENDENCY TO ECONOMY

It seems to me that this agreement is very simple and clear. The application of the same material is only a special case of condensation and the play on words is nothing but a condensation without substitutive formation. Condensation thus remains as the chief category. A compressing or —to be more exact—an economic tendency controls all these techniques.

As Prince Hamlet says: "Thrift, Horatio, thrift." It seems to be all matter of economy.

Let us examine this economy in individual cases. *"C'est le premier vol de l'aigle."* That is, the first flight of the eagle. Certainly, but it is a depredatious flight. Luckily, for the gist of this joke "vol" signifies flight as well as depredation. Has nothing been condensed and economized by this? Certainly, the entire second thought, and, to be sure, it was dropped without any substitution. The double sense of the word "vol" makes such substitution superfluous, or what is just as correct: the word "vol" contains the substitution for the repressed thought without the necessity of supplementing or varying the first sentence. Therein consists the benefit of the double meaning.

Another example: *Gold mine—gold spoon,* the enormous economy of expression the single word "gold" produces. It really tells the history of two generations in the life of some American families. The father made his fortune through hard toiling in the gold fields during the early pioneer days. The son was born with a golden spoon in his mouth; having been brought up as the son of a wealthy man, he becomes a chronic alcoholic and has to take the gold cure.

Thus, there is no doubt that the condensation in these examples produces economy and we shall demonstrate that the same is true in all cases. Where is the economy in such jokes as *"Rousseau—roux et sot,"* in which we first failed to find the prime factors in causing us to establish the technique of the manifold application of the same material? In such cases, condensation will naturally not cover the ground, but when we exchange it for the broader conception of "economy" we find no difficulty. What we save in such examples as those just given is quite obvious. We save ourselves the trouble of making a criticism, of forming a judgment. Both are contained in the names. The same is true in the *"livelihood"* example and the others thus far analyzed. Where one does not save much is in the example of *"I am in and you are out,"* at least the wording of a new answer is saved. The wording of the address, *"I am in,"* serves also for the answer. It is little, but in this little lies the wit. The manifold application of the same words in addressing and answering surely comes under the heading of economy. Note how Hamlet sums up the quick succession of the death of his father and the marriage of his mother:

> "the funeral baked meats
> Did coldly furnish forth the marriage tables."

But before we accept the "tendency to economize" as the universal character of wit and ask whence it originates, what it signifies, and how it gives origin to the resultant pleasure, we shall concede a doubt which may justly be considered. It may be true that every technique of wit shows the tendency to economize in expression, but the relationship is not reversible. Not every economy in expression or every brevity is witty on that account. We once raised the question when we still hoped to demonstrate the condensation process in every witticism, and at that we justly objected by remarking that a laconism is not necessarily wit. Hence, it must be a peculiar form of brevity and economy upon which the character of the wit depends, and just as long as we are ignorant of this peculiarity, the discovery of the common element in the technique of wit will bring us nearer a solution. Besides, we have the courage to acknowledge that the economies caused by the technique of wit do not impress us as very much. They remind one of the manner in which many a housewife economizes when she spends time and money to reach a distant market because the vegetables can there be had a cent cheaper. What does wit save by means of its technique? Instead of putting together a few new words, which, for the most part, could have been accomplished without any effort, it goes to the trouble of searching for the word which comprises both ideas. Indeed, it must often at first transform the expression of one of the ideas into an unusual form until it furnishes an associative connection with the second thought. Would it not have been simpler, easier, and really more economical to express both thoughts as they happen to come even if no agreement in expression results? Is not the economy in verbal expression more than abrogated through the expenditure of intellectual work? And who economized through it, whom does it benefit? We can temporarily circumvent these doubts by leaving them unsolved until later on. Are we really familiar enough with all the forms of techniques of wit? It will surely be safer to gather new examples and submit them to analysis.

PUNS

Indeed, we have not yet given consideration to one of the largest groups into which the techniques of wit may be divided. In this we have perhaps been influenced by the low estimate in which this form of wit is held. It embraces those jokes which are commonly called "puns." These are generally counted as the lowest form of wit, perhaps because they are "cheapest" and can be formed with the least effort. They really make the least demands on the technique of expression just as the actual play on words makes the most. Whereas in the latter, both meanings find expression in the identical word, and hence usually in a word used only once, in the pun it is enough if two words for both meanings resemble each other through some slight similarity in structure, in rhythmic consonance, in the community of several vowels, or in some other similar manner. The following examples illustrate these points:

"We are now fallen into that critical age wherein *censores* liberorum are become *censores librorum: Lectores, Lictores.*"

Professor Cromwell says that Rome in exchanging her religion changed *Jupiter* to *Jew Peter.*

It is related that some students, wishing to play a trick on Agassiz, the great naturalist, constructed an insect made up of parts taken from different bugs and sent it to him with the question, "What kind of a bug is this?" His answer was "Humbug."

K. Fischer has given much attention to this form of wit and insists upon making a sharp distinction between it and the "play on words" (p. 78). "A pun," he says, "is a bad play on words, for it does not play with the word as a word, but merely as a sound." The play on words, however, "transfers itself from the sound of the word into the word itself." On the other hand, he also classifies such jokes as "famillionaire," etc., with sound-wit. I see no necessity to follow him in this. In the plays on words also, the word serves us only as a sound to which this or that meaning attaches itself. Here, also, usage of language makes no distinction, and when it treats "puns" with disdain but play on words with a certain respect, it seems that these estimations are determined by others as technical viewpoints. One should bear in mind the forms of wit which are referred to as puns. There are persons who have the ability, when they are in a high-spirited mood, to reply with a pun for a long time to every sentence addressed to them. Brill [1] relates that at a gathering, someone spoke disparagingly of a certain drama and wound up by saying, *"It was so poor that the first act had to be rewritten." "And now it is rerotten,"* *added the punster of the gathering.*

At all events, we can already infer from the controversies about the line of demarcation between puns and play on words that the former cannot aid us in finding an entirely new technique of wit. Even if no claims are made for the pun that it utilizes the manifold application of the same material, the accent, nevertheless, falls upon the *rediscovering of the familiar* and upon the agreement between both words forming the pun. Thus, the latter is only a sub-species of the group which reaches its height in the real play on words.

DISPLACEMENTS

There are some witticisms, however, whose techniques baffle almost every attempt to classify them under any of the groups so far investigated. *It is related that while Heine and the poet Soulié were once chatting together in a Parisian drawing-room, there entered one of those Parisians whom one usually compared to Midas, but not alone on account of their money. He was soon surrounded by a crowd which treated him with the greatest*

[1] L. c., p. 339.

deference. "Look over there," said Soulié to Heine, "and see how the nineteenth century is worshipping the Golden Calf." Heine cast one glance upon the object of adoration and replied, as if correcting his friend: "Oh, he must be older than that" (K. Fischer, p. 82).

Wherein lies the technique of this excellent witticism? According to K. Fischer, it lies in the play on words. Thus, for example, he says, "the words 'Golden Calf' may signify Mammon as well as idol-worship—in the first case, the gold is paramount; in the second case, it is the animal picture. It may likewise serve to designate in a rather uncomplimentary way one who has very much money and very little brains." If we apply the test and take away the expression "Golden Calf," we naturally also abrogate the wit. We then cause Soulié to say, "Just see how the people are thronging about that blockhead only because he is rich." To be sure, this is no longer witty. Nor would Heine's answer be possible under these circumstances. But let us remember that it is not at all a matter of Soulié's witty comparison, but of Heine's retort, which is surely much more witty. We have then no right to disturb the phrase "the golden calf" which remains as a basis for Heine's words and the reduction can only be applied to the latter. If we dilate upon the words, "Oh, he must be older than that," we can only proceed as follows:

"Oh, he is no longer a calf; he is already a full-grown ox." Heine's wit is, therefore, based on the fact that he no longer took the "golden calf" metaphorically, but personally by referring it to the moneyed individual himself. If this double meaning is not already contained in the opinion of Soulié!

Let us see. We believe that we can state that this reduction has not altogether destroyed Heine's joke, but, on the contrary, it has left its essential element untouched. It reads as if Soulié were now saying, "Just see how the nineteenth century is worshipping the golden calf," and as if Heine were retorting, "Oh, he is no longer a calf. He is already an ox." And even in this reduced form, it is still a witticism. However, another reduction of Heine's words is not possible.

It is a pity that this excellent example contains such complicated technical conditions. And as it cannot aid us toward enlightenment, we shall leave it to search for another in which we imagine we can perceive a relationship with the former one.

It is a "bath" joke treating of the dread which some Jews are said to have for bathing. We demand no patent of nobility for our examples, nor do we make inquiries about their origin. The only qualifications we require are that they should make us laugh and serve our theoretical interest. It is to be remarked that both these demands are satisfied best by Jewish jokes.

Two Jews meet near a bathing establishment. "Have you taken a bath?" asked one. "How is that?" replies the other. "Is one missing?"

When one laughs very heartily about a joke, he is not in the best mood to investigate its technique. It is for this reason that some difficulties are experienced in delving into their analyses. "That is a comic misunderstanding" is the thought that comes to us. Yes, but how about the technique of this joke? Obviously, the technique lies in the double meaning of the word *take*. In the first case, the word is used in a colorless idiomatic sense, while in the second, it is the verb in its full meaning. It is, therefore, a case where the same word is taken now in the "full" and now in the "empty" sense (Group II, f). And if we replace the expression "take a bath" by the simpler equivalent "bathed," the wit disappears. The answer is no longer fitting. The joke, therefore, lies in the expression "take a bath."

This is quite correct, yet it seems that in this case, also, the reduction was applied in the wrong place, for the joke does not lie in the question, but in the answer, or rather in the counter-question: "How is that? Is there one missing?" Provided the same is not destroyed, the answer cannot be robbed of its wit by any dilation or variation. We also get the impression that in the answer of the second Jew, the overlooking of the bath is more significant than the misconception of the word "take." However, here, too, things do not look quite clear and we will, therefore, look for a third example.

Once more, we shall resort to a Jewish joke in which, however, the Jewish element is incidental only. Its essence is universally human. It is true that this example, too, contains undesirable complications, but luckily they are not of the kind so far which have kept us from seeing clearly.

In his distress, a needy man borrowed twenty-five dollars from a wealthy acquaintance. The same day, he was discovered by his creditor in a restaurant eating a dish of salmon with mayonnaise. The creditor reproached him in these words: "You borrow money from me and then order salmon with mayonnaise. Is that what you needed the money for?" "I don't understand you," responded the debtor, "when I have no money I can't eat salmon with mayonnaise. When I have money, I mustn't eat it. Well then, when shall I ever eat salmon with mayonnaise?"

Here, we no longer discover any double meaning. Even the repetition of the words "salmon with mayonnaise" cannot contain the technique of the witticism, as it is not the "manifold application of the same material," but an actual, identical repetition required by the context. We may be temporarily nonplussed in this analysis, and, as a pretext, we may wish to dispute the character of the wit in the anecdote which causes us to laugh. What else worthy of notice can be said about the answer of the poor man? It may be supposed that the striking thing about it is its logical character, but, as a matter of fact, the answer is illogical. The debtor endeavors to justify himself for spending the borrowed money on luxuries and asks, with some semblance of right, when he is to be allowed to eat salmon. But this is not at all the correct answer. The creditor does not blame him for eating salmon on the day that he borrowed the money, but reminds him that in his condition, he has no right to think of such luxuries at all. The poor *bon vivant* disregards this only possible meaning of the reproach, centers his answer on another point and acts as if he did not understand the reproach.

Is it possible that the technique of this joke lies in this deviation of the answer from the sense of reproach? A similar changing of the viewpoint—displacement of the psychic accent—may perhaps also be demonstrated in the two previous examples which we felt were related to this one. This can be successfully shown and solves the technique of these examples. Soulié calls Heine's attention to the fact that society worships the "golden calf" in the nineteenth century just as the Jewish nation once did in the desert. To this, an answer from Heine like the following would seem fit: "Yes, that is human nature. Centuries have changed nothing in it;" or he might have remarked something equally apposite. But Heine deviates in his manner from the instigated thought. Indeed, he does not answer at all. He makes use of the double meaning found in the phrase "golden calf" to go off on a tangent. He seizes upon one of the components of the phrase, namely, "the calf," and answers as if Soulié's speech placed the emphasis on it—"Oh, he is no longer a calf, etc." [1]

The deviation is much more evident in the bath joke. This example requires a graphic representation. The first Jew asks, "Have you taken a *bath*?" The emphasis lies upon the bath element. The second answers as if the query were: "Have you *taken* a bath?" The displacement would have been impossible if the question had been: "Bathed?" "What do you mean? I don't know what that means." However, the technique of the wit lies in the displacement of the emphasis from "to bathe" to "to take. [2]

Let us return to the example "salmon with mayonnaise," which is the purest of its kind. What is new in it will direct us into various paths. In the first place, we have to give a name to the mechanism of this newly discovered technique. I propose to designate it as *displacement,* for its most essential element, the deviation of the trend of thought, consists in

[1] Heine's answer is a combination of two wit-techniques—a displacement and an allusion—for he does not say directly: "He is an ox."
[2] The word "take," owing to its meanings, lends itself very well towards the formation of plays upon words, a pure example of which I wish to cite as a contrast to the displacement mentioned above. While walking with his friend, in front of a café, a well-known stock-plunger and bank director made this proposal: "Let us go in and take something." His friend held him back and said: "My dear sir, remember there are people in there."

displacing the psychic accent to another than the original theme. It is then incumbent upon us to find out the relationship of the technique of displacement to the expression of the witticism. Our example (salmon with mayonnaise) shows us that the displacement technique is absolutely independent of the verbal expression. It does not depend upon words, but upon the mental trend, and to abrogate it we are not helped by substitution so long as the sense of the answer is adhered to. The reduction is possible only when we change the mental trend and permit the gastronomist to answer directly to the reproach which he eluded in the conception of the joke. The reduced conception would then be: "What I like I cannot deny myself, and it is all the same to me where I get the money for it. Here you have my explanation as to why I happen to be eating salmon with mayonnaise today just after you have loaned me some money." But that would not be a witticism but a *cynicism*. It will be instructive to compare this joke with one which is closely allied to it in meaning.

A man who was addicted to drink supported himself in a small city by private teaching. His vice gradually became known and he lost most of his pupils in consequence. A friend of his took it upon himself to admonish him to reform. "Look here," he said, "you could have the best pupils in town if you would give up drinking. Why not do it?" "What are you talking about?" was the indignant reply. "I am teaching in order to be able to drink. Shall I give up drinking in order to get pupils?"

This joke, too, carries the stamp of logic which we have noted in the case of "salmon with mayonnaise," but it is no longer displacement-wit. The answer is a direct one. The cynicism, which is veiled there, is openly admitted here, "For me drink is the most important thing." The technique of this witticism is really very poor and cannot explain its effect. It lies merely in the change in order of the same material, or to be more exact, in the reversal of the means-and-end relationship between drink and teaching or getting pupils. As I gave no greater emphasis in the reduction to this factor of the expression, the witticism is somewhat blurred; it may be expressed as follows: "What a senseless demand to make. For me, drink is the most important thing and not the pupils. Private teaching is only a means to more drink." The wit is really dependent upon the expression.

In the bath wit, the dependence of the witticism upon the wording "have you taken a bath" is unmistakable and a change in the wording nullifies the joke. The technique in this case is quite complicated. It is a combination of double meaning (sub-group f) and displacement. The wording of the question admits a double meaning. The joke arises from the fact that the answer is given not in the sense expected by the questioner, but has a different subordinate sense. By making the displacement retrogressive, we are accordingly in position to find a reduction which leaves the double meaning in the expression and still does away with the wit.

"Have you taken a bath?" "Taken what? A bath? What is that?" But that is no longer a witticism. It is simply either a spiteful or playful exaggeration.

In Heine's joke about the "golden calf" the double meaning plays a quite similar part. It makes it possible for the answer to deviate from the instigated stream of thought—a thing which happens in the joke about "salmon and mayonnaise"—without any such dependence upon the wording. In the reduction, Soulié's speech and Heine's answer would be as follows: "It reminds one very much of the worship of the golden calf when one sees the people throng around that man simply because he is rich." Heine's answer would be: "That he is made so much of on account of his wealth is not the worst part. You do not emphasize enough the fact that his ignorance is forgiven on account of his wealth." Thus, while the double meaning would be retained, the displacement-wit would be eliminated.

Here, we may be prepared for the objection which might be raised, namely, that we are seeking to tear asunder these delicate differentiations which really belong together. Does not every double meaning furnish occasion for displacment and for a deviation of the stream of thought from one sense to another? And shall we agree that a "double meaning" and "displacement" should be designated as representatives of two entirely different types of wit? It is true that a relation between double meaning and displacement actually exists, but it has nothing to do with our differentiation of the techniques of wit. In cases of double meaning the wit contains nothing but a word capable of several interpretations which allows the hearer to find the transition from one thought to another, and which, with a little forcing, may be compared to a displacement. In the cases of displacement-wit, however, the witticism itself contains a stream of thought in which the displacement is brought about. Here the displacement belongs to the work which is necessary for its understanding. Should this differentiation not be clear to us, we can make use of the reduction method, which is an unfailing way for tangible demonstration. We do not deny, however, that there is something in this objection. It calls our attention to the fact that we cannot confuse the psychic processes in the formation of wit (the wit-work) with the psychic processes in the conception of the wit (the understanding-work). The object of our present investigation will be confined only to the former.[1]

[1] For the latter, see a later chapter. It will perhaps not be superfluous to add here a few words for a better understanding. The displacement regularly occurs between a statement and an answer, and turns the stream of thought to a direction different from the one started in the statement. The justification for separating the displacement from the double meaning is best seen in the examples where both are com-

Are there still other examples of the technique of displacement? They are not easily found, but the following witticism is a very good specimen. It also shows a lack of over-emphasized logic found in our former examples.

A horse-dealer, in recommending a saddle horse to his client, said: "If you mount this horse at four o'clock in the morning, you will be in Monticello at six-thirty in the morning." "What will I do in Monticello at six-thirty in the morning?" asked the client.

Here, the displacement is very striking. The horse-dealer mentions the early arrival in the small city only with the obvious intention of proving the efficiency of the horse. The client disregards the capacity of the animal, about which he evidently has no more doubts, and takes up only the data of the example selected for the test. The reduction of this joke is comparatively simple.

More difficulties are encountered by another example, the technique of which is very obscure. It can be solved, however, through the application of double meaning with displacement. The joke relates the subterfuge employed by a "schadchen" (Jewish marriage broker). It belongs to a class which will claim more of our attention later.

The "schadchen" had assured the suitor that the father of the girl was no longer living. After the engagement had been announced, the news leaked out that the father was still living and serving a sentence in prison. The suitor reproached the agent for deceiving him. "Well," said the latter, "what did I tell you? Do you call that living?"

The double meaning lies in the word "living," and the displacement consists in the fact that the "schadchen" avoids the common meaning of the word, which is a contrast to "death," and uses it in the colloquial sense: "You don't call that living." In doing this, he explains his former utterance as a double meaning, although this manifold application is here quite out of place. Thus far the technique resembles that of the "golden calf" and the "bath" jokes. Here, however, another factor comes into consideration which disturbs the understanding of the technique through its obtrusiveness. One might say that this joke is a "characterization-wit." It endeavors to illustrate by example the marriage agent's characteristic admixture of mendacious impudence and repartee. We shall learn that this is only the "show-side" of the façade of the witticism, that is, its sense. Its object serves a different purpose. We shall also defer our attempt at reduction.[1]

After these complicated examples, which are not at all easy to analyze,

---

joined, that is, where the wording of the statement admits of a double meaning which was not intended by the speaker, but which reveals in the answer the way to the displacement (see examples).

[1] See Chapter III.

it will be gratifying to find a perfectly pure and transparent example of "displacement-wit." *A beggar implored the help of a wealthy baron for a trip to Ostend, where he asserted the physicians had ordered him to take sea baths for his health. "Very well, I shall assist you," said the rich baron, "but is it absolutely necessary for you to go to Ostend, which is the most expensive of all watering-places?" "Sir," was the reproving reply, "nothing is too expensive for my health."* Certainly that is a proper attitude, but hardly proper for the supplicant. The answer is given from the viewpoint of a rich man. The beggar acts as if it were his own money that he was willing to sacrifice for his health, as if money and health concerned the *same* person.

NONSENSE AS A TECHNICAL MEANS

Let us take up again in this connection the instructive example of "salmon with mayonnaise." It also presents to us a side in which we noticed a striking display of logical work and we have learned from analyzing it that this logic concealed an error of thought, namely, a displacement of the stream of thought. Henceforth, even if only by way of contrast association, we shall be reminded of other jokes which, on the contrary, present clearly something contradictory, something nonsensical, or foolish. We shall be curious to discover wherein the technique of the witticism lies. I shall first present the strongest and at the same time the purest example of the entire group. Once more, it is a Jewish joke.

Ike was serving in the artillery corps. He was seemingly an intelligent lad, but he was unwieldy and had no interest in the service. One of his superiors, who was kindly disposed toward him, drew him aside and said to him: "Ike, you are out of place among us. I would advise you to buy a cannon and make yourself independent."

The advice, which makes us laugh heartily, is obvious nonsense. There are no cannons to be bought and an individual cannot possibly make himself independent, or establish himself as a fighting force, as it were. One cannot remain one minute in doubt but this advice is not just nonsense; it is witty nonsense and an excellent joke. By what means does the nonsense become a witticism?

We need not meditate very long. From the discussions of the authors in the Introduction, we can guess that sense lurks in such witty nonsense, and that this sense in nonsense transforms nonsense into wit. In our example, the sense is easily found. The officer who gives the artilleryman, Ike, the nonsensical advice pretends to be stupid in order to show Ike how stupidly he is acting. He imitates Ike as if to say, "I will now give you some advice which is exactly as stupid as you are." He enters into Ike's stupidity and makes him conscious of it by making it the basis of a proposition which must meet with Ike's wishes, for if Ike owned a cannon and took up the art of warfare on his own account, of what advantage would his intelligence and ambition be to him? How would he take care of the cannon and acquaint himself with its mechanism in order to meet the competition of other possessors of cannon?

I am breaking off the analysis of this example to show the same sense in nonsense in a shorter and simpler, though less glaring case of nonsense-wit.

"Never to be born would be best for mortal man." *"But,"* added the sages of the *Fliegende Blätter, "hardly one man in a hundred thousand has this luck."*

The modern appendix to the ancient philosophical saying is pure nonsense, and becomes still more stupid through the addition of the seemingly careful "hardly." But this appendix, in attaching itself to the first sentence, incontestably and correctly limits it. It can thus open our eyes to the fact that that piece of wisdom so reverently scanned, is neither more nor less than sheer nonsense. He who is not born of woman is not mortal; for him there exists no "good" and no "best." The nonsense of the joke, therefore, serves here to expose and present another bit of nonsense as in the case of the artilleryman. Here, I can add a third example which, owing to its context, scarcely deserves a detailed description. It serves, however, to illustrate the use of nonsense in wit in order to represent another element of nonsense.

A man about to go upon a journey intrusted his daughter to his friend, begging him to watch over her chastity during his absence. When he returned some months later, he found that she was pregnant. Naturally, he reproached his friend. The latter alleged that he could not explain this unfortunate occurrence. "Where has she been sleeping?" the father finally asked. "In the same room with my son," replied the friend. "How is it that you allowed her to sleep in the same room with your son after I had begged you so earnestly to take good care of her?" remonstrated the father. "Well," explained the friend, "there was a screen between them. There was your daughter's bed, and over there was my son's bed and between them stood the screen." "And suppose he went behind the screen? What then?" asked the parent. "Well, in that case," rejoined the friend thoughtfully, "it might be possible."

In this joke—aside from the other qualities of this poor witticism—we can easily get the reduction. Obviously, it would read like this: "You have no right to reproach me. How could you be so foolish as to leave your daughter in a house where she must live in the constant companionship of a young man? As if it were possible for a stranger to be responsible for the chastity of a maiden under such circumstances!" The seeming stupidity of the friend here also serves as a reflection of the stupidity of the father. By means of the reduction, we have eliminated the nonsense contained in the witticism as well as the witticism itself. We have not gotten rid of the "nonsense" element itself, as it finds another place in the context of the sentence after it has been reduced to its true meaning.

We can now also attempt the reduction of the joke about the cannon. The officer might have said: "I know, Ike, that you are an intelligent business man, but I must tell you that you are very stupid if you do not realize that one cannot act in the army as one does in business, where each one is out for himself and competes with the other. Military service demands subordination and co-operation."

The technique of the nonsense witticisms hitherto discussed really consists in advancing something apparently absurd or nonsensical which, however, discloses sense that serves to illustrate and represent some other actual absurdity and nonsense.

Has the employment of contradiction in the technique of wit always this meaning? Here is another example which answers this affirmatively. On an occasion when Phocion's speech was applauded, he turned to his friends and asked: *"Did I say something foolish?"*

This question seems paradoxical, but we immediately comprehend its meaning. "What have I said that has pleased this stupid crowd? I ought really to be ashamed of the applause, for if it appealed to these fools, it could not have been very clever after all."

Other examples teach us that absurdity is used very often in the technique of wit without serving at all the purpose of uncovering another piece of nonsense.

A well-known university teacher who was wont to spice richly with jokes his rather dry specialty, was once congratulated upon the birth of his youngest son, who was bestowed upon him at a rather advanced age. "Yes," said he to the well-wishers, "it is remarkable what mortal hands can accomplish." This reply seems especially senseless and out of place, for children are called the blessings of God in contrast to creations of mortal hands. But it soon dawns upon us that this answer has a sense and an obscene one at that. The point in question is not that the happy father wishes to appear stupid in order to make something else or some other persons appear stupid. The seemingly senseless answer causes us astonishment. It puzzles us, as the authors would have it. We have seen that the authors deduce the entire mechanism of such jokes from the change of the succession of "clearness and confusion." We shall try to form an opinion about this later. Here we content ourselves by remarking that the technique of this witticism consists in advancing such confusing and senseless elements.

The following joke of Lichtenberg's has an especially peculiar place in nonsense jokes.

"He was surprised that the two holes were cut in the pelts of cats just

where their eyes were located." It is certainly foolish to be surprised about something that is obvious in itself, something which is really the explanation of an identity. It reminds one of a seriously intended utterance of Michelet (*The Woman*) which, as I remember it, runs as follows: "*How beautifully everything is arranged by nature. As soon as the child comes into the world, it finds a mother who is ready to care for it.*" This utterance of Michelet's is really silly, but the one of Lichtenberg is a witticism, which makes use of the absurdity for some purpose. There is something behind it. What? At present, that is something we cannot discuss.

SOPHISTIC FAULTY THINKING

We have learned from two groups of examples that the wit-work makes use of deviations from normal thought, namely, *displacement* and *absurdity*, as technical means of presenting witty expressions. It is only just to expect that other faulty thinking may find a similar application. Indeed, a few examples of this sort can be cited.

A gentleman entered a shop and ordered a fancy cake, which, however, he soon returned, asking for some liqueur in its stead. He drank the liqueur, and was about to leave without paying for it. The shopkeeper held him back."*What do you want of me?*" *he asked.* "*Please pay for the liqueur,*" *said the shopkeeper.* "*But I have given you the fancy cake for it.*" "*Yes, but you have not paid for that either.*" "*Well, neither have I eaten it.*"

This little story also bears the semblance of logic which we already know as the suitable façade for faulty thinking. The error, obviously, lies in the fact that the cunning customer establishes a connection between the return of the fancy cake and its exchange for the liqueur, a connection which really does not exist. The state of affairs may be divided into two processes which, as far as the shopkeeper is concerned, are independent of each other. He first took the fancy cake and returned it, so that he owes nothing for it. He then took the liqueur, for which he owes money. One might say that the customer uses the relation "for it" in a double sense, or, to speak more correctly, by means of a double sense, he forms a relation which does not hold in reality.[1]

The opportunity now presents itself for making a not unimportant confession. We are here busying ourselves with an investigation of technique of wit by means of examples, and we ought to be sure that the examples which we have selected are really true witticisms. The facts are, however, that in a series of cases, we fall into doubt as to whether or not the example in question may be called a joke. We have no criterion at our

[1] A similar nonsense technique results when the joke aims to maintain a connection which seems to be removed through the special conditions of its content. A joke of this sort is related by J. Falke (l. c.): "*Is this the place where the Duke of Wellington spoke these words?*" "*Yes, this is the place; but he never spoke these words.*"

disposal before investigation itself furnishes one. Usage of language is unreliable and is itself in need of examination for its authority. To decide the question, we can rely on nothing else but a certain "feeling," which we may interpret by saying that in our judgment, the decision follows certain criteria which are not yet accessible to our knowledge. We shall naturally not appeal to this "feeling" for substantial proof. In the case of the last-mentioned example, we cannot help doubting whether we may present it as a witticism, as a sophistical witticism, or merely as a sophism. The fact is that we do not yet know wherein the character of wit lies.

On the other hand, the following example, which evinces, as it were, the complementary faulty thinking, is a witticism without any doubt. Again, it is a story of a marriage agent. *The agent is defending the girl he has proposed against the attacks of her prospective fiancé. "The mother-in-law does not suit me," the latter remarks. "She is a crabbed, foolish person." "That's true," replies the agent, "but you are not going to marry the mother-in-law, but the daughter." "Yes, but she is no longer young, and she is not pretty, either." "That's nothing: if she is not young or pretty, you can trust her all the more." "But she hasn't much money." "Why talk of money? Are you going to marry money? You want a wife, don't you?" "But she is a hunchback." "Well, what of that? Do you expect her to have no blemishes at all?"*

It is really a question of an ugly girl who is no longer young, who has a paltry dowry and a repulsive mother, and who is besides equipped with a pretty bad deformity, qualities which are not at all inviting to matrimony. The marriage agent knows how to present each individual fault in a manner to cause one to become reconciled to it, and then takes up the unpardonable hunchback as the one fault which can be excused in anyone. Here again, there is the semblance of logic which is characteristic of sophisms, and which serves to conceal the faulty thinking. It is apparent that the girl possesses nothing but faults, many of which can be overlooked, but one that cannot be passed by. The chances for the marriage become very slim. The agent acts as if he removed each individual fault by his evasions, forgetting that each leaves behind some depreciation which is added to the next one. He insists upon dealing with each factor individually, and refuses to combine them into a sum-total.

A similar omission forms the nucleus of another sophism which causes much laughter, though one can well question its right to be called a joke. *A. had borrowed a copper kettle from B., and upon returning it, was sued by B. because it had a large hole which rendered it unserviceable. His defense was this: "In the first place, I never borrowed any kettle from B., secondly, the kettle had a hole in it when I received it from B., thirdly, the kettle was in perfect condition when I returned it."* Each separate protest is good by itself, but taken together, they exclude each other. A. treats individually what must be taken as a whole, just as the marriage agent when he deals with the imperfections of the bride. One can also say that A. uses "and" where only an "either—or" is possible.

Another sophism greets us in the following marriage agent story. *The suitor objects because the bride has a short leg and therefore limps. The agent contradicts him. "You are wrong," he says. "Suppose you marry a woman whose legs are sound and straight. What do you gain by it? You are not sure from day to day that she will not fall down, break a leg, and then be lame for the rest of her life. Just consider the pain, the excitement, and the doctor's bill. But if you marry this one, nothing can happen. Here you have a finished job."*

Here the semblance of logic is very shallow, for no one will admit that a "finished misfortune" is to be preferred to a mere possibility of such. The error in the stream of thought will be seen more easily in a second example.

In the temple of Cracow, sat the great Rabbi N. praying with his disciples. Suddenly, he emitted a cry, and in response to his troubled disciples said: "The great Rabbi L. died just now in Lemberg." The congregation thereupon went into mourning for the deceased. In the course of the next day, travellers from Lemberg were asked how the rabbi had died, and what had caused his death. They knew nothing about the event, however, as, they said, they had left him in the best of health. Finally, it was definitely ascertained that the Rabbi of Lemberg had not died at the hour on which Rabbi N. had felt his death telepathically, and that he was still living. A stranger seized the opportunity to banter a pupil of the Cracow rabbi about the episode. "That was a glorious exhibition that your rabbi made of himself when he saw the Rabbi of Lemberg die," he said. "Why, the man is still living!" "No matter," replied the pupil. "To look from Cracow to Lemberg was wonderful anyhow."

Here the faulty thinking common to both of the last examples is openly shown. The value of fanciful ideas is unfairly matched against reality; possibility is made equivalent to actuality. To look from Cracow to Lemberg despite the miles between would have been an imposing telepathic feat, had it resulted in some truth, but the disciple gives no heed to that. It might have been possible that the Rabbi of Lemberg had died at the moment when the Rabbi of Cracow had proclaimed his death, but the pupil displaces the accent from the condition under which the teacher's act would be remarkable to the unconditional admiration of this act. *"In magnis rebus voluisse sat est"* is a similar point of view. Just as in this example, reality is sacrificed in favor of possibility, so in the foregoing example, the marriage agent suggests to the suitor that the possibility of the woman's becoming lame through an accident is a far more important consideration to be taken into account; whereas the question as to whether or not she is lame is put altogether into the background.

Another interesting group falls in with this one of sophistical faulty thinking, in which the faulty thinking may be designated as *automatic*. It is perhaps only a stroke of fate that all the examples which I shall cite for this new group are again stories referring to marriage agents.

The agent brought along an assistant to a conference about a bride. This assistant was to confirm his assertions. "She is as well built as a pine tree," said the agent. "Like a pine tree," repeated the echo. "She has eyes which one must appreciate." "Wonderful eyes," confirmed the echo. "She is cultured beyond words. She possesses extraordinary culture." "Wonderfully cultured," repeated the assistant. "However, one thing is true," confessed the agent. "She has a slight hunch on her back." "And what a hunch!" confirmed the echo.

The other stories are quite analogous to this one, but they are cleverer.

On being introduced to his prospective bride, the suitor was rather unpleasantly surprised, and drawing aside the marriage agent, he reproachfully whispered to him: "Why have you brought me here? She is ugly and old. She squints, has bad teeth and bleary eyes." "You can talk louder," interrupted the agent. "She is deaf, too."

A prospective bridegroom made his first call on his future bride in company with the agent, and while in the parlor waiting for the appearance of the family, the agent drew the young man's attention to a glass closet containing a handsome silver set. "Just look at these things," he said. "You can see how wealthy these people are." "But is it not possible that these articles were just borrowed for the occasion," inquired the suspicious young man, "so as to give the appearance of wealth?" "What an idea," answered the agent protestingly. "Who in the world would lend them anything?"

In all three cases, one finds the same thing. A person who reacts several times in succession in the same manner, continues in the same manner on the next occasion where it is inappropriate, and runs contrary to his intentions. Falling into the automatism of habit, he fails to adapt himself to the demands of the situation. Thus, in the first story, the assistant forgot that he was taken along in order to influence the suitor in favor of the proposed bride, and as he had thus far accomplished his task by emphasizing through repetition the excellencies attributed to the lady, he now emphasizes also her timidly conceded hunchback which he should have belittled.

The marriage agent in the second story is so fascinated by the failings and infirmities of the bride that he completes the list from his own knowledge, which it was certainly neither his business nor his intention to do. Finally, in the third story, he is so carried away by his zeal to convince the young man of the family's wealth, that in order to corroborate his proofs, he blurts out something which must upset all his efforts. Everywhere, the automatism triumphs over the appropriate variation of thought and expression.

That is all quite easy to understand, although it must cause confusion when it is called to our attention that these three stories could just as well be termed "comical" as "witty." Like every act of unmasking and self-betrayal, the discovery of the psychic automatism also belongs to technique of the comic. We suddenly see ourselves here confronted with the problem of the relationship of wit to the comic element—a subject which we endeavored to avoid (see the Introduction). Are these stories only "comical" and not "witty" also? Does the comic element employ here the same technical means as wit? And again, of what does the peculiar character of wit consist?

We must bear in mind that the technique of the group of witticisms examined last consists of nothing else but illustrations of "faulty thinking." We are forced to admit, however, that so far, the investigation has led us into more obscurity than enlightenment. Nevertheless, we do not abandon the hope of arriving at a result by means of a more thorough knowledge of the technique of wit, which may become the starting-point for further understanding.

UNIFICATION

The next examples of wit with which we wish to continue our investigation do not give us as much work. Their technique reminds us very much of what we already know. Here is one of Lichtenberg's jokes. *"January,"* he says, *"is the month in which one extends good wishes to his friends, and the rest are months in which the good wishes are not fulfilled."*

As these witticisms may be called clever rather than strong, and are effected by less forceful means, we shall reinforce the impression gained from them by further study.

"Human life is divided into two halves; during the first, one looks forward to the second, and during the second, one looks backward to the first."

"Experience consists in experiencing what one does not care to experience." (The last two examples were cited by K. Fischer.)

One cannot help being reminded by these examples of a group, treated of before, which is characterized by the "manifold application of the same material." The last example especially will cause us to ask why we have not inserted it there instead of presenting it here in a new connection.

"Experience" is described through its own terms, just as in some of the examples cited above. Neither would I be against this correction. However, I am of the opinion that the other two cases, which are surely similar in character, contain a different factor which is more striking and more important than the manifold application of the same words, which shows nothing here verging on double meaning. And what is more, I wish to emphasize that new and unexpected identities are here formed which show themselves in relations of ideas to one another, in relations of definitions to each other, or to a common third. I would call this process *unification*. Obviously, it is analogous to condensation by compression into similar words. Thus, the two halves of human life are described by the inter-relationship discovered between them: during the first part, one longs for the second, and in the second, one longs for the first. To speak more precisely, there were two relationships very similar to each other which were selected for description. This similarity of the relationship which corresponds to the similarity of the words that, just for this reason, might recall the manifold application of the same material—(looks forward) (looks backward).

In Lichtenberg's joke, January and the months contrasted with it are characterized again by a modified relationship to a third factor: these are good wishes which one receives in the first month, but are not fulfilled during the other months. The differentiation from the manifold application of the same material which is really related to double meaning is here quite clear.

A good example of unification-wit needing no explanation is the following:

J. B. Rousseau, the French poet, wrote an ode to posterity (à la postérité). Voltaire, thinking that the poor quality of the poem in no way justified its reaching posterity, wittily remarked, "This poem will not reach its destination." (K. Fischer).

The last example may remind us of the fact that it is essentially unification which forms the basis of the so-called repartee in wit. For ready repartee consists in using the defense for aggression and in "turning the tables" or in "paying with the same coin." That is, repartee consists in establishing an unexpected identity between attack and counter-attack.

For example, *a baker said to a tavern keeper, one of whose fingers was festering: "I guess your finger got into your beer." The tavern keeper replied: "You are wrong. One of your rolls got under my finger nail"* (Ueberhorst: *Das Komische*, II, 1900).

While Augustus was travelling through his domains, he noticed a man in the crowds who bore a striking resemblance to himself. He beckoned to him to come over and asked: *"Was your mother ever employed in my home?" "No, sire,"* replied the man, *"but my father was."*

While Duke Karl of Würtemberg was riding horseback, he met a dyer working at his trade. *"Can you color my white horse blue?" "Yes, sire,"* was the rejoinder, *"if the animal can stand the boiling."*

In this excellent repartee, which answers a foolish question with a condition that is equally impossible, there occurs another technical factor which would have been omitted if the dyer's reply had been: "No, sire, I am afraid that the horse could not stand being boiled."

Another peculiarly interesting technical means at the disposal of unification, is the addition of the conjunction "and." Such correlation signifies a connection which could not be understood otherwise. When Heine (*Harzreise*) says of the city of Göttingen, *"In general, the inhabitants of Göttingen are divided into students, professors, Philistines and cattle,"* we understand this combination exactly in the sense which he furthermore emphasized by adding: "These four social groups are distinguished little less than sharply." Again, when he speaks about the school where he had to submit *"to so much Latin, drubbing and geography,"* he wants to convey by this combination, which is made very conspicuous by placing the drubbing between the two studies, that the schoolboy's conception unmistakably described by the drubbing should be extended also to Latin and geography.

In Lipps's book, we find, among the examples of "witty enumeration" (Koordination) the following verse, which stands nearest to Heine's "students, professors, Philistines and cattle,"

"With a fork and with much effort, his mother pulled him from a mess."

"As if effort were an instrument like the fork," adds Lipps by way of explanation. But we get the impression that there is nothing witty in this sentence. To be sure, it is very comical, whereas Heine's co-ordination is undoubtedly witty. We shall, perhaps, recall these examples later when we shall no longer be forced to evade the problem of the relationship between wit and the comic.

REPRESENTATION THROUGH THE
OPPOSITE

We have remarked in the example of the Duke and the dyer that it would still have been a joke by means of unification had the dyer replied, "No, I fear that the horse could not stand being boiled." But his answer read: "Yes, if the horse could stand boiling." In substituting a "yes" for the "no" which rightly belonged there, we meet a new technical means of wit, the application of which we shall study in other examples.

This joke, which resembles the one we have just cited from K. Fischer, is somewhat simpler. *"Frederick the Great heard of a Silesian clergyman who had the reputation of communicating with spirits. He sent for him*

and received him with the following question: 'Can you call up ghosts?'
'At your pleasure, Your Majesty,' replied the clergyman, 'but they won't
come.' " Here, it is perfectly obvious that the wit lies in the substitution
of its opposite for the only possible answer, "No." To complete this substitution "but" had to be added to "yes," so that "yes" plus "but" gives
the equivalent for "no."

This "representation through the opposite," as we choose to call it,
serves the mechanism of wit in several ways. In the following cases, it
appears almost in its pure form:

"This woman resembles the Venus de Milo in many points. Like her,
she is extraordinarily old, has no teeth, and has white spots on the yellow
surface of her body" (Heine).

Here, ugliness is depicted by making it agree with the most beautiful.
Of course, these agreements consist of attributes expressed in double
meaning or of matters of slight importance. The latter applies to the second example.

"The attributes of the greatest men were all united in himself. Like
Alexander, his head was tilted to one side; like Caesar, he always had
something in his hair. He could drink coffee like Leibnitz, and once settled
in his armchair, he forgot eating and drinking like Newton, and like him,
had to be awakened. He wore a wig like Dr. Johnson, and like Cervantes,
the fly of his trousers was always open" (Lichtenberg: *The Great Mind*).

J. V. Falke's *Lebenserinnerungen an eine Reise nach Irland* (page
271) furnishes an exceptionally good example of "representation through
the opposite" in which the use of words of a double meaning plays absolutely no part. The scene is laid in a wax figure museum, like Mme. Tus-
saud's. A lecturer discourses on one figure after another to his audience,
which is composed of old and young people. *"This is the Duke of Welling-*
ton and his horse," he says. Whereupon a young girl remarks, *"Which is*
the duke and which is the horse?" "Just as you like, my pretty child," is
the reply. *"You pay your money and you take your choice."*

The reduction of this Irish joke would be: "It is gross impudence on
the part of the museum's management to offer such an exhibition to the
public. It is impossible to distinguish between the horse and the rider
(playful exaggeration), and it is for this exhibit that one pays one's hard-
earned money!" The indignant expression is now dramatized and applied
to a trivial occurrence. In the place of the entire audience, there appears
one woman and the riding figure becomes individually determined. It is
necessarily the Duke of Wellington, who is so very popular in Ireland.
But the insolence of the museum proprietor or lecturer who takes money
from the public and offers nothing in return, is represented by the opposite, through a speech, in which he extols himself as a conscientious business man, whose fondest desire is to respect the rights to which the public

is entitled through the admission fee. One then realizes that the technique of this joke is not very simple. In so far as a way is found to allow the swindler to assert his scrupulosity, it may be said that the joke is a case of "representation through the opposite." The fact, however, that he does it on an occasion where something different is demanded of him, and the fact that he replies in terms of commercial integrity when he is expected to discuss the similarity of the figures, shows that it is a case of displacement. The technique of the joke lies in the combination of both technical means.

OUTDOING-WIT

This example is closely allied to another small group which might be called "outdoing-wit." Here, "yes," which would be proper in the reduction, is replaced by "no," which, owing to its context, is equivalent to a still stronger "yes." The same mechanism holds true when the case is reversed. The contradiction takes the place of an exaggerated confirmation. An example of this nature is seen in the following epigram from Lessing.[1]

"The good Galatea! 'Tis said that she dyes her hair black, yet it was black when she bought it."

Lichtenberg's make-believe mocking defense of philosophy is another example.

"There are more things in heaven and earth than are dreamt of in your philosophy," Prince Hamlet had disdainfully declared. Lichtenberg well knew that this condemnation was by no means severe enough, in that it does not take into account all that can be said against philosophy. He therefore added the following: *"But there is also much in philosophy which is found neither in heaven nor on earth."* To be sure, his assertion supplements what was lacking in Hamlet's philosophical utterance, but in doing this, he adds another and still greater reproach.

More transparent still, because they show no trace of displacement, are two Jewish jokes, which are, however, of the coarse kind.

Two Jews were conversing about bathing. "I take a bath once a year," said one, *"whether I need one or not."*

It is clear that this boastful assurance of his cleanliness only betrays his state of uncleanliness.

A Jew noticed remnants of food on the beard of another. "I can tell you what you ate yesterday," he remarked. *"Well, let's hear it,"* said the other. *"Beans,"* said the first one. *"You are wrong,"* responded the other. *"I had beans the day before yesterday."*

The following example is an excellent "outdoing" witticism which can be traced easily to representation through the opposite.

[1] Following an example of the *Greek Anthology.*

The king condescended to pay a visit at a surgical clinic, and found the professor of surgery engaged in amputating a leg. He watched the various steps of the operation with interest and expressed his royal approval with these loud utterances: "Bravo, bravo, Professor." When the operation was over, the professor approached the king, bowed low and asked: "Does your majesty also command the amputation of the other leg?"

Whatever the professor may have thought during this royal applause surely could not have been expressed unchanged. His real thoughts were: "Judging by this applause, he must be under the impression that I am amputating the poor devil's diseased leg by order of the king and for his pleasure. To be sure, I have other reasons for performing this operation." But instead of expressing these thoughts, he goes to the king and says: "I have no other reasons but your majesty's order for performing this operation. The applause you accorded me has inspired me so much that I am only awaiting your majesty's command to amputate the other leg also." He thus succeeded in making himself understood by expressing the opposite of what he really thought but which he had to keep to himself. Such an expression of the opposite represents an incredible exaggeration or outdoing.

As we gather from these examples, representation through the opposite is a means frequently and effectively used in the technique of wit. We need not overlook, however, something else, namely, that this technique is by no means confined only to wit. When Marc Antony, after his long speech in the Forum had changed the mood of the mob listening to Caesar's obsequies, at last repeats the words,
"For Brutus was an honorable man,"
he well knows that the mob will scream the true meaning of his words at him, namely,
"They are traitors: nice honorable men!"
Or when someone transcribes a collection of unheard-of brutalities and cynicisms as expressions of "people with temperaments," this, too, is a representation through the opposite. However, this is no longer designated as wit, but as "irony." Indeed, the only technique that is characteristic of irony is representation through the opposite. Besides, one reads and hears about "ironical wit." Hence, there is no longer any doubt that technique alone is not capable of characterizing wit. There must be something else which we have not yet discovered. On the other hand, the fact that the reduction of the technique destroys the wit still remains uncontradicted. For the present, it may be difficult for us to unite for the explanation of wit the two strong points which we have already gained.

INDIRECT EXPRESSION

Since representation through the opposite belongs to the technical means of wit, we may also expect that wit could make use of its reverse, namely, the representation through the similar and cognate. Indeed, when we continue our investigation, we find that this forms the technique of a new and especially extensive group of thought-witticisms. We can describe the peculiarity of this technique much better if, instead of representation through the "cognate," we use the expression representation through "relationships and associations." We shall start with the last characteristic and illustrate it by an example.

INDIRECT EXPRESSION WITH
ALLUSION

It is an American anecdote and runs as follows: *By undertaking a series of risky schemes, two not very scrupulous business men had succeeded in amassing an enormous fortune and were now intent on forcing their way into good society. Among other things, they thought it advisable to have their portraits painted by the most prominent and most expensive painters in the city, men whose works were considered masterpieces. The costly pictures were exhibited for the first time at a great evening gathering, and the hosts themselves led the most prominent connoisseur and art critic to the wall of the salon on which both portraits were hanging side by side, in order to elicit from him a favorable criticism. He examined the portraits for a long time, then shook his head as if he were missing something. At length, he pointed to the bare space between the pictures, and asked: "And where is the Savior?"*

The meaning of this expression is clear. It is again the expression of something which cannot be represented directly. In what way does this "indirect expression" come about? By a series of very obvious associations and conclusions, let us work backwards from the verbal setting.

The query, *"where is the Savior?"* or *"where is the picture of the Savior?"* arouses the conjecture that the two pictures have reminded the speaker of a similar arrangement familiar to him as it is familiar to us. This arrangement, of which one element is here missing, shows the figure of the Savior between two other figures. There is only one such case: Christ hanging between the two thieves. The missing element is emphasized by the witticism, and the similarity rests in the figures at the right and left of the Savior, which are not mentioned in the jest. It can only mean that the pictures hanging in the drawing-room are likewise those of thieves. This is what the critic wished to, but could not say, "You are a pair of scoundrels," or more in detail, "What do I care about your portraits? You are a pair of scoundrels, that I know." And by means of a few associations and conclusive inferences, he has said it in a manner which we designate as "allusion."

We are immediately reminded that we have encountered the process of allusion before. Namely, in double meaning, when one of the two meanings expressed by the same word stands out very prominently because being used much oftener and more commonly, our attention is directed to it first, whereas the other meaning remains in the background because it is more remote—such cases we wished to describe as double meaning with allusion. In an entire series of examples which we have hitherto examined, we have remarked that their technique is not simple and we realized that the process of allusion was the factor that complicated it. For example, see the contradiction-witticism in which the congratulations on the birth of the youngest child are acknowledged by the remark that it is remarkable what human hands can accomplish.

In the American anecdote, we have the process of allusion without the double meaning, and we find that the character of this process consists in completing the picture through mental association. It is not difficult to guess that the utilized association can be of more than one kind. So as not to be confused by large numbers, we shall discuss only the most pronounced variations, and shall give only a few examples.

For example, Lichtenberg coined the saying: *"New baths heal well,"* which immediately reminds one of the proverb, *"New brooms clean well,"* whose first and last words, as well as whose whole sentence structure, is the same as in the first saying. It has undoubtedly arisen in the witty thinker's mind as an imitation of the familiar proverb. Thus Lichtenberg's saying is an allusion to the latter. By means of this allusion, something is suggested that cannot be frankly said, namely, that the efficacy of the baths taken as cures is due to other things beside the thermal springs whose attributes are the same everywhere.

The solution of the technique of another one of Lichtenberg's jokes is similar: *"The girl barely twelve modes old."* That sounds something like the chronological term *"twelve moons"* (*i.e.*, months), and may originally have been a mistake in writing, a permissible poetical expression. But there is a good deal of sense in designating the age of a feminine creature by the changing modes instead of by the changing of moons.

The connection of similarity may even consist of a single slight modification. This technique again runs parallel with a word-technique. Both kinds of witticisms create almost the identical impression, but they are more easily distinguishable by the processes of the wit-work.

The following is an example of such a word-witticism or pun. The great singer, Mary Wilt, who was famous not merely on account of the magnitude of her voice, suffered the mortification of having a title of a play, dramatized from the well-known novel of Jules Verne, serve as an allusion to her corpulency. *"Around the Wilt* (world) *in Eighty Days."*

Or: *"Every fathom a queen,"* which is a modification of the familiar Shakespearian quotation, *"Every inch a king,"* and served as an allusion to a prominent woman who was unusually big physically. There would really be no serious objection if one should prefer to classify this witticism as a substitution for condensation with modification (cf. tête-à-bête).

Discussing the hardships of the medical profession, namely, that physicians are obliged to read and study constantly because remedies and drugs once considered efficacious are later rejected as useless, and that despite the physician's best efforts, the patient often refuses to pay for the treatment, one of the doctors present remarked: *"Yes, every drug has its day,"* to which another added, *"But not every Doc gets his pay."* These two witty remarks are both modifications with allusion of the well-known saying, *"Every dog has his day."* But here, too, the technique could be described as fusion with modification.

If the modification contents itself with a change in letters, allusions through modifications are barely distinguishable from condensation with substitutive formation, as shown in this example: *"Mellingitis," the allusion to the dangerous disease meningitis, refers to the danger which the conservative members of a provincial borough in England thought impended if the socialist candidate Mellon were elected.*

The negative particles make very good allusions at the cost of very little changing. Heine referred to Spinoza as:

"My fellow *un*believer Spinoza."

"We, by the *U*ngrace of God, Laborers, Bondsmen, Negroes, Serfs," etc., is a manifesto (which Lichtenberg quotes no further) of these unfortunates who probably have more right to that title than kings and dukes have to the unmodified "by the Grace of God."

OMISSION

Finally *omission,* which is comparable to condensation without substitutive formation, is also a form of allusion. For in every allusion there is really something omitted, namely, the trend of thought that leads to the allusion. It is only a question of whether the gap, or the substitute in the wording of the allusion, which partly fills in the gap, is the more obvious element. Thus we come back through a series of examples from the very clear cases of omission to those of actual allusion.

Omission without substitution is found in the following example. There lived in Vienna a clever and bellicose writer whose sharp invectives had repeatedly brought him bodily assault from the hands of the persons he assailed. During a conversation about a new misdeed by one of his habitual opponents, someone said, *"When X. hears this, he will receive another box on the ear."* The technique of this wit shows in the first place the confusion about the apparent contradiction, for it is by no means clear to us why a box on one's ear should be the direct result of having heard something. The contradiction disappears if one fills in the gap by adding to the remark: *"then he will write such a caustic article against that person that, etc."* Allusions through omission and contradiction are thus the technical means of this witticism.

Heine remarked about someone: *"He praises himself so much that pastils for fumigation are advancing in price."* The omission can easily be filled in. What has been omitted is replaced by an inference which then strikes back as an allusion to the same. For self-praise has always carried an evil odor with it.

Once more we encounter the two Jews in front of the bathing establishment. *"Another year has passed by already,"* says one with a sigh.

These examples leave no doubt that the omission is meant as an allusion.

A still more obvious omission is contained in the next example, which is really a genuine and correct allusion-witticism. Subsequent to an artists' banquet, a joke book was given out in which, among others, the following most remarkable proverb could be read:

"A wife is like an umbrella, at worst one may also take a cab."

An umbrella does not afford enough protection from rain. The words *"at worst"* can mean only: when it is raining hard. A cab is a public conveyance. As we have to deal here with the figure of comparison, we shall put off the detailed investigation of this witticism until later on.

Heine's "Bäder von Lucca" contains a veritable wasps' nest of stinging allusions which make the most artistic use of this form of wit as polemics against the Count of Platen. Long before the reader can suspect this application, a certain theme, which hardly lends itself to direct representation, is preluded by allusions of the most varied material possible; *e.g.*, in Hirsch-Hyacinth's twisting of words: "You are too corpulent and I am too lean; you have too much imagination and I as much more business acumen; I am a *practicus* and you are a *diarrheticus,* in fine, 'You are altogether my *Antipodex'*—'*Venus Urinia,*' etc." Then the occurrences of which the poet speaks take a turn in which it first merely seems to show the impolite sportiveness of the poet, but soon it discloses the symbolic relation to the polemical intention, and in this way it also reveals itself as allusion. At last, the attack against Platen bursts forth, and now the allusions to the subject of the Count's love for men seethe and gush from each one of the sentences which Heine directs against the talent and the character of his opponent, *e.g.*:

"Even the Muses are not well disposed to him, he has at least the genius of speech in his power, or rather he knows how to violate him; for he lacks the free love of this genius, besides he must perseveringly run after this youth, and he knows only how to grasp the outer forms which, in spite of their beautiful rotundity, never express themselves nobly."

"He has the same experience as the ostrich, which considers itself sufficiently hidden when it sticks its head into the sand so that only its backside is visible. Our illustrious bird would have done better if he had stuck his backside into the sand, and had shown us his head."

Allusion is perhaps the commonest and most easily employed means of wit, and is at the basis of most of the short-lived witty productions which we are wont to weave into our conversation. They cannot bear being separated from their native soil nor can they exist independently. Once more, we are reminded by the process of allusion of that relationship which has already begun to confuse our estimation of the technique of wit. The process of allusion is not witty in itself; there are perfectly formed allusions which have no claims to this character. Only those allusions which show a "witty" element are witty, hence the characteristics of wit, which we have followed even into its technique, again escape us.

I have sometimes designated allusion as "indirect expression," and now recognize that the different kinds of allusion with representation through the opposite, as well as the techniques still to be mentioned, can be united into a single large group for which "indirect expression" would be the comprehensive name. *Errors of thought—unification—indirect representation*—are therefore designations for those viewpoints under which we can group the techniques of thought-wit with which we became familiar.

REPRESENTATION THROUGH THE MINUTE OR THE MINUTEST ELEMENT

On continuing the investigation of our material, we think that we recognize a new sub-group of indirect representation, which though sharply defined, can be illustrated only by few examples. It is that of representation through a minute or minutest element, and solves the problem by bringing the entire character to full expression through a minute detail. Correlation of this group with the mechanism of allusion is made possible when we consider that this triviality is connected with the thing to be presented and is really derived from it. For example:

A Jew who was riding in a train had made himself very comfortable; he had unbuttoned his coat, and had put his feet on the seat, when a fashionably dressed gentleman came in. The Jew immediately put on his best behavior and assumed a modest position. The stranger turned over the pages of a book, did some calculation, and pondered a moment and suddenly addressed the Jew: "I beg your pardon, how soon will we have Yom Kippur?" (Day of Atonement). "Oh, oh!" said the Jew, and put his feet back on the seat before he answered.

It cannot be denied that this representation through something minute is allied to the tendency of economy which we found to be the final common element in the investigation of the technique of word-wit.

The following example is much similar.

The doctor who had been summoned to help the baroness in her confinement declared that the critical moment had not yet arrived, and proposed to the baron that they play a game of cards in the adjoining room in the meantime. After a while, the doleful cry of the baroness reached the ears of the men. "Ah, mon Dieu, que je souffre!" The husband jumped up, but the physician stopped him saying, "That's nothing; let us play on." A little while later, the woman in labor was heard again: "My God, my God, what pains!" "Don't you want to go in, Doctor?" asked the baron. "By no means, it is not yet time," answered the doctor. At last, there rang from the adjacent room the unmistakable cry, "A-a-a-ai-e-e-e-e-e-e-E-E-E!" The physician quickly threw down the cards and said, "Now it's time."

How the pain causes the original nature to break through all the strata of education, and how an important decision is rightly made dependent upon a seemingly inconsequential utterance—both are shown in this good joke by the successive changes in the cries of this child-bearing lady of quality.

COMPARISON

Another kind of indirect expression of which wit makes use is *comparison*, which we have not discussed so far because an examination of comparison touches upon new difficulties, or rather it reveals difficulties which have made their appearance on other occasions. We have already admitted that in many of the examples examined, we could not banish all doubts as to whether they should really be counted as witty, and have recognized in this uncertainty a serious shock to the principles of our investigation. But in no other material do I feel this uncertainty greater and nowhere does it occur more frequently than in the case of comparison-wit. The feeling which usually tells me—and I dare say a great many others under the same conditions—this is a joke, this may be written down as witty before even the hidden and essential character of the wit has been uncovered—this feeling I lack most in witty comparisons. If I first have no hesitation in declaring the comparison as witty, then the next instant I seem to think that the pleasure I thus found was of a different quality than that which I am accustomed to ascribe to a joke. Moreover, the fact that witty comparisons but seldom evoke the explosive variety of laughter by which a good joke proves itself, makes it impossible for me to cast aside the existing doubts, even when I limit myself to the best and most effective examples.

That there are some especially good and effective examples of comparison, which in no way give the impression of wit, can be easily shown. A beautiful example of this kind which I have not yet tired of admiring, and the impression of which still clings to me, I shall not deny myself the pleasure of citing. It is a comparison with which Ferd. Lassalle concluded one of his famous pleas (*Die Wissenschaft und die Arbeiter*): "A man like myself who, as I explained to you, had devoted his whole life to the motto 'Die Wissenschaft und die Arbeiter' (Science and the Working-man), would receive the same impression from a condemnation which in the course of events confronts him *as would the chemist, absorbed in his scientific experiments, from the cracking of a retort. With a slight knitting of his brow at the resistance of the material, he would, as soon as the disturbance was quieted, calmly continue his labor and investigations.*"

One finds a rich assortment of pertinent and witty comparisons in the writings of Lichtenberg (Vol. II of the Göttingen edition, 1853). I shall take the material for our investigation from that source.

"It is almost impossible to carry the torch of truth through a crowd without singeing somebody's beard." This may seem witty, but on closer examination, one notices that the witty effect does not come from the comparison itself but from a secondary attribute of the same. For the expression "the torch of truth" is no new comparison, but one which has been used for a long time and which has degenerated into a fixed phrase, as always happens when a comparison has the luck to be absorbed into the common usage of speech. But whereas we hardly notice the comparison in the saying, "the torch of truth," its original full force is restored to it by Lichtenberg, since by building further on the comparison it results in a deduction. But the taking of blurred expressions in their full sense is already known to us as a technique of wit; it finds a place in the Manifold Applications of the Same Material. It may well be that the witty impression created by Lichtenberg's sentence is due only to its relation to this technique of wit.

The same explanation will undoubtedly hold good for another witty comparison by the same author.

"The man was not exactly a shining light, but a great illuminator. . . . He was a professor of philosophy."

To call a scholar a shining light, a *"lumen mundi,"* has long ceased to be an effective comparison, whether it be originally qualified as a witticism or not. But here the comparison was freshened up and its full force was restored to it by deducting a modification from it, and in this way setting up a second, new comparison. The way in which the second comparison came into existence seems to contain the condition of the witticism, and not the two comparisons themselves. This is a case of the same technique of wit as in the example of the torch.

The following comparison seems witty for another, though similarly classified reason: *"I look upon reviews as a kind of children's disease* which more or less attacks new-born books. There are cases on record where the healthiest succumbed to them, and the puniest have often survived them. Many never get this disease. Attempts have frequently been made to prevent the disease by means of *amulets of prefaces and dedications, or by coloring them up with pronunciamentos; but it does not always help."*

The comparison of reviews with children's diseases is based in the first place upon their susceptibility to attack shortly after they have seen the light of the world. Whether this makes it witty I do not trust myself to decide. But when the comparison is continued, it is found that the later fates of the new books may be represented within the scope of the same or by means of similar comparisons. Such a continuation of a comparison is undoubtedly witty, but we know already to what technique it owes its witty flavor; it is a case of *unification* or the establishment of an unexpected association. The character of the unification, however, is not changed by the fact that it consists here in a relationship with the first comparison.

DOUBT IN WITTY COMPARISONS

In a series of other comparisons, one is tempted to ascribe an indisputably existing witty impression to another factor which again in itself has nothing to do with the nature of the comparison. These are comparisons which are strikingly grouped, often contain a combination that sounds absurd, or comes into being as a result of such combinations. Most of Lichtenberg's examples belong to this group.

"It is a pity that one cannot see the *learned bowels* of the writers, in order to find out what they have eaten." *"The learned bowels"* is a confusing, really absurd attribute which is made clear only by the comparison. How would it be if the witty impression of this comparison should be referred entirely and fully to the puzzling character of their composition? This would correspond to one of the means of wit well known to us, namely, representation through absurdity.

Lichtenberg has produced another witticism by comparing imbibing of reading and educational material with imbibing of physical nourishment.

"He thought highly of *studying in his room* and was heartily in favor of *learned stable fodder."*

The same absurd or at least conspicuous attributes, which, as we are beginning to notice, are the real carriers of the wit, mark other comparisons of the same author.

"This is the weatherside of my moral constitution; here I can stand almost anything."

"Every person has also his *moral backside* which he does not show *except under the stress of necessity* and which he covers as long as possible with the *pants of good breeding*."

The "moral backside" is the striking attribute which exists here as a result of a comparison. But this is followed by a continuation of the comparison with a regular play on words ("necessity") and a second, still more unusual combination ("the pants of good breeding"), which is possibly witty in itself; for the pants become witty, as it were, because they are the pants of good breeding. We may, therefore, be surprised if the whole thing gives us the impression of a very witty comparison and we are beginning to notice that we are generally inclined in our estimation to extend a quality to the whole thing when it clings only to one part of it. Besides, the "pants of good breeding" remind us of a similar confusing verse of Heine:

"Until, at last, the buttons tore from the pants of my patience."

It is obvious that both of the last comparisons possess a character which one cannot find in all good, *i.e.*, fitting comparisons. One might say that they are in a large manner "debasing," for they place a thing of high category, an abstraction (good breeding, patience), side by side with a thing of a very concrete nature of a very low kind (pants). Whether this peculiarity has something to do with wit we shall have to consider in another connection. Let us attempt to analyze another example in which the degrading character is exceptionally well defined. In Nestroy's farce *"Einen Jux will er sich machen,"* the clerk, Weinberl, who resolves in his imagination how he will ponder over his youth when he has some day become a well-established merchant, says: *"When in the course of confidential conversation, the ice is chopped up before the warehouse of memory, when the portal of the storehouse of antiquity is unlocked again, and when the mattings of phantasy are stocked full with wares of yore."* These are certainly comparisons of abstractions with very common, concrete things, but the witticism depends—exclusively or only partially—upon the circumstance that a clerk makes use of these comparisons which are taken from the sphere of his daily occupation. But to bring the abstract in relation to the commonplace with which he is otherwise filled, is an act of *unification*. Let us revert to Lichtenberg's comparisons.

PECULIAR ATTRIBUTIONS

"The motives for our actions may be arranged like the thirty-two winds, and their names may be classified in a similar way, e.g., Bread-bread-glory or Glory-glory-bread."

As so often happens in Lichtenberg's witticisms, in this case, too, the impression of appropriateness, cleverness and ingenuity is so marked that our judgment of the character of the witty element is thereby misled. If something witty is intermingled in such an utterance with excellent sense, we probably are deluded into declaring the whole thing as an exceptional joke. Moreover, I dare say that everything that is really witty about it results from the strangeness of the peculiar combination bread-bread-glory. Thus, as far as wit is concerned, it is representation through absurdity.

The peculiar combination or absurd attribution can alone be represented as a product of a comparison.

Lichtenberg says: *"A twice-sleepy woman—a once-sleepy church pew."* Behind each one there is a comparison with a bed; in both cases, there is besides the comparison also the technical factor of *allusion*. Once it is an allusion to the soporific effect of sermons, and the second time to the inexhaustible theme of sex.

Having found hitherto that a comparison as often as it appears witty owes this impression to its connection with one of the techniques of wit known to us, there are nevertheless some other examples which seem to point to the fact that a comparison as such can also be witty.

This is Lichtenberg's characteristic remark about certain odes. "They are in poetry what Jacob Böhm's immortal writings are in prose—*they are a kind of picnic in which the author supplies the words and the readers the meaning."*

"When he *philosophizes,* he generally sheds *an agreeable moonlight* over his topics, which is in the main quite pleasant, but which does not show any one subject clearly."

Again, Heine's description: *"Her face resembled a kodex palimpsestus, where under the new block-lettered text of a church father peek forth the half-obliterated verses of an ancient Hellenic erotic poet."*

Or, the continued comparison with a very depreciating tendency, from the "Bäder von Lucca:"

"The Catholic priest is more like a clerk who is employed in a big business; the church, the big house at the head of which is the Pope, gives him a set salary. He works lazily like one who is not working for himself; he has many colleagues, and thus easily remains unnoticed in this big business enterprise. He is concerned only in the credit of the house and still more in its preservation, since he would be deprived of his livelihood if it went into bankruptcy. *The Protestant clergyman,* on the other hand, is his own boss and carries on the religious businesses on his own responsibility. He has no wholesale trade like his Catholic brother-tradesman, but deals merely at retail; and since he himself must understand it, he cannot afford to be lazy. He must praise his *articles of faith* to the people and must disparage the articles of his competitors. Like a true small tradesman, he stands in his retail store, full of envy of the industry of all large houses, particularly the large house in Rome which has so many

thousand bookkeepers and packers on its payroll, and which owns factories in all four corners of the world."

In the face of this, as in many other examples, we can no longer dispute the fact that a comparison may in itself be witty, and that the witty impression need not necessarily depend on one of the known techniques of wit. But we are entirely in the dark as to what determines the witty character of the comparison, since it certainly does not cling to the similarity as a form of expression of the thought, or to the operation of the comparison. We can do no better than include comparison among the different forms of "indirect representation" which are at the disposal of the technique of wit, but the problem, which confronted us more distinctly in the mechanism of comparison, than in the means of wit hitherto treated, must remain unsolved. There must surely be a special reason why the decision as to whether something is a witticism or not, presents more difficulties in cases of comparison than in other forms of expression.

This gap in our understanding, however, offers no ground for complaint that our first investigation has been unsuccessful. Considering the intimate connection which we had to be prepared to ascribe to the different qualities of wit, it would have been imprudent to expect, that we could fully explain one aspect of the problem before we had cast a glance over the others. We shall have to take up this problem at another place.

REVIEW OF THE TECHNIQUES OF WIT

Are we sure that none of the possible techniques of wit has escaped our investigation? Not exactly; but by a continued examination of new material, we can convince ourselves that we have become acquainted with the most numerous and most important technical means of wit-work—at least with as much as is necessary for formulating a judgment about the nature of this psychic process. At present no such judgment exists; on the other hand, we have come into possession of important indications, from the direction of which we may expect a further explanation of the problem. The interesting processes of condensation with substitutive formation, which we have recognized as the nucleus of the technique of word-wit, directed our attention to the dream-formation in whose mechanism the identical psychic processes were discovered. Thither also we are directed by the technique of the thought-wit, namely displacement, faulty thinking, absurdity, indirect expression and representation through the opposite—each and all are also found in the technique of dreams. The dream is indebted to displacement for its strange appearance, which hinders us from recognizing in it the continuation of our waking thoughts; the dream's use of absurdity and contradiction has cost it the dignity of a psychic product, and has misled the authors to assume that the determinants of dream-formation are: collapse of mental activity, cessation of criticism, morality and logic. Representation through the opposite is so common in dreams that even the popular, but entirely misleading, books on dream interpretation usually put it to good account. Indirect expression, the substitution for the dream-thought by an allusion, by a trifle or by a symbolism analogous to comparison, is just exactly what distinguishes the manner of expression of the dream from our waking thoughts.[1] Such a far-reaching agreement as found between the means of wit-work and those of dream-work can scarcely be accidental. To show those agreements in detail and to trace their motivations will be one of our future tasks.

[1] Cf. my *Interpretation of Dreams,* Chap. VI, *The Dream-Work.*

III

THE TENDENCIES OF WIT

NEAR the end of the preceding chapter as I was writing down Heine's comparison of the Catholic priest to an employee of a large business house, and the Protestant divine to an independent retail dealer, I felt an inhibition which nearly prevented me from using this comparison. I said to myself that among my readers probably there would be some who hold in veneration not only religion, but also its administration and personnel. These readers might take offense at the comparison and get into such an emotional state about it that it would take away all interest from the question whether the comparison seemed witty in itself or was witty only through its garnishings. In other examples, *e.g.*, the one mentioned above concerning the agreeable moonlight shed by a certain philosophy, there would be no worry that for some readers it might be a disturbing influence in our investigation. Even the most religious person would remain in the right mood to form a judgment about our problem.

It is easy to guess the character of the witticism by the kind of reaction that wit exerts on the hearer. Sometimes wit is wit for its own sake and serves no other particular purpose; then, again, it places itself at the service of such a tendency; *i.e.*, it becomes tendentious. Only that form of wit which has such a tendency runs the risk of ruffling people who do not wish to hear it.

Theo Vischer called wit without a tendency *"abstract"* wit; I prefer to call it *"harmless"* wit.

As we have already classified wit according to the material touched by its technique into word- and thought-wit, it is incumbent upon us to investigate the relation of this classification to the one just put forward. Word- and thought-wit on the one hand, and abstract- and tendency-wit on the other hand, bear no relation of dependence to each other; they are two entirely independent classifications of witty productions. Perhaps some one may have gotten the impression that harmless witticisms are preponderately word-witticisms, whereas the complicated techniques of thought-witticisms are mostly made to serve strong tendencies. There are harmless witticisms that operate through play on words and sound similarity, and just as harmless ones which make use of all means of thought-wit. Nor is it less easy to prove that tendency-wit as far as technique is concerned may be merely the wit of words. Thus, for example, witticisms that *"play"* with proper names often show an insulting and offending tendency, and yet they, too, belong to word-wit. Again, the most harmless of all jests are word-witticisms. Examples of this nature are the popular "shake-up" rhymes (Schüttelreime) in which the technique is represented through the manifold application of the same material with a very peculiar modification:

"Having been forsaken by *Dame Luck*, he degenerated into a *Lame Duck*."

Let us hope that no one will deny that the pleasure experienced in this kind of otherwise unpretentious rhyming is of the same nature as the one by which we recognize wit.

Good examples of abstract or harmless thought-witticisms abound in Lichtenberg's comparisons with which we have already become acquainted. I add a few more. *"They sent a small octavo to the University of Göttingen; and received back in body and soul a quarto"* (a fourth-form boy).

"In order to erect this building well, one must above all things lay a good foundation, and I know of no firmer than by laying immediately over every pro-layer a contra-layer."

"One man begets the thought, the second acts as its godfather, the third begets children by it, the fourth visits it on its death-bed, and the fifth buries it" (comparison with unification).

"Not only did he not believe in ghosts, but not once was he ever afraid of them." The witticism in this case lies exclusively in the absurd representation which puts what is usually considered less important in the comparative and what is considered more important in the positive degree. Divested of its dress it says: it is much easier to use our reason and make light of the fear of ghosts than to defend ourselves against this fear when the occasion presents itself. But this rendering is no longer witty; it is merely a correct and still too little respected psychological fact suggesting what Lessing expresses in his well-known words:

"Not all are free who mock their chains."

HARMLESS AND TENDENCY WIT

I shall take the opportunity presented here of clearing up what may still lead to a possible misunderstanding. "Harmless" or "abstract" wit should in no way convey the same meaning as "shallow" or "poor" wit. It is meant only to designate the opposite of the "tendency" wit to be described later. As shown in the aforementioned examples, a harmless jest, *i.e.*, a witticism without a tendency, can also be very rich in content and express something worth while. The quality of a witticism, however, is independent of the wit and represents the quality of the thought which is here expressed wittily by means of a special contrivance. To be sure, just as watch-makers are wont to enclose very good works in valuable cases, so it may likewise happen with wit that the best wit-contrivances are used to invest the richest thoughts.

Now, if we pay strict attention to the distinction between thought-content and the witty wording of thought-wit, we arrive at an insight which may clear up much uncertainty in our judgment of wit. For it turns out—astonishing as it may seem—that our enjoyment of a witticism is supplied by the combined impression of content and wit-activity, and that one of the factors is likely to deceive us about the extent of the other. It is only the reduction of the witticism that lays bare to us our mistaken judgment.

The same thing applies to word-wit. When we hear that *"experience consists simply of experiencing what one wishes he had not experienced,"* we are puzzled, and believe that we have learnt a new truth; it takes some time before we recognize in this disguise the platitude, "adversity is the school of wisdom." The excellent witticism which seeks to define "experience" by the almost exclusive use of the word "experience" deceives us so completely that we overestimate the content of the sentence. The same thing happens in many similar cases and also in Lichtenberg's unification-witticism about January, which expresses nothing but what we already know, namely, that New Year's wishes are as seldom realized as other wishes.

We find the contrary true of other witticisms, in which obviously what is striking and correct in the thought captivates us, so that we call the saying an excellent witticism, whereas it is only the thought that is brilliant while the wit-function is often weak. It is especially true of Lichtenberg's wit that the path of the thought is often of more value than its witty expression, though we unjustly extend the value of the former to the latter. Thus the remark about the "torch of truth" is hardly a witty comparison, but it is so striking that we are inclined to lay stress on the sentence as exceptionally witty.

Lichtenberg's witticisms are above all remarkable for their thought-content and their certainty of hitting the mark. Goethe has rightly remarked about this author that his witty and jocose thoughts positively conceal problems. Or perhaps it may be more correct to say that they touch upon the solutions of problems. When, for example, he presents as a witty thought:

"He always read *Agamemnon* instead of the German word *angenommen* (accepted), so thoroughly had he read Homer" (technically this is absurdity plus sound similarity of words). Thus he discovered nothing less than the secret of mistakes in reading.[1] The following joke, whose technique seemed to us quite unsatisfactory, is of a similar nature.

"He was surprised that there were two holes cut in the pelts of cats just where the eyes were located." The stupidity here exhibited is only seemingly so; in reality this ingenuous remark conceals the great problem of teleology in the structure of animals; it is not at all so self-evident that the eyelid cleft opens just where the cornea is exposed, until the science of evolution explains to us this coincidence.

Let us bear in mind that a witty sentence gave us a general impression in which we were unable to distinguish the amount of thought-content from the amount of wit-work; perhaps even a more significant parallel to it will be found later.

PLEASURE RESULTS FROM THE TECHNIQUE

For our theoretical explanation of the nature of wit, harmless wit must be of greater value to us than tendency-wit and shallow wit more than profound wit. Harmless and shallow plays on words present to us the problem of wit in its purest form, because of the good sense therein and because it has no tendency nor underlying philosophy to confuse the judgment. With such material our understanding can make further progress.

At the end of a dinner to which I had been invited, a pastry called Roulard was served; it was a culinary accomplishment which presupposed a good deal of skill on the part of the cook. "Is it home-made?" asked one of the guests. "Oh, yes," replied the host, "it is a Home-Roulard" (Home Rule).

This time we shall not investigate the technique of this witticism, but shall center our attention upon another, and most important factor. As I remember, this improvised joke delighted all the guests and made us laugh. In this case, as in countless others, the feeling of pleasure of the hearer cannot have originated from the tendency or the thought-content of the wit; so we are forced to connect the feeling of pleasure with the technique of wit. The technical means of wit which we have described, such as condensation, displacement, indirect expression, etc., have therefore the faculty to produce a feeling of pleasure in the hearer, although we cannot as yet see how they acquired that faculty. By such easy stages we get the second axiom for the explanation of wit; the first one states that the character of wit depends upon the mode of expression. Let us remember also that the second axiom has really taught us nothing new. It merely isolates a fact that was already contained in a discovery which

[1] Cf. my *Psychopathology of Everyday Life*.

we made before. For we recall that whenever it was possible to reduce the wit by substituting for its verbal expression another set of words, at the same time carefully retaining the sense, it not only eliminated the witty character but also the laughableness that constitutes the pleasure of wit.

At present we cannot go further without first coming to an understanding with our philosophical authorities.

The philosophers who consider wit as a part of the comic and deal with the latter itself in the field of æsthetics, characterize the æsthetic feeling through the following condition: that we are not thereby interested in or about the objects, that we do not need these objects to satisfy our great wants in life, but that we are satisfied with the mere contemplation of the same, and with the pleasure of the idea itself. "This pleasure, this mode of conception is purely æsthetical, it depends entirely on itself, its end is only itself and it fulfills no other end in life" (K. Fischer, p. 68).

We scarcely venture a contradiction to K. Fischer's words—perhaps we merely translate his thoughts into our own mode of expression—when we insist that the witty activity is, after all, not to be designated as aimless or purposeless, since it has for its aim the evocation of pleasure in the hearer. I doubt whether we are able to undertake anything which has no object in view. When we do not use our psychic apparatus for the fulfillment of one of our indispensable gratifications, we let it work for pleasure, and we seek to derive pleasure from its own activity. I suspect that this is really the condition which underlies all æsthetic thinking, but I know too little about æsthetics to be willing to support this theory. About wit, however, I can assert, on the strength of the two impressions gained before, that it is an activity whose purpose is to derive pleasure— be it intellectual or otherwise—from the psychic processes. To be sure, there are other activities which accomplish the same thing. They may be differentiated from each by the sphere of psychic activity from which they wish to derive pleasure, or perhaps by the methods which they use in accomplishing this. At present we cannot decide this, but we firmly maintain that at last we have established a connection between the technique of wit which is partly controlled by the tendency to economize, and the production of pleasure.

But before we proceed to solve the riddle of how the technical means of wit-work can produce pleasure in the hearer, we wish to mention that, for the sake of simplicity and more lucidity, we have altogether put aside all tendency witticisms. Still we must attempt to explain what the tendencies of wit are and in what manner wit makes use of these tendencies.

HOSTILE AND OBSCENE WIT

We are taught above all by an observation not to put aside tendency-wit when we are investigating the origin of the pleasure in wit. The pleasurable effect of harmless wit is usually of a moderate nature; all that it can be expected to produce in the hearer is a distinct feeling of satisfaction and a slight ripple of laughter; and as we have shown by fitting examples at least a part of this effect is due to the thought-content. The sudden irresistible outburst of laughter evoked by tendency-wit rarely follows wit without a tendency. As the technique may be identical in both, it is fair to assume that by virtue of its purpose, tendency-wit has at its disposal sources of pleasure to which harmless wit has no access.

It is now easy to survey wit-tendencies. Wherever wit is not a means to its end, *i.e.*, harmless, it puts itself in the service of but two tendencies which may themselves be united under one viewpoint; it is either *hostile* wit serving as an aggression, satire, or defense, or it is *obscene* wit serving as a sexual exhibition. Again, it is to be observed that the technical form of wit—be it a word- or thought-witticism—bears no relation to these two tendencies.

It is a much more complicated matter to show in what way wit serves these tendencies. In this investigation I wish to present first not the hostile but the exhibition wit. The latter has indeed very seldom been deemed worthy of an investigation, as if an aversion had transferred itself here from the material to the subject. However, we shall not allow ourselves to be misled thereby, for we shall soon touch upon a detail in wit which promises to throw light on more than one obscure point.

We all know what is meant by a "smutty" joke. It is the intentional bringing into prominence of sexual facts or relations through speech. However, this definition is no sounder than other definitions. A lecture on the anatomy of the sexual organs or on the physiology of reproduction need not, in spite of this definition, have anything in common with obscenity. It must be added that the smutty joke is directed toward a certain person who excites one sexually, and who becomes cognizant of the speaker's excitement by listening to the smutty joke, and thereby in turn becomes sexually excited. Instead of becoming sexually excited the listener may react with shame and embarrassment, which merely signifies a reaction against the excitement and indirectly an admission of the same. The smutty joke was originally directed against the woman and may be comparable to an attempt at seduction. If a man tells or listens to obscene jokes in male society, the original situation, which cannot be realized on account of social inhibitions, is thereby also represented. Whoever laughs at a smutty joke does the same as the spectator who laughs at a sexual aggression.

The sexual element which is at the basis of the obscene joke comprises more than that which is peculiar to both sexes, and goes beyond that which is common to both sexes, it is connected with all these things that cause shame, and includes the whole domain of the excrementitious. However, this was the sexual domain of childhood, where the imagination fancied a cloaca, so to speak, within which the sexual elements were either badly or not at all differentiated from the excrementitious.[1] In the whole mental domain of the psychology of the neuroses, the sexual still includes the excrementitious, and it is understood in the old, infantile sense.

The smutty joke is like a denudation of a person of the opposite sex toward whom the joke is directed. Through the utterance of obscene words the person attacked is forced to picture the parts of the body in question, or the sexual act, and is shown that the aggressor himself pictures the same thing. There is no doubt that the original motive of the smutty joke was the pleasure of seeing the sexual displayed.

It will only help to clarify the subject if here we go back to the fundamentals. One of the primitive components of our libido is the desire to see the sexual exposed. Perhaps this libido is in itself already a substitution for the desire to touch which is assumed to be the primary pleasure. As it often happens, the desire to see has here also replaced the desire to touch.[2] The libido for looking and touching is found in every person in two forms, active and passive, or masculine and feminine; and in accordance with the preponderance of sex characteristics it develops preponderately in one or the other direction. In young children one can readily observe the desire to exhibit themselves nude. If the germ of this desire does not experience the usual fate of stratification and repression, it develops into a mania for exhibitionism, a familiar perversion among grown-up men. In women the passive desire to exhibit is almost regularly covered by the masked reaction of sexual modesty; despite this, however, remnants of this desire may always be seen in women's dress. How flexible and variable convention and circumstances make that remaining portion of exhibitionism still allowed to women needs hardly be mentioned.

THE TRANSFORMATION OF THE SMUTTY JOKE INTO OBSCENE WIT

In the case of men a great part of this striving to exhibit remains as a part of his libido and serves to initiate the sexual act. If this striving asserts itself on first meeting the woman, it must make use of speech for two motives. First, in order to make itself known to the woman; and secondly, because the awakening of the imagination through speech puts the woman herself in a corresponding excitement and awakens in her the desire to passive exhibitionism. This speech of courtship is not yet smutty, but may pass over into the same. Wherever the yieldingness of the woman manifests itself quickly, smutty speech is short-lived, for it gives way to the sexual act. It is different if the rapid yielding of the woman cannot be

[1] Cf. *Three Contributions to the Theory of Sex.*
[2] *Moll's Kontrektationstrieb* (Untersuchungen über die Libido sexualis, 1898).

counted upon, but instead there appears the defense reaction. In that case the sexually exciting speech changes into obscene wit as its own end; as the sexual aggression is inhibited in its progress towards the act, it lingers at the evocation of the excitement and derives pleasure from the indications of the same in the woman. In this process the aggression changes its character in the same way as any libidinal impulse confronted by a hindrance; it becomes distinctly hostile and cruel, and utilizes the sadistical components of the sexual instinct against the hindrance.

Thus, the unyieldingness of the woman is, therefore, the next condition for the development of smutty wit; to be sure, this resistance must be of the kind to indicate merely a deferment and make it appear that further efforts will not be in vain. The ideal case of such resistance on the part of the woman usually results from the simultaneous presence of another man, a third person, whose presence almost excludes the immediate yielding of the woman. This third person soon becomes of the greatest importance for the development of the smutty wit, but above all the presence of the woman is almost indispensable. Among rural people or in the ordinary hostelry one can observe that not till the waitress or the hostess approaches the guests does the obscene wit come out; in a higher order of society just the opposite happens, here the presence of a woman puts an end to smutty talk. The men reserve this kind of conversation, which originally presupposed the presence of bashful women, until they are alone, "by themselves." Thus gradually the spectator, now turned the listener, takes the place of the woman as the object of the smutty joke, and through such a change the smutty joke already resembles the character of wit.

Henceforth, our attention may be centered upon two factors, first upon the rôle that the third person—the listener—plays, and secondly, upon the intrinsic conditions of the smutty joke itself.

Tendency-wit usually requires three persons. Besides the one who makes the wit there is a second person, who is taken as the object of the hostile or sexual aggression, and a third person in whom the purpose of the wit to produce pleasure is fulfilled. We shall later on inquire into the deeper motive of this relationship, for the present we shall adhere to the fact which states that it is not the maker of the wit who laughs about it and enjoys its pleasurable effect, but the idle listener. The same relationship exists among the three persons connected with the smutty joke. The process may be described as follows: As soon as the libidinal impulse of the first person, to gratify himself through the woman, is blocked, he immediately develops a hostile attitude towards this second person and takes the originally intruding third person as his confederate. Through the obscene speech of the first person the woman is exposed before the third person, who now as a listener is bribed by the easy gratification of his own libido.

It is curious that common people so thoroughly enjoy such smutty talk, and that it is a never-lacking activity of cheerful humor. It is also worthy of notice that in this complicated process which shows so many characteristics of tendency-wit, no formal demands, such as characterize wit, are made upon "smutty wit." To express the unveiled nudity affords pleasure to the first, and makes the third person laugh.

Not until we come to the refined and cultured social stratum does the formal determination of wit arise. The obscenity becomes witty and is tolerated only if it is witty. The technical means of which it mostly makes use is allusion, *i.e.*, substitution through a trifle, something which is only remotely related, which the listener reconstructs in his imagination as a full fledged and direct obscenity. The greater the disproportion between what is directly offered in the obscenity and what is necessarily aroused by it in the mind of the listener, the finer is the witticism and the higher it may venture in good society. Besides the coarse and delicate allusions, the witty obscenity also utilizes all other means of word- and thought-wit, as can be easily demonstrated by examples.

THE FUNCTION OF WIT IN THE SERVICE OF THE TENDENCY

It now becomes comprehensible what wit accomplishes through this service of its tendency. It makes possible the gratification of a craving (lewd or hostile) despite a hindrance which stands in the way; it eludes the hindrance and so derives pleasure from a source that has been inaccessible on account of the hindrance. The hindrance in the way is really nothing more than the higher degree of culture and education which correspondingly increases the inability of the woman to tolerate stark sex matters. The woman thought of as present in the final situation, is still considered present, or her influence acts as a deterrent to the men even in her absence. One often notices how cultured men are influenced by the company of girls of a lower station in life to change witty obscenities to broad smut.

The power which makes it difficult or impossible for the woman, and in a lesser degree for the man, to enjoy unveiled obscenities we call "repression," and we recognize in it the same psychic process which keeps from consciousness in severe nervous attacks, whole complexes of emotions with their resultant affects, and which has shown itself to be the principal factor in the causation of the so-called psychoneuroses. We acknowledge to culture and higher civilization an important influence in the development of repressions, and assume that under these conditions there has come about a change in our psychic organization which may also have been brought along as an inherited disposition. In consequence of it, what was once accepted as pleasureful is now counted unacceptable and is rejected by means of all the psychic forces. Owing to the repression brought about by civilization many primary pleasures are now disapproved by the censorship and lost. But the human psyche finds renunciation very difficult; hence we discover that tendency-wit furnishes us with a means to make the renunciation retrogressive and thus to regain what has been lost. When we laugh over a delicately obscene witticism, we laugh at the identical thing which causes laughter in the ill-bred man when he hears a coarse, obscene joke; in both cases the pleasure comes from the same source. The coarse, obscene joke, however, could not incite us to laughter, because it would cause us shame or would seem to us disgusting; we can laugh only when wit comes to our aid.

What we had presumed in the beginning seems to have been confirmed, namely, that tendency-wit has access to other sources of pleasure than harmless wit, in which all the pleasure is somehow dependent upon the technique. We can also reiterate that owing to our feelings we are in no position to distinguish in tendency-wit what part of the pleasure originates from the technique and what part from the tendency. *Strictly speaking, we do not know what we are laughing about.* In all obscene jokes we succumb to striking mistakes of judgment about the "goodness" of the joke as far as it depends upon formal conditions; the technique of these jokes is often very poor while their laughing effect is enormous.

INVECTIVES MADE POSSIBLE THROUGH WIT

We next wish to determine whether the rôle of wit in the service of the hostile tendency is the same.

Right from the start we meet with similar conditions. Since our individual childhood and the childhood of human civilization, our hostile impulses towards our fellow-beings have been subjected to the same restrictions and the same progressive repressions as our sexual strivings. We have not yet progressed so far as to love our enemies, or to extend to them our left cheek after we are smitten on the right. Furthermore, all moral codes about the subjection of active hatred bear even today the clearest indications that they were originally meant for a small community of clansmen. As we all may consider ourselves members of some nation, we permit ourselves for the most part to forget these restrictions in matters touching a foreign people. But within our own circles we have nevertheless made progress in the mastery of hostile emotions. Lichtenberg drastically puts it when he says: "Where nowadays one says, 'I beg your pardon,' formerly one had recourse to a cuff on the ear." Violent hostility, no longer tolerated by law, has been replaced by verbal invectives, and the better understanding of the concatenation of human emotions robs us, through its consequential *"Tout comprendre, c'est tout par-*

donner," more and more of the capacity to become angry at our fellow-man who is in our way. Having been endowed with a strong hostile disposition in our childhood, higher personal civilization teaches us later that it is undignified to use abusive language; even where combat is still permitted, the number of things which may be used as means of combat has been markedly restricted. Society, as the third and dispassionate party in the combat, to whose interest it is to safeguard personal safety, prevents us from expressing our hostile feelings in action; and hence, as in sexual aggression, there has developed a new technique of invectives, the aim of which is to enlist this third person against our enemy. By belittling and humbling our enemy, by scorning and ridiculing him, we directly obtain the pleasure of his defeat by the laughter of the third person, the inactive spectator.

We are now prepared for the rôle that wit plays in hostile aggression. Wit permits us to make our enemy ridiculous through that which we could not utter loudly or consciously on account of existing hindrances; in other words, *wit affords us the means of surmounting restrictions and of opening up otherwise inaccessible pleasure sources*. Moreover, the listener will be induced by the gain in pleasure to take our part, even if he is not altogether convinced—just as we on other occasions, when fascinated by harmless witticism, were wont to overestimate the substance of the sentence wittily expressed. "To prejudice the laughter in one's own favor" is a completely pertinent saying in the German language.

One may recall the Cincinnatus witticism given above. It is of an insulting nature, as if the author wished to shout loudly: "But the minister of agriculture is himself an ox!" But he, as a man of culture, could not put his opinion in this form. He therefore appealed to wit which assured his opinion a reception at the hands of the listeners which, in spite of its amount of truth, never would have been received if in an unwitty form. Brill cites an excellent example of a similar kind: *Wendell Phillips, according to a recent biography by Dr. Lorenzo Sears, was on one occasion lecturing in Ohio, and while on a railroad journey going to keep one of his appointments met in the car a number of clergymen returning from some sort of convention. One of the ministers, feeling called upon to approach Mr. Phillips, asked him, "Are you Mr. Phillips?" "I am, sir." "Are you trying to free the niggers?" "Yes, sir; I am an abolitionist." "Well, why do you preach your doctrines up here? Why don't you go over into Kentucky?" "Excuse me, are you a preacher?" "I am, sir." "Are you trying to save souls from hell?" "Yes, sir, that's my business." "Well, why don't you go there?"* The assailant hurried into the smoker amid a roar of unsanctified laughter. This anecdote nicely illustrates the tendency-wit in the service of hostile aggression. The minister's behavior was offensive and irritating, yet Wendell Phillips as a man of culture could not defend himself in the same manner as a common, ill-bred person would have done, and as his inner feelings must have prompted him to do. The only alternative under the circumstances would have been to take the affront in silence, had not wit showed him the way, and enabled him by the technical means of unification to turn the tables on his assailant. He not only belittled him and turned him into ridicule, but by his clever retort, "Well, why don't you go there?" fascinated the other clergymen, and thus brought them to his side.

Although the hindrance to the aggression which the wit helped to elude was in these cases of an inner nature—the æsthetic resistance against insulting—it may at other times be of a purely outer nature. So it was in the case when Augustus asked the stranger who had a striking resemblance to himself: "Was your mother ever in my home?" and he received the ready reply, "No, but my father was." The stranger would certainly have felled the imprudent inquirer who dared to make an ignominious allusion to the memory of his mother; but this imprudent person was Augustus, who may not be felled and not even insulted unless one wishes to pay for this revenge with his life. The only thing left was to swallow the insult in silence; but luckily wit pointed out the way of requiting the insult without personally imperiling one's self. It was accomplished simply by treating the allusion with the technical means of unification and employing it against the aggressor. The impression of wit is here so thoroughly determined by the tendency that in view of the witty rejoinder we are inclined to forget that the aggressor's question is itself made witty by allusion.

REBELLION AGAINST AUTHORITY THROUGH WIT

The prevention of abuse or insulting retorts through outer circumstances is so often the case, that tendency-wit is used with special preference as a weapon of attack or criticism of superiors who claim to be in authority. Wit then serves as a resistance against such authority and as an escape from its pressure. In this factor, too, lies the charm of caricature, at which we laugh even if it is badly done simply because we consider resistance to authority a great merit.

If we keep in mind that tendency-wit is so well adapted as a weapon of attack upon what is great, dignified, and mighty, that which is shielded by internal hindrances or external circumstance against direct disparagement, we are forced to a special conception of certain groups of witticisms which seem to occupy themselves with inferior and powerless persons. I am referring to the marriage-agent stories—with a few of which we have become familiar in the investigation of the manifold techniques of thought-wit. In some of these examples, "But she is deaf, too!" and "Who in the world would ever lend these people anything!" the agent was derided as a careless and thoughtless person who becomes comical because the truth escapes his lips automatically, as it were. But does on the one hand, what we have learned about the nature of tendency-wit, and on the other hand the amount of satisfaction in these stories, harmonize with the misery of the persons at whom the joke seems to be pointed? Are these worthy opponents of the wit? Or, is it not more plausible to suppose that the wit puts the agent in the foreground only in order to strike at something more important; does it, as the saying goes, strike the saddle pack, when it is meant for the mule? This conception can really not be rejected.

The above-mentioned interpretation of the marriage-agent stories admits of a continuation. It is true that I need not enter into them, that I can content myself with seeing the farcical in these stories, and can dispute their witty character. However, such subjective determination of wit actually exists. We have now become cognizant of it and shall later on have to investigate it. It means that only that is a witticism which I wish to consider as such. What may be wit to me, may be only an amusing story to another. But if a witticism admits of doubt, that can be due only to the fact that it possesses an obverse side, or another side which in our examples happens to be a façade of the comic, upon which one may be satisfied to bestow a single glance while another may attempt to peep behind. We also suspect that this façade is intended to dazzle the prying glance which is to say, that such stories have something to conceal.

At all events, if our marriage-agent stories are witticisms at all, they are all the better witticisms because, thanks to their façade, they are in a position to conceal not only what they have to say but also that they have something—forbidden—to say. But the continuation of the interpretation, which reveals this hidden part and shows that these stories which have a comical façade, are tendency-witticisms, would be as follows: Every one who allows the truth to escape his lips in an unguarded moment is really pleased to have rid himself of this thought. This is a correct and far-reaching psychological insight. Without the inner assent no one would allow himself to be overpowered by the automatism which here brings the truth to light.[1] The marriage agent is thus transformed from a ludicrous personage into an object deserving of pity and sympathy. How blest must be the man, able at last to unburden himself of the weight of dissimulation, if he immediately seizes the first opportunity to shout out the last fragment of truth! As soon as he sees that his case is lost, that the prospective bride does not suit the young man, he gladly betrays the secret that the girl has still another blemish which the young man had overlooked, or he makes use of the chance to present a conclusive argument in detail in order to express his contempt for the people who employ

[1] It is the same mechanism that controls "slips of the tongue" and other phenomena of self-betrayal. Cf. *The Psychopathology of Everyday Life.*

him: "Who in the world would ever lend these people anything!" The ludicrousness of the whole thing now reverts upon the parents—hardly mentioned in the story—who consider such deceptions justified to clutch a man for their daughter; it also reflects upon the wretched state of the girls who get married through such contrivances, and upon the want of dignity of the marriage contracted after such preliminaries. The agent is the right person to express such criticisms, for he is best acquainted with these abuses; but he may not raise his voice, because he is a poor man whose livelihood depends altogether on turning these abuses to his advantage. But the same conflict is found in the national spirit which has given rise to these and similar stories; for he is aware that the holiness of wedlock suffers severely by reference to some of the methods of marriage-making.

We recall also the observation made during the investigation of wit-technique, namely, that absurdity in wit frequently stands for derision and criticism in the thought behind the witticism, wherein the wit-work follows the dream-work. This state of affairs, we find, is here once more confirmed. That the derision and criticism are not aimed at the agent, who appears in the former examples only as the whipping boy of the joke, is shown by another series in which the agent, on the contrary, is pictured as a superior person whose dialectics are a match for any difficulty. They are stories whose façades are logical instead of comical—they are sophistic thought-witticisms. In one of them the agent knows how to circumvent the limping of the bride by stating that in her case it is at least "a finished job"; another woman with straight limbs would be in constant danger of falling and breaking a leg, which would be followed by sickness, pains, and doctor's fees—all of which can be avoided by marrying the one already limping. Again in another example the agent is clever enough to refute by good arguments each of the whole series of the suitor's objections against the bride; only to the last, the hunchback, which cannot be glossed over, he rejoins, "Do you expect her to have no blemishes at all?" as if the other objections had not left behind an important remnant. It is not difficult to pick out the weak points of the arguments in both examples, a thing which we have done during the investigation of the technique. But now something else interests us. If the agent's speech is endowed with such a strong resemblance of logic, which on more careful examination proves to be merely a semblance, then the truth must be lurking in the fact that the witticism adjudges the agent to be right. The thought does not dare to admit that he is right in all seriousness, and replaces it by the semblance which the wit brings forth; but here, as it often happens, the jest betrays the seriousness of it. We shall not err if we assume that all stories with logical façades really mean what they assert even if these assertions are deliberately falsely motivated. Only this use of sophism for the veiled presentation of the truth, endows it with the character of wit, which is mainly dependent upon the tendency. What these two stories wish to indicate is that the suitor really makes himself ridiculous when he collects together so sedulously the individual charms of the bride which are transient after all, and when he forgets at the same time that he must be prepared to take as his wife a human being with inevitable faults; whereas, the only virtue which might make tolerable marriage with the more or less imperfect personality of the woman— mutual attachment and willingness for affectionate adaptation—is not once mentioned in the whole affair.

Ridicule of the suitor as seen in these examples in which the agent quite correctly assumes the rôle of superiority, is much more clearly depicted in other examples. The more pointed the stories, the less wit-technique they contain; they are, as it were, merely borderline cases of wit with whose technique they have only the façade-formation in common. However, in view of the same tendency and the concealment of the same behind the façade, they obtain the full effect of wit. The poverty of technical means makes it clear also that many witticisms of that kind cannot dispense with the comic element of jargon which acts similarly to wit-technique, without great sacrifices.

The following is such a story, which with all the force of tendency-wit obviates all traces of that technique. *The agent asks: "What are you looking for in your bride?" The reply is: "She must be pretty, she must be rich, and she must be cultured." "Very well," was the agent's rejoinder. "But what you want will make three matches."* Here the reproach is no longer embodied in wit, but is made directly to the man.

In all the preceding examples the veiled aggression was still directed against persons; in the marriage-agent jokes it is directed against all the parties involved in the betrothal—the bridegroom, bride, and her parents. The object of attack by wit may equally well be institutions, persons, in so far as they may act as agents of these, moral or religious precepts, or even philosophies of life which enjoy so much respect that they can be challenged in no other way than under the guise of a witticism, and one that is veiled by a façade at that. No matter how few the themes upon which tendency-wit may play, its forms and investments are manifold. I believe that we shall do well to designate this species of tendency-wit by a special name. To decide what name will be appropriate is possible only after analyzing a few examples of this kind.

THE WITTY CYNICISM

I recall the two little stories about the impecunious gourmet who was caught eating "salmon with mayonnaise," and about the tippling tutor; these witty stories, which we have learned to regard as sophistical displacement-wit, I shall continue to analyze. We have learned since then that when the semblance of logic is attached to the façade of a story, the actual thought is as follows: The man is right; but on account of the opposing contradiction, I did not dare to admit the fact except for one point in which his error is easily demonstrable. The "point" chosen is the correct compromise between his right and his wrong; this is really no decision, but bespeaks the conflict within ourselves. Both stories are simply epicurean. They say, Yes, the man is right; nothing is greater than pleasure, and it is fairly immaterial in what manner one procures it. This sounds frightfully immoral, and perhaps it is, but fundamentally it is nothing more than the *"Carpe diem"* of the poet who refers to the uncertainty of life and the bareness of virtuous renunciation. If we are repelled by the idea that the man in the joke about "salmon with mayonnaise" is in the right, then it is merely due to the fact that it illustrates the sound sense of the man in indulging himself—an indulgence which seems to us wholly unnecessary. In reality each one of us has experienced hours and times during which he has admitted the justice of this philosophy of life and has reproached our system of morality for knowing only how to make claims upon us without reimbursing us. Since we no longer lend credence to the idea of a hereafter in which all former renunciations are supposed to be rewarded by gratification—(there are very few pious persons if one makes renunciation the password of faith)—*"Carpe diem"* becomes the first admonition. I am quite ready to postpone the gratification, but how do I know whether I shall still be alive tomorrow?

"Di doman' non c'e certezza." [1]

I am quite willing to give up all the paths to gratification interdicted by society, but am I sure that society will reward me for this renunciation by opening for me—even after a certain delay—one of the permitted paths? One can plainly tell what these witticisms whisper, namely, that the wishes and desires of man have a right to make themselves perceptible next to our pretentious and inconsiderate morality. And in our times it has been said in emphatic and striking terms that this morality is merely the selfish precept of the few rich and mighty who can gratify their desires at any time without deferment. As long as the art of healing has not succeeded in safeguarding our lives, and as long as the social organizations do not do more towards making conditions more agreeable, just so long cannot the voice within us which is striving against the demands of morality, be stifled. Every honest person finally makes this admission— at least to himself. The decision in this conflict is possible only through the roundabout way of a new understanding. One must be able to knit one's life so closely to that of others, and to form such an intimate iden-

[1] "There is nothing certain about tomorrow," Lorenzo de' Medici.

tification with others, that the shortening of one's own term of life becomes surmountable; one should not unlawfully fulfill the demands of
one's own needs, but should leave them unfulfilled, because only the
continuance of so many unfulfilled demands can develop the power to
recast the social order. But not all personal needs allow themselves to be
displaced in such a manner and transferred to others, nor is there a universal and definite solution of the conflict.

We now know how to designate the witticisms just discussed; they are
cynical witticisms, and what they conceal are cynicisms.

Among the institutions which cynical wit is wont to attack there is
none more important and more completely protected by moral precepts,
and yet more inviting of attack, than the institution of marriage. Most
of the cynical jokes are directed against it. For no demand is more personal than that made upon sexual freedom, and nowhere has civilization
attempted to exert a more stringent suppression than in the realm of
sexuality. For our purposes a single example suffices: the "Entries in the
Album of Prince Carnival" mentioned above.

"A wife is like an umbrella, at worst one may also take a cab."

We have already elucidated the complicated technique of this example;
it is a puzzling and seemingly impossible comparison which, however, as
we now see, is not in itself witty. It shows besides an allusion (cab = public conveyance), and as the strongest technical means it also shows an
omission which serves to make it still more unintelligible. The comparison
may be worked out in the following manner. A man marries in order to
guard himself against the temptations of sensuality, but it then turns out
that after all marriage does not afford sufficient gratification for one of
stronger needs, just as one takes along an umbrella for protection against
rain only to get wet in spite of it. In both cases one must search for better
protection; in one case one must take a public cab, in the other, women
procurable for money. Now the wit has almost entirely been replaced by
cynicism. That marriage is not the organization which can satisfy a man's
sexuality, one does not dare say loudly and frankly unless indeed he be
a Christian v. Ehrenfels,[1] or a Judge Lindsey, who is forced to it by the
love of truth and the zeal of reform. The strength of this witticism lies in
the fact that it has expressed the thought even though it had to be done
through all sorts of roundabout ways.

CYNICAL WITTICISMS AND SELF-CRITICISM

A particularly favorable case for tendency-wit results if the intended
criticism of the inner resistance is directed against one's own person, or,
more carefully expressed, against a person in whom one takes interest,
that is, a composite personality such as one's own people. This determina-

[1] See his essays in the *Politisch-anthropologische Revue*, II, 1903.

tion of self-criticism may make clear why it is that a number of the most excellent jokes of which we have shown here many specimens should have sprung into existence from the soil of Jewish national life. They are stories which were invented by Jews themselves and which are directed against Jewish peculiarities. The Jewish jokes made up by non-Jews are nearly all brutal buffooneries in which the wit is spared by the fact that the Jew appears as a comic figure to a stranger. The Jewish jokes which originate with Jews admit this, but they know their real shortcomings as well as their merits, and the interest of the person himself in the thing to be criticised produces the subjective determination of the wit-work which would otherwise be difficult to bring about. Incidentally I do not know whether one often finds a people that makes merry so unreservedly over its own shortcomings.

As an illustration I can point to the story cited above in which the Jew in the train immediately abandons all sense of decency of deportment as soon as he recognizes the new arrival in his coupé as his co-religionist. We have come to know this joke as an illustration by means of a detail—representation through a trifle; it is supposed to represent the democratic mode of thought of the Jew who recognizes no difference between master and servant, but unfortunately this also disturbs discipline and co-operation. Another especially interesting series of jokes presents the relationship between the poor and the rich Jews: their heroes are the "shnorrer," [1] and the charitable Jewish philanthropists. *The shnorrer, who was a regular Sunday-dinner guest at a certain house, appeared one day accompanied by a young stranger, who prepared to seat himself at the table. "Who is that?" demanded the host. "He became my son-in-law last week," was the reply, "and I have agreed to supply his board for the first year."* The tendency of these stories is always the same, and is most distinctly shown in the following story. *The shnorrer supplicates the Jewish philanthropic baron for money to take the "cure" at Ostend, as the physician has ordered him to take sea-baths for his ailment. The baron remarks that Ostend is an especially expensive resort, and that a less fashionable place would do just as well. But the shnorrer rejects that proposition by saying, "Herr Baron, nothing is too expensive for my health."* That is an excellent displacement-witticism which we could have taken as a model of its kind. The baron is evidently anxious to save his money, but the shnorrer replies as if the baron's money were his own, which he may then consider secondary to his health. One is forced to laugh at the insolence of the demand, but these jokes are exceptionally unequipped with a façade to becloud the understanding. The truth is that the shnorrer who mentally treats the rich man's money as his own, really possesses almost the right to this mistake, according to the sacred codes of the Jews. Naturally the resistance which

[1] An habitual beggar.

is responsible for this joke is directed against the sacred law which even the pious find very oppressive.

Another story relates *how on the steps of a rich man's house a shnorrer met one of his own kind. The latter counseled him to depart, saying, "Do not go up today, the Baron is out of sorts and refuses to give any one more than a dollar." "I will go up anyway," replied the first. "Why in the world should I make him a present of a dollar? Is he making me any presents?"*

This witticism makes use of the technique of absurdity by permitting the shnorrer to declare that the baron gives him nothing at the same moment in which he is preparing to beg him for the donation. But the absurdity is only apparent, for it is almost true that the rich man gives him nothing, since he is obligated by the mandate to give alms, and strictly speaking must be thankful that the shnorrer gives him an opportunity to be charitable. The ordinary, bourgeois conception of alms is at cross-purposes with the religious one; it openly revolts against the religious conception in the *story about the baron who, having been deeply touched by the shnorrer's tale of woe, rang for his servants and said: "Throw him out of the house; he is breaking my heart."* This obvious exposition of the tendency again creates a case of border-line wit. From the no longer witty complaint: "It is really no advantage to be a rich man among Jews. The wretched foreigners do not grant one the pleasure of one's own fortune," these last stories deviate only by the illustration of a single situation.

Other stories as the following, which, technically again present border-lines of wit, have their origin in a deeply pessimistic cynicism. *A patient whose hearing was defective consulted a physician who made the correct diagnosis, namely, that the patient probably drank too much whiskey and consequently was becoming deaf. He advised him to desist from drinking and the patient promised to follow his advice. Some time thereafter the doctor met him on the street and inquired in a loud voice about his condition. "Thank you, Doctor," was the reply, "there is no necessity for speaking so loudly, I have given up drinking whiskey and consequently I hear perfectly." Some time afterwards they met again. The doctor again inquired into his condition in the usual voice, but noticed that he did not make himself audible. "It seems to me that you are deaf again because you have returned to drinking whiskey," shouted the doctor in the patient's ear. "Perhaps you are right," answered the latter, "I have taken to drinking again, and I shall tell you why. As long as I did not drink I could hear, but all that I heard was not as good as the whiskey."* Technically this joke is nothing more than an illustration. The jargon and the ability of the *raconteur* must aid in the production of laughter. But behind it there lies the sad question, "Is not the man right in his choice?"

It is the manifold hopeless misery of the Jews to which these pessimistical stories allude, which prompted me to add them to tendency-wit.

CRITICAL AND BLASPHEMOUS WITTICISMS

Other jokes, cynical in a similar sense, and not only stories about Jews, attack religious dogmas and the belief in God Himself. The story about the "telepathic look of the rabbi," whose technique consisted in faulty thinking which made phantasy equal to reality (the conception of displacement is also tenable), is such a cynical or critical witticism directed against miracle-workers and also, surely, against belief in miracles. Heine is reported to have made a directly blasphemous joke as he lay dying. *When the kindly priest commended him to God's mercy and inspired him with the hope that God would forgive him his sins, he replied: "Bien sûr qu'il me pardonnera; c'est son métier."* That is a derogatory comparison; technically its value lies only in the allusion, for a métier—business or vocation—is plied either by a craftsman or a physician, and what is more he has only a single métier. The strength of the wit, however, lies in its tendency. The joke is intended to mean nothing else, but: "Certainly he will forgive me; that is what he is here for, and for no other purpose have I engaged him" (just as one retains one's doctor or one's lawyer). Thus, the helpless dying man is still conscious of the fact that he has created God for himself and has clothed Him with power in order to make use of Him as occasion arises. The so-called creature makes himself known as the Creator only a short time before his extinction.

SKEPTICAL WIT

To the three kinds of tendency-wit discussed so far—exhibitionistic or obscene wit, aggressive or hostile wit, and cynical wit (critical, blasphemous)—I desire to add a fourth and the most uncommon of all, whose character can be elucidated by a good example.

Two Jews met in a train at a Galician railway station. "Where are you traveling?" asked one. "To Cracow," was the reply. "Now see here, what a liar you are!" said the first one, bristling. "When you say that you are traveling to Cracow, you really wish me to believe that you are traveling to Lemberg. Well, but I am sure that you are really traveling to Cracow, so why lie about it?"

This precious story, which creates an impression of exaggerated subtlety, evidently operates by means of the technique of absurdity. The second Jew has put himself in the way of being called a liar because he has said that he is traveling to Cracow, which is his real goal! However, this strong technical means—absurdity—is paired here with another technique—representation through the opposite, for, according to the uncontradicted assertion of the first, the second one is lying when he speaks the truth, and speaks the truth by means of a lie. However, the more earnest content of this joke is the question of the conditions of truth; again the joke points to a problem and makes use of the uncertainty of one of our commonest notions. Does it constitute truth if one describes things as they are and does not concern himself with the way the hearers will interpret what one has said? Or is this merely Jesuitical truth, and does not the real truthfulness consist much more in having a regard for the hearer and of furnishing him an exact picture of his own mind? I consider jokes of this type sufficiently different from the others to assign them a special place. What they attack is not a person nor an institution, but the certainty of our very knowledge—one of our speculative gifts. Hence, the name "skeptical" witticism will be the most expressive for them.

In the course of our discussion of the tendencies of wit we have gotten perhaps many an elucidation and certainly found numerous incentives for further investigations. But the results of this chapter combine with those of the preceding chapter to form a difficult problem. If it be true that the pleasure created by wit is dependent upon the technique on one hand and upon the tendency on the other hand, under what common point of view can these two utterly different pleasure-sources of wit be united?

B. SYNTHESIS

IV

THE PLEASURE MECHANISM AND THE PSYCHOGENESIS OF WIT

WE can now definitely assert that we know from what sources the peculiar pleasure arises furnished us by wit. We know that we can be easily misled to mistake our sense of satisfaction experienced through the thought-content of the sentence for the actual pleasure derived from the wit, on the other hand, the latter itself has two intrinsic sources, namely, the wit-technique and the wit-tendency. What we now desire to ascertain is by what manner pleasure originates from these sources, and the mechanism of this resultant pleasure.

It seems to us that the desired explanation can be more easily ascertained in tendency-wit than in harmless wit. We shall therefore commence with the former.

The pleasure in tendency-wit results from the fact that a tendency, whose gratification would otherwise remain unfulfilled, is actually gratified. That such gratification is a source of pleasure is self-evident without further discussion. But the manner in which wit brings about gratification is connected with special conditions from which we may perhaps gain further information. Here two cases must be differentiated. The simpler case is the one in which the gratification of the tendency is opposed by an external hindrance which is eluded by the wit. This process we found, for example, in the reply which Augustus received to his query whether the mother of the stranger he addressed had ever sojourned in his home, and likewise in the question of the art critic who asked: "And where is the Savior?" when the two rich rogues showed him their portraits. In one case the tendency serves to answer one insult with another; in the other case it offers an affront instead of the demanded expert opinion; in both cases the tendency was opposed by purely external factors, namely, the powerful position of the persons who are the targets of the insult. Nevertheless it may seem strange to us that these and analogous tendency-witticisms have not the power to produce a strong effect of laughter no matter how much they may gratify us.

It is different, however, if no external factors but internal hindrances stand in the way of the direct realization of the tendency, that is, if an inner feeling opposes the tendency. This condition, according to our assumption, was present in the aggressive joke of Mr. N. and in the one of Wendell Phillips, in whom a strong inclination to use invectives was stifled by a highly developed æsthetic sense. With the aid of wit the inner resistances in these special cases were overcome and the inhibition removed. As in the case of external hindrances, the gratification of the tendency is made possible, and a suppression with its concomitant "psychic damming" is thus obviated. So far, the mechanism of the development of pleasure would seem to be identical in both cases.

At this place, however, we are inclined to feel that we should enter more deeply into the differentiation of the psychological situation between the cases of external and internal hindrance, as we have a faint notion that the removal of the inner hindrance might possibly result in a disproportionately higher contribution to pleasure. But I propose that we rest content here, that we be satisfied for the present with this one collection of evidence which adheres to what is essential to us. The only difference between the cases of outer and inner hindrances consists in the fact that here an already existing inhibition is removed, while there the formation of a new inhibition is avoided. We hardly resort to speculation when we assert that a *"psychic expenditure"* is required for the formation as well as for the retention of a psychic inhibition. Now if we find that in both cases the use of the tendency-wit produces pleasure, then it may be assumed *that such resultant pleasure corresponds to the economy of psychic expenditure.*

Thus we are once more confronted with the principle of *economy* which we noticed first in the study of the technique of word-wit. But whereas the economy we believed to have found at first was in the use of few or possibly the same words, we can here foresee an economy of psychic expenditure in general in a far more comprehensive sense, and we think it possible to come nearer to the nature of wit through a better determination of the as yet very obscure idea of "psychic expenditure."

A certain amount of haziness which we could not dissipate during the study of the pleasure mechanism in tendency-wit we accept as a slight punishment for attempting to elucidate the more complicated problem before the simpler one, or the tendency-wit before the harmless wit. We observe that *"economy in the expenditure of inhibitions or suppressions"* seems to be the secret of the pleasurable effect of tendency-wit, and we now turn to the mechanism of the pleasure in harmless wit.

While examining appropriate examples of harmless witticisms, in which we had no fear of false judgment through content or tendency, we were forced to the conclusion that the techniques of wit themselves are pleasure-sources; now we wish to ascertain whether the pleasure may be traced to the economy in psychic expenditure. In a group of these witticisms (plays on words) the technique consisted in directing the psychic focus upon the sound instead of upon the sense of the word, and in allowing the (acoustic) word-disguise to take the place of the meaning accorded to it by its relations to reality. We are really justified in assuming that great relief is thereby afforded to the psychic work, and that in the serious use of words we refrain from this convenient procedure only at the expense of a certain amount of exertion. We can observe that abnormal mental states, in which the possibility of concentrating psychic expenditure on one place is probably restricted, actually allow to come to the foreground word-sound associations of this kind rather than the significance of the words, and that such patients react in their speech with "outer" instead of "inner" associations. Also, in children who are still accustomed to treat the word as an object, we notice the inclination to look for the same meaning in words of the same or of similar sounds, which is a source of great amusement to adults. If we experience in wit an unmistakable pleasure, because through the use of the same or similar words we reach from one set of ideas to a distant other one (as in "Home-Roulard" from the kitchen to politics), we can justly refer this pleasure to the economy of psychic expenditure. The pleasure of the wit resulting from such a "short-circuit" appears greater the more remote and foreign the two series of ideas which become related through the same word are to each other, or the greater the economy in thought brought about by the technical means of wit. We may add that in this case wit makes use of a means of connection which is rejected by, and carefully avoided in serious thinking.[1]

[1] If I may be permitted to anticipate what later is discussed in the text, I can here throw some light upon the condition which seems to be authoritative in the usage of language when it is a question of calling a joke "good" or "poor." If by means of a double meaning or slightly modified word I have gotten from one idea to another by a short route, and if this does not also simultaneously result in senseful association between the two ideas, then I have made a "poor" joke. In this poor joke one word or the "point" forms the only existing association between the two widely separated ideas. The joke "Home-Roulard" used above is such an example. But a "good" joke results if the infantile expectation is right in the end and if with the similarity of the word another essential similarity in meaning is really simultaneously produced—as in the examples Traduttore—Traditore (translator—traitor), and Amantes—Amentes (lovers—lunatics). The two disparate ideas which are here linked by an outer association are held together besides by a senseful connection which expresses an important relationship between them. The outer association only replaces the inner connection; it serves to indicate the latter or to clarify it. Not only does "translator" sound somewhat similar to "traitor," but he is a sort of a traitor whose claims to that name are good. The same may be said of Amantes—Amentes. Not only do the words bear a resemblance, but the similarity between "love" and "lunacy" has been noted from time immemorial.

The distinction made here agrees with the differentiation, to be made later, be-

A second group of technical means of wit—unification, similar sounding words, manifold application, modification of familiar idioms, allusions to quotations—all evince one common character, namely, that one always discovers something familiar where one expects to find something new instead. To discover the familiar is pleasurable and it is not difficult to recognize such pleasure as economy-pleasure and to refer it to the economy of psychic expenditure.

That the discovery of the familiar—"recognition"—causes pleasure seems to be universally admitted. Groos says: [1] "Recognition is everywhere bound up with feelings of pleasure where it has not been made too mechanical (as perhaps in dressing . . .). Even the mere quality of acquaintanceship is easily accompanied by that gentle delight which Faust experiences when, after an uncanny experience, he steps into his study." If the act of recognition is so pleasureful, we may expect that man merges into the habit of practicing this activity for its own sake, that is, he experiments playfully with it. In fact, Aristotle recognized in the joy of rediscovery the basis of artistic pleasure, and it cannot be denied that this principle must not be overlooked even if it has not such a far-reaching significance as Aristotle assumes.

Groos then discusses the games, whose character consists of heightening the pleasure of rediscovery by putting hindrances in its path, or in other words by raising a "psychic dam" which is removed by the act of recognition. However, his attempted explanation leaves the assumption that recognition as such is pleasurable, in that he attributes the pleasure of recognition connected with these games to the pleasure in power, or to the surmounting of a difficulty. I consider this latter factor as secondary, and I find no occasion for abandoning the simpler explanation, that the recognition *per se, i.e.*, through the alleviation of the psychic expenditure, is pleasurable, and that the games founded upon this pleasure make use of the damming-mechanism merely in order to intensify their effect.

We know also that the source of pleasure in rhyme, alliteration, refrain, and other forms of repetition of similar sounding words in poetry, is due merely to the discovery of the familiar. A "sense of power" plays no perceptible rôle in these techniques, which show so marked an agreement with the "manifold application" in wit.

Considering the close connection between recognition and remembering, the assumption is no longer daring that there exists also a pleasure

---

tween a "witticism" and a "jest." However, it would not be correct to exclude examples like Home-Roulard from the discussion of the nature of wit. As soon as we take into consideration the peculiar pleasure of wit, we discover that the "poor" witticisms are by no means poor as witticisms, *i.e.*, they are by no means unsuited for the production of pleasure.

[1] *Die Spiele der Menschen*, 1899, p. 153.

in remembering, *i.e.*, that the act of remembering in itself is accompanied by a feeling of pleasure of a similar origin. Groos seems to have no objection to such an assumption, but he again deducts the pleasure of remembering from the "sense of power" in which he seeks—as I believe unjustly—the principal basis of pleasure in almost all games.

THE FACTOR OF ACTUALITY

The use of another technical expedient of wit, which has not yet been mentioned, is also dependent upon "the rediscovery of the familiar." I refer to the factor of *actuality* (dealing with actual persons, things, or events), which in many witticisms provides a prolific source of pleasure and explains several peculiarities in the life history of wit. There are witticisms which are entirely free from this condition, and in a treatise on wit it is incumbent upon us to make use of such examples almost exclusively. But we must not forget that we laughed perhaps more heartily over such perennial witticisms than over others; witticisms whose application now would be difficult, because they would require long commentaries, and even with that aid the former effect could not be attained. These latter witticisms contained allusions to persons and occurrences which were "actual" at the time, which had stimulated general interest and were endowed with tension. After the cessation of this interest, after the settlement of these particular affairs, the witticisms lost a part of their pleasurable effect, and a very considerable part at that. Thus, for example, the joke which my friendly host made when he called the dish that was being served a "Home-Roulard," seems to me by no means as good now as when the question of Home Rule was a continuous headline in the political columns of our newspaper. If I now attempt to express my appreciation of this joke by stating that this one word led us from the idea of the kitchen to the distant field of politics, and saved us a long mental detour, I should have been forced at that time to change this description as follows: "That this word led us from the idea of the kitchen to the very distant field of politics; but that our lively interest was all the keener because this question was constantly absorbing us." The same thing is true of another joke: *"This girl reminds me of Dreyfus; the army does not believe in her innocence,"* which has become blurred in spite of the fact that its technical means has remained unchanged. The confusion arising from the comparison with, and the double meaning of, the word "innocence" cannot do away with the fact that the allusion, which at that time touched upon a matter pregnant with excitement, now recalls an interest set at rest. The many irresistible jokes about the world war have sunk in our estimation in a very short time. "Gone with the Windsor," a condensation of the popular book, "Gone with the Wind," and the abdication of Edward VIII, now the Duke of Windsor, no longer evokes the mirth that it did a year ago.[1]

A great many witticisms in circulation reach a certain age or rather go through a course composed of a flourishing season and a mature season, and then sink into complete oblivion. The need that people feel to draw pleasure from their mental processes continually creates new witticisms which are supported by current interests of the day. The vitality of actual witticisms is not their own, it is borrowed by way of allusion from those other interests, the expiration of which determines the fate of the witticism. The factor of actuality which may be added as a transitory pleasure-source of wit, although it is productive in itself, cannot be simply put on the same basis as the rediscovery of the familiar. It is much more a question of a special qualification of the familiar which must be aided by the quality of freshness and recency and which has not been affected by forgetfulness. In the formation of the dream one also finds that there is a special preference for what is recent, and one cannot refrain from inferring that the association with what is recent is rewarded or facilitated by a special pleasure premium.

Unification, which is really nothing more than repetition in the sphere of mental association instead of in material, has been accorded an especial recognition as a pleasure-source of wit by G Th. Fechner.[2] He says: "In my opinion the principle of uniform connection of the manifold, plays the most important rôle in the field under discussion; it needs, however, the support of subsidiary determinations in order to drive across the threshold the pleasure with its peculiar character which the cases here belonging can furnish." [3]

In all of these cases of repetition of the same association or of the same word-material, of refinding the familiar and recent, we surely cannot be prevented from referring the pleasure thereby experienced to the economy in psychic expenditure; providing that this viewpoint proves fertile for the explanation of single facts as well as for bringing to light new generalities. We are fully conscious of the fact that we have yet to make clear the manner in which this economy results and also the meaning of the expression "psychic expenditure."

The third group of the technique of wit, mostly thought-wit, which includes false logic, displacement, absurdity, representation through the opposite, and other varieties, may seem at first sight to present special features and to be unrelated to the techniques of the discovery of the familiar, or the replacing of object-associations by word-associations. But

[1] Translator's example.
[2] *Vorschule der Aesthetik*, i, XVII.
[3] Chapter XVII has for its title: "Concerning senseful and witty comparisons, play on words, and similar cases, which have the character of enjoyment, merriment and laughter."

it will not be difficult to demonstrate that this group, too, shows an economy or facilitation of psychic expenditure.

It is quite obvious that it is easier and more convenient to turn away from a definite trend of thought than to stick to it; it is easier to mix up different things than to distinguish them; and it is particularly easier to travel over modes of reasoning unsanctioned by logic; finally in connecting words or thoughts it is especially easy to overlook the fact that such connections should result in sense. All this is indubitable and this is exactly what is done by the techniques of the wit in question. It will sound strange, however, to assert that such processes in the wit-work may produce pleasure, since outside of wit we can experience only unpleasant feelings of defense against all these kinds of inferior achievement of our mental activity.

WORD-PLEASURE AND PLEASURE IN NONSENSE

The "pleasure in nonsense," as we may call it for short, is, in the seriousness of our life, crowded back almost to the vanishing point. To demonstrate it we must enter into the study of two cases in one of which it is still visible and in the other becomes visible for the second time. I refer to the behavior of the learning child and to the behavior of the adult under unstable toxic influences. When the child learns to control the vocabulary of its mother tongue it apparently takes great pleasure in "experimenting playfully" with that material (Groos); it connects words without regard for their meaning in order to obtain pleasure from the rhyme and rhythm. Gradually the child is deprived of this pleasure until only the senseful connection of words is allowed him. But even in later life there is still a tendency to overstep the acquired restrictions in the use of words, a tendency which manifests itself in disfiguring the same by definite appendages, and in changing their forms by means of certain contrivances (reduplication, trembling speech), or even by developing an individual language for use in playing—efforts which reappear also among the insane of a certain category.[1]

I believe that whatever the motive which actuated the child when it began such playings, in his further development the child indulges in them fully conscious that they are nonsensical and derives pleasure from this stimulus which is interdicted by reason. He now makes use of play in order to withdraw from the pressure of critical reason. More powerful, however, are the restrictions which must develop in education along the lines of right thinking, and in the separation of reality from fiction, and it is for this reason that the resistance against the pressures of thinking and reality is far-reaching and persistent; even the phenomena of phan-

[1] Cf. Brill: Poetry as an Oral Outlet, Psychoanalytic Review, Vol. XVIII, No. 4, October, 1931.

tasy formation come under this point of view. The power of reason usually grows so strong during the later part of childhod and during that period of education which extends over the age of puberty, that the pleasure in "freed nonsense" rarely dares manifest itself. One fears to utter nonsense; but it seems to me that the inclination characteristic of boys to act in a contradictory and inexpedient manner is a direct outcome of this pleasure in nonsense. In pathological cases one often sees this tendency so accentuated that it again controls the speeches and answers of the pupils. In the case of some college students who merged into neuroses I could convince myself that the unconscious pleasure derived from the nonsense produced by them is just as much responsible for their mistakes as their actual igonarnce.

REPRODUCTION OF OLD LIBERTIES

The student does not give up his demonstrations against the pressures of thinking and reality whose domination becomes unceasingly intolerant and unrestricted. A good part of the tendency of students to skylarking is responsible for this reaction. Man is an "untiring pleasure seeker"—I can no longer recall which author coined this happy expression—and finds it extremely difficult to renounce pleasure once experienced. With the hilarious nonsense of "sprees," college cheers and songs, the student attempts to preserve that pleasure which results from freedom of thought, a freedom of which he is more and more deprived through scholastic discipline. Even much later, when as a mature alumnus he meets with others at scientific congresses and class reunions and feels himself a student again, he then reads again the comic college paper, which distorts the newly gained knowledge into the nonsensical, and thus, compensates him for the newly added mental inhibitions.

Reason, which has stifled the pleasure in nonsense, has become so powerful that not even temporarily can it be abandoned without a toxic agency. The change in the state of mind is the most valuable thing that alcohol offers man, and that is the reason why this "poison" is not equally indispensable for all people. The hilarious humor, whether due to endogenous origin or whether produced toxically, weakens the inhibiting forces, among which is reason, and thus, again makes accessible pleasure-sources, which are burdened by suppression. It is very instructive to see how the demand made upon wit sinks with the rise in spirits. The latter actually replace wit, just as wit must make an effort to replace the mental state in which the otherwise inhibited pleasure possibilities (pleasure in nonsense among the rest) assert themselves.

"With little wit and much comfort."

Under the influence of alcohol the adult again becomes a child who derives pleasure from the free disposal of his mental stream without being restricted by the pressure of logic.

We hope we have shown that the technique of absurdity in wit corresponds to a source of pleasure. We need hardly repeat that this pleasure results from the economy of psychic expenditure or alleviation from the pressure of reason.

On reviewing again the wit-technique classified under three headings, we notice that the first and last of these groups—the replacement of object-association by word-association, and the use of absurdity as a restorer of old liberties and as a relief from the pressure of intellectual upbringing—can be taken collectively. Psychic relief may in a way be compared to economy, which constitutes the technique of the second group. Alleviation of the already existing psychic expenditure, and economy in the yet to be offered psychic expenditure, are two principles from which all techniques of wit and with them all pleasure in these techniques can be deduced. The two forms of the technique and the resultant pleasures, correspond more or less in general to the division of wit into word- and thought-witticisms.

PLAY AND JEST

The preceding discussions have led us unexpectedly to an understanding of the history of the development of psychogenesis of wit which we shall now examine still further. We have become acquainted with the successive steps in wit, the development of which up to tendency-wit, will undoubtedly reveal new relationships between the different characters of wit. Antedating wit there exists something which we may designate as "play" or "jest." Play—we shall retain this name—appears in children while they are learning how to use words and connect thoughts; this playing is probably the result of an impulse which urges the child to exercise his capacities (Groos). During this process he experiences pleasurable effects which originate from the repetition of similarities, the rediscovery of the familiar, sound-associations, etc., which may be explained as an unexpected economy of psychic expenditure. Therefore it surprises no one that these resulting pleasures urge the child to practice playing and impel him to continue without regard for the meaning of words or the connections between sentences. Playing with words and thoughts, motivated by certain pleasures in economy, would thus be the first step of wit.

This playing is stopped by the growing strength of a factor which may well be called criticism or reason. The play is then rejected as senseless or as directly absurd, and by virtue of reason it becomes impossible. Only accidentally is it now possible to derive pleasure from those sources of rediscovery of the familiar, etc., which is explained by the fact that the maturing person has then merged into a playful mood which, as in the case of merriment in the child, removes inhibitions. In this way only is the old pleasure-giving playing made possible, but as men do not wish to wait for these propitious occasions and also hate to forego this pleasure, they seek means to make themselves independent of these pleasant states. The further development of wit is directed by these two impulses; the one striving to elude reason, and the other to substitute for the adult an infantile state of mind.

This gives rise to the second stage of wit, the *jest*. The object of the jest is to bring about the resultant pleasure of playing and at the same time appease the protesting reason which strives to suppress the pleasant feeling. There is but one way to accomplish this. The senseless combination of words or the absurd linking of thoughts must make sense after all. The whole process of wit production is therefore directed towards the discovery of words and thought constellations which fulfill these conditions. The jest makes use of almost all the technical means of wit. What distinguishes the jest from wit is the fact that the pith of the sentence withdrawn from criticism does not need to be valuable, new, or even good; it matters only that it can be expressed, even though what it may say is obsolete, superfluous, and useless. The most conspicuous factor of the jest is the gratification it affords by making possible that which reason forbids.

A mere jest is the following of Professor Kästner, who taught physics at Göttingen in the 16th century, and who was fond of making jokes. Wishing to enroll a student named Warr in his class, he asked him his age, and upon receiving the reply that he was thirty years of age he exclaimed: "Aha, so I have the honor of seeing the thirty years' War." [1] When asked what vocations his sons followed, Rokitansky jestingly answered: "Two are healing and two are howling," (two physicians and two singers). The reply was correct and therefore unimpeachable, but it added nothing to what is contained in the parenthetic expression. There is no doubt that the answer assumed another form only because of the pleasure which arises from the unification and assonance of both words.

I believe that we now see our way clear. In estimating the techniques of wit we were constantly disturbed by the fact that these are not peculiar to wit alone, and yet the nature of wit seemed to depend upon them, since their removal by means of reduction nullified the character as well as the pleasure of wit. Now we become aware that what we have described as techniques of wit—and which in a certain sense we shall have to continue to call so—are really the sources from which wit derives pleasure; nor does it strike us as strange that other processes draw from the same sources with the same object in view. The technique, however, which is

[1] Kleinpaul: *Die Rätsel der Sprache*, 1890.

peculiar to, and belongs to wit alone, consists in a process of safeguarding the use of this pleasure-forming means against the protest of reason which would obviate the pleasure. We can make few generalizations about this process. The wit-work, as we have already remarked, expresses itself in the selection of such word-material and such thought-situations as to permit the old play with words and thoughts to stand the test of reason; but to accomplish this end the cleverest use must be made of all the peculiarities of the stock of words and of all constellations of mental combinations. Later on perhaps we shall be in a position to characterize the wit-work by a definite attribute; for the present it must remain unexplained how our wit makes its advantageous selections. The tendency and capacity of wit to guard the pleasure-forming word and thought combinations against reason, already makes itself visible as an essential criterion in jests. From the beginning its object is to remove inner inhibitions and thereby, render productive those pleasure-sources which have become inaccessible, and we shall find that it remains true to this characteristic throughout the course of its entire development.

We are now in a position to prescribe a correct place for the factor "sense in nonsense," to which the authors ascribe so much significance in respect to the recognition of wit and the explanation of the pleasurable effect. The two firmly established points in the determination of wit—its tendency to carry through the pleasureful play, and its effort to guard it against the criticism of reason—make it perfectly clear why the individual witticism, even though it appear nonsensical from one point of view, must appear full of meaning or at least acceptable from another. How it accomplishes this is the business of the wit-work; if it is not successful it is relegated to the category of "nonsense." Nor do we find it necessary to deduce the resultant pleasure of wit from the conflict of feelings which emerge either directly or by way of "confusion and clearness," from the simultaneous sense and nonsense of the wit. There is just as little necessity for our delving deeper into the question how pleasure can come from the succession of that part of the wit considered senseless and from that part recognized as senseful. The psychogenesis of wit has taught us that the pleasure of wit arises from word-play or from the liberation of nonsense, and that the sense of wit is meant only to guard this pleasure against suppression through reason.

JEST AND WIT

Thus, the problem of the essential character of wit could almost be explained by means of the jest. We may follow the development of the jest until it reaches its height in the tendency-wit. The jest puts the tendency ahead when it is a question of supplying us with pleasure, and it is content when its utterance does not appear utterly senseless or insipid. But if this utterance is substantial and valuable, the jest changes into wit. A thought, which would have been worthy of our interest even when expressed in the most unpretentious form, is now invested in a form which must in itself excite our sense of satisfaction. Such an association we cannot help thinking has surely not come into existence unintentionally; we must make an effort to divine the intention at the bottom of the formation of wit. An incidental observation, made once before, will put us on the right track. We have already remarked that a good witticism gives us, so to speak, a general feeling of satisfaction without our being able to decide offhand which part of the pleasure comes from the witty form and which part from the excellent thought contained in the context. We are deceiving ourselves constantly about this division; sometimes we overvalue the quality of the wit on account of our admiration for the thought contained therein, and then again we overestimate the value of the thought on account of the pleasure afforded us by the witty investment. We know not what gives us pleasure, nor at what we are laughing. This uncertainty of our judgment, assuming it to be a fact, may have given the motive for the formation of wit in the literal sense. The thought seeks the witty disguise because it thereby recommends itself to our attention and can thus appear to us more important and valuable than it really is; but above all because this disguise fascinates and confuses our reason. We are apt to attribute to the thought the pleasure derived from the witty form, and we are not inclined to consider improper what has given us pleasure, and in this way deprive ourselves of a source of pleasure. For if wit makes us laugh, it has also established in us a mood most unfavorable to reason, and then that mood is forced upon us from one point which already suffices for play and which wit strives to displace by all means. Although we have maintained before that such wit is harmless, and is not yet to be designated as tendentious, we may not deny that, strictly speaking, it is the jest alone which shows no tendency; that is, it serves to produce pleasure only. For wit is really never purposeless even if the thought contained therein has no tendency and merely serves a theoretical, intellectual interest. Wit carries out its purpose in advancing the thought by magnifying it and by guarding it against reason. Here again it reveals its original nature in that it sets itself up against an inhibiting and restrictive power, or against the critical judgment.

The first use of wit, which goes beyond the mere production of pleasure, points to the road ahead of us. Wit is now recognized as a powerful psychic factor whose weight can decide the issue if it falls into this or that side of the scale. The great tendencies and impulses of our psychic life enlist its service for their own purposes. The original purposeless wit, which began as play, becomes related in a *secondary* manner to tendencies from which nothing that is formed in psychic life can escape for any length of time.

We already know what it can achieve in the service of the exhibitionistic, aggressive, cynical, and skeptical tendencies. In the case of obscene wit, which originated in the smutty joke, it makes a confederate of the third person who originally disturbed the sexual situation, by giving him pleasure through the utterance which causes the woman to be ashamed in his presence. In the case of the aggressive tendency, wit by the same means changes the original indifferent hearers into active haters and scorners, and in this way confronts the enemy with a host of opponents where formerly there was but one. In the first case it overcomes the inhibitions of shame and decorum by the pleasure premium which it offers. In the second case it overthrows the critical judgment which would otherwise have examined the dispute in question. In the third and fourth cases where wit is in the service of the cynical and skeptical tendency, it shatters the respect for institutions and truths in which the hearer had believed, first by strengthening the argument, and secondly by resorting to a new method of attack. Where the argument seeks to draw the hearer's reason to its side, wit strives to push aside this reason. There is no doubt that wit has chosen the way which is psychologically more efficacious.

THE DEVELOPMENT INTO TENDENCY-WIT

What impressed us in reviewing the achievements of tendency-wit was the effect it produced on the hearer. It is more important, however, to understand the effect produced by wit on the psychic life of the person who makes it, or more precisely expressed, on the psychic life of the person who conceives it. Once before we have expressed the intention, which we find occasion to repeat here, that we wish to study the psychic processes of wit in regard to its apportionment between two persons. We can assume for the present that the psychic process aroused by wit in the hearer is usually an imitation of the psychic processes of the wit producer. The outer inhibitions which are to be overcome in the hearer correspond to the inner inhibitions of the wit producer. In the latter the expectation of the outer hindrance exists, at least as an inhibiting idea. The inner hindrance, which is overcome in tendency-wit, is evident in some single cases; for example, in the Cincinnatus joke we can assume that it not only enables the hearer to enjoy the pleasure of the aggression through injuries, but it also makes it possible for him to produce the wit in the first place. Of the different kinds of inner inhibitions or suppressions one is especially worthy of our interest because it is the most far-reaching. We designate that form by the term "repression." It is characterized by the fact that it excludes from consciousness certain buried emotions and their products. We shall learn that tendency-wit itself is capable of liberating pleasure from sources that have undergone repression. If the overcoming of outer hindrances can be traced in the manner indicated above to inner inhibitions and repressions, we may say that tendency-wit proves more clearly than any other developmental stage of wit that the main character of wit-making is to set free pleasure by removing inhibitions. It reinforces the tendencies which it serves by bringing them assistance from repressed emotions; or it puts itself at the disposal of the repressed tendencies directly.

We may readily concede that these are the functions of tendency-wit, but we must nevertheless admit that we do not understand in what manner these functions can succeed in accomplishing their end. The power of tendency-wit consists in the pleasure derived from the sources of word-plays and liberated nonsense, and if one can judge from the impressions received from purposeless jests, one cannot possibly consider the amount of the pleasure so great as to attribute to it the power to annul deep-rooted inhibitions and repressions. As a matter of fact, we do not deal here with a simple propelling power, but rather with a more complicated mechanism. Instead of covering the long circuitous route through which I arrived at an understanding of this relationship, I shall endeavor to demonstrate it by a short synthetic route.

G. Th. Fechner has established the principle of aesthetic assistance or enhancement which he explains in the following words: *"From the unopposed concurrence of pleasurable states which individually accomplish little, there results a greater, often much greater resultant pleasure than corresponds to the sum of the pleasure values of the separate states, or a greater result than could be explained by the sum of the individual effects; in fact, the mere concurrence of this kind can result in a positive pleasure product, which overflows the threshold of pleasure where the individual factors are too weak to accomplish this. The only condition is that in comparison to others they must produce a greater sense of satisfaction."* [1] I am of the opinion that the theme of wit does not give us the opportunity to test the correctness of this principle which is demonstrable in many other artistic fields. But from wit we have learned something, which at least comes near this principle, namely that in a coöperation of many pleasure-producing factors we are in no position to assign to each one the resultant part which really belongs to it. But the situation assumed in the principle of assistance can be varied, and for these new conditions we can formulate the following combination of questions which are worthy of a reply. What usually happens if in one constellation there is a meeting of pleasurable and painful conditions? Upon what depends the result and the previous intimations of the result? Tendency-wit particularly shows these possibilities. There is one feeling or impulse which strives to liberate pleasure from a certain source and under unrestricted conditions certainly would liberate it, but there is another im-

[1] *Vorschule der Aesthetik,* Vol. 1, V, p. 51, 2nd Ed., Leipzig, 1897.

pulse which works against this development of pleasure, that is, which inhibits or suppresses it. The suppressing stream, as the result shows, must be somewhat stronger than the one suppressed, which however is by no means destroyed.

THE FORE-PLEASURE PRINCIPLE

But now there appears another impulse which strives to set free pleasure by this identical process, albeit from different sources, which acts like the suppressed stream. What can be the result in such a case? An example can make this clearer than this schematization. There is an impulse to insult a certain person, but this is so strongly opposed by a feeling of decorum and æsthetic culture that the impulse to insult must be crushed. If, for example, by virtue of some changed emotional state the insult should happen to break through, this insulting tendency would subsequently be painfully perceived. Therefore, the insult is omitted. There is a possibility, however, of making good wit from the words or thoughts which would have served in the insult; that is, pleasure can be set free from other sources without being hindered by the same suppression. But the second development of pleasure would have to be foregone if the insulting quality of the wit were not allowed to come out, and as the latter is allowed to come to the surface, it is connected with the new release of pleasure. Experience with tendency-wit shows that under such circumstances the suppressed tendency can become so strengthened by the aid of wit-pleasure as to overcome the otherwise stronger inhibition. One resorts to insults because wit is thereby made possible. But the satisfaction thus obtained is not produced by wit alone; it is incomparably greater, in fact it is by so much greater than the pleasure of the wit, that we must assume that the former suppressed tendency has succeeded in breaking through, perhaps without any discharge. Under these circumstances tendency-wit causes the most prolific laughter.

The investigation of the conditions of laughter will perhaps aid us in forming a clearer picture of the process of the help which wit gets against suppression. But we see even now that the case of tendency-wit is a special case of the principle of help. A possibility of the development of pleasure enters into a situation in which another pleasure possibility is so hindered that individually it would not result in pleasure. The result is a development of pleasure which is greater by far than the added possibility. The latter has acted, as it were, as an *alluring premium;* with the aid of a small sum of pleasure a very large and almost inaccessible amount is obtained. I have good grounds for thinking that this principle corresponds to an arrangement which holds true in many widely separated spheres of the psychic life, and I consider it appropriate to designate the pleasure serving to liberate the large sum of pleasure as *fore-pleasure* and the principle as the *principle of fore-pleasure*.

PLAY-PLEASURE AND REMOVAL-PLEASURE

The effect of tendency-wit may now be formulated as follows: It enters the service of tendencies in order to produce new pleasure by removing suppressions and repressions. This it does by using wit-pleasure as fore-pleasure. When we now review its development, we may say that wit has remained true to its nature from beginning to end. It begins as play in order to obtain pleasure from the free use of words and thoughts. As soon as the growing reason forbids this senseless play with words and thoughts, it turns to the jest or joke in order to hold to these sources of pleasure and in order to be able to gain new pleasure from the liberation of the absurd. In the rôle of harmless wit it assists the thoughts and fortifies them against the impugnment of the critical judgment, whereby it makes use of the principle of intermingling the pleasure-sources. Finally, it enters into the great struggling suppressed tendencies in order to remove inner inhibitions in accordance with the principle of fore-pleasure. Reason, critical judgment, and suppression, these are the forces which it combats in turn. It firmly holds on to the original word-pleasure sources, and beginning with the stage of the jest opens for itself new pleasure sources by removing inhibition. The pleasure which it produces, be it play-pleasure or removal-pleasure, can at all times be traced to the economy of psychic expenditure, in so far as such a conception does not contradict the nature of pleasure, and proves itself productive also in other fields.

The nonsense-witticisms, which have been somewhat slighted in this treatise, deserve a short supplementary comment.

In view of the significance attributed by our conception to the factor "sense in nonsense," one might be tempted to demand that every witticism should be a nonsense-joke. But this is not necessary, because only the play with thoughts inevitably leads to nonsense, whereas the other source of wit-pleasure, the play with words, makes this impression incidental and does not regularly invoke the criticism connected with it. The double root of wit-pleasure—from the play with words and thoughts, which corresponds to the most important division into word- and thought-witticisms—sets its face against a short formulation of general principles about wit as a tangible aggravation of difficulties. The play with words produces laughter, as is well known, in consequence of the factor of recognition described above, and therefore suffers suppression only in a small degree. The play with thoughts cannot be motivated through such pleasure: it has suffered a very energetic suppression and the pleasure which it can give is only the pleasure of released inhibitions. Accordingly one may say that wit-pleasure shows a kernel of the original play-pleasure and a shell of removal-pleasure. Naturally we do not grant that the pleasure in nonsense-wit is due to the fact that we have succeeded in making nonsense despite the suppression, while we do notice that the play with words gives us pleasure. Nonsense, which has remained fixed in thought-wit, acquires secondarily the function of stimulating our attention through confusion; it serves as a reinforcement of the effect of wit, but only when it is insistent, so that the confusion can anticipate the intellect by a definite fraction of time. That nonsense in wit may also be employed to represent a judgment contained within the thought has been demonstrated by the joke of Ike the artilleryman. But even this is not the primal signification of nonsense in wit.

A series of wit-like productions for which we have no appropriate name, but which may lay claim to the designation of "witty nonsense," may be added to the nonsense-jokes. They are very numerous, but I shall cite only two examples: As the fish was served to a guest at the table he put both hands twice into the mayonnaise and then ran them through his hair. Being looked at by his neighbor with astonishment, he seemed to have noticed his mistake and excused himself, saying, "Pardon me, I thought it was spinach."

Or: "Life is like a suspension bridge," said the one. "How is that?" asked the other. "How should I know?" was the answer.

These extreme examples produce an effect through the fact that they give rise to the expectation of wit, so that one makes the effort to find the hidden sense behind the nonsense. But none is found, they are really nonsense. Under that deception, it was possible for one moment to liberate the pleasure in nonsense. These witticisms are not altogether without tendencies, they furnish the narrator a certain pleasure in that they deceive and annoy the hearer. The latter then calms his anger by resolving that he himself should take the place of the narrator.

V

THE MOTIVES OF WIT AND WIT
AS A SOCIAL PROCESS

IT SEEMS superfluous to speak of the motives of wit, since the purpose of obtaining pleasure must be recognized as a sufficient motive of the wit-work. But on the one hand it is not impossible that still other motives participate in the production of wit, and on the other hand, in view of certain well-known experiences, the theme of the subjective determination of wit must be discussed.

Two things above all urge us to it. Though wit-making is an excellent means of obtaining pleasure from the psychic processes, we know that not all persons are equally able to make use of it. Wit-making is not at the disposal of all, in general there are but a few persons to whom one can point and say that they are witty. Here wit seems to be a special ability somewhere within the region of the old "psychic faculties," and this shows itself in its appearance as fairly independent of the other faculties such as intelligence, phantasy, memory, etc. A special talent or psychic determination permitting or favoring wit-making must be presupposed in all wit-makers.

I am afraid that we shall not get very far in the exploration of this theme. Only now and then do we succeed in proceeding from the understanding of a single witticism to the knowledge of the subjective determinations in the mind of the wit-maker. It is quite accidental that the example of wit with which we began our investigation of the wit-technique permits us also to gain some insight into the subjective determination of the witticism. I am referring to Heine's witticism, to which also Heymans and Lipps have paid attention.

"*I was sitting next to Solomon Rothschild and he treated me just as an equal, quite famillionaire.*"

Heine put this word in the mouth of a comical person, Hirsch-Hyacinth, collector, operator and tax appraiser from Hamburg, and valet of the aristocratic baron, Cristoforo Gumpelino (formerly Gumpel). Evidently the poet has experienced great pleasure in these productions, for he allows Hirsch-Hyacinth to talk big and puts in his mouth the most amusing and most candid utterances; he positively endows him with the practical wisdom of a Sancho Panza. It is a pity that Heine, as it seems, had no liking for this dramatic figure and that he drops the delightful character so soon. From many passages it would seem that the poet himself is speaking behind the transparent mask of Hirsch-Hyacinth, and we are quite convinced that this person is nothing but a parody of the poet himself. Hirsch tells of reasons why he has discarded his former name and now calls himself Hyacinth. "Besides I have the advantage," he continues, "of having an H on my seal already, and, therefore, I am in no need of having a new letter engraved." But Heine himself resorted to this economy when he changed his surname "Harry" to "Heinrich" at his baptism. Every one acquainted with the life of the poet will recall that in Hamburg, where one also meets the personage Hirsch-Hyacinth, Heine had an uncle of the same name, who played the greatest rôle in Heine's life as the wealthy member of the family. The uncle's name was likewise Solomon, just like the elderly Rothschild who treated the impecunious Hirsch on such a famillionaire basis. What seems to be merely a jest in the mouth of Hirsch-Hyacinth soon reveals a background of earnest bitterness when we attribute it to the nephew Harry-Heinrich. For he belonged to the family, nay, more, it was his earnest wish to marry a daughter of this uncle, but she refused him, and his uncle always treated him on a somewhat famillionaire basis, as a poor relative. His rich relatives in Hamburg always dealt with him condescendingly. I recall the story of one of his old aunts by marriage who, when she was still young and pretty, sat next to some one at a family dinner who seemed to her unprepossessing and whom the other members of the family treated shabbily. She did not feel herself called upon to be any more condescending towards him. Only many years later did she discover that the careless and neglected cousin was the poet Heinrich Heine. We know from many a record how keenly Heine suffered from these repulses at the hands of his wealthy relatives in his youth and during later years. The witticism "famillionaire" grew out of the soil of such a subjective emotional feeling.

One may suspect similar subjective determinations in many other witticisms of the great scoffers, but I know of no other example by which one can show this in such a convincing way. It is, therefore, hazardous to venture a more definite opinion about the nature of this personal determination. Furthermore, one is not inclined in the first place to claim similar complicated conditions for the origin of each and every witticism. Neither are the witty productions of other celebrated men better suited to give us the desired insight into the subjective determination of wit. In fact, one gets the impression that the subjective determination of wit production is oftentimes not unrelated to persons suffering from neurotic diseases, when, for example, one learns that Lichtenberg was a confirmed hypochondriac burdened with all kinds of eccentricities. The great majority of witticisms, especially those produced from current happenings, are anonymous; one might be inquisitive to know what kind of people they are who originate them. The physician occasionally has an opportunity to make a study of persons who, if not renowned wits, are recognized in their circle as witty and as originators of many passable witticisms; he is often surprised to find such persons showing dissociated personalities and a predisposition to nervous affections. However, owing to insufficient data, we certainly cannot maintain that such a psychoneurotic constitution is a regular or necessary subjective condition for wit-making.

A clearer case is afforded by Jewish witticisms which, as before mentioned, are made exclusively by Jews themselves, whereas Jewish stories of different origin rarely rise above the level of the comical strain or of brutal mockery. The determination for the self-participation here, as in Heine's joke "famillionaire," seems to be due to the fact that the person finds it difficult to express directly his criticism or aggression and is thus compelled to resort to by-ways.

Other subjective determinations or favorable conditions for wit-making are less shrouded in darkness. The motive for the production of harmless wit is usually the ambitious impulse to display one's spirit or to "show off." It is an impulse comparable to the impulse to sexual exhibition. The existence of numerous inhibited impulses whose suppression retains a certain degree of liability produces a most favorable disposition for the production of tendency-wit. Thus, certain single components of the sexual constitution may appear as motives for wit-formation. A whole series of obscene witticisms lead one to the conclusion that a person who gives origin to such wit conceals a desire to exhibit. Persons having a powerful sadistical component in their sexuality, which is more or less inhibited in life, are most successful with the tendency-wit of aggression.

THE IMPULSE TO IMPART WIT

The second fact which impels one to examine the subjective determination of wit is the common experience that nobody is satisfied with making wit for himself. Wit-making is inseparably connected with the desire to impart it; in fact, this impulse is so strong that it is often realized after overcoming strong objections. In the comic, too, one experiences pleasure by imparting it to another person; but this is not imperative; one can enjoy the comic alone when one happens on it. Wit, on the other hand, must be imparted. Apparently the process of wit-formation does not end with the witty inspiration. There remains something which strives to complete the mysterious process of wit-formation by imparting it.

We cannot conjecture, at first, what may have motivated the impulse to impart wit. But in wit we notice another peculiarity which again distinguishes it from the comic. If I encounter the latter, I can laugh heartily over it alone; I am naturally pleased if by imparting it to some one else I make him laugh too. In the case of wit, however, which accidentally occurs to me, which I have made, I cannot laugh over it in spite of the unmistakable feeling of pleasure which I experience in the witticism. It is possible that my need to impart the witticism to another is in some way connected with the resultant laughter, which is manifest in the other, but denied to me.

But why do I not laugh over my own joke? And what rôle does the other person play in it?

Let us consider the last query first. In the comic usually two persons come into consideration. Besides my own ego there is another person in whom I find something comic; if objects appear comical to me, it takes place by means of a sort of personification which is not uncommon in our emotional life. The comic process is satisfied with these two persons, the ego and the object person; there may also be a third person, but that is not obligatory. Wit as a play with one's own words and thoughts at first dispenses with an object person, but already, upon the first step of the jest, it demands another person to whom it can impart its result, if it has succeeded in safeguarding play and nonsense against the remonstrance of reason. This second person in wit does not, however, correspond to the object person, but to the third person who is the other person in the comic. It seems 'that in the jest the decision as to whether wit has fulfilled its task is left to the other person, as if the ego were not quite certain of its opinion in the matter. The harmless wit, too, is in need of the other person's support in order to ascertain whether it has accomplished its purpose. If wit enters the service of sexual or hostile tendencies, it can be described as a psychic process among three persons, just as in the comic, with the exception that there the third person plays a different rôle. The psychic process of wit is consummated here between the first person—the ego, and the third person—the stranger, and not, as in the comic, between the ego and the object person.

Also, in the case of the third person of wit, the wit is confronted with subjective determinations which can make the goal of the pleasure-stimulus unattainable. As Shakespeare states in *Love's Labor's Lost* (Act V, Scene 2):

> "A jest's prosperity lies in the ear
> Of him that hears it, never in the tongue
> Of him that makes it."

He whose thoughts run in sober channels is incompetent to declare whether or not the jest is a good one. He himself must be in a jovial, or at least indifferent state of mind, in order to become the third person of the jest. The same hindrance is present in the case of both harmless and tendency wit, but in the latter the antagonism to the tendency which wishes to serve wit appears as a new hindrance. The readiness to laugh about an excellent smutty joke cannot manifest itself if the exposure concerns an honored kinsman of the third person. In an assemblage of divines and pastors no one would dare to refer to Heine's comparison of Catholic and Protestant priests as retail dealers and employees of a wholesale business. In the presence of my opponent's friends the wittiest invectives with which I might assail him would not be considered witticisms but invectives, and in the minds of my hearers it would create not pleasure, but indignation. A certain amount of willingness or a certain indifference, the absence of all factors which might evoke strong feelings in opposition to the tendency, are absolute conditions for the participation of the third person in the completion of the wit process.

THE THIRD PERSON OF THE WITTICISM

Wherever such hindrances to the operation of wit fail, we see the phenomenon which we are now investigating, namely, that the pleasure which the wit has provided manifests itself more clearly in the third person than in the originator of the wit. We must be satisfied to use the expression "more clearly" where we should be inclined to ask whether the pleasure of the hearer is not more intensive than that of the wit producer, because we are obviously lacking the means of measuring and comparing it. We see, however, that the hearer shows his pleasure by means of explosive laughter after the first person, in most cases with a serious expression on his face, has related the joke. If I repeat a witticism which I have heard, I am forced, in order not to spoil its effect, to conduct myself during its recital exactly like him who made it. We may now put the question of whether we can draw conclusions concerning the psychic process of wit-formation from this determination of laughter over wit.

Now, it cannot be our intention to take into consideration everything that has been asserted and printed about the nature of laughter. We are deterred from this undertaking by the statement which Dugas, one of Ribot's pupils, put at the beginning of his book *Psychologie du rire*

(1902). *"Il n'est pas de fait plus banal et plus étudié que le rire, il n'en est pas qui ait eu le don d'exciter d'advantage la curiosité du vulgaire et celle des philosophes, il n'en est pas sur lequel on ait recueilli plus d'observations et bâti plus de théories, et avec cela il n'en est pas qui demeure plus inexpliqué, on serait tenté de dire avec les sceptiques qu'il faut être content de rire et de ne pas chercher à savoir pourquoi on rit, d'autant que peut-être le réflexion tue le rire, et qu'il serait alors contradictoire qu'elle en découvrit les causes."*

On the other hand, we must make sure to utilize for our purposes a view of the mechanism of laughter which fits our own realm of thought excellently. I refer to the attempted explanation of Herbert Spencer in his essay entitled *Physiology of Laughter*.[1]

According to Spencer laughter is a phenomenon of discharge of psychic irritation, and an evidence of the fact that the psychic utilization of this irritation has suddenly met with a hindrance. The psychological situation, which discharges itself in laughter, he describes in the following words: "Laughter naturally results only when consciousness is unawares transferred from great things to small—only when there is what we call a descending incongruity."[2]

In an almost analogous sense the French authors (Dugas) designate laughter as a *"détente,"* a manifestation of release of tension, and A. Bain's theory, "Laughter a relief from restraint," seems to me to approach Spencer's conceptions nearer than many authors would have us believe.

However, we experience the desire to modify Spencer's thought; to give a more definite meaning to some of the ideas and to change others. We would say that laughter arises when the sum of psychic energy, formerly used for the occupation of certain psychic channels, has become unutilizable so that it can experience free discharge. We know what criti-

---

[1] H. Spencer, *The Physiology of Laughter* (first published in *Macmillan's Magazine* for March, 1860), Essays, Vol. II, 1901.

[2] Different points in this declaration would demand an exhaustive inquiry into an investigation of the pleasure of the comic, a thing that other authors have already done, and which, at all events, does not touch our discussion. It seems to me that Spencer was not happy in his explanation of why the discharge happens to find just that path, the excitement of which results in the physical picture of laughter. I should like to add one single contribution to the subject of the physiological explanation of laughter, that is, to the derivation or interpretation of the muscular actions that characterize laughter—a subject that has been often treated before and since Darwin, but which has never been conclusively settled. According to the best of my knowledge the grimaces and contortions of the corners of the mouth that characterize laughter appear first in the satisfied and satiated nursling when he drowsily quits the breasts. There it is a correct motion of expression since it bespeaks the determination to take no more nourishment, an "enough," so to speak, or rather a "more than enough." This primal sense of pleasurable satiation may have furnished the smile, which ever remains the basic phenomenon of laughter, as the late͞r connection with the pleasurable processes of discharge.

cism such a declaration invites, but for our defense we dare cite a pertinent quotation from Lipps's treatise on *Komik und Humor*, an analysis which throws light on other problems besides the comic and humor. He says: "In the end individual psychological problems always lead us fairly deeply into psychology, so that fundamentally no psychological problem may be considered by itself" (p. 71). The terms "psychic energy," "discharge," and the treatment of psychic energy as a quantity have become habitual modes of thinking since I began to explain to myself philosophically the fact of psychopathology. Being of the same opinion as Lipps I have essayed to represent in my *Interpretation of Dreams* the unconscious psychic processes as real entities, and I have not represented the conscious contents as the "real psychic activity." [1] Only when I speak about the "investing energy cathexis of psychic channels," do I seem to deviate from the analogies that Lipps uses. The knowledge that I have gained about the fact that psychic energy can be displaced from one idea to another along certain association channels, and about the almost indestructible conservation of the traces of psychic processes, has actually made it possible for me to attempt such a representation of the unknown. In order to obviate the possibility of a misunderstanding I must add that I am making no attempt to proclaim that cells and fibers, or the neuron system in vogue nowadays, represent these psychic paths, even if such paths would have to be represented by the organic elements of the nervous system in a manner which cannot yet be indicated.

LAUGHTER AS A DISCHARGE

Thus, according to our assumption, the conditions for laughter are such that a sum of psychic energy hitherto employed in the cathexis [2] of some paths may experience free discharge. And since not all laughter (but surely the laughter of wit), is a sign of pleasure, we shall be inclined to refer this pleasure to the release of previously existing cathectic energy. When we see that the hearer of the witticism laughs, while the creator of the same cannot, then that must indicate that in the hearer a sum of damming energy has been released and discharged, whereas during the

[1] Cf. *The Interpretation of Dreams*, Chap. VII, also *On the Psychic Force*, etc., in the above cited book of Lipps (p. 123), where he says: "This is the general principle: The dominant factors of the psychic life are not represented by the contents of consciousness but by those psychic processes which are unconscious. The task of psychology, provided it does not limit itself to a mere description of the content of consciousness, must also consist of revealing the nature of these unconscious processes from the nature of the contents of consciousness and its temporal relationship. Psychology must itself be a theory of these processes. But such a psychology will soon find that there exist quite a number of characteristics of these processes which are unrepresented in the corresponding contents of consciousness.

[2] Cathexis, from the Greek *cathexo*, I occupy; the term refers to a sum of psychic energy, which occupies or invests objects or some particular channels.

wit formation, either in the release or in the discharge, inhibitions resulted. One can characterize the psychic processes in the hearer, in the
third person of the witticism, hardly more pointedly than by asserting
that he has bought the pleasure of the witticism with very little expenditure on his part. One might say that it is presented to him. The words of
the witticism which he hears necessarily produce in him that idea or
thought-connection whose formation in him was also resisted by great
inner hindrances. He would have had to make an effort of his own in order
to bring it about spontaneously like the first person, or he would have had
to put forth at least as much psychic expenditure to equalize the force
of the suppression or repression of the inhibition. This psychic expenditure he has saved himself; according to our former discussion, we should
say that his pleasure corresponds to this economy. Following our understanding of the mechanism of laughter we should be more likely to say
that the cathexis utilized in the inhibition has now suddenly become
superfluous and neutralized because a forbidden idea came into existence
by way of auditory perception, and is, therefore, ready to be discharged
through laughter. Essentially both statements amount to the same thing,
for the economized expenditure corresponds exactly to the now superfluous inhibition. The latter statement is more obvious, for it permits us
to say that the hearer of the witticism laughs with the amount of psychic
energy which was liberated by the suspension of inhibition cathexis; that
is, he laughs away, as it were, this amount of psychic energy.

WHY THE FIRST PERSON DOES NOT LAUGH

If the person in whom the witticism is formed cannot laugh, then it indicates, as we have just remarked, that we deal here with a deviation from
the process of the third person, which concerns either the suspension of
the inhibition cathexis or the discharge possibility of the same. But the
first of the two cases is inconclusive, as we must presently see. The inhibition cathexis in the first person must have also been suspended, for otherwise there would have been no witticism, the formation of which had to
overcome just such a resistance. It would have also been impossible for
the first person to have experienced the wit-pleasure, which we have indeed been forced to derive from the suspension of inhibition. But there
remains the second case, namely, that even though the first person experienced pleasure, he cannot laugh, because the possibility of discharge
is disturbed. In the production of laughter such discharge is essential; an
interruption in the possibility of discharge might result from the immediate attachment of the freed cathexis to some other endopsychic use. It is
well that we have become cognizant of this possibility; we shall soon pay
more attention to it. But still another condition leading to the same result
is possible in the first person of the wit. Perhaps, after all, no appreciable

amount of energy has been liberated, in spite of the successful release of inhibition cathexis. For in the first person of the wit, the wit-work actually proceeds in a way which must correspond to a certain amount of fresh psychic expenditure. Thus, the first person contributes the power which removes the inhibitions and which surely results in a gain of pleasure for himself; in the case of tendency-wit it is indeed a very big gain, since the fore-pleasure gained from the wit-work takes upon itself the further removal of inhibitions. But the expenditure of the wit-work is, in every case, derived from the gain which results from the removal of inhibitions; it is the same expenditure which escapes from the hearer of the witticism. To confirm what was said it may be added that the witticism loses its laughter effect in the third person, as soon as an expenditure of mental work is exacted of him. The allusions of the witticism must be striking, and the omissions easily supplemented; with the awakening of conscious interest in thinking, the effect of the witticism is regularly made impossible. Here lies the real distinction between wit and riddle. It may be that the psychic constellations during wit-work are not at all favorable to the free discharge of the energy gained. We are here in no position to gain a deeper understanding; our inquiry as to why the third person laughs we have been able to explain better than the question why the first person does not laugh.

At any rate, if we have well in mind these views about the conditions of laughter and about the psychic process in the third person, we have arrived at a place where we can satisfactorily elucidate an entire series of peculiarities which are familiar in wit, but which have not been understood. Before an amount of interlocked energy, capable of discharge, is to be liberated in the third person, there are several conditions which must be fulfilled, or which at least are desirable. 1. It must be assured that the third person really makes this cathexis expenditure. 2. Care must be taken that when the latter becomes freed, that it should find another psychic use instead of offering itself to motor discharge. 3. It can only be of advantage if the cathexis to be liberated in the third person is first strengthened and heightened. Certain processes of wit-work which we can gather together under the caption of secondary or auxiliary techniques serve all these purposes.

The first of these conditions determines one of the qualifications of the third person as hearer of the witticism. He must be in every way so completely in psychic harmony with the first person as to possess the same inner inhibitions which the wit-work has overcome in the first person. Whoever is focused on smutty jokes will not be able to derive pleasure from clever exhibitionistic wit. Mr. N.'s or Mr. Wendell Phillips' aggressions will not be understood by uncultured people who are wont to give free rein to pleasure gained by insulting others. Every witticism thus demands its own public, and to laugh over the same witticisms is proof of absolute psychic agreement. We have indeed arrived at a point where we are at liberty to examine even more thoroughly the process in the third person's mind. The latter must be able habitually to produce the same inhibition which the joke has surmounted in the first person, so that, as soon as he hears the joke, there awakens within him compulsively and automatically a readiness for this inhibition. This readiness for the inhibition, which I must conceive as a true expenditure analogous to the mobilization of an army, is simultaneously recognized as superfluous or as belated, and is thus immediately discharged in its nascent state through the channel of laughter.[1]

The second condition for the production of the free discharge, in which there is another utilization for the liberated energy, seems to me of far greater importance. It furnishes the theoretical explanation for the uncertainty of the effect of wit; if the thoughts expressed in the wit evoke very exciting ideas in the hearer (depending on the agreement or antagonism between the wit's tendencies and the train of thought dominating the hearer), the witty process either receives attention or is deprived of it. Of still greater theoretical interest, however, are a series of auxiliary wit-techniques, which obviously serve the purpose of diverting the attention of the listeners from the wit-process so as to allow the latter to proceed automatically. I advisedly use the term "automatically" rather than "unconsciously" because the latter designation might prove misleading. It is only a question of keeping the psychic process from getting more than its share of attention during the recital of the witticism, and the usefulness of these auxiliary techniques permits us to assume rightfully that it is just the occupation of attention which has a large share in the control, and in the fresh utilization of the freed cathexis.

THE AUTOMATISM OF THE WIT-PROCESS

It seems by no means easy to avoid the endopsychic utilization of energy that has become superfluous, for in our mental processes we are constantly in the habit of transferring such emotional outputs from one path to another without losing any of their energy through discharge. Wit prevents this in the following way. In the first place it strives for the shortest possible expression in order to expose fewer points of attack to the attention. Secondly, it strictly adheres to the condition of being easily understood (*v. s.*), for as soon as there is recourse to mental effort, or a demand for a choice between different mental paths, it imperils the effect, not only through the unavoidable mental expenditure, but also through the awakening of attention. Besides this, wit also makes use of the artifice of

---

[1] Heymans (*Zeitschrift für Psychol.*, XI) has used the viewpoint of the nascent state in a somewhat different connection.

diverting the attention, by offering something in the expression of the witticism which fascinates the hearer, while the liberation of inhibition cathexis and its discharge can take place undisturbed. The omissions in the wording of wit already carry out this intention. They impel us to fill in the gaps and in this way they keep the wit-process free from attention. The technique of the riddle, as it were, which attracts attention is here pressed into the service of the wit-work. The façade formations, which we have already discovered in many groups of tendency-wit, are still more effective. The syllogistical façades excellently fulfill the purpose of riveting the attention by an allotted task. While we begin to ponder wherein the given answer was lacking, we are already laughing; our attention has been surprised, and the discharge of the liberated inhibition cathexis has been effected. The same is true of witticisms possessing a comic façade in which the comic serves to assist the wit-technique. A comic façade promotes the effect of wit in more than one way; it makes possible not only the automatism of the wit-process by riveting the attention, but it also facilitates the discharge of wit by sending ahead a discharge from the comic. Here, the effect of the comic resembles that of a fascinating fore-pleasure, and we can thus understand why many witticisms are able to dispense entirely with the fore-pleasures produced by other means of wit, and make use of only the comic as a fore-pleasure. Among the true techniques of wit it is especially displacement and representation through absurdity which, besides other properties, also develop the deviation of attention so desirable for the automatic discharge of the wit-process.[1]

We already surmise, and later will be able to see it more clearly, that

[1] Through an example of displacement-wit I desire to discuss another interesting character of the technique of wit. The genial actress, Gallmeyer, when once asked how old she was, is said to have answered this unwelcome question with abashed and downcast eyes, by saying, "In Brünn." This is a very good example of displacement. Having been asked her age, she replied by naming the place of her birth, thus anticipating the next query, and in this manner she wishes to imply: "This is a question which I prefer to pass by." And still we feel that the character of the witticism does not here come to expression undimmed. The deviation from the question is too obvious; the displacement is much too conspicuous. Our attention understands immediately that it is a matter of an intentional displacement. In other displacement-witticisms the displacement is disguised and our attention is riveted by the effort to discover it. In one of the above mentioned displacement-witticisms, the reply to the recommendation of the horse—"What in the world should I do in Monticello at 6:30 in the morning?"—the displacement is also an obtrusive one, but as a substitute for it it acts upon the attention in a senseless and confusing manner, whereas in the interrogation of the actress we know immediately how to dispose of her displacement answer.

The so-called "facetious questions," which may make use of the best techniques, deviate from wit in other ways. An example of the facetious question with displacement is the following: "What is a cannibal who devours his father and mother?—Answer: An orphan.—And when he has devoured all his other relatives?—Sole-heir.—And where can such a monster ever find sympathy?—In the dictionary under S." The facetious questions are not full witticisms because the required witty answers cannot be guessed like the allusions, omissions, etc., of wit.

in this condition of deviation of attention we have disclosed no unessential characteristic of the psychic process in the hearer of wit. In conjunction with this, we can understand something more. First, how it happens that we rarely ever know in a joke why we are laughing, although by analytical investigation we can determine the cause. This laughing is the result of an automatic process which was first made possible by keeping our conscious attention at a distance. Secondly, we arrive at an understanding of that characteristic of wit as a result of which wit can exert its full effect on the hearer only when it is new and when it comes to him as a surprise. This property of wit, which causes wit to be short-lived and forever urges the production of new wit, is evidently due to the fact that it is inherent in the surprising or the unexpected, to succeed but once. When we repeat wit the awakened memory leads the attention to the first hearing. This also explains the desire to impart wit to others who have not heard it before, for the impression made by wit on the new hearer replenishes that part of the pleasure which has been lost by the lack of novelty. And an analogous motive probably impels the wit producer to impart his wit to others.

ELEMENTS FAVORING THE WIT-PROCESS

As elements favoring the wit-process, even if we can no longer consider them as conditions, I present in the third place those three technical aids to wit-work which are destined to increase the sums of energy to be discharged and thus enhance the effect of the wit. These technical aids also very often accentuate the attention directed to the wit, but they neutralize its influence by simultaneously fascinating it and impeding its movements. Everything that provokes interest and confusion exerts its influence in these two directions. This is especially true of the nonsense and contrast elements, and above all of the "contrast of ideas," which some authors consider the essential character of wit, but in which I see only a means to reinforce the effect of wit. All that is confusing evokes in the hearer that condition of distribution of energy which Lipps has designated as "psychic damming"; and, doubtless, he has a right to assume that the force of the "discharge" varies with the success of the damming process which precedes it. Lipps's exposition does not explicitly refer to wit, but to the comic in general, yet it seems quite probable that the discharge in wit, releasing a gush of inhibition energy, is brought to its height in a similar manner by means of the damming.

It now dawns upon us that the technique of wit is really determined by two kinds of tendencies, those which make possible the formation of wit in the first person, and those guaranteeing that the witticism produces in the third person as much pleasurable effect as possible. The Janus-like double-facedness of wit, which safeguards its original resultant pleasure against the impugnment of critical reason, belongs to the first tendency together with the mechanism of fore-pleasure; the other complications of the technique resulting from the conditions discussed in this chapter concern the third person of the witticism. Thus, wit in itself is a double-tongued villain, which serves two masters at the same time. Everything that aims at gaining pleasure is calculated by the witticism to arouse the third person, as if inner, unsurmountable inhibitions in the first person stood in the way of the same. Thus, one gets the full impression of the absolute necessity of this third person for the completion of the wit-process. But while we have succeeded in obtaining a good insight into the nature of this process in the third person, we feel that the corresponding process in the first person is still shrouded in darkness. So far, we have not succeeded in answering the first of our two questions: Why can we not laugh over wit made by ourselves? and: Why are we urged to impart our own witticisms to others? We can only suspect that there is an intimate connection between the two facts yet to be explained, and that we must impart our witticisms to others for the reason that we ourselves are unable to laugh over them. From our examinations of the conditions in the third person for pleasure gaining and pleasure discharging, we can draw the conclusion that in the first person the conditions for discharge are lacking, and that those for gaining pleasure are only incompletely fulfilled. Thus it is not to be disputed that we supplement our pleasure in that we attain the—to us impossible—laughter in the roundabout way, from the impression of the person who stimulated to laughter. Thus we laugh, so to speak, *par ricochet*, as Dugas expresses it. Laughter belongs to those manifestations of psychic states which are highly infectious; if I make some one else laugh by imparting my wit to him, I am really using him as a tool in order to arouse my own laughter. One can really notice that the person who at first recites the witticism with a serious mien later joins the hearer with a moderate amount of laughter. Imparting my witticisms to others may thus serve several purposes. First, it serves to give me the objective certainty of the success of the wit-work; secondly, it serves to enhance my own pleasure through the reaction of the hearer upon myself; thirdly, in the case of repeating a not original joke, it serves to remedy the loss of pleasure due to the lack of novelty.

ECONOMY AND TOTAL EXPENDITURE

At the end of these discussions about the psychic processes of wit, in so far as they are enacted between two persons, we can glance back to the factor of economy which impressed us as an important item in the psychological conception of wit since we offered the first explanation of wit-technique. Long ago we dismissed the nearest but also the simplest conception of this economy, where it was a matter of avoiding psychic expenditure in general by a maximum restriction in the use of words and by the production of associations of ideas. We had then already asserted that brevity and laconisms are not witty in themselves. The brevity of wit is a peculiar one; it has to be a "witty" brevity. The original pleasure gain produced by playing with words and thoughts resulted, to be sure, from simple economy in expenditure, but with the development of play into wit the tendency to economize also had to shift its goals, for whatever might be saved by the use of the same words or by avoiding new thought connections, would surely be of no account when compared to the colossal expenditure of our mental activity. We may be permitted to make a comparison between the psychic economy and a business enterprise. So long as the latter's transactions are very small, good policy demands that expenses be kept low and that the costs of operation be minimized as much as possible. The economy still follows the absolute height of the expenditure. Later on when the volume of business has increased, the importance of the business expenses dwindles; increases in the expenditure totals matter little so long as the transactions and returns can be sufficiently increased. Keeping down running expenses would be parsimonious; in fact, it would mean a direct loss. Nevertheless, it would be equally false to assume that with a very great expenditure there would be no more room for saving. The manager inclined to economize would now make an effort to save on particular things and would feel satisfied if the same establishment, with its costly upkeep, could reduce its expenses at all, no matter how small the saving would seem in comparison to the entire expenditure. In quite an analogous manner the detailed economy in our complicated psychic affairs remains a source of pleasure, as may be shown by everyday occurrences. Whoever used to have a gas lamp in his room, but now uses electric light, will experience for a long time a definite feeling of pleasure when he presses the electric light button; this pleasure continues as long as at that moment he remembers the complicated arrangements necessary to light the gas lamp. Similarly the economy of expenditure in psychic inhibition brought about by wit—small though it may be in comparison to the sum total of psychic expenditure—will remain a source of pleasure for us, because we thereby save a particular expenditure which we are wont to make, and which we were also ready to make this time. That the expenditure is expected and prepared for, is a factor which stands unmistakably in the foreground.

A localized economy, as the one just considered, will not fail to give us momentary pleasure, but it will not bring about a lasting alleviation so long as what has been saved here can be utilized in another place. Only when this disposal into a different path can be avoided, will the special economy be transformed into a general alleviation of the psychic expenditures. Thus, with clearer insight into the psychic processes of wit, we see that the factor of alleviation takes the place of economy. Obviously the former gives us the greater feeling of pleasure. The process in the first person of the witticism produces pleasure by removing inhibitions and by diminishing local expenditure; it does not, however, seem to come to rest until it succeeds through the intervention of the third person, in attaining general relief through discharge.

C. THEORETICAL PART

THE RELATION OF WIT TO DREAMS AND TO THE UNCONSCIOUS

AT THE end of the chapter which dealt with the elucidation of the technique of wit we asserted that the processes of condensation with and without substitutive formation, displacement, representation through absurdity, representation through the opposite, indirect representation, etc., all of which we found participating in the formation of wit, evinced a far-reaching agreement with the processes of "dream-work." We promised, at that time, first to examine more carefully these similarities, and secondly, so far as such indications point, to search for what is common to both wit and dreams. The discussion of this comparison would be much easier for us if we could assume that one of the subjects to be compared—the "dream-work"—were well known. But we shall probably do better not to take this assumption for granted. I received the impression that my book *The Interpretation of Dreams* created more "confusion" than "enlightenment" among my colleagues, and I know that the wider reading circles have contented themselves to reduce the contents of the book to a catchword, "Wish fulfillment"—a term easily remembered and easily abused.

However, in my continued occupation with the problems considered therein, for the study of which my practice as a psychotherapeutist affords me much opportunity, I found nothing that would impel me to change or improve on my ideas; I can therefore peacefully wait until the reader's comprehension has risen to my level, or until an intelligent critic has pointed out to me the basic faults in my conception. For the purposes of comparison with wit, I shall briefly review the most important features of dreams and dream-work.

We know dreams by the recollection, which usually seems fragmentary and which occurs upon awakening. It is then a structure made up mostly of visual or other sensory impressions, which represents to us a deceptive picture of an experience, and may be mingled with mental processes (the "knowledge" in the dream), and emotional manifestations. What we thus remember as a dream I call "the manifest dream-content." The latter is often altogether absurd and confused, at other times it is merely one part or another that is so affected. But even if it be entirely coherent, as in the case of some anxiety dreams, it stands out in our psychic life as something strange, for the origin of which one cannot account. Until recently the explanation for these peculiarities of the dream has been sought in the dream itself, in that it was considered roughly speaking an indication of a muddled, dissociated, and "sleepy" activity of the nervous elements.

As opposed to this view, I have shown that the excessively peculiar "manifest" dream-content can regularly be made comprehensible, and that it is a disfigured and changed transcription of certain correct psychic formations which deserve the name of "latent dream-thoughts." One gains an understanding of the latter by resolving the manifest dream-content into its component parts without regard for its apparent meaning, and then by following up the threads of associations which emanate from each one of the now isolated elements. These become interwoven and in the end lead to a structure of thoughts, which is not only entirely accurate, but also fits easily into the familiar associations of our psychic processes. During this "analysis" the dream-content loses all of the peculiarities so strange to us; but if the analysis is to be successful, we must firmly cast aside the critical objections which incessantly arise against the reproduction of the individual associations.

THE DREAM-WORK

From the comparison of the remembered manifest dream-content with the latent dream-thoughts thus discovered, there arises the conception of "dream-work." The entire sum of the transforming processes which have changed the latent dream-thought into the manifest dream is called the dream-work. The astonishment which formerly the dream evoked in us is now perceived to be due to the dream-work.

The function of the dream-work may be described in the following manner: A structure of thoughts, mostly very complicated, which has been built up during the day and not brought to settlement—a day remnant—clings firmly even during night to the energy which it had assumed —the underlying center of interest—and thus threatens to disturb sleep. This day remnant is transformed into a dream by the dream-work and in this way rendered harmless to sleep. But in order to make possible its employment by the dream-work, this day remnant must be capable of being cast into the form of a wish, a condition that is not difficult to fulfill. The wish emanating from the dream-thoughts forms the first step and later on the nucleus of the dream. Experience gained from analyses—not the theory of the dream—teaches us that with children a fond wish left from the waking state suffices to evoke a dream, which is coherent and senseful, but almost always short, and easily recognizable as a "wish fulfillment." In the case of adults the universally valid condition for the dream-creating wish seems to be that the latter should appear foreign to conscious thinking, that is, it should be a repressed wish, or that it should supply consciousness with reinforcement from unknown sources. Without the assumption of the unconscious activity in the sense used above, I should be at a loss to develop further the theory of dreams and to explain the material gleaned from experience in dream-analyses. The action of this unconscious wish upon the logical conscious material of dream-thoughts now results in the dream. The latter is thereby drawn down into the unconscious, as it were, or to speak more precisely, it is exposed to a treatment which usually takes place at the level of unconscious mental activity, and which is characteristic of this mental level. Only from the results of the "dream-work" have we thus far learned to know the qualities of this unconscious mental activity and its differentiation from the "fore-conscious" which is capable of consciousness.

THE UNCONSCIOUS

A novel and difficult theory that runs counter to our habitual modes of thinking can hardly gain in lucidity by a condensed exposition. I can therefore accomplish little more in this discussion than refer the reader to the detailed treatment of the unconscious in my *Interpretation of Dreams*, and also to Lipps's work, which I consider most important. I am aware that he who is under the spell of a good old philosophical training, or stands aloof from a so-called philosophical system, will oppose the assumption of the "unconscious psychic processes" in Lipps's sense and in mine, and will desire to prove the impossibility of it preferably by means of definitions of the term psychic. But definitions are conventional and changeable. I have often found that persons who dispute the unconscious on the grounds of its absurdity or impossibility have not received their impressions from those sources from which I, at least, have found it necessary to draw, in order to become aware of its existence. These opponents had never witnessed the effect of a posthypnotic suggestion, and they were immensely surprised at the evidence I imparted to them gleaned from my analysis of unhypnotized neurotics. They had never gained the conception of the unconscious as something which one does not really know, while cogent proofs force one to supplement this idea by saying that one understands by the unconscious something capable of conscious-ness, something concerning which one has not thought and which is not in the field of vision of consciousness. Nor had they attempted to convince themselves of the existence of such unconscious thoughts in their own psychic life by means of an analysis of one of their own dreams, and when I attempted this with them, they could perceive their own mental occurrences only with astonishment and confusion. I have also gotten the impression that these are essentially affective resistances which stand in the way of the acceptation of the "unconscious," and that they are based on the fact that no one is desirous of becoming acquainted with his unconscious, and it is most convenient to deny altogether its possibility.

CONDENSATION AND DISPLACEMENT IN THE DREAM-WORK

The dream-work, to which I return after this digression, subjects the thought material uttered in the optative mood to a very peculiar elaboration. First of all it proceeds from the optative to the indicative mood; it substitutes "it is" for "would it were!" This "it is" is destined to become part of an hallucinatory representation which I have called the "regression" of the dream-work. This regression represents the path from the mental images to the sensory perceptions of the same, or if one chooses to speak with reference to the still unfamiliar—not to be understood anatomically—topic of the psychic apparatus, it is the region of the thought-formation to the region of the sensory perception. Along this road which runs in an opposite direction to the course of development of psychic complications, the dream-thoughts gain in clearness; a plastic situation finally results as a nucleus of the manifest "dream picture." In order to arrive at such a sensory representation the dream-thoughts have had to experience tangible changes in their expression. But while the thoughts are changed back into mental images they are subjected to still greater changes, some of which are easily conceivable as necessary, while others are surprising. As a necessary secondary result of the regression, one understands that nearly all relationships within the thoughts which have organized the same are lost to the manifest dream. The dream-work takes over, as it were, only the raw material of the ideas for representation, and not the thought-relations which held each other in check; or at least it reserves the freedom of leaving the latter out of the question. On the other hand, there is a certain part of the dream-work which cannot be traced to the regression or to the recasting into mental images; it is just that part which is significant to us for the analogy to wit-formation. The material of the dream-thoughts experiences an extraordinary compression or *condensation* during the dream-work. The starting-points of this condensation are those points which are common to two or more dream-thoughts because they naturally pertain to both or because they are inevitable consequences of the contents of two or more dream-thoughts, and since these points do not regularly suffice for a prolific condensation new artificial and fleeting common points come into existence, and for this purpose preferably words are used which combine different meanings in their sounds. The newly framed common points of condensation enter as representatives of the dream-thoughts into the manifest dream-content, so that an element of the dream corresponds to a point of junction or intersection of the dream-thoughts, and with regard to the latter it must in general be called "over-determined." The process of condensation is that part of the dream-work which is most easily recognizable; it suffices to compare the recorded wording of a dream with the written dream-thoughts gained by means of analysis, in order to get a good impression of the productiveness of dream condensation.

It is not easy to convince one's self of the second great change that takes place in the dream-thoughts through the agency of the dream-work. I refer to that process which I have called the dream *displacement*. It manifests itself by the fact that what occupies the center of the manifest dream and is endowed with vivid sensory intensity has occupied a peripheral and secondary position in the dream-thoughts, and *vice versa*. This process causes the dream to appear out of proportion when compared with the dream-thoughts, and it is because of this displacement that it seems strange and incomprehensible to the waking state. In order that such a displacement should occur it must be possible for the cathexis to pass uninhibited from important to insignificant ideas—a process which in normal conscious thinking can only give the impression of "faulty thinking."

Transformation into expressive activity, condensation, and displacement are the three great functions which we can ascribe to the dream-work. A fourth, to which too little attention was given in *The Interpretation of Dreams*, does not come into consideration here for our purpose. In a consistent elucidation of the ideas dealing with the "topic of the psychic apparatus" and "regression," which alone can lend value to these working hypotheses, an effort would have to be made to determine at what stages of regression the various transformations of the dream-thoughts occur. As yet, no serious effort has been made in this direction, but at least we can speak definitely about displacement when we say that it must arise in the thought material while the latter is in the level of the unconscious processes. One will probably have to think of condensation as a process that extends over the entire course up to the outposts of the perceptive region, but in general it suffices to assume that there is a simultaneous activity of all the forces which participate in the formation of dreams. In view of the reserve which one must naturally exercise in the treatment of such problems, and in consideration of the inability to discuss here the main objections to these problems, I should like to trust somewhat to the assertion that the process of the dream-work which prepares the dream, is situated in the region of the unconscious. Roughly speaking, one can distinguish three general stages in the formation of the dream: first, the transference of the conscious day remnants into the unconscious, a transference in which the conditions of the sleeping state must co-operate; secondly, the actual dream-work in the unconscious; and thirdly, the regression of the elaborated dream material to the region of perception, whereby the dream becomes conscious.

The forces participating in the dream-formation may be recognized as the following: the wish to sleep; the sum of cathexis which still clings to the day remnants after the depression brought about by the state of sleep; the psychic energy of the unconscious wish forming the dream; and the opposing force of the *"censorship,"* which exercises its authority in our waking state, and is not entirely abolished during sleep. The task of dream-formation is, above all, to overcome the inhibition of the censorship, and it is just this task that is fulfilled by the displacement of the psychic energy within the material of the dream-thoughts.

THE FORMULA FOR WIT-WORK

Now we recall what caused us to think of the dream while investigating wit. We found that the character and activity of wit were bound up in certain forms of expression and technical means, among which the various forms of condensation, displacement, and indirect representation were the most conspicuous. But the processes which led to the same results—condensation, displacement, and indirect expression—we learned to know as peculiarities of dream-work. Does not this analogy almost force us to the conclusion that wit-work and dream-work must be identical at least in one essential point? I believe that the dream-work lies revealed before us in its most important characters, but in wit we find obscured just that portion of the psychic processes which we may compare with the dream-work, namely, the process of wit-formation in the first person. Shall we not yield to the temptation to construct this process according to the analogy of dream-formation? Some of the characteristics of dreams are so foreign to wit, that that part of the dream-work corresponding to them cannot be carried over to the wit-formation. The regression of the stream of thought to perception is certainly lacking as far as wit is concerned. However, the other two stages of dream-formation, the sinking of a foreconscious [1] thought into the unconscious, and the unconscious elaboration, would give us exactly the result which we might observe in wit if we assumed this process in wit-formation. Let us decide to assume that this is the proceeding of wit-formation in the case of the first person. *A foreconscious thought is left for a moment to unconscious elaboration and the results are forthwith grasped by the conscious perception.*

Before, however, we attempt to prove the details of this assertion, we wish to consider an objection which may jeopardize our assumption. We start with the fact that the techniques of wit point to the same processes which become known to us as peculiarities of dream-work. Now it is an

[1] Cf. *The Interpretation of Dreams,* Chapter VII.

easy matter to say in opposition that we would not have described the techniques of wit as condensation, displacement, etc., nor would we have arrived at such a comprehensive agreement in the means of representation of wit and dreams, if our previous knowledge of dream-work had not influenced our conception of the technique of wit; so that fundamentally we find that wit confirms only those expectations which we brought to it from our study of dreams. Such a genesis of agreement would be no certain guarantee of its stability beyond our preconceived judgment. No other author has really thought of considering condensation, displacement, and indirect expression as active factors of wit. This might be a possible objection, but nevertheless it would not be justified. It might just as well be said that in order to recognize the real agreement between dreams and wit our ordinary knowledge must be augmented by a specialized knowledge of dream-work. However, the decision will really depend only upon the question whether the examining critic can prove that such a conception of the technique of wit in the individual examples is forced, and that other nearer and farther-reaching interpretations have been suppressed in favor of mine; or whether the critic will have to admit that the expectations derived from the study of dreams can be really confirmed through wit. My opinion is that we have nothing to fear from such a critic and that our processes of reduction have confidently pointed out in which forms of expression we must search for the techniques of wit. That we designated these techniques by names which previously anticipated the result of the agreement between the technique of wit and the dream-work was our just prerogative, and really nothing more than an easily justified simplification.

There is still another objection which would not be vital, but which could not be so completely refuted. One might think that the techniques of wit that fit in so well considering the ends we have in view deserve recognition, but that they do not represent all possible techniques of wit or even all those in use. Also, that we have selected only the techniques of wit which were influenced by and would suit the pattern of the dream-work, whereas others ignored by us would have demonstrated that such an agreement was not common to all cases. I really do not trust myself to make the assertion that I have succeeded in explaining all the current witticisms with reference to their techniques, and I therefore admit the possibility that my enumeration of wit-techniques may show many gaps. But I have not purposely excluded from my discussion any form of technique that was clear to me, and I can affirm that the most frequent, the most essential, and the most characteristic technical means of wit have not eluded my attention.

WIT AS AN INSPIRATION

Wit possesses still another character which entirely corresponds to our conception of the wit-work as originally discovered in our study of dreams. It is true that it is common to hear one say "I *made* a joke," but one feels that one behaves differently during this process than when one pronounces a judgment or offers an objection. Wit shows in a most pronounced manner the character of an involuntary "inspiration" or a sudden flash of thought. A moment before one cannot tell what kind of joke one is going to make, though it lacks only the words to clothe it. One usually experiences something indefinable which I should like most to compare to an absence, or sudden drop of intellectual tension; then all of a sudden the witticism appears, usually simultaneously with its verbal investment. Some of the means of wit are also utilized in the expression of thought along other lines, as in the cases of comparison and allusion. I can intentionally will to make an allusion. In doing this I have first in mind (in the inner hearing) the direct expression of my thought, but as I am inhibited from expressing the same through some objection from the situation in question, I almost resolve to substitute the direct expression by a form of indirect expression, and then I utter it in the form of an allusion. But the allusion that comes into existence in this manner having been formed under my continuous control is never witty, no matter how useful it may be. On the other hand, the witty allusion appears without my having been able to follow up these preparatory stages in my mind. I do not wish to attribute too much value to this procedure, it is hardly conclusive, but it does agree well with our assumption, that in wit-formation a stream of thought is dropped for a moment which then suddenly emerges from the unconscious as a witticism.

Wit also evinces a peculiar behavior along the lines of association of ideas. Frequently it is not at the disposal of our memory when we look for it; on the other hand, it often appears unsolicited, and at places of our train of thought where we cannot understand its presence. Again, these are only minor qualities, but none the less they point to their unconscious origin.

Let us now collect the properties of wit whose formation can be referred to the unconscious. Above all, there is the peculiar brevity of wit which, though not an indispensable, is a marked and distinctive characteristic feature. When we first encountered it, we were inclined to see in it an expression of a tendency to economize, but owing to very evident objections we ourselves depreciated the value of this conception. At present we look upon it more as a sign of the unconscious elaboration which the thought of wit has undergone. The process of condensation which corresponds to it in dreams, we can correlate with no other factor than with the localization in the unconscious, and we must assume that the conditions for such condensations which are lacking in the foreconscious are present in the unconscious mental process.[1] It is to be expected that in the process of condensation some of the elements subjected to it become lost, while others which take over their cathexis are strengthened by it, or are built up too energetically. The brevity of wit, like the brevity of dreams, would thus be a necessary concomitant manifestation of the condensation which occurs in both cases; both times it is a result of the condensation process. The brevity of wit is indebted also to this origin for its peculiar character, which though not further established produces a striking impression.

THE UNCONSCIOUS AND THE INFANTILE

We have defined above the one result of condensation—the manifold application of the same material, play upon words, and similarity of sound—as a localized economy, and have also referred the pleasure produced by harmless wit to that economy. At a later place we have found that the original purpose of wit consisted in producing this kind of pleasure from words, a process which was permitted to the individual during the stage of playing, but which became banked in during the course of intellectual development or by rational criticism. Now we have decided upon the assumption that such condensations as serve the technique of wit originate automatically and without any particular purpose during the process of thinking in the unconscious. Have we not here two different conceptions of the same fact which seem to be incompatible with each other? I do not think so. To be sure, there are two different conceptions, which should be brought in unison, but they do not contradict each other. They are merely somewhat strange to each other, and as soon as we have established a relationship between them we shall probably gain in knowledge. That such condensations are sources of pleasure is in perfect accord with the supposition that they easily find in the unconscious the conditions necessary for their origin. On the other hand, we see the motivation for the sinking into the unconscious in the circumstance, that the pleasure-bringing condensation necessary to wit easily results there. Two other factors also, which upon first examination seem entirely foreign to each other and which are brought together quite accidentally, will be recognized on deeper investigation as intimately connected, and perhaps may be found to be substantially the same. I am referring to the two assertions that on the one hand wit could form such pleasure-bringing condensations

---

[1] Besides in the dream-work and the technique of wit I have been able to demonstrate condensation as a regular and significant process in another psychic occurrence, in the mechanism of normal (not purposive) forgetting. Singular impressions put difficulties in the way of forgetting; impressions in any way analogous are forgotten by becoming fused at their points of contact. The confusion of analogous impressions is one of the first steps in forgetting.

during its development in the stage of playing, that is, during the infancy of reason; and, on the other hand, that it accomplishes the same function on higher levels by submerging the thought into the unconscious. For the infantile is the source of the unconscious. The unconscious mental processes are no others than those which are solely produced during early infancy. The thought which sinks into the unconscious for the purpose of wit-formation only revisits there the old homestead of the former playing with words. The thought is put back for a moment into the infantile state in order to regain in this way childish pleasure-sources. If, indeed, one were not already acquainted with it from the investigation of the psychology of the neuroses, wit would surely impress one with the idea that the peculiar unconscious elaboration is nothing else but the infantile type of the mental process. But this peculiar infantile manner of thinking is by no means easy to grasp in the unconscious of the adult because it is usually corrected, so to say, in *statu nascendi*. However, it is successfully grasped in a series of cases, and then we always laugh about the "childish stupidity." In fact, every exposure of such an unconscious fact affects us in a "comical" manner.[1]

It is easier to comprehend the character of these unconscious mental processes in the utterances of patients suffering from various psychic disturbances. It is very probable that, following the assumption of Griesinger, we would be in a position to understand the deliria of the insane and to turn them to good account as valuable information, if we would not make the demands of conscious thinking upon them, but instead treat them as we do dreams by means of our art of interpretation.[2] In the dream, too, we were able to show the "return of psychic life to the embryonal state."[3]

In discussing the processes of condensation we have entered so deeply into the significance of the analogy between wit and dreams that we can here be brief. As we know that displacements in dream-work point to the influence of censorship of conscious thought, we will consequently be inclined to assume that an inhibiting force also plays a part in the formation of wit when we find the process of displacement among the techniques of wit. We also know that this is commonly the case; the endeavor of wit to revive the old pleasure in nonsense or the old pleasure in word-play meets with resistance in every normal state, a resistance which is

[1] Many of my patients while under psychoanalytic treatment are wont to prove regularly by their laughter that I have succeeded in demonstrating faithfully to their conscious perception the veiled unconscious; they laugh also when the content of what is disclosed does not at all justify this laughter. To be sure, it is conditional that they have approached this unconscious closely enough to grasp it when the physician has conjectured it and presented it to them.

[2] In doing this we must not forget to reckon with the distortion brought about by the censorship which is still active in the psychoses.

[3] *The Interpretation of Dreams.*

exerted by the protest of critical reason, and which must be overcome in each individual case. But a radical distinction between wit and dreams is shown in the manner in which the wit-work solves this difficulty. In the dream-work the solution of this task is brought about regularly through displacements and through the choice of ideas which are remote enough from those objectionable to secure passage through the censorship; the latter themselves are but offsprings of those whose psychic cathexis they have taken over through full transference. The displacements are, therefore, not lacking in any dream and are far more comprehensive. They not only include the deviations from the trend of thought, but also all forms of indirect expression, especially the substitution for an important but offensive element by one indifferent and seemingly harmless to the censorship, which then looks like a most remote allusion to the first; they also include substitution through symbols, comparisons, or trifles. It is not to be denied that parts of this indirect representation really originate in the foreconscious thoughts of the dream—as, for example, symbolical representation and representation through comparisons—because otherwise the thought would not have reached the state of the foreconscious expression. Such indirect expressions and allusions, whose reference to the original thought is easily detectable, are really permissible and customary means of expression even in our conscious thought. The dream-work, however, exaggerates the application of these means of indirect expression to an unlimited degree. Under the pressure of the censor any kind of association becomes good enough for substitution by allusion; the displacement from one element to any other is permitted. The substitution of the inner associations (similarity, causal connection, etc.) by the so-called outer associations (simultaneity, contiguity in space, assonance) is particularly conspicuous and characteristic of the dream-work.

THE DIFFERENCE BETWEEN DREAM-TECHNIQUE AND WIT-TECHNIQUE

All these means of displacement also occur as techniques of wit, but when they do occur they usually restrict themselves to those limits prescribed for their use in conscious thought; in fact, they may be lacking even though wit must regularly solve a task of inhibition. One can comprehend this retirement of the process of displacement in wit-work when one remembers that wit usually has another technique at its disposal through which it defends itself against inhibitions. Indeed, we have discovered nothing more characteristic of it than just this technique. For wit does not have recourse to compromises as does the dream, nor does it evade the inhibition; it insists upon retaining the play with words or nonsense unaltered, but thanks to the ambiguity of words and multiplicity of thought-relations, it restricts itself to the choice of cases in which this play or nonsense may appear at the same time admissible (jest) or sense-ful (wit). Nothing distinguishes wit from all other psychic formations better than this double-sidedness and this double-dealing; by emphasiz-ing the "sense in nonsense," the authors have approached nearest the understanding of wit, at least from this angle.

Considering the unexceptional predominance of this peculiar technique in overcoming inhibitions in wit, one might find it superfluous that wit should make use of the displacement-technique even in a single case. But on the one hand, certain kinds of this technique remain useful for wit as objects and sources of pleasure—as, for example, the real displacement (deviation of the trend of thought) which in fact shares in the nature of nonsense—and on the other hand one must not forget that the highest stage of wit, tendency-wit, must frequently overcome two kinds of inhibi-tions which oppose both itself and its tendency, and that allusion and dis-placements are qualified to facilitate this latter task.

The numerous and unrestricted application of indirect representation, of displacements, and especially of allusions in the dream-work, has a re-sult which I mention not because of its own significance but because it be-came for me the subjective inducement to occupy myself with the prob-lem of wit. If a dream analysis is imparted to one unfamiliar with the subject and unaccustomed to it, and the peculiar ways of allusions and displacements (objectionable to the waking thoughts but utilized by the dream-work) are explained, the hearer experiences an uncomfortable impression. He declares these interpretations to be "witty," but it seems obvious to him that these are not successful jokes but forced ones which run contrary to the rules of wit. This impression can be easily explained by the fact that the dream-work operates with the same means as wit, but in the application of the same, the dream exceeds the bounds which wit restricts. We shall soon learn that in consequence of the rôle of the third person, wit is bound by a certain condition which does not affect the dream.

IRONY—NEGATIVISM

Among those techniques which are common to both wit and dreams, representation through the opposite and the application of absurdity are especially interesting. The first belongs to the strongly effective means of wit as shown above in the examples of "out-doing wit." The representa-tion through the opposite, unlike most of the wit-techniques, is unable to withdraw itself from conscious attention. He who intentionally tries to make use of wit-work, as in the case of the "habitual wag," soon discovers that the easiest way to answer an assertion with a witticism is to concen-trate one's mind on the opposite of this assertion and trust to the chance flash of thought to brush aside the feared objection to this opposite, by means of a different interpretation. Maybe the representation through its opposite is indebted for such a preference to the fact that it forms the nucleus of another pleasurable mode of mental expression, for an understanding of which we do not have to consult the unconscious. I refer to *irony*, which is very similar to wit and is considered a sub-species of the comic. The essence of irony consists in imparting the very opposite of what one intended to express, but it precludes the anticipated contradiction by indicating through the inflections, concomitant gestures, and through slight changes in style—if it is done in writing—that the speaker himself means to convey the opposite of what he says. Irony is applicable only in cases where the other person is prepared to hear the reverse of the statement actually made, so that he cannot fail to be inclined to contradict. As a consequence of this condition, ironic expressions are particularly subject to the danger of being misunderstood. To the person who uses it, it gives the advantage of readily avoiding the difficulties to which direct expressions, as, for example, invectives, are subject. In the hearer it produces comic pleasure, probably by causing him to make preparations for contradiction, which are immediately found to be unnecessary. Such a comparison of wit with a form of the comical that is closely allied to it, might strengthen us in the assumption that the relation of wit to the unconscious is the peculiarity that also distinguishes it from the comical.[1]

In dream-work, representation through the opposite has a far more important part to play than in wit. The dream not only delights in representing a pair of opposites by means of one and the same composite image, but in addition it often changes an element from the dream-thoughts into its opposite, thus causing considerable difficulty in the work of interpretation. In the case of any element capable of having an opposite it is impossible to tell whether it is to be taken negatively or positively in the dream-thoughts.

I must emphasize that as yet this fact has by no means been understood. Nevertheless, it seems to give indications of an important characteristic of unconscious thinking which in all probability results in a process comparable to "judging." Instead of setting aside judgments, the unconscious forms "repressions." The repression may correctly be described as a stage intermediate between the defense reflex and condemnation.[2]

[1] The character of the comical which is referred to as its "dryness" also depends in the broadest sense upon the differentiation of the things spoken from the antics accompanying it.

[2] This very remarkable and still inadequately understood behavior of antagonistic relationships is probably not without value for the understanding of the symptom of negativism in neurotics and in the insane. Cf. the two latest works on the subject: Bleuler, "Über die negative Suggestibilität," *Psych.-Neurol. Wochenscrift*, 1904, and Otto Groos's *Zur Differential diagnostik negativistischer Phänomene*, also my review of the *Gegensinn der Urworte*, in *Jahrb. f. Psychoanalyse* II, 1910.

THE UNCONSCIOUS AS THE PSYCHIC STAGE OF THE WIT-WORK

Nonsense, or absurdity, which occurs so often in dreams and which has made them the object of so much contempt, has never really come into being as the result of an accidental shuffling of conceptual elements, but may in every case be proven to have been purposely admitted by the dream-work. Nonsense and absurdity are intended to express embittered criticism and scornful contradiction within the dream-thoughts. Absurdity in the dream-content thus stands for the judgment: "It's pure nonsense," expressed in dream-thoughts. In my *Interpretation of Dreams* I have placed great emphasis on the demonstration of this fact because I thought that I could in this manner most strikingly controvert the error expressed by many, that the dream is no psychic phenomenon at all—an error which bars the way to an understanding of the unconscious. Now we have learnt (in the analysis of certain tendency-witticisms) that nonsense in wit is made to serve the same purposes of expression. We also know that a non-sensical façade of a witticism is peculiarly adapted to enhance the psychic expenditure in the hearer and hence also to increase the amount to be discharged through laughter. Moreover, we must not forget that nonsense in wit is an end in itself, since the purpose of reviving the old pleasure in non-sense is one of the motives of the wit-work. There are other ways to regain the feeling of nonsense in order to derive pleasure from it; *caricature, exaggeration, parody,* and *travesty* utilize the same and thus produce "comical nonsense." If we subject these modes of expression to an analysis similar to the one used in studying wit, we shall find that there is no occasion in any of them for resorting to unconscious processes in our sense, for the purpose of getting explanations. We are now also in a position to understand why the "witty" character may be added as an embellishment to caricature, exaggeration, and parody; it is the manifold character of the performance upon the "psychic stage" [1] that makes this possible.

I am of the opinion that by transferring the wit-work into the system of the unconscious we have made a distinct contribution, since it makes it possible for us to understand the fact that the various techniques to which wit admittedly adheres are not its exclusive property. Many doubts, which have arisen in the beginning of our investigation of these techniques and which we were forced temporarily to leave, can now be conveniently cleared up. Hence, we shall give due consideration to the doubt which expresses itself in the assertion that the undeniable relation of wit to the unconscious is correct only for certain categories of tendency-wit, while we are ready to claim this relation for all forms and from all the stages of development. We may not shirk from testing this objection.

[1] An expression of G. T. Fechner's, which has acquired significance from the point of view of my conception.

We may assume that we deal with a sure case of wit-formation in the unconscious when it concerns witticisms that serve unconscious tendencies, or such as are strengthened by unconscious tendencies; that is, in most of the "cynical" witticisms. For in such cases the unconscious tendency draws the foreconscious thought down into the unconscious in order to remodel it there; a process to which the study of the psychology of the neuroses has added many analogies with which we are acquainted. But in the case of tendency-wit of other varieties, namely, harmless wit and the jest, this power seems to vanish and the relation of wit to the unconscious is an open question.

But now let us consider the case of the witty expression of a thought that is not without value in itself and that comes to the surface in the course of the association of mental processes. In order that this thought may become wit, it is of course necessary that it make a choice among the possible forms of expression in order to find the exact form that will bring along the gain in word-pleasure. We know from self-observation that this choice is not made by conscious attention, but the selection will certainly be better if the cathexis of the foreconscious thought sinks to the unconscious. For in the unconscious, as we have learnt from the dream-work, the paths of association emanating from a word are treated on a par with associations from objects. The cathexis from the unconscious presents by far the more favorable conditions for the selection of the expression. Moreover, we may assume without going farther that the possible expression which contains the gain in word-pleasure exerts a lowering effect on the still fluctuating self-command of the foreconscious, similar to that exerted in the first case by the unconscious tendency. As an explanation for the simpler case of the jest we may imagine that an ever-watchful intention of attaining the gain in word-pleasure seizes the opportunity offered in the foreconscious of again drawing the investing energy down into the unconscious, according to the familiar scheme.

I earnestly wish that it were possible for me on the one hand to present one decisive point in my conception of wit more clearly, and on the other hand to fortify it with cogent arguments. But as a matter of fact, it is not a question here of two failures, but of one and the same failure. I can give no clearer exposition because I have no further proof for my assumption. The latter developed from my study of the technique and from comparison with dream-work, and indeed from this one side only. I could then find that the dream-work as a whole fitted excellently the peculiarities of wit. This assumption is now accepted. If such a conclusion does not lead to a familiar, but rather a strange province, one that is novel to our modes of thought, the conclusion is called a "hypothesis," and the relation of the hypothesis to the material from which it was drawn is justly not accepted as "proof." The hypothesis is admitted as "proved" only if it can be reached by other ways and if it can be shown to be the juncture for other associations. But in view of the fact that our knowledge of unconscious processes has hardly begun, such proof cannot be had. Realizing then that we are on soil still virgin, we shall be content to project from our viewpoint of observation one narrow slender plank into the unexplored region.

We shall not build much on this foundation. If we correlate the different stages of wit to the mental dispositions favorable to them, we may say: The *jest* has its origin in the happy mood, which seems to have a peculiar tendency to lower the cathexis. The jest already makes use of all the characteristic techniques of wit and satisfies the fundamental conditions of the same through the choice of such an assortment of words or mental associations as will conform not only to the requirements for the production of pleasure, but also to the demands of the intelligent critic. We may conclude that the sinking of the mental energy to the unconscious stage, a process facilitated by the happy mood, has already taken place in the case of-the jest. The mood does away with this requirement in the case of *harmless* wit connected with the expression of a valuable thought; here we must assume a particular *personal adaptation* which finds it as easy to come to expression as it is for the foreconscious thought to sink for a moment into the unconscious. An ever watchful tendency to renew the original resultant pleasure of wit exerts thereby a lowering effect upon the still fluctuating foreconscious expression of the thought. Most people are probably capable of making jests when in a happy mood; aptitude for joking independent of the mood is found only in a few persons. Finally, the most powerful incentive for wit-work is the presence of strong tendencies which reach back into the unconscious and which indicate a particular fitness for witty productions; these tendencies might explain to us why the subjective conditions of wit are so frequently fulfilled in the case of neurotic persons. Even the most inapt person may become witty under the influence of strong tendencies.

DIFFERENCES BETWEEN WIT AND DREAMS

This last contribution, the explanation of wit-work in the first person, though still hypothetical, strictly speaking, ends our interest in wit. There still remains a short comparison of wit to the more familiar dream, and we may expect that, outside of the one agreement already considered, two such diverse mental activities should show nothing but differences. The most important difference lies in their social behavior. The dream is a perfectly asocial psychic product. It has nothing to tell to anyone else, having originated in an individual as a compromise between conflicting psychic forces it remains incomprehensible to the person himself and has therefore altogether no interest for anybody else. Not only does the dream find it unnecessary to place any value on intelligibleness, but it must even guard against being understood, as it would then be destroyed; it can only exist in disguised form. For this reason the dream may make use freely of the mechanism that controls unconscious thought processes to the extent of producing undecipherable distortions. Wit, on the other hand, is the most social of all those psychic functions whose aim is to gain pleasure. It often requires three persons, and the psychic process which it incites always requires the participation of at least one other person. It must therefore bind itself to the condition of intelligibleness; it may employ distortion made practicable in the unconscious through condensation and displacement, to no greater extent than can be deciphered by the intelligence of the third person. As for the rest, wit and dreams have developed in altogether different spheres of the psychic life, and are to be classed under widely separated categories of the psychological system. No matter how concealed, the dream is still a wish, while wit is a developed play. Despite its apparent unreality, the dream retains its relation to the great interests of life; it seeks to supply what is lacking through a regressive detour of hallucinations; and it owes its existence solely to the strong need for sleep during the night. Wit, on the other hand, seeks to draw a small amount of pleasure from the free and unencumbered activities of our psychic apparatus, and later to seize this pleasure as an incidental gain. It thus *secondarily* reaches to important functions relative to the outer world. The dream serves preponderantly to guard against pain, while wit serves to acquire pleasure; in these two aims all our psychic activities meet.

VII

WIT AND THE VARIOUS FORMS OF
THE COMIC

WE have approached the problems of the comic in an unusual manner. It appeared to us that wit, which is usually regarded as a sub-species of the comic, offered enough peculiarities to warrant our taking it directly under consideration, and thus it came about that we avoided discussing its relation to the more comprehensive category of the comic as long as it was possible to do so, yet we did not proceed without picking up on the way some hints that might be valuable for studying the comic. We found it easy to ascertain that the comic differs from wit in its social behavior. The comic is content with only two persons, one who finds the comical, and one in whom it is found. The third person to whom the comical may be imparted reinforces the comic process, but adds nothing new to it. In wit, however, this third person is indispensable for the completion of the pleasure-bearing process, while the second person may be omitted, especially when it is not a question of aggressive wit with a tendency. Wit is made, while the comical is found; it is found first of all in persons, and only later by transference may be seen also in objects, situations, and the like. We know, too, in the case of wit that it is not a strange person's, but one's own mental processes that contain the sources for the production of pleasure. In addition, we have heard that wit occasionally reopens inaccessible sources of the comic, and that the comic often serves wit as a façade to replace the fore-pleasure usually produced by the above described technique. All of this does not really point to a very simple relationship between wit and the comic. On the other hand, the problems of the comic have shown themselves to be so complicated, and have until now so successfully defied all attempts made by the philosophers to solve them, that we have not been able to justify the expectation of mastering it by a sudden stroke, so to speak, even if we approach it along the paths of wit. Incidentally we came provided with an instrument for investigating wit that had not yet been made use of by others; namely, the knowledge of dream-work. We have no similar advantage at our disposal for comprehending the comic, and we may therefore expect that we shall learn nothing about the nature of the comic other than that which we have already become aware of in wit; in so far as wit belongs to the comic and retains certain features of the same, unchanged or modified in its own nature.

THE NAÏVE

The species of the comic that is most closely allied to wit is the *naïve*. Like the comic the naïve is found universally and is not made as in the case of wit. The naïve cannot be made at all, while in the case of the pure comic the question of making or evoking the comical may be taken into account. The naïve must result without our intervention from the speech and actions of other persons who take the place of the *second* person in the comic or in wit. The naïve originates when one puts himself completely outside of inhibition, because it does not exist for him; that is, if he seems to overcome it without any effort. What conditions the function of the naïve is the fact that we are aware that the person does not possess this inhibition, otherwise we should not call it naïve but impudent, and instead of laughing we should be indignant. The effect of the naïve, which is irresistible, seems easy to understand. The expenditure of inhibition which we usually make suddenly becomes inapplicable when we hear the naïve and is discharged through laughter; as the removal of the inhibition is direct, and not the result of an incited operation, there is no need for a suspension of attention. We behave like the hearer in wit, to whom the economy of inhibition is given without any effort on his part.

Following our insight into the genesis of inhibitions, which we obtained while tracing the development of play into wit, it is not surprising to learn that the naïve is mostly found in children, although it may also be observed in uneducated adults, upon whom we look as children as far as their intellectual development is concerned. For the purposes of comparison with wit, naïve speech is naturally better adapted than naïve actions, for speech and not actions are the usual forms of expression employed by wit. It is significant, however, that naïve speeches, such as those of children, can without straining also be designated as "naïve witticisms." The points of agreement as well as demonstration between wit and naïveté will become clear to us upon consideration of a few examples.[1]

A little girl of three years was accustomed to hear from her German nurse the exclamatory word "Gesundheit" (God bless you!; literally, may you be healthy!) whenever she happened to sneeze. While suffering from a severe cold during which the profuse coughing and sneezing caused her considerable pain, she pointed to her chest and said to her father, "Daddy, Gesundheit hurts."

Another little girl of four years heard her parents refer to a Jewish ac-
___
[1] Given by the Editor.

*quaintance as a Hebrew, and on later hearing the latter's wife referred to
as Mrs. X, she corrected her mother, saying, "No, that is not her name; if
her husband is a Hebrew she is a Shebrew."*

In the first example the wit is produced through the use of a contiguous
association in the form of an abstract thought for the concrete action. The
child so often heard the word "Gesundheit" associated with sneezing that
she took it for the act itself. The second example may be designated
as word-wit formed by the technique of sound similarity. The child divided the word Hebrew into He-brew and having been taught the genders
of the personal pronouns, she naturally imagined that if the man is a Hebrew his wife must be a She-brew. Both examples could have originated
as real witticisms upon which we would have unwillingly bestowed a little
mild laughter. But as examples of naïveté they seem excellent and cause
loud laughter. But what is it here that produces the difference between
wit and naïveté? Apparently it is neither the wording nor the technique,
which is the same for both wit and the naïve, but a factor which at first
sight seems remote from both. It is simply a question whether we assume
that the speakers had the intention of making a witticism or whether we
assume that they—the children—wished to draw an earnest conclusion, a
conclusion held in good faith though based on uncorrected knowledge.
Only the latter case is one of naïveté. It is here that our attention is first
called to the mechanism in which the second person places himself into
the psychic process of the person who produces the wit.

The investigation of a third example will confirm this opinion. A
brother and a sister, the former ten and the latter twelve years old, produce a play of their own composition before an audience of uncles and
aunts. The scene represents a hut on the seashore. In the first act the two
dramatist-actors, a poor fisherman and his devoted wife, complain about
the hard times and the difficulty of getting a livelihood. The man decides
to sail over the wide ocean in his boat in order to seek wealth elsewhere,
and after a touching farewell the curtain is drawn. The second act takes
place several years later. The fisherman has come home rich with a big
bag of money and tells his wife, whom he finds waiting in front of the hut,
what good luck he has had in the far countries. His wife interrupts him
proudly, saying: "Nor have I been idle in the meanwhile," and opens the
hut, on whose floor the fisherman sees twelve large dolls representing children asleep. At this point of the drama the performers were interrupted by
an outburst of laughter on the part of the audience, a thing which they
could not understand. They stared dumbfounded at their dear relatives,
who had thus far behaved respectably and had listened attentively. The
explanation of this laughter lies in the assumption on the part of the audience that the young dramatists knew nothing as yet about the origin of
children, and were therefore in a position to believe that a wife would ac-

tually boast of bearing offspring during the prolonged absence of her husband, and that the husband would rejoice with her over it. But the results achieved by the dramatists on the basis of this ignorance may be designated as nonsense or absurdity.

These examples show that the naïve occupies a position midway between wit and the comic. As far as wording and contents are concerned, the naïve speech is identical with wit; it produces a misuse of words, a bit of nonsense, or an obscenity. But the psychic process of the first person or producer which, in the case of wit, offered us so much that was interesting and puzzling, is here entirely absent. The naïve person imagines that he is using his thoughts and expressions in a simple and normal manner; he has no other purpose in view, and receives no pleasure from his naïve production. All the characteristics of the naïve lie in the conception of the hearer, who corresponds to the third person in the case of wit. The producing person creates the naïve without any effort. The complicated technique, which in wit serves to paralyze the inhibition produced by critical reason, does not exist here, because the person does not possess this inhibition, and he can, therefore, readily produce the senseless or the obscene without any compromise. The naïve may be added to the realm of wit if it comes into existence after the important function of the censorship, as observed in the formula for wit-formation, has been reduced to zero.

If the affective determination of wit consists in the fact that both persons should be subject to about the same inhibitions or inner resistances, we may say now that the condition of the naïve consists in the fact that one person should have inhibitions which the other lacks. It is the person provided with inhibitions who understands the naïve, and it is he alone who gains the pleasure produced by the naïve. We can easily understand that this pleasure is due to the removal of inhibitions. Since the pleasure of wit is of the same origin—a kernel of word-pleasure and nonsense-pleasure, and a shell of removal- and release-pleasure—the similarity of this connection to the inhibition thus determines the inner relationship between the naïve and wit. In both cases pleasure results from the removal of inner inhibitions. But the psychic process of the recipient person (which in the naïve regularly corresponds with our ego, whereas in wit we may also put ourselves in place of the producing person) is by as much more complicated in the case of the naïve as it is simpler in the producing person in wit. For one thing, the naïve must produce the same effect upon the receiving person as wit does, this may be fully confirmed by our examples, for just as in wit the removal of the censorship has been made possible by the mere effort of hearing the naïve. But only a part of the pleasure created by the naïve admits of this explanation, in other cases of naïve utterances, even this portion would be endangered; as, for example, while listening to naïve obscenities. We would react to a naïve obscenity with the same indignation felt toward a real obscenity, were it not for the fact that another factor saves us from this indignation and at the same time furnishes the more important part of the pleasure derived from the naïve.

This other factor is the result of the condition mentioned before, namely, that in order to recognize the naïve we have to be cognizant of the fact that there are no inner inhibitions in the producing person. It is only when this is assured that we laugh instead of being indignant. Hence we take into consideration the psychic state of the producing person; we imagine ourselves in this same psychic state and endeavor to understand it by comparing it to our own. This putting ourselves into the psychic state of the producing person and comparing it with our own, results in an economy of expenditure which we discharge through laughter.

We might prefer the simpler explanation, namely, that when we reflect that the person has no inhibition to overcome, our indignation becomes superfluous; the laughing, therefore, results at the cost of economized indignation. In order to avoid this conception, which is, in general, misleading, I shall distinguish more sharply between two cases that I had treated as one in the above discussion. The naïve, as it appears to us, may either be in the nature of a witticism, as in our example, or an obscenity, or of anything generally objectionable; which becomes especially evident if the naïve is expressed not in speech but in action. This latter case is really misleading; for one might here assume, that the pleasure originates from the economized and transformed indignation. The first case, however, is the explanatory one. The naïve speech in the example "Hebrew" can produce the effect of a light witticism and give no cause for indignation; it is certainly the more rare, or the more pure and by far the more instructive case. In so far as we think that the child took the syllable "he" in "Hebrew" seriously, and without any additional reason identified it with the masculine personal pronoun, the increase in pleasure as a result of hearing it, has no longer anything to do with the pleasure of the wit. We shall now consider what has been said from two viewpoints, first how it came into existence in the mind of the child, and secondly, how it would occur to us. In following this comparison we find that the child has discovered an identity and has overcome barriers which exist in us, and by continuing still further it may express itself as follows: "If you wish to understand what you have heard, you may save yourself the expenditure necessary for holding these barriers in place." The expenditure which became freed by this comparison is the source of pleasure in the naïve, and is discharged through laughter; to be sure, it is the same expenditure which we would have converted into indignation if our understanding of the producing person, and in this case the nature of his utterance, had not precluded it. But if we take the case of the naïve joke as a model for the second case, viz., the objectionable naïve, we shall see that here, too, the economy in inhibition may originate directly from the comparison. That is, it is unnecessary for us to assume an incipient and then a strangulated indignation, an indignation corresponding to a different application of the freed expenditure, against which, in the case of wit, complicated defensive mechanisms are required.

SOURCE OF COMIC PLEASURE IN THE NAÏVE

This comparison and this economy of expenditure that occur, as the result of putting one's self into the psychic process of the producing person, can have an important bearing on the naïve, only if they do not belong to the naïve alone. As a matter of fact, we suspect that this mechanism which is so completely foreign to wit is a part—perhaps the essential part—of the psychic process of the comic. This aspect—it is perhaps the most important aspect of the naïve—thus represents the naïve as a form of the comic. Whatever is added to the wit-pleasure by the naïve speeches in our examples is "comical" pleasure. Concerning the latter, we might be inclined to make a general assumption, that this pleasure originates through an economized expenditure by comparing the utterance of some one else with our own. But since we are here in the presence of very broad views we shall first conclude our consideration of the naïve. The naïve would thus be a form of the comic, in so far as its pleasure originates from the difference in expenditure which results in our effort to understand the other person; and it resembles wit through the condition that the expenditure saved by the comparison must be an inhibition expenditure.[1]

Before concluding let us rapidly point out a few agreements and differences between the conceptions at which we have just arrived, and those that have been known for a long time in the psychology of the comic. The putting one's self into the psychic process of another and the desire to understand him is obviously nothing else than the so-called "comic burrowing" which has played a part in the analysis of the comic ever since the time of Jean Paul; the "comparing" of the psychic process of another with our own corresponds to a "psychological contrast," for which we here at last find a place, after we did not know what to do with it in wit. But in our explanation of comic pleasure we take issue with many authors who contend that this pleasure originates through the fluctuation of our attention to and fro between contrasting ideas. We are unable to see how such a mechanism could produce pleasure, and we point to the fact that in the comparing of contrasts there results a difference in ex-

---

[1] I have everywhere here identified the naïve with the naïve-comic, which is certainly not permissible in all cases. But it serves our purposes to study the characteristics of the naïve as seen in the "naïve joke" and the "naïve obscenity." It is our intention to proceed from here with the investigation of the nature of the comic.

penditure which, if not used for anything else, becomes capable of discharge and hence a source of pleasure.[1]

It is with misgiving only that we approach the problem of the comic. It would be presumptuous to expect from our efforts any decisive contribution to the solution of this problem after the works of a large number of excellent thinkers have not resulted in an explanation that is in every respect satisfactory. As a matter of fact, we intend simply to follow out into the province of the comic certain observations that have been found valuable in the study of wit.

OCCURRENCE AND ORIGIN OF THE COMIC

The comical appears primarily as an unintentional discovery in the social relations of human beings. It is found in persons—that is, in their movements, shapes, actions, and characteristic traits. In the beginning it is found probably only in their physical peculiarities and later on in their mental qualities, especially in the expression of the latter. Even animals and inanimate objects become comical as the result of a widely used method of personification. However, the comical can be considered apart from the person in whom it is found, if the conditions under which a person becomes comical can be discerned. Thus arises the comical situation, and this knowledge enables us to make a person comical at will by putting him into situations in which the conditions necessary for the comic are bound up with his actions. The discovery that it is in our power to make another person comical opens the way to unsuspected gains in comic pleasure, and forms the foundation of a highly developed technique. It is also possible to make one's self just as comical as others. The means which serve to make a person comical are transference into comic situations, imitations, disguise, unmasking, caricature, parody travesty, and the like. It is quite evident that these techniques may enter into the service of hostile or aggressive tendencies. A person may be made comical in order to render him contemptible or in order to deprive him of his claims to dignity and authority. But even if such a purpose were regularly at the bottom of all attempts to make a person comical this need not necessarily be the meaning of the spontaneous comic.

As a result of this superficial survey of the manifestations of the comic we can readily see that the comic originates from wide-spread sources, and that conditions so specialized as those found in the naïve cannot be expected in the case of the comic. In order to get a clue to the conditions

[1] Also Bergson (*Laughter, An Essay on the Meaning of the Comic,* translated by Brereton and Rothwell, The Macmillan Co., 1914) rejects with sound arguments this sort of explanation of comic pleasure, which has unmistakably been influenced by the effort to create an analogy to the laughing of a person tickled. The explanation of comic pleasure by Lipps, which might, in connection with his conception of the comic, be represented as an "unexpected trifle," is of an entirely different nature.

that are applicable to the comic the selection of the first example is most important. We will examine first the comic movement because we remember that the most primitive stage performance, the pantomime, uses this means to make us laugh. The answer to the question, "Why do we laugh at the actions of the clowns?", would be that their actions appear to us immoderate and inappropriate; that is, we really laugh over the excessive expenditure of energy. Let us look for the same condition outside of the manufactured comic, that is, under circumstances where it may unintentionally be found. The child's motions do not appear to us comical, even if he jumps and fidgets, but it is comical to see a little boy or girl follow with the tongue the movement of his pen-holder when he is trying to master the art of writing; we see in these additional motions a superfluous expenditure of energy which under similar conditions we save. In the same way we find it comical to see unnecessary motions or even marked exaggeration of expressive motions in adults. Among the genuinely comic cases we might mention the motions made by the bowler after he has released the ball while he is following its course as though he were still able to control it. All grimaces which exaggerate the normal expression of the emotions are comical, even if they are involuntary, as in the case of persons suffering from St. Vitus' dance (chorea). The impassioned movements of a modern orchestra leader will appear comical to every unmusical person, who cannot understand why they are necessary. Indeed, the comic element found in bodily shapes and physiognomy is a branch of the comic of motion, in that they are conceived as if they were the result of motion that has been carried too far or motion that is purposeless. Wide exposed eyes, a crook-shaped nose bent towards the mouth, handle-like ears, a hunch back, and all similar physical defects probably produce a comical impression only in so far as the movements that would be necessary to produce these features are imagined, whereby the nose and other parts of the body are pictured as more movable than they actually are. It is certainly comical if some one can "wiggle his ears," and it would undoubtedly be a great deal more comical if he could raise and lower his nose. A large part of the comical impression that animals make upon us is due to the fact that we perceive in them movements which we cannot imitate.

COMIC OF MOTION

But how does it come about that we laugh as soon as we have recognized that the actions of some one else are immoderate and inappropriate? I believe that we laugh because we compare the motions observed in others with those which we ourselves should produce if we were in their place. The two persons must naturally be compared in accordance with the same standard, but this standard is my own innervation expenditure connected with my idea of motion in the one case as well as the other. This assertion is in need of discussion and amplification.

What we are here putting into juxtaposition is, on the one hand, the psychic expenditure of a given idea, and on the other hand, the content of this idea. We maintain that the former is not primarily and principally independent of the latter—the content of the idea—particularly because the idea of something great requires a larger expenditure than the idea of something small. As long as we are concerned only with the idea of different coarse movements, we shall encounter no difficulties in the theoretical determination of our thesis or in establishing its proof through observation. It will be shown that in this case an attribute of the idea actually coincides with an attribute of the object conceived, although psychology warns us of confusions of this sort.

I obtain an idea of a definite coarse movement by performing this motion or by imitating it, and in so doing I set a standard for this motion in my feelings of innervation.[1]

Now if I perceive a similar more or less coarse motion in some one else, the surest way to the understanding—to apperception—of the same is to carry it out imitatively, and the comparison will then enable me to decide in which motion I expended more energy. Such an impulse to imitate certainly arises on perceiving a movement. But in reality I do not carry out the imitation any more than I still spell out words simply because I have learned to read by means of spelling. Instead of imitating the movement with my muscles I substitute the idea of the same through my memory traces of the expenditures necessary for similar motions. Perceiving, or "thinking," differs above all from acting or carrying out things, through the fact that it entails a very much smaller displacement of energy and keeps the main expenditure from being discharged. But how is the quantitative factor, the greater or lesser element of the movement perceived, given expression in the idea? And if the representation of the quantity is left off from the idea that is composed of qualities, how am I to differentiate the ideas of different big movements, how am I to compare them?

Here, physiology shows the way in that it teaches us that even while an idea is in the process of conception innervations proceed to the muscles, which naturally represent only a moderate expenditure. It is now easy to assume that this expenditure of innervation which accompanies the conception of the idea is utilized to represent the quantitative factor

[1] The recollection of this innervation expenditure will remain the essential part of the idea of this motion, and there will always be methods of thought in my psychic life in which the idea will be represented by nothing else but this expenditure. In other connections a substitute for this element may possibly be put in the form of other ideas, for instance the visual idea of the object of the motion, or it may be put in the form of the word-idea; and in certain types of abstract thought a sign instead of the full content itself may suffice.

of the idea, and that when a great motion is imagined it is greater than it would be in the case of a smaller one. The conception of greater motions would thus actually be greater, that is, it would be a conception accompanied by greater expenditure.

IDEATIONAL MIMICRY

Observation shows directly that human beings are in the habit of expressing the big and small things in their ideation content by means of a manifold expenditure or by means of a sort of *ideational mimicry*.

When a child or a person of the common people or one belonging to a certain race imparts or depicts something, one can easily observe that he is not content to make his ideas intelligible to the hearer through the choice of correct words alone, but that he also represents the contents of the same through his expressive motions. Thus, he designates the quantities and intensities of "a high mountain" by raising his hands over his head, and those of "a little dwarf" by lowering his hand to the ground. If he controlled the habit of depicting with his hands, he would nevertheless do it with his voice, and if he should also control his voice, one may be sure that in picturing something big he would distend his eyes, and in describing something little he would press his eyes together. It is not his own affects that he thus expresses, but it is really the content of what he imagines.

Shall we now assume that this need for mimicry is first aroused through the demand for imparting, whereas a good part of this manner of representation still escapes the attention of the hearer? I rather believe that this mimicry, though less vivid, exists even if all imparting is left out of the question, that it comes about when the person imagines for himself alone, or thinks of something in a graphic manner; that then such a person, just as in talking, expresses through his body the idea of big and small which manifests itself at least through a change of innervation in the facial expressions and sensory organs. Indeed, I can imagine that the bodily innervation which is consensual to the content of the idea conceived is the beginning and origin of mimicry for purposes of communication. For, in order to be in a position to serve this purpose, it is only necessary to increase it and make it conspicuous to the other. When I take the view that this "expression of the ideation content" should be added to the expression of the emotions, which are known as physical by-products of psychic processes, I am well aware that my observations which refer to the category of big and small do not exhaust the subject. I myself could add still other things, even before reaching to the phenomenon of tension through which a person physically indicates the accumulation of his attention and the *niveau* of abstraction upon which his thoughts happen to rest. I maintain that this subject is very important, and I believe that tracing the ideation mimicry in other fields of æsthetics would be just as useful for the understanding of the comic as it is here.

To return to the comic movement, I repeat that with the perception of a certain motion the impulse to conceive it will be given through a certain expenditure. In the "desire to understand," in the apperception of this movement I produce a certain expenditure, and I behave in this part of the psychic process just as if I put myself in the place of the person observed. Simultaneously I probably grasp the aim of the motion, and through former experiences I am able to estimate the amount of expenditure necessary to attain this aim. I thereby drop out of consideration the person observed and behave as if I myself wished to attain the aim of the motion. These two ideational possibilities depend on a comparison of the motion observed, with my own inhibited motion. In the case of an immoderate or inappropriate movement on the part of the other, my greater expenditure for understanding becomes inhibited in *statu nascendi* during the mobilization as it were, it is declared superfluous and stands free for further use or for discharge through laughing. If other favorable conditions supervened, this would be the nature of the origin of pleasure in comic movement—an innervation expenditure which, when compared with one's own motion, becomes an inapplicable surplus.

COMPARISON OF TWO KINDS OF EXPENDITURE AS PLEASURE-SOURCES

We now note that we must continue our discussion by following two different paths; first, to determine the conditions for the discharge of the surplus; secondly, to test whether the other cases of the comic can be conceived similarly to our conception of comic motion.

We shall turn first to the latter task and after considering comic movement and action we shall turn to the comic found in the psychic activities and peculiarities of others.

As an example of this kind we may consider the comical nonsense produced by ignorant students at examinations; it is more difficult, however, to give a simple example of peculiarities of character. We must not be confused by the fact that nonsense and foolishness which so often act in a comical manner are nevertheless not perceived as comical in all cases, just as the same things which once made us laugh because they seemed comical may appear later as contemptible and hateful. This fact, which we must not forget to take into account, simply points to the fact that besides the comparison familiar to us other relations come into consideration for the comic effect—conditions which we can investigate in other connections.

The comic found in the mental and psychic attributes of another person is apparently again the result of a comparison between him and my own ego. But it is remarkable that it is a comparison which has more often furnished the opposite result than in the case of comic movement and action. In the latter case is was comical if the other person exerted a greater expenditure than I believed necessary for me; in the case of psychic activity it is just the reverse, it is comical if the other person economizes in expenditure, which I consider indispensable, for nonsense and foolishness are nothing but inferior functions. In the first case I laugh because he makes it too difficult for himself, and in the latter case because he makes it too easy for himself. As to the comic effect, it is obviously only a question of the difference between the two cathexes expenditures—the one of empathy,[1] and the other of the ego—and not in whose favor this difference inclines. This peculiarity, which at first confuses our judgment, disappears, however, when we consider that it is in accord with our personal development towards a higher stage of culture to limit our muscular work and increase our mental work. By heightening our mental expenditure we produce a diminution of motion expenditure for the same activity. Our machines bear witness to this cultural success.[2]

Thus, it coincides with a uniform understanding that that person appears comical to us who puts forth too much expenditure in his physical activities and too little in his mental activities; and it cannot be denied that in both cases our laughing is the expression of a pleasurably perceived superiority which we adjudge to ourselves in comparison with him. If the relation in both cases becomes reversed, that is, if the somatic expenditure of the other is less and the psychic expenditure greater, then we no longer laugh, but are struck with amazement and admiration.[3]

COMIC OF SITUATION

The origin of the comic pleasure discussed here, that is, the origin of such pleasure in a comparison of the other person with one's own self in respect to the difference between the empathy expenditure and one's own expenditure—is genetically probably most important. It is certain, however, that it is not the only one. We have learned before to disregard any such comparison between the other person and one's self, and to obtain the pleasure-bringing difference from one side only, either from empathy, or from the processes in one's own ego, proving thereby that the feeling of superiority bears no essential relations to comic pleasure. A comparison is indispensable, however, for the origin of this pleasure, and we find this comparison between two energy expenditures which rapidly follow each other and refer to the same function. It is produced either in ourselves by way of empathy into the other, or we find it without any such

1 From the Greek *en—pathein*, to read oneself into another person or situation.
2 "What one has not in his head," as the saying goes, "he must have in his legs."
3 The problem has been greatly confused by the general conditions determining the comic, whereby the comic pleasure is seen to have its source now in a too-muchness and now in a not-enoughness. Cf. Lipps, l.c. p. 47.

relation in our own psychic processes. The first case, in which the other person still plays a part, though not in comparison with the ego, results when the pleasure-producing difference of cathexes expenditures comes into existence through outer influences which we can comprehend as a "situation," for which reason this species of comic is also called the "comic of the situation." The peculiarities of the person who furnishes the comic do not here come into essential consideration; we laugh when we admit to ourselves that had we been placed in the same situation we should have done the same thing. Here we draw the comic from the relation of the individual to the often all-too-powerful outer world, which is represented in the psychic processes of the individual by the conventions and necessities of society, and even by his bodily needs. A typical example of the latter is when a person engaged in an activity, which claims all his psychic forces, is suddenly disturbed by a pain or excremental need. The opposite case which furnishes us the comic difference through empathy, lies between the great interest which existed before the disturbance occurred and the minimum left for his psychic activity after the disturbance made its appearance. The person who furnishes us this difference again becomes comical through inferiority; but he is only inferior in comparison with his former ego and not in comparison with us, for we know that in a similar case we could not have behaved differently. It is remarkable, however, that we find this inferiority of the person only in the case of empathy, that is, we can only find it comical in the other, whereas we ourselves are conscious only of painful emotions when such or similar embarrassments happen to us. By keeping away the painful from our own person we are probably first enabled to enjoy as pleasurable that difference which resulted from the comparison of the changing cathexes.

COMIC OF EXPECTATION

The other source of the comic, which we find in our own transformations of cathexes, lies in our relations of the future, which we are accustomed to anticipate through our ideas of expectation. I assume that a quantitatively determined expenditure underlies our every idea of expectation, which in case of disappointment becomes diminished by a certain difference, and I again refer to the observations made before concerning "ideational mimicry." But it seems to me easier to demonstrate the real mobilized cathectic expenditure for the cases of expectation. It is well known concerning a whole series of cases that the manifestation of expectation is formed by motor preliminaries; this is first of all true of cases in which the expected events make demands on my motility, and these preparations are quantitatively determinable without anything further. If I am expecting to catch a ball thrown at me, I put my body in states of tension in order to enable me to withstand the collision with the ball, and the superfluous motions which I make if the ball turns out to be light make me look comical to the spectators. I allow myself to be misled by the expectation to exert an immoderate expenditure of motion. A similar thing happens if, for example, I lift out a basket of fruit which I took to be heavy but which was hollow and formed out of wax in order to deceive me. By its upward jerk my arm betrays the fact that I have prepared a superfluous innervation for this purpose and hence I am laughed at. In fact there is at least one case in which the expectation expenditure can be directly demonstrated by means of physiological experimentation with animals. In Pavlov's experiments with salivary secretions of dogs who, provided with salivary fistulæ, are shown different kinds of food, it is noticed that the amount of saliva secreted through the fistulæ depends on whether the conditions of the experiment have strengthened or disappointed the dogs' expectation to be fed with the food shown them.

Even where the thing expected lays claims only to my sensory organs, and not to my motility, I may assume that the expectation manifests itself in a certain motor emanation causing tension of the senses, and I may even conceive the suspension of attention as a motor activity which is equivalent to a certain amount of expenditure. Moreover, I can presuppose that the preparatory activity of expectation is not independent of the amount of the expected impression, but that I represent mimically the bigness and smallness of the same by means of a greater or smaller preparatory expenditure, just as in the case of imparting something and in the case of thinking when there is no expectation. The expectation expenditure naturally will be composed of many components, and also for my disappointment diverse factors will come into consideration; it is not only a question whether the realized event is perceptibly greater or smaller than the expected one, but also whether the expectation is worthy of the great interest which I had offered for it. In this manner I am instructed to consider, besides the expenditure for the representation of bigness and smallness (the conceptual mimicry), also the expenditure for the tension of attention (expectation expenditure), and in addition to these two expenditures there is in all cases the abstraction expenditure. But these other forms of expenditure can easily be reduced to the one of bigness and smallness, for what we call more interesting, more sublime, and even more abstract, are only particularly qualified special cases of what is greater. Let us add to this that, among other things, Lipps holds that the quantitative, not the qualitative, contrast is primarily the source of comic pleasure, and we shall be altogether content to have chosen the comic element of motion as the starting-point of our investigation.

In discussing Kant's thesis, "The comic is an expectation dwindled into nothing," Lipps made the attempt in his book, often cited here, to trace the comic pleasure altogether to expectation. Despite the many instructive and valuable results which this attempt brought to light, I should like to agree with the criticism expressed by other authors, namely, that Lipps has formulated a field of origin of the comic which is much too narrow, and that he could not subject its phenomena to his formula without much forcing.

CARICATURE

Human beings are not satisfied to enjoy the comic as they encounter it in life, but they aim to produce it intentionally. Thus, we discover more of the nature of the comic by studying the methods employed in producing the comic. Above all one can produce comical elements in one's personality for the amusement of others, by making one's self appear awkward or stupid. One then produces the comic exactly as if one were really so, by complying with the condition of comparison which leads to the difference of expenditure; but one does not make himself laughable or contemptible through this; indeed, under certain circumstances one can even secure admiration. The feeling of superiority does not come into existence in the other when he knows that the actor is only shamming, and this furnishes us a good new proof that the comic is independent in principle of the feeling of superiority.

To make someone else comical, the method most commonly employed is to transfer him into situations wherein he becomes comical regardless of his personal qualities, as a result of human dependence upon external circumstances, especially social factors; in other words, some one resorts to the comical situation. This transferring into a comic situation may be real as in practical jokes, such as placing the foot in front of one so that he falls like a clumsy person, or making some one appear stupid by utilizing his credulity to make him believe some nonsense, etc., or it can be feigned by means of speech or play. It is a good aid in aggression, in the service of which, production of the comic is wont to place itself, in order that the comic pleasure may be independent of the reality of the comic situation; thus every person is really defenseless against being made comical.

But there are still other means of making one comical which deserve special attention and which in part also show new sources of comic pleasure. *Imitation,* for example, belongs here; it accords the hearer an extraordinary amount of pleasure and makes its subject comical, even if it still keeps away from the exaggeration of caricature. It is much easier to fathom the comic effect of caricature than that of simple imitation. Caricature, parody and travesty like their practical counterpart unmasking, are directed against persons and objects who command authority and respect and who are exalted in some sense. These are procedures which tend to degrade.[1] In the transferred psychic sense, the exalted is equivalent to something great and I want to make the statement, or more accurately to repeat the statement, that psychic greatness like somatic greatness is exhibited by means of an increased expenditure. It needs little observation to ascertain that when I speak of the exalted I give a different innervation to my voice, I change my facial expression, and attempt to bring my entire bearing as it were into complete accord with the dignity of that which I present. I impose upon myself a dignified restriction, not much different than if I were coming into the presence of an illustrious personage, monarch, or prince of science. I can scarcely err when I assume that this added innervation of conceptual mimicry corresponds to an increased expenditure. The third case of such an added expenditure I readily find when I indulge in abstract trains of thought instead of in the concrete and plastic ideas. If I can now imagine that the mentioned processes for degrading the illustrious are quite ordinary, that during their activity I need not be on my guard and in whose ideal presence I may, to use a military formula, put myself "at ease," all that saves me the added expenditure of dignified restriction. Moreover, the comparison of this manner of presentation instigated by empathy with the manner of presentation to which I have been hitherto accustomed, which seeks to present itself at the same time, again produces a difference in expenditure which can be discharged through laughter.

As is known, caricature brings about the degradation by rendering prominent one feature, comic in itself, from the entire picture of the exalted object, a feature which would be overlooked if viewed with the entire picture. Only by isolating this feature can the comic effect be obtained which spreads in our memory over the whole picture. This has, however, this condition; the presence of the exalted element must not force us into a disposition of reverence. Where such a comical feature is really lacking, caricature then unhesitatingly creates it by exaggerating one that is not comical in itself. It is again characteristic of the origin of comic pleasure that the effect of the caricature is not essentially impaired through such a falsifying of reality.

UNMASKING

Parody and *travesty* accomplish the degradation of the exalted by other means; they destroy the uniformity between the attributes of persons familiar to us and their speech and actions; by replacing either the illustrious persons or their utterances by lowly ones. Therein they differ from caricature, but not through the mechanism of the production of the

---

[1] Degradation: A. Bain (*The Emotions and the Will*, 2nd Ed., 1865) states: "The occasion of the ludicrous is the degradation of some person of interest possessing dignity, in circumstances that excite no other strong emotion" (p. 248).

comic pleasure. The same mechanism also holds true in *unmasking*, which comes into consideration only where some one has attached to himself dignity and authority which in reality should be taken from him. We have seen the comic effect of unmasking through several examples of wit, for example, in the story of the fashionable lady who in her first labor-pains cries: "Ah, mon Dieu!" but to whom the physician paid no attention until she screamed: "A-a-a-ai-e-e-e-e-e-E-E-E!" Being now acquainted with the character of the comic, we can no longer dispute that this story is really an example of comical unmasking and has no just claim to the term witticism. It recalls wit only through the setting, through the technical means of "representation through a trifle"; here it is the cry which was found sufficient to indicate the point. The fact remains, however, that our feeling for the niceties of speech, when we call on it for judgment, does not oppose calling such a story a witticism. We can find the explanation for this in the reflection that usage of speech does not enter scientifically into the nature of wit so far as we have evolved it by means of this painstaking examination. As it is a function of the activities of wit to reopen hidden sources of comic pleasure, every artifice which does not bring to light the barefaced comic may in looser analogy be called a witticism. This is especially true in the case of unmasking, though in other methods of comic-making the appellation also holds good.[1]

In the mechanism of "unmasking" one can also utilize those processes of comic-making already known to us which degrade the dignity of individuals by calling attention to one of the common human frailties, but particularly to the dependence of his mental functions upon physical needs. Unmasking them becomes equivalent to the reminder: This or that one who is admired like a demigod is only a human being like you and me after all. Moreover, all efforts in this mechanism serve to lay bare the monotonous psychic automatism which is behind wealth and apparent freedom of psychic achievements. We have become acquainted with examples of such "unmasking" through the marriage agent's witticisms and at that time we felt doubt whether we could rightly count these stories as wit. Now we can decide with more certainty that the anecdote of the echo who reinforces all assertions of the marriage agent and in the end reinforces the latter's admission that the bride has a hunchback with the exclamation "And what a hunch!" is essentially a comic story, an example of unmasking of the psychic automatism. But here the comic story serves only as a façade; to any one who wishes to note the hidden meaning of the marriage agent, the whole remains a splendidly put together piece of wit. He who does not penetrate so far sees only the comic story. The same

---

[1] "Thus, every conscious and clever evocation of the comic is called wit, be it the comic of views or situations. Naturally we cannot use this view of wit here." Lipps, l. c., p. 78.

is true of the other witticism of the agent who, to refute an objection, finally confirms the truth through the exclamation: "But who in the world would lend them anything?" This is a comic unmasking which serves as a façade for a witticism. Still the character of the wit is here quite evident, as the speech of the agent is at the same time an expression through the opposite. In trying to prove that the people are rich he proves at the same time that they are not rich but very poor. Wit and the comic unite here and teach us that a statement may be simultaneously witty and comical.

We eagerly grasp the opportunity to return from the comic of unmasking to wit, for our real task is to explain the relation between wit and comic and not to determine the nature of the comic. Hence to the case of uncovering the psychic automatism, wherein our feeling left us in doubt as to whether the matter was comical or witty, we add another, the case of nonsense-wit, wherein likewise wit and the comic fuse. But our investigation will ultimately show us that in this second case the meeting of wit and comic may be theoretically deductable.

In the discussion of the techniques of wit we have found that giving free play to such modes of thinking as are common in the unconscious, which in consciousness are conceived only as "faulty thinking," furnishes the technical means of a great many witticisms. We had then doubted their witty character and were inclined to classify them simply as comic stories. We could come to no decision regarding our uncertainty because in the first place the real character of wit was not familiar to us. Later we found this character by following the analogy to the dream-work, as to the compromise formed by the wit-work between the demands of the rational critic and the impulse not to abandon the old word-pleasure and nonsense-pleasure. What thus came into existence as a compromise, when the foreconscious thought was left for a moment to unconscious elaboration, satisfied both demands in all cases, but it presented itself to the critic, in various forms and had to stand various criticisms from it. In one case wit succeeded in surreptitiously assuming the form of an unimportant but none the less admissible proposition; a second time it smuggled itself into the expression of a valuable thought. But within the outer limit of the compromise activity it made no effort to satisfy the critic, and defiantly utilizing the pleasure-sources at its disposal, it appeared before the critic as pure nonsense. It had no fear of provoking contradiction because it could rely on the fact that the hearer would decipher the distortion of the expression through the operation of his unconscious and thus give back to it its meaning.

Now in what case will wit appear to the critic as nonsense? Particularly when it makes use of those modes of thought, which are common in the unconscious, but forbidden in conscious thought; that is, when it resorts to faulty thinking. Some of the modes of thinking, of the unconscious, have also been retained in conscious thinking, for example, many forms of indirect expression, allusions, etc., even though their conscious use has to be much restricted. Using these techniques, wit will arouse little or no opposition on the part of the critic; but this only happens when it also uses that technical means with which conscious thought no longer cares to have anything to do. Wit can still further avoid offending, if it disguises the faulty thinking by investing it with a semblance of logic as in the story of the fancy cake and liqueur, salmon with mayonnaise, and similar ones. But should it present the faulty thinking undisguised, the critic is sure to protest.

THE MEETING OF WIT AND THE COMIC

In this case, something else comes to the aid of wit. The faulty thinking, which as a form of thinking of the unconscious, wit utilizes for its technique, appears comical to the critic, although this is not necessarily the case. The conscious giving of free play to the unconscious and to those forms of thinking which are rejected as faulty, furnishes a means for the production of comic pleasure. This can be easily understood, as a greater expenditure is surely needed for the production of the foreconscious cathexis than for the giving of free play to the unconscious. When we hear the thought which is formed like one from the unconscious we compare it to its correct form, and this results in a difference of expenditure which gives origin to comic pleasure. A witticism which makes use of such faulty thinking as its technique, and therefore appears absurd, can produce a comic impression at the same time. If we do not strike the trail of the wit, there remains to us only the comic or funny story.

The story of the borrowed kettle, which showed a hole on being returned, whereupon the borrower excused himself by stating that in the first place he had not borrowed the kettle; secondly, that it already had a hole when he borrowed it; and thirdly, that he had returned it intact without any hole, is an excellent example of a purely comic effect through giving free play to one's unconscious modes of thinking. Just this mutual neutralization of several thoughts, each of which is well motivated in itself, is the province of the unconscious. Corresponding to this, the dream in which the unconscious thoughts become manifest, also shows an absence of either —or.[1] These are expressed by putting the thoughts next to one another. In that dream example given in my *Interpretation of Dreams*,[2] which in spite of its complication I have chosen as a type of the work of interpretation, I seek to rid myself of the reproach that I have not removed the pains of a patient by psychic treatment. My arguments are: 1. she is herself to blame for her illness, because she does not wish to accept my solution, 2. her

[1] At the most this is inserted by the dreamer as an explanation.
[2] l. c., pp. 195–207.

pains are of organic origin, therefore none of my concern, 3. her pains are connected with her widowhood, for which I am certainly not to blame, 4. her pains resulted from an injection with a dirty syringe, which was given by another. All these motives follow one another just as though one did not exclude the other. In order to escape the reproach that it was nonsense I had to insert the words "either—or" instead of the "and" of the dream.

A similar comical story is the one which tells of a blacksmith in a Hungarian village who has committed a crime punishable by death; the burgomaster, however, decreed that not the smith but a tailor was to be hanged, as there were two tailors in the village but only one blacksmith, and the crime had to be expiated. Such a displacement of guilt from one person to another naturally contradicts all laws of conscious logic, but in no ways the mental trends of the unconscious. I am in doubt whether to call this story comic, and still I put the story of the kettle among the witticisms. Now I admit that it is far more correct to designate the latter as comic rather than witty. But now I understand how it happens that my feelings, usually so reliable, can leave me in the lurch as to whether this story be comic or witty. The case in which I cannot come to a conclusion through my feelings is the one in which the comic results through the uncovering of modes of thought which exclusively belong to the unconscious. A story of that kind can be comic and witty at the same time; but it will impress me as being witty even if it be only comic, because the use of the faulty thinking of the unconscious reminds me of wit, just as in the case of the arrangements for the uncovering of the hidden comic discussed before.

I must lay great stress upon making clear this most delicate point of my analysis, namely, the relation of wit to the comic, and will therefore supplement what has been said with some negative statements. First of all, I call attention to the fact that the case of the meeting of wit and comic treated here is not identical with the preceding one. I grant it is a fine distinction, but it can be drawn with certainty. In the preceding case the comic originated from the unmasking of the psychic automatism. This is in no way peculiar to the unconscious alone and it does not at all play a conspicuous part in the technique of wit. Unmasking appears only accidentally in relation to wit, in that it serves another technique of wit, namely, representation through the opposite. But in the case of giving free play to unconscious ways of thinking the union of wit and comic is an essential one, because the same method which is used by the first person in wit as the technique of releasing pleasure, will naturally produce comic pleasure in the third person.

We might be tempted to generalize this last case and seek the relation of wit to the comic in the fact that the effect of wit upon the third person follows the mechanism of comic pleasure. But there is no question about that; contact with the comic is not in any way found in all nor even in most witticisms; in most cases wit and the comic can be cleanly separated. As often as wit succeeds in escaping the appearance of absurdity, which is to say in most witticisms of double meaning or of allusion, one cannot discover any effect in the hearer resembling the comic. One can make the test with examples previously cited or with some new ones given here.

Congratulatory telegram to be sent to a gambler on his 70th birthday: *"Trente et quarante"* [1] (word-division with allusion).

Madame de *Maintenon* was called Madame de *Maintenant* (modification of a name).

We might further believe that at least all jokes with nonsense façades appear comical and must impress us as such. But I recall here the fact that such witticisms often have a different effect on the hearer, calling forth confusion and a tendency to rejection (see footnote, p. 212). Therefore, it evidently depends on whether the nonsense of the wit appears comical or common plain nonsense, and the conditions for this we have not yet investigated. Accordingly, we hold to the conclusion that wit, judging by its nature, can be separated from the comic, and that it unites with it on the one hand, only in certain special cases, on the other in the tendency to gain pleasure from intellectual sources.

In the course of these examinations concerning the relations of wit and the comic there revealed itself to us that distinction which we must emphasize as most significant, and which at the same time points to a psychologically important characteristic of the comic. We had to transfer to the unconscious the source of wit-pleasure; there is no occasion which can be discovered for the same localization of the comic. On the contrary, all analyses which we have made thus far indicate that the source of comic pleasure lies in the comparison of two expenditures, both of which we must adjudge to the foreconscious. Wit and the comic can above all be differentiated in the psychic localization; *wit is, so to speak, the contribution to the comic from the sphere of the unconscious.*

COMIC OF IMITATION

We need not blame ourselves for digressing from the subject, for the relation of wit to the comic really furnished the occasion which impelled us to examine the comic. But it is time for us to return to the point under discussion, to the treatment of the means which serve to produce the comic. We have advanced the discussion of caricature and unmasking, because from both of them we can borrow several points of similarity for the analysis of the comic of *imitation*. Imitation is mostly replaced by caricature, which is an exaggeration of certain otherwise not striking

---

[1] "Trente et quarante" is a gambling game.

traits, and also bears the character of degradation. Still this does not seem to exhaust the nature of imitation; it is incontestable that in itself it represents an extraordinarily rich source of comic pleasure, for we laugh particularly over faithful imitations. It is not easy to give a satisfactory explanation of this if we do not accept Bergson's view,[1] according to which the comic of imitation is put next to the comic produced by unmasking the psychic automatism. Bergson believes that everything gives a comic impression which manifests itself in the shape of a machine-like inanimate movement in the human being. His law is that "the attitudes, gestures, and movements of the human body are laughable in exact proportion as that body reminds us of a mere machine." He explains the comic of imitation by connecting it with a problem formulated by Pascal in his *Thoughts,* why is it that we laugh at the comparison of two faces that are alike although neither of them excites laughter by itself. "The truth is that a really living life should never repeat itself. Wherever there is repetition or complete similarity, we always suspect some mechanism at work behind the living." Analyze the impression you get from two faces that are too much alike, and you will find that you are thinking of two copies cast in the same mould, or two impressions of the same soul, or two reproductions of the same negative—in a word, of some manufacturing process or other. This deflection of life towards the mechanical is here the real cause of laughter. We might say it is the degradation of the human to the mechanical or inanimate. If we accept these winning arguments of Bergson, it is moreover not difficult to subject his view to our own formula. Taught by experience that every living being is different, and demands a definite amount of expenditure from our understanding, we find ourselves disappointed when, as a result of a perfect agreement or deceptive imitation, we need no new expenditure. But we are disappointed in the sense of being relieved, and the expenditure of expectation which has become superfluous is discharged through laughter. The same formula will also cover all cases of comic rigidity considered by Bergson, such as professional habits, fixed ideas, and modes of expression which are repeated on every occasion. All these cases aim to compare the expenditure of expectation with what is commonly required for the understanding, whereby the greater expectation depends on observation of individual variety and human plasticity. Hence in imitation the source of comic pleasure is not the comic of situation but that of expectation.

As we trace the comic pleasure in general to comparison, it is incumbent upon us to investigate also the comic element of comparison itself, which likewise serves as a means of producing the comic. Our interest in this question will be enhanced when we recall that in the case of comparison

---

[1] Bergson: Le Rire, essai sur la signification du comique.

the "feeling" as to whether something was to be classed as witty or merely comical often left us in the lurch.

The subject really deserves more attention than we can bestow upon it. The main quality for which we ask in comparison is whether it is pertinent, that is, whether it really calls our attention to an existing agreement between two different objects. The original pleasure in refinding the same thing (Groos), is not the only motive which favors the use of comparison. Besides this there is the fact that comparison is capable of a utilization which facilitates intellectual work; when for example, as is usually the case, one compares the less familiar to the more familiar, the abstract to the concrete, and explains through this comparison the more strange and the more difficult objects. With every such comparison, especially of the abstract to the concrete, there is a certain degradation and a certain economy in abstraction expenditure (in the sense of a conceptual mimicry), yet this naturally does not suffice to render prominent the character of the comic. The latter does not emerge suddenly from the freed pleasure of the comparison but comes gradually; there are many cases which only touch the comic, in which one might doubt whether they show the comic character. The comparison undoubtedly becomes comical when the *niveau* difference of the expenditure of abstraction between the two things compared becomes increased, if something serious and strange, especially of intellectual or moral nature is compared to something banal and lowly. The former release of pleasure and the contribution from the conditions of conceptual mimicry may perhaps explain the gradual change—which is determined by quantitative relations—from the universally pleasurable to the comic, which takes place during the comparison. I am certainly avoiding misunderstandings by emphasizing that I deduce the comic pleasure in the comparison, not from the contrast of the two things compared but from the difference of the two abstraction expenditures. The strange which is difficult to grasp, the abstract and really intellectually sublime, through its alleged agreement with a familiar lowly one, in the imagination of which every abstraction expenditure disappears, is now itself unmasked as something equally lowly. The comic of comparison thus becomes reduced to a case of degradation.

The comparison, as we have seen above, can now be witty without a trace of comic admixture, especially when it happens to evade the degradation. Thus, the comparison of Truth to a torch, which one cannot carry through a crowd without singeing somebody's beard, is pure wit, because it takes an obsolete expression ("The torch of truth") at its full value and not at all in a comical sense, and because the torch as an object does not lack a certain distinction, though it is a concrete object. However, a comparison may just as well be witty as comic, and what is more, one may be independent of the other, in that the comparison becomes an aid for certain techniques of wit, as, for example, unification or allusion. Thus Nestroy's above mentioned comparison of memory to a "Warehouse," is simultaneously comical and witty, first, on account of the extraordinary degradation to which the psychological conception must consent in the comparison to a "Warehouse," and secondly, because he who utilizes the comparison is a clerk, and in this comparison he establishes a rather un-expected unification between psychology and his vocation. Heine's verse, "until at last the buttons tore from the pants of my patience," seems at first an excellent example of a comic degrading comparison, but on closer reflection we must ascribe to it also the attribute of wittiness, since the comparison as a means of allusion strikes into the realm of the obscene and causes a release of pleasure from the obscene. Through a union not altogether incidental the same material also gives us a resultant pleasure which is at the same time comical and witty; it does not matter whether or not the conditions of the one promote the origin of the other, such a union acts confusingly on the "feeling" whose function it is to announce to us whether we have before us wit or the comic, and only a careful ex-amination independent of the disposition of pleasure can decide the question.

As tempting as it would be to trace these more intimate determinations of comic pleasure, the author must remember that neither his previous education nor his daily vocation justifies him in extending his investiga-tions beyond the spheres of wit, and he must confess that it is precisely the subject of comic comparison which makes him feel his incompetence

We are quite willing to be reminded that many authors do not recog-nize the clear notional and objective distinction between wit and comic, as we were impelled to do, and that they classify wit merely as "the comic of speech" or "of words." To test this view let us select one example of intentional and one of involuntary comic of speech and compare it with wit. We have already mentioned before that we are in a good position to distinguish comic from witty speech. "With a fork and with effort, his mother pulled him out of the mess," is only comical, but Heine's verse about the four castes of the population of Göttingen: "Professors, stu-dents, Philistines, and cattle," is exquisitely witty.

As an example of the intentional comic of speech I will take as a model Stettenheim's *Wippchen*. We call Stettenheim witty because he possesses the cleverness that evokes the comic. The wit which one "has," in con-tradistinction to the wit which one "makes," is indeed correctly condi-tioned by this ability. It is true that the letters of Wippchen are also witty in so far as they are interspersed with a rich collection of all sorts of witticisms, some of which very successful ones (as "festively undressed" when he speaks of a parade of savages), but what lends the peculiar character to these productions is not these isolated witticisms, but the superabundant flow of comic speech contained therein. Originally *Wipp-chen* was certainly meant to represent a satirical character, a modification of Freytag's Schmock, one of those uneducated persons who trade in the educational treasure of the nation and abuse it; but the pleasure in the comic effect experienced in representing this person seems gradually to have pushed to the background the author's satirical tendency. Wippchen's productions are for the most part "comic nonsense." The author has justly utilized the pleasant mood resulting from the accumulation of such achievements to present beside the altogether admissible material, all sorts of absurdities which would be intolerable in themselves. Wippchen's nonsense appears to be of a specific nature only on account of its special technique. If we look closer into some of these "witticisms," we find that some forms which have impressed their character on the whole production are especially conspicuous. Wippchen makes use mostly of compositions (fusions), of modifications of familiar expressions and quotations. He replaces some of the banal elements in these expressions by others which are usually more pretentious and more valuable. This naturally comes near to the techniques of wit.

THE COMIC OF SPEECH

Some of the fusions taken from the preface and the first pages are the following: *"Turkey's money is like the hay of the sea."* This is only a condensation of the two expressions, "Money like hay," "Money like the sands of the sea." Or: *"I am nothing but a leafless pillar which tells of a vanished splendor,"* which is a fusion of "leafless trunk" and "a pillar which, etc." Or: *"Where is Ariadne's thread which leads out of the Scylla of this Augean stable?"*, for which three different Greek myths contribute an element each.

The modifications and substitutions can be treated collectively without much forcing; their character can be seen from the following examples which are peculiar to Wippchen, they are regularly permeated by a different wording which is more fluent, most banal, and reduced to mere platitudes.

"To hang my paper and ink high." The saying: "To hang one's breadbasket high," expresses metaphorically the idea of placing one under difficult conditions. But why not stretch this figure to other material?

"Already in my youth Pegasus was alive in me." When the word "Pegasus" is replaced by "the poet," one can recognize it as an expression often used in autobiographies. Naturally "Pegasus" is not the proper word to replace the words "the poet," but it has thought associations to it and is a high-sounding word.

From Wippchen's other numerous productions some examples can be shown which present the pure comic. As an example of comic disillusionment the following can be cited: *"For hours the battle raged, finally it remained undecisive"*; an example of comical unmasking (of ignorance) is the following: *"Clio, the Medusa of history,"* or quotations like the following: *"Habent sua fata morgana."* But our interest is aroused more by the fusions and modifications because they recall familiar techniques of wit. We may compare them to such modification witticisms as the following: "He has a great future behind him," and Lichtenberg's modification witticisms such as: "New baths heal well," etc. Should Wippchen's productions having the same technique be called witticisms, or what distinguishes them from the latter?

It is surely not difficult to answer this. Let us remember that wit presents to the hearer a double face, and forces him to two different views. In nonsense-wit as those mentioned last, one view, which considers only the wording, states that they are nonsense; the other view, which, in obedience to suggestion, follows the road that leads through the hearer's unconscious, finds very good sense in these witticisms. In Wippchen's wit-like productions one of these views of wit is vacant, as if stunted. It is a Janus head with only one countenance developed. One would get nowhere should he be tempted to proceed by means of this technique to the unconscious. The condensations lead to no case in which the two fused elements really result in a new sense; they fall to pieces when an attempt is made to analyze them. As in wit, the modifications and substitutions lead to a customary and familiar wording, but they themselves tell us little else, as a rule nothing that is of any possible use. Hence, the only thing that remains to these "witticisms" is the nonsense view. Whether such productions, which have freed themselves from one of the most essential characters of wit, should be called "bad" wit or no wit at all, every one must decide as he feels inclined.

There is no doubt that such stunted wit produces a comic effect for which we can account in more than one way. Either the comic originates through the uncovering of the unconscious modes of thinking in a manner similar to the cases considered above, or the wit originates by comparison with perfect wit. Nothing prevents us from assuming that we here deal with a union of both modes of origin of the comic pleasure. It is not to be denied that it is precisely the inadequate dependence on wit which here shapes the nonsense into comic nonsense.

COMIC OF INADEQUACY

There are, of course, other quite apparent cases, in which such inadequacy produced by the comparison with wit, makes the nonsense irresistibly comic. The counterpart to wit, the riddle, can perhaps give us better examples for this than wit itself. A facetious question states: *What is this: It hangs on the wall and one can dry his hands on it? It would be a foolish riddle if the answer were: a towel. On the contrary this answer is rejected with the statement: No, it is a herring,—"But, for mercy's sake," is the objection, "a herring does not hang on the wall."—"But you can hang it there,"—"But who wants to dry his hands on a herring?"—"Well," is the soft answer, "you don't have to."* This explanation given through two typical displacements shows how much this question lacks of being a real riddle, and because of this absolute insufficiency it impresses one as irresistibly comic, rather than mere nonsensical foolishness. Through such means, that is, by not restricting essential conditions, wit, riddles, and other forms, which in themselves produce no comic pleasure, can be made into sources of comic pleasure.

It is not so difficult to understand the case of the unvoluntary comic of speech which we can perhaps find realized with as much frequency as we like in the poems of Frederika Kempner.[1]

ANTI-VIVISECTION

> Fraternal sentiment should urge us
> To champion the guinea-pig,
> For has it not a soul like ours,
> Although most likely not as big?

Or a conversation between a loving couple.

THE CONTRAST

> The young wife whispers "I'm so happy,"
> "And I!" chimes in her husband's voice,
> "Because your virtues, dearest help-mate,
> Reveal the wisdom of my choice."

There is nothing here which makes one think of wit. Doubtless, however, it is the inadequacy of these "poetic productions," as the very extraordinary clumsiness of the expressions which recall the most commonplace or newspaper style, the ingenious poverty of thoughts, the absence of every trace of poetic manner of thinking or speaking—it is all these inadequacies which make these poems comic. Nevertheless, it is not at all self-evident that we should find these poems comical; many similar productions we merely consider very bad, we do not laugh at them but are rather vexed with them. But here it is the great disparity in our demand of a poem which impels us to the comic conception; where this difference is less, we are inclined to criticise rather than laugh. The comic effect of Kempner's poetic productions is furthermore assured by the additional circumstances of the lady author's unmistakably good intentions, and by the fact that her helpless phrases disarm our feeling of mockery and

[1] Sixth Ed., Berlin, 1891.

anger. We are now reminded of a problem the consideration of which we have so far postponed. The difference of expenditure is surely the main condition of the comic pleasure, but observation teaches that such difference does not always produce pleasure. What other conditions must be added, or what disturbances must be checked in order that pleasure should result from the difference of expenditure? But before proceeding with the answers to these questions we wish to verify what was said in the conclusions of the former discussion, namely, that the comic of speech is not synonymous with wit, and that wit must be something quite different from speech comic.

As we are about to attack the problem just formulated, concerning the conditions of the origin of comic pleasure from the difference of expenditure, we may permit ourselves to facilitate this task so as to attain for ourselves some pleasure. To give a correct answer to this question would amount to an exhaustive presentation of the nature of the comic for which we are fitted neither by ability nor authority. We shall therefore again be content to elucidate the problem of the comic only so far as it distinctly separates itself from wit.

All theories of the comic were objected to by the critics on the ground that in defining the comic these theories overlooked the essential element of it. This can be seen from the following theories, with their objections. The comic depends on a contrasting idea; yes, in so far as this contrast affects one comically and in no other way. The feeling of the comic results from the dwindling away of an expectation; yes, if the disappointment does not prove to be painful. There is no doubt that these objections are justified, but they are overestimated if one concludes from them that the essential characteristic mark of the comic has hitherto escaped our conception. What depreciates the general validity of these definitions, are conditions, which are indispensable for the origin of the comic pleasure, but in which one must not necessarily search for the nature of comic pleasure. The rejection of the objections, and the explanations of the contradictions to the definitions of the comic, will become easy for us, only after we trace back comic pleasure to the difference resulting from a comparison of two expenditures. Comic pleasure and the effect by which it is recognized—laughter, can originate only when this difference is no longer utilizable and when it is capable of discharge. We gain no pleasurable effect, or at most only a flighty feeling of pleasure in which the comic does not appear, if the difference is put to other use as soon as it is recognized. Just as special precautions must be taken in wit, in order to guard against making new use of expenditure recognized as superfluous, so also can comic pleasure originate only under relations which fulfill this latter condition. The cases in which such differences of expenditure originate in our ideational life are therefore uncommonly numerous, while the cases in which the comic originates from them are comparatively very rare.

THE CONDITIONS OF ISOLATION OF THE COMIC

Two observations obtrude themselves upon the observer who reviews even only superficially the origin of comic pleasure from the difference of expenditure; first, that there are cases in which the comic appears regularly and as if necessarily; and, in contrast to these cases, others in which this depends on the conditions of the case and on the viewpoint of the observer. But secondly, that unusually large differences very often triumph over unfavorable conditions, so that the comic feeling originates in spite of it. In reference to the first point one may set up two classes, the inevitable comic and the accidental comic, although one will have to be prepared from the beginning to find exceptions in the first class to the inevitableness of the comic. It would be tempting to follow the conditions which are essential to each class.

What is important in the second class are the conditions, of which one may be designated as the "isolation" of the comic case. A closer analysis reveals something like the following relations:

a) The favorable condition for the origin of comic pleasure is brought about by a general happy disposition in which "one is in the mood for laughing." In happy toxic states almost everything seems comic, which probably results from a comparison with the expenditure in normal conditions. For wit, the comic, and all similar methods of gaining pleasure from the psychic activities, are nothing but ways to regain this happy state—euphoria—from one single point, when it does not exist as a general disposition of the psyche.

b) A similar favorable condition is produced by the expectation of the comic or by putting one's self in the right mood for comic pleasure. Hence when the intention to make things comical exists and when this feeling is shared by others, the differences required are so slight that they probably would have been overlooked had they been experienced in unpremeditated occurrences. He who decides to attend a comic lecture or a farce at the theater is indebted to this intention for laughing over things which in his everyday life would hardly produce in him a comic effect. He finally laughs at the recollection of having laughed, at the expectation of laughing, and at the appearance of the one who is to present the comic, even before the latter makes the attempt to make him laugh. It is for this reason that people later admit that they are ashamed of that which made them laugh at the theater.

c) Unfavorable conditions for the comic result from the kind of psychic activity which may occupy the individual at the moment. Imaginative or mental activity tending towards serious aims disturbs the discharging capacity of the cathexis which the activity needs for its own displacements, so that only unexpected and great differences of expenditure can break through to form comic pleasure. All manner of mental processes far enough removed from the obvious to cause a suspension of ideational mimicry are unfavorable to the comic; in abstract contemplation there is hardly any room left for the comic, except when this form of thinking is suddenly interrupted.

d) The occasion for releasing comic pleasure vanishes when the attention is directly fixed on the comparison which is capable of giving rise to the comic. Under such circumstances the comic force is lost from that which is otherwise sure to produce a comic effect. A movement or a mental activity cannot become comical to him whose interest is fixed at the time of comparing this movement with a standard which distinctly presents itself to him. Thus the examiner does not see the comical in the nonsense produced by the student in his ignorance; he is simply annoyed by it, whereas the offender's classmates who are more interested in his chances of passing the examination than in what he knows, laugh heartily over the same nonsense. The teacher of dancing or gymnastics seldom has any eyes for the comic movements of his pupils, and the preacher entirely loses sight of humanity's defects of character, which the writer of comedy brings out with so much effect. The comic process cannot stand examination by the attention, it must be able to proceed absolutely unnoticed in a manner similar to wit. But for good reasons, it would contradict the nomenclature of "conscious processes" which I have used in *The Interpretation of Dreams,* if one wished to call it of necessity *unconscious.* It rather belongs to the *foreconscious,* and one may use the fitting name "automatic" for all those processes which are enacted in the foreconscious, and dispense with the attention cathexis which is connected with consciousness. The process of comparison of the expenditures must remain automatic if it is to produce comic pleasure.

e) It is exceedingly disturbing to the comic if the case from which it originates gives rise at the same time to a marked release of affect. The discharge of the affective difference is then as a rule excluded. Affects, disposition, and the attitude of the individual in occasional cases make it clear that the comic comes or goes with the viewpoint of the individual person; that only in exceptional cases is there an absolute comic. The dependence or relativity of the comic is therefore much greater than that of wit, which never happens but is regularly made, and at its production one may already give attention to the conditions under which it finds acceptance. But affective development is the most intensive of the conditions which disturb the comic, the significance of which is well known.[1] It is, therefore, said that the comic feeling comes most in tolerably indif-

[1] "You may well laugh, that no longer concerns you."

ferent cases which evince no strong feelings or interests. Nevertheless, it is just in cases with affective release that one may witness the production of a particularly strong expenditure-difference in the automatism of discharge. When Colonel Butler answers Octavio's admonitions with "bitter laughter," exclaiming:

"Thanks from the house of Austria!"

his bitterness has thus not prevented the laughter which results from the recollection of the disappointment which he believes he has experienced; and on the other hand, the magnitude of this disappointment could not have been more impressively depicted by the poet than by showing it capable of effecting laughter in the midst of the storm of unchained affects. It is my belief that this explanation may be applicable in all cases in which laughing occurs on other than pleasurable occasions, and in conjunction with exceedingly painful or tense affects.

f) If we also mention that the development of the comic pleasure can be promoted by means of any other pleasurable addition to the case which acts like a sort of contact-effect (after the manner of the fore-pleasure principle in the tendency-wit), then we have discussed surely not all the conditions of comic pleasure, yet enough of them to serve our purpose. We then see that for these conditions, as well as for the inconstancy and dependence of the comic effect, no other assumption so easily lends itself as this one which traces the comic pleasure from the discharge of a difference, which under many conditions can be diverted to a different use than discharge.

It still remains to give a thorough consideration of the comic of the sexual and the obscene, but we shall only skim over it with a few observations. Here, too, we shall take the act of exposing one's body as the starting-point. An accidental exposure produces a comical effect on us, because we compare the ease with which we attained the enjoyment of this view with the great expenditure otherwise necessary for the attainment of this object. The case thus comes nearer to the naïve-comic, but it is simpler than the latter. In every case of exhibitionism in which we are made spectators—or, in the case of the smutty joke hearers—we play the part of the third person, and the person exposed is made comical. We have heard that it is the purpose of wit to replace obscenity and in this manner to reopen a source of comic pleasure that has been lost. On the contrary, spying out an exposure, forms no example of the comic for the one spying, because the effort he exerts thereby abrogates the condition of comic pleasure; the only thing remaining is the sexual pleasure in what is seen. If the peeper relates to another what he has seen, the person looked at again becomes comical, because the viewpoint that predominates is that the expenditure was omitted which would have been necessary for the concealment of the private parts. At all events, the sphere of the sexual or obscene offers the richest opportunities for gaining comic pleasure beside the pleasurable sexual stimulation, as it exposes the person's dependence on his physical needs (degradation) or it can uncover behind the spiritual love the physical demands of the same (unmasking).

THE PSYCHOGENESIS OF THE COMIC

An invitation to seek the understanding of the comic in its psychogenesis comes surprisingly from Bergson's well written and stimulating book *Laughter*. Bergson, whose formula for the conception of the comic character has already become known to us—"mechanization of life," "the substitution of something mechanical for the natural"—reaches by obvious associations from automatism to the automaton, and seeks to trace a series of comic effects to the blurred memories of children's toys. In this connection he reaches this viewpoint, which, to be sure, he soon drops; he seeks to trace the comic to the after-effect of childish pleasure. "Perhaps we ought even to carry simplification still further, and, going back to our earliest recollection, try to discover in the games that amused us as children the first faint traces of the combinations that make us laugh as grown-up persons." . . . "Above all, we are too apt to ignore the childish element, so to speak, latent in most of our joyful emotions" (p. 67). As we have now traced wit to that childish playing with words and thoughts which is prohibited by the rational critic, we must be tempted to trace also these infantile roots of the comic, conjectured by Bergson.

As a matter of fact we meet a whole series of conditions which seem most promising, when we examine the relation of the comic to the child. The child itself does not by any means seem comic to us, although its character fulfills all conditions which, in comparison to our own, would result in a comic difference. Thus we see the immoderate expenditure of motion as well as the slight psychic expenditure, the control of the psychic activities through bodily functions, and other features. The child gives us a comic impression only when it does not behave as a child but as an earnest grown-up, and even then it affects us only in the same manner as other persons in disguise; but as long as it retains the nature of the child our perception of it furnishes us a pure pleasure, which perhaps recalls the comic. We call it naïve in so far as it displays to us the absence of inhibitions, and we call naïve-comic those of its utterances which in another we would have considered obscene or witty.

On the other hand the child lacks all feeling for the comic. This sentence seems to say no more than that this comic feeling, like many others, first makes its appearance in the course of psychic development; and that would by no means be remarkable, especially since we must admit that it shows itself distinctly even during years which must be accredited to childhood. Nevertheless it can be demonstrated that the assertion that the child lacks feeling for the comic has a deeper meaning than one would suppose. In the first place it will readily be seen that it cannot be different, if our conception is correct, that the comic feeling results from a difference of expenditure produced in the effort to understand the other. Let us again take comic motion as an example. The comparison which furnishes the difference reads as follows, when put in conscious formulæ: "So he does it," and: "So I would do it," or "So I have done it." But the child lacks the standard contained in the second sentence, it understands simply through imitation; it just does it. Education of the child furnishes it with the standard: "So you shall do it," and if it now makes use of the same in comparisons, the nearest conclusion is: "He has not done it right, and I can do it better." In this case it laughs at the other, it laughs at him with a feeling of superiority. There is nothing to prevent us from tracing this laughter also to a difference of expenditure; but according to the analogy with the examples of laughter occurring in us we may conclude that the comic feeling is not experienced by the child when it laughs as an expression of superiority. It is a laughter of pure pleasure. In our own case whenever the judgment of our own superiority occurs we smile rather than laugh, or if we laugh, we are still able to distinguish clearly this conscious realization of our superiority from the comic which makes us laugh.

It is probably correct to say that in many cases which we perceive as "comical" and which we cannot explain, the child laughs out of pure pleasure, whereas the child's motives are clear and assignable. If for instance, some one slips on the street and falls, we laugh because this impression—we know not why—is comical. The child laughs in the same case out of a feeling of superiority or out of joy over the calamity of others. It amounts to saying: "You fell, but I did not." Certain pleasure motives of the child seem to be lost for us grown-ups, but as a substitute for these we perceive under the same conditions the "comic" feeling.

THE INFANTILE AND THE COMIC

If we were permitted to generalize, it would seem very tempting to transfer the desired specific character of the comic into the awakening of the infantile, and to conceive the comic as a regaining of "lost infantile laughter." One could then say, "I laugh every time over a difference of expenditure between the other and myself, when I discover in the other the child." Or expressed more precisely, the whole comparison leading to the comic would read as follows:

"He does it this way—I do it differently—
He does it just as I did when I was a child."

This laughter would thus result every time from the comparison between the ego of the grown-up and the ego of the child. The uncertainty itself of the comic difference, causing now the lesser and now the greater expenditure to appear comical to me, would correspond to the infantile condition; the comic therein is actually always on the side of the infantile.

This is not contradicted by the fact that the child itself as an object of comparison does not make a comic impression on me but a purely pleasurable one, nor by the fact that this comparison with the infantile produces a comic effect only when any other use of the difference is avoided. For the conditions of the discharge come thereby into consideration. Everything that confines a psychic process in an association of ideas works against the discharge of the surplus cathexis and directs the same to other utilization; whatever isolates a psychic act favors the discharge. By consciously focussing on the child as the person of comparison, the discharge necessary for the production of comic pleasure therefore becomes impossible; only in foreconscious energetic states is there a similar approach to the isolation which we may moreover also ascribe to the psychic processes in the child. The addition to the comparison: "Thus, I have also done it as a child," from which the comic effect would emanate, could come into consideration for the average difference only when no other association could obtain control over the freed surplus.

If we still continue with our attempt to find the nature of the comic in the foreconscious association of the infantile, we have to go a step further than Bergson and admit that the comparison resulting in the comic, need not necessarily awake old childish pleasure and play, but that it is enough if it touches the childish nature in general, perhaps even childish pain. Herein we deviate from Bergson, but remain consistent with ourselves, when we connect the comic pleasure not with remembered pleasure but always with a comparison. This is possible, for cases of the first kind comprise in a measure those which are regularly and irresistibly comic. Let us now draw up the scheme of the comic possibilities instanced above. We stated that the comic difference would be found either

(a) through a comparison between the other and one's self, or (b) through a comparison altogether within the other, or (c) through a comparison altogether within one's self.

In the first case the other would appear to me as a child, in the second he would put himself on the level of a child, and in the third I would find the child in myself. To the first class belong the comic of movement, of forms, of psychic activity, and of character. The infantile corresponding to it would be the urge for motion and the inferior mental and moral development of the child, so that the fool would perhaps become comical to me by reminding me of a lazy child, and the bad person by reminding me of a naughty child. The only time one might speak of a childish pleasure lost to grown-ups would be where the child's own motion pleasure came into consideration.

The second case, in which the comic altogether depends on empathy, comprises numerous possibilities such as the comic situation, exaggeration (caricature), imitation, degradation, and unmasking. It is under this head that the presentation of infantile viewpoints mostly takes place. For the comic situation is largely based on embarrassment, in which we feel again the helplessness of the child. The worst of these embarrassments, the disturbance of other activities through the imperative demands of natural wants, corresponds to the child's lack of control of the physical functions. Where the comic situation acts through repetitions it is based on the pleasure of constant repetition peculiar to the child (asking questions, telling stories), through which it makes itself a nuisance to grown-ups. Exaggeration, which also affords pleasure even to the grown-up in so far as it is justified by his reason, corresponds to the characteristic want of moderation in the child, and its ignorance of all quantitative relations which it later really learns to know as qualitative. To keep within bounds, to practice moderation even in permissible feelings is a late fruit of education, and is gained through opposing inhibitions of the psychic activity acquired in the same association. Wherever this association is weakened, as in the unconscious of dreams and in the mono-ideation of the psychoneuroses, the want of moderation of the child again makes its appearance.

The understanding of comic imitation has caused us many difficulties so long as we left out of consideration the infantile factor. But imitation is the child's best art and is the impelling motive of most of its playing. The child's ambition is not so much to distinguish himself among his equals as to imitate the big fellows. The relation of the child to the grown-up determines also the comic of degradation, which corresponds to the lowering of the grown-up in the life of the child. Few things can afford the child greater pleasure than when the grown-up lowers himself to his level, disregards his superiority, and plays with the child as its equal. The alleviation which furnishes the child pure pleasure is a debasement used by the adult as a means of making things comic and as a source of comic pleasure. As for unmasking, we know that it is based on degradation.

The infantile determination of the third case, the comic of expectation, presents most of the difficulties; this really explains why those authors who put this case to the foreground in their conception of the comic, found no occasion to consider the infantile factor in their studies of the comic. The comic of expectation is farthest from the child's thoughts, the ability to understand this is the latest quality to appear in him. Most of those cases which produce a comic effect in the grown-up are probably felt by the child as a disappointment. One can refer, however, to the blissful expectation and gullibility of the child, in order to understand why one considers himself as comical "as a child," when he succumbs to comic disappointment.

If the preceding remarks produce a certain probability that the comic feeling may be translated into the thought that everything is comic which does not fit the grown-up, I still do not feel bold enough—in view of my whole position to the problem of the comic—to defend this last proposition with the same earnestness as those that I formulated before. I am unable to decide whether the lowering to the level of the child is only a special case of comic degradation, or whether everything comical fundamentally depends on the degradation to the level of the child.[1]

HUMOR

An examination of the comic, however superficial it may be, would be most incomplete if it did not devote at least a few remarks to the consideration of *humor*. There is so little doubt as to the essential relationship between the two that a tentative explanation of the comic must furnish at least one component for the understanding of humor. It does not matter how much appropriate and important material was presented as an appreciation of humor, which, as one of the highest psychic functions, enjoys the special favor of thinkers, we still cannot elude the temptation to express its essence through an approach to the formulæ given for wit and the comic.

We have heard that the release of painful emotions is the strongest hindrance to the comic effect. Just as aimless motion causes harm, stupidity mischief, and disappointment pain;—the possibility of a comic effect ends, at least for him who cannot defend himself against such pain, who is himself affected by it or must participate in it, whereas he who is unconcerned shows by his behavior that the situation of the case in question contains everything necessary to produce a comic effect. Humor is thus a means to gain pleasure despite the painful affects which disturb it; it acts as a substitute for this affective development, and takes its place. If we are in a situation which tempts us to liberate painful affects according to our habits, and motives then urge us to suppress these affects in *statu nascendi*, we have the conditions for humor. In the cases just cited the person affected by misfortune, pain, etc., could obtain humoristic pleasure while the disinterested party laughs over the comic pleasure. We can only say that the pleasure of humor results at the cost

---

[1] That comic pleasure has its source in the "quantitative contrast," in the comparison of big and small, which ultimately also expresses the essential relation of the child to the grown-up, would indeed be a peculiar coincidence if the comic had nothing else to do with the infantile.

of this discontinued liberation of affect; it originates through the *econo-mized expenditure of affect.*[1]

THE ECONOMY IN EXPENDITURE OF AFFECT

Humor is the most self-sufficient of the comic forms; its process consummates itself in one single person and the participation of another adds nothing new to it. I can enjoy the pleasure of humor originating in myself without feeling the necessity of imparting it to another. It is not easy to tell what happens during the production of humoristic pleasure in a person; but one gains a certain insight by investigating these cases of humor which have emanated from persons with whom we have entered into a sympathetic understanding. By sympathetically understanding the humoristic person in these cases one gets the same pleasure. The coarsest form of humor, the so-called humor of the gallows or grim-humor (*Galgenhumor*), may enlighten us in this regard. The rogue, on being led to execution on Monday, remarked: "Yes, this week is beginning well." This is really a witticism, as the remark is quite appropriate in itself, on the other hand it is displaced in the most nonsensical fashion, as there can be no further happening for him this week. But it required humor to make such wit, that is, to overlook what distinguished the beginning of this week from other weeks, and to deny the difference which could give rise to motives for very particular emotional feelings. The case is the same when on the way to the gallows he requests a neckerchief for his bare neck, in order to guard against taking cold, a precaution which would be quite praiseworthy under different circumstances, but becomes exceedingly superfluous and indifferent in view of the impending fate of this same neck. We must say that there is something like greatness of soul in this *blague,* in this clinging to his usual nature and in deviating from that which would overthrow and drive this nature into despair. This form of grandeur of humor thus appears unmistakably in cases in which our admiration is not inhibited by the circumstances of the humoristic person.

In Victor Hugo's *Ernani* the bandit who entered into a conspiracy against his king, Charles I, of Spain (Charles V, as the German Emperor), falls into the hands of his most powerful enemy; he foresees his fate; as one convicted of high treason his head will fall. But this prospect does not deter him from introducing himself as a hereditary Grandee of Spain and from declaring that he has no intention of waiving any prerogative belonging to such personage. A Grandee of Spain could appear before his royal master with his head covered. Well:

> "Nos têtes ont le droit
> De tomber couvertes devant de toi." [2]

[1] Cf. Freud: *Der Humor*, Gesam. Schriften Vol. XI, p. 402, Int. Psychoanal. Verlag.
[2] "Our heads have the right to fall covered before thee."

This is excellent humor and if we do not laugh on hearing it, it is because our admiration covers the humoristic pleasure. In the case of the rogue who did not wish to take cold on the way to the gallows we roar with laughter. The situation which should have driven this criminal to despair might have evoked in us intense pity, but this pity is inhibited because we understand that he who is most concerned is quite indifferent to the situation. As a result of this understanding, the expenditure for pity, which was already prepared in us, became inapplicable and we laughed it off. The indifference of the rogue, which we notice has cost him a great expenditure of psychic labor, infects us, as it were.

Economy of sympathy is one of the most frequent sources of humoristic pleasure. Mark Twain's humor usually follows this mechanism. When he tells us about the life of his brother, how, as an employee in a large road-building enterprise, he was hurled into the air through a premature explosion of a blast, to come to earth again far from the place where he was working, feelings of sympathy for this unfortunate are invariably aroused in us. We should like to inquire whether he sustained no injury in this accident; but the continuation of the story that the brother lost a half-day's pay for being away from the place he worked diverts us entirely from sympathy and makes us almost as hard-hearted as that employer, and just as indifferent to the possible injury to the victim's health. Another time Mark Twain presents us his pedigree, which he traces back almost as far as one of the companions of Columbus. But after describing the character of this ancestor, whose entire possessions consisted of several pieces of linen each bearing a different mark, we cannot help laughing at the expense of the stored-up piety, a piety which characterized our frame of mind at the beginning of this family history. The mechanism of humoristic pleasure is not disturbed by our knowing that this family history is a fictitious one, and that this fiction serves a satirical tendency to expose the embellishments which result in imparting such pedigrees to others; it is just as independent of the conditions of reality as the manufactured comic. Another of Mark Twain's stories relates how his brother constructed for himself subterranean quarters into which he brought a bed, a table, and a lamp, and that as a roof he used a large piece of sail-cloth with a hole through the centre; how during the night after the room was completed, a cow being driven home, fell through the opening in the ceiling on to the table and extinguished the lamp; how his brother helped patiently to hoist the animal out and to rearrange everything; how he did the same thing when the same disturbance was repeated the following night; and then every succeeding night; such a story becomes comical through repetition. But Mark Twain closes with the information that on the forty-sixth night when the cow again fell through, his brother finally remarked that the thing was beginning to grow monotonous; and here we can no longer restrain our humoristic pleasure for we had long expected to hear how the brother would express his anger over this chronic *malheur*. The slight humor which we draw from our own life we usually produce at the expense of anger instead of irritating ourselves.

The excellent humoristic effect of a character like that of the fat knight, Sir John Falstaff, is based on economized contempt and indignation. To be sure, we recognize in him the unworthy glutton and fashionably dressed swindler, but our condemnation is disarmed through a whole series of factors. We understand that he knows himself to be just as we estimate him; he impresses us through his wit; and besides that, his physical deformity produces a contact-effect in favor of a comic conception of his personality instead of a serious one; as if our demands for morality and honor must recoil from such a big stomach. His activities are altogether harmless and are almost excused by the comic lowness of those he deceives. We admit that the poor devil has a right to live and enjoy himself like anyone else, and we almost pity him because in the principal situation we find him a puppet in the hands of one much his superior. It is for this reason that we cannot bear him any grudge and turn all we economize in him in indignation into comic pleasure, which he otherwise provides. Sir John's own humor really emanates from the superiority of an ego which neither his physical nor his moral defects can rob of its joviality and security.

On the other hand, the courageous knight, Don Quixote de la Mancha, is a figure who possesses no humor, and in his seriousness furnishes us a pleasure which can be called humoristic, although its mechanism shows a decided deviation from that of humor. Originally Don Quixote is a purely comic figure, a big child whose fancies from his books on knighthood have gone to his head. It is known that at first the poet wanted to show only that phase of his character, and that the creation gradually outgrew the author's original intentions. But after the poet endowed this ludicrous person with the profoundest wisdom and noblest aims and made him the symbolic representation of an idealism, a man who believed in the realization of his aims, who took duties seriously and promised literally, he ceased to be a comic personality. Like humoristic pleasure, which results from a prevention of emotional feelings, it originates here through the disturbance of comic pleasure. However, in these examples we already depart perceptibly from the simple cases of humor.

FORMS OF HUMOR

The forms of humor are extraordinarily varied according to the nature of the emotional feeling which is economized in favor of humor, as sympathy, anger, pain, compassion, etc. This series seems incomplete because the sphere of humor undergoes a constant enlargement, as often as an artist or writer succeeds in mastering humoristically the, as yet, unconquered emotional feelings and in making them, through artifices similar to those in the above example, a source of humoristic pleasure. Thus, some artists have worked wonders in gaining humor at the expense of fear and disgust. The manifestations of humor are above all determined by two peculiarities, which are connected with the conditions of its origin. In the first place, humor may appear fused with wit or any other form of the comic; whereby it has for its task the removal of a possible emotional development which would form a hindrance to the pleasurable effect. Secondly, it can entirely or only partially abolish this emotional development, which is really more frequently the case, because the simpler function and the different forms of "broken" [1] humor, results in that humor which smiles under its tears. It withdraws from the affect a part of its energy and gives it instead the additional humoristic ring.

As was noticed from former examples, the humoristic pleasure gained through subsequent sympathy results from a special technique resembling displacement, through which the liberation of affect held ready is checked and the cathexis is deflected to other, and not often, to matters of secondary importance. This does not help us, however, to understand the process by which the displacement from the development of affect proceeds in the humoristic person himself. We see that the recipient imitates the producer of the humor in his psychic processes, but we discover nothing thereby concerning the forces which make this process possible in the latter.

When, for example, somebody succeeds in disregarding a painful affect because he holds before himself the greatness of the world's interest as a contrast to his own smallness, we can only say that we see in this no function of humor, but one of philosophic thinking, and we gain no pleasure even if we put ourselves into his train of thought. The humoristic displacement is, therefore, just as impossible in the light of conscious attention as in the comic comparison; like the latter it is connected with the condition to remain in the foreconscious—that is to say, to remain automatic.

One reaches some solution of humoristic displacement if one considers it in the light of a defense process. The defense processes are the psychic correlates of the flight reflex and follow the task of guarding against the origin of pain from inner sources. In fulfilling this task they serve the psychic occurrence as an automatic adjustment, which, to be sure, finally proves harmful and, therefore, must be subjected to the control of the conscious thinking. A definite form of this defense, the failure of repression, I have demonstrated as the effective mechanism in the origin of the psychoneuroses. Humor can now be conceived as the loftiest of these de-

[1] A term which is used in quite a different sense in the *Aesthetik* of Theo. Vischer.

fense functions. It disdains to withdraw from conscious attention the ideas which are connected with the painful affect, as repression does, and it, thus, overcomes the defense automatism. It brings this about by finding the means to withdraw the energy from the ready held pain release, and through discharge changes the same into pleasure. It is even credible that it is again the connection with the infantile that puts at humor's disposal the means for this function. Only in childhood did we experience intensively painful affects over which today as grown-ups we would laugh, just as a humorist laughs over his present painful affects. The elevation of his ego, which is evidenced by the humoristic displacement—the translation of which would nevertheless read: I am too big to have these causes affect me painfully—he could find in the comparison of his present ego with his infantile ego. This conception is to some extent confirmed by the rôle which falls to the infantile in the neurotic processes of repression.

THE RELATION OF HUMOR TO WIT AND COMIC

On the whole, humor is closer to the comic than wit. Like the former its psychic localization is in the foreconscious, whereas wit, as we had to assume, is formed as a compromise between the unconscious and the foreconscious. On the other hand, humor has no share in the peculiar nature in which wit and the comic meet, a peculiarity which perhaps we have not hitherto emphasized strongly enough. It is a condition for the origin of the comic that we be induced to apply—either *simultaneously or in rapid succession*—to the same thought function two different modes of ideas, between which the "comparison" then takes place and the comic difference results. Such differences originate between the expenditure of the stranger and one's own, between the usual expenditure and the emergency expenditure, between an anticipated expenditure and one which has already occurred.[1]

The difference between two forms of conception resulting simultaneously, which work with different expenditures, comes into consideration in wit, in respect to the hearer. The one of these two conceptions, by taking the hints contained in wit, follows the train of thought through the unconscious, while the other conception remains on the surface and presents the witticism like any wording from the foreconscious which has become conscious. Perhaps it would not be considered an unjustified statement if we should refer the pleasure of the witticism heard to the difference between these two forms of presentation.

Concerning wit, we here repeat our former statement concerning its

---

[1] If one does not hesitate to do some violence to the conception of expectation, one may ascribe—according to the process of Lipps—a very large sphere of the comic to the comic of expectation; but probably the most original cases of the comic which result through a comparison of a strange expenditure with one's own, will fit least into this conception.

Janus-like double-facedness, a simile we used when the relation between wit and the comic still appeared to us unsettled.[1]

The character thus put into the foreground becomes indistinct when we deal with humor. To be sure, we feel the humoristic pleasure where an emotional feeling is evaded, which we might have expected as a pleasure usually belonging to the situation; and in so far humor really falls under the broadened conception of the comic of expectation. But in humor it is no longer a question of two different kinds of ideas having the same content. The fact that the situation comes under the domination of a painful emotional feeling which should have been avoided, puts an end to possible comparison with the nature of the comic and of wit. The humoristic displacement is really a case of that different kind of utilization of a freed expenditure, which proved to be so dangerous for the comic effect.

FORMULÆ FOR WIT, COMIC AND HUMOR

Now, that we have reduced the mechanism of humoristic pleasure to a formula analogous to the formula of comic pleasure and of wit, we are at the end of our task. It has seemed to us that the pleasure of wit originates from an *economy of expenditure in inhibition,* of the comic from an *economy of expenditure in thought,* and of humor from an *economy of expenditure in feeling.* All three modes of activity of our psychic apparatus derive pleasure from economy. All three present methods strive to bring back from the psychic activity a pleasure which has really been lost in the development of this activity. For the euphoria which we are thus striving to obtain is nothing but the state of a bygone time, in which we were wont to defray our psychic work with slight expenditure. It is the state of our childhood in which we did not know the comic, were incapable of wit, and did not need humor to make us happy.

---

[1] The characteristic of the "double face" naturally did not escape the authors. Mélinaud, from whom I borrowed the above expression, conceives the condition for laughing in the following formula: "Ce qui fait rire, c'est qui est à la fois, d'un côté, absurde et de l'autre, familier" ("Pourquoi rit-on?" *Revue de deux mondes,* February, 1895). This formula fits in better with wit than with the comic, but it really does not altogether cover the former. Bergson (l. c., p. 96) defines the comic situation by the "reciprocal interference of series," and states: "A situation is invariably comic when it belongs simultaneously to two altogether independent series of events and is capable of being interpreted in two entirely different meanings at the same time." According to Lipps the comic is "the greatness and smallness of the same."

FIVE

TOTEM AND TABOO

THE SAVAGE'S DREAD OF INCEST

PRIMITIVE man is known to us by the stages of development through which he has passed: that is, through the inanimate monuments and implements which he has left behind for us, through our knowledge of his art, his religion and his attitude towards life, which we have received either directly or through the medium of legends, myths and fairy tales; and through the remnants of his ways of thinking that survive in our own manners and customs. Moreover, in a certain sense he is still our contemporary: there are people whom we still consider more closely related to primitive man than to ourselves, in whom we therefore recognize the direct descendants and representatives of earlier man. We can thus judge the so-called savage and semi-savage races; their psychic life assumes a peculiar interest for us, for we can recognize in their psychic life a well-preserved, early stage of our own development.

If this assumption is correct, a comparison of the psychology of primitive races as taught by folklore, with the psychology of the neurotic as it has become known through psychoanalysis, will reveal numerous points of correspondence and throw new light on subjects that are more or less familiar to us.

For outer as well as for inner reasons, I am choosing for this comparison those tribes which have been described by ethnographists as being most backward and wretched: the aborigines of the youngest continent, namely Australia, whose fauna has also preserved for us so much that is archaic and no longer to be found elsewhere.

The aborigines of Australia are looked upon as a peculiar race which shows neither physical nor linguistic relationship with its nearest neighbours, the Melanesian, Polynesian and Malayan races. They do not build houses or permanent huts; they do not cultivate the soil or keep any domestic animals except dogs; and they do not even know the art of pottery. They live exclusively on the flesh of all sorts of animals which they kill in the chase, and on the roots which they dig. Kings or chieftains are unknown among them, and all communal affairs are decided by the elders in assembly. It is quite doubtful whether they evince any traces of religion in the form of worship of higher beings. The tribes living in the interior who have to contend with the greatest vicissitudes of life owing to a scarcity of water, seem in every way more primitive than those who live near the coast.

We surely would not expect that these poor naked cannibals should be moral in their sex life according to our ideas, or that they should have imposed a high degree of restriction upon their sexual impulses. And yet we learn that they have considered it their duty to exercise the most searching care and the most painful rigour in guarding against incestuous sexual relations. In fact their whole social organization seems to serve this object or to have been brought into relation with its attainment.

Among the Australians the system of *Totemism* takes the place of all religious and social institutions. Australian tribes are divided into smaller *septs* or clans, each taking the name of its *totem*. Now what is a totem? As a rule it is an animal, either edible or harmless, or dangerous and feared; more rarely the totem is a plant or a force of nature (rain, water), which stands in a peculiar relation to the whole clan. The totem is first of all the tribal ancestor of the clan, as well as its tutelary spirit and protector; it sends oracles and, though otherwise dangerous, the totem knows and spares its children. The members of a totem are therefore under a sacred obligation not to kill (destroy) their totem, to abstain from eating its meat or from any other enjoyment of it. Any violation of these prohibitions is automatically punished. The character of a totem is inherent not only in a single animal or a single being but in all the members of the species. From time to time festivals are held at which the members of a totem represent or imitate, in ceremonial dances, the movements and characteristics of their totems.

The totem is hereditary either through the maternal or the paternal line (maternal transmission probably always preceded and was only later supplanted by the paternal). The attachment to a totem is the foundation of all the social obligations of an Australian: it extends on the one hand beyond the tribal relationship, and on the other hand it supersedes consanguineous relationship.[1]

The totem is not limited to district or to locality; the members of a totem may live separated from one another and on friendly terms with adherents of other totems.[2]

[1] Frazer, *Totemism and Exogamy*, Vol. I, p. 53. "The totem bond is stronger than the bond of blood or family in the modern sense."

[2] This very brief extract of the totemic system cannot be left without some elucidation and without discussing its limitations. The name Totem or Totam was first learned from the North American Indians by the Englishman, J. Long, in 1791. The subject has gradually acquired great scientific interest and has called forth a copious literature. I refer especially to *Totemism and Exogamy* by J. G. Frazer, 4 vols., 1910, and the books and articles of Andrew Lang (*The Secret of Totem*, 1905). The credit

And now, finally, we must consider that peculiarity of the totemic system which attracts the interest of the psychoanalyst. Almost everywhere where the totem prevails, there also exists the law that *the members of the same totem are not allowed to enter into sexual relations with each other; that is, that they cannot marry each other.* This represents the *exogamy* which is associated with the totem.

This sternly maintained prohibition is very remarkable. There is nothing to account for it in anything that we have hitherto learned from the conception of the totem or from any of its attributes; that is, we do not understand how it happened to enter the system of totemism. We are therefore not astonished if some investigators simply assume that at first exogamy—both as to its origin and to its meaning—had nothing to do with totemism, but that it was added to it at some time without any deeper association, when marriage restrictions proved necessary. However that may be, the association of totemism and exogamy exists, and proves to be very strong.

Let us elucidate the meaning of this prohibition through further discussion.

(*a*) The violation of the prohibition is not left to what is, so to speak, an automatic punishment, as is the case with other violations of the pro-

---

for having recognized the significance of totemism for the ancient history of man belongs to the Scotchman, J. Ferguson MacLennan (*Fortnightly Review*, 1869–70). Exterior to Australia, totemic institutions were found and are still observed among North American Indians, as well as among the races of the Polynesian Islands group, in East India, and in a large part of Africa. Many traces and survivals otherwise hard to interpret lead to the conclusion that totemism also once existed among the aboriginal Aryan and Semitic races of Europe, so that many investigators are inclined to recognize in totemism a necessary phase of human development through which every race has passed.

How then did prehistoric man come to acquire a totem; that is, how did he come to make his descent from this or that animal foundation of his social duties and, as we shall hear, of his sexual restrictions as well? Many different theories have been advanced to explain this, a review of which the reader may find in Wundt's *Voelkerpsychologie* (Vol. II: *Mythus und Religion*).

I promise soon to make the problem of totemism a subject of special study in which an effort will be made to solve it by applying the psychoanalytic method. (Cf. The fourth chapter of this work.)

Not only is the theory of totemism controversial, but the very facts concerning it are hardly to be expressed in such general statements as were attempted above. There is hardly an assertion to which one would not have to add exceptions and contradictions. But it must not be forgotten that even the most primitive and conservative races are, in a certain sense, old, and have a long period behind them during which whatsoever was aboriginal with them has undergone much development and distortion. Thus among those races who still evince it, we find totemism today in the most manifold states of decay and disintegration; we observe that fragments of it have passed over to other social and religious institutions; or it may exist in fixed forms but far removed from its original nature. The difficulty then consists in the fact that it is not altogether easy to decide what in the actual conditions is to be taken as a faithful copy of the significant past and what is to be considered as a secondary distortion of it.

hibitions of the totem (*e.g.*, not to kill the totem animal), but is most energetically avenged by the whole tribe as if it were a question of ward‑ing off a danger that threatens the community as a whole or a guilt that weighs upon all. A few sentences from Frazer's book [1] will show how seri‑ously such trespasses are treated by these savages who, according to our standard, are otherwise very immoral.

"In Australia the regular penalty for sexual intercourse with a person of a forbidden clan is death. It matters not whether the woman is of the same local group or has been captured in war from another tribe; a man of the wrong clan who uses her as his wife is hunted down and killed by his clansmen, and so is the woman; though in some cases, if they succeed in eluding capture for a certain time, the offense may be condoned. In the Ta-Ta-thi tribe, New South Wales, in the rare cases which occur, the man is killed, but the woman is only beaten or speared, or both, till she is nearly dead; the reason given for not actually killing her being that she was probably coerced. Even in casual amours the clan prohibitions are strictly observed; any violations of these prohibitions 'are regarded with the utmost abhorrence and are punished by death' (Howitt)."

(*b*) As the same severe punishment is also meted out for temporary love affairs which have not resulted in childbirth, the assumption of other motives, perhaps of a practical nature, becomes improbable.

(*c*) As the totem is hereditary and is not changed by marriage, the re‑sults of the prohibition, for instance in the case of maternal heredity, are easily perceived. If, for example, the man belongs to a clan with the totem of the Kangaroo and marries a woman of the Emu totem, the children, both boys and girls, are all Emu. According to the totem law incestuous relations with his mother and his sister, who are Emu like himself, are therefore made impossible for a son of this marriage.[2]

(*d*) But we need only a reminder to realize that the exogamy connected with the totem accomplishes more; that is, aims at more than the preven‑tion of incest with the mother or the sisters. It also makes it impossible for the man to have sexual union with all the women of his own group, with a number of females, therefore, who are not consanguineously related to him, by treating all these women like blood relations. The psycholog‑ical justification for this extraordinary restriction, which far exceeds any‑thing comparable to it among civilized races, is not, at first, evident. All

---

[1] Frazer, *l.c.*, p. 54.

[2] But the father, who is a Kangaroo, is free—at least under this prohibition—to com‑mit incest with his daughters, who are Emu. In the case of paternal inheritance of the totem the father would be Kangaroo as well as the children; then incest with the daughters would be forbidden to the father and incest with the mother would be left open to the son. These consequences of the totem prohibition seem to indicate that the maternal inheritance is older than the paternal one, for there are grounds for assuming that the totem prohibitions are directed first of all against the incestuous desires of the son.

we seem to understand is that the rôle of the totem (the animal) as ancestor is taken very seriously. Everybody descended from the same totem is consanguineous; that is, of one family; and in this family the most distant grades of relationship are recognized as an absolute obstacle to sexual union.

Thus, these savages reveal to us an unusually high grade of incest dread or incest sensitiveness, combined with the peculiarity, which we do not very well understand, of substituting the totem relationship for the real blood relationship. But we must not exaggerate this contradiction too much, and let us bear in mind that the totem prohibitions include real incest as a special case.

In what manner the substitution of the totem group for the actual family has come about remains a riddle, the solution of which is perhaps bound up with the explanation of the totem itself. Of course it must be remembered that with a certain freedom of sexual intercourse, extending beyond the limitations of matrimony, the blood relationship, and with it also the prevention of incest, becomes so uncertain that we cannot dispense with some other basis for the prohibition. It is, therefore, not superfluous to note that the customs of Australians recognize social conditions and festive occasions at which the exclusive conjugal right of a man to a woman is violated.

The linguistic customs of these tribes, as well as of most totem races, reveal a peculiarity which undoubtedly is pertinent in this connection. For the designations of relationship of which they make use do not take into consideration the relationship between two individuals, but between an individual and his group; they belong, according to the expression of L. H. Morgan, to the "classifying" system. That means that a man not only calls his begetter "father" but also every other man who, according to the tribal regulations, might have married his mother and thus, become his father; he calls "mother" not only the woman who bore him, but also every other woman who might have become his mother without violation of the tribal laws; he calls "brothers" and "sisters" not only the children of his real parents, but also the children of all the persons named who stand in the parental group relation with him, and so on. The kinship names which two Australians give each other do not, therefore, necessarily point to a blood relationship between them, as they would have to according to the custom of our language; they signify much more the social than the physical relations. An approach to this classifying system is perhaps to be found in our nursery, when the child is induced to greet every male and female friend of the parents as "uncle" and "aunt," or it may be found in a transferred sense when we speak of "Brothers in Apollo," or "Sisters in Christ."

The explanation of this linguistic custom, which seems so strange to us,

is simple if looked upon as a remnant and indication of those marriage
institutions which the Rev. L. Fison has called "group marriage," characterized by a number of men exercising conjugal rights over a number
of women. The children of this group marriage would then rightly look
upon each other as brothers and sisters although not born of the same
mother, and would take all the men of the group for their fathers.

Although a number of authors, as, for instance, B. Westermarck in his
History of Human Marriage, oppose the conclusions which others have
drawn from the existence of group-relationship names, the best authorities on the Australian savages are agreed that the classificatory relationship names must be considered as survivals from the period of group
marriages. And, according to Spencer and Gillen,[1] a certain form of group
marriage can be established as still existing today among the tribes of
the Urabunna and the Dieri. Group marriage therefore preceded individual marriage among these races, and did not disappear without leaving
distinct traces in language and custom.

But if we replace individual marriage, we can then grasp the apparent
excess of cases of incest shunning which we have met among these same
races. The totem exogamy, or prohibition of sexual intercourse between
members of the same clan, seemed the most appropriate means for the
prevention of group incest; and this totem exogamy then became fixed
and long survived its original motivation.

Although we believe we understand the motives of the marriage restrictions among the Australian savages, we have still to learn that the
actual conditions reveal a still more bewildering complication. For there
are only a few tribes in Australia which show no other prohibition besides
the totem barrier. Most of them are so organized that they fall into two
divisions which have been called marriage classes, or phratries. Each of
these marriage groups is exogamous and includes a majority of totem
groups. Usually each marriage group is again divided into two subclasses
(subphratries), and the whole tribe is therefore divided into four classes;
the subclasses thus standing between the phratries and the totem groups.

The typical and very often intricate scheme of organization of an Australian tribe is shown in the diagram opposite:

The twelve totem groups are brought under four subclasses and two
main classes. All the divisions are exogamous.[2] The subclass c forms an
exogamous unit with e, and the subclass d with f. The success or the tendency of these arrangements is quite obvious; they serve as a further
restriction on the marriage choice and on sexual freedom. If there were
only these twelve totem groups—assuming the same number of people in
each group—every member of a group would have $1\frac{1}{12}$ of all the women

[1] *The Native Tribes of Central Australia* (London, 1899).
[2] The number of totems is arbitrarily chosen.

of the tribe to choose from. The existence of the two phratries reduces this number to $\frac{6}{12}$ or $\frac{1}{2}$; a man of the totem ^{a} can only marry a woman from groups 1 to 6. With the introduction of the two subclasses the selection sinks to $\frac{3}{12}$ or $\frac{1}{4}$; a man of the totem ^{a} must limit his marriage choice to a woman of the totems 4, 5, 6.

The historical relations of the marriage classes—of which there are found as many as eight in some tribes—are quite unexplained. We only see that these arrangements seek to attain the same object as the totem exogamy, and even strive for more. But whereas the totem exogamy makes

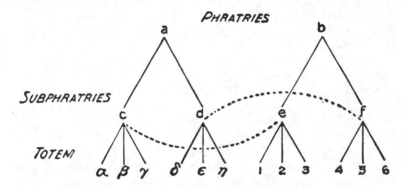

the impression of a sacred statute which sprang into existence, no one knows how, and is therefore a custom, the complicated institutions of the marriage classes, with their subdivisions and the conditions attached to them, seem to spring from legislation with a definite aim in view. They have perhaps taken up afresh the task of incest prohibition because the influence of the totem was on the wane. And while the totem system is, as we know, the basis of all other social obligations and moral restrictions of the tribe, the importance of the phratries generally ceases when the regulation of the marriage choice at which they aimed has been accomplished.

In the further development of the classification of the marriage system there seems to be a tendency to go beyond the prevention of natural and group incest, and to prohibit marriage between more distant group relations, in a manner similar to the Catholic church, which extended the marriage prohibitions always in force for brothers and sisters, to cousins, and invented for them the grades of spiritual kinship.[1]

It would hardly serve our purpose to go into the extraordinarily intricate and unsettled discussion concerning the origin and significance of the marriage classes, or to go more deeply into their relation to totemism. It is sufficient for our purposes to point out the great care expended by

[1] Article *Totemism* in *Encyclopedia Britannica*, eleventh edition, 1911 (A. Lang).

the Australians as well as by other savage people to prevent incest.[1] We must say that these savages are even more sensitive to incest than we, perhaps because they are more subject to temptations than we are, and hence, require more extensive protection against it.

But the incest dread of these races does not content itself with the creation of the institutions described, which, in the main, seem to be directed against group incest. We must add a series of "customs" which watch over the individual behaviour to near relatives in our sense, which are maintained with almost religious severity and of whose object there can hardly be any doubt. These customs or custom prohibitions may be called "avoidances." They spread far beyond the Australian totem races. But here again I must ask the reader to be content with a fragmentary excerpt from the abundant material.

Such restrictive prohibitions are directed in Melanesia against the relations of boys with their mothers and sisters. Thus, for instance, on Lepers Island, one of the New Hebrides, the boy leaves his maternal home at a fixed age and moves to the "clubhouse," where he regularly sleeps and takes his meals. He may still visit his home to ask for food, but if his sister is at home he must go away before he has eaten; if no sister is about, he may sit down to eat near the door. If brother and sister meet by chance in the open, she must run away or turn aside and conceal herself. If the boy recognizes certain footprints in the sand as his sister's, he is not to follow them, nor is she to follow his. He will not even mention her name and will guard against using any current word if it forms part of her name. This avoidance, which begins with the ceremony of puberty, is strictly observed for life. The reserve between mother and son increases with age and generally is more obligatory on the mother's side. If she brings him something to eat she does not give it to him herself but puts it down before him, nor does she address him in the familiar manner of mother and son, but uses the formal address. Similar customs obtain in New Caledonia. If brother and sister meet, she flees into the bush and he passes by without turning his head toward her.[2]

On the Gazelle Peninsula in New Britain a sister, beginning with her marriage, may no longer speak with her brother, nor does she utter his name but designates him by means of a circumlocution.[3]

In New Mecklenburg some cousins are subject to such restrictions, which also apply to brothers and sisters. They may neither approach each

[1] Storfer has recently drawn special attention to this point in his monograph: *Parricide as a Special Case. Papers on Applied Psychic Investigation*, No. 12 (Vienna, 1911).

[2] R. H. Codrington, *The Melanesians*, also Frazer *Totemism and Exogamy*, Vol. I, p. 77.

[3] Frazer, *l.c.*, II, p. 124, referring to Kleintischen: *The Inhabitants of the Coast of the Gazelle Peninsula*.

other, shake hands, nor give each other presents, though they may talk to each other at a distance of several paces. The penalty for incest with a sister is death through hanging.[1]

These rules of avoidance are especially severe in the Fiji Islands where they concern not only consanguineous sisters but group sisters as well.

To hear that these savages hold sacred orgies in which persons of just these forbidden degrees of kinship seek sexual union would seem still more peculiar to us, if we did not prefer to make use of this contradiction to explain the prohibition instead of being astonished at it.[2]

Among the Battas of Sumatra these laws of avoidance affect all near relationships. For instance, it would be most offensive for a Battan to accompany his own sister to an evening party. A brother will feel most uncomfortable in the company of his sister even when other persons are also present. If either comes into the house, the other prefers to leave. Nor will a father remain alone in the house with his daughter any more than the mother with her son. The Dutch missionary who reported these customs added that unfortunately he had to consider them well founded. It is assumed without question by these races that a man and a woman left alone together will indulge in the most extreme intimacy, and as they expect all kinds of punishments and evil consequences from consanguineous intercourse they do quite right to avoid all temptations by means of such prohibitions.[3]

Among the Barongos in Delagoa Bay, in Africa, the most rigorous precautions are directed, curiously enough, against the sister-in-law, the wife of the brother of one's own wife. If a man meets this person who is so dangerous to him, he carefully avoids her. He does not dare to eat out of the same dish with her; he speaks only timidly to her, does not dare to enter her hut, and greets her only with a trembling voice.[4]

Among the Akamba (or Wakamba) in British East Africa, a law of avoidance is in force which one would have expected to encounter more frequently. A girl must carefully avoid her own father between the time of her puberty and her marriage. She hides herself if she meets him on the street and never attempts to sit down next to him, behaving in this way right up to her engagement. But after her marriage no further obstacle is put in the way of her social intercourse with her father.[5]

The most widespread and strictest avoidance, which is perhaps the most interesting one for civilized races is that which restricts the social relations between a man and his mother-in-law. It is quite general in Australia, but it is also in force among the Melanesian, Polynesian and

---

[1] Frazer, l.c., II, p. 131, referring to P. G. Peckel in *Anthropes*, 1908.
[2] Frazer, l.c., II, p 147, referring to the Rev. L. Fison.
[3] Frazer, l.c., II, p. 189.
[4] Frazer, l.c., II, p. 388, referring to Junod.
[5] Frazer, l.c., II, p. 424.

Negro races of Africa as far as the traces of totemism and group relationship reach, and probably further still. Among some of these races similar
prohibitions exist against the harmless social intercourse of a wife with
her father-in-law, but these are by far not so constant or so serious. In a
few cases both parents-in-law become objects of avoidance.

As we are less interested in the ethnographic dissemination than in the
substance and the purpose of the mother-in-law avoidance, I will here also
limit myself to a few examples.

On the Banks Islands these prohibitions are very severe and painfully
exact. A man will avoid the proximity of his mother-in-law as she avoids
his. If they meet by chance on a path, the woman steps aside and turns
her back until he is passed, or he does the same.

In Vanna Lava (Port Patterson) a man will not even walk behind his
mother-in-law along the beach until the rising tide has washed away the
trace of her footsteps. But they may talk to each other at a certain distance. It is quite out of the question that he should ever pronounce the
name of his mother-in-law, or she his.[1]

On the Solomon Islands, beginning with his marriage, a man must
neither see nor speak with his mother-in-law. If he meets her he acts as if
he did not know her and runs away as fast as he can in order to hide
himself.[2]

Among the Zulu Kaffirs custom demands that a man should be ashamed
of his mother-in-law and that he should do everything to avoid her company. He does not enter a hut in which she is and when they meet, he or
she goes aside, she perhaps hiding behind a bush while he holds his shield
before his face. If they cannot avoid each other and the woman has nothing with which to cover herself, she at least binds a bunch of grass around
her head in order to satisfy the ceremonial requirements. Communication
between them must either be made through a third person or else they may
shout at each other at a considerable distance if they have some barrier
between them as, for instance, the enclosure of a kraal. Neither may utter
the other's name.[3]

Among the Basogas, a Negro tribe living in the region of the Nile
sources, a man may talk to his mother-in-law only if she is in another
room of the house and is not visible to him. Moreover, this race abominates incest to such an extent as not to let it go unpunished even among
domestic animals.[4]

Whereas all observers have interpreted the purpose and meaning of the
avoidances between near relatives as protective measures against incest,

---

[1] Frazer, l.c., II, p. 76.
[2] Frazer, l.c., II, p. 113, referring to C. Ribbie: *Two Years among the Cannibals of
the Solomon Islands*, 1905.
[3] Frazer, l.c., II, p. 385.
[4] Frazer, l.c., II, p. 461.

different interpretations have been given for those prohibitions which concern the relationship with the mother-in-law. It was quite incomprehensible why all these races should manifest such great fear of temptation on the part of the man for an elderly woman, old enough to be his mother.[1]

The same objection was also raised against the conception of Fison who called attention to the fact that certain marriage class systems show a gap in that they make marriage between a man and his mother-in-law theoretically not impossible and that a special guarantee was therefore necessary to guard against this possibility.

Sir J. Lubbock, in his book *The Origin of Civilization,* traces back the behaviour of the mother-in-law toward the son-in-law to the former "marriage by capture." "As long as the capture of women actually took place, the indignation of the parents was probably serious enough. When nothing but symbols of this form of marriage survived, the indignation of the parents was also symbolized and this custom continued after its origin had been forgotten." Crawley has found it easy to show how little this tentative explanation agrees with the details of actual observation.

E. B. Tylor thinks that the treatment of the son-in-law on the part of the mother-in-law is nothing more than a form of "cutting" on the part of the woman's family. The man counts as a stranger, and this continues until the first child is born. But even if no account is taken of cases in which this last condition does not remove the prohibition, this explanation is subject to the objection that it does not throw any light on the custom dealing with the relation between mother-in-law and son-in-law, thus overlooking the sexual factor, and that it does not take into account the almost sacred loathing which finds expression in the laws of avoidance.[2]

A Zulu woman who was asked about the basis for this prohibition showed great delicacy of feeling in her answer: "It is not right that he should see the breasts which nursed his wife." [3]

It is known that also among civilized races the relation of son-in-law and mother-in-law belongs to one of the most difficult sides of family organization. Although laws of avoidance no longer exist in the society of the white races of Europe and America, much quarrelling and displeasure would often be avoided if they did exist and did not have to be re-established by individuals. Many a European will see an act of high wisdom in the laws of avoidance which savage races have established to preclude any understanding between two persons who have become so closely related. There is hardly any doubt that there is something in the psychological situation of mother-in-law and son-in-law which furthers hostilities

[1] *v.* Crawley: *The Mystic Rose* (London, 1902), p. 405.

[2] Crawley, *l.c.,* p. 407.

[3] Crawley, *l.c.,* p. 401, referring to Leslie: *Among the Zulus and Amatongas,* 1875.

between them and renders living together difficult. The fact that the witticisms of civilized races show such a preference for this very mother-in-law theme seems to me to point to the fact that the emotional relations between mother-in-law and son-in-law are controlled by components which stand in sharp contrast to each other. I mean that the relation is really "ambivalent"; that is, it is composed of conflicting feelings of tenderness and hostility.

A certain part of these feelings is evident. The mother-in-law is unwilling to give up the possession of her daughter; she distrusts the stranger to whom her daughter has been delivered, and shows a tendency to maintain the dominating position, to which she became accustomed at home. On the part of the man, there is the determination not to subject himself any longer to any foreign will, his jealousy of all persons who preceded him in the possession of his wife's tenderness, and, last but not least, his aversion to being disturbed in his illusion of sexual over-valuation. As a rule such a disturbance emanates for the most part from his mother-in-law who reminds him of her daughter through so many common traits but who lacks all the charm of youth, such as beauty and that psychic spontaneity which makes his wife precious to him.

The knowledge of hidden psychic feelings which psychoanalytic investigation of individuals has given us, makes it possible to add other motives to the above. Where the psycho-sexual needs of the woman are to be satisfied in marriage and family life, there is always the danger of dissatisfaction through the premature termination of the conjugal relation, and the monotony in the wife's emotional life. The ageing mother protects herself against this by living through the lives of her children, by identifying herself with them and making their emotional experiences her own. Parents are said to remain young with their children, and this is, in fact, one of the most valuable psychic benefits which parents derive from their children. Childlessness thus eliminates one of the best means to endure the necessary resignation imposed upon the individual through marriage. This emotional identification with the daughter may easily go so far with the mother that she also falls in love with the man her daughter loves, which leads, in extreme cases, to severe forms of neurotic ailments on account of the violent psychic resistance against this emotional predisposition. At all events the tendency to such infatuation is very frequent with the mother-in-law, and either this infatuation itself or the tendency opposed to it joins the conflict of contending forces in the psyche of the mother-in-law. Very often it is just this harsh and sadistic component of the love emotion which is turned against the son-in-law in order better to suppress the forbidden tender feelings.

The relation of the husband to his mother-in-law is complicated through similar feelings which, however, spring from other sources. The path of object selection has normally led him to his love object through the image of his mother and perhaps his sister; in consequence of the incest barriers his preference for these two beloved persons of his childhood has been deflected and he is then able to find their image in strange objects. He now sees the mother-in-law taking the place of his own mother and of his sister's mother, and there develops a tendency to return to the primitive selection, against which everything in him resists. His incest dread demands that he should not be reminded of the genealogy of his love selection; the actuality of his mother-in-law, whom he had not known all his life like his mother so that her picture can be preserved unchanged in his unconscious, facilitates this rejection. An added mixture of irritability and animosity in his feelings leads us to suspect that the mother-in-law actually represents an incest temptation for the son-in-law, just as it not infrequently happens that a man falls in love with his subsequent mother-in-law before his inclination is transferred to her daughter.

I see no objection to the assumption that it is just this incestuous factor of the relationship which motivates the avoidance between son- and mother-in-law among savages. Among the explanations for the "avoidances" which these primitive races observe so strictly, we would therefore give preference to the opinion originally expressed by Fison, who sees nothing in these regulations but a protection against possible incest. This would also hold good for all the other avoidances between those related by blood and by marriage. There is only one difference, namely, in the first case the incest is direct, so that the purpose of the prevention might be conscious; in the other case, which includes the mother-in-law relation, the incest would be a phantasy temptation brought about by unconscious intermediary links.

We have had little opportunity in this exposition to show that the facts of folk-psychology can be seen in a new light through the application of the psychoanalytic point of view, for the incest dread of savages has long been known as such, and is in need of no further interpretation. What we can add to the further appreciation of incest dread is the statement that it is a subtle infantile trait and is in striking agreement with the psychic life of the neurotic. Psychoanalysis has taught us that the first object selection of the boy is of an incestuous nature and that it is directed to the forbidden objects, the mother and the sister; psychoanalysis has taught us also the methods through which the maturing individual frees himself from these incestuous attractions. The neurotic, however, regularly presents to us a piece of psychic infantilism; he has either not been able to free himself from the childlike conditions of psycho-sexuality, or else he has returned to them (inhibited development and regression). Hence, the incestuous fixations of the libido still play or again are playing the main rôle in his unconscious psychic life. We have gone so far as to declare that the relation to the parents instigated by incestuous longings is the central complex of the neurosis. This discovery of the significance of incest for the neurosis naturally meets with the most general incredulity on the part of the grown-up, normal man; a similar rejection will also meet the researches of Otto Rank, which show in even larger scope to what extent the incest theme stands in the centre of poetical interest and how it forms the material of poetry in countless variations and distortions. We are forced to believe that such a rejection is above all the product of man's deep aversion to his former incest wishes which have since succumbed to repression. It is, therefore, of importance to us to be able to show that man's incest wishes, which later are destined to become unconscious, are still felt to be dangerous by savage races who consider them worthy of the most severe defensive measures.

II

TABOO AND THE AMBIVALENCE OF
EMOTIONS

I

TABOO is a Polynesian word, the translation of which provides difficulties for us because we no longer possess the idea which it connotes. It was still current with the ancient Romans: their word "sacer" was the same as the taboo of the Polynesians. The ἄγος of the Greeks and the Kodaush of the Hebrews must also have signified the same thing which the Polynesians express through their word taboo and what many races in America, Africa (Madagascar), North and Central Asia express through analogous designations.

For us the meaning of taboo branches off into two opposite directions. On the one hand it means to us, sacred, consecrated: but on the other hand it means, uncanny, dangerous, forbidden, and unclean. The opposite for taboo is designated in Polynesian by the word *noa* and signifies something ordinary and generally accessible. Thus something like the concept of reserve inheres in taboo; taboo expresses itself essentially in prohibitions and restrictions. Our combination of "holy dred" would often express the meaning of taboo.

The taboo restrictions are different from religious or moral prohibitions. They are not traced to a commandment of a god, but really they themselves impose their own prohibitions; they are differentiated from moral prohibitions by failing to be included in a system which declares abstinences in general to be necessary and gives reasons for this necessity. The taboo prohibitions lack all justification and are of unknown origin. Though incomprehensible to us they are taken as a matter of course by those who are under their dominance.

Wundt [1] calls taboo the oldest unwritten code of law of humanity. It is generally assumed that taboo is older than the gods and goes back to the pre-religious age.

[1] *Voelkerpsychologie*, II. Band: *Mythus und Religion*, 1906, II, p. 308.

As we are in need of an impartial presentation of the subject of taboo before subjecting it to psychoanalytic consideration I shall now cite an excerpt from the article *Taboo* in the *Encyclopaedia Britannica* written by the anthropologist Northcote W. Thomas: [1]

"Properly speaking, taboo includes only (a) the sacred (or unclean) character of persons or things, (b) the kind of prohibition which results from this character, and (c) the sanctity (or uncleanliness) which results from a violation of the prohibition. The converse of taboo in Polynesia is 'noa' and allied forms which mean 'general' or 'common.' . . .

"Various classes of taboo in the wider sense may be distinguished: 1. natural or direct, the result of 'mana' mysterious (power) inherent in a person or thing; 2. communicated or indirect, equally the result of 'mana' but (*a*) acquired or (*b*) imposed by a priest, chief or other person; 3. intermediate, where both factors are present, as in the appropriation of a wife to her husband. The term taboo is also applied to ritual prohibitions of a different nature; but its use in these senses is better avoided. It might be argued that the term should be extended to embrace cases in which the sanction of the prohibition is the creation of a god or spirit, *i.e.*, to religious interdictions as distinguished from magical, but there is neither automatic action nor contagion in such a case, and a better term for it is religious interdiction.

"The objects of the taboo are many: 1. direct taboos aim at (*a*) protection of important persons—chiefs, priests, etc.—and things against harm; (*b*) safeguarding of the weak—women, children and common people generally—from the powerful mana (magical influence) of chiefs and priests; (*c*) providing against the dangers incurred by handling or coming in contact with corpses, by eating certain food, etc.; (*d*) guarding the chief acts of life—births, initiation, marriage and sexual functions—against interference; (*e*) securing human beings against the wrath or power of gods and spirits; [2] (*f*) securing unborn infants and young children, who stand in a specially sympathetic relation with their parents, from the consequence of certain actions, and more especially from the communication of qualities supposed to be derived from certain foods. 2. Taboos are imposed in order to secure against thieves the property of an individual, his fields, tools, etc."

Other parts of the article may be summarized as follows. Originally the punishment for the violation of a taboo was probably left to an inner, automatic arrangement. The violated taboo avenged itself. Wherever the taboo was related to ideas of gods and demons an automatic punishment was expected from the power of the godhead. In other cases, probably as a result of a further development of the idea, society took over the punish-

[1] Eleventh Edition; this article also gives the most important references.
[2] This application of the taboo can be omitted as not originally belonging in this connection.

ment of the offender, whose action has endangered his companions. Thus man's first systems of punishment are also connected with taboo.

"The violation of a taboo makes the offender himself taboo." The author goes on to say that certain dangers resulting from the violation of a taboo may be exercised through acts of penance and ceremonies of purification.

A peculiar power inherent in persons and ghosts, which can be transmitted from them to inanimate objects is regarded as a source of the taboo. This part of the article reads as follows: "Persons or things which are regarded as taboo may be compared to objects charged with electricity; they are the seat of tremendous power which is transmissible by contact, and may be liberated with destructive effect if the organisms which provoke its discharge are too weak to resist it; the result of a violation of a taboo depends partly on the strength of the magical influence inherent in the taboo object or person, partly on the strength of the opposing mana of the violator of the taboo. Thus, kings and chiefs are possessed of great power, and it is death for their subjects to address them directly; but a minister or other person of greater mana than common, can approach them unharmed, and can in turn be approached by their inferiors without risk. . . . So, too, indirect taboos depend for their strength on the mana of him who opposes them; if it is a chief or a priest, they are more powerful than those imposed by a common person."

The fact that a taboo is transmissible has surely given rise to the effort of removing it through expiatory ceremonies.

The author states that there are permanent and temporary taboos. The former comprise priests and chiefs as well as the dead and everything that has belonged to them. Temporary taboos attach themselves to certain conditions such as menstruation and child-bed, the status of the warrior before and after the expedition, the activities of fishing and of the chase, and similar activities. A general taboo may also be imposed upon a large district like an ecclesiastical interdict, and may then last for years.

If I judge my readers' impressions correctly, I dare say that after hearing all that was said about taboo they are far from knowing what to understand by it and where to store it in their minds. This is surely due to the insufficient information I have given and to the omission of all discussions concerning the relation of taboo to superstition, to belief in the soul, and to religion. On the other hand I fear that a more detailed description of what is known about taboo would be still more confusing; I can therefore assure the reader that the state of affairs is really far from clear. We may say, however, that we deal with a series of restrictions which these primitive races impose upon themselves; this and that is forbidden without any apparent reason; nor does it occur to them to question this matter, for they subject themselves to these restrictions as a matter of course and are convinced that any transgression will be punished automatically in the most severe manner. There are reliable reports that innocent transgressions of such prohibitions have actually been punished automatically. For instance, the innocent offender who had eaten from a forbidden animal became deeply depressed, expected his death and then actually died. The prohibitions mostly concern matters which are capable of enjoyment such as freedom of movement and unrestrained intercourse; in some cases they appear very ingenious, evidently representing obstinences and renunciations; in other cases their content is quite incomprehensible, they seem to concern themselves with trifles and give the impression of ceremonials. Something like a theory seems to underlie all these prohibitions, it seems as if these prohibitions are necessary because some persons and objects possess a dangerous power which is transmitted by contact with the object so charged, almost like a contagion. The quantity of this dangerous property is also taken into consideration. Some persons or things have more of it than others and the danger is precisely in accordance with the charge. The most peculiar part of it is that any one who has violated such a prohibition assumes the nature of the forbidden object as if he had absorbed the whole dangerous charge. This power is inherent in all persons who are more or less prominent, such as kings, priests and the newly born, in all exceptional physical states such as menstruation, puberty and birth, in everything sinister like illness and death and in everything connected with these conditions by virtue of contagion or dissemination.

However, the term "taboo" includes all persons, localities, objects and temporary conditions which are carriers or sources of this mysterious attribute. The prohibition derived from this attribute is also designated as taboo, and lastly taboo, in the literal sense, includes everything that is sacred, above the ordinary, and at the same time dangerous, unclean and mysterious.

Both this word and the system corresponding to it express a fragment of psychic life which really is not comprehensible to us. And indeed it would seem that no understanding of it could be possible without entering into the study of the beliefs in spirits and demons which is so characteristic of these low grades of culture.

Now why should we take any interest at all in the riddle of taboo? Not only, I think, because every psychological problem is well worth the effort of investigation for its own sake, but for other reasons as well. It may be surmised that the taboo of Polynesian savages is after all not so remote from us as we were at first inclined to believe; the moral and customary prohibitions which we ourselves obey may have some essential relation to this primitive taboo the explanation of which may in the end throw light upon the dark origin of our own "categorical imperative."

We are, therefore, inclined to listen with keen expectations when an investigator like W. Wundt gives his interpretation of taboo, especially as he promises to go back to the very roots of the taboo concepts.[1]

Wundt states that the idea of taboo "includes all customs which express dread of particular objects connected with cultic ideas or of actions having reference to them." [2]

On another occasion he says: "In accordance with the general sense of the word we understand by taboo every prohibition laid down in customs or manners or in expressly formulated laws, not to touch an object or to take it for one's own use, or to make use of certain proscribed words. . . ." Accordingly there would not be a single race or stage of culture which had escaped the injurious effects of taboo.

Wundt then shows why he finds it more practical to study the nature of taboo in the primitive states of Australian savages rather than in the higher culture of the Polynesian races. In the case of the Australians he divides taboo prohibitions into three classes according as they concern animals, persons or other objects. The animal taboo, which consists essentially of the taboo against killing and eating, forms the nucleus of Totemism.[3] The taboo of the second class, which has human beings for its object, is of an essentially different nature. To begin with, it is restricted to conditions which bring about an unusual situation in life for the person tabooed. Thus young men at the feast of initiation, women during menstruation and immediately after delivery, newly born children, the diseased and especially the dead, are all taboo. The constantly used property of any person, such as his clothes, tools and weapons, is permanently taboo for everybody else. In Australia the new name which a youth receives at his initiation into manhood becomes a part of his most personal property, it is taboo and must be kept secret. The taboos of the third class, which apply to trees, plants, houses and localities, are more variable and seem only to follow the rule that anything which for any reason arouses dread or is mysterious, becomes subject to taboo.

Wundt himself has to acknowledge that the changes which taboo undergoes in the richer culture of the Polynesians and in the Malayan Archipeligo are not very profound. The greater social differentiation of these races manifests itself in the fact that chiefs, kings and priests exercise an especially effective taboo and are themselves exposed to the strongest taboo compulsion.

But the real sources of taboo lie deeper than in the interests of the privileged classes: "They begin where the most primitive and at the same time the most enduring human impulses have their origin, namely,

[1] *Voelkerpsychologie, Religion und Mythus,* p. 300.
[2] *l.c.,* p. 237.
[3] Cf. Chapter I.

in the fear of the effect of demonic powers." [1] "The taboo, which originally was nothing more than the objectified fear of the demonic power thought to be concealed in the tabooed object, forbids the irritation of this power and demands the placation of the demon whenever the taboo has been knowingly or unknowingly violated."

The taboo then gradually became an autonomous power which has detached itself from demonism. It becomes the compulsion of custom and tradition and finally the law. "But the commandment concealed behind taboo prohibitions which differ materially according to place and time, had originally the meaning: Beware of the wrath of the demons."

Wundt therefore teaches that taboo is the expression and evolution of the belief of primitive races in demonic powers, and that later taboo has dissociated itself from this origin and has remained a power simply because it was one by virtue of a kind of a psychic persistence and in this manner it became the root of our customs and laws. As little as one can object to the first part of this statement I feel, however, that I am only voicing the impression of many of my readers if I call Wundt's explanation disappointing. Wundt's explanation is far from going back to the sources of taboo concepts or to their deepest roots. For neither fear nor demons can be accepted in psychology as finalities defying any further deduction. It would be different if demons really existed; but we know that, like gods, they are only the product of the psychic powers of man; they have been created from and out of something.

Wundt also expresses a number of important though not altogether clear opinions about the double meaning of taboo. According to him the division between *sacred* and *unclean* does not yet exist in the first primitive stages of taboo. For this reason these conceptions entirely lack the significance which they could only acquire later on when they came to be contrasted. The animal, person or place on which there is a taboo is demonic, that is, not sacred, and therefore not yet, in the later sense, unclean. The expression taboo is particularly suitable for this undifferentiated and intermediate meaning of the demonic, in the sense of something which may not be touched, since it emphasizes a characteristic which finally adheres both to what is sacred and to the unclean, namely, the dread of contact. But the fact that this important characteristic is permanently held in common points to the existence of an original agreement here between these two spheres which gave way to a differentiation only as the result of further conditions through which both finally developed into opposites.

The belief associated with the original taboo, according to which a demonic power concealed in the object avenges the touching of it or its forbidden use by bewitching the offender was still an entirely objectified

[1] *l.c.,* p. 307.

fear. This had not yet separated into the two forms which it assumed at a more developed stage, namely, awe and aversion.

How did this separation come about? According to Wundt, this was done through the transference of taboo prohibitions from the sphere of demons to that of theistic conceptions. The antithesis of sacred and unclean coincides with the succession of two mythological stages the first of which did not entirely disappear when the second was reached but continued in a state of greatly lowered esteem which gradually turned into contempt. It is a general law in mythology that a preceding stage, just because it has been overcome and pushed back by a higher stage, maintains itself next to it in a debased form so that the objects of its veneration become objects of aversion.[1]

Wundt's further elucidations refer to the relation of taboo to lustration and sacrifice.

2

He who approaches the problem of taboo from the field of psychoanalysis, which is concerned with the study of the unconscious part of the individual's psychic life, needs but a moment's reflection to realize that these phenomena are by no means foreign to him. He knows people who have individually created such taboo prohibitions for themselves, which they follow as strictly as savages observe the taboos common to their tribe or society. If he were not accustomed to call these individuals "compulsion neurotics" he would find the term "taboo disease" quite appropriate for their malady. Psychoanalytic investigation has taught him the clinical etiology and the essential part of the psychological mechanism of this compulsion disease, so that he cannot resist applying what he has learnt there to explain corresponding manifestations in folk psychology.

There is one warning to which we shall have to give heed in making this attempt. The similarity between taboo and compulsion disease may be purely superficial, holding good only for the manifestations of both without extending into their deeper characteristics. Nature loves to use identical forms in the most widely different biological connections as, for instance, for coral stems and plants and even for certain crystals or for the formation of certain chemical precipitates. Assuredly would it be both premature and unprofitable to base conclusions relating to inner relationships upon the correspondence of merely mechanical conditions. We shall bear this warning in mind without, however, giving up our intended comparison on account of the possibility of such confusions.

The first and most striking correspondence between the compulsion prohibitions of neurotics and taboo lies in the fact that the origin of

[1] l.c., p. 313.

these prohibitions is just as unmotivated and enigmatic. They have appeared at some time or other and must now be retained on account of an unconquerable anxiety. An external threat of punishment is superfluous, because an inner certainty (a conscience) exists that violation will be followed by unbearable disaster. The very most that compulsion patients can tell us is the vague premonition that some person of their environment will suffer harm if they should violate the prohibition. Of what the harm is to consist is not known, and this inadequate information is more likely to be obtained during the later discussions of the expiatory and defensive actions than when the prohibitions themselves are being discussed.

As in the case of taboo, the nucleus of the neurotic prohibition is the act of touching, whence we derive the name "touching phobia" or *délire de toucher*. The prohibition extends not only to direct contact with the body but also to the figurative use of the phrase as "to come into contact" or "be in touch with some one or something." Anything that leads the thoughts to what is prohibited and thus calls forth mental contact is just as much prohibited as immediate bodily contact; this same extension is also found in taboo.

Some prohibitions are easily understood from their purpose but others strike us as incomprehensible, foolish and senseless. We designate such commands as "ceremonials" and we find that taboo customs show the same variations.

Obsessive prohibitions possess an extraordinary capacity for displacement; they make use of almost any form of connection to extend from one object to another and then in turn make this new object "impossible," as one of my patients aptly puts it. This impossibility finally lays an embargo upon the whole world. The compulsion neurotics act as if the "impossible" persons and things were the carriers of a dangerous contagion which is ready to displace itself through contact to all neighbouring things. We have already emphasized the same characteristics of contagion and transference in the description of taboo prohibitions. We also know that any one, who has violated a taboo by touching something which is taboo, becomes taboo himself, and no one may come into contact with him.

I shall put side by side two examples of transference or, to use a better term, displacement, one from the life of the Maori, and the other from my observation of a woman suffering from a compulsion neurosis:

"For a similar reason a Maori chief would not blow on a fire with his mouth; for his sacred breath would communicate its sanctity to the fire, which would pass it on to the meat in the pot, which would pass it on to the man who ate the meat which was in the pot, which stood on the fire, which was breathed on by the chief; so that the eater, infected by the chief's breath conveyed through these intermediaries, would surely die." [1]

My patient demanded that a utensil which her husband had purchased and brought home should be removed lest it make the place where she lived impossible. For she had heard that this object was bought in a store which was situated, let us say, in Stag Street. But as the word "stag" was the name of a friend now in a distant city, whom she had known in her youth under her maiden name and whom she now found "impossible," that name was taboo, and the object bought in Vienna was just as taboo as this friend with whom she did not want to come in contact.

Compulsion prohibitions, like taboo prohibitions, entail the most extraordinary renunciations and restrictions of life, but a part of these can be removed by carrying out certain acts which now also must be done because they have acquired a compulsive character (obsessive acts); there is no doubt that these acts are in the nature of penances, expiations, defence reactions, and purifications. The most common of these obsessive acts is washing with water (washing obsession). A part of the taboo prohibitions can also be replaced in this way, that is to say, their violation can be made good through such a "ceremonial," and here too lustration through water is the preferred way.

Let us now summarize the points in which the correspondence between taboo customs and the symptoms of compulsion neurosis are most clearly manifested: 1. In the lack of motivation of the commandments, 2. in their enforcement through an inner need, 3. in their capacity for displacement and in the danger of contagion from what is prohibited, 4. and in the causation of ceremonial actions and commandments which emanate from the forbidden.

However, psychoanalysis has made us familiar with the clinical history as well as the psychic mechanism of compulsion neurosis. Thus, the history of a typical case of touching phobia reads as follows: In the very beginning, during the early period of childhood, the person manifested a strong pleasure in touching himself, the object of which was much more specialized than one would be inclined to suspect. Presently the carrying out of this very pleasurable act of touching was opposed by a prohibition from without. [2] The prohibition was accepted because it was supported by strong inner forces; [3] it proved to be stronger than the impulse which wanted to manifest itself through this act of touching. But due to the primitive psychic constitution of the child this prohibition did not succeed in abolishing the impulse. Its only success lay in repressing the impulse (the pleasure of touching) and banishing it into the un-

---

[1] Frazer, *The Golden Bough*, II: *Taboo and the Perils of the Soul*, 1911, p. 136.
[2] Both the pleasure and the prohibition referred to touching one's own genitals.
[3] The relation to beloved persons who impose the prohibition.

conscious. Both the prohibition and the impulse remained; the impulse because it had only been repressed and not abolished, the prohibition, because if it had ceased, the impulse would have broken through into consciousness and would have been carried out. An unsolved situation, a psychic fixation, had thus been created and now everything else emanated from the continued conflict between prohibition and impulse.

The main characteristic of the psychic constellation which has thus gone under fixation lies in what one might call the ambivalent behaviour [1] of the individual to the object, or rather to an action regarding it. The individual constantly wants to carry out this action (the act of touching), he sees in it the highest pleasure, but he may not carry it out, and he even abominates it. The opposition between these two streams cannot be easily adjusted because—there is no other way to express it—they are so localized in the psychic life that they cannot meet. The prohibition becomes fully conscious, while the surviving pleasure of touching remains unconscious, the person knowing nothing about it. If this psychological factor did not exist the ambivalence could neither maintain itself so long nor lead to such subsequent manifestations.

In the clinical history of the case we have emphasized the appearance of the prohibition in early childhood as the determining factor, but for the further elaboration of the neurosis this rôle is played by the repression which appears at this age. On account of the repression which has taken place, which is connected with forgetting (amnesia), the motivation of the prohibition that has become conscious remains unknown, and all attempts to unravel it intellectually must fail, as the point of attack cannot be found. The prohibition owes its strength—its compulsive character—to its association with its unknown counterpart, the hidden and unabated pleasure, that is to say, to an inner need into which conscious insight is lacking. The transferability and reproductive power of the prohibition reflect a process which harmonizes with the unconscious pleasure and is very much facilitated through the psychological determinants of the unconscious. The pleasure of the impulse constantly undergoes displacement in order to escape the blocking which it encounters and seeks to acquire surrogates for the forbidden in the form of substitutive objects and actions. For the same reason the prohibition also wanders and spreads to the new aims of the proscribed impulse. Every new advance of the repressed libido is answered by the prohibition with a new severity. The mutual inhibition of these two contending forces creates a need for discharge and for lessening the existing tension, in which we may recognize the motivation for the compulsive acts. In the neurosis there are distinctly acts of compromise which on the one hand may be regarded as proofs of remorse and efforts to expiate and

[1] To use an excellent term coined by Bleuler.

similiar actions; but on the other hand they are at the same time substitutive actions which recompense the impulse for what has been forbidden. It is a law of neurotic diseases that these obsessive acts serve the impulse more and more and come nearer and nearer to the original and forbidden act.

We may now make the attempt to study taboo as if it were of the same nature as the compulsive prohibitions of our patients. It must naturally be clearly understood that many of the taboo prohibitions which we shall study are already secondary, displaced and distorted, so that we shall have to be satisfied if we can shed some light upon the earliest and most important taboo prohibitions. We must also remember that the differences in the situation of the savage and of the neurotic may be important enough to exclude complete correspondence and prevent a point by point transfer from one to the other such as would be possible if we were dealing with exact copies.

First of all it must be said that it is useless to question savages as to the real motivation of their prohibitions or as to the genesis of taboo. According to our assumption they must be incapable of telling us anything about it since this motivation is "unconscious" to them. But following the model of the compulsive prohibition we shall construct the history of taboo as follows: Taboos are very ancient prohibitions which at one time were forced upon a generation of primitive people from without, that is, they probably were forcibly impressed upon them by an earlier generation. These prohibitions concerned actions for which there existed a strong desire. The prohibitions maintained themselves from generation to generation, perhaps only as the result of a tradition set up by paternal and social authority. But in later generations they have perhaps already become "organized" as a piece of inherited psychic property. Whether there are such "innate ideas" or whether these have brought about the fixation of the taboo by themselves or by co-operating with education no one could decide in the particular case in question. The persistence of taboo teaches, however, one thing, namely, that the original pleasure to do the forbidden still continues among taboo races. They therefore assume an *ambivalent attitude* toward their taboo prohibitions; in their unconscious they would like nothing better than to transgress them but they are also afraid to do it; they are afraid just because they would like to transgress, and the fear is stronger than the pleasure. But in every individual of the race the desire for it is unconscious, just as in the neurotic.

The oldest and most important taboo prohibitions are the two basic laws of *totemism:* namely, not to kill the totem animal, and to avoid sexual intercourse with totem companions of the other sex.

It would, therefore, seem that these must have been the oldest and strongest desires of mankind. We cannot understand this and therefore we cannot use these examples to test our assumptions as long as the meaning and the origin of the totemic system is so wholly unknown to us. But the very wording of these taboos and the fact that they occur together will remind any one who knows the results of the psychoanalytic investigation of individuals, of something quite definite which psycho-analysts call the central point of the infantile wish life and the nucleus of the later neurosis.[1]

All other varieties of taboo phenomena which have led to the attempted classifications noted above become unified if we sum them up in the following sentence: The basis of taboo is a forbidden action for which there exists a strong inclination in the unconscious.

We know, without understanding it, that whoever does what is pro-hibited and violates the taboo, becomes himself taboo. But how can we connect this fact with the other, namely that the taboo adheres not only to persons who have done what is prohibited, but also to persons who are in exceptional circumstances, as well as to these circumstances themselves and to impersonal things? What can this dangerous attribute be which always remains the same under all these different conditions? Only one thing, namely, the propensity to arouse the ambivalence of man and to tempt him to violate the prohibition.

An individual, who has violated a taboo, becomes himself taboo be-cause he has the dangerous property of tempting others to follow his example. He arouses envy; why should he be allowed to do what is prohibited to others? He is therefore really *contagious*, in so far as every example incites to imitation and, therefore, he himself must be avoided.

But a person may become permanently or temporarily taboo without having violated any taboos, for the simple reason that he is in a con-dition which has the property of inciting the forbidden desires of others and of awakening the ambivalent conflict in them. Most of the excep-tional positions and conditions have this character and possess this dangerous power. The king or chieftain arouses envy of his prerogatives; everybody would perhaps like to be king. The dead, the newly born, and women when they are incapacitated, all act as incitements be-cause of their peculiar helplessness, while the individual who has just reached sexual maturity tempts through the promise of a new pleasure. Therefore, all these persons and all these conditions are taboo, for one must not yield to the temptations which they offer.

Now, too, we understand why the forces inherent in the "mana" of various persons can neutralize one another so that the mana of one individual can partly cancel that of the other. The taboo of a king is too strong for his subject because the social difference between them

[1] See Chapter IV: *Totemism*, etc.

is too great. But a minister, for example, can become the harmless mediator between them. Translated from the language of taboo into the language of normal psychology this means: the subject who shrinks from the tremendous temptation which contact with the king creates for him can brook the intercourse of an official, whom he does not have to envy so much and whose position perhaps seems attainable to him. The minister, on his part, can moderate his envy of the king by taking into consideration the power that has been granted to him. Thus, smaller differences in the magic power that lead to temptation are less to be feared than exceptionally big differences.

It is equally clear how the violation of certain taboo prohibitions becomes a social danger which must be punished or expiated by all the members of society lest it harm them all. This danger really exists if we substitute the known impulses for the unconscious desires. It consists in the possibility of imitation, as a result of which society would soon be dissolved. If the others did not punish the violation they would perforce become aware that they want to imitate the evil doer.

Though the secret meaning of a taboo prohibition cannot possibly be of so special a nature as in the case of a neurosis, we must not be astonished to find that touching plays a similar rôle in taboo prohibition as in the *délire de toucher*. To touch is the beginning of every act of possession, of every attempt to make use of a person or thing.

We have interpreted the power of contagion which inheres in the taboo as the property of leading into temptation, and of inciting to imitation. This does not seem to be in accord with the fact that the contagiousness of the taboo is above all manifested in the transference to objects which thus themselves become carriers of the taboo.

This transferability of the taboo reflects what is found in the neurosis, namely, the constant tendency of the unconscious impulse to become displaced through associative channels upon new objects. Our attention is thus drawn to the fact that the dangerous magic power of the mana corresponds to two real faculties, the capacity of reminding man of his forbidden wishes, and the apparently more important one of tempting him to violate the prohibition in the service of these wishes. Both functions reunite into one, however, if we assume it to be in accord with a primitive psychic life that with the awakening of a memory of a forbidden action there should also be combined the awakening of the tendency to carry out the action. Memory and temptation then again coincide. We must also admit that if the example of a person who has violated a prohibition leads another to the same action, the disobedience of the prohibition has been transmitted like a contagion, just as the taboo is transferred from a person to an object, and from this to another.

If the violation of a taboo can be condoned through expiation or penance, which means, of course, a *renunciation* of a possession or a liberty, we have the proof that the observance of a taboo regulation was itself a renunciation of something really wished for. The omission of one renunciation is cancelled through a renunciation at some other point. This would lead us to conclude that, as far as taboo ceremonials are concerned, penance is more primitive than purification.

Let us now summarize what understanding we have gained of taboo through its comparison with the compulsive prohibition of the neurotic. Taboo is a very primitive prohibition imposed from without (by an authority) and directed against the strongest desires of man. The desire to violate it continues in the unconscious; persons who obey the taboo have an ambivalent feeling toward what is affected by the taboo. The magic power attributed to taboo goes back to its ability to lead man into temptation; it behaves like a contagion, because the example is contagious, and because the prohibited desire becomes displaced in the unconscious upon something else. The expiation for the violation of a taboo through a renunciation proves that a renunciation is at the basis of the observance of the taboo.

3

We may ask what we have gained from the comparison of taboo with compulsion neurosis and what value can be claimed for the interpretation we have given on the basis of this comparison? Our interpretation is evidently of no value unless it affords an advantage not to be had in any other way and unless it affords a better understanding of taboo than was otherwise possible. We might claim that we have already given proof of its usefulness in what has been said above; but we shall have to try to strengthen our proof by continuing the explanation of taboo prohibitions and customs in detail.

But we can avail ourselves of another method. We can shape our investigation so as to ascertain whether a part of the assumptions which we have transferred from the neurosis to the taboo, or the conclusions at which we have thereby arrived can be demonstrated directly in the phenomena of taboo. We must decide, however, what we want to look for. The assertion concerning the genesis of taboo, namely, that it was derived from a primitive prohibition which was once imposed from without, cannot, of course, be proved. We shall therefore seek to confirm those psychological conditions for taboo with which we have become acquainted in the case of compulsion neurosis. How did we gain our knowledge of these psychological factors in the case of neurosis? Through the analytical study of the symptoms, especially the compulsive actions, the defense reactions and the obsessive commands. These mechanisms gave every indication of having been derived from *ambivalent* impulses or tendencies, they either represented simultaneously the wish and counter-wish or they served preponderantly one of the two contrary tendencies. If we should now succeed in showing that ambivalence, *i.e.*, the sway of contrary tendencies, exists also in the case of taboo regulations or if we should find among taboo mechanisms some which like neurotic obsessions give simultaneous expression to both currents, we would have established what is practically the most important point in the psychological correspondence between taboo and compulsion neurosis.

We have already mentioned that the two fundamental taboo prohibitions are inaccessible to our analysis because they belong to totemism; another part of the taboo rules is of secondary origin and cannot be used for our purpose. For among these races taboo has become the general form of law giving and has helped to promote social tendencies which are certainly younger than taboo itself, as for instance, the taboos imposed by chiefs and priests to insure their property and privileges. But there still remains a large group of laws which we may undertake to investigate. Among these I lay stress on those taboos which are attached (*a*) to enemies, (*b*) to chiefs, and (*c*) to the dead; the material for our investigation is taken from the excellent collection of J. G. Frazer in his great work, *The Golden Bough*.[1]

(a) The Treatment of Enemies

Inclined as we may have been to ascribe to savage and semi-savage races uninhibited and remorseless cruelty towards their enemies, it is of great interest to us to learn that with them, too, the killing of a person compels the observation of a series of rules which are associated with taboo customs. These rules are easily brought under four groups; they demand 1. reconciliation with the slain enemy, 2. restrictions, 3. acts of expiation, and purifications of the manslayer, and 4. certain ceremonial rites. The incomplete reports do not allow us to decide with certainty how general or how isolated such taboo customs may be among these races, but this is a matter of indifference as far as our interest in these occurrences is concerned. Still, it may be assumed that we are dealing with widespread customs and not with isolated peculiarities.

The reconciliation customs practised on the island of Timor, after a victorious band of warriors has returned with the severed heads of the vanquished enemy, are especially significant because the leader of the expedition is subject to heavy additional restrictions. "At the solemn entry of the victors, sacrifices are made to conciliate the souls of the enemy; otherwise one would have to expect harm to come to the victors. A dance is given and a song is sung in which the slain enemy is mourned

[1] Third Edition, Part II: *Taboo and the Perils of the Soul*, 1911.

and his forgiveness is implored: 'Be not angry,' they say, 'because your head is here with us; had we been less lucky, our heads might have been exposed in your village. We have offered the sacrifice to appease you. Your spirit may now rest and leave us at peace. Why were you our enemy? Would it not have been better that we should remain friends? Then your blood would not have been spilt and your head would not have been cut off.' " [1]

Similar customs are found among the Palu in Celebes; the Gallas sacrifice to the spirits of their dead enemies before they return to their home villages. [2]

Other races have found methods of making friends, guardians and protectors out of their former enemies after they are dead. This consists in the tender treatment of the severed heads, of which many wild tribes of Borneo boast. When the See-Dayaks of Sarawak bring home a head from a war expedition, they treat it for months with the greatest kindness and courtesy and address it with the most endearing names in their language. The best morsels from their meals are put into its mouth, together with titbits and cigars. The dead enemy is repeatedly entreated to hate his former friends and to bestow his love upon his new hosts because he has now become one of them. It would be a great mistake to think that any derision is attached to this treatment, horrible though it may seem to us. [3]

Observers have been struck by the mourning for the enemy after he is slain and scalped, among several of the wild tribes of North America. When a Choctaw had killed an enemy he began a month's mourning during which he submitted himself to serious restrictions. The Dakota Indians mourned in the same way. One authority mentions that the Osaga Indians after mourning for their own dead mourned for their foes as if they had been friends. [4]

Before proceeding to the other classes of taboo customs for the treatment of enemies, we must define our position in regard to a pertinent objection. Both Frazer as well as other authorities may well be quoted against us to show that the motive for these rules of reconciliation is quite simple and has nothing to do with "ambivalence." These races are dominated by a superstitious fear of the spirits of the slain, a fear which was also familiar to classical antiquity, and which the great British dramatist brought upon the stage in the hallucinations of Macbeth and Richard the Third. From this superstition all the reconciliation rules as well as the restrictions and expiations which we shall discuss

---

[1] Frazer, *l.c.*, p. 166.
[2] Paulitschke, *Ethnography of North-east Africa.*
[3] Frazer *Adonis, Attis, Osiris,* p. 248, 1907; referring to Hugh Low, *Sarawak* (London, 1848).
[4] J. O. Dorsay, see Frazer, *Taboo,* etc., p. 181.

later can be logically deduced; moreover, the ceremonies included in the fourth group also argue for this interpretation, since the only explanation of which they admit is the effort to drive away the spirits of the slain which pursue the manslayers.[1] Besides, the savages themselves directly admit their fear for the spirits of their slain foes and trace back the taboo customs under discussion to this fear.

This objection is certainly pertinent and if it were adequate as well we would gladly spare ourselves the trouble of our attempt to find a further explanation. We postpone the consideration of this objection until later and for the present merely contrast it to the interpretation derived from our previous discussion of taboo. All these rules of taboo lead us to conclude that other impulses besides those that are merely hostile find expression in the behaviour towards enemies. We see in them manifestations of repentance, of regard for the enemy, and of a bad conscience for having slain him. It seems that the commandment, Thou shalt not slay, which could not be violated without punishment, existed also among these savages, long before any legislation was received from the hands of a god.

We now return to the remaining classes of taboo rules. The *restrictions* laid upon the victorious manslayer are unusually frequent and are mostly of a serious nature. In Timor (compare the reconciliation customs mentioned above) the leader of the expedition cannot return to his house under any circumstances. A special hut is erected for him in which he spends two months engaged in the observance of various rules of purification. During this period he may not see his wife or nourish himself; another person must put his food in his mouth.[2] Among some Dayak tribes warriors returning from a successful expedition must remain sequestered for several days and abstain from certain foods; they may not touch iron and must remain away from their wives. In Logea, an island near New Guinea, men who have killed an enemy or have taken part in the killing, lock themselves up in their houses for a week. They avoid every intercourse with their wives and friends, they do not touch their victuals with their hands, and live on nothing but vegetable foods which are cooked for them in special dishes. As a reason for this last restriction it is alleged that they must smell the blood of the slain, otherwise they would sicken and die. Among the Toaripi- or Motumotu-tribes in New Guinea a manslayer must not approach his wife and must not touch his food with his fingers. A second person must feed him with special food. This continues until the next new moon.

I avoid the complete enumeration of all the cases of restrictions of the

[1] Frazer, *Taboo*, pp. 166–174. These ceremonies consist of hitting shields, shouting, bellowing and making noises with various instruments, etc.
[2] Frazer, *Taboo*, p. 166, referring to S. Mueller, *Reisen en Onderzoekingen in den Indischen Archipel*. (Amsterdam, 1857).

victorious slayer mentioned by Frazer, and emphasize only such cases in which the character of taboo is especially noticeable or where the restriction appears in connection with expiation, purification and ceremonial.

Among the Monumbos in New Guinea a man who has killed an enemy in combat becomes "unclean," the same word being employed which is applied to women during menstruation or confinement. For a considerable period he is not allowed to leave the men's club-house, while the inhabitants of his village gather about him and celebrate his victory with songs and dances. He must not touch any one, not even his wife and children; if he did so they would be afflicted with boils. He finally becomes clean through washing and other ceremonies.

Among the Natchez in North America young warriors who had procured their first scalp were bound for six months to the observance of certain renunciations. They were not allowed to sleep with their wives or to eat meat, and received only fish and maize pudding as nourishment. When a Choctaw had killed and scalped an enemy he began a period of mourning for one month, during which he was not allowed to comb his hair. When his head itched he was not allowed to scratch it with his hand but used a small stick for this purpose.

After a Pima Indian had killed an Apache he had to submit himself to severe ceremonies of purification and expiation. During a fasting period of sixteen days he was not allowed to touch meat or salt, to look at a fire or to speak to any one. He lived alone in the woods, where he was waited upon by an old woman who brought him a small allowance of food; he often bathed in the nearest river, and carried a lump of clay on his head as a sign of mourning. On the seventeenth day there took place a public ceremony through which he and his weapons were solemnly purified. As the Pima Indians took the manslayer taboo much more seriously than their enemies and, unlike them, did not postpone expiation and purification until the end of the expedition, their prowess in war suffered very much through their moral severity or what might be called their piety. In spite of their extraordinary bravery they proved to be unsatisfactory allies to the Americans in their wars against the Apaches.

The detail and variations of these expiatory and purifying ceremonies after the killing of an enemy would be most interesting for purposes of a more searching study, but I need not enumerate any more of them here because they cannot furnish us with any new points of view. I might mention that the temporary or permanent isolation of the professional executioner, which was maintained up to our time, is a case in point. The position of the "free-holder" in mediæval society really conveys a good idea of the "taboo" of savages.[1]

[1] For these examples see Frazer, *Taboo*, pp. 165–170, "Manslayers Tabooed."

The current explanation of all these rules of reconciliation, restriction, expiation and purification, combines two principles, namely, the extension of the taboo of the dead to everything that has come into contact with him, and the fear of the spirit of the slain. In what combination these two elements are to explain the ceremonial, whether they are to be considered as of equal value or whether one of them is primary and the other secondary, and which one, is nowhere stated, nor would this be an easy matter to decide. In contradistinction to all this we emphasize the unity which our interpretation gains by deducing all these rules from the ambivalence of the emotion of savages towards their enemies.

(b) The Taboo of Rulers

The behaviour of primitive races towards their chiefs, kings, and priests, is controlled by two principles which seem rather to supplement than to contradict each other. They must both be guarded and be guarded against.[1]

Both objects are accomplished through innumerable rules of taboo. Why one must guard against rulers is already known to us; because they are the bearers of that mysterious and dangerous magic power which communicates itself by contact, like an electric charge, bringing death and destruction to any one not protected by a similar charge. All direct or indirect contact with this dangerous sacredness is therefore avoided, and where it cannot be avoided a ceremonial has been found to ward off the dreaded consequences. The Nubas in East Africa, for instance, believe that they must die if they enter the house of their priest-king, but that they escape this danger if, on entering, they bare the left shoulder and induce the king to touch it with his hand. Thus we have the remarkable case of the king's touch becoming the healing and protective measure against the very dangers that arise from contact with the king; but it is probably a question of the healing power of the intentional touching on the king's part in contradistinction to the danger of touching him, in other words, of the opposition between passivity and activity towards the king.

Where the healing power of the royal touch is concerned we do not have to look for examples among savages. In comparatively recent times the kings of England exercised this power upon scrofula, whence it was called "The King's Evil." Neither Queen Elizabeth nor any of her successors renounced this part of the royal prerogative. Charles I is said to have healed a hundred sufferers at one time, in the year 1633. Under his dissolute son Charles II, after the great English revolution had passed, royal healings of scrofula attained their greatest vogue.

[1] Frazer, *Taboo*, p. 132. "He must not only be guarded, he must also be guarded against."

This king is said to have touched close to a hundred thousand victims of scrofula in the course of his reign. The crush of those seeking to be cured used to be so great that on one occasion six or seven patients suffered death by suffocation instead of being healed. The skeptical king of Orange, William III, who became king of England after the banishment of the Stuarts, refused to exercise the spell; on the one occasion when he consented to practise the touch, he did so with words: "May God give you better health and more sense." [1]

The following account will bear witness to the terrible effect of touching by virtue of which a person, even though unintentionally, becomes active against his king or against what belongs to him. A chief of high rank and great holiness in New Zealand happened to leave the remains of his meal by the roadside. A young slave came along, a strong healthy fellow, who saw what was left over and started to eat it. Hardly had he finished when a horrified spectator informed him of his offence in eating the meal of the chief. The man had been a strong, brave warrior, but as soon as he heard this he collapsed and was afflicted by terrible convulsions, from which he died towards sunset of the following day. [2] A Maori woman ate a certain fruit and then learned that it came from a place on which there was a taboo. She cried out that the spirit of the chief whom she had thus offended would surely kill her. This incident occurred in the afternoon, and on the next day at twelve o'clock she was dead. [3] The tinder box of a Maori chief once cost several persons their lives. The chief had lost it, and those who found it used it to light their pipes. When they learned whose property the tinder box was they all died of fright. [4]

It is hardly astonishing that the need was felt to isolate dangerous persons like chiefs and priests, by building a wall around them which made them inaccessible to others. We surmise that this wall, which originally was constructed out of taboo rules, still exists to-day in the form of court ceremony.

But probably the greater part of this taboo of the rulers cannot be traced back to the need of guarding against them. The other point of view in the treatment of privileged persons, the need of guarding them from dangers with which they are threatened, has had a distinct share in the creation of taboo and therefore of the origin of court etiquette.

The necessity of guarding the king from every conceivable danger arises from his great importance for the weal and woe of his subjects. Strictly speaking, he is a person who regulates the course of the world; his people have to thank him not only for rain and sunshine, which

[1] Frazer, *The Magic Art*, I, p. 368.
[2] *Old New Zealand*, by a Pakeha Maori (London, 1884), see Frazer, *Taboo*, p. 135.
[3] W. Brown, *New Zealand and Its Aborigines* (London, 1845) Frazer, *l.c.*
[4] Frazer, *l.c.*

allow the fruits of the earth to grow, but also for the wind which brings the ships to their shores and for the solid ground on which they set their feet.[1]

These savage kings are endowed with a wealth of power and an ability to bestow happiness which only gods possess; certainly in later stages of civilization none but the most servile courtiers would play the hypocrite to the extent of crediting their sovereigns with the possession of attributes similar to these.

It seems like an obvious contradiction that persons of such perfection of power should themselves require the greatest care to guard them against threatening dangers, but this is not the only contradiction revealed in the treatment of royal persons on the part of savages. These races consider it necessary to watch over their kings to see that they use their powers in the right way; they are by no means sure of their good intentions or of their conscientiousness. A strain of mistrust is mingled with the motivation of the taboo rules for the king. "The idea that early kingdoms are despotisms," says Frazer,[2] "in which the people exist only for the sovereign, is wholly inapplicable to the monarchies we are considering. On the contrary, the sovereign in them exists only for his subjects: his life is only valuable so long as he discharges the duties of his position by ordering the course of nature for his people's benefit. So soon as he fails to do so, the care, the devotion, the religious homage which they had hitherto lavished on him cease and are changed into hatred and contempt; he is ignominiously dismissed and may be thankful if he escapes with his life. Worshipped as a god one day, he is killed as a criminal the next. But in this changed behaviour of the people there is nothing capricious or inconsistent. On the contrary, their conduct is quite consistent. If their king is their god he is, or should be, also their preserver; and if he will not preserve them he must make room for another who will. So long, however, as he answers their expectations, there is no limit to the care which they take of him, and which they compel him to take of himself. A king of this sort lives hedged in by ceremonious etiquette, a network of prohibitions and observances, of which the intention is not to contribute to his dignity, much less to his comfort, but to restrain him from conduct which, by disturbing the harmony of nature, might involve himself, his people, and the universe in one common catastrophe. Far from adding to his comfort, these observances, by trammelling his every act, annihilate his freedom and often render the very life, which it is their object to preserve, a burden and sorrow to him."

One of the most glaring examples of thus fettering and paralysing a

[1] Frazer, *Taboo. The Burden of Royalty*, p. 7.
[2] *l.c.*, p. 7.

holy ruler through taboo ceremonial seems to have been reached in the
life routine of the Mikado of Japan, as it existed in earlier centuries.
A description which is now over two hundred years old [1] relates: "He
thinks that it would be very prejudicial to his dignity and holiness to
touch the ground with his feet; for this reason when he intends to go
anywhere, he must be carried thither on men's shoulders. Much less
will they suffer that he should expose his sacred person to the open air,
and the sun is not thought worthy to shine on his head. There is such
a holiness ascribed to all the parts of his body that he dares to cut
off neither his hair, nor his beard, nor his nails. However, lest he should
grow too dirty, they may clean him in the night when he is asleep; because they say that what is taken from his body at that time, hath been
stolen from him, and that such a theft does not prejudice his holiness or
dignity. In ancient times, he was obliged to sit on the throne for some
hours every morning, with the imperial crown on his head; but to sit
altogether like a statue without stirring either hands or feet, head or
eyes, nor indeed any part of his body, because by this means it was
thought that he could preserve peace and tranquillity in his empire;
for if unfortunately, he turned himself on one side or other, or if he
looked a good while towards any part of his dominion, it was apprehended that war, famine, fire or some other great misfortune was near
at hand to desolate the country."

Some of the taboos to which barbarian kings are subject vividly recall
the restrictions placed on murderers. On Shark Point at Cape Padron
in Lower Guinea (West Africa), a priest-king called Kukulu lives alone
in a woods. He is not allowed to touch a woman or to leave his house
and cannot even rise out of his chair, in which he must sleep in a sitting
position. If he should lie down the wind would cease and shipping would
be disturbed. It is his function to keep storms in check, and in general,
to see to an even, healthy condition of the atmosphere.[2] The more powerful a king of Loango is, says Bastian, the more taboos he must observe.
The heir to the throne is also bound to them from childhood on; they
accumulate abut him while he is growing up, and by the time of his
accession he is suffocated by them.

Our interest in the matter does not require us to take up more space
to describe more fully the taboos that cling to royal and priestly dignity.
We merely add that restrictions as to freedom of movement and diet
play the main rôle among them. But two examples of taboo ceremonial
taken from civilized nations, and therefore from much higher stages of

[1] Kaempfer, *History of Japan*, see in Frazer, *l.c.*, p. 3.
[2] Bastian, *The German Expedition to the Coast of Loango* (Jena 1874), cited by
Frazer, *l.c.*, p. 5.

culture, will indicate to what an extent association with these privileged persons tends to preserve ancient customs.

The *flamen Dialis*, the high-priest of Jupiter in Rome, had to observe an extraordinarily large number of taboo rules. He was not allowed to ride, to see a horse or an armed man, to wear a ring that was not broken, to have a knot in his garments, to touch wheat flour or leaven, or even to mention by name a goat, a dog, raw meat, beans and ivy; his hair could only be cut by a free man and with a bronze knife, his hair combings and nail parings had to be buried under a lucky tree; he could not touch the dead, go into the open with bare head, and similar prohibitions. His wife, the *flaminica*, also had her own prohibitions: she was not allowed to ascend more than three steps on a certain kind of stairs and on certain holidays she could not comb her hair; the leather for her shoes could not be taken from any animal that had died a natural death but only from one that had been slaughtered or sacrificed; when she heard thunder she was unclean until she had made an expiatory sacrifice.[1]

The old kings of Ireland were subject to a series of very curious restrictions, the observance of which was expected to bring every blessing to the country while their violation entailed every form of evil. The complete description of these taboos is given in the *Book of Rights*, of which the oldest manuscript copies bear the dates 1390 and 1418. The prohibitions are very detailed and concern certain activities at specified places and times; in some cities, for instance, the king cannot stay on a certain day of the week, while at some specified hour this or that river may not be crossed, or again there is a plain on which he cannot camp a full nine days, etc.[2]

Among many savage races the severity of the taboo restrictions for the priest-kings has had results of historic importance which are especially interesting from our point of view. The honour of being a priest-king ceased to be desirable; the person in line for the succession often used every means to escape it. Thus, in Cambodia, where there is a fire and water king, it is often necessary to use force to compel the successor to accept the honour. On Niue or Savage Island, a coral island in the Pacific Ocean, monarchy actually came to an end because nobody was willing to undertake the responsible and dangerous office. In some parts of West Africa a general council is held after the death of the king to determine upon the successor. The man on whom the choice falls is seized, tied and kept in custody in the fetish house until he has declared himself willing to accept the crown. Sometimes the presumptive successor to the throne finds ways and means to avoid the intended honour; thus it is related of a certain chief that he used to go armed day and night

[1] Frazer, *l.c.*, p. 13.
[2] Frazer, *l.c.*, p. 11.

and resist by force every attempt to place him on the throne.[1] Among the Negroes of Sierra Leone the resistance against accepting the kingly honour was so great that most of the tribes were compelled to make strangers their kings.

Frazer makes these conditions responsible for the fact that in the development of history a separation of the original priest-kingship into a spiritual and a secular power finally took place. Kings, crushed by the burden of their holiness, became incapable of exercising their power over real things and had to leave this to inferior but executive persons who were willing to renounce the honours of royal dignity. From these there grew up the secular rulers, while the spiritual over-lordship, which was now of no practical importance, was left to the former taboo kings. It is well known to what extent this hypothesis finds confirmation in the history of old Japan.

A survey of the picture of the relations of primitive peoples to their rulers gives rise to the expectation that our advance from description to psychoanalytic understanding will not be difficult. These relations are of an involved nature and are not free from contradictions. Rulers are granted great privileges which are practically cancelled by taboo prohibitions in regard to other privileges. They are privileged persons, they can do or enjoy what is withheld from the rest through taboo. But in contrast to this freedom they are restricted by other taboos which do not affect the ordinary individual. Here, therefore, is the first contrast, which amounts almost to a contradiction, between an excess of freedom and an excess of restriction as applied to the same persons. They are credited with extraordinary magic powers, and contact with their person or their property is therefore feared, while on the other hand the most beneficial effect is expected from these contacts. This seems to be a second and an especially glaring contradiction; but we have already learned that it is only apparent. The king's touch, exercised by him with benevolent intention, heals and protects; it is only when a common man touches the king or his royal effects that the contact becomes dangerous, and this is probably because the act may recall aggressive tendencies. Another contradiction which is not so easily solved is expressed in the fact that great power over the processes of nature is ascribed to the ruler and yet the obligation is felt to guard him with especial care against threatening dangers, as if his own power, which can do so much, were incapable of accomplishing this. A further difficulty in the relation arises because there is no confidence that the ruler will use his tremendous power to the advantage of his subjects as well as for his own protection; he is therefore distrusted and surveillance over him is considered to be justi-

[1] A. Bastian, *The German Expedition to the Coast of Loango,* cited by Frazer, *l.c.,* p. 18.

fied. The taboo etiquette, to which the life of the king is subject, simultaneously serves all these objects of exercising a tutelage over the king, of guarding him against dangers and of guarding his subjects against danger which he brings to them.

We are inclined to give the following explanation of the complicated and contradictory relation of the primitive peoples to their rulers. Through superstition as well as through other motives, various tendencies find expression in the treatment of kings, each of which is developed to the extreme without regard to the other. As a result of this, contradictions arise at which the intellect of savages takes no more offence than a highly civilized person would as long as it is only a question of religious matters or of "loyalty."

That would be so far so good; but the psychoanalytic technique may enable us to penetrate more deeply into the matter and to add something about the nature of these various tendencies. If we subject the facts as stated to analysis, just as if they formed the symptoms of a neurosis, our first attention would be directed to the excess of anxious worry which is said to be the cause of the taboo ceremonial. The concurrence of such excessive tenderness is very common in the neurosis and especially in the compulsion neurosis upon which we are drawing primarily for our comparison. We now thoroughly understand the origin of this tenderness. It occurs wherever, besides the predominant tenderness, there exists a contrary but unconscious stream of hostility, that is to say, wherever the typical case of an ambivalent affective attitude is realized. The hostility is then cried down by an excessive increase of tenderness which is expressed as anxiety and becomes compulsive because otherwise it would not suffice for its task of keeping the unconscious opposition in a state of repression. Every psychoanalyst knows how infallibly this anxious excess of tenderness can be resolved even under the most improbable circumstances, as for instance, when it appears between mother and child, or in the case of affectionate married people. Applied to the treatment of privileged persons this theory of an ambivalent feeling would reveal that their veneration, their very deification, is opposed in the unconscious by an intense hostile tendency, so that, as we had expected, the situation of an ambivalent feeling is here realized. The distrust which certainly seems to contribute to the motivation of the royal taboo, would be another direct manifestation of the same unconscious hostility. Indeed the ultimate issues of this conflict show such a diversity among different races that we would not be at a loss for examples in which the proof of such hostility would be much easier. We learn from Frazer [1] that the savage Timmes of Sierra Leone reserve the right to administer a beating to their elected king on the evening before his coro-

[1] l.c., p. 18, citing Zwefel et Monstier, *Voyage aux Sources du Niger*, 1880.

nation, and that they make use of this constitutional right with such thoroughness that the unhappy ruler sometimes does not long survive his accession to the throne; for this reason the leaders of the race have made it a rule to elect some man against whom they have a particular grudge. Nevertheless, even in such glaring cases the hostility is not acknowledged as such, but is expressed as if it were a ceremonial.

Another trait in the attitude of primitive races towards their rulers recalls a mechanism which is universally present in mental disturbances, and is openly revealed in the so-called delusions of persecution. Here the importance of a particular person is extraordinarily heightened and his omnipotence is raised to the improbable in order to make it easier to attribute to him the responsibility for everything painful which happens to the patient. Savages really do not act differently towards their rulers when they ascribe to them power over rain and shine, wind and weather, and then dethrone or kill them because nature has disappointed their expectation of a good hunt or a ripe harvest. The prototype which the paranoiac reconstructs in his persecution mania, is found in the relation of the child to its father. Such omnipotence is regularly attributed to the father in the imagination of the son, and distrust of the father has been shown to be intimately connected with the highest esteem for him. When a paranoiac names a person of his acquaintance as his "persecutor," he thereby elevates him to the paternal succession and brings him under conditions which enable him to make him responsible for all the misfortune which he experiences. Thus this second analogy between the savage and the neurotic may allow us to surmise how much in the relation of the savage to his ruler arises from the infantile attitude of the child to its father.

But the strongest support for our point of view, which seeks to compare taboo prohibitions with neurotic symptoms, is to be found in the taboo ceremonial itself, the significance of which for the status of kinship has already been the subject of our previous discussion. This ceremonial unmistakably reveals its double meaning and its origin from ambivalent tendencies if only we are willing to assume that the effects it produces are those which it intended from the very beginning. It not only distinguishes kings and elevates them above all ordinary mortals, but it also makes their life a torture and an unbearable burden and forces them into a thraldom which is far worse than that of their subjects. It would thus be the correct counterpart to the compulsive action of the neurosis, in which the suppressed impulse and the impulse which suppresses it meet in mutual and simultaneous satisfaction. The compulsive action is nominally a protection against the forbidden action; but we would say that actually it is a repetition of what is forbidden. The word "nominally" is here applied to the conscious whereas the word "actually" applies to the unconscious instance of the psychic life. Thus also the taboo ceremonial of kings is nominally an expression of the highest veneration and a means of guarding them; actually it is the punishment for their elevation, the revenge which their subjects take upon them. The experiences which Cervantes makes Sancho Panza undergo as governor on his island have evidently made him recognize this interpretation of courtly ceremonial as the only correct one. It is very possible that this point would be corroborated if we could induce kings and rulers of today to express themselves on this point.

Why the emotional attitude towards rulers should contain such a strong unconscious share of hostility is a very interesting problem which, however, exceeds the scope of this book. We have already referred to the infantile father-complex; we may add that an investigation of the early history of kingship would bring the decisive explanations. Frazer has an impressive discussion of the theory that the first kings were strangers who, after a short reign, were destined to be sacrificed at solemn festivals as representatives of the deity; but Frazer himself does not consider his facts altogether convincing.[1] Christian myths are said to have been still influenced by the after-effects of this evolution of kings.

(c) The Taboo of the Dead

We know that the dead are mighty rulers: we may be surprised to learn that they are regarded as enemies.

Among most primitive people the taboo of the dead displays, if we may keep to our infection analogy, a peculiar virulence. It manifests itself in the first place, in the consequences which result from contact with the dead, and in the treatment of the mourners for the dead. Among the Maori any one who had touched a corpse or who had taken part in its interment, became extremely unclean and was almost cut off from intercourse with his fellow beings; he was, as we say, boycotted. He could not enter a house, or approach persons or objects without infecting them with the same properties. He could not even touch his food with his own hands, which were now unclean and therefore quite useless to him. His food was put on the ground and he had no alternative except to seize it as best he could, with his lips and teeth, while he held his hands behind on his back. Occasionally he could be fed by another person who helped him to his food with outstretched arms so as not to touch the unfortunate one himself, but this assistant was then in turn subjected to almost equally oppressive restrictions. Almost every village contained some altogether disreputable individual, ostracized by society, whose wretched existence depended upon people's charity. This creature

[1] Frazer, *The Magic Art and the Evolution of Kings*, 2 vols., 1911 (*The Golden Bough*).

alone was allowed within arm's length of a person who had fulfilled the last duty towards the deceased. But as soon as the period of segregation was over and the person rendered unclean through the corpse could again mingle with his fellow-beings, all the dishes which he had used during the dangerous period were broken and all his clothing was thrown away.

The taboo customs after bodily contact with the dead are the same all over Polynesia, in Melanesia, and in a part of Africa; their most constant feature is the prohibition against handling one's food and the consequent necessity of being fed by somebody else. It is noteworthy that in Polynesia, or perhaps only in Hawaii,[1] priest-kings were subject to the same restrictions during the exercise of holy functions. In the taboo of the dead on the Island of Tonga the abatement and gradual abolition of the prohibitions through the individual's own taboo power are clearly shown. A person who touched the corpse of a dead chieftain was unclean for ten months; but if he was himself a chief, he was unclean for only three, four, or five months, according to the rank of the deceased; if it was the corpse of the idolized head-chief even the greatest chiefs become taboo for ten months. These savages are so certain that any one who violates these taboo rules must become seriously ill and die, that according to the opinion of an observer, they have never yet dared to convince themselves of the contrary.[2]

The taboo restrictions imposed upon persons whose contact with the dead is to be understood in the transferred sense, namely the mourning relatives such as widows and widowers, are essentially the same as those mentioned above, but they are of greater interest for the point we are trying to make. In the rules hitherto mentioned we see only the typical expression of the virulence and power of diffusion of the taboo; in those about to be cited we catch a gleam of the motives, including both the ostensible ones and those which may be regarded as the underlying and genuine motives.

Among the Shuswap in British Columbia widows and widowers have to remain segregated during their period of mourning; they must not use their hands to touch the body or the head and all utensils used by them must not be used by any one else. No hunter will want to approach the hut in which such mourners live, for that would bring misfortune; if the shadow of one of the mourners should fall on him he would become ill. The mourners sleep on thorn bushes, with which they also surround their beds. This last precaution is meant to keep off the spirit of the deceased; plainer still is the reported custom of other North American tribes where the widow, after the death of her husband, has to wear a

---

[1] Frazer, *Taboo*, p. 148, etc.
[2] W. Mariner, *The Natives of the Tonga Islands*, 1818; see Frazer, *l.c.*, p. 140.

kind of trousers of dried grass in order to make herself inaccessible to the approach of the spirit. Thus it is quite obvious that touching "in the transferred sense" is after all understood only as bodily contact, since the spirit of the deceased does not leave his kin and does not desist from "hovering about them," during the period of mourning.

Among the Agutainos, who live on Palawan, one of the Philippine Islands, a widow may not leave her hut for the first seven or eight days after her husband's death, except at night, when she need not expect encounters. Whoever sees her is in danger of immediate death and therefore she herself warns others of her approach by hitting the trees with a wooden stick with every step she takes; these trees all wither. Another observation explains the nature of the danger inherent in a widow. In the district of Mekeo, British New Guinea, a widower forfeits all civil rights and lives like an outlaw. He may not tend a garden, or show himself in public, or enter the village or go on the street. He slinks about like an animal, in the high grass or in the bushes, and must hide in a thicket if he sees anybody, especially a woman, approaching. This last hint makes it easy for us to trace back the danger of the widower or widow to the danger of temptation. The husband who has lost his wife must evade the desire for a substitute; the widow has to contend with the same wish, and besides this, she may arouse the desire of other men because she is without a master. Every such satisfaction through a substitute runs contrary to the intention of mourning and would cause the anger of the spirit to flare up.[1]

One of the most surprising, but at the same time one of the most instructive taboo customs of mourning among primitive races is the prohibition against pronouncing the *name* of the deceased. This is very widespread, and has been subjected to many modifications with important consequences.

Aside from the Australians and the Polynesians, who usually show us taboo customs in their best state of preservation, we also find this prohibition among races so far apart and unrelated to each other as the Samojedes in Siberia and the Todas in South India, the Mongolians of Tartary and the Tuaregs of the Sahara, the Aino of Japan and the Akamba and Nandi in Central Africa, the Tinguanes in the Philippines and the inhabitants of the Nikobari Islands and of Madagascar and Borneo.[2] Among some of these races the prohibition and its consequences hold good only for the period of mourning while in others it remains per-

---

[1] The same patient whose "impossibilities" I have correlated with taboo (see above, p. 829) acknowledged that she always became indignant when she met anybody on the street who was dressed in mourning. "Such people should be forbidden to go out!" she said.

[2] Frazer, *l.c.*, p. 353.

manent; but in all cases it seems to diminish with the lapse of time after the death.

The avoidance of the name of the deceased is as a rule kept up with extraordinary severity. Thus, among many South American tribes, it is considered the gravest insult to the survivors to pronounce the name of the deceased in their presence, and the penalty set for it is no less than that for the slaying itself.[1] At first it is not easy to guess why the mention of the name should be so abominated, but the dangers associated with it have called into being a whole series of interesting and important expedients to avoid this. Thus the Masai in Africa have hit upon the evasion of changing the name of the deceased immediately upon his death; he may now be mentioned without dread by this new name, while all the prohibitions remain attached to the old name. It seems to be assumed that the ghost does not know his new name and will not find it out. The Australian tribes on Adelaide and Encounter Bay are so consistently cautious that when a death occurs almost every person who has the same name as the deceased or a very similar one, exchanges it for another. Sometimes by a further extension of the same idea as seen among several tribes in Victoria and in North America all the relatives of the deceased change their names regardless of whether their names resemble the name of the deceased in sound. Among the Guaycuru in Paraguay the chief used to give new names to all the members of the tribe, on such sad occasions, which they then remembered as if they had always had them.[2]

Furthermore, if the deceased had the same name as an animal or object, etc., some of the races just enumerated thought it necessary to give these animals and objects new names, in order not to be reminded of the deceased when they mentioned them. Through this there must have resulted a never ceasing change of vocabulary, which caused a good deal of difficulty for the missionaries, especially where the interdiction upon a name was permanent. In the seven years which the missionary Dobrizhofer spent among the Abipons in Paraguay, the name for jaguar was changed three times and the words for crocodile, thorns and animal slaughter underwent a similar fate.[3] But the dread of pronouncing a name which has belonged to a deceased person extends also to the mention of everything in which the deceased had any part, and a further important result of this process of suppression is that these races have no tradition or any historical reminiscences, so that we encounter the greatest difficulties in investigating their past history. Among a number of these primitive races compensating customs have also been estab-

---

[1] Frazer, *l.c.,* p. 352, etc.
[2] Frazer, *l.c.,* p. 357, citing an old Spanish observer, 1732.
[3] Frazer, *l.c.,* p, 360.

lished in order to re-awaken the names of the deceased after a long period of mourning; they are bestowed upon children who were regarded as reincarnations of the dead.

The strangeness of this taboo on names diminishes if we bear in mind that the savage looks upon his name as an essential part and an important possession of his personality, and that he ascribes the full significance of things to words. Our children do the same, as I have shown elsewhere, and therefore they are never satisfied with accepting a meaningless verbal similarity, but consistently conclude that when two things have identical names a deeper correspondence between them must exist. Numerous peculiarities of normal behaviour may lead civilized man to conclude that he too is not yet as far removed as he thinks from attributing the importance of things to mere names and feeling that his name has become peculiarly identified with his person. This is corroborated by psychoanalytic experiences, where there is much occasion to point out the importance of names in unconscious thought activity.[1] As was to be expected, the compulsion neurotics behave just like savages in regard to names. They show the full "complex sensitiveness" towards the utterance and hearing of special words (as do also other neurotics) and derive a good many, often serious, inhibitions from their treatment of their own name. One of these taboo patients whom I knew, had adopted the avoidance of writing down her name for fear that it might get into somebody's hands who thus would come into possession of a piece of her personality. In her frenzied faithfulness, which she needed to protect herself against the temptations of her phantasy, she had created for herself the commandment, "not to give away anything of her personality." To this belonged first of all her name, then by further application her handwriting, so that she finally gave up writing.

Thus it no longer seems strange to us that savages should consider a dead person's name as a part of his personality and that it should be subjected to the same taboo as the deceased. Calling a dead person by name can also be traced back to contact with him, so that we can turn our attention to the more inclusive problem of why this contact is visited with such a severe taboo.

The nearest explanation would point to the natural horror which a corpse inspires, especially in view of the changes so soon noticeable after death. Mourning for a dead person must also be considered as a sufficient motive for everything which has reference to him. But horror of the corpse evidently does not cover all the details of taboo rules, and mourning can never explain to us why the mention of the dead is a severe insult to his survivors. On the contrary, mourning loves to preoccupy itself with the deceased, to elaborate his memory, and preserve

[1] Stekel, *Abraham*.

it for the longest possible time. Something besides mourning must be
made responsible for the peculiarities of taboo customs, something which
evidently serves a different purpose. It is this very taboo on names
which reveals this still unknown motive, and if the customs did not tell
us about it we would find it out from the statements of the mourning
savages themselves.

For they do not conceal the fact that they fear the presence and the
return of the spirit of a dead person; they practise a host of ceremonies
to keep him off and banish him.[1] They look upon the mention of his
name as a conjuration which must result in his immediate presence.[2]
They, therefore, consistently do everything to avoid conjuring and awakening a dead person. They disguise themselves in order that the spirit
may not recognize them,[3] they distort either his name or their own, and
become infuriated when a ruthless stranger incites the spirit against
his survivors by mentioning his name. We can hardly avoid the conclusion that they suffer, according to Wundt's expression, from the fear of
"his soul now turned into a demon." [4]

With this understanding we approach Wundt's conception who, as
we have heard, sees the nature of taboo in the fear of demons.

The assumption which this theory makes, namely, that immediately
after death the beloved member of a family becomes a demon, from
whom the survivors have nothing but hostility to expect, so that they
must protect themselves by every means from his evil desires, is so
peculiar that our first impulse is not to believe it. Yet almost all competent authors agree as to this interpretation of primitive races. Westermarck,[5] who, in my opinion, gives altogether too little consideration to
taboo, makes this statement: "On the whole facts lead me to conclude
that the dead are more frequently regarded as enemies than as friends
and that Jevons and Grant Allen are wrong in their assertion that it
was formerly believed that the malevolence of the dead was as a rule
directed only against strangers, while they were paternally concerned

[1] Frazer, *l.c.*, p. 353, cites the Tuaregs of the Sahara as an example of such an acknowl-
edgment.
[2] Perhaps this condition is to be added: as long as any part of his physical remains
exist. Frazer, *l.c.*, p. 372.
[3] *On the Nikobar Islands*, Frazer, *l.c.*, p. 382.
[4] Wundt, *Religion and Myth*, Vol. II, p. 49.
[5] *The Origin and Development of Moral Conceptions*, see section entitled "Attitude
Towards the Dead," Vol. II, p. 424. Both the notes and the text show an abundance
of corroborating and often very characteristic testimony, *e.g.*, the Maori believed
that "the nearest and most beloved relatives changed their nature after death and
bore ill-will even to their former favourites." The Austral Negroes believe that every
dead person is for a long time malevolent; the closer the relationship the greater the
fear. The Central Eskimos are dominated by the idea that the dead come to rest very
late and that at first they are to be feared as mischievous spirits who frequently hover
about the village to spread illness, death and other evils. (Boas.)

about the life and welfare of their descendants and the members of their clan."

R. Kleinpaul has written an impressive book in which he makes use of the remnants of the old belief in souls among civilized races to show the relation between the living and the dead.[1] According to him too, this relation culminates in the conviction that the dead, thirsting for blood, draw the living after them. The living did not feel themselves safe from the persecutions of the dead until a body of water had been put between them. That is why it was preferred to bury the dead on islands or to bring them to the other side of a river: the expressions "here" and "beyond" originated in this way. Later moderation has restricted the malevolence of the dead to those categories where a peculiar right to feel rancour had to be admitted, such as the murdered who pursue their murderer as evil spirits, and those who, like brides, had died with their longings unsatisfied. Kleinpaul believes that originally, however, the dead were all vampires, who bore ill-will towards the living, and strove to harm them and deprive them of life. It was the corpse that first furnished the conception of an evil spirit.

The hypothesis that those whom we love best turn into demons after death obviously allows us to put a further question. What prompted primitive races to ascribe such a change of sentiment to the beloved dead? Why did they make demons out of them? According to Westermarck this question is easily answered.[2] "As death is usually considered the worst calamity that can overtake man, it is believed that the deceased are very dissatisfied with their lot. Primitive races believe that death comes only through being slain, whether by violence or by magic, and this is considered already sufficient reason for the soul to be vindictive and irritable. The soul presumably envies the living and longs for the company of its former kin; we can therefore understand that the soul should seek to kill them with diseases in order to be re-united with them. . . .

". . . A further explanation of the malevolence ascribed to souls lies in the instinctive fear of them, which is itself the result of the fear of death."

Our study of psychoneurotic disturbances points to a more comprehensive explanation, which includes that of Westermarck.

When a wife loses her husband, or a daughter her mother, it not infrequently happens that the survivor is afflicted with tormenting scruples, called "obsessive reproaches" which raise the question whether she herself has not been guilty through carelessness or neglect, of the death of the beloved person. No recalling of the care with which she nursed the

[1] R. Kleinpaul: *The Living and the Dead in Folklore, Religion and Myth,* 1898.
[2] *l.c.,* p. 426.

invalid, or direct refutation of the asserted guilt can put an end to the torture, which is the pathological expression of mourning and which in time slowly subsides. Psychoanalytic investigation of such cases has made us acquainted with the secret mainsprings of this affliction. We have ascertained that these obsessive reproaches are in a certain sense justified and therefore are immune to refutation or objections. Not that the mourner has really been guilty of the death or that she has really been careless, as the obsessive reproach asserts; but still there was something in her, a wish of which she herself was aware, which was not displeased with the fact that death came, and which would have brought it about sooner had it been strong enough. The reproach now reacts against this unconscious wish after the death of the beloved person. Such hostility, hidden in the unconscious behind tender love, exists in almost all cases of intensive emotional allegiance to a particular person, indeed it represents the classic case, the prototype of the ambivalence of human emotions. There is always more or less of this ambivalence in everybody's disposition; normally it is not strong enough to give rise to the obsessive reproaches we have described. But where there is abundant predisposition for it, it manifests itself in the relation to those we love most, precisely where you would least expect it. The disposition to compulsion neurosis which we have so often taken for comparison with taboo problems, is distinguished by a particularly high degree of this original ambivalence of emotions.

We now know how to explain the supposed demonism of recently departed souls and the necessity of being protected against their hostility through taboo rules. By assuming a similar high degree of ambivalence in the emotional life of primitive races such as psychoanalysis ascribes to persons suffering from compulsion neurosis, it becomes comprehensible that the same kind of reaction against the hostility latent in the unconscious behind the obsessive reproaches of the neurotic should also be necessary here after the painful loss had occurred. But this hostility, which is painfully felt in the unconscious in the form of satisfaction with the demise, experiences a different fate in the case of primitive man: the defence against it is accomplished by displacement upon the object of hostility, namely, the dead. We call this defence process, frequent both in normal and diseased psychic life, a *projection*. The survivor will deny that he has ever entertained hostile impulses toward the beloved dead; but now the soul of the deceased entertains them and will try to give vent to them during the entire period of mourning. In spite of the successful defence through projection, the punitive and remorseful character of this emotional reaction manifests itself in being afraid, in self-imposed renunciations and in subjection to restrictions which are partly disguised as protective measures against the hostile demon. Thus we find again that taboo has grown out of the soil of an ambivalent emotional attitude. The taboo of the dead also originates from the opposition between the conscious grief and the unconscious satisfaction at death. If this is the origin of the resentment of spirits it is self-evident that just the nearest and formerly most beloved survivors have to fear it most.

As in neurotic symptoms, the taboo regulations also evince opposite feelings. Their restrictive character expresses mourning, while they also betray very clearly what they are trying to conceal, namely, the hostility towards the dead, which is now motivated as self-defence. We have learnt to understand part of the taboo regulations as temptation fears. A dead person is defenceless, which must act as an incitement to satisfy hostile desires entertained against him; this temptation has to be opposed by the prohibition.

But Westermarck is right in not admitting any difference in the savage's conception between those who have died by violence and those who have died a natural death. As will be shown later,[1] in the unconscious mode of thinking even a natural death is perceived as murder; the person was killed by evil wishes. Any one interested in the origin and meaning of dreams dealing with the death of dear relatives such as parents and brothers and sisters will find that the same feeling of ambivalence is responsible for the fact that the dreamer, the child, and the savage all have the same attitude towards the dead.[2]

A little while ago we challenged Wundt's conception, which explains the nature of taboo through the fear of demons, and yet we have just agreed with the explanation which traces back the taboo of the dead to a fear of the soul of the dead after it has turned into a demon. This seems like a contradiction, but it will not be difficult for us to explain it. It is true that we have accepted the idea of demons, but we know that this assumption is not something final which psychology cannot resolve into further elements. We have, as it were, exposed the demons by recognizing them as mere projections of hostile feelings which the survivor entertains toward the dead.

The double feeling—tenderness and hostility—against the deceased, which we consider well founded, endeavours to assert itself at the time of bereavement as mourning and satisfaction. A conflict must ensue between these contrary feelings, and as one of them, namely the hostility, is altogether or for the greater part unconscious, the conflict cannot result in a conscious difference in the form of hostility or tenderness as, for instance, when we forgive an injury inflicted upon us by some one we love. The process usually adjusts itself through a special psychic

1 Cf. Chap. III.
2 See: Freud *The Interpretation of Dreams.*

mechanism, which is designated in psychoanalysis as *projection*. This unknown hostility, of which we are ignorant and of which we do not wish to know, is projected from our inner perception into the outer world and is thereby detached from our own person and attributed to the other. Not we, the survivors, rejoice because we are rid of the deceased, on the contrary, we mourn for him; but now, curiously enough, he has become an evil demon who would rejoice in our misfortune and who seeks our death. The survivors must now defend themselves against this evil enemy; they are freed from inner oppression, but they have only succeeded in exchanging it for an affliction from without.

It is not to be denied that this process of projection, which turns the dead into malevolent enemies, finds some support in the real hostilities of the dead which the survivors remember and with which they really can reproach the dead. These hostilities are harshness, the desire to dominate, injustice, and whatever else forms the background of even the most tender relations between men. But the process cannot be so simple that this factor alone could explain the origin of demons by projection. The offences of the dead certainly motivate in part the hostility of the survivors, but they would have been ineffective if they had not given rise to this hostility and the occasion of death would surely be the least suitable occasion for awakening the memory of the reproaches which justly could have been brought against the deceased. We cannot dispense with the unconscious hostility as the constant and really impelling motive. This hostile tendency towards those nearest and dearest could remain latent during their lifetime, that is to say, it could avoid betraying itself to consciousness either directly or indirectly through any substitutive formation. However, when the person who was simultaneously loved and hated died, this was no longer possible, and the conflict became acute. The mourning originating from the enhanced tenderness, became on the one hand more intolerant of the latent hostility, while on the other hand it could not tolerate that the latter should not give origin to a feeling of pure gratification. Thus there came about the repression of the unconscious hostility through projection, and the formation of the ceremonial in which fear of punishment of demons finds expression. With the termination of the period of mourning, the conflict also loses its acuteness so that the taboo of the dead can be abated or sink into oblivion.

4

Having thus explained the basis on which the very instructive taboo of the dead has grown up, we must not miss the opportunity of adding a few observations which may become important for the understanding to taboo in general.

The projection of unconscious hostility upon demons in the taboo of the dead is only a single example from a whole series of processes to which we must grant the greatest influence in the formation of primitive psychic life. In the foregoing case the mechanism of projection is used to settle an emotional conflict; it serves the same purpose in a large number of psychic situations which lead to neuroses. But projection is not specially created for the purpose of defence, it also comes into being where there are no conflicts. The projection of inner perceptions to the outside is a primitive mechanism which, for instance, also influences our sense-perceptions, so that it normally has the greatest share in shaping our outer world. Under conditions that have not yet been sufficiently determined even inner perceptions of ideational and emotional processes are projected outwardly, like sense perceptions, and are used to shape the outer world, whereas they ought to remain in the inner world. This is perhaps genetically connected with the fact that the function of attention was originally directed not towards the inner world, but to the stimuli streaming in from the outer world, and only received reports of pleasure and pain from the endopsychic processes. Only with the development of the language of abstract thought through the association of sensory remnants of word representations with inner processes, did the latter gradually become capable of perception. Before this took place primitive man had developed a picture of the outer world through the outward projection of inner perceptions, which we, with our reinforced conscious perception, must now translate back into psychology.

The projection of their own evil impulses upon demons is only a part of what has become the world system ("Weltanschauung") of primitive man which we shall discuss later as "animalism." We shall then have to ascertain the psychological nature of such a system formation and the points of support which we shall find in the analysis of these system formations will again bring us face to face with the neurosis. For the present we merely wish to suggest that the "secondary elaboration" of the dream content is the prototype of all these system formations.[1] And let us not forget that beginning at the stage of system formation there are two origins for every act judged by consciousness, namely the systematic, and the real but unconscious origin.[2]

Wundt[3] remarks that "among the influences which myth everywhere ascribes to demons the evil ones preponderate, so that according to the religions of races evil demons are evidently older than good demons." Now it is quite possible that the whole conception of demons was derived

---

[1] See: *The Interpretation of Dreams.*
[2] The projection creations of primitive man resemble the personifications through which the poet projects his warring impulses out of himself, as separated individuals.
[3] *Myth and Religion*, p. 129.

from the extremely important relation to the dead. In the further course of human development the ambivalence inherent in this relation then manifested itself by allowing two altogether contrary psychic formations to issue from the same root, namely, the fear of demons and of *ghosts*, and the reverence for ancestors.[1] Nothing testifies so much to the influence of mourning on the origin of belief in demons as the fact that demons were always taken to be the spirits of persons not long dead. Mourning has a very distinct psychic task to perform, namely, to detach the memories and expectations of the survivors from the dead. When this work is accomplished the grief, and with it the remorse and reproach, lessens, and therefore also the fear of the demon. But the very spirits which at first were feared as demons now serve a friendlier purpose; they are revered as ancestors and appealed to for help in times of distress.

If we survey the relation of survivors to the dead through the course of the ages, it is very evident that the ambivalent feeling has extraordinarily abated. We now find it easy to suppress whatever unconscious hostility towards the dead there may still exist without any special psychic effort on our part. Where formerly satisfied hate and painful tenderness struggled with each other, we now find piety, which appears like a cicatrice and demands: *De mortuis nil nisi bonum*. Only neurotics still blur the mourning for the loss of their dear ones with attacks of compulsive reproaches which psychoanalysis reveals as the old ambivalent emotional feeling. How this change was brought about, and to what extent constitutional changes and real improvement of familiar relations share in causing the abatement of the ambivalent feeling, need not be discussed here. But this example would lead us to assume *that the psychic impulses of primitive man possessed a higher degree of ambivalence than is found at present among civilized human beings. With the decline of this ambivalence the taboo, as the compromise symptom of the ambivalent conflict, also slowly disappeared*. Neurotics who are compelled to reproduce this conflict, together with the taboo resulting from it, may be said to have brought with them an atavistic remnant in the form of an archaic constitution the compensation of which in the interest of cultural demands entails the most prodigious psychic efforts on their part.

As this point we may recall the confusing information which Wundt offered us about the double meaning of the word taboo, namely, holy and unclean (see above). It was supposed that originally the word taboo

[1] In the psychoanalysis of neurotic persons who suffer, or have suffered, in their childhood from the fear of ghosts, it is often not difficult to expose these ghosts as the parents. Compare also in this connection the communication of P. Haeberlin, *Sexual Ghosts* (*Sexual Problems*, Feb. 1912), where it is a question of another erotically accentuated person, but where the father was dead.

did not yet mean holy and unclean but signified something demonic, something which may not be touched, thus emphasizing a characteristic common to both extremes of the later conception; this persistent common trait proves, however, that an original correspondence existed between what was holy and what was unclean, which only later became differentiated.

In contrast to this, our discussion readily shows that the double meaning in question belonged to the word taboo from the very beginning and that it serves to designate a definite ambivalence as well as everything which has come into existence on the basis of this ambivalence. Taboo is itself an ambivalent word and by way of supplement we may add that the established meaning of this word might of itself have allowed us to guess what we have found as the result of extensive investigation, namely, that the taboo prohibition is to be explained as the result of an emotional ambivalence. A study of the oldest languages has taught us that at one time there were many such words which included their own contrasts so that they were in a certain sense ambivalent, though perhaps not exactly in the same sense as the word taboo.[1] Slight vocal modifications of this primitive word containing two opposite meanings later served to create a separate linguistic expression for the two opposites originally united in one word.

The word taboo has had a different fate; with the diminished importance of the ambivalence which it connotes, it has itself disappeared, or rather, the words analogous to it have vanished from the vocabulary. In a later connection I hope to be able to show that a tangible historic change is probably concealed behind the fate of this conception; that the word at first was associated with definite human relations which were characterized by great emotional ambivalence from which it expanded to other analogous relations.

Unless we are mistaken, the understanding of taboo also throws light upon the nature and origin of *conscience*. Without stretching ideas we can speak of a taboo conscience and a taboo sense of guilt after the violation of a taboo. Taboo conscience is probably the oldest form in which we meet the phenomenon of conscience.

For what is "conscience"? According to linguistic testimony it belongs to what we know most surely; in some languages its meaning is hardly to be distinguished from consciousness.

Conscience is the inner perception of objections to definite wish impulses that exist in us; but the emphasis is put upon the fact that this rejection does not have to depend on anything else, that it is sure of itself. This becomes even plainer in the case of a guilty conscience,

[1] Compare my article on Abel's *Gegensinn der Urworte* in the *Jahrbuch für Psychoanalytische und Psychopathologische Forschungen*, Bd. II, 1910.

where we become aware of the inner condemnation of such acts which realized some of our definite wish impulses. Confirmation seems superfluous here; whoever has a conscience must feel in himself the justification of the condemnation, and the reproach for the accomplished action. But this same character is evinced by the attitude of savages towards taboo. Taboo is a command of conscience, the violation of which causes a terrible sense of guilt which is as self-evident as its origin is unknown.[1]

It is, therefore, probable that conscience also originates on the basis of an ambivalent feeling from quite definite human relations which contain this ambivalence. It probably originates under conditions which are in force both for taboo and the compulsion neurosis, that is, one component of the two contrasting feelings is unconscious and is kept repressed by the compulsive domination of the other component. This is confirmed by many things which we have learned from our analysis of neurosis. In the first place the character of compulsion neurotics shows a predominant trait of painful conscientiousness which is a symptom of reaction against the temptation which lurks in the unconscious, and which develops into the highest degrees of guilty conscience as their illness grows worse. Indeed, one may venture the assertion that if the origin of guilty conscience could not be discovered through compulsion neurotic patients, there would be no prospect of ever discovering it. This task is successfully solved in the case of the individual neurotic, and we are confident of finding a similar solution in the case of races.

In the second place we cannot help noticing that the sense of guilt contains much of the nature of anxiety; without hesitation it may be described as "conscience phobia." But fear points to unconscious sources. The psychology of the neuroses taught us that when wish feelings undergo repression their libido becomes transformed into anxiety. In addition we must bear in mind that the sense of guilt also contains something unknown and unconscious, namely the motivation for the rejection. The character of anxiety in the sense of guilt corresponds to this unknown quantity.

If taboo expresses itself mainly in prohibitions it may well be considered self-evident, without remote proof from the analogy with neurosis that it is based on a positive, desireful impulse. For what nobody desires to do does not have to be forbidden, and certainly whatever is expressly forbidden must be an object of desire. If we applied this plausible theory to primitive races we would have to conclude that among their strongest temptations were desires to kill their kings and priests,

---

[1] It is an interesting parallel that the sense of guilt resulting from the violation of a taboo is in no way diminished if the violation took place unwittingly (see examples above), and that even in the Greek myth the guilt of Oedipus is not cancelled by the fact that it was incurred without his knowledge and will and even against them.

to commit incest, to abuse their dead and the like. That is not very probable. And if we should apply the same theory to those cases in which we ourselves seem to hear the voice of conscience most clearly we would arouse the greatest contradiction. For there we would assert with the utmost certainty that we did not feel the slightest temptation to violate any of these commandments, as for example, the commandment: Thou shalt not kill, and that we felt nothing but repugnance at the very idea.

But if we grant the testimony of our conscience the importance it claims, then the prohibition—the taboo as well as our moral prohibitions —becomes superfluous, while the existence of a conscience, in turn, remains unexplained and the connection between conscience, taboo and neurosis disappears. The net result of this would then be our present state of understanding unless we view the problem psychoanalytically.

But if we take into account the following results of psychoanalysis, our understanding of the problem is greatly advanced. The analysis of dreams of normal individuals has shown that our own temptation to kill others is stronger and more frequent than we had suspected and that it produces psychic effects even where it does not reveal itself to our consciousness. And when we have learnt that the obsessive rules of certain neurotics are nothing but measures of self-reassurance and self-punishment erected against the reinforced impulse to commit murder, we can return with fresh appreciation to our previous hypothesis that every prohibition must conceal a desire. We can then assume that this desire to murder actually exists and that the taboo as well as the moral prohibition are psychologically by no means superfluous but are, on the contrary, explained and justified through our ambivalent attitude towards the impulse to slay.

The nature of this ambivalent relation so often emphasized as fundamental, namely, that the positive underlying desire is unconscious, opens the possibility of showing further connections and explaining further problems. The psychic processes in the unconscious are not entirely identical with those known to us from our conscious psychic life, but have the benefit of certain notable liberties of which the latter are deprived. An unconscious impulse need not have originated where we find it expressed; it can spring from an entirely different place and may originally have referred to other persons and relations, but through the mechanism of *displacement*, it reaches the point where it comes to our notice. Thanks to the indestructibility of unconscious processes and their inaccessibility to correction, the impulse may be saved over from earlier times to which it was adapted to later periods and conditions in which its manifestations must necessarily seem foreign. These are all only hints, but a careful elaboration of them would show how important they may become for the understanding of the development of civilization.

In closing these discussions we do not want to neglect to make an observation that will be of use for later investigations. Even if we insist upon the essential similarity between taboo and moral prohibitions, we do not dispute that a psychological difference must exist between them. A change in the relations of the fundamental ambivalence can be the only reason why the prohibition no longer appears in the form of a taboo.

In the analytical consideration of taboo phenomena we have hitherto allowed ourselves to be guided by their demonstrable agreements with compulsion neurosis; but as taboo is not a neurosis but a social creation we are also confronted with the task of showing wherein lies the essential difference between the neurosis and a product of culture like the taboo.

Here again, I will take a single fact as my starting point. Primitive races fear a punishment for the violation of a taboo, usually a serious disease or death. This punishment threatens only him who has been guilty of the violation. It is different with the compulsion neurosis. If the patient wants to do something that is forbidden to him he does not fear punishment for himself, but for another person. The person is usually indefinite, but, by means of analysis, is easily recognized as some one very near and dear to the patient. The neurotic therefore acts as if he were altruistic, while primitive man seems egotistical. Only if retribution fails to overtake the taboo violator spontaneously does a collective feeling awaken among savages that they are all threatened through the sacrilege, and they hasten to inflict the omitted punishment themselves. It is easy for us to explain the mechanism of this solidarity. It is a question of fear of the contagious example, the temptation to imitate, that is to say, of the capacity of the taboo to infect. If some one has succeeded in satisfying the repressed desire, the same desire must manifest itself in all his companions; hence, in order to keep down this temptation, this envied individual must be despoiled of the fruit of his daring. Not infrequently the punishment gives the executors themselves an opportunity to commit the same sacrilegious act by justifying it as an expiation. This is really one of the fundamentals of the human code of punishment which rightly presumes the same forbidden impulses in the criminal and in the members of society who avenge his offence.

Psychoanalysis here confirms what the pious were wont to say, that we are all miserable sinners. How then shall we explain the unexpected nobility of the neurosis which fears nothing for itself and everything for the beloved person?

Psychoanalytic investigation shows that this nobility is not primary. Originally, that is to say at the beginning of the disease, the threat of punishment pertained to one's own person; in every case the fear was for one's own life; the fear of death being only later displaced upon another beloved person. The process is somewhat complicated but we have a complete grasp of it. An evil impulse—a death wish—towards the beloved person is always at the basis of the formation of a prohibition. This is repressed through a prohibition, and the prohibition is connected with a certain act which by displacement usually substitutes the hostile for the beloved person, and the execution of this act is threatened with the penalty of death. But the process goes further and the original wish for the death of the beloved other person is then replaced by fear for his death. The tender altruistic trait of the neurosis therefore merely *compensates* for the opposite attitude of brutal egotism which is at the basis of it. If we designate as social these emotional impulses which are determined through regard for another person who is not taken as a sexual object, we can emphasize the withdrawal of these social factors as an essential feature of the neurosis, which is later disguised through over-compensation.

Without lingering over the origin of these social impulses and their relation to other fundamental impulses of man, we will bring out the second main characteristic of the neurosis by means of another example. The form in which taboo manifests itself has the greatest similarity to the touching phobia of neurotics, the *délire de toucher*. As a matter of fact this neurosis is regularly concerned with the prohibition of sexual touching and psychoanalysis has quite generally shown that the motive power which is deflected and displaced in the neurosis is of sexual origin. In taboo the forbidden contact has evidently not only sexual significance but rather the more general one of attack, of acquisition and of personal assertion. If it is prohibited to touch the chief or something that was in contact with him it means that an inhibition should be imposed upon the same impulse which on other occasions expresses itself in suspicous surveillance of the chief and even in physical ill-treatment of him before his coronation (see above). *Thus the preponderance of sexual components of the impulse over the social components is the determining factor of the neurosis.* But the social impulses themselves came into being through the union of egotistical and erotic components into special entities.

From this single example of a comparison between taboo and compulsion neurosis it is already possible to guess the relation between individual forms of the neurosis and the creations of culture, and in what respect the study of the psychology of the neurosis is important for the understanding of the development of culture.

In one way the neuroses show a striking and far-reaching correspondence with the great social productions of art, religion and philosophy, while again they seem like distortions of them. We may say that hysteria is a caricature of an artistic creation, a compulsion neurosis, a caricature of a religion, and a paranoiac delusion a caricature of a philosophic system. In the last analysis this deviation goes back to the fact that the neuroses are asocial formations; they seek to accomplish by private means what arose in society through collective labour. In analysing the impulse of the neuroses one learns that motive powers of sexual origin exercise the determining influence in them, while the corresponding cultural creations rest upon social impulses and on such as have issued from the combination of egotistical and sexual components. It seems that the sexual need is not capable of uniting men in the same way as the demands of self-preservation; sexual satisfaction is in the first place the private concern of the individual.

Genetically the asocial nature of the neurosis springs from its original tendency to flee from a dissatisfying reality to a more pleasurable world of phantasy. This real world which neurotics shun is dominated by the society of human beings and by the institutions created by them; the estrangement from reality is at the same time a withdrawal from human companionship.

III

ANIMISM, MAGIC AND THE OMNIPOTENCE OF THOUGHT

I

It is a necessary defect of studies which seek to apply the point of view of psychoanalysis to the mental sciences that they cannot do justice to either subject. They therefore confine themselves to the rôle of incentives and make suggestions to the expert which he should take into consideration in his work. This defect will make itself felt most strongly in an essay such as this which tries to treat of the enormous sphere called animism.[1]

Animism in the narrower sense is the theory of psychic concepts, and in the wider sense, of spiritual beings in general. Animatism, the animation theory of seemingly inanimate nature, is a further subdivision which also includes animatism and animism. The name animism, formerly applied to a definite philosophic system, seems to have acquired its present meaning through E. B. Tylor.[2]

What led to the formulation of these names is the insight into the very remarkable conceptions of nature and the world of those primitive races known to us from history and from our own times. These races populate the world with a multitude of spiritual beings which are benevolent or malevolent to them, and attribute the causation of natural processes to these spirits and demons; they also consider that not only animals and plants, but inanimate things as well are animated by them. A third and perhaps the most important part of this primitive "nature philosophy" seems far less striking to us because we ourselves are not yet far enough removed from it, though we have greatly limited the existence of spirits

[1] The necessary crowding of the material also compels us to dispense with a thorough bibliography. Instead of this the reader is referred to the well-known works of Herbert Spencer, J. G. Frazer, A. Lang, E. B. Tylor and W. Wundt, from which all the statements concerning animism and magic are taken. The independence of the author can manifest itself only in the choice of the material and of opinions.
[2] E. B. Tylor, *Primitive Culture*, Vol. I, p. 425, fourth ed., 1903. W. Wundt, *Myth and Religion*, Vol. II, p. 173, 1906.

and today explain the processes of nature by the assumption of impersonal physical forces. For primitive people believe in a similar "animation" of human individuals as well. Human beings have souls which can leave their habitation and enter into other beings; these souls are the bearers of spiritual activities and are, to a certain extent, independent of the "bodies." Originally souls were thought of as being very similar to individuals; only in the course of a long evolution did they lose their material character and attain a high degree of "spiritualization." [1]

Most authors incline to the assumption that these soul conceptions are the original nucleus of the animistic system, that spirits merely correspond to souls that have become independent, and that the souls of animals, plants and things were formed after the analogy of human souls.

How did primitive people come to the peculiarly dualistic fundamental conceptions on which this animistic system rests? Through the observation, it is thought, of the phenomena of sleep (with dreams) and death, which resembles sleep, and through the effort to explain these conditions, which affect each individual so intimately. Above all, the problem of death must have become the starting point of the formation of the theory. To primitive man the continuation of life—immortality—would be self-evident. The conception of death is something accepted later, and only with hesitation, for even to us it is still devoid of content and unrealizable. Very likely discussions have taken place over the part which may have been played by other observations and experiences in the formation of the fundamental animistic conceptions such as dream imagery, shadows and reflections, but these have led to no conclusion. [2]

If primitive man reacted to the phenomena that stimulated his reflection with the formation of conceptions of the soul, and then transferred these to objects of the outer world, his attitude will be judged to be quite natural and in no way mysterious. In view of the fact that animistic conceptions have been shown to be similar among the most varied races and in all periods, Wundt states that these "are the necessary psychological product of the myth-forming consciousness, and primitive animism may be looked upon as the spiritual expression of man's natural state in so far as this is at all accessible to our observation." [3] Hune has already justified the animation of the inanimate in his *Natural History of Religions,* where he said: "There is a universal tendency among mankind to conceive all beings like themselves and to transfer to every ob-

---

[1] Wundt, *l.c.*, Chapter IV: *Die Seelenvorstellungen.*
[2] Compare, besides Wundt and H. Spencer and the instructive articles in the *Encyclopedia Britannica,* 1911 (*Animism, Mythology,* and so forth).
[3] *l.c.*, p. 154.

ject those qualities with which they are familiarly acquainted and of which they are intimately conscious." [1]

Animism is a system of thought, it gives not only the explanation of a single phenomenon, but makes it possible to comprehend the totality of the world from one point, as a continuity. Writers maintain that in the course of time three such systems of thought, three great world systems came into being: the animistic (mythological), the religious, and the scientific. Of these animism, the first system, is perhaps the most consistent and the most exhaustive, and the one which explains the nature of the world in its entirety. This first world system of mankind is now a psychological theory. It would go beyond our scope to show how much of it can still be demonstrated in the life of today, either as a worthless survival in the form of superstition, or in living form, as the foundation of our language, our belief, and our philosophy.

It is in reference to the successive stages of these three world systems that we say that animism in itself was not yet a religion but contained the prerequisites from which religions were later formed. It is also evident that myths are based upon animistic foundations, but the detailed relation of myths to animism seem unexplained in some essential points.

2

Our psychoanalytic work will begin at a different point. It must not be assumed that mankind came to create its first world system through a purely speculative thirst for knowledge. The practical need of mastering the world must have contributed to this effort. We are therefore not astonished to learn that something else went hand in hand with the animistic system, namely the elaboration of directions for making one's self master of men, animals and things, as well as of their spirits. S. Reinach [2] wants to call these directions, which are known under the names of "sorcery and magic," the strategy of animism. With Mauss and Hubert, I should prefer to compare them to a technique. [3]

Can the conceptions of sorcery and magic be separated? It can be done if we are willing on our own authority to put ourselves above the vagaries of linguistic usage. Then sorcery is essentially the art of influencing spirits by treating them like people under the same circumstances, that is to say by appeasing them, reconciling them, making them more favourably disposed to one, by intimidating them, by depriving them of their power and by making them subject to one's will; all that is accomplished through the same methods that have been found effective with living people. Magic, however, is something else; it does not

---

[1] See Tylor, *Primitive Culture*, Vol. I, p. 477.
[2] *Cultes, Mythes et Religions*, Vol. II: *Introduction*, p. XV, 1909.
[3] *Année Sociologique*, Seventh Vol., 1904.

essentially concern itself with spirits, and uses special means, not the ordinary psychological method. We can easily guess that magic is the earlier and the more important part of animistic technique, for among the means with which spirits are to be treated there are also found the magic kind,[1] and magic is also applied where spiritualization of nature has not yet, as it seems to us, been accomplished.

Magic must serve the most varied purposes. It must subject the processes of nature to the will of man, protect the individual against enemies and dangers, and give him the power to injure his enemies. But the principles on whose assumptions the magic activity is based, or rather the principle of magic, is so evident that it was recognized by all authors. If we may take the opinion of E. B. Tylor at its face value it can be most tersely expressed in his words: "mistaking an ideal connection for a real one." We shall explain this characteristic in the case of two groups of magic acts.

One of the most widespread magic procedures for injuring an enemy consists of making an effigy of him out of any kind of material. The likeness counts for little, in fact any object may be "named" as his image. Whatever is subsequently done to this image will also happen to the hated prototype; thus if the effigy has been injured in any place he will be afflicted by a disease in the corresponding part of the body. This same magic technique, instead of being used for private enmity, can also be employed for pious purposes and can thus be used to aid the gods against evil demons. I quote Frazer:[2] "Every night when the sun-god Ra in ancient Egypt sank to his home in the glowing west he was assailed by hosts of demons under the leadership of the archfiend Apepi. All night long he fought them, and sometimes by day the powers of darkness sent up clouds even into the blue Egyptian sky to obscure his light and weaken his power. To aid the sun-god in this daily struggle, a ceremony was daily performed in his temple at Thebes. A figure of his foe Apepi, represented as a crocodile with a hideous face or a serpent with many coils, was made of wax, and on it the demon's name was written in green ink. Wrapt in a papyrus case, on which another likeness of Apepi had been drawn in green ink, the figure was then tied up with black hair, spat upon, hacked with a stone knife and cast on the ground. There the priest trod on it with his left foot again and again, and then burned it in a fire made of a certain plant of grass. When Apepi himself had thus been effectively disposed of, waxen effigies of each of his principal demons, and of their fathers, mothers, and children, were made and burnt in the same way. The service accompanied by the recitation

---

[1] To frighten away a ghost with noise and cries is a form of pure sorcery; to force him to do something by taking his name is to employ magic against him.
[2] *The Magic Art*, II, p. 67.

of certain prescribed spells, was repeated not merely morning, noon and night, but whenever a storm was raging or a heavy rain had set in, or black clouds were stealing across the sky to hide the sun's bright disk. The fiends of darkness, clouds and rain, felt the injury inflicted on their images as if it had been done to themselves; they passed away, at least for a time and the beneficent sun-god shone out triumphant once more." [1]

There is a great mass of magic actions which show a similar motivation, but I shall lay stress upon only two, which have always played a great rôle among primitive races and which have been partly preserved in the myths and cults of higher stages of evolution: the art of causing rain and fruitfulness by magic. Rain is produced by magic means, by imitating it, and perhaps also by imitating the clouds and storm which produce it. It looks as if they wanted to "play rain." The Ainos of Japan, for instance, make rain by pouring out water through a big sieve, while others fit out a big bowl with sails and oars as if it were a ship, which is then dragged about the village and gardens. But the fruitfulness of the soil was assured by magic means by showing it the spectacle of human sexual intercourse. To cite one out of many examples; in some part of Java, the peasants used to go out into the fields at night for sexual intercourse when the rice was about to blossom in order to stimulate the rice to fruitfulness through their example.[2] At the same time it was feared that proscribed incestuous relationships would stimulate the soil to grow weeds and render it unfruitful.[3]

Certain negative rules, that is to say magic precautions, must be put into this first group. If some of the inhabitants of a Dayak village had set out on a hunt for wild-boars, those remaining behind were in the meantime not permitted to touch either oil or water with their hands, as such acts would soften the hunters' fingers and would let the quarry slip through their hands.[4] Or when a Gilyak hunter was pursuing game in the woods, his children were forbidden to make drawings on wood or in the sand, as the paths in the thick woods might become as intertwined as the lines of the drawing and the hunter would not find his way home.[5]

The fact that in these as in a great many other examples of magic influence, distance plays no part, telepathy is taken as a matter of course—will cause us no difficulties in grasping the peculiarity of magic.

There is no doubt about what is considered the effective force in all

[1] The Biblical prohibition against making an image of anything living hardly sprang from any fundamental rejection of plastic art, but was probably meant to deprive magic, which the Hebraic religion proscribed, of one of its instruments. Frazer, l.c., p. 87, note.
[2] The Magic Art, II, p. 98.
[3] An echo of this is to be found in the Oedipus Rex of Sophocles.
[4] The Magic Art, p. 120.
[5] l.c., p. 122.

these examples. It is the *similarity* between the performed action and the expected happening. Frazer therefore calls this kind of magic *imitative* or *homœopathic*. If I want it to rain I only have to produce something that looks like rain or recalls rain. In a later phase of cultural development, instead of these magic conjurations of rain, processions are arranged to a house of god, in order to supplicate the saint who dwells there to send rain. Finally also this religious technique will be given up and instead an effort will be made to find out what would influence the atmosphere to produce rain.

In another group of magic actions the principle of similarity is no longer involved, but in its stead there is another principle the nature of which is well brought out in the following examples.

Another method may be used to injure an enemy. You possess yourself of his hair, his nails, anything that he has discarded, or even a part of his clothing, and do something hostile to these things. This is just as effective as if you had dominated the person himself, and anything that you do to the things that belong to him must happen to him too. According to the conception of primitive men a name is an essential part of a personality; if therefore you know the name of a person or a spirit you have acquired a certain power over its bearer. This explains the remarkable precautions and restrictions in the use of names which we have touched upon in the essay on taboo.[1] In these examples similarity is evidently replaced by relationship.

The cannibalism of primitive races derives its more sublime motivation in a similar manner. By absorbing parts of the body of a person through the act of eating we also come to possess the properties which belonged to that person. From this there follow precautions and restrictions as to diet under special circumstances. Thus a pregnant woman will avoid eating the meat of certain animals because their undesirable properties, for example, cowardice, might thus be transferred to the child she is nourishing. It makes no difference to the magic influence whether the connection is already abolished or whether it had consisted of only one very important contact. Thus, for instance, the belief in a magic bond which links the fate of a wound with the weapon which caused it can be followed unchanged through thousands of years. If a Melanesian gets possession of the bow by which he was wounded he will carefully keep it in a cool place in order thus to keep down the inflammation of the wound. But if the bow has remained in the possession of the enemy it will certainly be kept in close proximity to a fire in order that the wound may burn and become thoroughly inflamed. Pliny, in his *Natural History*, xxviii, advises spitting on the hand which has caused the injury if one regrets having injured some one; the pain of

[1] See preceding chapter, p. 850.

the injured person will then immediately be eased. Francis Bacon, in his *Natural History,* mentions the generally accredited belief that putting a salve on the weapon which has made a wound will cause this wound to heal of itself. It is said that even today English peasants follow this prescription, and that if they have cut themselves with a scythe they will from that moment on carefully keep the instrument clean in order that the wound may not fester. In June, 1902, a local English weekly reported that a woman called Matilde Henry of Norwich accidentally ran an iron nail into the sole of her foot. Without having the wound examined or even taking off her stocking she bade her daughter to oil the nail thoroughly in the expectation that then nothing could happen to her. She died a few days later of tetanus [1] in consequence of postponed antisepsis.

The examples from this last group illustrate Frazer's distinction between *contagious* magic and *imitative* magic. What is considered as effective in these examples is no longer the similarity, but the association in space, the contiguity, or at least the imagined contiguity, or the memory of its existence. But since similarity and contiguity are the two essential principles of the processes of association of ideas, it must be concluded that the dominance of associations of ideas really explains all the madness of the rules of magic. We can see how true Tylor's quoted characteristic of magic: "mistaking an ideal connection for a real one," proves to be. The same may be said of Frazer's idea, who has expressed it in almost the same terms: "men mistook the order of their ideas for the order of nature, and hence imagined that the control which they have, or seem to have, over their thoughts, permitted them to have a corresponding control over things." [2]

It will at first seem strange that this illuminating explanation of magic could have been rejected by some authors as unsatisfactory.[3] But on closer consideration we must sustain the objection that the association theory of magic merely explains the paths that magic travels, and not its essential nature, that is, it does not explain the misunderstanding which bids it put psychological laws in place of natural ones. We are apparently in need here of a dynamic factor; but while the search for this leads the critics of Frazer's theory astray, it will be easy to give a satisfactory explanation of magic by carrying its association theory further and by entering more deeply into it.

First, let us examine the simpler and more important case of imitative magic. According to Frazer this may be practised by itself, whereas contagious magic as a rule presupposes the imitative.[4] The motives which

[1] Frazer, *The Magic Art,* pp. 201-3.
[2] *The Magic Art,* p. 420.
[3] Compare the article *Magic* (N. T. W.), in the *Encyclopedia Britannica,* 11th Ed.
[4] *l.c.,* p. 54.

impel one to exercise magic are easily recognized; they are the wishes of men. We need only assume that primitive man had great confidence in the power of his wishes. At bottom everything which he accomplished by magic means must have been done solely because he wanted it. Thus in the beginning only his wish is accentuated.

In the case of the child which finds itself under analogous psychic conditions, without being as yet capable of motor activity, we have elsewhere advocated the assumption that it at first really satisfies its wishes by means of hallucinations, in that it creates the satisfying situation through centrifugal excitements of its sensory organs.[1] The adult primitive man knows another way. A motor impulse, the will, clings to his wish and this will which later will change the face of the earth in the service of wish fulfillment is now used to represent the gratification so that one may experience it, as it were, through motor hallucination. Such a *representation* of the gratified wish is altogether comparable to the *play* of children, where it replaces the purely sensory technique of gratification. If play and imitative representation suffice for the child and for primitive man, it must not be taken as a sign of modesty, in our sense, or of resignation due to the realization of their impotence; on the contrary, it is the very obvious result of the excessive valuation of their wish, of the will which depends upon the wish and of the paths the wish takes. In time the psychic accent is displaced from the motives of the magic act to its means, namely to the act itself. Perhaps it would be more correct to say that primitive man does not become aware of the overvaluation of his psychic acts until it becomes evident to him through the means employed. It would also seem as if it were the magic act itself which compels the fulfilment of the wish by virtue of its similarity to the object desired. At the stage of animistic thinking there is as yet no way of demonstrating objectively the true state of affairs, but this becomes possible at later stages when, though such procedures are still practised, the psychic phenomenon of scepticism already manifests itself as a tendency to repression. At that stage men will acknowledge that the conjuration of spirits avails nothing unless accompanied by belief, and that the magic effect of prayer fails if there is no piety behind it.[2]

The possibility of a contagious magic which depends upon contiguous association will then show us that the psychic valuation of the wish and the will has been extended to all psychic acts which the will can command. We may say that at present there is a general over-valuation of

---

[1] Formulation of two principles of psychic activity, *Jahrb. für Psychoanalyt. Forschungen*, Vol. III, 1912, p. 2.

[2] The King in *Hamlet* (Act III, Scene 4):
    "My words fly up, my thoughts remain below,
    Words without thoughts never to heaven go."

all psychic processes, that is to say there is an attitude towards the world which according to our understanding of the relation of reality to thought must appear like an over-estimation of the latter. Objects as such are overshadowed by the ideas representing them; what takes place in the latter must also happen to the former, and the relations which exist between ideas are also postulated as to things. As thought does not recognize distances and easily brings together in one act of consciousness things spatially and temporally far removed, the magic world also puts itself above spatial distance by telepathy, and treats a past association as if it were a present one. In the animistic age the reflection of the inner world must obscure that other picture of the world which we believe we recognize.

Let us also point out that the two principles of association, similarity and contiguity, meet in the higher unity of contact. Association by contiguity is contact in the direct sense, and association by similarity is contact in the transferred sense. Another identity in the psychic process which has not yet been grasped by us is probably concealed in the use of the same word for both kinds of associations. It is the same range of the concept of contact which we have found in the analysis of taboo.[1]

In summing up we may now say that the principle which controls magic, and the technique of the animistic method of thought, is "Omnipotence of Thought."

3

I have adopted the term "Omnipotence of Thought" from a highly intelligent man, a former sufferer from compulsion neurosis, who, after being cured through psychoanalytic treatment, was able to demonstrate his efficiency and good sense.[2] He had coined this phrase to designate all those peculiar and uncanny occurrences which seemed to pursue him just as they pursue others afflicted with his malady. Thus if he happened to think of a person, he was actually confronted with this person as if he had conjured him up; if he inquired suddenly about the state of health of an acquaintance whom he had long missed he was sure to hear that this acquaintance had just died, so that he could believe that the deceased had drawn his attention to himself by telepathic means; if he uttered a half meant imprecation against a stranger, he could expect to have him die soon thereafter and burden him with the responsibility for his death. He was able to explain most of these cases in the course of the treatment, he could tell how the illusion had originated, and what he himself had contributed towards furthering his superstitious expecta-

[1] Compare Chapter II.
[2] Remarks upon a case of Compulsion Neurosis, *Jahrb. für Psychoanalyt. und Psychopath. Forschungen,* Vol. I, 1909.

tions.[1] All compulsion neurotics are superstitious in this manner and often against their better judgment.

The existence of omnipotence of thought is most clearly seen in compulsion neurosis, where the results of this primitive method of thought are most often found or met in consciousness. But we must guard against seeing in this a distinguishing characteristic of this neurosis, for analytic investigation reveals the same mechanism in the other neuroses. In every one of the neuroses it is not the reality of the experience but the reality of the thought which forms the basis for the symptom formation. Neurotics live in a special world in which, as I have elsewhere expressed it, only the "neurotic standard of currency" counts, that is to say, only things intensively thought of or affectively conceived are effective with them, regardless of whether these things are in harmony with outer reality. The hysteric repeats in his attacks and fixates through his symptoms, occurrences which have taken place only in his phantasy, though in the last analysis they go back to real events or have been built up from them. The neurotic's guilty conscience is just as incomprehensible if traced to real misdeeds. A compulsion neurotic may be oppressed by a sense of guilt which is appropriate to a wholesale murderer, while at the same time he acts towards his fellow beings in a most considerate and scrupulous manner, a behaviour which he evinced since his childhood. And yet his sense of guilt is justified: it is based upon intensive and frequent death wishes which unconsciously manifest themselves towards his fellow beings. It is motivated from the point of view of unconscious thoughts, but not of intentional acts. Thus the omnipotence of thought, the over-estimation of psychic processes as opposed to reality, proves to be of unlimited effect in the neurotic's affective life and in all that emanates from it. But if we subject him to psychoanalytic treatment, which makes his unconscious thoughts conscious to him he refuses to believe that thoughts are free and is always afraid to express evil wishes lest they be fulfilled in consequence of his utterance. But through this attitude as well as through the superstition which plays an active part in his life, he reveals to us how close he stands to the savage, who believes he can change the outer world by a mere thought of his.

The primary obsessive actions of these neurotics are really altogether of a magical nature. If not magic they are at least anti-magic and are destined to ward off the expectation of evil with which the neurosis is wont to begin. Whenever I was able to pierce these secrets, it turned out that the content of this expectation of evil was death. According to Schopenhauer the problem of death stands at the beginning of every

[1] We seem to attribute the character of the "uncanny" to all such impressions which seek to confirm the omnipotence of thought and the animistic method of thought in general, though our judgment has long rejected it.

philosophy; we have heard that the formation of the soul conception and of the belief in demons which characterize animism, are also traced back to the impression which death makes upon man. It is hard to decide whether these first compulsive and protective actions follow the principle of similarity, or of contrast, for under the conditions of the neurosis they are usually distorted through displacement upon some trifle, upon some action which in itself is quite insignificant.[1] The protective formulæ of the compulsion neurosis also have a counterpart in the incantations of magic. But the evolution of compulsive actions may be described by pointing out how these actions begin as a spell against evil wishes which are very remote from anything sexual, only to end up as a substitute for forbidden sexual activity, which they imitate as faithfully as possible.

If we accept the evolution of man's conceptions of the universe mentioned above, according to which the *animistic* phase is *succeeded* by the *religious,* and this in turn by the *scientific,* we have no difficulty in following the fortunes of the "omnipotence of thought" through all these phases. In the animistic stage man ascribes omnipotence to himself; in the religious he has ceded it to the gods, but without seriously giving it up, for he reserves to himself the right to control the gods by influencing them in some way or other in the interest of his wishes. In the scientific attitude towards life there is no longer any room for man's omnipotence; he has acknowledged his smallness and has submitted to death as to all other natural necessities in a spirit of resignation. Nevertheless, in our reliance upon the power of the human spirit which copes with the laws of reality, there still lives on a fragment of this primitive belief in the omnipotence of thought.

In retracing the development of libidinous impulses in the individual from its mature form back to its first beginnings in childhood, we at first found an important distinction which is stated in the *Three contributions to the Theory of Sex.* The manifestations of sexual impulses can be recognized from the beginning, but at first they are not yet directed to any outer object. Each individual component of the sexual impulse works for a gain in pleasure and finds its gratification in its own body. This stage is called *autoerotism* and is distinguished from the stage of object selection.

In the course of further study it proved to be practical and really necessary to insert a third stage between these two or, if one prefers, to divide the first stage of autoerotism into two. In this intermediary stage, the importance of which increases the more we investigate it, the sexual impulses which formerly were separate, have already formed into a unit and have also found an object; but this object is not external and foreign

[1] The following discussions will yield a further motive for this displacement upon a trivial action.

to the individual, but is his own ego, which is formed at this period. This new stage is called *narcism*, in view of the pathological fixation of this condition which may be observed later on. The individual acts as if he were in love with himself; for the purposes of our analysis the ego impulses and the libidinous wishes cannot yet be separated from each other.

Although this narcistic stage, in which the hitherto dissociated sexual impulses combine into a unity and take the ego as their object, cannot as yet be sharply differentiated, we can already surmise that the narcistic organization is never altogether given up again. To a certain extent man remains narcistic, even after he has found outer subjects for his libido, and the objects on which he bestows it represent, as it were, emanations of the libido which remain with his ego and which can be withdrawn into it. The state of being in love, so remarkable psychologically, and the normal prototype of the psychoses, corresponds to the highest stage of these emanations, in contrast to the state of self-love.

This high estimation of psychic acts found among primitives and neurotics, which we feel to be an overestimation, may now appropriately be brought into relation to narcism, and interpreted as an essential part of it. We would say that among primitive people thinking is still highly sexualized and that this accounts for the belief in the omnipotence of thought, the unshaken confidence in the capacity to dominate the world and the inaccessibility to the obvious facts which could enlighten man as to his real place in the world. In the case of neurotics a considerable part of this primitive attitude had remained as a constitutional factor, while on the other hand the sexual repression occurring in them has brought about a new sexualization of the processes of thought. In both cases, whether we deal with an original libidinous investment of thought or whether the same process has been accomplished regressively, the psychic results are the same, namely, intellectual narcism and omnipotence of thought.[1]

If we may take the now established omnipotence of thought among primitive races as a proof of their narcism, we may venture to compare the various evolutionary stages of man's conception of the universe with the stages of the libidinous evolution of the individual. We find that the animistic phase corresponds in time as well as in content with narcism, the religious phase corresponds to that stage of object finding which is characterized by dependence on the parents, while the scientific stage has its full counterpart in the individual's state of maturity where, hav-

[1] It is almost an axiom with writers on this subject that a sort of "Solipsism or Berkleyanism" (as Professor Sully terms it as he finds it in the child) operates in the savage to make him refuse to recognize death as a fact.—Marett, *Pre-animistic Religion; Folklore*, Vol. XI, 1900, p. 178.

ing renounced the pleasure principle and having adapted himself to reality, he seeks his object in the outer world.[1]

Only in one field has the omnipotence of thought been retained in our own civilization, namely in art. In art alone it still happens that man, consumed by his wishes, produces something similar to the gratification of these wishes, and this playing, thanks to artistic illusion, calls forth effects as if it were something real. We rightly speak of the magic of art and compare the artist with a magician. But this comparison is perhaps more important than it claims to be. Art, which certainly did not begin as art for art's sake, originally served tendencies which today have for the greater part ceased to exist. Among these we may suspect various magic intentions.[2]

4

Animism, the first conception of the world which man succeeded in evolving, was therefore psychological. It did not yet require any science to establish it, for science sets in only after we have realized that we do not know the world and that we must therefore seek means of getting to know it. But animism was natural and self-evident to primitive man; he knew how the things of the world were constituted, and as man conceived himself to be. We are therefore prepared to find that primitive man transferred the structural relations of his own psyche to the outer world,[3] and on the other hand we may make the attempt to transfer back into the human soul what animism teaches about the nature of things.

Magic, the technique of animism, clearly and unmistakably shows the tendency of forcing the laws of psychic life upon the reality of things, under conditions where spirits did not yet have to play any rôle, and could still be taken as objects of magic treatment. The assumptions of magic are therefore of older origin than the spirit theory, which forms the nucleus of animism. Our psychoanalytic view here coincides with a theory of R. R. Marett, according to which animism is preceded by a pre-

---

[1] We merely wish to indicate here that the original narcism of the child is decisive for the interpretation of its character development and that it precludes the assumption of a primitive feeling of inferiority for the child.

[2] S. Reinach, L'Art et la Magie, in the collection Cultes, Mythes et Religions, Vol. I, pp. 125–136. Reinach thinks that the primitive artists who have left us the scratched or painted animal pictures in the caves of France did not want to "arouse" pleasure, but to "conjure things." He explains this by showing that these drawings are in the darkest and most inaccessible part of the caves and that representations of feared beasts of prey are absent. "Les modernes parlent souvent, par hyperbole, de la magie du pinceau ou du ciseau d'un grand artiste et, en général, de la magie de l'art. Entendu en sense propre, qui est celui d'une constrainte mystique exercée par la volonté de l'homme sur d'autres volontés ou sur les choses, cette expression n'est plus admissible; mais nous avons vu qu'elle était autrefois rigoureusement vraie, du moins dans l'opinion des artistes" (p. 136).

[3] Recognized through so-called endopsychic perceptions.

animistic stage the nature of which is best indicated by the name Animatism (the theory of general animation). We have practically no further knowledge of pre-animism, as no race has yet been found without
conceptions of spirits.[1]

While magic still retains the full omnipotence of ideas, animism has
ceded part of this omnipotence to spirits and thus has started on the way
to form a religion. Now what could have moved primitive man to this
first act of renunciation? It could hardly have been an insight into the
incorrectness of his assumptions, for he continued to retain the magic
technique.

As pointed out elsewhere, spirits and demons were nothing but the projection of primitive man's emotional impulses;[2] he personified the
things he personified his affects, populated the world with them and then
rediscovered his inner psychic processes outside himself, quite like the
ingenious paranoiac Schreber, who found the fixations and detachments
of his libido reflected in the fates of the "God-rays," which he invented.[3]

As on a former occasion,[4] we want to avoid the problem as to the origin
of the tendency to project psychic processes into the outer world. It is
fair to assume, however, that this tendency becomes stronger where the
projection into the outer world offers psychic relief. Such a state of affairs can with certainty be expected if the impulses struggling for omnipotence have come into conflict with each other, for then they evidently
cannot all become omnipotent. The morbid process in paranoia actually
uses the mechanism of projection to solve such conflicts which arise in
the psychic life. However, it so happens that the model case of such a
conflict between two parts of an antithesis is the ambivalent attitude
which we have analysed in detail in the situation of the mourner at the
death of one dear to him. Such a case appeals to us as especially fitted to
motivate the creation of projection formations. Here again we are in
agreement with those authors who declare that evil spirits were the first
born among spirits, and who find the origin of soul conceptions in the
impression which death makes upon the survivors. We differ from them
only in not putting the intellectual problem which death imposes upon
the living into the foreground, instead of which we transfer the force
which stimulates inquiry to the conflict of feelings into which this situation plunges the survivor.

---

[1] R. R. Marett, *Pre-animistic Religion* in *Folklore*, Vol. XI, No. 2, 1900.—comp.
Wundt, *Myth and Religion*, Vol. II, p. 171.
[2] We assume that in this early narcistic stage feelings from libidinal and other
sources of excitement are perhaps still indistinguishably combined with each other.
[3] Schreber, *Denkwürdigkeiten eines Nervenkranken*, 1903.—Freud, Psychoanalytic
Observations concerning an autobiographically described case of Paranoia, *Jahrbuch
für Psychoanalyt. Forsch.*, Vol. III, 1911.
[4] Schreber, p. 59.

The first theoretical accomplishment of man, the creation of spirits, would therefore spring from the same source as the first moral restrictions to which he subjects himself, namely, the rules of taboo. But the fact that they have the same source should not prejudice us in favour of a simultaneous origin. If it really were the situation of the survivor confronted by the dead which first caused primitive man to reflect, so that he was compelled to surrender some of his omnipotence to spirits and to sacrifice a part of the free will of his actions, these cultural creations would be a first recognition of the ἀνάγκη, which opposes man's narcism. Primitive man would bow to the superior power of death with the same gesture with which he seems to deny it.

If we have the courage to follow our assumptions further, we may ask what essential part of our psychological structure is reflected and reviewed in the projection formation of souls and spirits. It is then difficult to dispute that the primitive conception of the soul, though still far removed from the later and wholly immaterial soul, nevertheless shares its nature and therefore looks upon a person or a thing as a duality, over the two elements of which the known properties and changes of the whole are distributed. This origin duality, we have borrowed the term from Herbert Spencer,[1] is already identical with the dualism which manifests itself in our customary separation of spirit from body, and whose indestructible linguistic manifestations we recognize, for instance, in the description of a person who faints or raves as one who is "beside himself." [2]

The thing which we, just like primitive man, project in outer reality, can hardly be anything else but the recognition of a state in which a given thing is present to the senses and to consciousness, next to which another state exists in which the thing is *latent*, but can reappear, that is to say, the co-existence of perception and memory, or, to generalize it, the existence of unconscious psychic processes next to conscious ones.[3] It might be said that in the last analysis the "spirit" of a person or thing is the faculty of remembering and representing the object, after he or it has been withdrawn from conscious perception.

Of course we must not expect from either the primitive or the current conception of the "soul" that its line of demarcation from other parts should be as marked as that which contemporary science draws between conscious and unconscious psychic activity. The animistic soul, on the contrary, unites determinants from both sides. Its flightiness, and mobility, its faculty of leaving the body, of permanently or temporarily taking possession of another body, all these are characteristics which remind us

---

[1] *Principles of Sociology*, Vol. I.
[2] *l.c.*, p. 179.
[3] Compare my short paper: *A note on the Unconscious in Psychoanalysis*, in the *Proceedings of the Society for Psychical Research*, Part LXVI, Vol. XXVI, 1912.

unmistakably of the nature of consciousness. But the way in which it keeps itself concealed behind the personal appearance reminds us of the unconscious; today we no longer ascribe its unchangeableness and indestructibility to conscious but to unconscious processes and look upon these as the real bearers of psychic activity.

We said before that animism is a system of thought, the first complete theory of the world; we now want to draw certain inferences through psychoanalytic interpretation of such a system. Our everyday experience is capable of constantly showing us the main characteristics of the "system." We dream during the night and have learnt to interpret the dream in the daytime. The dream can, without being untrue to its nature, appear confused and incoherent; but on the other hand it can also imitate the order of impressions of an experience, infer one occurrence from another, and refer one part of its contents to another. The dream succeeds more or less in this, but hardly ever succeeds so completely that an absurdity or a gap in the structure does not appear somewhere. If we subject the dream to interpretation we find that this unstable and irregular order of its components is quite unimportant for our understanding of it. The essential part of the dream is the dream thoughts, which have, to be sure, a significant, coherent order. But their order is quite different from that which we remember from the manifest content of the dream. The coherence of the dream thoughts has been abolished and may either remain altogether lost or can be replaced by the new coherence of the dream content. Besides the condensation of the dream elements there is almost regularly a re-grouping of the same which is more or less independent of the former order. We say in conclusion, that what the dream-work has made out of the material of the dream thoughts has been subjected to a new influence, the so-called "secondary elaboration," the object of which evidently is to do away with the incoherence and incomprehensibility caused by the dream-work, in favour of a new "meaning." This new meaning which has been brought about by the secondary elaboration is no longer the meaning of the dream thoughts.

The secondary elaboration of the product of the dream-work is an excellent example of the nature and the pretensions of a system. An intellectual function in us demands the unification, coherence and comprehensibility of everything perceived and thought of, and does not hesitate to construct a false connection if, as a result of special circumstances, it cannot grasp the right one. We know such system formation not only from the dream, but also from phobias, from compulsive thinking and from the types of delusions. The system formation is most ingenious in delusional states (paranoia) and dominates the clinical picture, but it also must not be overlooked in other forms of neuropsychoses. In every case we can show that a re-arrangement of the psychic material takes place, which may often be quite violent, provided it seems comprehensible from the point of view of the system. The best indication that a system has been formed then lies in the fact that each result of it can be shown to have at least two motivations, one of which springs from the assumptions of the system and is therefore eventually delusional—and a hidden one which, however, we must recognize as the real and effective motivation.

An example from a neurosis may serve as illustration. In the chapter on Taboo I mentioned a patient whose compulsive prohibitions correspond very neatly to the taboo of the Maori.[1] The neurosis of this woman was directed against her husband and culminated in the defence against the unconscious wish for his death. But her manifest systematic phobia concerned the mention of death in general, in which her husband was altogether eliminated and never became the object of conscious solicitude. One day she heard her husband give an order to have his dull razors taken to a certain shop to have them sharpened. Impelled by a peculiar unrest she went to the shop herself, and on her return from this reconnoitre she asked her husband to lay the razors aside for good because she had discovered that there was a warehouse of coffins and funeral accessories next to the shop he mentioned. She claimed that he had intentionally brought the razors into permanent relation with the idea of death. This was then the systematic motivation of the prohibition, but we may be sure that the patient would have brought home the prohibition relating to the razors even if she had not discovered this warehouse in the neighbourhood. For it would have been sufficient if on her way to the shop she had met a hearse, a person in mourning, or somebody carrying a wreath. The net of determinants was spread out far enough to catch the prey in any case, it was simply a question whether she should pull it in or not. It could be established with certainty that she did not mobilize the determinants of the prohibition in other circumstances. She would then have said it had been one of her "better days." The real reason for the prohibition of the razor was, of course, as we can easily guess, her resistance against a pleasurably accentuated idea that her husband might cut his throat with the sharpened razors.

In much the same way a motor inhibition, an abasia or an agoraphobia, becomes perfected and detailed if the symptom once succeeds in representing an unconscious wish and of imposing a defence against it. All the patient's remaining unconscious phantasies and effective reminiscences strive for symptomatic expression through this outlet, when once it has been opened, and range themselves appropriately in the new order within the sphere of the disturbance of gait. It would therefore be a futile and really foolish way to begin to try to understand the symptomatic struc-

[1] pp. 828 ff.

ture, and the details of, let us say, an agoraphobia, in terms of its basic assumptions. For the whole logic and strictness of connexion is only apparent. Sharper observation can reveal, as in the formation of the façade in the dream, the greatest inconsistency and arbitrariness in the symptom formation. The details of such a systematic phobia take their real motivation from concealed determinants which must have nothing to do with the inhibition in gait; it is for this reason that the form of such a phobia varies so and is so contradictory in different people.

If we now attempt to retrace the system of animism with which we are concerned, we may conclude from our insight into other psychological systems that "superstition" need not be the only and actual motivation of such a single rule or custom even among primitive races, and that we are not relieved of the obligation of seeking for concealed motives. Under the dominance of an animistic system it is absolutely essential that each rule and activity should receive a systematic motivation which we today call "superstitious." But "superstition," like "anxiety," "dreams," and "demons," is one of the preliminaries of psychology which have been dissipated by psychoanalytic investigation. If we get behind these structures, which like a screen conceal understanding, we realize that the psychic life and the cultural level of savages have hitherto been inadequately appreciated.

If we regard the repression of impulses as a measure of the level of culture attained, we must admit that under the animistic system too, progress and evolution have taken place, which unjustly have been underestimated on account of their superstitious motivation. If we hear that the warriors of a savage tribe impose the greatest chastity and cleanliness upon themselves as soon as they go upon the war-path,[1] the obvious explanation is that they dispose of their refuse in order that the enemy may not come into possession of this part of their person in order to harm them by magical means, and we may surmise analogous superstitious motivations for their abstinence. Nevertheless the fact remains that the impulse is renounced and we probably understand the case better if we assume that the savage warrior imposes such restrictions upon himself in compensation, because he is on the point of allowing himself the full satisfaction of cruel and hostile impulses otherwise forbidden. The same holds good for the numerous cases of sexual restriction while he is preoccupied with difficult or responsible tasks.[2] Even if the basis of these prohibitions can be referred to some association with magic, the fundamental conception of gaining greater strength by foregoing gratification of desires nevertheless remains unmistakable, and besides the magic rationalization of the prohibition, one must not neglect its hygienic root.

[1] Frazer, *Taboo and the Perils of the Soul*, p. 158.
[2] Frazer, *l.c.*, p. 200.

When the men of a savage tribe go away to hunt, fish, make war, or collect valuable plants, the women at home are in the meantime subjected to numerous oppressive restrictions which, according to the savages themselves, exert a sympathetic effect upon the success of the faraway expedition. But it does not require much acumen to guess that this element acting at a distance is nothing but a thought of home, the longing for the absent, and that these disguises conceal the sound psychological insight that the men will do their best only if they are fully assured of the whereabouts of their guarded women. On other occasions the thought is directly expressed without magic motivation, that the conjugal infidelity of the wife thwarts the absent husband's efforts.

The countless taboo rules to which the women of savages are subject during their menstrual periods are motivated by the superstitious dread of blood which in all probability actually determines it. But it would be wrong to overlook the possibility that this blood dread also serves æsthetic and hygienic purposes which in every case have to be covered by magic motivations.

We are probably not mistaken in assuming that such attempted explanations expose us to the reproach of attributing a most improbable delicacy of psychic activities to contemporary savages.

But I think that we may easily make the same mistake with the psychology of these races who have remained at the animistic stage that we made with the psychic life of the child, which we adults understood no better and whose richness and fineness of feeling we have therefore so greatly undervalued.

I want to consider another group of hitherto unexplained taboo rules because they admit of an explanation with which the psychoanalyst is familiar. Under certain conditions it is forbidden to many savage races to keep in the house sharp weapons and instruments for cutting.[1] Frazer cites a German superstition that a knife must not be left lying with the edge pointing upward because God and the angels might injure themselves with it. May we not recognize in this taboo a premonition of certain "symptomatic actions" [2] for which the sharp weapon might be used by unconscious evil impulses?

[1] Frazer, *l.c.*, p. 237.
[2] Cf. *The Psychopathology of Everyday Life*.

THE INFANTILE RECURRENCE OF TOTEMISM

THE reader need not fear that psychoanalysis, which first revealed the regular over-determination of psychic acts and formations, will be tempted to derive anything so complicated as religion from a single source. If it necessarily seeks, as in duty bound, to gain recognition for one of the sources of this institution, it by no means claims exclusiveness for this source or even first rank among the concurring factors. Only a synthesis from various fields of research can decide what relative importance in the genesis of religion is to be assigned to the mechanism which we are to discuss; but such a task exceeds the means as well as the intentions of the psychoanalyst.

I

The first chapter of this book made us acquainted with the conception of totemism. We heard that totemism is a system which takes the place of religion among certain primitive races in Australia, America, and Africa, and furnishes the basis of social organization. We know that in 1869 the Scotchman MacLennan attracted general interest to the phenomena of totemism, which until then had been considered merely as curiosities, by his conjecture that a large number of customs and usages in various old as well as modern societies were to be taken as remnants of a totemic epoch. Science has since then fully recognized this significance of totemism. I quote a passage from the *Elements of the Psychology of Races* by W. Wundt (1912), as the latest utterance on this question: [1] "Taking all this together it becomes highly probable that a totemic culture was at one time the preliminary stage of every later evolution as well as a transition stage between the state of primitive man and the age of gods and heroes."

It is necessary for the purposes of this chapter to go more deeply into the nature of totemism. For reasons that will be evident later I here give

[1] p. 139.

preference to an outline by S. Reinach, who in the year 1900 sketched the following *Code du Totémisme* in twelve articles, like a catechism of the totemic religion: [1]

1. Certain animals must not be killed or eaten, but men bring up individual animals of these species and take care of them.

2. An animal that dies accidentally is mourned and buried with the same honours as a member of the tribe.

3. The prohibition as to eating sometimes refers only to a certain part of the animal.

4. If pressure of necessity compels the killing of an animal usually spared, it is done with excuses to the animal and the attempt is made to mitigate the violation of the taboo, namely the killing, through various tricks and evasions.

5. If the animal is sacrificed by ritual, it is solemnly mourned.

6. At specified solemn occasions, like religious ceremonies, the skins of certain animals are donned. Where totemism still exists, these are totem animals.

7. Tribes and individuals assume the names of totem animals.

8. Many tribes use pictures of animals as coats of arms and decorate their weapons with them; the men paint animal pictures on their bodies or have them tatooed.

9. If the totem is one of the feared and dangerous animals it is assumed that the animal will spare the members of the tribe named after it.

10. The totem animal protects and warns the members of the tribe.

11. The totem animal foretells the future to those faithful to it and serves as their leader.

12. The members of a totem tribe often believe that they are connected with the totem animal by the bond of common origin.

The value of this catechism of the totem religion can be more appreciated if one bears in mind that Reinach has here also incorporated all the signs and clews which lead to the conclusion that the totemic system had once existed. The peculiar attitude of this author to the problem is shown by the fact that to some extent he neglects the essential traits of totemism, and we shall see that of the two main tenets of the totemistic catechism he has forced one into the background and completely lost sight of the other.

In order to get a more correct picture of the characteristics of totemism we turn to an author who has devoted four volumes to the theme, combining the most complete collection of the observations in question with the most thorough discussion of the problems they raise. We shall remain

[1] *Revue Scientifique*, October, 1900 reprinted in the four volume work of the author, *Cultes, Mythes et Religions*, 1908, Tome I, p. 17.

indebted to J. G. Frazer, the author of *Totemism and Exogamy*,[1] for the pleasure and information he affords, even though psychoanalytic investigation may lead us to results which differ widely from his.[2]

"A totem," wrote Frazer in his first essay,[3] "is a class of material objects which a savage regards with superstitious respect, believing that there exists between him and every member of the class an intimate and altogether special relation. The connection between a person and his totem is mutually beneficent; the totem protects the man and the man shows his respect for the totem in various ways, by not killing it if it be an animal, and not cutting or gathering it if it be a plant. As distinguished from a fetich, a totem is never an isolated individual but always a class of objects, generally a species of animals or of plants, more rarely a class of inanimate natural objects, very rarely a class of artificial objects."

At least three kinds of totem can be distinguished:

1.   The tribal totem which a whole tribe shares and which is hereditary from generation to generation,

2.   The sex totem which belongs to all the masculine or feminine members of a tribe to the exclusion of the opposite sex, and

3.   The individual totem which belongs to the individual and does not descend to his successors.

[1] 1910.

[2] But it may be well to show the reader beforehand how difficult it is to establish the facts in this field.

In the first place those who collect the observations are not identical with those who digest and discuss them; the first are travellers and missionaries, while the others are scientific men who perhaps have never seen the objects of their research.—It is not easy to establish an understanding with savages. Not all the observers were familiar with the languages but had to use the assistance of interpreters or else had to communicate with the people they questioned in the auxiliary language of pidgin-English. Savages are not communicative about the most intimate affairs of their culture and unburden themselves only to those foreigners who have passed many years in their midst. From various motives they often give wrong or misleading information (Compare Frazer, *The Beginnings of Religion and Totemism Among the Australian Aborigines; Fortnightly Review*, 1905; *Totemism and Exogamy*, Vol. I, p. 150).—It must not be forgotten that primitive races are not young races but really are as old as the most civilized, and that we have no right to expect that they have preserved their original ideas and institutions for our information without any evolution or distortion. It is certain, on the contrary, that far-reaching changes in all directions have taken place among primitive races, so that we can never unhesitatingly decide which of their present conditions and opinions have preserved the original past, having remained petrified, as it were, and which represent a distortion and change of the original. It is due to this that one meets the many disputes among authors as to what proportion of the peculiarities of a primitive culture is to be taken as a primary, and what as a later and secondary manifestation. To establish the original conditions, therefore, always remains a matter of construction. Finally, it is not easy to adapt oneself to the ways of thinking of primitive races. For like children, we easily misunderstand them, and are always inclined to interpret their acts and feelings according to our own psychic constellations.

[3] *Totemism* (Edinburgh, 1887), reprinted in the first volume of his great study, *Totemism and Exogamy*.

The last two kinds of totem are comparatively of little importance compared to the tribal totem. Unless we are mistaken they are recent formations and of little importance as far as the nature of the taboo is concerned.

The tribal totem (clan totem) is the object of veneration of a group of men and women who take their name from the totem and consider themselves consanguineous offspring of a common ancestor, and who are firmly associated with each other through common obligations towards each other as well as by the belief in their totem.

Totemism is a religious as well as a social system. On its religious side it consists of the relations of mutual respect and consideration between a person and his totem, and on its social side it is composed of obligations of the members of the clan towards each other and towards other tribes. In the later history of totemism these two sides show a tendency to part company; the social system often survives the religious and conversely remnants of totemism remain in the religion of countries in which the social system based upon totemism had disappeared. In the present state of our ignorance about the origin of totemism we cannot say with certainty how these two sides were originally combined. But there is on the whole a strong probability that in the beginning the two sides of totemism were indistinguishable from each other. In other words, the further we go back the clearer it becomes that a member of a tribe looks upon himself as being of the same genus as his totem and makes no distinction between his attitude towards the totem and his attitude towards his tribal companions.

In the special description of totemism as a religious system, Frazer lays stress on the fact that the members of a tribe assume the name of their totem and also as a *rule believe that they are descended from it*. It is due to this belief that they do not hunt the totem animal or kill or eat it, and that they deny themselves every other use of the totem if it is not an animal. The prohibitions against killing or eating the totem are not the only taboos affecting it; sometimes it is also forbidden to touch it and even to look at it; in a number of cases the totem must not be called by its right name. Violation of the taboo prohibitions which protect the totem is punished automatically by serious disease or death.[1]

Specimens of the totem animals are sometimes raised by the clan and taken care of in captivity.[2] A totem animal found dead is mourned and buried like a member of the clan. If a totem animal had to be killed it was done with a prescribed ritual of excuses and ceremonies of expiation. The tribe expected protection and forbearance from its totem. If it

---

[1] Compare the chapter on Taboo.
[2] Just as today we still have the wolves in a cage at the steps of the Capitol in Rome and the bears in the pit at Berne.

was a dangerous animal (a beast of prey or a poisonous snake), it was assumed that it would not harm, and where this assumption did not come true the person attacked was expelled from the tribe. Frazer thinks that oaths were originally ordeals, many tests as to descent and genuineness being in this way left to the decision of the totem. The totem helps in case of illness and gives the tribe premonitions and warnings. The appearance of the totem animal near a house was often looked upon as an announcement of death. The totem had come to get its relative.[1]

A member of a clan seeks to emphasize his relationship to the totem in various significant ways; he imitates an exterior similarity by dressing himself in the skin of the totem animal, by having the picture of it tatooed upon himself, and in other ways. On the solemn occasions of birth, initiation into manhood or funeral obsequies this identification with the totem is carried out in deeds and words. Dances in which all the members of the tribe disguise themselves as their totem and act like it, serve various magic and religious purposes. Finally there are the ceremonies at which the totem animal is killed in a solemn manner.[2]

The social side of totemism is primarily expressed in a sternly observed commandment and in a tremendous restriction. The members of a totem clan are brothers and sisters, pledged to help and protect each other; if a member of the clan is slain by a stranger the whole tribe of the slayer must answer for the murder and the clan of the slain man shows its solidarity in the demand for expiation for the blood that has been shed. The ties of the totem are stronger than our ideas of family ties, with which they do not altogether coincide, since the transfer of the totem takes place as a rule through maternal inheritance, paternal inheritance possibly not counting at all in the beginning.

But the corresponding taboo restriction consists in the prohibition against members of the same clan marrying each other or having any kind of sexual intercourse whatsoever with each other. This is the famous and enigmatic *exogamy* connexion with totemism. We have devoted the whole first chapter of this book to it, and therefore need only mention here that this exogamy springs from the intensified incest dread of primitive races, that it becomes entirely comprehensible as a security against incest in group marriages, and that at first it accomplishes the avoidance of incest for the younger generation and only in the course of further development becomes a hindrance to the older generation as well.[3]

To this presentation of totemism by Frazer, one of the earliest in the literature on the subject, I will now add a few excerpts from one of the latest summaries. In the *Elements of the Psychology of Races,* which

---

[1] Like the legend of the white woman in many noble families.
[2] *l.c.,* p. 35. See the discussion of sacrifice further on.
[3] See Chapter I.

appeared in 1912, W. Wundt says: [1] "The totem animal is considered the ancestral animal. 'Totem' is therefore both a group name and a birth name and in the latter aspect this name has at the same time a mythological meaning. But all these uses of the conception play into each other and the particular meanings may recede so that in some cases the totems have become almost a mere nomenclature of the tribal divisions, while in others the idea of the descent or else the cultic meaning of the totem remains in the foreground. . . . The conception of the totem determines the *tribal* arrangement and the *tribal organization*. These norms and their establishment in the belief and feelings of the members of the tribe account for the fact that originally the totem animal was certainly not considered merely a name for a group division but that it usually was considered the progenitor of the corresponding division. . . . This accounted for the fact that these animal ancestors enjoyed a cult. . . . This animal cult expresses itself primarily in the attitude towards the totem animal, quite aside from special ceremonies and ceremonial festivities: not only each individual animal but every representative of the same species was to a certain degree a sanctified animal; the member of the totem was forbidden to eat the flesh of the totem animal or he was allowed to eat it only under special circumstances. This is in accord with the significant contradictory phenomenon found in this connexion, namely, that under certain conditions there was a kind of ceremonial consumption of the totem flesh. . . ."

". . . But the most important social side of this totemic tribal arrangement consists in the fact that it was connected with certain rules of conduct for the relations of the groups with each other. The most important of these were the rules of conjugal relations. This tribal division is thus connected with an important phenomenon which first made its appearance in the totemic age, namely with exogamy."

If we wish to arrive at the characteristics of the original totemism by shifting through everything that may correspond to later development or decline, we find the following essential facts: *The totems were originally only animals and were considered the ancestors of single tribes. The totem was hereditary only through the female line; it was forbidden to kill the totem* (or to eat it, which under primitive conditions amounts to the same thing); *members of a totem were forbidden to have sexual intercourse with each other.*[2]

---

[1] p. 116.

[2] The conclusion which Frazer draws about totemism in his second work on the subject (*The Origin of Totemism; Fortnightly Review,* 1899) agrees with this text: "Thus, totemism has commonly been treated as a primitive system both of religion and of society. As a system of religion it embraces the mystic union of the savage with his totem; as a system of society it comprises the relations in which men and women of the same totem stand to each other and to the members of other totemic

It may now seem strange to us that in the *Code du totémisme* which
Reinach has drawn up the one principal taboo, namely exogamy, does
not appear at all while the assumption of the second taboo, namely the
descent from the totem animal, is only casually mentioned. Yet, Reinach
is an author to whose work in this field we owe much and I have chosen
his presentation in order to prepare us for the differences of opinion
among the authors, which will now occupy our attention.

2

The more convinced we became that totemism had regularly formed
a phase of every culture, the more urgent became the necessity of arriving at an understanding of it and of casting light upon the riddle
of its nature. To be sure, everything about totemism is in the nature
of a riddle; the decisive questions are the origin of the totem, the motivation of exogamy (or rather of the incest taboo which it represents)
and the relation between the two, the totem organization and the incest
prohibition. The understanding should be at once historical and psychological; it should inform us under what conditions this peculiar institution developed and to what psychic needs of man it has given expression.

The reader will certainly be astonished to hear from how many different points of view the answer to these questions has been attempted
and how far the opinions of expert investigators vary. Almost everything
that might be asserted in general about totemism is doubtful; even the
above statement of it, taken from an article by Frazer in 1887, cannot
escape the criticism that it expresses an arbitrary preference of the
author and would be challenged today by Frazer himself, who has repeatedly changed his view on the subject.[1]

It is quite obvious that the nature of totemism and exogamy could be
most readily grasped if we could get into closer touch with the origin of
both institutions. But in judging the state of affairs we must not forget
the remark of Andrew Lang, that even primitive races have not preserved
these original forms and the conditions of their origin, so that we are

---

groups. And corresponding to these two sides of the system are two rough-and-ready
tests or canons of totemism: first, the rule that a man may not kill or eat his totem
animal or plant, and second, the rule that he may not marry or cohabit with a
woman of the same totem" (p. 101). Frazer then adds something which takes us
into the midst of the discussion about totemism: "Whether the two sides—the religious and the social—have always coexisted or are essentially independent, is a
question which has been variously answered."

[1] In connection with such a change of opinion Frazer made this excellent statement:
"That my conclusions on these difficult questions are final, I am not so foolish as
to pretend. I have changed my views repeatedly, and I am resolved to change them
again with every change of the evidence, for like a chameleon the inquirer should
shift his colours with the shifting colours of the ground he treads." Preface to Vol. I,
Totemism and Exogamy, 1910.

altogether dependent upon hypotheses to take the place of the observation we lack.[1] Among the attempted explanations some seem inadequate from the very beginning in the judgment of the psychologist. They are altogether too rational and do not take into consideration the effective character of what they are to explain. Others rest on assumptions which observation fails to verify; while still others appeal to facts which could better be subjected to another interpretation. The refutation of these various opinions as a rule hardly presents any difficulties; the authors are, as usual, stronger in the criticism which they practice on each other than in their own work. The final result as regards most of the points treated is a *non liquet*. It is therefore not surprising that most of the new literature on the subject, which we have largely omitted here, shows the unmistakable effort to reject a general solution of totemic problems as unfeasible. (See, for instance, B. Goldenweiser in the *Journal of American Folklore*, XXIII, 1910. Reviewed in the *Britannica Year Book*, 1913.) I have taken the liberty of disregarding the chronological order in stating these contradictory hypotheses.

(a) The Origin of Totemism

The question of the origin of totemism can also be formulated as follows: How did primitive people come to select the names of animals, plants and inanimate objects for themselves and their tribes? [2]

The Scotchman, MacLennan, who discovered totemism and exogamy for science,[3] refrained from publishing his views of the origin of totemism. According to a communication of Andrew Lang [4] he was for a time inclined to trace totemism back to the custom of tatooing. I shall divide the accepted theories of the derivation of totemism into three groups, (α) nominalistic, (β) sociological, (γ) psychological.

(α) *The Nominalistic Theories*

The information about these theories will justify their summation under the headings I have used.

Garcilaso de La Vega, a descendant of the Peruvian Incas, who wrote the history of his race in the seventeenth century, is already said to have traced back what was known to him about totemic phenomena to the need of the tribes to differentiate themselves from each other by means

---

[1] "By the nature of the case, as the origin of totemism lies far beyond our powers of historical examination or of experiment, we must have recourse as regards this matter, to conjecture," Andrew Lang, *Secret of the Totem*, p. 27.—"Nowhere do we see absolutely primitive man, and a totemic system in the making," p. 29.

[2] At first probably only animals.

[3] *The Worship of Animals and Plants* (*Fortnightly Review*, 1869–1870). *Primitive Marriage*, 1865; both works reprinted in *Studies in Ancient History*, 1876; second edition, 1886.

[4] *The Secret of the Totem*, 1905, p. 34.

of names.[1] The same idea appears centuries later in the *Ethnology* of A. K. Keane where totems are said to be derived from heraldic badges through which individuals, families and tribes wanted to differentiate themselves.[2]

Max Müller expresses the same opinion about the meaning of the totem in his *Contributions to the Science of Mythology*.[3] A totem is said to be, 1. a mark of the clan, 2. a clan name, 3. the name of the ancestor of the clan, 4. the name of the object which the clan reveres. J. Pikler wrote later, in 1899, that men needed a permanent name for communities and individuals that could be preserved in writing. . . . Thus totemism arises, not from a religious, but from a prosaic everyday need of mankind. The giving of names, which is the essence of totemism, is a result of the technique of primitive writing. The totem is of the nature of an easily represented writing symbol. But if savages first bore the name of an animal they deduced the idea of relationship from this animal.[4]

Herbert Spencer,[5] also, thought that the origin of totemism was to be found in the giving of names. The attributes of certain individuals, he showed, had brought about their being named after animals so that they had come to have names of honour or nicknames which continued in their descendants. As a result of the indefiniteness and incomprehensibility of primitive languages, these names are said to have been taken by later generations as proof of their descent from the animals themselves. Totemism would thus be the result of a mistaken reverence for ancestors.

Lord Avebury (better known under his former name, Sir John Lubbock) has expressed himself quite similarly about the origin of totemism, though without emphasizing the misunderstanding. If we want to explain the veneration of animals we must not forget how often human names are borrowed from animals. The children and followers of a man who was called bear or lion naturally made this their ancestral name. In this way it came about that the animal itself came to be respected and finally venerated.

Fison has advanced what seems an irrefutable objection to such a derivation of the totem name from the names of individuals.[6] He shows from conditions in Australia that the totem is always the mark of a group of people and never of an individual. But if it were otherwise, if the totem was originally the name of a single individual, it could never, with the system of maternal inheritance, descend to his children.

[1] *Ibid.*

[2] *Ibid.*

[3] According to Andrew Lang.

[4] Pikler and Somló, *The Origin of Totemism*, 1901. The authors rightly call their attempt at explanation a "Contribution to the materialistic theory of History."

[5] *The Origin of Animal Worship* (*Fortnightly Review*, 1870). *Principles of Psychology*, Vol. I, §§ 169 to 176.

[6] *Kamilaroi and Kurnai*, p. 165, 1880 (Lang, *Secret of the Totem*, etc.).

The theories thus far stated are evidently inadequate. They may explain how animal names came to be applied to primitive tribes but they can never explain the importance attached to the giving of names which constitutes the totemic system. The most noteworthy theory of this group has been developed by Andrew Lang in his books, *Social Origins*, 1903, and *The Secret of the Totem*, 1905. This theory still makes naming the centre of the problem, but it uses two interesting psychological factors and thus may claim to have contributed to the final solution of the riddle of totemism.

Andrew Lang holds that it does not make any difference how clans acquired their animal names. It might be assumed that one day they awoke to the consciousness that they had them without being able to account from where they came. *The origin of these names had been forgotten.* In that case they would seek to acquire more information by pondering over their names, and with their conviction of the importance of names they necessarily came to all the ideas that are contained in the totemic system. For primitive men, as for savages of today and even for our children,[1] a name is not indifferent and conventional as it seems to us, but is something important and essential. A man's name is one of the main constituents of his person and perhaps a part of his psyche. The fact that they had the same names as animals must have led primitive men to assume a secret and important bond between their persons and the particular animal species. What other bond than consanguinity could it be? But if the similarity of names once led to this assumption it could also account directly for all the totemic prohibitions of the blood taboo, including exogamy.

"No more than these three things—a group animal name of unknown origin; belief in a transcendental connexion between all bearers, human and bestial, of the same name; and belief in the blood superstitions—were needed to give rise to all the totemic creeds and practices, including exogamy" (*Secret of the Totem*, p. 126).

Lang's explanation extends over two periods. It derives the totemic system of psychological necessity from the toten names, on the assumption that the origin of the naming has been forgotten. The other part of the theory now seeks to clear up the origin of these names. We shall see that it bears an entirely different stamp.

This other part of the Lang theory is not markedly different from those which I have called "nominalistic." The practical need of differentiation compelled the individual tribes to assume names and therefore they tolerated the names which every tribe ascribed to the other. This "naming from without" is the peculiarity of Lang's construction. The fact that the names which thus originated were borrowed from animals is not further remarkable and need not have been felt by primitive men as abuse or derision.

[1] See the chapter on Taboo.

Besides, Lang has cited numerous cases from later epochs of history in which names given from without that were first meant to be derisive were accepted by those nicknamed and voluntarily borne (The Guises, Whigs and Tories). The assumption that the origin of these names was forgotten in the course of time connects this second part of the Lang theory with the first one just mentioned.

(β) *The Sociological Theories*

S. Reinach, who successfully traced the relics of the totemic system in the cult and customs of later periods, though attaching from the very beginning only slight value to the factor of descent from the totem animal, once made the casual remark that totemism seemed to him to be nothing but *"une hypertrophie de l'instinct social."* [1]

The same interpretation seems to permeate the new work of E. Durkheim, *Les Formes Élémentaires de la Vie Religieuse; Le Systéme Totémique en Australie,* 1912. The totem is the visible representative of the social religion of these races. It embodies the community, which is the real object of veneration.

Other authors have sought a more intimate reason for the share which social impulses have played in the formation of totemic institutions. Thus A. C. Haddon has assumed that every primitive tribe originally lived on a particular plant or animal species and perhaps also traded with this food and exchanged it with other tribes. It then was inevitable that a tribe should become known to other tribes by the name of the animal which played such weighty rôle with it. At the same time this tribe would develop a special familiarity with this animal, and a kind of interest for it which, however, was based upon the psychic motive of man's most elementary and pressing need, namely, hunger. [2]

The objections against this most rational of all the totem theories are that such a state of the food supply is never found among primitive men and probably never existed. Savages are the more omnivorous the lower they stand in the social scale. Besides, it is incomprehensible how such an exclusive diet could have developed an almost religious relation to the totem, culminating in an absolute abstention from the revered food.

The first of the three theories about the origin of totemism which Frazer stated, was a psychological one. We shall report it elsewhere.

Frazer's second theory, which we will discuss here, originated under the infl nce of an important publication by two investigators of the inhabitants of Central Australia. [3]

[1] *l.c.,* Vol. I, p. 41.
[2] *Address to the Anthropological Section, British Association,* Belfast, 1902. According to Frazer, *l.c.,* Vol. IV, p. 50.
[3] *The Native Tribes of Central Australia,* by Baldwin Spencer and H. J. Gillen, London, 1891.

Spencer and Gillen describe a series of peculiar institutions, customs, and opinions of a group of tribes, the so-called Arunta nation, and Frazer subscribes to their opinion that these peculiarities are to be looked upon as characteristics of a primary state and that they can explain the first and real meaning of totemism.

In the Arunta tribe itself (a part of the Arunta nation) these peculiarities are as follows:

1. They have the division into totem clans but the totem is not hereditary but is individually determined (as will be shown later).

2. The totem clans are not exogamus, and the marriage restrictions are brought about by a highly developed division into marriage classes which have nothing to do with the totems.

3. The function of the totem clan consists of carrying out a ceremony which in a subtle magic manner brings about an increase of the edible totem. (This ceremony is called *Intichiuma*.)

4. The Aruntas have a peculiar theory about conception and re-birth. They assume that the spirits of the dead who belonged to their totem wait for their re-birth in definite localities and penetrate into the bodies of the women who pass such a spot. When a child is born the mother states at which spirit abode she thinks she conceived her child. This determines the totem of the child. It is further assumed that the spirits (of the dead as well as of the re-born) are bound to peculiar stone amulets, called *Churinga*, which are found in these places.

Two factors seem to have induced Frazer to believe that the oldest form of totemism had been found in the institution of the Aruntas. In the first place the existence of certain myths which assert that the ancestors of the Aruntas always lived on their totem animal, and that they married no other women except those of their own totem. Secondly, the apparent disregard of the sexual act in their theory of conception. People who have not yet realized that conception was the result of the sexual act might well be considered the most backward and primitive people living today.

Frazer, in having recourse to the *Intichiuma* ceremony to explain totemism, suddenly saw the totemic system in a totally different light as a thoroughly practical organization for accomplishing the most natural needs of man. (Compare Haddon above.[1]) The system was simply an extraordinary piece of "co-operative magic." Primitive men formed what might be called a magic production and consumption club. Each totem clan undertook to see to the cleanliness of a certain article of food. If it were a question of inedible totems like harmful animals, rain, wind, or similar objects, it was the duty of the totem clan to dominate this part of nature

---

[1] There is nothing vague or mystical about it, nothing of that metaphysical haze which some writers love to conjure up over the humblest beginnings of human speculation but which is utterly foreign to the simple, sensuous, and concrete modes of the savage. (*Totemism and Exogamy*, I., p. 117).

and to ward off its injuriousness. The efforts of each clan were for the good of all the others. As the clan could not eat its totem or could eat only a very little of it, it furnished this valuable product for the rest and was in turn supplied with what these had to take care of as their social totem duty. In the light of this interpretation furnished by the *Intichiuma* ceremony, it appeared to Frazer as if the prohibition against eating the totem had misled observers to neglect the more important side of the relation, namely the commandment to supply as much as possible of the edible totem for the needs of others.

Frazer accepted the tradition of the Aruntas that each totem clan had originally lived on its totem without any restriction. It then became difficult to understand the evolution that followed through which savages were atisfied to ensure the totem for others while they themselves abstained from eating it. He then assumed that this restriction was by no means the result of a kind of religious respect, but came about through ⁺he observation that no animal devoured its own kind, so that this break in he identification with the totem was injurious to the power which savages sought to acquire over the totem. Or else it resulted from the endeavour to make the being favourably disposed by sparing it. Frazer did not conceal the difficulties of this explanation from himself,[1] nor did he dare to indicate in what way the habit of marrying within the totem, which the myths of the Aruntas proclaimed, was converted into exogamy.

Frazer's theory based on the *Intichiuma,* stands or falls with the recognition of the primitive nature of the Arunta institutions. But it seems impossible to hold to this in the face of the objections advanced by Durkheim [2] and Lang.[3] The Aruntas seem on the contrary to be the most developed of the Australian tribes and to represent rather a dissolution stage of totemism than its beginning. The myths that made such an impression on Frazer because they emphasize, in contrast to prevailing institutions of today, that the Aruntas are free to eat the totem and to marry within it, easily explain themselves to us as wish phantasies, which are projected into the past, like the myths of the Golden Age.

(γ) *The Psychological Theories*

Frazer's first psychological theories, formed before his acquaintance with the observations of Spencer and Gillen, were based upon the belief in an "outward soul." [4] The totem was meant to represent a safe place of refuge where the soul is deposited in order to avoid the dangers which threaten it. After primitive man had housed his soul in his totem, he him-

[1] *l.c.,* p. 120.
[2] *L'Année Sociologique,* Vols. I, V, VIII, and elsewhere. See especially the chapter, *Sur le Totémisme,* Vol. V, 1901.
[3] *Social Origins and the Secret of the Totem.*
[4] *The Golden Bough,* Vol. II, p. 332.

self became invulnerable and he naturally took care himself not to harm the bearer of his soul. But as he did not know which individual of the species in question was the bearer of his soul, he was concerned in sparing the whole species. Frazer himself later gave up this derivation of totemism from the belief in souls.

When he became acquainted with the observations of Spencer and Gillen, he set up the other social theory which has just been stated, but he himself then saw that the motive from which he had derived totemism was altogether too "rational" and that he had assumed a social organization for it which was altogether too complicated to be called primitive.[1] The magic coöperative companies now appeared to him rather as the fruit than as the germ of totemism. He sought a simpler factor for the derivation of totemism in the shape of a primitive superstition behind these forms. He then found this original factor in the remarkable conception theory of the Aruntas.

As already stated, the Aruntas establish no connection between conception and the sexual act. If a woman feels herself to be a mother it means that at that moment one of the spirits from the nearest spirit abode who has been watching for a re-birth, has penetrated into her body and is born as her child. This child has the same totem as all the spirits that lurk in that particular locality. But if we are willing to go back a step further and assume that the woman originally believed that the animal, plant, stone, or other object which occupied her fancy at the moment when she first felt herself pregnant had really penetrated into her and was being born through her in human form, then the identity of a human being with his totem would really be founded on the belief of the mother, and all the other totem commandments (with the exception of exogamy) could easily be derived from this belief. Men would refuse to eat the particular animal or plant because it would be just like eating themselves. But occasionally they would be impelled to eat some of their totem in a ceremonial manner because they could thus strengthen their identification with the totem, which is the essential part of totemism. W. H. R. Rivers' observations among the inhabitants of the Banks Islands seemed to prove men's direct identification with their totems on the basis of such a conception theory.[2]

The ultimate sources of totemism would then be the ignorance of savages as to the process of procreation among human beings and animals; especially their ignorance as to the rôle which the male plays in fertilization. This ignorance must be facilitated by the long interval which is interposed between the fertilizing act and the birth of the child or the sensa-

---

[1] "It is unlikely that a community of savages should deliberately parcel out the realm of nature into provinces, assign each province to a particular band of magicians, and bid all the bands to work their magic and weave their spells for the common good." *Totemism and Exogamy*, Vol. IV, p. 57.

[2] *Totemism and Exogamy*, Vol. II, p. 89, and IV, p. 59.

tion of the child's first movements. Totemism is therefore a creation of the feminine mind and not of the masculine. The sick fancies of the pregnant woman are the roots of it. Anything indeed that struck a woman at that mysterious moment of her life when she first knows herself to be a mother might easily be identified by her with the child in her womb. Such maternal fancies, so natural and seemingly so universal, appear to be the root of totemism.[1]

The main objection to this third theory of Frazer's is the same which has already been advanced against his second, sociological theory. The Aruntas seem to be far removed from the beginnings of totemism. Their denial of fatherhood does not apparently rest upon primitive ignorance; in many cases they even have paternal inheritance. They seem to have sacrificed fatherhood to a kind of a speculation which strives to honour the ancestral spirits.[2] Though they raise the myth of immaculate conception through a spirit to a general theory of conception, we cannot for that reason credit them with ignorance as to the conditions of procreation any more than we could the old races who lived during the rise of the Christian myths.

Another psychological theory of the origin of totemism has been formulated by the Dutch writer, G. A. Wilcken. It establishes a connection between totemism and the migration of souls. "The animal into which, according to general belief, the souls of the dead passed, became a blood relative, an ancestor, and was revered as such." But the belief in the soul's migration to animals is more readily derived from totemism than inversely.[3]

Still another theory of totemism is advanced by the excellent American ethnologists, Franz Boas, Hill-Tout, and others. It is based on observations of totemic Indian tribes and asserts that the totem is originally the guardian spirit of an ancestor who has acquired it through a dream and handed it on to his descendants. We have already heard the difficulties which the derivation of totemism through inheritance from a single individual offers; besides, the Australian observations seem by no means to support the tracing back of the totem to the guardian spirit.[4]

Two facts have become decisive for the last of the psychological theories as stated by Wundt; in the first place, that the original and most widely known totem object was an animal, and secondly, that the earliest totem animals corresponded to animals which had a soul.[5] Such animals as birds, snakes, lizards, mice are fitted by their extreme mobility, their flight

---

[1] *Totemism and Exogamy*, Vol. IV, p. 63.
[2] "That belief is a philosophy far from primitive," Andrew Lang, *Secret of the Totem*, p. 192.
[3] Frazer, *Totemism and Exogamy*, Vol. IV, p. 45.
[4] Frazer, *l.c.*, p. 48.
[5] Wundt, *Elemente der Völker-Psychologie*, p. 190.

through the air, and by other characteristics which arouse surprise and fear, to become the bearers of souls which leave their bodies. The totem animal is a descendant of the animal transformations of the spirit-soul. Thus, with Wundt totemism is directly connected with the belief in souls or with animism.

(b) and (c) The Origin of Exogamy and Its Relation to Totemism

I have put forth the theories of totemism with considerable detail and yet I am afraid that I have not made them clear enough on account of the condensation that was constantly necessary. In the interest of the reader I am taking the liberty of further condensing the other questions that arise. The discussions about the exogamy of totem races become especially complicated and untractable, one might even say confused, on account of the nature of the material used. Fortunately the object of this treatise permits me to limit myself to pointing out several guide-posts and referring to the frequently quoted writings of experts in the field for a more thorough pursuit of the subject.

The attitude of an author to the problems of exogamy is of course not independent of the stand he has taken toward one or the other of the totem theories. Some of these explanations of totemism lack all connection with exogamy so that the two institutions are entirely separated. Thus we find here two opposing views, one of which clings to the original likelihood that exogamy is an essential part of the totemic system while the other disputes such a connection and believes in an accidental combination of these two traits of the most ancient cultures. In his later works Frazer has emphatically stood for this latter point of view.

"I must request the reader to bear constantly in mind that the two institutions of totemism and exogamy are fundamentally distinct in origin and nature though they have accidentally crossed and blended in many tribes." (*Totemism and Exogamy* I, Preface XII.)

He warns directly against the opposite view as being a source of endless difficulties and misunderstandings. In contrast to this, many authors have found a way of conceiving exogamy as a necessary consequence of the basic views on totemism. Durkheim [1] has shown in his writings how the taboo, which is attached to the totem, must have entailed the prohibition against putting a woman of the same totem to sexual uses. The totem is of the same blood as the human being and for this reason the blood ban (in reference to defloration and menstruation) forbids sexual intercourse with a woman of the same totem. [2] Andrew Lang, who here agrees with Durkheim, goes so far as to believe that the blood taboo was not necessary to bring about the prohibition in regard to the women of the same tribe. [3]

[1] *L'année Sociologique*, 1898–1904.
[2] See Frazer's *Criticism of Durkheim, Totemism and Exogamy*, p. 101.
[3] *Secret*, etc., p. 125.

The general totem taboo which, for instance, forbids any one to sit in the shadow of the totem tree, would have sufficed. Andrew Lang also contends for another derivation of exogamy (see below) and leaves it in doubt how these two explanations are related to each other.

As regards the temporal relations, the majority of authors subscribe to the opinion that totemism is the older institution and that exogamy came later.[1]

Among the theories which seek to explain exogamy independently of totemism only a few need be mentioned in so far as they illustrate different attitudes of the authors towards the problem of incest.

MacLennan [2] had ingeniously guessed that exogamy resulted from the remnants of customs pointing to earlier forms of female rape. He assumed that it was the general custom in ancient times to procure women from strange tribes so that marriage with a woman from the same tribe gradually became "improper because it was unusual." He sought the motive for the exogamous habit in the scarcity of women among these tribes, which had resulted from the custom of killing most female children at birth. We are not concerned here with investigation whether actual conditions corroborate MacLennan's assumptions. We are more interested in the argument that these premises still leave it unexplained why the male members of the tribe should have made these few women of their blood inaccessible to themselves, as well as in the manner in which the incest problem is here entirely neglected.[3]

Other writers have on the contrary assumed, and evidently with more right, that exogamy is to be interpreted as an institution for the prevention of incest.[4]

If we survey the gradually increasing complication of Australian marriage restrictions we can hardly help agreeing with the opinion of Morgan, Frazer, Hewitt and Baldwin Spencer,[5] that these institutions bear the stamp of "deliberate design," as Frazer puts it, and that they were meant to do what they have actually accomplished. "In no other way does it seem possible to explain in all its details a system at once so complex and so regular." [6]

It is of interest to point out that the first restrictions which the introduction of marriage classes brought about affected the sexual freedom of the younger generation, in other words, incest between brothers and

---

[1] See Frazer, *l.c.*, Vol. IV, p. 75: "The totemic clan is a totally different social organism from the exogamous class, and we have good grounds for thinking that it is far older."

[2] *Primitive Marriage*, 1865.

[3] Frazer, *l.c.*, p. 73 to 92.

[4] Compare Chapter I.

[5] Morgan, *Ancient Society*, 1877.—Frazer *Totemism and Exogamy*, Vol. IV, p. 105.

[6] Frazer, *l.c*, p. 106.

sisters and between sons and mothers, while incest between father and daughter was only abrogated by more sweeping measures.

However, to trace back exogamus sexual restrictions to legal intentions does not add anything to the understanding of the motive which created these institutions. From what source, in the final analysis, springs the dread of incest which must be recognized as the root of exogamy? It evidently does not suffice to appeal to an instinctive aversion against sexual intercourse with blood relatives, that is to say, to the fact of incest dread, in order to explain the dread of incest, if social experience shows that, in spite of this instinct, incest is not a rare occurrence even in our society, and if the experience of history can acquaint us with cases in which incestuous marriage of privileged persons was made the rule.

Westermarck [1] advanced the following to explain the dread of incest: "that an innate aversion against sexual intercourse exists between persons who live together from childhood and that this feeling, since such persons are as a rule consanguineous, finds a natural expression in custom and law through the abhorrence of sexual intercourse between those closely related." Though Havelock Ellis disputed the instinctive character of this aversion in the *Studies in the Psychology of Sex*, he otherwise supported the same explanation in its essentials by declaring: "The normal absence of the manifestation of the pairing instinct where brothers and sisters or boys and girls living together from childhood are concerned, is a purely negative phenomenon due to the fact that under these circumstances the antecedent conditions for arousing the mating instinct must be entirely lacking. . . . For persons who have grown up together from childhood, habit has dulled the sensual attraction of seeing, hearing and touching and has led it into a channel of quiet attachment, robbing it of its power to call forth the necessary erotic excitement required to produce sexual tumescence."

It seems to me very remarkable that Westermarck looks upon this innate aversion to sexual intercourse with persons with whom we have shared childhood as being at the same time a psychic representative of the biological fact that inbreeding means injury to the species. Such a biological instinct would hardly go so far astray in its psychological manifestation as to affect the companions of home and hearth who in this respect are quite harmless, instead of the blood relatives who alone are injurious to procreation. And I cannot resist citing the excellent criticism which Frazer opposes to Westermarck's assertion. Frazer finds it incomprehensible that sexual sensibility today is not at all opposed to sexual intercourse with companions of the hearth and home while the dread of incest, which is said to be nothing but an offshoot of this reluctance, has

[1] *Origin and Development of Moral Conceptions*, Vol. II: Marriage (1909). See also there the author's defence against familiar objections.

nowadays grown to be so overpowering. But other remarks of Frazer's go deeper and I set them down here in unabbreviated form because they are in essential agreement with the arguments developed in my chapter on Taboo.

"It is not easy to see why any deep human instinct should need reinforcement through law. There is no law commanding men to eat and drink, or forbidding them to put their hands in the fire. Men eat and drink and keep their hands out of the fire instinctively, for fear of natural, not legal penalties, which would be entailed by violence done to these instincts. The law only forbids men to do what their instincts incline them to do; what nature itself prohibits and punishes it would be superfluous for the law to prohibit and punish. Accordingly we may always safely assume that crimes forbidden by law are crimes which many men have a natural propensity to commit. If there were no such propensity there would be no such crimes, and if no such crimes were committed, what need to forbid them? Instead of assuming therefore, from the legal prohibition of incest, that there is a natural aversion to incest we ought rather to assume that there is a natural instinct in favour of it, and that if the law represses it, it does so because civilized men have come to the conclusion that the satisfaction of these natural instincts is detrimental to the general interests of society." [1]

To this valuable argument of Frazer's I can add that the experiences of psychoanalysis make the assumption of such an innate aversion to incestuous relations altogether impossible. They have taught, on the contrary, that the first sexual impulses of the young are regularly of an incestuous nature and that such repressed impulses play a rôle which can hardly be overestimated as the motive power of later neuroses.

The interpretation of incest dread as an innate instinct must therefore be abandoned. The same holds true of another derivation of the incest prohibition which counts many supporters, namely, the assumption that primitive races very soon observe the dangers with which inbreeding threatened their race and that they therefore had decreed the incest prohibition with a conscious purpose. The objections to this attempted explanation crowd upon each other.[2] Not only must the prohibition of incest be older than all breeding of domestic animals from which men could derive experience of the effect of inbreeding upon the characteristics of the breed, but the harmful consequences of inbreeding are not established beyond all doubt even today and in man they can be shown only with difficulty. Besides, everything that we know about contemporaneous savages makes it very improbable that the thoughts of their far-removed ancestors should already have been occupied with preventing injury to

[1] *l.c.*, p. 97.
[2] Compare Durkheim, *La Prohibition de l'Inceste* (*L'année Sociologique*, I, 1896–7).

their later descendants. It sounds almost ridiculous to attribute hygienic and eugenic motives such as have hardly yet found consideration in our culture, to these children of the race who lived without thought of the morrow.[1]

And finally it must be pointed out that a prohibition against inbreeding as an element weakening to the race, which is imposed from practical hygienic motives, seems quite inadequate to explain the deep abhorrence which our society feels against incest. This dread of incest, as I have shown elsewhere,[2] seems to be even more active and stronger among primitive races living to-day than among the civilized.

In inquiring into the origin of incest dread it could be expected that here also there is the choice between possible explanations of a sociological, biological, and psychological nature in which the psychological motives might have to be considered as representative of biological forces. Still, in the end, one is compelled to subscribe to Frazer's resigned statement, namely, that we do not know the origin of incest dread and do not even know how to guess at it. None of the solutions of the riddle thus far advanced seems satisfactory to us.[3]

I must mention another attempt to explain the origin of incest dread which is of an entirely different nature from those considered up to now. It might be called an historic explanation.

This attempt is associated with a hypothesis of Charles Darwin about the primal social state of man. From the habits of the higher apes Darwin concluded that man, too, lived originally in small hordes in which the jealousy of the oldest and strongest male prevented sexual promiscuity. "We may indeed conclude from what we know of the jealousy of all male quadrupeds, armed, as many of them are, with special weapons for battling with their rivals, that promiscuous intercourse in a state of nature is extremely improbable. . . . If we therefore look back far enough into the stream of time and judging from the social habits of man as he now exists, the most probable view is that he originally lived in small communities, each with a single wife, or if powerful, with several, whom he jealously defended against all other men. Or he may not have been a social animal and yet have lived with several wives, like the gorilla; for all the natives agree that only the adult male is seen in a band; when the young male grows up a contest takes place for mastery, and the strongest, by killing and driving out the others, establishes himself as the head of the community (Dr. Savage in the Boston *Journal of Natural History*, Vol.

---

[1] Charles Darwin says about savages: "They are not likely to reflect on distant evils to their progeny."

[2] See Chapter I.

[3] "Thus the ultimate origin of exogamy and with it the law of incest—since exogamy was devised to prevent incest—remains a problem nearly as dark as ever."—*Totemism and Exogamy*, I, p. 165.

V, 1845–7). The younger males being thus driven out and wandering about would also, when at last successful in finding a partner, prevent too close breeding within the limits of the same family." [1]

Atkinson [2] seems to have been the first to recognize that these conditions of the Darwinian primal horde would in practice bring about the exogamy of the young men. Each one of those driven away could found a similar horde in which, thanks to jealousy of the chief, the same prohibition as to sexual intercourse obtained, and in the course of time these conditions would have brought about the rule which is now known as law: no sexual intercourse with the members of the horde. After the advent of totemism the rule would have changed into a different form: no sexual intercourse within the totem.

Andrew Lang [3] declared himself in agreement with this explanation of exogamy. But in the same book he advocates the other theory of Durkheim which explains exogamy as a consequence of the totem laws. It is not altogether easy to combine the two interpretations; in the first case exogamy would have existed before totemism; in the second case it would be a consequence of it. [4]

3

Into this darkness psychoanalytic experience throws one single ray of light.

The relation of the child to animals has much in common with that of primitive man. The child does not yet show any trace of the pride which afterwards moves the adult civilized man to set a sharp dividing line between his own nature and that of all other animals. The child unhesitatingly attributes full equality to animals; he probably feels himself more closely related to the animal than to the undoubtedly mysterious adult, in the freedom with which he acknowledges his needs.

Not infrequently a curious disturbance manifests itself in this excellent understanding between child and animal. The child suddenly begins to

---

[1] *The Origin of Man,* Vol. II, Chap. 20, pp. 603–4.

[2] *Primal Law,* London, 1903 (with Andrew Lang, *Social Origins*).

[3] *Secret of the Totem,* pp. 114, 143.

[4] "If it be granted that exogamy existed in practice, on the lines of Mr. Darwin's theory, before the totem beliefs lent to the practice a *sacred* sanction, our task is relatively easy. The first practical rule would be that of the jealous sire: 'No males to touch the females in my camp,' with expulsion of adolescent sons. *In efflux of time that rule, becoming habitual,* would be, 'No marriages within the local group.' Next let the local groups receive names such as Emus, Crows, Opossums, Snipes, and the rule becomes, 'No marriage within the local group of animal name; no Snipe to marry a Snipe.' But, if the primal groups were not exogamous they would become so as soon as totemic myths and taboos were developed out of the animal, vegetable, and other names of small local groups."—*Secret of the Totem,* p. 143. [The italics above are mine.]—In his last expression on the subject (*Folklore,* December, 1911), Andrew Lang states, however, that he has given up the derivation of exogamy out of the "general totemic" taboo.

fear a certain animal species and to protect himself against seeing or touching any individual of this species. There results the clinical picture of an *animal phobia*, which is one of the most frequent among the psychoneurotic diseases of this age and perhaps the earliest form of such an ailment. The phobia is as a rule in regard to animals for which the child has until then shown the liveliest interest and has nothing to do with the individual animal. In cities the choice of animals which can become the object of phobia is not great. They are horses, dogs, cats, more seldom birds, and strikingly often very small animals like bugs and butterflies. Sometimes animals which are known to the child only from picture books and fairy stories become objects of the senseless and inordinate anxiety which is manifested with these phobias; it is seldom possible to learn the manner in which such an unusual choice of anxiety has been brought about. I am indebted to Dr. Karl Abraham for the report of a case in which the child itself explained its fear of wasps by saying that the colour and the stripes of the body of the wasp had made it think of the tiger of which, from all that it had heard, it might well be afraid.

The animal phobias have not yet been made the object of careful analytical investigation, although they very much merit it. The difficulties of analysing children of so tender an age have probably been the motive of such neglect. It cannot therefore be asserted that the general meaning of these illnesses is known, and I myself do not think that it would turn out to be the same in all cases. But a number of such phobias directed against larger animals have proved accessible to analysis and have thus betrayed their secret to the investigator. In every case it was the same: the fear at bottom was of the father, if the children examined were boys, and was merely displaced upon the animal.

Every one of any experience in psychoanalysis has undoubtedly seen such cases and has received the same impression from them. But I can refer to only a few detailed reports on the subject. This is an accident of the literature of such cases, from which the conclusion should not be drawn that our general assertion is based on merely scattered observation. For instance I mention an author, M. Wulff of Odessa, who has very intelligently occupied himself with the neuroses of childhood. He tells, in relating the history of an illness, that a nine-year-old boy suffered from a dog phobia at the age of four. "When he saw a dog running by on the street he wept and cried: 'Dear dog, don't touch me, I will be good.'" By "being good" he meant "not to play violin any more" (to practice onanism).[1]

The same author later sums up as follows: "His dog phobia is really his fear of the father displaced upon the dog, for his peculiar expression:

[1] M. Wulff, *Contributions to Infantile Sexuality, Zentralbl. f. Psychoanalyze,* 1912, II, No. I, p. 15.

'Dog, I will be good'—that is to say, I will not masturbate—really refers to the father who has forbidden masturbation." He then adds something in a note which fully agrees with my experience and at the same time bears witness to the abundance of such experiences: "Such phobias (of horses, dogs, cats, chickens and other domestic animals) are, I think, at least as prevalent as *pavor nocturnus* in childhood, and usually reveal themselves in the analysis as a displacement of fear from one of the parents to animals. I am not prepared to assert that the wide-spread mouse and rat phobia has the same mechanism."

I reported the "Analysis of the Phobia of a Five-year-old Boy"[1] which the father of the little patient had put at my disposal. It was a fear of horses as a result of which the boy refused to go on the street. He expressed his apprehension that the horse would come into the room and bite him. It proves that this was meant to be the punishment for his wish that the horse should fall over (die). After assurances had relieved the boy of his fear of his father, it proved that he was fighting against wishes whose content was the absence (departure or death) of the father. He indicated only too plainly that he felt the father to be his rival for the favour of the mother, upon whom his budding sexual wishes were by dark premonitions directed. He therefore had the typical attitude of the male child to its parents which we call the "Œdipus complex" in which we recognize the central complex of the neuroses in general. Through the analysis of "little John" we have learnt a fact which is very valuable in relation to totemism, namely, that under such conditions the child displaces a part of its feelings from the father upon some animal.

Analysis showed the paths of association, both significant and accidental in content, along which such a displacement took place. It also allowed one to guess the motives for the displacement. The hate which resulted from the rivalry for the mother could not permeate the boy's psychic life without being inhibited; he had to contend with the tenderness and admiration which he had felt for his father from the beginning, so that the child assumed a double or ambivalent emotional attitude towards the father and relieved himself of this ambivalent conflict by displacing his hostile and anxious feelings upon a substitute for the father. The displacement could not, however, relieve the conflict by bringing about a smooth division between the tender and the hostile feelings. On the contrary, the conflict was continued in reference to the object to which displacement has been made and to which also the ambivalence spreads. There is no doubt that little John had not only fear, but respect and interest for horses. As soon as his fear was moderated he identified himself with the feared animal; he jumped around like a horse, and now

[1] Gesammelte Schriften, Vol. VIII, English translation in Collected Papers, Vol. III.

it was he who bit the father.[1] In another stage of solution of the phobia he did not scruple to identify his parents with other large animals.[2]

We may venture the impression that certain traits of totemism return as a negative expression in these animal phobias of children. But we are indebted to S. Ferenczi for a beautiful individual observation of what must be called a case of positive totemism in the child.[3] It is true that with the little Arpád, whom Ferenczi reports, the totemic interests do not awaken in direct connection with the Œdipus complex, but on the basis of a narcistic premise, namely, the fear of castration. But whoever looks attentively through the history of little John will also find there abundant proof that the father was admired as the possessor of large genitals and was feared as threatening the child's own genitals. In the Œdipus as well as in the castration complex the father plays the same rôle of feared opponent to the infantile sexual interests. Castration and its substitute through blinding is the punishment he threatens.[4]

When little Arpád was two and a half years old he once tried, while at a summer resort, to urinate into the chicken coop, and on this occasion a chicken bit his penis or snapped at it. When he returned to the same place a year later he became a chicken himself, was interested only in the chicken coop and in everything that occurred there, and gave up human speech for cackling and crowing. During the period of observation, at the age of five, he spoke again, but his speech was exclusively about chickens and other fowl. He played with no other toy and sang only songs in which there was something about poultry. His behaviour towards his totem animal was subtly ambivalent, expressing itself in immoderate hating and loving. He loved best to play killing chickens. "The slaughtering of poultry was quite a festival for him. He could dance around the animals' bodies for hours at a time in a state of intense excitement." [5] But then he kissed and stroked the slaughtered animal, and cleaned and caressed the chicken effigies which he himself had ill-used.

Arpád himself saw to it that the meaning of his curious activity could not remain hidden. At times he translated his wishes from the totemic method of expression back into that of everyday life. "Now I am small, now I am a chicken. When I get bigger I shall be a fowl. When I am bigger still, I shall be a cock." On another occasion he suddenly expressed the wish to eat a "potted mother" (by analogy, potted fowl). He was

---

[1] *l.c.,* p. 41.

[2] "The Phantasy of the Giraffe," *l.c.,* p. 30.

[3] S. Ferenczi, *Contributions to Psychoanalysis,* p. 204, translated by Ernest Jones (Badger, Boston, 1916).

[4] Compare the communications of Reitler, Ferenczi, Rank, and Eder about the substitution of blindness in the Œdipus myth for castration. *Intern. Zeitschrift f. ärtzl. Psychoanalyze,* 1913, I, No. 2.

[5] Ferenczi, *l.c.,* p. 209.

very free with open threats of castration against others, just as he himself had received them on account of onanistic preoccupation with his penis.

According to Ferenczi there was no doubt as to the source of his interest in the activities of the chicken yard: "The continual sexual activity between cock and hen, the laying of eggs and the creeping out of the young brood" [1] satisfied his sexual curiosity which really was directed towards human family life. His object wishes have been formed on the model of chicken life when we find him saying to a woman neighbour: "I am going to marry you and your sister and my three cousins and the cook; no, instead of the cook I'll marry my mother."

We shall be able to complete our consideration of these observations later; at present we will only point out two traits that show a valuable correspondence with totemism: the complete identification with the totem animal,[2] and the ambivalent affective attitude towards it. In view of these observations we consider ourselves justified in substituting the father for the totem animal in the male's formula of totemism. We then notice that in doing so we have taken no new or especially daring step. For primitive men say it themselves and, as far as the totemic system is still in effect today, the totem is called ancestor and primal father. We have only taken literally an expression of these races which ethnologists did not know what to do with and were therefore inclined to put it into the background. Psychoanalysis warns us, on the contrary, to emphasize this very point and to connect it with the attempt to explain totemism.[3]

The first result of our substitution is very remarkable. If the totem animal is the father, then the two main commandments of totemism, the two taboo rules which constitute its nucleus—not to kill the totem animal and not to use a woman belonging to the same totem for sexual purposes—agree in content with the two crimes of Œdipus, who slew his father and took his mother to wife, and also with the child's two primal wishes whose insufficient repression or whose re-awakening forms the nucleus of perhaps all neuroses. If this similarity is more than a deceptive play of accident it would perforce make it possible for us to shed light upon the origin of totemism in prehistoric times. In other words, we should succeed in making it probable that the totemic system resulted from the conditions underlying the Œdipus complex, just as the animal phobia of "little John" and the poultry perversion of "little Arpád" resulted from it. In order to trace this possibility we shall in what follows study a peculiarity

[1] Ferenczi, l.c., p. 212.
[2] Frazer finds that the essence of totemism is in this identification: "Totemism is an identification of a man with his totem." *Totemism and Exogamy*, IV, p. 5.
[3] I am indebted to Otto Rank for the report of a case of dog phobia in an intelligent young man whose explanation of how he acquired his ailment sounds remarkably like the totem theory of the Aruntas mentioned above. He had heard from his father that his mother at one time during her pregnancy had been frightened by a dog.

of the totemic system or, as we may say, of the totemic religion, which until now could hardly be brought into the discussion.

4

W. Robertson Smith, who died in 1894, was a physicist, philologist, Bible critic, and archæologist, a many-sided as well as keen and free-thinking man, expressed the assumption in his work, *The Religion of the Semites,*[1] published in 1889, that a peculiar ceremony, the so-called *totem feast,* had, from the very beginning, formed an integral part of the totemic system. For the support of this supposition he had at his disposal at that time only a single description of such an act from the year 500 A.D.; he knew, however, how to give a high degree of probability to his assumption through his analysis of the nature of sacrifice among the old Semites. As sacrifice assumes a godlike person we are dealing here with an inference from a higher phase of religious rite to its lowest phase in totemism.

I shall now cite from Robertson Smith's excellent book [2] those statements about the origin and meaning of the sacrificial right which are of great interest to us; I shall omit the only too numerous tempting details as well as the parts dealing with all later developments. In such an excerpt it is quite impossible to give the reader any sense of the lucidity or of the argumentative force of the original.

Robertson Smith shows that sacrifice at the altar was the essential part of the rite of old religions. It plays the same rôle in all religions, so that its origin must be traced back to very general causes whose effects were everywhere the same.

But the sacrifice—the holy action κατζογέη (sacrificium ἱερουργία)—originally meant something different from what later times understood by it: the offering to the deity in order to reconcile him or to incline him to be favourable. The profane use of the word was afterwards derived from the secondary sense of self-denial. As is demonstrated, the first sacrifice was nothing else but "an act of social fellowship between the deity and his worshippers."

Things to eat and drink were brought as sacrifice; man offered to his god the same things as those on which he himself lived, flesh, cereals, fruits, wine and oil. Only in regard to sacrificial flesh did there exist restrictions and exceptions. The god partakes of the animal sacrifices with his worshippers while the vegetable sacrifices are left to him alone. There is no doubt that animal sacrifices are older and at one time were the only forms of sacrifice. The vegetable sacrifices resulted from the offering of the first-fruits and correspond to a tribute to the lord of the soil and the land. But animal sacrifice is older than agriculture.

[1] *The Religion of the Semites,* Second Edition, London, 1907.
[2] *Ibid.*

Linguistic survivals make it certain that the part of the sacrifice destined for the god was looked upon as his real food. This conception became offensive with the progressive dematerialization of the diety, and was avoided by offering the deity only the liquid part of the meal. Later the use of fire, which made the sacrificial flesh ascend in smoke from the altar, made it possible to prepare human food in such a way that it was more suitable for the deity. The drink sacrifice was originally the blood of the sacrificed animals; wine was used later as a substitute for the blood. Primitive man looked upon wine as the "blood of the grape," as our poets still call it.

The oldest form of sacrifice, older than the use of fire and the knowledge of agriculture, was therefore the sacrifice of animals, whose flesh and blood the god and his worshippers ate together. It was essential that both participants should receive their shares of the meal.

Such a sacrifice was a public ceremony, the celebration of a whole clan. As a matter of fact all religion was a public affair; religious duty was a part of the social obligation. Sacrifice and festival go together among all races; each sacrifice entails a holiday and no holiday can be celebrated without a sacrifice. The sacrificial festival was an occasion for joyously transcending one's own interests and emphasizing social community and community with god.

The ethical power of the public sacrificial feast was based upon primal conceptions of the meaning of eating and drinking in common. To eat and drink with some one was at the same time a symbol and a confirmation of social community and of the assumption of mutual obligations; the sacrificial eating gave direct expression to the fact that the god and his worshippers are communicants, thus confirming all their other relations. Customs that today still are in force among the Arabs of the desert prove that the binding force resulting from the common meal is not a religious factor but that the subsequent mutual obligations are due to the act of eating itself. Whoever has shared the smallest bite with such a Bedouin, or has taken a swallow of his milk, need not fear him any longer as an enemy, but may be sure of his protection and help. Not indeed, forever, strictly speaking this lasts only while it may be assumed that the food partaken remains in the body. So realistically is the bond of union conceived; it requires repetition to strengthen it and make it endure.

But why is this binding power ascribed to eating and drinking in common? In the most primitive societies there is only one unconditional and never failing bond, that of kinship. The members of a community stand by each other jointly and severally, a kin is a group of persons whose life is so bound into a physical unity that they can be considered as parts of a common life. In case of the murder of one of this kin they therefore do not say: the blood of so and so has been spilt, but our blood has been spilt. The Hebraic phrase by which the tribal relation is acknowledged is: "Thou art my bone and my flesh." Kinship therefore signifies having part in a general substance. It is natural then that it is based not only upon the fact that we are a part of the substance of our mother who has borne us, and whose milk nourished us, but also that the food eaten later through which the body is renewed, can acquire and strengthen kinship. If one shared a meal with one's god the conviction was thus expressed that one was of the same substance as he; no meal was therefore partaken with any one recognized as a stranger.

The sacrificial repast was therefore originally a feast of the kin, following the rule that only those of kin could eat together. In our society the meal unites the members of the family; but the sacrificial repast has nothing to do with the family. Kinship is older than family life; the oldest families known to us regularly comprised persons who belonged to various bonds of kinship. The men married women of strange clans and the children inherited the clan of the mother; there was no kinship between the man and the rest of the members of the family. In such a family there was no common meal. Even today savages eat apart and alone, and the religious prohibitions of totemism as to eating often make it impossible for them to eat with their wives and children.

Let us now turn to the sacrificial animal. There was, as we have heard, no meeting of the kin without animal sacrifice, but, and this is significant, no animal was slaughtered except for such a solemn occasion. Without any hesitation the people ate fruits, game and the milk of domestic animals, but religious scruples made it impossible for the individual to kill a domestic animal for his own use. There is not the least doubt, says Robertson Smith, that every sacrifice was originally a clan sacrifice, and that the *killing of a sacrificial animal* originally belonged to those acts which were *forbidden to the individual and were only justified if the whole kin assumed the responsibility*. Primitive men had only one class of actions which were thus characterized, namely, actions which touched the holiness of the kin's common blood. A life which no individual might take and which could be sacrificed only through the consent and participation of all the members of the clan was on the same plane as the life of a member of the kin. The rule that every guest of the sacrificial repast must partake of the flesh of the sacrificial animal, had the same meaning as the rule that the execution of a guilty member of the kin must be performed by the whole kin. In other words: the sacrificial animal was treated like one of kin; *the sacrificing community, its god, and the sacrificial animal were of the same blood,* and the members of a clan.

On the basic of much evidence Robertson Smith identifies the sacrificial animal with the old totem animal. In a later age there were two kinds of sacrifices, those of domestic animals which usually were also eaten, and the unusual sacrifice of animals which were forbidden as being unclean. Further investigation then shows that these unclean animals were holy and that they were sacrificed to the gods to whom they were holy, that these animals were originally identified with the gods themselves and that at the sacrifice the worshippers in some way emphasized their blood relationship to the god and to the animal. But this difference between usual and "mystic" sacrifices does not hold good for still earlier times. Originally all animals were holy, their meat was forbidden and might be eaten only on solemn occasions, with the participation of the whole kin. The slaughter of the animal amounted to the spilling of the kin's blood and had to be done with the same precautions and assurances against reproach.

The taming of domestic animals and the rise of cattle-breeding seems everywhere to have put an end to the pure and rigorous totemism of earliest times.[1] But such holiness as still clung to domestic animals in what was now a "pastoral" religion, is sufficiently distinct for us to recognize its totemic character. Even in late classical times the rite in several localities prescribed flight for the sacrificer after the sacrifice, as if to escape revenge. In Greece the idea must once have been general that the killing of an ox was really a crime. At the Athenian festival of the Bouphonia a formal trial, to which all the participants were summoned, was instituted after the sacrifice. Finally it was agreed to put the blame for the murder upon the knife, which was then cast into the sea.

In spite of the dread which protects the life of the animal as being of kin, it became necessary to kill it from time to time in solemn conclave, and to divide its flesh and blood among the members of the clan. The motive which commands this act reveals the deepest meaning of the essence of sacrifice. We have heard that in later times every eating in common, the participation in the same substance which entered into their bodies, established a holy bond between the communicants; in oldest time this meaning seemed to be attached only to participation in the substance of a holy sacrifice. *The holy mystery of the sacrificial death was justified in that only in this way could the holy bond be established which united the participants with each other and with their god.*[2]

This bond was nothing else but the life of the sacrificial animal which lived on its flesh and blood and was shared by all the participants by means of the sacrificial feast. Such an idea was the basis of all the *blood bonds* through which men in still later times became pledged to each other. The thoroughly realistic conception of consanguinity as an identity of

---

[1] "The inference is that the domestication to which totemism leads (when there are any animals capable of domestication) is fatal to totemism." Jevons, *Introduction to the History of Religion*, 1911, fifth edition, p. 120.

[2] *l.c.*, p. 313.

substance makes comprehensible the necessity of renewing it from time to time through the physical process of the sacrificial repast.

We will now stop quoting from Robertson Smith's train of thought in order to give a condensed summary of what is essential in it. When the idea of private property came into existence sacrifice was conceived as a gift to the deity, as a transfer from the property of man to that of the god. But this interpretation left all the peculiarities of the sacrificial ritual unexplained. In oldest times the sacrificial animal itself had been holy and its life inviolate; it could be taken only in the presence of the god, with the whole tribe taking part and sharing the guilt in order to furnish the holy substance through the eating of which the members of the clan assured themselves of their material identity with one another and with the deity. The sacrifice was a sacrament, and the sacrificial animal itself was one of the kin. In reality it was the old totem animal, the primitive god himself through the slaying and eating of whom the members of the clan revived and assured their similarity with the god.

From this analysis of the nature of sacrifice Robertson Smith drew the conclusion that the periodic killing and eating of the totem before the period when the *anthropomorphic deities were venerated* was an important part of totem religion. The ceremonial of such a totem feast was preserved for us, he thought, in the description of a sacrifice in later times. Saint Nilus tells of a sacrificial custom of the Bedouins in the desert of Sinai towards the end of the fourth century A.D. The victim, a camel, was bound and laid upon a rough altar of stones; the leader of the tribe made the participants walk three times around the altar to the accompaniment of song, inflicted the first wound upon the animal and greedily drank the spurting blood; then the whole community threw itself upon the sacrifice, cut off pieces of the palpitating flesh with their swords and ate them raw in such haste that in a short interval between the rise of the morning star, for whom this sacrifice was meant, and its fading before the rays of the sun, the whole sacrificial animal, flesh, skin, bones, and entrails, were devoured. According to every testimony this barbarous rite, which bespeaks great antiquity, was not a rare custom but the general original form of the totem sacrifice, which in later times underwent the most varied modifications.

Many authors have refused to grant any weight to this conception of the totem feast because it could not be strengthened by direct observation at the stage of totemism. Robertson Smith himself has referred to examples in which the sacramental meaning of sacrifices seems certain, such as the human sacrifices of the Aztecs and others which recall the conditions of the totem feast, the bear sacrifices of the bear tribe of the *Ouataouaks* in America, and the bear festival of the Ainus in Japan. Frazer has given a full account of these and similar cases in the two divisions of his great work that have last appeared.[1] An Indian tribe in California which reveres the buzzard, a large bird of prey, kills it once a year with solemn ceremony, whereupon the bird is mourned and its skin and feathers preserved. The Zuni Indians in New Mexico do the same thing with their holy turtle.

In the *Intichiuma* ceremonies of Central Australian tribes a trait has been observed which fits in excellently with the assumptions of Robertson Smith. Every tribe that practises magic for the increase of its totem, which it cannot eat itself, is bound to eat a part of its totem at the ceremony before it can be touched by the other tribes. According to Frazer the best example of the sacramental consumption of the otherwise forbidden totem is to be found among the Bini in West Africa, in connexion with the burial ceremony of this tribe.[2]

But we shall follow Robertson Smith in the assumption that the sacramental killing and the common consumption of the otherwise forbidden totem animal was an important trait of the totem religion.[3]

5

LET us now envisage the scene of such a totem meal and let us embellish it further with a few probable features which could not be adequately considered before. Thus we have the clan, which on a solemn occasion kills its totem in a cruel manner and eats it raw, blood, flesh, and bones. At the same time the members of the clan disguised in imitation of the totem, mimic it in sound and movement as if they wanted to emphasize their common identity. There is also the conscious realization that an action is being carried out which is forbidden to each individual and which can only be justified through the participation of all, so that no one is allowed to exclude himself from the killing and the feast. After the act is accomplished the murdered animal is bewailed and lamented. The death lamentation is compulsive, being enforced by the fear of a threatening retribution, and its main purpose is, as Robertson Smith remarks on an analogous occasion, to exculpate oneself from responsibility for the slaying.[4]

But after this mourning there follows loud festival gaiety accompanied by the unchaining of every impulse and the permission of every gratification. Here we find an easy insight into the nature of the *holiday*.

A holiday is a permitted, or rather a prescribed excess, a solemn violation of a prohibition. People do not commit the excesses, which at all times

---

[1] *The Golden Bough,* Part V; *Spirits of the Corn and of the Wild,* 1912, in the chapters: "Eating the God and Killing the Divine Animal."

[2] Frazer, *Totem and Exogamy,* Vol. II, p. 590.

[3] I am not ignorant of the objections to this theory of sacrifice as expressed by Marillier, Hubert, Mauss and others, but they have not essentially impaired the theories of Robertson Smith.

[4] *Religion of the Semites,* Second Edition, 1907, p. 412.

have characterized holidays, as a result of an order to be in a holiday mood, but because in the very nature of a holiday there is excess; the holiday mood is brought about by the release of what is otherwise forbidden.

But what has mourning over the death of the totem animal to do with the introduction of this holiday spirit? If men are happy over the slaying of the totem, which is otherwise forbidden to them, why do they also mourn it?

We have heard that members of a clan become holy through the consumption of the totem and thereby also strengthen their identification with it and with each other. The fact that they have absorbed the holy life with which the substance of the totem is charged may explain the holiday mood and everything that results from it.

Psychoanalysis has revealed to us that the totem animal is really a substitute for the father, and this really explains the contradiction that it is usually forbidden to kill the totem animal, that the killing of it results in a holiday and that the animal is killed and yet mourned. The ambivalent emotional attitude which today still marks the father complex in our children and so often continues into adult life also extended to the father substitute of the totem animal.

But if we associate the translation of the totem as given by psychoanalysis, with the totem feast and the Darwinian hypothesis about the primal state of human society, a deeper understanding becomes possible and a hypothesis is offered which may seem fantastic but which has the advantage of establishing an unexpected unity among a series of hitherto separated phenomena.

The Darwinian conception of the primal horde does not, of course, allow for the beginning of totemism. There is only a violent, jealous father who keeps all the females for himself and drives away the growing sons. This primal state of society has nowhere been observed. The most primitive organization we know, which today is still in force with certain tribes, is *associations of men* consisting of members with equal rights, subject to the restrictions of the totemic system, and founded on matriarchy, or descent through the mother.[1] Can the one have resulted from the other, and how was this possible?

By basing our argument upon the celebration of the totem we are in a position to give an answer: "One day [2] the expelled brothers joined forces, slew and ate the father, and thus put an end to the father horde. Together they dared and accomplished what would have remained impossible for them singly. Perhaps some advance in culture, like the use of a new weapon, had given them the feeling of superiority. Of course

[1] For a recent contribution compare *The Whole House of the Chilkat*, by G. T. Emmons (*American Museum Journal*, Vol. XVI, No. 7). [Translator's note.]

[2] The reader will avoid the erroneous impression which this exposition may call forth by taking into consideration the concluding sentence of the subsequent chapter.

these cannibalistic savages ate their victim. This violent primal father had surely been the envied and feared model for each of the brothers. Now they accomplished their identification with him by devouring him and each acquired a part of his strength. The totem feast, which is perhaps mankind's first celebration, would be the repetition and commemoration of this memorable, criminal act with which so many things began, social organization, moral restrictions and religion.[1]

In order to find these results acceptable, quite aside from our supposition, we need only assume that the group of brothers banded together were dominated by the same contradictory feelings towards the father which we can demonstrate as the content of ambivalence of the father complex in all our children and in neurotics. They hated the father who stood so powerfully in the way of their sexual demands and their desire for power, but they also loved and admired him. After they had satisfied their hate by his removal and had carried out their wish for identification with him, the suppressed tender impulses had to assert themselves.[2] This took place in the form of remorse, a sense of guilt

[1] The seemingly monstrous assumption that the tyrannical father was overcome and slain by a combination of the expelled sons has also been accepted by Atkinson as a direct result of the conditions of the Darwinian primal horde. "A youthful band of brothers living together in forced celibacy, or at most in polyandrous relation with some single female captive. A horde as yet weak in their impubescence they are, but they would, when strength was gained with time, inevitably wrench by combined attacks, renewed again and again, both wife and life from the paternal tyrant" (*Primal Law*, pp. 220–1). Atkinson, who spent his life in New Caledonia and had unusual opportunities to study the natives, also refers to the fact that the conditions of the primal horde which Darwin assumes can easily be observed among herds of wild cattle and horses and regularly lead to the killing of the father animal. He then assumes further that a disintegration of the horde took place after the removal of the father through embittered fighting among the victorious sons, which thus precluded the origin of a new organization of society; "An ever recurring violent succession to the solitary paternal tyrant by sons, whose parricidal hands were so soon again clenched in fratricidal strife" (p. 228). Atkinson, who did not have the suggestions of psychoanalysis at his command and did not know the studies of Robertson Smith, finds a less violent transition from the primal horde to the next social stage in which many men live together in peaceful accord. He attributes it to maternal love that at first only the youngest sons and later others too remain in the horde, who in return for this toleration acknowledge the sexual prerogative of the father by the restraint which they practise towards the mother and towards their sisters.

So much for the very remarkable theory of Atkinson, its essential correspondence with the theory here expounded, and its point of departure which makes it necessary to relinquish so much else.

I must ascribe the indefiniteness, the disregard of time interval, and the crowding of the material in the above exposition to a restraint which the nature of the subject demands. It would be just as meaningless to strive for exactness in this material as it would be unfair to demand certainty here.

[2] This new emotional attitude must also have been responsible for the fact that the deed could not bring full satisfaction to any of the perpetrators. In a certain sense it had been in vain. For none of the sons could carry out his original wish of taking the place of the father. But failure is, as we know, much more favourable to moral reaction than success.

was formed which coincided here with the remorse generally felt. The dead now became stronger than the living had been, even as we observe it today in the destinies of men. What the fathers' presence had formerly prevented they themselves now prohibited in the psychic situation of "subsequent obedience" which we know so well from psychoanalysis. They undid their deed by declaring that the killing of the father substitute, the totem, was not allowed, and renounced the fruits of their deed by denying themselves the liberated women. Thus they created two fundamental taboos of totemism out of the *sense of guilt of the son,* and for this very reason these had to correspond with the two repressed wishes of the Œdipus complex. Whoever disobeyed became guilty of the two only crimes which troubled primitive society.[1]

The two taboos of totemism with which the morality of man begins are psychologically not of equal value. One of them, the sparing of the totem animal, rests entirely upon emotional motives; the father had been removed and nothing in reality could make up for this. But the other, the incest prohibition, had, besides, a strong practical foundation. Sexual need does not unite men; it separates them. Though the brothers had joined forces in order to overcome the father, each was the other's rival among the women. Each one wanted to have them all to himself like the father, and in the fight of each against the other the new organization would have perished. For there was no longer any one stronger than all the rest who could have successfully assumed the rôle of the father. Thus there was nothing left for the brothers, if they wanted to live together, but to erect the incest prohibition—perhaps after many difficult experiences—through which they all equally renounced the women whom they desired, and on account of whom they had removed the father in the first place. Thus they saved the organization which had made them strong and which could be based upon the homo-sexual feelings and activities which probably manifested themselves among them during the time of their banishment. Perhaps this situation also formed the germ of the institution of the mother right discovered by Bachofen, which was then abrogated by the patriarchal family arrangement.

On the other hand the claim of totemism to be considered the first attempt at a religion is connected with the other taboo which protects the life of the totem animal. The feelings of the sons found a natural and appropriate substitute for the father in the animal, but their compulsory treatment of it expressed more than the need of showing remorse. The surrogate for the father was perhaps used in the attempt to assuage the burning sense of guilt, and to bring about a kind of reconciliation

---

[1] "Murder and incest, or offences of like kind against the sacred law of blood are in primitive society the only crimes of which the community as such takes cognizance . . ." *Religion of the Semites,* p. 419.

with the father. The totemic system was a kind of agreement with the father in which the latter granted everything that the child's phantasy could expect from him, protection, care, and forbearance, in return for which the pledge was given to honour his life, that is to say, not to repeat the act against the totem through which the real father had perished. Totemism also contained an attempt at justification. "If the father had treated us like the totem we should never have been tempted to kill him." Thus totemism helped to gloss over the real state of affairs and to make one forget the event to which it owed its origin.

In this connection some features were formed which henceforth determined the character of every religion. The totem religion had issued from the sense of guilt of the sons as an attempt to palliate this feeling and to conciliate the injured father through subsequent obedience. All later religions prove to be attempts to solve the same problem, varying only in accordance with the stage of culture in which they are attempted and according to the paths which they take; they are all, however, reactions aiming at the same great event with which culture began and which ever since has not let mankind come to rest.

There is still another characteristic faithfully preserved in religion which already appeared in totemism at this time. The ambivalent strain was probably too great to be adjusted by any arrangement, or else the psychological conditions are entirely unfavourable to any kind of settlement of these contradictory feelings. It is certainly noticeable that the ambivalence attached to the father complex also continues in totemism and in religions in general. The religion of totemism included not only manifestations of remorse and attempts at reconciliation, but also serves to commemorate the triumph over the father. The gratification obtained thereby creates the commemorative celebration of the totem feast at which the restrictions of subsequent obedience are suspended, and makes it a duty to repeat the crime of parricide through the sacrifice of the totem animal as often as the benefits of this deed, namely, the appropriation of the father's properties, threaten to disappear as a result of the changed influences of life. We shall not be surprised to find that a part of the son's defiance also reappears, often in the most remarkable disguises and inversions, in the formation of later religions.

If thus far we have followed, in religion and moral precepts—but little differentiated in totemism—the consequences of the tender impulses towards the father as they are changed into remorse, we must not overlook the fact that for the most part the tendencies which have impelled to parricide have retained the victory. The social and fraternal feelings on which this great change is based, henceforth for long periods exercises the greatest influence upon the development of society. They find expression in the santification of the common blood and in the emphasis upon the solidarity of life within the clan. In thus ensuring each other's lives the brothers express the fact that no one of them is to be treated by the other as they all treated the father. They preclude a repetition of the fate of the father. The socially established prohibition against fratricide is now added to the prohibition against killing the totem, which is based on religious grounds. It will still be a long time before the commandment discards the restrictions to members of the tribe and assumes the simple phraseology: Thou shalt not kill. At first the *brother clan* has taken the place of the *father horde* and was guaranteed by the blood bond. Society is now based on complicity in the common crime, religion on the sense of guilt and the consequent remorse, while morality is based partly on the necessities of society and partly on the expiation which this sense of guilt demands.

Thus psychoanalysis, contrary to the newer conceptions of the totemic system and more in accord with older conceptions, bids us argue for an intimate connection between totemism and exogamy as well as for their simultaneous origin.

6

I am under the influence of many strong motives which restrain me from the attempt to discuss the further development of religions from their beginning in totemism up to their present state. I shall follow out only two threads as I see them appearing in the weft with especial distinctness: the motive of the totem sacrifice and the relation of the son to the father.[1]

Robertson Smith has shown us that the old totem feast returns in the original form of sacrifice. The meaning of the rite is the same: sanctification through participation in the common meal. The sense of guilt, which can only be allayed through the solidarity of all the participants, has also been retained. In addition to this there is the tribal deity in whose supposed presence the sacrifice takes place, who takes part in the meal like a member of the tribe, and with whom identification is effected by the act of eating the sacrifice. How does the god come into this situation which originally was foreign to him?

The answer might be that the idea of god had meanwhile appeared— no one knows whence—and had dominated the whole religious life, and that the totem feast, like everything else that wished to survive, had been forced to fit itself into the new system. However, psychoanalytic investigation of the individual teaches with especial emphasis that god is in every case modelled after the father and that our personal relation to god is dependent upon our relation to our physical father, fluctuating and changing with him, and that god at bottom is nothing but an exalted

---

[1] Compare *Transformations and Symbols of the Libido*, by C. G. Jung, in which some dissenting points of view are represented.

father. Here also, as in the case of totemism, psychoanalysis advises us to believe the faithful, who call god father just as they called the totem their ancestor. If psychoanalysis deserves any consideration at all, then the share of the father in the idea of a god must be very important, quite aside from all the other origins and meanings of god upon which psychoanalysis can throw no light. But then the father would be represented twice in primitive sacrifice, first as god, and secondly as the totem-animal-sacrifice, and we must ask, with all due regard for the limited number of solutions which psychoanalysis offers, whether this is possible and what the meaning of it may be.

We know that there are a number of relations of the god to the holy animal (the totem and the sacrificial animal): 1. Usually one animal is sacred to every god, sometimes even several animals. 2. In certain, especially holy, sacrifices, the so-called "mystical" sacrifices, the very animal which had been sanctified through the god was sacrificed to him.[1] 3. The god was often revered in the form of an animal, or from another point of view, animals enjoyed a godlike reverence long after the period of totemism. 4. In myths the god is frequently transformed into an animal, often into the animal that is sacred to him. From this the assumption was obvious that the god himself was the animal, and that he had evolved from the totem animal at a later stage of religious feeling. But the reflection that the totem itself is nothing but a substitute for the father relieves us of all further discussion. Thus the totem may have been the first form of the father substitute and the god a later one in which the father regained his human form. Such a new creation from the root of all religious evolution, namely, the longing for the father, might become possible if in the course of time an essential change had taken place in the relation to the father and perhaps also to the animal.

Such changes are easily divined even if we disregard the beginning of a psychic estrangement from the animal as well as the distintegration of totemism through animal domestication. The situation created by the removal of the father contained an element which in the course of time must have brought about an extraordinary increase of longing for the father. For the brothers who had joined forces to kill the father had each been animated by the wish to become like the father and had given expression to this wish by incorporating parts of the substitute for him in the totem feast. In consequence of the pressure which the bonds of the brother clan exercised upon each member, this wish had to remain unfulfilled. No one could or was allowed to attain the father's perfection of power, which was the thing they had all sought. Thus the bitter feeling against the father which had incited to the deed could subside in the course of time, while the longing for him grew, and an ideal could arise

[1] Robertson Smith, *Religion of the Semites*, Second Edition, 1907.

having as a content the fullness of power and the freedom from restriction of the conquered primal father, as well as the willingness to subject themselves to him. The original democratic equality of each member of the tribe could no longer be retained on account of the interference of cultural changes; in consequence of which there arose a tendency to revive the old father ideal in the creation of gods through the veneration of those individuals who had distinguished themselves above the rest. That a man should become a god and that a god should die, which today seems to us an outrageous presumption, was still by no means offensive to the conceptions of classical antiquity.[1] But the deification of the murdered father from whom the tribe now derived its origin, was a much more serious attempt at expiation than the former covenant with the totem.

In this evolution I am at a loss to indicate the place of the great maternal deities who perhaps everywhere preceded the paternal deities. But it seems certain that the change in the relation to the father was not restricted to religion but logically extended to the other side of human life influenced by the removal of the father, namely, the social organization. With the institution of paternal deities the fatherless society gradually changed into a patriarchal one. The family was a reconstruction of the former primal horde and also restored a great part of their former rights to the fathers. Now there were patriarchs again but the social achievements of the brother clan had not been given up and the actual difference between the new family patriarchs and the unrestricted primal father was great enough to ensure the continuation of the religious need, the preservation of the unsatisfied longing for the father.

The father therefore really appears twice in the scene of sacrifice before the tribal god, once as the god and again as the totem-sacrificial-animal. But in attempting to understand this situation we must beware of interpretations which superficially seek to translate it as an allegory, and which forget the historical stages in the process. The twofold presence of the father corresponds to the two successive meanings of the scene. The ambivalent attitude towards the father as well as the victory of the son's tender emotional feelings over his hostile ones, have here found plastic expression. The scene of vanquishing the father, his greatest degradation, furnishes here the material to represent his highest triumph. The meaning which sacrifice has quite generally acquired is found in the fact that in the very same action which continues the memory of this misdeed it offers satisfaction to the father for the ignominy put upon him.

[1] "To us moderns, for whom the breach which divides the human and divine has deepened into an impassable gulf, such mimicry may appear impious, but it was otherwise with the ancients. To their thinking gods and men were akin, for many families traced their descent from a divinity, and the deification of a man probably seemed as little extraordinary to them as the canonization of a saint seems to a modern Catholic." Frazer, *The Golden Bough,* I; *The Magic Art and the Evolution of Kings,* II, p. 177.

In the further development the animal loses its sacredness and the sacrifice its relation to the celebration of the totem; the rite becomes a simple offering to the deity, a self-deprivation in favour of the god. God himself is now so exalted above man that he can be communicated with only through a priest as intermediary. At the same time the social order produces godlike kings who transfer the patriarchal system to the state. It must be said that the revenge of the deposed and reinstated father has been very cruel; it culminated in the dominance of authority. The subjugated sons have used the new relation to disburden themselves still more of their sense of guilt. Sacrifice, as it is now constituted, is entirely beyond their responsibility. God himself has demanded and ordained it. Myths in which the god himself kills the animal that is sacred to him, which he himself really is, belong to this phase. This is the greatest possible denial of the great misdeed with which society and the sense of guilt began. There is an unmistakable second meaning in this sacrificial demonstration. It expresses satisfaction at the fact that the earlier father substitute has been abandoned in favour of the higher conception of god. The superficial allegorical translation of the scene here roughly corresponds with its psychoanalytic interpretation by saying that the god is represented as overcoming the animal part of his nature.[1]

But it would be erroneous to believe that in this period of renewed patriarchal authority the hostile impulses which belong to the father complex had entirely subsided. On the contrary, the first phases in the domination of the two new substitutive formations for the father, those of gods and kings, plainly show the most energetic expression of that ambivalence which is characteristic of religion.

In his great work, *The Golden Bough,* Frazer has expressed the conjecture that the first kings of the Latin tribes were strangers who played the part of a deity and were solemnly sacrificed in this rôle on specified holidays. The yearly sacrifice (self-sacrifice is a variant) of a god seems to have been an important feature of Semitic religions. The ceremony of human sacrifice in various parts of the inhabited world makes it certain that these human beings ended their lives as representatives of the deity. This sacrificial custom can still be traced in later times in the substitution of an inanimate imitation (doll) for the living person. The theanthropic god sacrifice into which unfortunately I cannot enter with the same thoroughness with which the animal sacrifice has been treated

---

[1] It is known that the overcoming of one generation of gods by another in mythology represents the historical process of the substitution of one religious system by another, either as the result of conquest by a strange race or by means of a psychological development. In the latter case the myth approaches the "functional phenomena" in H. Silberer's sense. That the god who kills the animal is a symbol of the libido, as asserted by C. G. Jung (*l.c.*), presupposes a different conception of the libido from that hitherto held, and at any rate seems to me questionable.

throws the clearest light upon the meaning of the older forms of sacrifice. It acknowledges with unsurpassable candour that the object of the sacrificial action has always been the same, being identical with what is now revered as a god, namely with the father. The question as to the relation of animal to human sacrifice can now be easily solved. The original animal sacrifice was already a substitute for a human sacrifice, for the solemn killing of the father, and when the father substitute regained its human form, the animal substitute could also be retransformed into a human sacrifice.

Thus, the memory of that first great act of sacrifice had proved to be indestructible despite all attempts to forget it, and just at the moment when men strove to get as far away as possible from its motives, the undistorted repetition of it had to appear in the form of the god sacrifice. I need not fully indicate here the developments of religious thought which made this return possible in the form of rationalizations. Robertson Smith who is, of course, far removed from the idea of tracing sacrifice back to this great event of man's primal history, says that the ceremony of the festivals in which the old Semites celebrated the death of a deity were interpreted as "a commemoration of a mythical tragedy" and that the attendant lament was not characterized by spontaneous sympathy, but displayed a compulsive character, something that was imposed by the fear of a divine wrath.[1] We are in a position to acknowledge that this interpretation was correct, the feelings of the celebrants being well explained by the basic situation.

We may now accept it as a fact that in the further development of religions these two inciting factors, the son's sense of guilt and his defiance, were never again extinguished. Every attempted solution of the religious problem and every kind of reconciliation of the two opposing psychic forces gradually fall to the ground, probably under the combined influence of cultural changes, historical events, and inner psychic transformations.

The endeavour of the son to put himself in place of the father god, appeared with greater and greater distinctness. With the introduction of agriculture the importance of the son in the patriarchal family increased. He was emboldened to give new expression to his incestuous libido which found symbolic satisfaction in labouring over mother earth. There came into existence figures of gods.like Attis, Adonis, Tammuz, and others, spirits of vegetation as well as youthful divinities who enjoyed the favours of maternal deities and committed incest with the mother in defiance of

[1] *Religion of the Semites,* pp. 412–413. "The mourning is not a spontaneous expression of sympathy with the divine tragedy, but obligatory and enforced by fear of supernatural anger. And a chief object of the mourners is *to disclaim responsibility for the god's death*—a point which has already come before us in connection with theanthropic sacrifices, such as the 'ox-murder at Athens.' "

the father. But the sense of guilt which was not allayed through these creations, was expressed in myths which visited these youthful lovers of the maternal goddesses with short life and punishment through castration or through the wrath of the father god appearing in animal form. Adonis was killed by the boar, the sacred animal of Aphrodite; Attis, the lover of Cybele, died of castration.[1] The lamentation for these gods and the joy at their resurrection have gone over into the ritual of another son which divinity was destined to survive long.

When Christianity began its entry into the ancient world it met with the competition of the religion of Mithras and for a long time it was doubtful which deity was to be the victor.

The bright figure of the youthful Persian god has eluded our understanding. Perhaps we may conclude from the illustrations of Mithras slaying the steers that he represented the son who carried out the sacrifice of the father by himself and thus released the brothers from their oppressing complicity in the deed. There was another way of allaying this sense of guilt and this is the one that Christ took. He sacrificed his own life and thereby redeemed the brothers from primal sin.

The theory of primal sin is of Orphic origin; it was preserved in the mysteries and thence penetrated into the philosophic schools of Greek antiquity.[2] Men were the descendants of Titans, who had killed and dismembered the young Dionysos-Zagreus; the weight of this crime oppressed them. A fragment of Anaximander says that the unity of the world was destroyed by a primordial crime and everything that issued from it must carry on the punishment for this crime.[3] Although the features of banding together, killing, and dismembering as expressed in the deed of the Titans very clearly recall the totem sacrifice described by St. Nilus—as also many other myths of antiquity, for example, the death of Orpheus himself—we are nevertheless disturbed here by the variation according to which a youthful god was murdered.

In the Christian myth man's original sin is undoubtedly an offence against God the Father, and if Christ redeems mankind from the weight of original sin by sacrificing his own life, he forces us to the conclusion

[1] The fear of castration plays an extraordinarily big rôle in disturbing the relations to the father in the case of our youthful neurotics. In Ferenczi's excellent study we have seen how the boy recognized his totem in the animal which snaps at his little penis. When children learn about ritual circumcision they identify it with castration. To my knowledge the parallel in the psychology of races to this attitude of our children has not yet been drawn. The circumcision which was so frequent in primordial times among primitive races belongs to the period of initiation in which its meaning is to be found; it has only secondarily been relegated to an earlier time of life. It is very interesting that among primitive men circumcision is combined with or replaced by the cutting off of the hair and the drawing of teeth, and that our children, who cannot know anything about this, really treat these two operations as equivalents to castration when they display their fear of them.

[2] Reinach, *Cultes, Mythes, et Religions*, II, p. 75.

[3] "Une sorte pe péché proethnique," *l.c.*, p. 76.

that this sin was murder. According to the law of retaliation which is deeply rooted in human feeling, a murder can be atoned only by the sacrifice of another life; the self-sacrifice points to a blood-guilt.[1] And if this sacrifice of one's own life brings about a reconciliation with god, the father, then the crime which must be expiated can only have been the murder of the father.

Thus, in the Christian doctrine mankind most unreservedly acknowledges the guilty deed of primordial times because it now has found the most complete expiation for this deed in the sacrificial death of the son. The reconciliation with the father is the more thorough because simultaneously with this sacrifice there follows the complete renunciation of woman, for whose sake mankind rebelled against the father. But now also the psychological fatality of ambivalence demands its rights. In the same deed which offers the greatest possible expiation to the father, the son also attains the goal of his wishes against the father. He becomes a god himself beside or rather in place of his father. The religion of the son succeeds the religion of the father. As a sign of this substitution the old totem feast is revived again in the form of communion in which the band of brothers now eats the flesh and blood of the son and no longer that of the father, the sons thereby identifying themselves with him and becoming holy themselves. Thus through the ages we see the identity of the totem feast with the animal sacrifice, the theanthropic human sacrifice, and the Christian eucharist, and in all these solemn occasions we recognize the aftereffects of that crime which so oppressed men but of which they must have been so proud. At bottom, however, the Christian communion is a new setting aside of the father, a repetition of the crime that must be expiated. We see how well justified is Frazer's dictum that "the Christian communion has absorbed within itself a sacrament which is doubtless far older than Christianity."[2]

7

A process like the removal of the primal father by the band of brothers must have left ineradicable traces in the history of mankind and must have expressed itself the more frequently in numerous substitutive formations the less it itself was to be remembered.[3] I am avoiding the tempta-

[1] The suicidal impulses of our neurotics regularly prove to be self-punishments for death wishes directed against others.

[2] *Eating the God*, p. 51. . . . Nobody familiar with the literature on this subject will assume that the tracing back of the Christian communion to the totem feast is an idea of the author of this book.

[3] Ariel in *The Tempest:*

> Full fathom five thy father lies:
> Of his bones are coral made;
> Those are pearls that were his eyes;
> Nothing of him that doth fade
> But doth suffer a sea-change
> Into something rich and strange. . . .

tion of pointing out these traces in mythology, where they are not hard to find, and am turning to another field in following a hint of S. Reinach in his suggestive treatment of the death of Orpheus.[1]

There is a situation in the history of Greek art which is strikingly familiar even if profoundly divergent, to the scene of a totem feast discovered by Robertson Smith. It is the situation of the oldest Greek tragedy. A group of persons, all of the same name and dressed in the same way, surround a single figure upon whose words and actions they are dependent, to represent the chorus and the original single impersonator of the hero. Later developments created a second and a third actor in order to represent opponents in playing, and off-shoots of the hero, but the character of the hero as well as his relation to the chorus remains unchanged. The hero of the tragedy had to suffer; this is today still the essential content of a tragedy. He had taken upon himself the so-called "tragic guilt," which is not always easy to explain; it is often not a guilt in the ordinary sense. Almost always it consisted of a rebellion against a divine or human authority and the chorus accompanied the hero with their sympathies, trying to restrain and warn him, and lamented his fate after he had met with what was considered fitting punishment for his daring attempt.

But why did the hero of the tragedy have to suffer, and what was the meaning of his "tragic" guilt? We will cut short the discussion by a prompt answer. He had to suffer because he was the primal father, the hero of that primordial tragedy the repetition of which here serves a certain tendency, and the tragic guilt is the guilt which he had to take upon himself in order to free the chorus of theirs. The scene upon the stage came into being through purposive distortion of the historical scene or, one is tempted to say, it was the result of refined hypocrisy. Actually, in the old situation, it was the members of the chorus themselves who had caused the suffering of the hero; here, on the other hand, they exhaust themselves in sympathy and regret, and the hero himself is to blame for his suffering. The crime foisted upon him, namely, presumption and rebellion against a great authority, is the same as that which in the past oppressed the colleagues of the chorus, namely, the band of brothers. Thus the tragic hero, though still against his will, is made the redeemer of the chorus.

When one bears in mind the suffering of the divine goat Dionysos in the performance of the Greek tragedy and the lament of the retinue of goats who identified themselves with him, one can easily understand how the almost extinct drama was revived in the Middle Ages in the Passion of Christ.

In closing this study, which has been carried out in extremely con-

[1] La Mort d'Orphée, *Cultes, Mythes, et Religions*, Vol. II, p. 100.

densed form, I want to state the conclusion that the beginnings of religion, ethics, society, and art meet in the Œdipus complex. This is in entire accord with the findings of psychoanalysis, namely, that the nucleus of all neuroses as far as our present knowledge of them goes is the Œdipus complex. It comes as a great surprise to me that these problems of racial psychology can also be solved through a single concrete instance, such as the relation to the father. Perhaps another psychological problem must be included here. We have so frequently had occasion to show the ambivalence of emotions in its real sense, that is to say the coincidence of love and hate towards the same object, at the root of important cultural formations. We know nothing about the origin of this ambivalence. It may be assumed to be a fundamental phenomenon of our emotional life. But the other possibility seems to me also worthy of consideration: that ambivalence, originally foreign to our emotional life, was acquired by mankind from the father complex,[1] where psychoanalytic investigation of the individual today still reveals the strongest expression of it.[2]

Before closing we must take into account that the remarkable convergence reached in these illustrations, pointing to a single inclusive relation, ought not to blind us to the uncertainties of our assumptions and to the difficulties of our conclusions. Of these difficulties I will point out only two which must have forced themselves upon many readers.

In the first place it can hardly have escaped any one that we base everything upon the assumption of a psyche of the mass in which psychic processes occur as in the psychic life of the individual. Moreover, we let the sense of guilt for a deed survive for thousands of years, remaining effective in generations which could not have known anything of this deed. We allow an emotional process such as might have arisen among generations of sons that had been ill-treated by their fathers, to continue to new generations which had escaped such treatment by the very removal of the father. These seem indeed to be weighty objections and any other explanation which can avoid such assumptions would seem to merit preference.

But further consideration shows that we ourselves do not have to carry the whole responsibility for such daring. Without the assumption of a mass psyche, or a continuity in the emotional life of mankind which per-

---

[1] That is to say, the parent complex.
[2] I am used to being misunderstood and therefore do not think it superfluous to state clearly that in giving these deductions I am by no means oblivious of the complex nature of the phenomena which give rise to them; the only claim made is that a new factor has been added to the already known or still unrecognized origins of religion, morality, and society, which was furnished through psychoanalytic experience. The synthesis of the whole explanation must be left to another. But it is in the nature of this new contribution that it could play none other than the central rôle in such a synthesis, although it will be necessary to overcome great affective resistances before such importance will be conceded to it.

mits us to disregard the interruptions of psychic acts through the transgression of individuals, social psychology could not exist at all. If psychic processes of one generation did not continue in the next, if each had to acquire its attitude towards life afresh, there would be no progress in this field and almost no development. We are now confronted by two new questions: how much can be attributed to this psychic continuity within the series of generations, and what ways and means does a generation use to transfer its psychic states to the next generation? I do not claim that these problems have been sufficiently explained or that direct communication and tradition, of which one immediately thinks, are adequate for the task. Social psychology is in general little concerned with the manner in which the required continuity in the psychic life of succeeding generations is established. A part of the task seems to be performed by the inheritance of psychic dispositions which, however, need certain incentives in the individual life in order to become effective. This may be the meaning of the poet's words: Strive to possess yourself of what you have inherited from your ancestors. The problem would appear more difficult if we could admit that there are psychic impulses which can be so completely suppressed that they leave no traces whatsoever behind them. But that does not exist. The greatest suppression must leave room for distorted substitutions and their resulting reactions. But in that case we may assume that no generation is capable of concealing its more important psychic processes from the next. For psychoanalysis has taught us that in his unconscious psychic activity every person possesses an apparatus which enables him to interpret the reactions of others, that is to say, to straighten out the distortions which the other person has affected in the expression of his feelings. By this method of unconscious understanding of all customs, ceremonies, and laws which the original relation to the primal father had left behind, later generations may also have succeeded in taking over this legacy of feelings.

There is another objection which the analytic method of thought itself might raise.

We have interpreted the first rules of morality and moral restrictions of primitive society as reactions to a deed which gave the authors of it the conception of crime. They regretted this deed and decided that it should not be repeated and that its execution must bring no gain. This creative sense of guilt has not become extinct with us. We find its asocial effects in neurotics producing new rules of morality and continued restrictions, in expiation for misdeeds committed, or as precautions against misdeeds to be committed.[1] But when we examine these neurotics for the deeds which have called forth such reactions, we are disappointed. We do not find deeds, but only impulses and feelings which sought evil but which

[1] Compare Chapter II.

were restrained from carrying it out. Only psychic realities and not actual ones are at the basis of the neurotics' sense of guilt. It is characteristic of the neurosis to put a psychic reality above an actual one and to react as seriously to thoughts as the normal person reacts only towards realities.

May it not be true that the case was somewhat the same with primitive men? We are justified in ascribing to them an extraordinary over-valuation of their psychic acts as a partial manifestation of their narcistic organization.[1] According to this the mere impulses of hostility towards the father and the existence of the wish phantasy to kill and devour him may have sufficed to bring about the moral reaction which has created totemism and taboo. We should thus escape the necessity of tracing back the beginning of our cultural possession, of which we rightly are so proud, to a horrible crime which wounds all our feelings. The causal connection, which stretches from that beginning to the present time, would not be impaired, for the psychic reality would be of sufficient importance to account for all those consequences. It may be agreed that a change has really taken place in the form of society from the father horde to the brother clan. This is a strong argument, but it is not conclusive. The change might have been accomplished in a less violent manner and still have conditioned the appearance of the moral reaction. As long as the pressure of the primal father was felt, the hostile feelings against him were justified and repentance at these feelings had to wait for another opportunity. Of as little validity is the second objection, that everything derived from the ambivalent relation to the father, namely taboos, and rules of sacrifice, is characterized by the highest seriousness and by complete reality. The ceremonials and inhibitions of compulsion neurotics exhibit this characteristic too and yet they go back to a merely psychic reality, to resolution and not to execution. We must beware of introducing the contempt for what is merely thought or wished which characterizes our sober world where there are only material values, into the world of primitive man and the neurotic, which is full of inner riches only.

We face a decision here which is really not easy. But let us begin by acknowledging that the difference which may seem fundamental to others does not, in our judgment, touch the most important part of the subject. If wishes and impulses have the full value of fact for primitive man, it is for us to follow such a conception intelligently instead of correcting it according to our standard. But in that case we must scrutinize more closely the prototype of the neurosis itself which is responsible for having raised this doubt. It is not true that compulsion neurotics, who today are under the pressure of over-scrupulousness, defend themselves only against the psychic reality of temptations and punish themselves for impulses which they have only felt. A piece of historic reality is also involved; in their

[1] See Chapter III.

childhood these persons had nothing but evil impulses and as far as their childish impotence permitted they put them into action. Each of these over-good persons had a period of badness in his childhood, and a perverse phase as a fore-runner and a premise of the latter over-morality. The analogy between primitive men and neurotics is therefore much more fundamentally established if we assume that with the former, too, the psychic reality, concerning whose structure there is no doubt, originally coincided with the actual reality, and that primitive men really did what according to all testimony they intended to do.

But we must not let our judgment about primitive men be influenced too far by the analogy with neurotics. Differences must also be taken into account. Of course the sharp division between thinking and doing as we draw it does not exist either with savages or with neurotics. But the neurotic is above all inhibited in his actions; with him the thought is a complete substitute for the deed. Primitive man is not inhibited, the thought is directly converted into the deed, the deed is for him, so to speak, rather a substitute for the thought, and for that reason I think we may well assume in the case we are discussing, though without vouching for the absolute certainty of the decision, that "In the beginning was the deed."

SIX

THE HISTORY OF THE
PSYCHOANALYTIC MOVEMENT

I

If in what follows, I bring any contribution to the history of the psychoanalytic movement, nobody must be surprised at the subjective nature of this paper, nor at the rôle which falls to me therein. For psychoanalysis is my creation; for ten years I was the only one occupied with it, and all the annoyance which this new subject caused among my contemporaries has been hurled upon my head in the form of criticism. Even today, when I am no longer the only psychoanalyst, I feel myself justified in assuming that nobody knows better than I what psychoanalysis is, wherein it differs from other methods of investigating the psychic life, what its name should cover, or what might better be designated as something else.

In the year 1909, when I was first privileged to speak publicly on psychoanalysis in an American university, fired by this momentous occasion for my endeavors, I declared that it was not I who brought psychoanalysis into existence. I said that it was Josef Breuer, who had merited this honor at a time when I was a student and busy working for my examinations (1880–1882).[1] Since then, well-intentioned friends have frequently repeated that I at that time expressed my gratitude to Breuer out of all due proportion. They maintained that, as on previous occasions, I should have dignified Breuer's "cathartic procedure" as a mere preliminary to psychoanalysis, and should have claimed that psychoanalysis itself only began with my rejection of the hypnotic technique and my introduction of free association. Now it is really a matter of indifference whether one considers that the history of psychoanalysis started with the cathartic method or only with my modification of the same. I enter into this uninteresting question only because some of my opponents of psychoanalysis are wont to recall, now and then, that the art of psychoanalysis did not originate with me at all, but with Breuer. Naturally, this only happens to be the case when their attitude permits

[1] "On Psychoanalysis." Five lectures given on the occasion of the twentieth anniversary of Clark University, Worcester, Mass., dedicated to Stanley Hall. Second edition, 1912. Published simultaneously in English in the American Journal of Psychology, March, 1910; translated into Dutch, Hungarian, Polish and Russian.

them to find in psychoanalysis something that is noteworthy; on the other hand, when they set no limit to their repudiation of psychoanalysis, then psychoanalysis is always indisputably my creation. I have never yet heard that Breuer's great part in psychoanalysis had brought him an equal measure of insult and reproach. As I have recognized long since that it is the inevitable fate of psychoanalysis to arouse opposition and to embitter people, I have come to the conclusion that I must surely be the originator of all that characterizes psychoanalysis. I add, with satisfaction, that none of the attempts to belittle my share in this much disdained psychoanalysis has ever come from Breuer himself, or could boast of his support.

The content of Breuer's discovery has been so often presented that a detailed discussion of it here may be omitted.[1] Its fundamental fact is that the symptoms of hysterical patients depend upon impressive, but forgotten scenes of their lives (traumata). The therapy founded thereon was to cause the patients to recall and reproduce these experiences under hypnosis (catharsis), and the fragmentary theory deduced from it was that these symptoms corresponded to an abnormal use of undischarged sums of excitement (conversion). In his theoretical contribution to the "Studies in Hysteria," Breuer, wherever obliged to mention the term *conversion*, has always added my name in parenthesis, as though his first attempt at a theoretical formulation was my spiritual property. I think this allotment refers only to the nomenclature, whilst the conception itself occurred to us both at the same time.

It is also well known that Breuer, after his first experience with it, allowed the cathartic treatment to remain dormant for a number of years and only resumed it after I urged him to do so, on my return from Charcot. He was then an internist and taken up with a rather busy medical practice. I had become a physician quite reluctantly, but was, at that time, impelled by a strong motive to help nervous patients, or, at least, to learn to understand something of their conditions. I had placed reliance on physical therapy and found myself helpless in the face of the disappointments that I had with W. Erb's "Electrotherapy," so rich in advice and indications. If I did not, at that time, pilot myself independently to the opinion later announced by Moebius, that the successes of electrotherapy in nervous disorders are the results of suggestion, it was mainly due to the fact that these promised successes failed to materialize. The treatment by suggestion in deep hypnosis seemed to offer me at that time sufficient compensation for the loss of confidence in electrical therapy. I learned this treatment through the extremely impressive demonstrations of Liébault and Bernheim. But the investigation under hypnosis with

[1] Cf. Breuer and Freud: Studies in Hysteria, translated by A. A. Brill, Monograph Series of the Journal of Nervous and Mental Diseases.

which I became acquainted through Breuer, I found, owing to its automatic manner of working and the simultaneous gratification of one's eagerness for knowledge, much more attractive than the monotonous and violent suggestive command which was devoid of every possibility of inquiry.

As one of the latest achievements of psychoanalysis, we have lately been admonished to put the actual conflict and the cause of the illness into the foreground of analysis. This is exactly what Breuer and I did in the beginning of our work with the cathartic method. We guided the patient's attention directly to the traumatic scene in which the symptom had arisen, we endeavored to find therein the psychic conflict, and to free the repressed affect. We thus discovered the procedure characteristic of the psychic processes of the neuroses which I later named *regression*. The associations of the patients went back from the scene to be explained, to earlier experiences, and forced the analysis which was to correct the present, to occupy itself with the past. This regression led even further backwards. At first, it went quite regularly to the time of puberty. Later, however, such failures as gaps in the understanding tempted the analytic work further back into the years of childhood which had, hitherto, been inaccessible to every sort of investigation. This regressive direction became an important characteristic of the analysis. It was proved that psychoanalysis could not clear up anything actual, except by going back to something in the past. It even proved that every pathological experience presupposes an earlier one, which, though not in itself pathological, lent a pathological quality to the later occurrence. But the temptation to stop short at the known actual cause was so great, that even in later analyses I yielded to it. In the case of the patient called "Dora," carried out in 1899,[1] the scene which caused the outbreak of the actual illness was known to me. I tried uncounted times to analyze this experience, but all that I could receive to my direct demands was the same scanty and broken description. Only after a long detour, which led through the earliest childhood of the patient, a dream appeared in the analysis of which the hitherto forgotten details of the scene were remembered, and this made possible the understanding and solution of the actual conflict.

From this one example, it may be seen how misleading is the admonition just mentioned, and how much of a scientific regression it is to follow the advice of neglecting the regression in the analytic technique.

The first difference of opinion between Breuer and myself came to light on a question of the more intimate psychic mechanism of hysteria. He still favored a physiological theory, so to speak, and wished to explain the psychic splitting of hysterics through the non-communication of various psychic states (or states of consciousness, as we then called them). He

[1] Gesammelte Schriften Bd. VIII, Translation in Collected Papers, Vol. III, Hogarth Press.

thus created the theory of the "hypnoid states," the effects of which were supposed to push the unassimilated foreign bodies into the "waking consciousness." I formulated this situation less scientifically. I perceived everywhere tendencies and strivings analogous to those of everyday life, and conceived the psychic splitting itself as a result of a repelling process, which I at that time called "defense," and later "regression." I made a short-lived attempt to reconcile the two mechanisms, but as experience showed me always the same and only thing, my defense theory soon stood in opposition to his hypnoid theory.

I am quite certain, however, that this difference of opinion had nothing to do with the parting of the ways which occurred between us soon thereafter. The latter had a deeper reason, but it happened in such a manner that at first, I did not understand it, and only later did I learn from many good indications how to interpret it. It will be recalled that Breuer had stated, concerning his first famous patient, that "the sexual element in her make-up was astonishingly undeveloped" and had never contributed anything to her very marked morbid picture.[1] I have always wondered why the critics of my theory of the sexual etiology of the neuroses have not often opposed it with this assertion of Breuer, and up to this day, I do not know whether in this reticence I am to see a proof of their discretion, or of their lack of observation. Whoever will reread the history of Breuer's patient in the light of the experience we have gained since then, will have no difficulty in understanding the symbolism of the snakes and her rigidity, and the paralysis of the arm; and by taking into account also the situation at the sick-bed of the father, he will easily guess the actual meaning of that symptom-formation. His opinion as to the part sexuality played in the psychic life of that girl will then differ greatly from that of her physician. To cure the patient, Breuer utilized the most intensive suggestive *rapport*, which may serve as prototype of that which we call "transference." Now I have strong reasons for thinking that after the removal of the symptoms, Breuer must have discovered the sexual motivations of this transference by new signs, but that the general nature of this unexpected phenomenon escaped him, so that he stopped his investigation right there, as though hit by "an untoward event." He did not furnish me with any direct information about this, but at different times he gave me enough clues to justify this deduction. Later, when I emphasized more and more the significance of sexuality in the etiology of the neuroses, Breuer was the first to show me those reactions of resentful rejection, with which it was my lot to become so familiar later on, but which at that time I had not yet recognized as my inevitable destiny.

The fact that a gross sexual, tender or inimical, transference occurs in every treatment of a neurosis, although this is neither desired nor induced

[1] Breuer and Freud, l.c., p. 14.

by either party, has always seemed to me the most unshakable proof that the forces of the neuroses originate in the sexual life. This argument has by no means received the serious consideration it deserved, for if it had, there would have been no arguments. For my own conviction, it has remained the decisive factor beside and above the special results of the analytic work.

I felt some solace for the poor reception of the sexual etiology of the neuroses even among the closer circle of my friends (an empty space soon formed itself about my person) in the thought that I had taken up the fight for a new and original idea. But, one day my memories grouped themselves in such a way as to disturb this satisfaction. However, in return I obtained an excellent insight into the origin of our activities and into the nature of our knowledge. The idea for which I was held responsible had not at all originated with me. It had come to me from three persons, for whose opinions I entertained the deepest respect: from *Breuer* himself, from *Charcot*, and from *Chrobak*, the gynecologist of our university, probably the most prominent of our Vienna physicians. All three men had imparted to me an insight which, strictly speaking, they had not themselves possessed. Two of them denied their communication to me when later I reminded them of it; the third (Charcot) would have also done so had it been granted me to see him again. But these identical communications, received without my grasping them, had lain dormant within me, until one day they awoke apparently as an original discovery.

One day, while I was a young hospital doctor, I was accompanying Breuer on a walk through the town when a man came up to him and urgently desired to speak to him. I fell back, and when Breuer was free again, he told me in his kindly-teacher-like manner, that this was the husband of a patient who had brought some news about her. The wife, he added, behaved in so conspicuous a manner when in company, that she had been turned over to him for treatment as a nervous case. He ended with the remark: "Those are always secrets of the alcove." Astonished, I asked him what he meant and he explained to me the word, alcove (conjugal-bed), for he did not realize how strange this matter appeared to me.

A few years later at one of Charcot's evening receptions, I found myself near the venerated teacher who was just relating to Brouardel a very interesting history from the day's practice. I did not hear the beginning clearly, but gradually the story obtained my attention. It was the case of a young married couple from the far East. The wife was a great sufferer and the husband was impotent, or exceedingly awkward. I heard Charcot repeat: *"Tâchez donc, je vous assure vous y arriverez."* Brouardel, who spoke less distinctly, must have expressed his astonishment that such symptoms as those of the young wife should have appeared as a result of such circumstances, for Charcot said suddenly and with great vivacity:

"*Mais, dans des cas pareils, c'est toujours la chose génital, toujours—toujours—toujours.*" And while saying that, he crossed his hands in his lap and jumped up and down several times, with the vivacity peculiar to him. I know that for a moment I was almost paralyzed with astonishment, and I said to myself, "Yes, but if he knows this, why does he never say so?" But the impression was soon forgotten; brain anatomy and the experimental induction of hysterical paralyses absorbed all my interests.

A year later, when I had begun my medical activities in Vienna, as a *Privatdozent* of nervous diseases, I was as innocent and ignorant in all that concerned the etiology of the neuroses as could only be expected of a promising academician. One day I received a friendly call from Chrobak, who asked me to take a patient to whom he could not give sufficient time in his new capacity as lecturer at the university. I reached the patient before he did and learned that she suffered from senseless attacks of anxiety, which could only be alleviated by the most exact information as to the whereabouts of her physician at any time of day. When Chrobak appeared, he took me aside and disclosed to me that the patient's anxiety was due to the fact that although she had been married eighteen years, she was still a *virgo intacta*, that her husband was utterly impotent. In such cases there is nothing that the physician can do but cover up the domestic misfortune with his reputation, and he must bear it if people shrug their shoulders and say, "He is not a good doctor if in all these years he has not been able to cure her." He added, "The only prescription for such troubles is the one well-known to us, but which we cannot prescribe. It is:

Penis normalis
dosim
Repetatur!"

I had never heard of such a prescription and would like to have shaken my head at my patron's cynicism.

I have certainly not uncovered the illustrious origins of this wicked idea in order to shove the responsibility for it on others. I know well that it is one thing to express an idea once or several times in the form of a rapid *aperçu*, and quite another to take it seriously and literally to lead it through all opposing details and conquer a place for it among accepted truths. It is the difference between a light flirtation and a righteous marriage with all its duties and difficulties. *Épouser les idées* (to be wedded to ideas) is, at least in French, a quite common figure of speech.

Of the other contributions that were added to the cathartic method through my efforts, which thus transformed it into psychoanalysis, I emphasize the following: the theories of repression and resistance, the installation of the infantile sexuality, and the method of dream interpretation for the understanding of the unconscious.

The theory of repression I certainly worked out independently. I knew of no influence that directed me in any way to it, and I long considered this idea to be original until O. Rank showed us the passage in Schopenhauer's "The World as Will and Idea," where the philosopher is struggling for an explanation for insanity.[1] What he states there concerning the striving against the acceptance of a painful piece of reality agrees so completely with the content of my theory of repression, that once again, I must be grateful to my not being well read, for the possibility of making a discovery. To be sure, others have read this passage and overlooked it without making this discovery and perhaps the same would have happened to me if, in former years, I had taken more pleasure in reading philosophical authors. In later years I denied myself the great pleasure of reading Nietzsche's works, with the conscious motive of not wishing to be hindered in the working out of my psychoanalytic impressions by any preconceived ideas. I have, therefore, to be prepared—and am so gladly —to renounce all claim to priority in those many cases in which the laborious psychoanalytic investigations can only confirm the insights intuitively won by the philosophers.

The theory of repression is the pillar upon which the edifice of psychoanalysis rests. It is really the most essential part of it, and yet, it is nothing but the theoretical expression of an experience which can be repeatedly observed whenever one analyses a neurotic without the aid of hypnosis. One is then confronted with a resistance which opposes and blocks the analytic work by causing failures of memory. This resistance was always covered by the use of hypnosis; the history of psychoanalysis proper, therefore, starts with the technical innovation of the rejection of hypnosis. The theoretical value of the fact, that this resistance is connected with an amnesia, leads unavoidably to that concept of unconscious psychic activity which is peculiar to psychoanalysis, and distinguishes it markedly from the philosophical speculations about the unconscious. It may, therefore, be said that the psychoanalytic theory endeavors to explain two experiences, which result in a striking and unexpected manner during the attempt to trace back the morbid symptoms of a neurotic to their source in his life-history; viz., the facts of transference and of resistance. Every investigation which recognizes these two facts and makes them the starting-points of its work may call itself psychoanalysis, even if it leads to other results than my own. But whoever takes up other sides of the problem and deviates from these two assumptions will hardly escape the charge of interfering with the rights of ownership, if he insists upon calling himself a psychoanalyst.

[1] Zentralblatt für Psychoanalyse, 1911, Vol. I, p. 69.

I would very energetically oppose any attempt to count the principles of repression and resistance as mere assumptions instead of results of psychoanalysis. Such assumptions of a general psychological and biological nature exist, and it would be quite to the point to deal with them elsewhere, but the principle of repression is an acquisition of the psychoanalytic work, won by legitimate means, as a theoretical extract from very numerous experiences. Just such an acquisition, but of much later days, is the theory of the infantile sexuality, of which no account was taken during the first years of tentative analytic investigation. At first, it was merely noticed that the effect of actual impressions had to be traced back to the past. However, "the seeker often found more than he bargained for." One was lured further and further back into the past and one finally hoped to be permitted to tarry in the period of puberty, the epoch of the traditional awakening of the sexual impulses. In vain the tracks led still further backward into childhood and into its earliest years. On the way down there an obstacle had to be overcome, which was almost fatal for this young science. Under the influence of the theory of traumatic hysteria, following Charcot, one was easily inclined to regard as real and as of etiological importance the accounts of patients who traced back their symptoms to passive sexual occurrences in the first years of childhood— speaking frankly, to seductions. When this etiology broke down through its own unlikelihood, and through the contradiction of well-established circumstances, there followed a period of absolute helplessness. The analysis had led by the correct path to such infantile sexual traumas, and yet, these were not true. Thus, the basis of reality had been lost. At that time, I would gladly have dropped the whole thing, as did my esteemed predecessor, Breuer, when he made his unwelcome discovery. Perhaps I persevered only because I had no longer any choice of beginning something else. Finally, I reflected that after all no one has a right to despair if he has been disappointed in his expectations; one must merely revise them. If hysterics trace back their symptoms to imaginary traumas, then this new fact signifies that they create such scenes in phantasy, and hence psychic reality deserves to be given a place next to actual reality. This was soon followed by the conviction that these phantasies were intended to hide the autoerotic activities of the early years of childhood, to embellish and raise them to a higher level, and now the whole sexual life of the child came to light behind these phantasies.

In this sexual activity of the first years of childhood, the congenital constitution could finally also attain its rights. Disposition and experience here became associated into an inseparable etiological unity, insofar as the disposition raised certain impressions to inciting and fixed traumas, which otherwise would have remained altogether banal and ineffectual, whilst the experiences evoked factors from the disposition which, without them, would have remained dormant and, perhaps, undeveloped. The last word in the question of traumatic etiology was later on spoken by Abraham, when he drew attention to the fact that the very peculiar nature of the child's sexual constitution is prone to provoke sexual experiences of a peculiar kind—that is to say, traumas.[1]

My formulations concerning the sexuality of the child were founded at first almost exclusively on the results of the analyses of adults, which led back into the past. I lacked the opportunity of direct observations on the child. It was, therefore, an extraordinary triumph when, years later, my discoveries were successfully confirmed for the greater part by direct observation and analyses of very young children, a triumph that gradually became tarnished on reflecting that the discovery was of such a nature that one really ought to be ashamed of having made it. The deeper one penetrated into the observations on the children, the more self-evident this fact became, and the more strange, too, became the circumstances that such pains had been taken to overlook it.

To be sure, so certain a conviction of the existence and significance of the infantile sexuality can be obtained only if one follows the path of analysis, if one goes back from the symptoms and peculiarities of neurotics to their ultimate sources, the discovery of which then explains what is explicable in them, and permits modifying whatever can be changed. I understand that one can arrive at different conclusions if, as was recently done by C. G. Jung, one first forms a theoretical conception of the nature of the sexual instinct and then tries to explain thereby the life of the child. Such a conception can only be selected arbitrarily or with regard to secondary considerations, and runs the danger of becoming inadequate to the sphere for which it was to be utilized. To be sure, the analytic way also leads to certain final difficulties and obscurities in regard to sexuality and its relation to the whole life of the individual; but these cannot be set aside by speculations; they must wait till solutions will be found by other observations or by observations in other spheres.

I shall briefly discuss the history of dream-interpretation. It came to me as the first-fruits of the technical innovation when, following a dim presentiment, I had decided to replace hypnosis with free associations. It was not the understanding of dreams towards which my curiosity was originally directed. I do not know of any influences which had guided my interest to this or inspired me with any helpful expectations. Before Breuer and I stopped collaborating, I had only just time to tell him in one sentence that I now knew how to translate dreams. During the development of these discoveries, the symbolism of the language of dreams was about the last thing which became known to me, since the associations

---

[1] Klinische Beiträge zur Psychoanalyse aus den Jahren 1907–1920, Intern. Psychoanalyt. Bibliothek, Vd. X, 1921.

of the dreamer offer but little help for the understanding of symbols. As I have held fast to the habit of first studying things themselves before looking them up in books, I was, therefore, able to establish for myself the symbolism of dreams before I was directed to it by the work of Sherner. It was only later that I came to value fully this mode of expression in dreams. This was partly due to the influence of the works of Steckel, who at first did very meritorious work, but later became most perfunctory. The close connection between the psychoanalytic interpretation of dreams and the once so highly esteemed art of dream interpretation of the ancients only became clear to me many years afterwards. The most characteristic and significant portion of my dream theory, namely, the reduction of the dream distortion to an inner conflict, to a sort of inner dishonesty, I found later in an author to whom medicine, but not philosophy was unknown. I refer to the engineer, J. Popper, who had published his work, "Phantasies of a Realist," under the name of Lynkeus.

The interpretation of dreams became a solace and support to me in those difficult first years of analysis, when I had to master at the same time the technique, the clinical material, and the therapy of the neuroses; when I was entirely isolated and in the confusion of problems and the accumulation of difficulties, I often feared lest I should lose my orientation and my confidence. It often took a long time before the test of my assumption, that a neurosis must become comprehensible through analysis, was seen by the perplexed patient, but the dreams, which might be regarded as analogous to the symptoms, almost regularly confirmed this assumption.

Only because of these successes was I able to persevere. I have, therefore, acquired the habit of measuring the grasp of a psychological worker by his attitude to the problem of dream interpretation, and I have noticed with satisfaction that most of the opponents of psychoanalysis avoided this field altogether, or if they ventured into it, they behaved most awkwardly. The analysis of myself, the need of which soon became apparent to me, I carried out by the aid of a series of my own dreams, which led me through all the happenings of my childhood years. Even today, I am of the opinion that in the case of a prolific dreamer and a person not too abnormal this sort of analysis may be sufficient.

By unfurling this developmental history, I believe I have shown better than I could have done by a systematic presentation of the subject what psychoanalysis really is. The peculiar nature of my findings I did not at first recognize. I sacrificed unhesitatingly my budding popularity as a physician and a growing practice in nervous diseases because I searched directly for the sexual origin of their neuroses. In this way, I also gained a number of experiences which definitely confirmed my conviction of the practical importance of the sexual factor. I appeared once unsuspiciously as a speaker at the Vienna Neurological Society, then under the presidency of Krafft-Ebing, expecting to be compensated by the interest and recognition of my colleagues for my material losses, which I voluntarily incurred. I treated my discoveries as ordinary contributions to science and hoped that others would treat them in the same way. But the silence which followed my lectures, the void that formed about my person, and the insinuations directed at me, made me realize gradually that statements concerning the rôle of sexuality in the etiology of the neuroses cannot hope to be treated like other communications. I realized that henceforth I belonged to those who, according to Hebbel's expression, "have disturbed the world's sleep," and that I could not count upon being treated objectively and with toleration. But as my conviction of the general accuracy of my observations and the conclusions grew and grew, and as my faith in my own judgment and my moral courage were by no means small, there could be no doubt about the issue of this situation. I was imbued with the conviction that it fell to my lot to discover particularly important connections, and was prepared to accept the fate which sometimes accompanies such discoveries.

This fate I pictured to myself as follows: I should probably succeed in sustaining myself through the therapeutic successes of the new procedure, but science would take no notice of me during my lifetime. Some decades later, someone would surely stumble upon the same, now untimely things, compel their recognition and thus, bring me to honor as a forerunner, whose misfortune was inevitable. Meanwhile, I arrayed myself as comfortably as possible like Robinson Crusoe on my lonely island. When I look back to those lonely years, from the perplexities and pressure of the present, it seems to me like a beautiful and heroic era. The "splendid isolation" was not lacking in advantages and in charms, I did not have to read any of the medical literature or listen to any ill-informed opponents. I was subject to no influences, and no pressure was brought to bear on me. I learned to restrain speculative tendencies and, following the unforgotten advice of my master, Charcot, I looked at the same things again and again until they, themselves, began to talk to me. My publications, for which I found shelter despite some difficulty, could safely remain far behind my state of knowledge. They could be postponed as long as I pleased. *The Interpretation of Dreams*, for example, was completed in all essentials in the beginning of 1896, but was not written down until the summer of 1899. The analysis of "Dora" was finished at the end of 1899. The history of her illness was completed in the next two weeks, but was not published until 1905. In the meantime, my writings were not reviewed in the medical periodicals, or if an exception was made, they were always treated with scornful or pitying condescension. Now and then, a colleague would refer to me in one of his publications, in very short and unflattering terms, such as "unbalanced," "extreme," or "very odd." It happened once that an assistant at the clinic in Vienna asked me for permission to attend one of my courses. He listened very attentively and said nothing, but after the last lecture he offered to accompany me home. During this walk, he informed me that, with the knowledge of his chief, he had written a book against my views, but regretted very much that he had only become better acquainted with them through my lectures. Had he known these before, he would have written very differently. He had, indeed, inquired at the clinic whether he had not better first read *The Interpretation of Dreams,* but had been advised against it, as it was not worth the trouble. As he now understood it, he compared the solidity of the structure of my theory with that of the Catholic Church. In the interests of his soul's salvation, I will assume that this remark contained a bit of recognition. But he concluded by saying that it was too late to alter anything in his book, as it was already printed. This particular colleague did not consider it necessary later on to tell the world something of the change in his opinions of my psychoanalysis. On the contrary, as a permanent reviewer of a medical journal, he chose rather to follow its development with facetious comments.

Whatever personal sensitiveness I possessed was blunted in those years, to my advantage. I was saved, however, from becoming embittered by a circumstance that does not come to the assistance of all lonely discoverers. Such a person usually torments himself with a need to discover the cause of the lack of sympathy or of the rejection from his contemporaries, and perceives them as a painful contradiction against the certainty of his own conviction. That did not trouble me, for the psychoanalytic principles enabled me to understand this attitude of my environment as a necessary consequence of fundamental analytic theories. If it was true that the connections I had discovered were kept from the knowledge of the patients by inner affective resistances, then these resistances would be sure to manifest themselves also in normal persons as soon as the repressed material is conveyed to them from the outside. It was not strange that they should know how to motivate their affective rejections of my ideas on intellectual grounds. This happened just as often in the patients, and the arguments advanced—arguments are as common as blackberries, as Falstaff's speech puts it—were just the same and not exactly brilliant. The only difference was that with patients, one had the means of bringing pressure to bear in order to induce them to recognize and overcome their resistances, but in the case of those seemingly normal, such help had to be omitted. How to force these normal people to examine the subject in a cool and scientifically objective manner was an insoluble problem, the solution of which was best left to time. In the history of science it has often been possible to verify that the very assertion which, at first, called forth only opposition, received recognition a little later without the necessity of bringing forward any new proofs.

That I have not developed any particular respect for the opinion of the world or any desire for intellectual compliance during those years when I alone represented psychoanalysis, will surprise no one.

II

BEGINNING with the year 1902, a number of young doctors gathered around me with the expressed intention of learning, practising, and spreading psychoanalysis. The impetus for this came from a colleague who had himself experienced the beneficial effects of the analytic therapy. We met on regular evenings at my home and discussed subjects according to certain rules. The guests endeavored to orient themselves in this strange and new realm of investigation and to interest others in it. One day a young graduate of the technical school was admitted to our circle through a manuscript which showed very unusual understanding. We induced him to go through college and the university, and then devote himself to the non-medical application of psychoanalysis. Thus, the little society acquired in him a zealous and reliable secretary, and I gained in Otto Rank a most faithful helper and collaborator.

The little circle soon expanded, and in the course of the next few years changed its composition often. On the whole, I could say to myself that in the wealth and variety of talent our circle was hardly inferior to the staff of any clinical teacher. From the very beginning, it included those men who later were to play a considerable, if not always an agreeable, part in the history of the psychoanalytic movement. But these developments could not be imagined at that time. I was satisfied and I believe I did all I could to convey to the others what I knew and had experienced. There were only two inauspicious circumstances which at last estranged me inwardly from this circle. I could not succeed in establishing among the members that friendly relation which should obtain among men doing the same difficult work, nor could I crush out the quarrels about the priority of discoveries, for which there were ample opportunities under these conditions of working in common. The difficulties of teaching the practice of psychoanalysis, which are particularly great, and are often to blame for the present dissension among psychoanalysts, already made themselves felt in this Viennese private psychoanalytic society. I, myself, did not venture to present an as yet incomplete technique, or a theory which was still in the making, with that authority which might have spared the others many a pitfall and ultimate derailment. The self-reliance of mental workers, their early independence of the teacher, is always gratifying psychologically, but a scientific gain only results when certain, not too frequently occurring, personal conditions are also fulfilled in the workers. For psychoanalysis in particular a long and severe discipline and training in self-control is really necessary. In view of the courage displayed by devotion to a subject so ridiculed and poor in prospects, I was disposed to tolerate among the members much to which I would otherwise have objected. Besides, the circle included not only physicians, but other cultured men, such as authors and artists, who had recognized something significant in psychoanalysis. *The Interpretation of Dreams,* the book on *Wit,* and other writings had already shown that the principles of psychoanalysis cannot be restricted to the medical field, but are capable of application to various other mental sciences.

In 1907 the situation suddenly changed at one stroke, contrary to all expectations. It appeared that psychoanalysis had unobtrusively awakened interest and had gained some friends, and that there were even some scientific workers who were ready to admit their allegiance to it. A communication from Bleuler had already acquainted me with the fact that my works were studied and applied in Burghölzli.[1] In January 1907, the first man connected with the Zürich Clinic, Dr. Eitingon, visited me in Vienna. Other visitors soon followed, thus leading to a lively exchange of ideas. Finally, on the invitation of Dr. C. G. Jung, at that time still an assistant physician at Burghölzli, the first meeting took place at Salzburg, in the spring of 1908, where the friends of psychoanalysis from Vienna, Zürich, and other places met together. The result of this first psychoanalytic congress was the founding of a periodical, which began to appear in 1909, under the name of "Jahrbuch für Psychoanalytische und Psychopatholgische Forschungen," published by Bleuler and Freud, and edited by Jung. A close comradeship in the work of Vienna and Zürich found expression in this publication.

I have repeatedly acknowledged with gratitude the great efforts of the Zürich School of Psychiatry in the spreading of psychoanalysis, especially those of Bleuler and Jung, and I do not hesitate to do the same today, even under such changed circumstances. It was certainly not the partisanship of the Zürich School, which at that time first directed the attention of the scientific world to the subject of psychoanalysis. The latency period had just come to an end and everywhere psychoanalysis was becoming the object of constantly increasing interest. But whilst in all the other places this manifestation of interest resulted first in nothing but a violent and emphatic repudiation of the subject, in Zürich, on the contrary, the dominant feeling was that of agreement. In no other place could such a compact little gathering of adherents be found, nor a public

[1] The Clinic of Psychiatry, Zürich.

clinic placed at the service of psychoanalytic investigation, or a clinical teacher who considered the principles of psychoanalysis as an integral part of the teaching of psychiatry. The Zürich group became, as it were, the nucleus of the little band who were fighting for the recognition of psychoanalysis. Only in Zürich was there a possible opportunity to learn the new art and to apply it in practice. Most of my present day followers and co-workers came to me by way of Zürich, even those who might have found, geographically speaking, a shorter road to Vienna than to Switzerland. Vienna lies in an eccentric position from western Europe, which houses the great centers of our culture. For many years Vienna has been much affected by strong prejudices. The representatives of all the most prominent nations gather in Switzerland, which is very active mentally, and an infective lesion there was sure to be of great importance for the dissemination of the "psychic epidemic," as Hoche of Freiburg has called psychoanalysis.

According to the testimony of a colleague who was a witness of the developments at Burghölzli, it may be asserted that psychoanalysis awakened interest there very early. In Jung's work on occult phenomena, published in 1902, there was already an allusion to dream-interpretation. Ever since 1903 or 1904, according to my informant, psychoanalysis has stood in the foreground. After the establishment of personal relations between Vienna and Zürich, a society was also founded in Burghölzli in 1907, which discussed the problems of psychoanalysis at regular meetings. In the bond that united the Vienna and Zürich schools, the Swiss were by no means mere recipients. They had already produced important scientific work, the results of which were of much use to psychoanalysis. The association experiment, started by the Wundt School, had been interpreted by them in the psychoanalytic sense and had proved itself useful in unexpected ways. Thus, it had become possible to get rapid experimental confirmation of psychoanalytic facts, and to demonstrate experimentally to beginners certain relationships which the analyst would only have been able to talk about. The first bridge leading from experimental psychology to psychoanalysis had thus been constructed.

In psychoanalytic treatment, however, the association experiment enables one to make only a preliminary, qualitative analysis of the case; it offers no essential contribution to the technique, and is really not indispensable in the work of analysis. Of more importance, however, was another discovery of the Zürich School, or rather, of its two leaders, Bleuler and Jung. The former pointed out that a great many purely psychiatric cases can be explained by the same psychoanalytic processes as those used in dreams and in the neuroses (Bleuler's "Freudsche Mechanismen") and Jung successfully applied the analytic method of interpretation in the strangest and most obscure phenomena of dementia praecox, the origin of which then appeared quite clear when correlated with the life and interests of the patient. From that time on, it became impossible for the psychiatrists to ignore psychoanalysis. Bleuler's great work on *Schizophrenie* (1911) in which the psychoanalytic points of view are placed on an equal footing with the systematic clinical one, completed this success.

I will not omit pointing out a divergence which was already at that time noticeable in the direction of the two schools. As early as 1897, I had published the analysis of a case of schizophrenia which showed, however, paranoid trends, so that its solution could not have anticipated the results of Jung's analyses. But to me the important element had not been the interpretation of the symptoms, but rather the psychic mechanisms of the disease, and above all, the similarity of this mechanism with the one already known in hysteria. No light had been thrown at that time on the difference between these two maladies. I was then already working toward a theory of the libido in the neuroses, which was to explain all neurotic as well as psychotic appearances on the basis of abnormal drifts of the libido. The Swiss investigators lacked this point of view. So far as I know, Bleuler, even today, adheres to an organic causation for the forms of dementia praecox, and Jung, whose book on this malady appeared in 1907; [1] upheld the toxic theory of the same at the Congress at Salzburg in 1908, which though not excluding it, goes far beyond the libido theory. On this same point, he came to grief later (1912), in that he then used too much of the material which he refused altogether previously.

A third contribution from the Swiss School, which is probably to be ascribed entirely to Jung, I do not value as highly as do others who are not in as close contact with it. I speak of the theory of the complexes, which grew out of the "Diagnostische Assoziationsstudien" (1906-1910). It has neither produced a psychological theory in itself, nor has it been easy to insert it into the context of the psychoanalytic principles. On the other hand, the word, "complex," has gained for itself the right of citizen-ship in psychoanalysis, as a convenient and often an indispensable term for descriptive summaries of psychologic facts. None other among the names and designations, newly coined as a result of psychoanalytic needs, has attained such widespread popularity; but no other term has been so misapplied to the detriment of clear thinking. In psychoanalytic diction, one often spoke of the "return of the complex," when "the return of the repression" was intended to be conveyed, or one became accustomed to saying "I have a complex against him," when more correctly he should have said "a resistance."

In the years following 1907 when the schools of Vienna and Zürich

---

[1] Jung: *The Psychology of Dementia Praecox*, translated by A. A. Brill, Monograph Series.

were united, psychoanalysis received that extraordinary impetus, the signs of which are still discernible today. This is shown by the spread of psychoanalytic literature and by the increase in the number of doctors who desire to practise or learn it, as well as by the mass of attacks upon it at congresses and learned societies. It has wandered into the most distant countries; it shocked psychiatrists everywhere, and has gained the attention of the cultured laity and workers in other scientific fields. Havelock Ellis, who has followed its development with sympathy without ever calling himself its adherent, wrote, in 1911, in a paper for the Australasian Medical Congress: "Freud's psychoanalysis is now championed and carried out not only in Austria and in Switzerland, but in the United States, in England, India, Canada, and, I doubt not, in Australasia."[1] A doctor from Chile (probably a German) appeared at the International Congress in Buenos Ayres in 1910, and spoke on behalf of the existence of infantile sexuality and praised the results of psychoanalytic therapy in obsessions.[2] An English neurologist in Central India informed me through a distinguished colleague who came to Europe, that the cases of Mohammedan Indians, on whom he had practised analysis, showed no other etiology of their neuroses than our European patients.

The introduction of psychoanalysis into North America took place under particularly glorious auspices. In the autumn of 1909, Jung and myself were invited by President Stanley Hall, of Clark University, to take part in the celebration of the twentieth anniversary of the opening of Clark University, by giving some lectures in German. We found, to our great astonishment, that the unprejudiced men of that small but respected pedagogic-philosophical university knew all the psychoanalytic writings and had honored them in their lectures to their students. Thus, even in prudish America one could, at least in academic circles, discuss freely and treat scientifically all those things that are regarded as offensive in life. The five lectures that I improvised at Worcester then appeared in English in the American Journal of Psychology; later on, they were printed in German under the title, "Über Psychoanalyse." Jung lectured on diagnostic association studies and on "conflicts in the psychic life of the child."[3] We were rewarded for it with the honorary degree of LL.D. During this week of celebration at Worcester, psychoanalysis was represented by five persons. Besides Jung and myself, there were Ferenczi, who had joined me as travelling-companion, Ernest Jones, then of Toronto University (Canada), now in London, and A. A. Brill, who was already practising psychoanalysis in New York.

---

[1] Havelock Ellis, "The Doctrines of the Freudian School."
[2] G. Greve, "Sobre Psicologia y Psicoterapia de ciertos Estados angustiosos." See Zentralblatt für Psychoanalyse, Vol. I, p. 594.
[3] Translated by A. A. Brill, American Journal of Psychology, Vol. X.

The most noteworthy personal relationship which resulted at Worcester was that established with James J. Putnam, teacher of neuropathology at Harvard University. For years he had expressed a disparaging opinion of psychoanalysis, but now he befriended it and recommended it to his countrymen and his colleagues in numerous lectures, rich in content and fine of form. The respect which he enjoyed in America, owing to his character, his high moral standard and his keen love for truth, was very helpful to the cause of psychoanalysis and protected it against the denunciations to which it might otherwise have early succumbed. Yielding too much to the great ethical and philosophic bent of his nature, Putnam later required of psychoanalysis what, to me, seems an impossible demand. He wished that it should be pressed into the service of a certain moral philosophical conception of the universe; but Putnam has remained the chief prop of the psychoanalytic movement in his native land.

For the diffusion of this movement, Brill and Jones deserve the greatest credit. With a self-denying industry, they constantly brought under the notice of their countrymen, through their works, the easily observable fundamental principles of psychoanalysis of everyday life, of the dream and of the neuroses. Brill has strengthened these influences by his medical activities and his translations of my writings: Jones, by illuminating lectures and clever discussions at the American Congresses.[1] The lack of a rooted scientific tradition and the lesser rigidity of official authority have been of decided advantage to the impetus given to psychoanalysis in America by Stanley Hall. It was characteristic there from the beginning that professors, heads of insane asylums, as well as independent practitioners, all showed themselves equally interested in psychoanalysis. But just for this very reason it is clear that the fight for psychoanalysis must be fought to a decisive end, where the greater resistance has been met with, namely, in the countries of the old cultural centers.

Of the European countries, France has so far shown herself the least receptive towards psychoanalysis, although creditable writings by the Zürich physician, A. Maeder, have opened up for the French reader an easy path to its principles. The first indications of interest came from provincial France. Moricheau-Beauchant (Poitiers) was the first Frenchman who openly accepted psychoanalysis. Régis and Hesnard (Bordeaux) have lately tried (1913) to overcome the prejudices of their countrymen by an exhaustive and senseful presentation of the subject, which takes exception only to symbolism. In Paris itself, there still appears to reign the conviction (given such oratorical expression at the London Congress in

---

[1] The collected publications of these two authors have appeared in book form: Brill, "Psychoanalysis, Its Theories and Practical Applications," 1912, 2nd edition, 1914, 3rd edition, 1922, Saunders, Philadelphia, and E. Jones's "Papers on Psychoanalysis," 1913, Wood and Company, New York.

1913 by Janet) that everything good in psychoanalysis only repeats, with slight modifications, the views of Janet—everything else in psychoanalysis being bad. Janet himself had to stand at this Congress a number of corrections from Ernest Jones, who was able to reproach him for his lack of knowledge of the subject. We cannot, however, forget the credit due Janet for his works on the psychology of the neuroses, although we must repudiate his claims.

Italy, after many promising starts, ceased to take further interest. Owing to personal connections, psychoanalysis gained an early hearing in Holland: Van Emden, Van Ophuijsen, Van Renterghem ("Freud en zijn school") and the two doctors Stärke are busy in Holland, particularly on the theoretical side.[1] The interest in psychoanalysis in scientific circles in England developed very slowly, but the indications are that just here, favored by the English liking for the practical and their passionate championship of justice, a flourishing future awaits psychoanalysis.

In Sweden, P. Bjerre, successor to Wetterstand, has, at least temporarily, given up hypnotic suggestion in favor of analytic treatment. A. Vogt (Christiania) honored psychoanalysis already in 1907 in his "Psykiatriens gruntraek," so that the first text-book on psychiatry that took any notice of psychoanalysis was written in Norwegian. In Russia, psychoanalysis is very generally known and widespread; almost all my writings, as well as those of other advocates of analysis, are translated into Russian. But a deeper grasp of the analytic teaching has not yet shown itself in Russia. The contributions written by Russian physicians and psychiatrists are not at present noteworthy. Only Odessa possesses a trained psychoanalyst in the person of M. Wulff. The introduction of psychoanalysis into the science and literature of Poland is due chiefly to the endeavors of L. Jekels. Hungary, geographically so near to Austria, scientifically so foreign to it, has given to psychoanalysis only one co-worker, S. Ferenczi, but such an one as is worth a whole society.

The standing of psychoanalysis in Germany can be described in no other way than to state that it is the cynosure of all scientific discussion, and evokes from physicians as well as from the laity, opinions of decided rejection, which, so far, have not come to an end, but which, on the contrary, are constantly renewed and strengthened. No official seat of learning has, so far, admitted psychoanalysis. Successful practitioners who apply it are few. Only a few institutions, such as that of Binswanger in Kreuzlingen (on Swiss soil) and Marcinowski's in Holstein, have opened their doors to psychoanalysis. In the critical city of Berlin, we have K. Abraham, one of the most prominent representatives of psychoanalysis.

---

[1] The first official recognition that psychoanalysis and dream interpretation received was extended to them by the psychiatrist, Jelgersma, rector of the University of Leyden, in his rectorship address February 1, 1914.

He was formerly an assistant of Bleuler. One might wonder that this state of things has thus continued for a number of years without any change, if it was not known that the above account merely describes the superficial appearances. One must not overestimate the significance of the rejection of psychoanalysis by the official representatives of science, the heads of institutions, as well as their young following. It is easy to understand why the opponents loudly raise their voices whilst the followers, being intimidated, keep silent. Many of the latter, whose first contributions to analysis raised high expectations, later withdrew from the movement under the pressure of circumstances. But the movement itself strides ahead quietly. It is always gaining new supporters among psychiatrists and the laity. It constantly increases the number of readers of psychoanalytic literature and thus forces the opponents to a more violent attempt at defense. In the course of these years, I have read, perhaps a dozen times, in the reports of the transactions of certain congresses and of meetings of scientific societies, or in reviews of certain publications, that psychoanalysis was now dead, that it was finally overcome and settled. The answer to all this would have to read like the telegram from Mark Twain to the newspaper that falsely announced his death: "The report of my death is grossly exaggerated." After each of these death-notices, psychoanalysis has gained new followers and co-workers and has created for itself new organs. Surely to be reported dead is an advance over being treated with dead silence!

Hand in hand with its territorial expansion just described, psychoanalysis became enlarged with regard to its contents through its encroaching upon fields of knowledge outside of the study of the neuroses and psychiatry. I will not treat in detail the development of this part of our branch of science since this was excellently done by Rank and Sachs (in Löwenfeld's "Grenzfragen") [1] which presents exhaustively just these achievements in the work of analysis. Besides, here everything is in inchoate form, hardly worked out, mostly only preliminary and sometimes only in the stage of an intention. Every honest thinker will find herein no grounds for reproach. There is a tremendous amount of problems for a small number of workers, whose chief activity lies elsewhere, who are obliged to attack the special problems of the new science with only amateurish preparation. These workers, hailing from the psychoanalytic field, make no secret of their dilettantism; they only desire to be guides and temporary occupants of the places of those specialists to whom they recommend the analytic technique and principles until the latter are ready to take up this work themselves. That the results aimed at are, even now, not at all insignificant, is due partly to the fruitfulness of the psy-

[1] An English translation has now appeared in the Nervous and Mental Disease Monograph Series, No. 23.

choanalytic method, and partly to the circumstance that already, there are a few investigators who, without being physicians, have made the application of psychoanalysis to the mental sciences their lifework.

Most of these psychoanalytic applications can be traced, as is easily understood, to the impetus given by my early analytic works. The analytic examinations of nervous patients and neurotic manifestations of normal persons drove me to the assumption of psychological relationships which, most certainly, could not be limited only to that field. Thus, analysis presented us not only with the explanation of pathological occurrences, but also showed us their connection with normal psychic life, and uncovered undreamed-of relations between psychiatry and a variety of other sciences dealing with activities of mind. Thus, certain typical dreams furnished the understanding of many myths and fairy tales. Riklin and Abraham followed this hint and began those investigations about myths which have found their completion in the works of Rank on Mythology, works which do full justice to all the requirements of the specialist. The prosecution of dream-symbology led to the very heart of the problem of mythology, folk-lore (Jones, Storfer) and of religious abstraction. At one of the psychoanalytic congresses, the audience was deeply impressed when a student of Jung pointed out the similarity of the phantasy-formation of schizophrenics with the cosmogonies of primitive times and peoples. In a later elaboration, no longer free from objection, yet very interesting, Jung made use of mythological material in an attempt to harmonize the neurotic with religious and mythological phantasies.

Another path led from the investigation of dreams to the analysis of poetic creations and finally, to the analysis of authors and artists themselves. Very soon, it was discovered that the dreams invented by writers stand in the same relation to analysis as do genuine dreams.[1] The conception of the unconscious psychic activity enabled us to get the first glimpse into the nature of the poetic creativeness. The valuation of the emotional feelings, which we were forced to recognize while studying the neuroses, enabled us to recognize the sources of artistic productions and brought up the problem as to how the artist reacts to those stimuli and with what means he disguises his reactions.[2] Most psychoanalysts with wide interests have furnished contributions from their works for the treatment of these problems, which are among the most attractive in the application of psychoanalysis. Naturally, here also, opposition was not lacking from those who are not acquainted with analysis, and expressed itself with the same lack of understanding and passionate rejection as on

[1] Cf. Freud: "Der Wahn und die Träume" in W. Jensen's "Gradiva."
[2] Rank, "Der Künstler," analyses of poets by Sadger, Reik and others, my little monograph on "Leonardo da Vinci," translated by Brill, Dodd Mead and Co., New York; also Abraham's "Analysis of Segantini."

the native soil of psychoanalysis. For it was to be expected as a matter of course, that everywhere psychoanalysis penetrates, it would have to go through the same struggle with the natives. However, these attempted invasions have not yet stirred up interest in all fields which will, in the future, be open to them. Among the strictly scientific applications of analysis to literature, the deep work of Rank on the theme of incest easily ranks first. Its content is certain to evoke the greatest unpopularity. Philological and historical works on the basis of psychoanalysis are few, at present. I myself dared to venture to make the first attempt into the problems of the psychology of religion in 1910, when I compared religious ceremonials with neurotic ceremonials. In his work on the "piety of the Count of Zinsendorf," as well as in other contributions, the Rev. Dr. Pfister, of Zürich, has succeeded in tracing back religious zealotism to perverse eroticism. In the recent works of the Zürich School, one is more likely to find that religion becomes injected into the analysis rather than rationally explained by it.

In my four essays on "Totem and Taboo" I made the attempt to discuss the problems of race psychology by means of analysis. This should lead us directly to the origins of the most important institutions of our civilization, such as state regulations, morality, religion, as well as to the origins of the interdiction of incest and of conscience. To what extent the relations thus obtained will be proof to criticism cannot be determined today.

My book on Wit furnished the first examples of the application of analytic thinking to esthetic themes. Everything else is still waiting for workers who can expect a rich harvest in this very field. We are lacking here in workers from these respective specialties, and in order to attract such, Hans Sachs founded in 1912 the journal *Imago*, edited by himself and Rank. Hitschmann and v. Winterstein made a beginning with the psychoanalytic elucidation of philosophical systems and personalities. The continuation and deeper treatment of the same is much to be desired.

The revolutionary findings of psychoanalysis concerning the psychic life of the child, the part played therein by the sexual instinct (v. Hug-Helmuth) and the fate of such participation of sexuality which becomes useless for the purpose of propagation, naturally drew attention to pedagogics and instigated the effort to push the analytical viewpoint into the foreground of this sphere. Recognition is due to the Rev. Pfister for having begun this application of analysis with honest enthusiasm and for having brought it to the notice of ministers and educators.[1] He succeeded in winning over a number of Swiss pedagogues as sympathizers in this work. It is said that some preferred to remain circumspectly in the background.

[1] "Die Psychoanalytische Methode," 1913, Vol. 1 of the Pedagogium, Meumann and Messner. English translation by Dr. C. R. Payne. Moffat Yard & Co., New York.

A portion of the Vienna analysts seem to have landed in their retreat from psychoanalysis on a sort of medical pedagogy. (Adler and Furtmüller, "Heilen und Bilden," 1913.)

I have attempted in these incomplete suggestions to indicate the, as yet, hardly visible wealth of associations which have sprung up between medical psychoanalysis and other fields of science. There is material for the work of a whole generation of investigators, and I doubt not that this work will be done when once the resistance to psychoanalysis as such has been overcome.[1]

To write the history of the resistances, I consider, at present, both fruitless and inopportune. It would not be very glorious for the scientific men of our day. But I will add at once that it has never occurred to me to rail against the opponents of psychoanalysis merely because they were opponents, not counting a few unworthy individuals, fortune hunters and plunderers, such as in time of war are always found on both sides. For I knew how to account for the behavior of these opponents and had besides discovered that psychoanalysis brings to light the worst in every man. But I decided not to answer my opponents and, so far as I had influence, to keep others from polemics. The value of public or literary discussions seemed to me very doubtful under the particular conditions in which the fight over psychoanalysis took place. The value of majorities at congresses or society meetings was certainly doubtful, and my confidence in the honesty and distinction of my opponents was always slight. Observation shows that only very few persons are capable of remaining polite, not to speak of objective, in any scientific dispute, and the impression gained from a scientific quarrel was always a horror to me. Perhaps this attitude of mine has been misunderstood, perhaps I have been considered as good-natured or so intimidated that it was supposed no further consideration need be shown me.

This is a mistake. I can revile and rave as well as any other, but I am not able to render into literary form the expressions of the underlying affects, and therefore I prefer to abstain entirely.

Perhaps in many respects it might have been better had I permitted free vent to my own passions and to those about me. We have all heard the interesting attempt at an explanation of the origin of psychoanalysis from its Viennese milieu. Janet did not scorn to make use of it as late as 1913, although, no doubt, he is proud of being a Parisian. This *aperçu* says that psychoanalysis, especially the assertion that the neuroses can be traced back to disturbances in the sexual life, could only have originated in a city like Vienna, in an atmosphere of sensuality and immorality not to be found in other cities, and that it thus represents only a reflection,

---

[1] Cf. my two essays in Scientia, Vol. XIV, 1913, "Das Interesse an der Psychoanalyse." Gesammelte Schriften.

the theoretical projection, as it were, of these particular Viennese conditions. Well, I certainly am no local patriot, but this theory has always seemed to be especially nonsensical, so nonsensical that sometimes I was inclined to assume that the reproaching of the Vienna spirit was only a euphemistic substitution for another one which one did not care to bring up publicly. If the assumptions had been of the opposite kind, we might be inclined to listen. But even if we assume that there might be a city whose inhabitants have imposed upon themselves special sexual restrictions and at the same time, show a peculiar tendency to severe neurotic maladies, then such a town might well furnish the soil on which some observer might get the idea of connecting these two facts and of deducting the one from the other. But neither assumption fits Vienna. The Viennese are neither more abstemious nor yet more nervous than dwellers in any other metropolis. Sex matters are a little freer; prudishness is less than in the cities of western and northern Europe that are so proud of their chastity. Our supposed observer would, more likely, be led astray by the particular conditions prevailing in Vienna than be enlightened as to the cause of the neuroses.

But Vienna has done everything possible to deny her share in the origin of psychoanalysis. Nowhere else is the inimical indifference of the learned and cultured circles so clearly evident to the psychoanalyst.

Perhaps I am somewhat to blame for this by my policy of avoiding widespread publicity. If I had caused psychoanalysis to occupy the medical societies of Vienna with noisy sessions, with an unloading of all passions, wherein all reproaches and invectives carried on the tongue or in the mind would have been expressed, then perhaps the ban against psychoanalysis might, by now, have been removed and its standing no longer might have been that of a stranger in its native city. As it is, the poet may be right when he makes Wallenstein say:

> "Yet this the Viennese will not forgive me,
> That I did them out of a spectacle."

The task to which I am unequal, namely, that of reproaching the opponents "suaviter in modo" for their injustice and arbitrariness, was taken up by Bleuler in 1911 and carried out in most honorable fashion in his work, *Freud's Psychoanalysis: a Defense and a Criticism*. It would be so entirely natural for me to praise this work, critical in two directions, that I hasten to tell what there is in it I object to. This work appears to me to be still very partisan, too lenient to the mistakes of our opponents, and altogether too severe to the shortcomings of our followers. This characterization of it may explain why the opinion of a psychiatrist of such high standing, of such indubitable ability and independence, has not had greater influence on his colleagues. The author of *Affectivity* (1906) must not be surprised if the influence of a work is not determined by the value of its argument but by the tone of its affect. Another part of this influence—the one on the followers of psychoanalysis—Bleuler himself destroyed later on by bringing into prominence in 1913, in his *Criticism of the Freudian School,* the obverse side of his attitude to psychoanalysis. Therein, he takes away so much from the structure of the psychoanalytic principles that our opponents may well be satisfied with the assistance of this defender. It was not new arguments or better observations that served Bleuler as a guidance for these verdicts, but only the reference to his own knowledge, the inadequacy of which the author no longer admits as in his earlier writings. Here, an almost irreparable loss seemed to threaten psychoanalysis. However, in his last utterance (*Die Kritiken der Schizophrenie,* 1914) on the occasion of the attacks made upon him owing to his introduction of psychoanalysis into his book on "Schizophrenie," Bleuler rises to what he himself terms a "haughty presumption": "But now I will assume a haughty presumption; I consider that the many psychologies to date have contributed mighty little to the explanation of the connection between psychogenetic symptoms and diseases, but that the depth psychology ('tiefen Psychologie') furnishes us a part of the psychology still to be created, which the physician needs in order to understand his patients and to heal them rationally; and I even believe that in my 'Schizophrenie' I have taken a very small step towards this." The first two assertions are surely correct, the latter may be an error.

Since by the "depth psychology" psychoanalysis alone is to be understood, we may, for the present, remain satisfied with this admission.

III

"Cut it short!
On doomsday 'twon't be worth a farthing!"
Goethe

Two years after the first congress, the second private congress of psychoanalysts took place at Nuremberg, March, 1910. During the interval,
whilst I was still under the impression of the favorable reception in America, the growing hostility in Germany and the unexpected support through
the acquisition of the Zürich School, I had conceived a project which I
was able to carry out at this second congress, with the help of my friend
S. Ferenczi. I had in mind to organize the psychoanalytic movement, to
transfer its center to Zürich and place it under a head who would take
care of its future. As this found much opposition among the adherents of
psychoanalysis, I will explain my motives more fully. Thus I hope to
justify myself, even if it turns out that my action was not a very wise one.

I judged that the association with Vienna was no recommendation, but
rather an obstacle for the new movement. A place like Zürich, in the heart
of Europe, where an academic teacher had opened his institution to psychoanalysis, seemed to me much more promising. Moreover, I assumed
that my own person was a second obstacle. The estimate put upon my
personality was utterly confused by the favor or dislike from different
factions. I was either compared to Darwin and Kepler or reviled as a
paralytic. I, therefore, desired to push into the background not only the
city whence psychoanalysis emanated, but also my own personality.
Furthermore, I was no longer young; I saw a long road before me and I
felt oppressed by the idea that it had fallen to my lot to become a leader
in my advanced age. Yet I felt that there must be a leader. I knew only
too well what mistakes lay in wait for him who would undertake the
practice of psychoanalysis, and hoped that many of these might be
avoided if we had an authority who was prepared to guide and admonish.
Such authority naturally devolved upon me in view of the indisputable
advantage of fifteen years' experience. It was now my desire to transfer
this authority to a younger man who would, quite naturally, take my

place on my death. I felt that this person could be only C. G. Jung, for Bleuler was of my own age. In favor of Jung were his conspicuous talents, the contributions he had already made to analysis, his independent position and the impression of energy which his personality always made. He also seemed prepared to enter into friendly relations with me, and to give up, for my sake, certain race prejudices which he had so far permitted himself to indulge. I had no notion then that in spite of the advantages enumerated, this was a very unfortunate choice; that it concerned a person who, incapable of tolerating the authority of another, was still less fitted to be himself an authority, one whose energy was devoted to the unscrupulous pursuit of his own interests.

The formation of an official organization I considered necessary because I feared the abuses to which psychoanalysis would be subjected, once it should achieve popularity. I felt that there should be a place that could give the dictum: "With all this nonsense, analysis has nothing to do; this is not psychoanalysis." It was decided that at the meeting of the local groups which together formed the international organization, instruction should be given how psychoanalysis should be practised, that physicians should be trained there and that the local society should, in a way, stand sponsor for them. It also appeared to me desirable that the adherents of psychoanalysis should meet for friendly intercourse and mutual support, inasmuch as official science had pronounced its great ban and boycott against physicians and institutions practising psychoanalysis.

This and nothing else I wished to attain by the founding of the "International Psychoanalytic Association." Perhaps it was more than could possibly be attained. Just as my opponents learned that it was not possible to stem the new movement, so I had to learn, by experience, that it would not permit itself to be led along the particular path which I had laid out for it. The motion made by Ferenczi at the Nuremberg Congress was seconded. Jung was elected president and Riklin was chosen as secretary. It was also decided to publish a correspondence journal through which the central association was "to foster and further the science of psychoanalysis as founded by Freud both as pure psychology, as well as in its application to medicine and the mental sciences, and to promote assistance among the members in all their efforts to acquire and to spread psychoanalytic knowledge." The members of the Vienna group alone firmly opposed the project with passionate excitement. Adler expressed his fear that "a censorship and limitation of scientific freedom" was intended. The Viennese finally gave in, after having gained their point that Zürich should not be raised to the center of the association, but that the center should be the home city of the president, who was to be elected for two years.

At this congress, three local groups were constituted: one in Berlin under the chairmanship of Abraham, one in Zürich, whose chairman became the president of the central association, and one in Vienna, the chairmanship of which I relinquished to Adler. A fourth group in Budapest could not be formed until later. On account of illness, Bleuler had been absent from the congress. Later, he evinced considerable hesitation about entering the association and, although he let himself be persuaded to do so by my personal representations, he resigned a short time afterwards, owing to disagreements at Zürich. This severed the connection between the Zürich group and the Burghölzli institution.

Another result of the Nuremberg Congress was the founding of the *Zentralblatt für Psychoanalyse,* which caused a reconciliation between Adler and Stekel. It had originally been intended as an opposing tendency and was to win back for Vienna the hegemony threatened by the election of Jung. But when the two founders of the journal, under pressure of the difficulty of finding a publisher, assured me of their friendly intentions and as guarantee of their attitude gave me the right to veto, I accepted the editorship and worked vigorously for this new organ, the first number of which appeared in September, 1910.

I will not continue the history of the Psychoanalytic Congress. The third one took place at Weimar, September, 1911, and even surpassed the previous ones in spirit and scientific interest. J. J. Putnam, who was present at this meeting, later expressed in America his satisfaction and his respect for the "mental attitude" of those present and quoted words which I was supposed to have used in reference to the latter: "They have learned to endure a bit of truth." As a matter of fact, anyone who has attended scientific congresses must have received a lasting impression in favor of the Psychoanalytic Association. I myself had presided over two former congresses. I thought it best to give every lecturer ample time for his paper and left the discussions of these lectures to take place later as a sort of private exchange of ideas. Jung, who presided over the Weimar meeting, re-established the discussions after each lecture, which had not, however, proved disturbing at that time.

Two years later, in September, 1913, quite another picture was presented by the congress at Munich which is still vividly recalled by those who were present. It was presided over by Jung in an unamiable and incorrect fashion: the lecturers were limited as to time and the discussion dwarfed the lectures. Through a malicious mood of chance, the evil genius of Hoche had taken up his residence in the same house in which the analyists held their meetings. Hoche could easily have convinced himself that his characterization of these psychoanalysts, as a sect blindly and meekly following their leader, was true *ad absurdum.* The fatiguing and unedifying proceedings ended in the re-election of Jung as president of the International Psychoanalytic Association, which fact Jung accepted, although two-fifths of those present refused him their support. We took leave from one another without feeling the need to meet again!

About the time of this third Congress, the condition of the International Psychoanalytic Association was as follows: The local groups at Vienna, Berlin and Zürich had constituted themselves already at the congress at Nuremberg in 1910. In May, 1911, a group, under the chairmanship of Dr. L. Seif, was added at Munich. In the same year, the first American local group was formed under the chairmanship of A. A. Brill under the name of "The New York Psychoanalytic Society." At the Weimar Congress, the founding of a second American group was authorized. This came into existence during the next year as "The American Psychoanalytic Association." It included members from Canada and all America; Putnam was elected president and Ernest Jones was made secretary. Just before the congress at Munich in 1913, a local group was founded at Budapest under the leadership of S. Ferenczi. Soon afterwards, Jones, who settled in London, founded the first English group. The number of members of the eight groups then in existence could not, of course, furnish any standard for the computation of the non-organized students and adherents of psychoanalysis.

The development of the periodical literature of psychoanalysis is also worthy of a brief mention. The first periodical publications serving the interests of analysis were the *Schriften zur angewandten Seelenkunden* which have appeared irregularly since 1907 and have reached the fifteenth volume.[1] They published writings by Freud, Riklin, Jung, Abraham, Rank, Sadger, Pfister, M. Graf, Jones, Storfer and Hug-Helmuth. The founding of the *Imago,* to be mentioned later, has somewhat lowered the value of this form of publication. After the meeting at Salzburg, 1908, the *Jahrbuch für psychoanalytische und psychopathologische Forschungen* was founded, which appeared under Jung's editorship for five years, and it has now reappeared under new editorship and under the slightly changed title of *Jahrbuch der Psychoanalyse.* It no longer wishes to be, as in former years, merely an archive for collecting works of psychoanalytic merit, but it wishes to justify its editorial task by taking due notice of all occurrences and all endeavors in the field of psychoanalysis. As mentioned before, *Das Zentralblatt für Psychoanalyse* started by Adler and Stekel after the founding of the "International Association" (Nuremberg, 1910), went through in a short time a very varied career. Already in the tenth issue of the first volume, there was an announcement that in view of scientific difference of opinion with the editors, Dr. Adler had decided voluntarily to withdraw his collaboration. This placed the entire editorship in the hands of Dr. Stekel (summer of 1911). At the

---

[1] *Dreams and Myths, Wish-Fulfilment and Fairy Tales, Myth of a Birth of the Hero,* in this series are translated in the Monograph Series.

Weimar Congress, the *Zentralblatt* was raised to the official organ of the "International Association," and by increasing the annual dues, it was made accessible to all members. Beginning with the third number of the second year (winter, 1912) Stekel alone became responsible for the contents of the journal. His behavior, which is difficult to explain in public, forced me to sever all my connections with this journal and to give psychoanalysis in all haste a new organ, the *International Journal for Medical Psychoanalysis (Internationale Zeitschrift für Ärztliche Psychoanalyse)*. With the help of almost all my collaborators and the new publisher H. Heller, the first number of this new journal made its appearance in January, 1913, to take the place of the *Zentralblatt* as the official organ of the "International Psychoanalytic Association."

Meanwhile, Dr. Hanns Sachs and Dr. Otto Rank founded early in 1912 a new journal, *Imago* (published by Heller), whose only aim is the application of psychoanalysis to mental sciences. *Imago* has now reached the middle of its third year and enjoys the increasing interest of readers who are not medically interested in psychoanalysis.

Apart from these four periodical publications (*Schriften z. Angewandten Seelenkunde, Jahrbuch, Intern. Zeitschrift,* and *Imago*) other German and foreign journals have contributed works that can claim a place in psychoanalytic literature. The *Journal of Abnormal Psychology* published by Morton Prince, as a rule, contains many good analytical contributions. In the winter of 1913, Dr. White and Dr. Jelliffe started a journal exclusively devoted to psychoanalysis, *The Psychoanalytic Review*, which took into account the fact that most physicians in America interested in psychoanalysis did not master the German language.

I am now obliged to speak of two secessions which have taken place among the followers of psychoanalysis. The first of these took place in the interval between the founding of the association in 1910 and the Congress at Weimar, 1911; the second took place after this and came to light in Munich in 1913. The disappointment which they caused me might have been avoided if more attention had been paid to the mechanisms of those who undergo analytical treatment. I was well aware that anyone might take flight on first approach to the unlovely truths of analysis; I myself had always asserted that anyone's understanding may be suspended by one's own repressions (through the resistances which sustain them), so that in his relation to psychoanalysis he cannot get beyond a certain point. But I had not expected that anyone who had mastered analysis to a certain depth could renounce this understanding and lose it. And yet, daily experience with patients had shown that the total rejection of all knowledge gained through analysis may be brought about by any deeper stratum of particularly strong resistance. Even if we succeed through laborious work in causing such a patient to grasp parts of analytic knowledge and handle these as his own possessions, it may well happen that under the domination of the next resistance, he will throw to the winds all he has learned and will defend himself as in his first days of treatment. I had to learn that this can happen among psychoanalysts, just as among patients during treatment.

It is no enviable task to write the history of these two secessions, partly because I am not impelled to it by strong personal motives—I had not expected gratitude nor am I to any active degree revengeful—and partly because I know that I hereby lay myself open to the invectives of opponents manifesting but little consideration, and at the same time, I regale the enemies of psychoanalysis with the long wished-for spectacle of seeing the psychoanalysts tearing each other to pieces. I had to exercise much control to keep myself from fighting with the opponents of psychoanalysis, and now I feel constrained to take up the fight with former followers or such as still wish to be called so. I have no choice: to keep silent would be comfortable or cowardly, but it would hurt the subject more than the frank uncovering of the existing evils. Anyone who has followed the growth of scientific movements will know that quite similar disturbances and dissentions took place in all of them. It may be that elsewhere they are more carefully concealed. However, psychoanalysis, which denies many conventional ideas, is also more honest in these things.

Another very palpable inconvenience lies in the fact that I cannot altogether avoid going into an analytic elucidation. Analysis is not, however, suitable for polemic use; it always presupposes the consent of the one analyzed and the situation of a superior and subordinate. Therefore, he who wishes to use analysis with polemic intent must offer no objection if the person so analyzed will, in his turn, use analysis against him, and if the discussion merges into a state in which the awakening of a conviction in an impartial third party is entirely excluded. I shall, therefore, make here the smallest possible use of analysis, thereby limiting my indiscretion and aggression against my opponents, and I will also add that I base no scientific criticism on this means. I have nothing to do with the possible substance of truths in the theories to be rejected, nor am I seeking to refute the same. This task may be left to other able workers in the field of psychoanalysis, and some of it has already been done. I only desire to show that these theories deny the basic principles of analysis—I will show in what points—and for this reason, should not be known under this name. I shall, therefore, use analysis only to make clear how these deviations from analysis could take place among analysts. At the parting places I am, of course, obliged to defend the just rights of psychoanalysis with purely critical remarks.

Psychoanalysis has found as its first task the explanation of the neuroses; it has taken the two facts of resistance and transference as starting points, and by bearing in mind the third fact of amnesia in the theories of repression, it has given justification to the sexual motive forces of the neuroses, and of the unconscious. Psychoanalysis has never claimed to give a perfect theory of the human psychic life, but has only demanded that its discoveries should be used for the completion and correction of knowledge we have gained elsewhere. But Alfred Adler's theory goes far beyond this goal. It pretends to explain with one stroke the behavior and character of men as well as their neurotic and psychotic maladies. As a matter of fact, Adler's theory is more adequate to any other field than to that of the neuroses, which he still puts in the first place because of the history of it origin. I had the opportunity of studying Dr. Adler many years and have never denied him the testimonial of having a superior mind, especially endowed speculatively. As proof of the "persecution" which he claims to have suffered at my hands, I can only say that after the formation of the Association, I handed over to him the leadership of the Vienna group. It was only after urgent requests from all the members of the society that I could be prevailed upon to resume the presidency at the scientific proceedings. When I had recognized Dr. Adler's slight talent for the estimation of the unconscious material, I expected that he would know how to discover the connections between psychoanalysis and psychology and the biological bases of the impulses, a discovery to which he was entitled, in a certain sense, through his valuable studies about the inferiority of organs. He really did bring out something, but his work makes the impression as if—to speak in his own jargon—it were intended to prove that psychoanalysis was wrong in everything and that the significance of the sexual impelling forces could only be due to gullibility about the assertions of neurotics. Of the personal motive of his work I may also speak publicly, since he himself revealed it in the presence of a small circle of members of the Vienna group. "Do you believe," he remarked, "that it is such a great pleasure for me to stand in your shadow my whole life?" To be sure, I see nothing objectionable in the fact that a younger man should frankly admit an ambition which one might, in any case, suspect as one of the incentives of his work. But even under the domination of such a motive, a man should know how to avoid being "unfair" as designated by the English with their fine social tact. We Germans have only a much coarser word at our disposal to convey this idea. How little Adler has succeeded in not being unfair is shown by the great number of mean outbursts of anger which distort his writings, and by the feeling of an ungovernable mania for priority which pervades his work. At the Vienna Psychoanalytic Society, we once heard him claim for himself the priority for the viewpoints of the "unity of the neuroses" and the "dynamic conception" of the same. This was a great surprise for me, as I had always believed that I had represented these two principles before I had ever known Adler.[1]

This striving of Adler for a place in the sun has brought about, however, one result, which must be considered beneficial to psychoanalysis. When I was obliged to bring about Adler's resignation from the editorial staff of the *Zentralblatt*, after the appearance of his irreconcilable scientific antagonisms, Adler also left the Vienna group and founded a new society to which he first gave the tasteful name "Society for Free Psychoanalysis." But the outside public, unacquainted with analysis, is evidently as little skilled in recognizing the difference between the views of two psychoanalysts, as are Europeans in recognizing the tints between two Chinese faces. The "free" psychoanalysis remained in the shadow of the "official" and "orthodox" one, and was treated only as an appendage of the latter. Then Adler took the step for which we are thankful. He severed all connection with psychoanalysis and named his teachings "The Individual Psychology." There is much space on God's earth, and anyone who can is surely justified in tumbling about upon it uninhibited; but it is not desirable to continue living under one roof when people no longer understand one another and no longer get on together. Adler's "Individual Psychology" is now one of the many psychological movements opposed to psychoanalysis, and its further development lies outside our interests.

Adler's theory was, from the very beginning, a "system," which psychoanalysis was careful not to become. It is also an excellent example of a "secondary elaboration" as seen, for example, in the process which the waking thought produces in dream material. In this case the dream material is replaced by the material recently acquired from psychoanalytic studies, which is then relegated to the viewpoint of the ego, and brought under the familiar categories of the same. It is then translated, twirled, and as thoroughly misunderstood as happens in dream formation. Adler's theory is thus characterized less by what it asserts than by what it denies. It consequently consists of three elements of quite dissimilar value: first, good contributions to the psychology of the ego, which are superfluous but admissible; secondly, translations of analytical facts into new jargon, and thirdly, distortions and twistings of these facts when they do not fit into his ego theories. The elements of the first kind have never been ignored by psychoanalysis, although they required no special attention. Psychoanalysis has a greater interest in showing that all ego strivings are mixed with libidinal components. Adler's theory emphasizes the counterpart to it; namely, that all libidinal feeling contains an admixture of egotism. This would have been a palpable gain if Adler had not made use

[1] Adler's "Inferiority of Organs," translated by Jelliffe, appears as Monograph 24. His "Nervous Character," translated by Glueck and Lind, published by Moffat Yard & Co., New York.

of this assertion to deny, every time, the libidinal feelings in favor of the impelling ego components. His theory thus does exactly what all patients do, and what our conscious thinking always does; it rationalizes, as Jones would say, in order to conceal the unconscious motives. Adler is so consistent in this, that he considers the desire to dominate the woman, to be on the top, as the mainspring of the sexual act. I do not know if he has upheld this monstrous idea in his writings.

Psychoanalysis early recognized that every neurotic symptom owes its existence to some compromise. The symptom must, therefore, also take some account of the demands of the ego, which controls the repression by offering it some advantages, some useful application; otherwise, it would suffer the same fate as the original impulse which the ego must ward off. The term, "morbid gain," expresses this state of affairs. One might even be justified in differentiating the ego's primary gain, which must already be active in the beginning, from a "secondary" gain, which appears in connection with other intentions of the ego, when the symptom is about to assert itself. It has also long been known in analysis that the withdrawal of this morbid gain, or the cessation of the same as a result of some real change, constitutes one of the mechanisms of curing the symptom. On these relationships, which are easily verified and clearly understood, Adler's theory puts the greatest emphasis, while it entirely overlooks the fact that on innumerable occasions the ego makes a virtue out of necessity in submitting to the most undesirable symptom forced upon it, because of the use it can make of it, e.g., when the ego accepts anxiety as a means to security. Here, the ego plays the absurd part of the clown in the circus, who, through his gestures, wishes to convey to the spectators the impression that all changes in the ring are taking place at his command. But only the youngest among the spectators believe him.

For the second part of Adler's theory, psychoanalysis must stand security as for its own possessions. For it is nothing but psychoanalytic knowledge, which the author had from all the sources opened to him during ten years of our joint work, which he later marked as his own after changing the nomenclature. For instance, I, myself, consider "security" a better word than "protective measure," which I considered using, but cannot find in it any new meaning. Similarly, one will find in Adler's statements a great many well known features if one will replace his expressions "feigned" (fingiert) "fictive," and "fiction," by the original words, "to phantasy" and "phantasy." This identity would be emphasized by psychoanalysis, even if the author had not for many years participated in our common work.

The third part of Adler's theory, the misinterpretations and distortions of the disagreeable facts of psychoanalysis, contains that which definitely severs "Individual Psychology" from psychoanalysis. As is known, the principle of Adler's system states that it is the object of the self-assertion of the individual, his "will to power" in the form of the "masculine protest," to manifest itself domineeringly in the conduct of life, in character formation, and in the neurosis. This "masculine protest," the Adlerian motor, is, however, nothing else but the repression detached from its psychological mechanism, which is, moreover, sexualized in addition. This is hardly in keeping with Adler's vaunted expulsion of sexuality from its place in psychic life. The "masculine protest" certainly exists, but in constituting it as the motor of the psychic life, observation has only played the part of the springboard, which one leaves in order to raise one's self. Let us consider one of the most fundamental situations of infantile wishing, namely, the child's desire to observe the sexual act between adults. When the life-history of such persons is later subjected to analysis, it is found that at that moment, the minor spectator was swayed by two feelings; one, in the case of a boy, to put himself in the place of the active man, and the other, the opposing feeling, to identify himself with the suffering woman. Both strivings conjointly exhaust the pleasure that might have resulted from this situation. Only the first feeling can come under the head of the "masculine protest," if this idea is to retain any meaning at all. The second feeling, whose fate Adler either ignores or does not know, is really the one which assumes greater importance in the later neurosis. Adler has so thoroughly transplanted himself into the jealous restrictions of the ego, that he takes account only of those impulsive feelings which are agreeable to the ego and furthered by it; but the case of the neurosis, which opposes these strivings, lies beyond his horizon.

Adler's most serious deviations from the reality of observation and his deepest confusion of ideas have arisen in his attempt to correlate the basic principle of his theory with the psychic life of the child, an attempt which has become inevitable in psychoanalysis. The biological, social, and physiological meanings of "masculine" and "feminine" have thereby merged into a hopeless mixture. It is quite impossible to assume—and easily disproved by observation—that the masculine or feminine child builds his plan of life on an original depreciation of the feminine sex; nor is it conceivable that a child can take as his guiding principle the wish: "I will be a real man." In the beginning, the child has no inkling of the significance of the difference in sex; more likely he starts with the assumption that both sexes possess the same (male) genital. He does not begin his sexual investigation with the problem of sex differentiation and is far from entertaining any social depreciation of the woman. There are women in whose neurosis the wish to be a man has never played any part. What we know of the "masculine protest" is easily traceable to a disturbance in the primary narcissism caused by the castration threat; that is, by the first hindrances to the sexual activity. All dispute as to the psychogenesis of the neuroses must ultimately be decided in the sphere of the neuroses of childhood. Careful analysis of a neurosis of the early years of childhood puts an end to all errors and doubts as to the etiology of the neuroses and as to the part played by the sexual instinct. That is why Adler, in his criticism of Jung's "Conflicts of the Child's Mind" was obliged to resort to the imputation that the material of the case must have been arranged to conform to some tendency, "probably by the father." [1]

I will not linger any longer on the biological side of Adler's theory, and will not examine whether the actual inferiority of organs or the subjective feeling of the same (one often cannot tell which) is really capable of sustaining the foundation of Adler's system. May I only be permitted to remark that this concept would make the neurosis a by-product of stunting in general, whereas observation teaches that an excessively large number of ugly, misshapen, crippled, and wretched creatures fail to react to their deficiencies by developing a neurosis. Nor will I discuss the interesting information that the sense of inferiority goes back to infantile feelings. This shows in what disguise the factor of infantilism, so much emphasized in psychoanalysis, returns in Adler's Individual Psychology. On the other hand, I feel obliged to emphasize how all psychological acquisitions of psychoanalysis have been thrown to the winds by Adler. In his book, *The Nervous Character,* the unconscious still appears as a psychological peculiarity, but without any relation to his system. Later, he declared, quite logically, that it was a matter of indifference to him whether any conception be conscious or unconscious. From the very beginning Adler never evinced any understanding for the principle of repressions. While reviewing a lecture before the Vienna Society in 1911, he said: "On the strength of a case, I wish to point out that the patient had never repressed his libido, against which he continually tried to secure himself." [2] Soon thereafter, at a discussion in Vienna Adler said: "If you ask whence comes the repression, you are told: from culture. But if you ask whence comes culture, the reply is: from the repression. So you see it is only a question of a play on words." A small fragment of the wisdom used by Adler to unmask the defensive tricks of his "nervous character" might have sufficed to show him the way out of this pettifogging argument. There is nothing mysterious about it, except that culture depends upon the acts of repression of former generations, and that each new generation is required to retain this culture by carrying out the same repressions. I have heard of a child who considered himself fooled and began to cry because to the question: "Where do eggs come from?", he received the

---

[1] Zentralb., Vol. I, p. 122, See "Analytical Psychology," Moffat Yard and Co., New York.
[2] Korrespondenzbl., No. 5, Zurich, April, 1911.

answer, "Eggs come from hens,"; and to the further question: "Where do the hens come from?", the information was: "From the eggs," and yet, this was not a play upon words. On the contrary, the child had been told the truth.

Just as pitiful and devoid of substance is all that Adler asserted about the dream—the shibboleth of psychoanalysis. First, he considered the dream as a turning from the masculine to the feminine line, which is simply a translation of the wish-fulfillment theory of dreams into the language of the "masculine protest." Later, he found that the essence of the dream lies in the fact that it enables man to realize unconsciously what is denied him consciously. Adler must also be credited with priority of confounding the dream with the latent dream-thoughts, on the cognition of which rests his idea of "prospective tendency." Maeder followed him in this, later on. In doing so, he readily overlooks the fact that every interpretation of the dream, which really tells nothing comprehensible in its manifest appearance, rests upon the same dream-interpretations, whose assumptions and conclusions he is disputing. Concerning resistance, Adler asserts that it serves to strengthen the patient against the physician. This is certainly correct; it is as much to say that it serves the resistance. But whence this resistance originates, and how it happens that its phenomena serve the patient's interest, these questions, as if of no interest for the ego, are not further discussed by Adler. The detailed mechanisms of symptoms and phenomena, the motivation of the variety of diseases and morbid manifestations, find no consideration whatever in Adler, since everything is equally subservient to the "masculine protest," to self-assertion and to the exaltation of the personality. The system is complete at the expense of an extraordinary amount of new interpretation. Yet, it has not contributed a single new observation. I believe that I have succeeded in showing that his system has nothing whatever in common with psychoanalysis.

The view of life which one obtains from Adler's system is founded entirely upon the impulse of aggression. It leaves no room at all for love. One might wonder that such a cheerless aspect of life should have received any notice whatever; but we must not forget that humanity, oppressed by its sexual needs, is prepared to accept anything, if only the "overcoming of sexuality" is held out as bait.

The secession of Adler's faction was finished before the Congress at Weimar which took place in 1911, while the one of the Swiss School began after this date. Strangely enough, the first indications of it were found in some remarks by Riklin in popular articles printed in Swiss journals, from which the general public learned, even before Riklin's closest colleagues, that psychoanalysis had succeeded in overcoming some regrettable mistakes, which discredited it. In 1912, Jung boasted, in a letter to me from America, that his modifications of psychoanalysis had overcome the resistances to it in many persons, who hitherto wanted to know nothing about it. I replied that this was nothing to boast about, that the more he sacrificed of the hard won truths of psychoanalysis, the less resistances he would encounter. This modification, for the introduction of which the Swiss were so proud, again was nothing more or less than the theoretical suppression of the sexual factor. I admit that from the very beginning, I have regarded this "progress" as a too far-reaching adaptation to the demands of actuality.

These two retrogressive movements, tending away from psychoanalysis, which I shall now compare, also resemble each other in the fact that they were seeking to obtain a favorable opinion by means of certain lofty points of view, as if they were *sub specie aeternitatis*. In the case of Adler, this rôle is played by the relativity of all knowledge, and the right of the personality to construct artificially the substance of knowledge to suit the individual; while Jung insists on the cultural historical right of youth to throw off any fetters that tyrannical old age with ossified views would forge for it. These arguments require some repudiation. The relativity of all our knowledge is a consideration which may be used as an argument against any other science, as well as against psychoanalysis. It originates from well-known reactionary currents of the present day, which are inimical to science, and strives to give the appearance of superiority to which we are not entitled. Not one among us can guess what may be the ultimate judgment of mankind about our theoretical efforts. There are examples to show that what was rejected by the next three generations was corrected by the fourth, and thus changed into recognition. There is nothing else for the individual to do but to defend, with all his strength, his conviction based on experience after he has carefully listened to his own criticisms and has given some attention to the criticisms of his opponents. Let him be content to conduct his affair honestly and not assume the office of judge, which must be reserved for the remote future. To emphasize personal arbitrariness in scientific matters is bad; it evidently is an attempt to deny to psychoanalysis the value of a science, which, to be sure, has already been depreciated by the previous remark. Anyone who highly regards scientific thinking will rather seek for means and methods to restrict if possible, the factor of personal and artificial arbitrariness, wherever it still plays too large a part. Besides, one must remember that all zeal to defend is out of place. Adler does not take these arguments seriously. They are only meant to be used against his opponents, respecting, however, his own theories. They have not prevented Adler's own followers from hailing him as the Messiah, for whose appearance waiting humanity had been prepared by so and so many forerunners. The Messiah is surely no longer anything relative.

Jung's argument *ad captandam benevolentiam* rests on the all too optimistic assumption that the progress of humanity, of civilization, and of knowledge has always continued in an unbroken line, as if there had never been any epigones, reactions, and restorations after every revolution, as if there had been no races, who, through a retrogression, rejected the gain of former generations. The approach to the standpoint of the masses, the giving up of an innovation that has proved unpopular, make it improbable from the beginning that Jung's correction of psychoanalysis could justly claim to be a liberation for youth. Finally, it is not the years of the doer that decide this, but the character of the deed.

Of the two movements under consideration here, Adler's is undoubtedly the more important. Though radically false, it is, nevertheless, characterised by consistency and coherence, and it is still founded on the theory of the instincts. On the other hand, Jung's modification has slackened the connection between the phenomena and the instinctive-life; besides as its critics (Abraham, Ferenczi, Jones) have already pointed out, it is so unintelligible, muddled and confused, that it is not easy to take any attitude towards it. Wherever one touches it, one must be prepared to be told that one has misunderstood it, and it is impossible to know how one can arrive at a correct understanding of it. It represents itself in a peculiarly vacillating manner, since at one time it calls itself "a quite tame deviation, not worthy of the row which has arisen about it" (Jung); yet, at another time, it calls itself a new message of salvation which is to begin a new epoch in psychoanalysis; indeed, a new philosophy of life for everything else.

When one thinks of the disagreements between Jung's various private and public utterances, one is obliged to ask to what extent this is due to his own lack of clearness and how much to a lack of sincerity. It must be admitted, however, that the representatives of the new theory find themselves in a difficult position. They are now disputing things which they, themselves, formerly defended and what is more, this dispute is not based on new observations, which might have taught them something fresh, but rather on a different interpretation which makes them see things in a different light than before. It is for this reason that they are unwilling to give up their connection with psychoanalysis, as the representatives of which they first became known to the world, and prefer to proclaim that psychoanalysis has changed. At the Congress of Munich, I was obliged to clear up this confusion and did so by declaring that I could not recognize the innovation of the Swiss School as a legitimate continuation and further development of the psychoanalysis which originated with me. Outside critics (like Furtmüller) had already recognized this state of affairs and Abraham truly states that Jung is in full retreat from psychoanalysis. I am naturally perfectly willing to admit that anyone has the right to think and write what he likes, but he has not right to give it out as something different from what it really is.

Just as Adler's researches brought something new into psychoanalysis, a contribution to the ego-psychology, and then wished to be paid only too dearly for this gift by repudiating all the fundamental analytic principles, so in the same way Jung and his adherents have based their fight against psychoanalysis upon a new contribution to the same. They have traced in detail (what Pfister did before them) how the material of the sexual ideas, originating in the family complex and in incestuous object selection, can be used to represent the highest ethical and religious interests of mankind—that is, they have explained a remarkable case of sublimation of the erotic instinctual forces and their transformation into strivings that can no longer be called erotic. All this was in perfect agreement with all the expectations of psychoanalysis, and would have agreed very well with the conception that in the dream and in the neurosis, one sees the regressive dissolutions of these and of all other sublimations. But the world would have indignantly exclaimed that they were sexualizing ethics and religion. I cannot help assuming finally that these discoverers found themselves quite unequal to the storm of indignation they had to face. Perhaps, the storm began to rage also in their own bosoms. The previous theological history of so many of the Swiss workers is as important in their attitude to psychoanalysis as the socialistic record of Adler for the development of his "psychology." One is reminded of Mark Twain's famous story about the vicissitudes of his watch and of the speculative remark with which he ends it: "And he used to wonder what became of all the unsuccessful tinkers and gunsmiths and shoemakers and blacksmiths; but nobody could ever tell him."

I will encroach upon the realm of parables and will assume that in a certain society there lived an upstart who boasted of descent from a very noble family not locally known. But it so happened that it was proved to him that his parents were living somewhere in the neighborhood and were very simple people indeed. Only one way out remained to him and he seized upon it. He could no longer deny his parents, but he asserted that they were very aristocratic by origin, but were much reduced in circumstances, and secured for them at some obliging office a document showing their descent. It seems to me that the Swiss workers had been obliged to act in a similar manner. If ethics and religion could not be sexualized, but must be regarded as something "higher" from the very beginning, and as their origin from the family and Œdipus complexes seemed undeniable, then there was only one way out: the complexes themselves could not from the beginning have had the significance which they seemed to express, but must have that higher "anagogic" sense (to use Silberer's nomenclature) which adapts them for proper use in the abstract streams of thought, of ethics, and religious mysticism.

I am quite prepared to be told again that I have misunderstood the contents and object of the New-Zürich School theory, but I wish to protest from the beginning against being held responsible for those contradictions to my theories that have arisen from the publications of this school. The burden of responsibility rests on them, not on me. In no other way can I make comprehensible to myself the ensemble of Jung's innovations or grasp their connection. All the changes which Jung has brought into psychoanalysis originated from his intention to eliminate all that is objectionable in the family complexes, in order that it may not be found again in religion and ethics. The sexual libido was replaced by an abstract idea, concerning which it may be said that it remained equally mysterious and incomprehensible alike to fools and wise. The Œdipus complex, we are told, has only a "symbolical" sense, the mother therein representing the unattainable which must be renounced in the interests of cultural development. The father who is killed in the Œdipus myth represents the "inner" father, from whose influence we must free ourselves in order to become independent. No doubt, other portions of the material of sexual ideas will, in time, surely undergo similar new interpretations. In place of the conflict between erotic strivings adverse to the ego and the self-assertion, we are given the conflict between the "life-task" and the "psychic laziness." The neurotic feeling of guilt corresponds to the reproach of not properly fulfilling one's life-task. Thus, a new religio-ethical system was founded, which exactly like Adler's, was forced to new interpretations, distortions and eliminations of the actual results of analysis. As a matter of fact, they have caught a few cultural overtones from the symphony of life, but once more have failed to hear the most powerful melody of the impulses.

In order to hold this system together, it was necessary to draw away entirely from the observations and technique of psychoanalysis. Now and then, the enthusiasm for the higher cause even permits a total disregard for scientific logic, as for instance, when Jung maintains that the "Œdipus complex" is not "specific" enough for the etiology of the neuroses, and ascribed this specificity to laziness; that is, to the most universal quality of animate and inanimate bodies! It is, moreover, remarked that the "Œdipus complex" only represents a content in which the psychic forces of the individual are measured, and is not in itself a force, like the "psychic laziness." The study of the individual man has shown and always will show that the sexual complexes are alive in him in their original sense. That is why the study of the individual was pushed back by Jung and replaced by the conclusions drawn from the study of racial history. As the study of the early childhood of man offers the greatest likelihood of encountering the original and undisguised meaning of these misinterpreted complexes, Jung made it a rule to direct as little as possible of the therapy to this past and to place the greatest emphasis on the return to the current conflict, where, however, the essential thing is not at all the incidental and personal, but rather the general or the "non-fulfillment of the life-task." We know, however, that the actual conflict of the neurotic becomes comprehensible and capable of solution only if it can be traced back to the patient's past history, and by following the path which his libido took when his neurosis started.

How the New Zürich therapy has shaped itself under such tendencies, I can convey by means of reports of a patient who was himself forced to experience it. "Not the slightest consideration was given at this time to the past or the transference. Whenever I thought that the latter was touched, it was explained as a mere symbol of the libido. The moral teachings, which were very beautiful, I followed faithfully, but I did not advance one step. This was more distressing to me than to the physician, but how could I help it? Instead of freeing me analytically, each session made new and tremendous demands on me, on which fulfillment the overcoming of the neurosis was supposed to depend. Some of these demands were: inner concentration by means of introversion, religious meditation, living with my wife in loving devotion, etc. It was almost beyond my power, since it really amounted to a radical transformation of the whole spiritual man. I left the analysis as a poor sinner with the strongest feelings of contrition and the very best resolutions, but at the same time, with the deepest discouragement. All that this physician recommended any clergyman would have advised, but where was I to find the strength?" It is true that the patient had also heard that an analysis of the past and of the transference should precede this process. He was, however, told that he had already had enough of that. But since it had not helped him, it seems to me that it is just to conclude that the patient had not had enough of this first sort of analysis. Not in any case has the superimposed treatment, which no longer has the slightest claim to call itself psychoanalysis, helped. It is a matter of wonder that the men of Zürich should have taken the long detour via Vienna to reach Berne, which is so near to them, where Dubois cures neuroses by ethical encouragement, but with much greater indulgence.[1]

The total disagreement evinced by this new movement with psychoanalysis naturally also shows itself in its attitude towards repression,

[1] I know the objections which may be advanced against the use of a patient's statements and I will, therefore, expressly state that my informant is as trustworthy as he is capable of expressing judgment. He gave me this information without any solicitation on my part and I use this communication without asking his consent because I cannot admit that any psychoanalytical technique should claim the protection of discretion.

which Jung hardly mentions any more in his writings, in the miscon-
struction of the dream, which, like Adler who ignores the psychology of
the dream, Jung confuses with the latent dream-thoughts, and also in the
lack of understanding of the unconscious. In brief, this disagreement is
seen in all the essential points of psychoanalysis. When Jung tells us that
the incest-complex is only "symbolic," that it has "no real existence,"
that the savage cannot possibly feel any desire towards the old hag, but
prefers a young and pretty woman, one is tempted to assume that "symbolic" and "no real existence" simply mean to him that which is designated in psychoanalysis—with regard to its expression and pathogenic
effects—as "existing unconsciously," expressions which thus remove the
apparent contradiction.

If one bears in mind that the dream is something different from the
latent dream-thoughts which it elaborates, one will not wonder that the
patients dream of those things with which their minds have been filled
during the treatment, be it the "life-task" or being "above" or "below."
To be sure, the dreams of those analyzed can be directed in the same
manner as dreams can be influenced by stimuli applied experimentally.
One may determine a part of the material that occurs in the dream, but
this changes nothing in the nature and mechanism of the dream. Nor do
I believe that the so-called "biographical" dream occurs outside of analysis. On the other hand, if we analyze dreams which appeared before treatment, or if one considers what the dreamer adds to the stimuli suggested
to him during the treatment, or if one avoids putting to him such tasks,
then one may convince himself how far removed it is from the dream to
offer tentative solutions of the life-task. For the dream is nothing but another form of thinking; the understanding of this form can never be
gained from the content of its thoughts, only the appreciation of the
dream-work will lead to it.

An effective refutation of Jung's misconceptions of psychoanalysis and
his deviations from it is not difficult. Any analysis carried out in accordance with the rules, especially any analysis of a child, strengthens the convictions on which the theory of psychoanalysis rests and repudiates the
new interpretations of Adler's and Jung's systems. Jung, himself, before
he became enlightened, carried out such an analysis of a child and published it.[1] It remains to be seen if he will undertake a new interpretation
of this case with the help of another "uniform trend of the facts," to use
an expression which Adler used in this connection.

The view that the sexual representation of "higher" ideas in the dream
and in the neurosis is nothing but an archaic mode of expression, is naturally irreconcilable with the fact that in the neuroses these sexual com-

[1] *Experiences Concerning the Psychic Life of the Child*, translated by A. A. Brill,
American Journal of Psychology, April, 1910

plexes prove to be the carriers of those quantities of libido which have been withdrawn from real life. If it were only a question of sexual jargon, nothing could thereby be altered in the economy of the libido itself. Jung admits this himself in his *Darstellung der psychoanalytischen Theorie,* and formulates, as a therapeutic task, that the libido cathexis should be withdrawn from these complexes. But this can never be accomplished by turning away from them and urging that they be sublimated, but only by the most exhaustive occupation with them, and by making them fully conscious. The first bit of reality with which the patient must deal is his illness. Any effort to spare him this task points to the physician's incapacity to help him to overcome his resistances, or to the physician's fear of the results of his work.

I should like to say in conclusion that Jung, by his "modifications" of psychoanalysis has furnished us a counterpart of Lichtenberg's famous knife. He has changed the hilt and has inserted a new blade into it, and because the same trademark is engraved on it, we are required to regard the instrument as the former one.

On the contrary, I believe that I have shown that the new theory which desires to replace psychoanalysis, signifies an abandonment of analysis and a secession from it. Some may perhaps be inclined to fear that this defection perforce signifies a greater misfortune for the fate of psychoanalysis than any other, because it had emanated from persons who once played so great a part in the psychoanalytic movement, and did so much to advance it. I do not share this apprehension.

Men are strong so long as they represent a strong idea. They become powerless when they oppose it. Psychoanalysis will be able to bear this loss and will gain new adherents for those lost. I can only conclude with the wish that fate may grant an easy ascension to those whose sojourn in the underworld of psychoanalysis has become uncomfortable. May it be vouchsafed to the others to bring to a happy conclusion their works in the depth.

INDEX

NOTE

My thanks are herewith expressed to Mr. John J. Trounstine, who, in addition to arranging the following index, has relieved me of the burden of reading proof on the text.

A. A. B.

INDEX